Blue Book Pool Cues™
3rd Edition

by Brad Simpson

$39.95
Publisher's Softcover
Suggested List Price

Publisher's Limited
Edition Hardcover
Suggested List Price - $99.95

3rd EDITION BLUE BOOK OF POOL CUES™

This book is the result of continuous pool cue research performed by attending and/or participating in trade shows, billiard tournaments, auctions, and also communicating with cuemakers, contributing editors, dealers, collectors, historians, and other knowledgeable industry professionals worldwide each year. This book represents an analysis of prices for which collectible pool cues have actually been selling at an average retail level. Although every reasonable effort has been made to compile an accurate and reliable guide, prices may vary significantly (especially auction prices) depending on such factors as the locality of the sale, the number of sales we were able to consider, and economic conditions. Accordingly, no representation can be made that the cues listed may be bought or sold at prices indicated, nor shall the author or publisher be responsible for any error made in compiling and recording such prices and related information.

Copyright © 2005 Blue Book Publications, Inc.
All Rights Reserved.

Blue Book Publications, Inc.
8009 34th Avenue South, Suite 175
Minneapolis, MN 55425 U.S.A.
Orders Only: 800-877-4867
Phone: 952-854-5229
Fax: 952-853-1486
Email: bluebook@bluebookinc.com
Website: http://www.bluebookinc.com

Published and printed in the United States of America
ISBN 1-886768-52-8

No part of this publication may be reproduced in any form whatsoever, by photograph, mimeograph, fax transmission or any other mechanical or electronic means. Nor can it be broadcast or transmitted, by translation into any language, nor by electronic recording or otherwise, without the express written permission from the publisher—except by a reviewer, who may quote brief passages for critical articles and/or reviews.

The percentage breakdown of a cue's condition factor with respective values per condition is a trademark copyrighted by Blue Book Publications, Inc. Any unauthorized usage of these systems for the evaluation of pool cue values is expressly forbidden by the publisher.

ABOUT THE COVER & CREDITS

The ten cues featured on the cover of this third edition were selected to represent some of the finest work among the 1,000+ cues photographed for the book. They span a period of 88 years of craftsmanship, from the Brunswick Model 360 (c.1915) to three cues making their debut in 2003.

Front cover, from top to bottom:
"Banana Stan" has many of the unique design trademarks which can be found in cues by **David Paul Kersenbrock**: engraved silver and asymmetrical inlay work, and engraved designs on the ivory joint. White sapphires are inlaid in the "broken" bird's-eye points in a cocobolo forearm. The flattop radial pin he designed over 20 years ago has become one of the standard choices among contemporary cuemakers. Courtesy - Wu Collection.
Mike Lambros created the ivory "Dragon" cue in 2003. Its abalone fire breathers wind around the cue from top to bottom, interrupted only by a lizard skin wrap. Courtesy - Randy Welty.
"The Hustler" cue is a collaboration between **pfd Studios** and scrimshaw artist **Sandra Brady**. The cue commemorating the movie was begun in 2000 and completed for the 2002 International Cue Collectors Show in Ruidoso, New Mexico. After designing the random filmstrip layout for the cue, **Paul Drexler** sent the cue to Sandra Brady to scrim ivory "film frames" using scenes selected from actual movie stills. Stylized "movie premiere" arc lights of 18-karat gold with sterling silver rays were then added around the forearm of the cue, which was hand-signed by **Paul Newman**. It was auctioned for the "Hole in the Wall Gang" in 2004 (see pages 22-25).
A veneered six-point, ivory-jointed **Gus Szamboti** cue; perhaps the rarest and most desirable to collectors among his classic designs; he only made a few. It was built in 1988 and was one of the last ten cues Gus completed. Courtesy of Mark Kulungian.
The ivory-sleeved "Two Sisters" cue is one of a pair built and engraved by **Joel Hercek** in 2003. The cue, like its "Sister" has both prophets and angels as a part of its heavenly design, with the full-spliced blank Joel is known for at its heart. The design was inspired by Michelangelo's Sibyls and putti painted for the Sistine Chapel. Courtesy - Wu Collection.
The background of ring components was photographed at **South West Cues** by Sue Bachmen.

Back cover, top to bottom:
Samsara featured the "Eye of the Tiger" at the 2003 Showcase at the Ritz; their unique designs were among the highlights of the L.A. cue extravaganza. Decorating the base of the cue's eight points and butt sleeve are a combination of ivory, tiger-eye, Crazy Lace stone and ebony inlays. The wrap area has textured black leather, snakewood and ivory inlays. The snakewood and ebony Intarsia design in the butt sleeve is called a "Double Fantail."
One of the fanciest **Herman Rambow** cues ever made, this cue has both the owner's name and "Made by Rambow" handwritten under the finish. The first "name" American custom cuemaker of the 20th century, Rambow's influence continues to be felt 80 years later. Courtesy - Wu Collection.
Ernie Gutierrez created his "Feather" design Ginacue for the Smithsonian cue collection using snakewood, ebony, pink ivorywood, and ivory. The designs Ernie created 40 years ago are often copied but seldom equaled.
The **Brunswick-Balke-Collender** Model 360 with its multiple butterfly splices extending into the shaft is as much in demand now as it was 90 years ago—although the price has gone up 1000%. Courtesy - Kulungian Collection.
One of **Tad Kohara**'s 'ultimate' creations is this 28-point ivory and ebony cue with its ornate ringwork and almost iridescent bird's-eye forearm. Tad uses ivory only in special cues. Courtesy - Cheng Collection.
Cue photos and background photo of **Barry Szamboti**'s workshop by Peter Andrew Hangarter.

3rd Edition *Blue Book of Pool Cues* Credits:
Production Manager & Art Director - Clint H. Schmidt
Assistant Art Director - Zachary R. Fjestad
Cover Layout, Lettering, Digital Imaging, and Art Direction - Clint H. Schmidt
Cover and Color Section Design - Brad Simpson, Sue Bachmen, and Clint H. Schmidt
Principal Color Section and Cover Photography - Peter Andrew Hangarter
Copyeditor - Stacy M. Knutson
Executive Assistant Editor - Carol Simpson
Printer - Von Hoffmann, Eldridge, IA

CONTENTS

Title Page 1
Publisher's Note & Copyright/About the Cover & Credits 2
Table of Contents 3
Acknowledgements & Dedication 4
Contributing Editors 5
BBP General Information 6
Meet the Staff 7
Publisher's Overview 8
Foreword & A Word About the Author 9
The PCIII Overview by Carol Simpson 10
How To Use This Book 11-12
Tracking Your Cue Through the Book 13
Collecting Pool Cues by Deno Andrews 14-17
Scuffers & Cue Accessories by Tom Shaw 18-21
The Hustler Cue by James Yonge 22-25
Wanted Dead or Alive/Correspondence & Appraisals 26
Glossary 27-28
Condition Factors 29
Levels of Intricacy 30
How to Use the Level of Intricacy Grading 31
The Pool Cue Catscan 32
Cue Gallery 33-96
A-Z sections 97-888
Trademark Index 889-900
Organizations 901
Periodicals Listing 902
Buy/Sell/Trade 903-904
Index 905-912

ACKNOWLEDGEMENTS & DEDICATION

Special thanks to my mother Carol for taking a ten-month break from her retirement to help with this book. She did everything short of co-authoring this third edition. I also want to thank the other people who offered moral support when I had to take over this project. When things go wrong you find out who your real friends are. These friends include: Dale Deebs, Randy Ewing, Lars Jensen, Rich Junk, John McCarthy, David Thompson, and Gene Troken, among others. Thank you Deno Andrews, Gian Calise, Penny Davis-Shaffer, Tom Shaw, and James Yonge for your writing contributions to this book. And to Dick Abbott, Deno Andrews, William Grassley, Mark Kulungian, and Roy Malott for help with the thousands of cue prices in this book. Thanks to Victor Stein and Paul Rubino for allowing me unlimited access to the information gathered from *The Billiard Encyclopedia* (the only reference book on cues I've ever used). That information helped me get the first two editions off the ground. They also were involved in introducing me to many of the people in this industry. Clint Schmidt has done an excellent job of laying this book out and updating the graphics and Stacy Knutson has been great at editing and making last-minute corrections. Thanks to Steve Fjestad, editor and publisher at Blue Book Publications, Inc., for being in on this project from the very beginning. He helped make the project happen by agreeing to publish the first edition of this book when it was just an idea, by later publishing the second edition of *The Billiard Encyclopedia* and by publishing the second, and now third edition of the *Blue Book of Pool Cues*. To Mark Wilson, who piqued my interest in the sport. Mark's personal instruction greatly improved my ability and enjoyment of the game. The Matchroom, a pool room run by Mark in the early 1990s, was the best environment for enjoying the game that I have ever encountered. Mark wrote articles in the first two editions of this book, and also provided the image of his friend Frank Stellman, "Sailor." Thanks again to Mark Kulungian for taking excellent photographs of his collection, which appear in many of the deceased makers sections and in the color section. He has also been very helpful with the pricing of this material. Tom Foley of Foley Studio here in Galesburg took time out of his busy schedule to take my portrait for the foreword, as well as portraits of my mom, Carol, and my friend Penny Davis-Shaffer. And thanks to Adam Powell and Michael Wynkoop for constantly taking time away from their posts at Simpson Ltd. to help with photography and computer glitches. I would also like to thank the following people for providing information, cues, photographs, advice, support, and their time. I could not have completed this third edition, or future editions, without them.

Robin Adair
Richard Akimoto
Bruce Baker
Barry M Barash
Bob Barnett
Ryan Birkenfeld
Dwaine Bowman
Joe Brown
James Carter
Bill Chapin
Charles Cheng
Steve Cherne
Ron Clark
Cathy Corbin
Cathy Cox
Don Daly
Scott Dunning
Debra Foss
James Germany
Randy Goettlicher
John Gozales
Rick Goulden
Sean Granahan
Mark Griffin
Dan Gronich
Jared Halcomb
Mark Hammerl
Tom Heller
Lucky Hishinuma
Allen Hopkins
Len Jaszewski
Joe Kerr
Bridget C. Lake
Dr. Robert Leonard
Richard Machniak
Doug Maddox
Tom Madsen
Tony Martino
Stephen Mayhew
John McChesney
David N. McCrery III
Kathy McFarland
Chris Miele
Henry K. Miller
Steve Miller
Chuck Montaqu
Rob Montgomery
Rory Mueller
Jay Nelsion
Joe Nielsen
Sarah Nielsen
Keith Notham
Ed O'Connell
Barbara Knowles-Olson
Jim Oswald
Tom Peck
Joe Pena
Bob Price
Will Prout
Gerald Quist
Rick Rogers
Joe Salazar
Steven R. Sawyer
Rick Schryack
Mike Schutzius
Valient Seu
Thomas C. Shaw
Joe Shugart
Delbert Sielschott
Robert C. Simpson
Scott Smith
Mark & Connie Stellinga
Larry Stone
Richard Story
Thomas Tidd
Steve Tipton
George Tutka
Audie Wallace
Keith Walton
Dan Weis
R.W. Welty
Debbie Wilson
Roy Yamane
Jerry Zebrowski

Additional Photo Credits:
Dick Abbott: Samsara Twisted Sisters color photo
Deno Andrews: Photos for article on cue collecting
Ashi: Gugino cues
Sue Bachmen: Various cuemaker and logo photos
Coleman Collection: Rauenzahn cues
Dennis Fitch: The Kulungian collection
Tom Foley, Foley Studio: Brad Simpson, Carol Simpson, Penny Davis-Shaffer photos
Peter Andrew Hangarter: Principal photography
Highlights Phtography: Ron Haley cues
Joe Koontz: Blue Grass cues
Nandon Studios: Michael Morgan cues
Adam Powell, Simpson LTD: Various cue photos
Carol Simpson, Simpson LTD: Various cuemaker and logo photos
Thompson Photographics: Richard Black photos
Tintype, Mark Jones: Durbin photos
Jeff Willings: Joel Hercek photos
Jim Yonge: Photographs for "The Hustler Cue"
Carl Yusuf: Michael Morgan cues

Pricing Editors: In order to insure the accuracy of the prices in this book, the following people viewed and/or edited prices before this book went to press.

Dick Abbott   Deno Andrews   William Grassley   Mark Kulungian   Roy Malott

This book is dedicated to the memory of the cuemakers we have lost since the publishing of the second edition of the Blue Book of Pool Cues.

CONTRIBUTING EDITORS

Deno Andrews began playing carom billiards at the early age of five. He was instructed by his grandfather, a champion billiardist who was close friends with Willie Hoppe, Jake Schaefer Jr. and many other champions of the game. After his grandfather's death, Deno continued to play billiards for many years. During his teen years, Deno began to learn the craft of cuemaking by working for Ray Schuler for two summers. Deno started to compete at billiards around 1989-1990. Around the same time that he began competing, Deno worked for Cognoscenti Cues, which was, at that point, a start-up company. Working side-by-side with Joe Gold for several years, Deno learned the complete cuemaking process, while having the flexibility to compete at billiards. During his roughly 10 years on the road, Deno built what is considered to be the largest collection of Rambow cues in the world. He acquired most of them from retiring old-timers of the game who had purchased their cues directly from Rambow himself. As his cue collecting interests shifted to more contemporary works, Deno was able to use some of his Rambow holdings to build a more diverse cue collection. Deno also maintains a large collection of billiards-related paper, including 19th and early 20th century magazines, catalogs, newspapers, and one of the most comprehensive antiquarian billiards book collections in the country.

Deno's unique contribution to the *Blue Book of Pool Cues* project was to oversee the Chicago area cuemakers' chapters, both living and deceased. His knowledge as a collector and historian, and his experience in making cues, as well as his relationships with contemporary cuemakers, have allowed him to contribute accurate and updated details to the cuemaker biographies. Deno also contributed an article on building a cue collection. Deno holds a BA from DePaul University.

When asked how he discovered his passion for cues, Gian Calise will speak of his first mentor in pool, a player named Greg Ford. As Gian tells the story, Ford sold his pickup truck to pay for an early Joss cue made by Dan Janes. It was the first two-piece cue Gian ever saw, and from that moment forward, he felt a love and fascination for the functional art of the cuemaker. Gian has bought and sold cues as a collector for more than 20 years. In the photo, he is seen with cues from Bill Schick, Ned Morris, Jim Buss, Mike Webb and Pete Ohman.

Gian is a graduate of the University of Rhode Island, and has now realized one of his dreams by participating in the editorial process of the third edition of the *Blue Book of Pool Cues*. "I've always wanted to show my respect for those who have brought cuemaking to the magnificent art form it is today. The craft requires a harmony of aesthetic and practical talents, combined with an understanding of traditional methods and modern innovations in woodworking. Those who have developed the 'feel' for this art provide us with a functional beauty that endures."

Penny Davis-Shaffer is a writer, a lover of music, and mother of two, who enjoys cooking and entertaining friends. She recently graduated with an Associates Degree in Marketing/Mid-Management and currently resides in Galesburg, Illinois, where she was born and raised.

She was a contributing editor, doing rewrites on biographies of George Balabushka, Harold Morey, Joe Marchant, John "Jack" Madden, Jim Olms, Reiper Manufacturing, Isadore Rutzisky, and The Mace, along with being a driving force and friend behind the author, Brad Simpson

GENERAL INFORMATION

While many of you have probably dealt with our company for years, it may be helpful for you to know a little bit more about our operation, including information on how to contact us regarding our various titles, software programs, and other informational services.

Blue Book Publications, Inc.
8009 34th Avenue South, Suite 175
Minneapolis, MN 55425 USA
Phone: 952-854-5229 • Orders Only (domestic and Canada): 800-877-4867
Fax: 952-853-1486 (available 24 hours a day)
Website: http://www.bluebookinc.com
Email: bluebook@bluebookinc.com. Please refer to individual email addresses listed below with phone extension numbers.

To find out the latest information on our products (including availability and pricing) and related consumer services, and up-to-date industry information (trade show recaps with photos/captions, upcoming events, feature articles, etc.), please check our website, as it is updated on a regular basis. Surf us – you'll have fun!

Since our phone system is equipped with voicemail, you may also wish to know extension numbers, which have been provided below:

Ext. 10 - Beth Marthaler (bethm@bluebookinc.com)	Ext. 16 - John Allen (johna@bluebookinc.com)
Ext. 11 - Katie Sandin (katies@bluebookinc.com)	Ext. 17 - Zach Fjestad (zachf@bluebookinc.com)
Ext. 12 - John Andraschko (johnand@bluebookinc.com)	Ext. 18 - Tom Stock (toms@bluebookinc.com)
Ext. 13 - S.P. Fjestad (stevef@bluebookinc.com)	Ext. 19 - Cassandra Faulkner (cassandraf@bluebookinc.com)
Ext. 15 - Clint Schmidt (clints@bluebookinc.com)	Ext. 22 - Stacy Knutson (stacyk@bluebookinc.com)

Additionally, an automated after-hours message service is available for ordering. All orders are processed within one business day of receiving them, assuming payment and order information is correct. Depending on the product, we typically ship either UPS, Media Mail, or Priority Mail. Expedited shipping services are also available domestically for an additional charge. Please contact us directly for an expedited shipping quotation.

Online subscriptions and individual downloading services for the *Blue Book of Gun Values*, *Blue Book of Modern Black Powder Arms*, *Blue Book of Airguns*, *Blue Book of Electric Guitars*, *Blue Book of Acoustic Guitars*, and the *Blue Book of Guitar Amplifiers* are also available.

As this edition goes to press, the following titles/products are currently available, unless otherwise specified:

Blue Book of Gun Values, 26th Edition by S.P. Fjestad (ISBN 1-886768-55-2 1,934 pages)
Parker Gun Identification & Serialization, compiled by Charlie Price and edited by S.P. Fjestad (ISBN 1-886768-37-4)
4th Edition Blue Book of Modern Black Powder Arms by John Allen & Dennis Adler *(ISBN: 1-886768-46-3)*
5th Edition Blue Book of Airguns by Dr. Robert Beeman & John Allen (ISBN 1-886768-56-0)
Blue Book 3-Pack CD-ROM (includes the contents of the 26th Edition *Blue Book of Gun Values*, 4th Edition *Blue Book of Modern Black Powder Arms* and 5th Edition *Blue Book of Airguns*)
The Nethercutt Collection - The Cars of San Sylmar by Dennis Adler (ISBN: 1-886768-53-6)
Blue Book of Electric Guitars, 9th Edition, by Zach Fjestad, edited by S.P. Fjestad (ISBN 1-886768-57-9)
Blue Book of Acoustic Guitars, 9th Edition, by Zach Fjestad, edited by S.P. Fjestad (ISBN 1-886768-58-7)
Blue Book of Guitar Amplifiers, 2nd Edition, by Zach Fjestad, edited by S.P. Fjestad (ISBN 1-886768-42-0)
Blue Book of Guitars CD-ROM
Blue Book of Guitar Amplifiers CD-ROM

If you would like to get more information about any of the above publications/products, simply check our website: www.bluebookinc.com.

We would like to thank all of you for your business in the past – you are the reason we are successful. Our goal remains the same – to give you the best products, the most accurate and up-to-date information for the money, and the highest level of customer service available in today's marketplace. If something's right, tell the world over time. If something's wrong, please tell us immediately – we'll make it right.

MEET THE STAFF

Many of you may be familiar with our names and/or have spoken with us on the phone, but don't know what we look like. Our pictures are presented here so you can match our faces with our names.

S.P. Fjestad – Publisher/Author of *Blue Book of Gun Values*.

Tom Stock – CFO

John B. Allen – Author & Associate Editor Arms Division

Cassandra Faulkner – Executive Assistant Editor

John Andraschko – Technology Director

Beth Marthaler – Operations Manager

Katie Sandin – Operations

Stacy Knutson – Proofreader/Operations

Clint Schmidt – Art Director

Zachary R. Fjestad – Author/Editor Guitar & Amp Division

Bitey – Floor/wall/tight spaces Division Manager (unseen by most employees)

PUBLISHER'S OVERVIEW

Author & Publisher S.P. Fjestad, shown with one millionth copy of the *Blue Book of Gun Values*.

As a publishing company, Blue Book Publications, Inc. has published scores of books on firearms, guitars, airguns, cars, and pool cues. Every book/edition has its own story and unique DNA once the project is off the press. Most go really well, even though they never go exactly the way you think or plan for. This one did not start well, but did manage to pull out of its tailspin at the end. Work on this third edition began in earnest during Christmas 2003. Brad Simpson decided a co-author would be needed on this newest edition, since he was spending much of his time in Asia working on other projects. Unfortunately, all the original deadlines for spring and summer 2004 were missed, and we were unable to make the first of many scheduled publishing release dates.

It became evident to both Brad and myself that if this book was ever going to be published, he'd have to take over manuscript responsibilities (including contacting all the existing manufacturers) as well as image selection, and finish this large project on his own. To his credit, Brad took over a difficult situation, and with the help of his mom, Carol Simpson, both of them soldiered through the grim publishing battlefield, and were not only able to survive, but actually managed to rally their resources and complete this project on time.

So what's new in this third edition? Almost everything. Maybe the most noticeable difference is the size! It's now 912 pages, over 50% more pages than the second edition, and is physically almost twice as big. In addition, the paper stock has been changed to a matte enamel to give you better resolution for the hundreds of enhanced black and white images. A completely new 64-page Cue Gallery color section featuring some of the world's finest cues has also been included. But the most important and significant improvement is easily the additional amount of cuemakers, number of individual cues and their images, and up-to-date values on both new and vintage collectible cues. Without question, the Trademark Index is the most comprehensive listing of cue manufacturers and trademarks with contact information ever published.

Don't miss the editorial on scuffers and accessories provided by veteran billiard journalist Thomas C. Shaw. Deno Andrews has written a comprehensive article on the collecting of pool cues, and James Yonge has provided an interesting article on the creation of the "Hustler" cue. With the help of Paul Newman, his wife Joanne Woodward and a host of talented people, this unique cue was sold at auction to benefit the Hole-In-the-Wall Gang camps, which provide free summer camps for children stricken with cancer.

Special thanks go out to Carol Simpson, for without her help you probably wouldn't have this book in your hands. An author herself, with great typing and computer skills, only Carol will be able to tell us how many hours she has logged on this project. Even when in Asia, Carol and Brad kept the production going and at the end, not only did they meet the publisher's deadlines, but they were also able to vastly improve the amount of information in this new third edition.

Also, Brad's main contributing editors, Gian Calise, Deno Andrews, and Penny Davis-Shaffer, deserve a round of applause for helping Brad track down and provide information on many additional cuemakers and their cues. Even though some of these makers may only manufacture 10 or so cues a year, at least you'll have the information needed to make the right decisions when buying, selling, or trading their cues.

Thank you for your patience on this project. It was the longest, hardest road I've ever been on while pursuing the collectible information necessary to publish a credible book. We appreciate the support you've given us in the past. As in any other hobby/sport, get educated first, know what to look for (and how much to spend on it), and above all else, have some fun and rack 'em up on a regular basis.

Sincerely,

S.P. Fjestad
Publisher
Blue Book of Pool Cues

PS - Don't forget that this book is also available on CD-ROM, by individual download, or by online subscription. Good information never sleeps!

FOREWORD

Brad Simpson, author of the *Blue Book of Pool Cues*.

When I started on the First Edition *Blue Book of Pool Cues* over ten years ago I tried to put together the best team possible for the project. Victor Stein and Paul Rubino had written and published the *Billiard Encyclopedia*, the best book ever written on the subject of billiards, and I was lucky enough to recruit them as editors and contributors for the *Blue Book of Pool Cues*. Paul Goodwin was the best firearms photographer in the world, and he brought a photography talent that the pool cue industry had never seen. This team helped me produce two editions in less than four years.

When the publisher asked me to start a third edition in 2003, I declined. I was unable to put the original team back together, and I was busy with other projects in both the United States and Thailand. I agreed to help find someone to take over the project, and started making inquiries within the billiards industry. Not long after, a new potential co-author flew to Thailand to convince me that they were the right person to revise the Third Edition. The credentials seemed more than adequate, so I helped put together the agreement and turned over my Second Edition manuscript for revisions. This was a great opportunity for a new author to take over the future course of this project, but it was an opportunity wasted. After three missed deadlines, and no revised manuscript, I chose to take over the project rather than let it die.

I returned from Thailand to collect what I could from the Third Edition project. There were hundreds of pictures with no captions, a box full of raw submitted data that had never been entered, and a manuscript that was about 15% revised, at best. On top of this, the information was already a year old and it would take almost another year to be ready for publication. It would have been easier just to start from scratch, but most of the resources and budget had already been used. And the cue industry had worked hard to provide what was there.

My mother, Carol, who has written four books and had just retired from 33 years of teaching, volunteered to help. She came with me to retrieve the original material. She organized the material from the box we brought home, and entered all of that data. She entered data at Valley Forge, sent most of the emails, and entered most of the data that came back. She also organized the indexes, the Cue Gallery, and edited everything before it was submitted to the publisher. Deno Andrews called soon after I took over the project to see how I liked the article he had written and submitted. I hadn't even received it. He resent the article to me and then offered to revise the data from many of the cuemakers in the Chicago area, which he did. Gian Calise also offered to help in any way that he could. He improved many of the revisions that had been made to the manuscript I received, and he also interviewed Ernie Gutierrez for a new Ginacue biography. My friend Penny Davis-Shaffer rewrote other revised material that was not up to our standards.

I personally called every cuemaker in the Trademark Index, revised what I could over the phone, wrote most of the cue descriptions, and entered almost all of the prices. Then the prices were edited by cue experts including Dick Abbott, Deno Andrews, Gian Calise, Bill Grassley, and Mark Kulungian. We have all tried to make this book as accurate as possible.

I was lucky to have the support behind me that I did. The pool cue industry wanted this book to happen, so they threw their support behind me. A new team created the momentum that led to the completion of this project. And the contributions of the previous team can still be seen.

As I write this, the revised "A to Z" text has been submitted, the Cue Gallery has been submitted, articles by Deno Andrews, Jim Yonge, and Tom Shaw are complete and most of the rest of the book is ready to print. I haven't been back to Thailand for months - this is the longest time I have spent in America in years. Now I am sitting in the upper deck of a 747 somewhere over Siberia, writing on a laptop. I'll be back in Bangkok in a matter of hours. All is good. ■

PCIII OVERVIEW

I recall the day when my son, Brad Simpson, author of the *Blue Book of Pool Cues*, First and Second Editions, told me that he was going to have to complete the Third Edition by himself due to some unfortunate circumstances related to a guest co-authorship agreement that went awry. I immediately said, "I'll help!" As the author of four of my own books on a completely unrelated subject, as well as numerous published travel articles, I thought, "Why not!" My past experiences with writing and publishing surely would be good preparation for the task ahead. Wrong! They say hindsight is 20/20, and had I known then what I know now, I might not have said "yes" so quickly. My books and travel articles were totally reliant upon me for information. No one else contributed a single page or thought. The *Blue Book of Pool Cues*, on the other hand, depended upon over three hundred cuemakers and billiard industry professionals for information. I had to get used to asking many people to meet deadlines and submit information and photos in a timely fashion. Most were ready, willing, and able to comply. In the end, very few were told that they were too late. But the good news is, the book is finally being published, and I learned so much from the experience!

Brad and I made a trip to California to gather materials and begin trying to put the many pieces of the unwritten manuscript together. I pride myself on being organized, so the task of going through someone else's papers, CDs, notes, etc. should have been pretty easy, or so I thought. I found that things were not as ready to be organized as I had hoped. There were piles of papers waiting to be alphabetized and many cue, cue logo, cue ID and cuemaker images that had to be cataloged. Much of the information was on CD-ROMs and had to be printed and coordinated. Some information was very sketchy at best. There were multiple copies of some cuemaker files. From the end of 2004 through mid-September of 2005, my family room looked as though it has been hit by a hurricane. Thank goodness I am married to a very patient man, my husband of 40 years, and Brad's father, Robert Simpson. I think he was just as anxious as me to see this project finally completed.

When Brad and I could see the amount of work that had, and had not, been done for the Third Edition, we first needed to come up with a system to get in touch with each of the over three hundred cuemakers who would be included in the new book. Thank goodness for the Internet and email! It became my task to contact as many folks as possible using my computer. If you browse through the Cuemaker Index, you will note that there are a large number of listings with websites and email addresses, and most of them actually read their email fairly regularly. The Internet was really a great tool for this huge information-gathering project. I contacted everyone with email at least two to three times, and sometimes more than that. Most of the cuemakers who answered my requests for updated information were excited to see that the book was back on track for publication, after a false start a couple of years ago.

I traveled with Brad to the Allen Hopkins show in Valley Forge, Pennsylvania in March of 2005 and was very excited to meet many of the people in the billiard industry face to face. I knew many of the names, and could finally put a face with them. With laptop in hand, Brad and I gathered information as we interviewed many of the cuemakers in attendance, and updated their biographies and cue specifications in person. Brad did the talking, and I did the typing. We were pleasantly surprised that nearly everyone there was happy that we had picked up the project and were going to see to it that the Third Edition would be completed in a timely fashion. Most were very helpful, and we appreciated that they were so understanding of the situation and the circumstances that had brought us to this point. And most of them could see my drive and determination to keep this project moving along steadily, to its fruition.

Fast forward to the end of July of 2005, and a meeting with the publisher. By this time, every cuemaker with an email address had finally been contacted via email at least twice, with many that were contacted a half dozen times or more, and information was pouring in from all around the United States, Canada, Europe and Asia. Brad was busy telephoning everyone to make sure everything was as up to date as possible. He was also writing descriptions for hundreds of new cues that would be pictured in the new book. Finally, we could see the light at the end of the tunnel! The A to Z sections were ready to be submitted to the publisher, along with cuemaker photos, logos, and cue IDs. Every letter was finalized by the end of August or first few days of September. The publisher began sending back completed sections for final edit. There would be front materials to gather and indexes to check for the most up-to-date contact information we had at our disposal. With any luck, the entire project would be finished on time.

Senior Contributing Editor, Carol Simpson

I really felt like the book was finally coming together when, one evening in mid-September, Brad and I, along with Penny Davis-Shaffer, met at Billiards on Main, a new upscale pool hall in Galesburg, Illinois, where Brad and his father like to shoot 9-ball and sometimes play in weekly tournaments. A friend and photographer, Tom Foley of Foley Studio, Galesburg, came to the hall and did a photo shoot with the perfect backdrop for a book about pool cues.

By the last half of the month of September of 2005, it was time for me, Carol Simpson the traveler, writer, retired elementary teacher, wife and mother, and small business owner, to get back to life as usual. The hectic life of gathering information from over three hundred cuemakers and getting a manuscript ready for publication was finally accomplished. Now there would be time for my favorite pastime, traveling. As someone who has been to Europe at least fifteen times, Australia and islands in the South Pacific six times, Thailand eight times, plus trips to Rio de Janeiro, Mexico, Canada, multiple cruises, not to mention all fifty states in the USA, it was challenging to stay home for such a long period of time! My bags are packed, my ticket is in hand, and I'm ready to see the world once again.

Nothing would please me more than to have you, the reader, say that this book is a job well done. We know that there are probably errors and omissions, but please know that we did our best to gather the most complete and up-to-date information we possibly could, so that this book could finally be published. Enjoy reading this Third Edition of the *Blue Book of Pool Cues*!

HOW TO USE THIS BOOK

Also see "Tracking Your Cue Through the Book" on page 13.

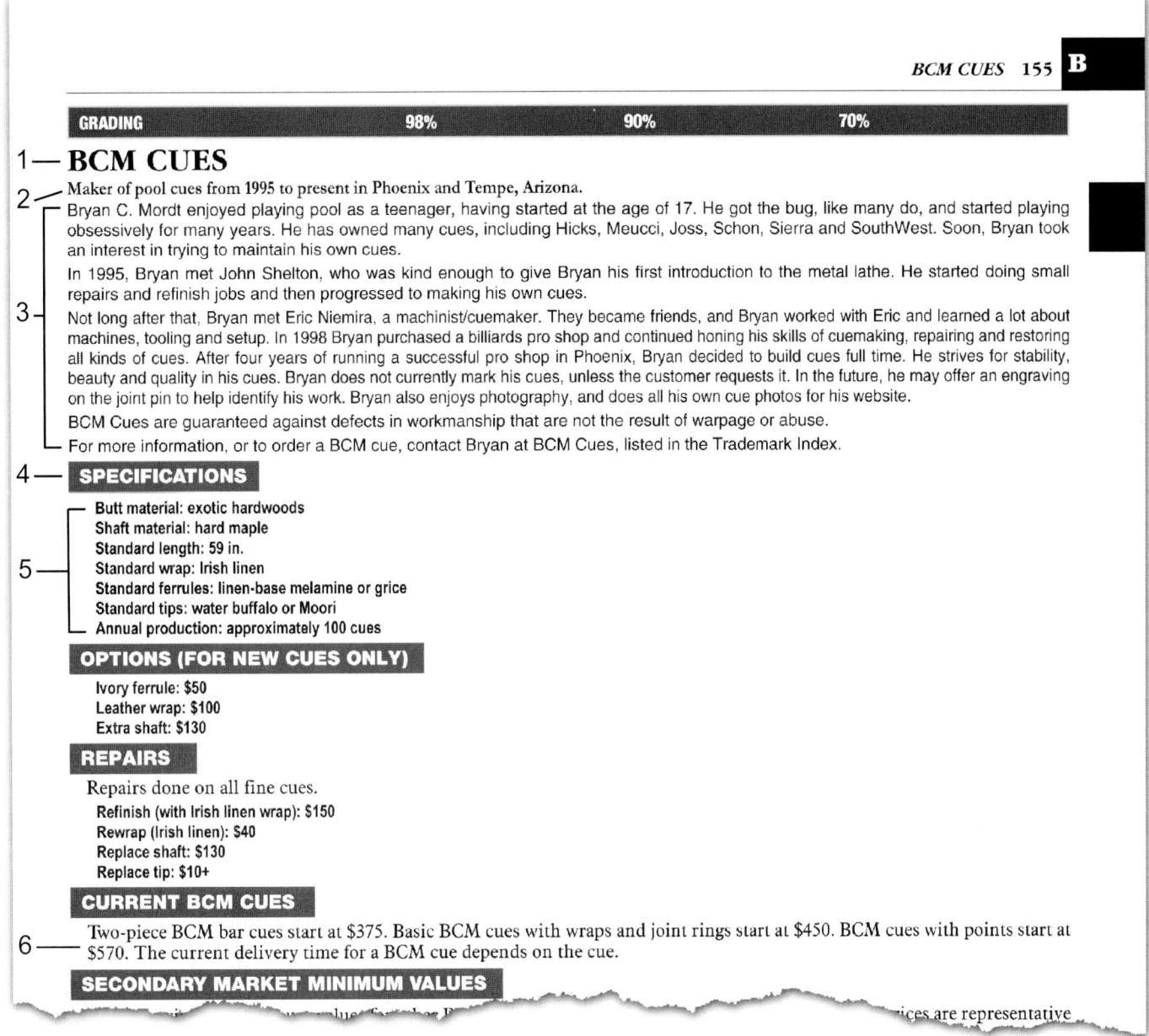

1. **Maker name.** The maker names are listed alphabetically throughout the book. The first step in locating your cue is to identify the maker and then look up the corresponding entry for that maker.
2. **Dates/locations.** This line states the time period in which the maker created cues and also the location(s) where they made the cues. Any available distribution information will also be listed here.
3. **History.** This section will have one or more paragraphs describing the maker's history and background, and any other relevant information. This section may also include information on any guarantees that come with the maker's cues, and will tell you to refer to the Trademark Index for contact information.
4. **Category heading.** Category headings, such as "Specifications," "Options," "Repairs," and "Current Cues," are in grey boxes with white text. "Specifications" describes the standard specifications on cues by that maker, as well as how many cues the maker produces each year. "Options" lists other options, with pricing, that are available from that maker, and "Repairs" specifies what types of repairs the maker does (including pricing), if any. "Current Cues" and similar headings describe the cues that are available from the maker, and may include specific examples along with images and pricing (see next page).
5. **List.** This type of font indicates a list of some sort, generally of specifications, repairs, or price modifications.
6. **Supporting text.** The text under the category heading gives more specific information about the category and/or the cues by that particular maker.

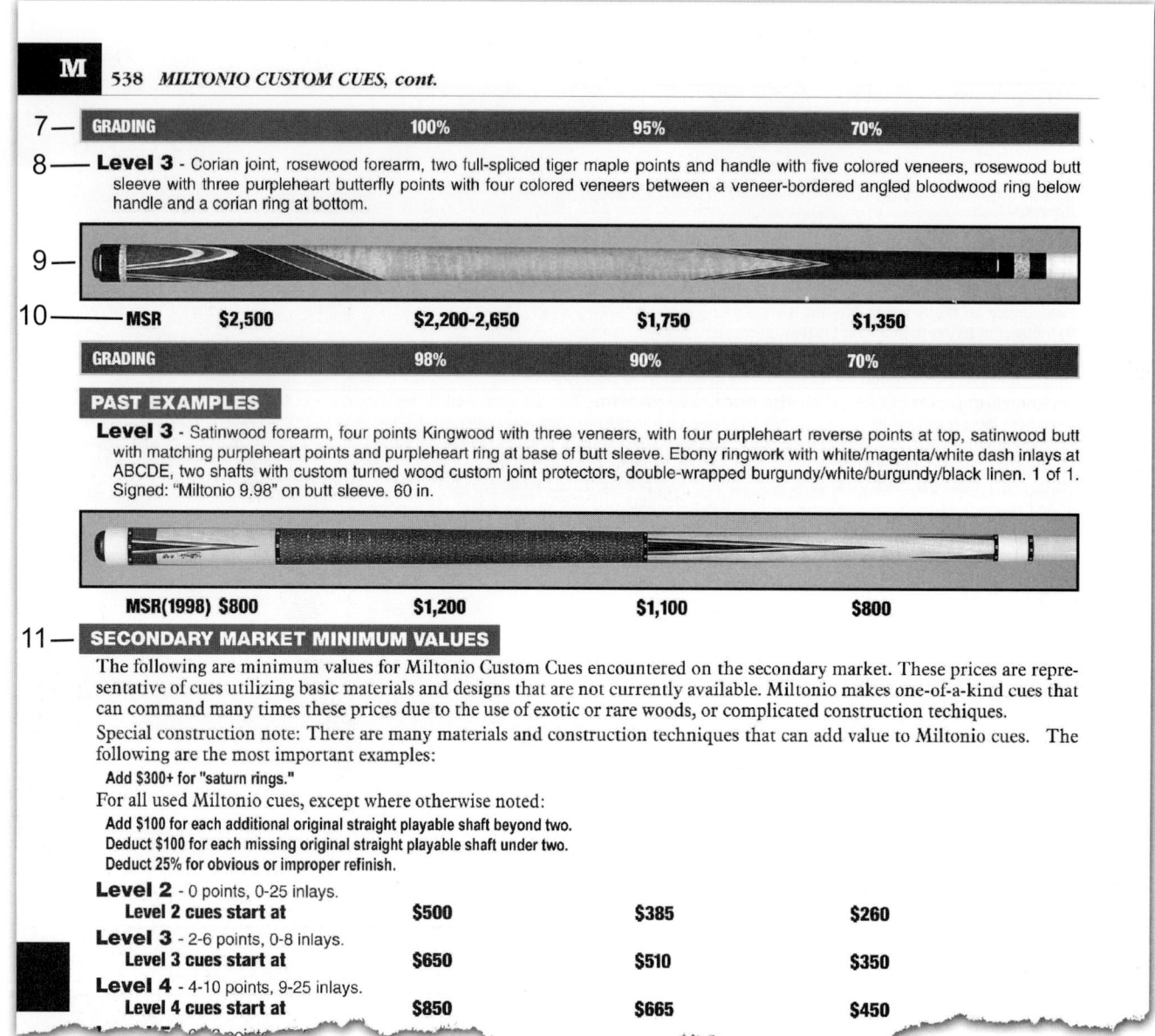

7. **Grading bar.** This bar will be one of two types: 100%-95%-70% or 98%-90%-70%. The first type is for current cues, while the second type is for used, vintage, and secondary market cues. Both work in the same way. For a current, brand new, perfect condition cue, check the price from the 100% column. Or, for a vintage cue in approximately 90% of its original condition, check the price in the corresponding column.
8. **Cue name and description.** These entries, along with the images and pricing, make up the bulk of the book. The first part of the entry specifies the model name, or the level of the cue if no model name is available. Immediately following the model name is a detailed description of the cue. You will need to look under the appropriate category name and then search for your cue name in order to get the information and pricing you are looking for.
9. **Image.** An image of the cue is provided if one is available.
10. **MSR and pricing.** Underneath the image (if any) is the MSR (manufacturer suggested retail) of the cue as well as its value in various conditions.
11. **Secondary Market Minimum Values.** This category gives the minimum retail values that collectors can expect for cues with the minimum specifications shown (see "Levels of Intricacy" and "How to Use the Level of Intricacy Grading" on pages 30 and 31 for more information).

TRACKING YOUR CUE THROUGH THE BOOK

I chose an older Joss West cue by Bill Stroud as an example to evaluate using the Level of Intricacy Grading System. This cue is in about 95% original condition with two original shafts. It's a beautiful cue that plays great.

First look up the listing for Joss West. You can see in his listing the different types of identification markings, and when they were used. This cue has the earliest type of marking, a "JW" with the "W" being sideways. That means it was made between 1972 and 1980. The earliest Joss West cues had spliced points, but close inspection shows this cue has inlaid points. Although the cue has mitered veneers, the tips of the points are rounded. That narrows down the time it was made even more, as Bill started experimenting with inlaid points in about 1980. The cue was probably made right around 1980, when Bill was in Colorado Springs, Colorado.

Since this exact cue is not pictured in the book, we go straight to the Level of Intricacy Grading System. Counting the 28 inlays in this cue determines that it fits into the Level 5 category, with 98% examples of second-hand Joss West cues starting at $2,400. It falls closer to base Level 5 than to base Level 6, which requires over 50 inlays, and 98% examples start at $3,500. The fact that the four largest inlays are ivory windows adds about 10%, and add $175 for an original leather wrap. Deduct a little for the condition being a little less than 98% and you are in the $2,750 range. I think that is a fair value for the cue.

This cue is fairly easy to evaluate using the Level of Intricacy Grading System because it is a fairly traditional design with fairly simple inlay work. Looking at actual examples in the A to Z listings in this book will show how materials and designs affect values relative to basic starting points in the Level of Intricacy price lines. Remember, those prices are for the least valuable cues that can be encountered within those parameters.

Level 5 Joss West cues can be worth five figures, with the right materials and designs. Many one-of-a-kind custom cues can be worth far more than the starting prices based on the Level of Intricacy. The more exotic the cue, the harder it is to evaluate. As cues enter the art market, the more the price is determined by the emotions of the buyer and seller, with recent prices reaching six figures.

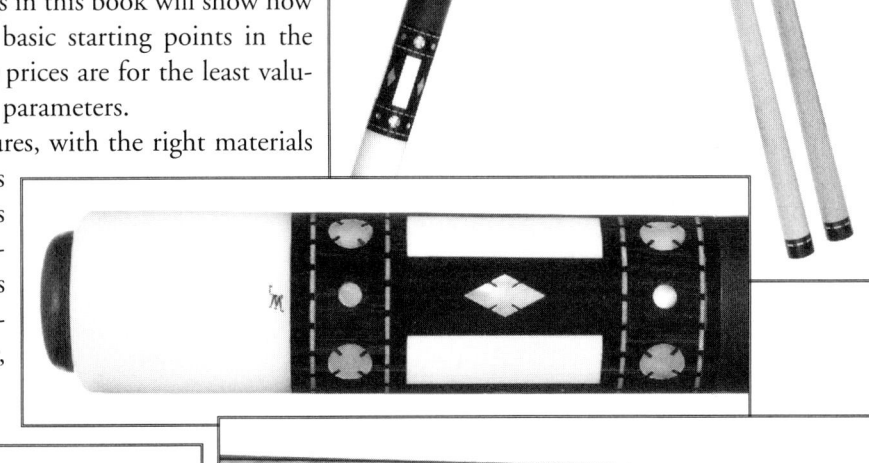

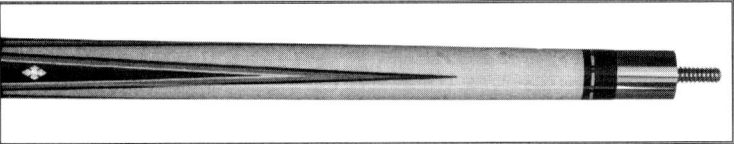

ADDITIONAL CONSIDERATIONS

Although there are hundreds of pages of specific cue models and pricing, this book is not a simple "hold-your-hand" pricing guide. In theory, for cues that are not pictured, you should be able to identify the trademark name or signature off the butt cap or forearm of the cue (where applicable), and also be able to figure out the level of intricacy and the cue's condition. This will lead you to a price that represents the least amount the cue could be worth, based on these three factors.

All values in this text assume original condition. If your cue has been repaired or altered in any way, this could reduce its value by 20-50% or more, depending on the severity of the repair or alteration. Please take this into consideration when pricing your cue. If you own a current *Blue Book of Pool Cues* and you still have questions, please refer to page 26.

Conditions below 70% may be encountered, but are obviously much less desirable, and are therefore not specifically addressed. Additionally, vintage cues in greater than 98% condition are so rare that these are not specifically addressed either. Cues in the 100% condition category are assumed to have not been previously sold at retail and to have a factory warranty.

Collecting Pool Cues

by Deno Andrews

People collect billiard cues for various reasons, which are as diverse as cue collectors themselves. Regardless of the reason for building a collection, one thought almost all collectors share is that we want our collections to grow bigger and better. This chapter explores the art of collection building by analyzing the methods and philosophies of some of the world's foremost cue collectors. A number of reliable collection-building maxims, or fundamental principles, are the result of this study. Incorporating these principles may certainly help you start a great cue collection, or take your existing collection to the next level. For the purpose of this article, consider the difference between having a collection and being a collector. Having a small number of random cue sticks can certainly by definition be considered a collection, although the owner of such a collection may not consider him- or herself a collector.

COLLECT THAT WHICH YOU LIKE

I think of collectors as people who put great thought or passion into defining collection criteria to help focus their collections. That is not to say that those criteria need to be very definitive, as they are established by the collectors themselves. Establishing criteria for your collection is an art in itself. As your tastes or interests change, so will your cue collecting criteria. Some collectors narrow their criteria while others may be more diverse in their acquisitions. For example, one criterion for my collection limits my acquisitions of Herman Rambow cues to those produced before 1960 that are in original condition with the exception of tips and ferrules (meaning not restored or refinished). In contrast, a friend and fellow collector, Jon Spiegel, who is the United States Manager for Granito Cloth, will collect virtually any out-of-the-ordinary cue, regardless of originality, as long as it has a solid and good-feeling hit. Mark and Connie Stellinga, the country's premier collecting duo with regard to billiard-related antiquities, focus a large part of their cue collection on primarily "pre-1910 American cues and always hope for pre-1890 examples, particularly the more ornate and rare examples." Each collector's criteria are valid and simply help define which cues best fit into their collection. Defining criteria for your collection, no matter how wide or narrow, will help you to accomplish one thing—collecting cues you like. Collecting what you like is a maxim that spans all areas of collecting, from pool cues to Persian rugs. For many collectors, it is the basis for making a decision to add another cue to their collection.

INVEST IN QUALITY

Whenever I give the advice to buy what you like, the inevitable retort is "But I like a lot of stuff." At this point just about any collector must make a decision about the direction of their collecting. You must decide between owning a great number of cues, or a number of great cues. At one point, collectors Michael and Teri McDermott had a large number of production-quality cues. Michael admits that he "bought 'production' cues not realizing the difference between a custom and production cue." However, Michael had played with a Tad cue that appealed to him. Later, the owner of that Tad cue offered to sell it to him for $950, but Michael did not have the

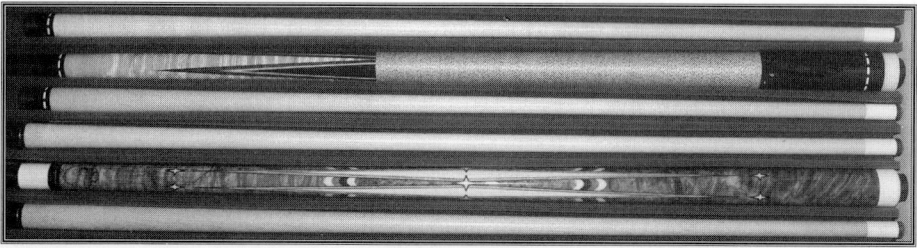

Certain collectors focus on more contemporary works while others favor classic cue stock designs. Collect that which you like.

money to purchase the cue. Michael recalls, "I was unable to buy the cue and I started selling all my cues for cash. From that point on I only would buy a custom cue with value to me, not just buy cues to buy." All of Michael's funds were tied up in cues that he had little regard for when balanced against his love of that Tad cue. Michael learned the hard way, as we all have at some point in building our collections that "ten $100 cues were worth a lot less than a single $1000 custom cue. Quality not quantity." Michael and Teri's experience illustrates how important it is to invest in quality. Whether you collect for investment or aesthetics, or even playability, quality cue sticks will outperform in virtually every category. Quality cue sticks will appreciate in value, will be more visually pleasing, and in most cases will outperform production-quality cues.

As the areas of quality, condition, and value are covered at length in other parts of this publication, I will limit my thoughts on this subject. If you ask ten cue collectors the meaning of quality, you will hear ten different answers. Some collectors consider quality to be in the craftsmanship and hit of the cue, while others put an emphasis on the aesthetic quality of the cue. I asked Ron Sakahara, an architect and astute cue collector, what advice he would give to people building their collections. He responded by writing "Be aware of the 'original conditions' of a classic older collectible cue. It is very tempting to many novice collectors to go out and have a classic cue refinished and lower its value." I would urge anyone who owns a collectible cue to think twice before having any work done to it, as you cannot replace that originality which is lost when work is done to a cue. There are other valid points of view regarding this issue that advocate restoration work on older collectibles. Mark Stellinga believes that "Professional restoration of a good [to great] original condition collectible or antique cue may detract value for the 'original condition enthusiast,' but it will greatly enhance the value to collectors who admire cues for their sheer beauty." So when faced with the decision to either purchase a restored cue, or to have restoration work done to a cue you own, please consider what you value about the cue and take great care in making your decision. Making a decision that may negatively affect your collection is contrary to the point of this article. Remember that while value is constantly fluctuating, originality can only diminish when work is done to cues. Other serious collectors are your best measure when faced with the decision to have work done to a collectible cue.

WORK FROM A PLAN AND BUY DIRECT FROM THE SOURCE WHENEVER POSSIBLE

Whatever your definition of quality is, those cues typically have large price tags attached to them. There are hundreds cuemakers in the United States making nice cues, but only a fraction of them are producing collectible-quality cues. Like the price of any product, the market price of a cue reacts to the economic laws of supply and demand. Cuemakers producing the highest quality cues are doing so in very limited numbers, as many of them work alone. Furthermore, these quality products attract the most serious buyers, creating a more than adequate demand. Joel Hercek, a master cuemaker outside of Chicago, is producing such high quality full-splice cues that his six-year waiting list is more than worth the wait for one of his traditional masterpieces. Several other cuemakers are backlogged for years as well, which makes their pre-existing works sought after on the secondary market. Combine quality work and waiting lists for what is already a very limited output and you have the perfect formula for high-priced cues that rapidly appreciate in value. With the exception of a few people, most collectors do not have the means to instantly acquire large cue collections. Serious collections are typically built over a number of years because of economic consider-

...quality cue sticks will outperform in virtually every category...

Get on the waiting lists of cue makers who are in high demand as their work typically appreciates in value immediately upon delivery.

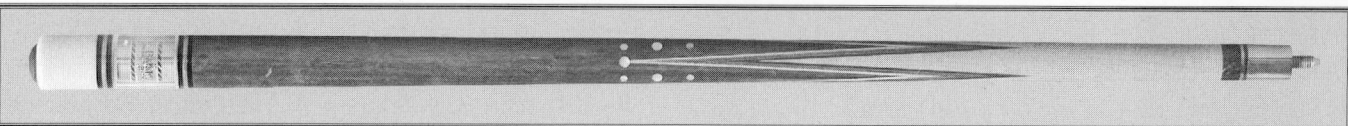

Rare full splice, no wrap, Palmer cue which belonged to American artist Robert Kipniss.

ations and a limited pool of collectible-quality cues on the market from which to choose. This is where the disciplined and long-term thinking collector has an advantage over the remainder of the cue-buying public.

I believe that to be successful at building a collection rather than simply maintaining an existing one, a collector would do well to have a multi-year plan. First, decide on approximately how much money annually you can dedicate to building your collection. If you want to purchase cues from contemporary cuemakers, it is best to order them directly from the source. Once you make a list of the cuemakers' work you would like to collect, contact each cuemaker and learn how their waiting lists work. You will soon discover that one cuemaker will have a one-year back log; another will have a two-year wait, another with a three-year wait, and so on. You can get on these lists for little or no deposit money. This strategy virtually guarantees you one or two quality collectible cues annually directly from the source (no middleman costs), and those cues can be truly customized to your specifications. Also, there will never be any question as to the authenticity or provenance of the cues. Finally, getting to know the cuemakers personally and having that story of collaboration with the artist makes collectible cues even more valuable for you. You need not use your entire annual budget on this strategy, as you will always want to have funds available for that potential opportunity that awaits us all at the billiard room, trade show, or tournament. But planning your collection over several years will allow you, within ten years' time, to build a collection that would land you in the top one percent of cue collectors without taking out a second mortgage on your house.

Great cues can always be found...

ENJOY THE HUNT

Purchasing cues from the source is not always possible because a large number of collectible cues were made by cuemakers who are no longer working or who are deceased. Finding cues in this category can be difficult, again because of supply and demand. I interviewed Will Prout about collecting in general and asked how he built his vast collection of cues. Before reporting his answer, you need to know something about Will. By my estimation, he is the epitome of the collector mentality. His collections go way beyond cue sticks and range from antique cars to pachinko machines. Will's response to my question was that he "found the 'hunt' to be as much fun as the purchase, and personally rewarding to add each cue to the collection one at a time...." He went on to say "Great cues can always be found, but sometimes the price of the cue may not be in line with your view of the value, and it may take several cue finds before you make the leap for a purchase." There are a number of ways older cues can be found. One of the quickest methods to acquire an older collectible cue is to purchase it from a dealer. However, only a handful of dealers in the United States stock a number of older collectibles, so expect to pay a premium for their services. Most of my Rambow collection was acquired over a 10-year period of purchasing cues from older billiard players around the country at three-cushion billiard tournaments. Older players who purchased cues from the original cuemakers continue to be a great source for cues. So many of the older collectible cues were purchased for less than $100, and older players notoriously played with a single cue their whole lives. When selling their

These two CAM cues show the work of young cuemaker Chad McLennon.

cues, older players would typically sell to a collector rather than a dealer. Collectors will pay more money for their cues and the player will know that the next owner will appreciate the cue's quality. Antique stores can also be a great potential source for cue sticks. I recently purchased a 19th-century English billiard cue with a matched tubular metal case from a Chicago antique store for $125. At that price, this cue and case were perfect for trading up for something that fits my collection criteria. Mark Stellinga informed me that a large number of their collectible cues were included in antique table purchases. Discovering a true collectible outside of the normal venues makes acquiring the cue even more rewarding especially if you can buy the cue far below the market value.

NETWORK

Finally, I suggest getting to know cuemakers and other collectors throughout the country. A misconception about collecting is that collectors are in competition with each other. While there are exceptions, nothing is further from the truth. Most collectors have specific tastes and strict criteria, so what appeals to one collector may not appeal to the next. Knowing other collectors can prove to be a great source for cues that fit into your collection, especially if they know you and your collecting criteria. One great way to meet other collectors would be to attend an event like the International Cue Collector's Show. Collectors and cuemakers alike exhibit their cues, and Mr. Prout "encourage[s] anyone contemplating growing their collection to come to the show. Speaking with others that have collections can provide great networking and sources for growing your cue collection, and provide a great way to get ideas on what to collect and how to collect, as well as storing and display of cues." In addition, it is not a bad idea to get to know some of the dealers. It is in your best interest to supply reputable dealers with a list of your criteria and your budget so that you may get an opportunity at a piece before it "goes public." Being open to others about what you are in the market for will typically yield much better results than silently searching the marketplace. Cue collecting is no different than any other business; networking creates opportunity.

In conclusion, consider how these maxims can help you build your collection. Buying cues that you like helps keep your collection focused on your tastes rather than collecting what the public may consider valuable. Investing in quality will be the difference between cues that will appreciate over time and those that will not. Having a plan and buying from the source whenever possible allows you to spread out your quality acquisitions over time and within a reasonable budget, all the while building a world-class collection. Enjoy the hunt, and remember to network with other collectors, dealers, and players.

Great collections are typically not built in a short period of time. Most of today's serious collectors have built their collections slowly and cautiously, sometimes spanning a good part of their lives. Whether you collect for sheer enjoyment or as an investment, it is my hope that some or all of the principals herein will help you in your journey to build a bigger and better cue stick collection. ∎

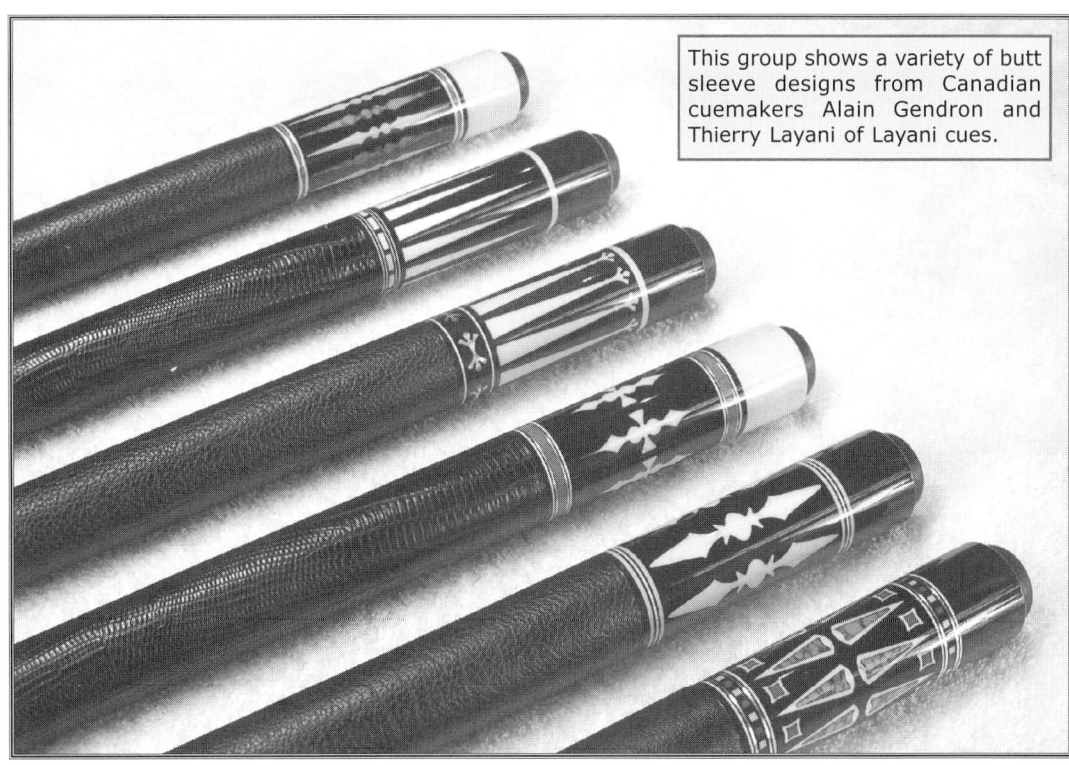

This group shows a variety of butt sleeve designs from Canadian cuemakers Alain Gendron and Thierry Layani of Layani cues.

Scuffers and Cue Accessories

Tom Shaw

Dealers, museums, collectors and cuemakers will all advise you not to alter a collectible cue. No cleaning, sanding (ouch!), or polishing - they can all make the cue drop in value. At the very most, and even this is debatable, a collectible cue can be sent back to the artist for cleaning about once every century or so.

But even collectors usually have one or two prize cues that they actually use and some precautions are in order.

A cue glove (Fig. 1) helps many players generate a smoother stroke, but it also keeps body oils from transferring to the shaft, which is bare wood and very vulnerable to moisture and dirt. Using a piece of smooth leather to burnish the shaft is a good idea. Burnishing temporarily seals the cells, or pores, that were cut open during the wood turning process when the shaft was created. Open wood cells are oil and dust traps.

Washing your hands before picking up a cue, collectible or not, is something all players should do. Chalk dust accumulates in pool cloth, and hand washing - and thorough drying - every hour or so is a good habit to acquire.

Most serious players will tell you that the most important part of a cue is the tip, so it's not surprising that most of the attention of accessory makers has focused on that item.

The cue tip, the "business" part of the cue, has a domed top usually slightly pre-scuffed straight out of the box. Domed tops have been standard for a bit over one hundred years from the original French tips imported in the late 1800s, and with tips manufactured by Cue Tipper and Tweeten Fibre Company in the early 1900s.

Hit enough balls and the tip forms a smooth, hard, and slightly flattened surface. It then won't hold chalk well, becomes less effective when you want to apply cue ball spin, and can lead to miscues.

METAL FILES & SANDPAPER

During the nineteenth century and more than half of the twentieth century the solution to a smooth or flat tip was to use a simple metal file or coarse sandpaper. Metal files, usually cross-cut but sometimes single-cut, were carried by players in their cue cases or back pockets. In New York City the file was usually a half-round, but elsewhere a flat file was favored. Room owners kept one behind the counter but were reluctant to let anyone use it on their house cues. Most big city rooms had a well-known "tip man" who was said to wield a file with uncommon skill.

Sometime in the 1940s (or perhaps the late 1930s; the company itself is unsure) Tweeten Fibre Co. began making a tip tool shaped like a tube cut in half lengthwise. It held a strip of sandpaper and was called a Tip Shaper. The design was so basic, inexpensive and useful that they're still sold in large numbers today.

Fig 1

THE BRAD SCUFFER

Howard Reinhart, an auto industry engineer who held the patent on ethyl, used in gasoline, and was one of the passengers on the first commercial transatlantic flight, was also an avid pool player. He invented a tenon machine, pop-in cue tips made from a mixture of ground leather and plastic, and the world's first purpose-made non-sandpaper tip scuffer (Fig. 2).

The scuffer was made from steel knockouts from an auto industry freeze plug mold and the early (and collectible) models were painted blue to inhibit rusting.

Reinhart called his company Brilliard Research And Development, Inc. (B.R.A.D., Inc.) and the scuffer became widely known as "the Brad scuffer."

In 1979 Houston's International Billiards bought the company and began producing the scuffer in stainless steel, made the grit finer, and imprinted "B.R.A.D." on the back.

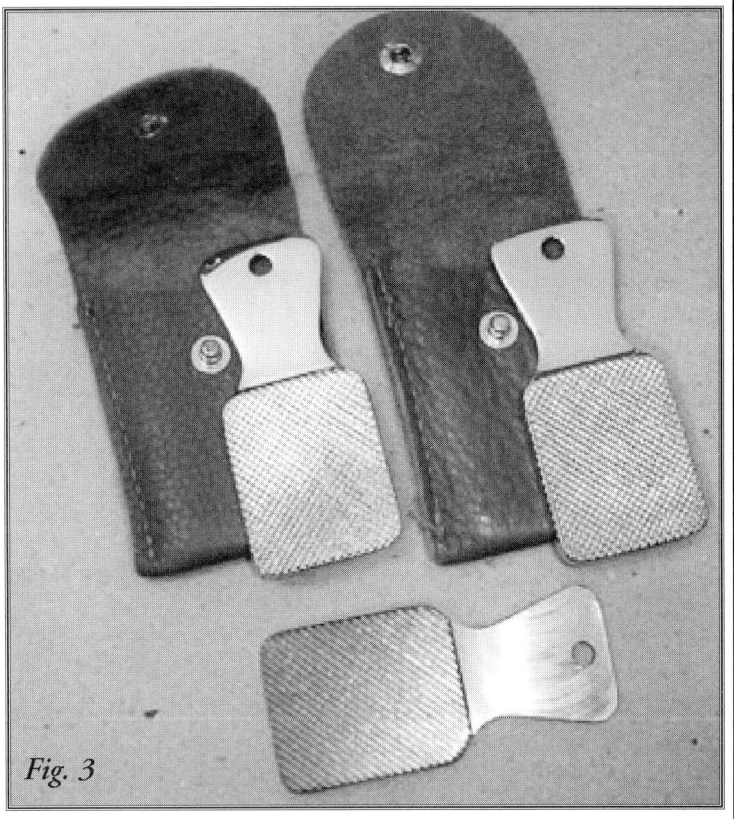

Fig. 3

LOU BUTERA'S TIP TAPPER

On a summer night in 1974 Rich Poliquin left his favorite poolroom and got into his car. He'd forgotten that his tip file was still in his back pocket and the tang ripped his leather car seat.

Poliquin owned a small steel company in California and had access to a machine shop. He cut the tang short and flattened it, and then cut off most of the file, rounding the corners. The resulting file did the job and easily fit in a pocket or cue case. He made ten and sent them to a Chicago tournament with a friend who promised to give them to ten top players and get their reactions.

> ...Tip Tappers found their way into the hands of Hollywood stars...

Everyone raved about the tool and Poliquin struck a deal with Lou Butera to endorse it. They added a hole so it could be kept on a key chain and widened the handle. Over a handshake they agreed on a one-year relationship, and Lou Butera's Tip Tapper was born (Fig. 3). It quickly became ubiquitous at tournaments and poolrooms around the country.

Tip Tappers found their way into the hands of Hollywood stars, including Paul Newman, and each had their names engraved on the backside. A few presentation models were gold plated.

The verbal agreement is still in force, and a new version is being developed.

THE CUE CUBE

Fig 2

Like many tip tools and cue accessories, the Cue Cube (Fig. 4) was made by someone who wanted a tool for themselves. Others in their local poolroom wanted one and it turned into a business.

In the late 1970s and early 1980s the Cue Cube was sold only in Milwaukee.

Fig 4

In 1982 the "company" was purchased and, at the suggestion of some pro players, the curvature and grit roughness were modified, though the cube shape, aluminum base, and silicon carbide material were retained.

The cube has come out in a great many variations, some discontinued today and difficult to get. They include various colors, a cube on a keychain, cubes in boxes, a Cue Cube-Shaft Slicker (burnisher) combination, and highly polished silver, black and gold versions.

WILLARD'S

Jim Willard was another man involved in the metal machining industry who had a love for pool, and in 1985 he started producing the popular Willard's cue tip shaper/scuffer (Fig. 5). Similar to the B.R.A.D. scuffer in its use of stainless steel and bonded abrasive material, Willard added a dimple, either the size of a nickel radius or a dime radius for the tip, and a bottle opener/screwdriver, calling it The Sportsman. Most players used it by placing it on the floor, stepping on the bottle opener end, placing their tip in the dimple, and twisting.

He later developed a circular model that included the dimple with abrasive, and a cut-out along the edge for comparing the final tip to either a nickel or dime radius.

Willard's experimented with different designs, materials and colors over the years, including a Universal Tool with a shaper at one end and a Lou Butera's Tip Tapper at the other. They also made a popular machined tip and ferrule replacement tool.

THE PORCUPINE TAPPER AND TIP-PIK

Another classic tip accessory that came out just before The Color of Money (1986) is the Porcupine Tapper. Developed and sold locally in North Carolina, the rights were purchased by Glen Sadler in 1987.

Originally the needles of the tapper were made outside of New York City, shipped to an undisclosed location where they were molded into a lead base, then shipped to Pennsylvania where the shell was made, and finally sent to Raleigh, NC where the metal was chrome plated.

The company later expanded to produce joint protectors, a tip burnisher (for the sides of tips to keep them from mushrooming) and even a line of cues.

A very similar device, the Tip-Pik was developed by Tony Long in Virginia in 1988. The company buys needles, the most difficult-to-obtain part of the tool, in cases of hundreds of thousands whenever they're available. They've also offered solid brass models, a keychain Tip-Pik and various other permutations.

CREATIVE INVENTIONS

In 1987 California's Joe Porper started making cue accessories for his company, Creative Inventions. A long-

Fig 5

time serious pool player, Porper began producing tip trimmers, shapers, scuffers, burnishers and combinations and variations of all of the above.

OTHER ACCESSORIES

After The Color of Money dozens of tip tools were invented and promoted. Although the limited-production variations on earliest designs, mentioned above, are the most collectible, any item with a short production run or from a defunct company is desireable.

As cue games became more popular, overseas American-made accessories were imported and sometimes copied for local production. The same player needs existed and local entrepreneurs created cue products to meet those needs.

Silicone became a popular item in the 1980s because it was slippery. It was impregnated into cloth, mixed in powder and blended into liquids, all to be applied to cue shafts to promote a smoother stroke.

Burnishing "tools" (usually simply small pieces of leather) became popular and their non-destructive quality made them excellent cue accessories. They're also used on the sides of cue tips to harden and strengthen the tip, making it more resistant to mushrooming.

"Cue papers" - small rectangles of plastic with ridges set to three levels of coarseness - promised not to harm the cue shaft like sandpaper. They were easily washable and reusable, but the three-step process proved to be only mildly popular.

Cuemakers generally still advise owners to just keep the cue clean, and use a damp cloth followed by rapid rubbing with a dry cloth on a regular basis. The damp cloth will clean any dirt that has accumulated to the point of creating bumps but it doesn't thoroughly scour the pores. This isn't altogether bad because it contributes slightly to building the patina.

Wood bleach (a different formula than household bleach) is used by some cuemakers to whiten the shaft before it's sold. Shaft whiteness has varied in popularity over the last forty years so it's not advisable to whiten the shaft unless you're about to sell the cue during a period when white is in demand. It's never advisable for a collectible cue. (A naturally darker shaft frequently means closer age rings and possibly a higher mineral content in the wood, producing a generally firmer shaft and firmer hit. Some players believe that signifies quality.)

Household bleach is commonly used to whiten older ferrules.

Chemist-pool players have created a wide range of products to treat the shaft and butt, and it seems that any advancement in automotive finishes or the space industry quickly find themselves being used on cues. Some of these are used by cuemakers to finish or polish the cue butt, but many are available to consumers as shaft cleaners and polishers.

...household bleach is commonly used to whiten older ferrules...

Small accessory kits are sold to repair dings, and most consist of some moistener and a sandpaper smoother. The moistener swells the compressed area and the sandpaper is used to make it flush with the rest of the shaft. A steam iron will do the swelling trick, if you watch your aim.

I saw one player repair a very serious dent with an epoxy glue, and another with Bond-O, the automotive dent filler. They filed it smooth. Neither looked good but if I closed my eyes I couldn't feel where the dent had been.

Cue joints aren't very vulnerable. The protruding pin is tougher than the wood around it. Joint protectors aren't a bad idea but players got along without them for hundreds of years.

A few manufacturers build scuffers into their joint protectors, making it easier to justify buying them. Custom cue makers often make matching joint protectors for their cues and they can add a great deal to a cue on display.

Two final accessories that a player should seriously consider are a bridge head and a cue holder. Having a favorite, non-abrasive and well-maintianed bridge head—one that slips on a house cue—will help your game and guarantee your cue shaft won't be scratched. A cue holder that can be secured to a pub table or chair arm is far better than leaning your cue against a wall or chair. ∎

THE HUSTLER CUE

by James A. Yonge

The movie "The Hustler" is one of my favorite movies. This movie was the first time I remember seeing Paul Newman act, and I become a fan. The movie and Paul Newman's drive to help children is where my first inspiration for a cue came from. I felt a need to thank Paul for his generosity and his creative powers, and by his example I decided to create an item that could be auctioned off to benefit his favorite charity. That charity, The Hole-In-The-Wall Gang Camp, is for children with life-threatening illnesses like cancer. It costs about $2000 per child, all expenses paid, for a week at the camp. I have learned how this really gives the children a sense of hope, belonging and joy. Thank you to Paul and Joanne Woodward for all the great work they have done to help children with cancer.

THE CONCEPT FOR THE CUE

I knew I wanted the cue to have the old movie "sprocket feed film" look. I wanted the film to wrap around the butt end of the cue to just under the joint of the cue. I then decided to have ivory inlaid to create the look of the copy portion of the frame. I envisioned in the frame area picture portraits scrimshawed in, depicting the cast members of the original "Hustler" movie: Paul Newman, Jackie Gleason, George C. Scott, Piper Laurie and Willie Mosconi. On the cue I took the liberty to use color images scrimshawed on versus the black and white film images from the original movie. It was also my goal to have an old friend's picture scimshawed onto the cue. He helped make this movie great and, in my opinion, his talent on the billiard table, his choice of shots to film and his instructions on stance and execution made the film extremely realistic. He was the great Willie Mosconi, professional billiard player. Willie and this movie inspired me to learn and enjoy the game of billiards. In the final editing of the movie Willie was never actually shown facing the camera (this was edited out). On the cue Willie is shown facing front as he was prior to the editing of the movie. A special "thank you" to my friend Charlie Urzitti must be made; Charlie sent me a great picture of Willie from his archive of photos. Jackie Gleason was an accomplished pool player in his own right and, per Jackie, he did shoot his own shots during filming.

CHOOSING THE CUEMAKER

Next, I needed to take my concepts and find a cuemaker who had the ability to create a cue using my ideas. There are a great many talented cuemakers here in the USA and choosing one was very difficult.

I chose Paul Drexler of pdf Studios. Paul and I had been friends during our gun collecting days and I was impressed with Paul's cuemaking skills. It was his cuemaking ability, not just our friendship, that made him my choice for cuemaker. Plus Paul really understood my

Scrimshaw image of Paul Newman

Scrimshaw image of Jackie Gleason

concepts for the cue. Paul makes great playing cues and equally creates artwork out of his cues. For the materials to be used on the cue, Paul decided on black ebony for the butt and mammoth ivory for the inlays. We did not want to use modern-day elephant ivory because we are both active conservationists. We decided on sterling silver for the scrollwork on the cue and in the sprocket areas as well. During one of our many calls about the cue I told Paul I wanted to depict the lights that were used to aim intense light in the air during grand openings of movies. Drexler didn't miss a beat and said he could do it. Thus, the two 18-karat-gold lights were created with scrollwork in silver creating the illusion of shining lights, above the artwork frames on the cue. A special note of thanks is due here to Paul's wife, Ellen, who did a great deal of the work with programming needed to make these pieces of cue art. She also worked on many other aspects of the cue's development.

THE SCRIMSHAW ARTIST

Speaking of artwork, I then needed to find a person to scrimshaw the scenes into the ivory on the cue. After viewing many shows and searching on the Internet, I, along with Paul, chose a fantastic scrimshaw artist, Sandra Brady. Sandra understood what I wanted and I sent her a great deal of old pictures from the movie. Many thanks go to Brad Morris for sending the pictures.

I chose the pictures and decided on where each was to be scrimshawed. Sandra did a great job of capturing the scenes and actors. She was a dream to work with and she really did help create a beautiful piece of cue artistry. Looking at pictures of the cue you will see she really captured Paul and Jackie Gleason. It was Paul Drexler's cue-making ability and Sandra's scrimshaw talent that made my idea for the cue become reality. Sandra worked miracles and put a great deal of heart and soul into this project. Paul Newman then autographed the cue for me after viewing the semi-finished cue. Paul Drexler then applied the final clear coats to the cue.

I want to thank Predator Cues, who made the shafts for the cue, as well as Allen McCarthy. His high-tech cue shafts added the state-of-the-art playability I was hoping to achieve. Predator shafts are all I have played with for many years and I have not found a shaft to equal it.

THE CUE CASE

During the build of the cue I had been looking for a suitable case to house the cue. After a great amount of time and effort, I still could not decide on a case. In my mind it had to be unique and be as artistic as the cue. Then luck came my way in the form of Mike Massey, world trick-shot artist and television personality. Mike and I have been friends for many years, and during one of our get-togethers he showed me one of the most unique cue cases I have ever seen. An artist by the name of Mel Larson had built a case for Mike that was outstanding. So I contacted Mel and asked if he was interested in helping me with regards to the auction. Mel said

Paul Newman looks at the Hustler cue

Scrimshaw artist Sandra Brady

Jim Yonge and Sandra Brady, with Paul and Ellen Drexler

Jim Yonge with case maker, Mel Larson

he had a case he had just finished and would donate it to the charity. It was a hand-carved case in the shape of a shark made out of exotic (lace) wood and real shark teeth with an eight-ball in its mouth. We were so close to the auction event that Kathy and I had decided to use Mel's case on the next cue build. We had not mentioned the case for the advertisement of auction items. However, Mel Larson surprised us and drove up to Connecticut with this beautiful case. Mel's cases are one-of-a-kind art pieces that take hundreds of hours of work to finish. Our intent was to show the case and use it for The Color of Money Cue. That all changed after the auction and really by chance.

THE AUCTION

Paul Newman and Joanne Woodward founded The Hole-In-The-Wall Gang Camp, which is located in Connecticut. The auction was held in Connecticut at the beautiful Polo Club, which is close to the camp location. The auction is an annual event with all proceeds going to The Hole-in-the-Wall Gang Camp. In the past, the auctioneer was the late Tony Randall, who really gave his all for the children and the camp.

At this event they had another excellent actor named Jay Sanders. Jay gave new meaning to the word "auctioneer"—it was a treat watching him work the crowd and really connect. The Hustler cue was viewed by the prospective bidders prior to the auction and this set the stage nicely for the actual bidding. Jay started the auction with various items such as trips to Europe, in-ground pools, and many other fantastic items. The cue came up and the action was great—there were actually two key bidders. The winning bidder was a businessman from Connecticut and the other bidder was from Florida. During the bidding I mentioned that Mike Massey would give a private lesson to the winning bidder. The person who won the bid, Walter Racquet, was very pleased with the cue and really enjoyed contributing to the camp. It was because of Walter and some great friends that we added more money to the camp.

After the auction we were taking pictures of the various

Winning bidder, Walter Racquet

people who participated in the auction. A great guy named John Lee had come up and asked to buy the Mel Larson Shark case. I explained we were going to auction it on the next charity auction sometime next year. He explained that it was to be a birthday gift for Walter, the high bidder on the hustler cue. I gave him a price that was comparable to what it would sell for in an art gallery. He said, "Sold." The cue and case brought in just under $50,000 for the charity. Needless to say my wife and I were extremely pleased with this outcome. I would like to say thank you to my wife of 34 years, Kathy. She really supported me throughout this project. From start to finish it took almost two and a half years to finish.

THE CAMP SUCCESSES

Just to give you an idea of statistics on what Paul inspired and began (from information obtained from The Hole-in-the-Wall Gang Camp newsletter): "The Hole-in-the-Wall Gang Camps have spread rapidly throughout the United States and internationally. In 2004 alone, more than 13,000 children had a good old-fashioned summer camp experience and it was fully paid for." It is my hope to see this number grow to 20,000 or greater by 2008. There are a great number of volunteers who make this camp and others like it successful. There is always a need for more people like Paul and Joanne with big hearts and good ideas about helping others. If you would like to help in any way please be a contributor in either your time or money. Anyone interested should call the camp or go online to www.holeinthewallgang.org." ■

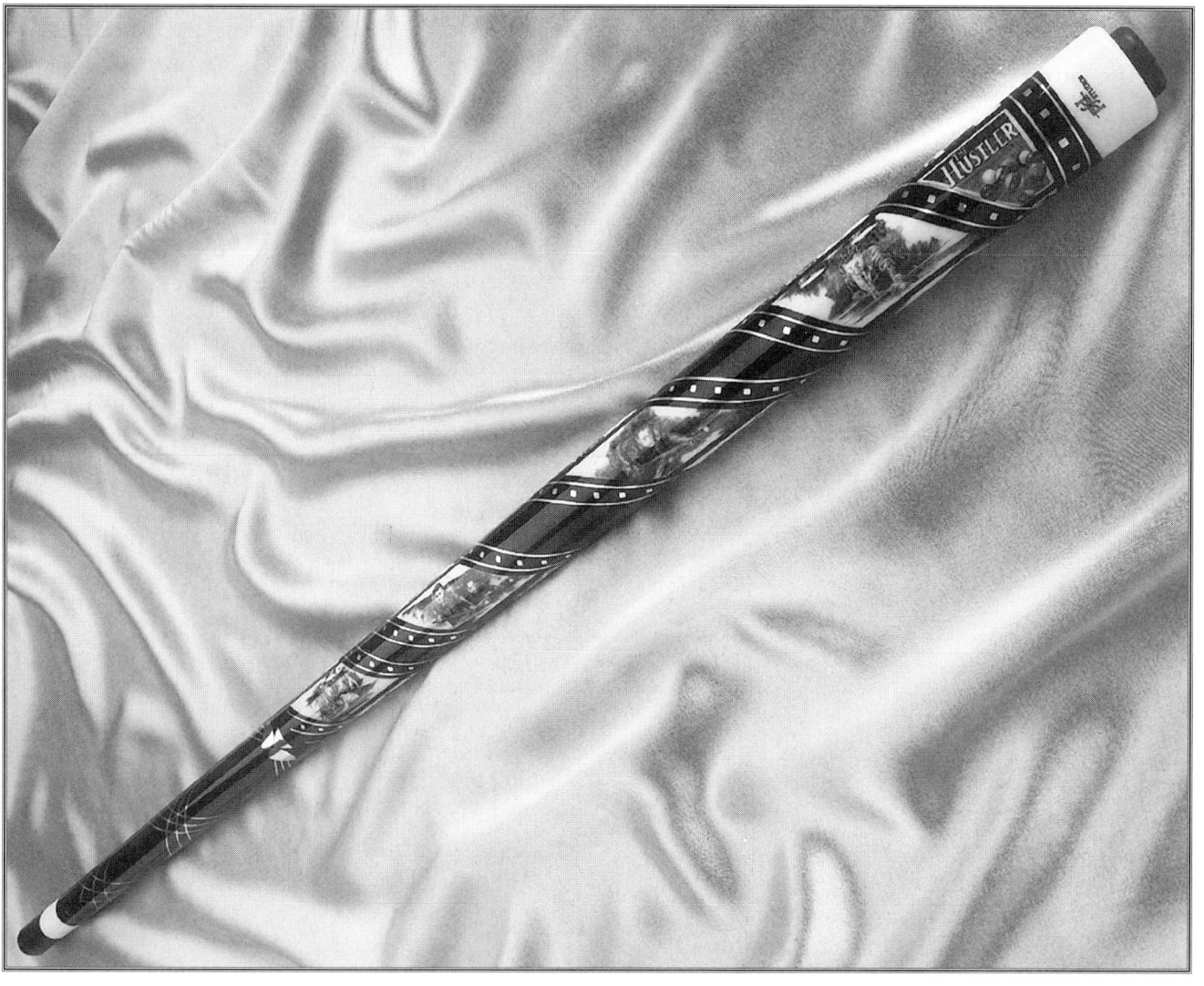

WANTED
DEAD OR ALIVE

Cues and cuemakers for inclusion in the fourth edition of the *Blue Book of Pool Cues*.

Rewards paid for:
Publishable portraits of legendary cuemakers
Publishable catalogues of old cues
Any old advertising or letterheads with publishable logos from the past

If you are a cuemaker, please email or send the following:
A high resolution digital portrait
Your logo in a large digital format
Your name, address, phone number, fax, website address, and email
A brief biography, specs, and prices (written in a Word document and emailed as an attachment is best)
High resolution digital images of four to six cues from joint to bumper (flat!) on a white background, with prices and descriptions

Send info to:
Brad Simpson
132 South Seminary St.
Galesburg, IL 61401
Phone: 309-335-0440 • Fax: 309-342-5730
www.cuebook.com • email: simpsonb@gallatinriver.net • In Thailand: Phone: 011-669-918-9895 Email: bradinbangkok@yahoo.com

I reserve the right to use or refuse any information or photos as I see fit. People who submit information on other cuemakers will be credited in the acknowledgements section of the *Blue Book of Pool Cues*.

CORRESPONDENCE/APPRAISAL

As with any ongoing publication, certain models and variations will not be included within the scope of the text. As expanded research uncovers model variations and new companies, the book's body of text will always have some "grey areas." Not believing in ivory towers and one-way traffic, this author offers a mechanism for the consumer to get further information about models not listed in these pages. No book can ever be totally complete in a collectible field as broad as this one. For that reason, I am offering correspondence and appraisal inquiries to help you obtain additional information on items not listed or even help with questions on the data and prices provided.

To make sure I can assist you with any correspondence, please include good quality photos of the specimen in question, any information available about that particular specimen, including manufacturer, model (if any), materials, specifications, and unusual or other discernible features that will assist us with identifying your cue. The charge for this comprehensive research program is $100 per cue. In addition to payment, be sure to include both your address and phone number, giving me an option as to how to contact you for best service. To keep up with this constant onslaught of mail, I have a network of both dealers and collectors who can assist me (if necessary) in answering most of your questions within this time frame.

Remember, the charge for this research service is $100 per cue and payment (PayPal, personal check, cashier's check or money order) must accompany your correspondence. Your letters will be answered in a FIFO system (first in - first out) as quickly as possible. Thank you for your patience.

All correspondence regarding information and appraisals should be directed to:
Brad Simpson
132 South Seminary St.
Galesburg, IL 61401
Email/PayPal: simpsonb@gallatinriver.net • http://www.cuebook.com

GLOSSARY

Applied image - points, patterns, or pictures on cues that are achieved with decals instead of inlaid or spliced materials.

Balance point - the point at which the cue, when put together, will balance horizontally.

Blank - a spliced rod used to make the forearm or butt section of a cue.

Break-jump cue - a cue that has a joint above the handle so that when the handle section is removed, the cue is the ideal length for jumping balls.

Bumper - a rubber piece under the butt cap that prevents damage when the cue is rested on the floor or bumped on the end.

Butt - the section of a two-piece cue that includes the forearm, the handle, and the butt sleeve.

Butt cap - a protective piece on the back end of a cue.

Butt collar - the decorative ring at the butt end of the joint of a two-piece cue.

Butt sleeve - the section of the cue between the handle and the butt cap.

Check - a rectangular piece created when decorative rings are made.

Dot - a round inlay.

Ferrule - a protective tube, sometimes capped, at the end of the shaft that prevents the shaft from splitting under the tip.

Hustler - a slang term for a custom two-piece cue designed to look like a bar cue taken off the rack.

Inlay - a decorative piece that is cut to fit into a pocket on a cue.

Joint - the connecting component between the butt and the shaft that allows the cue to be broken down into two pieces.

Joint collar - a sleeve at the joint that protects the wood from splitting.

Laminated - to reinforce by stacking layers of glued materials, usually wood.

Melamine - a synthetic material that resembles the look and playability of ivory.

Micarta - a synthetic material made by soaking layers of linen in a phenolic resin.

Mother-of-pearl - the material derived from the inside of shells, often seen as inlay material.

Notched diamond - an inlay commonly seen on cues, that is created with a four-sided diamond shape with notches cut into each of the four sides.

Pantograph - a machinist's tool used to manually cut inlays and pockets for inlays.

Pedigree - whatever documentation and proven history accompanies a cue.

Phenolic - a synthetic material used in cues because of its strength and weight.

Points - originally used to strengthen cues via a v-cut splice, now they are often decorative, sometimes achieved by inlay or even decals.

Ring - a cylindrical component of the cue, sometimes decorative, sometimes structural, usually at the joint and above and below the wraps and/or butt sleeves.

Shaft - the thinner front half of a two-piece cue that is tapered and includes the tip and ferrule.

Shaft collar - a sometimes decorative ring that reinforces the joint on the shaft.

Sneaky Pete - a slang term for a two-piece custom cue designed to look like a one-piece bar cue taken off the rack.

Veneer - a wood laminate vertically applied to points and inlays to create a horizontal line.

Window - a term used to describe a large symmetrical inlay, usually in the butt sleeve.

Wrap - a material applied to the handle for grip, usually irish linen or leather.

WOODS

Bird's-eye maple - a maple with a figured grain that creates eye-like circles in the wood.

Black palm - a very dark wood from palm trees found in Southeast Asia, having straight grain.

Bloodwood - a reddish-brown wood from South America, so named because the sap from the tree is blood red.

Bocote - an orange-colored wood from Mexico with a distinctive wavy grain.

Bubinga - a reddish-brown hardwood from Africa.

Burls - the circular grain patterns in exotic woods.

Cocobolo - a very durable brownish-orange hardwood from Mexico.

Ebony - an almost black wood, usually from Africa. Usually used on the butt because of its weight and density.

Gabon ebony - a black ebony from Africa that is very dense and heavy.

Holly - a very light, almost white, hardwood.

Kingwood - a violet-streaked Brazilian hardwood.

Macassar ebony - a black ebony with reddish-brown streaks, found in Southeast Asia.

Maple - a light durable hardwood usually from Canada or the northern United States.

Morado - another name for pauferro.

Padauk - an orange to brown straight-grain hardwood that grows in central and tropical West Africa.

Pauferro - a brown tight-grained hardwood.

Pink ivorywood - a very dense, very rare, pink hardwood from Africa with grain that resembles the grain in ivory.

Purpleheart (amaranth) - a purple-colored hardwood, usually with straight grain, that grows from Mexico to Southern Brazil.

Quilted maple - a type of maple with quilted patterns in the grain.

Redwood burl - a reddish wood that is very strong and resistant to decay.

Rock maple - a very hard, very straight-grained hardwood from Canada, usually used to make shafts.

Rosewood - a dark red to brown hardwood with black graining that can be found in South America and East India.

Satinwood - a light-colored, close-grained, yellowish wood from India and Sri Lanka.

Snakewood - a very dense East Indian hardwood, with grain that resembles the scales on the skin of a snake, and which comes from a climbing shrub.

Teakwood - a durable yellowish-brown wood from teak trees that is very resistant to warping.

Tulipwood - a heavy pinkish-brown hardwood from Brazil with irregular multi-colored streaks.

Wildwoods™ - hardwoods impregnated with a variety of colors, using a patented and trademarked technique.

Zebrawood - named because of its zebra-striped grain pattern, this hardwood grows in West Africa.

EXPLANATION OF ABCDE TERMINOLOGY

"A" is above the wrap, "B" is below the wrap, and "C," "D," and "E" refer to different points in the butt sleeve, which can change depending on the cuemaker. This terminology refers to decorative rings.

CONDITION FACTORS

100%: Virtually new condition, straight butt and shafts, no nicks, dings, or scratches, possibly never chalked.
98%: Almost no observable wear, perhaps extremely light finish scratching, near 100% except for chalk on tip, ferrules, and shaft. It is slightly lower than mint (in other words, it's been played).
95%: Very light observable wear, has seen a fair amount of use, perhaps light finish scratching, close to mint.
90%: Straight and playable, but has light wear on the shafts, finish, wrap, ferrules, and tips from plenty of play.
70%: Noticeable wear on most areas, possible warping on shafts, chips and dings, possible cracks in non-vital areas, shows plenty of use, still very playable but may make noise, possibly ready for repair or a restoration.
Note: For lesser condition cues, price is based on the value of a mint restored example, minus the time and cost to restore a cue to this condition. (Refer to repairs for this determination.)

A Few Words on Condition: All cues start out 100%, but end up in a variety of conditions. Their conditions reflect how much they have been used, the care they have received, the temperatures and humidities they have been exposed to, their age, etc. With normal use, the tip of a cue is the first component to show signs of use. From the first time it is chalked, you can see that it has been played. Since tips need reshaping occasionally, they slowly get shorter. Also, the compression from hitting balls causes mushrooming (you should always make sure the tip is securely fastened). The ferrule will start to show chalk discoloration with very little use. Some ferrules show discoloration sooner than others, ivory being a good example. Many players are very careful not to get chalk on their ferrules, which is a good idea (especially with ivory). If the ferrule is a different diameter than the shaft, the cue has probably been exposed to a harsh change in temperature or humidity (if it has, the cue may also be warped, or have other serious problems). Also, make sure the ferrule has no cracks. Wear on the shaft usually starts as chalk discoloration coming back from the ferrule. Even without any visible wear, a shaft may be warped. Some players follow through their shots to the point of bending the shaft. This breaks down the fibers in the wood, eventually making the shaft very malleable. Extreme temperature can warp a shaft with no apparent wear. If the shaft taper gets thinner as it comes back from the ferrule, chances are someone has been sanding the shaft too heavily. Always look for cracks in the wood on each side of the shaft and butt collars. This is a sure sign of abuse, and is very expensive to fix. Cracks in the joint collar are not as serious, but can still be expensive to fix. Also, look to see that there are no nicks in the edges of the joint faces (the main reason to invest in joint protectors). After a cue has seen a lot of use, the finish may start to wear off of the forearm. Look for nicks and/or dings in this area (from banging the cue on the edge of the table). At the base of the forearm, look for a sharp, even edge that meets the wrap (this is the best place to look for signs of refinishing). Every wrap wears differently, and the wear will show where the cue has been gripped. This is usually a little forward of the center. Leather wraps tend to change in color with wear, while linen wraps will fray and become coarse. Sanding and starching is a good temporary fix for linen, while dye can restore the color of worn leather. The butt end of a cue will usually show more wear than the forearm, as the back end seems to be exposed to more potential abuse. Look at the butt cap to see if the cue has been banged on the floor. The wear on the bumper is also a tell-tale sign. Look to make sure that the inlays and rings are flush. If you can feel them, they may have expanded. This can be a sign of internal damage as well. When inlays have expanded so much that they are coming out and/or cracking the wood they are seated in, the cue has serious problems. Try to determine if a cue has been repaired, restored, or had shafts replaced (very important on vintage material). Look for components that do not match in terms of wear, age, finish, etc. Oil finishes were common on older cues. Lacquer was very popular more recently. Urethanes and automotive finishes are very popular today. Obviously, if you see a current finish on an older cue, something is wrong.

LEVELS OF INTRICACY

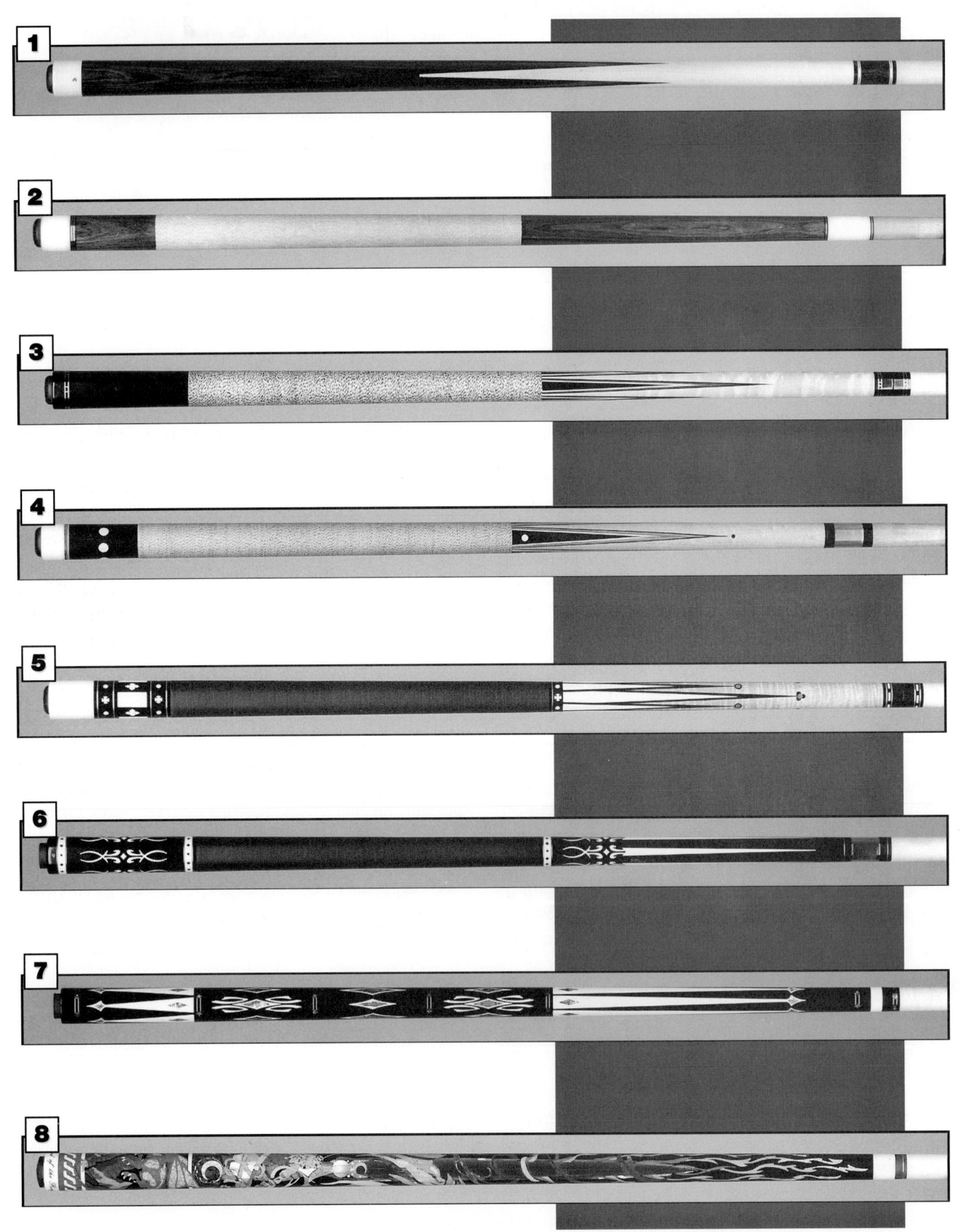

HOW TO USE THE LEVEL OF INTRICACY GRADING

LEVEL OF INTRICACY GRADING DEFINITIONS

Level 1	4 Points	(Hustler)
Level 2	0 Points	0-25 Inlays
Level 3	2-6 Points	0-8 Inlays
Level 4	4-10 Points	9-25 Inlays
Level 5	0-12 Points	26-50 Inlays
Level 6	0-12 Points	51-75 Inlays
Level 7	0-12 Points	76-125 Inlays
Level 8	4 or more Points	126 or more Inlays

If it were possible to show a picture of every model and one-of-a-kind cue ever made, it would be very easy to evaluate them. Since this is impossible, a system has to be used to help evaluate cues where no specific picture is available. There are many aspects that are important in determining a cue's value. Usually, the most important aspects are: who made it, how intricate (fancy) the cue is, and what condition it is in. The Level of Intricacy Grading system was developed to help the reader evaluate a cue the way the experts do. All the reader has to do is know who made the cue, figure out what Level of Intricacy grade the cue fits into (graphics are included in each section), look under the proper condition column, and progress from there based on the construction, features, artistry, etc.

This system works best on simple cues, and becomes more difficult as cues progress in complexity. For example, a Level 1 cue is a two-piece bar cue. There is very little variation in Level 1 cues because they are almost all designed to look like house cues, and very rarely incorporate exotic materials. Level 2 cues will have a solid forearm with no points. Most Level 2 cues will be made of maple, but many other hardwoods may be used, and many inlays are possible. Level 3 cues will have points, and up to eight inlays. Most Level 3 cues are bird's-eye maple with ebony or rosewood points and butt sleeves, but many other combinations of materials are possible, and inlays will affect the value somewhat.

Basic Level 1, 2, and 3 cues will be the easiest to evaluate under this system because of the relative lack of variety at these Levels of Intricacy. If a starting price is given for a certain maker's Level 1 (hustler) cue, one pretty much knows what that cue is worth. With Level 2 cues, the value is going to be relatively predictable also. Although many different woods may be used in a Level 2 cue, unless the cue has many inlays, the value of all but the most exotic woods or ivory would be a small fraction of the intrinsic value of the basic cue itself. The same is true of a Level 3 cue, with the points being the additional variable. Where there are exotic materials involved, the articles in the front of this book will help the reader determine how this may affect the value.

It becomes more difficult to determine values as the Level of Intricacy increases, especially past Level 4. At this point, many different inlays and point designs may be used. The articles in the front of this book will explain what types of inlays (sharp and intricate versus round and simple) add the most value to a cue. The articles also explain that certain original one-of-a-kind custom cues will have artistic value that can not be determined by any book.

Minimum values for cues have been determined with the help of top collectors and dealers in the market. Maximum values (a price ceiling) are not included for several reasons. Number one is that the market is increasing too fast to be able to do this. Also, it is impossible to know what the upper limit for a certain cuemaker is unless you know the actual sale and resale prices of every cue they ever made.

By giving minimum values for the most basic cues based on their complexity, and then giving the reader the information about the cuemaker, the cue, and what characteristics add value to those cues, the *Blue Book of Pool Cues* makes it easier for many more collectors and players to feel confident about purchasing a cue.

THE POOL CUE CATSCAN

The one-minute Vintage Pool Cue Catscan.

Over the years, one of the most frequently asked questions I receive is "What do you look for when examining a collectible cue for originality, condition, and other important factors?" No easy question, and no easy answer. While there is simply no substitute for the experience gained running cues through your hands, hopefully the following pointers will assist you while inspecting your next potential purchase.

Look at the colors! If the colors are wrong, the condition probably isn't right. Knowing the correct color of the finish (and/or other materials) of a particular cue is absolutely vital. The wood finish is color critical, and typically the older the cue, the darker the wood should be or more yellow the finish and ivory components should be. Often times old oil finishes will become blue from years of accumulated chalk residue. If the colors in the veneers have bled together, this is often a sign of a poor restoration. Once you determine that a cue has been refinished, there is no telling how serious of a restoration is hiding underneath.

Roll the cue on a flat surface to see if it is straight! Although warpage on a vintage cue is not the end of the world, it does indicate that the wood has moved, which could mean internal problems. Hit a ball to see if it makes any noise to make sure. And look for any cracks in the wood.

Scrutinize the markings and decals (if any). Stamps or engraving should typically be sharp and distinctive. Look for consistency and any signs of "thinning" or irregularity of finish color around decals, as this indicates probable refinishing, as does finish over deep dings, or rounded edges in the wood on either side of the wrap.

Alterations. Is the cue all original? If not, what's been altered? Depending on the nature of these alterations/modifications, the price has to be adjusted accordingly (as in downward). Make sure all of the shafts are identical in construction and age (many thirty year old cues have twenty year old replacement shafts). Use your instincts here - if something doesn't seem right, but you can't put your finger on it, your conscience is silently telling you "Notta."

Does the condition factor "add up" overall? Know how finishes wear, and where this condition loss would naturally accumulate through years of normal (and possible abnormal) usage. A Balabushka in less than average condition with mint shafts and a clean wrap simply doesn't add up - chances are they've been refinished or replaced. This also includes ferrule material and fit.

Since many older cues used ivory, modern synthetic ferrules on a vintage cue are a dead giveaway that someone has been performing surgery.

60 seconds - time's up! Hope your catscan was thorough, addressing all of the issues above. If not, take some more time - you might want to scan those troublesome areas twice to make sure another "doctor" doesn't tell you there's something wrong with the patient at a later date. With a little practice, you'll be able to zone in on these factors almost instantly, and then determine if the C-notes and fractionals are worth spending.

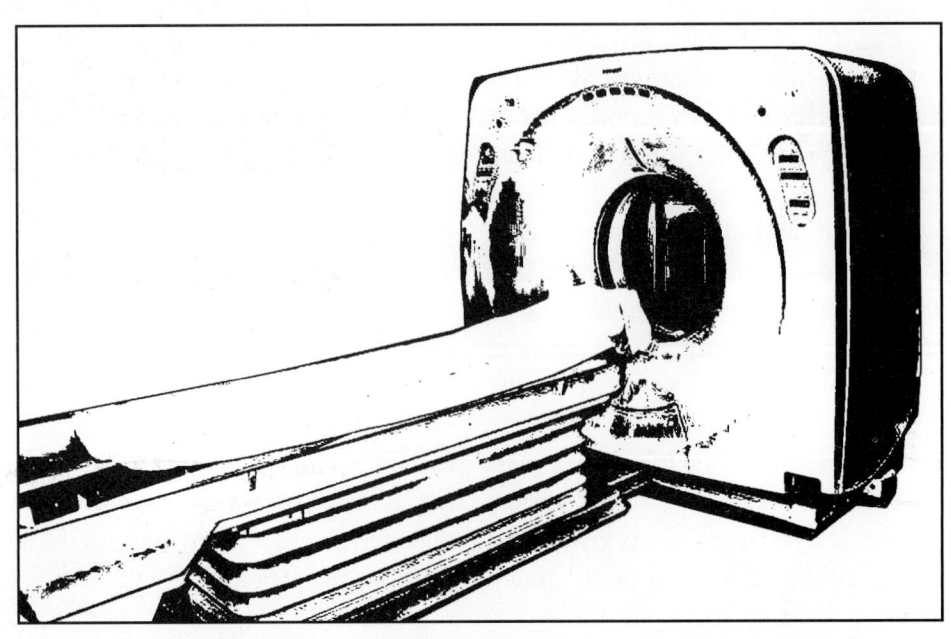

Adam: A group of unique designs by Richard Helmstetter of Adam Cues. Some feature butterfly splices and wood screws in the shafts.

AE: The third cue in this group of AE Cues is made of ebony and sterling silver and retails for $12,500.

J. Alan: Four cues from J. Alan showing some of the different butt sleeve lengths available

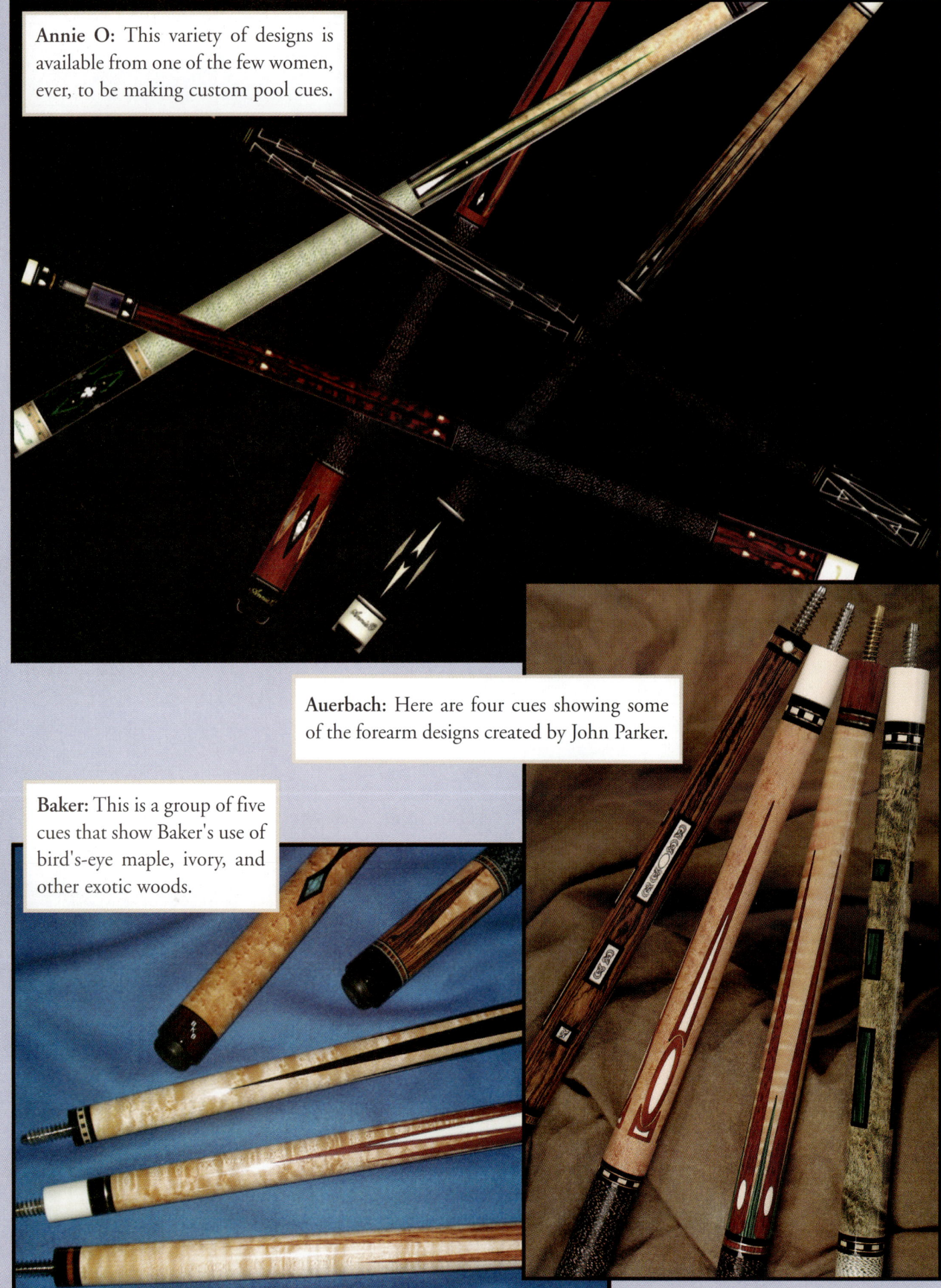

Annie O: This variety of designs is available from one of the few women, ever, to be making custom pool cues.

Auerbach: Here are four cues showing some of the forearm designs created by John Parker.

Baker: This is a group of five cues that show Baker's use of bird's-eye maple, ivory, and other exotic woods.

Balabushka: This is a fantastic grouping of some of the different styles of work by George Balabuska, including an original shipping tube.

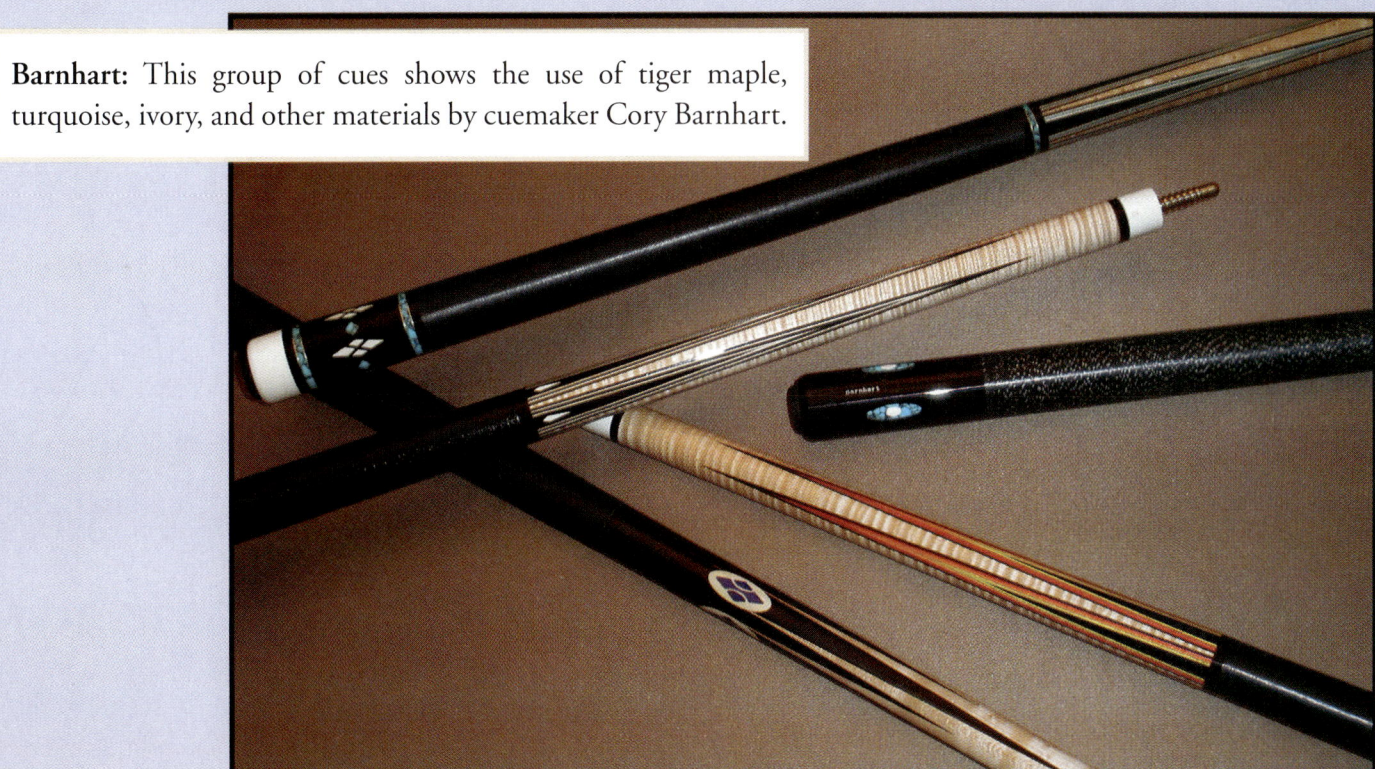

Barnhart: This group of cues shows the use of tiger maple, turquoise, ivory, and other materials by cuemaker Cory Barnhart.

Barringer: Here we note a variety of designs by cuemaker, and cue component dealer, Joe Barringer.

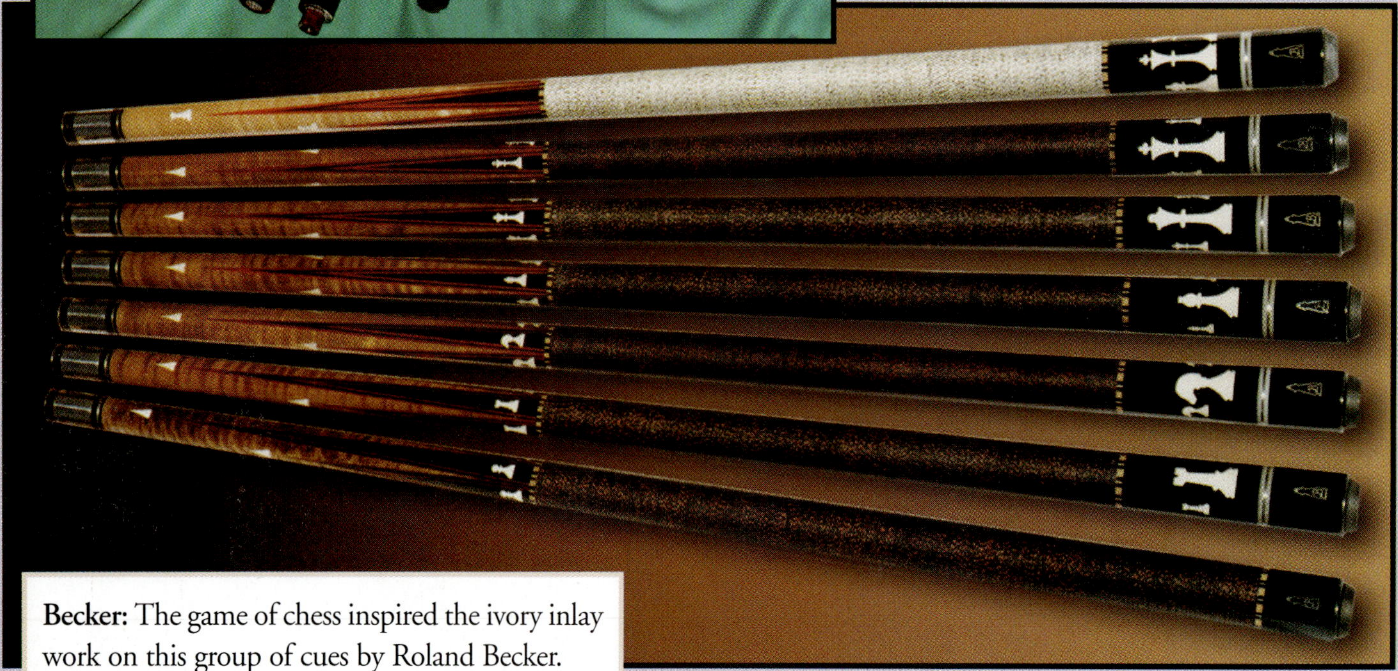

Becker: The game of chess inspired the ivory inlay work on this group of cues by Roland Becker.

Bender: The "Hawaiian cue" by Mike Bender features beautiful beach scenery scrimshawed in color on ivory.

Black: This group demonstrates how Richard Black views the cue as a functional art form.

Bludworth: This group of one-of-a-kind cues by Leonard and Donald Bludworth feature unique designs made from exotic materials.

Blue Grass: Richard Harris crafted this group of one-of-a-kind Blue Grass cues in his shop in Winchester, Ohio.

Bourque (Doug): These cues are all one-of-a-kind creations made from exotic materials by cuemaker Doug Bourque.

Brunswick: Intricate splices, butterfly points, colorful veneers, and unusual wraps have been found on Brunswick cues for over one hundred years.

Buss (Jim): The middle cue by Jim Buss is one of two identical cues, the other one of which was commissioned for the collection of the Smithsonian Institute.

Cameron: In the background are some of the exotic materials that Barry Cameron used to create this group of cues.

Cantando: You see two different types of identification marks on the butt caps in this group of cues by Art Cantando.

Capone: Three different types of available joints are pictured in this group of one-of-a-kind cues by cuemaker Michael Capone.

Carmeli: You will notice three different designs of ivory points in this group of Ariel Carmeli cues.

Casanova: Extensive use of ivory can be seen in this group of cues of Paul Casanova.

Chudy: The bottom two cues in this group by Richard Chudy are examples of his "Dancing Wings" design in different exotic materials.

CK: Real gold is used in all of these cues by Chester Krick of CK Cues.

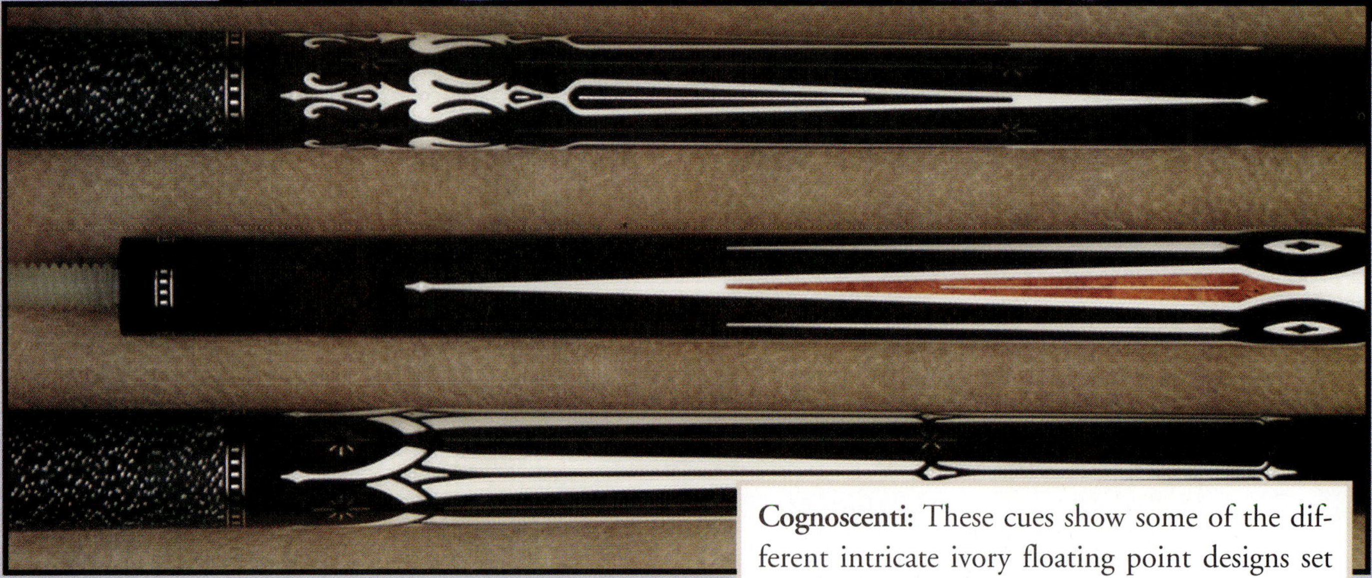

Cognoscenti: These cues show some of the different intricate ivory floating point designs set in ebony by Joe Gold of Cognoscenti Cues.

Coker: In the upper left you can see an identification signature that appears on cues made by Tom and Grady Coker.

Corsair: Roger Korsiak continues the cuemaking tradition that his father, Hank, started decades ago at Corsair cues.

Coster: Fancy Coster cues such as these are extremely rare, with not many more than a dozen believed to exist.

Cousins: The cue at the top shows the identification mark that is typical on Cousins cues.

Dayton: Long sharp points and ivory inlays are trademarks of the work of Paul Dayton.

Cues by David: These unique one-of-a-kind custom cues are the work of David Whitsell.

Dishaw: These cues are the work of American Cuemaker's Association President and Billiard Congress of America Board Member, Dan Dishaw.

Diveney: These two cues show examples of butterfly splices that Pat Diveney puts in the butts of his hustler cues.

Downey: This group of cues by Troy Downey range in price from $795 to $2295.

DP: These four DP cues by Dale Perry are each priced at $3500.

Durbin: This is a group of cues by Michael Durbin showing a variety of designs and exotic materials.

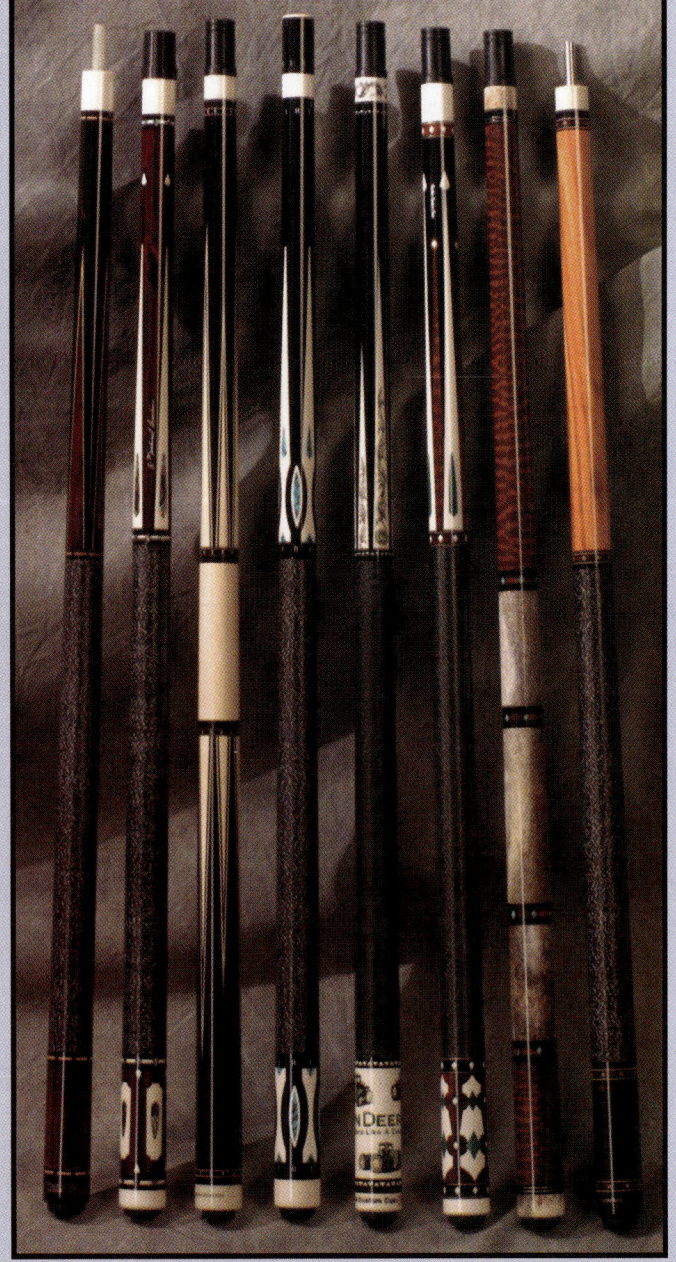

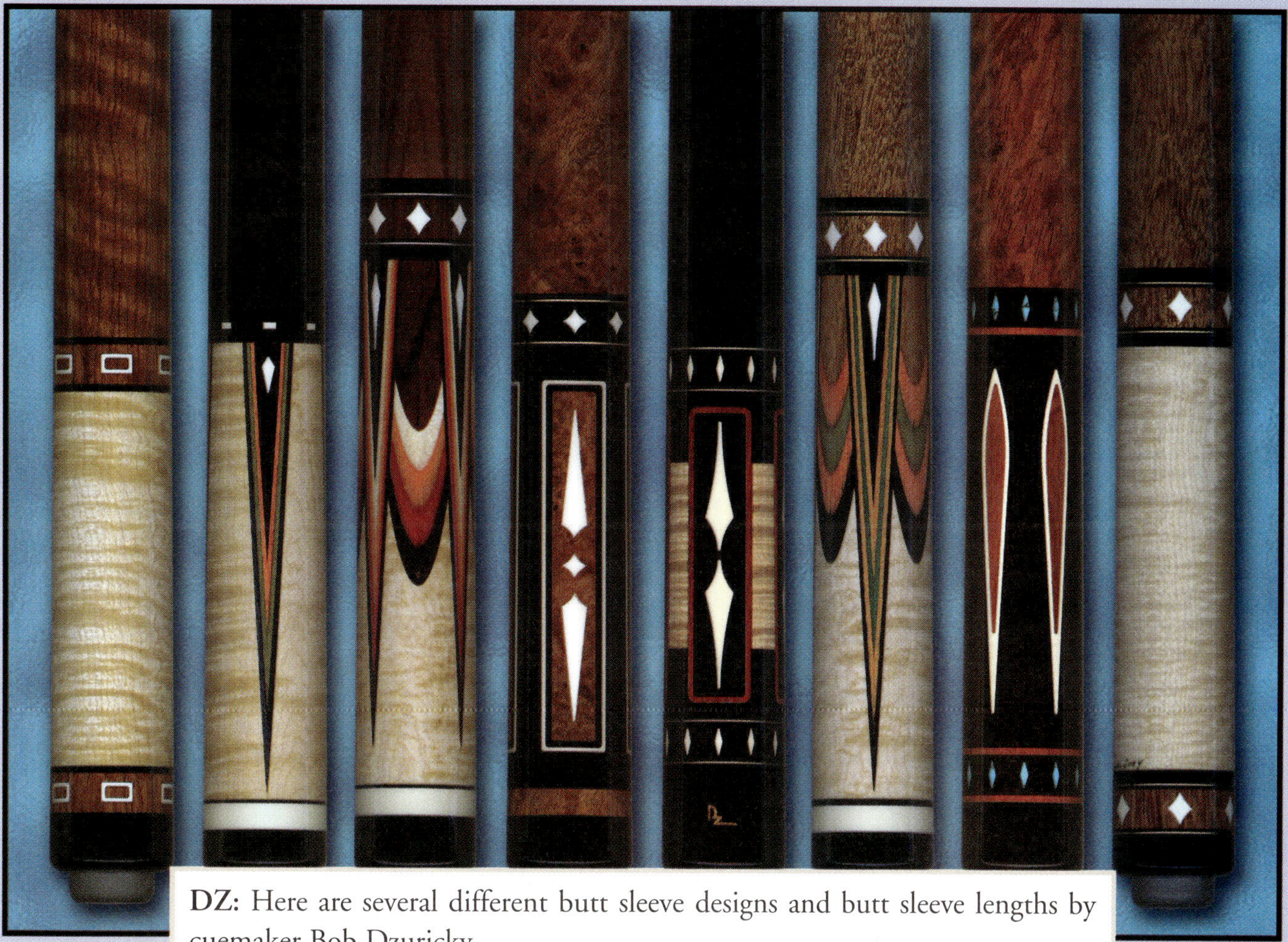

DZ: Here are several different butt sleeve designs and butt sleeve lengths by cuemaker Bob Dzuricky.

Espiritu: The "Zig" cue at top, and the "Zag" cue below it, have hundreds of pieces inlaid by cuemaker Russ Espiritu.

Fanelli: Paul Fanelli is famous for unique butterfly splices, as shown on the butt sleeves of these six one-of-a-kind cues.

Farris: Two different kinds of joints can be seen on this pair of one-of-a-kind cues by Ed Farris.

Fry: Colored plastics and glitter bands were often seen on cues made by Doc Fry.

Gilbert: Here you can see some very intricate ivory inlay work that is typical of the work of Andy Gilbert.

Ginacue: Handles and forearms of ivory can be seen on high-end cues made by Ernie Gutierrez.

Gulyassy: This cue was made by Mike Gulyassy to commemorate the 2004 World Poker Tour.

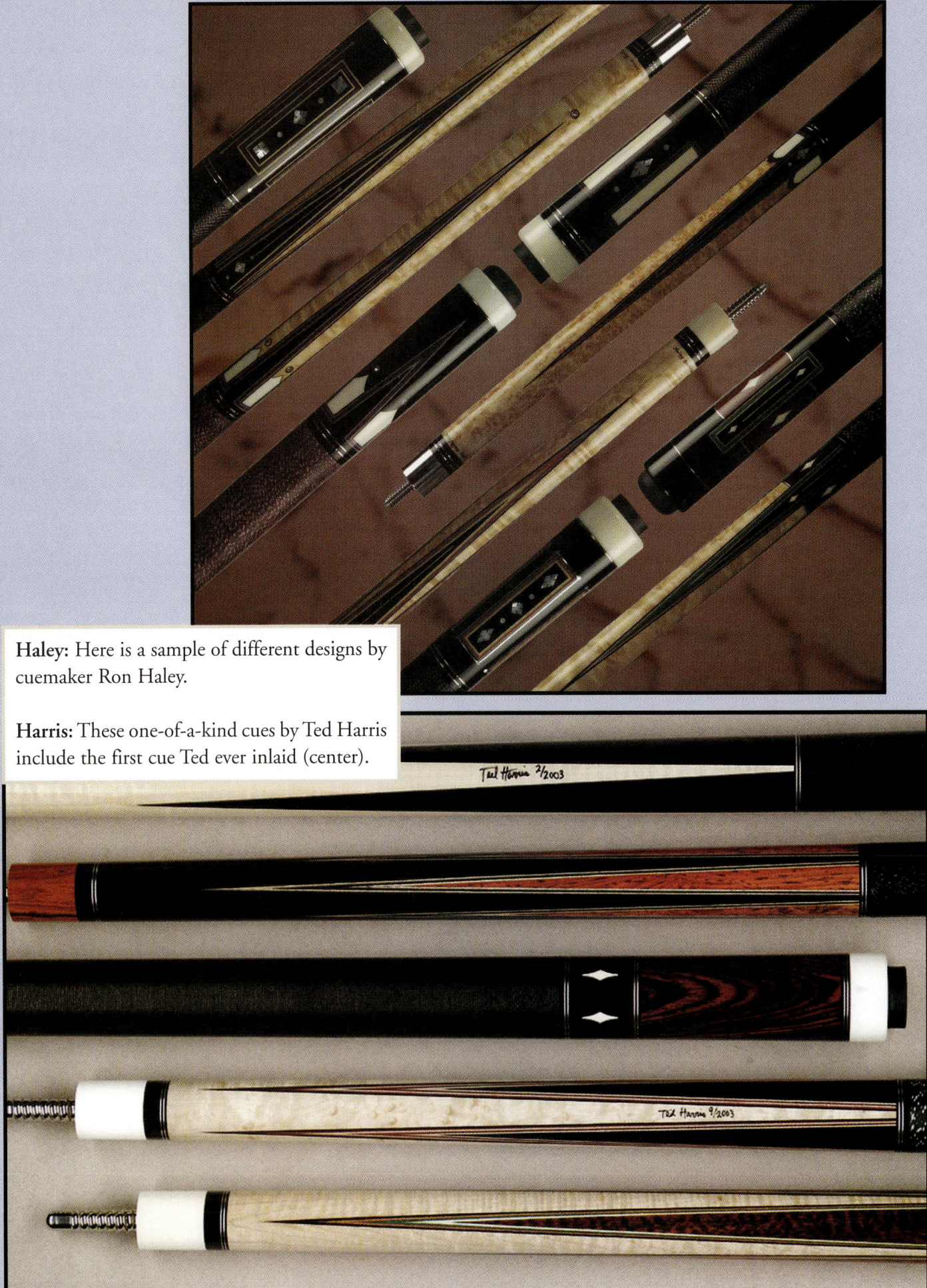

Haley: Here is a sample of different designs by cuemaker Ron Haley.

Harris: These one-of-a-kind cues by Ted Harris include the first cue Ted ever inlaid (center).

Hercek: The butt sleeves of these cues feature very intricate ivory inlay work into ebony, by Joel Hercek.

Hightower: Gemstones, including genuine rubies, are inlaid in the two center cues by Chris Hightower, who is also known for selling machinery built for cuemakers.

Horn: This group of cues shows a variety of work by the late Verl Horn.

Hunter (Bob): This group of ebony cues by champion pool player Bob Hunter features intricate floating points of ivory inlaid with exotic stone.

Hunter (Wes): Native American designs inspire the inlay work of cuemaker Wes Hunter.

Jackson: A unique color scene of a pool player is featured on the one-of-a-kind Jackson cue at center.

Jacoby: These one-of-a-kind and limited edition Jacoby cues range in price from $950 to $3900.

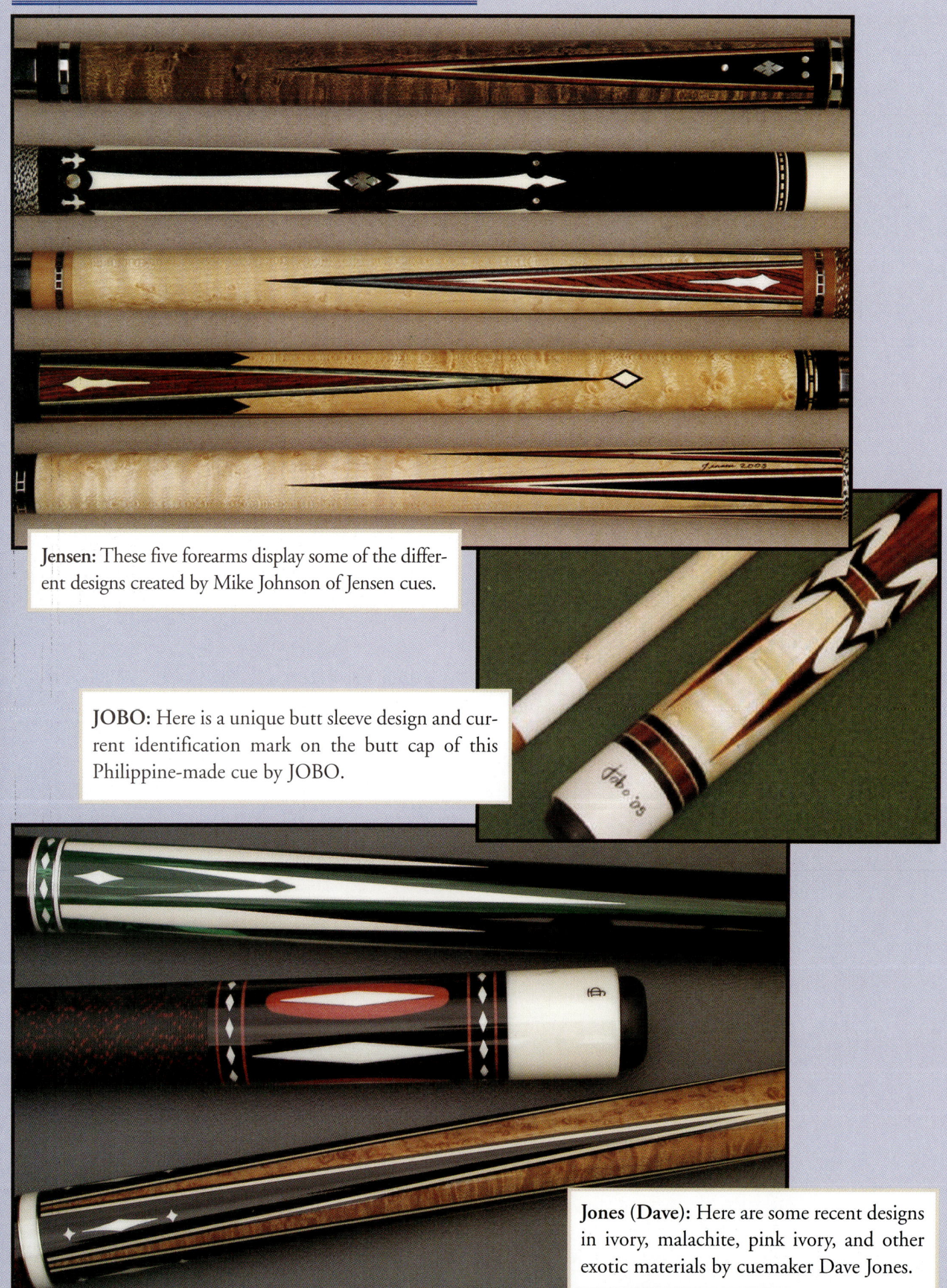

Jensen: These five forearms display some of the different designs created by Mike Johnson of Jensen cues.

JOBO: Here is a unique butt sleeve design and current identification mark on the butt cap of this Philippine-made cue by JOBO.

Jones (Dave): Here are some recent designs in ivory, malachite, pink ivory, and other exotic materials by cuemaker Dave Jones.

Josey: Redstone inlays are used for the hearts and diamonds in the "Gambler cue" at the center of this group by Keith Josey.

Joss: This group of cues by Dan Janes of Joss cues includes rare one-of-a-kind and limited edition examples.

Josswest: These three butt sleeves show a few of the unique ring and inlay designs created by Bill Stroud, maker of Josswest cues.

Judd: Intricate inlays in turquoise, ivory, silver, and multi-colored exotic woods create the southwestern designs characteristic of cues made by Judd Fuller.

Kersenbrock: The inlay work of David Kersenbrock features very unique designs executed in the most exotic materials.

Kikel: David Kikel achieves some of the most intricate inlay work available without the aid of CNC equipment.

Klein: These four cues by Steve Klein are priced from $325 to $1300. The center cue features a rainbow splice in patriotic red, white, and blue.

Klickcue: These three cues by Chris Klindt feature five snakewood points in the forearm and five reverse snakewood points in the butt sleeves.

Lambros: The ivory dragon cue (second from the bottom) by Mike Lambros is one of the most intricate and unique art cues ever created.

Lanz: The bottom cue in this group by Richard Lanz features both traditional and butterfly snakewood points in a snakewood forearm.

Laube: Eddie Laube cues are easily identifiable by the gold-colored band that has his name and address on it.

Lebow: The butt sleeve design on this unique $4000 Sheldon Lebow cue features silver, ebony, snakewood, and amboyna burl rings and mammoth ivory inlays.

Legend: Legend cues are one of the lines distributed by DMI Sports and are priced from $60 to $500.

Longoni: Longoni has been making fine pool and billiard cues in Italy for over 50 years.

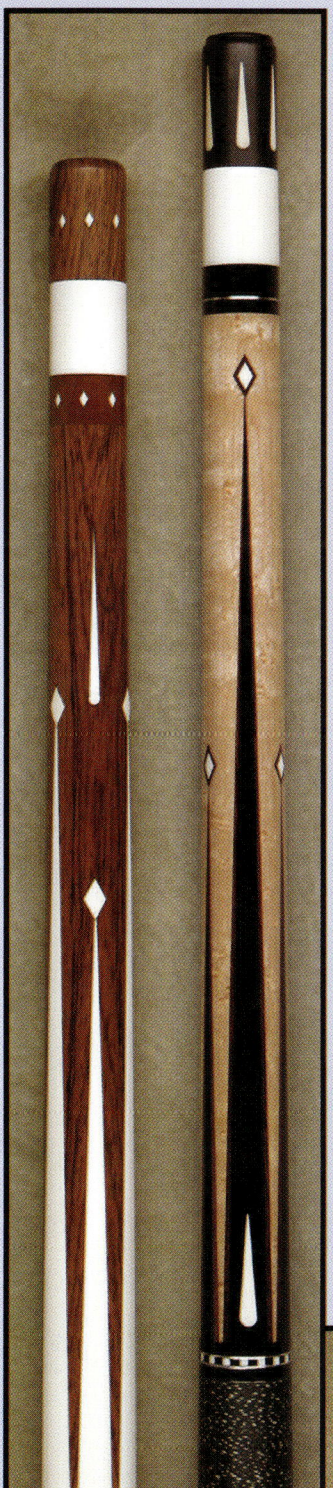

L.T.D. Cues: Here are two one-of-a-kind ivory jointed custom cues by Washington state cuemaker Dale Teague.

Mace (Rick Howard): Two of the identification markings that can be found on Mace cues by Rick Howard can be seen in this grouping of six cues.

Manzino: Extensive use of ivory can be seen in this group of one-of-a-kind cues by Bob Manzino.

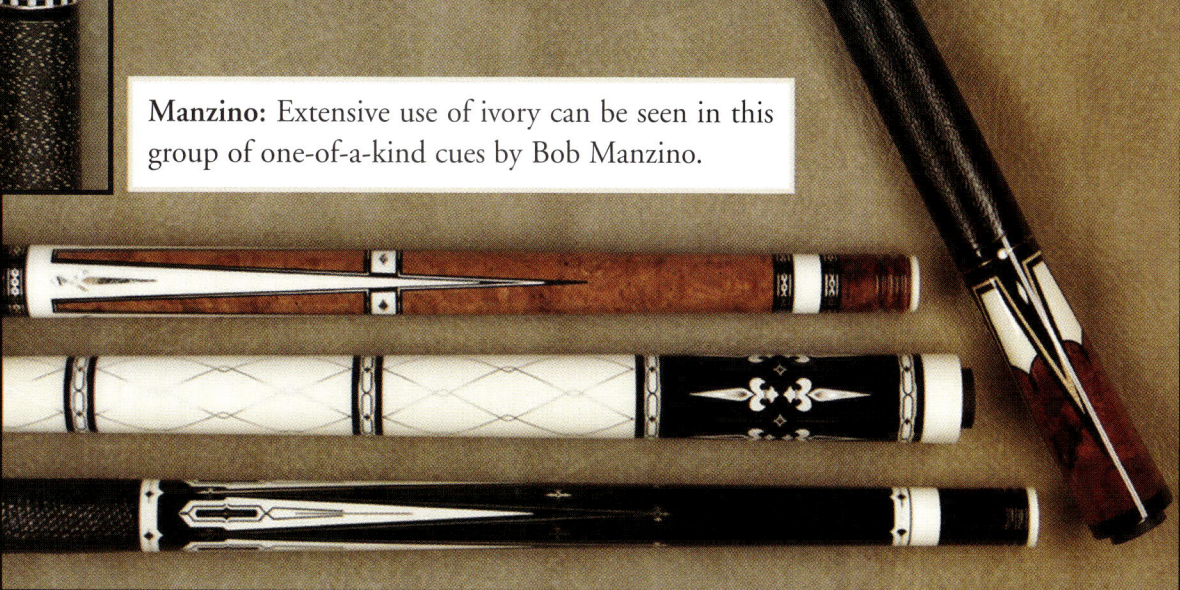

Mariposa: Kyle Van den Bosch used butterfly splices and wood screws to create his unique Mariposa cues.

Martin: This typical Harvey Martin pool cue is in a rare original Martin case.

Martinez: Three different types of joints can be seen in this group of cues by Ernie Martinez.

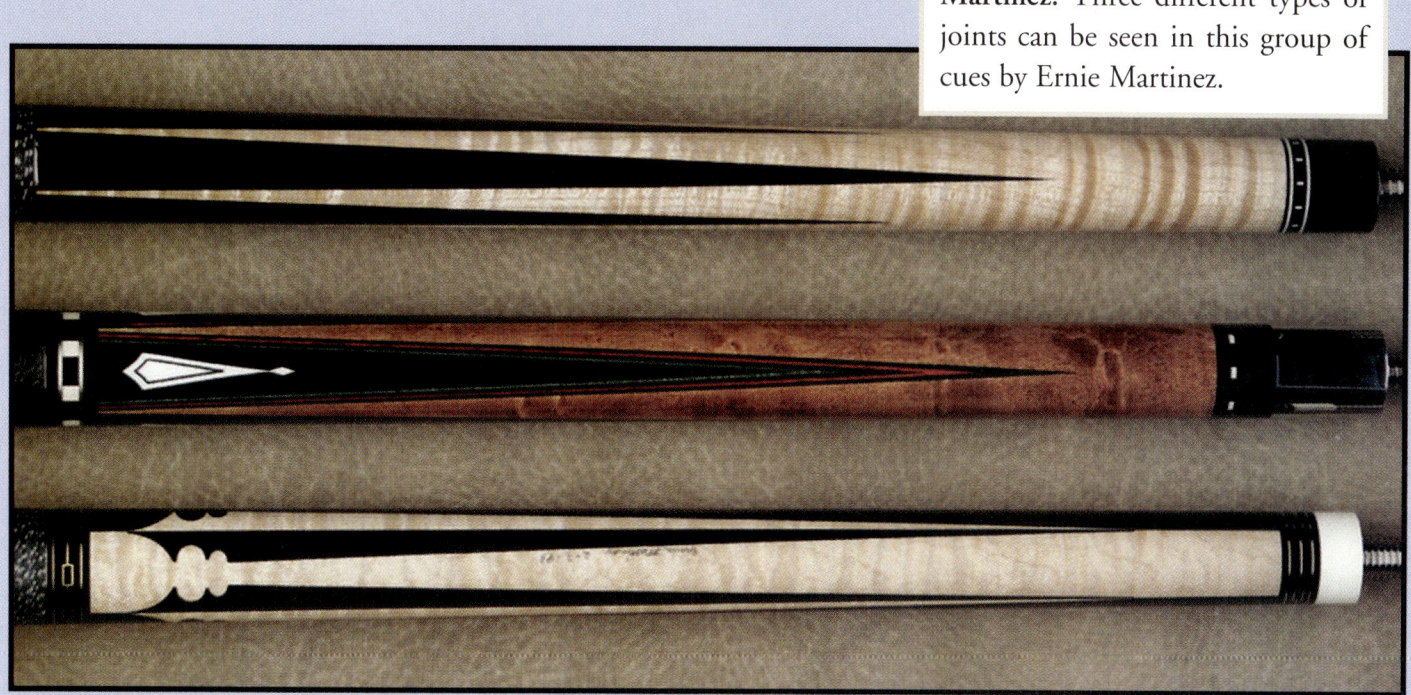

McDaniel: This group of cues displays some of the recent high-end designs available from cuemaker Bill McDaniel.

McDermott: These are some of the fancier cues that have been offered by Wisconsin cue manufacturer McDermott.

McWorter: The "Regal," the "Spaniard," the "Pinnacle," the "Deco," and the "Victorian" are all one-of-a-kind cues by cuemaker Jerry McWorter.

Michael Morgan: All of the inlay work on these five Michael Morgan cues was done by hand by Michael Miller on a manual pantograph.

Michaels: Here are eight different butt sleeve designs by Michael Kratochvill of Racine, Wisconsin.

Mid West: These six cues by Steve Morris display interesting silversmithing and unique bumpers that are found on Mid West cues.

Miltonio: Milt Hyman is known for his butterfly splices, "Saturn Rings" and long "Super Points" on his Miltonio cues.

Minnesota Fats: This line of cues distributed by DMI Sports commemorates legendary hustler Minnesota Fats.

Morris: Two different kinds of identification markings can be seen on the butt caps of these six Ned Morris cues.

Mottey: A variety of different styles ranging from traditional to contemporary are available from Pittsburgh cuemaker Paul Mottey.

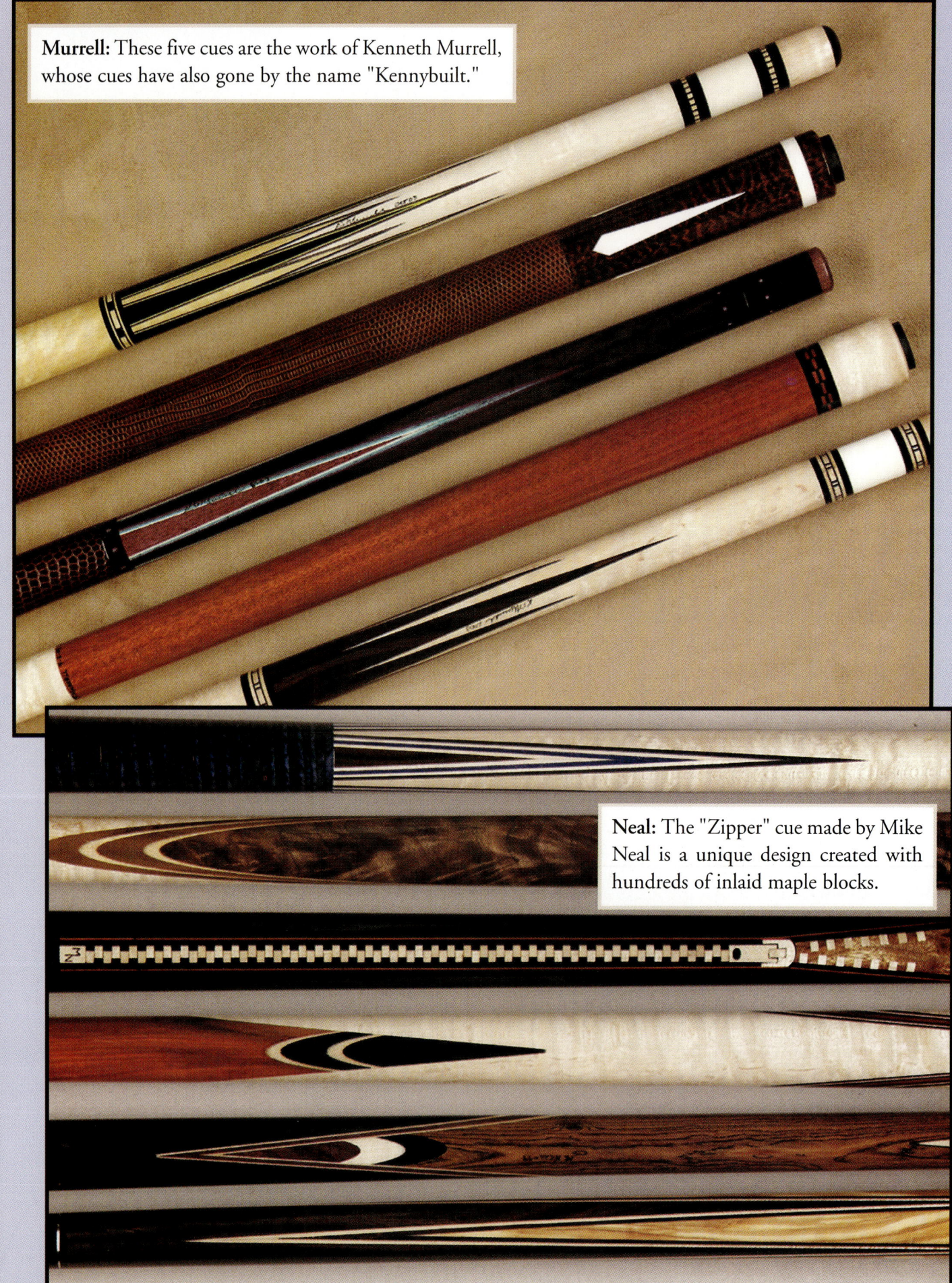

Murrell: These five cues are the work of Kenneth Murrell, whose cues have also gone by the name "Kennybuilt."

Neal: The "Zipper" cue made by Mike Neal is a unique design created with hundreds of inlaid maple blocks.

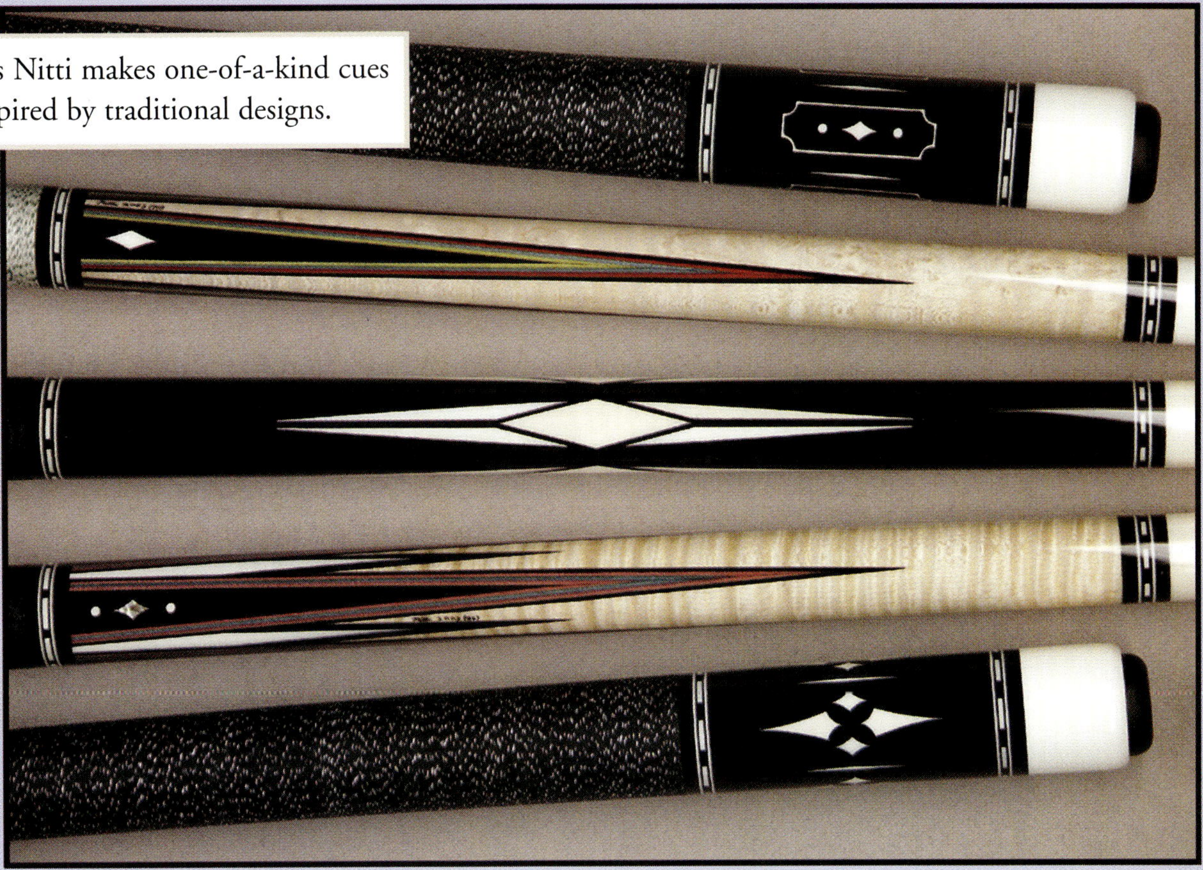

Nitti: Chris Nitti makes one-of-a-kind cues that are inspired by traditional designs.

Olivier: The red, white, and blue scrimshawed $3000 "Patriot" cue is one of three one-of-a-kind versions by cuemaker Jerry Olivier.

Olney: These five cues exhibit a range of early to contemporary work by Jeff Olney.

Omega DPK: David Kersenbrock made cues for Omega DPK in a suburb of Chicago from the late 1980s to the mid-1990s.

Omen: Here are a few interesting butt sleeve designs by cuemaker Peter Ohman of Omen cues.

Palmer: This group shows some of the more collectible models made by Palmer in the late 1960s and early 1970s.

Panther: J & J America distributes two different lines of Panther cues.

Paradise: These four Frank Paradise cues include a custom cue that was presented to Bob Hope by Willie Mosconi.

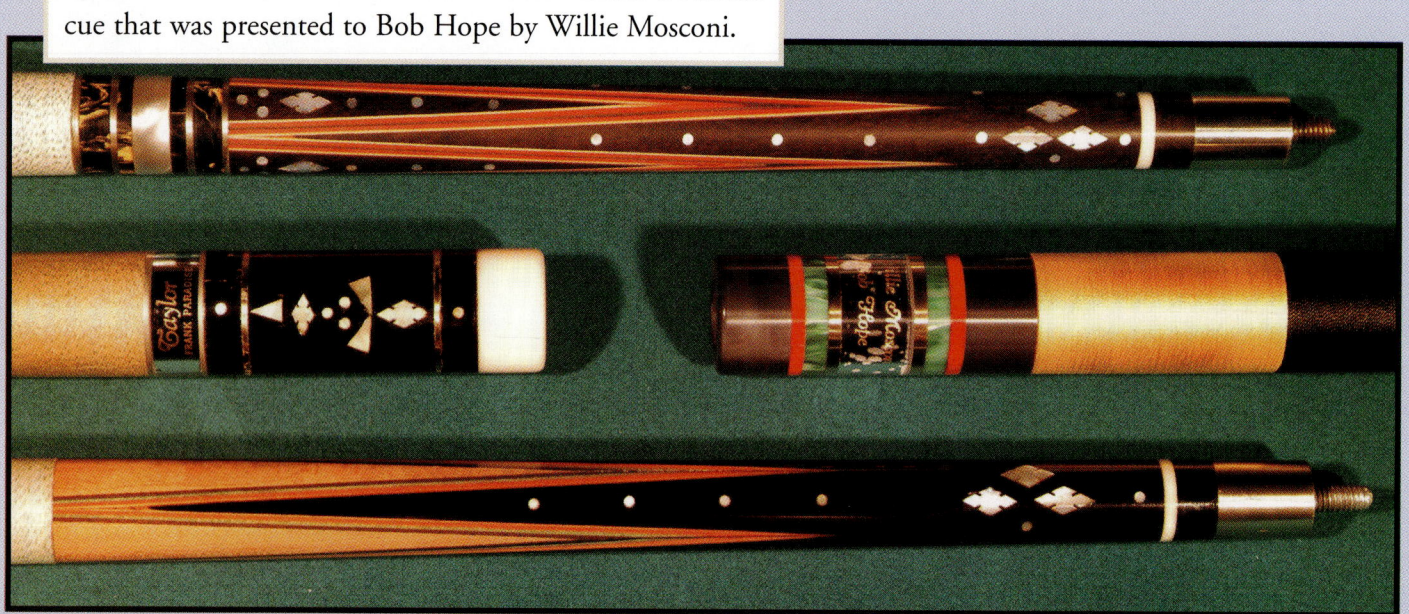

Pechauer: The top three cues shown are one-of-a-kind creations by Joe Pechauer of J. Pechauer cues and are priced from $4000 to $6000.

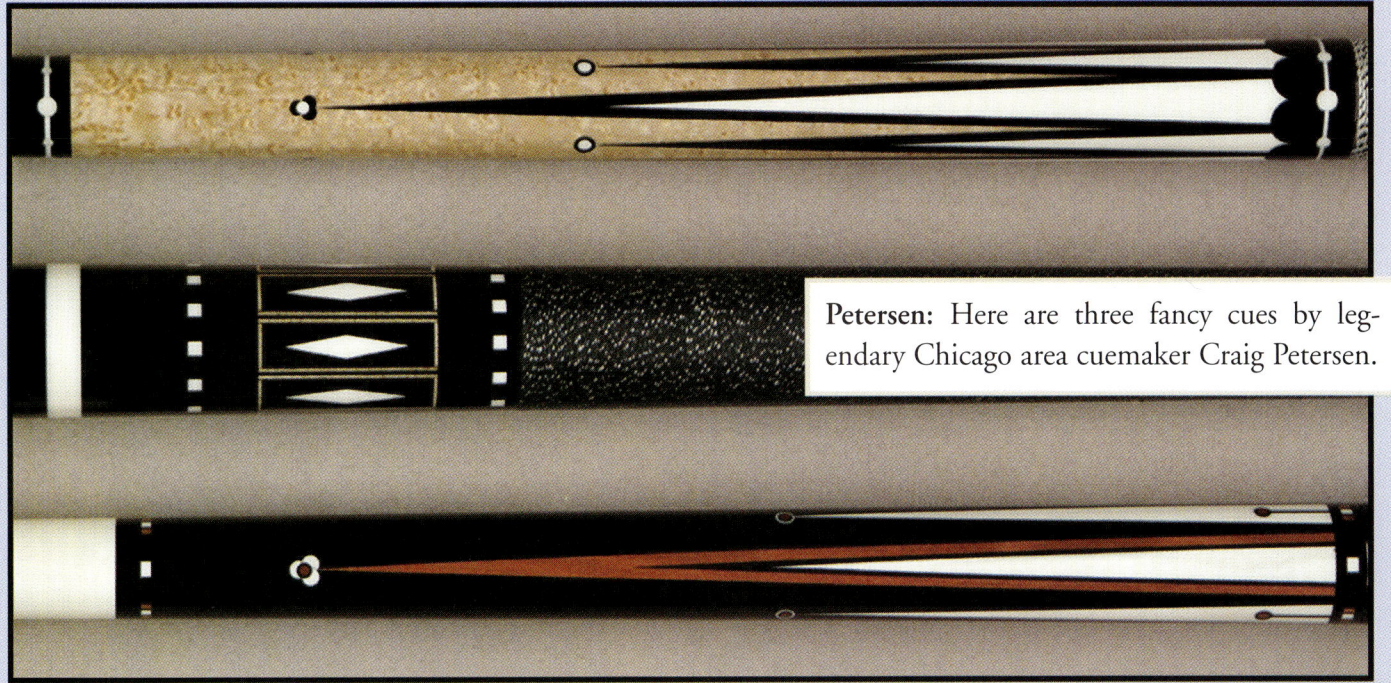

Petersen: Here are three fancy cues by legendary Chicago area cuemaker Craig Petersen.

pfd Studios: Paul and Ellen Drexler create unique images from intricate inlays in their high-end cues for pfd Studios.

Phillippi: This group of five Phillippi cues range in price from $1800 at top to $6000 at bottom.

Prather: Here are five different varieties of spliced point designs in different exotic materials from Prather cues.

Prince: Tim Prince crafted these six cues in his workshop in Glendale Heights, Illinois.

Rambow: The center cue, by Herman Rambow, was presented to Jackie Gleason by Willie Mosconi during the making of the movie "The Hustler."

Rauenzahn: Four different types of joints available from Jerry Rauenzahn can be seen in this group of four cues.

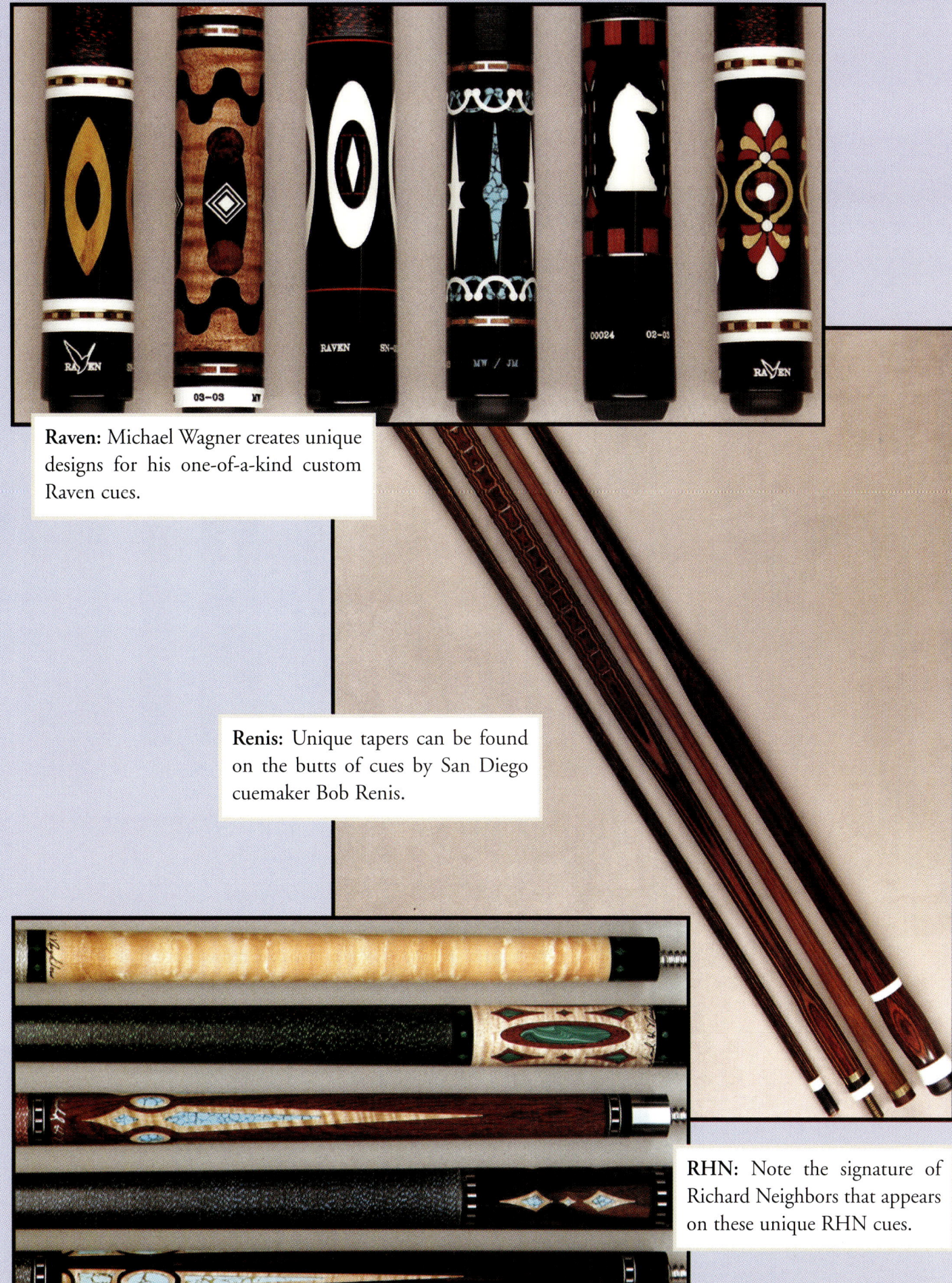

Raven: Michael Wagner creates unique designs for his one-of-a-kind custom Raven cues.

Renis: Unique tapers can be found on the butts of cues by San Diego cuemaker Bob Renis.

RHN: Note the signature of Richard Neighbors that appears on these unique RHN cues.

Ricco: Ricco Cervantes started Ricco Custom Cues which is now in the hands of his son, Marco Cervantes.

Samsara: The "Twisted Sisters" collection, by cuemakers Dave Doucette and Jim Stadum of Samsara cues, consists of three one-of-a-kind custom cues named Bertha, Mary Jane, and Liz.

Rikard: Note the Toeboy signature, a nickname for William Rikard, which often appears on Rikard Custom Cues.

Sanko: This group of eight custom cues displays the work of Florida cuemaker Joe Sanko.

Schick: Bill Schick creates one-of-a-kind custom cues from his shop in Shreveport, Louisiana.

Schon: Milwaukee-based Schon cues currently specializes in limited edition and one-of-a-kind custom cues.

Schrager: California cuemaker Bert Schrager specializes in unique one-of-a-kind custom cues featuring extensive use of ivory.

Schuler: The middle Schuler cue was made by the late Ray Schuler for famous billiards author Robert Byrne.

Searing: This Dennis Searing custom cue and custom case were for legendary pool player Steve "The Miz" Mizerak.

Shaman: Two different types of butt cap identification marks can be seen in this group of Shaman cues made by Robert Smith.

Sherm: Unique designs utilizing exotic materials can be seen in this group of one-of-a-kind Sherm cues by Sherm Adamson.

Showcase: These one-of-a-kind Showcase cues feature unique shafts with back sections that match the designs on the butts.

Showman: These cues by Florida cuemaker John Showman are inspired by the designs of legendary cuemakers from the past.

Shurtz: These five one-of-a-kind cues by Shurtz Cues are priced from $1350 to $3000.

Smith (Mark): This group of cues by Mark Smith features inlays of turquoise, ivory and silver.

Southeast: The top Southeast cue by Nat Green has over 624 inlays including 120 rubies set in 14-karat gold.

South West: The tradition started by ACA Hall of Fame cuemaker Jerry Franklin continues in these contemporary South West cues.

Spain: Burton Spain full-spliced blanks can be seen on each side of this group of finished Burton Spain cues.

Stacey: These one-of-a-kind custom cues by Mike Stacey range in price from $800 to $1895.

Star Cue Co: Abe Rich has been making one-of-a-kind custom cues for decades in his Star Cue Company shop in Miami, Florida.

Blue Book of Pool Cues™ - Third Edition 87

Szamboti (Barry): The top cue pictured is the 100th cue ever made by cuemaker Barry Szamboti.

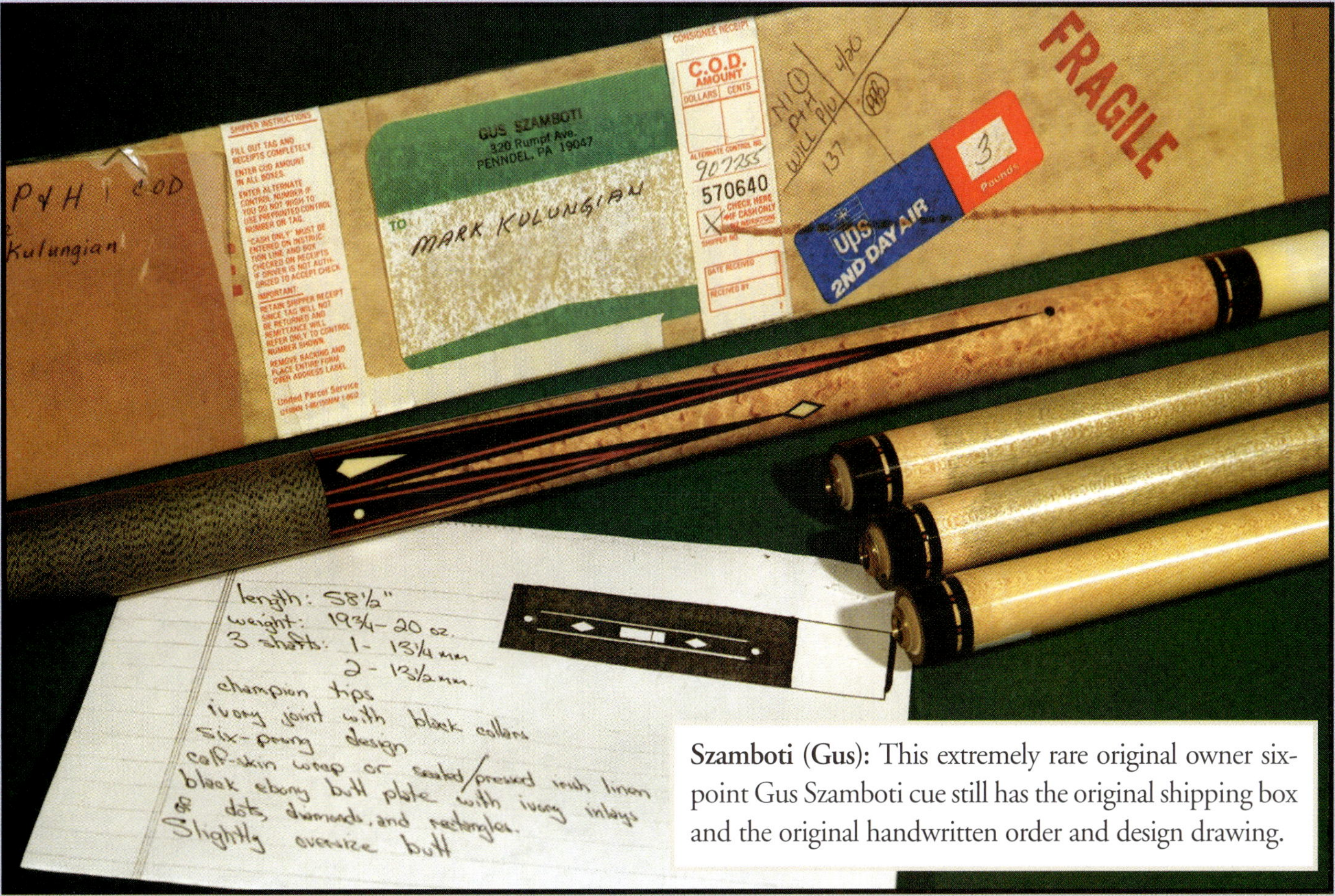

Szamboti (Gus): This extremely rare original owner six-point Gus Szamboti cue still has the original shipping box and the original handwritten order and design drawing.

Tad: This group of Tad cues represents a range of work from the 1960s to the new millennium.

Tascarella: Pete Tascarella makes custom cues in the tradition of legendary cuemaker and friend George Balabushka.

Taylor: These six custom Taylor cues are all one-of-a-kind examples using ivory and ebony, made by Kent Taylor.

Terbrock: The unique designs of these four cues show the work of Jerry Terbrock.

Tibbitts: Georgia cuemaker Danny Tibbitts specializes in intricate custom cues.

Tice: David Tice cues feature intricate splices and showcase the natural beauty of the exotic woods that he uses.

Tillis: Rocky Tillis was a legendary cuemaker who inspired many contemporary Florida cuemakers.

Viking: Pictured are some of the unique designs available from Viking Cues in Madison, Wisconsin.

Wayne (Thomas): Unique artistic designs are the trademark of Alaska cuemaker Thomas Wayne.

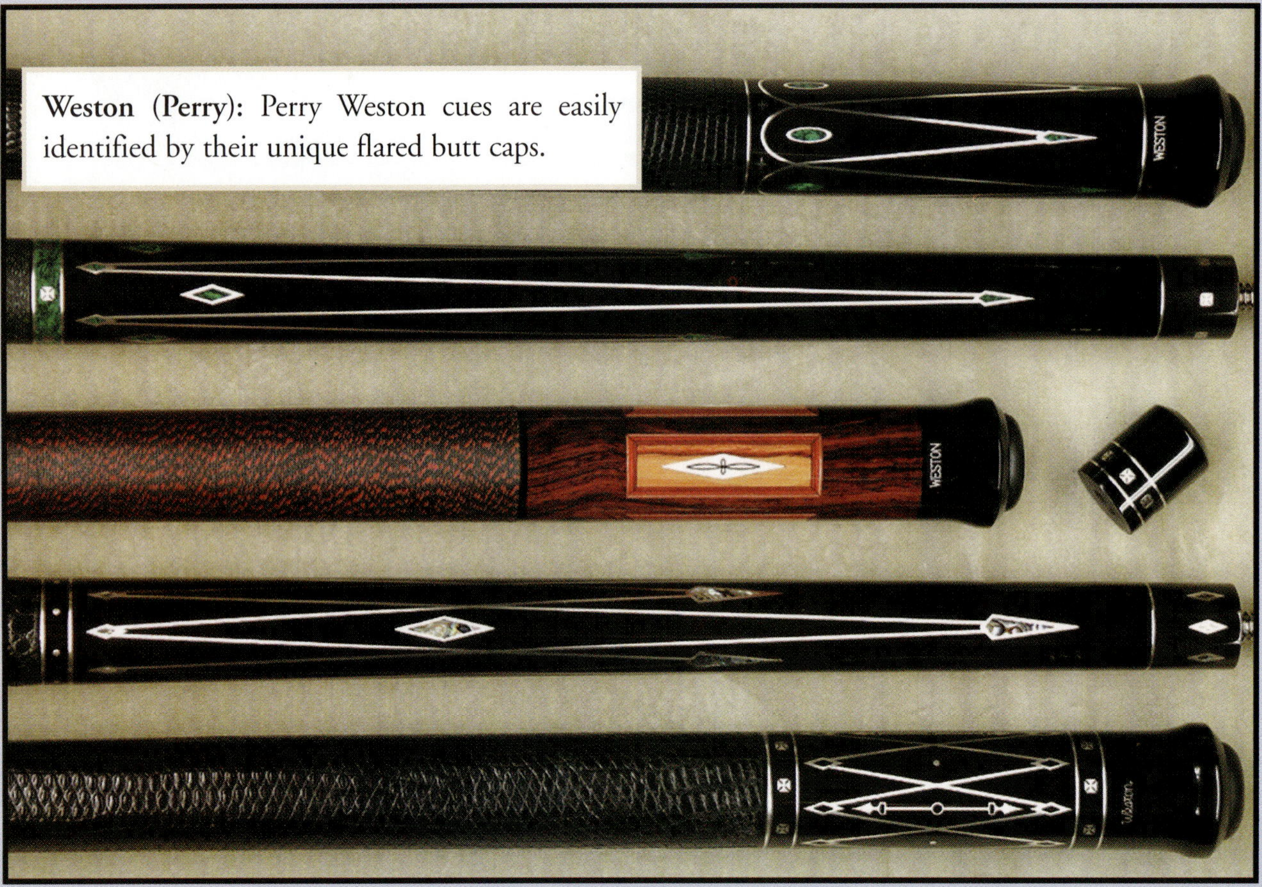

Weston (Perry): Perry Weston cues are easily identified by their unique flared butt caps.

Weston (Skip): The short-spliced blank in the center shows the precision work done by cuemaker Skip Weston.

White: After apprenticing for Paul Mottey, Pittsburgh cuemaker Jim White is now making cues of his own.

Woodworth: These two ivory jointed cues by William Woodworth show the signatures on the forearm that identify Woodworth cues.

Young: Chicago cuemaker Ed Young shares his shop with legendary cuemaker David Kersenbrock.

Zylr: Kerry Zeiler prefers simple cues out of exotic materials that stress playability over intricacy.

Balsis: This is a group of cues made by different cuemakers for the legendary pool player Joe Balsis.

Champion Cues: These cues were made by legendary cuemakers for, and used by, different champions of the past.

Madiera Del Rey: The Madiera Del Rey collection features the work of nine different cuemakers using exotic wood from the same board.

Pro's Cues: Here is a group of custom cues made for some of the top contemporary professional players.

Tuxedo Group: Tony Martino commissions today's finest cuemakers to create one-of-a-kind ebony and ivory cues for his "Tuxedo Collection."

A SECTION

ABEAR CUES

Maker of pool cues from 1984 to 2003 in Arlington, Texas.

Steve Hebert began building one-of-a-kind cues in 1984, and continued to make cues for 17 years (his last cue was made in 2003). Steve's work was known for his use of exotic bones, ivory and horns. Abear Cues were featured on the cover of American Cueist Magazine in 1994. Since then Steve has moved from Arlington, Texas to Salem, Oregon. Steve now works for the Oregon Department of Transportation. He plans to resume cuemaking in Oregon in the future, after taking a few years off.

SPECIFICATIONS

Butt material: hardwoods
Shaft material: rock maple
Standard length: 58 in.
Standard wrap: Irish linen
Point construction: short splice

GRADING

	98%	90%	70%

SECONDARY MARKET MINIMUM VALUES

The following are minimum values for Abear cues encountered on the secondary market. These prices are representative of the cues using the most basic materials and designs that were offered. Abear offered one-of-a-kind cues which can command many times these prices due to the use of exotic materials and artistry.

Special construction note: There are many materials and construction techniques that can add value to Abear cues.

For all used Abear cues, except where otherwise noted:

Add $100 for each additional original straight playable shaft beyond two.
Deduct $150 for missing original straight playable shaft.
Add $75 each for ivory ferrules.
Add $100 for leather wrap.
Add $200+ for each ivory point.
Deduct 25% for obvious or improper refinish.

Level 2 - 0 points, 0-25 inlays.
Level 2 cues start at	$500	$385	$265

Level 3 - 2-6 points, 0-8 inlays.
Level 3 cues start at	$750	$575	$385

Level 4 - 4-10 points, 9-25 inlays.
Level 4 cues start at	$1,000	$785	$550

Level 5 - 0-12 points, 26-50 inlays.
Level 5 cues start at	$1,400	$1,100	$750

AC CUES

For more information, see listing for Ariel Carmeli Cues.

ACTION CUES

Pool cues manufactured in China from 1997 to present by CueStix International Inc. of Lafayette, Colorado.

CueStix is a wholesale billiards distributor which has manufactured the Action cue brand since 1997. The cues are made in China under specifications determined by CueStix, and imported and exclusively distributed to authorized retailers. Many Action cues feature painted designs, and some have short-spliced or inlaid points. All cues have resin butt caps and rubber bumpers. Many have stainless steel joints and a 5/16 size pin with 18 pitch threads. In 2003 CueStix introduced the "Athena Series by Action," designed specifically for women players. Athena cues come in a shorter length (57 inches versus the standard 58 inches) with smaller diameter shafts (12.5 inches versus the standard 13 inches), and include an extension which will screw into a removable butt cap. Hustler cues, Break Jump cues, and a Junior Series (48 and 52 inches) are also offered.

Action cues are easily identified by the "Action " logo in script on the butt cap. CueStix will honor a manufacturer's warranty for parts and workmanship for one year from the date of purchase, excluding warping. At this time no repairs are offered for Action cues. Photos of current examples of Action cues can be viewed on the CueStix website. If you have an Action cue that needs further identification or would like information regarding ordering a new Action cue from an authorized retailer, contact CueStix International Inc., listed in the Trademark Index.

SPECIFICATIONS

Butt material: hardwoods
Shaft material: rock maple

98 ACTION CUES, cont.

GRADING	98%	90%	70%

Standard length: 58 in.
Lengths available: 57 to 58 in.
Standard finish: polyurethane
Standard butt Cap: resin
Standard wrap: Irish linen
Point construction: short spliced
Standard joint: Implex
Joint type: flat-faced
Joint screw thread: 5/16-18
Standard number of shafts: one
Standard taper: 8 to 10 in. pro
Standard ferrules: fiber
Standard tip: proprietary
Standard tip width: 13 mm

CURRENT ACTION CUES

Action cues currently produces a line of over 80 cues ranging in price from $39 to $115 retail. Basic two-piece cues with no wrap start at $39. Hustlers start at $49. Cues with points and wrap start at $89.

SECONDARY MARKET MINIMUM VALUES

The following are minimum values for Action cues encountered on the secondary market. These prices are representative of cues using basic materials and designs that are not necessarily available at present.

Special construction note: There are many materials and construction techniques that can add value to Action cues.

For all used Action cues, except where otherwise noted:

Deduct 50% for missing original straight playable shaft.
Deduct 15% for obvious or improper refinish.

Level 1 - Hustler.
	98%	90%	70%
Level 1 cues start at	$35	$25	$15

Level 2 - 0 points, 0-25 inlays.
Level 2 cues start at	$30	$25	$15

Level 3 - 2-6 points, 0-8 inlays.
Level 3 cues start at	$60	$45	$25

Level 4 - 4-10 points, 9-25 inlays.
Level 4 cues start at	$75	$60	$35

Level 6 - 0-12 points, 51-75 inlays.

ADAM CUSTOM CUES

Maker of pool cues from 1970 to present in Japan. Distributed in the United States by Competition Sports of Farmingdale, New York.

Richard Helmstetter

In 1960 Richard Helmstetter made his first cue in a night school woodworking class. Shortly afterwards, Richard heard about a cuemaker named Rollie Welch, and soon he was on a bus to North Milwaukee. On Friday nights after his classes were over, Richard made shafts for Rollie in exchange for the use of Rollie's lathe. Later in the weekend Richard could work on his own cues; he bought Brunswick one-piece cues, cut them in half, and put in a joint. It was at this time that Richard met Gordon Hart, who wanted to set up a cue shop in the basement of his new pool room in Stoughton, Wisconsin. A deal was struck: if Richard helped Gordon set up the shop, Richard would have a "permanent" part-time job there while he finished his degree at the University of Wisconsin-Madison.

In 1965, Richard took an armload of cues to the annual Johnson City tournament and sold every one of them. It was in Johnson City that he heard about a fellow in Chicago building quality blanks. Soon Gordon and Richard were buying blanks from this man, Burton Spain, to use in their cues. After graduating from college in 1966, Richard moved to Washington, D.C. to start Helmstetter Cues. (Gordon Hart went on to establish Viking Cues.) His namesake company established Richard's reputation as an accomplished craftsman. A year later Richard was offered the opportunity to set up a cuemaking facility for the National Tournament Chalk Company in Chicago. With the combined talents of Richard and other soon-to-be-important cuemakers, National was making high quality cues.

In 1968, Richard met Dave Forman, who was importing two lines of cues which he manufactured in Japan. Dave enlisted Richard to improve and expand his Japanese cuemaking facility. In October of 1969, Richard moved to Japan to begin this project. Richard bought new machinery for the facility and had kilns custom made for drying wood. Two years later, Adam Custom Cues was born, named after

| GRADING | 98% | 90% | 70% |

Dave Forman's first grandson. The twelve models available in 1970 were entirely handmade. By 1973, 60 models were available. Now that Adam-Japan produces thousands of cues a year, the cues are built using state-of-the-art machinery. Adam is now using sixth generation equipment. Some early prototype cues are still handmade.

Richard started producing wood-screw billiard cues during the 1970s, which soon became popular with the world's leading three-cushion billiards players. From the mid-1970s until the early 1990s, the Carl Conlon and CCS ("Carl Conlon Special") and Adam/CCS carom cues were sold in Europe. In 1976, Adam Custom Cues successfully introduced the John Spencer and Harry Harbottle ("HH") lines of snooker cues. Other lines manufactured by Adam over the past 30 years include Julio Stamboulini, Raymond Calvert, Bob Weir, Buffalo, By Helmstetter, Lisciotti, and the Superstar Signature Series—all of which are easily identifiable by visible logos and/or signatures, and are discontinued. "Bob Weir" cues were a private label Adam production cue made for a Texan by that name whose only brush with cuemaking was designing the "flying W" logo embossed on the cues. According to Richard, they were made for three to four years in the 1980s; fewer than 1000 cues were imported from Japan to Texas. Currently Adam-Japan manufactures three lines of cues: Adam, Helmstetter, and the George Balabushka series. The Balabushka cues are made by Adam under license from the Balabushka family in designs similar to what George himself might have made before he passed on in 1975. If your cue has "George Balabushka" on the forearm, it was made by Adam-Japan. These cues are now distributed by Competition Sports Corp.

Despite his status as a seminal figure in cuemaking, Richard Helmstetter is best known for his contributions to the golf world. He returned to live in the United States in 1986, when he joined Callaway Golf, where he is Senior Executive Vice President and Chief of New Products. Richard is the creator of the famed "Big Bertha" driver and Fairway Woods. He still continues to do cue design work for Adam-Japan. Richard's world travels and product development contacts at Callaway have proven helpful to Adam, from sourcing woods to discovering new high-tech materials and machinery.

Collectors are becoming interested in many of the early Adam and Helmstetter cues, particularly those with wood screws. If you have an Adam cue that needs further identification or repair, contact Competition Sports, listed in the Trademark Index.

For more information, please refer to listings for Julio Stambolini Cues, and Bob Weir Cues.

SPECIFICATIONS

Butt material: hardwoods
Shaft material: rock maple
Standard length: 58 in.
Point construction: short splice and full splice
Standard wrap: Irish linen
Standard number of shafts: one

DISCONTINUED ADAM CUES

The following cues are from Adam's first catalogue, circa 1970. They were named after popular cars of the time.

Level 2 R/A-1 "Adam Ltd." - Rosewood forearm, rosewood butt sleeve with a black plastic-bordered metal ring at bottom.

| MSR | N/A | $350 | $275 | $190 |

Level 2 R/A-2 "Adam AMX" - Rosewood forearm, rosewood butt sleeve with a black plastic-bordered red pearlized plastic ring at bottom.

| MSR | N/A | $300 | $230 | $165 |

Level 2 R/A-3 "Cutlass" - Rosewood forearm, rosewood butt sleeve with a thick black plastic-bordered metal ring at bottom.

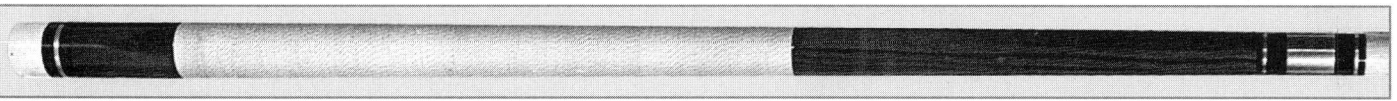

| MSR | N/A | $365 | $275 | $180 |

Level 4 R/A-4 "Tempest" - Maple forearm with ebony dots above the points, full-spliced rosewood handle with four points up and down, maple butt with ebony dots below the points.

| MSR | N/A | $360 | $270 | $175 |

ADAM CUSTOM CUES, cont.

GRADING	98%	90%	70%

Level 2 R/A-5 "Firebird" - Rosewood forearm, pearlized blue plastic butt sleeve with black plastic and metal rings at top and bottom.

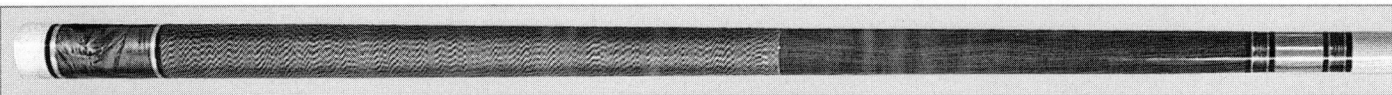

MSR	N/A	$340	$275	$175

Level 3 R/A-6 "Cougar" - Maple forearm, four rosewood points with four colored veneers, rosewood butt sleeve with a black plastic-bordered metal ring at bottom.

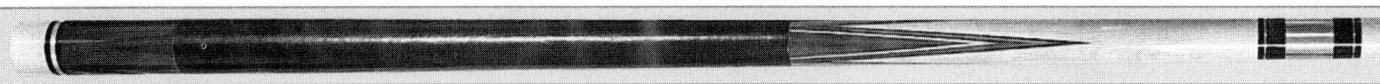

MSR	N/A	$400	$325	$215

Level 3 R/A-7B "Rambow Leather" - Maple forearm, four rosewood points with four colored veneers and a mother-of-pearl dot in each point, leather wrap, rosewood butt sleeve with four mother-of-pearl dots.

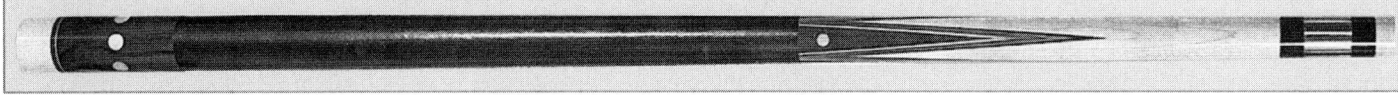

MSR	N/A	$500	$395	$265

Level 3 R/A-7W "Rambow Linen" - Maple forearm, four rosewood points with four colored veneers and a mother-of-pearl dot in each point, rosewood butt sleeve with four mother-of-pearl dots.

MSR	N/A	$490	$385	$255

Level 4 R/A-8 "Adam XR7" - Ebony forearm with mother-of-pearl dots and notched, diamond-shaped inlays, ebony butt sleeve with mother-of-pearl dots and notched diamond-shaped inlays between black plastic and metal rings at top and bottom.

MSR	N/A	$395	$295	$185

Level 3 R/A-9 "Grand Prix" - Maple forearm, four rosewood points with four colored veneers, green pearlized plastic butt sleeve with black plastic and metal rings at top and bottom.

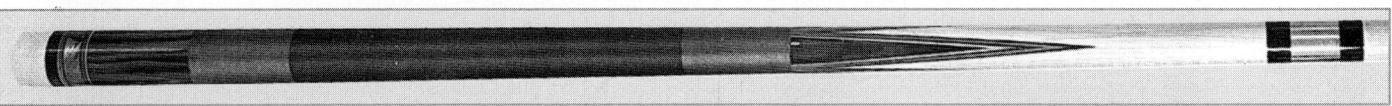

MSR	N/A	$375	$295	$195

Level 3 R/A-10 "Le Mans" - Maple forearm, four ebony points with four colored veneers, ebony butt sleeve with pearlized plastic rings towards bottom.

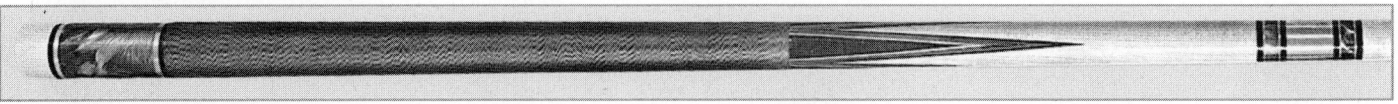

MSR	N/A	$415	$335	$230

Level 4 R/A-11 "Riviera" - Maple forearm, four ebony points with four colored veneers, ebony butt sleeve with mother-of-pearl dots between metal rings at top and bottom.

MSR	N/A	$565	$445	$295

GRADING	98%	90%	70%

Level 4 R/A-12 "Eldorado" - Maple forearm, four ebony points with four colored veneers with mother-of-pearl dots above and below a mother-of-pearl notched diamond-shaped inlay in each point, ebony butt sleeve with mother-of-pearl dots alternating with mother-of-pearl notched diamond-shaped inlays between metal rings at top and bottom.

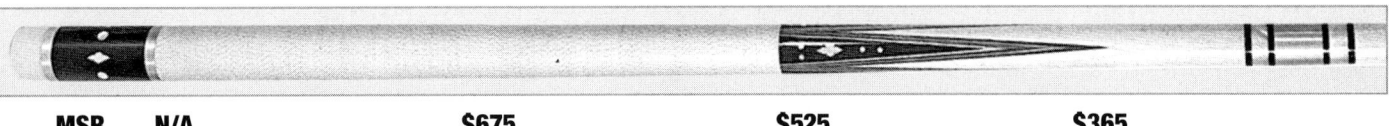

MSR	N/A	$675	$525	$365

MID-1970S TO EARLY 1980S CUES

The following cues were produced by Adam from the mid-1970s through the early 1980s. All came with a stainless steel joint, and one shaft with composition ferrules. The first 12 cues shown were named after major international airlines, and the rest were named after top international hotels, famous aircraft, and rockets.

Level 2 N/B-1 "Delta" - Rosewood forearm with mother-of-pearl-bordered ebony dots alternating with mother-of-pearl dots above wrap, rosewood butt sleeve with mother-of-pearl-bordered ebony dots alternating with mother-of-pearl dots above a pearlized plastic ring at bottom.

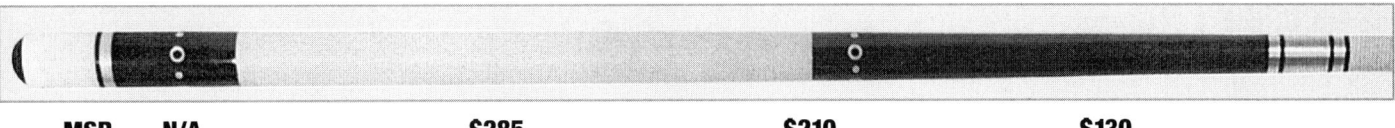

MSR	N/A	$285	$210	$130

Level 2 N/B-2 "Olympic" - Rosewood forearm with three rows of progressively larger mother-of-pearl dots above wrap, black plastic butt sleeve with a pearlized plastic ring between rows of large mother-of-pearl dots above and below.

MSR	N/A	$435	$330	$200

Level 2 N/B-3 "Cathay" - Walnut forearm with a row of ebony-bordered mother-of-pearl dots between rows of ebony dots above wrap, pearlized blue plastic butt sleeve with a pearlized plastic ring between rows of large mother-of-pearl dots above and below.

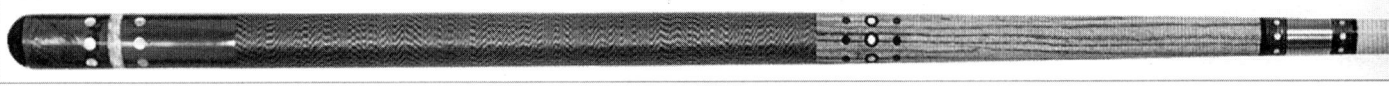

MSR	N/A	$395	$295	$190

Level 6 N/B-4 "Sabena" - Maple forearm, four rosewood points with four colored veneers and an ebony dot within a mother-of-pearl flower-shaped inlay between three progressively smaller mother-of-pearl dots above and below in each point, rosewood butt sleeve with ebony dots within mother-of-pearl flower-shaped inlays between three progressively smaller mother-of-pearl dots above and below alternating with mother-of-pearl dots above white windows set in black at bottom.

MSR	N/A	$610	$475	$320

Level 4 N/B-5 "Varig" - Maple forearm, four rosewood points with four colored veneers and a white rectangle-shaped inlay in each, rosewood butt sleeve with four white rectangle-shaped inlays between white windows set in black at top and bottom.

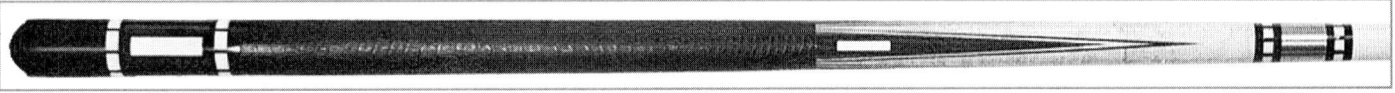

MSR	N/A	$450	$340	$210

Level 6 N/B-6 "Lufthansa" - Rosewood forearm, four rosewood points with four colored veneers and a concentric ebony and mother-of-pearl dot between a pattern of mother-of-pearl dots above and below in each point, rosewood butt sleeve with large mother-of-pearl dots bordered by a ring of small mother-of-pearl dots between progressively smaller mother-of-pearl dots above and below alternating with smaller mother-of-pearl dots between mother-of-pearl windows set within single rows of mother-of-pearl dots set in black at top and bottom.

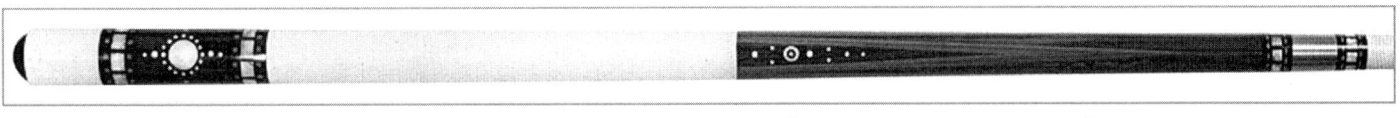

MSR	N/A	$785	$575	$345

ADAM CUSTOM CUES, cont.

GRADING	98%	90%	70%

Level 6 N/B-7 "Continental" - Rosewood forearm, four rosewood points with four colored veneers and a concentric ebony and mother-of-pearl dot between a pattern of mother-of-pearl dots above and below in each point, black plastic butt sleeve with concentric ebony and mother-of-pearl dots connected by a mother-of-pearl line between pearlized white plastic windows set in black at top and bottom.

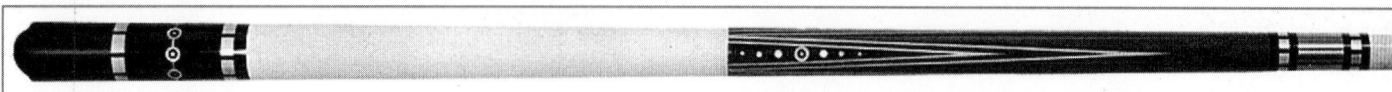

MSR	N/A	$495	$395	$275

Level 6 N/B-8 "United" - Maple forearm, four rosewood points with four colored veneers and two mother-of-pearl flower-shaped inlays alternating with three small mother-of-pearl dots in each point, rosewood butt sleeve with vertical pairs of pearl flower-shaped inlays alternating with three small rows of mother-of-pearl dots.

MSR	N/A	$850	$615	$415

Level 6 N/B-9 "Iberia" - Rosewood forearm with rows of mother-of-pearl dots and notched diamond-shaped inlays, rosewood butt sleeve with vertical rows of mother-of-pearl dots alternating with pearl windows between rows of mother-of-pearl blocks at top and bottom.

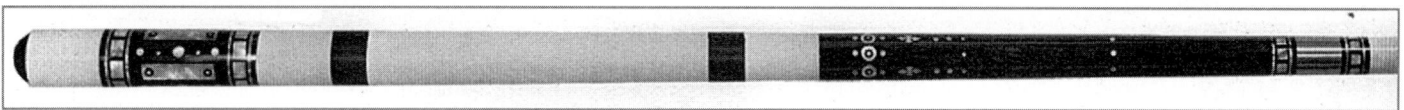

MSR	N/A	$825	$620	$395

Level 6 N/B-10 "Alitalia" - Maple forearm, four rosewood points with four veneers and a series of mother-of-pearl dots in each point, white plastic butt sleeve with sets of black plastic circles within black plastic rings and white plastic blocks.

MSR	N/A	$785	$615	$410

Level 6 N/B-11 "Quantas" - Maple forearm, four cocobolo points with two veneers and mother-of-pearl dots above and below a mother-of-pearl notched diamond-shaped inlay in each point, cocobolo butt sleeve with vertical rows of mother-of-pearl dots alternating with pearl windows between rows of mother-of-pearl blocks at top and bottom.

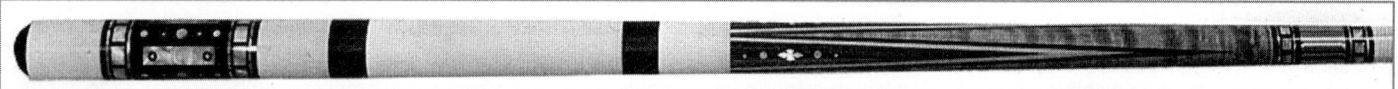

MSR	N/A	$875	$675	$465

Level 5 N/B-12 "Pan American" - Maple forearm, four rosewood points with two veneers and mother-of-pearl dots above and below a mother-of-pearl notched diamond-shaped inlay in each point, rosewood butt sleeve with mother-of-pearl dots above and below a mother-of-pearl notched diamond-shaped inlay in each of four maple-bordered windows between rows of mother-of-pearl blocks at top and bottom.

MSR	N/A	$860	$655	$445

Level 2 A/H-1 "Ambassador" - Maple forearm, maple butt sleeve.

MSR	N/A	$165	$125	$80

Level 2 A/H-1L "Ambassador Leather" - Maple forearm, leather wrap, maple butt sleeve.

MSR	N/A	$195	$145	$90

ADAM CUSTOM CUES, cont. 103

GRADING	98%	90%	70%

Level 2 A/H-2 "Americana" - Maple forearm, maple butt sleeve with four colored pearlized plastic rings at bottom.

MSR	N/A	$175	$135	$80

Level 3 A/H-6 "Dorado" - Maple forearm, four rosewood points with four colored veneers, rosewood butt sleeve.

MSR	N/A	$215	$165	$105

Level 3 A/H-7 "Carlton" - Maple forearm, four ebony points with four colored veneers, ebony butt sleeve.

MSR	N/A	$210	$160	$100

Level 2 A/H-8 "Blackstone" - Ebony forearm with mother-of-pearl notched diamond-shaped inlays within mother-of-pearl dots above wrap, rosewood butt sleeve with mother-of-pearl notched diamond-shaped inlays alternating with mother-of-pearl dots between metal rings at top and bottom.

MSR	N/A	$265	$215	$130

Level 5 A/H-10 "Ritz" - Maple forearm, four rosewood points with four colored veneers and mother-of-pearl notched diamond-shaped inlays within mother-of-pearl dots in each point, rosewood butt sleeve with mother-of-pearl notched diamond-shaped inlays alternating with two rows of mother-of-pearl dots between metal rings at top and bottom.

MSR	N/A	$415	$315	$205

Level 5 A/H-11 "Drake" - Maple forearm, three long and three short ebony points with ebony and mother-of-pearl dots, maple butt sleeve with ebony and mother-of-pearl dots within four veneered ebony windows between ebony and veneer rings at top and bottom.

MSR	N/A	$645	$485	$310

Level 4 A/H-12 "Century" - Maple forearm, four rosewood points with four colored veneers and a mother-of-pearl notched diamond-shaped inlay in each point going up and four rosewood points with four colored veneers coming down, ebony butt sleeve with sets of four mother-of-pearl dots surrounding each of four mother-of-pearl notched diamond-shaped inlays.

MSR	N/A	$795	$600	$380

Level 2 A/H-20 "Sands" - Solid bocote butt.

MSR	N/A	$280	$215	$130

ADAM CUSTOM CUES, cont.

GRADING	98%	90%	70%

Level 2 A/H-21 "Flamingo" - Bocote forearm, bocote butt sleeve with colored pearlized plastic rings at bottom.

MSR	N/A	$270	$205	$130

Level 2 A/H-22 "Stardust" - Ebony forearm with a series of mother-of-pearl dots, ebony butt sleeve with a series of mother-of-pearl dots above plastic and metal rings at bottom.

MSR	N/A	$385	$285	$175

Level 2 A/H-23 "Sahara" - Maple forearm with a series of ebony and mother-of-pearl dots, rosewood butt sleeve with a series of mother-of-pearl and ebony dots between plastic and metal rings at top and bottom.

MSR	N/A	$365	$275	$170

Level 6 A/H-24 "Monaco" - Maple forearm, four rosewood points with four colored veneers and a series of mother-of-pearl and ebony dots in each point, rosewood butt sleeve with a series of mother-of-pearl and ebony dots above plastic and metal rings at bottom.

MSR	N/A	$600	$455	$290

Level 7 A/H-25 "St. Moritz" - Maple forearm with a series of mother-of-pearl and ebony dots above the points, four rosewood points with four colored veneers and a series of mother-of-pearl and ebony dots in each point, rosewood butt sleeve with a series of mother-of-pearl and ebony dots between plastic and metal rings at top and bottom.

MSR	N/A	$885	$655	$410

Level 5 A/H-26 "Monte Carlo" - Maple forearm with a series of mother-of-pearl and ebony dots above the points, four rosewood points with four colored veneers and a series of mother-of-pearl and ebony dots surrounding a mother-of-pearl notched, diamond-shaped inlay in each point, maple butt sleeve with four mother-of-pearl notched, diamond-shaped inlays set in veneer-bordered ebony windows between plastic and veneer rings at top and bottom.

MSR	N/A	$815	$620	$405

Level 2 A/H-30 "Spartan" - Hardwood forearm, hardwood butt sleeve.

MSR	N/A	$165	$130	$80

Level 2 A/H-31 "Sabre" - Rosewood forearm, tulipwood handle, rosewood butt sleeve.

MSR	N/A	$220	$165	$105

ADAM CUSTOM CUES, cont. 105

GRADING	98%	90%	70%

Level 2 A/H-32 "Super Sabre" - Rosewood forearm, tulipwood handle with wrap, rosewood butt sleeve.

MSR	N/A	$255	$195	$110

Level 2 A/H-33 "Nike" - Maple forearm, maple butt sleeve with white and black plastic rings at bottom.

MSR	N/A	$185	$145	$85

Level 2 A/H-34 "Concorde" - Maple forearm, maple butt sleeve with metal and white plastic rings at bottom.

MSR	N/A	$160	$125	$75

Level 3 A/H-35 "Foxbat" - Maple forearm, four ebony points with two veneers, ebony butt sleeve with metal and white plastic rings at bottom.

MSR	N/A	$275	$215	$130

Level 7 A/H-36 "Corsair" - Maple forearm with ebony-bordered mother-of-pearl dots above wrap, four long rosewood points with three veneers and mother-of-pearl dots and notched, diamond-shaped inlays with a maple splice at top alternating with three maple points with three veneers, ebony butt sleeve with four mother-of-pearl notched, diamond-shaped inlays each set in veneer-bordered ebony windows between rows of mother-of-pearl dots and metal rings.

MSR	N/A	$1,150	$850	$510

Level 7 A/H-37 "Galaxie" - Stained maple forearm with ebony-bordered mother-of-pearl dots above wrap, three long rosewood points with three colored veneers and mother-of-pearl dots and notched, diamond-shaped inlays with a maple splice at top alternating with three maple points with three colored veneers, rosewood butt sleeve with four mother-of-pearl notched diamond-shaped inlays each set in colored veneer-bordered rosewood windows between rows of mother-of-pearl dots and metal rings.

MSR	N/A	$1165	$865	$540

Level 7 A/H-38 "Phantom" - Rosewood forearm with a pattern of mother-of-pearl dots and notched diamond-shaped inlays, rosewood butt sleeve with four mother-of-pearl notched diamond-shaped inlays each set in colored veneer-bordered ebony windows between rows of mother-of-pearl dots and metal rings.

MSR	N/A	$750	$565	$350

Level 2 A/H-40 "Atlas" - Solid hardwood butt.

MSR	N/A	$160	$125	$75

GRADING	98%	90%	70%

Level 2 A/H-41 "Apollo" - Solid rosewood butt.

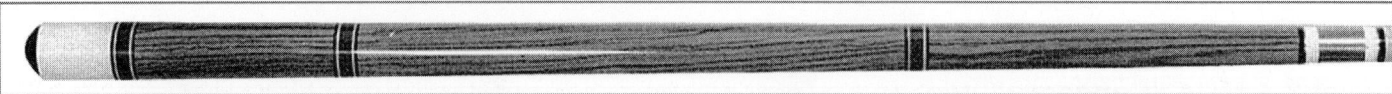

| MSR | N/A | $210 | $160 | $100 |

Level 2 A/H-42 "Gemini" - Bocote forearm with a rosewood ring within black and white plastic rings at bottom, bocote handle with a rosewood ring within black and white plastic rings at bottom, bocote butt sleeve with a rosewood ring within black and white plastic rings at bottom.

| MSR | N/A | $275 | $205 | $130 |

Level 2 A/H-43 "Mercury" - Rosewood forearm with a bocote ring within black and white plastic rings at bottom, rosewood handle with a bocote ring within black and white plastic rings at bottom, rosewood butt sleeve with a bocote ring within black and white plastic rings at bottom.

| MSR | N/A | $300 | $230 | $145 |

Level 2 A/H-44 "Eagle" - Rosewood forearm with mother-of-pearl dots set in a rosewood ring within black and white plastic rings above wrap, rosewood butt sleeve with ebony and mother-of-pearl dots set between mother-of-pearl dots set in a rosewood ring within black and white plastic rings at top and bottom.

| MSR | N/A | $325 | $255 | $160 |

Level 2 A/H-45 "Hercules" - Carved hardwood butt with large rosewood dots and shield-shaped inlays.

| MSR | N/A | $565 | $335 | $270 |

Level 2 A/H-46 "Saturn" - Carved rosewood butt with large mother-of-pearl dots and shield-shaped inlays.

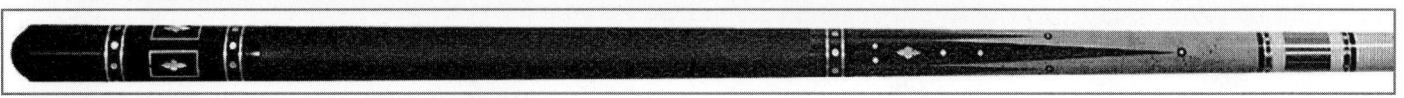

| MSR | N/A | $545 | $415 | $260 |

Level 4 A/H-47 "Regal" - Maple forearm with rows of mother-of-pearl dots set within metal rings above wrap, three long ebony points with mother-of-pearl dots and notched diamond-shaped inlays and an ebony-bordered mother-of-pearl dot at the tip alternating with three short ebony points with an ebony-bordered mother-of-pearl dot at the tip, ebony butt sleeve with four mother-of-pearl notched diamond-shaped inlays each set in veneer-bordered ebony windows between rows of mother-of-pearl dots set within metal rings.

| MSR | N/A | $900 | $685 | $420 |

TWIN JOINT PROFESSIONAL CUES

The following Twin Joint Professional series cues featured a piloted stainless steel joint that had a necked down screw with two different thread dimensions. Maple stitching was featured on the butt and shaft collars. Extra shafts were available for $100 each.

ADAM CUSTOM CUES, cont.

GRADING	98%	90%	70%

Level 2 TJ-1 - Burgundy-stained maple forearm, burgundy-stained maple butt sleeve.

MSR (1996) $180	$165	$130	$80

Level 2 TJ-2 - Grey-stained bird's-eye maple forearm, grey-stained bird's-eye maple butt sleeve.

MSR (1996) $200	$175	$135	$85

Level 2 TJ-3 - Burgundy-stained maple forearm with laminated strips of tulipwood, burgundy-stained maple butt sleeve with laminated strips of tulipwood.

MSR (1996) $232	$200	$155	$95

Level 2 TJ-4 - Light-stained bird's-eye maple forearm, light-stained bird's-eye maple butt sleeve with four black "X"-shaped inlays.

MSR (1996) $268	$250	$195	$125

Level 2 TJ-5 - Light green-stained bird's-eye maple forearm, white butt sleeve with four black-bordered abalone windows above black and white checks within black rings at bottom.

MSR (1996) $272	$255	$200	$125

Level 2 TJ-6 - Light grey-stained bird's-eye maple forearm, black butt sleeve with four stylized light grey-stained bird's-eye maple windows with a black-bordered white dot at the center of each.

MSR (1996) $276	$260	$205	$130

Level 2 TJ-7 - Bird's-eye maple forearm, bird's-eye maple butt sleeve with a ring pattern of bird's-eye maple triangles set in purpleheart between thin purpleheart rings at top and bottom.

MSR (1996) $308	$260	$200	$125

Level 2 TJ-8 - Bird's-eye maple forearm with black and white checks within nickel silver rings set in purpleheart above wrap, purpleheart butt sleeve with a ring of diagonal maple and ebony windows between black and white checks within nickel silver rings.

MSR (1996) $320	$280	$205	$135

Level 3 TJ-9 - Bird's-eye maple forearm, four cocobolo points, cocobolo butt sleeve with four white dots each surrounded by a hollow white triangle.

MSR (1996) $328	$300	$225	$140

ADAM CUSTOM CUES, cont.

GRADING	98%	90%	70%

Level 3 TJ-10 - Bird's-eye maple forearm, four ebony points with four colored veneers, ebony butt sleeve with black and white rings at bottom.

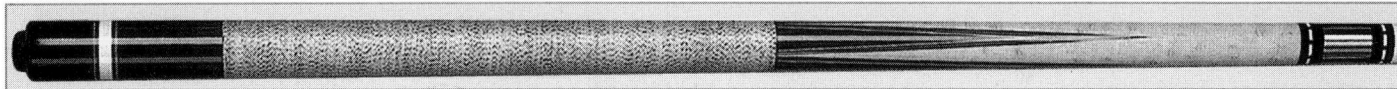

MSR (1996) $360	$325	$235	$150

Level 3 TJ-11 - Bird's-eye maple forearm, three long and three short ebony points, ebony butt sleeve with a ring of black and white checks within nickel silver rings at bottom.

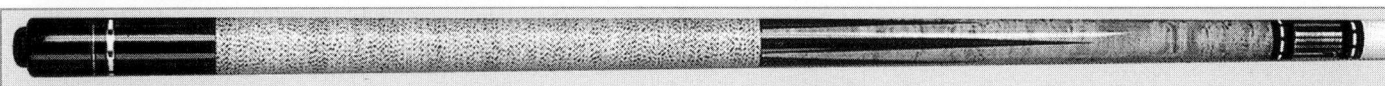

MSR (1996) $364	$330	$240	$155

Level 3 TJ-12 - Maple forearm, four bocote points with three colored veneers, bocote butt sleeve with four mother-of-pearl dots alternating with laminations of three colored veneers.

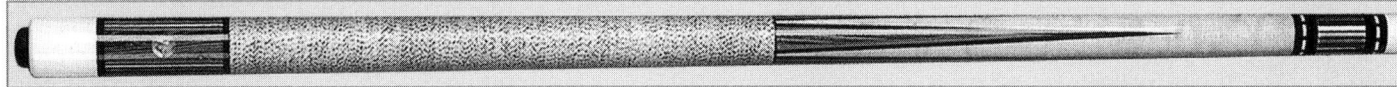

MSR (1996) $368	$335	$245	$155

Level 3 TJ-13 - Grey-stained bird's-eye maple forearm, four ebony points with three colored veneers, ebony butt sleeve with black-bordered mother-of-pearl dots set in a white ring towards bottom.

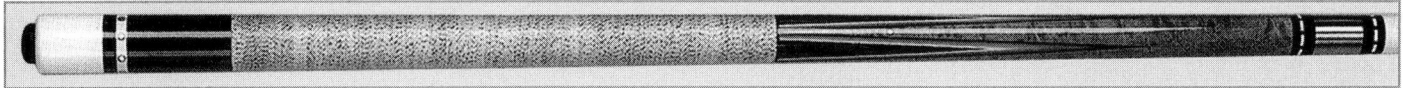

MSR (1996) $380	$345	$250	$160

Level 3 TJ-14 - Maple forearm with an ebony diamond-shaped inlay above each short point, two long and two short ebony points with single colored veneers, ebony butt sleeve with four ebony diamond-shaped inlays set in a red-bordered maple ring.

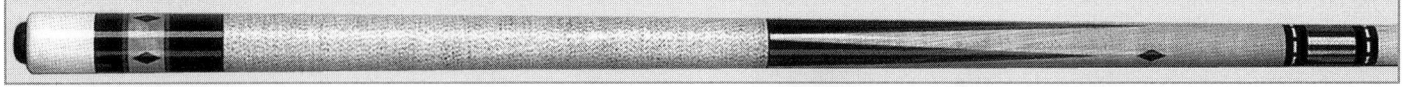

MSR (1996) $416	$365	$260	$170

Level 4 TJ-15 - Dark-stained bird's-eye maple forearm with a thick ring of ebony above wrap, four ebony points with a white stylized diamond-shaped inlay between two small white squares in each point, ebony butt sleeve with four white stylized diamond-shaped inlays each between two small white squares.

MSR (1996) $428	$375	$280	$175

Level 2 TJ-16 - Bird's-eye maple forearm with four floating intricate four-point ebony stars with a black-bordered white dot within a red oval in the center of each, bird's-eye maple butt sleeve with four intricate, four-point ebony stars with a black-bordered white dot within a red oval in the center of each.

MSR (1996) $440	$380	$285	$180

Level 3 TJ-17 - Bird's-eye maple forearm, four ebony points with four colored veneers and a long white diamond-shaped inlay in each, ebony butt sleeve with four long white diamond-shaped inlays between double white dash rings above and below.

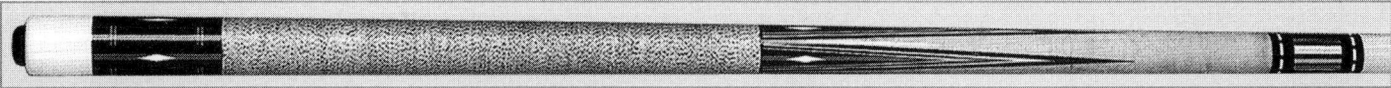

MSR (1996) $440	$385	$290	$190

ADAM CUSTOM CUES, cont. 109

GRADING	98%	90%	70%

Level 4 TJ-18 - Bird's-eye maple forearm with mother-of-pearl dots between the points, four ebony points with four colored veneers and a mother-of-pearl notched diamond-shaped inlay in each, ebony butt sleeve with four mother-of-pearl notched diamond-shaped inlays alternating with four mother-of-pearl dots.

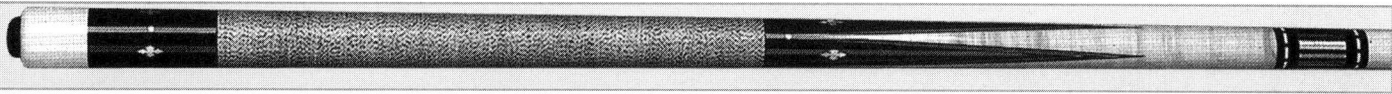

MSR (1996) $448	$395	$300	$195

Level 4 TJ-19 - Light-stained bird's-eye maple forearm, four tulipwood points with four colored veneers, cocobolo butt sleeve with four white, diamond-shaped inlays within ebony ovals set in stylized tulipwood windows within a thick ebony ring.

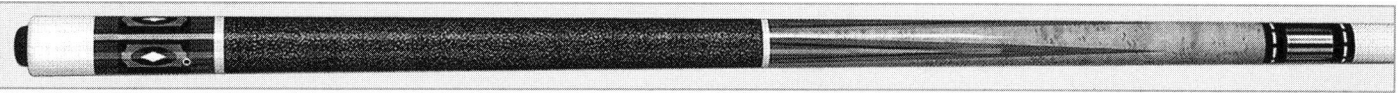

MSR (1996) $452	$400	$305	$190

Level 4 TJ-20 - Dark-stained bird's-eye maple forearm with black-bordered mother-of-pearl dots within a white ring above the wrap and a black-bordered mother-of-pearl dot above each long point, three long and three short ebony points, ebony butt sleeve with long ebony rectangles alternating with long dark-stained bird's-eye maple rectangles between black-bordered mother-of-pearl dots within white rings above and below.

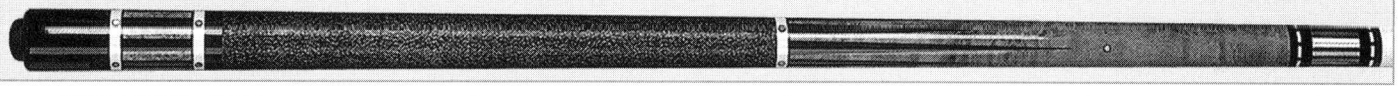

MSR (1996) $460	$405	$310	$195

Level 3 TJ-21 - Grey-stained bird's-eye maple forearm with black and white checks within nickel silver rings above wrap, four black-bordered white points, ebony butt sleeve with long ebony rectangles each inlaid with a white diamond-shaped inlay alternating with long white rectangles between black and white checks within nickel silver rings above and below.

MSR (1996) $504	$450	$340	$210

Level 5 TJ-22 - Bird's-eye maple forearm, three long ebony points with a mother-of-pearl notched diamond-shaped inlay in each and a black-bordered mother-of-pearl dot at the tip of each alternating with three short ebony points with a mother-of-pearl dot in each and an ebony dot at the tip of each, ebony butt sleeve with six mother-of-pearl notched diamond-shaped inlays alternating with six long thin maple windows between mother-of-pearl dots above and below each window.

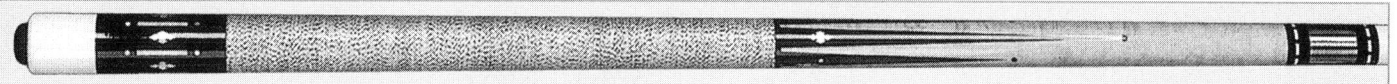

MSR (1996) $544	$500	$380	$235

Level 5 TJ-23 - Bird's-eye maple forearm, four ebony points with four colored veneers and an ebony diamond-shaped inlay at the tip of each with a notched mother-of-pearl diamond-shaped inlay between two mother-of-pearl dots above and below in each point, ebony butt sleeve with four sets of mother-of-pearl notched diamond-shaped inlays between two mother-of-pearl dots above and below alternating with four mother-of-pearl dots above black and white checks within nickel silver rings below.

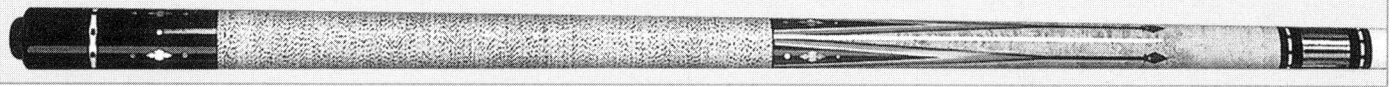

MSR (1996) $572	$515	$390	$250

Level 4 TJ-24 - Grey-stained bird's-eye maple forearm, four short rosewood points with four colored veneers spliced over four long ebony points with a notched mother-of-pearl diamond-shaped inlay between two mother-of-pearl dots above and below in each point, rosewood butt sleeve with four mother-of-pearl diamond-shaped inlays alternating with four mother-of-pearl dots in a thick ebony ring.

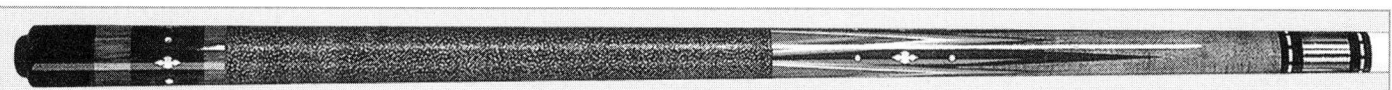

MSR (1996) $604	$550	$420	$265

ADAM CUSTOM CUES, cont.

GRADING		98%	90%	70%

Level 5 TJ-25 - Bird's-eye maple forearm with six stylized tulipwood hexagons between the points each inlaid with a black-bordered mother-of-pearl dot, six ebony points with a white diamond-shaped inlay in each, ebony butt sleeve with six stylized tulipwood hexagons set over long maple bars each inlaid with a black-bordered mother-of-pearl dot alternating with six white diamond-shaped inlays between white rings at top and bottom.

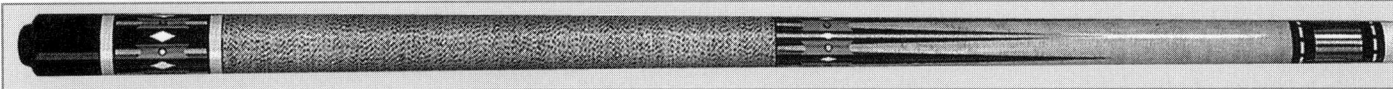

MSR (1996) $668	$565	$425	$270

Level 4 TJ-26 - Bird's-eye maple forearm with four rosewood diamond-shaped inlays between points, four ebony points with two colored veneers and a mother-of-pearl arch in each point, ebony butt sleeve with four downward-pointing ebony points with two colored veneers and a mother-of-pearl arch in each point alternating with four rosewood diamond-shaped inlays set over long maple bars.

MSR (1996) $708	$625	$475	$300

HELMSTETTER H SERIES CUES

The following Helmstetter H Series cues featured a stainless steel joint and maple stitching on the butt and shaft collars. Each cue had the Helmstetter signature on the forearm. Extra shafts were available for $100 each.

Level 2 H-1 - Grey-stained bird's-eye maple forearm with white dashes set in a black ring above wrap, grey-stained bird's-eye maple butt sleeve with four mother-of-pearl notched diamond-shaped inlays set in rosewood ovals alternating with rosewood bars between white dashes set in black rings above and below.

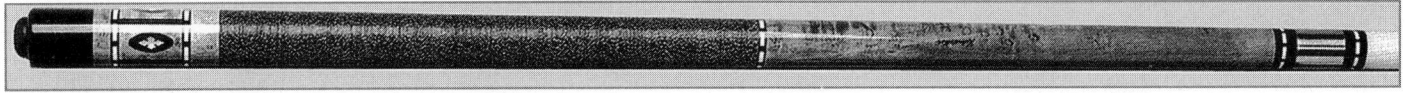

MSR (1996) $320	$300	$225	$140

Level 3 H-2 - Grey-stained bird's-eye maple forearm, four ebony points with four colored veneers, ebony butt sleeve with black-bordered mother-of-pearl dots set in a white ring at bottom.

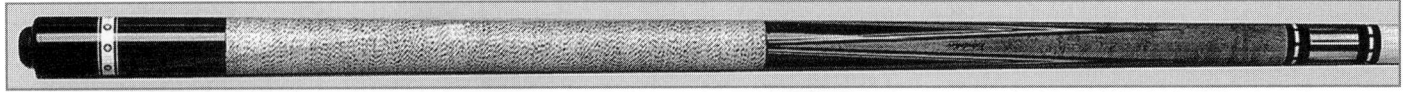

MSR (1996) $380	$350	$265	$165

Level 4 H-3 - Bird's-eye maple forearm, four ebony points with three colored veneers and a white stylized arrowhead-shaped inlay in each, ebony butt sleeve with four downward-pointing white stylized arrowhead-shaped inlays alternating with four upward-pointing white stylized arrowhead-shaped inlays above three colored rings at bottom.

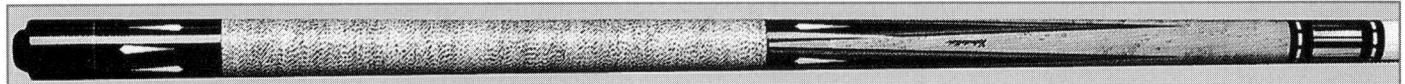

MSR (1996) $440	$400	$300	$190

Level 5 H-4 - Stained bird's-eye maple forearm, three short ebony points alternating with three long ebony points with a four-piece white diamond-shaped inlay in each, ebony butt sleeve with four, four-piece white diamond-shaped inlays alternating with four white diamond-shaped inlays above a white ring at bottom.

MSR (1996) $450	$415	$320	$205

Level 4 H-5 - Bird's-eye maple forearm with white dashes set in an ebony ring above wrap and a black ebony dot above each long point, three short ebony points with a mother-of-pearl dot in each alternating with three long ebony points with a mother-of-pearl notched diamond-shaped inlay in each, ebony butt sleeve with three mother-of-pearl notched diamond-shaped inlays alternating with three mother-of-pearl dots between white dashes set in ebony rings above and below.

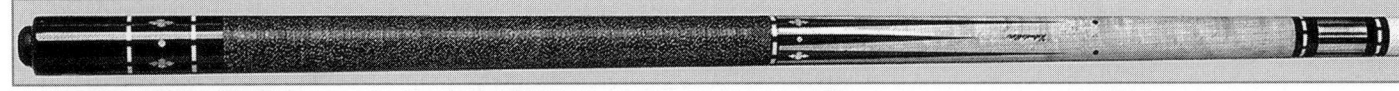

MSR (1996) $520	$475	$360	$230

ADAM CUSTOM CUES, cont. 111

GRADING	98%	90%	70%

Level 5 H-6 - Bird's-eye maple forearm, three short ebony points with two colored veneers spliced over three long ebony points with a four-piece white diamond-shaped inlay in each, ebony butt sleeve with four, four-piece white diamond-shaped inlays set in red veneer rectangles above a thin red ring at bottom.

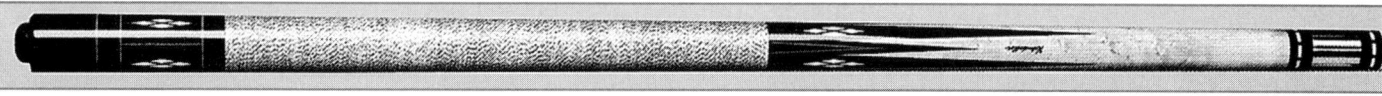

MSR (1996)	$580	$525	$345	$255

Level 3 H-7 - Stained bird's-eye maple forearm, four white points with a thick black veneer, white butt sleeve with four stylized windows set in a thick ebony ring between white dashes set in ebony rings above and below.

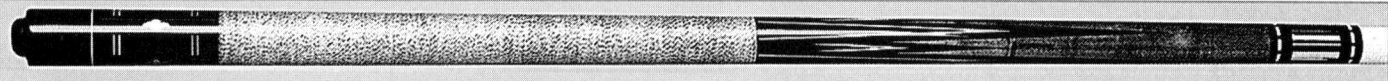

MSR (1996)	$460	$425	$325	$215

Level 3 H-8 - Grey-stained bird's-eye maple forearm, three long ebony points with two colored veneers spliced over three short ebony points with two colored veneers, ebony butt sleeve with three mother-of-pearl notched diamond-shaped inlays between pairs of long maple dash rings above and below.

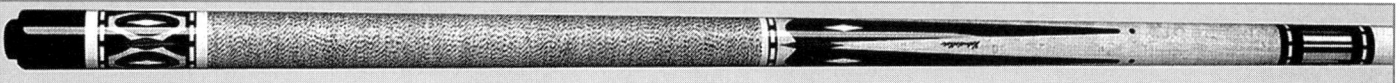

MSR (1996)	$550	$500	$380	$240

Level 4 H-9 - Bird's-eye maple forearm with an ebony dot above each point and four large rosewood diamond-shaped inlays between the point bases and white dashes set in an ebony ring above wrap, four floating ebony points with a white diamond-shaped inlay in each, white butt sleeve with four white diamond-shaped inlays set in ebony ovals within maple octagons divided by four large rosewood diamond-shaped inlays between white dashes set in ebony rings above and below.

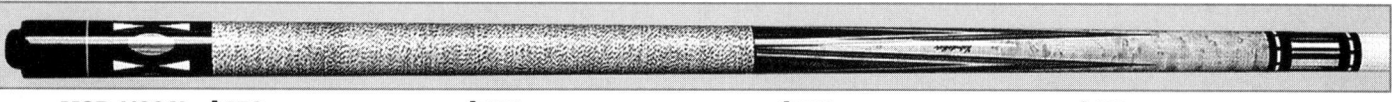

MSR (1996)	$900	$825	$625	$400

Level 4 H-10 - Bird's-eye maple forearm, four rosewood points with four colored veneers, rosewood butt sleeve with four tulipwood ovals alternating with four pairs of inward-pointing white triangles.

MSR (1996)	$450	$400	$300	$190

Level H-11 - Bird's-eye maple forearm, three long ebony points with a mother-of-pearl notched diamond-shaped inlay in each spliced over three short ebony points, ebony butt sleeve with six ebony hexagons with a mother-of-pearl notched diamond-shaped inlay set in every other one within a maple ring at bottom.

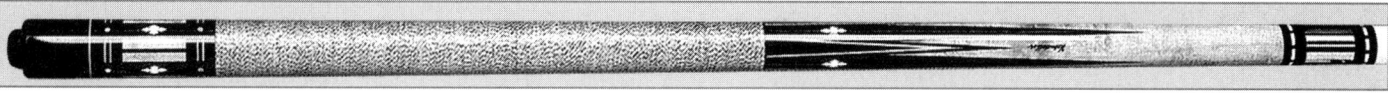

MSR (1996)	$550	$500	$375	$235

Level H-12 - Bird's-eye maple forearm, three short ebony points with two colored veneers spliced over three long ebony points with a mother-of-pearl notched diamond-shaped inlay in each, ebony butt sleeve with three mother-of-pearl notched diamond-shaped inlays alternating with three pairs of long thin maple windows between rings of long maple dashes alternating with mother-of-pearl dots above and below.

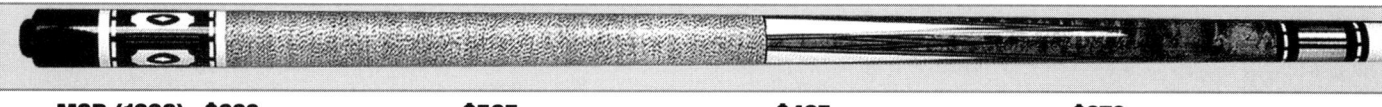

MSR (1996)	$580	$525	$400	$250

Level H-13 - Stained bird's-eye maple forearm, three long white points with three colored veneers spliced over three short grey-stained bird's-eye maple points with three colored veneers, white butt sleeve with three white diamond-shaped inlays set in ebony ovals within white stylized windows alternating with three pairs of blue veneers in a thick ebony ring between white dashes set in ebony rings above and below.

MSR (1996)	$620	$565	$425	$270

| GRADING | 98% | 90% | 70% |

HELMSTETTER 97 SERIES CUES

The following Helmstetter 97 Series cues featured a stainless steel joint with a double nickel/silver ring design and interchangeable shafts. All cues featured standard Irish linen wraps and Le Pro tips.

Level 2 97-1 - Rosewood forearm, rosewood butt sleeve with a pair of nickel silver rings set in black at bottom. Also available in natural bird's-eye maple and cherry-stained bird's-eye maple.

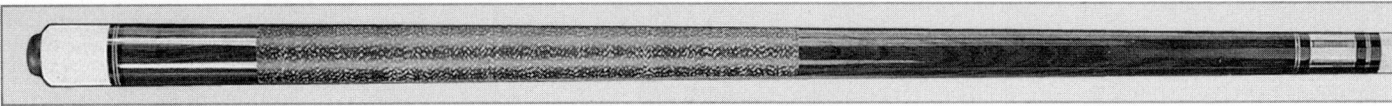

| MSR (1997) $140 | $100 | $75 | $45 |

Level 3 97-4 - Bird's-eye maple forearm, four black rosewood points, black rosewood butt sleeve with a pair of nickel silver rings set in black within maple in middle.

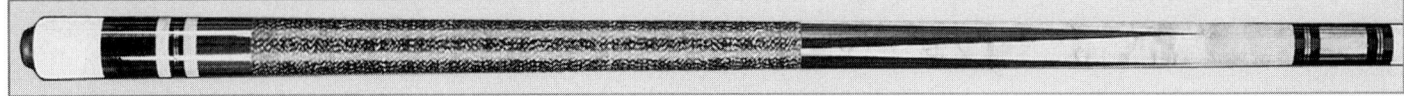

| MSR (1997) $170 | $125 | $95 | $60 |

Level 4 97-5 - Rosewood forearm, four rosewood points with four colored veneers and a mother-of-pearl diamond-shaped inlay in each, rosewood butt sleeve with four mother-of-pearl diamond-shaped inlays between pairs of nickel silver rings set in black rings at top and bottom.

| MSR (1997) $190 | $140 | $105 | $65 |

Level 5 97-6 - Bird's-eye maple forearm, four ebony points with four colored veneers and a mother-of-pearl diamond-shaped inlay in each, ebony butt sleeve with four mother-of-pearl diamond-shaped inlays alternating with mother-of-pearl dots above and below and between with a pair of nickel silver rings set in black at bottom.

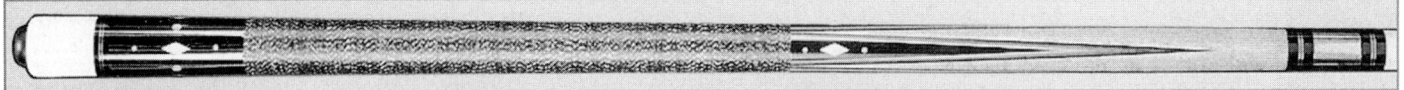

| MSR (1997) $220 | $160 | $125 | $75 |

Level 3 97-7 - Bocote forearm, four ebony points with four colored veneers and an abalone diamond-shaped inlay in each, ebony butt sleeve with four large abalone dots inlaid in middle above a thin red ring at bottom.

| MSR (1997) $240 | $170 | $130 | $80 |

Level 4 97-8 - Smoke-stained bird's-eye maple forearm, four cerosite points with thick ebony veneers and an ebony gun-sight-shaped inlay in each, ebony butt sleeve with four intricate ebony inlaid cerosite windows between pairs of nickel silver rings set in black rings at top and bottom.

| MSR (1997) $260 | $185 | $140 | $90 |

Level 4 97-9 - Bird's-eye maple forearm, four ebony points with four colored veneers and a mother-of-pearl notched diamond-shaped inlay in each, maple butt sleeve with eight yellow veneer lines alternating with mother-of-pearl notched diamond- and dot-shaped inlays set in a thick ebony ring between pairs of nickel silver rings set in black rings at top and bottom.

| MSR (1997) $280 | $200 | $150 | $90 |

ADAM CUSTOM CUES, cont. 113

GRADING	98%	90%	70%

Level 4 97-10 - Bird's-eye maple forearm, four long ebony points with green-stained maple and ebony veneers with a mother-of-pearl diamond-shaped inlay between a mother-of-pearl dot above and two mother-of-pearl dots below in each long point alternating with four short ebony points with green-stained maple and ebony veneers, ebony butt sleeve with four mother-of-pearl diamond-shaped inlays set in ebony shield-shaped inlays within maple windows and a green veneer box pattern between pairs of nickel silver rings set in black rings at top and bottom.

| MSR (1997) $330 | $240 | $180 | $110 |

Level 5 97-11 - Bird's-eye maple forearm, four long ebony points with a mother-of-pearl diamond-shaped inlay between a mother-of-pearl dot above and below alternating with four short ebony points with a mother-of-pearl dot in each, ebony butt sleeve with four mother-of-pearl diamond-shaped inlays between mother-of-pearl dots above and below alternating with four large white windows between pairs of nickel silver rings set in black rings at top and bottom.

| MSR (1997) $340 | $245 | $190 | $115 |

Level 4 97-12 - Smoke-stained bird's-eye maple forearm, four long cerosite points with stained maple and ebony veneers with an ebony gun-sight-shaped inlay in each alternating with four short maple points with stained maple and ebony veneers, ebony butt sleeve with eight stylized cerosite windows between mother-of-pearl dots set in purpleheart within pairs of nickel silver rings above and below.

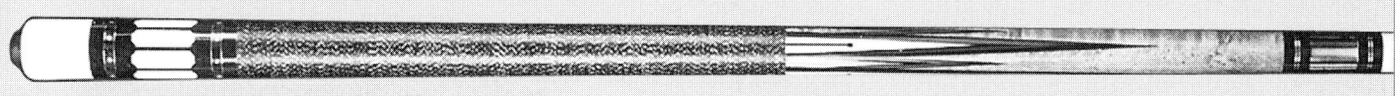

| MSR (1997) $350 | $250 | $195 | $120 |

Level 4 97-13 - Bird's-eye maple forearm, four long ebony points with four colored veneers alternating with four maple butterfly-spliced points with two colored veneers, ebony butt sleeve with four two-piece maple windows hollowed in an oval shape alternating with four red veneer lines between pairs of nickel silver rings above and below.

| MSR (1997) $395 | $285 | $215 | $135 |

Level 4 97-14 - Smoke-stained bird's-eye maple forearm with a thick bird's-eye maple ring above wrap, four rosewood points with thick ebony veneers and an ebony diamond-shaped inlay at the tip of each and between the base of each, maple butt sleeve with four rosewood windows alternating with four ebony-bordered diamond-shaped inlays framed in an ebony box pattern.

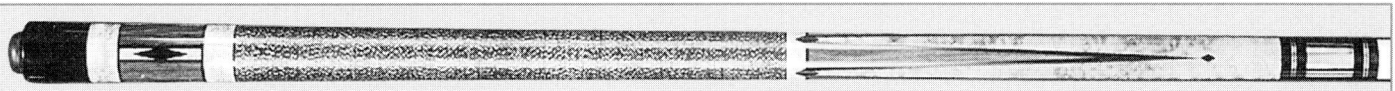

| MSR (1997) $415 | $300 | $230 | $140 |

Level 4 97-15 - Rosewood forearm with a nickel silver ring set in black above wrap, four Mozambique points with a mother-of-pearl diamond-shaped inlay set in an ebony spear-shaped inlay in each, Mozambique butt sleeve with four mother-of-pearl diamond-shaped inlays set in an ebony spear-shaped inlays between nickel silver rings set in black at top and bottom.

| MSR (1997) $440 | $315 | $240 | $150 |

Level 5 97-16 - Bird's-eye maple forearm with a purpleheart ring above wrap, four ebony points with an intricate four-piece Ivorine diamond-shaped inlay in each alternating with four ebony-bordered Ivorine four-point-star-shaped inlays, ebony butt sleeve with four intricate four-piece Ivorine diamond-shaped inlays alternating with four Ivorine four-point-star-shaped inlays above a thick maple ring between purpleheart rings at top and bottom.

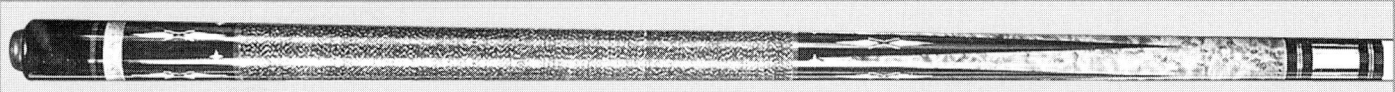

| MSR (1997) $425 | $305 | $225 | $140 |

GRADING	98%	90%	70%

Level 5 97-17 - Bird's-eye maple forearm, four cocobolo points with four colored veneers and a mother-of-pearl notched diamond-shaped inlay set between a mother-of-pearl dot above and below in each with a small mother-of-pearl dot within an ebony diamond-shaped inlay at the tip of each point, ebony butt sleeve with four mother-of-pearl notched diamond-shaped inlays set between mother-of-pearl dots above and below alternating with four mother-of-pearl dots above ebony and Ivorine checks within a pair of nickel silver rings at bottom.

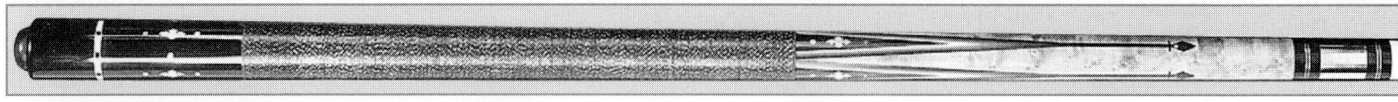

MSR (1997)	$520	$380	$295	$180

HELMSTETTER 98 SERIES

The following Helmstetter 98 Series cues featured a stainless steel joint with a checked burgundy-stained maple ring design, and interchangeable shafts. All cues featured standard Irish linen wraps and Le Pro tips.

Level 2 98-1 - Purpleheart forearm, purpleheart butt sleeve.

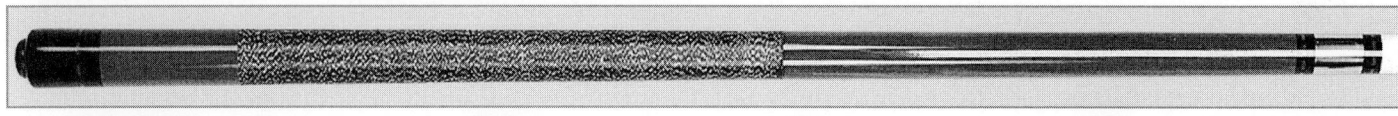

MSR (1998)	$120	$90	$70	$40

Level 4 98-2 - Smoke-stained maple forearm, four ebony points with four colored veneers and a pearlized plastic diamond-shaped inlay between two pearlized plastic dots in each point, ebony butt sleeve with four sets of pearlized plastic diamond-shaped inlays between two pearlized plastic dots set between rows of burgundy-stained maple checks above and below.

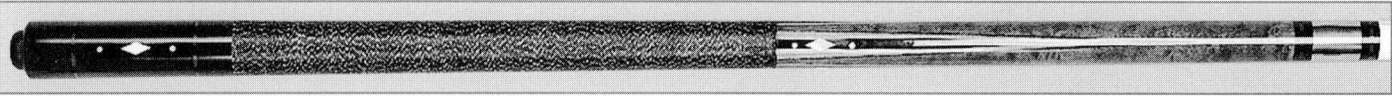

MSR (1998)	$220	$175	$135	$80

Level 5 98-3 - Maple forearm, four ebony points with four colored veneers and a pearlized plastic oval-shaped inlay between two pearlized plastic dots in each point, ebony butt sleeve with four sets of pearlized plastic oval-shaped inlays between two pearlized plastic dots alternating with four tall maple windows set between rows of burgundy-stained maple checks above and below.

MSR (1998)	$230	$180	$135	$85

Level 5 98-4 - Maple forearm, four purpleheart points with four colored veneers and a pearlized plastic oval-shaped inlay between two ebony dots in each point, purpleheart butt sleeve with four sets of pearlized plastic oval-shaped inlays between two ebony dots alternating with four tall ebony windows inlaid with pairs of pearlized plastic dots set between rows of purpleheart checks above and below.

MSR (1998)	$270	$200	$155	$95

Level 5 98-5 - Purpleheart forearm, four ebony points with four colored veneers and a pearlized plastic notched diamond-shaped inlay between two pearlized plastic dots in each point, ebony butt sleeve with four sets of pearlized plastic notched diamond-shaped inlays between two pearlized plastic dots alternating with four stylized purpleheart windows with three ebony dots in each set between rows of purpleheart checks above and below.

MSR (1998)	$310	$225	$170	$100

ADAM CUSTOM CUES, cont. 115

GRADING	98%	90%	70%

Level 4 98-6 - Smoke-stained maple forearm, three long hardwood points with ebony veneers and a pearlized plastic dot in each alternating with three short hardwood points with ebony veneers, hardwood butt sleeve with six pearlized plastic notched diamond-shaped inlays set in a maple- and ebony-bordered ebony ring with rows of six pearlized plastic dots above and below set between rows of burgundy-stained maple checks at top and bottom.

| MSR (1998) | $310 | $225 | $175 | $105 |

Level 4 98-7 - Smoke-stained maple forearm, six ebony points with a pearlized plastic dot in each, ebony butt sleeve with three white diamond-shaped inlays set between a pair of pearlized plastic dots alternating with three pearlized plastic notched square-shaped inlays.

| MSR (1998) | $340 | $240 | $185 | $115 |

Level 4 98-8 - Smoke-stained maple forearm, three long ebony points with a pearlized plastic dot in each alternating with three short ebony points with a pearlized plastic dot in each, ebony butt sleeve with six stylized smoke-stained maple windows inlaid with three ebony dots each set between rows of six pearlized plastic dots above and below.

| MSR (1998) | $350 | $250 | $190 | $120 |

Level 4 98-9 - Smoke-stained maple forearm, three long ebony points with two colored veneers and a pearlized plastic dot in each alternating with three short ebony points with two colored veneers and a a pearlized plastic dot in each, ebony butt sleeve with six white diamond-shaped inlays set between rows of six pearlized plastic dots within maple veneers above and below.

| MSR (1998) | $360 | $255 | $195 | $120 |

Level 5 98-10 - Smoke-stained maple forearm, eight long ebony points with a pearlized plastic dot in each, ebony butt sleeve with eight hardwood windows inlaid with pairs of ebony dots within burgundy-stained maple checked borders set between rows of six pearlized plastic dots above and below.

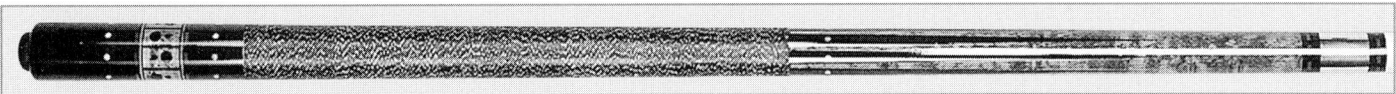

| MSR (1998) | $370 | $260 | $200 | $125 |

HELMSTETTER TJ SERIES

The following Helmstetter TJ Series cues featured a stainless steel joint with a patented double-threaded design, nickel/silver ringed collars, and interchangeable shafts. All cues featured standard Irish linen wraps and Le Pro tips.

Level 2 TJ-27 - Smoke-stained maple forearm, ebony butt sleeve with four large white-bordered tulipwood diamond-shaped inlays.

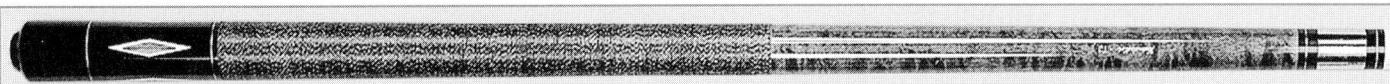

| MSR (1999) | $220 | $175 | $130 | $80 |

Level 2 TJ-28 - Stained maple forearm, stained maple butt sleeve with intricate ebony-bordered white diamond-shaped inlays between tulipwood rings at top and bottom.

| MSR (1999) | $230 | $185 | $140 | $85 |

ADAM CUSTOM CUES, cont.

GRADING	98%	90%	70%

Level 4 TJ-29 - Maple forearm, four ebony points with a large white inlay in each, ebony butt sleeve with eight large white inlays.

MSR (1999) $250	$195	$150	$90

Level 3 TJ-30 - Stained maple forearm, four ebony points with three colored veneers, ebony butt sleeve.

MSR (1999) $260	$200	$155	$95

Level 3 TJ-31 - Smoke-stained maple forearm, four burgundy-stained maple points with two colored veneers and a white diamond-shaped inlay in each, burgundy-stained maple butt sleeve with four white diamond-shaped inlays.

MSR (1999) $290	$220	$160	$100

Level 3 TJ-32 - Smoke-stained maple forearm, four cocobolo points with three colored veneers, ebony butt sleeve with four white diamond-shaped inlays set in white-bordered ebony windows.

MSR (1999) $300	$225	$165	$110

Level 4 TJ-33 - Stained maple forearm, three long ebony points with a white four-point-star-shaped inlay in each alternating with three short ebony points, ebony butt sleeve with four white and tulipwood-bordered white diamond-shaped inlays alternating with four white four-point-star-shaped inlays below a tulipwood ring at top.

MSR (1999) $340	$250	$190	$120

ADAM CUSTOM SERIES CUES

The following Adam Custom series cues featured Irish linen wrap on all but A1 and A2. Implex joints are standard except for A1, which has an invisible joint and A4 and A6-A7 cues, which have stainless steel joints.

Level 1 A1 - Maple forearm, four rosewood points and butt sleeve.

MSR (1999) $75	$55	$45	$25

Level 2 A2 - One-piece rosewood butt.

MSR (1999) $60	$45	$35	$20

Level 2 A3 - Rosewood forearm, rosewood butt sleeve.

MSR (1999) $65	$45	$35	$20

Level 2 A4 - Rosewood forearm, rosewood butt sleeve with a steel-bordered black ring at bottom.

MSR (1999) $70	$50	$40	$20

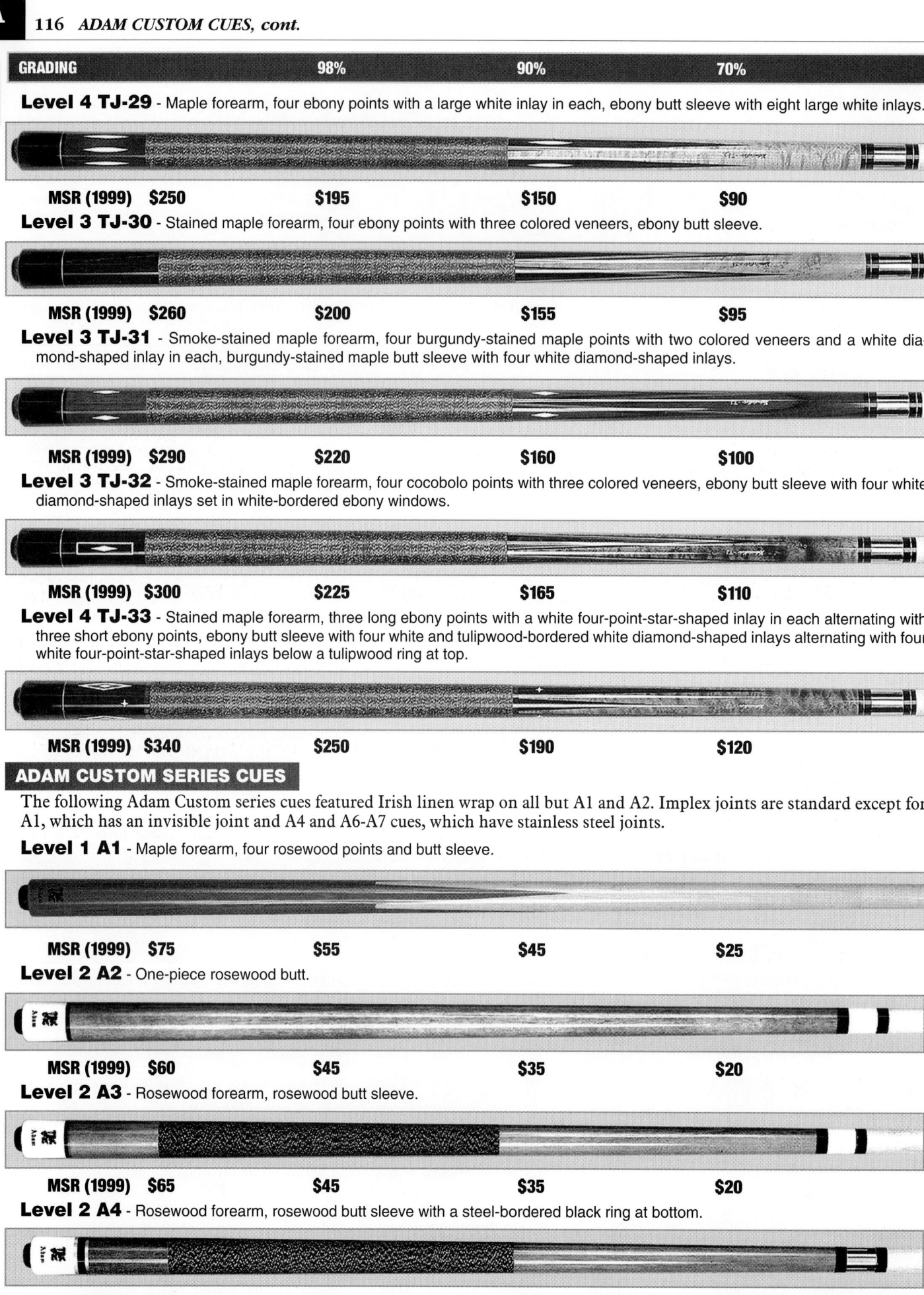

ADAM CUSTOM CUES, cont.

GRADING	98%	90%	70%

Level 2 A5 - Stained bird's-eye maple forearm and butt sleeve. Irish linen wrap. Available in blue, smoke gray, natural, red, or green stain.

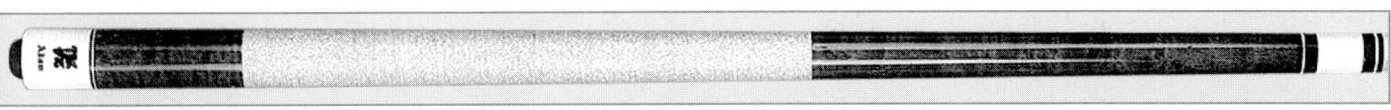

MSR (1999) $120	$80	$60	$35

Level 2 A6 - Stained bird's-eye maple forearm and butt sleeve. Stainless steel joint. Available in brown, smoke gray, natural, or multi-color stain.

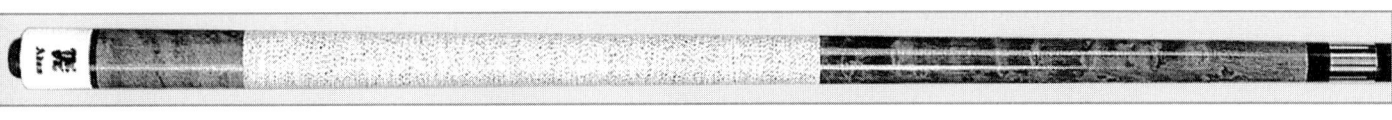

MSR (1999) $140	$100	$75	$45

Level 2 A7 - Smoke-stained bird's-eye maple forearm with joint and extra wrap above wrapped handle, smoke-stained bird's-eye maple butt sleeve.

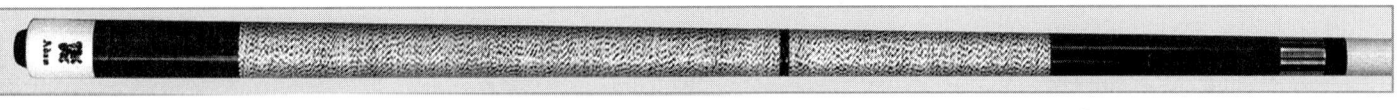

MSR (1999) $150	$105	$80	$50

Adam Deluxe Custom Designs DX Series Cues - The Adam Deluxe Custom Designs DX Series cues were available in eight models (DX-1 through DX-8). All featured a stainless steel joint and steel rings on the butt and shaft collars. All cues had stained bird's-eye maple forearms and butt sleeves. Each cue had applied images on the points and butt sleeve that looked like inlays, but were less expensive to produce, resulting in an inexpensive yet intricate cue. The example shown is typical; all had an MSR of $140 in 2004.

Level 3 DX-1 - Natural-stained bird's-eye maple forearm, four ebony points with two colored veneers and an intricate patterned applied image in each, ebony butt sleeve with an intricate repeated pattern applied image similar to the ones in the points between steel rings set in ebony at top and bottom.

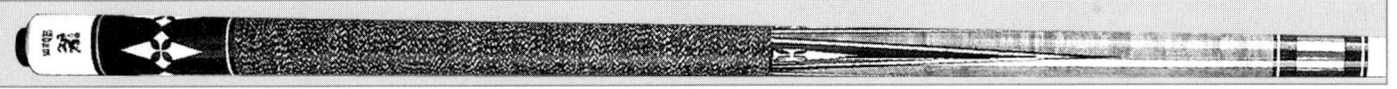

MSR (2004) $140	$110	$85	$50

SECONDARY MARKET MINIMUM VALUES

The following are minimum values for other Adam cues encountered on the secondary market. These prices are representative of cues using basic materials and designs that are not currently available. Adam has offered one-of-a-kind cues that can command higher prices due to the use of exotic materials or unique designs or rarity. Early models and limited editions are becoming collectible, and can also command many times these prices.

Special construction note: There are many materials and construction techniques that can add value to Adam cues. (Please refer to chapters in the front of the book). The following are the most important examples:

Add up to 500% for custom cues made by R.C. Helmstetter that are signed and dated.
Add 200%+ for handmade prototype cues.
Add 50%+ for limited edition and signature cues made by Helmstetter.

For all used Adam cues, except where otherwise noted:

Add $75+ for each additional original straight playable shaft (standard with one).
Deduct $80 for missing original straight playable shaft.
Add $75 each for ivory ferrules.
Add $85 for leather wrap.
Deduct 30% for obvious or improper refinish.
Add 25% for totally original finish, wrap, shaft, and ferrules for cues from first Adam catalog (c. 1970).
Add 20% for totally original finish, wrap, shaft, and ferrules for early cues from airline/hotel/aircraft series c.1975-1982.

Level 1 - 4 points, hustler.

Level 1 cues start at	$75	$60	$35

Level 2 - 0 points, 0-25 inlays.

Level 2 cues start at	$65	$50	$30

Level 3 - 2-6 points, 0-8 inlays.

Level 3 cues start at	$135	$100	$60

GRADING	98%	90%	70%
Level 4 - 4-12 points, 9-25 inlays.			
Level 4 cues start at	$275	$210	$130
Level 5 - 0-12 points, 26-50 inlays.			
Level 5 cues start at	$400	$305	$190
Level 6 - 0-12 points, 51-75 inlays.			
Level 6 cues start at	$550	$425	$260

GUS ADAMS

Maker of pool cues in the Los Angeles, California area in the 1950s.

In addition to building cues, Gus operated a billiard supply store in the Los Angeles area.

SHERM ADAMSON

Maker of Sherm cues. For more information see listing for Sherm Custom Cues.

ADVANCED ACCURACY CUES

Line of American-made pool cues distributed from 1995 to present, currently made in Dorsey, Illinois. In 1995 professional pool player and instructor Mark Wilson started to develop a line of cues totally focused on the cue's performance. The result was Advanced Accuracy Cues, built for maximum playability. After working with several cuemakers (Doug Patrick, J. Pechauer) over the years, Mark teamed up in 2002 with J. Michael Durbin, who is now crafting the line of true custom-fitted cues distributed by Mark. Mike Durbin also makes custom pool cues under his own company name, Durbin Custom Cues.

The cues are built by hand to suit each customer's hand size and height. Custom shaft sizes, cue lengths, and weights are offered at no extra charge. Inspired by Joe Gold of Cognoscenti, they exclusively use a G-10 glass epoxy joint pin, which they believe allows more "feel." All components are made by Mike except for the tips and bumpers. Cues are clearly marked "Mark Wilson's Advanced Accuracy Cues." Three standard models are offered, and one-of-a-kind custom cues are also available. The current order time for a custom fitted cue is three months. Repairs are done on Advanced Accuracy Cues only; call for prices.

If you would like to order a new Advanced Accuracy cue, contact Advanced Accuracy Cues, listed in the Trademark Index.

For more information, please refer to the listing for "DURBIN CUSTOM CUES."

SPECIFICATIONS

Butt material: hardwood
Shaft material: rock maple
Standard length: custom
Lengths available: 55 to 61 in.
Standard finish: urethane
Standard joint screw: 3/8-10
Standard joint: G-10 glass epoxy
Standard joint type: flat face
Balance point: custom
Point construction: short splice or inlaid
Standard wrap: Irish linen
Standard butt cap: LBM
Standard number of shafts: one
Standard ferrule: Aegis II
Other ferrule options: ivory
Standard tip: Le Pro
Standard bumper: rubber, screw-in
Annual production: 50 cues

OPTIONS (FOR NEW CUES ONLY)

Extra shaft: $125
Ivory joint: $150
Ivory butt cap: $240
Ivory ferrule: $75
Layered tip: $15

CURRENT ADVANCED ACCURACY CUES

Currently three models are available: the Ball Crusher Break Jump cue for $400, the Shot Maker 2020 for $500, and the top-of-the-line cue with veneered points, the Rack Runner 2040 for $700. Custom Advanced Accuracy Cues start at $800.

ADVANCED ACCURACY CUES, cont.

GRADING	98%	90%	70%

SECONDARY MARKET MINIMUM VALUES

The following are minimum values for other Advanced Accuracy cues encountered on the secondary market.
Special construction note: There are many materials and construction techniques that can add value to Advanced Accuracy cues.
For all used Advanced Accuracy cues, except where otherwise noted:

- Add $100 for each additional original straight playable shaft beyond one.
- Deduct $125 for missing original straight playable shaft.
- Add $65 each for ivory ferrules.
- Deduct 20% for obvious or improper refinish.

Level 2 - 0 points, 0-25 inlays.
Level 2 cues start at	$350	$245	$185

Level 3 - 2-6 points, 0-8 inlays.
Level 3 cues start at	$600	$475	$325

Level 4 - 4-12 points, 9-25 inlays.
Level 4 cues start at	$700	$550	$375

Level 5 - 0-12 points, 26-50 inlays.
Level 5 cues start at	$1,000	$800	$550

AE CUES

Maker of pool cues from 1992 to present in Aurora, Colorado.

Bruce Kuhn and Jeff Fugal became neighbors and friends in 1978. They've shared a variety of common interests, including playing pool. Jeff attended college for a short time after high school, and then apprenticed in a machine shop where he first worked as a machinist, and later as a tool grinder and tool maker. His father was a custom cabinet maker.

Cue Signature

1992 to 1994

Bruce Kuhn & Jeff Fugal

Bruce grew up working in his father's well-equipped shop, learning how to use wood- and metal-working tools and equipment. His father was self-employed, and Bruce helped him build everything from furniture to a tractor. Even while he studied for his degree in business management, and later worked in corporate management, he continued to do custom woodworking and mechanical work.

One day Bruce and Jeff visited Bill Stroud's cue shop to buy custom cues from him, and emerged with the idea of building their own cues. They started out in 1990 by doing cue repairs, and analyzing the top cues in the market. Soon they began to develop their own designs and construction techniques. After two years of cue building and testing, the first AE cue was offered for sale in 1992. Originally, the name "AE Cues" was derived from Aardvark Enterprises, and a few early cues had an aardvark cut into the butt cap. The AE name and logo have remained, but "Aardvark Enterprises" has been dropped in favor of "Artistic Engineering," which Jeff and Bruce feel is a more accurate reflection of their cues. All AE Cues are easily identified by the AE logo that has been cut into the butt cap of every cue since AE Cue's inception. To help with identification, since 1996 a signature and date have been put under the wrap of every cue. An individual serial number was also stamped under the rubber bumper on earlier cues, which can be seen by removing the bumper with an Allen wrench. Today, Bruce and Jeff make approximately 100 cues per year without the help of employees. They have been making cues full time since 1994, and they moved their business from Bruce's garage to a commercial building in 2000. Construction techniques have been evolving since AE Cue's beginning. Both Bruce and Jeff are perfectionists and bring their own skills and talents to the partnership, resulting in a cue showing the best that both have to offer while having to meet the exacting standards of each.

All AE cues are guaranteed indefinitely to the original owner against construction defects that are not the result of warping, natural material movement or cracking, or abuse. If you have an AE cue that needs further identification or repair, or would like to talk to Bruce or Jeff about ordering a new cue, contact AE Cues, listed in the Trademark Index.

SPECIFICATIONS

Butt material: hardwoods
Shaft material: rock maple
Standard length: 58 in.
Special lengths available: 56 to 62 in.
Standard finish: two-part urethane
Joint screw: Uni-Loc radial
Standard joints: linen phenolic or stainless steel
Joint type: flat face (phenolic) or piloted (stainless steel)
Point construction: short splice or inlaid
Standard wrap: Irish linen
Standard butt cap: linen phenolic

| GRADING | 100% | 95% | 70% |

Standard number of shafts: two
Standard taper: 10.5 in. straight pro taper
Ferrules: melamine
Standard tip: Talisman pigskin laminate
Tip widths available: 11 to 13.75 mm
Annual production: 100 cues

OPTIONS (FOR NEW CUES ONLY)

Leather wrap: $100
Lizard wrap: $175
Ivory joint: $150
Ivory butt cap: $250
Ivory ferrule: $50
Extra shaft: $150+

REPAIRS

Repairs done on most fine cues.
Refinish (with leather wrap): $300+
Refinish (with Irish linen wrap): $200+
Rewrap (leather): $150
Rewrap (lizard): $225
Rewrap (linen): $50
Replace ivory butt cap: $250 + refinish
Replace shaft: $150+
Replace ivory ferrule: $85
Replace tip: $15+
Replace layered Tip: $20+

CURRENT AE CUES

AE cues currently start at $650 for a basic two-piece cue with or without points. AE Cues currently specializes in one-of-a-kind or limited edition custom cues. The current delivery time for a custom cue is four to twelve months.

The following AE cues can be ordered as shown or customized to suit the desires of the customer.

Level 2 - Ebony forearm with a ring of ivory dots and spears above wrap, three ebony butt sleeves with rings of ivory dots and spears at top and bottom.

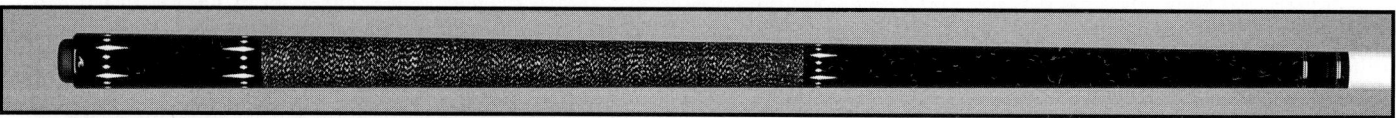

| MSR | $900 | $800-1,000 | $665 | $500 |

Level 3 - Bird's-eye maple forearm with turquoise set in sterling silver rings above wrap, three long and three short ebony points, ebony butt sleeve with turquoise set in sterling silver rings at top and bottom.

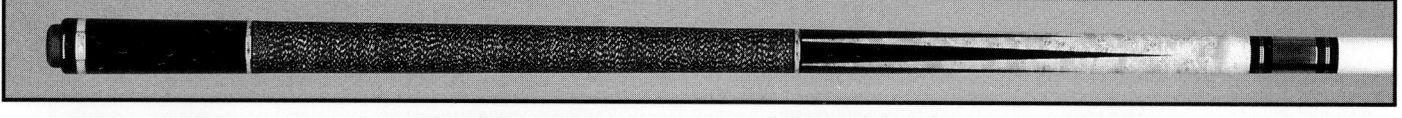

| MSR | $900 | $800-1,000 | $665 | $500 |

Level 3 - Ebony forearm with an ebony ring above wrap, three long and three short myrtle burl points, myrtle burl butt sleeve with six ebony lines between an ebony ring below wrap and ivory blocks set in ebony at bottom.

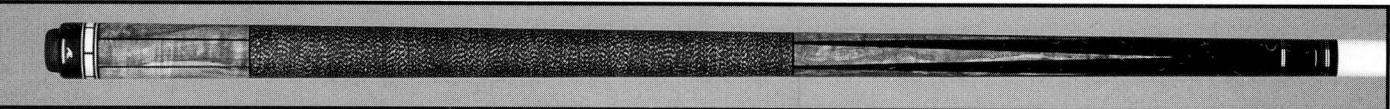

| MSR | $1,000 | $900-1,100 | $745 | $550 |

GRADING	100%	95%	70%

Level 4 - Quilted maple forearm with a ring of purpleheart and ebony and maple above wrap, three long and three short purpleheart points with two veneers, purpleheart butt sleeve with six pairs of large ivory opposing spear-shaped inlays alternating with six smaller ivory diamond-shaped inlays between rings of purpleheart and ebony and maple at top and bottom.

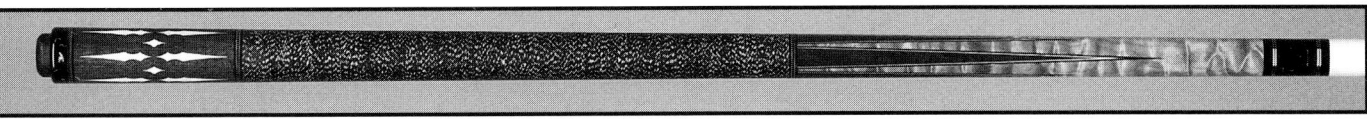

MSR	$1,300	$1,200-1,450	$950	$675

Level 4 - Tiger maple forearm with a sterling silver ring set in ebony above wrap, four ebony points with two veneers and an ivory rectangle-shaped inlay in each, ebony butt sleeve with eight large intricate ivory inlays alternating with eight smaller ivory rectangle-shaped inlays between a sterling silver ring set in ebony below wrap and ivory blocks set in ebony and sterling silver rings at bottom.

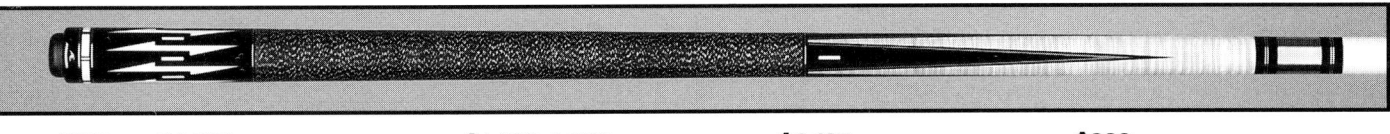

MSR	$1,500	$1,400-1,650	$1,125	$800

Level 4 - Tiger maple forearm with a red veneer set in an ebony ring above wrap, four long and four short ebony points with an ivory diamond-shaped inlay in each, leather wrap, ebony butt sleeve with eight large ivory diamond-shaped inlays alternating with eight smaller ivory diamond-shaped inlays between red veneers set in ebony rings at top and bottom.

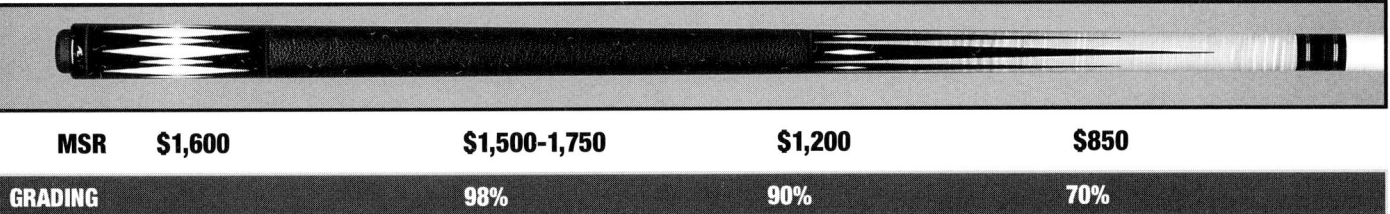

MSR	$1,600	$1,500-1,750	$1,200	$850

GRADING	98%	90%	70%

SECONDARY MARKET MINIMUM VALUES

The following are minimum prices for other AE Cues encountered on the secondary market. These prices include cues using basic materials and designs that may not be currently available. Simple "cut-down"-style hustler cues are no longer produced; current hustler cues are custom made, cored four-point cues with no veneers. Jeff and Bruce make many one-of-a-kind cues that can command premium prices due to fine detail work or the use of exotic materials such as precious metals, shells, stone, rare woods and burls.

Special construction note: There are many materials and construction techniques that can add value to AE cues. The following are the most important examples:

Add $500+ for ivory points.
Add $750+ for ivory butt sleeve.

For all used AE Cues, except where otherwise noted:

Add $150+ for each additional original straight playable shaft (standard with two).
Deduct $150 for missing original straight playable shaft.
Add $150+ for ivory joint.
Add $100+ for leather wrap.
Add $50 for each ivory ferrule.

Level 1 – Hustler.
Level 1 cues start at	$350	$275	$175

Level 2 - 0 points, 0-25 inlays.
Level 2 cues start at	$450	$365	$250

Level 3 - 2-6 points, 0-8 inlays.
Level 3 cues start at	$600	$465	$325

Level 4 - 4-12 points, 9-25 inlays.
Level 4 cues start at	$1,000	$815	$600

Level 5 - 0-12 points, 26-50 inlays.
Level 5 cues start at	$1,400	$1,075	$750

Level 6 - 0-12 points, 51-75 inlays.
Level 6 cues start at	$2,000	$1,600	$1,100

Level 7 - 0-12 points, 76-125 inlays.
Level 7 cues start at	$2,500	$1,950	$1,350

GRADING	98%	90%	70%
Level 8 - 0-16 points, 126-200 inlays.			
Level 8 cues start at	$3,750	$2,900	$1,900

AKERS CUES

Maker of pool cues from 2003 to present in Mediapolis, Iowa.

Bill Akers started making cues in 2003. He has always enjoyed the game of pool and his background in woodworking brought him to becoming a cuemaker. He strives for playability and quality in his cues. He is always looking for new and improved products and is always experimenting with new construction techniques.

Bill works out of a small shop in the back of his house. It is equipped with a standard lathe for doing butt caps, collars, and pins. He has a taper machine for shafts, butts, and billets, and a pantograph for doing inlays.

2003 to present

Bill Akers

Bill's cues can be identified by his signature with the month and year, usually in the point, but sometimes in or just above the buttcap. All of his cues are custom order, made from scratch.

Akers cues are guaranteed for life on construction defects that are not the result of warpage or abuse.

If you are interested in talking to Bill Akers about a new cue or cue that needs to be repaired, you can contact him at Akers Cues, which is listed in the Trademark Index.

SPECIFICATIONS

Butt material: hardwoods
Shaft material: rock maple
Standard length: 58 in.
Standard wrap: Irish linen
Standard ferrules: Ivorine-3
Standard tip: Le Pro
Annual production: fewer than 30 cues

OPTIONS (FOR NEW CUES ONLY)

Ivory ferrule: $75
Ivory joint: $175
Leather wrap: $100+
Extra shaft: $100
Ivory buttcap: $275

REPAIRS

Repairs done on all fine cues.
Refinish (with Irish linen wrap): $150
Rewrap (Irish linen): $40
Replace shaft: $100
Replace tip: $10+

CURRENT AKERS CUES

Two-piece Akers bar cues cues start at $200. Basic Akers cues with wraps and joint rings start at $325. Akers cues with points start at $425. One-of-a-kind custom Akers cues start at $550. The current delivery time for an Akers cue is three to six months, depending on the intricacy of the cue.

SECONDARY MARKET MINIMUM VALUES

The following are minimum values for other Akers cues encountered on the secondary market. These prices are representative of cues utilizing basic materials and designs that are not necessarily available at present. Bill has offered one-of-a-kind cues that can command many times these prices due to the use of exotic materials and artistry.

Special construction note: There are many materials and construction techniques that can add value to Akers cues.

For all used Akers cues, except where otherwise noted:

Add $75 for each additional original straight playable shaft beyond one.
Deduct $100 for missing original straight playable shaft.
Add $50 each for ivory ferrules.

GRADING	98%	90%	70%

Add $60 for leather wrap.
Deduct 20% for obvious or improper refinish.

	98%	90%	70%
Level 1 - Hustler.			
Level 1 cues start at	$175	$135	$90
Level 2 - 0 points, 0-25 inlays.			
Level 2 cues start at	$300	$235	$160
Level 3 - 2-6 points, 0-8 inlays.			
Level 3 cues start at	$400	$315	$215
Level 4 - 4-10 points, 9-25 inlays.			
Level 4 cues start at	$500	$390	$270
Level 5 - 0-12 points, 26-50 inlays.			
Level 5 cues start at	$700	$545	$375

J. ALAN CUES

Maker of pool cues from 1998 to present in Jonesboro, Arkansas.

Jeff Smith has a background in woodworking, machining, custom knife making, and woodcarving. He has always loved buying and trading cues, and has enjoyed owning high quality cues. This has lead to an interest in cue construction and repair, materials, and, finally, cuemaking. He learned from Billy Webb, Alex Brick, Chris Hightower, and Ken Churchill. Jerry Franklin, Mike Bender, and David Paul Kersenbrock have all inspired Jeff's work.

If you are interested in talking to Jeff Smith about a new cue or cue that needs repaired, you can contact him at J. Alan Cues, listed in the Trademark Index.

SPECIFICATIONS

Butt material: hardwoods
Shaft material: rock maple or laminated maple
Standard length: 58 in.
Lengths available: any up to 60 in.
Standard finish: automotive clearcoat
Balance point: 18 in. from butt
Standard butt cap: linen phenolic
Standard wrap: Irish linen
Point construction: short splice
Standard joint: linen phenolic
Joint type: flat-faced
Joint screw thread: 3/8-10
Standard number of shafts: one
Standard taper: pro
Standard ferrules: micarta
Other ferrule options: linen melamine
Standard tip: Le Pro
Standard tip width: 13 mm
Tip widths available: up to 14 mm
Annual production: fewer than 15 cues

OPTIONS (FOR NEW CUES ONLY)

Special length: no charge
Layered tip: $20
Ivory butt cap: $200
Ivory joint: $150
Ivory ferrule: $50
Joint protectors: $25+
Extra shaft: $85

REPAIRS

Repairs done on all fine cues.
Refinish (with Irish linen wrap): $150
Rewrap (Irish linen): $40
Clean and press linen wrap: $20
Replace ivory ferrule: $50
Replace tip: $10 Le Pro
Replaced layered tip: $25
Replace fiber/linen ferrule: $25

124 J. ALAN CUES, cont.

| GRADING | 98% | 90% | 70% |

SECONDARY MARKET MINIMUM VALUES

The following are minimum values for other J. Alan cues encountered on the secondary market. These prices are representative of cues using basic materials and designs that are not necessarily available at present. Jeff has offered one-of-a-kind cues that can command many times these prices due to the use of exotic materials and artistry.

Special construction note: There are many materials and construction techniques that can add value to J. Alan cues.

For all used J. Alan cues, except where otherwise noted:
- Add $70 for each additional original straight playable shaft beyond one.
- Deduct $85 for missing original straight playable shaft.
- Add $40 each for ivory ferrules.
- Deduct 25% for obvious or improper refinish.

Level 1 - Hustler.
	98%	90%	70%
Level 1 cues start at	$150	$120	$80

Level 2 - 0 points, 0-25 inlays.
Level 2 cues start at	$225	$175	$115

Level 3 - 2-6 points, 0-8 inlays.
Level 3 cues start at	$300	$235	$160

Level 4 - 4-10 points, 9-25 inlays.
Level 4 cues start at	$375	$290	$190

Level 5 - 0-12 points, 26-50 inlays.
Level 5 cues start at	$550	$480	$285

CHIP ALBERY CUSTOM CUES

Maker of pool cues from 1995 to present in Sun Lakes, Arizona.

Richard "Chip" Albery Jr. has always enjoyed working with wood. The process of creating a pool cue was a well-guarded secret that intrigued him. He wanted to learn how to make a cue with a hit and proper balance that he would enjoy using. Chip developed his own cue-building techniques after working with Phoenix Custom Cues, Dale Teague, and, more recently, with Prather Cues. Chip has blended some of their techniques with his own to form a distinctive method of building a high quality custom cue. He is currently working with Prather Cue on a handbook for cuemakers.

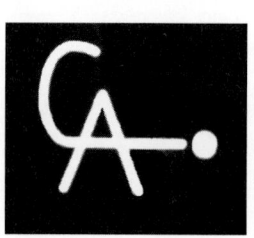

Present Day

Chip Albery

Albery Custom Cues are marked with a logo that is milled into every butt cap and filled with colored putty. Chip strives to make a cue that plays well because of balance and hit properties, and one that will stand out among the many cues available today. He uses exotic woods such as curly teak, black palm, and desert ironwood and also creates special inlay patterns that are unique to Albery Custom Cues. Each Albery cue is custom and no two are alike.

Chip's shop consists of several lathes which are modified for cue construction. He has a one-man shop that is equipped with saws, compressor, HVLP spray gun and industrial buffer for finishing the cues. Chip keeps a two-year supply of wood in stock to assure dimensional stability due to low moisture content.

Chip Albery cues are guaranteed for life against manufacturing defects that are not the result of warpage or abuse, and the cues are guaranteed for one year against warpage due to wood movement. If you are interested in talking to Richard "Chip" Albery Jr. about a new cue or cue that needs to be repaired, you can contact him at Albery Custom Cues, listed in the Trademark Index.

SPECIFICATIONS

Butt material: hardwoods
Shaft material: rock maple
Standard length: 58 in.
Standard wrap: Irish linen
Standard ferrules: Aegis II
Standard tip: tiger laminated tip
Annual production: approximately 50 cues

CHIP ALBERY CUSTOM CUES, cont.

GRADING	98%	90%	70%

OPTIONS (FOR NEW CUES ONLY)
Ivory ferrule: $50
Leather wrap: $65
Extra shaft: $125

REPAIRS
Repairs done on all fine cues.
Refinish with Irish linen wrap: $200
Rewrap with Irish linen: $35
Replace shaft: $150
Replace tip: $15+

CURRENT ALBERY CUES
Basic two-piece Albery hustler cues start at $150. Basic Albery cues with a wrap and joint collars start at $250. Basic Albery cues with points start at $450. One-of-a-kind custom Albery cues start at $600.

SECONDARY MARKET MINIMUM VALUES
The following are minimum values for other Albery cues encountered on the secondary market. These prices are representative of cues using basic materials and designs that are not necessarily available at present. Chip has offered one-of-a-kind cues that can command many times these prices due to the use of exotic materials and artistry.

Special construction note: There are many materials and construction techniques that can add value to Albery cues.

For all used Albery cues, except where otherwise noted:
Add $100 for each additional original straight playable shaft beyond one.
Deduct $125 for missing original straight playable shaft.
Add $40 each for ivory ferrules.
Deduct 20% for obvious or improper refinish.

	98%	90%	70%
Level 1 - Hustler.			
Level 1 cues start at	$125	$110	$85
Level 2 - 0 points, 0-25 inlays.			
Level 2 cues start at	$200	$160	$115
Level 3 - 2-6 points, 0-8 inlays.			
Level 3 cues start at	$375	$300	$200
Level 4 - 4-10 points, 9-25 inlays.			
Level 4 cues start at	$500	$400	$275
Level 5 - 0-12 points, 26-50 inlays.			
Level 5 cues start at	$650	$525	$350

ALDREN CUES

Maker of pool cues from 2001 to present in Rapid City, South Dakota.

Jim Aldren started playing pool in 1968 while studying electrical engineering at the South Dakota School of Mines and Technology in Rapid City, South Dakota. He's been playing pool in the South Dakota local area over the past 30 years. Jim works at a large electronics company as a senior manufacturing engineer, where he supports many computer-controlled machines and manufacturing processes. Many of the jigs and tooling, including the CNC currently being used in his shop, were designed and built using pieces of excess manufacturing equipment from work. His engineering background and interests in pool and woodworking led to building the first cues when he and his former partner, Stan Hawkins, started Black Hawk Custom Cues in 1994. In 2001, Jim sold his interest

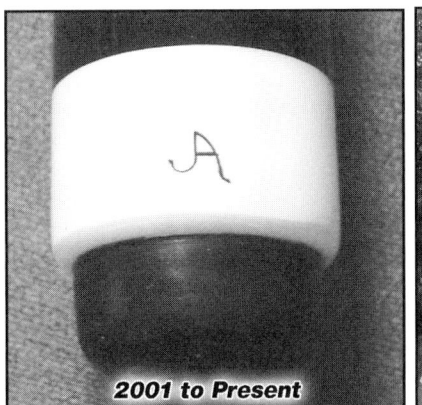
2001 to Present

Jim Aldren

in BHCC and started Aldren Cues. He has been building made-to-order cues ever since. Jim continues to perfect his process through continuous improvement in equipment, tooling and techniques. The process of building a well-executed cue is as exciting to Jim as it is to a satisfied customer who is involved in the design of their own personal cue. Jim has created a quick-release extension for many wheelchair-confined pool players. This extension is designed to attach directly through the butt of their normal shooting cue.

If you are interested in talking to Jim Aldren about a new cue or cue that needs to be repaired, you can contact him at Aldren Cues, listed in the Trademark Index.

126 ALDREN CUES, cont.

GRADING	98%	90%	70%

SPECIFICATIONS

Butt material: hardwoods
Shaft material: rock maple
Standard length: 58 in.
Lengths available: any up to 60 in.
Standard finish: one-part acrylic, UV cure
Balance point: custom
Standard butt cap: linen based
Standard wrap: Irish linen
Point construction: short splice or inlaid
Standard joint: stainless steel
Joint screw thread: Uni-Loc
Standard number of shafts: one
Standard taper: custom
Standard ferrules: Aegis
Standard tip: laminated
Standard tip width: 13 mm
Tip widths available: any up to 14 mm
Annual production: fewer than 40 cues

OPTIONS (FOR NEW CUES ONLY)

Special length: no charge
Ivory butt cap: $200
Ivory joint: $125
Ivory ferrule: $75
Joint protectors: $20+
Extra shaft: $100
13 in. extension for butt with QR: $40

CURRENT ALDREN CUES

Basic two-piece Aldren hustler cues start at $160. Basic Aldren cues with a wrap and joint collars start at $350. Basic Aldren cues with points start at $500. One-of-a-kind custom cues start at $750. Aldren cues over $500 come with two shafts.

SECONDARY MARKET MINIMUM VALUES

The following are minimum values for other Aldren cues encountered on the secondary market. These prices are representative of cues using basic materials and designs that are not necessarily available at present. Jim has offered one-of-a-kind cues that can command many times these prices due to the use of exotic materials and artistry.

Special construction note: There are many materials and construction techniques that can add value to Aldren cues.

For all used Aldren cues, except where otherwise noted:
- Add $75 for each additional original straight playable shaft beyond one.
- Deduct $100 for missing original straight playable shaft.
- Add $50 each for ivory ferrules.
- Deduct 15% for obvious or improper refinish.

	98%	90%	70%
Level 1 - Hustler.			
Level 1 cues start at	$125	$110	$85
Level 2 - 0 points, 0-25 inlays.			
Level 2 cues start at	$300	$245	$175
Level 3 - 2-6 points, 0-8 inlays.			
Level 3 cues start at	$400	$325	$225
Level 4 - 4-10 points, 9-25 inlays.			
Level 4 cues start at	$550	$450	$300
Level 5 - 0-12 points, 26-50 inlays.			
Level 5 cues start at	$750	$600	$400

ALLEN'S CUSTOM CUES

Maker of pool cues from 1975 to present in Hawthorne, California.

Gary Allen became interested in woodworking after taking a course in high school. After graduation, he went on to work in a machine shop, with Dale Patten as his supervisor.

Gary left his machine shop job to start work in a pool room. One day in 1975 his former supervisor came in with a cue he had made. This prompted Gary to leave his current position and start making pool cues. For the next five years Gary worked full time with Dale Patten making Richie Florence cues, and continued to make cues with Dale on a part-time basis for the next ten years.

He then worked with Tim Padgett for a year. In 1990 Gary decided it was time to start his own line of cues. He had been wanting to do this for many years, and knew it was time to follow his dream.

Allen cues are easily identifiable by the "Allen" logo which appears on butt caps. Gary is proud that his cues are made the "old-fashioned way," without the aid of a CNC machine. All of his work is done by hand on a lathe in his home-based shop. For special inlays he uses a pantograph. Gary makes his own short blanks and makes some full-spliced cues with traditional and butterfly points. He likes to design and make one-of-a-kind custom cues, and specializes in tailoring the length, weight, balance, taper, and joint to the desires of the customer. Gary uses available exotic hardwoods and offers a variety of joint types, including a joint screw made of wood. Butt caps are offered in three colors of Delrin, which he prefers for its durability. In 2002, he changed his standard finish from a two-part urethane to the less toxic butyl acetate lacquer.

Allen cues are guaranteed against construction defects that are not the result of warping or abuse. If you would like to talk to Gary regarding an order, or have an Allen cue that needs further identification or repair, contact Allen's Custom Cues, listed in the Trademark Index.

SPECIFICATIONS

Butt material: hardwoods
Shaft material: rock maple
Standard length: 58 in.
Lengths available: any
Standard finish: butyl acetate lacquer
Standard joint screw: 5/16-18
Standard joint: stainless steel
Standard joint type: piloted
Balance point: custom
Point construction: short splice
Standard wrap: Irish linen
Standard butt cap: Delrin
Standard number of shafts: one
Standard taper: 10 in. straight
Standard ferrules: melamine
Standard tip: Le Pro
Tip widths available: any
Annual production: approximately 12 cues

OPTIONS (FOR NEW CUES ONLY)

Leather or cork wrap: $150
Ivory joint: $150
Ivory points: $75 and up per point
Joint protectors: $10 to $100 each
Ivory butt cap: $300
Ivory ferrules: $100
Extra shaft: $125

REPAIRS

Repairs done on most fine cues.
Refinish (with leather wrap): $250
Refinish (with Irish linen wrap): $150
Rewrap (leather): $150
Rewrap (linen): $45
Replace Delrin butt cap: $60
Replace shaft: $125
Replace ferrule: $35 and up
Replace Ivory ferrule: $100

CURRENT ALLEN'S CUES

Allen's cues over $1,000 come with two shafts. The estimated delivery time for an Allen custom cue is approximately 12 weeks.

128 ALLEN'S CUSTOM CUES, cont.

GRADING	98%	90%	70%

SECONDARY MARKET MINIMUM VALUES

The following are minimum prices for Allen's cues encountered on the secondary market. These prices are representative of cues using basic materials and designs that may not be currently available. Gary also offers one-of-a-kind cues that can command many times these prices due to the use of exotic materials such as gold and silver wire, abalone, mother-of-pearl, and ivory.

Special construction note: There are many materials and construction techniques that can add value to Allen's cues.

For all used Allen's cues, except where otherwise noted:
- Add $75+ for each additional original straight playable shaft beyond one.
- Deduct $100 for missing original straight playable shaft.

Level 1 - 4 points, hustler.

	98%	90%	70%
Level 1 cues start at	$150	$135	$120

Level 2 - 0 points, 0-25 inlays.

Level 2 cues start at	$400	$340	$290

Level 3 - 2-6 points, 0-8 inlays.

Level 3 cues start at	$600	$500	$425

Level 4 - 4-10 points, 9-25 inlays.

Level 4 cues start at	$1000	$800	$725

Level 5 - 0-12 points, 26-50 inlays.

Level 5 cues start at	$1200	$1000	$900

Level 6 - 0-12 points, 51+ inlays.

Level 6 cues start at	$1,550	$1,375	$1,200

AMOS CUES & REPAIRS

Maker of pool cues in Oak Brook Terrace, Illinois.

If you have an Amos cue that needs further identification or repair, or would like to order a new cue, write to Amos Custom Cues, listed in the Trademark Index.

BRADY ANDRESEN

Maker of Braden Cues. Refer to listing for Braden Cues.

AO CUSTOM CUES

Maker of pool cues from 1998 to present in Annie O's Billiard Pro Shop in Houston, Texas.

Identification Marks

Anne Mayes

Anne Mayes started playing pool at the age of 17. In 1975 she was offered sponsorship on the women's pro tour, won her first event, the Southeastern Open, and was invited to play in the U.S. Open. Anne played on the pro tour whenever work permitted, and from 1983 to 1986 was a top-ten-ranked player. From 1986 to 1994 she worked full time in management for the Engineering Division at Texaco, and had to put pool on hold. In 1995 she was laid off and was able to start playing again on the WPBA tour for two years. In late 1996 she had to retire from the tour once again, this time due to poor health. Her next job was the creation of the magazine "Billiard & Dart News" in 1997. After a year and a half of struggling to build circulation, she decided she would be much happier crafting custom cues. With the help of friends, Annie O's Billiard Pro Shop opened in June, 1998. She started by buying a lathe for repairs. With advice from Jim Buss, Jerry Olivier, and other cuemakers, she quickly learned to make cues. In 2003 Anne moved from suite three in her building to suite one. That move doubled her floor space to accommodate $52,000 worth of cuemaking equipment that she had purchased. She now has three lathes, a knee mill, a CNC lathe, and a CNC mill which she designed and had custom built. Anne's drafting and engineering background, and her CAD software and systems design experience have proved useful.

Anne has used three different types of identifying marks since she started making cues. The first cues were signed "Annie O" from 1998 to 2000. She then started engraving "AO" on the butt caps from 2000 to 2003. From 2003 to present, Anne has engraved "AO Cues," followed by a serial number, on the butt caps. She keeps a record of each serial numbered cue to help with future identification and to help increase the owner's chances of recovery in case of theft.

Anne makes all cue components except for the pins and shaft inserts. Most of her cues are custom ordered. She offers a choice of three of her own proprietary shafts as options for her cues. The newest is the AO NT35 Flat-Laminated shaft, made from 35 flat nothern hard rock maple laminations, the same as a tree normally grows. A large selection of hardwoods and exotic woods are offered at the same price as maple: bocote, bloodwood, bubinga, cocobolo and other rosewoods, gabon or macassar ebony, holly, kingwood, padauk, purpleheart, black palm, satinwood, tulipwood, and zebrawood. Burls, snakewood, pink ivorywood, and wildwoods are also available at an additional charge. AO Cues are guaranteed against manufacturing defects while still owned by the original owner. If you have an AO

AO CUSTOM CUES, cont. 129

| GRADING | 98% | 90% | 70% |

cue that needs further identification or repair, or would like to order a new AO cue, contact Anne Mayes at Annie O's Billiard Pro Shop, which is listed in the Trademark Index.

SPECIFICATIONS

Butt material: hardwoods
Shaft material: rock maple or 35-layer laminated maple
Standard length: 58 in.
Lengths available: 40 to 60 in.
Standard finish: three-part polyurethane
Balance point: 17 to 18 in. from butt
Standard butt cap: linen-based phenolic
Standard wrap: Irish linen
Point construction: short splice or inlaid
Standard joint: phenolic
Joint type: flat-faced
Joint pin thread: 3/8-10
Standard number of shafts: one
Standard taper: custom
Standard ferrules: linen-based melamine
Annual production: 80 to 100 cues

OPTIONS (FOR NEW CUES ONLY)

Ivory butt cap: $200
Ivory joint: $125
Extra shaft: $150
Extra laminated shaft: $175+
Ivory ferrule: $50
Ivory points: $60 Each
Leather wrap: $75
Inlays: $20+ each
Custom joint protectors: $50

REPAIRS

Repairs done on all fine cues.
Refinish with Irish linen: $150
Refinish with leather wrap: $175
Rewrap (Irish linen): $50
Clean and press linen wrap: $20
Rewrap (leather): $75
Replace shaft: $150+
Replace butt cap: $30
Replace Ivory butt cap: $150+
Replace LBF ferrule: $25+
Replace tip: $10 to $35

CURRENT AO CUES

Basic two-piece AO hustler cues start at $350. Basic AO cues with a wrap and joint collars start at $350. Basic AO cues with points start at $450. One-of-a-kind custom AO cues start at $700. The estimated delivery time for an AO custom cue is two to five months.

SECONDARY MARKET MINIMUM VALUES

The following are minimum values for AO Cues encountered on the secondary market. These prices are representative of cues using basic materials and designs that may no longer be available.

For all used AO Cues, except where otherwise noted:
Add $125+ for each additional original straight playable shaft beyond one.
Deduct $125 for missing original straight playable shaft.
Add $50 each for ivory ferrules.

Level 2 - 0 points, 0-25 inlays.
	98%	90%	70%
Level 2 cues start at	$275	$115	$140

Level 3 - 2-6 points, 0-8 inlays.
	98%	90%	70%
Level 3 cues start at	$350	$270	$185

AO CUSTOM CUES, cont.

GRADING	98%	90%	70%
Level 4 - 4-10 points, 9-25 inlays.			
Level 4 cues start at	$450	$350	$235
Level 5 - 0-12 points, 26-50 inlays.			
Level 5 cues start at	$750	$585	$385
Level 6 - 0-12 points, 51-75 inlays.			
Level 6 cues start at	$1,250	$975	$650
Level 7 - 0-12 points, 76-125 inlays.			
Level 7 cues start at	$1,600	$1,450	$850
Level 8 - 0-16 points, 126-200 inlays.			
Level 8 cues start at	$2,000	$1,600	$1,100

AP CUES

Maker of pool cues from 2002 to present in Los Angeles, California.

Andrew Park started playing pool in his teen years and got hooked on the game very quickly. Over the many years of playing pool, he collected a few top-notch cues (Tad, Szamboti, Ginacue, Southwest) and loved the way they were not overly extravagant, but elegant. An engineer by trade, Andrew is a craftsman at heart, who has always enjoyed working with wood in his spare time. It was just a matter of time before he started making cues as a hobby. He made cues for

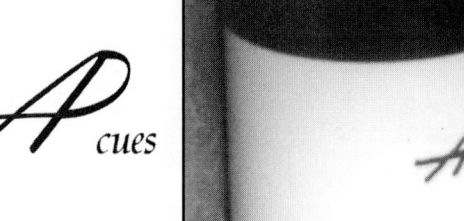

2002 to Present

Andrew Park

himself and then friends and family. He thought the cues played surprisingly well. From there on, Andrew decided to become a part-time cuemaker. He started by selling some hustler-type cues, but since then has moved on to more elaborate ones. AP Cues is a home-based company that produces fewer than 25 cues per year. All cues are one of a kind. Andrew started without the bigger machinery some other cuemakers use, so he learned how to do a lot of hand work. In 2005 he purchased a four-axis CNC machine for inlay work. He believes his passion for the game of pool and pride in his workmanship are the keys to making cues that look beautiful and play well. Andrew makes all the cue components except tips, joint screws, and bumpers. Cues can be identified by the "APcues" or "AP" logo on the cue, and some cues have "Andrew Park" hand-signed on the butt cap.

If you are interested in talking to Andrew Park about a new cue or cue that needs to be repaired, you can contact him at AP Cues, which is listed in the Trademark Index.

SPECIFICATIONS

Butt material: hardwoods
Shaft material: rock maple
Standard length: 58 in.
Lengths available: any
Standard finish: two-part polyurethane
Balance point: 1 in. above wrap
Standard butt cap: linen phenolic
Standard wrap: Irish linen
Point construction: short splice
Standard joint: linen phenolic
Joint type: flat-faced
Joint screw thread: 3/8-10
Standard number of shafts: one
Standard taper: 10 in. pro
Standard ferrules: linen phenolic
Standard tip: Le Pro
Standard tip width: 13 mm
Tip widths available: any
Annual production: fewer than 25 cues

OPTIONS (FOR NEW CUES ONLY)

Moori tip: $50
Ivory butt cap: $200+
Ivory joint: $150
Ivory ferrule: $75
Leather wrap: $100
Extra shaft: $125

AP CUES, cont. **131**

GRADING	98%	90%	70%

REPAIRS

Repairs done on all fine cues.
- Refinish (with Irish linen wrap): $150
- Refinish (with leather wrap): $200
- Rewrap (Irish linen): $50
- Rewrap (leather): $100
- Replace shaft: $125
- Replace ivory ferrule: $100
- Replace butt cap: $50
- Replace ivory butt cap: $225
- Replace Le Pro/triangle tip: $25
- Replaced Moori tip: $50
- Replace fibre/linen ferrule: $30

CURRENT AP CUES

Andrew Park makes basic two-piece cues with wraps and joint rings that start at $350. AP cues with points start at $650. The current delivery time for an AP cue is six to nine months.

SECONDARY MARKET MINIMUM VALUES

The following are minimum values for other AP cues encountered on the secondary market. These prices are representative of cues using basic materials and designs that are not necessarily available at present. Andrew has offered one-of-a-kind cues that can command many times these prices due to the use of exotic materials and artistry.

Special construction note: There are many materials and construction techniques that can add value to AP cues.

For all used AP cues, except where otherwise noted:
- Add $100 for each additional original straight playable shaft beyond one.
- Deduct $125 for missing original straight playable shaft.
- Add $65 each for ivory ferrules.
- Add $50 for leather wrap.
- Deduct 20% for obvious or improper refinish.

Level 1 - Hustler.
	98%	90%	70%
Level 1 cues start at	$150	$120	$85

Level 2 - 0 points, 0-25 inlays.
Level 2 cues start at	$300	$235	$160

Level 3 - 2-6 points, 0-8 inlays.
Level 3 cues start at	$550	$475	$285

Level 4 - 4-10 points, 9-25 inlays.
Level 4 cues start at	$700	$545	$375

Level 5 - 0-12 points, 26-50 inlays.
Level 5 cues start at	$1,000	$785	$550

Level 6 - 0-12 points, 51-75 inlays.
Level 6 cues start at	$1,500	$1,195	$800

ARNOT Q'S CUSTOM CUES

Maker of pool cues from 1994 to present in West Palm Beach, Florida.

Arnot Q. Wadsworth spent over twenty years in the wood industry, working as a logger and in a sawmill. He loved the game of pool, and even tried to play on the pro tour. But he didn't feel he was good enough to win against the pros. He was always interested in cues, and knew that with his knowledge of wood combined with the two years of formal training in a machine shop when he was younger, he could be a cuemaker. Arnot was a hands-on worker in the sawmill, but a disabling back injury left him unable to continue to his satisfaction. This was his chance to make cues. When his wife urged him to go for it, he made the commitment to devote himself to cuemaking. Arnot bought all of the necessary equipment, and began experimenting with different construction techniques.

Arnot ultimately developed a unique way of making cues. He uses a short splice, but he adds the splice after he has attached the handle. The V cuts actually go from the forearm into the handle section. The points continue below the wrap, adding extra strength to the butt half of the cue. Arnot did all inlay work on a manual pantograph until 1999, when he started using a CNC machine. He likes to do chain link designs in the rings, and does not believe in sacrificing structural integrity for the sake of aesthetics. Arnot has also developed his own laminated shafts called the TerminatorShaftT3. They are made from blanks with 28 horizontal layers. When turned, a finished shaft will have about 22 laminations at the joint.

Although the first 50 or so cues Arnot made had no identification marks, he has since been marking every cue. Less expensive cues have had an "Arnot Q" label on the butt cap, while he has cut the logo into the butt caps of more expensive cues. Late in 1998, Arnot started to sign and date every cue on the forearm, with a few signatures appearing on the butt cap instead. Arnot operates a large website for his business, which is updated every day and includes an up-to-date listing of many current cuemakers.

132 ARNOT Q'S CUSTOM CUES, cont.

| GRADING | 98% | 90% | 70% |

Arnot Cues are guaranteed for life against manufacturing defects that are not the result of warpage or abuse. If you have an Arnot cue that needs further identification or repair, or would like to order a new cue, contact Arnot Q's, listed in the Trademark Index.

SPECIFICATIONS

Butt material: hardwoods
Shaft material: laminated maple (TerminatorShaftT3™)
Standard length: 58 in.
Lengths available: any up to 64 in.
Standard finish: UV catalyzed epoxy
Balance point: 18 in. from butt
Standard butt cap: double black linen-based fiber
Standard wrap: Irish linen
Point construction: short splice, full splice, or inlaid
Standard joint: double black linen-based fiber
Joint type: flat-faced
Standard number of shafts: one
Standard taper: 12 in. modified pro
Standard ferrules: melamine
Annual production: fewer than 150 cue

OPTIONS (FOR NEW CUES ONLY)

Ivory butt cap: $30
Ivory joint: $150
Extra shaft: $79+
Extra TerminatorShaftT3™: $149
Ivory ferrule: $90
Exotic wood joint protectors: $105

REPAIRS

Repairs done on all fine cues.
Refinish with Irish linen: $150
Rewrap (Irish linen): $50
Rewrap (leather): $150
Replace shaft: $79-149
Replace 5/16-14, 5/16-18, or 3/8-10 joint screw: $30
Replace plastic, LBF, or Ivorine-3 butt cap: $50
Replace ivory ferrule: $90
Replace Aegis, melamine, Ivorine-3, or LBF ferrule: $30+

CURRENT ARNOT CUES

Basic Arnot cues with a wrap and joint collars start at $400. Basic Arnot cues with points start at $649. The estimated delivery time for an Arnot cue is eight weeks to six months, depending on complexity.

SECONDARY MARKET MINIMUM VALUES

The following are minimum values for Arnot Cues encountered on the secondary market. These prices are representative of cues using basic materials and designs that are not currently available. Arnot has offered one-of-a-kind cues that can command many times these prices due to the use of exotic materials and artistry.

Special construction note: There are many materials and construction techniques that can add value to Arnot cues. The following are the most important examples:

Add $250+ for chain link ring work.

For all used Arnot cues, except where otherwise noted:
Add $100 for each additional original straight playable shaft beyond one.
Deduct $100 for missing original straight playable shaft.
Add $80 each for ivory ferrules.
Deduct 20% for obvious or improper refinish.

	98%	90%	70%
Level 2 - 0 points, 0-25 inlays.			
Level 2 cues start at	$350	$275	$185
Level 3 - 2-6 points, 0-8 inlays.			
Level 3 cues start at	$500	$375	$235
Level 4 - 4-10 points, 9-25 inlays.			
Level 4 cues start at	$650	$500	$345
Level 5 - 0-12 points, 26-50 inlays.			
Level 5 cues start at	$850	$665	$445

ARNOT Q'S CUSTOM CUES, cont. 133

GRADING	98%	90%	70%
Level 6 - 0-12 points, 51-75 inlays.			
Level 6 cues start at	$1,250	$975	$650
Level 7 - 0-12 points, 76-125 inlays.			
Level 7 cues start at	$1,600	$1,250	$875

AUERBACH CUSTOM CUES

Maker of pool cues from 1990 to present in Tulsa, Oklahoma.

Identification Marks

John Parker

John Parker and Jim Auerbach have been partners in several business ventures since 1979. Jim worked for Boeing Aircraft Company as a quality control manager. When he retired in 1990, he and John established the Auerbach Custom Cue Company. Jim was responsible for designing several of the CNC programs to make cues. He enjoyed cutting the inlay pockets and their parts. John's father was a cabinet maker, and John started helping him when he was about ten years old. He learned how to use machinery while in the US Navy, and has been the only craftsman for Auerbach Custom Cues. Jim passed away on Mother's Day, May 13, of 2001, and he left the cuemaking shop to John.

John makes everything except tips and bumpers, and he has made many of his own screws. He also makes his own checkered rings. John has an eight-foot by six-foot heated and humidity-controlled room full of 54 different species of exotic hardwoods for future cues. Each Auerbach cue is a one of a kind. John can make short-spliced points or CNC-inlaid points. The purchaser of one of his cues can select ivory, gem stones and exotic woods and also specify length, weight, balance, and many other components of a custom made cue. Purchasing a pool cue is a matter of personal preference. John has on many occasions engraved the owner's name or initials on different parts of the cue. When asked why he has not changed the name of the company since Jim's death, he says he will leave the name Auerbach Custom Cues in place in honor of his friend. Had it not been for Jim, John would not be doing what he does now.

John also makes furnishings such as oak ball racks and wine racks for local pool rooms.

The first 38 Auerbach cues had no ID markings. Most of those are in the Tulsa, Oklahoma area. After that, Auerbach cues were easily identified by a reverse "R" logo on the butt caps of the cues. Red logos were on more basic cues and gold logos were on custom cues. After Jim Auerbach died, John started using a "JA" logo on the butt caps. This logo design was the idea of Duane Remick, a painter who worked in the shop who set up John's spray booth for finishing cues. Duane also made a few cues in the shop, a few of which were signed "Duane Remick."

John makes a few simple inexpensive cues for local players that are marked "Oakie Q's," most of which stay in the Tulsa area. He also specializes in difficult repairs on cues that are barely salvageable.

The butts of Auerbach cues are guaranteed for a year to the original buyer, and longer if the failure is clearly due to a manufacturer's defect. There is no guarantee offered on shafts. If you have an Auerbach cue that needs further identification or repair, or would like to order a new cue, contact Auerbach Cues, which is listed in the Trademark Index.

SPECIFICATIONS

Butt material: hardwoods
Shaft material: rock maple
Standard length: 58 in.
Lengths available: any up to 62 in.
Standard finish: polyurethane
Balance point: 1 in. above wrap
Standard butt cap: phenolic
Standard wrap: Irish linen
Point construction: short splice or inlaid
Standard joint: phenolic
Joint type: flat-faced
Joint screw thread: 3/8-10
Standard number of shafts: one
Standard taper: Auerbach custom
Standard ferrules: fiber
Standard tip: Le Pro
Standard tip width: 13 mm
Tip widths available: 10 to 14 mm
Annual production: 200+ cues

GRADING	100%	95%	70%

OPTIONS (FOR NEW CUES ONLY)

Special length: no charge
Ivory butt cap: $150
Ivory joint: $100
Ivory ferrule: $60
Ivory points: $100
Leather wrap: $75
Joint protectors: $50
Extra shaft: $80+

REPAIRS

Repairs done on all fine cues.
Refinish (with Irish linen wrap): $140
Refinish (with leather wrap): $175
Rewrap (Irish linen): $40
Rewrap (leather): $75
Clean and press linen wrap: $30
Replace shaft: $80+
Replace ivory ferrule: $60
Replace phenolic butt cap: $40
Replace ivory butt cap: $150
Replace tip: $10+
Replace fiber/linen ferrule: $25

CURRENT AUERBACH CUES

Auerbach Hustler cues start at $100. Plain Oakie Q cues start at $180. Plain Auerbach cues with a wrap and joint rings start at $200. Auerbach cues with points start at $400.

AUERBACH CUES

The following Auerbach cues can be ordered as shown or modified to suit the desires of the customer.

Level 2 - Bird's-eye maple forearm with sycamore and ebony checks set in silver rings above wrap, bird's-eye maple butt sleeve with sycamore and ebony checks set in silver rings at top and bottom.

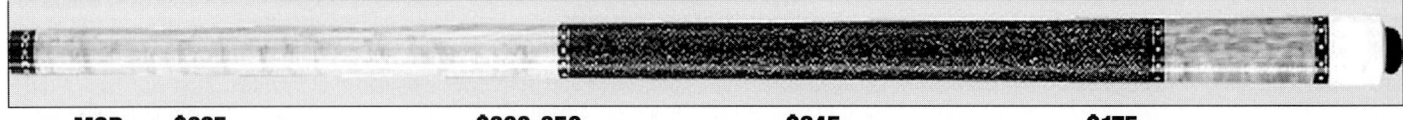

| MSR | $325 | $300-350 | $245 | $175 |

Level 2 - Bird's-eye maple forearm with floating ebony-bordered malachite windows above ivory and ebony checks set in silver rings above wrap, bird's-eye maple butt sleeve with ebony-bordered malachite windows between ivory and ebony checks set in silver rings at top and bottom.

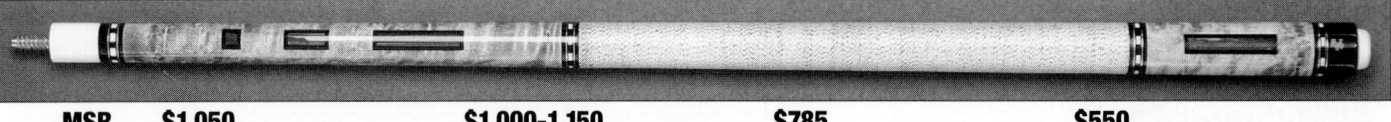

| MSR | $1,050 | $1,000-1,150 | $785 | $550 |

Level 4 - Cocobolo forearm with cocobolo checks set in silver rings above wrap, four triple-milled corian/ebony/tulipwood points with an ebony diamond-shaped inlay in each, cocobolo butt sleeve with four ebony diamond-shaped inlays set corian-bordered tulipwood windows between cocobolo checks set in silver rings at top and bottom.

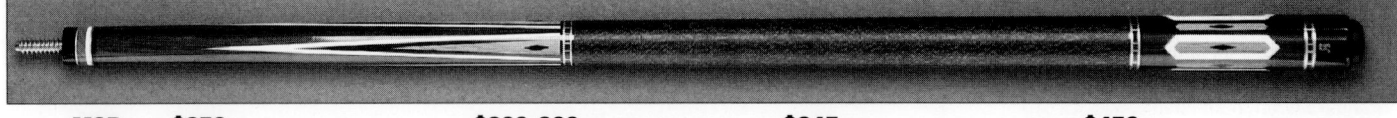

| MSR | $850 | $800-900 | $645 | $450 |

Level 4 - Tiger maple forearm with purple heart checks set in silver rings above wrap, five long purpleheart points with an ivory ellipse-shaped inlay in each alternating with five short malachite points, tiger maple butt sleeve with five ivory ellipse-shaped inlays set in purpleheart windows alternating with five malachite diamond-shaped inlays between purpleheart checks set in silver rings at top and bottom.

| MSR | $1,200 | $1,100-1,350 | $900 | $650 |

AUERBACH CUSTOM CUES, cont. **135**

GRADING	98%	90%	70%

SECONDARY MARKET MINIMUM VALUES

The following are minimum values for other Auerbach cues encountered on the secondary market. These prices are representative of cues using basic materials and designs that are not necessarily available at present. Jim and John have offered one-of-a-kind cues that can command many times these prices due to the use of exotic materials and artistry.

Special construction note: There are many materials and construction techniques that can add value to Auerbach cues.

For all used Auerbach cues, except where otherwise noted:
- Add $85 for each additional original straight playable shaft beyond one.
- Deduct $100 for missing original straight playable shaft.
- Add $50 each for ivory ferrules.
- Add $50 for leather wrap.
- Deduct 20% for obvious or improper refinish.

	98%	90%	70%
Level 1 - Hustler.			
Level 1 cues start at	$85	$70	$45
Level 2 - 0 points, 0-25 inlays.			
Level 2 cues start at	$165	$130	$85
Level 3 - 2-6 points, 0-8 inlays.			
Level 3 cues start at	$350	$285	$195
Level 4 - 4-10 points, 9-25 inlays.			
Level 4 cues start at	$500	$340	$265
Level 5 - 0-12 points, 26-50 inlays.			
Level 5 cues start at	$750	$585	$395
Level 6 - 0-12 points, 51-75 inlays.			
Level 6 cues start at	$1,250	$985	$650

AXIOM CUES

Maker of pool cues from 2003 to present in Palm Harbor, Florida.

David Miller's father, Harold Miller, started the company Cobra Cues. Just prior to Harold's passing in 2003, David started the concept of Axiom Billiards. David continues Axiom today, bringing the customer a high quality, low-priced cue. The company strives to make a fine quality cue in its class, at an affordable price. The cues are manufactured in China. Axiom cues all have the company logo on the butt. Axiom has licensed a line of cues that feature WWE (World Wrestling Entertainment) stars. They will be WWE cues, and will not be marked with the Axiom logo.

Axiom offers a two-year, no-risk warranty to dealers, which covers manufacturer's defects in workmanship and craftsmanship.

If you are interested in talking to David Miller about a new cue or a cue that needs to be repaired, you can contact him at Axiom Billiard Supplies Inc., which is listed in the Trademark Index.

SPECIFICATIONS

- Butt material: maple
- Shaft material: Canadian hard rock maple
- Standard length: 58 in.
- Standard wrap: Irish linen
- Standard ferrules: fiber
- Standard tip: Le Pro
- Annual production: 50,000 cues

OPTIONS

Extra shaft: $19.99+

CURRENT AXIOM CUES

Axiom Cues range in price from $45 to $400.

SECONDARY MARKET MINIMUM VALUES

The following are minimum values for other Axiom cues encountered on the secondary market. These prices are representative of cues using basic materials and designs.

Special construction note: There are materials and construction techniques that can add value to Axiom cues.

For all used Axiom cues, except where otherwise noted:
- Deduct $20+ for missing original straight playable shaft.
- Deduct 20% for obvious or improper refinish.

AXIOM CUES, cont.

GRADING	98%	90%	70%
Level 1 - Hustler.			
Level 1 cues start at	$30	$20	$10
Level 2 - 0 points, 0-25 inlays.			
Level 2 cues start at	$30	$20	$10
Level 3 - 2-6 points, 0-8 inlays.			
Level 3 cues start at	$65	$50	$30
Level 4 - 4-10 points, 9-25 inlays.			
Level 4 cues start at	$85	$65	$40

B SECTION

BAKER CUSTOM CUES

Maker of pool cues from 2000 to present in Oklahoma City, Oklahoma.

Buddy K. Baker began playing pool in his early teens and he has enjoyed playing ever since. As a teen he learned the art of leatherwork while in school. Later on, in 1979, he took up the art of leatherwork as a part-time hobby while working at his full-time job for General Motors. There was such a high demand for the elite craftsmanship in his leatherwork that he bagan selling many different items. Buddy always had the knack for learning new hobbies and his passion has always been for the sport of billiards. He began collecting billiard cues in the early 1990s, not as an investment but because he admired the beauty and craftsmanship of cues. He later became a dealer in the billiard industry. As a dealer, he was introduced to Verl Horn, who lived in Buddy's home state, and immediately became a dealer for Horn Cues. Buddy visited with Verl Horn frequently and watched him work on cues periodically. He witnessed cues in various stages of cue building, which sparked his interest in learning the art of custom cue building. From there, Buddy watched Verl construct his cues while taking notes. The billiard industry was saddened by the unfortunate loss of Verl Horn in 1999. Buddy learned a lot from Verl but never built a cue with him. Over the next year, he received pointers from various other cuemakers. He constructed his first hustler cue in 2000 and began building custom cues in 2001.

Buddy Baker

Baker Custom Cues have a "BKB" identification on the buttcap. All custom cues are numbered as they are completed. For more information on Baker Custom Cues, or to order a new cue from Buddy, please refer to the listing in the Trademark Index.

SPECIFICATIONS

Butt material: hardwoods
Shaft material: rock maple
Standard length: 58 in.
Lengths available: any
Standard wrap: Irish linen
Standard finish: urethane
Standard joint: phenolic
Joint type: flat faced
Standard tip width: 13 mm
Standard tip: Triangle
Standard number of shafts: one
Standard ferrules: melamine
Annual production: 15 cues

OPTIONS (FOR NEW CUES ONLY)

Special length: no charge
Ivory ferrule: $60
Custom joint protectors: $35 per set
Ivory joint: $150
Ivory butt cap: $250
Extra shaft: $125
Layered tip: $15

REPAIRS

Repairs done on all fine cues.
Refinish (with Irish linen wrap): $150
Rewrap (Irish linen): $50
Replace shaft: $125
Replace ivory ferrule: $80
Replace fiber/linen ferrule: $30
Replace ivory butt cap: $300
Replace tip: $10
Replace layered tip: $15

CURRENT BAKER CUES

Two-piece Baker hustler cues start at $225. Basic Baker cues with wraps and joint rings start at $275. Baker cues with spliced points start at $550. The current delivery time for a Baker cue is about six months.

138 BAKER CUSTOM CUES, cont.

GRADING	100%	95%	70%

CURRENT EXAMPLES

The following Baker cues can be ordered as shown, modified to suit the desires of the customer, or new designs can be created.

Level 1 "Hustler" - Maple forearm, four full-spliced bocote points and handle.

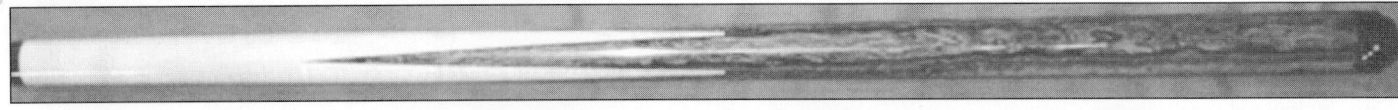

MSR	$225	$200-250	$165	$125

Level 2 - Bocote forearm with a metal ring above wrap, bocote butt sleeve with a metal ring below wrap.

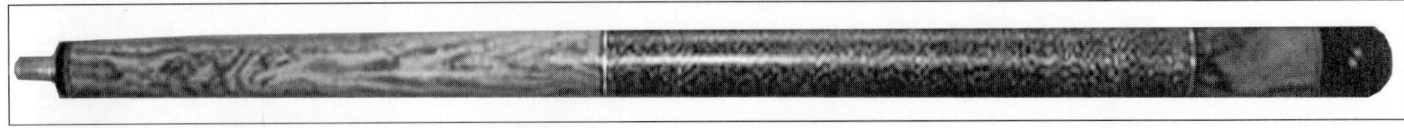

MSR	$275	$250-300	$205	$150

Level 3 - Black palm forearm with a holly ring above wrap, four intricate floating holly-bordered ebony points, black palm butt sleeve with a holly ring below wrap.

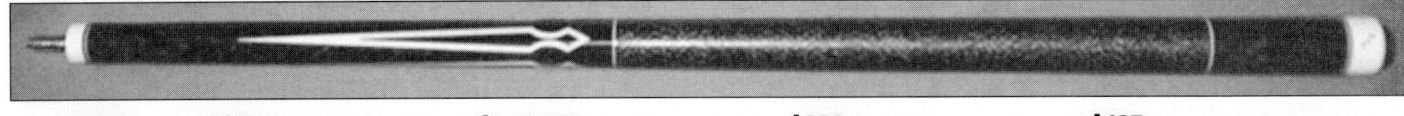

MSR	$350	$325-385	$260	$185

Level 3 - Cocobolo forearm with an ebony ring above wrap, four curly maple points, cocobolo butt sleeve with four short reverse curly maple points below an ebony ring below wrap.

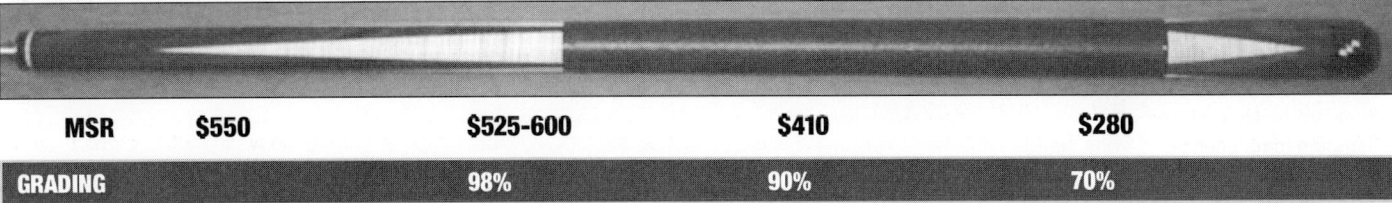

MSR	$550	$525-600	$410	$280

GRADING	98%	90%	70%

SECONDARY MARKET MINIMUM VALUES

The following are minimum values for Baker cues encountered on the secondary market. These prices are representative of cues using basic materials and designs. Buddy has offered one-of-a-kind cues that can command many times these prices due to the use of exotic materials and artistry.

Special construction note: There are many materials and construction techniques that can add value to Baker cues.

For all used Baker cues, except where otherwise noted:
- Add $100 for each additional original straight playable shaft beyond one.
- Deduct $125+ for missing original straight playable shaft.
- Add $50 each for ivory ferrules.
- Deduct 20% for obvious or improper refinish.

Level 1 - Hustler.
Level 1 cues start at	$200	$160	$115

Level 2 - 0 points, 0-25 inlays.
Level 2 cues start at	$250	$195	$135

Level 3 - 2-6 points, 0-8 inlays.
Level 3 cues start at	$500	$385	$260

Level 4 - 4-10 points, 9-25 inlays.
Level 4 cues start at	$600	$495	$320

Level 5 - 0-12 points, 26-50 inlays.
Level 5 cues start at	$850	$675	$450

GEORGE BALABUSHKA

Maker of pool cues from 1959 to 1975 in Brooklyn, New York.

George Balabushka

His name having been synonymous with the finest cue craftsmanship for over 40 years, George Balabushka has often been referred to as the "Stradivarius" of cue makers, a title which accurately suggests the rarity and allure of the cues he created. As a boy of 12, he arrived in New York speaking only Russian, as did his parents and younger sister. Born 'Gregory Balabushka', the immigration officials on Ellis Island erred in translating his passport, and 'Gregory' became 'George' Balabushka. His first loves being music and woodworking, George played the accordion professionally with an accordion orchestra throughout the 1930's and 1940's, while also building accordions during that time. Still in his teens, George took a job crafting wooden toys, and later created children's furniture for the Playtime Woodworking Company.

While at Playtime, George married Josephine in 1941, and a few years later the couple moved to Brooklyn to raise their family, sons Gregory and George both being named for their father. As many cue makers have discovered, woodworking has its hazards. Those risks brought about the loss of most of George's left index finger to a band saw. George's love of playing pool, and the loss of his forefinger on his bridge hand, presented a serious complication. But, George's resourcefulness afforded him a solution and he assembled a very convincing plastic surrogate using a wooden mold. The prosthesis attached to the finger stub and enabled him to continue to play the game with friends, with most people never realizing he wore it.

George began making cues in 1959 when he and partner Frank McGowan purchased a poolroom at 50th and 5th in Brooklyn. His first cues were adaptations of Brunswick Titlists - a familiar starting point for many cuemakers. At that time he was one of only a handful of custom cue makers in the United States. After producing just a few dozen cues a year for several years, the desire for Balabushka's cues increased and he sold his interest in the poolroom and began to develop cues full time. By 1964, George converted his garage into a shop, complete with heating and air conditioning. The shop was simple and compact, with just enough space for a small Atlas metal lathe, a saw, and a drill press. Cue shafts and butts in various stages of completion occupied any remaining space.

Almost every distinguished player of the era, from Joe Balsis to Willie Mosconi, wished to possess a Balabushka. Although he retailed a number of cues to movie stars, he preferred clients who were talented players. Most Balabushka cues were unadorned but their reputation was founded on their composition and on the way they hit, both solid. George was both practical and meticulous. He developed his cues to be efficient and durable, and fancied materials that met his high standards. Cue pieces were machined or excised for the most precise fit possible. The sound the cue made was as significant to him as the way it played. George painstakingly selected woods, and procured the most superior blanks he could acquire. Preferring straight grain maple for the blanks because of its natural structural stability, gave way to why most Balabushka cues have straight-grain maple forearms. However, there are instances in which the forearms have noticeable figuring. Burton Spain contended to have made George a few curly maple blanks, and Szamboti granted a small quantity of special orders for figured blanks.

There are three significant styles of Balabushka cues. Balabushka initially began making cues with Brunswick Titlist blanks, and persisted to make them throughout his cue making career, although not as regularly after acquiring blanks from Spain and Szamboti. Early cues had nylon wraps or no wraps, but eventually George modified them to Cortland #9 Irish linen. The cues were predominantly rosewood, but models in ebony can be located. Acquiring one of these early cues requires caution, as original Titlist blanks are still available for replication by unscrupulous cue-makers. Although the initial cues are the most frequently plagiarized, they are still exceedingly sought-after, as Balabushka completed much of his finest pieces during this time. He particularly enjoyed working with Titlist blanks, as they included a full splice and did not involve a cut between the wrap and forearm. In the early sixties plastic rings were prevalent and George experimented with them in butt sleeves, generally red or blue metallic-looking polyester.

In 1966, due to Titlist's declining quality, George began searching for a product comparable to the earlier Titlist blanks, when he received notice from Burton Spain proposing the sale of his premium blanks. Having a greater selection with which to work, Balabushka introduced decorative rings above the wrap; most prevalent was ebony with phenolic checks between two silver rings (commonly called Bushka rings), with no rings in the butt sleeve. Responding to a catalog inquiry in the late sixties, George declared that all of the cues he manufactured were one of a kind and ranged in price from $70 to $140. He requisitioned twelve blanks each month from Spain over four years, totaling 550 to 600 blanks. It is believed that about half the estimated 1100 to 1200 Balabushka cues made had Spain forearms, thereby being the most frequently encountered. Spain implemented assorted woods and veneer combinations, the most customary being four veneers of black, orange, green, and white, though Spain also vended some of his famous five-veneer blanks, referring to George as a "bedrock of quality." In 1970, Spain sold his cue business to John Davis, who continued to supply the same Spain-style blanks to Balabushka for almost two years. Davis, who only assembled prongs part-time, stated that he sold approximately 100 blanks to Balabushka.

By early 1973, George found a new source from which to purchase blanks: Gus Szamboti. The stunning Szamboti blanks ushered in the third and final chapter in Balabushka's career. According to Barry Szamboti, his father completed less than 125 blanks for George, the majority having a straight grained maple forearm with four ebony points. Though George thought the straight-grained maple blanks superior, a small number of bird's-eye blanks were requested by customers and occasionally what appeared to be a straight grain blank would expose a small number of bird's-eyes when turned down. The four veneers were typically black, mahogany, green, and white, however several were recognized to include orange veneers in lieu of the mahogany.

During this period George created his most intricate and possibly most superb cues, although even elaborate Balabushka cues show elegance with restraint. It was rumored that George completed cues with blanks he prepared himself, though it was thought to have been John Davis. The superiority of the points and the veneers were akin to those from Brunswick, with the maple veneers working into the ebony grain. George had sparse equipment with which to operate in his garage, and therefore opted to acquire blanks from individuals who were paramount at creating them, making it unlikely that he prepared many - or any - of his own. When George died in 1975 at the age of 63 he was at the pinnacle of his influence as a cue maker.

GEORGE BALABUSHKA, cont.

Balabushka cues present several common characteristics, and although ivory joints and butt caps may be encountered, the greater part of his cues had piloted stainless steel joints and white Delrin butt caps with a very identifiable auburn bumper purchased from Brunswick. Cortland Irish Linen was the customary wrap, but George's leather wraps, which are incredibly scarce, are among several of the best ever finished by anyone. Rings of colored plastic, nickel silver, and wood were frequently used, as were inlays of mother-of-pearl dots and notched diamonds. Maple windows in the butt sleeve were also a characteristic, and these often had only one burl. Ivory inlays were rarely applied, and were almost always semi-circles around maple windows. Early Balabushka cues were oil polished while it is believed that George sprayed lacquer on his later cues.

Millions were introduced to the notion of rare and collectible cues when Paul Newman gave Tom Cruise a Balabushka cue in "The Color of Money," immortalizing Balabushka cues as the most sought-after cues ever designed. The movie producers were fearful that a real Balabushka might get damaged during the filming of the scene where Tom Cruise twirls it, so the cue used was one of two made by Joss Cues for the film. This cue, the model J-18, exhibited the distinctive Balabushka style, but could be exchanged by an identical model if broken …virtually impossible with an original Balabushka. (How disappointing that Balabushka did not benefit from the posthumous recognition when the Oscar-winning film made him the most renowned cue maker in history.)

Original George Balabushka cues do not have his signature on the forearm. There are licensed reproductions distributed by Competition Sports. There are far more Balabushkas in circulation today than could have possibly been produced. It becomes even more difficult to differentiate the genuine from the counterfeit when old cues are refinished to look "new" - thereby eradicating their patina, their age properties, and much of their worth. Balabushka cues in original form are becoming more difficult to find, and therefore quickly increasing in value. Cues with provenance and authentication are also more esteemed. Insist on verification by a renowned expert, or get a voucher that offers a money-back guarantee if the cue can not be authenticated by an expert. Recommended experts include Pete Tascarella, Bill Schick, Paul Rubino, Barry Szamboti, Richard Black, Bill Stroud, and Ernie Gutierrez, all of whom are cuemakers listed in the Trademark Index, as well as Mark Kulungian, who can be found in the Buy, Sell, Trade Index. (Please be aware that most experts will charge a fee for authentication services.) The author, Brad Simpson, is also an expert at authenticating original George Balabushka cues.

Note: Due to the rarity of George Balabushka cues and increasing interest, prices are on the rise. Fewer original examples are surfacing, and collectors are holding on to the ones they have. Unique examples with pedigree (original boxes, receipts, etc.), and cues made for top professional players (with convincing documentation), are bringing the highest prices.

SPECIFICATIONS

- Butt materials: hardwoods
- Shaft material: rock maple
- Standard length: 57 1/2 in.
- Standard taper: 10 1/2 in. straight
- Standard joint: stainless steel
- Standard joint screw: 5/16-14
- Joint type: piloted
- Standard wrap: Cortland Irish linen
- Number of shafts: two
- Standard ferrules: ivory
- Standard butt cap: white Delrin
- Total production: approximately 1,100 to 1,200 cues

OPTIONS

- Leather wrap (very rare)
- Nylon wrap (very early and extremely rare)
- Linen melamine or phenolic resin ferrules
- Ivory joint (very rare)
- Ivory butt cap (extremely rare)
- Delrin insert for butt cap (extremely rare)

KNOWN BALABUSHKA EXAMPLES

Special construction note: There are many materials and construction techniques that can add value to George Balabushka cues. The following are the most important examples:

- Add $1,000+ for leather wrap.
- Add $1,000+ for each original straight playable shaft beyond two.
- Deduct 20% for each missing original straight playable shaft under two.
- Add 35%+ for original box.
- Add 40%+ for original documentation (original receipt from George Balabushka).
- Add 15%+ for authentication (letter by recognized expert).
- Deduct 30% for obvious or inappropriate refinish.
- Add 25%+ for totally original finish, wrap, shafts, and ferrules.

TITLIST BLANK CUES (1959-1975)

Most of the following cues were made from 1959 to 1966 at an average rate of approximately 20 to 60 cues per year, although Titlist blank cues were made until 1975. The earliest examples may have nylon wrap, and most will have plain black phenolic joint rings. Later examples may have a yellow fiber ring (similar to that used by Doc Fry). Although rare, some may have no wrap, and examples with carved handles are known. Flat-topped pins were used on some cues in the early to mid-1960s. Pricing is given for cues in original condition except as noted.

GEORGE BALABUSHKA, cont.

GRADING	98%	90%	70%

Level 3 - Maple forearm, four full-spliced ebony points and handle with four colored veneers.

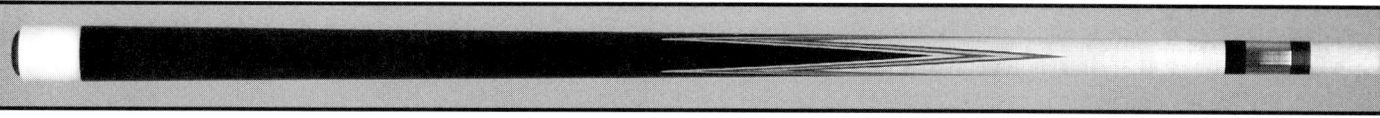

| Cues start at | $7,000 | $6,000 | $5,000 |

Level 3 - Maple forearm, four rosewood points with four colored veneers, Cortland Irish linen wrap, rosewood butt sleeve.

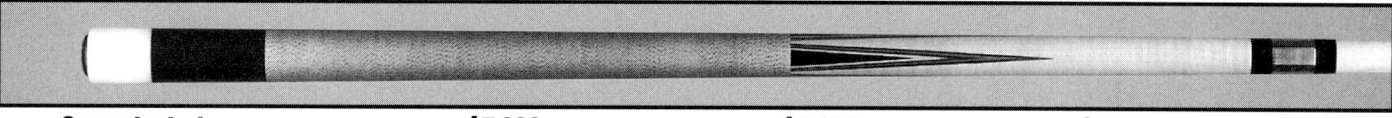

| Cues start at | $7,000 | $6,000 | $5,000 |

Level 3 - Maple forearm, four rosewood points with four colored veneers, Cortland Irish linen wrap, black plastic butt sleeve with bird's-eye maple bands and colored slotted veneers, eight mother-of-pearl dots in zigzag pattern.

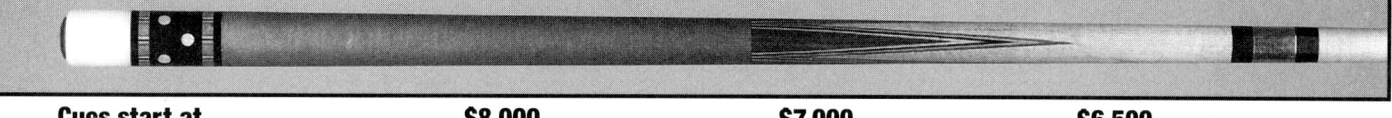

| Cues start at | $8,000 | $7,000 | $6,500 |

Level 3 - Maple forearm, four rosewood points with four colored veneers, Cortland Irish linen wrap, butt sleeve made of rings of plastic with glitter foil bordered by silver metal and black fiber rings.

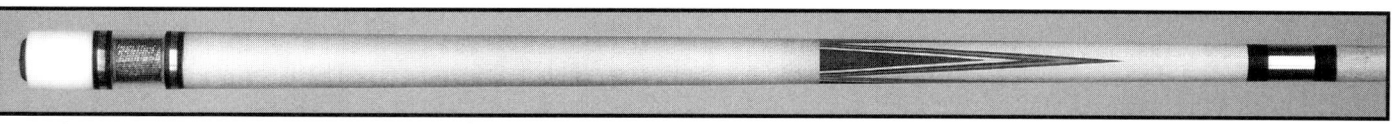

| Cues start at | $9,500 | $8,000 | $6,500 |

Level 3 - Maple forearm, four rosewood points with four colored veneers, butt sleeve made of rings of plastic with glitter foil bordered by silver metal and black fiber rings, silk wrap. Black linen joint and shaft collars with yellow plastic ring.

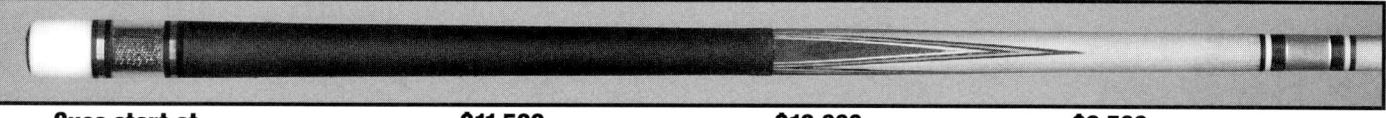

| Cues start at | $11,500 | $10,000 | $8,500 |

Level 3 - Black linen joint and shaft collars with yellow plastic ring, maple forearm, four rosewood points with four colored veneers, end of butt sleeve has three rings of nylon plastic, carved handle.

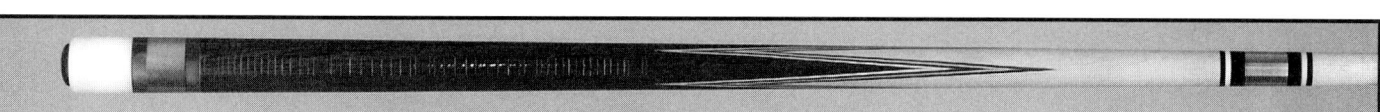

| Cues start at | $9,500 | $8,000 | $6,500 |

Level 3 - Maple forearm, four rosewood points with four colored veneers, Cortland Irish linen wrap, black nylon plastic butt sleeve with silver metal ringwork.

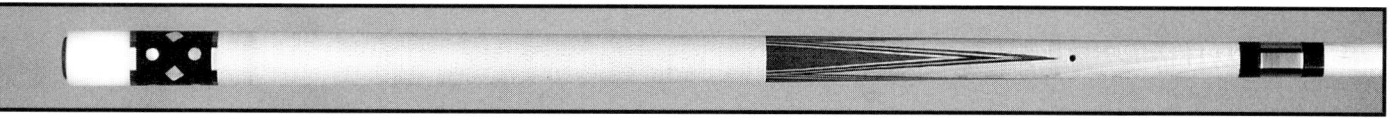

| Cues start at | $8,500 | $7,500 | $5,700 |

Level 4 - Maple forearm, four rosewood points with four colored veneers, ebony butt sleeve with mother-of-pearl inlays: four notched diamonds and eight dots. Six rings above Cortland linen wrap of silver metal, black fiber and white linen, black linen joint and shaft collars with nickel silver ring.

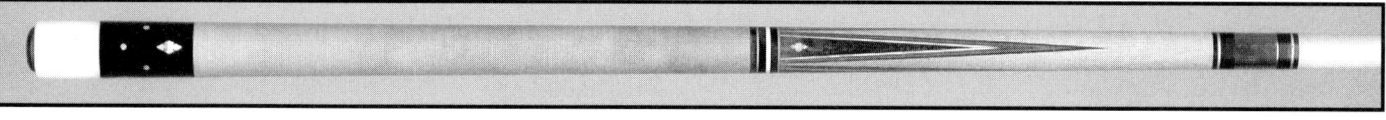

| Cues start at | $12,000 | $10,000 | $8,000 |

| GRADING | 98% | 90% | 70% |

BURTON SPAIN/JOHN DAVIS BLANK CUES (1966-1971)

The following cues were made from 1966 to 1971, at an average rate of 100 to 145 cues per year. These cues usually have fancier black phenolic or plain white joint collars. The maximum estimated production for cues with these blanks is 675.

Level 4 - Maple forearm, four rosewood points with four colored veneers, ebony butt sleeve with mother-of-pearl nameplate.

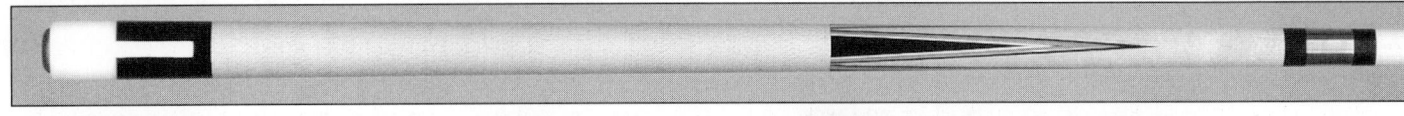

| Cues start at | $8,500 | $7,500 | $6,500 |

Level 4 - Maple forearm, four ebony points with five colored veneers, leather wrap, ebony butt sleeve with slotted maple veneers at top and bottom.

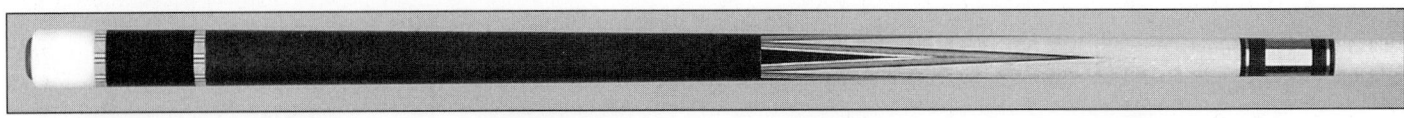

| Cues start at | $11,500 | $9,500 | $8,000 |

Level 3 - Maple forearm with seven rings above wrap, four ebony points with four colored veneers, black plastic butt sleeve with bands of red nylon plastic at top and bottom with four mother-of-pearl notched diamonds.

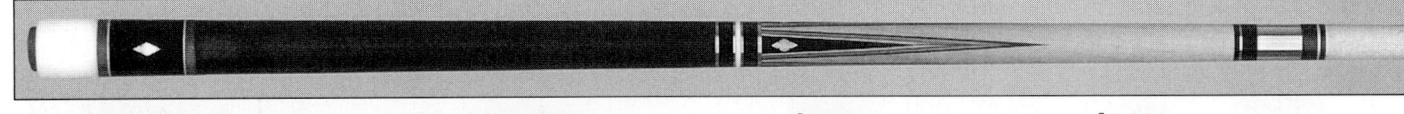

| Cues start at | $10,500 | $8,500 | $7,000 |

Level 4 - Maple forearm, four ebony points with four colored veneers, Cortland Irish linen wrap, black plastic butt sleeve with mother-of-pearl inlays and silver-colored rings at top and bottom.

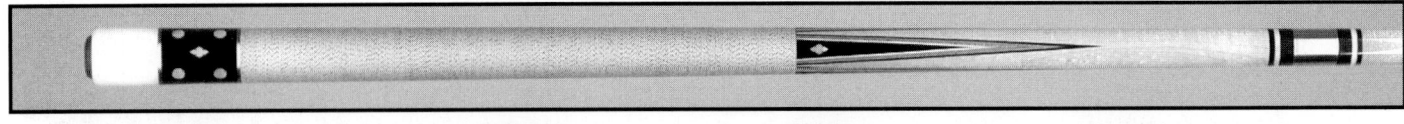

| Cues start at | $10,000 | $8,200 | $6,500 |

Level 4 - Maple forearm with four ebony points with four colored veneers, row of three notched mother-of-pearl diamonds in each point, Cortland Irish linen wrap, ebony butt sleeve with four mother-of-pearl notched diamonds.

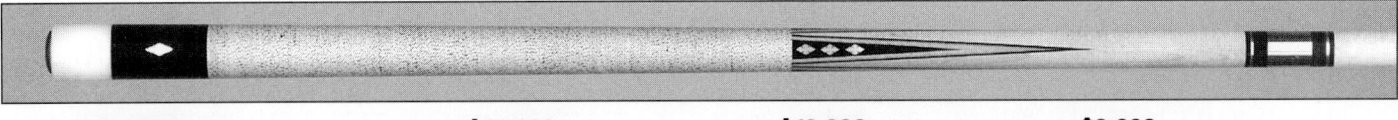

| Cues start at | $15,000 | $12,000 | $9,000 |

Level 4 - Maple forearm with white linen and nickel silver rings above wrap, four ebony points with four colored veneers, notched mother-of-pearl diamond and two dots in each point, leather wrap, ebony butt sleeve with four mother-of-pearl notched diamonds alternating with four dots.

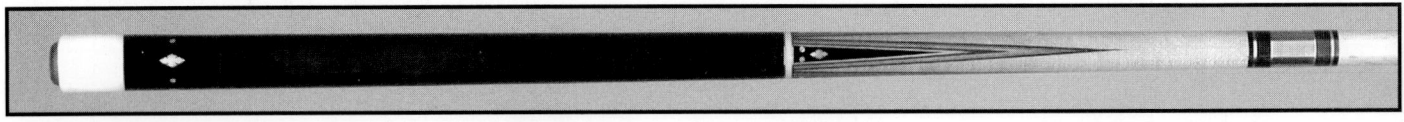

| Cues start at | $12,500 | $11,000 | $9,500 |

Level 4 - Black linen joint and shaft collars with nickel silver ring, maple forearm, four ebony points with four colored veneers, two mother-of-pearl dots and one notched diamond, Cortland Irish linen wrap, ebony butt sleeve has three rings of nylon plastic, separated by plastic rings, four mother-of-pearl notched diamonds alternating with four dots.

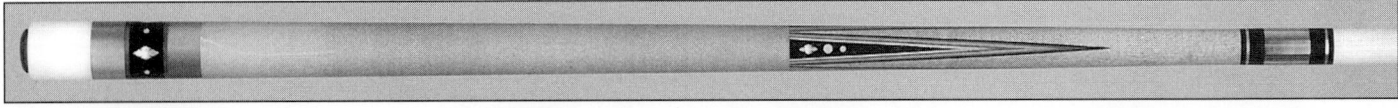

| Cues start at | $12,500 | $10,000 | $9,000 |

GRADING	98%	90%	70%

Level 4 - Black linen joint and shaft collars with nickel silver ring, maple forearm, four rosewood points with four colored veneers, three small mother-of-pearl dots, Cortland Irish linen wrap, rosewood butt sleeve (rare) has four sets of mother-of-pearl diamonds and dots alternating with four dots.

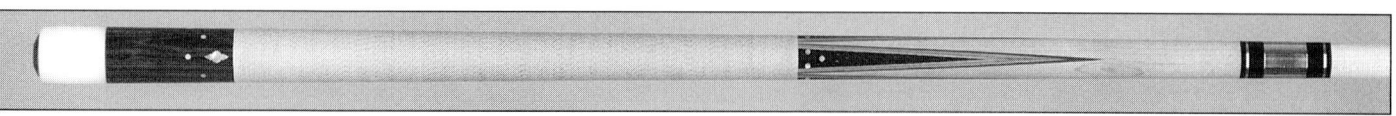

Cues start at	$12,000	$10,500	$8,500

Level 4 - Black linen joint and shaft collars with nickel silver ring, maple forearm, four ebony points with four colored veneers, one mother-of-pearl notched diamond, black linen and nickel silver ring above wrap inlaid with eight mother-of-pearl dots, ebony butt sleeve has a ring of eight mother-of-pearl dots with rings of nylon plastic above and below and four mother-of-pearl notched diamonds.

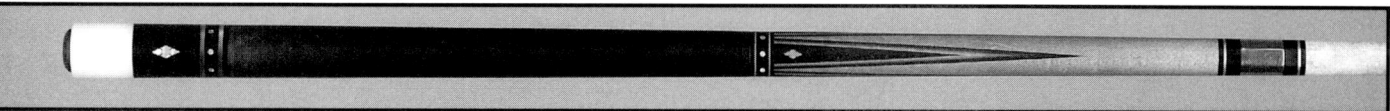

Cues start at	$13,000	$11,000	$9,000

Level 5 - Black linen joint and shaft collars with nickel silver ring, maple forearm, four ebony points with four colored veneers, one mother-of-pearl notched diamond and three dots in each point, white linen fiber ring with two nickel silver rings and two black linen rings above wrap, Cortland Irish linen wrap, black plastic butt sleeve with four mother-of-pearl notched diamonds each surrounded by four mother-of-pearl dots, and silver colored rings at the top and bottom.

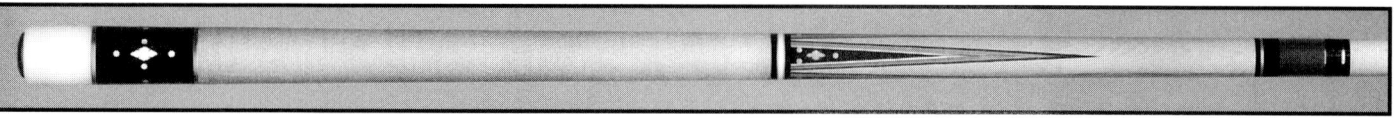

Cues start at	$25,000	$22,000	$19,000

Level 5 - Black linen joint and shaft collars with nickel silver ring, maple forearm, four ebony points with four colored veneers, one mother-of-pearl notched diamond and three dots in each point, white linen fiber ring with slotted veneers and two nickel silver rings above wrap, Cortland Irish linen wrap, ebony butt sleeve has two gold foil rings bordering maple "railroad track" two-diamond veneer strips alternating with mother-of-pearl notched diamonds.

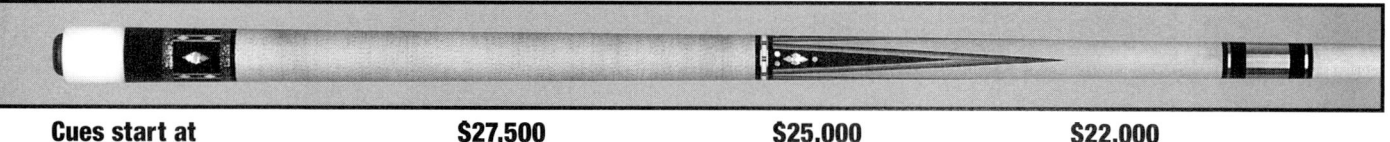

Cues start at	$27,500	$25,000	$22,000

GUS SZAMBOTI BLANK CUES

The following cues were made from 1971 to 1975, with a total production of approximately 125 cues. Most examples feature black linen joints with nickel silver rings at the joint and shaft collars.

Level 4 - Maple forearm, four ebony points with four colored veneers and mother-of-pearl notched diamonds and/or dots, Cortland Irish linen wrap, ebony butt sleeve with mother-of-pearl dots and/or notched diamonds and ringwork at top.

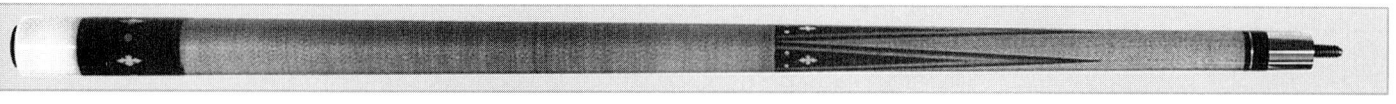

Cues start at	$15,000	$13,500	$10,500

Level 4 - Maple forearm with ring above wrap, four ebony points with four colored veneers and mother-of-pearl notched diamonds and/or dots, ebony butt sleeve with mother-of-pearl dots and/or notched diamonds.

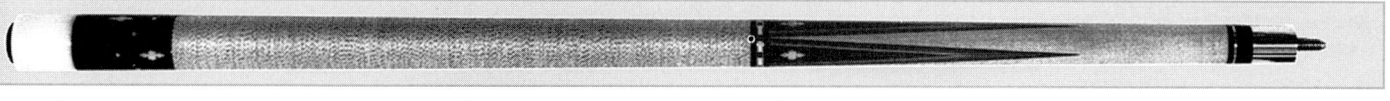

Cues start at	$18,000	$16,000	$13,000

GEORGE BALABUSHKA, cont.

GRADING	98%	90%	70%

Level 5 (Early 1970s) - Maple forearm with maple and ebony "Bushka" ring above wrap, four ebony points with four colored veneers, Cortland Irish linen wrap, ebony butt sleeve with four maple windows and eight maple arch inlays between them.

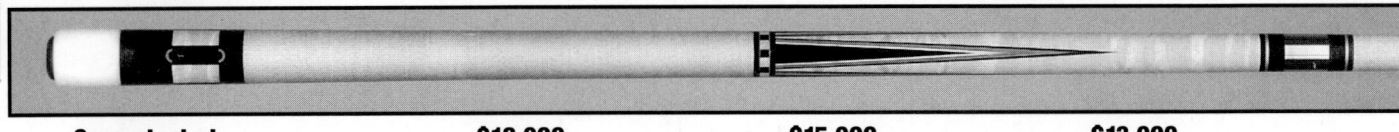

Cues start at	$18,000	$15,000	$13,000

Level 5 - Maple forearm, four ebony points with four colored veneers and mother-of-pearl notched diamonds and/or dots, Cortland Irish linen wrap, ebony butt sleeve with gold foil rings at top and bottom around four maple three-diamond veneer strips and mother-of-pearl notched diamonds.

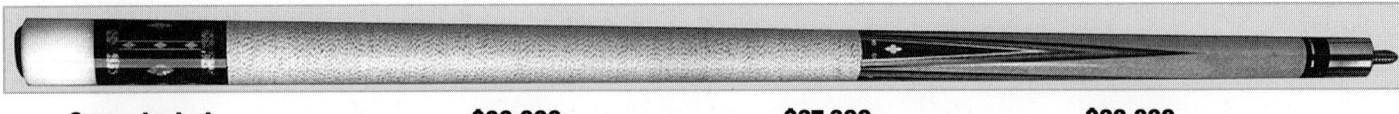

Cues start at	$30,000	$27,000	$22,000

Level 5 (Early 1970s) - Black linen joint and shaft collars with nickel silver ring, maple forearm with maple and ebony "Bushka" ring above wrap, four ebony points with four colored veneers, Cortland Irish linen wrap, ebony butt sleeve with four maple windows and eight maple arch inlays between them.

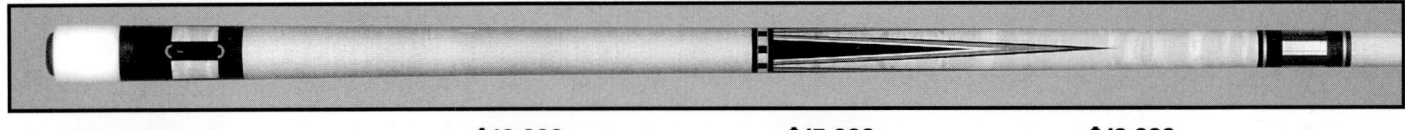

Cues start at	$18,000	$15,000	$13,000

Level 6 - Maple forearm with maple and nine rings above wrap, four ebony points with four colored veneers and one mother-of-pearl notched diamond surrounded by five dots, leather wrap, ebony butt sleeve with four notched mother-of-pearl inlays with 20 dots.

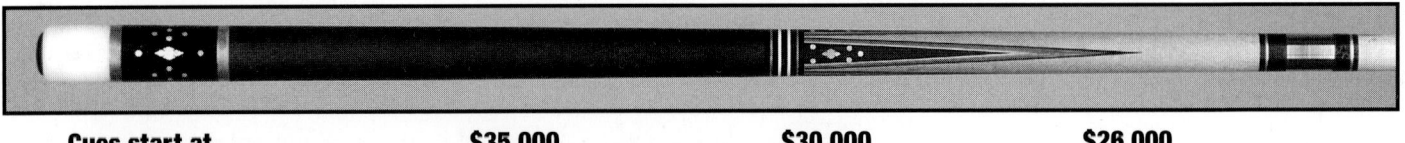

Cues start at	$35,000	$30,000	$26,000

TITLIST BLANK GEORGE BALABUSHKA CUES (1959-1975)

The following are minimum prices for other George Balabushka cues encountered on the secondary market. These prices are representative of cues using the most basic materials and designs that were available. George specialized in one-of-a-kind cues that can command many times these prices due to the use of exotic materials and artistry. Early variations are becoming very collectible, and can also command many times these prices. George Balabushka cues will be further covered in future editions.

Level 3 - 2-6 points, 0-8 inlays.
Level 3 cues start at	$7,000	$6,000	$5,000

Level 4 - 4-10 points, 9-25 inlays.
Level 4 cues start at	$8,500	$7,500	$6,000

Level 5 - 0-12 points, 26-50 inlays.
Level 5 cues start at	$13,000	$10,500	$8,000

BURTON SPAIN/JOHN DAVIS BLANK GEORGE BALABUSHKA CUES (1966-1972)

Level 3 - 2-6 points, 0-8 inlays.
Level 3 cues start at	$9,000	$7,500	$6,000

Level 4 - 4-10 points, 9-25 inlays.
Level 4 cues start at	$10,500	$8,500	$7,000

Level 5 - 0-12 points, 26-50 inlays.
Level 5 cues start at	$13,500	$12,000	$9,750

Level 6 - 0-12 points, 51-75 inlays.
Level 6 cues start at	$18,000	$13,500	$11,000

GUS SZAMBOTI BLANK GEORGE BALABUSHKA CUES (1973-1975)

Level 3 - 2-6 points, 0-8 inlays.
Level 3 cues start at	$10,800	$9,250	$7,500

GRADING	98%	90%	70%
Level 4 - 4-10 points, 9-25 inlays.			
Level 4 cues start at	$14,500	$10,500	$8,500
Level 5 - 0-12 points, 26-50 inlays.			
Level 5 cues start at	$17,000	$15,000	$11,500
Level 6 - 0-12 points, 51-75 inlays.			
Level 6 cues start at	$25,000	$18,500	$13,000

BALICINI CUES

Pool cues manufactured by McDermott Cue Manufacturing Inc. and distributed by Balicini Marketing Group from 1994 to 1995 in Atlanta, Georgia, and later distributed by McDermott Cue Manufacturing Inc.

The Balicini cue was a joint effort between the Balicini Marketing Group and McDermott Cue Mfg. Inc. McDermott manufactured the cues and Balicini marketed and distributed them. The idea was to produce a good playing cue for people who wanted something more durable than wood. Made almost entirely of carbon fiber, the Balicini cue was almost indestructible, even in the hands of the most abusive players. Early cues had a finish over the shaft which required a glove for comfortable play. This was later solved by sanding the shafts smooth and not applying a finish.

Production was stopped in 1995, but then resumed for a time in the late 1990s. McDermott honors the warranties on Balicini cues. If you have a Balicini cue that needs repair, contact McDermott Cue Mfg. Inc., which is listed in the Trademark Index.

SPECIFICATIONS

Butt material: carbon fiber
Shaft material: carbon fiber
Standard length: 58 in.
Standard wrap: Irish linen
Joint type: flat faced
Joint screw: 3/8-10
Standard number of shafts: one
Total production: several thousand

SECONDARY MARKET MINIMUM VALUES

For all used Balicini cues:
Add $50 for each additional original straight playable shaft (standard with one).
Deduct $80 for missing original straight playable shaft.
Deduct 20% for obvious or improper refinish.

Level 2 - 0 points, 0-25 inlays.			
Level 2 cues start at	$210	$120	$80

FRANK BALL CUSTOM CUES

Maker of pool cues from 1987 to 2003 in West Palm Beach, Florida.

Frank Ball was a woodworker all of his life, doing carpentry and making custom furniture. He played a lot of pool when he was younger. One day in the mid-1980s his son Randy accompanied Frank to a local cuemaker's shop to have a minor repair done. On the way home, Frank told his son that he thought he would enjoy making cues. He already had much of the equipment and was familiar with the necessary materials. By 1987 Frank had made his first cue. Early Frank Ball cues had 5/16-18 piloted stainless steel joints and Delrin butt caps. A dozen or so had "Frank Ball" laser engraved on the buttcaps. Frank changed to a black linen phenolic butt cap in 1997, and changed to a 3/8-10 flat-faced linen phenolic butt cap in 1998.

Frank made everything in his cues by hand except for the tips, screws, and bumpers in his one-man shop. He made his own short-spliced blanks, or could inlay points with a manual pantograph if the customer preferred. Frank tried to select the best woods he could find and would always use A+ grade pure white maple for his shafts. He only used ivory in a couple of his cues. He made a bumper that can be unscrewed so that a 22-inch extension can be screwed into the back of the cue for greater reach on long shots. Although there are no identification marks, Frank Ball cues made up until the late 1990s can be identified by their unique joint rings with black and white triple-stacked veneers. He stopped using these in his last four to five years of cuemaking, preferring to use a more modern type of ring. Frank was retired and made cues part-time primarily for enjoyment, with most of his cues being sold to local players. He made 10 to 20 cues each year, so his total production over 15 years was fewer than 300 cues. Frank spent 70 to 80 hours building each cue, and during the last five years all the cues he made were custom orders. The cues Frank made from 2000 on are considered to be his best work. Frank died in April of 2002, about a month after making his last cue.

If you have a Frank Ball cue needing identification, contact Grovers Billiards in West Palm Beach, listed in the Buy, Sell, Trade Index. Many Frank Ball cues were sold through Grovers.

SPECIFICATIONS

Butt material: hardwoods
Shaft material: rock maple
Standard length: 58 in.
Lengths available: any

146 FRANK BALL CUSTOM CUES, cont.

GRADING	98%	90%	70%

Standard finish: cattelized urethane
Balance point: custom
Standard butt cap: black linen phenolic
Standard wrap: Irish linen
Point construction: short splice or pantographed
Standard joint: linen phenolic
Joint type: flat faced or piloted
Joint screw: 3/8-10 or 5/16-18
Standard number of shafts: two
Standard taper: custom
Standard ferrules: Aegis
Standard tip width: 13 mm
Standard tip: Le Pro
Total production: fewer than 300 cues

SECONDARY MARKET MINIMUM VALUES

The following are minimum values for Frank Ball Custom Cues encountered on the secondary market. These prices are representative of cues using materials and designs that are not currently available. Frank has offered one-of-a-kind cues that can command many times these prices due to the use of exotic materials and artistry.

Special construction note: There are many materials and construction techniques that can add value to Frank Ball cues.

For all used cues, except where otherwise noted:
  Add $75 for each additional original straight playable shaft beyond two.
  Deduct $100 for each missing original straight playable shaft under two.
  Add $50 for leather wrap.
  Deduct 20% for obvious or improper refinish.

	98%	90%	70%
Level 1 - 4 points, hustler.			
Level 1 cues start at	$150	$125	$75
Level 2 - 0 points, 0-25 inlays.			
Level 2 cues start at	$225	$175	$120
Level 3 - 2-6 points, 0-8 inlays.			
Level 3 cues start at	$550	$435	$350
Level 4 - 4-10 points, 9-25 inlays.			
Level 4 cues start at	$650	$525	$425
Level 5 - 0-12 points, 26-50 inlays.			
Level 5 cues start at	$800	$650	$525
Level 6 - 0-12 points, 51-75 inlays.			
Level 6 cues start at	$1,200	$875	$700

BARBER CUSTOM CUES

Maker of pool cues from 1983 to present, in Texas, Louisiana, Saucier, Mississippi, and currently believed to be in Florida.

1990 to Present Day

David Barber grew up playing pool. Both his father and uncle were excellent players, and they started teaching David when he was fourteen years old. In 1971, David made his first pool cue in his high school shop class. He continued to enjoy the game, and pursued a career as a welder and machinist in the Texas oil fields. After receiving a $350 custom cue in 1977, David thought that he could do a better job making a cue. That same year, he started repairing and making hustler cues as a hobby. David enjoyed repairing cues, and he would take them apart to learn how they were made. He bought a few of the best cues made at the time, just to dissect them. Using what he had learned, he made his first cue from scratch in 1983.

David constantly improved his cuemaking through the 1980s, while continuing to work full time as a pipe welder. He made many hustler cues and quite a few custom cues, most of which had "DB" cut into the butt cap. His wife was from Shreveport, Louisiana, and they would often go there to visit her family. David would spend time in the pool rooms there, and he ended up meeting Bill Schick. They quickly became friends, and, although Bill has never formally taught David how to make cues, Bill has given him a lot of helpful advice over the years.

In 1990, David started cutting his "D over B" logo into the butt cap of every cue he made. He finally retired from the welding business in 1995 so he could start making cues full time. He still enjoys doing repairs, especially on custom cues by legendary makers.

In 1997, Fred "Creole Freddie" Yates joined Barber Custom Cues as a partner. Fred and David have been friends since high school (although they went to competing schools and played football on opposing teams). Over the years, Fred had promoted tournaments and was co-owner of Snap magazine with Rick Boling, but his favorite occupation has always been cuemaking.

David and Fred made almost 100 cues a year together until Fred left in early 1999. Fred usually started the construction process of a cue, both worked on the cues together, and then David applied the finish. David now does all work on his own. He is proud that all work is done by hand, without the aid of

GRADING	98%	90%	70%

CNC equipment. Hustler cues are still available from Barber Custom Cues, but he also makes his own full-spliced blanks. Exotic wood hustler cues have become very popular, and David says that purpleheart is probably the favorite. Four joints are available on Barber cues, and David makes shafts with four pie-shaped laminations that are available as an option. Most cues come with one shaft, but those over $550 come with two. Le Pro tips used to be standard on all Barber cues, but David now swears by "Sumo" tips, imported from Japan. He offers a unique leather wrap as an option, which is wound on in a 1/8-inch-wide strand. David is very proud of the playability of his cues.

SPECIFICATIONS

Butt material: hardwoods
Shaft material: rock maple
Standard length: 58 in.
Lengths available: any
Standard finish: Dishler 20/20
Balance point: 1 1/2 in. above wrap
Standard butt cap: linen micarta
Standard wrap: Irish linen
Point construction: short splice
Standard joint: linen micarta
Standard pin: 3/8-7 radial stainless steel
Joint type: flat faced
Standard number of shafts: one
Standard taper: 11 in. pro
Standard ferrules: linen micarta
Standard tip: Sumo
Annual production: fewer than 100 cues

OPTIONS (FOR NEW CUES ONLY)

Wound leather wrap: $60
Special length: $50
Extra shaft: $80+
Laminated shaft: $165
Ivory ferrule: $60
Joint protectors: $40

REPAIRS

Repairs done on most fine cues.
Refinish: $150+
Rewrap (Irish linen): $35
Replace joint (stainless steel): $60
Replace joint (ivory): by quote
Replace shaft: $80+
Replace ivory ferrule: $60

CURRENT BARBER CUES

Barber cues over $550 come with two shafts. The current delivery time for a Barber custom cue is two to six months depending on the intricacy of the cue.

PAST EXAMPLES

Level 3 - Bird's-eye maple forearm with a black and white dash ring above wrap, four long purpleheart points with two re-cut veneers of black and ivory, curly maple handle, purpleheart butt sleeve with black and white dash rings at top and bottom.

MSR (1998) $600+	$900	$750	$500

SECONDARY MARKET MINIMUM VALUES

The following are minimum values for Barber Custom Cues encountered on the secondary market. These prices are representative of cues using basic materials and designs that are not currently available. Barber has offered one-of-a-kind cues that can command many times these prices due to the use of exotic materials and artistry.

Special construction note: There are many materials and construction techniques that can add value to Barber cues. The following are the most important examples:

Add $100+ for ivory joint.
Add $200+ for ivory butt cap.

For all used Barber cues, except where otherwise noted:

Add $80 for each additional original straight playable shaft beyond one.
Deduct $80 for missing original straight playable shaft.
Add $60 each for ivory ferrules.
Add $50 for wound leather wrap.
Deduct 30% for obvious or improper refinish.

BARBER CUSTOM CUES, cont.

GRADING	98%	90%	70%
Level 1 - 4 points, hustler.			
Level 1 cues start at	$250	$185	$125
Level 2 - 0 points, 0-25 inlays.			
Level 2 cues start at	$300	$225	$150
Level 3 - 2-6 points, 0-8 inlays.			
Level 3 cues start at	$400	$300	$225
Level 4 - 4-10 points, 9-25 inlays.			
Level 4 cues start at	$600	$450	$325
Level 5 - 0-12 points, 26-50 inlays.			
Level 5 cues start at	$900	$750	$600
Level 6 - 0-12 points, 51-75 inlays.			
Level 6 cues start at	$1250	$1100	$900

BARENBRUGGE CUES

Maker of pool cues from 1995 to present in Apache Junction, Arizona.

The cue bug bit Dave Barenbrugge in 1995 when he ran into an old friend, cuemaker Jim Olms, in an Ohio billiards hall. Jim showed Dave a cue he had built and told him about the work he was doing. Shortly after this encounter, Dave did some research and announced his decision to build cues. He was able to talk Dennis Dieckman into letting him apprentice at his "Cueniversity" for nearly two years. In 1998 he completed his first cue and moved to Arizona. For several years he called his business "Precision Cue Design."

In describing his cues, Dave states, "I build what some would consider a plain cue because they aren't loaded with inlays. Most of my energy is focused on the design that I spent almost eight years doing research and development on. My cues are distinctly different from most others." He starts with a perfectly square "mother" piece for the forearm and does all the splicing from there; four deep 'V'-spliced points underlaying with the butterfly points overlaying. The entire process to hand splice one forearm blank requires over two dozen separate gluing and milling operations and many months. Dave manufctures every piece himself from raw materials except the tips, pins, and bumpers. Joint screws can be stainless steel or titanium. He cuts his own veneers from various hardwoods instead of buying the pre-dyed ones. All pairs of shafts are weight matched.

Barenbrugge cues are guaranteed against construction defects that are not the result of abuse, misuse, warpage and normal wear and tear. They will be repaired or replaced as long as Dave is alive.

For more information or to purchase a cue, please refer to Barenbrugge Cues, which is listed in the Trademark Index.

Dave Barenbrugge

SPECIFICATIONS

Butt material: hardwoods
Shaft material: Northern Michigan maple
Standard Llength: 58 in.
Standard wrap: leather
Point construction: short splice under butterfly splices
Joint type: flat face
Joint screw thread: .360 x 11 tpi
Joint protectors: standard
Standard number of shafts: two
Standard ferrules: LBM threaded

OPTIONS (FOR NEW CUES ONLY)

Special length: $500
Ivory joint: $200
Ivory butt cap: $300
Ivory ferrule: $125
Leather wrap: $300
Extra shaft: $300

REPAIRS

Repairs done on Barenbrugge cues only. Contact Barenbrugge cues for repair pricing.

CURRENT BARENBRUGGE CUES

Basic exotic wood Barenbrugge cues with wraps and joint rings start at $2,500. Basic exotic wood Barenbrugge cues with butterfly points start at $4,000. The current delivery time for a Barenbrugge cue is 18 to 24 months.

GRADING	98%	90%	70%

SECONDARY MARKET MINIMUM VALUES

The following are minimum values for Barenbrugge cues encountered on the secondary market. These prices are representative of cues using basic materials and designs that are not necessarily available at present. Dave Barenbrugge has offered one-of-a-kind cues that can command many times these prices due to the use of exotic materials and artistry.

There are many materials and construction techniques that can add value to Barenbrugge cues.

For all used Barenbrugge cues, except where otherwise noted:
- Add $150 for each additional original straight playable shaft beyond two.
- Deduct $300 for each missing original straight playable shaft under two.
- Add $75 each for ivory ferrules.
- Add $100 for leather wrap.
- Deduct 20% for obvious or improper refinish.

Level 2 - 0 points, 0-25 inlays.

Level 2 cues start at	$2,250	$1,800	$1,250

Level 3 - 2-6 points, 0-8 inlays.

Level 3 cues start at	$3,500	$2,850	$2,000

BARKLEY CUSTOM CUES

Maker of pool cues from 1991 to present in Joplin, Missouri.

Present Day

Jim Barkley's family was in the vending business for over 25 years before Jim started making cues. He was exposed to pool when he worked for the business as a kid, repairing tables and maintaining the bar cues. He learned how to put ferrules and tips on cues in the 1960s. Jim had learned the tool and die business before opening his own business, a machine shop. Jim owned the machine shop for about 20 years and he had as many as 35 employees. When he sold the business, he had free time to return to some of the bars and pool rooms he had worked in as a boy. He noticed there were a lot of cues in need of repair so he started doing repairs part time to have something to do. It wasn't long before he was making his own cues and no longer fully retired.

Jim now builds cues in his new one-man shop that he moved to in 2004. It is a 50 by 100 foot building with five lathes, a Bridgeport mill, two pantographs, table saws, sanders, polishers, band saws, etc. All work is done by hand, without the aid of CNC. Inlays are done on manual pantographs. Jim is also well known for repairs and restorations and he is not afraid to take on cues that need serious work. He most enjoys creating one-of-a-kind custom cues built to the specifications of the customer. Many of his cues have intricate ringwork and inlays, and come with ornate custom joint protectors. He can make his own veneers if the color he is looking for is not available. Several high end Barkley cues were featured in the 2004 Pool Cues Calendar. Jim also makes his own two-piece bar cues from scratch.

All Barkley cues can be easily identified by the "Jim Barkley" script logo with the year of completion engraved on the butt cap or signed on the forearm. Jim is a voting member of the American Cuemaker's Association.

Barkley cues are guaranteed for life to the original owner against construction defects that are not the result of warpage or abuse. If you would like to order a new Barkley cue, or have a cue that you would like Jim to repair or restore, contact Barkley Custom Cues, which is listed in the Trademark Index.

SPECIFICATIONS

Butt material: hardwoods
Shaft material: rock maple
Lengths available: 57 to 60 in.
Standard wrap: Irish linen
Point construction: short splice and inlaid
Standard joint: Uni-Loc
Standard number of shafts: one
Standard ferrules: Ivor-X
Annual production: fewer than 50 cues

OPTIONS (FOR NEW CUES ONLY)

Special length: no charge
Stacked leather wrap: $150
Extra shaft: $175+

REPAIRS

Repairs done on all fine cues.

150 BARKLEY CUSTOM CUES, cont.

GRADING	98%	90%	70%

Refinish (with Irish linen wrap): $200+
Refinish (with leather wrap): $300+
Rewrap (Irish linen): $40
Rewrap (leather): $100+
Replace shaft: $175+
Replace Ivor-X ferrule: $35

CURRENT BARKLEY CUES

Basic two-piece Barkley hustler cues start at $750. Basic two-piece Barkley cues with wraps and joint rings start at $1,000. Barkley cues with points start at $1,800. One-of-a-kind custom Barkley cues start at $4,000.

SECONDARY MARKET MINIMUM VALUES

The following are minimum values for Barkley cues encountered on the secondary market. These prices are representative of cues using basic materials and designs that are not necessarily available at present. Jim has offered one-of-a-kind cues that can command many times these prices due to the use of exotic materials and artistry.

Special construction note: There are many materials and construction techniques that can add value to Barkley cues.

For all used Barkley cues, except where otherwise noted:
- Add $150 for each additional original straight playable shaft beyond one.
- Deduct $175+ for missing original straight playable shaft.
- Add $50 each for ivory ferrules.
- Add $50 for leather wrap.
- Deduct 20% for obvious or improper refinish.

Level 1 - Hustler.
	98%	90%	70%
Level 1 cues start at	$400	$315	$215

Level 2 - 0 points, 0-25 inlays.
Level 2 cues start at	$750	$585	$400

Level 3 - 2-6 points, 0-8 inlays.
Level 3 cues start at	$1,200	$950	$650

Level 4 - 4-10 points, 9-25 inlays.
Level 4 cues start at	$1,500	$1,175	$800

Level 5 - 0-12 points, 26-50 inlays.
Level 5 cues start at	$2,000	$1,600	$1,100

Level 6 - 0-12 points, 51-75 inlays.
Level 6 cues start at	$3,000	$2,400	$1,650

BARNET CUES

Maker of pool cues in Olathe, Kansas.

Jerry Barnet has been building pool and billiard cues out of the well-known Shooters poolroom in the Kansas City suburb of Olathe for a number of years. He produces hustler cues and also some short-spliced and butterfly-spliced cues.

For more information or to order a cue, contact Barnett Cues, which is listed in the Trademark Index.

BARNHART CUES

Maker of pool cues from 1995 to present in Martinsburg, West Virginia.

As a young boy, Cory Barnhart worked for his father at their family's excavating business. At the age of 15, he got a job working for a custom cabinet builder. At 16 he began working for a custom home builder. By the time Cory graduated from high school, he had already built a custom home on his own for a local buyer.

Cory began doing simple cue repairs in 1994, and in 1995 he built his first cue. He learned a lot through trial and error, but was helped along the way by a number of cuemakers, including Chester Krick, Dennis Deickman, Dan Dishaw and Jim Buss. Mike Webb and Chris Hightower were also influential in Cory's learning of the trade. Cory's work is inspired by Szamboti, Kersenbrock, and Richard Black.

Cory Barnhart

BARNHART CUES, cont.

GRADING	100%	95%	70%

Cory experimented with several different designs until he was satisfied that he had built a durable cue that played well. In 2003, he was inducted into the American Cuemaker's Association. Cory Barnhart hosts pool tournaments for various charities and is also in the process of planning for other tournaments on the East coast of the United States.

Barnhart Cues are usually signed under the wrap, but Cory will sign or engrave what the customer wants. His cues are guaranteed for life against construction defects that are not the result of warpage or abuse. For more information, or to order a Barnhart Cue, contact Cory at Barnhart Cues, listed in the Trademark Index.

SPECIFICATIONS

- Butt material: hardwoods
- Shaft material: rock maple
- Standard length: 58 ½ in.
- Standard wrap: any
- Standard finish: acrylic urethane
- Balance point: custom
- Point construction: short splice
- Standard joint: phenolic
- Standard butt cap: phenolic
- Joint type: flat face
- Joint screw thread: 7.5 radial
- Joint protectors: standard
- Standard number of shafts: one
- Standard taper: custom
- Standard tip width: 13 mm
- Standard tip: Triangle
- Standard ferrules: ¾ in. Aegis II
- Annual production: more than 50 cues

OPTIONS (FOR NEW CUES ONLY)

- Special length: no charge
- Ivory joint: $150
- Ivory ferrule: $50
- Ivory butt cap: $250
- Leather wrap: $75
- Extra shaft: $100+

REPAIRS

Repairs done on all fine cues.
- Refinish (with Irish linen wrap): $150
- Refinish (with leather wrap): $225
- Rewrap (Irish linen): $50
- Rewrap (leather): $100
- Clean and press linen wrap: $25
- Replace shaft: $100+
- Replace ivory ferrule: $50+
- Replace tip: $15
- Replace fiber/linen ferrule: $30+

CURRENT BARNHART CUES

Two-piece Barnhart bar cues start at $250. Basic Barnhart cues with wraps and joint rings start at $500. Barnhart cues with points start at $625. The current delivery time for a Barnhart Cue depends upon the design of the cue.

CURRENT EXAMPLES

The following Barnhart cues can be ordered as shown, modified to suit the desires of the customer, or new designs can be created.

Level 1 - Maple forearm, four full-spliced bocote points and handle.

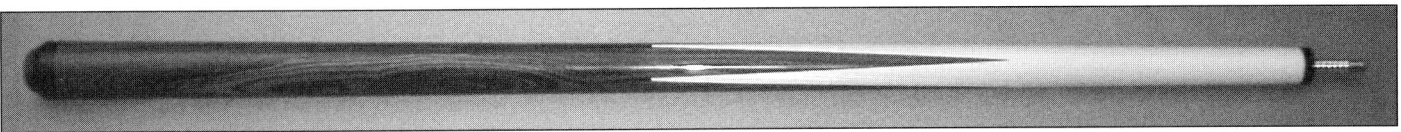

MSR	$250	$225-250	$185	$140

BARNHART CUES, cont.

GRADING	100%	95%	70%

Level 2 - Bocote forearm, bocote butt sleeve with a metal ring at bottom.

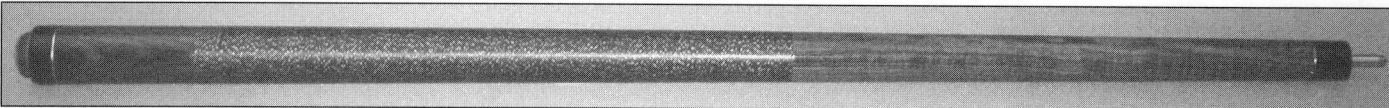

MSR	$400	$375-435	$310	$230

Level 2 "Jump/Break" - Bird's-eye maple forearm with a jump/break joint above wrap, purpleheart handle.

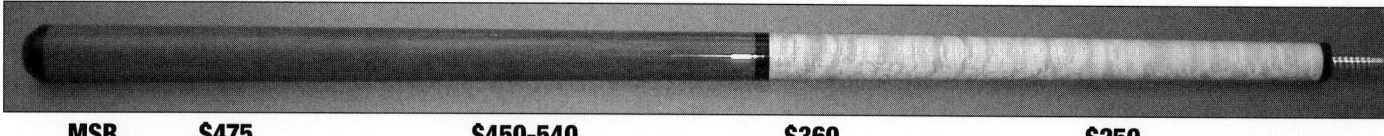

MSR	$475	$450-540	$360	$250

Level 3 - Bird's-eye maple forearm, four bird's-eye maple butterfly points with two colored veneers, ebony butt sleeve with four ivory dots set in turquoise ovals.

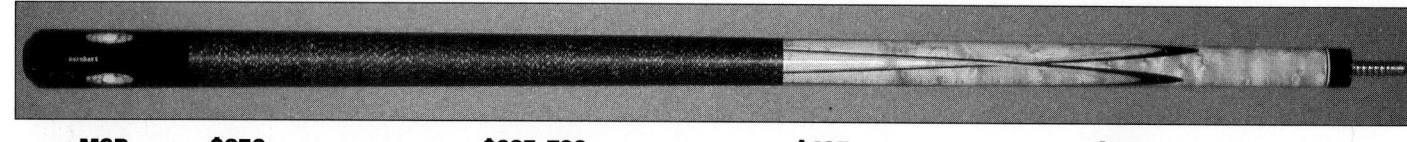

MSR	$650	$625-700	$495	$350

Level 3 - Curly maple forearm, five ebony points with four colored veneers, leather wrap, ebony butt sleeve.

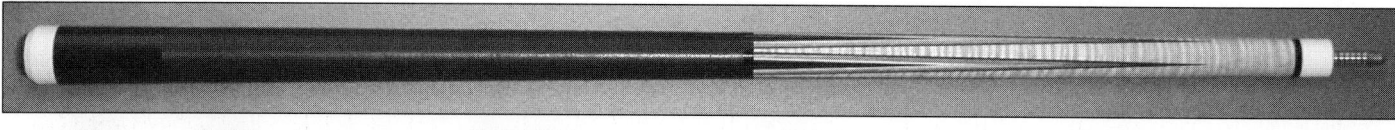

MSR	$725	$700-825	$575	$400

Level 4 - Curly maple forearm, five ebony points with four colored veneers and an ivory spear-shaped inlay in each, leather wrap, ebony butt sleeve with five ivory diamond-shaped inlays.

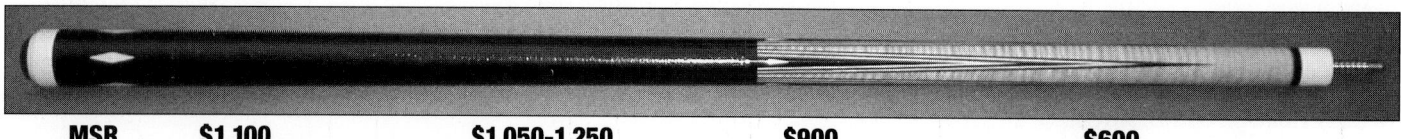

MSR	$1,100	$1,050-1,250	$900	$600

Level 4 - Bird's-eye maple forearm with turquoise set in metal rings above wrap, five ebony points with four colored veneers, leather wrap, ebony butt sleeve with five four-piece ivory diamond-shaped inlays alternating with five turquoise squares between turquoise set in metal rings above and below.

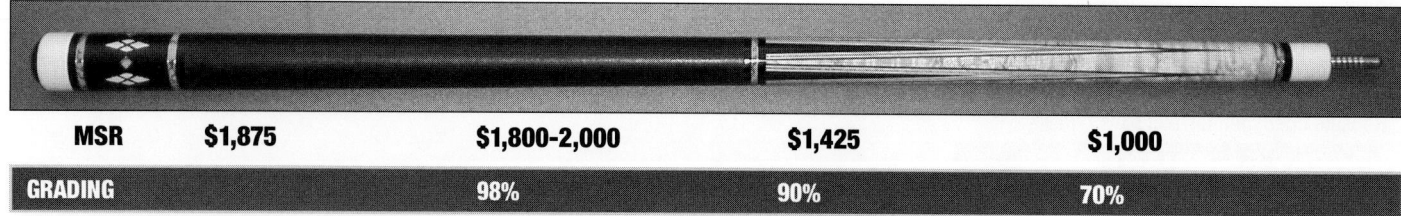

MSR	$1,875	$1,800-2,000	$1,425	$1,000
GRADING		98%	90%	70%

SECONDARY MARKET MINIMUM VALUES

The following are minimum values for other Barnhart cues encountered on the secondary market. These prices are representative of cues using basic materials and designs that are not necessarily available at present. Cory has offered one-of-a-kind cues that can command many times these prices due to the use of exotic materials and artistry.

Special construction note: There are many materials and construction techniques that can add value to Barnhart cues.

For all used Barnhart cues, except where otherwise noted:

- Add $75 for each additional original straight playable shaft beyond one.
- Deduct $100+ for missing original straight playable shaft.
- Add $40 each for ivory ferrules.
- Add $50 for leather wrap.
- Deduct 20% for obvious or improper refinish.

Level 1 - Hustler.

Level 1 cues start at	$200	$165	$120

GRADING	98%	90%	70%
Level 2 - 0 points, 0-25 inlays.			
Level 2 cues start at	$350	$275	$190
Level 3 - 2-6 points, 0-8 inlays.			
Level 3 cues start at	$500	$395	$270
Level 4 - 4-10 points, 9-25 inlays.			
Level 4 cues start at	$700	$545	$375
Level 5 - 0-12 points, 26-50 inlays.			
Level 5 cues start at	$1,000	$825	$600
Level 6 - 0-12 points, 51-75 inlays.			
Level 6 cues start at	$1,400	$1,150	$850

BARRINGER CUES

Maker of pool cues from 1976 to 2005 in Las Vegas, Nevada, and from 2005 to present in New Smyrna Beach, Florida.

Born and raised in Brooklyn, New York, Joe Barringer had an opportunity at a very early age to learn from some of the best players of the 1960s. By 1976, he was playing in top form. Joe was playing everywhere in Brooklyn, and getting a reputation as a good player.

By 1976, Joe was looking for that perfect cue. He agrees with the philosophy, "If you want something done right, you do it yourself." And so he did. He invested in an old lathe and various other woodworking tools and was turning out his first cue by late 1976. Cue production steadily improved as Joe learned techniques and acquired various materials to work with. At this time, cuemaking was more of a hobby than the business enterprise it has become today. It was, and still is, a labor of love.

Joe's favorite cues are all natural and made entirely of wood. He has four large lathes in his shop, which he has modified to his exact specifications and each one is set up to do specific tasks with precision and accuracy. Joe has two inlay machines. Most of his inlays are still done with a pantograph, and he has two table saws, a jointer, planer, sliding compound mitre saw and other equipment for spraying.

Present Day

In 2000, Joe started selling some of his fine exotic wood and hard maple to other cue builders, as well as supplying various component parts. In 2003, he opened his company, Cue Components. Cue builders from all over the world have purchased products from his website.

Joe currently only uses two style joint pins in his cues: a brass 3/8-11, and a black rolled G-10, which is a Barringer exclusive. Joe's cues offer a hit that is hard to duplicate. Early cues have the 3/8-10 pins, and later cues have the radial pin. Today he only uses the 3/8-11 and his exclusive black G-10 pin. Beginning with 2004, both his brass 3/8-11 and his black G-10 pin sport serial numbers for authenticity, value and provenance of each cue.

Joe also builds a fine jump/break cue. He uses purpleheart and maple with a Uni-Loc joint for quick release action on the butt end, and a purpleheart shaft with a serial numbered radial pin.

Current order time for a new Barringer Cue is about three years. He is no longer taking custom orders, but is building cues to his own specifications and creativity.

If you are interested in talking to Joe Barringer about a new cue or a cue that needs to be repaired, you can contact him at Barringer Cues, listed in the Trademark Index.

SPECIFICATIONS

Butt material: hardwoods
Shaft material: hard maple
Standard finish: urethane gloss and satin
Standard length: 58 to 60 in.
Standard wrap: Irish linen
Balance point: 18 to 19 in.
Standard joint: phenolic
Standard ferrules: melamine
Standard tip: Moori

OPTIONS (FOR NEW CUES ONLY)

Ivory ferrule: $60
Ivory joint: $125
Ivory butt: $150+
Leather stack wrap: $165
Extra shaft: $150

GRADING	100%	95%	70%

CURRENT BARRINGER CUES

Barringer hustler cues start at $250. Basic Barringer cues with wraps and joint rings start at $400. Barringer cues with points start at $700. The current delivery time for a Barringer cue is about three years.

CURRENT EXAMPLES

The following Barringer cues can be ordered as shown, modified to suit the desires of the customer, or new designs can be created.

Level 1 "Sneaky Pete" - Maple forearm, four full-spliced cocobolo points and handle, maple butt sleeve with a cocobolo ring at bottom.

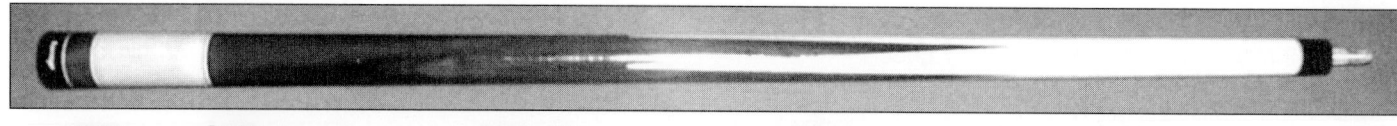

MSR	$250	$225-275	$185	$135

Level 2 "Jump/Break" - Purpleheart forearm with a Uni-Loc jump/break joint above handle, hard maple handle, purpleheart butt sleeve.

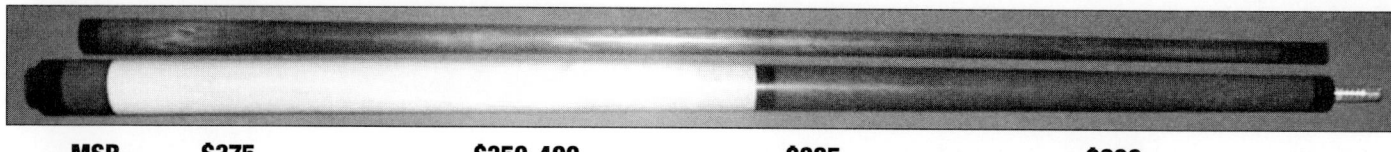

MSR	$375	$350-400	$285	$200

Level 2 - Bocote forearm, bird's-eye maple handle, bocote butt sleeve.

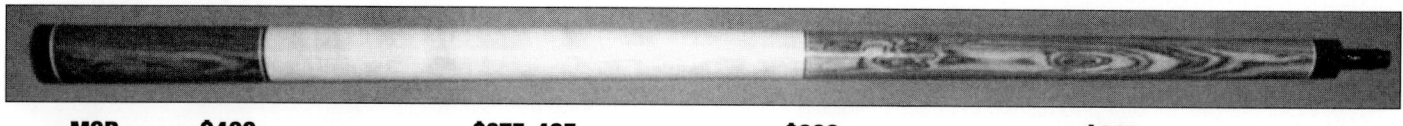

MSR	$400	$375-435	$300	$215

Level 3 - Ebony forearm, three long and three short maple points, maple butt sleeve with a thick ebony ring at bottom.

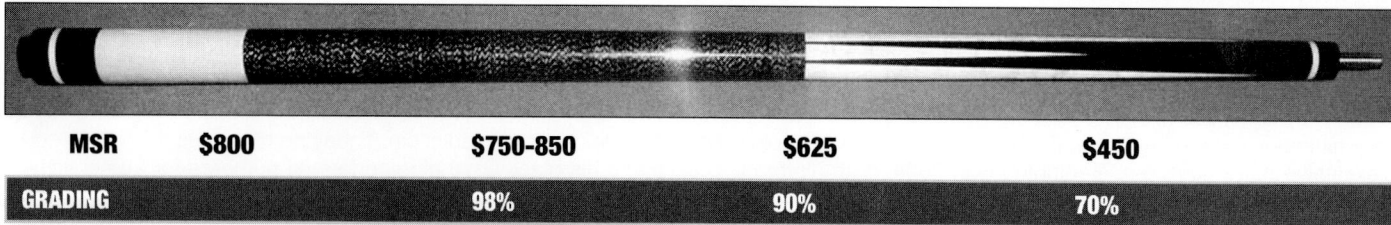

MSR	$800	$750-850	$625	$450

GRADING	98%	90%	70%

SECONDARY MARKET MINIMUM VALUES

The following are minimum values for other Barringer cues encountered on the secondary market. These prices are representative of cues using basic materials and designs that are not necessarily available at present. Barringer has offered one-of-a-kind cues that can command many times these prices due to the use of exotic materials and artistry.

Special construction note: There are many materials and construction techniques that can add value to Barringer cues.

For all used Barringer cues, except where otherwise noted:

- Add $150 for each additional original straight playable shaft beyond two.
- Deduct $125 for missing original straight playable shaft.
- Add $50 each for ivory ferrules.
- Add $75 for leather wrap.
- Deduct 20% for obvious or improper refinish.

Level 1 - Hustler.

Level 1 cues start at	$250	$200	$135

Level 2 - 0 points, 0-25 inlays.

Level 2 cues start at	$375	$300	$200

Level 3 - 2-6 points, 0-8 inlays.

Level 3 cues start at	$600	$475	$325

Level 4 - 4-10 points, 9-25 inlays.

Level 4 cues start at	$850	$675	$450

Level 5 - 0-12 points, 26-50 inlays.

Level 5 cues start at	$1,150	$925	$650

| GRADING | 98% | 90% | 70% |

BCM CUES

Maker of pool cues from 1995 to present in Phoenix and Tempe, Arizona.

Bryan C. Mordt enjoyed playing pool as a teenager, having started at the age of 17. He got the bug, like many do, and started playing obsessively for many years. He has owned many cues, including Hicks, Meucci, Joss, Schon, Sierra and SouthWest. Soon, Bryan took an interest in trying to maintain his own cues.

In 1995, Bryan met John Shelton, who was kind enough to give Bryan his first introduction to the metal lathe. He started doing small repairs and refinish jobs and then progressed to making his own cues.

Not long after that, Bryan met Eric Niemira, a machinist/cuemaker. They became friends, and Bryan worked with Eric and learned a lot about machines, tooling and setup. In 1998 Bryan purchased a billiards pro shop and continued honing his skills of cuemaking, repairing and restoring all kinds of cues. After four years of running a successful pro shop in Pheonix, Bryan decided to build cues full time. He strives for stability, beauty and quality in his cues. Bryan does not currently mark his cues, unless the customer requests it. In the future, he may offer an engraving on the joint pin to help identify his work. Bryan also enjoys photography, and does all his own cue photos for his website.

BCM Cues are guaranteed against defects in workmanship that are not the result of warpage or abuse.

For more information, or to order a BCM cue, contact Bryan at BCM Cues, listed in the Trademark Index.

SPECIFICATIONS

Butt material: exotic hardwoods
Shaft material: hard maple
Standard length: 59 in.
Standard wrap: Irish linen
Standard ferrules: linen-base melamine or grice
Standard tips: water buffalo or Moori
Annual production: approximately 100 cues

OPTIONS (FOR NEW CUES ONLY)

Ivory ferrule: $50
Leather wrap: $100
Extra shaft: $130

REPAIRS

Repairs done on all fine cues.
Refinish (with Irish linen wrap): $150
Rewrap (Irish linen): $40
Replace shaft: $130
Replace tip: $10+

CURRENT BCM CUES

Two-piece BCM bar cues start at $375. Basic BCM cues with wraps and joint rings start at $450. BCM cues with points start at $570. The current delivery time for a BCM cue depends on the cue.

SECONDARY MARKET MINIMUM VALUES

The following are minimum values for other BCM cues encountered on the secondary market. These prices are representative of cues using basic materials and designs that are not necessarily available at present. Brian has offered one-of-a-kind cues that can command many times these prices due to the use of exotic materials and artistry.

Special construction note: There are many materials and construction techniques that can add value to BCM cues.

For all used BCM cues, except where otherwise noted:

Add $100 for each additional original straight playable shaft beyond one.
Deduct $130+ for missing original straight playable shaft.
Add $40 each for ivory ferrules.
Add $50 for leather wrap.
Deduct 20% for obvious or improper refinish.

Level 1 - Hustler.
	98%	90%	70%
Level 1 cues start at	$325	$250	$165

Level 2 - 0 points, 0-25 inlays.
Level 2 cues start at	$400	$315	$220

Level 3 - 2-6 points, 0-8 inlays.
Level 3 cues start at	$500	$385	$265

Level 4 - 4-10 points, 9-25 inlays.
Level 4 cues start at	$650	$515	$350

Level 5 - 0-12 points, 26-50 inlays.
Level 5 cues start at	$900	$700	$475

MARK BEAR CUSTOM CUES

Maker of pool cues from 1994 to present in Fredericksburg, Virginia.

Present Day

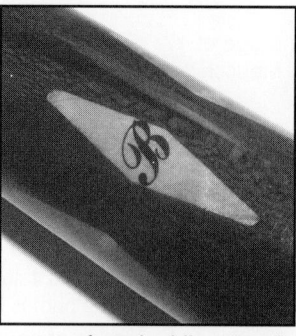

Mark Bear

Mark Bear became interested in the game of pool while attending college. It quenched his competitive drive and was a natural, yet safer, replacement for his love of racing four-wheeled motocross. It was during those racing years that Mark learned his way around a machine shop. That machine shop knowledge, coupled with an art background throughout high school and college, made his love for the functional art of cues begin to grow rapidly. The ambition to make and repair cues was fueled further by the progression of his pool game. Mark then began purchasing the materials and equipment to make this goal possible. In 1994 he made his first cue and, over the course of that year, slowly improved upon its design. After that year, confident with the design and performance of his cues, he began showing them locally and regionally to players. Bear Cues was born. Over the years, Mark has constantly improved upon his designs and construction techniques with the latest being what he calls the "Modern Day Full Splice." This is based on the tried and true Brunswick Titlist design. Mark Bear Custom Cues is truly a one-man shop where everything is made in-house, with the exception of the tips, bumpers and some screws. Every cue is one-of-a-kind and truly handmade.

If you are interested in talking to Mark Bear about a new cue or a cue that needs to be repaired, you can contact him at Mark Bear Custom Cues, listed in the Trademark Index.

SPECIFICATIONS

Butt material: hardwoods
Shaft material: rock maple
Standard length: 58 in.
Lengths available: any
Standard finish: UV
Balance point: custom
Standard wrap: linen
Point construction: full splice, short splice or butterfly
Standard number of shafts: one
Standard taper: custom
Standard ferrules: melamine
Standard tip: Triangle
Standard tip width: 13 mm
Tip widths available: any
Annual production: fewer than 60 cues

OPTIONS (FOR NEW CUES ONLY)

Ivory butt cap: $250
Ivory butt sleeve: $700
Ivory joint: $150
Ivory ferrule: $50
Ivory points: $600
Leather wrap: $100
Joint protectors: $50
Extra shaft: $100

REPAIRS

Repairs done on all fine cues.
Refinish (with Irish linen wrap): $100
Refinish (with leather wrap): $150
Rewrap (Irish linen): $40
Rewrap (leather): $100
Clean and press linen wrap: $10
Restore leather wrap: $10
Replace shaft: $100

GRADING	98%	90%	70%

Replace ivory ferrule: $75
Replace butt cap: $40
Replace ivory butt cap: $250
Replace tip: $10
Replaced layered tip: $20+
Replace fiber/linen ferrule: $30

CURRENT MARK BEAR CUES

Basic Mark Bear two-piece hustler cues start at $250. Two-piece Mark Bear cues with wraps and joints start at $450. Cues with short spliced points start at $500. Eight-point Mark Bear short spliced cues start at $700. Cues with full-spliced butterfly points start at $850. Mark Bear cues with full-spliced points and veneers start at $950. The current delivery time for a custom Mark Bear cue is at least six months depending on the intricacy of the cue.

SECONDARY MARKET MINIMUM VALUES

The following are minimum prices for Mark Bear Cues encountered on the secondary market. These prices are representative of cues using basic materials and designs that may not be currently available. Mark Bear also offers one-of-a-kind cues that can command in excess of these prices due to the use of exotic materials or special construction techniques.

Special construction note: There are many materials and construction techniques that can add value to Mark Bear cues.

For all used Mark Bear cues, except where otherwise noted:
- Add $80 for each additional original straight playable shaft beyond one.
- Deduct $100 for missing original straight playable shaft.
- Add $40 each for Ivory ferrules.
- Add $50 for leather wrap.
- Deduct 20% for obvious or improper refinish.

	98%	90%	70%
Level 1 - 4 points, hustler.			
Level 1 cues start at	$200	$150	$125
Level 2 - 0 points, 0-25 inlays.			
Level 2 cues start at	$400	$300	$200
Level 3 - 2-6 points, 0-8 inlays.			
Level 3 cues start at	$450	$375	$235
Level 4 - 4-12 points, 9-25 inlays.			
Level 4 cues start at	$800	$600	$500
Level 5 - 0-12 points, 26-50 inlays.			
Level 5 cues start at	$1,200	$1,000	$850
Level 6 - 0-12 points, 51-75 inlays.			
Level 6 cues start at	$1,500	$1,200	$1,000
Level 7 - 0-16 points, 76-125 inlays.			
Level 7 cues start at	$2,000	$1,600	$1,250

AL BECKELHIMER

Maker of Star City Cues. Refer to Star City Cues for information.

BECKER CUSTOM CUES

Maker of pool cues since 1995 in Ft. Collins, Colorado, presently in Pierce, Colorado.

Roland Becker began working in the billiard machine shop at Woodward Governor right out of high school in 1972. He went through a two-year apprentice program at Woodward about five years after high school. He has worked as a tooling machinist for the past 15 years, but has been in the machining trade for the last 30 years. The precision and attention to detail of making and designing high quality plastic injection molds has helped Roland in the making of his one-of-a-kind quality cues. He has always enjoyed working with wood, but wood brings out his allergies, from extreme skin rash to asthma attacks. Therefore, cue making will remain a hobby and be limited as to the number of cues put out each year. Roland does not use CNC. He uses all manual tools in his cuemaking.

Becker credits two people with inspiring his work. Burt Kellerman, a cue collector in Denver, saw the potential Roland had and kept giving him challenges. The other person was the late Jerry Franklin of South West Cues. Jerry and Roland talked at length, and when Jerry found out Roland's background, he asked him to make some patterns for their pantograph. Getting with Jerry's brother Gary, he has made several of their patterns.

Roland tries to exceed his customer's expectations in his cuemaking. Appearance and performance of his cues are of extreme importance to Roland, and all of his cues are one-of-a-kind. They can be identified by the king chess piece with a B in the middle, to be found on the butt cap. If you have a Becker cue that needs further identification or repair, or would like to talk to Roland about ordering a new cue, contact Becker Custom Cues, which is listed in the Trademark Index.

158 BECKER CUSTOM CUES, cont.

GRADING	100%	95%	70%

SPECIFICATIONS

Butt material: hardwoods
Shaft material: hard rock maple
Standard length: 58 in.
Standard wrap: Irish linen
Standard ferrules: Ivorine-3
Standard joint: stainless steel
Standard tip: Le Pro
Annual production: fewer than 30 cues

OPTIONS (FOR NEW CUES ONLY)

Ivory ferrule: $50
Leather wrap: $50
Extra shaft: $65

REPAIRS

Repairs done on all fine cues.
Refinish (with Irish linen wrap): $125
Rewrap (Irish linen): $35
Replace shaft: $60+
Replace tip: $10+

CURRENT BECKER CUES

Two-piece Becker bar cues start at $150. Basic Becker cues with wraps and joint rings start at $200. Roland can add points to his basic cues for $20 per point and $20 per veneer. The current delivery time for a Becker cue is about eight months to one year, depending on the cue.

CURRENT EXAMPLES

The following Becker cues can be ordered as shown, modified to suit the desires of the customer, or new designs can be created.

Level 4 - Curly maple forearm with maple and ebony checks above wrap, four ebony points with three colored veneers and an ivory diamond-shaped inlay in each and at the tip of each point, curly maple butt sleeve with maple and ebony checks below wrap above four large ivory diamond-shaped inlays above a metal ring at bottom.

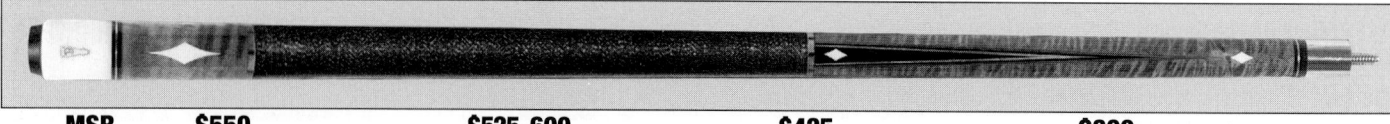

MSR	$550	$525-600	$425	$300

Level 4 - Ivory joint, ebony forearm, four gold-bordered ebony floating elliptical points with a gold arrowhead-shaped inlay at the upper and lower tip of each point, ebony butt sleeve with four gold-bordered ebony floating elliptical windows with a gold arrowhead-shaped inlay at the upper and lower tip of each above a metal ring at bottom, ivory butt cap.

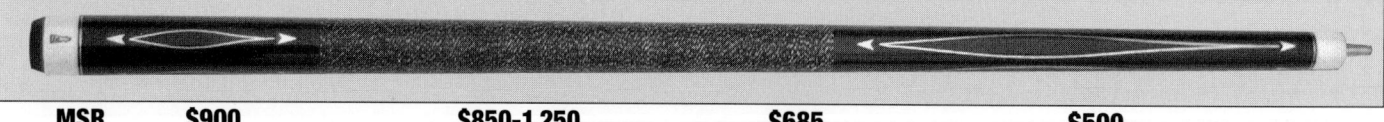

MSR	$900	$850-1,250	$685	$500

Level 3 - Ivory joint, bird's-eye maple forearm with maple/ebony/ivory checks above wrap, three long and three short ivory points with three ebony veneers and a famous cuemaker's signature in each, ebony butt sleeve with six ebony-bordered ivory windows with a famous cuemaker's signature in each between maple/ebony/ivory check rings at top and bottom.

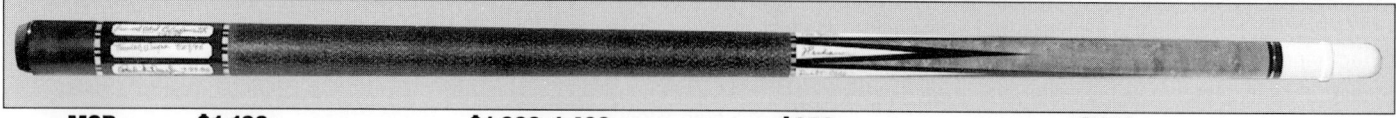

MSR	$1,100	$1,000-1,400	$850	$650

Level 3 - Ivory joint, ebony forearm with maple/ebony/ivory checks above wrap, three long and three short ivory points with three colored veneers and an ebony sword inlaid in each and an ivory heart-shaped spearhead at the tip of each point, ebony butt sleeve with six ivory windows with an ebony sword-shaped inlay in each between maple/ebony/ivory check rings at top and bottom.

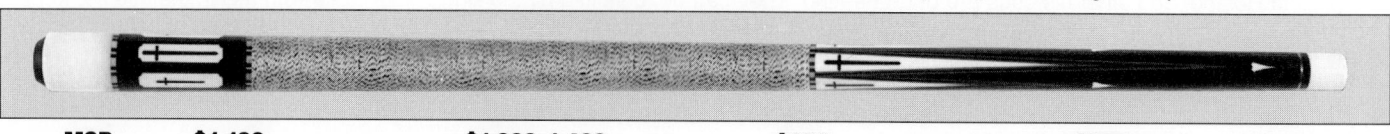

MSR	$1,100	$1,000-1,400	$850	$650

BECKER CUSTOM CUES, cont. **159**

GRADING	98%	90%	70%

SECONDARY MARKET MINIMUM VALUES

The following are minimum values for Becker cues encountered on the secondary market. These prices are representative of cues using basic materials and designs that are not necessarily available at present. Roland has offered one-of-a-kind cues that can command many times these prices due to the use of exotic materials and artistry.

Special construction note: There are many materials and construction techniques that can add value to Becker cues.

For all used Becker cues, except where otherwise noted:
- Add $50 for each additional original straight playable shaft beyond one.
- Deduct $65+ for missing original straight playable shaft.
- Add $40 each for ivory ferrules.
- Add $40 for leather wrap.
- Deduct 15% for obvious or improper refinish.

Level 1 - Hustler.
Level 1 cues start at	$125	$100	$65

Level 2 - 0 points, 0-25 inlays.
Level 2 cues start at	$180	$140	$95

Level 3 - 2-6 points, 0-8 inlays.
Level 3 cues start at	$250	$195	$135

Level 4 - 4-10 points, 9-25 inlays.
Level 4 cues start at	$350	$275	$185

Level 5 - 0-12 points, 26-50 inlays.
Level 5 cues start at	$500	$390	$270

BELLA SERA CUSTOM CUES, LLC

Maker of pool cues since 2001 in Shreveport, Louisiana.

Wayne Anderson began working in the billiard industry in 1985, making cue cases for "It's George" in Mike Roberts' garage. Mike "Cosmo" Gray joined the company shortly thereafter. With the success of the cases, Mr. Roberts decided to add pool cues to their product line. "It's George" shared a space with Bill Schick, one of the top cuemakers in the country. He trained them and helped set up their cuemaking operation. Wayne and Mike made cues for "It's George" from 1990 to 1995, when they left with Mr. Schick to work at his new shop until 2000.

In 2001, Wayne and Cosmo became partners in Bella Sera Custom Cues. They still adhere to the highest standards using the "handmade" methods they learned from years of experience as cuemaking apprentices. Obtaining only the finest hand-selected woods and using no computerized equipment enables them to give each cue their personal touch. Quality and playability are most important for Wayne and Cosmo. In 2004 Wayne became a member of the ACA. Bella Sera Custom Cues can be readily identified by the "Bella Sera" logo engraved on the butt sleeve of each cue.

Bill Lunsford, Wayne Anderson, and Mike "Cosmo" Gray

If you are interested in talking to Wayne Anderson, Mike (Cosmo) Gray, or Sales Manager Bill Lunsford about a new cue or a cue that needs to be repaired, you can contact them at Bella Sera Cues LLC, listed in the Trademark Index.

SPECIFICATIONS

Butt material: hardwoods
Shaft material: rock maple
Standard length: 58 in.
Lengths available: any
Standard finish: automotive clear coat
Balance point: custom
Standard butt cap: phenolic
Standard wrap: Irish linen
Point construction: short splice
Standard joint: stainless steel
Delrin joint protectors: standard
Standard number of shafts: one
Standard taper: custom
Standard ferrules: phenolic
Standard tip: Triangle

BELLA SERA CUSTOM CUES, LLC, cont.

GRADING	98%	90%	70%

Standard tip width: 13 mm
Tip widths available: any
Annual production: approximately 40 cues

OPTIONS (FOR NEW CUES ONLY)

Special length: no charge
Layered tip: $30
Ivory joint: $125+
Ivory ferrule: $80+
Leather wrap: $75+
Phenolic joint protectors: no charge
Extra shaft: $50

REPAIRS

Repairs done on Bella Sera cues only.
Refinish (with Irish linen wrap): $100
Refinish (with leather wrap): $165
Rewrap (Irish linen): $35
Rewrap (leather): $85
Replace shaft: $100
Replace ivory ferrule: $80+
Replace butt cap: varies
Replace tip: $10
Replaced layered tip: $35
Replace fiber/linen ferrule: $35

CURRENT BELLA SERA CUES

Basic two-piece Bella Sera hustler cues start at $175. Two-piece Bella Sera cues with wraps and joint rings start at $275. Basic Bella Sera cues with points start at $500. One-of-a-kind custom Bella Sera cues start at $900. Bella Sera cues over $1,000 come with two shafts.

SECONDARY MARKET MINIMUM VALUES

The following are minimum values for Bella Sera cues encountered on the secondary market. These prices are representative of cues using basic materials and designs that are not necessarily available at present. Bella Sera has offered one-of-a-kind cues that can command many times these prices due to the use of exotic materials and artistry.

Special construction note: There are many materials and construction techniques that can add value to Bella Sera cues.

For all used Bella Sera cues, except where otherwise noted:
- Add $45 for each additional original straight playable shaft beyond one.
- Deduct $50 for missing original straight playable shaft.
- Add $50 each for ivory ferrules.
- Add $50 for leather wrap.
- Deduct 25% for obvious or improper refinish.

	98%	90%	70%
Level 1 - Hustler.			
Level 1 cues start at	$150	$120	$85
Level 2 - 0 points, 0-25 inlays.			
Level 2 cues start at	$250	$190	$135
Level 3 - 2-6 points, 0-8 inlays.			
Level 3 cues start at	$450	$350	$240
Level 4 - 4-10 points, 9-25 inlays.			
Level 4 cues start at	$600	$475	$325
Level 5 - 0-12 points, 26-50 inlays.			
Level 5 cues start at	$1,000	$795	$550
Level 6 - 0-12 points, 51-75 inlays.			
Level 6 cues start at	$1,350	$1,050	$700

BENDER CUES

Maker of pool cues since 1988, currently in Delta Junction, Alaska.

Mike Bender and Tracy Dunham

Michael J. Bender grew up in the Chicago suburb of Arlington Heights, Illinois. At a young age, he became interested in the things his father made in his shop at home. After high school, Mike went to gunsmithing school for one year, and was involved in competitive rifle shooting. Mike was a five-time All-American rifle shooter while attending the University of Eastern Kentucky and later at graduate school in Richmond, Kentucky. Shooting was very competitive and stressful, and he found that the one activity that provided a complete diversion from the stress was playing pool. Soon, he was playing many hours a week. As an industrial technology major, Mike regularly worked in the machine shops at college. One day, he decided to make his own two-piece cue from a house cue. When he brought the completed cue into the local pool room, he immediately started getting requests for cue repair work.

It was at the University of Eastern Kentucky where Mike met his wife, artist Tracy Dunham. After college, the two moved to Chicago, where Mike worked for eight years making full-size prototype printing presses. He continued to do cue repair work on the side, which is how he met Ed Boado, a cue collector and businessman.

In 1989, the two started Omega Cues. While at Omega, Mike learned from David Kersenbrock, who joined the company soon after it was founded. Tracy also worked at Omega, and was responsible for designing some of the shop's most beautiful cues. Mike and Tracy collaborated on many elaborate cues while at Omega, but they were not happy with big city life.

In 1992, they moved to the interior of Alaska to start Bender Cues in Delta Junction. Mike's machining skills won Bender Cues a first place award for "Best Execution" just one year later, at the 1993 American Cuemakers Convention in Baltimore. They exhibited at the cue shows in 1995, 1998, and 1999. Today, Mike and Tracy make 50 cues per year. Tracy does most of the design and inlay work. Her inlay pieces are cut using a World War II vintage Gorton pantograph. In 2003 they switched from a two-part urethane to a UV cure finish. Hustler cues are no longer offered; only about 12 were made before they were discontinued several years ago.

Bender cues are easily identifiable by the "M. J. Bender Alaska" or the newer "Dunham-Bender Alaska" identification mark on the joint screw. Inlays and points are radially arranged in multiples of five. Mike was the first to do multiple re-splice points in 1994, which are one of Bender's signature designs. They make every component in the cue except for the tip and the bumper. If you have a Bender cue that needs repair, or would like to talk to Mike and Tracy about the design of a new cue, contact Bender Cues, listed in the Trademark Index.

For more information on Mike Bender and Tracy Dunham, please refer to the listing for the "Omega/dpk Cue Company."

Mike and Tracy currently specialize in one-of-a-kind custom cues. The following cues are representations of the work of Bender Cues. These cues can be ordered as shown, modified to suit the desires of the customer, or new designs can be created. The current delivery time for a Bender cue is approximately two years.

SPECIFICATIONS

Butt material: hardwoods
Shaft material: rock maple
Standard length: 58 in.
Lengths available: any
Standard finish: UV cure
Joint screw: 3/8-14
Standard joint collars: linen phenolic with ebony and silver stitching
Joint type: flat face
Balance point: 19 to 19 1/2 in. from butt
Point construction: short splice
Standard wrap: Irish linen
Standard butt cap: phenolic
Standard number of shafts: two
Standard taper: custom
Standard ferrules: linen phenolic
Standard tip: Sumo
Tip widths available: any
Annual production: fewer than 50 cues

OPTIONS (FOR NEW CUES ONLY)

Leather wrap: $200
Calf skin and exotic leather wrap: $300
Ivory joint: $200
Joint protectors: standard
Ivory butt cap: $250
Ivory ferrules: $75 each
Extra shaft: $200
Extra shaft with ivory ferrule: $275

162 BENDER CUES, cont.

GRADING	100%	95%	70%

REPAIRS

Repairs done on most fine cues.
 Refinish (with linen wrap): $200
 Rewrap (leather): $400+
 Replace shaft: $200+
 Replace ivory ferrule: $75
 Replace phenolic butt cap: $250 (includes butt refinish and rewrap)
 Replace Ivory butt cap: $500 (includes butt refinish and rewrap)

CURRENT EXAMPLES

These cues are from the Bender brochure c. 1998-1999. Cues in these designs are still being produced. Cues come with linen phenolic ferrules and joint protectors standard. Ivory ferrules and joints are custom options.

Level 4 #1 - Ebony forearm with a ring of sterling silver-bordered ebony bars above wrap, five long ebony points with single holly veneers spliced over five short holly points, ebony butt sleeve with five long reverse ebony points with single holly veneers spliced over five short reverse holly points between rings of sterling silver-bordered ebony bars at top and bottom.

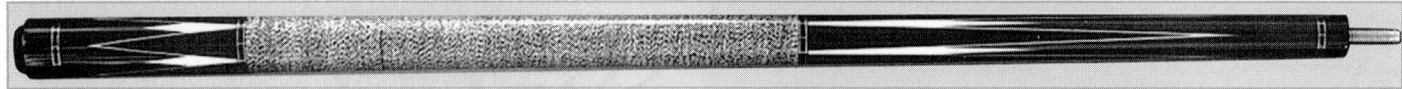

| MSR | $1,800 | $1,650-1,950 | $1,600 | $1,450 |

Level 4 #2 - Ebony forearm with a ring of sterling silver bordered ebony bars above wrap, five long sharkwood points with four colored veneers spliced over five short holly points, ebony butt sleeve with five long reverse sharkwood points with four colored veneers spliced over five short reverse holly points between rings of sterling silver bordered ebony bars at top and bottom.

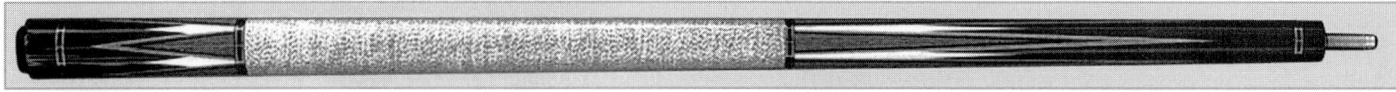

| MSR | $2,300 | $1,750-2,450 | $1,700 | $1,550 |

Level 4 #4 - Ivory joint, ebony forearm with an intricate sterling silver rosary ring set in ebony above wrap, five long ebony points with single holly veneers spliced over five short holly points, ebony handle with five long reverse ebony points with single holly veneers spliced over five short reverse holly points at top above five long ebony points with single holly veneers spliced over five short holly points at bottom, ebony butt sleeve with five long reverse ebony points with single holly veneers spliced over five short reverse holly points between intricate sterling silver rosary rings set in ebony at top and bottom.

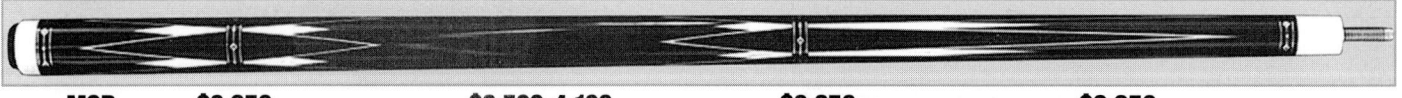

| MSR | $3,950 | $3,500-4,100 | $3,250 | $2,950 |

Level 4 #5 - Ivory joint cocobolo forearm with an intricate sterling silver rosary ring set in cocobolo above wrap, five long sharkwood points with single holly veneers spliced over five short holly points, cocobolo butt sleeve with five long reverse sharkwood points with single holly veneers spliced over five short reverse holly points between intricate sterling silver rosary rings set in ebony at top and bottom.

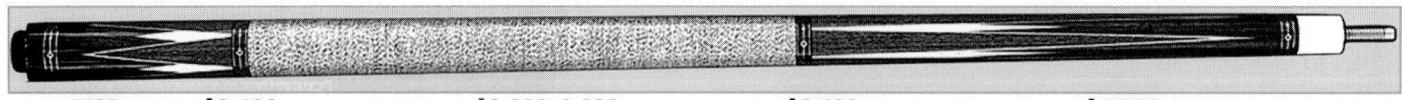

| MSR | $2,400 | $2,200-2,600 | $2,100 | $1,850 |

Level 4 #6 - Ebony forearm with a ring of sterling silver bordered ebony bars above wrap, five long purpleheart points with single holly veneers spliced over five short ebony points with single holly veneers, ebony butt sleeve with five long reverse purpleheart points with single holly veneers spliced over five short reverse ebony points with single holly veneers between rings of sterling silver bordered ebony bars at top and bottom.

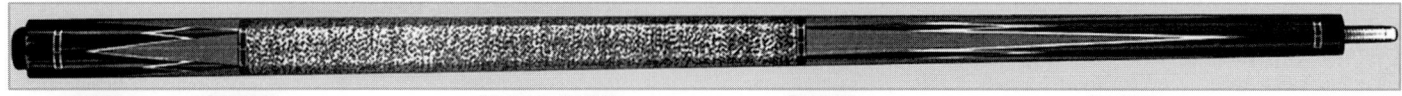

| MSR | $1,950 | $1,950-2,200 | $1,850 | $1,750 |

Level 4 #8 - Ebony forearm with a ring of sterling silver bordered ebony bars above wrap, five long cocobolo points spliced over five short bird's-eye maple points, ebony butt sleeve with five long reverse cocobolo points spliced over five short reverse bird's-eye maple points between rings of sterling silver bordered ebony bars at top and bottom, ivory ferrules.

| MSR | $1,350 | $1,350-1,750 | $1,300 | $1,150 |

BENDER CUES, cont. 163

GRADING	100%	95%	70%

TWO SHAFTS WITH IVORY FERRULES AND JOINT PROTECTORS STANDARD

The following Bender cues come with two shafts with ivory ferrules and joint protectors standard.

Level 4 "Ivory Dagger" - Ebony forearm, five ivory inlaid dagger points with silver-bezelled filigree engraved ivory ellipses, matching floating points and inlays in ebony butt sleeve, floating ivory/silver/mother-of-pearl rosary rings; ebony handle; ivory joint and butt cap.

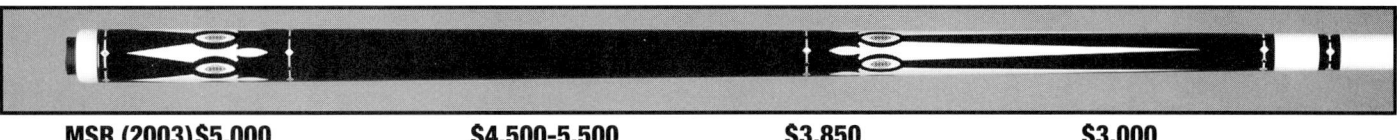

MSR (2003) $5,000	$4,500-5,500	$3,850	$3,000

SPECIAL INTEREST CUES

The following represent some of the finest one-of-a-kind Bender cues.

Level 8 "Miguelet" - Inspired by the flintlock of an antique firearm, an 18th century Spanish miguelet. Curly African blackwood forearm and butt sleeve with five inlaid ivory points in the nose and five in the butt sleeve. Ivory inlays, with the design at the base of each point is composed of multiple layers of mother-of-pearl, gold-lipped mother-of-pearl, silver and abalone with silver and ebony stringing.; over 800 inlays total. The floating rosary rings repeat the finial motif in the points with silver-bordered mother-of-pearl dots alternating with a silver dot along the silver line. Leather wrap, ivory joint and butt cap, matching inlaid joint protectors.

MSR (2003) $25,000	$25,000-27,000	$23,000	$20,000

Level 8 "Cabin Fever (Lanai Petroglyphs)" - Curly koa forearm with six points of ivory with blue veneer, matching reverse points in koa butt sleeve, curly koa handle. Double ivory bands above and below wrap scrimshawed with palm trees and other Hawaiian motifs by Tracy Dunham, abalone and silver ring work, ivory joint. Engraved on ivory butt cap: "Cabin Fever 1998 – Lanai Petroglyphs"

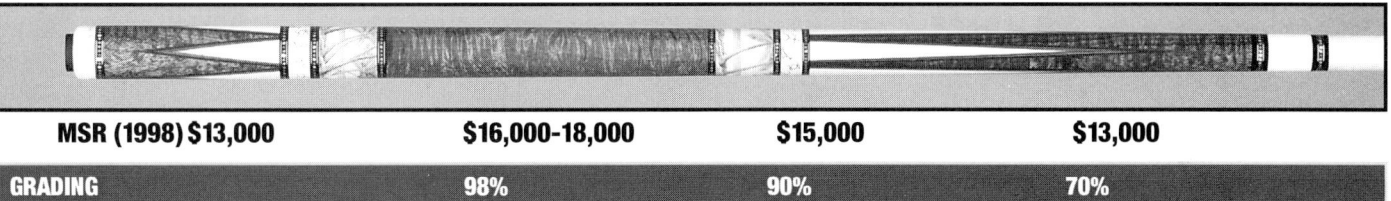

MSR (1998) $13,000	$16,000-18,000	$15,000	$13,000

GRADING	98%	90%	70%

SECONDARY MARKET MINIMUM VALUES

The following are minimum prices for other Bender Cues encountered on the secondary market. These prices are representative of cues using basic materials and designs that may not be currently available. Bender Cues currently specializes in one-of-a-kind cues that can command many times these prices due to the use of exotic materials and artistry.

Special construction note: There are many materials and construction techniques that can add value to Bender cues. . The following are the most important examples:

Add $600+ for ivory points.
Add $200+ for ivory butt cap.

For all used Bender cues:

Add $100+ for each additional original straight playable shaft (standard with two).
Deduct $125 for each missing original straight playable shaft.
Add $175+ for ivory joint.
Add $100+ for leather wrap.
Add $60+ for each ivory ferrule.

Level 1 - 4 points, hustler.

Level 1 cues start at	$500	$400	$300

Level 2 - 0 points, 0-25 inlays.

Level 2 cues start at	$900	$775	$650

Level 3 - 2-6 points, 0-8 inlays.

Level 3 cues start at	$1050	$925	$750

Level 4 - 4-10 points, 9-25 inlays.

Level 4 cues start at	$1,500	$1,300	$1000

Level 5 - 0-12 points, 26-50 inlays.

Level 5 cues start at	$1,950	$1,650	$1,300

GRADING	98%	90%	70%
Level 6 - 0-12 points, 51-75 inlays.			
Level 6 cues start at	$2,500	$2,100	$1,650
Level 7 - 0-12 points, 76-125 inlays.			
Level 7 cues start at	$4,000	$3,000	$2,000
Level 8 - 4 or more points, 126+ inlays.			
Level 8 cues start at	$6,000	$5,000	$4,000

MATT K. BENDER

Maker of pool cues from 1988 to 1996 in Wauconda, Illinois.

Matt Bender credits his brother, Mike, for teaching him most of what he learned about cue making. Matt worked at Omega/dpk from 1991 to 1996, where he built cues with David Kersenbrock after Mike and his wife left to form their own company in Alaska. Matt also briefly worked for Joe Gold at Cognoscenti. Retired from cue maiking since 1996, he ran a shop in the Chicago area building furniture and restoring antiques. In early 2004 he moved back to Wauconda, where he lives just a half mile from the former Omega shop.

If you have Omega/dpk cues for which you need information or authentication, contact Bender Cues, which is listed in the Trademark Index.

For more information on Matt L. Bender, please refer to the listing for the "Omega/dpk Cue Company."

BENSON CUE

Maker of pool cues from 1975 to present in Kennewick, Washington.

Richard Benson

Thirty years ago, Richard Benson was a pool player in Washington state who needed a new cue. He was unable to find a manufactured cue that played the way he liked and he didn't know any of the handful of custom cue makers around at that time, so he set out to make his own. With some of the skills he had learned in high school woodworking, Richard was able to complete his first cue in 1975. Today, Richard makes between 100 and 200 cues per year with the help of his son, Chris. All work is done by hand, and they make every component except the tips, bumpers, and screws, which are custom made to their specifications.

Beginning in 1994, when Richard returned to cuemaking after a one-year break, all Benson cues were stamped "Benson" on the forearm, just below the joint. Current cues are marked "R. Benson". 1994 was the year he made 35 improvements in the design and construction of Benson cues from the top to the bottom. Richard continues to introduce improvements to his cues. Benson cues feature their own custom taper, which Richard developed. They can be finished in oil, lacquer, or polyurethane, whichever the customer prefers. A variety of joints, butt caps, and other components are also available for custom orders. He is always trying to create new designs for one-of-a-kind cues. Many cues have been made using a chess motif, one of his favorites. Richard prides himself on quick repair work, turning down repairs if he cannot do them in a reasonable amount of time. Richard and Chris try to make durable, good-looking cues that play well, at a fair price.

Benson cues are guaranteed indefinitely against construction defects that are not the result of warpage or abuse. If you have a Benson cue that needs further identification or repair, or would like to talk to Richard about ordering a new Benson cue, contact Benson Cue Company, listed in the Trademark Index.

SPECIFICATIONS

Butt material: hardwoods
Shaft material: rock maple
Standard length: 58 in.
Lengths available: any up to 60 in.
Standard finish: lacquer
Joint screw: 3/8-10
Standard joint: stainless steel
Joint type: flat face
Balance point: 17-1/2 in. from butt cap
Point construction: short splice
Standard wrap: Irish linen
Standard butt cap: linen phenolic or implex plastic
Standard number of shafts: one
Standard taper: custom
Standard ferrules: linen micarta
Standard tip: Triangle
Tip widths available: any up to 15 mm
Annual production: fewer than 200 cues

OPTIONS (FOR NEW CUES ONLY)

Leather wrap: $50

GRADING	98%	90%	70%

Ivory joint: $200+
Joint protector for butt: standard
Ivory butt cap: $250
Ivory ferrules: $50 each
Extra shaft: $150

REPAIRS

Repairs done on most fine cues – call for prices.
Replace shaft: $150

CURRENT BENSON CUES

Two-piece Benson hustler cues start at $200. Basic Benson cues with joints and wraps start at $400. Benson cues with points start at $550. One-of-a-kind custom Benson cues start at $750. The current delivery time for a Benson cue is approximately 10 weeks, depending on the intricacy of the cue.

SECONDARY MARKET MINIMUM VALUES

The following are minimum prices for Benson cues encountered on the secondary market. These prices are representative of cues using basic materials and designs that may not be currently available. Richard also offers one-of-a-kind cues that can command many times these prices due to the use of exotic materials and artistry.

Special construction note: There are many materials and construction techniques that can add value to Benson cues. Inlay materials used may include 24K gold or ,999 pure silver, exotic woods, ivory, and shell (abalone or mother-of-pearl).

For all used Benson cues, except where otherwise noted:
Add $100+ for each additional original straight playable shaft (standard with one).
Deduct $125 for missing original straight playable shaft.
Deduct 25% for obvious or improper refinish.

Level 1 - 4 points, hustler.
Level 1 cues start at	$175	$135	$90

Level 2 - 0 points, 0-25 inlays.
Level 2 cues start at	$325	$265	$175

Level 3 - 2-6 points, 0-8 inlays.
Level 3 cues start at	$450	$365	$250

Level 4 - 4-10 points, 9-25 inlays.
Level 4 cues start at	$700	$565	$385

Level 5 - 0-12 points, 26-50 inlays.
Level 5 cues start at	$1,250	$985	$650

Level 6 - 0-12 points, 51-75 inlays.
Level 6 cues start at	$1,500	$1,200	$800

Level 7 - 0-12 points, 76-125 inlays.
Level 7 cues start at	$1,850	$1,450	$1,000

BLACK BOAR INDUSTRIES

Maker of pool cues from 1988 to present in College Park, Maryland.

Early or simple cues

Present Day

Tony Scianella

Raymond and Anthony (Tony) Sciannella purchased a billiard supply business in 1985, and quickly found themselves interested in the cues they were selling. It seemed to them that most cues were made about the same. They believed that scientific research and engineering could lead to a better type of construction and that they could make better cues if they tried.

BLACK BOAR INDUSTRIES, cont.

GRADING	98%	90%	70%

Anthony's son, Anthony Jr., who has a master's degree in electrical engineering and had experience with motion control devices, was involved from the beginning in 1988 until 1999. He developed custom software and operating CNC equipment, a job now taken over by his father, Tony. A friend and billiard historian, Vincent Sangmeister, was also a member of the team that designed the first set of Black Boar cues. The four started by designing and building equipment to test and build Black Boar cues. They found that they did not like the idea of the three-piece butt, so they designed a solid bird's-eye maple butt with spliced points that continued under the wrap, and a butt sleeve that went over the one piece of maple.

The first cues were completed in 1988. After the first 120 or so cues were made, it was decided that rock maple would be used for the butt, as it is much less prone to warping, and the bird's-eye maple in the forearm would be sleeved on, thereby stabilizing it, with the point design and butt sleeve remaining the same.

Early Black Boar cues are easily identifiable by a small boar head logo on a white Delrin butt cap, which was used from 1988 until 1994. The logo was changed to a "BB Custom" logo on a black linen cap (often mistaken for ebony) in 1994, signifying some design changes to the cues. Cues made before this time usually had four points, but in 1994 six points became standard, with eight-point cues also being available. They also developed a new ivory joint, which is sleeved over stainless steel; it is the standard joint still currently used.

In the past, Raymond and Tony specialized in custom making cues to the designs of specific customers. The length, weight, taper, resonant pitch, etc., were adjusted to suit the size and playing style of the customer. They now prefer to make cues of their own designs, made to a variety of specifications, and put them on the market. They started making cues because they loved the engineering and design aspects of cuemaking, and their cues stress playability over aesthetics. When inlays are done, ivory, abalone, and silver are the most common materials used. They used to make their own Black Boar tips, but they found them to be inconsistent like others. Then they developed a means of testing tips for consistent compression qualities. Anthony now purchases Triangle tips, using only the one in ten that meets his standards.

Anthony has worked alone in the shop since 2000. Beginning in late 2002, eight points with pronged ivory and exotic wraps became the standard Black Boar cue. In the early days, Black Boar made 200 cues each year priced between $400 and $600. In the 1990s when they reduced their production to 50 per year, cue prices were $1200 and up. Now that he is only building less than a dozen cues per year, prices and demand for older Black Boar cues are increasing steadily.

Tony continues to make constant improvements in the engineering of Black Boar cues, based on studies of the physics of cue performance using high speed photography and his own custom diagnostic equipment. His philosophy is, "let the cue do the work."

Tony is proud that he makes every component of Black Boar cues, except the tip. Black Boar cues are guaranteed indefinitely against construction defects that are not the result of warpage or abuse. If you have a Black Boar cue that needs further identification or repair, or would like to talk to Tony about ordering a new Black Boar cue, contact Black Boar Industries, listed in the Trademark Index.

SPECIFICATIONS

Butt material: hardwoods
Shaft material: rock maple
Standard length: 58 in.
Lengths available: 58 in. to 60 in.
Standard finish: epoxy and urethane
Standard joint screw: 5/16-14 piloted
Standard joint: ivory over stainless steel
Standard joint type: piloted
Point construction: custom splice
Standard wrap: lizard
Standard butt cap: one-piece, eight-point ivory
Standard number of shafts: two
Standard ferrules: ivory
Standard tip: Black Boar selected Triangle
Tip widths available: any
Annual production: fewer than 12 cues

CURRENT BLACK BOAR CUES

Black Boar currently specializes in one-of-a-kind custom eight-point cues, and custom Black Boar cue prices start at $4,800. The current delivery time for a custom Black Boar cue is about three years.

SECONDARY MARKET MINIMUM VALUES

Black Boar currently specializes in one-of-a-kind custom eight-point cues. The following are minimum prices for Black Boar cues encountered on the secondary market. These prices are representative of early cues utilizing basic materials and designs that may not be currently available. Black Boar currently offers one-of-a-kind cues that can command many times these prices due to the use of exotic materials and artistry.

Special construction note: There are many materials and construction techniques that can add value to Black Boar cues.

For all used Black Boar cues, except where otherwise noted:

Add $200 for each additional original straight playable shaft (standard with two).
Deduct $200 for each missing original straight playable shaft.
Add $150 for leather or lizard wrap.

Level 3 - 2-6 points, 0-8 inlays.

	98%	90%	70%
Level 3 cues start at	$1,200	$1,050	$800

GRADING	98%	90%	70%
Level 4 - 4-10 points, 9-25 inlays.			
Level 4 cues start at	$1,300	$1,100	$950
Level 5 - 0-12 points, 26-50 inlays.			
Level 5 cues start at	$1,600	$1300	$975
Level 6 - 0-12 points, 51-75 inlays.			
Level 6 cues start at	$4,000	$3,300	$2,350
Level 7 - 0-12 points, 76-125 inlays.			
Level 7 cues start at	$6,500	$5,200	$3,500
Level 8 - 4-20 points, 126 or more inlays.			
Level 8 cues start at	$8,500	$6,750	$4,500

BLACKCREEK CUSTOM CUES

Maker of pool cues from 1998to 2003 in Red Bud, Illinois, and from 2003 to present in Smithton, Illinois.

Travis Niklich began playing pool at age 19, being taught by BCA instructor Mark Wilson. Travis became fascinated with how cues were made. He worked in his father's wood shop starting at age eight. He attended several pool competitions and was interested in the on-site repairs and construction of cues. Travis started repairing cues at the age of 21 and decided to start making cues within six months. He was inducted into the American Cuemakers Association at the age of 24, in March of 2002. Andy Gilbert and Ron Haley have inspired Travis and helped him learn the trade.

Travis likes to make traditional style cues, especially with butterfly splices. He makes everything except for the screw, the tip, and the bumper. Travis makes his own short splice blanks with a manual pantograph in his one man shop. If he gets a CNC machine, it will be for inlays only. He prefers to make cues that are not too elaborate. Scrimshaw is available from a local artist. Travis only uses the radial joint pin with phenolic, ivory, or wood collars. Travis will not make a cue with a stainless steel joint. He makes cues part time when away from his full time job as a pressman for a St. Louis newspaper. Blackcreek Cues can be identified the "Travis Niklich" signature and date.

Black Creek cues are guaranteed for life against material and workmanship defects that are not the result of warpage or abuse.

If you are interested in talking to Travis Niklich about a new cue or cue that needs to be repaired, you can contact him at Blackcreek Custom Cues, listed in the Trademark Index.

Travis Niklich

SPECIFICATIONS

Butt material: hardwoods
Shaft material: rock maple
Standard length: 58 in.
Lengths available: any up to 60 in.
Standard finish: PPG
Balance point: 1-2 in. above wrap
Standard butt cap: phenolic
Standard wrap: Irish linen
Point construction: short splice
Standard joint: phenolic
Joint type: flat faced
Joint screw thread: radial pin
Standard number of shafts: two
Standard taper: custom
Standard ferrules: LBM
Other ferrule options: ivory
Standard tip: Le Pro
Standard tip width: 13 mm
Tip widths available: 12-14 mm
Other tips available: any
Annual production: fewer than 50 cues

OPTIONS (FOR NEW CUES ONLY)

Special length: no charge
Moori tip: $30
Ivory butt cap: $200
Short ivory joint: $75
Long ivory joint: $150
Ivory ferrule: $50
Leather wrap: $100

168 BLACKCREEK CUSTOM CUES, cont.

GRADING	100%	95%	70%

Lizard wrap: $250
Extra shaft: $100
Butterfly points: $100+

REPAIRS

Repairs done on all fine cues.
Refinish (with Irish linen wrap): $125
Refinish (with leather wrap): $200
Rewrap (Irish linen): $35
Rewrap (leather): $100
Clean and press linen wrap: $15
Replace shaft: $100+
Replace ivory ferrule: $60
Replace tip: $10
Replaced layered tip: $20+
Replace fiber/linen ferrule: $30

CURRENT BLACKCREEK CUES

Basic two-piece Blackcreek cues with wraps and joint rings start at $575. One-of-a-kind custom Blackcreek cues start at $800. The current delivery time for a Blackcreek cue is four to six months.

CURRENT EXAMPLES

The following Blackcreek cues can be ordered as shown, modified to suit the desires of the customer, or new designs can be created.

Level 3 "Titlist by Blackcreek" - Ivory joint, maple forearm with nickel silver ring work above wrap, four rosewood points with four colored veneers, rosewood butt sleeve with nickel silver ring work below wrap and above an ivory ring inscribed with "Titlist by Blackcreek" and date.

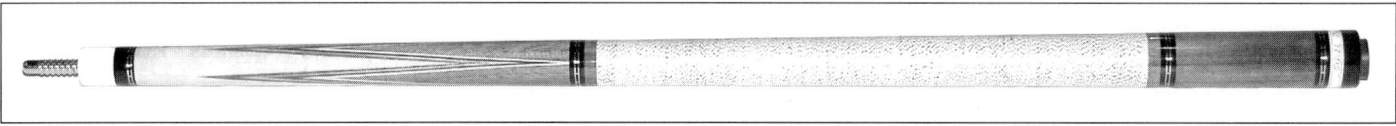

MSR	$1,500	$1,400 -1,750	$1,125	$800

Level 3 - Ivory joint, curly maple forearm with nickel silver ring work above wrap, four ebony points with two colored veneers, ebony butt sleeve with four ivory propeller-shaped inlays set between nickel silver ring work at top and bottom.

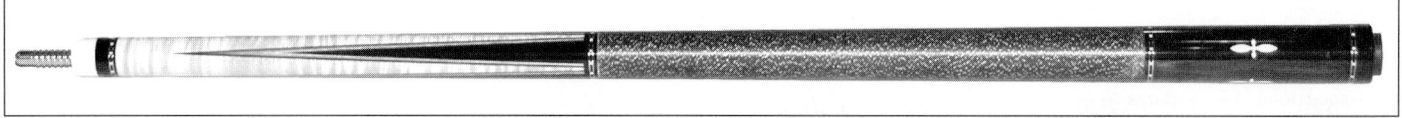

MSR	$1,150	$1,100 -1,250	$875	$600

Level 3 - Ivory joint, curly maple forearm with nickel silver ring work above wrap, four ebony points with two colored veneers and an ivory diamond-shaped inlay in each, ebony butt sleeve with four ivory diamond-shaped inlays alternating with four smaller ivory diamond-shaped inlays set between nickel silver ring work at top and bottom.

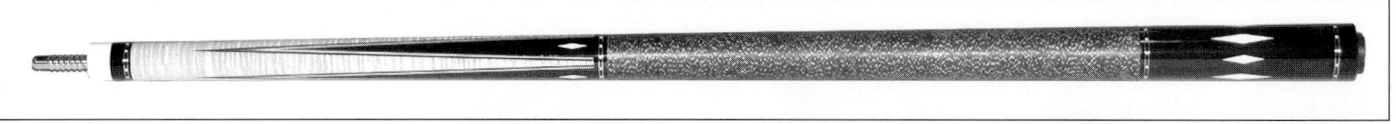

MSR	$1,300	$1,200 -1,450	$975	$700

Level 4 - Ivory joint, bird's-eye maple forearm with nickel silver ring work above wrap, three ebony points with four colored veneers and an ivory diamond-shaped inlay in each alternating with three short ebony butterfly points with four colored veneers and a smaller ivory diamond-shaped inlay in each, pigskin wrap, ebony butt sleeve with three ivory diamond-shaped inlays alternating with three smaller ivory diamond-shaped inlays set between nickel silver ring work at top and bottom.

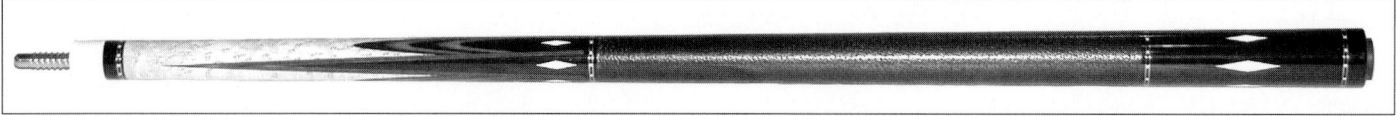

MSR	$1,500	$1,400 -1,750	$1,125	$800

GRADING	100%	95%	70%

Level 5 - Ivory joint, African blackwood forearm with nickel silver ring work above wrap, four snakewood points with an ivory diamond-shaped inlay in each, African blackwood butt sleeve with three rows of varying sized ivory diamond-shaped inlays set between nickel silver ring work at top and bottom.

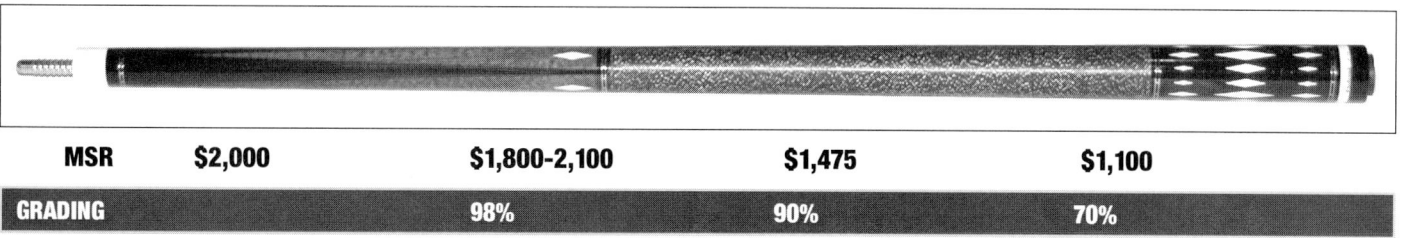

MSR	$2,000	$1,800-2,100	$1,475	$1,100

GRADING	98%	90%	70%

SECONDARY MARKET MINIMUM VALUES

The following are minimum values for other Blackcreek cues encountered on the secondary market. These prices are representative of cues using basic materials and designs that are not necessarily available at present. Travis has offered one-of-a-kind cues that can command many times these prices due to the use of exotic materials and artistry.

Special construction note: There are many materials and construction techniques that can add value to Blackcreek cues.

For all used Blackcreek cues, except where otherwise noted:
- Add $75 for each additional original straight playable shaft beyond two.
- Deduct $100 for missing original straight playable shaft.
- Add $45 each for ivory ferrules.
- Add $50 for leather wrap.
- Deduct 20% for obvious or improper refinish.

Level 1 - Hustler.
Level 1 cues start at	$200	$215	$125

Level 2 - 0 points, 0-25 inlays.
Level 2 cues start at	$400	$320	$220

Level 3 - 2-6 points, 0-8 inlays.
Level 3 cues start at	$600	$465	$315

Level 4 - 4-10 points, 9-25 inlays.
Level 4 cues start at	$700	$545	$365

Level 5 - 0-12 points, 26-50 inlays.
Level 5 cues start at	$1,000	$785	$550

BLACK HAWK CUSTOM CUES

Maker of pool cues from 1994 to present in Rapid City, South Dakota.

Stan Hawkins and Jim Aldren met at the manufacturing engineering department of a large electronics company where both were working. They both liked to play pool and had a background in high-tech manufacturing. Jim had a woodworking hobby and often talked about cues, wood, and machining techniques. Stan had been a carpenter and was getting tired of sending cues away to be repaired. Stan bought a lathe and started doing repair work in 1991. They were both playing on the same pool league team, and started talking about making cues. In 1994 they founded Black Hawk Custom Cues, Inc.

Early Black Hawk cues were hustler cues or one-piece plain bird's-eye maple butts. The first twenty or so that Stan made were not marked. About the next 30 cues had "SH" on the butt caps, with the following cues being unmarked. After about six months, Stan and Jim created the Black Hawk logo, which has appeared on all Black Hawk cues made since. Their focus on playability led them to develop their own very stiff taper.

Stan and Jim made almost 100 cues a year part time, while maintaining their full time engineering jobs. Most cues were custom orders made to individual specifications. Among their popular cues was a one-piece butt with no wrap, using select pieces of exotic woods. In 1999 they started building micro electronics into their cues to serialize them and identify the original owners. Stan and Jim regularly use CNC equipment in the engineering department they work at during weekdays, and installed similar equipment in their shop while making cues on weekends and weekday evenings.

In 2001 Jim Aldren sold Stan his interest in Black Hawk and started Aldren Cues. Stan continues to make Black Hawk cues. Stan guarantees the cues for life against manufacturing defects that are not the result of warpage or abuse. If you have a Black Hawk cue that needs further identification or repair, or would like to order a new Black Hawk cue, contact Stan Hawkins at Black Hawk Custom Cues, listed in the Trademark Index.

For more information, please refer to the listing for Aldren Cues.

170 BLACK HAWK CUSTOM CUES, cont.

GRADING	98%	90%	70%

SPECIFICATIONS

Butt material: hardwoods
Shaft material: rock maple
Standard length: 58 in.
Lengths available: any up to 62 in.
Standard finish: two-part urethane
Balance point: 1 in. above wrap
Standard butt cap: linen phenolic
Standard wrap: Irish linen
Point construction: short splice
Standard joint: linen phenolic
Joint type: flat faced
Joint screw: radial pin
Standard number of shafts: one
Standard taper: custom
Standard ferrules: Aegis
Tip widths available: 12-1/2 mm up
Standard tip: Le Pro
Annual production: 65-100 cues

OPTIONS (FOR NEW CUES ONLY)

Special length: $50 per shaft
Ivory joint: $100
Extra shaft: $60
Ivory ferrule: $50

REPAIRS

Repairs done on select cues.
Rewrap (Irish linen): $42
Replace joint (ivory): $150
Replace ivory butt cap: $200
Replace ivory ferrule: $75
Replace Aegis ferrule: $20-30
Replace tip: $10-25

CURRENT BLACK HAWK CUES

The current delivery time for a Black Hawk custom cue is three to four months.

SECONDARY MARKET MINIMUM VALUES

The following are minimum values for Black Hawk custom cues encountered on the secondary market. These prices are representative of cues using basic materials and designs that are not currently available. Black Hawk has offered one-of-a-kind cues that can command many times these prices due to the use of exotic materials and artistry.

Special construction note: There are many materials and construction techniques that can add value to Black Hawk cues. The following are the most important examples:

Add $75+ for ivory joint.

For all used Black Hawk cues, except where otherwise noted:

Add $50 for each additional original straight playable shaft beyond one.
Deduct $60 for each missing original straight playable shaft under two.
Add $40 each for ivory ferrules.
Deduct 20% for obvious or improper refinish.

Level 1 - 4 points, hustler.

	98%	90%	70%
Level 1 cues start at	$175	$135	$100

Level 2 - 0 points, 0-25 inlays.

Level 2 cues start at	$250	$195	$150

Level 3 - 2-6 points, 0-8 inlays.

Level 3 cues start at	$350	$275	$225

Level 4 - 4-10 points, 9-25 inlays.

Level 4 cues start at	$450	$375	$300

Level 5 - 0-12 points, 26-50 inlays.

Level 5 cues start at	$675	$525	$400

Level 6 - 0-12 points, 51-75 inlays.

Level 6 cues start at	$900	$775	$625

BLACK HEART CUSTOM CUES

Maker of pool cues from 1987 to present in Peru, Illinois

1987 to Present Day

Jerry Eick

Jerry Eick grew up in the small town of Ottowa, Illinois. The town had a local pool hall where Jerry loved to play snooker, and became one of the best players in town. Jerry was a very defensive player who became very accomplished at safeties. For this, he earned the nickname "Black Heart."

After high school Jerry went into the service and gave up playing pool. Many years later, while Jerry was working as an engineer, his daughter started dating a good pool player. Jerry became interested in the game and began playing again. He immediately became interested in cues and started selling cues as a hobby. By the early eighties, he was also doing repairs.

When Jerry decided to start making cues he took several of his favorite cues and cut them in half to see how they were made and made engineering-type drawings of all of the measurements. With limited knowledge from his high school shop class and some advice from a few top cuemakers, he made his first cue in 1986. The first few cues he made were in the local area, and the local players referred to them as Black Heart cues. That year, Jerry decided to use that name and put a Black Heart logo on the cues. At this time he did not know how to do inlay work so he drew black hearts on the butt caps with India ink. Although he now does an array of different types of inlays, he still applies the Black Heart logos with India ink as a matter of tradition.

Jerry now has six lathes in his shop and makes just under 50 cues a year, working on a part-time basis. He prides himself on his repair work and has done over 2000 repairs a year. Jerry makes everything in Black Heart cues except for the screws and bumpers. All inlay work is done by hand on a pantograph and there are no plans for getting a CNC machine. Points can be spliced or pantographed by hand. Jerry likes to use buck horn for ferrules and joints, and also can use woods in the joints and butt caps. He retired in July of 2005 and now concentrates on making cues full time.

When a customer orders a custom Black Heart cue, Jerry fills out a chart starting from the tip and going to the bumper, which will include design, materials, specifications etc. Since 1995, he has serial numbered all cues internally and kept a record of every one. Black Heart Custom Cues are guaranteed for life against manufacturing defects that are not the result of warping or abuse. If you have a Black Heart cue that needs further identification or repair, or would like to order a new cue, contact Black Heart Custom Cues, listed in the Trademark Index.

SPECIFICATIONS

Butt material: hardwoods
Shaft material: rock maple and flat laminated
Standard length: 58 in.
Lengths available: any
Standard finish: urethane enamel
Balance point: 1 in. above wrap
Standard butt cap: Atlas ivory substitute
Standard wrap: Irish linen or leather
Point construction: short splice or pantographed
Standard joint: Atlas ivory substitute
Joint type: flat faced
Joint screw: 3/8-10
Standard number of shafts:- One
Standard taper: 12 in. modified pro
Standard ferrules: Atlas ivory substitute
Standard tip width: 13 mm
Standard tip: Buffalo
Annual production: fewer than 50 cues

OPTIONS (FOR NEW CUES ONLY)

Special length: $25
Ivory ferrule: $50
Ivory butt cap: $100
Ivory joint: $100
Buck horn ferrule: $50
Extra shaft: $100+
Leather wrap: $75

BLACK HEART CUSTOM CUES, cont.

| GRADING | 98% | 90% | 70% |

REPAIRS

Repairs done on all fine cues. Basic Black Heart hustler cues and two-piece cues with wraps and joints start at $300. Black Heart cues with points start at $525. One-of-a-kind custom Black Heart cues start at $600. The current delivery time for a Black Heart custom cue is six to eight months.

Rewrap (Irish linen): $30
Replace shaft: $100+
Replace joint (ivory): $100
Replace buck horn ferrule: $50
Replace ivory ferrule: $50

SECONDARY MARKET MINIMUM VALUES

The following are minimum values for Black Heart Custom Cues encountered on the secondary market. These prices are representative of cues using basic materials and designs that are not currently available. Black Heart has offered one-of-a-kind cues that can command many times these prices due to the use of exotic materials and artistry.

Special construction note: There are many materials and construction techniques that can add value to cues. The following are the most important examples:

Add $100+ for each ivory point.

For all used Black Heart cues, except where otherwise noted:

Add $90 for each additional original straight playable shaft beyond one.
Deduct $100 for missing original straight playable shaft.
Add $40 each for ivory ferrules.
Deduct 20% for obvious or improper refinish.

Level 1 - 4 points, hustler.
| Level 1 cues start at | $225 | $175 | $115 |

Level 2 - 0 points, 0-25 inlays.
| Level 2 cues start at | $250 | $195 | $130 |

Level 3 - 2-6 points, 0-8 inlays.
| Level 3 cues start at | $450 | $350 | $235 |

Level 4 - 4-10 points, 9-25 inlays.
| Level 4 cues start at | $550 | $425 | $285 |

Level 5 - 0-12 points, 26-50 inlays.
| Level 5 cues start at | $800 | $625 | $425 |

RICHARD BLACK CUSTOM CRAFTED CUES

Maker of pool cues from 1974 to present in Humble, Texas.

In the early seventies, Richard Black was one of the more successful stockbrokers in the Houston area. He was also a fan of billiards. In his home, he regularly held black-tie pool tournaments for his business associates. These tournaments became so well-known that a story, "The Fanciest Game in Town," was written in Texas Magazine, and a picture from one of the tournaments was featured on the cover. At one of these tournaments, Richard

1980 to Present Day

Richard Black

gave away a Joss Cue, made by Dan Janes. Richard was so fascinated with the artistry of this cue that he decided to try to make one himself. That was 1974. This first attempt was not up to Richard's personal standards, but his persistence would not let him quit until he could make a cue of which he was proud.

By 1976, he loved cuemaking so much that he decided to give up stockbrokering to pursue making cues full-time. Although Richard is self-taught, he has been inspired by the work of the late George Balabushka. Richard's cues are the same length, same taper, and most have used the same joint screw as Balabushka cues. The exceptions were made from 1980 to 1983, when Richard used a 5/16-18 joint screw. Other changes in Richard Black cues include the following. Cues made before 1980 were not signed, but had these characteristics: the first cues made in 1975 were four-point, four veneer cues with flat-faced, stainless steel joints. These cues had a maple band in the joint rings with four ebony checks. In 1976, the same rings were used, but the joint was changed to the piloted type that Richard has used ever since. In 1977, the number of ebony checks in the joint rings was increased to six. In 1980, this number was increased again to eight. In mid-1983, Richard went back to the 5/16-14 joint pin and started using the nickel silver joint rings that have appeared on most Richard Black cues made since. Richard has also made joints of ivory (piloted and flat faced), brass, micarta, water buffalo horn, and phenolic. He has also used 3/8-10 and a few 3/8-8 joint screws. One of the unique features on a Richard Black cue is the tip. He has them custom made and they are not offered for sale (he will only put them on the cues he makes).

Since most of the early cues were not signed, sometimes identification of these cues can be difficult. With Balabushka dimensions, many having Szamboti blanks, some of these cues have been misrepresented as Balabushkas by unscrupulous individuals. The fact that some of these cues were purchased as Balabushkas by fairly knowledgeable collectors is a testament to the quality of Richard's work. If there is doubt, Richard is the best person to contact, as he can identify all of his early cues. Almost all Richard Black cues have been signed on the forearm since 1980. If Richard knew that he was custom-making a cue for a specific individual, he would sign the cue and also include the date that the cue was finished on the forearm. If he knew or sensed that the cue was being purchased for resale, he would sign the cue but not date it. Of course, he was not always correct in his assessment of the situation, so this rule does not hold true 100% of the time.

Richard has been one of the more creative cuemakers of our time. He has made some limited edition cues which are of special interest to collectors. Among these were the "Helmet" cues, which were identified by an ivory helmet, like the one in his former logo, inlaid in the butt sleeve. These were all four-point cues made in the early nineties. There was also the 20th Anniversary Cue, of which 20 were made in 1994, featuring an ebony butt heavily decorated with ivory and sterling silver. The "Pinnacle" limited edition cue was made from 1983 to 1990 with 39 being made. In early 1996, Richard started to date and add a serial number to all one-of-a kind-cues and cues over $2,500. A four-digit number appears on the joint screw, the butt screw, and under the wrap of these cues. The first two digits represent the year of completion, and the last two digits are the number of the cue. Richard was one of five custom cuemakers who designed cues for Joss Cues' (Dan Janes) 1998 "Collector Series" cues. In 1999 on Richard's 25th anniversary of cuemaking he celebrated by making twenty-five 25th Anniversary Cues.

He refers to cues as "functional art," which may be the most appropriate term for what he makes. Richard has won awards, including "Best of Show" for his "Ambassador" cue at the 1993 American Cuemakers Association Show. His cues have received quite a bit of publicity. For example, the cue "Ewa Mataya" held on the cover of the New York Times Magazine was a Black cue. Richard is one of ten cue makers who have donated a cue to the National Museum of American History-Smithsonian Institution, Washington, D.C. at the curator's request. Richard's "El Blanco Grande" was acquired by a foreign cue collector and it is currently on display in a private museum in Japan. Richard also held a one-man show at the Art Museum of Southeast Texas titled "The Art of Cue" which ran from March to May of 2005. The exhibition featured over 30 high art cues priced for tens of thousands of dollars in Beaumont, Texas.

Richard believes in promoting the field of custom cuemaking to the level of recognition it deserves. To this end, he has served on the Board for the Academy of American Cue Art, and displayed cues in their shows held in Los Angeles and New York. He was one of the first cue makers to inlay jewels in his cues and was commanding $25,000 or more for his finest showcase cues over a decade ago. Current cue prices start at $1200 and special collector cues can be priced at $35,000 or more.

All Richard Black cues are guaranteed indefinitely against playability defects that are not the result of abuse. If you have a question about an old Richard Black cue, or would like to talk to Richard about the design of a new one, contact Richard Black Custom Crafted Cues, listed in the Trademark Index.

SPECIFICATIONS

Butt material: hardwoods
Shaft material: rock maple
Standard length: 57-1/2 in.
Lengths available: any
Standard finish: polyurethane
Joint screw: 5/16-14
Standard joint: stainless steel
Joint type: piloted
Balance point: 18-1/2 in. from butt
Point construction: short splice
Standard wrap: Irish linen
Standardbutt cap: Delrin
Standard number of shafts: two
Standard taper: 10-1/2 in. straight
Standard ferrules: ivory
Standard tip: custom
Tip widths available: any under 14 mm
Annual production: fewer than 50 cues

OPTIONS (FOR NEW CUES ONLY)

Leather wrap: $125
Ivory joint: $200+
Joint protectors: no charge
Flat face joint: no charge
Phenolic joint: no charge
5/16-18 joint screw: no charge
3/8-8 joint screw: no charge
3/8-10 joint screw: no charge
Extra shaft: $195

174 RICHARD BLACK CUSTOM CRAFTED CUES, cont.

GRADING	100%	95%	70%

Special length: no charge up to 60 in.
Aegis ferrules: deduct $50 per shaft

REPAIRS

Repairs done only on Richard Black cues, or cues by past masters such as Balabushka, Szamboti, Rambow, Martin, Paradise, Doc Fry, etc.

- Refinish (with leather wrap): $240
- Refinish (with linen wrap): $195
- Rewrap (leather): $125
- Rewrap (linen): $80
- Replace shaft: $195
- Replace ivory ferrule: $90
- Replace Delrin butt cap: $40
- Replace ivory butt cap: $200-400

CURRENT RICHARD BLACK CUES

Basic Richard Black cues start at $1,200. Richard currently specializes in one-of-a-kind custom cues that start at $10,000. Richard Black will guarantee a delivery time when an order is placed. Most cues can be delivered within three months.

CURRENT EXAMPLES

The following cues are representations of the work of Richard Black from his current brochure and price list. These cues can be ordered as shown, modified to suit the desires of the customer, or new designs can be created. Each cue comes with two shafts, ivory ferrules, and joint protectors.

Level 3 "Four Point" - Bird's-eye maple forearm, four ebony points with four colored veneers, ebony butt sleeve. (Points and butt sleeve available in rosewood or bocote at no extra charge.)

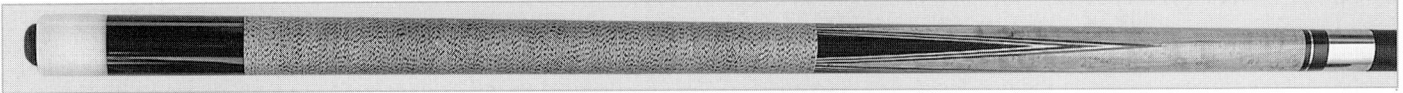

MSR	$1,200	$1,100-1,250	$895	$650

Level 3 "Four Window" - Bird's-eye maple forearm, four ebony points with four colored veneers, ebony butt sleeve with four maple windows. (Points and butt sleeve available in rosewood or bocote at no extra charge.)

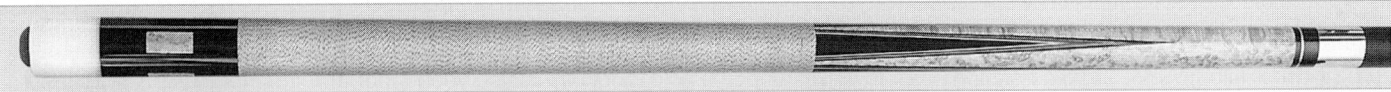

MSR	$1,250	$1,125-1,300	$925	$700

Level 3 "Hoppe" - Bird's-eye maple forearm, four ebony points with four colored veneers, ebony butt sleeve with an ivory ring above a short butt cap.

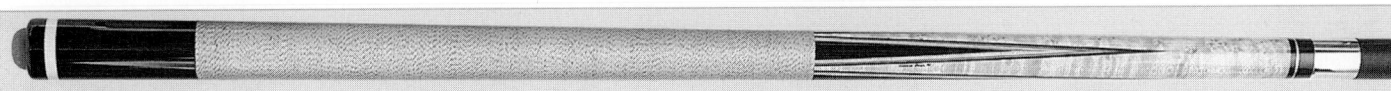

MSR	$1,350	$1,100-1,375	$1050	$800

Level 4 "Split Diamond" - Bird's-eye maple forearm, four ebony points with four colored veneers and an ivory diamond in each point, checked rings above and below wrap and above butt cap, ebony butt sleeve with four ivory diamonds separated into three pieces.

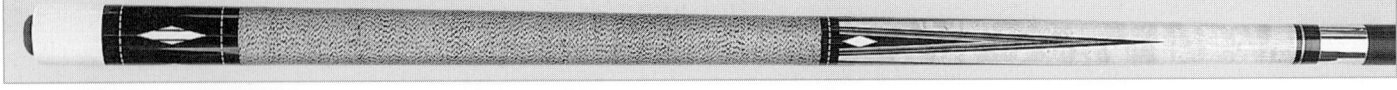

MSR	$1,500	$1,300-1,550	$1,175	$975

Level 4 "New Phoenix" - Stained bird's-eye maple forearm, four rosewood points with four colored veneers and an ivory "gun sight" in each point, rosewood butt sleeve with inlaid pattern of exotic woods and ivory.

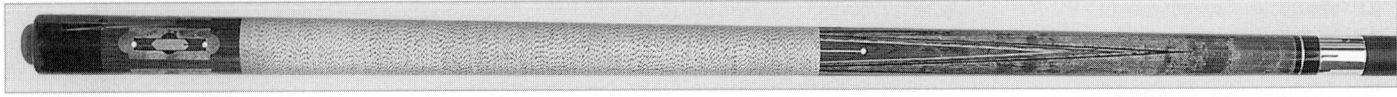

MSR	$1,600	$1,300-1,650	$1,250	$1,025

RICHARD BLACK CUSTOM CRAFTED CUES, cont. 175

GRADING	98%	90%	70%

Level 4 "Shanin II" - Stained bird's-eye maple forearm, with three floating ivory inlays, three floating rosewood points with an ivory inlay in each point, checked rosewood rings above and below wrap and above butt cap, butt sleeve with six exotic wood windows each with an ivory diamond-shaped inlay.

MSR	$1,650	$1,325-1,700	$1,275	$1,050

Level 5 "Bushka" - Bird's-eye maple forearm, four ebony points with four colored veneers and mother-of-pearl dots and notched diamond-shaped inlays, rings of ebony and ivory checks between nickel silver rings above and below wrap, ebony butt sleeve with mother-of-pearl dots and notched diamond-shaped inlays.

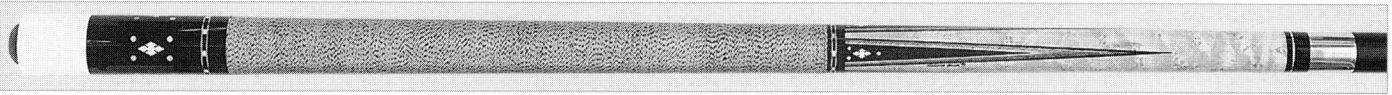

MSR	$1,700	$1,400-1,850	$1,350	$1150

Level 5 "Black Baron" - Stained bird's-eye maple forearm, four ebony points with double black and white veneers and inlaid ivory "gun sights," ivory inlaid rings above and below wrap, ebony butt sleeve with large ivory windows and ivory diamonds between veneers.

MSR	$1,800	$1,450-1,950	$1,450	$1,300

Level 5 "Pendleton Plus" - Bird's-eye maple forearm, four ebony points with four colored veneers and mother-of-pearl notched diamonds and dots, rings of checked ivory and snakewood between nickel silver above and below wrap and above butt cap, ebony butt sleeve with snakewood windows inlaid with mother-of-pearl dots and notched diamond-shaped inlays.

MSR	$2,750	$2,225-2,950	$2,150	$1,750

Level 5 "Madison" - Bird's-eye maple forearm, six long and six short floating points of intricately inlaid ivory within silkwood within ebony, ebony butt sleeve with eight ivory bordered diamond-shaped inlays inlaid over eight silkwood windows.

MSR	$3,200	$2,800-3,450	$2,675	$2,400

Level 5 "Double Oval" - Bird's-eye maple forearm, four ebony points with four colored veneers, scrimmed ivory ovals bordered by ebony and silver between points, checked rings between nickel silver rings above and below wrap and above butt cap, ebony butt sleeve with four scrimmed ivory ovals bordered by ebony and silver inlaid between four silver bordered red ovals.

MSR	$4,000	$3,500-4,500	$3,450	$3,000

Level 5 "Silver Crown" - Ivory joint, stained bird's-eye maple forearm, four long and four short scrimmed ivory points with double black ebony veneers and ebony and ivory dots on tips, scrimmed ivory butt sleeve with heavily engraved silver rings and windows, ivory butt cap.

MSR	$8,500	$7,000-9,500	$6,750	$5,000

DISCONTINUED RICHARD BLACK CUES

The following is a limited edition Helmet cue from the early 1990s. These cues were all one-of-a-kind, four-point cues in a variety of materials and designs. They were signed and dated by Richard on the forearms, and are easily identifiable by the ivory helmet logos on their butt sleeves above the butt caps.

| GRADING | 98% | 90% | 70% |

Level 3 Helmet - Bird's-eye maple forearm, four hardwood points with or without veneers, hardwood butt sleeve with or without inlays.

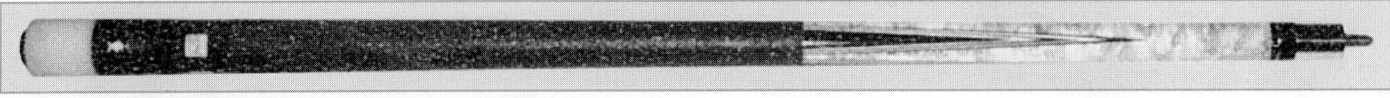

| MSR (1991) $450+ | $1,150 | $925 | $600 |

SPECIAL INTEREST CUES

The following is a selection of important and/or unique works by Richard Black. Richard's limited edition and one-of-a-kind cues come standard with two shafts with ivory ferrules and a custom Whitten case with the 'RB' logo. Most have one of Richard's special caps carved to match the cue protecting the pin.

Level 5 "30th Anniversary" - Ebony forearm, wrap, and butt sleeve with inlays of ebony, ivory, and silver overlapping ovals, ivory medallion engraved with limited edition number and "30th Anniversary Richard Black", silver and ivory ring work. Black phenolic 5/16-14 piloted joint, inlaid custom butt cap protector. Includes special commemorative Whitten case. One of edition of 30.

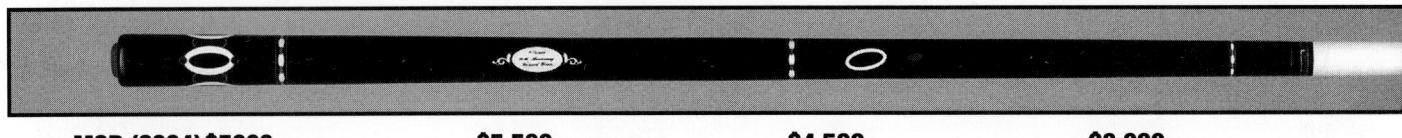

| MSR (2004) $5000 | $5,500 | $4,500 | $3,000 |

Level 7 "Athena #2" - Number two of a limited edition. Bocote forearm, ebony handle with silver and abalone inlays, cocobolo butt with full-spliced and butterfly splices incorporating English ash, cacique and holly., buttfly splices in shafts. Joint and shaft collars are buffalo horn; matching custom joint protector.

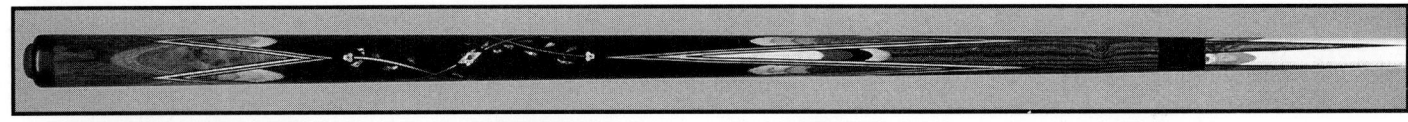

| MSR (1998) $15,000 | $17,500 | $13,500 | $9,500 |

SECONDARY MARKET MINIMUM VALUES

The following are minimum prices for other Richard Black cues encountered on the secondary market. These prices are representative of cues using basic materials and designs that may not be currently available. Richard currently specializes in one-of-a-kind cues that can command many times these prices due to the use of exotic materials and artistry.

Special construction note: There are many materials and construction techniques that can add value to Richard Black cues. The following are the most important examples:

- Add $1,000+ for ivory points.
- Add $800+ for ivory butt sleeve.
- Add 100%+ for precious metals and stones.
- Add 50%+ for 1975 production.
- Add 30%+ for 1976-1979 production.

For all used Richard Black cues:

- Add $150+ for each additional original straight playable shaft (standard with two).
- Deduct $200 for each missing original straight playable shaft.
- Add $150+ for ivory joint (except where otherwise noted).
- Add $50+ for leather wrap (except where otherwise noted).

Level 1 - 4 points, hustler.
| Level 1 cues start at | $500 | $440 | $375 |

Level 2 - 0 points, 0-25 inlays.
| Level 2 cues start at | $600 | $500 | $425 |

Level 3 - 2-6 points, 0-8 inlays.
| Level 3 cues start at | $950 | $775 | $600 |

Level 4 - 4-10 points, 9-25 inlays.
| Level 4 cues start at | $1,200 | $975 | $900 |

Level 5 - 0-12 points, 26-50 inlays.
| Level 5 cues start at | $3,000 | $2,450 | $1,750 |

Level 6 - 0-12 points, 51-75 inlays.
| Level 6 cues start at | $5,000 | $3,950 | $2,750 |

Level 7 - 0-12 points, 76-125 inlays.
| Level 7 cues start at | $7,500 | $6,000 | $4,000 |

GRADING	98%	90%	70%
Level 8 - 4-20 points, 126+ inlays.			
Level 8 cues start at	$9,500	$7,450	$5,000

SAMUEL BLATT

Maker of pool cues in New York and New Jersey from 1923 until the 1960s.

The Blatt family has been involved in the billiard business for more than 90 years, beginning in 1913 when Samuel Blatt worked for the New York Billiard Table Company on New York's Bowery. Samuel's experience grew beyond cuemaking and repair when he learned the art of making ivory balls from established master and proprietor of the New York Billiard Table Company, Isadore Rutzisky.

In the year 1923, Samuel opened his own cue repair and ball turning business, Sam Blatt & Son. Located in Freehold, New Jersey, Samuel sold his one-piece cues to poolrooms, often salvaging their old cues for two-piece conversions, a common practice at that time. Ron Blatt recalled his Grandfather Samuel's first shop as being a converted one-car garage behind the family residence where he would expertly turn ivory balls and also buckhorn ferrules. Ron's memories include his grandmother's refusal to let either of them back into the house until they had brushed all the white buckhorn shavings from their clothes. Samuel was one of the last craftsmen of buckhorn ferrules in his era. When he died in the early 1960s, a time when many were using fiber ferrules, Samuel had a pending order for 5000 buckhorn ferrules from Brunswick.

Samuel Blatt and Isadore Rutzisky c. 1920

The family business that Samuel Blatt started as a small shop in 1923 grew in the early 1930s when his sons Mel and Maurice opened their own billiard store on Washington Avenue in New York City. A decade later, they went on to start the M. Blatt Company with a store located on Broad Street in Trenton, New Jersey. A short time after that, in 1946, they opened a second store at Blatt Billiards' current location on Broadway in New York. It is the last surviving billiard company of that era in New York.

The Blatt Company continued to produce cues into the 1950s, employing a cuemaker who formerly served the Columbia Table Company also located (prior to its demise) on New York's Bowery where Samuel got his start. Cues that were made by Blatt were never marked and were predominantly two-piece conversion cues crafted from house cues.

Presently, Blatt's cuemaker is James Scott, a former employee of Palmer Cues, who still uses the original machines he ran when he worked for Palmer in Elizabeth, New Jersey. While he occasionally services the old Palmer cues that he built in the 1960s, James builds shafts and does cue repair work two days per week for Blatt's retail customers. The company Samuel Blatt started in the 1920s has thrived; its services are now worldwide and have graced many major tournaments including the U.S. Open Straight Pool Championships.

Today, Blatt Billiards is located at 809 Broadway. The six-floor factory and the showrooms house some of the finest antique, custom, and contemporary pool tables in the world. The Blatt workshops are staffed with artisans and cabinetmakers gathered from around the globe. They use skills and construction techniques of a bygone era to create tables of uncompromising quality and beauty. Several hundred constantly changing antique tables are always on display, and their ability to accurately and tastefully preserve the artistry and authenticity of these rarities is why Blatt Billiards is recognized as one of the foremost experts of antique tables.

The cue department has changed a little since the days of Sam Blatt. Because of their expertise in woodworking, Blatt has an extensive array of antique and custom cue racks on display. Snooker and three-cushion cues are available, and a full line of pool cues by today's most popular companies are always in stock. This year, with the coming on board of Victor Stein, author of The Billiard Encyclopedia, Blatt Billiards has greatly expanded its custom cue section, and the inventory is ever-changing.

LES BLEVINS

Maker of pool cues in the 1990s in Kentucky.

Les Blevins made cues from the 1990s until about 2000. Les still has all of his equipment and hopes to start making cues again in the future.

SPECIFICATIONS

Butt material: hardwoods
Shaft material: rock maple
Standard length: 58 in.
Standard butt cap: linen phenolic
Standard wrap: Irish linen
Point construction: short splice
Standard joint: linen phenolic
Joint type: flat faced
Joint screw: 3/8-11

SECONDARY MARKET MINIMUM VALUES

The following are minimum values for Les Blevins cues encountered on the secondary market. These prices are representative of cues using basic materials and designs that are not necessarily available at present. Les offered one-of-a-kind cues that can command many times these prices due to the use of exotic materials and artistry.

Special construction note: There are many materials and construction techniques that can add value to Les Blevins cues.

For all used Blevins cues, except where otherwise noted:

GRADING	98%	90%	70%

Add $75 for each additional original straight playable shaft beyond one.
Deduct $100 for missing original straight playable shaft.
Add $50 each for ivory ferrules.
Add $50 for leather wrap.
Deduct 25% for obvious or improper refinish.

	98%	90%	70%
Level 2 - 0 points, 0-25 inlays.			
Level 2 cues start at	$300	$240	$165
Level 3 - 2-6 points, 0-8 inlays.			
Level 3 cues start at	$500	$395	$275
Level 4 - 4-10 points, 9-25 inlays.			
Level 4 cues start at	$650	$525	$350

BLUDWORTH CUES

Maker of pool cues from 1988 to present, currently in Leakey, Texas.

Leonard Bludworth was born into a well-known sailing family in the Houston, Texas area. He competed in sailing and archery as a boy and he learned to make arrows and fishing poles. At 14, Leonard started playing pool. He soon became obsessed with the game, and dropped out of school. He worked in a shipyard and played pool in the Houston area, eventually playing on the road and in tournaments.

At the age of 23, Leonard was hospitalized for nine months after a shipyard accident. When he was released, he returned to playing pool. Although he wound up playing on the pro tour, he was not quite good enough to make enough money at it. He did put his own tips on, and was soon putting tips on for other players. He saw the need for someone to follow the pro tour and do cue repairs for the players.

In 1977, Leonard bought some equipment and planned to go to a couple of consecutive tournaments with his wife, Janice, to see if the idea was profitable. The first outing was so successful that it was 14 ½ months before they came back home. Leonard had found a way to attend all the major tournaments and make as much money as the top players. He continued to do repairs on the road, learning how the top players wanted their cues to hit. Leonard also promoted some pro tournaments with the help of Grady Mathews. During this time, Leonard invented and marketed a ball cleaner, which proved very successful. Leonard also was the head equipment coordinator (the tournament setup guy) for the mens' pro billiard tour for about eight years or so.

Donald Bludworth and Leonard Bludworth

Buddy Hall was one of Leonard's best customers on the road, as well as his best friend. Buddy was always happy with the way Leonard could make his cue play, so he asked Leonard to make cues. Leonard said no at first, and later on accepted the offer, and started Bludworth Custom Cues in 1981-82. As a player and friend of the top players in the business, he was able to design his cues with playability as the primary concern. Through the custom cue business, Leonard also designed and marketed lathes, and eventually CNC mills, to other cuemakers.

After seven years, Leonard and his son, Donald, were making more than one thousand Bludworth cues a year. By this time, Leonard was ready to slow down. In 1993, he left Houston and bought a ranch in west Texas. Donald stayed in Houston to run Bludworth Custom Cues. Donald soon bought out Leonard and his mom, Janice, in March of 1994 and operated it until about 1999. Leonard built a new shop on the new property, and founded Precision Custom Cues. The name was later changed to Bludworth Fine Billiard Cues and now Bludworth Cues. They plan to stick with the current name from here on.

Leonard refuses to make a cue with a stainless steel joint, as he does not like the way they hit. He still maintains Bludworth Billiard Products, which includes the ball cleaner, the cuemaking machinery, and offers personal training by Leonard and Donald for cuemakers worldwide. Leonard says he's constantly designing and building new machines to keep up with the changing times. His customers demand the best equipment possible. Leonard and Donald have several videos and DVDs on cue repair and cue making.

In the spring of 1992, Leonard helped to found the American Cuemakers Association.

Today Leonard makes about 80 Bludworth cues a year. The slower pace gives him more time to spend with his 20 grandchildren and 2 great-gandchildren.

Custom cues with inlays of precious metals and stones are a specialty of Leonard's. Leonard calls his current edition of cues the "Connoisseur Collection." All cues have flat-faced joints and custom a Bludworth stainless steel pin with .348 x 11.5 thread. Black leather wrap and two shafts with linen ferrules are standard. Most are ebony with inlayed points of malachite or turqouise, accented with silver and ivory inlays. All include a Whitten case, and most are signed "BLUD" and dated. He also builds traditional spliced cues. These are the same style of cues that he first built many years ago. Leonard has a lot of fun building these cues.

Donald came back in early 2005 as a full partner. Donald teaches CAD drawing and cue design. He also helps Leonard build all models of cues and really likes to be creative with the CNC machinery. The shop is still in the same location and has expanded to 2880 square feet. Bludworth cues are easily identifiable by the red dot in the butt cap. Current cues often feature a lot of Sterling silver inlays.

Bludworth Billiard cues are guaranteed indefinitely against construction defects that are not the result of warpage or abuse. If you have a Bludworth Billiard cue that needs further identification or repair, or would like to talk to Leonard about ordering a new cue, contact Bludworth Billiard Cues, listed in the Trademark Index.

| GRADING | 98% | 90% | 70% |

SPECIFICATIONS

Butt material: hardwoods
Shaft material: rock maple
Standard length: 58 in.
Lengths available: any
Standard finish: PPG
Standard joint: phenolic
Standard thread: .348 x 11.5
Joint type: flat-faced wood-to-wood
Balance point: 1-1/8 in. above wrap
Point construction: short splice or inlaid
Standard wrap: Irish linen
Standard butt cap: phenolic
Standard number of shafts: two
Standard taper: 12-1/2 in. straight
Standard ferrules: linen phenolic
Standard tip: Champion
Tip widths available: any
Annual production: about 80

OPTIONS (FOR NEW CUES ONLY)

Ivory joint: $225
Joint protectors: $40+
Ivory butt cap: $240
Ivory ferrule: $100
Extra shaft: $150+

REPAIRS

Repairs done on most fine cues.
Refinish (with leather wrap): $225
Refinish (with Irish linen wrap)- $160
Rewrap (leather): $150
Rewrap (linen): $45
Replace shaft (linen ferrule): $150
Replace shaft (ivory ferrule): $225
Replace ivory ferrule: $100
Replace Champion tip: $25

The current delivery time for a Bludworth cue is approximately 90 days, depending on the intricacy of the cue.

CURRENT BLUDWORTH CUES

Basic Bludworth cues with spliced points start at $2,200. One-of-a-kind Bludworth Connoisseur Collection cues start at $3,000.

SECONDARY MARKET MINIMUM VALUES

The following are minimum prices for Bludworth cues encountered on the secondary market. These prices are representative of cues using basic materials and designs that may not be currently available. Leonard currently specializes in one-of-a-kind cues that can command many times these prices due to the use of exotic materials and artistry.

Special construction note: There are many materials and construction techniques that can add value to Bludworth cues. The following are the most important examples:

Add $100+ for each ivory point.

For all used Bludworth cues, except where otherwise noted:

Add $125+ for each additional original straight playable shaft (standard with two).
Deduct $160 for each missing original straight playable shaft.
Add $200+ for ivory joint.
Add $100+ for leather wrap.
Add $60+ for each ivory ferrule.

Level 2 - 0 points, 0-25 inlays.

	98%	90%	70%
Level 2 cues start at	$300	$260	$175

Level 3 - 2-6 points, 0-8 inlays.

	98%	90%	70%
Level 3 cues start at	$600	$335	$300

Level 4 - 4-10 points, 9-25 inlays.

	98%	90%	70%
Level 4 cues start at	$700	$525	$375

GRADING	98%	90%	70%
Level 5 - 0-12 points, 26-50 inlays.			
Level 5 cues start at	$950	$725	$550
Level 6 - 0-12 points, 51-75 inlays.			
Level 6 cues start at	$1,300	$1,050	$800

BLUE GRASS CUES

Maker of pool cues from 1990 to 1994 in Greenup, Kentucky, from 1994 to 2003 in Hillsboro, Ohio and from 2003 to present in Winchester, Ohio.

Richard Harris was born in Cincinnati in 1957 and grew up near the town of Mowrystown, Ohio and graduated from Lynchburg High School (1975). He earned a degree in Business and Mathematics from Shawnee State University (1988). Richard first became interested in pool in 1974, when his dad bought an old Brunswick pool table with leather pockets, and set it up in the back of their television repair shop. He liked the game because he could beat all his friends. Richard was a good shot maker but knew nothing about playing the game. Then a man

Marked joint protectors

Richard Harris

named Elwood Patrick brought his television over to be repaired. While Richard's father was working on the television, Elwood took Richard back to the pool table for a few games. The last game they played, Elwood drew the cue ball back about twelve inches for shape on the eight ball. Richard was fascinated with the move, as he didn't know it was possible. Elwood showed him how it was done and Richard has been hooked on pool ever since. Richard's most memorable time playing pool was in Lexington, Kentucky in early 1990. Most of the pros were in town for a big tournament and some of them came over to Steepletons pool hall for their weekly nine-ball tournament on Thursday nights. Richard lived in Lexington at the time and Steepletons was his home court. Richard beat Keith McCready and Johnny Archer back to back, to win the tournament.

Not long after that, Richard started making cues. A friend of his had a lathe and other quipment and wanted him to experiment making cues. He thought it might be fun, so he started working on the project. Like playing pool, this fascinated Richard. He couldn't believe that trying to make cues could be so difficult. Working with a retired machinist, Charlie Rose, for about six months and extensively researching cues, he made several test models before finally coming up with the cue that Richard was proud to call his own. While prefecting the cues, Richard and his family were living in Greenup County, Kentucky, and he needed a name for the cues. The name Blue Grass Cues (Kentucky is the Blue Grass State) was finally settled on. Although they no longer live in Kentucky, and the cues have become popularly known as Richard Harris Cues, Blue Grass Cues remains the name of his cues.

Richard has been interested in the making of cues for a long time. In 1981, he and his wife, Donna, visited McDermott's first new factory. Through the mid-1980s, a friend, Darrel Bumgardner, from Huntington, West Virginia, always had a bounty of cues that Richard would look over very carefully. He noticed a distinct difference in the cues that were made by Paul Mottey. Richard thought the craftsmanship in the Mottey cues was excellent. When Richard started making cues, he knew exactly the direction he wanted to go. He liked the hit of a flat face, wood-to-wood joint, like the McDermott, which he played with for years, and he liked the craftsmanship of the cues made by hand.

In 2003, the Harris family built a new shop and home and now reside in Winchester, Ohio. Richard still believes in the old fashioned way of making cues—no computerized equipment, just hard work and lots of time. Richard and Donna make every part of the cue except the tips and bumpers. Richard will hand sand the shafts, machine his own screws and even make his own ferrules from blocks of micarta. Every part of a Blue Grass Cue is truly custom made. Richard's greatest concern is the playability of his cues.

Blue Grass cues are easily identifiable by the "Richard Harris" signature that has appeared on the forearms or the butt sleeves on almost every cue that has been made since the early nineties. Since 1992, Richard has put serial numbers under the bumpers of his custom cues.

In 2004, Blue Grass Cues started taking orders online. In less than 6 months they were backed up more than five years. Richard quit taking new orders effective January 2005.

Blue Grass Cues are guaranteed for life against manufacturing defects that are not the result of warpage or abuse. If you have a Blue Grass cue that needs further identification or repair, contact Blue Grass Cues, listed in the Trademark Index.

SPECIFICATIONS

Butt material: hardwoods
Shaft material: hard rock maple
Standard length: 58 in.
Lengths available: 58 in. to 59 in.
Standard finish: clear coat
Balance point: 18 in. to 19 in. from butt
Standard butt cap: linen phenolic
Standard wrap: Irish linen
Point construction: short splice

GRADING	98%	90%	70%

Standard joint: linen phenolic
Joint type: flat faced
Joint screw: 3/8-11
Standard number of shafts: two
Standard taper: Harris pro
Standard ferrules: micarta
Other Ferrule Options- Ivory
Standard tip width: 13 mm
Tip widths available: 12.75 mm to 13.5 mm
Standard tip: Talisman pro medium
Annual production: fewer than 50 cues plus hustler cues

OPTIONS (FOR NEW CUES ONLY)

Option pricing depends entirely on the design and cost of the individual cue, refer to their website.

REPAIRS

Repairs done on Blue Grass cues only. Repair pricing depends upon the individual cue.

CURRENT BLUE GRASS CUES

Basic two-piece Blue Grass hustler cues start at $500 with one shaft. Blue Grass cues with wraps and joint rings start at $1,000. Blue Grass cues with points start at $1,500. One-of-a-kind custom Blue Grass cues start at $2,500. Blue Grass Cues is not taking new cue orders at this time.

PAST EXAMPLES

The following cues are representative examples that are not currently available for order from Blue Grass Cues.

Level 2 - Maple forearm with a block ring above wrap, maple butt sleeve with block rings at top and bottom.

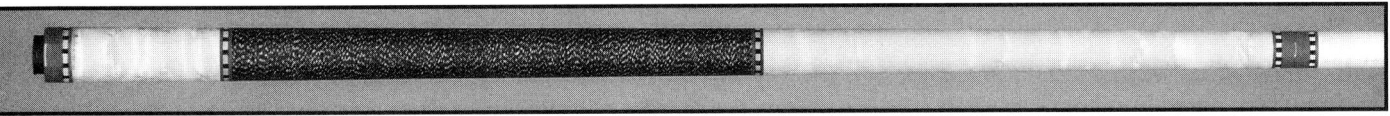

MSR (2004) $1,000	$1,000-1,200	$785	$550

Level 3 - Bird's-eye maple forearm with block rings above wrap, three long and three short rosewood points, rosewood butt sleeve with block rings at top and bottom.

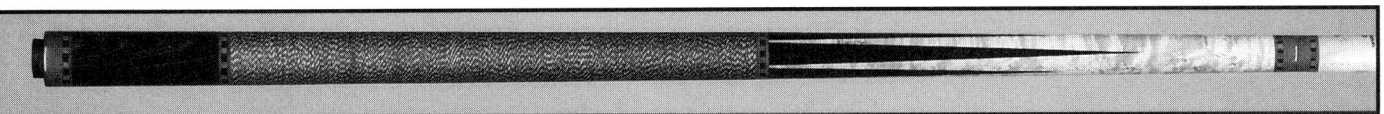

MSR (2004) $1,500	$1,500-1,700	$1,175	$800

SECONDARY MARKET MINIMUM VALUES

The following are minimum values for other Blue Grass cues encountered on the secondary market. These prices are representative of cues using basic materials and designs that are not currently available. Blue Grass Cues has offered one-of-a-kind cues that can command many times these prices due to the use of exotic materials and artistry.

Special construction note: There are many materials and construction techniques that can add value to Blue Grass cues. The following are the most important examples:

Add $150 for stainless steel joint.
Add $250 for ivory joint.

For all used cues, except where otherwise noted:

Add $100 for each additional original straight playable shaft beyond two.
Deduct $150 for each missing original straight playable shaft under two.
Add $50 each for ivory ferrules.
Deduct 25% for obvious or improper refinish.

Level 1 - 4 points, hustler.

Level 1 cues start at	$400	$300	$200

Level 2 - 0 points, 0-25 inlays.

Level 2 cues start at	$850	$675	$450

Level 3 - 2-6 points, 0-8 inlays.

Level 3 cues start at	$1,250	$1,000	$700

Level 4 - 4-10 points, 9-25 inlays.

Level 4 cues start at	$1,500	$1,185	$800

GRADING	98%	90%	70%
Level 5 - 0-12 points, 26-50 inlays.			
Level 5 cues start at	$2,500	$1,950	$1,350
Level 6 - 0-12 points, 51-75 inlays.			
Level 6 cues start at	$4,000	$3,250	$2,250

BOB'S CUES

Maker of pool cues from 1983 to 1993 in Canton, MI.

Robert Parsons made cues for about ten years, from about 1983 to 1993. Other projects and commitments have kept him from making more cues since that time, but he hopes to return to his hobby as he gets closer to retirement. A master toolmaker by trade, Bob went back to school to become an engineer. He enjoys working with his hands, loves the game of pool, and still loves cues. His finished products were designed for simple execution, solid functionality, and done in classic designs. Bob's cues all have hidden markings under the wrap, along with engraved inserts in shafts. Bob has kept records of each one. All are serialized and signed.

For more information, refer to Bob's Cues in the Trademark Index.

SPECIFICATIONS

Butt material: hardwoods
Shaft material: rock maple
Standard length: 58 in.
Lengths encountered: 58 in. to 58 1/2 in.
Standard butt cap: Delrin
Standard wrap: Irish linen
Point construction: short splice
Standard joint: stainless steel
Joint type: piloted
Joint screw: 5/16-14
Standard number of shafts: two
Standard ferrules: Aegis or Ivorine II
Total production: fewer than 300 cues

SECONDARY MARKET MINIMUM VALUES

The following are minimum values for other Bob's cues encountered on the secondary market. These prices are representative of cues using basic materials and designs that are not necessarily available at present. Bob's has offered one-of-a-kind cues that can command many times these prices due to the use of exotic materials and artistry.

Special construction note: There are many materials and construction techniques that can add value to Bob's cues.

For all used Bob's cues, except where otherwise noted:

Add $100 for each additional original straight playable shaft beyond two.
Deduct $150 for each missing original straight playable shaft under two.
Add $65 each for ivory ferrules.
Add $200 for ivory joint (rare).
Deduct 15% for obvious or improper refinish.

Level 1 - Hustler.			
Level 1 cues start at	$400	$300	$190
Level 2 - 0 points, 0-25 inlays.			
Level 2 cues start at	$500	$375	$225
Level 3 - 2-6 points, 0-8 inlays.			
Level 3 cues start at	$700	$520	$300
Level 4 - 4-10 points, 9-25 inlays.			
Level 4 cues start at	$1,000	$725	$400

BourQue CUES

Maker of pool cues from 1997 to present in Sanford, Maine.

Dan Bourque has been playing pool for many years, starting at age four in his father's pool room. He was barely big enough to make a shot, standing on a soda box, dragging it around the table. He played with a special cue given to him by his father. He helped his father repair tables and cues for many years.

Dan Bourque designed, developed, and patented the "Tunable Pro Joint" which is designed to transfer the hit vibration from the shaft to the butt of the cue. A BourQue Cue is designed for playability first, and beauty second. Dan currently works a retirement schedule. Only a limited number of cues are being made and sold.

There are about three hundred BourQue cues that have been made, ranging in retail prices from $700 to $5000. Most are plain with two basic woods used by Dan: cocobolo and African ebony. BourQue cues do not have points.

Dan Bourque

BourQue CUES, cont.

GRADING	98%	90%	70%

All cues are naturally weighted without the use of weight bolts. Basic cues have Uni-Loc joints. High end cues have the Tunable Pro Joint and the One-Step extension. Most BourQue cues are finished with a natural wood high polish finish.

Dan Bourque is the inventor of the One-Step pool cue extension (Patent #5749788 & #415,231, #D444,519) that screws on the back, goes over the bumper, and becomes part of the cue. The licensed holders are Cuetec Cues (The Smart Extension) and The Mezz Cue (The Pro Extension). The Extension should be used, when needed, like a bridge. A 6 in. extension on the end of a cue will give you 15% more table reach. Using the extension in conjunction with a bridge gives the player a tremendous reach difference.

If you are interested in talking to Dan about a new cue or cue that needs to be repaired, you can contact him at BourQue Cues, listed in the Trademark Index.

SPECIFICATIONS

Butt material: hardwoods
Shaft material: rock maple
Standard length: 59 in.
Lengths available: 57 in. to 59 in.
Standard wrap: Irish linen
Standard joint: Atlas Ivorine
Joint type: tunable pro joint
Standard rings: Atlas nickel silver with ABS
Standard tip: Triumph

CURRENT BOURQUE CUES

Basic two-piece BourQue cues start at 750. One-of-a-kind custom BourQue cues start at $1,000. The current delivery time for a BourQue cue is about two to three months.

SECONDARY MARKET MINIMUM VALUES

The following are minimum values for BourQue cues encountered on the secondary market. These prices are representative of cues using basic materials and designs that are not necessarily available at present. Dan has offered one-of-a-kind cues that can command many times these prices due to the use of exotic materials and artistry.

Special construction note: There are many materials and construction techniques that can add value to Dan Bourque cues.

For all used Dan Bourque cues, except where otherwise noted:
  Add $100 for each additional original straight playable shaft beyond two.
  Deduct $150 for missing original straight playable shaft.
  Deduct 20% for obvious or improper refinish.

Level 2 - 0 points, 0-25 inlays.
  Level 2 cues start at $700 / $545 / $375

Level 5 - 0-12 points, 26-50 inlays.
  Level 5 cues start at $1,000 / $785 / $550

Level 6 - 0-12 points, 51-75 inlays.
  Level 6 cues start at $1,500 / $1,175 / $800

BOURQUE CUSTOM MADE CUES

Maker of pool cues from 1971 to Present in Sandusky, Ohio.

Douglas Bourque has been making cues part-time since 1971. After replacing tips for local players, he decided to apply his experience with machine tools to the art of cuemaking. Since his early cues are not marked, they can be difficult to identify. Cues made since early 1997 will have a "fleur-de-lis" logo on the butt cap. Doug has been constantly improving the design of his cues. He was an excellent player as a teenager, but stopped playing consistently until 1996. Doug specializes in one-of-a-kind custom cues, which have usually taken from four to six weeks to

1997 to Present Day

Douglas Bourque

deliver. He only likes to make a limited number of cues per year, so he has not advertised. Instead of accepting orders for special designs, Doug prefers to create his own designs, which he offers for sale when completed. Since retiring from his full-time job at Ford Motor Company in 1993, Doug is able to spend six days a week in his shop. Doug did all of his work by hand, until 1997, when he added CNC machinery. With his CAD-CAM equipment, Doug is able to make much fancier cues than before. Doug makes all his cue components except the stainless steel joints and inserts. Now that he is creating more intricate cues, he is only producing about 20 cues per year.

Bourque cues are guaranteed indefinitely against construction defects that are not the result of warpage or abuse. If you have a Bourque cue that needs repair, or would like to talk to Doug about the design of a one-of-a-kind custom cue, contact Bourque Custom Made Cues, listed in the Trademark Index.

184 BOURQUE CUSTOM MADE CUES, cont.

| GRADING | 98% | 90% | 70% |

SPECIFICATIONS

Butt material: hardwoods
Shaft material: rock maple
Standard length: 58 in.
Lengths available: any up to 60 in.
Standard finish: high gloss polymer
Joint screw: 5/16-14
Standard joint: stainless steel
Joint type: piloted
Balance point: above top of wrap
Point construction: short slice
Standard wrap: Irish linen
Standard butt cap: phenolic or woods to match butt
Standard number of shafts: two (one prior to 1998)
Standard taper: custom
Standard ferrules: linen-based phenolic
Standard tip: water buffalo
Tip widths available: any
Joint protectors: standard
Annual production: fewer than 20 cues

OPTIONS

Options pricing depends on the cue. Call for prices.

REPAIRS

Repairs done on Bourque cues only. Call for prices.

CURRENT BOURQUE CUES

Doug Bourque is not taking orders for cues at this time.

PAST EXAMPLES

The following cues are representations of the work of Douglas Bourque.

Level 3 - Bird's-eye maple forearm with linen ring above handle, four cocobolo points, one-piece cocobolo handle and butt sleeve.

| MSR (1999) $425 | $700 | $550 | $350 |

Level 3 - Bird's-eye maple forearm, four bocote points, bocote butt sleeve with a pair of alternating ebony and maple dash rings.

| MSR (1999) $375 | $550 | $460 | $325 |

Level 3 - Bird's-eye maple forearm, three long points with three colored veneers and an ivory-bordered ebony dot at the end of each and three short ebony points with two colored veneers and an ivory-bordered ebony dot at the end of each, bird's-eye maple butt sleeve with four ebony diamond-shaped inlays alternating with four ebony spade-shaped inlays between rings of nickel silver within ebony at top and bottom.

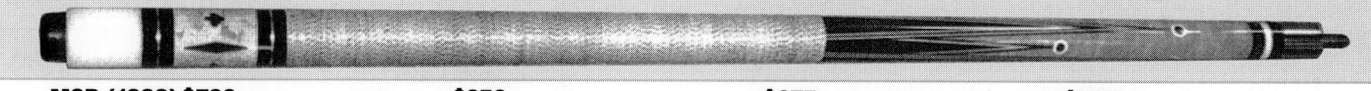

| MSR (1999) $700 | $850 | $675 | $450 |

Level 4 - Kingwood forearm, four floating micarta points, tiger maple handle with three rows of intricate ebony inlays, kingwood butt sleeve with four intricate micarta inlays.

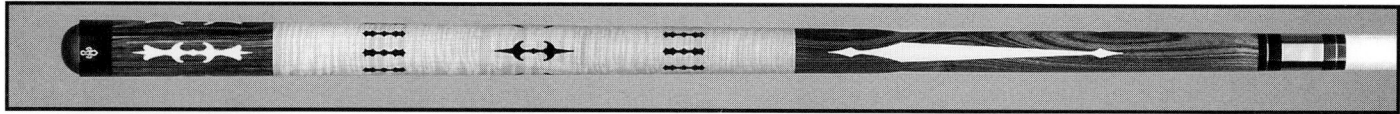

| MSR (2003) $750 | $1,000 | $800 | $550 |

BOURQUE CUSTOM MADE CUES, cont. 185

GRADING	98%	90%	70%

Level 4 - Ivory joint, ebony forearm with an ivory ring with malachite inlays above wrap, four floating ivory bordered malachite points above pairs of ivory arc-shaped inlays, black and white ringtail lizard wrap, ebony butt sleeve with ivory oval shaped inlays set within silver rings between ivory rings with ebony oval shaped inlays at top and bottom.

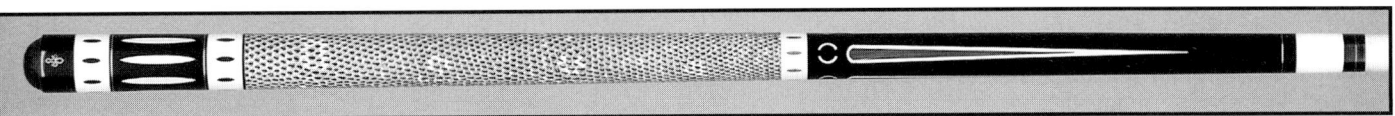

MSR (2003) $3,300	$3,500	$2,700	$1,800

Level 5 - Thuya burl forearm with a metal ring above wrap, four floating micarta points with sets of malachite spear-shaped and diamond-shaped inlays in each, thuya burl butt sleeve with intricate micarta and malachite inlays between metal rings at top and bottom.

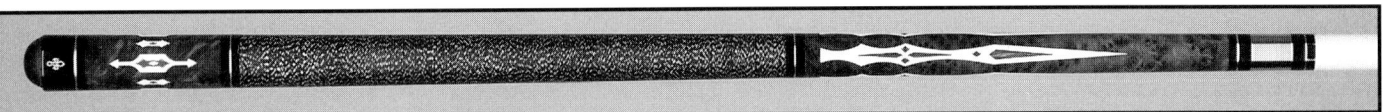

MSR (2003) $1,400	$1,650	$1,300	$850

Level 5 - Ivory joint, ebony forearm with an ebony-inlayed ivory ring above wrap and multiple intricate ivory inlays, four intricate floating ivory points with an ivory bordered ebony diamond-shaped inlay at the tip of each, black and white ringtail lizard wrap, ivory butt sleeve with intricate ivory and turquoise inlays set in ebony windows between rings of turquoise inlays within silver rings at top and bottom.

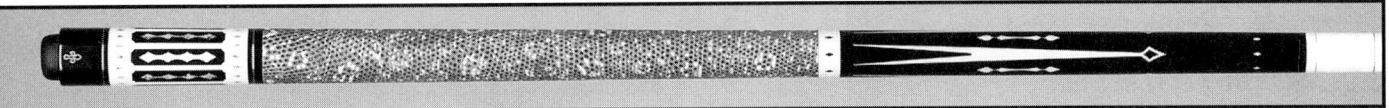

MSR (2003) $3,900	$4,000	$3,100	$2,100

Level 4 - Amboyna burl forearm with a metal ring above wrap, four ebony points with multi-colored veneers and an ivory bordered turquoise spear-shaped inlays in each, lizard wrap, amboyna burl butt sleeve with intricate turquoise inlaid ivory inlays between metal rings at top and bottom.

MSR (2003) $1,800	$2,000	$1,550	$1,050

Level 7 - Redwood burl forearm with a metal ring above wrap, four ebony points with multi-colored veneers and an ivory-bordered turquoise spear-shaped inlay in each, brown ringtail lizard wrap, redwood burl butt sleeve with intricate turquoise and ivory inlays between rings of itricate ivory and turquoise inlays at top and bottom.

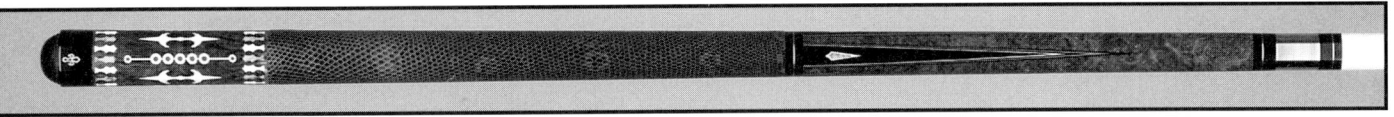

MSR (2003) $2,000	$2,150	$1,700	$1,150

SECONDARY MARKET MINIMUM VALUES

The following are minimum prices for other Bourque cues encountered on the secondary market. These prices are representative of cues using basic materials and designs that may not be currently available. Doug also offers one-of-a-kind cues that can command many times these prices due to the use of exotic materials and artistry.

Special construction note: There are many materials and construction techniques that can add value to Bourque cues. The following are the most important examples:

Add $100+ for ivory joint.
Add 100%+ for all ebony and ivory construction.

For all used Bourque cues:

Add $100+ for each additional original straight playable shaft (standard with one).
Deduct $100 if without original straight playable shaft.
Add $75+ for leather wrap.

Level 1 - 4 points, hustler.

Level 1 cues start at	$350	$275	$185

Level 2 - 0 points, 0-25 inlays.

Level 2 cues start at	$400	$315	$215

GRADING	98%	90%	70%
Level 3 - 2-6 points, 0-8 inlays.			
Level 3 cues start at	$500	$390	$265
Level 4 - 4-10 points, 9-25 inlays.			
Level 4 cues start at	$750	$575	$390
Level 5 - 0-12 points, 26-50 inlays.			
Level 5 cues start at	$1,000	$825	$600
Level 6 - 0-12 points, 51-75 inlays.			
Level 6 cues start at	$1,500	$1,200	$850

BRADEN CUES

Maker of pool cues in Oxnard, California.

Brady Andresen was a Bert Schrager apprentice for several months and shared a shop with Bert. Brady now has his own shop in Oxnard, California. Brady's cues can be identified by the script 'Braden' logo on the butt cap.

If you are interested in talking to Brady about a new cue or cue that needs to be repaired, you can contact him at Braden Cues, listed in the Trademark Index.

BRELAND CUES

Maker of pool cues from 1994 to present in Okeechobee, Florida.

Dale Breland

Dale Breland was a good pool player with a woodworking hobby. He made some custom furniture part time. Dale did cue repair work for years and his customers kept asking him to make cues for them. He finally started making cues part time in 1994, when he was still working as a wire lathe contractor, and has been building them full-time since 1999. Early Breland cues were unmarked, but Dale started signing them on the forearm by 1995. A few of Dale's early cues had stainless steel joints. He now uses a wood tenon instead of the metal screw he used to join the handle to the forearm until 1997. Aegis ferrules were used until 1998, when they were discontinued in favor of Ivorine 3. Dale owns his own pool room in Okeechobee, which he opened in 1997. It features a back bar that Dale built out of Pennsylvania red oak.

Dale moved to Fort Meyers, Florida in 2001. He built a 1,500-square-foot shop with a couple lathes, a band saw for cutting veneers, a manual pantograph, etc. Dale was diagnosed with pancreatic cancer in 2002. He spent over a month in the hospital and lost fifty-five pounds. This slowed down his cuemaking for a while, but he is now almost fully recovered. Dale now makes under 100 cues a year by hand in his one man shop, many of which are hustler cues for local players. He likes to use exotic woods in the butt caps, which are marked "Breland". Dale's "Native American Series" feature Native American materials, themes, and colors. These cues include beadwork, wraps made of lacework, and Native American images. Breland Cues are guaranteed for life against manufacturing defects that are not the result of warpage or abuse. If you have a Breland cue that needs further identification or repair, or would like to order a new Breland cue, contact Breland Cues, listed in the Trademark Index.

SPECIFICATIONS

Butt material: hardwoods
Shaft material: rock maple
Standard length: 58 1/2 in.
Lengths available: 58 in. to 60 in.
Standard finish: PPG 3-part catalyzed urethane
Balance point: custom
Standard butt cap: linen phenolic
Standard wrap: Irish linen
Point construction: pantographed or short spliced
Standard joint: linen phenolic
Joint type: flat faced
Joint screw: 3/8-10
Standard number of shafts: one
Standard taper: 12 in. straight
Standard ferrules: Ivorine 3
Standard tip width: 13 mm
Standard tip: Triangle
Annual production: fewer than 100 cues

OPTIONS (FOR NEW CUES ONLY)

Leather wrap: $75+
Special length: no charge
Ivory butt cap: $125+
Ivory joint collar: $90+

GRADING	98%	90%	70%

Joint protectors: $35+
Extra shaft: $110
Ivory ferrule: $50
Moori tip: $30

REPAIRS

Repairs done on all fine cues.

CURRENT BRELAND CUES

Basic two-piece hustler cues start at $200. Cues with wraps and joint rings start at $450. Breland Cues with points start at $650. One-of-a-kind custom cues also start at $650. Breland cues also offers the "Native American Series," a line of forty cues ranging in price from $1,000 to $3,000. The average delivery time for a Breland cue is three to four months.

SECONDARY MARKET MINIMUM VALUES

The following are minimum values for Breland Cues encountered on the secondary market. These prices are representative of cues using basic materials and designs that are not currently available. Breland Cues has offered one-of-a-kind cues that can command many times these prices due to the use of exotic materials and artistry.

Special construction note: There are many materials and construction techniques that can add value to Breland cues. The following are the most important examples:

- Add $400+ for ivory points.
- Add $125 for ivory joint.
- Add $150 for ivory butt cap.

For all used Breland cues, except where otherwise noted:

- Add $75 for each additional original straight playable shaft beyond two.
- Deduct $100 for each missing original straight playable shaft under two.
- Add $40 each for ivory ferrules.
- Add $50 for leather wrap.
- Deduct 20% for obvious or improper refinish.

Level 1 - 4 points, hustler.

	98%	90%	70%
Level 1 cues start at	$175	$145	$90

Level 2 - 0 points, 0-25 inlays.

Level 2 cues start at	$400	$325	$225

Level 3 - 2-6 points, 0-8 inlays.

Level 3 cues start at	$600	$465	$325

Level 4 - 4-10 points, 9-25 inlays.

Level 4 cues start at	$800	$675	$450

Level 5 - 0-12 points, 26-50 inlays.

Level 5 cues start at	$1000	$800	$550

BRICK CUE CO.

Maker of pool cues from 1996 to 2002 in Memphis, Tennessee, from 2002 to 2003 in Old Hickory, Tennessee, and from 2003 to present in Madison, Tennessee.

Alex Brick has been playing pool for over 40 years. He learned to use machinery in his high school shop class. Alex's brother is a carpenter, and Alex has helped him over the years. He learned about cuemaking from his college friend, Bill McDaniel. Retired, in 1996 Alex started making cues part time out of a shop in his house. Alex was influenced by David Kersenbrock's ideas on cue making and has tried to emulate the stiff hit of David's cues.

Alex had to move his shop into a local pool room in 1998. In 2002 he moved to Old Hickory, Tennessee and worked running a CNC router in a furniture factory. In 2003, Alex went to work helping long-time friend Joe Blackburn at JOB Billiard Pro Shop. Alex can now be found working at JOB Billiards in Madison, Tennessee.

Alex Brick

Alex likes to use distinctive silver joint rings, but never metal joints. Old Brick cues are signed on the forearms, followed by the number of the cue for the month and year. Brick cues made since 2000 can be identified by the AB logo with a circle around it. He is currently building only five or so cues per year.

BRICK CUE CO., cont.

| GRADING | 98% | 90% | 70% |

Brick Cues are guaranteed for life against manufacturing defects that are not the result of warpage or abuse. If you have a Brick cue that needs further identification or repair, or would like to order a new Brick cue, contact the Brick Cue Co., listed in the Trademark Index.

SPECIFICATIONS

Butt material: hardwoods
Shaft material: rock maple
Standard length: 58 in.
Lengths available: 57 to 57.5 in.
Standard balance point: 2-2.5 in. above wrap
Standard butt cap: linen phenolic
Standard wrap: Irish linen
Point construction: short splice
Standard joint: linen phenolic
Joint type: flat faced
Joint screw: 3/8-10
Standard number of shafts: two
Standard ferrules: melamine
Standard tip: LePro
Annual production: fewer than ten cues

OPTIONS (FOR NEW CUES ONLY)

Ivory butt cap: $225
Ivory joint: $125
Ivory ferrule: $75
Extra shaft: $125

REPAIRS

Repairs done on all fine cues.
Refinish with linen wrap: $150
Rewrap Irish linen: $45
Rewrap leather: $100
Replace shaft: $125+
Replace ivory ferrule: $75

CURRENT BRICK CUES

Basic two-piece Brick bar cues start at $175. Brick cues with wraps and joints start at $375. Brick cues with points start at $600. One-of-a-kind custom Brick cues start at $900. The current delivery time for a Brick cue is eight to ten weeks.

SECONDARY MARKET MINIMUM VALUES

The following are minimum values for Brick cues encountered on the secondary market. These prices are representative of cues using basic materials and designs that are not currently available. has offered one-of-a-kind cues that can command many times these prices due to the use of exotic materials and artistry.

Special construction note: There are many materials and construction techniques that can add value to Brick cues. The following are the most important examples:

Add $200+ for ivory butt cap.
Add $125 for ivory joint.

For all used Brick cues, except where otherwise noted:

Add $100 for each additional original straight playable shaft beyond two.
Deduct $125 for each missing original straight playable shaft under two.
Add $75 each for ivory ferrules.
Deduct 20% for obvious or improper refinish.

	98%	90%	70%
Level 1 - 4 points, hustler.			
Level 1 cues start at	$155	$125	$85
Level 2 - 0 points, 0-25 inlays.			
Level 2 cues start at	$350	$275	$185
Level 3 - 2-6 points, 0-8 inlays.			
Level 3 cues start at	$500	$395	$275
Level 4 - 4-10 points, 9-25 inlays.			
Level 4 cues start at	$650	$510	$350

GRADING	98%	90%	70%

OLIVER BRIGGS
Maker of pool cues in Boston, Massachusetts c. 1910.

Oliver L. Briggs was a manufacturer of pool cues and billiard tables in Boston in the early 1900s. Examples of their cues are extremely rare, and known examples have butterfly splicing. Cues can be identified by the name "OL BRIGGS" stamped into the end of the butt sleeve.

PAST EXAMPLES

Level 3 Circa 1910- Maple forearm with two full-spliced hardwood butterfly points with two veneers above two butterfly spliced hardwood points with two veneers. Black rubber bumper, no butt cap. Wooden joint collar, long brass pin in shaft, black linen twine wrap.

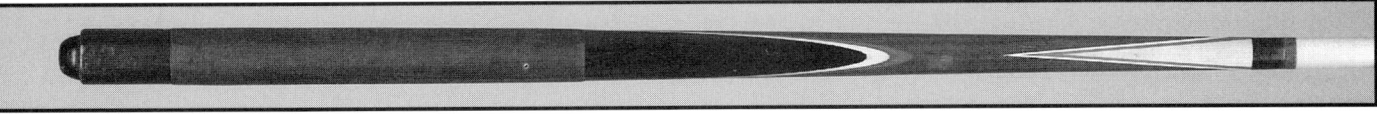

Level 3 cues start at	$1,150	$875	$550

JAMES BRUMFIELD
Maker of JB Cues. Refer to JB Cues for information.

BRUNSWICK BILLIARDS
Maker of pool cues for over 100 years; founded 1845 in Cincinnati, Ohio, currently distributing cues from Bristol, Wisconsin.

BBC decal labels used from 1890 until 1940s. All eagles are gold., circle color evolves.

White c.late 1800s-early 1900s	Red c.1906-1920	Gold (red field) c.1921-1925	Green (red or yellow field) c. 1926-1939

Brunswick Billiards began in the Cincinnati wood shop of John M. Brunswick in 1845. It eventually became the largest manufacturer of billiard tables and equipment in the world, merging with companies run by Julius Balke and H. W. Collender. Brunswick started manufacturing and importing cues as early as the mid-1800s, and had started making its own cues by the end of the century.

Early Brunswick-Balke-Collender (BBC) cues are especially collectible, with the complex and beautiful Model 360 with its many butterfly splices being one of the most desirable cues. It was the most expensive of the early models and was often awarded at tournaments of the time. Most examples have rosewood points, but ebony was occasionally used. Collectors also look for the model 26-1/2, which featured a full-spliced butt, with four veneers on each point. Brunswick also introduced the "Merry Widow" (a cue without points) and the term is still used to describe similar cues today.

By the early 1920s, Herman Rambow was involved in cuemaking at Brunswick. He invented the "Hub Cue," which featured an ivory joint above the wrap, and a bell-shaped ivory ferrule. Rambow also used the bell ferrule on some of his own cues into the 1940s. Brunswick was the first to make the "Hub" in the 1920s, and today they are sought after by collectors as a very important historical cue. Most of these early cues were sold with a "Brunswick Balke Collender" decal on the butt sleeve, which are particularly prized when they remain intact on the cues. (See examples shown.) Some restored cues have replicas of the early decals, which changed in color and small details over the decades.

In the 1930s, Brunswick introduced "Master Stroke" cues. Around 1940 the first "Willie Hoppe" Titlist and Professional cues debuted. This popular cue was produced until 1962, and earlier examples are especially sought-after. The one-piece Titlist was the favorite cue for conversions to two-piece custom cues by George Balabushka, Frank Paradise, Gus Szamboti and scores of others, whereas Rambow preferred to customize the Titlist "Professional." Over the years, Brunswick has made hundreds of models of cues, all of which are desirable to collectors. Collectors gladly pay a premium for older, pre-1960 BBC cues in good original condition, as they are becoming increasingly rare.

BBC became the Brunswick Corporation in 1960. Since the 1960s, the company has concentrated on table manufacturing and other billiards accessories. Until a few years ago they distributed several lines of Brunswick cues made by other manufacturers. The Magnum and Diamond series cues were manufactured by Joss Cues Ltd. and previously carried the Joss name. The Corvette series is aimed at Corvette aficionados and is manufactured under a licensing agreement with General Motors. The Ewa Mataya Lawrence series and Jimmy Caras series cues honored players with a long standing relationship with Brunswick. Brunswick currently distributes two "house" cues.

For more information, please refer to the listings for George Balabushka and Herman Rambow.

190 BRUNSWICK BILLIARDS, cont.

GRADING	98%	90%	70%

SPECIFICATIONS
Butt material: hardwoods
Shaft material: rock maple
Standard length: 57 in. only
Standard finish: polyurethane
Joint screw: 5/16-14
Joint type: flat face, brass insert
Point construction: inlaid
Standard wrap: Irish linen
Standard cutt cap: plastic
Standard number of shafts: one
Standard taper: 12 in. pro
Standard ferrules: plastic
Standard tip: Le Pro

CURRENT BRUNSWICK CUES

Brunswick currently offers four American made cues. The one-piece "Tru Balance" cue retails for $45. The "Heritage Cue" retails for $49. The "Centennial Cue" retails for $129. And the "Master Stroke Cue" retails for $209. All are usually available for immediate delivery.

DISCONTINUED EXAMPLES

The following "Gold Crown" Series cues featured piloted phenolic joints and Irish linen wraps. Each cue came with one shaft featuring an Aegis ferrule, a Brunswick soft cue case, and metal joint protectors. Extra "Gold Crown" Series shafts were available for $80 each.

Level 2 GC1 - Dark morado forearm, dark morado butt sleeve with four intricate pequia-amarello mirrored image crown-shaped inlays.

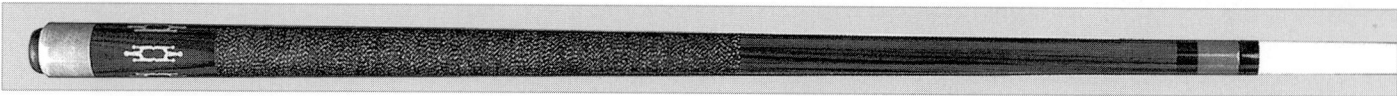

MSR (1996) $260	$210	$190	$125

Level 2 GC2 - Bird's-eye maple forearm with European pearl crown-shaped inlays set in purple dyed scepters above wrap, bird's-eye maple butt sleeve with four purple bordered European pearl crown-shaped inlays below wrap.

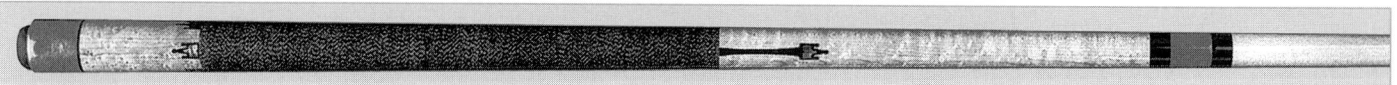

MSR (1996) $350	$275	$240	$175

Level 3 GC3 - Bird's-eye maple forearm, four two-piece morado points that form crowns at the base of each, bird's-eye maple butt sleeve with eight small purple dyed maple hourglass shaped inlays between thick morado rings at top and bottom.

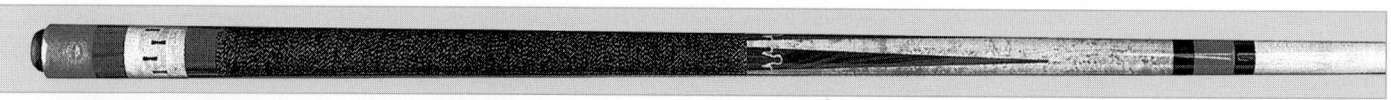

MSR (1996) $440	$335	$295	$220

Level 4 GC4 - Bird's-eye maple forearm, four intricate ebony floating points that each form a "B," bird's-eye maple butt sleeve with four purple bordered gold lip pearl mirrored image crown-shaped inlays alternating with four morado diamond-shaped inlays.

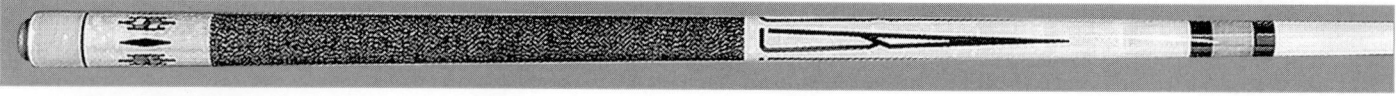

MSR (1996) $530	$400	$355	$275

Level 5 GC5 - Bird's-eye maple forearm, four ebony points with two colored veneers and a European pearl dot above and below a European pearl diamond-shaped inlay in each point, ebony butt sleeve with four intricate hollow pequia-amarello inlays with a pequia-amarello hourglass-shaped inlay above and below each alternating with four gold pearl-lipped European pearl diamond-shaped inlays.

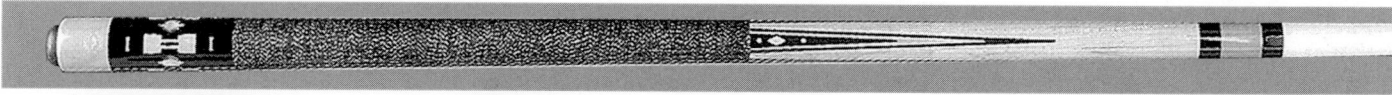

MSR (1996) $620	$475	$425	$310

BRUNSWICK BILLIARDS, cont. 191

GRADING	98%	90%	70%

Level 5 GC6 - Bird's-eye maple forearm, three long and three short ebony bordered white points, ebony butt sleeve with four European pearl diamond-shaped inlays set in a series of intricate white inlays alternating with four large iridescent abalone diamond-shaped inlays.

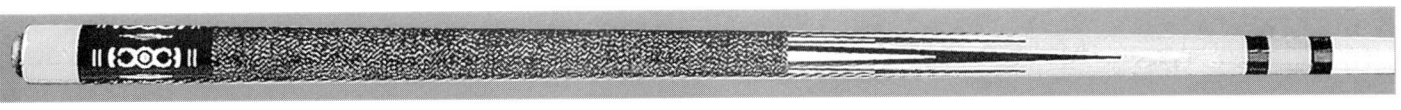

MSR (1996) $710	$545	$485	$350

MAJESTIC SERIES

The following Majestic Series cues featured piloted stainless steel joints and maple checked black collars. Each cue came with one shaft with a linen-based phenolic ferrule, a Brunswick soft case, and joint protectors. Irish linen wrap was available for $20 extra, except for the MJ-JB-CHAR, which had standard Irish linen wrap. Extra shafts were available for $50 each. The Majestic was offered in a choice of stain colors: burgundy, blue, purple, brown, black, and charcoal gray.

Level 2 MJ Series (MJ-BRW shown) - Stained bird's-eye maple one-piece butt with a maple checked black ring above butt cap. Available in burgundy, blue, purple, red, brown, black, charcoal grey.

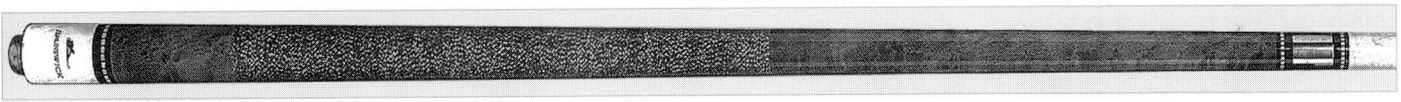

MSR (1996) $130	$100	$95	$60

Level 2 MJ-JB-CHAR - Charcoal stained bird's-eye maple forearm with a joint above the wrap to break down into a jump cue, charcoal stained bird's-eye maple butt sleeve with a maple checked black ring above butt cap.

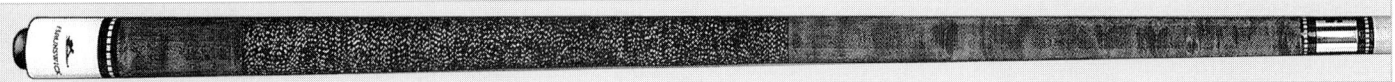

MSR (1996) $150	$125	$95	$80

EWA MATAYA LAWRENCE SERIES

The following Ewa Mataya Lawrence Series cues featured 3/8-10 flat-faced wood to wood joints and standard leather wraps. These cues each featured a unique interchangeable weight bolt system, allowing for custom weighting from 18 to 21 ounces. Extra weight bolts cost $5.00 each. Each cue came with one shaft. Extra shafts were available for $90.

Level 2 EWA-1 - Cocobolo forearm, cocobolo butt sleeve.

MSR (1999) $252	$200	$160	$100

Level 4 EWA-2 - Bird's-eye maple forearm, four ebony points with two black dots set in a hardwood inlay within an intricate white window in each point, bird's-eye maple butt sleeve with four pairs of black dots each set in hardwood inlays within four intricate white windows.

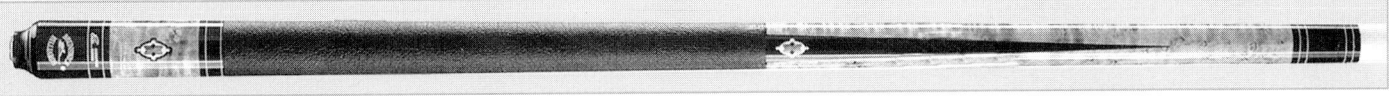

MSR (1999) $394	$300	$260	$200

Level 4 EWA-3 - Bird's-eye maple forearm, four intricate floating cocobolo points with two colored veneers above intricate ebony bordered two-piece cocobolo "S"-shaped scroll inlays, black butt sleeve with four intricate ebony bordered two-piece cocobolo "S"-shaped scroll inlays.

MSR (1999) $683	$500	$425	$300

JIMMY CARAS SERIES

The following Jimmy Caras Series cues featured piloted stainless steel joints engraved with the Brunswick logo and Irish linen wraps. These cues each featured a unique interchangeable weight bolt system, allowing for custom weighting from 18 to 21 ounces. Extra weight bolts were $3.00 each. Each cue came with one shaft, except for the JC-4 which comes with two. Extra shafts were available for $85 each.

GRADING	98%	90%	70%

Level 4 JC-1 - Maple forearm, four ebony points with a white diamond-shaped inlay in each, maple butt sleeve with four maple- and ebony-bordered intricate ebony diamond-shaped inlays between an ebony ring at top and bottom.

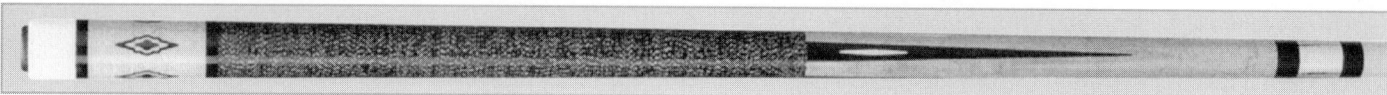

MSR (1999) $360	$285	$235	$175

Level 4 JC-2 - Stained bird's-eye maple forearm, six ebony points with a white diamond-shaped inlay in each, ebony butt sleeve with six white oval shaped inlays alternating above and below an intricate maple ring.

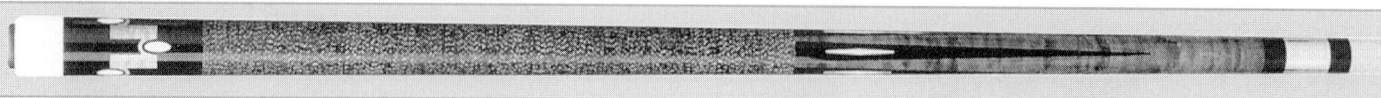

MSR (1999) $460	$365	$300	$225

Level 4 JC-3 - Stained bird's-eye maple forearm, four intricate black bordered floating white maple points alternating with four intricate black bordered white maple arrowhead shaped inlays, ebony butt sleeve with four bocote notched diamond-shaped inlays within rows of four white diamond-shaped inlays between rows of four intricate bocote checks above and below.

MSR (1999) $575	$425	$345	$285

Level 4 JC-4 - Stained bird's-eye maple forearm, four intricate black bordered floating bocote points with a white diamond-shaped inlay in each above an intricate black bordered bocote crown shaped inlay, ebony butt sleeve with four intricately black bordered white rectangles set in bocote windows alternating with four white diamond-shaped inlays between rows of white checks above and below. (Included 2 shafts, deluxe leather case, and a certificate of authenticity personally signed by Jimmy Caras. Each cue is numbered 001 to 200 on the joint.)

MSR (1999) $1200	$1000	$775	$500

CORVETTE SERIES

The following Corvette Series cues featured piloted stainless steel joints and Irish linen wraps. These cues each featured a uniquely interchangeable weight bolt system, allowing for custom weighting from 18 to 21 ounces. Extra weight bolts were $3.00 each. Corvette Series cues came with a nylon case embroidered with an emblem matching the one that appears on the butt sleeve. Each cue came with one shaft; extra shafts were available for $85 each.

Level 2 1995 - Stained maple forearm with the applied image of a yellow 1995 Corvette ZR-1, stained maple butt sleeve with the applied image of the Chevrolet Corvette ZR-1 emblem.

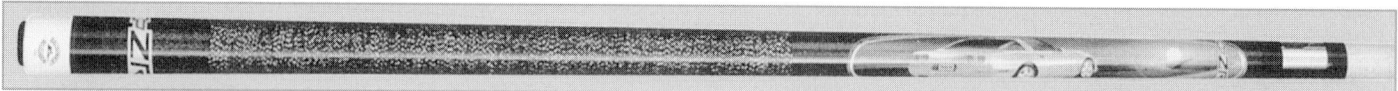

MSR (1999) $265	$200	$165	$135

Level 2 1967 - Stained maple forearm with the applied image of a light blue 1967 Corvette, stained maple butt sleeve with the applied image of the crossed flags emblem.

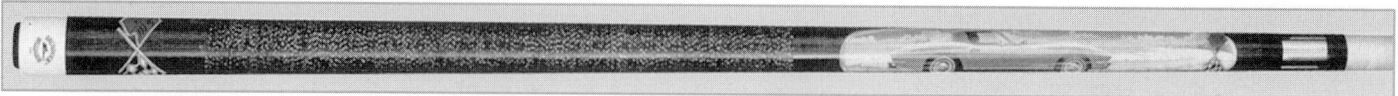

MSR (1999) $265	$200	$170	$135

Level 2 1953 - Stained maple forearm with the applied image of a white 1953 Corvette, stained maple butt sleeve with the applied image of the Chevrolet Corvette crossed flags emblem.

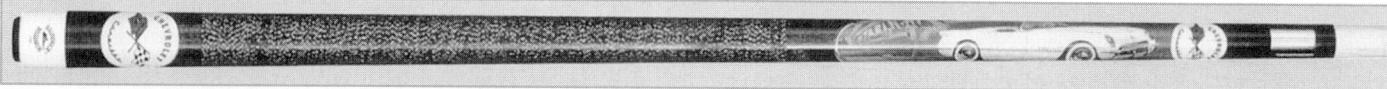

MSR (1999) $265	$200	$170	$135

BRUNSWICK BILLIARDS, cont. 193

GRADING	98%	90%	70%

MAGNUM SERIES

The following Magnum Series cues featured piloted stainless steel joints with plain black collars and Irish linen wraps. These cues each featured a uniquely designed interchangeable weight bolt system, accessible by removing the threaded bumper, allowing for custom weighting from 18 to 21 ounces. Extra weight bolts were available for $3.00 each. Each cue came with one shaft featuring an Aegis ferrule. Extra shafts were available for $85 each.

Level 2 MAG-1 - Stained bird's-eye maple forearm, stained bird's-eye maple butt sleeve.

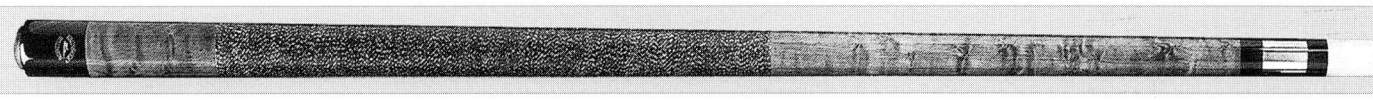

MSR (1999) $189	$145	$120	$90

Level 2 MAG-2 - Light charcoal stained bird's-eye maple forearm, ebony butt sleeve with four large hollow bocote diamond-shaped inlays alternating with four pairs of green dashes.

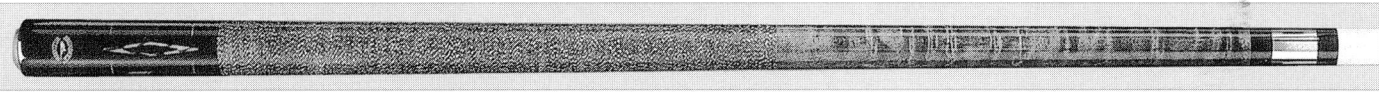

MSR (1999) $216	$155	$130	$100

Level 2 MAG-3 - Light charcoal stained bird's-eye maple forearm, ebony butt sleeve with four European pearl notched squares between maple rings at top and bottom.

MSR (1999) $242	$170	$145	$120

Level 3 MAG-4 - Stained bird's-eye maple forearm, four ebony points with single veneers, stained bird's-eye maple butt sleeve with four European pearl notched diamond-shaped inlays set in ebony windows over a pair of thin ebony rings.

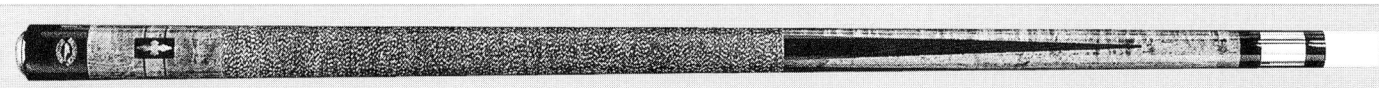

MSR (1999) $357	$250	$220	$195

Level 3 MAG-5 - Stained bird's-eye maple forearm, four bocote points with ebony veneers, bocote butt sleeve with four ebony bordered European pearl diamond-shaped inlays between thin ebony bordered maple rings above and below.

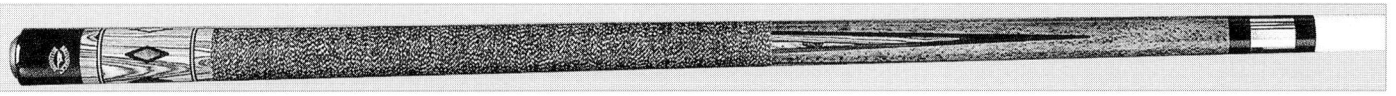

MSR (1999) $410	$285	$245	$200

Level 3 MAG-6 - Stained bird's-eye maple forearm, four ebony- and white-bordered floating purpleheart points, maple butt sleeve with long white diamond-shaped inlays set in purpleheart windows alternating with purpleheart bars between thick purple heart rings at top and bottom.

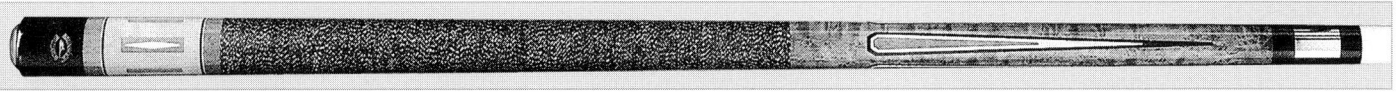

MSR (1999) $462	$325	$280	$225

DIAMOND SERIES

The following Diamond Series cues featured piloted stainless steel joints with plain black collars and Irish linen wraps. These cues each featured a uniquely designed interchangeable weight bolt system, accessible by removing the threaded bumper, allowing for custom weighting from 18 to 21 ounces. Extra weight bolts were available for $3.00 each. Each cue came with one shaft featuring an Aegis ferrule. Extra shafts were available for $85 each.

Level 2 Diamond # 1 - Dark grey-stained maple forearm, dark grey stained maple butt sleeve with six brown-stained maple diamond-shaped inlays.

MSR (1999) $252	$185	$160	$125

GRADING	98%	90%	70%

Level 2 Diamond # 2 - Brown-stained maple forearm, brown-stained maple butt sleeve with six black bordered European pearl diamond-shaped inlays.

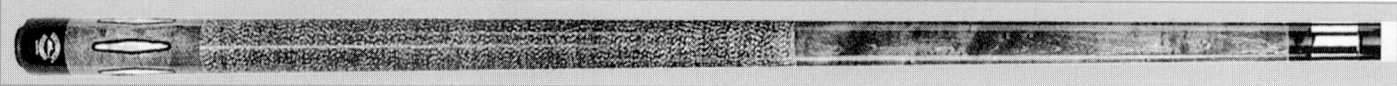

MSR (1999) $258	$190	$165	$125

Level 2 Diamond # 3 - Maple forearm, maple butt sleeve with six cocobolo and maple bordered European pearl diamond-shaped inlays.

 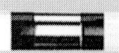

MSR (1999) $263	$195	$170	$135

Level 2 Diamond # 4 - Dark grey-stained maple forearm, black butt sleeve with four white diamond-shaped inlays alternating with four red-bordered European pearl oval-shaped inlays.

MSR (1999) $268	$200	$175	$140

Level 2 Diamond # 5 - Brown-stained maple forearm with three intricate black-bordered white diamond-shaped inlays, brown-stained maple butt sleeve with six intricate white-bordered ebony diamond-shaped inlays.

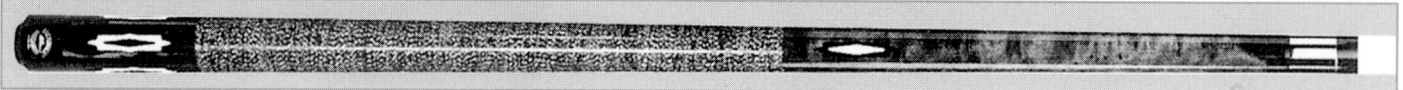

MSR (1999) $273	$205	$180	$140

Level 2 Diamond # 6 - Brown-stained maple forearm with three black bordered European pearl diamond-shaped inlays, black butt sleeve with six white and black-bordered European pearl diamond-shaped inlays.

MSR (1999) $279	$210	$185	$145

OPAL SERIES

The following Opal Series cues featured 3/8-10 flat faced wood to wood joints with plain black collars. They featured a unique interchangeable weight bolt system, allowing for custom weighting from 18 to 21 ounces, with available extra weight bolts available for $3.00 each. Each cue came with one shaft with a 6 in. to 8 in. pro taper. Extra shafts were $90. The cues came with or without linen wraps in a choice of stain colors: red, sapphire blue, silver gray, dark amethyst, topaz, and emerald green.

Level 2 Opal - One-piece stained maple butt; available in ruby red, blue, silver, amethyst, green

MSR (1999) $160	$125	$105	$80

Level 2 Opal-with wrap - Stained maple forearm and butt sleeve, linen wrap. Available in same colors as "opal" above.

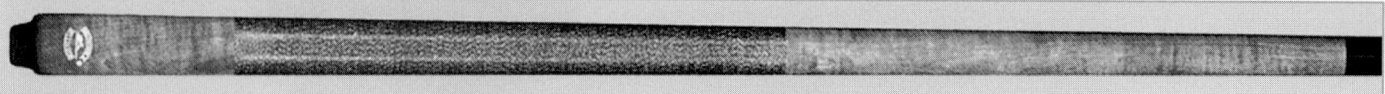

MSR (1999) $180	$150	$125	$90

SECONDARY MARKET MINIMUM VALUES

The following are minimum values for other Brunswick cues encountered on the secondary market.

Note: Due to the rarity of early Brunswick cues (turn-of-the-century era into the 1920s) and increasing interest, prices are on the rise. Fewer original examples are surfacing, and collectors are holding on to the ones they have. Unique examples with pedigree, and cues made for top professional players are bringing the highest prices.

GRADING	98%	90%	70%

Special construction note: There are many materials and construction techniques that can add value to Brunswick cues. The following are the most important examples:

Add 25%+ for early cues with original "Brunswick Balke Collender" decal label.
Add $200+ for ivory joint.
Add $300+ for ivory butt cap.
Add $75+ for each ivory ferrule.
Deduct 50% for pre-1960 cues with modifications, or inappropriate or obvious refinishing.

Level 1 - 4 points, hustler.
Level 1 cues start at $105 $35 $30

Level 2 - 0 points, 0-25 inlays.
Level 2 cues start at $215 $80 $60

Level 3 - 2-6 points, 0-8 inlays.
Level 3 cues start at $365 $125 $85

Level 4 - 4-10 points, 9-25 inlays.
Level 4 cues start at $425 $175 $110

Level 5 - 0-12 points, 26-50 inlays.
Level 5 cues start at $540 $250 $165

Level 6 - 0-12 points, 51-75 inlays.
Level 6 cues start at $775 $325 $215

SPECIAL INTEREST CUES: BRUNSWICK BALKE COLLENDER MODELS C. PRE-1900

The following Brunswick Balke Collender cues were popular one-piece cues from the latter half of the 1800s. Hardwoods encountered are usually rosewood or ebony, but cocobolo, amaranth, mahogany, sabacue, coraline, zebrawood, dagaine, and sapote were also used. Butterfly spliced cues were referred to as "Vignaux" style, while pointed spliced cues were referred to as "Berger" style. The names were references to popular players of the time that used each type of cue. All valuations assuming original condition.

Level 3 "No. 10" - One-piece maple shaft and forearm, two full-spliced hardwood butterfly points and butt sleeve.

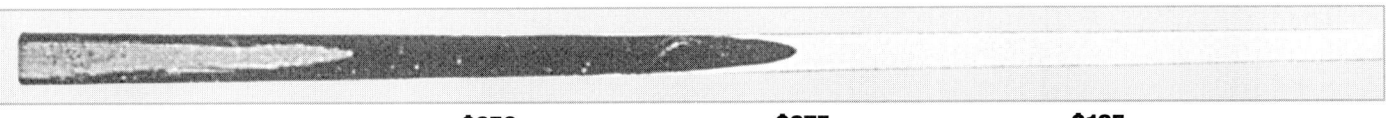

            $650 $375 $185

Level 3 "No. 11" - One-piece maple shaft and forearm, two full-spliced hardwood butterfly points and butt sleeve with a turned handle.

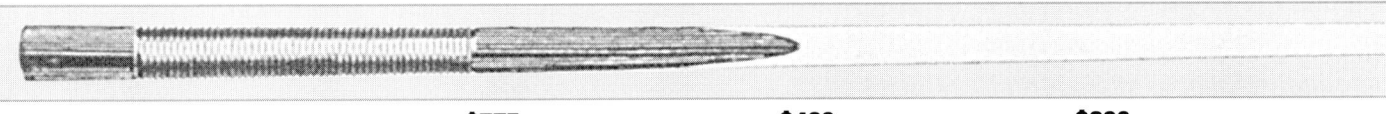

            $775 $420 $200

Level 3 "No. 12" - One-piece maple shaft and forearm, two full-spliced hardwood butterfly points and butt sleeve with a hammered handle.

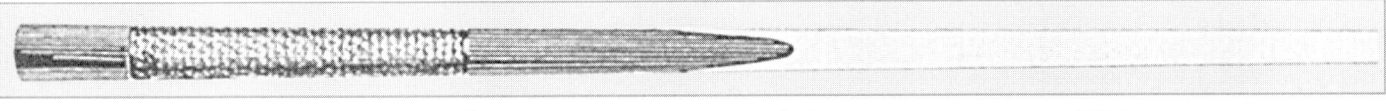

            $815 $410 $200

Level 3 "No. 13" - One-piece maple shaft and forearm, two full-spliced hardwood butterfly points and butt sleeve with a fluted handle.

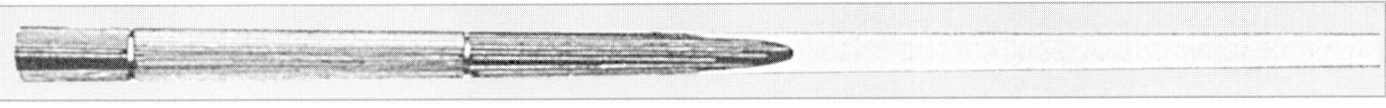

            $775 $420 $265

Level 3 "No. 14" - One-piece maple shaft and forearm, two full-spliced hardwood butterfly points and butt sleeve with a corrugated handle.

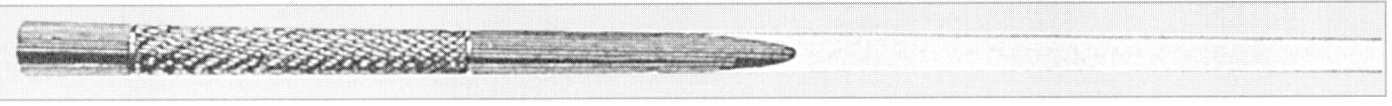

            $850 $465 $255

| GRADING | 98% | 90% | 70% |

Level 3 "No. 15" - One-piece maple shaft and forearm, two full-spliced hardwood butterfly points and butt sleeve with a spiral handle.

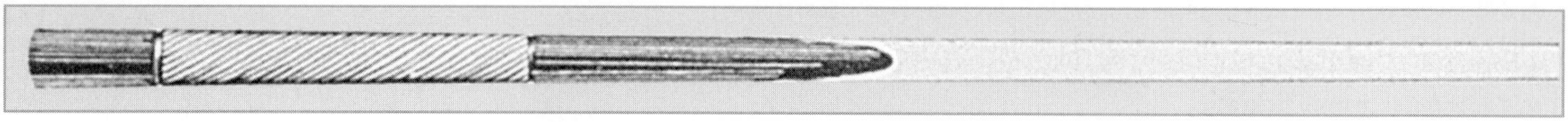

$800 $450 $215

Level 3 "No. 16" - One-piece maple shaft and forearm, two full-spliced hardwood butterfly points and butt sleeve with a checkered handle.

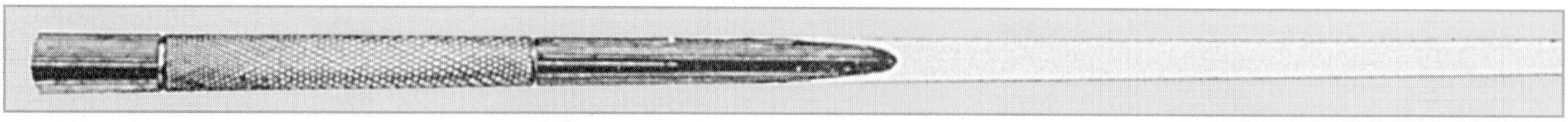

$800 $415 $265

Level 3 "No. 20" - One-piece maple shaft and forearm, four full-spliced hardwood points and butt sleeve.

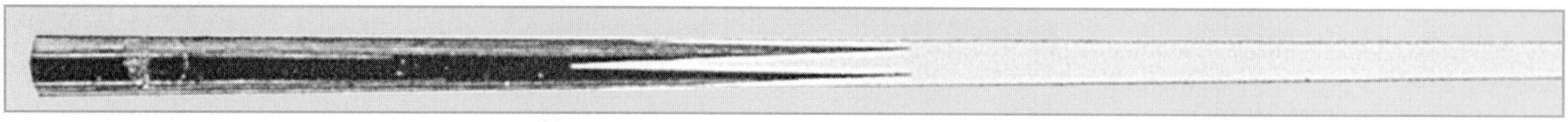

$875 $500 $285

Level 3 "No. 21" - One-piece maple shaft and forearm, four full-spliced hardwood points and butt sleeve with a turned handle.

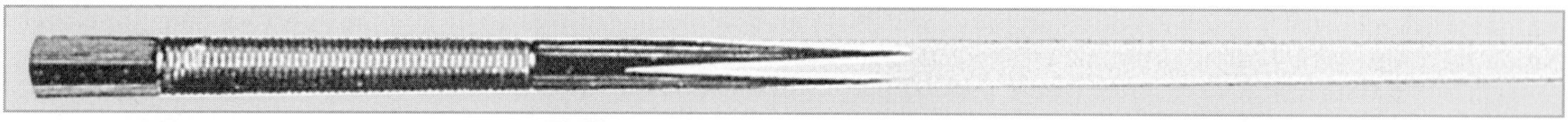

$975 $465 $285

Level 3 "No. 22" - One-piece maple shaft and forearm, four full-spliced hardwood points and butt sleeve with a hammered handle.

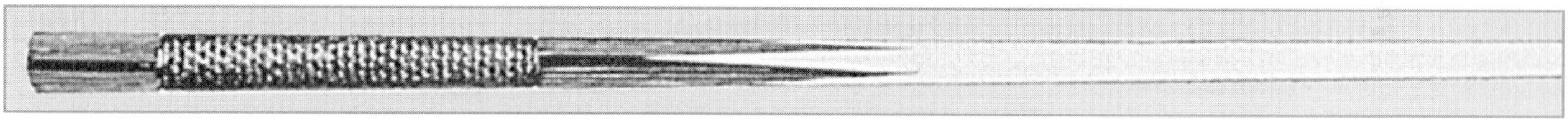

$950 $475 $285

Level 3 "No. 23" - One-piece maple shaft and forearm, four full-spliced hardwood points and butt sleeve with a fluted handle.

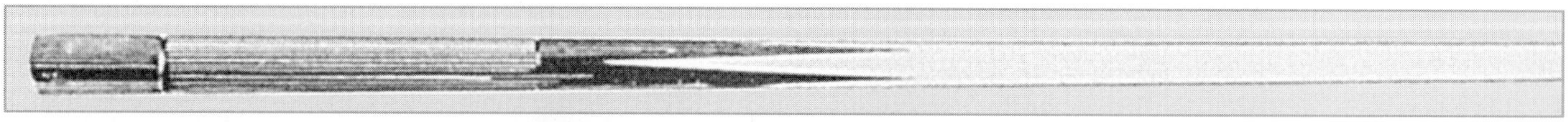

$965 $485 $305

Level 3 "No. 24" - One-piece maple shaft and forearm, four full-spliced hardwood points and butt sleeve with a corrugated handle.

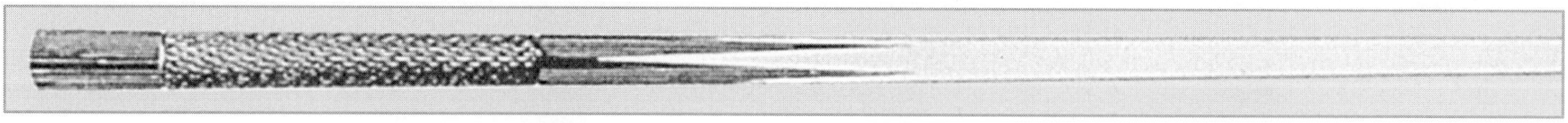

$950 $470 $295

Level 3 "No. 25" - One-piece maple shaft and forearm, four full-spliced hardwood points and butt sleeve with a spiral handle.

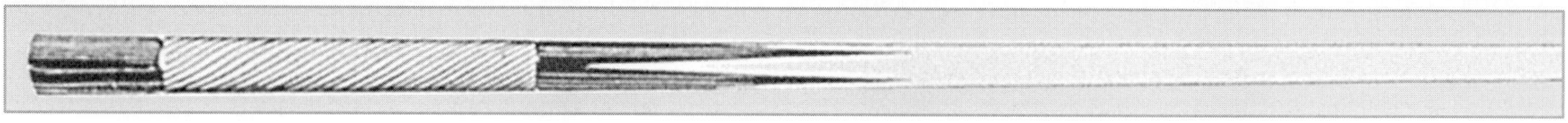

$945 $475 $325

Level 3 "No. 26" - One piece maple shaft and forearm, four full-spliced hardwood points and butt sleeve with a checkered handle.

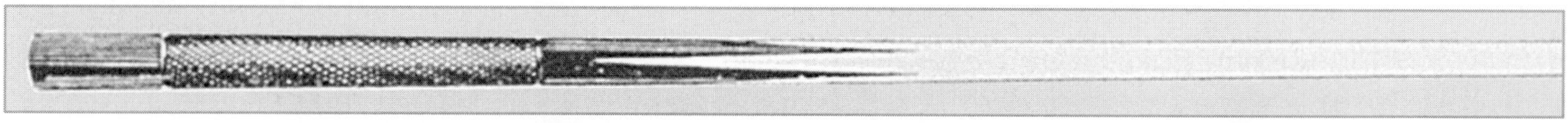

$985 $475 $325

GRADING	98%	90%	70%

Level 3 "No. 27" - One piece maple shaft and forearm, four full-spliced hardwood points and butt sleeve with a Chinese style carved handle.

$1,250 $800 $500

Level 3 "No. 30" - One piece maple shaft and forearm, four full-spliced hardwood points with four veneers above two butterfly spliced hardwood points and butt sleeve with three veneers.

$1,850 $1,200 $800

Level 3 "No. 31" - One piece maple shaft and forearm, four full-spliced hardwood points butt sleeve.

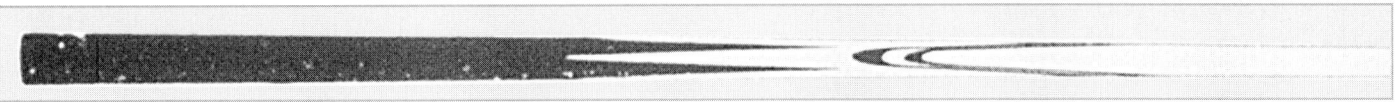

$2,250 $1,550 $1,100

SPECIAL INTEREST CUES: BRUNSWICK MODELS C. 1912 - 1929

Most two-piece cues of this era had a long brass pin in the shaft screwing directly into wood with an ivory collar. Cues that started as one-piece cues often had joints added to convert them to two-piece cues. Cues were available unwrapped or in a choice of wraps (eg. silk or linen twine) for a small additional charge.

Level 2 (No. 28) "Merry Widow" - Rosewood shaft with two butterfly spliced maple points and ivory ferrule, ivory joint, rosewood forearm, silk wrap, rosewood butt sleeve with original "Brunswick Balke Collender" decal at bottom.

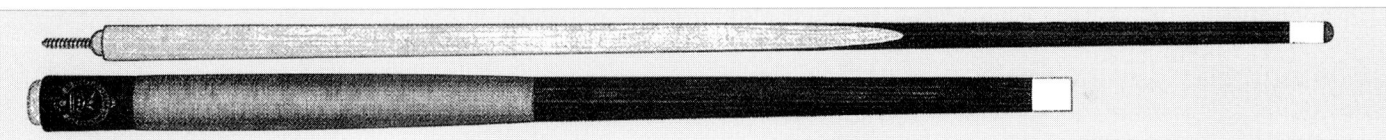

MSR (1915) $5.25 $2,500 $1,500 $1,050

Level 2 "Hub Cue" - Bell shaped ivory ferrule, ivory joint, ebony or rosewood forearm with ivory joint above wrap, ebony or rosewood butt sleeve with original "Brunswick Balke Collender" decal at bottom, ivory butt cap.

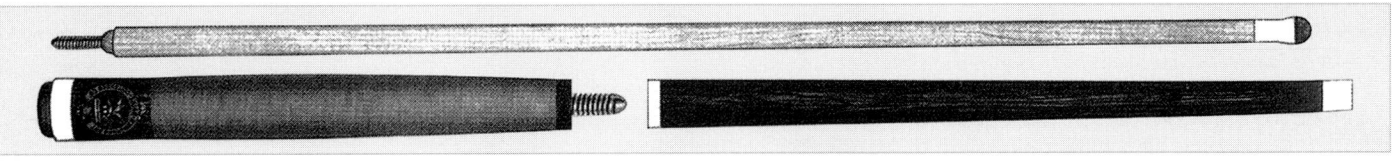

$5,700 $3,850 $2,500

Level 1 "Model 26-1/2" - One-piece maple front, four rosewood points and butt sleeve with two veneers on points and original "Brunswick Balke Collender" decal at bottom.

MSR (1914) $2.75 $4,750 $3,450 $2,700

Level 8 "Model 36" - One-piece ebony front with ivory ferrule, four series of four full-spliced ebony points with two veneers and inlaid rainbow shaped colored veneers between points, ebony butt sleeve with triangular mother-of-pearl name plate with two veneers and original "Brunswick Balke Collender" decal at bottom.

MSR (1915) $10.00 $13,500 $7,500 $3,500

GRADING	98%	90%	70%

Level 1 "Model 204" - Rosewood shaft with two butterfly-spliced maple points and ivory ferrule, ivory joint, four rosewood points, silk wrap, rosewood butt sleeve with original "Brunswick Balke Collender" decal.

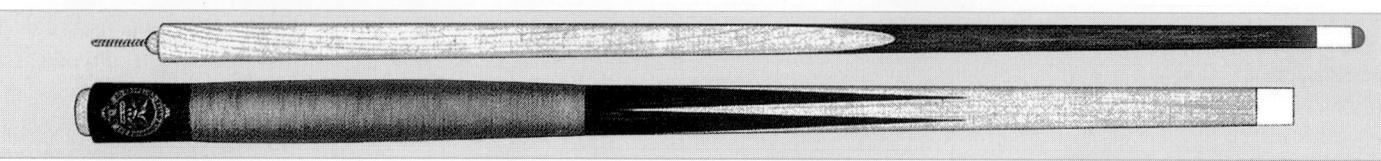

MSR (1915) $4.25	$2,200	$1,250	$800

Level 1 "Model 205 - Eisenmeister" - Spliced maple and hardwood shaft with ivory ferrule, four exotic hardwood points and butt sleeve with original "Brunswick Balke Collender" decal at bottom, ivory ferrule, braided "Eisenmeister" wrap.

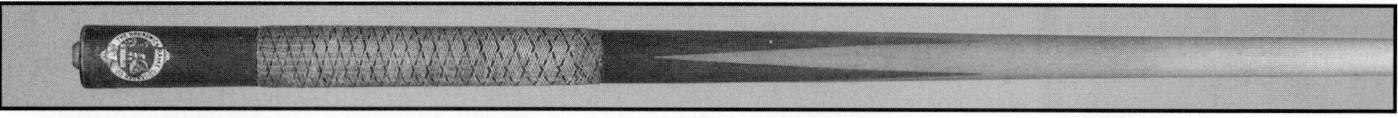

MSR (1916) $4.50	$1000	$550-800	$400

Level 8 "Model 360" - Ebony - Ebony shaft with ivory ferrule and a pair of full-spliced ebony points with two veneers and inlaid rainbow-shaped colored veneers between points spliced into double maple butterfly points, ivory joint rings in shaft and butt, four series of four full-spliced ebony points with two veneers and inlaid rainbow-shaped colored veneers between points, ebony butt sleeve with triangular mother-of-pearl name plate with two veneers and original Brunswok-Balke-Collener red and gold decal .

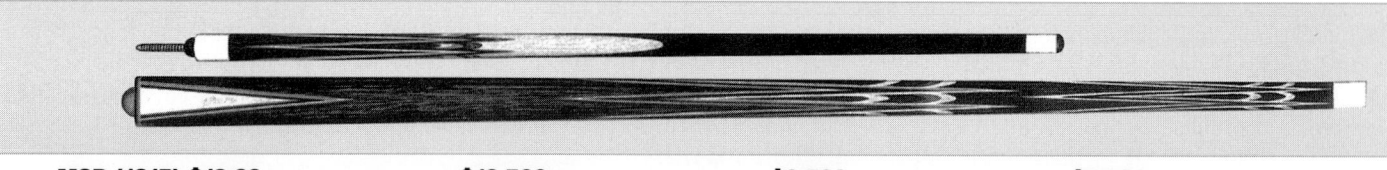

MSR (1915) $13.00	$12,500	$9,500	$6,500

SPECIAL INTEREST CUES: BRUNSWICK BALKE COLLENDER MODELS C. 1950 - 1965

The following Brunswick Balke Collender Cues were popular models from before WWII until the 1960s. Hardwoods encountered are usually rosewood or ebony, but other hardwoods were used.

For all used early Brunswick cues:
  Add 20%+ for each additional original straight playable shaft (standard with one).
  Deduct 40%+ for missing original straight playable shaft.

For all used other early used Brunswick cues, except where otherwise noted:
  Add $50+ for each additional original straight playable shaft (standard with one).
  Add $200+ for leather wrap.
  Deduct 50% for obvious or improper refinish.

Level 3 "Challenger" - Black fiber ferrule, one-piece maple shaft and forearm, four full-spliced hardwood points and butt sleeve with "Brunswick CHALLENGER" decal at bottom.

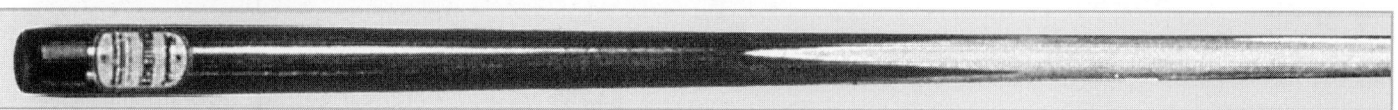

MSR (1950) $2.45	$400	$235	$165

Level 3 "Tru-Balance" - Buck horn ferrule, one-piece maple shaft and forearm, four full-spliced hardwood points and butt sleeve with "Brunswick TRU BALANCE" decal at bottom.

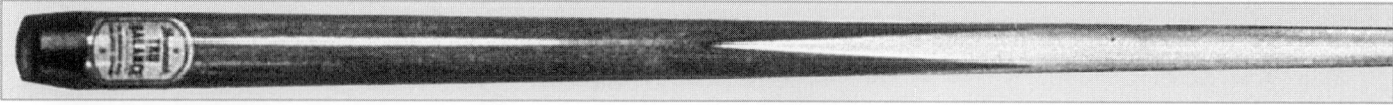

MSR (1950) $3.10	$375	$275	$175

Level 3 "Willie Hoppe Titlist" - Buck horn ferrule, one-piece maple shaft and forearm, four full-spliced hardwood points and butt sleeve with four colored veneers and green "Brunswick Willie Hoppe TITLIST CUE" decal at bottom, large rubber bumper. (Also availavble as a two-piece cue.)

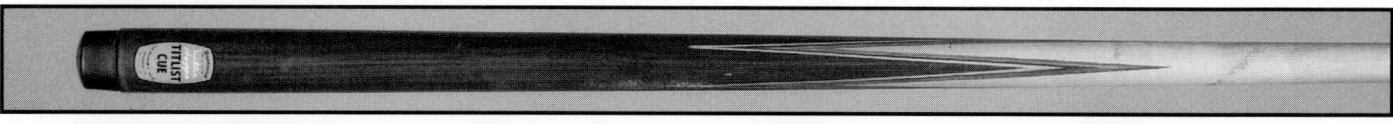

MSR (1950) $5.50	$500	$400	$250

GRADING	98%	90%	70%

"Master Stroke" - Maple forearm, four full-spliced hardwood points, ivory ferrule, leather wrap, hardwood butt sleeve with "Brunswick MASTER STROKE" decal at bottom. Also available as a one-piece cue.

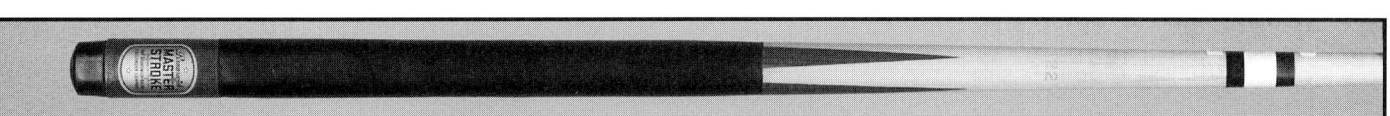

| MSR (1950) $8.95 | $550 | $400 | $285 |

Level 3 "Willie Hoppe Professional Cue" c. 1940's - Ivory ferrule, maple Titlist forearm, four full-spliced hardwood points with four colored veneers, black leather wrap, hardwood butt sleeve with light blue "Brunswick Willie Hoppe PROFESSIONAL CUE" decal above ivory "Hoppe" ring and thin black butt plate, large black rubber bumper.

| | $1,050 | $800 | $475 |

Level 3 "Willie Hoppe Professional Cue" c. 1950 - Ivory ferrule, maple Titlist forearm, four full-spliced hardwood points with four colored veneers, black leather wrap, hardwood butt sleeve with light blue "Brunswick Willie Hoppe PROFESSIONAL CUE" decal above thin black butt plate (no bumper).

| MSR (1950) $13.95 | $950 | $700 | $450 |

BRYLES CUES

Maker of pool cues in Delta, Pennsylvania.

If you have a Bryles cue that needs further identification or repair, or would like to order a new Bryles cue, contact Bryles Cues, listed in the Trademark Index.

BOB BURGOYNE

Maker of Q Works cues. Refer to listing for Q Works for information.

GEORGE BUSS

Refer to listing for GB Custom Cues

JIM BUSS CUSTOM CUES

Maker of pool cues from 1986 to 1997 in Houston, Texas, and from 1997 to present in Overland, Missouri.

Jim Buss was born on November 23, 1942 in Boone, Iowa. His father loved woodworking, and he completely remodeled the house, added rooms, built furniture, etc. He also made custom cabinets for some of the more affluent homes in town. Jim picked up his father's love of woodworking and enjoyed trying his hand at many of his own projects. Jim enjoyed designing his project, planning how to make it, and then making it. What he didn't enjoy was sanding the wood in preparation for a finish. When Jim was in high school, he discovered the wood lathe. This gave him a whole new perspective on the art of woodworking.

Present Day

Jim Buss

Jim had other hobbies at that time. He enjoyed being a ham radio operator and a photographer. He also enjoyed camping and was active in Boy Scouts, attaining the rank of Eagle Scout with a Bronze Palm.

In 1961 Jim finished high school and started college at Iowa State University, in Ames. His love of electronics guided him into selecting electrical engineering as his major.

Jim got introduced to the game of pool on his first day at Iowa State. While in the student union, he heard the sound of someone breaking a rack of balls and wondered what that wonderful sound was. This was a life-changing experience, as pool has ruled his life ever since.

Jim's first cue was a Hoppe Cue sold by Brunswick. One day he decided to modify his cue and he drilled some holes in his stick and glued in some rhinestones. By today's standards, that would look pretty tacky—but it was pretty enough that someone stole it!

Jim began working with cues that had been thrown in the trash at a pool hall. He would take them home and cut them apart. He was trying to figure out how the cues were made. He realized that it was a very complex procedure, and one that Jim thought he would never be able to do. Making a cue required machinery that Jim had never used before.

Jim graduated as an electrical engineer and began working for McDonnel Aircraft Company. His first assignment was to design an umbilical cable for one of the Gemini astronauts for doing a space walk. From this assignment, he went on to design the power distribution system for the Skylab program. After that, he was assigned to work on classified Air Force Space Systems.

Jim had to move to Sunnyvale, California for his new Air Force project. On a day off, he drove to North Hollywood and met cue maker Bert Schrager, who had agreed to put a new ferrule on Jim's cue. Jim watched Bert work on a metal lathe and got a tour of Bert's machine shop. At that point, Jim knew that he definitely wanted to be able to make cues some day. But that "someday" was still over ten years away.

In 1982, Jim moved to Houston, Texas to do support work for NASA and the space shuttle program. He still had dreams about making cues but realized that it was a very complicated job. He set a goal for himself: that he would be making cues that pro players would like to use by the time he could retire. This was nine years away. Within one year, he was realizing his dream, and a local pro player was using one of his cues. He was eight years ahead of his goal.

Since that time, Jim has been experimenting with cue making, creating more and more complicated designs, and pushing himself to perfect his techniques and to develop new ones.

In July of 1994, Jim was elected President of the American Cuemaker's Association. A few years later, he moved back to the Midwest, to the St. Louis area, to make cues as a full-time job. Jim was offered a job with Boeing that he couldn't refuse, so he now has two jobs and could not be happier. He has an 8 to 4:30 weekday job with Boeing. He works evenings, Saturdays, and Sundays building cues. Jim plans to retire from Boeing soon to become a full-time cue maker once again.

Although he shares his shop with his brother George, they both make cues entirely on their own, with no work being shared. Jim makes everything on his cues except for the tips, bumpers and screws. He makes his one-of-a-kind cues one at a time, instead of in batches, and he takes many extra steps to ensure that everything is done right. Although the early Jim Buss cues are unmarked, Jim started signing and dating all of his cues, including his hustler cues, in 1993. He will make a cue to any specification the customer desires and can make any common joint type they request at no additional charge. He was one of a few cuemakers to be invited to make a cue to be put on display at the Smithsonian in 1999.

If you order a custom Jim Buss cue and are unhappy with it when it arrives, you can return it for a full refund, minus shipping. Jim Buss cues are guaranteed indefinitely against construction defects that are not the result of warpage or abuse, and Jim will replace the cue, if necessary. If you have a Jim Buss cue that needs further identification or repair, or would like to talk to Jim about ordering a new cue, contact Jim Buss Custom Cues, which is listed in the trademark index.

SPECIFICATIONS

Butt material: hardwoods
Shaft material: rock maple
Standard length: 58 in.
Lengths available: any up to 62 in.
Standard finish: high-gloss acrylic urethane
Joint screw threads: radial, 3/8-10, or 5/16-14?
Standard joint: phenolic or stainless
Balance point: custom
Point construction: short splice
Standard wrap: Irish linen
Standard butt cap: phenolic
Standard number of shafts: two
Standard taper: 8-10 in. pro
Standard ferrules: linen-based melamine
Standard tip width: 13 mm
Tip widths available: any
Standard tip: Le Pro
Annual production: fewer than 75 cues

OPTIONS (FOR NEW CUES ONLY)

Leather wrap: $100+
Ivory joint: $150
Ivory butt cap: $250
Ivory ferrule: $75
Ivory butt sleeve: $1,000+
Ivory points: $300+ each

GRADING	100%	95%	70%

Ivory ferrule: $75
Ivory butt sleeve: $1,000+
Ivory points: $300+ each
Extra shaft: $125
Special lengths: $50+
Joint protectors: $250+
Layered tip: $15-30

REPAIRS

Repairs done on all fine American-made cues.
Refinish (with leather wrap): $200
Refinish (with Irish linen wrap): $125
Rewrap (leather): $125
Rewrap (linen): $40
Replace butt cap: $50+
Replace ivory butt cap: $250
Replace shaft: $125+
Replace ferrule: $20
Replace ivory ferrule: $85
Replace tip: $10+
Replace layered tip: $15-30

CURRENT JIM BUSS CUES

Jim Buss makes two-piece huster cues with one shaft that start at $400. Basic Jim Buss cues with a wraps and joint rings start at $800. Jim Buss cues with points start at $900.

CURRENT JIM BUSS EXAMPLES

The following cues can be ordered as shown, or modified to suit the desires of the customer.

Level 1 - Purple heart joint, maple forearm, four tulipwood points and handle with segmented purple heart rings above a tulipwood ring at bottom.

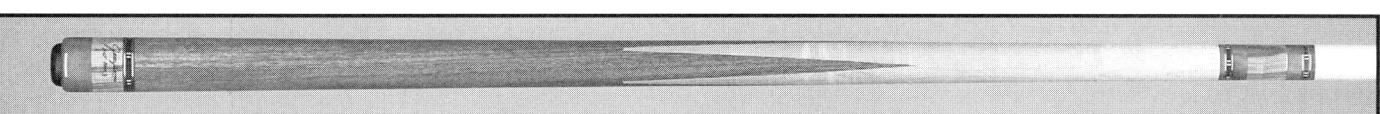

MSR	$800	$750-850	$615	$450

Level 2 - Purple heart joint, tulipwood forearm with a segmented purple heart ring above handle, purple heart handle, tulipwood butt sleeve with segmented purple heart rings at top and bottom.

MSR	$800	$750-850	$615	$450

Level 3 - Cocobolo joint, bird's-eye maple forearm with a cocobolo ring set within metal rings above wrap, four cocoblo points with four colored veneers, brown leather wrap, cocobolo butt sleeve with cocobolo rings set within metal rings at top and bottom.

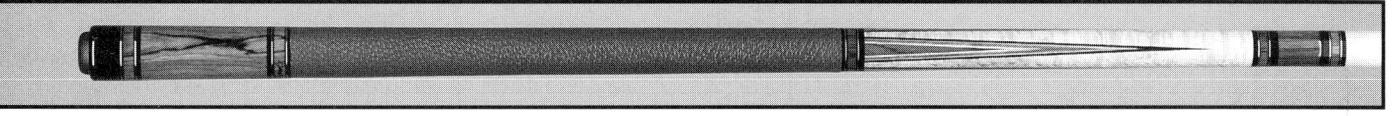

MSR	$950	$900-1,000	$725	$500

Level 3 - Desert ironwood joint, bird's-eye maple forearm with a desert ironwood ring set within brass rings set in black rings above wrap, four long desert ironwood points with four colored veneers alternating with four short desert ironwood points with a desert ironwood bordered maple arrowhead shaped inlay at the tip of each, desert ironwood butt sleeve with desert ironwood rings set within brass rings set in black rings at top and bottom.

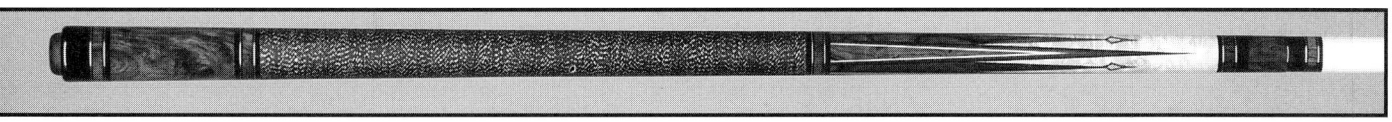

MSR	$1,600	$1,500-1,650	$1,200	$850

202 JIM BUSS CUSTOM CUES, cont.

GRADING	100%	95%	70%

Level 3 - Bird's-eye maple forearm with a desert ironwood ring set within brass rings set in black rings above wrap, four long desert ironwood points with four colored veneers alternating with four short ebony points, ebony butt sleeve with desert ironwood windows set between desert ironwood rings set within brass rings set in black rings at top and bottom.

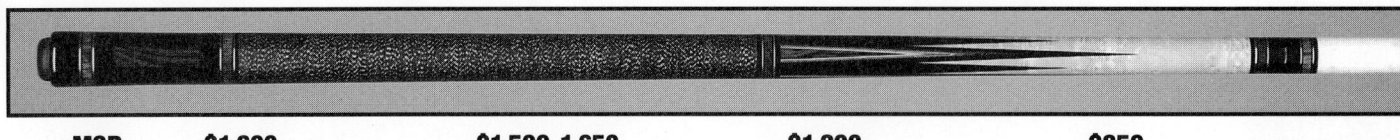

MSR	$1,600	$1,500-1,650	$1,200	$850

Level 4 - Pink ivory joint, ebony forearm with a pink ivory ring set within brass rings set in black rings above wrap, four long ebony points with four pink ivory and ebony veneers and a pink ivory spear-shaped inlay at the tip of each alternating with four short pink ivory points with a pink ivory-bordered ebony spear-shaped inlay at the tip of each, ebony butt sleeve with pink ivory and ebony inlays set between pink ivory rings set within brass rings set in black rings at top and bottom.

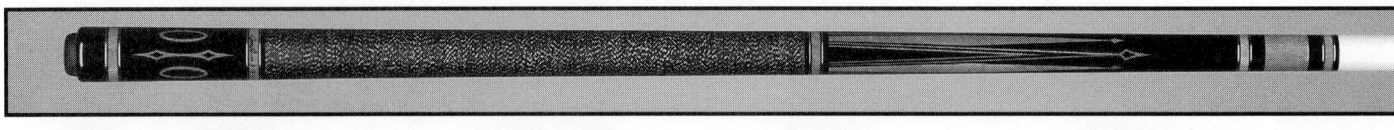

MSR	$2,000	$1,800-2,150	$1,550	$1,100

Level 5 - Bird's-eye maple forearm with a segmented purple heart ring set within brass rings set in black rings above wrap, four long ebony points with ebony bordered ivory spear-shaped inlay at the tip of each alternating with four short curly purple heart points, ebony butt sleeve with ivory and purple heart inlays set between purple heart rings set within brass rings set in black rings at top and bottom.

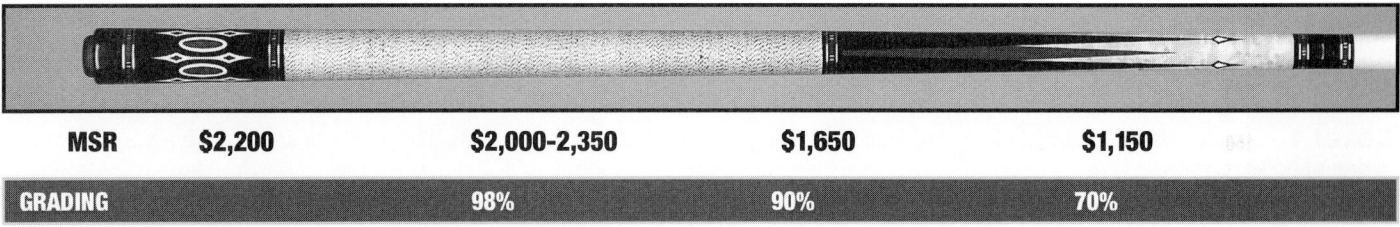

MSR	$2,200	$2,000-2,350	$1,650	$1,150

GRADING	98%	90%	70%

SECONDARY MARKET MINIMUM VALUES

The following are minimum prices for Jim Buss cues encountered on the secondary market. These prices are representative of cues using basic materials and designs that may not be currently available. Jim also offers one-of-a-kind cues that can command many times these prices due to the use of exotic materials and artistry.

Special construction note: There are many materials and construction techniques that can add value to Jim Buss cues. The following are the most important examples:

Add $200+ for each ivory joint.

For all used Jim Buss cues:

Add $75+ for each additional original straight playable shaft (standard with two).
Deduct $100 for each missing original straight playable shaft.
Add $100+ for ivory joint.
Add $50+ for leather wrap.
Add $50 for each ivory ferrule.
Deduct 25% for obvious or improper refinish.

Level 1 - 4 points, hustler.
Level 1 cues start at	$300	$185	$130

Level 2 - 0 points, 0-25 inlays.
Level 2 cues start at	$650	$515	$335

Level 3 - 2-6 points, 0-8 inlays.
Level 3 cues start at	$700	$550	$375

Level 4 - 4-10 points, 9-25 inlays.
Level 4 cues start at	$1,100	$845	$600

Level 5 - 0-12 points, 26-50 inlays.
Level 5 cues start at	$1,500	$1,275	$900

Level 6 - 0-12 points, 51-75 inlays.
Level 6 cues start at	$2,200	$1,700	$1,150

| GRADING | 98% | 90% | 70% |

CHRIS BYRNE CUSTOM CUES

Maker of pool cues from 1994 to present in Englewood, Colorado.

Chris Byrne of Englewood, Colorado has been making cues since 1994. Originally from Atlanta, Georgia, Chris started making cues as a hobby after moving to Colorado and meeting a friend who had a metal lathe. While playing in the Colorado State Games, Chris met Dan Breggin of Colorado Cues. After showing Dan his cues and talking throughout the tournament, they became friends. Dan hired Chris to help build cues in his shop, and this experience helped Chris in his cuemaking abilities. Chris also learned a lot from Leonard Bludworth.

Chris Byrne has developed his own cue-building style, after getting valuable advice from Dan and Leonard. He is now building cues in a newly renovated 1200-square-foot shop. The shop is outfitted with all modern equipment, with the exception of a 1942 Groton pantograph. Most of the equipment used is hand-built by Chris himself. Chris makes about 20 cues a year, and they are all special orders. You can identify Chris's cues by a styleized "cb" logo on the butt cap. Playability is of the utmost importance in his cues, and he also strives for perfection in all aspects of construction and finishing. Chris Byrne Cues are guaranteed for life against manufacturing defects that are not the result of warpage or abuse.

If you have a Chris Byrne cue that needs further identification or repair, or would like to talk to Chris about the design and specifications you have in mind for a custom-made cue, contact Chris Byrne Custom Cues, listed in the trademark index.

SPECIFICATIONS

Butt material: hardwoods
Shaft material: rock maple
Standard length: 59 in.
Standard butt cap: phenolic
Standard joints: phenolic
Standard wrap: Irish linen
Standard ferrule: melamine
Annual production: approximately 20 cues

OPTIONS FOR NEW CUES

Ivory ferrule: $50
Ivory joint: $150
Ivory butt cap: $225
Leather wrap: $75
Extra Shaft: $100

REPAIRS:

Repair prices are based on the condition of the cue.

CURRENT CHRIS BYRNE CUES

Basic two-piece Chris Byrne hustler cues start at $225. Basic two-piece Chris Byrne cues with wraps and joint rings start at $400. Chris Byrne cues with points start at $550. One-of-a-kind custom Chris Byrne cues start at $850.

SECONDARY MARKET MINIMUM VALUES

The following are minimum values for other Chris Byrne cues encountered on the secondary market. These prices are representative of cues using basic materials and designs that are not necessarily available at present. Chris has offered one-of-a-kind cues that can command many times these prices due to the use of exotic materials and artistry.

Special construction note: There are many materials and construction techniques that can add value to Chris Byrne cues.

For all used Chris Byrne cues, except where otherwise noted:
- Add $75 for each additional original straight playable shaft beyond one.
- Deduct $100 for missing original straight playable shaft.
- Add $40 each for ivory ferrules.
- Add $50 for leather wrap.
- Deduct 20% for obvious or improper refinish.

Level 1 - Hustler.
	98%	90%	70%
Level 1 cues start at	$200	$160	$110

Level 2 - 0 points, 0-25 inlays.
Level 2 cues start at	$350	$470	$185

Level 3 - 2-6 points, 0-8 inlays.
Level 3 cues start at	$500	$385	$260

Level 4 - 4-10 points, 9-25 inlays.
Level 4 cues start at	$650	$500	$335

Level 5 - 0-12 points, 26-50 inlays.
Level 5 cues start at	$850	$665	$450

NOTES

CADILLAC CUSTOM CUES

Maker of pool cues from 1971 to present in Wilmington, Delaware.

Joe Mazlewski began making cues in Wilmington, Delaware in 1971. He had his own Paradise cue repaired several times, and he thought he could do a better job at repairing it. He started buying equipment in 1970 when cuemaking equipment was more difficult to get. Joe's father had watched Frank Paradise and his helpers work in his shop, and taught him how the equipment was set up and how to go about making the cues. Joe still makes everything by hand, without the aid of CNC. He makes every component except for the tip, the screws, and the bumper. Cadillac cues tend to feature more traditional simple designs, and no two cues are exactly alike. Early Cadillac cues were 57 inches, but Joe increased the length to 58 inches in the eighties.

Joe doesn't take many orders any more as his production has slowed down and he is doing a lot of repair work and restorations on antique cues. He has a large stock of the old wraps, plastics, metals, and old ivory suitable for restorations.

Cadillac cues will have identification markings by request only. Most are completely unmarked. Cadillac cues are guaranteed for the original owner against construction defects that are not the result of warpage or abuse.

If you are interested in talking to Joe Mazlewski about a new cue or cue that needs to be repaired, you can contact him at Cadillac Custom Cues, listed in the Trademark Index.

SPECIFICATIONS

- Butt material: hardwoods
- Shaft material: maple
- Standard length: 58 in.
- Lengths available: any up to 63 in.
- Standard finish: urethane
- Balance point: custom
- Standard butt cap: plastic
- Standard wrap: Irish linen
- Point construction: short splice
- Standard joint: stainless steel
- Joint type: piloted
- Standard joint screw thread: 5/16-14
- Standard number of shafts: one
- Standard taper: 12 in. pro
- Standard ferrules: lucite
- Standard tip: Le Pro
- Standard tip width: 13 mm
- Annual production: fewer than 50 cues

OPTIONS (FOR NEW CUES ONLY)

- Leather wrap: $65+
- Extra shaft: $75+

REPAIRS

Repairs done on all fine cues.
- Refinish (with Irish linen wrap): $100+
- Rewrap (Irish linen): $35
- Rewrap (leather): $65+
- Replace shaft: $65+
- Replace ivory ferrule: $75+
- Replace fiber/linen ferrule: $20+

CURRENT CADILLAC CUES

Basic Cadillac hustler cues start at $150. Basic two-piece cues with joints and wraps cues start at $250. The current delivery time for a Cadillac cue is one to six months, depending on the intricacy of the cue.

SECONDARY MARKET MINIMUM VALUES

The following are minimum values for Cadillac cues encountered on the secondary market. These prices are representative of cues utilizing basic materials and designs that are not necessarily available at present. Joe has offered one-of-a-kind cues that can command many times these prices due to the use of exotic materials and artistry.

Special construction note: There are many materials and construction techniques that can add value to Cadillac cues.

For all used Cadillac cues, except where otherwise noted:
- Add $65 for each additional original straight playable shaft beyond one.
- Deduct $75+ for missing original straight playable shaft.

CADILLAC CUSTOM CUES, cont.

GRADING	98%	90%	70%

Add $50 each for ivory ferrules.
Add $50 for leather wrap.
Deduct 25% for obvious or improper refinish.

Level 1 - Hustler.
Level 1 cues start at	$125	$100	$65

Level 2 - 0 points, 0-25 inlays.
Level 2 cues start at	$200	$160	$110

Level 3 – 2-6 points, 0-8 inlays.
Level 3 cues start at	$300	$235	$165

Level 4 - 4-10 points, 9-25 inlays.
Level 4 cues start at	$500	$395	$275

CAM CUSTOM CUES

Maker of pool cues from 2004 to present in Guthrie, Oklahoma.

Chad McLennan started playing pool as soon as he could hold a cue. His grandfather had played pool his entire life and was eager to show Chad the ropes. All of his life, Chad had been an artistic person, and had always been interested in creating things with his hands. He is also a skilled jazz trumpet musician.

At age 24, Chad became interested in the art and craft of pool cues. He got his first lathe from Jeff Prather of Prather Cues. It was an old belt-driven Atlas lathe that he still uses today. Chad began his woodworking experience by making joint protectors, which he has turned into the successful "Billiard King Joint Protectors" business.

Chad's interest in building cues drove him to study countless videos, read numerous books, and do extensive research into creating cues. He was fortunate in that he could watch local cue builders at their craft.

Chad is proud of his cues for their "old school" qualities. He cuts each and every point by hand and makes every one of his cue components, except the tips, screws and bumpers. Chad is a young cuemaker. At only 26 years old when he finished his first cue, he is relatively new to the pool cue business. He rates his cues as comparable to some of the best in the business.

CAM cues are guaranteed for life against construction defects that are not the result of warpage or abuse.

If you are interested in talking to Chad about a new cue or cue that needs to be repaired, you can contact him at Cam Custom Cues, listed in the Trademark Index.

Chad McLennan

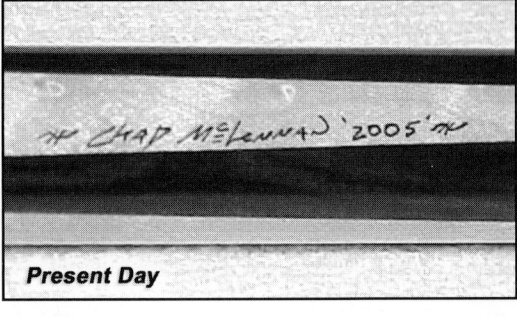

Present Day

SPECIFICATIONS

Butt material: hardwoods
Shaft material: rock maple
Standard length: 58 in.
Lengths available: any within reason
Standard finish: urethane
Balance point: three to four fingers above the wrap
Standard butt cap: phenolic
Standard wrap: leather
Point construction: short splice
Standard joint: stainless steel
Other joints offered: stainless steel
Joint type: flat faced
Joint screw thread: radial pin
Joint protectors: standard
Standard number of shafts: two
Standard taper: pro taper
Standard ferrules: Aegis

GRADING	98%	90%	70%

Standard tip: Triangle
Standard tip width: 13 mm
Tip widths available: 12-14 mm
Standard bumper: no. 1 black bumper
Annual production: fewer than 50 cues

OPTIONS (FOR NEW CUES ONLY)

Please call for all option prices.

REPAIRS

Repairs done on all fine cues.
- Refinish (with Irish linen wrap): $125
- Refinish (with leather wrap): $175
- Rewrap (Irish linen): $35
- Rewrap (leather): $65
- Clean and press linen wrap: $15
- Restore leather wrap: $15
- Replace shaft: $100+
- Replace ivory ferrule: $50
- Replace butt cap: $45
- Replace ivory butt cap: $125
- Replace tip: $15
- Replaced layered tip: $35

CURRENT CAM CUSTOM CUES

Basic two-piece CAM cues with wraps and joint rings start at $400. CAM cues with points start at $500. One-of-a-kind custom CAM cues start at $600. The average order time for a CAM Custom Cue is six to twelve months.

SECONDARY MARKET MINIMUM VALUES

The following are minimum values for Cam cues encountered on the secondary market. These prices are representative of cues utilizing basic materials and designs that are not necessarily available at present. WHO has offered one-of-a-kind cues that can command many times these prices due to the use of exotic materials and artistry.

Special construction note: There are many materials and construction techniques that can add value to CAM cues.

For all used CAM cues, except where otherwise noted:
- Add $75 for each additional original straight playable shaft beyond two.
- Deduct $100 for each missing original straight playable shaft under two.
- Add $40 each for ivory ferrules.
- Add $50 for leather wrap.
- Deduct 20% for obvious or improper refinish.

Level 2 - 0 points, 0-25 inlays.

Level 2 cues start at	$300	$235	$165

Level 3 - 2-6 points, 0-8 inlays.

Level 3 cues start at	$400	$315	$210

Level 4 - 4-10 points, 9-25 inlays.

Level 4 cues start at	$550	$470	$285

Level 5 - 0-12 points, 26-50 inlays.

Level 5 cues start at	$850	$665	$450

CAMERON CUSTOM CUES

Maker of pool cues from 1994 to present in Clinton, Connecticut.

Barry Cameron's pool interests started in the early 1970s, while working in a pool hall in Warner Robins, Georgia. He worked and played pool for about four years and became fairly proficient at the game that he still loves.

Barry's interests in pool had to be put aside for a stint in the U.S. Navy, followed by college, and then family. In the early 1990s, Barry's pool interests resurfaced and he started playing in local tournaments. He was an above average player who was often asked for advice about pool cues and the finer points of the game. It was then that Barry saw the need for affordable, quality pool cue work. He spent the next two years doing repairs and learning about cues and what players liked about the different ones available.

Barry purchased a lathe and spent a lot of time experimenting with different exotic woods and joint styles. He was looking for the right combination of joint, wood, shaft and construction to give a solid hit that he wanted to achieve. He finally produced cues that sold quickly, and gave the look and feel he was looking for. Playability is his primary goal. His mission statement is

Barry Cameron

| GRADING | 98% | 90% | 70% |

"For the player of the sport." Barry purchased additional equipment and now produces about 20-30 cues per year. He enjoys experimenting and learning more with each cue he makes. Barry has a small shop with miscellaneous equipment, including four lathes. One of those is primarily for taking to tournaments for doing cue repairs.

Cameron Cues can be identified by his signature on the butt cap, usually in silver or gold.

Cameron Cues are guaranteed against defects in materials and workmanship. If you want to talk to Barry about ordering a new Cameron cue, or have a Cameron cue that needs further identification or repair, contact Cameron Custom Cues, listed in the Trademark Index.

SPECIFICATIONS

Butt material: hardwoods
Shaft material: maple
Standard length: 58 in.
Standard wrap: Irish linen
Standard ferrules: linen-based melamine
Standard tip: Moori
Annual production: more than 24 cues

OPTIONS (PRICING FOR NEW CUES)

Ivory ferrule: $40 each
Leather wrap: $30+
Extra shaft: $75

REPAIRS (FOR WORK DONE ON ALL FINE CUES)

Refinish with Irish linen wrap- $90+
Rewrap with Irish linen- $45
Replace shaft: $125+
Replace tip: $10+

CURRENT CAMERON CUES

Basic Cameron cues with wraps and joint rings start at $500. Cameron cues with points start at $600. One-of-a-kind Cameron custom cues start at $600. The average delivery time for a Cameron Custom Cue is three to four months.

SECONDARY MARKET MINIMUM VALUES

The following are minimum values for Cameron cues encountered on the secondary market. These prices are representative of cues utilizing basic materials and designs that are not necessarily available at present. Barry has offered one-of-a-kind cues that can command many times these prices due to the use of exotic materials and artistry.

Special construction note: There are many materials and construction techniques that can add value to Cameron cues.

For all used Cameron cues, except where otherwise noted:

Add $100 for each additional original straight playable shaft beyond one.
Deduct $125 for missing original straight playable shaft.
Add $35 each for ivory ferrules.
Deduct 20% for obvious or improper refinish.

	98%	90%	70%
Level 2 - 0 points, 0-25 inlays.			
Level 2 cues start at	$400	$315	$220
Level 3 - 2-6 points, 0-8 inlays.			
Level 3 cues start at	$500	$385	$260
Level 4 - 4-10 points, 9-25 inlays.			
Level 4 cues start at	$650	$515	$350
Level 5 - 0-12 points, 26-50 inlays.			
Level 5 cues start at	$850	$675	$450
Level 6 - 0-12 points 51-75 inlays.			
Level 6 cues start at	$1,000	$800	$575

PETE CAMPBELL CUES

Maker of pool cues from 1990 to present in Wrentham, Massachusetts.

During high school, Courtney Campbell got a job at an ice cream shop where the workers wore shirts with their names on them. The first day on the job, Courtney did not have his own shirt, so he borrowed one with the name "Pete" on it. When his friends saw this, they started calling him by that name. This nickname stuck, and today it is the name Courtney has chosen for his cues.

Courtney started playing pool after college, while working as a plant manager. Courtney could see that the plant was going to be closing in a few years, so he started accumulating equipment and doing some cue repairs.

By 1990, he had made his first cue. Although the first thirty or so Pete Campbell cues made were unmarked, in 1992 Courtney started signing them on the forearm. In 1994, Courtney created a stylized "P.C." logo which has appeared on many of the cues he has made since. Either the signature or the logo is currently available, whichever the customer prefers.

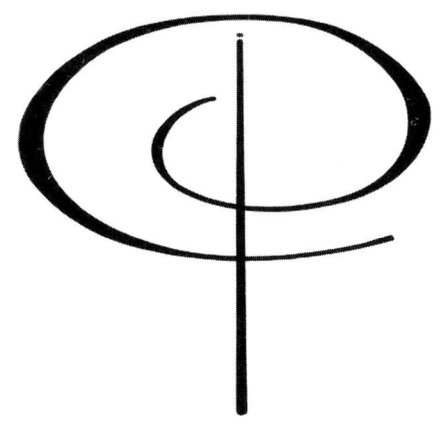

In the past, Courtney made about thirty cues a year in his one-man shop. He has slowed down, and is mainly doing repairs now. The work is done by hand and he makes everything except the tips, bumpers, and screws. Most of his cues are sold locally and the players who purchase them are involved in the designs. Courtney has experimented with different construction methods, materials, and adhesives. Many of these cues have reference numbers under the wraps. He keeps a file on each of these cues so that he can follow the long-term effects of this experimentation. Playability is stressed as the most important aspect of Pete Campbell cues. Courtney and the customer will often play with cues during different stages of construction to fine-tune the specifications before they are completed. Courtney also makes a 41 in. jump cue, of his own design, which uses a purpleheart shaft with a 13 mm tip.

All Pete Campbell cues are guaranteed indefinitely against construction defects that are not the result of warpage or abuse. If you have a Pete Campbell cue that needs further identification or repair, or would like to talk to Courtney about ordering a new Pete Campbell cue, contact Pete Campbell Cues, listed in the Trademark Index.

Courtney "Pete" Campbell

SPECIFICATIONS

Butt material: hardwoods
Shaft material: rock maple
Standard length: 59 in.
Lengths available: any
Standard finish: P.P.G.-D.C. 1100
Joint ccrew: 3/8-10
Standard joint: phenolic
Joint type: flat faced
Balance point: 18 in. to 18 ½ in. from the butt
Point construction: short splice
Standard wrap: Irish linen
Standard butt cap: black phenolic
Standard number of shafts: one
Standard taper: 11 in. straight
Standard ferrules: fiber
Standard tip: Le Pro
Tip widths available: any up to 14 mm
Annual production: fewer than 20 cues

OPTIONS (FOR NEW CUES ONLY)

Ivory joint: $100
Joint protectors: $45 per set
Ivory ferrules: $50 each
Extra shaft: $90+

REPAIRS

Repairs done on most fine cues.

Refinish (with Irish linen wrap): $100
Rewrap (linen): $45
Replace phenolic butt cap: $35
Replace Delrin butt cap: $35
Replace shaft: $90+
Replace ferrule: $25
Replace ferrule: $60
Replace tip: $10

GRADING	98%	90%	70%

CURRENT PETE CAMPBELL CUES

The current delivery time for a Pete Campbell cue is approximately six to eight months.

SECONDARY MARKET MINIMUM VALUES

The following are minimum prices for Pete Campbell cues encountered on the secondary market. These prices are representative of cues utilizing basic materials and designs that may not be currently available. Courtney also offers one-of-a-kind cues that can command many times these prices due to the use of exotic materials and artistry.

Special construction note: There are many materials and construction techniques that can add value to Pete Campbell cues.

For all used Pete Campbell cues, except where otherwise noted:

- Add $75+ for each additional original straight playable shaft (standard with two).
- Deduct $90 for each missing original straight playable shaft.
- Add $80+ for ivory joint.
- Add $40+ for each ivory ferrule.

Level 1 - 4 points, hustler.

Level 1 cues start at	$200	$155	$105

Level 2 - 0 points, 0-25 inlays.

Level 2 cues start at	$350	$270	$185

Level 3 - 2-6 points, 0-8 inlays.

Level 3 cues start at	$400	$300	$220

Level 4 - 4-10 points, 9-25 inlays.

Level 4 cues start at	$650	$510	$345

Level 5 - 0-12 points, 26-50 inlays.

Level 5 cues start at	$1,000	$790	$550

CANTANDO CUSTOM CUES

Maker of pool cues from 1997 to present in Huntington Valley, Pennsylvania.

Art Cantando played a lot of pool when he was a teenager, many years ago. When it was time to make a living, he went into the car repair business with his family. He then started his own successful business. Along the way, he learned leather carving. He carved animals on gun cases and holsters and the like.

When Art retired, he decided to pursue another field, cue making. His goal was to build a good playing cue. He talked to Barry Szamboti, who he knew, and who had put tips on cues for him. Art bought a lathe and began doing his own tip work. This led to making cues. Art owes his success to friends Tony Scianella from Black Boar, Jeff Prather, and most of all Barry Szamboti.

Cantando cues are guaranteed for life against construction defects that are not the result of warpage or abuse. If you are interested in talking to Art Cantando about a new cue or cue that needs to be repaired, you can contact him at Cantando Custom Cues, listed in the Trademark Index.

Art Cantando

SPECIFICATIONS

Butt material: hardwoods
Shaft material: rock maple
Standard length: 58 in.
Lengths available: any
Standard finish: two-stage acrylic clear coat
Balance point: 15 to 16 ½ in. from the butt
Standard butt cap: Ivorine
Standard wrap: Irish linen
Point construction: short splice
Standard joint: stainless steel
Joint type: any
Joint screw thread: 5/16-14
Joint protectors: standard
Standard number of shafts: two
Standard taper: 10 in. pro taper
Standard ferrules: linen based melamine
Standard tip: Le Pro
Tip widths available: any
Annual production: fewer than 12 cues

CANTANDO CUSTOM CUES, cont.

GRADING	98%	90%	70%

OPTIONS (FOR NEW CUES ONLY)
Special length: $50+
Ivory butt cap: $300
Ivory joint: $250
Ivory ferrule: $65
Extra shaft: $150

REPAIRS
Repairs done on all fine cues.
Rewrap (Irish linen): $50
Rewrap (leather): $150
Replace melamine ferrule: $30
Replace Le Pro tip: $10

CURRENT ART CANTANDO CUES
Basic two piece Art Cantando bar cues start at $400. Basic Art Cantando cues with wraps and joint rings start at $800. Art Cantando cues with points start at $950. The current delivery time for an Art Cantando cue is about eighteen months.

PAST EXAMPLES
The following cues represent the work of Art Cantando.

Level 1 - Maple forearm, four full spliced cocobolo points and handle.

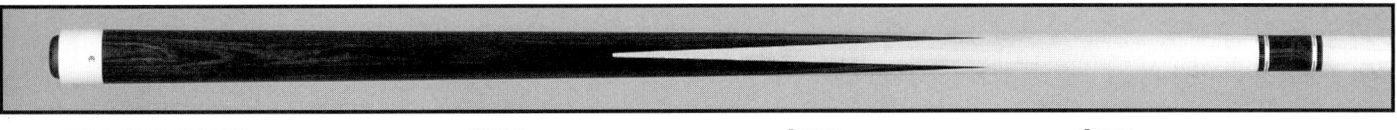

MSR (2003) $350	$500	$395	$275

Level 5 - Bird's-eye maple forearm, four ebony points with veneers and intricate ivory inlays in each, leather wrap, ebony butt sleeve with intricate ivory inlays between ivory dashes at top and bottom.

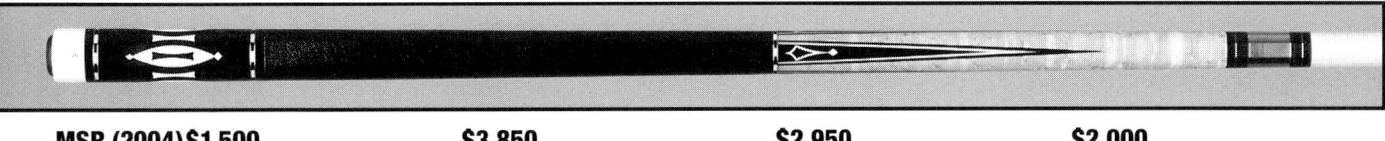

MSR (2004) $1,500	$3,850	$2,950	$2,000

SECONDARY MARKET MINIMUM VALUES
The following are minimum values for other Art Cantando cues encountered on the secondary market. These prices are representative of cues utilizing basic materials and designs that are not necessarily available at present. Art has offered one-of-a-kind cues that can command many times these prices due to the use of exotic materials and artistry.

Special construction note: There are many materials and construction techniques that can add value to Art Cantando cues.

For all used Art Cantando cues, except where otherwise noted:
- Add $100 for each additional original straight playable shaft beyond two.
- Deduct $150 for each missing original straight playable shaft under two.
- Add $50 each for ivory ferrules.
- Add $200 for ivory joint.
- Deduct 20% for obvious or improper refinish.

Level 1 - Hustler.

Level 1 cues start at	$500	$385	$265

Level 2 - 0 points, 0-25 inlays.

Level 2 cues start at	$1,100	$865	$600

Level 3 - 2-6 points, 0-8 inlays.

Level 3 cues start at	$1,250	$975	$650

Level 4 - 4-10 points, 9-25 inlays.

Level 4 cues start at	$1,650	$1,300	$900

Level 5 - 0-12 points, 26-50 inlays.

Level 5 cues start at	$2,000	$1,650	$1,200

CAPONE CUES

Maker of pool cues from 1993 to 2005 in Mercerville, New Jersey, currently in Poolesville, Maryland.

Michael Capone began playing pool as a teenager. While he was at Rutgers University studying mechanical engineering in the early 1990s, he and his cousins opened a pool room in New Jersey. While at the room, there was a need for repair work and he would often send cues out for those repairs, but was unhappy with the amount of time this took.

Michael had a woodworking hobby since he was young and had an old lathe in the basement, so he decided to start doing some basic repairs himself. He rebuilt the old lathe and began doing more difficult work, eventually making hustler cues by putting joints in house cues. In 1993 he purchased his main lathe, which is still in use today. Soon he was ordering blanks and components and making his own cues.

Michael Capone

When he graduated from college, he became more serious, learning how to make his own blanks in 1994. Over the years, Michael has improved his skills and added state-of-the-art equipment to his shop. In March of 1996, Michael was accepted into the American Cuemakers Association, at the age of 24. Other members were impressed with the quality of his work at such a young age, and with only a few years of experience.

Capone cues have gone through many improvements in design. Michael believes that playability is the most important aspect of a pool cue. He likes to make cues to specific weight requirements using wood selection, as opposed to adding metal screws. He specially designs and builds the handle and forearm core of his cues for stability and playability. Michael also makes cues with exotic wood handles for players who like the feeling of an unwrapped cue. He makes over 20 separate cuts on each shaft, and threads the ferrules. The wrap area is cut in after the cue is completely finished, so that the Irish linen or leather is perfectly flush.

In 1997, Michael changed the joint screw to a 3/8 x 7.5 radial pin, which features the Capone Custom Cues logo engraved on the top of it. This screw offers more thread contact than the earlier 3/8 x 10 pin. Also in 1997, Michael introduced the inlay work which is featured in the cues created today. Although Michael does do some CNC inlay work, he still prefers to build cues with spliced points. The majority of cues feature 4, 6, or 8 points with multiple veneers. His cues have become known for how well the points and veneers are executed. He likes the cues to reflect the natural beauty of the many exotic woods that are used in their construction. He is considered, by his customers and peers, to be one of the best in the business for leather, lizard, and other exotic wraps. Michael makes every part of his cues except for the tips, bumpers, and screws.

Michael makes between 125 and 150 cues a year, and does repair work. Capone cues are guaranteed indefinitely against construction defects that are not the result of warpage or abuse. If you have a Capone cue that needs further identification or repair, or would like to talk to Michael about ordering a new cue, contact Capone Cues, listed in the Trademark Index.

SPECIFICATIONS

Butt material: hardwoods
shaft material: rock maple
Standard length: 58 in.
Lengths available: any under 60 in.
Standard finish: catalyzed urethane
Joint screw: radial pin
Standard joint: linen phenolic
Joint type: flat faced
Balance point: 19 to 19 1/2 in. from the butt
Point construction: short splice or inlaid
Standard wrap: Irish linen
Standard butt cap: linen phenolic
Standard number of shafts: two
Joint protectors: standard
Standard taper: custom
Standard ferrules: melamine
Standard tip: Triangle
Tip widths available: any under 14 mm
Annual production: fewer than 150 cues

OPTIONS (FOR NEW CUES ONLY)

Leather wrap: $100
Ivory joint: $200
Ivory butt cap: $300
Ivory ferrules: $50
Extra shaft: $125

CAPONE CUES, cont. 213

GRADING	100%	95%	70%

REPAIRS
Repairs done on most fine cues.
- Refinish (with leather wrap): $200
- Refinish (with Irish linen wrap): $125
- Rewrap (leather): $75
- Rewrap (linen): $40
- Replace phenolic butt cap: $40
- Replace ivory butt cap: $300+
- Replace shaft: $125+
- Replace ferrule: $35
- Replace ivory ferrule: $75
- Replace tip: $15+

CURRENT CAPONE CUES
Basic two-piece cues with wraps and joint rings start at $700. Cues with points start at $1,000. The current delivery time for a Capone custom cue is approximately three to six months.

CURRENT EXAMPLES
The following cues are currently available from Capone Cues. They can be ordered as shown, or modified to suit the desires of the customer.

Level 2- Cocobolo forearm with checked ring above wrap, cocobolo butt sleeve with checked rings at top and bottom.

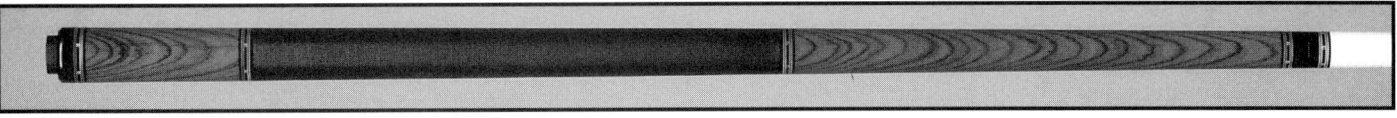

MSR	$750	$700-850	$575	$400

Level 3- Bird's-eye maple forearm, three long and three short ebony points with veneers and an ivory diamond-shaped inlay in each, leather wrap, ebony butt sleeve.

MSR	$1,350	$1,200-1,500	$1,000	$700

Level 4- Bird's-eye maple forearm with silver rings above wrap, four ebony points with veneers and an ivory spear-shaped inlay in each, ebony butt sleeve with ivory dots and spear-shaped inlays between silver rings at top and bottom.

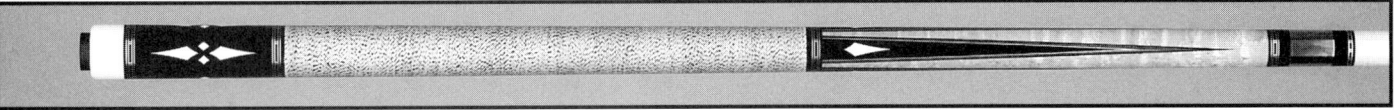

MSR	$1,350	$1,200-1,500	$1,000	$700

Level 3- Ivory joint, bird's-eye maple forearm, three long and three short cocobolo points with veneers, lizard wrap, cocobolo butt sleeve with an ivory ring at bottom.

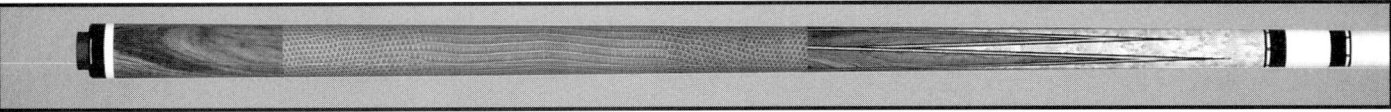

MSR	$1,700	$1,600-1,850	$1,300	$900

Level 3- Ebony forearm with an ivory inlaid ring above wrap, three long and three short thuya burl points with veneers, lizard wrap, thuya burl butt sleeve with ivory inlaid rings at top and bottom.

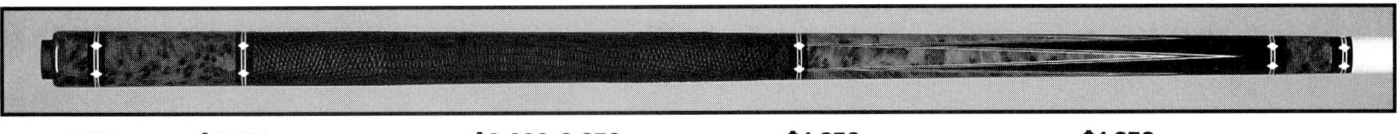

MSR	$2,100	$2,000-2,250	$1,650	$1,250

214 CAPONE CUES, cont.

GRADING	100%	95%	70%

Level 4 - Bird's-eye maple forearm with an ivory dash ring above wrap, four long ebony points with veneers and an ivory spear-shaped inlay in each alternating with four short ebony points, lizard wrap, ebony butt sleeve with ivory dots and spear-shaped inlays between ivory dash rings at top and bottom.

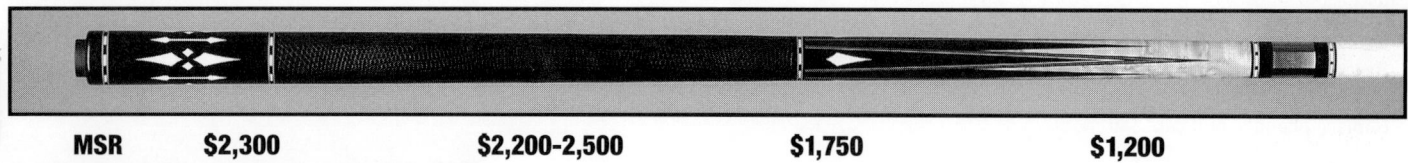

MSR	$2,300	$2,200-2,500	$1,750	$1,200

SPECIAL INTEREST EXAMPLES

The following cue was made for the "Tuxedo Collection" in 2003. The collection is comprised of cues made of ebony, ivory, and silver with black wraps.

Level 6 "Tuxedo" - Ebony forearm with silver and ivory inlaid rings above wrap, six ivory points with intricate tips, leather wrap, ebony butt sleeve with silver inlaid ivory diamond-shaped inlays with intricate tips between ivory inlaid silver rings at top and bottom.

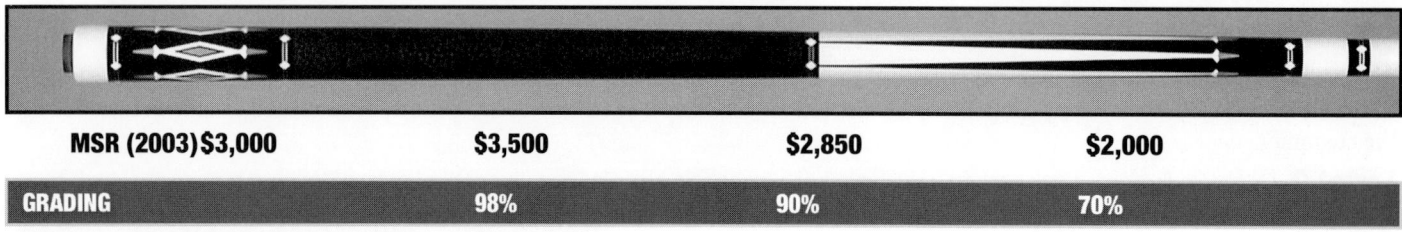

MSR (2003)	$3,000	$3,500	$2,850	$2,000

GRADING	98%	90%	70%

SECONDARY MARKET MINIMUM VALUES

The following are minimum prices for Capone cues encountered on the secondary market. These prices are representative of cues utilizing basic materials and designs that may not be currently available. Michael also offers one-of-a-kind cues that can command many times these prices due to the use of exotic materials and artistry.

Special construction note: There are many materials and construction techniques that can add value to Capone cues.

For all used Capone cues, except where otherwise noted:
- Add $95+ for each additional original straight playable shaft (standard with one).
- Deduct $125+ for missing original straight playable shaft.
- Add $70+ for leather wrap
- Deduct 25% for obvious or improper refinish.

Level 1 - 4 points, hustler.
Level 1 cues start at	$250	$195	$135

Level 2 - 0 points, 0-25 inlays.
Level 2 cues start at	$600	$465	$325

Level 3 - 2-6 points, 0-8 inlays.
Level 3 cues start at	$900	$695	$475

Level 4 - 4-10 points, 9-25 inlays.
Level 4 cues start at	$1,100	$875	$600

Level 5 - 0-12 points, 26-50 inlays.
Level 5 cues start at	$1,400	$1,090	$750

Level 6 - 0-12 points, 51-75 inlays.
Level 6 cues start at	$1,800	$1,400	$975

ARIEL CARMELI CUSTOM CUES

Maker of pool cues from 1994 to present in Santa Anna, California.

Ariel Carmeli made custom furniture before working at Best Billiards in Santa Anna, California. All of the employees there learn to do minor cue repairs as a service to their customers. Ariel enjoyed working on cues, and he admired the artistry and craftsmanship that went into them. Several of the top cuemakers visited Best Billiards, giving Ariel the opportunity to question them about repair and construction techniques. He found that all of the top cuemakers have different ways of doing things, each believing that theirs is the best. Ariel had his own ideas about making cues, a culmination of the advice he had received plus the experience he had doing repairs. He started making cues in the Best Billiards shop in 1994.

Ariel makes about 100 cues a year. Carmeli cues are made to specifications of the individual customer, with a variety of lengths, weights, butt diameters, woods, and joint types available. All components are threaded on and glued with an epoxy that is so strong it can be drilled and tapped without chipping. Ariel presses his own Triangle tips, and would like to use Moori tips if they again become readily

GRADING	98%	90%	70%

available in the United States. He has developed his own unique taper which is almost straight for the first 9 inches. Early Carmeli cues were unmarked, but in 1997 Ariel started laser engraving an "AC" within a circle on the butt caps.

Carmeli cues are guaranteed for life against manufacturing defects that are not the result of warpage or abuse. If you have a Carmeli cue that needs further identification or repair, or would like to order a new Carmeli cue, contact Carmeli Custom Cues, listed in the Trademark Index.

SPECIFICATIONS

Butt material: hardwoods
Shaft material: rock maple
Standard length: 58 in.
Lengths available: up to 61 in.
Standard finish: acrylic urethane
Balance point: about 1 in. above wrap
Standard butt cap: any
Standard wrap: Irish linen
Point construction: short splice
Standard joint: any
Joint type: any
Joint screw: any
Standard number of shafts: two
Standard taper: custom
Standard ferrules: Aegis
Tip widths available: any
Standard tip: pressed Triangle
Annual production: more than 100 cues

CURRENT CARMELI CUES

The current delivery time for a Carmeli custom cue is seven to eight months.

SECONDARY MARKET MINIMUM VALUES

The following are minimum values for Carmeli custom cues encountered on the secondary market. These prices are representative of cues utilizing basic materials and designs that are not currently available. Carmeli Custom Cues has offered one-of-a-kind cues that can command many times these prices due to the use of exotic materials and artistry.

Special construction note: There are many materials and construction techniques that can add value to Carmeli cues. The following are the most important examples:

Add $500+ for ivory points
Add $75+ for ivory joint.

For all used Carmeli cues, except where otherwise noted:

Add $85 for each additional original straight playable shaft beyond two.
Deduct $125 for each missing original straight playable shaft under two.
Add $50 each for ivory ferrules.
Add $100 for leather wrap.
Deduct 25% for obvious or improper refinish.

Level 1 - 4 points, hustler.
Level 1 cues start at	$250	$195	$135

Level 2 - 0 points, 0-25 inlays.
Level 2 cues start at	$450	$350	$235

Level 3 - 2-6 points, 0-8 inlays.
Level 3 cues start at	$700	$545	$375

Level 4 - 4-10 points, 9-25 inlays.
Level 4 cues start at	$900	$595	$475

Level 5 - 0-12 points, 26-50 inlays.
Level 5 cues start at	$1,250	$975	$650

Level 6 - 0-12 points, 51-75 inlays.
Level 6 cues start at	$1,550	$1,225	$850

CARTER CUSTOM CUES

Maker of pool cues from 1998 to present in Owensboro, Kentucky.

Chad Carter has been building custom cues part time since 1998 in Owensboro, Kentucky. His work is influenced by Jerry Franklin of Southwest Cues. Carter has been playing pool for about fifteen years. He grew up making guns and gun barrels which are a lot like cues, and he has a business background in banking.

Carter Custom Cues are signed "Carter" plus the year made.

If you are interested in talking to Chad Carter about a new cue or cue that needs to be repaired, you can contact him at Carter Custom Cues, listed in the Trademark Index.

Chad Carter

Present day

SPECIFICATIONS

Butt material: hardwoods
Shaft material: rock maple
Standard length: 58 in.
Lengths available: 56 in. to 61 in.
Standard finish: Dupont Chromaclear
Balance point: 19 ¼ in. from the butt
Standard butt cap: linen phenolic
Standard wrap: Irish linen
Point construction: short splice
Standard joint: linen phenolic
Joint type: flat faced
Standard joint screws: 3/8-11, radial, 5/16-14
Standard number of shafts: two
Standard taper: 10 in. pro
Standard ferrules: linen based
Standard tip: Moori
Standard tip width: 13 mm
Tip Widths available: from 11.5 to 14 mm
Annual production: approximately 20 cues

OPTIONS (FOR NEW CUES ONLY)

Special length: no charge
Layered tip: no charge
Ivory butt cap: $200
Ivory joint: $125
Ivory ferrule: $50
Extra shaft: $75

REPAIRS

Repairs done on all fine cues.
Refinish (with Irish linen wrap): $100
Rewrap (Irish linen): $35
Clean and press linen wrap: $15
Replace shaft: $75+
Replace ivory ferrule: $65
Replace butt cap: $35+
Replace ivory butt cap: $200
Replace tip: $10+
Replaced Layered tip: $20+
Replace fiber/linen ferrule: $35

CURRENT CARTER CUSTOM CUES

Basic two-piece Carter hustler cues start at $225. Simple Carter cues with wraps and joint rings start at $325. Carter cues with points start at $400. One-of-a-kind custom Carter cues start at $550. There is a four-month delivery time for a Chad Carter cue.

SECONDARY MARKET MINIMUM VALUES

The following are minimum values for other Carter Custom cues encountered on the secondary market. These prices are representative of cues utilizing basic materials and designs that are not necessarily available at present. Chad has offered one-of-a-kind cues that can command many times these prices due to the use of exotic materials and artistry.

Special construction note: There are many materials and construction techniques that can add value to Carter Custom cues.

For all used Carter Custom cues, except where otherwise noted:
Add $50 for each additional original straight playable shaft beyond two.

CARTER CUSTOM CUES, cont. 217

GRADING	98%	90%	70%

Deduct $75 for each missing original straight playable shaft under two.
Add $40 each for ivory ferrules.
Deduct 20% for obvious or improper refinish.

Level 1 - Hustler.
   Level 1 cues start at $175 $140 $90

Level 2 - 0 points, 0-25 inlays.
   Level 2 cues start at $250 $200 $135

Level 3 - 2-6 points, 0-8 inlays.
   Level 3 cues start at $350 $275 $185

Level 4 - 4-10 points, 9-25 inlays.
   Level 4 cues start at $450 $350 $235

Level 5 - 0-12 points, 26-50 inlays.
   Level 5 cues start at $650 $515 $350

CASANOVA CUES

Maker of pool cues from 1997 to present, starting in Newport Beach, California, and now in Corona del Mar, California.

Paul Casanova started playing pool and wanted a new cue. He didn't know anything about them, so he began to learn. He soon became a collector, and one day asked Judd to teach him how to make cues. Paul Casanova began making cues in Newport Beach, California in 1997. He is now located in Corona del Mar, California and continues his part time business. Judd Fuller, Richard Black, and Ernie Gutierrez are among makers whose work has inspired Paul.

If you are interested in talking to Paul Casanova about a new cue or cue that needs to be repaired, you can contact him at Casanova Cues, listed in the Trademark Index.

SPECIFICATIONS

Butt material: hardwoods
Shaft material: Canadian rock maple
Standard length: 58 in.
Standard finish: chromaclear
Balance point: 1 1/2 in. above handle
Standard wrap: leather or nylon
Standard joint: linen phenolic
Joint type: flat faced
Joint screw thread: 3/8 x 10
Standard number of shafts: two
Standard taper: pro
Standard ferrules: ivory
Standard tip: Talisman
Standard tip width: 13 mm
Annual production: 15

OPTIONS (FOR NEW CUES ONLY)

Most options priced on an individual basis, depending on the cue.
   Special length: no charge
   Layered tip: no charge
   Ivory ferrule: no charge
   Leather wrap: no charge

REPAIRS

Repairs done on Casanova cues only. Prices depend on the cue.

CURRENT CASANOVA CUES

The current delivery time for a Casanova cue is between seven and eight months.

SECONDARY MARKET MINIMUM VALUES

The following are minimum values for other Casanova cues encountered on the secondary market. These prices are representative of cues utilizing basic materials and designs that are not necessarily available at present. Paul has offered one-of-a-kind cues that can command many times these prices due to the use of exotic materials and artistry.

Special construction note: There are many materials and construction techniques that can add value to Casanova cues.

For all used Casanova cues, except where otherwise noted:
   Add $100 for each additional original straight playable shaft beyond two.
   Deduct $150 for missing original straight playable shaft.

GRADING	98%	90%	70%

Add $50 each for ivory ferrules.
Add $50 for leather wrap.
Deduct 20% for obvious or improper refinish.

	98%	90%	70%
Level 2 - 0 points, 0-25 inlays.			
Level 2 cues start at	$550	$470	$285
Level 3 - 2-6 points, 0-8 inlays.			
Level 3 cues start at	$700	$535	$365
Level 4 - 4-10 points, 9-25 inlays.			
Level 4 cues start at	$850	$665	$450
Level 5 - 0-12 points, 26-50 inlays.			
Level 5 cues start at	$1,150	$900	$625
Level 6 - 0-12 points, 51-75 inlays.			
Level 6 cues start at	$1,450	$1,150	$835

MARCO CERVANTES

Maker of Ricco Custom Cues, for more information see Ricco Custom Cues.

RICCO CERVANTES

Former maker of Ricco Custom Cues. For more information see Ricco Custom Cues.

THIERRY CHEVRON

Maker of TC Cues. For more information see TC Cues.

JOE CHILDS CUSTOM POOL CUES

Maker of pool cues in Mount Holly, Arkansas.
If you have a Joe Childs cue that needs further identification or repair, or would like to order a new Joe Childs cue, contact Joe Childs Custom Pool Cues, listed in the Trademark Index.

CHILTON CUSTOM CUES

Maker of pool cues from 1993 to present in South St. Paul, Minnesota.

Dale "Flying Eagle" Chilton began playing pool at the age of seven. He also got into woodworking as a hobby at a young age. In 1983, Dale suffered a serious back injury while working. This left him unable to do the kind of work he was used to. His injury led him into the health care field, and he started his own company soon after. He continued to play pool, and he built cedar cabinets as a hobby. He enjoyed league pool and, in 1990, won an award for running three consecutive racks in a league tournament. About this time, Dale combined his love of pool and his woodworking hobby to build aromatic cedar pool cue cases.

In 1993, Dale decided to start making custom cues. The first cues had 3/8-10 joint screws, a few of which had ACME threads. From the beginning, Dale started marking his cues with a "Chilton" logo with three concentric "C"s, representing Chilton Custom Cues. Early cues used blanks that Dale bought, but he soon learned to make his own.

Many construction improvements have been made to Chilton cues since Dale started. In 1993, he started to use thread on collars and cap thread on ferrules. In 1995, Dale started using laminated shafts, which he prefers to be very stiff and, soon after, he switched to the Uni-Loc joint. All Chilton cues use a Uni-Loc pin unless the customer requests something different. Dale has made many custom cues suited to the specifications of the specific player.

In March of 1996, Dale's shop burned down. After this incident, Dale bought better equipment and returned to cuemaking with an even better product. About 20 cues made after the fire were signed on the forearm to show how proud Dale was of his improved cues. Since then Dale is again putting the three concentric "C"s on the butt caps. In 1997, Dale started putting a laminated dowel through the center of the butts, and he believes this improves the hit. Dale makes approximately 90 cues per year. He does all of his own inlay work by hand on a pantograph, and all components are threaded on.

Dale makes a jump cue called the Flying Eagle 2, because it has two tips for two different types of jump shots (very short or very long). All Flying Eagle 2 cues have an aluminum Uni-Loc pin and should weigh less than 6 ounces.

Dale makes a complete cue package. With just one butt, you can get a break shaft and shooting shaft that attach to the Uni-Loc pin he uses. There is also an extension handle that adds 13 inches to the cue in a matter of seconds, for long reach shots. A complete package, including the butt, the two shafts, and the extension handle, starts at $500. Individual shafts, butt and extension handle can be purchased, with prices ranging from $80 to $120. Dale also sells Flying Eagle instructional videos at $20.

Dale is still involved in health care, and donated eleven $700 cues to Kirby Puckett's Children's Heart Fund Celebrity Pool Tournament, which all ended up in the hands of professional sports figures who have donated time to the charity. Dale would like to play on the pro tour, but may have to leave that up to his son, Dale Jr., who was playing pretty well by the age of four. Dale Jr. helped Dale make a cue for him and Dale has made cues for some other kids. Dale Jr., now a teenager, helps in the shop and can do almost all of the jobs except spraying the finish. He also gives free jump lessons at tournaments while his dad works on cue repairs. Dale's teenage daughter, Katrina, is also interested in pool and plays in an adult league. Dale's wife Julie plays on the Flying Eagles pool team, which has done very well in tournaments. The game of pool is a family affair for the Chiltons.

CHILTON CUSTOM CUES, cont. **219**

GRADING	98%	90%	70%

If you have a Chilton cue that needs further identification or repair, or would like to talk to Dale about ordering a new cue, contact Chilton Custom Cues listed in the Trademark Index.

SPECIFICATIONS

Butt material: hardwoods
Shaft material: laminated rock maple
Standard length: 59 in.
Lengths available: any
Standard finish: polyurethane
Standard joint screw: Uni-Loc
Standard joint: stainless steel or titanium
Standard joint type: piloted
Balance point: custom
Point construction: short splice
Standard wrap: Irish linen
Standard butt cap: double black linen phenolic
Standard number of shafts: two
Standard taper: custom
Standard ferrules: Ivorine 3
Standard tip: Triangle
Tip widths available: any
Annual production: approximately 90 cues

OPTIONS (FOR NEW CUES ONLY)

Leather wrap: $80
Ivory joint: $225
Joint protectors: standard
Ivory butt cap: $300
Ivory ferrules: $45 each
Extra shaft: $70+

REPAIRS

Repairs done on Chilton cues only.
Refinish (with leather wrap): $140
Refinish (with Irish linen wrap): $100
Rewrap (leather): $80
Rewrap (linen): $40
Replace butt cap: $35
Replace ivory butt cap: $300
Replace shaft: $70+
Replace Ivorine 3 ferrule: $20+ Tip
Replace Le Pro tip: $8
Replace Triangle tip: $10
Replace Porper laminated tip: $15
Shaft cleaning: $10

CURRENT CHILTON CUES

Basic two-piece Chilton hustler cues start at $300. Basic two-piece Chilton cues with wraps and joint rings start at $350. The current delivery time for a Chilton custom cue is approximately four months.

SECONDARY MARKET MINIMUM VALUES

The following are minimum prices for Chilton cues encountered on the secondary market. These prices are representative of cues utilizing basic materials and designs that may not be currently available. Dale also offers one-of-a-kind cues that can command many times these prices due to the use of exotic materials and artistry.

Special construction note: There are many materials and construction techniques that can add value to Chilton cues.

For all used Chilton cues, except where otherwise noted:
Add $60+ for each additional original straight playable shaft (standard with two)
Deduct $70 for each missing original straight playable shaft.
Add $40 for each ivory ferrule
Add $50 for leather wrap
Deduct 20% for obvious or improper refinish.

Level 1 - 4 points, hustler.

	98%	90%	70%
Level 1 cues start at	$275	$215	$145

GRADING	98%	90%	70%
Level 2 - 0 points, 0-25 inlays.			
Level 2 cues start at	$325	$255	$175
Level 3 - 2-6 points, 0-8 inlays.			
Level 3 cues start at	$450	$345	$235
Level 4 - 4-10 points, 9-25 inlays.			
Level 4 cues start at	$550	$425	$290
Level 5 - 0-12 points, 26-50 inlays.			
Level 5 cues start at	$750	$585	$395
Level 6 - 0-12 points, 51-75 inlays.			
Level 6 cues start at	$975	$765	$525

CHRIS' CUES

Maker of pool cues from 2001 to present in Anna, Illinois.

Chris Whitaker began building cues in January 2001 in Anna, Illinois. He has been a competitive pool player since the early 1980s. The business was started because of a need for cue repairs in Chris's area of Southern Illinois. What began as repair work has developed into cuemaking. His work has been influenced by Mike Durbin.

Chris makes his custom cues by hand, out of exotic hardwoods. He does not use CNC. He also does not use any stain, so the natural beauty of the wood can be appreciated. He began doing inlays in 2002. Chris usually has some of his cues in stock and can ship them right out. Each cue is different and showcases the natural beauty of the wood.

If you are interested in talking to Chris Whitaker about a new cue or cue that needs to be repaired, you can contact him at Chris' Cues, listed in the Trademark Index.

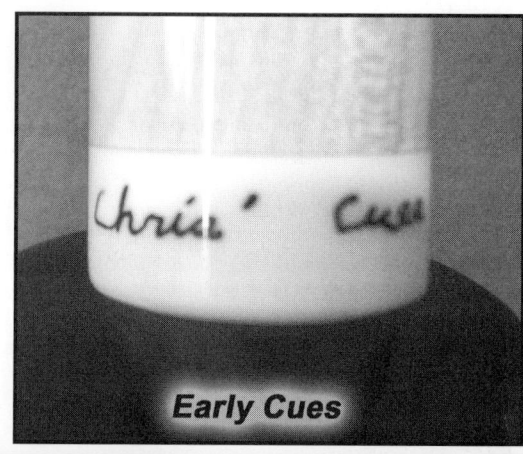
Early Cues

Chris Whitaker

Present day

SPECIFICATIONS

Butt material: hardwoods
Shaft material: rock maple
Standard length: 59 in.
Lengths available: any
Standard finish: PPG Automotive Clear Coat
Balance point: 18 To 20 in. from butt
Standard butt cap: linen based
Standard wrap: Irish linen
Point construction: short splice or inlaid
Standard joint: linen based
Joint type: flat faced wood-to-wood
Joint screw thread: 3/8-10
Joint protectors: standard
Standard number of shafts: one
Standard taper: custom
Standard ferrules: 1 in. Ivor-X
Standard tip: Talisman Pro Medium
Standard tip width: 13 mm
Tip widths available: any
Annual production: fewer than 30 cues

OPTIONS (FOR NEW CUES ONLY)

Special length: no charge
Ivory butt cap: $240
Ivory joint: $180
Ivory ferrule: $75
Ivory points: $120+ each
Extra shaft: $100+
Extra Matrix shaft: $150

REPAIRS

Repairs done on all fine cues.

GRADING	98%	90%	70%

Refinish (with Irish linen wrap): $100
Rewrap (Irish linen): $30
Replace shaft: $100
Replace Matrix shaft: $150
Replace ivory ferrule: $75 plus tip
Replace butt cap: $50+
Replace ivory butt cap: $240
Replace tip: $10 to $55
Replaced layered tip: $15+
Replace fiber/linen ferrule: $20 plus tip

CURRENT CHRIS' CUES

Basic two-piece Chris' hustler cues start at $250. Simple Chris' cues with wraps and joint rings as well as one-of-a-kind custom Chris' cues without points start at $350. Chris' cues with points start at $590. Chris' cues can be special ordered with a nine to twelve month average delivery time.

SECONDARY MARKET MINIMUM VALUES

The following are minimum values for other Chris' cues encountered on the secondary market. These prices are representative of cues utilizing basic materials and designs that are not necessarily available at present. Chris Whitaker has offered one-of-a-kind cues that can command many times these prices due to the use of exotic materials and artistry.

Special construction note: There are many materials and construction techniques that can add value to Chris' cues.

For all used Chris' cues, except where otherwise noted:

Add $75 for each additional original straight playable shaft beyond two.
Deduct $100+ for missing original straight playable shaft.
Add $50 each for ivory ferrules.
Deduct 15% for obvious or improper refinish.

	98%	90%	70%
Level 1 - Hustler.			
Level 1 cues start at	$200	$160	$110
Level 2 - 0 points, 0-25 inlays.			
Level 2 cues start at	$300	$235	$165
Level 3 - 2-6 points, 0-8 inlays.			
Level 3 cues start at	$500	$385	$265
Level 4 - 4-10 points, 9-25 inlays.			
Level 4 cues start at	$600	$465	$325
Level 5 - 0-12 points, 26-50 inlays.			
Level 5 cues start at	$850	$675	$450

RICHARD CHUDY CUSTOM CUES

Maker of pool cues from 1988 to present in Pleasant Hill, California.

Richard Chudy

Richard Chudy began playing pool while studying painting and sculpture at Wayne State University, in Detroit, Michigan. While there, he got a job at a billiard supply company, where he specialized in table repair. The company had always repaired cues and, in 1972, they started making them. They gradually went from putting joints in Titlists and adding Burton Spain components to making their own butts and shafts. Richard was active in the development of their cuemaking operation, and continued to make cues with the company for local pool and billiard players until 1977. During this time, he was also showing his art at local galleries.

In 1977, he was offered a position at a family business in northern California. Richard and his wife had visited the area before and knew they wanted to live there, so he accepted immediately. After moving, Richard continued painting, sculpture, and playing pool. By the mid-eighties, he was doing some table and cue repairs and started to accumulate cuemaking equipment. Around 1988, Richard made his first cue in California, and he found that cuemaking was an outlet for his artistic expression.

Early Richard Chudy cues are identifiable by a 5/16-18 flat face joint with a black Delrin or brass insert in the shaft and a French polish finish. Very early cues were all hustler cues, or cues with solid forearms. In 1990, Richard changed to a new 3/8-10 stainless steel joint. He developed a new technique for treating the wood threads in the shaft so they were deeper and made more surface contact with the joint screw than traditional shafts. At the 1993 A.C.A. show in Baltimore, Richard introduced the current "RC3" logo which then appeared on the butt caps, and moved to within the points in 1996. In 1994, Richard further improved his joint with a custom-made modified 3/8 in. flat trough screw with even more wood contact than before, and created textured joints and rings a year later. In 1997, a G-10 glass epoxy joint pin became an option, and he introduced twisted wire work into his work for the "Gallery of American Cue Art." In 1998 Richard was one of a

| GRADING | 100% | 95% | 70% |

handful of cuemakers invited to make a cue for a 1999 exhibit at the Smithsonian. In 2000 Richard started coring the butt sections with a conical tapered solid maple rod which the joint and butt cap are threaded onto. All other parts are threaded as well.

In 2001 he started constructing his cues with inlaid points instead of short spliced points. In 2003 Richard changed his ring design. The first ring design, which was produced from 1995 to 2000, was a 12-segment, 1/8 in. long design. The rings matched the veneers on the points. From 2000 through 2003 the veneer matching ring became a standardized sterling silver 12-segment design that evolved into a 24-segment sterling silver ring from 2003 to present. In 2005, Richard started using a carbon fiber joint pin.

He is currently a member of the board of the American Cuemakers Association, a position he was elected to in 1996. Richard makes less than 100 cues per year in his one-man shop. He makes every component of his cues except for the tips, bumpers, and screws, which are custom made to his specifications. Ferrules are capped and threaded for playability, which is the primary concern with Richard Chudy cues. Richard avoids plastics and acrylics, choosing to use only linen phenolics and micartas in conjunction with hardwoods. He uses his painting background to artistically combine the colored woods that are commonly used in Richard Chudy cues.

Richard estimates that half his time is spent acquiring the right materials, with an emphasis on wood selection. He inspects wood for aesthetics and for its natural resonance, which affects how the cues that are made with it will play. The wood is carefully weighed and assembled with aluminum, titanium, or steel screws, so that added weights are avoided in achieving the customer's desired weight. Richard slowly finishes the cues in several coats of hand-rubbed Imron. On higher end cues, two shafts and a set of black Delrin joint protectors are included.

Richard Chudy cues are guaranteed indefinitely against construction defects that are not the result of warpage or abuse. If you have a Richard Chudy cue that needs further identification or repair, or would like to talk to Richard about ordering a new cue, contact Richard Chudy Custom Cues, listed in the Trademark Index.

SPECIFICATIONS

Butt material: hardwoods
Shaft material: rock maple
Standard length: 58 in.
Lengths available: any
Standard finish: Imron
Joint screw: 3/8-10 modified
Standard joint: linen phenolic
Joint type: flat face
Balance point: 1-1/2 in above the wrap
Point construction: inlaid
Standard wrap: Irish linen
Standard butt cap: linen phenolic
Standard number of shafts: two
Standard taper: 14 in. modified pro
Standard ferrules: linen phenolic
Standard tip: Triangle
Tip widths available: any
Annual production: fewer than 100 cues

OPTIONS

Options are quoted on an individual basis, depending on the cue.

REPAIRS

Repairs are quoted on an individual basis, depending on the cue.

CURRENT RICHARD CHUDY CUES

Basic two-piece cues with wraps and joint rings start at $1,000. Richard Cudy cues with points start at $1,500. The current delivery time for a Richard Chudy cue is approximately three to five months.

CURRENT EXAMPLES

The following Richard Chudy cues can be ordered as shown, modified to suit the desires of the customer, or new designs can be created.

Level 2 - Bird's-eye maple forearm, bird's-eye maple butt sleeve.

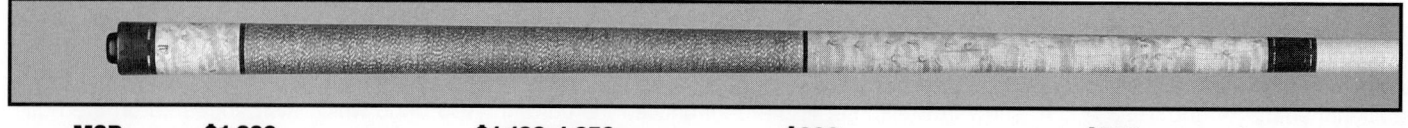

| MSR | $1,200 | $1,100-1,350 | $900 | $650 |

GRADING	100%	95%	70%

Level 3 - Cocobolo forearm with a sterling silver inlaid ring above wrap, three long and three short bird's-eye maple points with single side veneers, leather wrap, cocobolo butt sleeve with Sterling silver inlaid rings at top and bottom.

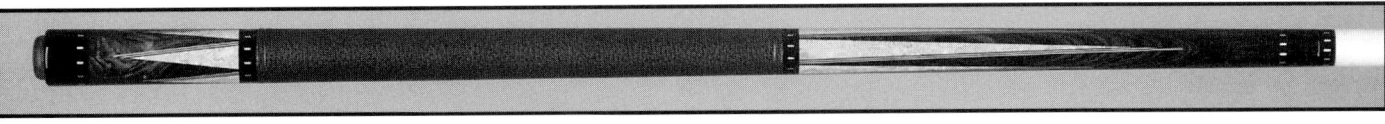

MSR	$1,950	$1,850-2,100	$1,450	$1,000

Level 4 "Dancing Wings" - Cocobolo forearm, five intricate two-piece ivory and gold burl floating points, leather wrap, cocobolo butt sleeve with five intricate two-piece ivory and gold burl reverse floating points within sterling silver inlaid rings at top and bottom.

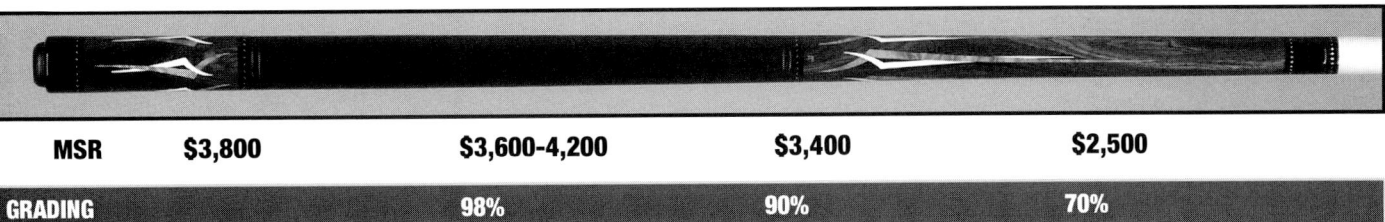

MSR	$3,800	$3,600-4,200	$3,400	$2,500

GRADING	98%	90%	70%

PAST EXAMPLES

The following Richard Chudy cues are typical examples that may be encountered as shown or with variations in materials and designs.

Level 3 - Cocobolo forearm, four bird's-eye maple points, doe skin wrap, short cocobolo butt sleeve decorative rings at bottom.

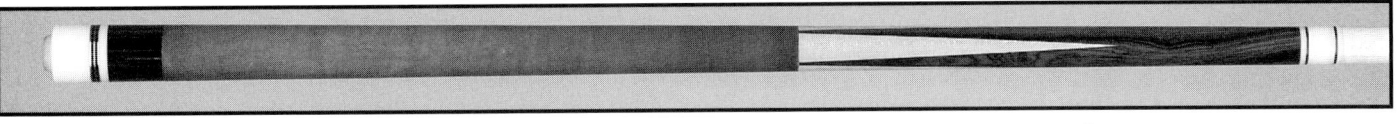

MSR (1988) $450	$1,000	$975	$550

Level 3 - Olive wood forearm with a purple heart and olive wood checked ring above wrap, three long and three short purple heart points with single side veneers, olive wood butt sleeve with purple heart and olive wood checked rings at top and bottom.

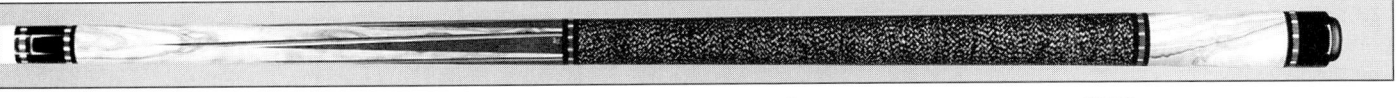

MSR (1998) $800	$1,250	$975	$650

Level 4 - Ivory joint, ebony forearm, five intricate two-piece ivory floating points, leather wrap, ebony butt sleeve with five intricate two-piece windows within sterling silver inlaid rings at top and bottom.

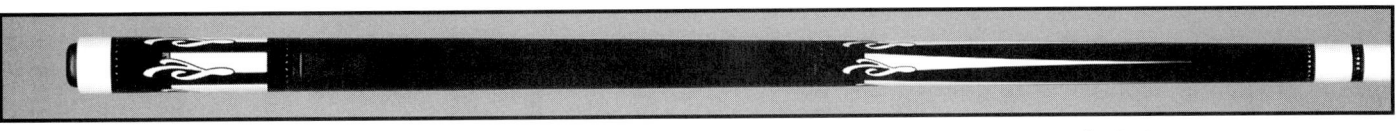

MSR (2001) $2,500	$3,750	$2,950	$1,950

SECONDARY MARKET MINIMUM VALUES

The following are minimum prices for other Richard Chudy cues encountered on the secondary market. These prices are representative of cues utilizing basic materials and designs that may not be currently available. Richard currently specializes in one-of-a-kind cues that can command many times these prices due to the use of exotic materials and artistry.

Special construction note: There are many materials and construction techniques that can add value to Richard Chudy cues.

For all used Richard Chudy cues, except where otherwise noted:
- Add $100+ for each additional original straight playable shaft beyond two.
- Deduct $150 for each missing original straight playable shaft under two.
- Add $200+ for ivory joint.
- Add $95+ for leather wrap.
- Add $75+ for each ivory ferrule.
- Deduct 25% for obvious or improper refinish.

Level 1 - 4 points, hustler.
Level 1 cues start at	$350	$270	$185

Level 2 - 0 points, 0-25 inlays.
Level 2 cues start at	$750	$570	$395

GRADING	98%	90%	70%
Level 3 - 2-6 points, 0-8 inlays.			
Level 3 cues start at	$950	$745	$500
Level 4 - 4-10 points, 9-25 inlays.			
Level 4 cues start at	$1,400	$1,100	$750
Level 5 - 0-12 points, 26-50 inlays.			
Level 5 cues start at	$3,500	$2,800	$2,000

CK CUSTOM CUES

Maker of pool cues from 1995 to present in East Peoria, Illinois.

Chester Krick was an avid pool player in his early teens. He also loved woodworking. In the 1980s, he owned a small woodworking shop, making furniture and antique reproductions. His first cue was factory made. It played alright, but he thought that he could improve it. He worked on it and basically ruined it trying to make it play better. But from that experience, he thought he could build a better cue. He did a lot of research about how to make cues, but information was, and still is, scarce. He finally stumbled across an Internet article about a cue maker named Dennis Dieckman, who was willing to sell information about the art of cue building. Chester called him and visited his shop in Michigan, and after several hours of conversation, decided that he could build cues.

Chester bought a lathe and started making and repairing cues in 1995. He learned by trail and error. It was and still is his goal to make a cue that plays well. The decorative aspect of the cue is secondary. Chester wanted to make two-piece cues that hit like a one-piece clue. He decided that a flat-face wood-to-wood joint was the best way to minimize the hardware at the joint. His first cues were not very fancy, but they hit pretty well. After making about every possible mistake, his cues improved in both function and decoration.

In 1996, Chester built a small website with photos of his cues and outlined his philosophy on cue making. To his surprise, lots of orders started coming in for his custom cues. At that point, he went full time into building cues and started reinvesting profits into better equipment. He got a hobby-type CNC machine to do inlays, but it wasn't long before he built his own CNC inlay machine. This machine was more industrial and did a better job with accuracy. Chester didn't know how to program CNC codes, so he bought a CAD program and taught himself how to draw inlays using Autocad. He then got a program that converted the drawings into machine code, and he was then off and running, making his own inlays on a machine that he had made himself.

Chester decided that he would not keep what he knew about cue making a secret. He offered to tutor students in how to build cues. Steve Klein was one of the first aspiring cue makers who worked with Chester. Steve is kind enough to give Chester a lot of credit for helping him to become a first rate cue maker. Chester has made many other friends and contacts through sharing of cue information, such as Dave Barenbrugge from Arizona. Dave and Chester have both benefited by sharing information.

Chester Krick's proudest day as a cue maker came in July of 2002 when Sonny Tan won the Singapore National 8 ball championship using a CK Custom Cue. He actually borrowed the cue from the original customer, and practiced with it for only two weeks before winning the National title. Chester has had an increase in demand for his cues since the day Sonny won using a CK Custom Cue.

For the past two years, Chester has designed and developed a new joint pin called the Supra™, and is now in the process of getting his product patented and trademarked.

If you are interested in talking to Chester Krick about a new cue or cue that needs to be repaired, you can contact him at CK Custom Cues, listed in the Trademark Index.

SPECIFICATIONS

Butt material: hardwoods
Shaft material: rock maple
Standard length: 58 in.
Lengths available: 29 in.
Standard finish: epoxy, car coat
Balance point: 19.5 in from the butt
Standard butt cap: phenolic
Standard wrap: Irish linen
Point construction: short splice or CNC
Standard joint: Supra™ joint pin
Joint type: flat faced wood-to-wood
Joint screw thread: 3/8 x 11 Supra™
Standard number of shafts: two
Standard taper: .440
Standard ferrules: Ivorine 3
Other ferrule options: ivory
Standard tip: LePro
Standard tip width: 13 mm
Tip widths available: 12 mm to 14 mm
Annual production: fewer than 40 cues

OPTIONS (FOR NEW CUES ONLY)

Layered tip: $25
Ivory butt cap: $175
Ivory butt sleeve: $450

GRADING	100%	95%	70%

Ivory joint: $100
Ivory ferrule: $65
Ivory points: $600
Ivory handle: $2000
Leather wrap: $125
Lizard wrap: $200
Joint protectors: $45
Extra shaft: $200

REPAIRS

Repairs done on CK Custom cues only. Repairs priced individually, depending on the cue.

CURRENT CK CUES

Basic two-piece CK hustler cues start at $200. Basic two piece CK cues with wraps and joint rings start at $400. CK cues with points start at $550. Eight point CK cues start at $750. One-of-a-kind custom CK cues start at $800. The current delivery time for a CK cue is about five months.

CURRENT EXAMPLES

Level 5 - Bird's-eye maple forearm with a ring of maple blocks set in blue veneers above wrap, four ebony points with four veneers and a turquoise diamond-shaped inlay in each and an ebony outlined turquoise spear-shaped inlay at the tip of each point, ebony butt sleeve with 28 turquois inlays set between maple blocks set in blue veneer rings at top and bottom.

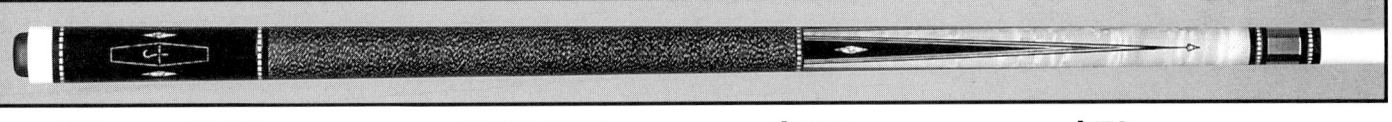

MSR	$1,450	$1,350-1,600	$1,075	$750

Level 5 - Bird's-eye maple forearm, four bloodwood points with four veneers and three ivory dot-shaped inlays in each point, bloodwood butt sleeve with four sets of three ivory inlays alternating with four ebony rectangles above twelve ivory diamond-shaped inlays set in a ring of ebony within pairs of blue and black veneer rings at bottom.

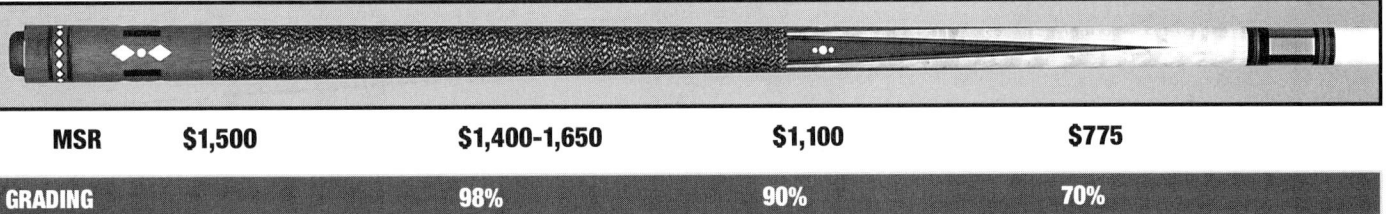

MSR	$1,500	$1,400-1,650	$1,100	$775

GRADING	98%	90%	70%

SECONDARY MARKET MINIMUM VALUES

The following are minimum values for other CK cues encountered on the secondary market. These prices are representative of cues utilizing basic materials and designs that are not necessarily available at present. Chester has offered one-of-a-kind cues that can command many times these prices due to the use of exotic materials and artistry.

Special construction note: There are many materials and construction techniques that can add value to CK cues.

For all used CK cues, except where otherwise noted:
Add $125 for each additional original straight playable shaft beyond two.
Deduct $200 for each missing original straight playable shaft under two.
Add $50 each for ivory ferrules.
Add $75 for leather wrap.
Deduct 20% for obvious or improper refinish.

Level 2 - 0 points, 0-25 inlays.
Level 2 cues start at	$350	$275	$185

Level 3 - 2-6 points, 0-8 inlays.
Level 3 cues start at	$500	$385	$265

Level 4 - 4-10 points, 9-25 inlays.
Level 4 cues start at	$750	$595	$400

Level 5 - 0-12 points, 26-50 inlays.
Level 5 cues start at	$1,200	$945	$650

Level 6 - 0-12 points, 51-75 inlays.
Level 6 cues start at	$1,600	$1,250	$850

GALE CLARK CUES

GRADING	98%	90%	70%

GALE CLARK CUES

Maker of pool cues since 1988, originally in Galesburg, Illinois and currently in Arvada, Colorado.

Gale Clark began making cues in 1988 with a friend of his, who was an excellent pool player. They began in a closet with just one lathe, by taking apart cues and learning how they were made. Gale was a machinist at the time, and, in the early 1990s, he built a shop in Galesburg, Illinois, and began building and selling low-end cues with the ambition of becoming a custom designer and builder. Circumstances took Gale and his wife to Colorado, where he worked for Showcase Cues for a couple of years.

Gale opened his own shop and started working with beautiful exotic woods and inlays and tried to build the perfect hitting cue. He enjoyed cue making for four years, until an unfortunate auto accident sidelined him for a time. Two years ago, Gale decided to start building custom hustler cues at a shop in his home. His hustler logo is a brass diamond in the butt cap. The points are usually either purple heart or bubinga.

Gale Clark cues are guaranteed for one year against product defects. If you have a Gale Clark cue that needs further identification or repair, or would like to talk to Gale about ordering a new cue, contact Gale Clark Cues, listed in the Trademark Index.

Gale Clark

SPECIFICATIONS

Butt material: hardwoods
Shaft material: hard maple
Standard length: 58 in.
Standard finish: three-part urethane
Joint screw: 3/8-10
Standard joint: phenolic
Joint type: flat faced
Standard ferrules: phenolic
Standard tip: Triumph
Standard bumper: 1 in. x 5/8 rubber
Annual production: approximately 120

OPTIONS (FOR NEW CUES ONLY)

Extra shaft: $110

REPAIRS

Repairs done on Gale Clark Cues only. Repairs priced on an individual basis, depending on the cue.

CURRENT GALE CLARK CUES

Basic two-piece Gale Clark hustler cues start at $175. The average order time for a Gale Clark Custom Hustler Cue is three weeks.

SECONDARY MARKET MINIMUM VALUES

The following are minimum values for other Gale Clark cues encountered on the secondary market. These prices are representative of cues utilizing basic materials and designs that are not necessarily available at present. Gale has offered one-of-a-kind cues that can command many times these prices due to the use of exotic materials and artistry.

Special construction note: There are many materials and construction techniques that can add value to Gale Clark cues.

For all used Gale Clark cues, except where otherwise noted:

Add $90 for each additional original straight playable shaft beyond one.
Deduct $110 for missing original straight playable shaft.
Add $50 each for ivory ferrules.
Deduct 20% for obvious or improper refinish.

Level 1 - Hustler.
Level 1 cues start at	$150	$120	$80

Level 2 - 0 points, 0-25 inlays.
Level 2 cues start at	$300	$235	$160

Level 3 - 2-6 points, 0-8 inlays.
Level 3 cues start at	$450	$350	$235

Level 4 - 4-10 points, 9-25 inlays.
Level 4 cues start at	$550	$425	$285

Level 5 - 0-12 points, 26-50 inlays.
Level 5 cues start at	$750	$585	$395

CLASSIC CUSTOM CUE

Maker of pool cues from 1997, in Crossville, Tennessee, to present in Fairfield Glade, Tennessee.

Fascination with cues began early for Bill Gibbs. He bought his first cue for $7 in 1967. In 1979, he acquired his first Balabushka, which was the start of a cue collection that eventually contained seven Szambotis and two Balabushkas. In 1984, Bill was invited to meet Gus Szamboti and tour his shop. About that same time, he started using a South West cue for his game of 9-ball. Mr. Szamboti's craftsmanship and the playability of the South West made an indelible impression on Bill. Since 1973, Bill had been repairing and building guitars. In 1985, he invented a guitar-related product and moved to Nashville, Tennessee to pursue becoming a master luthier while marketing his new product. Bill's passion for pool and cues had to be put aside for the next 11 years.

In 1997, both of Bill's parents were diagnosed with terminal illnesses, so Bill relocated in order to assist them. Needing a break from growing responsibilities, Bill attended the first "Derby City Classic." At the close of the tournament, he ran into old friends Gary Spaeth and Sherm Adamson. Sherm invited Bill to come see his shop and gave him a cue to start playing with again. That kindness rekindled Bill's passion for cues and pool. With Sherm's friendship, Bill was able to realize a lifelong dream: building a cue. After the first cue, Sherm encouraged him to build three more apprentice cues and allowed him to work in his shop when time and travel allowed.

In the next two years, while working with Sherm, Bill acquired the machinery specific to cue construction. Today, after a total of seven years repairing and building custom cues, Bill Gibbs is now doing work for his own company, Classic Custom Cue. Sherm and Bill remain best friends and continue to work on each others' projects, when asked to.

Bill Gibbs guarantees his cues indefinately against construction defects that are not the result of warpage or abuse. If you are interested in talking to Bill Gibbs about a new cue or cue that needs to be repaired, you can contact him at Classic Custom Cue, listed in the Trademark Index.

SPECIFICATIONS

Butt material: hardwoods
Shaft material: rock maple
Standard length: 57 ¾ in.
Lengths available: any
Standard finish: urethane/UV
Balance point: forward weighted
Standard butt cap: phenolic
Standard wrap: linen
Point construction: short splice
Standard joint: phenolic
Joint type: flat-faced
Joint screw thread: fadial 3/8-10
Joint protectors standard: on butt only
Standard number of shafts: one
Standard ferrules: phenolic
Standard tip: Triangle
Standard tip width: 12.8 mm
Tip widths available: any
Annual production: approximately 60

OPTIONS (FOR NEW CUES ONLY)

Special length: no charge
Moori tip: $25
Ivory butt cap: $300
Ivory joint: $200
Ivory ferrule: $50
Leather wrap: $50
Extra shaft: $150

REPAIRS

Repairs done on all fine cues.
Refinish (with Irish linen wrap): $130
Refinish (with leather wrap): $160
Rewrap (Irish linen): $50
Rewrap (leather): $85
Clean and press linen wrap: $20
Replace shaft: $150
Replace ivory ferrule: $75
Replace butt cap: $45
Replace ivory butt cap: $300
Replace Triangle tip: $17
Replaced Moori tip: $40
Replace fiber/linen/ferrule: $45

CURRENT CLASSIC CUES

The current delivery time for a Classic Custom Cue is nine weeks.

GRADING	98%	90%	70%

SECONDARY MARKET MINIMUM VALUES

The following are minimum values for other Classic cues encountered on the secondary market. These prices are representative of cues utilizing basic materials and designs that are not necessarily available at present. Bill has offered one-of-a-kind cues that can command many times these prices due to the use of exotic materials and artistry.

Special construction note: There are many materials and construction techniques that can add value to Classic cues.

For all used Classic cues, except where otherwise noted:
- Add $100 for each additional original straight playable shaft beyond one.
- Deduct $150 for missing original straight playable shaft.
- Add $45 each for ivory ferrules.
- Add $40 for leather wrap.
- Deduct 20% for obvious or improper refinish.

Level 2 - 0 points, 0-25 inlays.

Level 2 cues start at	$400	$315	$210

Level 3 - 2-6 points, 0-8 inlays.

Level 3 cues start at	$600	$475	$325

Level 4 - 4-10 points, 9-25 inlays.

Level 4 cues start at	$750	$595	$400

Level 5 - 0-12 points, 26-50 inlays.

Level 5 cues start at	$1,000	$785	$550

CLAWSON CUES

Maker of Predator shafts and distributor of Predator cues from 1994 to present in Jacksonville, Florida.
For more information on Predator cues, see Predator Cues in the P section of this book, or refer to Predator Cues in the Trademark Index.

COGNOSCENTI CUES

Maker of pool cues from 1989 to present in Chicago, Illinois.

Joe Gold

Joe Gold has been known as one of the top pool players in the Chicago area for years. On the weekends, for 10-15 years, Joe would go to some of the top tournaments in the country. During the week, Joe worked as a contractor and cabinet maker in high-end homes around Chicago. As a hobby, Joe did some gunsmithing and made parts for the motorcycles he raced. He has always been an aficionado of fine things and has collected such things as high performance autos and motorcycles, Swiss watches, precious metals and gemstones. With his background in fabrication, his ability as a player and his eye for detail, Joe believed that he could make a cue that would look and play better than anything that was then available.

In 1988, Joe went to his friend, Craig Petersen, and ordered a custom cue with the agreement that Joe could witness every step of its construction. After learning the basics of cue construction by watching his cue being built, Joe started to accumulate the necessary equipment to make cues. Joe hired an engineering firm in Chicago to help with the development of his cue design. He chose the name "Cognoscenti," which is a term used to describe people who recognize and appreciate the finest things. Soon thereafter the first Cognoscenti cue was built.

Although most Cognoscenti cues are not marked, they have always been easy to recognize. They were the first and only cues (for several years) to feature a G-10 glass epoxy joint screw. This material flexes more in harmony with, and is closer in weight to, wood rather than steel or brass. By reducing the weight at the joint and using a material that played more like wood, Joe Gold was able to balance and weight Cognoscenti cues to his design without compromising playability. At the same time, in its application for a joint pin, G-10 is as strong as steel and gives the cues a very unique look. The same is true of the optional Grade 5 titanium screw. Another feature that makes Cognoscenti cues easy to recognize is the design of the decorative rings. Early Cognoscenti cues featured notched wooden rings while all Cognoscenti cues today have ebony rings with exactly thirty stitches of .999 fine silver. These rings may also appear just above the wrap, and at the top and bottom of the butt sleeves, always with exactly thirty silver stitches. The only cues Joe has made that have identification marks have "Cognoscenti" on the titanium joint screw. The standard length of Joe's cues is 57 1/2 in., and Joe refuses to make a cue any longer than that. He played with a 57 ½ in. cue for years, and insists that shorter cues play better.

Joe also believes that being a better player allows him to make better playing cues. Cognoscenti cues are proof of Joe's philosophy. There are many variations of Cognoscenti desgins, the first being a basic cue with no points. The other variations each have different floating point designs. From there, the exotic materials used and the number and types of inlays added allow for infinite possibilities. Joe insists on perfect execution. Any flaw on a Cognoscenti means the cue is cut in pieces and thrown away. Demand for new custom designed Cognoscenti cues exceeds production output, so there is currently a three year wait list. Joe will indefinitely fix any construction defects on Cognoscenti cues that are not the result of abuse. If you have a Cognoscenti cue that needs repair, or would like to talk to Joe about the design of a new cue, contact Cognoscenti Cues, listed in the Trademark Index.

COGNOSCENTI CUES, cont. 229

GRADING	100%	95%	70%

SPECIFICATIONS

Butt material: hardwoods
Shaft material: rock maple
Standard length: 57 1/2 in.
Lengths available: 57 ½ in.
Standard finish: Imron 16-20 coats
Joint screw: G-10 glass epoxy
Standard joint: linen phenolic
Joint type: flat faced
Balance point: custom
Point construction: inlaid
Standard wrap: Irish linen
Standard butt cap: phenolic
Standard number of shafts: two
Standard taper: 8 in. straight
Standard ferrules: wound linen
Tip widths available: any under 14 mm
Annual production: fewer than 50 cues

OPTIONS (FOR NEW CUES ONLY)

Grade 5 titanium joint screw: $125
Extra shaft: $300

REPAIRS

Repairs done only on Cognoscenti Cues.
Refinish (with linen wrap): $300
Rewrap (linen): $60
Replace shaft: $300

CURRENT EXAMPLES

Joe currently specializes in one-of-a-kind custom designed cues. The following cues are representations of the work of Joe Gold. The current delivery time for a cue depends upon the intricacy of the cue.

Level 8 - Ivory and phenolic joint, ebony forearm with one-of-a-kind floating ivory points detailed with inlaid Amboyna burl wood and ivory lines, sub-point area detailed with ivory and Amboyna burl wood saber-tooth-like inlays, handle is three pieces of amboyna burl wood ebony butt sleeve with sub-point detail inlays replicated, rings are thirty stitches of silver-framed by solid silver rings, ivory butt cap.

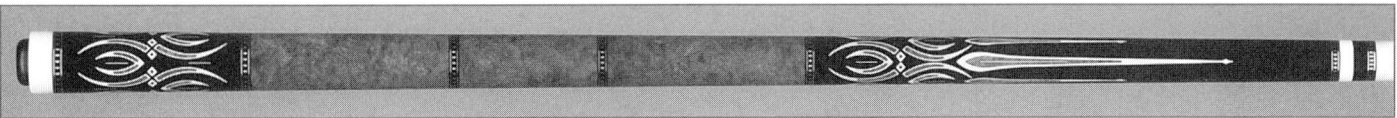

MSR	$22,500	$20,000-23,000	$18,500	$12,500

Level 8 - Ivory and phenolic joint, ebony forearm with one-of-a-kind floating ivory spear-headed points detailed with inlaid turquiose points, ovals, and diamond shapes, alternating with ivory and turquiose ovals with a line above and two 18-karat white gold starbursts framing D-color VS1 Russian-cut diamonds, ebony butt sleeve with short spear-headed ivory and turquoise point design mimicking the forearm design, between the short points are ivory and turquoise ovals with two more 18-karat and diamond starbursts. Total of 20 D-VS1 diamonds weighing one carat. Rings are thirty stitches of silver framed by solid silver rings, ivory butt cap.

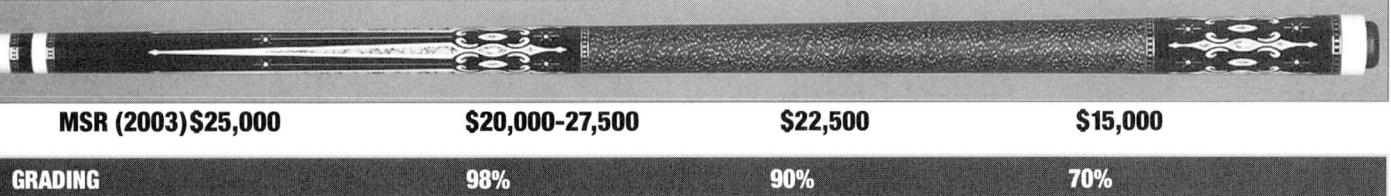

MSR (2003) $25,000	$20,000-27,500	$22,500	$15,000

GRADING	98%	90%	70%

PAST EXAMPLES

Level 2 - Phenolic joint, amaranth (purple heart) forearm, highly figured curly maple handle and amaranth butt sleeve. Rings are wood notched, phenolic butt cap.

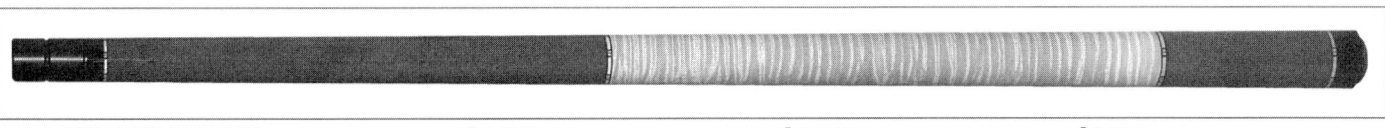

MSR (1991) $1,100	$2,250	$1,775	$1,275

GRADING	98%	90%	70%

Level 4 - Natural brown linen phenolic joint, maple forearm with early-design cocobolo floating points, ovals, and double lines, maple butt sleeve with floating cocobolo points and wood notched deco rings, natural brown linen phenolic butt cap.

MSR (1992) $1,500	$3,200	$2,900	$1,500

Level 5 - Phenolic joint, ebony forearm with fancy floating ivory points with spearheads re-cut with ebony inlays and ivory lines, ivory ovals with ebony diamonds inside, short ivory points between the long points, butt sleeve features re-sized forearm design, rings are 30-stich silver with silver frame ring on each side, phenolic butt cap.

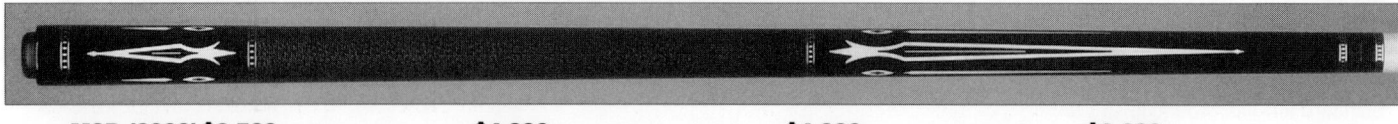

MSR (2002) $3,500	$4,200	$4,000	$2,200

Level 7 - Phenolic joint, ebony forearm with intricate floating ivory points each inlayed with silver lines and ebony dot framed in silver, between the ivory points in the forearm are skeleton points, with starbursts, of thirteen silver pieces each, highly figured bird's-eye maple handle, ebony butt sleeve with forearm design replicated, rings are floating 30-piece stitched silver, phenolic butt cap. Cue is pre-CNC.

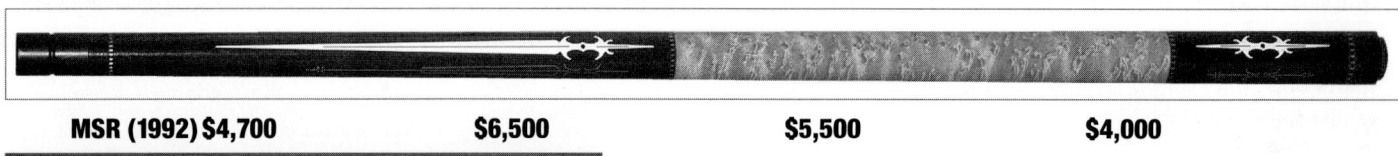

MSR (1992) $4,700	$6,500	$5,500	$4,000

SECONDARY MARKET MINIMUM VALUES

The following are minimum prices for Cognoscenti cues encountered on the secondary market. These prices are representative of cues utilizing basic materials and designs that may not be currently available. Joe currently specializes in one-of-a-kind cues that can command many times these prices due to the use of exotic materials and artistry, and the limited number of cues being produced annually.

Special construction note: There are many materials and construction techniques that can add value to Cognoscenti cues.

For all used Cognoscenti cues, except where otherwise noted:
- Add $200+ for each additional original straight playable shaft beyond two.
- Deduct $300 for each missing original straight playable shaft under two.
- Add $300+ for leather wrap.
- Add $300+ for notched wood rings.
- Add $500+ for cues with exotic wood handles.

Level 2 - 0 points, 0-25 inlays.
Level 2 cues start at	$1,600	$1,295	$900

Level 3 - 2-6 points, 0-8 inlays.
Level 3 cues start at	$1,900	$1,595	$1200

Level 4 - 4-10 points, 9-25 inlays.
Level 4 cues start at	$2,250	$1,850	$1,400

Level 5 - 0-12 points, 26-50 inlays.
Level 5 cues start at	$2,750	$2,250	$1,700

Level 6 - 0-12 points, 51-75 inlays.
Level 6 cues start at	$3,500	$2,800	$2,000

Level 7 - 0-12 points, 76-125 inlays.
Level 7 cues start at	$4,500	$3,650	$2,500

Level 8 - 0-12 points, 126+ inlays.
Level 8 cues start at	$7,500	$6,000	$4,000

COKER CUES

Maker of pool cues from 1990 to present in Sacramento, California.

Grady and Tom Coker

Tom Coker manufactured jewelry for fifteen years until he had to quit after suffering a massive heart attack. He took it easy for about three years after that, and played a lot of golf. Tom and his wife played pool as a hobby, and Tom missed making things. Tom told a friend that he was thinking about trying to make cues for himself and his wife for something to do. His friend told him he was crazy, that cuemaking was the most difficult form of woodworking. Considered a perfectionist by his friends, Tom was committed to making the best cues he could possibly make. After countless hours and investing over ten thousand dollars in equipment and materials, Tom turned out a couple of cues he was happy with. He loved making cues more than anything he had ever done, and he was so far in at that point that he made the commitment to start making cues full time.

Early Coker cues were unmarked and can be difficult to identify. In 1995, Tom started signing "Coker Cues" in the forearms followed by the month and the last two digits of the year it was completed. In 1996, Coker cues started to feature bumpers that have "Coker" molded into them. Tom used a polyurethane finish until 1998, when he switched to a superior polyester finish. In early 2003, Tom switched to an ultra-violet finish.

Today Tom splices his own blanks and has made two-, three-, four-, five-, six-, eight-, and ten-point cues with the help of his son, Grady. Tom is known for being able to inlay a customer's profile into the base of his floating points. Tom has found that it was much easier to make jewelry. Since the latter part of 2003, Tom's wife, Michi, has had responsibility for all of the CNC designing and inlaying of floating points, point inlays, and butt and sleeve inlays. Tom and Grady make everything in Coker cues except for the tips and screws. They also makes components for other cuemakers.

Coker cues are guaranteed for life against manufacturing defects that are not the result of warpage or abuse. If you have a Coker cue that needs further identification or repair, or would like to order a new Coker cue, contact Coker Cues, listed in the Trademark Index.

SPECIFICATIONS

Butt material: hardwoods
Shaft material: rock maple
Standard length: 58 in.
Lengths available: any
Standard finish: UV clear
Standard balance point: 17 in. from butt
Standard butt cap: linen phenolic
Standard wrap: Irish linen
Point construction: short splice
Standard joint: linen phenolic
Joint type: flat faced
Joint ccrew: 3/8-10
Standard number of shafts: two
Standard taper: custom
Standard ferrules: linen phenolic
Tip widths available: any
Standard tip: Triangle
Annual production: approximately 300

OPTIONS (FOR NEW CUES ONLY)

Leather wrap: $70
Special length: no charge
Ivory joint: $150
Extra shaft: $50

REPAIRS

Repairs done on all fine cues.
Refinish (with linen wrap): $100
Rewrap (Irish linen): $30
Rewrap (leather): $70
Replace joint (ivory): $175
Replace shaft: $80
Replace ivory ferrule: $80

CURRENT COKER CUES

Two-piece Coker bar cues start at $220. Basic Coker cues with wraps and joint rings start at $400. Coker cues with points start at $500. The current delivery time for a Coker cue is four to six months, depending upon intricacy of the cue.

232 COKER CUES, cont.

GRADING	98%	90%	70%

SECONDARY MARKET MINIMUM VALUES

The following are minimum values for Coker cues encountered on the secondary market. These prices are representative of cues utilizing basic materials and designs that are not currently available. Coker has offered one-of-a-kind cues that can command many times these prices due to the use of exotic materials and artistry.

Special construction note: There are many materials and construction techniques that can add value to Coker cues. The following are the most important examples:

Add $100+ for ivory joint.

For all used Coker cues, except where otherwise noted:

Add $45 for each additional original straight playable shaft beyond two.
Deduct $50 for each missing original straight playable shaft under two.
Add $45 each for ivory ferrules.
Add $45 for leather wrap.
Deduct 25% for obvious or improper refinish.

Level 1 - 4 points, hustler.
Level 1 cues start at	$200	$160	$110

Level 2 - 0 points, 0-25 inlays.
Level 2 cues start at	$350	$275	$185

Level 3 - 2-6 points, 0-8 inlays.
Level 3 cues start at	$450	$350	$235

Level 4 - 4-10 points, 9-25 inlays.
Level 4 cues start at	$565	$425	$285

Level 5 - 0-12 points, 26-50 inlays.
Level 5 cues start at	$800	$650	$435

COMPETITION SPORTS CORP

Formerly known as Adam Custom Cues. Maker of pool cues from 1997 to present in Japan. Distributed in the United States by Competition Sports Corp of Farmingdale, New York.

In 1997, Don Spetkar renamed Adam USA to Competition Sports. Richard Helmstetter was concentrating on his involvement with Callaway Golf which had started in 1986. Don and Helmstetter's partner, Dave Forman, continued to import Adam cues as well as several other lines. Don Spetcar became the sole owner in 2004. The company imports and distributes several lines of cues, and also makes cases, accessories, and tables as well. If you wish to order a new cue distributed by Competion Sports Corp, or have a cue distributed by Competition Sports Corp that is in need of repair or further identification, contact Competition Sports Corp, listed in the Trademark Index.

SPECIFICATIONS

Butt material: hardwoods
Shaft material: rock maple
Standard length: 58 in.
Point construction: short splice or full splice
Standard wrap: Irish linen
Standard number of shafts: one

OPTIONS (FOR NEW CUES ONLY)

Leather wrap: $120
Special length: $80
Extra shaft: $40 to $120

REPAIRS

Repairs done on all fine cues.

Rewrap (linen): $80
Rewrap (leather): $120
Replace butt cap: $60
Replace joint: $60
Replace shaft: $60+
Replace ivory ferrule: $100+

CURRENT COMPETITON SPORTS CORP CUES

Competition Sports Corp currently distributes the George Balabushka series (shown), the Hall of Fame series, the All Star series, Karella cues, and the Willie Mosconi Collector Series, among others. Most cues are available for immediate delivery.

COMPETITION SPORTS CORP., cont.

GRADING	100%	95%	70%

CURRENT EXAMPLES

The following "George Balabushka" series cues have a 5/16 piloted stainless steel joint with nickel silver rings in the black linen collars. The butt caps and ferrules are of Ceromeld, and the tips are Le Pro. Each cue carries a reproduced signature of George Balabushka on the forearm. One shaft is standard; extra shafts are available for $120 each. There were formerly 20 models. Several hundred GB series cues are produced each year in Japan.

Level 3 GB-1 - Maple forearm, four rosewood points with four colored veneers, rosewood butt sleeve.

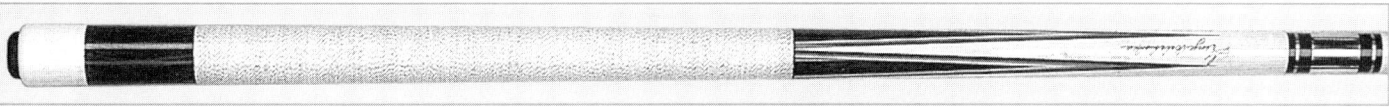

MSR	$440	$335-440	$295	$200

Level 3 GB-2 - Natural stained bird's-eye maple forearm, four rosewood points with four colored veneers, ebony butt sleeve.

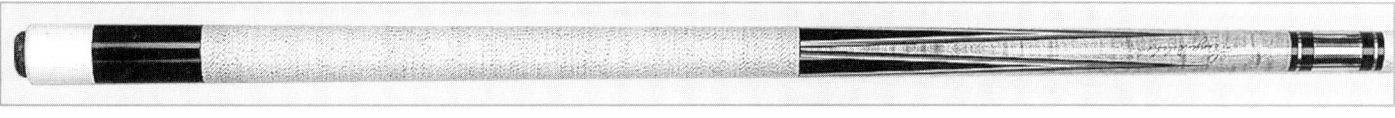

MSR	$500	$350-500	$315	$225

Level 3 GB-3 - Natural stained bird's-eye maple forearm, four rosewood points with four colored veneers and a mother-of-pearl notched diamond-shaped inlay in each, rosewood butt sleeve with four mother-of-pearl notched diamond-shaped inlays.

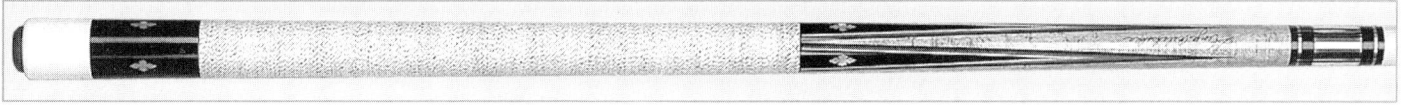

MSR	$550	$375-550	$340	$250

Level 3 GB-4 - Natural stained bird's-eye maple forearm, four rosewood points with thick ebony and maple veneers, ebony butt sleeve with mother-of-pearl dots set in ebony within thin maple rings between white and black dashes within nickel silver rings above and below (Bushka rings).

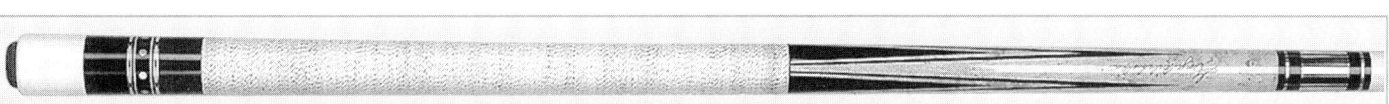

MSR	$620	$435-620	$395	$275

Level 4 GB-5 - Natural stained bird's-eye maple forearm, four bocote points with bocote and ebony veneers, bocote butt sleeve with four mother-of-pearl notched diamond-shaped inlays alternating with four sets of three-piece maple and bocote windows within three-piece maple and bocote dashes set in ebony above and below.

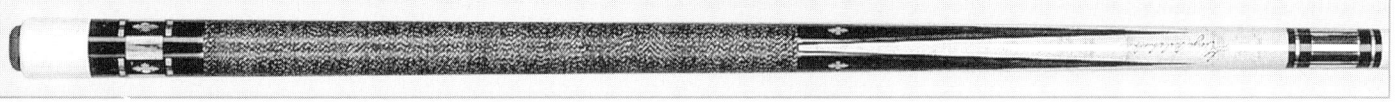

MSR	$680	$435-680	$400	$295

Level 3 GB-6 - Natural stained bird's-eye maple forearm with white and black dashes within nickel silver rings above wrap, three long ebony points with a white diamond-shaped inlay in each spliced over three short ebony points, ebony butt sleeve with three white diamond-shaped inlays above two bands of white and black dashes within three nickel silver rings below (Bushka rings).

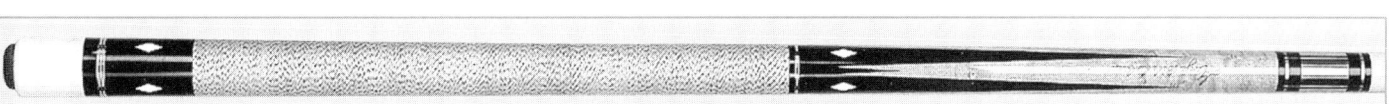

MSR	$750	$525-750	$450	$340

Level 4 GB-7 - Natural stained bird's-eye maple forearm, four rosewood points with four colored veneers and a small white diamond-shaped inlay in each, ebony butt sleeve with four white diamond-shaped inlays alternating with four maple "X"-shaped inlays between maple bordered red rings above and below.

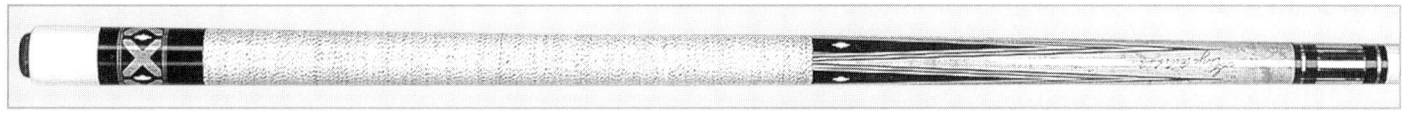

MSR	$800	$630-800	$550	$350

GRADING	100%	95%	70%

Level 4 GB-8 - Natural stained bird's-eye maple forearm, four ebony points with colored veneers and a mother-of-pearl notched diamond-shaped inlay between a mother-of-pearl dot above and below in each point, ebony butt sleeve with four mother-of-pearl notched diamond-shaped inlays alternating with four pairs of mother-of-pearl dots above and below between thin red rings above and below.

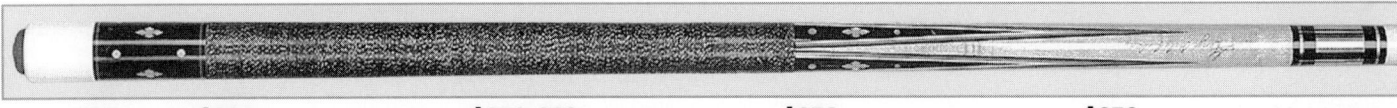

MSR	$600	$350-600	$350	$250

Level 4 GB-9 - Natural stained bird's-eye maple forearm, four ebony points with maple and ebony veneers and a mother-of-pearl notched diamond-shaped inlay in each, ebony butt sleeve with four mother-of-pearl notched diamond-shaped inlays between white and ebony dashes within nickel silver rings above and below (Bushka rings).

MSR	$650	$375-650	$375	$250

GRADING	98%	90%	70%

SECONDARY MARKET MINIMUM VALUES

The following are minimum values for other Competition Sports cues encountered on the secondary market. These prices are representative of cues utilizing basic materials and designs that may not be currently available.

Special construction note: There are many materials and construction techniques that can add value to Competition Sports Corp cues. For all used Competition Sports Corp cues, except where otherwise noted:

Add $35+ for each additional original straight playable shaft beyond one.
Deduct $60+ for missing original straight playable shaft.
Deduct 15% for obvious or improper refinish.

Level 1 - 4 points, hustler.
Level 1 cues start at	$60	$50	$25

Level 2 - 0 points, 0-25 inlays.
Level 2 cues start at	$60	$45	$25

Level 3 - 2-6 points, 0-8 inlays.
Level 3 cues start at	$120	$95	$55

Level 4 - 4-12 points, 9-25 inlays.
Level 4 cues start at	$175	$135	$80

CORLISS CUE

Maker of pool cues from 1994 to present in Juno Isles, Florida.

Neil Corliss is a cue maker in Juno Isles, Florida who began building cues in 1994. What started as a hobby is now a part time job, mainly for enjoyment. Neil spent a large portion of his time in yacht building as a master wood craftsman. He is happy to do all kinds of repairs on all makes of fine cues, but refinishing and rewrapping leather is a specialty. Neil has over twenty-five varieties of leathers and he has worked long and hard to perfect his leather wraps. As a result, Neil does a lot of leather wraps on his new cues and he does a lot of leather rewraps on other cues. Neil's own cues tend to feature more traditional designs, as Neil makes everything except the tips, bumpers, and screws by hand, without the aid of CNC. In 2004 Neil started coring the handles an forearms of his cues with laminated maple rods.

Corliss cues are signed on the forearm "Neil Corliss" followed by a number and the year of completion, and the same marks are engraved under the bumpers. Neil keeps a record of all the cues he makes and who all of the original owners are. Corliss cues are guaranteed for life to the original owner against construction defects that are not the result of warpage or abuse. If you are interested in talking to Neil M. Corliss Sr. about a new cue or cue that needs to be repaired, you can contact him at Corliss Cue, listed in the Trademark Index.

SPECIFICATIONS

Butt material: hardwoods
Shaft material: rock maple
Standard length: 58 in.
Standard finish: two-part acrylic
Balance point: 18 in. from butt
Standard butt cap: phenolic
Standard wrap: Irish linen
Point construction: short splice
Standard joint: stainless steel
Joint type: piloted
Standard joint screw thread: 5/16–18
Standard number of shafts: one
Standard taper: modified pro

| GRADING | 98% | 90% | 70% |

Standard ferrules: Aegis
Standard tip: Le Pro
Tip widths available: any
Annual production: about 25

OPTIONS (FOR NEW CUES ONLY)

Ivory butt cap: $175
Ivory joint: $85
Ivory ferrule: $60
Leather wrap: $80+
Joint protectors: $40+
Extra shaft: $100+

REPAIRS

Repairs done on all fine cues.
    Refinish (with Irish linen wrap): $100
    Refinish (with leather wrap): $140+
    Rewrap (Irish linen): $40
    Rewrap (leather): $80+
    Replace shaft: $100+
    Replace ivory ferrule: $60

CURRENT CORLISS CUES

Basic Corliss two-piece bar cues start at $100. Basic Corliss cues with wraps and joint rings start at $300. Corliss cues with points start at $450. Corliss cues require an average order time of two to six weeks to complete.

SECONDARY MARKET MINIMUM VALUES

The following are minimum values for other Corliss cues encountered on the secondary market. These prices are representative of cues utilizing basic materials and designs that are not necessarily available at present. Neal has offered one-of-a-kind cues that can command many times these prices due to the use of exotic materials and artistry.

Special construction note: There are many materials and construction techniques that can add value to Corliss cues.

For all used Corliss cues, except where otherwise noted:
    Add $70 for each additional original straight playable shaft beyond one.
    Deduct $100+ for missing original straight playable shaft.
    Add $50 each for ivory ferrules.
    Add $70+ for leather wrap.
    Deduct 20% for obvious or improper refinish.

	98%	90%	70%
Level 1 - Hustler.			
Level 1 cues start at	$85	$70	$45
Level 2 - 0 points, 0-25 inlays.			
Level 2 cues start at	$250	$195	$130
Level 3 - 2-6 points, 0-8 inlays.			
Level 3 cues start at	$400	$315	$215
Level 4 - 4-10 points, 9-25 inlays.			
Level 4 cues start at	$500	$390	$265
Level 5 - 0-12 points, 26-50 inlays.			
Level 5 cues start at	$750	$575	$390

CORSAIR CUSTOM CUES

Maker of pool cues from 1968 to present in Huntington Beach, California.

Hank Korsiak

Roger Korsiak

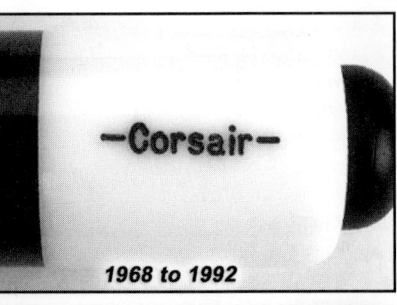
1968 to 1992

1992 to Present day

Henry "Hank" Korsiak was born in 1920 in New York City. He grew up in Brooklyn and began playing billiards at the age of ten. Hank moved to California in 1953 and worked as an aerospace design engineer. He continued to play billiards, and after having to install a tip and ferrule on a house cue during a tournament in the late sixties, he started doing repair work. He became well-known for repairing broken cues in such a way that they played better than they did before.

By 1968, Hank made his first cue. The first cues he made are identifiable by a brass 5/16 in. joint screw which was in the shaft. Shortly after that he started putting the screw in the butt and, in 1972, he started using a stainless screw instead of brass. Early cues were styled with thick, large, bold designs, consisting of patterns created from geometric shapes. "Rose Blossom" cues, with large circular inlays surrounded by smaller dots, are among the rarest and most valuable Corsair cues.

Around 1970, Hank introduced the all-black phenolic cue. He is believed to be the first and only maker ever to design and produce cues entirely out of this material. This type of cue soon became very popular for Corsair and customers soon nicknamed it the "Black Beauty." Early Black Beauty cues were made of a wood-grained black phenolic that almost looked like ebony. This material was unavailable after 1984, when black phenolic with more of a granite look was used instead.

From 1976 to 1992, Hank's three sons began making some cues. Each started in succession during this time. They made cues that were not as fancy as Hank's and were responsible for only about two percent of the production for those years. These cues are internally marked as to who made them, and only Corsair Custom Cues can verify the maker.

In about 1980, a deeper-set, full-thickness bumper permanently replaced the thin-set, shallow-based bumper that had been used on all Corsair cues up to that point. Around that time, Hank also began to engrave "-CORSAIR-" in the butt caps.

Cues made in the sixties and seventies and most of the eighties were finished with a French polish. In the late eighties, Hank started using urethane coatings. In late December of 1992, after 24+ years of custom cuemaking, Hank passed away. It is estimated that he made approximately 6,000 cues during his lifetime, all of which have become collectible.

Today, Corsair Custom Cues is run by Hank's son, Roger Korsiak. Roger makes and repairs cues with the same approach developed by his father, the majority of new cues being one-of-a-kind originals. Roger learned cue making from his father for thirteen years before he died. All work is done by hand, and no stains are used, so all woods display their natural colors. After Hank's death, Roger began marking the cues "*CORSAIR*" to avoid any confusion among customers and collectors. He now makes between six and ten cues per year.

Letters of authenticity, appraisal, and identification of the original maker are available for collectors who own early Corsair cues. If you have a Corsair cue that needs further identification or repair, or would like to talk to Roger about ordering a new Corsair cue, contact Corsair Custom Cues, listed in the Trademark Index.

SPECIFICATIONS

Butt material: hardwoods or linen phenolic
Shaft material: rock maple
Standard length: 58 in.
Lengths available: any
Standard finish: polyurethane
Joint screw: 5/16-18
Standard joint: 7075 aluminum
Joint type: piloted
Balance point: 18 to 19 in. from butt
Point construction: short splice
Standard wrap: Irish linen
Standard butt cap: Delrin
Standard number of shafts: one
Standard taper: 12-1/2 in. pro
Standard ferrules: fiber
Standard tip: Le Pro
Tip widths available: 9 mm – 14 mm
Annual production: fewer than 15 cues

CORSAIR CUSTOM CUES, cont. 237

GRADING	100%	95%	70%

OPTIONS (FOR NEW CUES ONLY)
Custom joint protectors: $45
Extra shaft: $90
Ivory joint: $100
Ivory ferrule: $50
Ivory butt cap: $200

REPAIRS
Repairs done on most fine cues.
Refinish (with linen wrap): $100
Refinish (with leather wrap): $100
Rewrap (linen): $50
Clean and press linen wrap: $15
Clean Leather wrap: $15
Replace shaft: $90
Replace ivory ferrule: $60
Replace tip: $10
Replace fiber ferrule: $10
Replace butt cap: $20
Replace ivory butt cap: $225
Replace layered tip: $10, if tip is provided

CURRENT CORSAIR CUES
The average order time for one of Roger's Corsair custom cues is three months.

CURRENT EXAMPLES
The following are current examples of Corsair cues by Roger Korsiak. These cues can be ordered as shown, modified to suit the desires of the customer, or new designs can be created.

Level 1 - Maple forearm, four full spliced ebony points and handle.

MSR	$310	$295-350	$235	$165

Level 2 "Black Beauty" - Black phenolic forearm, black phenolic butt sleeve with white fiber rings above and below.

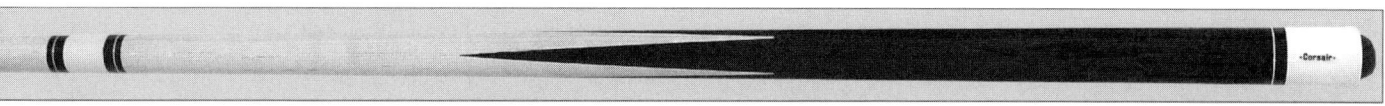

MSR	$550	$500-600	$400	$290

Level 2 - Curly koa forearm, curly koa butt sleeve with curly koa and maple checks set in black phenolic rings at bottom.

MSR	$600	$575-650	$465	$325

Level 2 "Black Beauty" - Black phenolic forearm with rows of graduated aluminum dots, black phenolic butt sleeve with aluminum dots set within aluminum rings above and below.

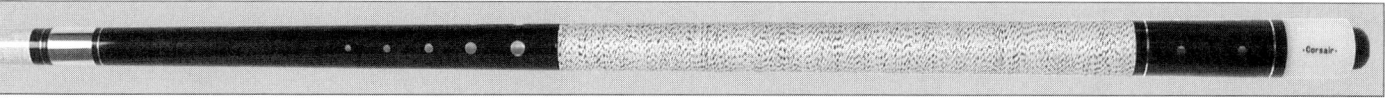

MSR	$650	$600-700	$480	$345

Level 2 - Bird's-eye maple forearm, bird's-eye maple butt sleeve with rosewood and maple checks set in black phenolic rings at top and bottom.

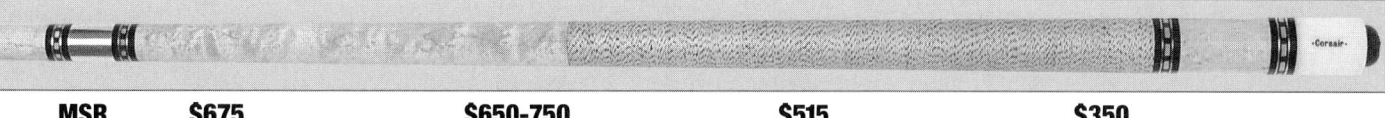

MSR	$675	$650-750	$515	$350

| GRADING | 98% | 90% | 70% |

PAST EXAMPLES (BY HANK KORSIAK)

The following cues are representations of Hank's work. These cues can be encountered as shown, modified to suit the desires of the original customer, or new designs can be encountered.

Level 1- Maple forearm, four full spliced purple heart points with wrap and butt cap.

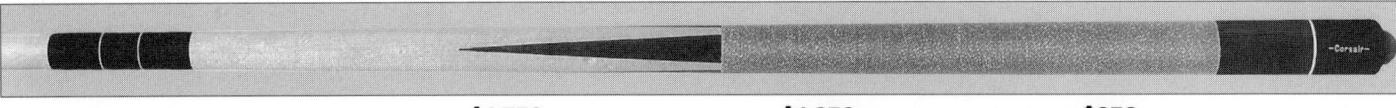

| | $1,550 | $1,250 | $850 |

Level 2- Ivory joint, bird's-eye maple forearm, bird's-eye maple butt sleeve with maple and paduk ring work at bottom.

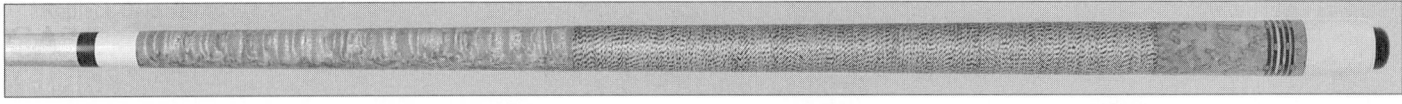

| | $1,950 | $1,600 | $1,150 |

Level 2- Bubinga forearm with maple/bubinga/black phenolic/Delrin/aluminum ring work above wrap, black phenolic butt sleeve with maple/bubinga/black phenolic/Delrin/aluminum ring work at top and bottom.

| MSR (1984) $500 | $2,750 | $2,250 | $1,600 |

Level 2 "Black Beauty"- Black phenolic shaft collar, black phenolic forearm, bird's-eye maple handle, black phenolic butt sleeve with an aluminum ring at bottom.

| MSR (1985) $475 | $3,250 | $2,650 | $1,900 |

Level 2 "Black Beauty"- Black phenolic shaft collar, black phenolic forearm with ebony and micarta ring work above wrap, black phenolic butt sleeve with ebony and white micarta ring work at top and bottom.

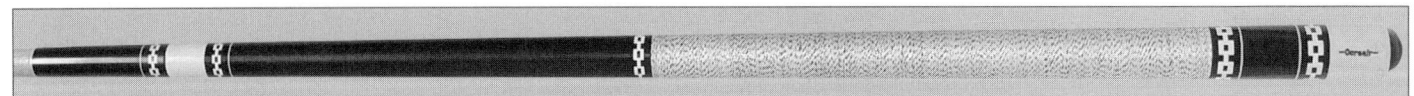

| | $3,500 | $2,850 | $2,000 |

Level 2 "Rose Blossom Black Beauty"- Black phenolic forearm with graduated aluminum dots above maple/micarta/rosewood/phenolic/aluminum ring work above wrap, black phenolic butt sleeve with aluminum dots in a "Rose Blossom" pattern between maple/micarta/rosewood/phenolic/aluminum ring work at top and bottom.

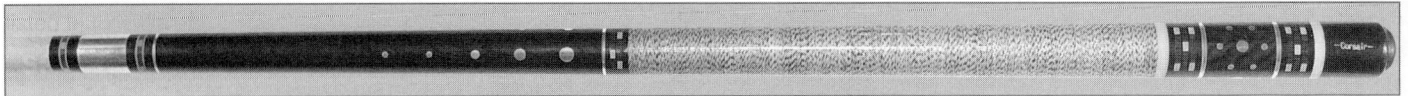

| | $5,500 | $4,400 | $3,000 |

Level 3 "Titlist"- Maple forearm, four rosewood points with four colored veneers, ebony butt sleeve with aluminum/Delrin/black phenolic ring work at center and top and bottom.

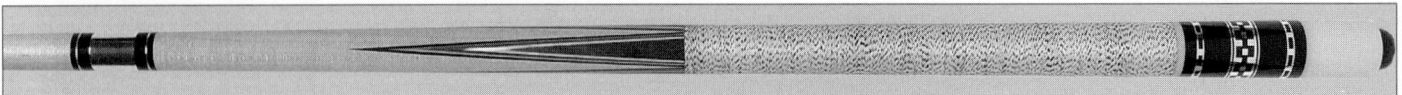

| | $3,750 | $2,950 | $2,000 |

Level 4- Ivory joint, bird's-eye maple forearm, four long and four short ebony bordered ivory points with an ivory diamond-shaped inlay at the tip of each, ebony butt sleeve with ivory diamond-shaped inlays within ebony and ivory ring work above and below.

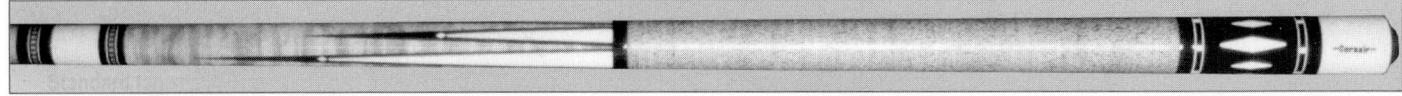

| | $6,500 | $5,250 | $3,500 |

CORSAIR CUSTOM CUES, cont. 239

GRADING	98%	90%	70%

PAST EXAMPLES (BY ROGER KORSIAK)

Level 2 "Black Beauty" - Black phenolic shaft collar, black phenolic forearm with ebony and micarta ring work above wrap, black phenolic butt sleeve with ebony and white micarta ring work at top and bottom.

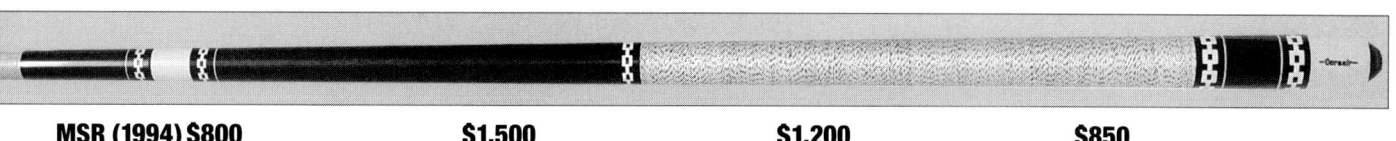

MSR (1994) $800	$1,500	$1,200	$850

SECONDARY MARKET MINIMUM VALUES (BY HANK KORSIAK)

The following are minimum prices for other early Corsair cues encountered on the secondary market. These prices are representative of cues utilizing basic materials and designs that were available. Hank also made one-of-a-kind cues that can command many times these prices due to the use of exotic materials and artistry.

Special construction note: There are many materials and construction techniques that can add value to early Corsair cues. The following are the most important examples:

  Add $1,000+ for ivory points.
  Add $750+ for "Rose Blossom" designs on cues.
  Add $500+ for solid black phenolic construction ("Black Beauty" cues).

Level 2 - 0 points, 0-25 inlays.

Level 2 cues start at	$1,650	$1,325	$950

Level 3 - 2-6 points, 0-8 inlays.

Level 3 cues start at	$2,350	$1,875	$1,350

Level 4 - 4-10 points, 9-25 inlays.

Level 4 cues start at	$2,800	$2,350	$1,775

Level 5 - 0-12 points, 26-50 inlays.

Level 5 cues start at	$3,500	$2,850	$2,100

SECONDARY MARKET MINIMUM VALUES (BY ROGER KORSIAK)

The following are minimum prices for later Corsair (by Roger Korsiak) cues encountered on the secondary market. These prices are representative of cues utilizing basic materials and designs that may not be currently available. Roger also offers one-of-a-kind cues that can command many times these prices due to the use of exotic materials and artistry.

Special construction note: There are many materials and construction techniques that can add value to Corsair cues.

For all used Corsair cues, except where otherwise noted:

  Add $75+ for each additional original straight playable shaft beyond one.
  Deduct $90 for missing original straight playable shaft.
  Add $250+ for ivory joint.
  Add $100+ for leather wrap.
  Add $65+ for each ivory ferrule.
  Add $35+ for 3" or longer black sleeve on shaft.
Deduct 25% for obvious or improper refinish.

Level 2 - 0 points, 0-25 inlays.

Level 2 cues start at	$450	$360	$250

Level 3 - 2-6 points, 0-8 inlays.

Level 3 cues start at	$700	$565	$400

Level 4 - 4-10 points, 9-25 inlays.

Level 4 cues start at	$950	$795	$625

FRANK COSTER

Maker of pool cues from 1982 to 1991 in Catasauqua, Pennsylvania, a suburb of Allentown.

Frank Coster was a tool and die maker for Western Electric in Allentown, Pennsylvania. He enjoyed playing checkers and pool as a hobby, and was a member of an Allentown pool league team. Frank retired from Western Electric in 1981, after more than thirty years of work there. One year later, in 1982, he made his first cue. Frank did all of his work by hand in his one-man shop. He blueprinted all of his designs and inlays.

Coster cues most often encountered will have bird's-eye maple forearms and butt sleeves with Irish linen wraps. Frank sold many of his cues out of Jordan Lanes in Allentown, the home base for his pool league team. He priced them for the local league players, charging relatively little compared to comparably skilled cuemakers of the time. Although he loved to make fancy cues, only about 10% of Coster cues encountered will be fancy, and these cues demand a premium. Fancy Coster cues often were decorated with very intricate ivory inlays shaped like gears. He always put inlays at the tips of the points.

| GRADING | 98% | 90% | 70% |

People who knew Frank remember the shop he had in his basement where he hung hundreds of pieces of wood to age for years, dating each one when he put it up. He had a nine-foot Brunswick Gold Crown in his shop and many trophies he had won in pool and checker tournaments. Frank was very well liked by the people for whom he made cues, one of them being Allen Hopkins. Friends remember him as a quiet man who was very precise and neat. He finished his last cue in April of 1991. Frank died one month later on May 12.

Coster cues were not marked, but are identifiable by their unique designs and flat faced joint with a brass insert in the shaft. If you have a Frank Coster cue that needs further identification or repair, contact Hercek Fine Billiard Cues or Szamboti Cues Inc., listed in the Trademark Index.

SPECIFICATIONS

Butt material: hardwoods
Shaft material: rock maple
Standard length: 58 in.
Joint type: flat faced with brass insert
Standard wrap: Irish linen
Total production: approximately 130

KNOWN FRANK COSTER EXAMPLES

The following cues are a representation of the work of Frank Coster. These cues can be encountered as shown, modified to suit the desires of the original customer, or more elaborate designs can be encountered. Frank Coster cues are most often encountered in the Northeastern United States.

Level 2 - Bird's-eye maple forearm, bird's-eye maple butt sleeve.

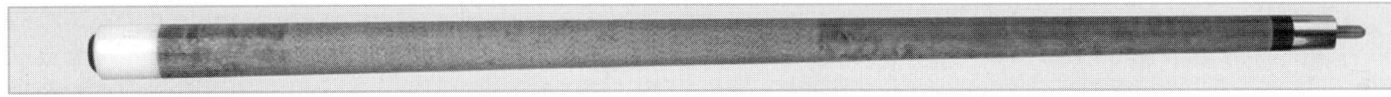

| Orig. Retail $140 | $2,750 | $2,245 | $1,500 |

Level 4 - Stained bird's-eye maple forearm, floating ebony barbells with ebony bordered ivory dots at each end, ebony butt sleeve with stained maple barbells with ebony bordered ivory dots at each end alternating with ivory notched diamond-shaped inlays.

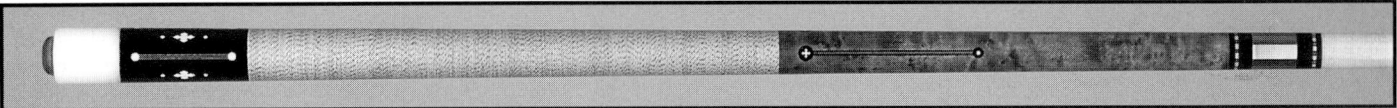

| $14,000 | $11,500 | $8,000 |

Level 5 - Stained bird's-eye maple forearm with an ivory inlaid ebony band at bottom, stained maple points with veneers and an ebony bordered ivory dots at the tip of each, ebony butt sleeve with stained maple barbells with ebony bordered ivory dots at each end alternating with ivory notched diamond- and dot-shaped inlays.

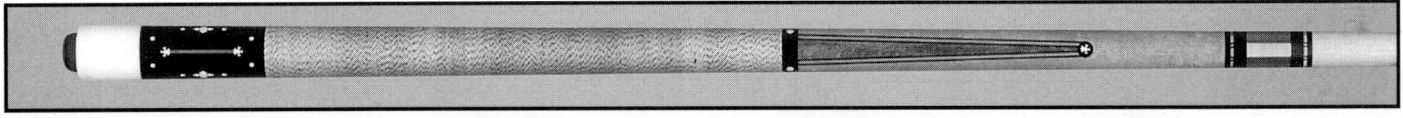

| $16,000 | $12,350 | $8,500 |

Level 6 - Stained bird's-eye maple forearm with an ivory inlaid ebony band at bottom, stained maple points with veneers and ebony-bordered ivory dots with ebony tips, ebony butt sleeve with stained maple windows with ivory dots at each corner surrounding ivory gear-shaped inlays with ivory dash rings above and below.

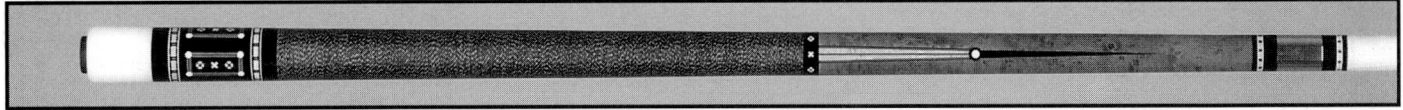

| $20,000 | $16,500 | $12,500 |

Level 6 - Stained bird's-eye maple forearm, floating ebony points with ivory dots and gears alternating with ebony barbells with ebony bordered ivory dots at each end, ebony butt sleeve with ivory dots surrounding rows of ivory gear-shaped inlays.

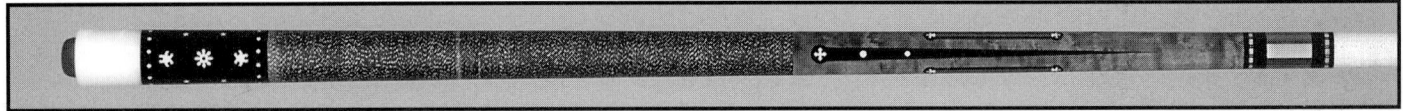

| $20,000 | $16,500 | $12,500 |

FRANK COSTER, cont. 241

| GRADING | 98% | 90% | 70% |

Level 6 - Stained bird's-eye maple forearm, floating ebony bordered stained maple windows with a barbell in each and ebony bordered ivory stars at each end, ebony butt sleeve with ivory dots surrounding ivory gear-shaped inlays.

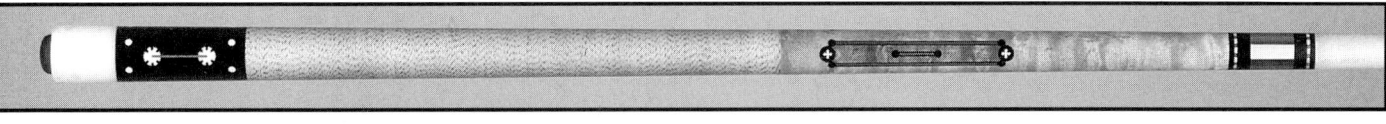

| | $20,000 | $16,500 | $12,500 |

Level 6 - Stained bird's-eye maple forearm with an ivory inlaid ebony band at bottom, stained maple points with veneers and ebony-bordered ivory dots with ebony tips alternating with floating ebony and ivory barbells, ebony butt sleeve with ivory notched diamond-shaped inlays within check rings and rings of ivory dots above and below.

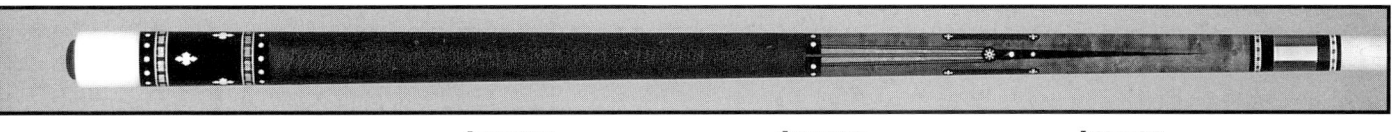

| | $22,000 | $17,500 | $13,500 |

Level 6 - Stained bird's-eye maple forearm with an ivory inlaid ebony band at bottom, stained maple points with veneers and ebony bordered ivory dots with ebony tips alternating with floating ebony and ivory barbells, ebony butt sleeve with stained maple windows with ebony bordered ivory dots and gears surrounded by ivory dots.

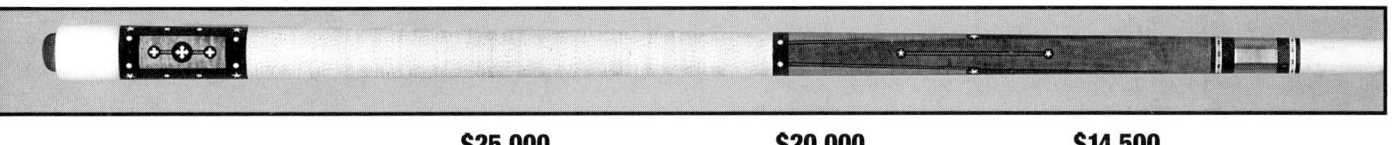

| | $25,000 | $20,000 | $14,500 |

Level 6 - Stained bird's-eye maple forearm with a thick ivory inlaid ebony band at bottom, stained maple points with veneers and ebony bordered ivory dots with ebony tips alternating with ivory inlaid ebony points, ebony butt sleeve with ivory notched diamond-shaped inlays within check rings and rings of ivory dots above and below.

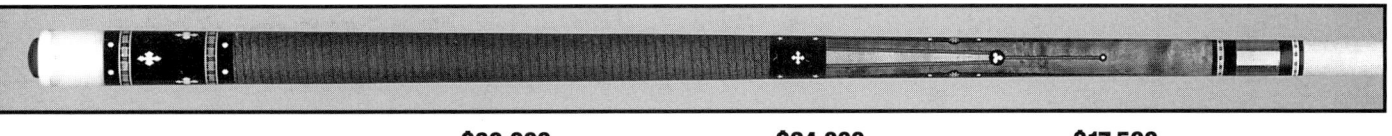

| | $30,000 | $24,000 | $17,500 |

SECONDARY MARKET MINIMUM VALUES

The following are minimum prices for other Coster cues encountered on the secondary market. These prices are representative of Coster cues utilizing the most basic materials and designs that were available. Frank also offered one-of-a-kind cues that can command many times these prices due to the use of exotic materials and artistry. Frank Coster cues will be further covered in future editions.

Note: Due to the rarity of Frank Coster cues and increasing interest, prices are on the rise. Fewer original examples are surfacing, and collectors are holding on to the ones they have. Unique examples with pedigree, and cues made for top professional players are bringing the highest prices.

Special construction note: There are many materials and construction techniques that can add value to Frank Coster cues. For all used Coster cues, except where otherwise noted:

- Add $200+ for each additional original straight playable shaft (standard with one).
- Deduct $350 for missing original straight playable shaft.
- Add $300+ for ivory joint.
- Add $200+ for leather wrap.
- Deduct 30% for obvious or improper refinish.

Level 2 - 0 points, 0-25 inlays.
| Level 2 cues start at | $2,500 | $1,950 | $1,350 |

Level 3 - 2-6 points, 0-8 inlays.
| Level 3 cues start at | $10,000 | $8,000 | $5,500 |

Level 4 - 4-10 points, 9-25 inlays.
| Level 4 cues start at | $14,000 | $11,000 | $7,500 |

Level 5 - 0-12 points, 26-50 inlays.
| Level 5 cues start at | $20,000 | $16,000 | $11,000 |

Level 6 - 0-12 points, 51-75 inlays.
| Level 6 cues start at | $25,000 | $19,500 | $13,500 |

| GRADING | 98% | 90% | 70% |

COUSIN'S CUSTOM CUES

Maker of pool cues from 1991 to present in Liverpool, New York.

Gary Wright made his first pool cue in 1991. Gary was an engineer and factory manager with General Electric. In 1992, after nineteen years with G.E., Gary was laid off. His cousin, Ed Wright, who had encouraged him to start making cues, responded, "Great! Now you'll have more time to make pool cues!"

That year, with Gary handling construction and Ed handling sales, Cousin's Custom Cues produced around 50 cues. Although there were no exterior logos, they were marked "G.R. Wright" under the linen wraps. With his experience in woodworking, Gary spends much of his time selecting and seasoning wood. Shaft wood is stored for six to eight months before it is cut. He developed his own taper that makes the shafts as stiff as possible. Cousin's cues stress the beauty of natural woods instead of stains or colored materials, and ivory is never used.

If you have a Cousin's cue that needs further identification or repair, or would like to talk to Gary or Ed about ordering a new cue, contact Cousin's Custom Cues, listed in the Trademark Index.

SPECIFICATIONS

Butt material: hardwoods
Shaft material: rock maple
Standard length: 58 in.
Standard joint screw: 3/8-10
Standard joint: linen phenolic
Joint type: flat faced
Balance point: 1 ½ in. above wrap
Standard wrap: Irish linen
Standard taper: custom
Annual production: approximately 200

SECONDARY MARKET MINIMUM VALUES

The following are minimum values for other Cousins cues encountered on the secondary market. These prices are representative of cues utilizing basic materials and designs that are not necessarily available at present. Cousins has offered one-of-a-kind cues that can command many times these prices due to the use of exotic materials and artistry.

Special construction note: There are many materials and construction techniques that can add value to Cousins cues.

For all used Cousins cues, except where otherwise noted:

Add $100 for each additional original straight playable shaft beyond one.
Deduct $150 for missing original straight playable shaft.
Add $40 each for ivory ferrules.
Add $50 for leather wrap.
Deduct 15% for obvious or improper refinish.

	98%	90%	70%
Level 2 - 0 points, 0-25 inlays.			
Level 2 cues start at	$400	$320	$225
Level 3 - 2-6 points, 0-8 inlays.			
Level 3 cues start at	$600	$465	$320
Level 4 - 4-10 points, 9-25 inlays.			
Level 4 cues start at	$700	$535	$365
Level 5 - 0-12 points, 26-50 inlays.			
Level 5 cues start at	$950	$735	$500

CRAMER CUES

Maker of pool cues in Albany, Oregon.

If you are interested in talking to Jeff Cramer about a new cue or cue that needs to be repaired, you can contact him at Cramer Cues, listed in the Trademark Index.

CRYSTAL LEISURE

Wholesale Distributor of pool cues in Englewood, Colorado.

If you have a Crystal Leisure cue that needs further identification or repair, or would like to order a new Crystal Leisure cue, contact Crystal Leisure, listed in the Trademark Index.

CUE MASTER

Maker of pool cues from 1987 to present in Spokane, Washington.

James Wough grew up in Los Angeles, California. After returning from four tours in Vietnam, he headed up to Montana. Four years later, in 1974, James moved to Spokane, Washington. He started to play pool as a means of entertainment. With a lathe at home and a woodworking hobby, he naturally did his own cue repair. After a stroke in 1987, he started making cues as part of his rehabilitation.

With little equipment and no desire to buy blanks, James has always made very simple cues without points, except for a few hustler cues. Although his early hustlers were made from scratch, he eventually settled on cutting nice one-piece cues in half. All inlays were done entirely by hand until the summer of 1996, when he got his first manual pantograph. He refuses to use ivory on his cues. He prefers to

GRADING	98%	90%	70%

use an oil finish, but he usually uses a spray lacquer, as his customers seem to prefer a higher gloss finish. James specializes in custom making cues to suit the specifications of the player. Cue Master cues tend to be balanced a little further forward than most cues.

James offers a money back guarantee on new cues if the customer is unhappy. James used to make custom Cue Master cues, on which he tried to keep the price under $300. After retiring from his job running a tennis racket company in 1998, James stopped making custom cues so he could devote more time creating websites and running his own website, http://www.cuemaster.com. He now makes hustler cues only, from scratch, making full splices with bocote or rosewood butts. He tries to match the grain in the shaft wood to the butt of the cue, making the joint even less conspicuous. Aside from making cues, James also designs web sites for Internet advertisers, with an emphasis on the billiards industry.

If you have a Cue Master cue that needs further identification or repair, or would like to talk to James about ordering a new cue, contact Cue Master, listed in the Trademark Index.

SPECIFICATIONS

Butt material: hardwoods
Shaft material: rock maple
Standard length: 58 in.
Lengths available: any
Standard finish: lacquer
Joint wcrew: 3/8-10
Standard joint: hidden
Joint type: flat faced
Balance point: custom
Standard wrap: Irish linen if wanted
Standard number of shafts: one
Standard taper: 9 in. pro
Standard ferrules: M.P. ivory
Standard tip: Chandivert
Tip widths available: any, up to 14 mm
Annual production: 100-150 cues

CUE MASTER CUES

The following are minimum prices for Cue Master cues encountered on the secondary market. These prices are representative of cues utilizing basic materials and designs that may not be currently available. James has offered one-of-a-kind cues that can command many times these prices due to the use of exotic materials and artistry.

Special construction note: There are many materials and construction techniques that can add value to Cue Master cues.

For all used Cue Master cues, except where otherwise noted:
- Add $75+ for each additional original straight playable shaft beyond one.
- Deduct $85 for missing original straight playable shaft.
- Deduct 20% for obvious or improper refinish.

Level 1 - 4 points, hustler.
Level 1 cues start at	$155	$125	$85

Level 2 - 0 points, 0-25 inlays.
Level 2 cues start at	$275	$215	$145

THE CUE MASTERS

Makers of pool cues from 2001 to present in Calliham, Texas.

Present day

Jim and Tom Haskin

Tom and Jimmy Haskin began making cues in 2001. It started as a hobby when they saw that there was a demand for quality cues in their area. Tom and Jimmy use hands-on and great care to make their quality cues. Playability is their ultimate goal. Their small shop has up-to-date equipment, with several lathes and also a CNC machine for inlay work. They also have a facility for doing finishing work.

GRADING	98%	90%	70%

Current Cue Masters cues can be identified by an "H" on the butt cap. Early models were personally signed with the name "Haskin." The Cue Masters are guaranteed against structural defects for the life of the original owner. Normal wear and tear, neglect or abuse are not covered. Customers can return their new cues within 90 days for a full refund minus shipping and handling, if they are not happy with their purchase.

If you are interested in talking to Tom and Jimmy about a new cue or cue that needs to be repaired, you can contact them at The Cue Masters, listed in the Trademark Index.

SPECIFICATIONS

Butt material: hardwoods
Shaft material: rock maple
Standard length: 58 in.
Standard butt cap: Phenolic
Standard wrap: Irish linen
Standard joint: wood-to-wood
Joint screw thread: 3/8-10
Standard ferrules: Aegis II
Standard tip: Le Pro
Annual production: approximately 100

OPTIONS (FOR NEW CUES ONLY)

Ivory ferrule: $80
Leather wrap: $110
Extra shaft: $75

REPAIRS

Repairs done on all American-made cues.
Refinish (with Irish linen wrap) $125+
Rewrap (Irish linen): $35
Replace shaft: $125
Replace tip: $12

CURRENT CUE MASTER CUES

Basic two-piece Cue Masters bar cues start at $275. Cue Masters cues with wraps and joint rings start at $395. Cue Masters cues with points start at $495.

SECONDARY MARKET MINIMUM VALUES

The following are minimum values for other Cue Masters cues encountered on the secondary market. These prices are representative of cues utilizing basic materials and designs that are not necessarily available at present. Tom and Jimmy have offered one-of-a-kind cues that can command many times these prices due to the use of exotic materials and artistry.

Special construction note: There are many materials and construction techniques that can add value to Cue Masters cues.

For all used Cue Masters cues, except where otherwise noted:
Add $100 for each additional original straight playable shaft beyond one.
Deduct $125 for missing original straight playable shaft.
Add $60 each for ivory ferrules.
Add $50 for leather wrap.
Deduct 20% for obvious or improper refinish.

Level 1 - Hustler.
	98%	90%	70%
Level 1 cues start at	$225	$175	$115

Level 2 - 0 points, 0-25 inlays.
Level 2 cues start at	$350	$270	$185

Level 3 - 2-6 points, 0-8 inlays.
Level 3 cues start at	$425	$325	$220

Level 4 - 4-10 points, 9-25 inlays.
Level 4 cues start at	$500	$385	$260

Level 5 - 0-12 points, 26-50 inlays.
Level 5 cues start at	$700	$550	$365

CUES BY DAVID

Maker of pool cues from 1989 to present in Newport Beach, California.

David Whitsell began building cues in 1989 in Newport Beach, California. He was inspired by the work of Dan and Jeff Prather, Verl Horn, and Joe Porper. There is a 14-week average wait for David's custom cues. His love of the artistry in some cues, as well as time spent in pool rooms, got him interested in this business. He spent time as an apprentice to the Prathers. Early on his business was named "Pool Tools."

If you are interested in talking to David Whitsell about a new cue or cue that needs to be repaired, you can contact him at Cues By David, listed in the Trademark Index.

SPECIFICATIONS

- Butt material: hardwoods
- Shaft material: rock maple
- Standard length: 58 in.
- Lengths available: 57 in. to 64 in.
- Standard finish: automotive clear coat
- Balance point: custom
- Standard butt cap: linen-based fiber
- Standard wrap: Irish linen
- Point construction: short splice or inlaid
- Standard joint: stainless steel
- Joint type: piloted
- Joint screw thread: 5/16-14
- Joint protectors: standard
- Standard number of shafts: one
- Standard taper: custom
- Standard ferrules: linen-based fiber
- Standard tip: Moori
- Standard tip width: 13 mm
- Tip widths available: 9 mm – 14 mm
- Standard bumper: 7/8 black rubber
- Annual production: approximately 70

OPTIONS (FOR NEW CUES ONLY)

- Special length: $50+
- Layered tip: $40
- Ivory butt cap: $200
- Ivory butt sleeve: $400
- Ivory joint: $150
- Ivory ferrule: $70
- Ivory points: $800
- Ivory handle: $1500
- Leather wrap: $150
- Joint protectors: $25+
- Extra shaft: $125+
- Custom case: $500+

REPAIRS

Repairs done on all American made cues.

- Refinish (with Irish linen wrap): $175
- Refinish (with leather wrap): $325
- Rewrap (Irish linen): $40
- Rewrap (leather): $150
- Restore leather wrap: $20+
- Replace shaft: $125+
- Replace ivory ferrule: $75
- Replace butt cap: $55
- Replace ivory butt cap: $200
- Replace tip: $20 - $50
- Replaced layered tip: $40
- Replace fiber/linen ferrule: $40

CURRENT CUES BY DAVID CUES

Basic two-piece Cues By David bar cues start at $350. Basic Cues By David cues with wraps and joint rings start at $400. Cues By David cues with points and one-of-a-kind Cues By David custom cues start at $500. The current delivery time for a Cues By David cue is fourteen weeks.

CUES BY DAVID CUES

GRADING	98%	90%	70%

The following are minimum values for other Cues By David cues encountered on the secondary market. These prices are representative of cues utilizing basic materials and designs that are not necessarily available at present. David has offered one-of-a-kind cues that can command many times these prices due to the use of exotic materials and artistry.

Special construction note: There are many materials and construction techniques that can add value to Cues By David cues.

For all used Cues By David cues, except where otherwise noted:
- Add $100+ for each additional original straight playable shaft beyond one.
- Deduct $120+ for missing original straight playable shaft.
- Add $50 each for ivory ferrules.
- Add $100 for leather wrap.
- Deduct 20% for obvious or improper refinish.

Level 1 - Hustler.

	98%	90%	70%
Level 1 cues start at	$275	$225	$150

Level 2 - 0 points, 0-25 inlays.

Level 2 cues start at	$350	$270	$185

Level 3 - 2-6 points, 0-8 inlays.

Level 3 cues start at	$450	$350	$240

Level 4 - 4-10 points, 9-25 inlays.

Level 4 cues start at	$600	$465	$315

Level 5 - 0-12 points 26-50 inlays.

Level 5 cues start at	$900	$715	$485

CUESPORT

Maker of pool cues from 1965 to present in Southfield, Masachussetts.

Cuesport was founded in 1965 by Fred Mali to build Mali cues. In 1998, Peter Balner joined the company, and a new line of Palmer cues was planned.

For information on Cuesport cues made for Henry W.T. Mali & Co., Inc., refer to Mali Cues.

CUETEC

Maker of pool cues in China and Taiwan. Distributed by J-S Sales Company in Mt. Vernon, New York.

Cuetec cues are made in China and Taiwan, and are distributed by J-S Sales, a company with many years of experience in the billiards industry. Cuetec shafts are made of maple, with clear fiberglass bonded to the surface. The butts on the "Signature," "Tournament," and "Professional" series cues are made of maple, with fiberglass bonded to the surface. The "Graphite" series cues have maple butts with graphite bonded to the surface. The "Classic" and "Traditional" series cues feature butts made of bird's-eye maple, with applied images of inlays and points, with clear fiberglass bonded to the surface. Jump break cues are also available, as are one-piece cues which are color-coded to identify their weight.

Cuetec cues are easily identifiable by the "Cuetec" logo on the butt sleeve or forearm. If you have a Cuetec cue that needs further identification or repair, or would like to talk to someone about ordering a new Cuetec cue, contact J-S Sales, listed in the Trademark Index.

SPECIFICATIONS

Butt material: synthetic over wood
Shaft material: clear fiberglass over maple
Standard length: 58 in.
Lengths available: 58 in. or 60 in.
Standard wrap: Irish linen
Standard number of shafts: one

CURRENT CUETEC CUES

Cuetec currently manufactures several series of cues. The Classic Series consists of four cues priced at $169. The Allison Fisher Series consists of three cues priced from $145 to $199. The Graphite Series consists of four cues priced from $159 to $179. The Jump/Break Series consists of four cues priced from $179 to $220. The Mahogany Series consists of six cues priced at $159.99. The Midnight Series consists of seven cues priced from $150 to $300. The Natural Series consists of six cues priced at $159.99. The Earl Strickland Signature Series consists of six cues priced at $139. The Starlight Six Prong Series consists of seven cues

GRADING	98%	90%	70%

priced from $139 to $149. The Thunderbolt Series consists of eight cues with leather wraps priced at $300. The Vortex Series consists of three cues with leather wraps priced at $300. Cuetec cues are available for immediate delivery.

SECONDARY MARKET MINIMUM VALUES

The following are minimum prices for Cuetec cues encountered on the secondary market.
For all used Cuetec cues, except where otherwise noted:
- Add $60+ for each additional original straight playable shaft beyond one.
- Deduct $55 for missing original straight playable shaft.
- Add $50+ for leather wrap.

	98%	90%	70%
Level 1 - 4 points, hustler.			
Level 1 cues start at	$100	$80	$50
Level 2 - 0 points, 0-25 inlays.			
Level 2 cues start at	$125	$100	$70

DAVID CZARNECKI
Maker of Zar Cues, for information refer to Zar Cues.

NOTES

D SECTION

DANBUILT CUSTOM CUES

Maker of pool cues from 1992 to 1996 as Danbuilt Custom Cues and from 1996 to present as Dishaw Custom Cues in Syracuse, New York. For more information, refer to Dishaw Custom Cues.

JOHN DAVIS CUSTOM CUES

Maker of pool cues from 1964 to 1975 and 2005 to present in Chicago, Illinois.

John Davis

John Davis has been a tool and die maker for most of his career. Following high school, John entered the tool and die field as an apprentice and has worked his way up to Shop Lead Man at Finzer Roller in Chicago, Illinois. John had a number of hobbies back then, one of which was pocket billiards. In the early 1960s, John visited Burton Spain's shop to have his Hoppe cue repaired. The two hit it off and soon began a partnership that would span many years. With John's knowledge of machinery and Burt's experience in woodworking, the two of them made a great team. John built many of the custom machines and fixtures used in their cuemaking process. Together the two turned out beautiful handmade custom cues and supplied blanks to many of the world's top cuemakers, including George Balabushka. In 1970 Burton Spain took a break from cuemaking to fix up some Greystone houses he and his father had bought. John purchased the business from Burton Spain and continued on his own until 1974. During that time, John continued to build blanks for cuemakers while concurrently building his own cues. In addition to cuemaking, John had a full-time job and a new family, all of which took a toll on him. As a result, John sold the cuemaking business back to Burton Spain in 1974. Although John stuck to his full-time job as a tool and die maker, he and Burton stayed friends and golf partners until Burt's untimely death. For the next 30 years, John separated himself from cuemaking but never completely abandoned the notion of returning to the craft he loved.

In 2004, John decided to get back into cuemaking and started to build his new cue shop from scratch. Some of the pieces of equipment John set up were the very machines he used back in the late 1960s and early 1970s. Several of the machines were acquired from Joel Hercek, who was retooling his shop and sold many of the items back to John, including a shaft machine John and Burton had built in the 1960s. The future looks bright for John Davis. He is starting back up where he left off and already has a following for his traditional cues with timeless designs.

If you are interested in talking to John Davis about a new cue or cue that needs to be repaired, you can contact him at John Davis Cues, listed in the Trademark Index.

SPECIFICATIONS

- Butt material: hardwoods
- Shaft material: rock maple
- Standard length: 57 in.- 58 in.
- Lengths available: 57 in. - 60 in.
- Standard finish: custom
- Joint screw: 5/16-14 or 3/8-10
- Standard joint: stainless steel
- Joint type: piloted or flat faced
- Joint protectors: standard
- Balance point: custom
- Point construction: full splice
- Standard wrap: Irish linen
- Standard butt cap: Delrin
- Standard number of shafts: two
- Standard taper: Spain Taper
- Standard ferrules: ivory
- Standard tip: leather
- Tip widths available: 11 mm - 15 mm
- Annual production: 40 cues

OPTIONS (FOR NEW CUES ONLY)

- Leather wrap: $200
- Ivory joint: $225
- Ivory butt cap: $400
- Extra shaft: $175+

REPAIRS:

Repairs considered on a cue-by-cue basis.

GRADING	98%	90%	70%

CURRENT DAVIS CUES

John Davis cues with full-spliced points start at $1,500. John is currently focusing more on splice work than inlay work. His new cues can feature fancy butterfly splices in addition to his full splice point construction. Pricing can vary depending on the complexity of a design. Fancy spliced cues are priced on a case-by-case basis.

PAST EXAMPLES

Level 3 Stainless steel joint, cocobolo forearm with four points of ebony, orange, blue, and white veneers, nylon wrap, black/silver/orange decorative rings at joint and butt sleeve (2).

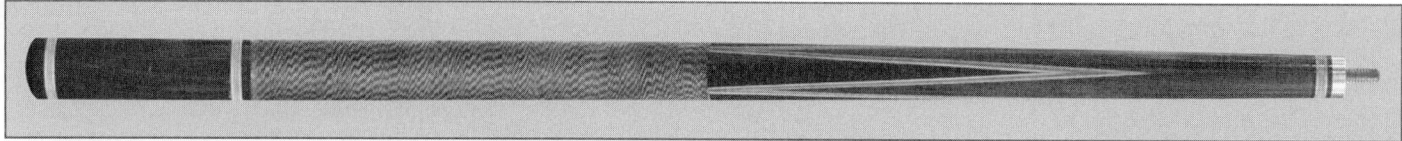

| MSR (1965-67) $300 | $2,400 | $2,100 | $1,300 |

Level 3 - Stainless steel joint, maple forearm, four ebony points with four colored veneers, nylon wrap, ebony butt sleeve, pearlized plastic/black/silver decorative ring work at joint, above wrap and in middle of butt sleeve.

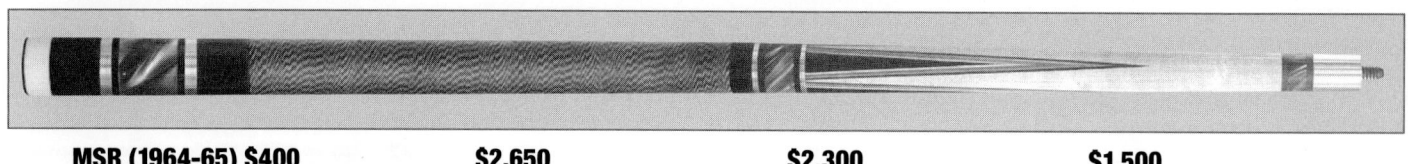

| MSR (1964-65) $400 | $2,650 | $2,300 | $1,500 |

JOHN DAVIS CUSTOM CUES

The following are minimum prices for other Davis cues encountered on the secondary market. These prices are representative of cues utilizing basic materials and designs that may not be currently available.

For all used Davis cues, except where otherwise noted:
- Add $175+ for each additional original straight playable shaft (standard with two).
- Deduct $175 for each missing original straight playable shaft.
- Add $250+ for ivory joint.
- Add $400+ for ivory butt cap.
- Add $250+ for leather wrap.
- Add $50+ for each ivory ferrule.
- Deduct up to 40% for obvious or improper refinish.

Level 3 - 2-6 points, 0-8 inlays.
| Level 3 cues start at | $2,400 | $2,100 | $1,300 |

Level 4 - 4-10 points, 9-25 inlays.
| Level 4 cues start at | $3,500 | $3,000 | $1,800 |

GARY DAWKINS

Maker of GD Cues. For more information, see GD Cues.

DAYTON CUSTOM CUES

Maker of pool cues from 1988 to present in Fort Pierce, Florida.

Paul Dayton started playing pool while in high school in 1960, in Scotia, New York. His first cue was a Brunswick "Willie Hoppe" Titleist. He thought it was too fat in the butt so he turned it down on the high school's lathe, wrapped it with fishing line, and refinished it. After seeing an old cue with the owner's name engraved in an inlaid mother-of-pearl plaque, Paul found a large shell and did the same to his cue. His friends wanted the same custom inlay on their cues and Paul was in business until he ran out of pearl.

1994 to Present Day

Paul Dayton

After graduating from high school, Paul joined the Air Force. He then went to college and got a degree in biochemistry, got married, and started a career as an epidemiologist with the New York State Health Department. In his spare time Paul was restoring antiques and repairing cues. He had bought a roll of Irish linen and some mother-of-pearl inlays from Pete Balner when he picked up a custom cue from Palmer in Elizabeth, New Jersey. By 1974, Paul was so busy with other things that he sold his Balabushka for $100 and stayed away from pool for the next 14 years.

Paul began playing pool again in 1988. He bought a used cue, but was unhappy with the way it hit. He put an ivory ferrule, phenolic rings, and a steel joint on it to improve the hit. Still not satisfied, Paul made a new shaft on his wood lathe. Next he made a cue from scratch, using old lumber he bought at country auctions. It was not terribly pretty, but Paul was very happy with the way it hit. It finally dawned on Paul that after 28 years of customizing and repairing cues, what he really wanted to do was make his own custom cues.

Paul purchased a small machinist's lathe and started making much nicer cues. With the proceeds, he began to buy more tooling, wood, and a bigger lathe. He started to phase out his antique restoration business so he could make cues full time. On early cues, Paul inlaid points by hand with an X-acto knife, a Dremel tool, chisels, and a file. Most cues were marked with a stylized "pd" on the butt cap from 1988 until 1994, when Paul began to sign and date most cues on the forearm or butt sleeve. Paul and his wife moved to Florida, built a house, and built a shop which was finished in 1996. That year, Paul started to use short spliced blanks. In 2000, Paul stopped putting dates on his cues, leaving only the signature. He still did all of the his inlay work by hand with an X-acto knife, a Dremel tool, chisels, and a file. In 2002, Paul bought a CNC machine, strictly for inlay work. Paul's inlays are of natural materials such as ivory, mother-of-pearl, and exotic woods. He travels to central Ontario to select the maple for his shafts and forearms. He also has a small selection of 100-year-old shaft wood obtained from trees that were salvaged from the bottom of the Great Lakes. Paul dyes his own veneers, creating a limitless array of colors. A steel or aluminum screw at the end of a tenon on the handle is used in the joining of the butt sections of a Dayton custom cue. Shafts, seasoned for years, are cut every six months until stable. Only thermoset plastics such as linen- and canvas-based fiber, and melamine are used. Metal rings may be of aluminum, nickel silver, sterling silver, or brass, depending on weight, balance, and design constraints. Paul makes everything except for the screws, steel joints, bumpers, and tips by hand in his one-man shop.

Dayton Custom Cues are guaranteed for life against manufacturing defects that are not the result of warpage or abuse.

If you are interested in talking to Paul Dayton about a new cue or cue that needs to be repaired, you can contact him at Dayton Cues, listed In the Trademark Index.

SPECIFICATIONS

Butt material: hardwoods
Shaft material: rock maple
Standard length: 58 in.
Lengths available: any up to 64 in.
Standard wrap: Irish linen
Standard finish: catalyzed urethane
Balance point: custom
Standard butt cap: linen phenolic
Point construction: short splice
Standard joints: linen phenolic or steel
Joint type: flat faced
Joint screw: radial pin
Standard taper: custom
Standard number of shafts: two
Standard ferrules: phenolic
Standard tip: Talisman Medium Pro
Standard tip width: 13 mm
Annual production: approximately 80 cues

OPTIONS (FOR NEW CUES ONLY)

Ivory ferrule: $70
Leather wrap: $100
Water buffalo horn joint: $125
Ivory joint: $100
Extra shaft: $125

REPAIRS

Repairs done on Dayton Cues only. Repair prices depend on the individual cue.

CURRENT DAYTON CUES

Two-piece Dayton Hustler cues start at $275. Basic Dayton cues with wraps and joint rings start at $400. Dayton cues with points start at $650. One-of-a-kind custom Dayton cues start at $1,350. Ivory ferrules are standard on Dayton cues over $1,000. The current delivery time for a Dayton cue is eight to twelve weeks, depending on the intricacy of the cue.

CURRENT EXAMPLES

The following cues are currently available from Dayton Custom Cues. They can be ordered as shown, or modified to suit the desires of the customer.

DAYTON CUSTOM CUES, cont.

GRADING	100%	95%	70%

Level 2 - Bird's-eye maple forearm with an ebony and ivory stitched ring above wrap, bird's-eye maple butt sleeve with ebony and ivory stitched rings at top and bottom.

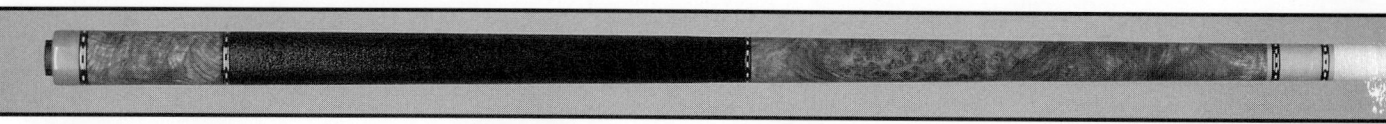

MSR	$850	$800-1,000	$700	$550

Level 3 - Ivory joint, tiger maple forearm, four ebony points with four veneers, leather wrap, ebony butt sleeve with ivory ring at bottom.

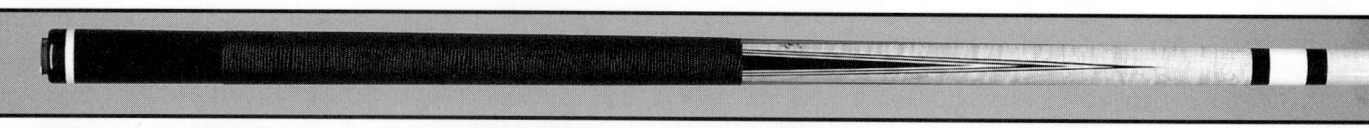

MSR	$1,100	$1,000-1,200	$850	$600

Level 3 - Ebony forearm with an ivory and purpleheart ring above wrap, three long and three short purpleheart points with three veneers, leather wrap, ebony butt sleeve with three long and three short reverse purpleheart points with three veneers between ivory and purpleheart rings at top and bottom

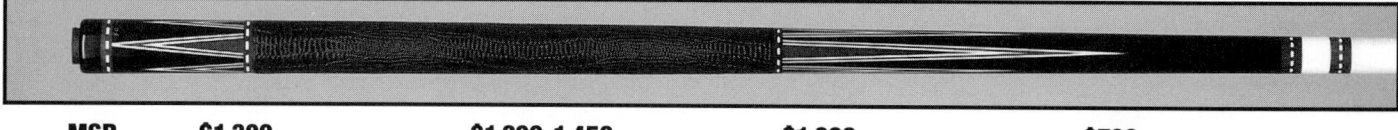

MSR	$1,300	$1,200-1,450	$1,000	$700

Level 3 - Honey-stained tiger maple forearm with an ivory and snakewood stitched ring above wrap, four snakewood points with two veneers, leather wrap, honey stained tiger maple butt sleeve with ivory and snakewood stitched rings at top and bottom.

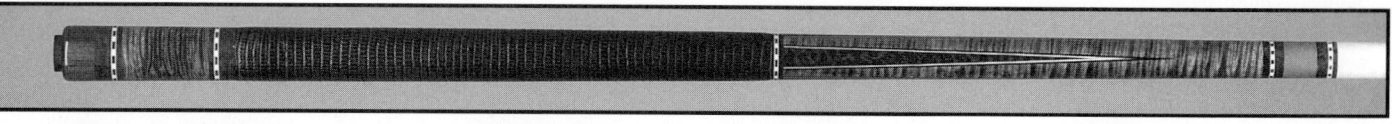

MSR	$1,900	$1,800-2,100	$1,450	$1,000

Level 4 - Bird's-eye maple forearm with ivory and turquoise and ebony rings above ivory stitched rings above wrap, four ebony points with four veneers and an ivory diamond-shaped inlay in each, ebony butt sleeve with eight ivory diamond-shaped inlays between ivory stitched rings at top and bottom.

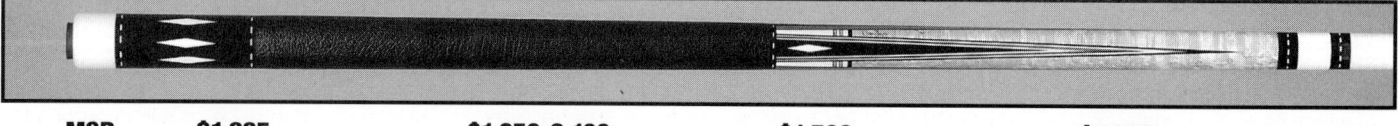

MSR	$1,995	$1,850-2,100	$1,500	$1,050

Level 4 - Ivory joint, honey-stained curly maple forearm with an Ivory block ring above wrap, four ebony points with four veneers and an ivory spear-shaped inlay in each, honey-stained curly maple butt sleeve with pairs of opposing ivory spear-shaped inlays alternating with hollow ivory windows between ivory block rings at top and bottom.

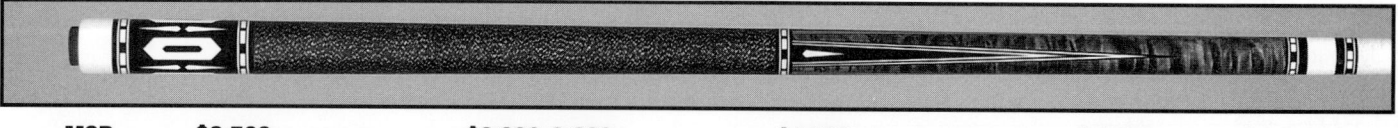

MSR	$2,500	$2,200-2,600	$1,800	$1,300

Level 4 - Ebony forearm with ebony and ivory and turquoise rings above an ebony and ivory stitched ring above wrap, three long and three short amboyna burl points with two veneers and an ivory diamond-shaped inlay in each, ebony butt sleeve with ebony and ivory and turquoise rings below an ebony and ivory stitched ring below wrap with three long and three short amboyna burl reverse points with two veneers and an ivory diamond-shaped inlay in each above an ivory stitched ring at bottom.

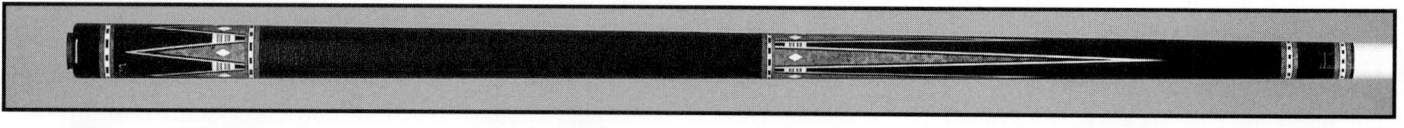

MSR	$2,750	$2,600-2,800	$2,150	$1,400

GRADING	98%	90%	70%

SECONDARY MARKET MINIMUM VALUES

The following are minimum values for other Dayton Custom Cues encountered on the secondary market. These prices are representative of cues utilizing basic materials and designs that are not currently available. Paul Dayton has offered one-of-a-kind cues that can command many times these prices due to the use of exotic materials and artistry.

Special construction note: There are many materials and construction techniques that can add value to Dayton cues.

For all used Dayton cues, except where otherwise noted:
- Add $100 for each additional original straight playable shaft beyond two.
- Deduct $125+ for each missing original straight playable shaft under two.
- Add $50 each for ivory ferrules.
- Add $50 for leather wrap.
- Deduct 20% for obvious or improper refinish.

	98%	90%	70%
Level 1 - Hustler. Level 1 cues start at	$250	$200	$140
Level 2 - 0 points, 0-25 inlays. Level 2 cues start at	$375	$295	$200
Level 3 - 2-6 points, 0-8 inlays. Level 3 cues start at	$600	$475	$325
Level 4 - 4-10 points, 9-25 inlays. Level 4 cues start at	$750	$585	$400
Level 5 - 0-12 points, 26-50 inlays. Level 5 cues start at	$1,100	$875	$600
Level 6 - 0-12 points, 51-75 inlays. Level 6 cues start at	$1,400	$1,150	$800

DG CUES

Maker of pool cues from 1999 to present in Rockaway, New Jersey.

Some of Don Gaudreau's earliest memories are of spending time in the shop with his father, a pattern-maker by trade. Don grew up appreciating the intricacies of pattern making and wanting to learn more about the precision work his father was doing. If his father was in the shop, Don was underfoot, watching and learning.

When he started playing pool, it was only natural that Don thought about making cues. The more involved in the game Don got, the more his curiosity about cuemaking grew. He finally started experimenting by doing repair work on his own cues and, then, those of his friends. As time went on, Don began to do more complex repair work and soon he started to make one-of-a-kind display cases for high end cues.

Around 1995, Don discovered the Super Billiards Expo at Valley Forge. He looked around at the expo and realized cue making was something he wanted to learn. He admired the quality and workmanship of every cue he saw. However, one particular maker stood out—Richard Black. Each time he ran into him, Don asked Mr. Black questions about cue making and soon Mr. Black took Don under his wing. Don has since learned a great deal from his mentor and friend.

The millennium marked a good year for DG Cues. After much trial and error, Don had finally believed he had a cue he could introduce to the market. He started out by selling to a few friends, and word of the quality of his cues soon spread. Now he sells cues and display cases mainly through word of mouth. Don stands behind his products and always tries to go the extra mile to make sure each and every customer is happy with their investment.

If you are interested in talking to Don Gaudreau about a new cue or cue that needs to be repaired, you can contact him at DG Cues, listed in the Trademark Index.

SPECIFICATIONS

Butt material: hardwoods
Shaft material: rock maple
Standard length: 58-1/2 in.
Lengths available: any
Standard finish: polyurethane
Balance point: 18.5 in. from the butt
Standard butt cap: linen-based phenolic
Standard wrap: Irish linen
Point construction: short splice
Standard joint: stainless steel
Other joints offered: various
Joint type: piloted
Joint screw thread: 5/16-14
Standard number of shafts: two
Standard taper: 10.5 in. straight
Standard ferrules: ivory

DG CUES, cont.

| GRADING | 98% | 90% | 70% |

Standard tip: custom
Standard tip width: 13 mm
Tip widths available: any up to 14 mm
Annual production: fewer than 50 cues

OPTIONS (FOR NEW CUES ONLY)

Special length: no charge
Ivory butt cap: $250
Ivory joint: $150
Leather wrap: $85+
Extra shaft: $125

REPAIRS

Repairs done on all fine cues.
Refinish (with Irish linen wrap): $150+
Rewrap (Irish linen): $45
Rewrap (leather): $85+
Clean and press linen wrap: $25
Replace shaft: $125
Replace ivory ferrule: $75
Replace butt cap: $50+
Replace ivory butt cap: $250
Replace tip: $10+
Replace fiber/linen ferrule: $25+

CURRENT DG CUES

Two-piece DG bar cues start at $250. Basic DG cues with wraps and joint rings start at $350. DG cues with points start at $600. The current delivery time for a DG cue is three to six months.

SECONDARY MARKET MINIMUM VALUES

The following are minimum values for DG cues encountered on the secondary market. These prices are representative of cues utilizing basic materials and designs that are not necessarily available at present. DG Cues has offered one-of-a-kind cues that can command many times these prices due to the use of exotic materials and artistry.

Special construction note: There are many materials and construction techniques that can add value to DG cues.

For all used DG cues, except where otherwise noted:
Add $100 for each additional original straight playable shaft beyond two.
Deduct $125 for each missing original straight playable shaft under two.
Add $50 each for ivory ferrules.
Add $50 for leather wrap.
Deduct 20% for obvious or improper refinish.

	98%	90%	70%
Level 1 - Hustler.			
Level 1 cues start at	$200	$165	$120
Level 2 - 0 points, 0-25 inlays.			
Level 2 cues start at	$300	$240	$165
Level 3 - 2-6 points, 0-8 inlays.			
Level 3 cues start at	$500	$395	$265
Level 4 - 4-10 points, 9-25 inlays.			
Level 4 cues start at	$650	$525	$350
Level 5 - 0-12 points, 26-50 inlays.			
Level 5 cues start at	$900	$700	$475
Level 6 - 0-12 points, 51-75 inlays.			
Level 6 cues start at	$1,200	$950	$650

DIAMOND CUE CO.

Maker of pool cues in the mid-1980s in Colonia, New Jersey.
Cues by Andrew Diamond are easily recognizable by their logos featuring a "D" in a diamond on the butt caps, and their blue bumpers.

SPECIFICATIONS

Butt material: hardwoods
Shaft material: rock maple
Standard length: 58 in.
Standard wrap: Irish linen

GRADING	98%	90%	70%

SECONDARY MARKET MINIMUM VALUES

The following are minimum values for Diamond Cues encountered on the secondary market. These prices are representative of cues utilizing basic materials and designs that are not currently available. Diamond Cues offered one-of-a-kind cues that can command many times these prices due to the use of exotic materials and artistry.

Special construction note: There are many materials and construction techniques that can add value to Diamond cues.

For all used Diamond cues, except where otherwise noted:
- Add $75 for each additional original straight playable shaft beyond one.
- Deduct $125 for missing original straight playable shaft.
- Add $50 each for ivory ferrules.
- Add $75 for leather wrap.
- Deduct 30% for obvious or improper refinish.

	98%	90%	70%
Level 2 - 0 points, 0-25 inlays. Level 2 cues start at	$250	$190	$120
Level 3 - 2-6 points, 0-8 inlays. Level 3 cues start at	$300	$230	$145
Level 4 - 4-10 points, 9-25 inlays. Level 4 cues start at	$375	$285	$180
Level 5 - 0-12 points, 26-50 inlays. Level 5 cues start at	$500	$380	$240

DENNIS DIECKMAN

Maker of pool cues from 1973 to present currently in Manchester, Michigan.

Dennis Dieckman

Dennis Dieckman decided to become a cuemaker in 1971 while attending the University of Michigan. He was there on the G.I. Bill, after spending three years in Vietnam. A player since the age of seven, he spent more time playing pool at the student union than studying at the library. It was at the union that Dennis met Carl Conlon, who taught him the game of three cushion billiards and was one of the inspiring people in his life. During this time, Dennis began making chess and backgammon boards, and started acquiring woodworking machines and tools. He also traveled to Chicago to meet Eddie Laube, who was instrumental in Dennis becoming a cuemaker.

In 1973, Dennis bought a lathe and made his first three cues. These cues were 57 in. long and had stainless steel joints with 5/16-18 screws and black phenolic rings at the joints and in the butt sleeves. One butt was red oak, one was walnut, and one was mahogany. The shafts were cut from house cues with 3/4 in. black ferrules. Dennis sold them for $50 each.

In the summer of 1975, Dennis moved to Virginia, and in 1977, moved to Omaha, Nebraska. In both locations, he set up shop and made cues and game boards. Dennis estimates that during those years he made approximately 100-150 hustler cues, which were essentially house cues that were cut in half and fitted with 5/16-18 screws that went into a shaft insert. These cues were primarily sold at regional flea markets for $40 to $75.

From November of 1978, to May of 1979, Dennis was at North Hollywood Billiards studying three cushion billiards under Frank Torres and studying cuemaking under Bert Schrager.

On September 5th, 1979, back in Omaha, after his second day of classes at Creighton University Law School, Dennis received a phone call offering him a job running a pool room in Ann Arbor, Michigan. He left school to take the position. In December of the same year, he bought a nice lathe and, by the spring of 1980, he set up shop in Ann Arbor. That summer he was offered a job as a golf pro at the University of Michigan golf course, something he had always wanted to do.

For the next nine years, Dennis played and taught golf in the summers, and made cues during the winters. Approximately 95% of these cues were for three cushion billiards, a game Dennis played around the country at tournament level since his days in college. The early cues, made before 1982 or so, had 3/8 in. wood-to-wood joints, inspired by Bert Schrager. After that, he started using 1/2 in. wood screws, usually on bird's-eye maple cues with brown phenolic butt caps and white ABS joint collars on the butts only. They were generally 54 in. to 56 in. long with 10 mm to 11.5 mm tips, short ferrules, and perfect conical tapers from butt cap to ferrule. These cues sold from $125 to $200. In 1983, Dennis made his first cue with butterfly points. This cue, as well as the other butterfly spliced cues he made before 1989, had disappearing points. During these years, he estimates that he made an average of two to three dozen cues a year, most of which were three cushion cues. Many of these cues were made for some of the top billiards players in the country.

In the summer of 1989, Dennis moved back to Ann Arbor, Michigan with the help of his old friend Steve Titus. Steve was Dennis's first cuemaking student, and was the creator of the laminated Predator shafts, which Dennis was heavily involved in.

In the winter of 1989-90, Dennis decided to start making cues full time, and has been doing so ever since. In 1990, Dennis made his first video on the art of cuemaking and made his first cue with traditional "pointed" points. In 1991, he helped to found the American

GRADING	98%	90%	70%

Cuemakers Association, and was one of nine makers present at the first meeting. In 1992, Dennis completed the sixth and final video in his first series of cuemaking videos. The same year, he began selling blanks and bird's-eye maple to other cuemakers.

1993 was spent searching for a more permanent location for his shop and, by the end of the year, he found it. After three months of interior construction on an outbuilding outside his new house, he had a shop he was proud to work in. With four metal working lathes, a wood working lathe, a spray room, an office, 30 feet of benches to work on, a sleeping loft, a pantograph, a milling machine, and at least 75 butts turned to .050 oversize, Dennis can deliver a finished custom cue in as little as two to four months.

In January of 1994, Dennis sat down and looked at all six of the cuemaking videos he had made, and was appalled to the point that he set out to re-do them. In the fall of 1994, he started writing a column on cuemaking in the First National Billiard Exchange. By mid-1995, he completed the first seven videos in his second edition, which were much better than the first. He estimates that approximately 250 people are making cues as a result of his instruction. In November of 1995, Dennis started writing a book on cuemaking, titled "From the Tree to the Cue" which he hopes to complete before he dies. A text-only version is now available in disk. During 1993, 1994, and 1995, his cue production was low because of these other projects. He increased his cue production to about forty cues in 1996.

Dennis has dramatically slowed his cuemaking down to spend more time teaching and making videos. He maintains his "Cueniversity" which is limited to a maximum of six students a year. Dennis now makes about twelve pool cues a year, and has stopped making billiard cues. He will still make a custom cue, but only for past customers. He absolutely refuses to use ivory in any cue. Dennis's cues stress the natural beauty of the wood, and are designed to be played. Faces of people and characters are common inlay themes. In 1998 Dennis was invited to create a cue for a 1999 Smithsonian exhibit. If you have a Dieckman cue that needs repair, or would like to talk to Dennis about a one-of-a-kind custom cue, contact Dennis Dieckman, listed in the Trademark Index.

SPECIFICATIONS
Butt material: hardwoods
Shaft material: rock maple

POINT CONSTRUCTION: BUTTERFLY SPLICE
Options (By Quote):

REPAIRS
Repairs done only on Dennis Dieckman cues (By Quote).

CURRENT DENNIS DIECKMAN CUES
Dennis Dieckman butterfly cues with two-weight matched shafts from 15-year-old Michigan maple and wooden jointed screws start at $1,750. Dennis plans to have about a dozen cues available each December.

PAST EXAMPLES
The following cues are representations of the work of Dennis Dieckman. Today, similar designs can be created.

Level 3 - Bird's-eye maple core, four purpleheart points with maple and purpleheart veneers, thin rosewood butt sleeve with four maple windows.

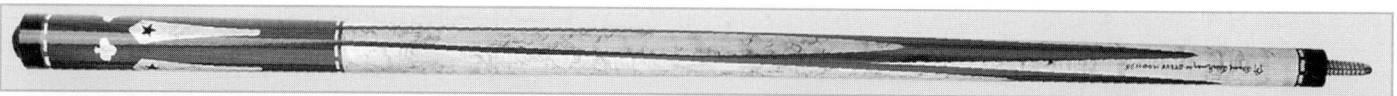

MSR (1996) $800	$1,500	$1,175	$800

Level 3 - Bird's-eye maple core with a pair of paduak and wenge veneered full splices that also appear on the shaft, two cocobolo points with maple and paduak veneers, maple butt sleeve with a pair of paduak and wenge veneered full splices.

MSR (1996) $1,400	$2,750	$2,150	$1,500

Level 4 - Bird's-eye maple core, four bird's-eye maple points with paduak veneers, paduak butt sleeve with four ebony star-shaped inlays each set in a bird's-eye maple spear above four bird's-eye maple club-shaped inlays all between maple checks at top and bottom.

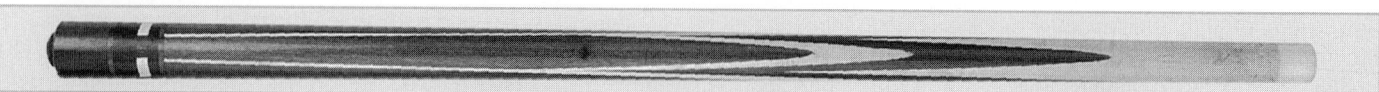

MSR (1996) $1,000	$2,250	$1,850	$1,350

SECONDARY MARKET MINIMUM VALUES
The following are minimum prices for other Dennis Dieckman cues encountered on the secondary market. These prices are representative of cues utilizing basic materials and designs that may not be currently available. Dennis also offers one-of-a-kind cues that can command many times these prices due to the use of exotic materials and artistry.

GRADING	98%	90%	70%

Special construction note: There are many materials and construction techniques that can add value to Dennis Dieckman cues. For all used Dieckman cues, except where otherwise noted:
- Add $100 for each additional original straight playable shaft beyond two.
- Deduct $150 for each missing original straight playable shaft under two.
- Deduct 25% for obvious or improper refinish.

Level 1 - 4 points, hustler.
Level 1 cues start at	$300	$235	$160

Level 2 - 0 points, 0-25 inlays.
Level 2 cues start at	$700	$545	$375

Level 3 - 2-6 points, 0-8 inlays.
Level 3 cues start at	$1,000	$825	$600

Level 4 - 4-10 points, 9-25 inlays.
Level 4 cues start at	$1,250	$975	$650

Level 5 - 0-12 points, 26-50 inlays.
Level 5 cues start at	$1,650	$1,275	$850

Level 6 - 0-12 points, 51-75 inlays.
Level 6 cues start at	$2,000	$1,585	$1,100

DAN DISHAW HANDCRAFTED CUES

Maker of pool cues from 1992 to 1996 as Danbuilt Custom Cues, and from 1996 to present as Dishaw Custom Cues, in Syracuse, New York.

1992 to 1996

1996 to Present Day

Dan Dishaw

Dan Dishaw grew up close to a pool hall, with a father who was a good player. Dan started playing at a very early age. He continued to play pool through college, where he majored in biochemistry and math. Dan also was involved in music, and he played several instruments. Right out of college, he did some construction work, restoring old hotels in Buffalo. Soon he was working as a pattern maker, making full-size wood models for castings, and making custom cabinets as a hobby. One day, he repaired a guitar of his, and decided to start doing some instrument repairs. Before long, he was doing all the repairs for three local music stores, specializing in wood stringed instruments. He enjoyed working with musical instruments, so when one of the music stores went out of business, he decided to open his own store. Dan's 25 years in building and restoring vintage stringed instruments has given him the ability to select and work with woods from all over the world.

In the late 1980s, Dan bought a small company that made flight cases for musical instruments and called it Danbuilt. As a pool player, Dan saw the need for a heavy-duty flight case for pool cues, so Danbuilt started making them. He put a pool table in his shop in the early 1990s, and began playing more. When he had a cue repaired, he was disappointed with the job because he knew he could do better. So, he bought an old lathe and started doing cue repairs as a hobby. In 1992, he made his first three cues. As a result of showing these cues, Dan got orders for well over two dozen more. Today, Dan's cues are sold worldwide.

Early Danbuilt cues are easily recognizable by the Danbuilt logo on the butt cap. In the summer of 1996, Dan started signing his cues "Dishaw" on the forearm instead, and renamed his cue company Dishaw Custom Cues, to avoid confusion with his case company. Early cues were fairly plain, but the more recent cues may feature overlapping points and elaborate inlay work. He believes that his experience with wood musical instruments gives him a different approach to cue construction.

Dan is a member of the American Cuemakers Association, and in 1997 was appointed the Vice President. He now serves as President of the ACA, after having been elected by the Board of Directors in September of 2000. Dan serves on a number of committees.

Dishaw Custom Cues is one of the founding members of the American Billiard Manufacturers Association, and is also a member of the Billiard Congress of American, and exhibits at all BCA trade shows. In April of 2003, Dan was elected to the BCA Board of Directors, where he also serves on several committees.

Dan is a participating cue artist at the prestigious Gallery of American Cue Art, held at the New York City Athletic Club. He also shows at the International Cue Collectors Show. He has just been voted President of the Academy of American Cue Art for 2005-06.

Dan makes about 100 cues a year in the shop he has built under his music store. Dishaw Custom cues are indefinitely guaranteed against construction defects that are not the result of warpage or abuse. If you have a Danbuilt cue that needs further identification or repair, or would like to talk to Dan about ordering a new cue or receiving a free color brochure, contact Dishaw Custom Cues, listed in the Trademark Index.

DAN DISHAW HANDCRAFTED CUES, cont.

| GRADING | 100% | 95% | 70% |

SPECIFICATIONS

Butt material: exotic woods and ivory
Shaft material: rock maple
Standard length: 58 in.
Lengths available: any up to 59 in.
Standard finish: 3-part catalyzed urethane clearcoat
Joint screw: radial pin
Standard joint: flat face
Joint type: phenolic
Joint protectors: standard
Balance point: 1 ½ in. above wrap
Point construction: short splice
Standard wrap: Irish linen
Standard butt cap: linen phenolic
Standard number of shafts: two
Standard taper: 12 in. pro
Standard ferrules: Aegis II
Standard tips: Le Pro or Triangle
Tip widths available: any
Annual production: fewer than 100 cues

OPTIONS (FOR NEW CUES ONLY)

Leather wrap: $150
Ivory joint: $150
Joint protectors: $100+
Ivory butt cap: $250
Ivory ferrules: $100 Each
Ivory butt sleeve: $500
Ivory points: $800
Ivory handle: $3000
Layered tip: $30
Extra shaft: $165

REPAIRS

Repairs done on most fine cues.
Refinish (with leather wrap): $350
Refinish (with Irish linen wrap): $240
Rewrap (leather): $150
Rewrap (linen): $40
Clean and press linen wrap: $20
Restore leather wrap: $35
Replace butt cap: $125
Replace ivory butt cap: $300
Replace shaft: $165
Replace Aegis II ferrule: $40
Replace ivory ferrule: $125
Replace Le Pro tip: $10
Replace layered tip: $30

CURRENT DISHAW CUES

Basic Dishaw cues with wraps and joint rings start at $800. Dishaw cues with points start at $1,100. The current delivery time for a Dishaw cue is approximately six months.

CURRENT EXAMPLES

The following Dishaw cues can be ordered as shown, modified to suit the desires of the customer, or new designs can be created.

Level 2 "Break Cue" - Zircoti forearm with an ivory dash ring set in metal rings above wrap, stained bird's-eye maple handle, zircoti butt sleeve with ivory dash rings set in metal rings at top and bottom.

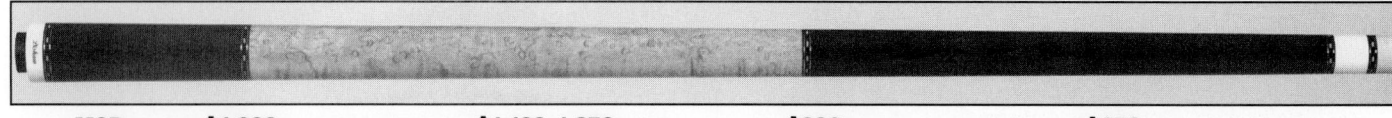

| MSR | $1,200 | $1,100-1,250 | $890 | $650 |

DAN DISHAW HANDCRAFTED CUES, cont. 259

GRADING		98%	90%	70%

Level 4 "Titlist" - Ivory joint, maple forearm, four rosewood points with four colored veneers and an ivory diamond-shaped inlay set in an ebony oval in each point, leather wrap, rosewood butt sleeve with four ivory diamond-shaped inlays set in ebony ovals.

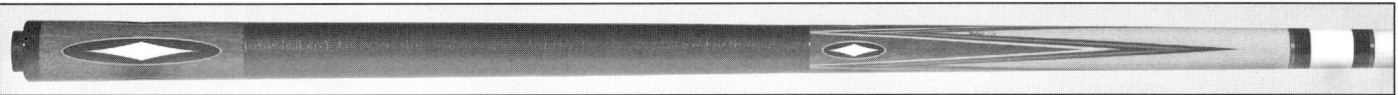

MSR	$2,200	$2,000-2,350	$1,700	$1,350

Level 5 "Oasis in Cocobolo" - Bird's-eye maple forearm with ebony and ivory ring work above wrap, three long cocobolo points with a cocobolo-bordered synthetic ivory spear-shaped inlay at the tip of each point alternating with three short ebony points with two veneers and a synthetic ivory diamond-shaped inlay in each point, leather wrap, bird's-eye maple butt sleeve with four synthetic ivory diamond-shaped inlays set in holly-bordered cocobolo ovals alternating with columns of ebony and cocobolo between ebony and ivory ring work at top and bottom.

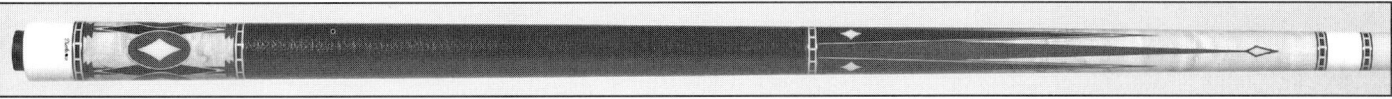

MSR	$2,700	$2,500-2,950	$2,050	$1,550

Level 5 "Oasis in Ebony and Burl" - Ebony forearm with ebony and ivory ring work above wrap, three long amboynia burl points with an amboyna burl-bordered synthetic ivory spear-shaped inlay at the tip of each point alternating with three short synthetic ivory points with two veneers and an ebony-bordered synthetic ivory diamond-shaped inlay in each point, leather wrap, ebony butt sleeve with four synthetic ivory diamond-shaped inlays set in holly-bordered amboynia burl ovals alternating with columns of holly-bordered ebony and amboynia burl between ebony and ivory ring work at top and bottom.

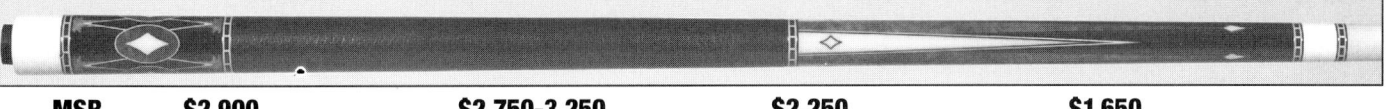

MSR	$2,900	$2,750-3,250	$2,250	$1,650

Level 4 "Butterfly" - Ivory joint, ebony forearm with an ebony and ivory dash ring above wrap, three long Sterling silver bordered ivory points with stylized tips alternating with three short holly and ebony butterfly points, leather wrap, ebony butt sleeve with three reverse sterling silver-bordered ivory points with three veneers and stylized tips alternating with three short holly and ebony reverse butterfly points, ivory butt cap.

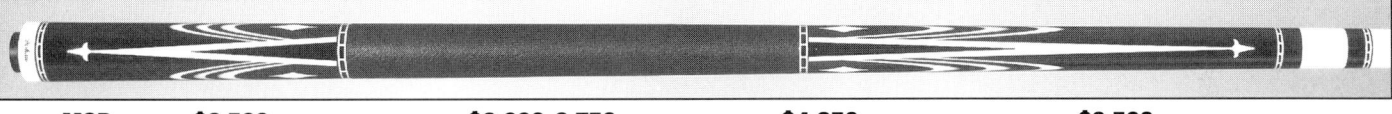

MSR	$6,500	$6,000-6,750	$4,850	$3,500

Level 5 "White Stiletto" - Ivory joint, purpleheart forearm with an intricate ivory/sterling silver/purpleheart ring above handle, three long sterling silver-bordered ivory points with stylized tips and sterling silver inlays alternating with three short sterling silver-bordered ivory points with stylized tips and six overlapping ivory inlays with sterling silver tips, three-section ivory handle seperated by intricate ivory/sterling silver/purpleheart rings, purpleheart butt sleeve with three long sterling silver-bordered ivory points with stylized tips and sterling silver inlays alternating with three short sterling silver-bordered ivory points with stylized tips and six overlapping ivory inlays with sterling silver tips between intricate ivory/sterling silver/purpleheart rings at top and bottom, ivory butt cap.

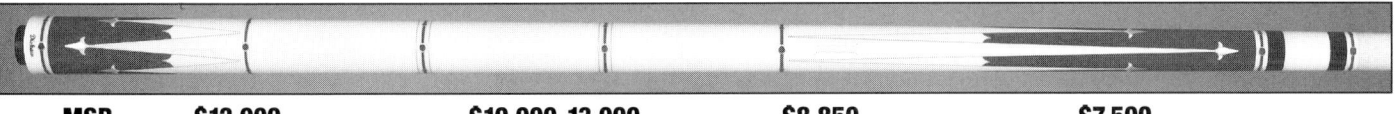

MSR	$12,000	$10,000-13,000	$8,850	$7,500

SECONDARY MARKET MINIMUM VALUES

The following are minimum prices for other Dishaw and Danbuilt cues encountered on the secondary market. These prices are representative of cues utilizing basic materials and designs that may not be currently available. Dan currently specializes in one-of-a-kind cues that can command many times these prices due to the use of exotic materials and artistry.

Special construction note: There are many materials and construction techniques that can add value to Dishaw and Danbuilt cues. The following are the most important examples:

Add $1,000+ for ivory points.

For all used Dishaw or Danbuilt cues, except where otherwise noted:

Add $125+ for each additional original straight playable shaft beyond two.
Deduct $165 for each missing original straight playable shaft under two.
Add $125+ for ivory joint.
Add $100+ for leather wrap.
Add $75+ for each ivory ferrule.
Deduct 25% for obvious or improper refinish.

GRADING	98%	90%	70%
Level 2			
Level 2 cues start at	$750	$570	$385
Level 3			
Level 3 cues start at	$1,000	$795	$550
Level 4			
Level 4 cues start at	$1,200	$950	$650
Level 5			
Level 5 cues start at	$2,000	$1,600	$1,150
Level 6			
Level 6 cues start at	$3,250	$2,500	$1,700

DIVENEY CUES

Maker of pool cues from 1999 to present in West Liberty, Iowa.

Pat Diveney has loved the game of pool all of his life. At about the age of twelve, a friend asked him to go shoot pool, and Pat became an instant fan. He bought his first cue at age nineteen, and he still has that cue today. Pat started doing cue repair work in the mid-1990s at local tournaments and selling other brands of cues. He thought that a lot of the cues he was repairing could have been made better, so he asked a co-worker to show him how to to use the lathe at his workplace. Pat sold his collection of antique Harley Davidsons and bought the equipment necessary to make cues. He made his first cue in 1999, and he learned by trial and error how to make cues for playability. Dave Jacoby, Paul Dayton, Nubs Wagner, and Mike Durbin gave Pat tips along the way. He admires the work of Jeff Hicks.

Pat has a one-man shop, but gets a little help from his sons. His shop is in the garage of his house, but he has never had a car in it. In 2004 he increased the size to make room for a couple of mills, inlay machines, and saws. Now the garage is 30 ft. by 34 ft. Pat strives for a good, deep finish on his cues. He uses the best materials he can find. Pat believes the tip, the ferrule and the joint are the three most important components in getting the balance and hit the customer wants. The hit of the cue is of foremost importance to Pat.

Pat Diveney is best known for his butterfly hustler cues. He started building them because customers wanted custom hustler cues, and he wanted to do something no one else was doing. Pat hopes to someday be remembered as a legendary cuemaker.

Diveney cues are easily identifiable by the "P Diveney" signature that has usually appeared on the forearms on almost all of his cues. Special cues will be signed "Patrick G Diveney." In 2005, Pat started using custom molded bumpers with "PD" within a circular "Q".

Diveney cues are guaranteed to be straight upon delivery. Pat guarantees his cues against construction defects that are not the result of warpage or abuse for the life of the cue. If you are interested in talking to Pat about a new cue or cue that needs to be repaired, you can contact him at Diveney Cues, listed in the Trademark Index.

Pat Diveney

Molded Bumper

Present day

SPECIFICATIONS

Butt material: exotic hardwoods
Shaft material: rock maple
Standard length: 58 in.
Lengths available: any
Standard finish: automotive urethane
Balance point: about 1 ½ in. above wrap
Standard butt cap: linen phenolic
Standard wrap: Irish linen
Point construction: short splice or full splice
Standard joint: linen phenolic
Joint type: flat faced
Joint screw: radial wood pin
Standard number of shafts: one
Standard taper: pro
Standard ferrules: Ivorine linen
Tip widths available: any up to 14 mm
Standard tip: Triangle
Annual production: fewer than 100 cues

DIVENEY CUES, cont.

GRADING	100%	95%	70%

OPTIONS (FOR NEW CUES ONLY)
Special length: no charge
Ivory ferrule: $55
Ivory butt cap: $150+
Ivory joint: $100+
Leather wrap: $75
Stacked leather wrap: $200+
Extra shaft: $75+

REPAIRS
Repairs done on all fine cues.
  Refinish (with Irish linen wrap): $150
  Refinish (with leather wrap): $200
  Rewrap (Irish linen): $45
  Rewrap (leather): $75+
  Replace butt cap: $65
  Replace shaft: $125+
  Replace triangle tip: $10
  Replace melamine ferrule: $25

CURRENT DIVENEY CUES
Basic two-piece hustler cues start at $175. Basic two-piece cues with wraps and joint rings start at $350. Cues with points start at $475. The current delivery time for a Diveney cue is two to three months.

CURRENT EXAMPLES
The following Diveney cues can be ordered as shown, or modified to suit the desires of the customer.

Level 1 "Butterfly Hustler" - Maple forearm, four full-spliced bloodwood points and handle with a six colored laminate reverse butterfly point.

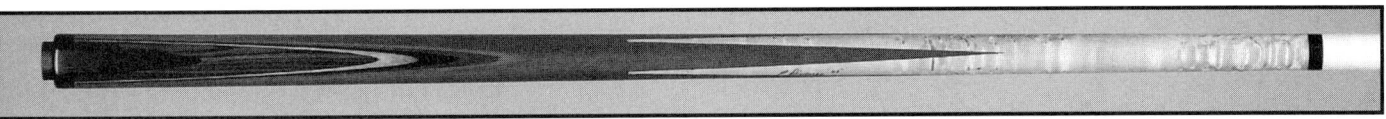

MSR	$310	$300-350	$235	$165

Level 1 "Break Jump" - Maple forearm with a break/jump joint above handle, four full-spliced bocote points and handle with a four-colored laminate reverse butterfly point.

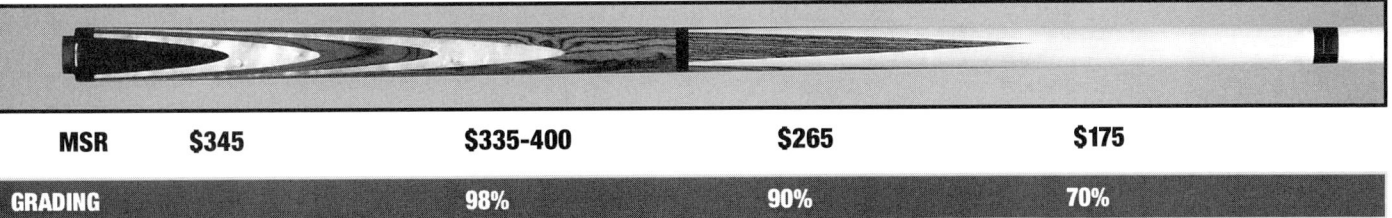

MSR	$345	$335-400	$265	$175

GRADING	98%	90%	70%

SECONDARY MARKET MINIMUM VALUES
The following are minimum values for other Diveney cues encountered on the secondary market. These prices are representative of cues utilizing basic materials and designs that are not necessarily available at present. Pat Diveney has offered one-of-a-kind cues that can command many times these prices due to the use of exotic materials and artistry.

Special construction note: There are many materials and construction techniques that can add value to Diveney cues.

For all used Diveney cues, except where otherwise noted:
  Add $100 for each additional original straight playable shaft beyond one.
  Deduct $125 for missing original straight playable shaft.
  Add $45 each for ivory ferrules.
  Add $50 for leather wrap.
  Deduct 20% for obvious or improper refinish.

Level 1 - Hustler.
  Level 1 cues start at $150 $120 $85
Level 2 - 0 points, 0-25 inlays.
  Level 2 cues start at $300 $235 $165

GRADING	98%	90%	70%
Level 3 - 2-6 points, 0-8 inlays.			
Level 3 cues start at	$400	$300	$225
Level 4 - 4-10 points, 9-25 inlays.			
Level 4 cues start at	$550	$435	$300
Level 5 - 0-12 points, 26-50 inlays.			
Level 5 cues start at	$850	$675	$450

DAVE DOUCETTE

Maker of Samsara Cues, for information refer to Samsara Cues.

DOWNEY CUSTOM CUES

Maker of pool cues from 1998 to present in Lincoln, Nebraska.

Troy Downey was raised on a cattle ranch in central Nebraska, in Custer County, and he started playing a little pool in college. His first cue was an Adam and he was particular about its appearance. He was often sending it off to be repired, but got tired of having to do that, so he started to do some of his own cue repairs. Troy's interest in cue making was sparked. He also had an interest in how to do an adequate job of restoring cues. At first, Troy's repair jobs were all done by hand until he gained access to a small sanding lathe in 1987, which made the work easier.

In 1988 Troy started using a Clausing lathe and began to do joint work and replacing of shaft and butt collars along with butt plates. Now, Troy realizes that those were pretty simple repairs, but he was happy with the way things were going.

In 1989 T&K Cue Repair was founded, which was named after Troy and his wife, Kristi. By this time, Troy was doing repairs for people from far and near, rather than just people around Lincoln, Nebraska.

In 1991, Rory Mueller approached Troy about doing repair work for his company. For the next seven years, that is what Troy did. He was then able to buy equipment and start making Downey Custom Cues.

There are two individuals that have been instrumental in Troy's success. Tom Madsen (Tom's Q-Sticks) helped him with the purchase of the Clausing lathe. Rory Mueller took a chance on Troy's cue making ability and bought the equipment that Troy now uses.

All cue components that Downey uses are core drilled, including the handle, making for a more stable cue. The points on Downey cues are flat milled. Troy's first cues had his initials, TSD and the year they were made. At present, cues are marked with his last name, and the month and year made (Downey 05/05).

Downey custom cues and Mueller cues are guaranteed against any construction defects that are not the result of warpage or abuse for thirty days. If you have a Downey or Mueller cue that needs repair, or would like to talk to someone about ordering a new Downey cue, contact Troy Downey at Mueller Sporting Goods, listed in the Trademark Index.

SPECIFICATIONS

Butt material: hardwoods
Shaft material: maple
Standard wrap: Irish linen
Standard length: 58 in.
Lengths available: any up to 58-50 in.
Standard finish: polyurethane
Joint screw: 3/8 radial
Standard joint: phenolic
Joint type: flat face
Joint protectors: standard
Standard butt cap: phenolic
Balance point: 18.5 in.
Point construction: inlaid
Standard number of shafts: two
Standard taper: 12-1/2 in.
Standard ferrules: Aegis
Standard tip width: 13 mm
Standard tips: Talisman, Everest, Triangle, or Moori
Annual production: 125 cues

OPTIONS (FOR NEW CUES ONLY)

Special lengths: $75
Extra shaft: $125

DOWNEY CUSTOM CUES, cont. 263

GRADING	100%	95%	70%

Ivory joint: $150
Ivory ferrules: $55
Custom joint protectors: $50+
Ivory butt cap: $275
Textured leather wrap: $55
Stacked leather wrap: $100

REPAIRS

Repairs done on all fine cues.
  Refinish (with Irish linen wrap): $125
  Refinish (with leather): $150
  Rewrap (linen): $35
  Rewrap (leather): $55
  Clean and press linen wrap: $20
  Replace linen phenolic butt cap: $30
  Replace ivory butt cap: $275
  Replace shaft: $125+
  Replace linen ferrule: $25
  Replace ivory ferrule: $55
  Replace tip: $10+

CURRENT DOWNEY CUES

Basic Downey cues with wraps and joint rings start at $179. Downey cues with points start at $650. One-of-a-kind custom Downey cues start at $1500. The current delivery time for a Downey custom cue is about twelve to sixteen weeks.

CURRENT EXAMPLES – DOWNEY CUSTOM CUES

The following cues are representations of the work of Downey Custom Cues. These cues can be ordered as shown or modified to suit the desires of the customer.

Level 2 - Curly maple forearm with cocobolo ringwork above handle, cocobolo handle, curly maple butt sleeve with cocobolo ringwork at top and bottom.

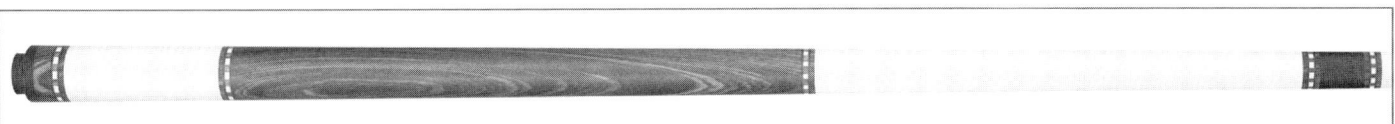

MSR	$585	$500-585	$410	$300

Level 2 - Cocobolo forearm with cocobolo ringwork set in brass rings above handle, three-piece curly maple handle seperated by cocobolo rings, cocobolo butt sleeve with cocobolo ringwork set in brass rings at top and bottom.

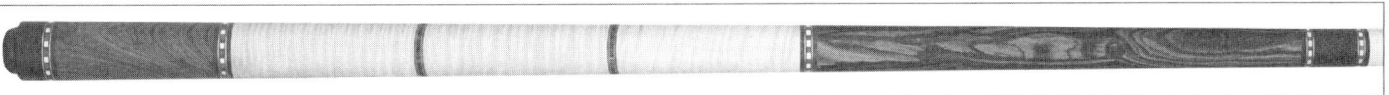

MSR	$630	$540-630	$435	$320

Level 3 - Ebony forearm with colored veneer rings above handle, four curly maple points with colored veneers, curly maple butt sleeve with colored veneer rings set in ebony at top and bottom.

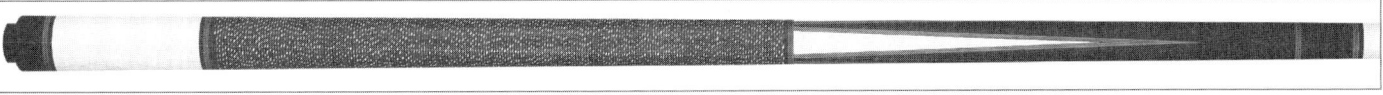

MSR	$775	$675-775	$545	$400

Level 4 - Bird's-eye maple forearm with cocobolo ringwork above wrap, four cocobolo points with two veneers and a holly-bordered ebony eliptical diamond-shaped inlay in each point, stacked leather wrap, cocobolo butt sleeve with four holly-bordered ebony elliptical diamond-shaped inlays alternating with four smaller holly-bordered ebony eliptical diamond-shaped inlays cocobolo ringwork at top and bottom.

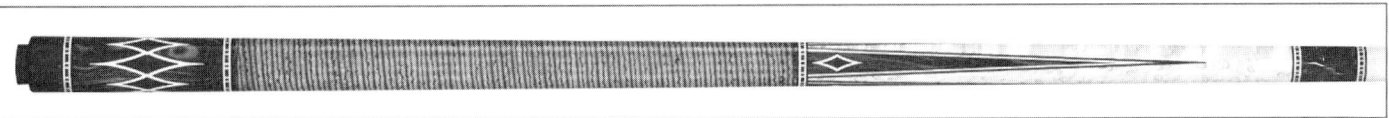

MSR	$975	$850-975	$685	$500

GRADING	100%	95%	70%

Level 4 - Curly maple forearm with cocobolo ringwork set in brass rings above wrap, six cocobolo points with a holly eliptical diamond-shaped inlay in each point, cocobolo butt sleeve with six holly eliptical diamond-shaped inlays between cocobolo ringwork set in brass rings at top and bottom.

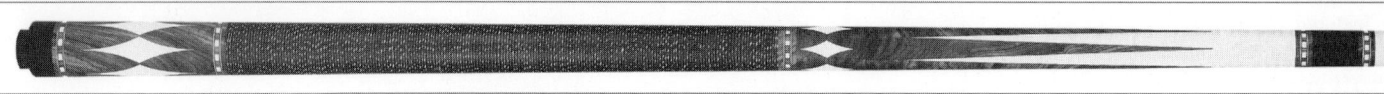

MSR	$1,040	$910-1,040	$735	$535

Level 4 - Ebony forearm with tulipwood and ebony ringwork above wrap, five intricate floating tulipwood points with ivory inlaid in an ebony oval-shaped inlay in each point, ebony butt sleeve with five intricate reverse floating tulipwood points with ivory inlaid in an ebony oval-shaped inlay in each point between tulipwood and ebony ringwork at top and bottom.

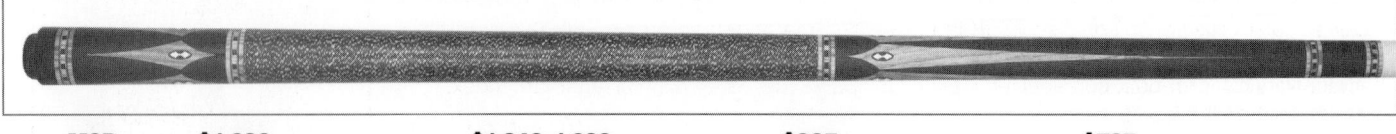

MSR	$1,390	$1,240-1,390	$995	$725

Level 8 - Curly maple forearm with blue and green veneer ring work above wrap, three long and three short points with three colored veneers and a nine-piece ivory and mother-of-pearl diamond-shaped inlay set between a pair of three-piece ivory/ebony/mother-of-pearl ovals in each point, ebony butt sleeve with six nine-piece ivory and mother of pearl diamond-shaped inlays set between pairs of three-piece ivory/ebony/mother of pearl ovals between blue and green veneer ringwork at top and bottom. A limited edition of ten numbered cues.

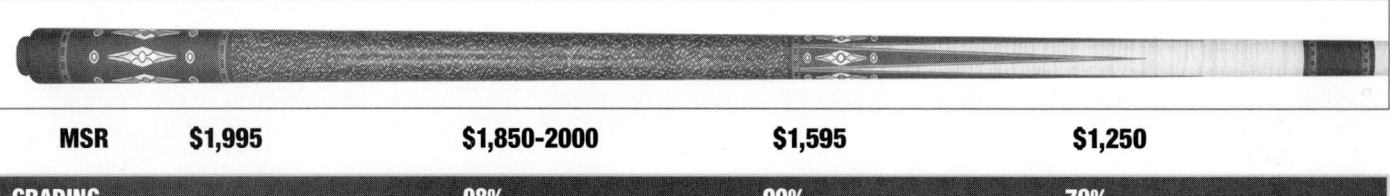

MSR	$1,995	$1,850-2000	$1,595	$1,250

GRADING	98%	90%	70%

SECONDARY MARKET MINIMUM VALUES

The following are minimum values for other Downey cues encountered on the secondary market. These prices are representative of cues utilizing basic materials and designs that are not necessarily available at present. Troy has offered one-of-a-kind cues that can command many times these prices due to the use of exotic materials and artistry.

Special construction note: There are many materials and construction techniques that can add value to Downey cues.

For all used Downey Custom Cues:
   Add $40+ for each additional original straight playable shaft (standard with one).
   Deduct $55 for missing original straight playable shaft.
   Deduct 25% for obvious or improper refinish.

Level 2 0 points, 0-25 inlays.
   Level 2 cues start at $165 $130 $85
Level 3 - 2-6 points, 0-8 inlays.
   Level 3 cues start at $500 $385 $260
Level 4 - 4-10 points, 9-25 inlays.
   Level 4 cues start at $650 $510 $345
Level 5 - 0-12 points, 26-50 inlays.
   Level 5 cues start at $850 $675 $465
Level 6 - 0-12 points, 51-75 inlays.
   Level 6 cues start at $1,150 $925 $650

DON DOYON CUSTOM CUES

GRADING	98%	90%	70%

Maker of pool cues from 1993 to 2003 in Augusta, Maine.

Don Doyon started playing pool at an early age and became serious about playing in the late eighties. A master cabinetmaker for over 20 years, Don decided to make himself a pool table in 1989. After some of the players in his local area saw the table, people started placing orders for their own Don Doyon custom table. After realizing that he could combine his work and his hobby, and find a receptive market, Don decided to start making cues in 1993. He stopped making cues in 2003 after rupturing two discs. Don still has all of his equipment and materials, and he may start making cues again if his health improves.

Don Doyon cues are easily identifiable by the "Don Doyon" signature and a serial number for further identification. "Don Doyon" under a clear acrylic window in the butt was also done. All work was done by hand in Don's one-man shop. Although basic cues came with only one shaft, cues with inlay work came with two.

Don Doyon cues may be personalized with the owners name engraved on the butt cap, or under a clear acrylic ring in the butt sleeve or above the wrap. If you have a Don Doyon cue that needs further identification or repair, contact Don Doyon Custom Cues, listed in the Trademark Index.

Identification

SPECIFICATIONS

Butt material: hardwoods
Shaft material: rock maple
Standard length: 58 in.
Lengths available: any
Standard finish: catalyzed urethane
Joint screw: 5/16-18
Standard joint: stainless steel
Joint type: piloted
Balance point: 18 in. from the butt
Point construction: short splice
Standard wrap: Irish linen
Standard butt cap: Delrin
Standard number of shafts: one
Standard taper: 10 in. pro
Standard ferrules: M.P. ivory substitute
Standard tip: Le Pro
Tip widths available: 10 mm to 14 mm
Total production: approximately 250

Don Doyon

PAST EXAMPLES

Don specialized in making one-of-a-kind custom cues designed by the customer. The following cues are representations of the work of Don Doyon Custom Cues. These cues can be encountered as shown, modified to suit the desires of the customer, or different designs can be encountered.

Level 2 Model # 1 - Bird's-eye maple forearm with cherry dots and an ivory-colored ring above wrap, bird's-eye maple butt sleeve with cherry dots between silver-bordered ivory rings at top and bottom.

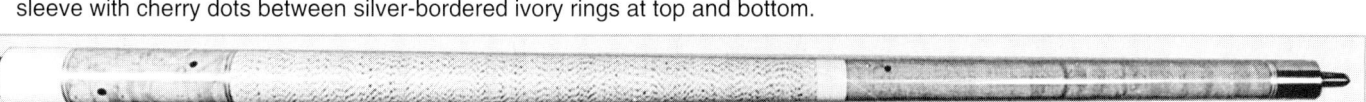

MSR (1999) $250	$350	$270	$185

Level 4 Model # 1A - Delrin joint, teakwood forearm, four Corian points with a Corian diamond-shaped inlay with ebony dots at top and bottom at the top of each point alternating with four Corian diamond-shaped inlays, teakwood butt sleeve with six Corian diamond-shaped inlays.

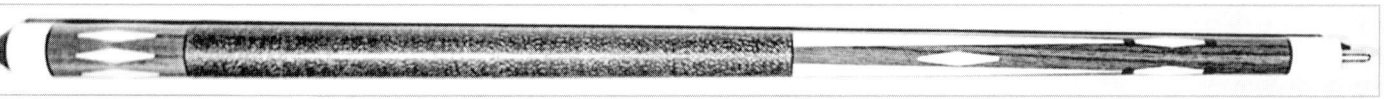

MSR (1999) $400	$550	$415	$275

Level 4 Model # 2A - Stained bird's-eye maple forearm with four ebony diamond-shaped inlays above points and a nickel silver-bordered red ring above wrap, four long and four short ebony points with two colored veneers, ebony butt sleeve with eight ebony diamond-shaped inlays between nickel silver-bordered red rings above and below.

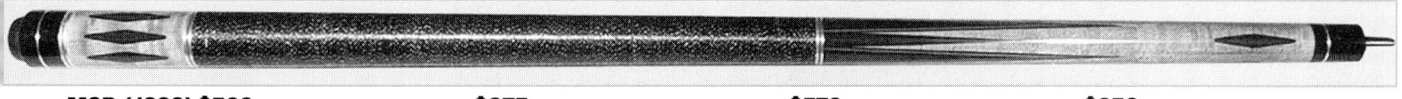

MSR (1999) $500	$675	$570	$350

GRADING	98%	90%	70%

Level 2 Model # 3 - Ivory substitute joint, stained maple forearm, stained maple butt sleeve.

MSR (1999) $250	$325	$250	$165

Level 2 Model # 3A - Red oak forearm with an ivory-colored ring above wrap, red oak butt sleeve with wenge and maple checks at top and bottom.

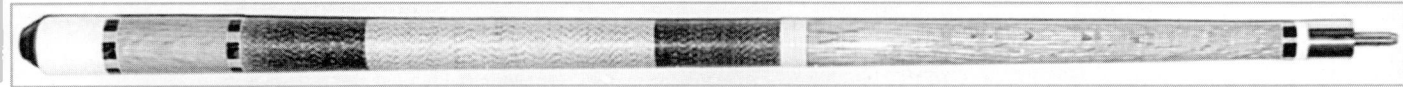

MSR (1999) $290	$350	$270	$185

Level 2 Model # 4 - Ivory joint, purpleheart forearm with black bordered ivory rings above wrap, two purpleheart points with ebony veneers and an ivory diamond-shaped inlay in each alternating with two purpleheart points with ebony veneers and an ebony and ivory barbell-shaped inlay in each, purpleheart butt sleeve with four ivory diamond-shaped inlays within ebony bordered purpleheart windows between inlaid ivory barbell rings within ebony above and below.

MSR (1999) $550	$750	$575	$385

Level 3 Model # 4A - Ash forearm, four padauk points with three colored veneers, ash butt sleeve with ivory colored/wenge/maple/padauk rings at top and bottom.

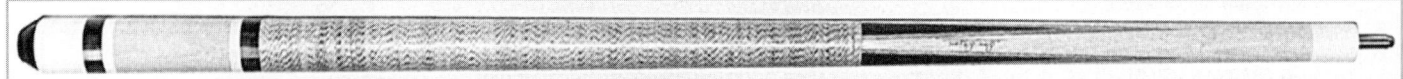

MSR (1999) $400	$565	$435	$290

Level 5 Model # 5 - Ivory joint with inlaid cocobolo bars, bird's-eye maple forearm with tall ebony and ivory checks within black bordered 14-karat gold rings above wrap, four long ivory points with ebony veneers alternating with four short cocobolo points, cocobolo butt sleeve with six large ivory windows between tall ebony and ivory checks between black bordered 14-karat gold rings within cocobolo above and below, ivory butt cap.

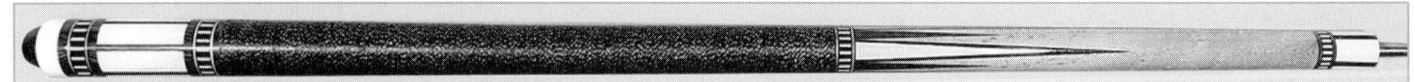

MSR (1999) $2,500	$3,000	$2,400	$1,700

Level 2 Model # 5A - Ivory joint, bird's-eye maple forearm with a red-bordered nickel silver ring above wrap, four long cocobolo points with two colored veneers alternating with four short ivory points with two colored veneers and an ebony dot at the tip of each, cocobolo butt sleeve with eight ivory diamond-shaped inlays between red bordered nickel silver rings at top and bottom, silver ring in black delrin above butt cap, ivory butt cap.

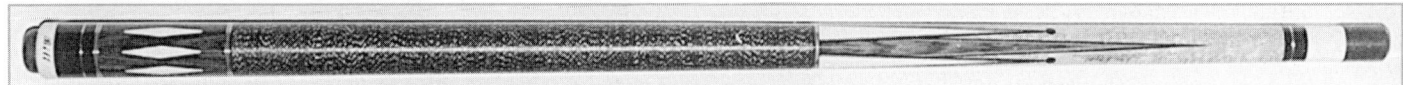

MSR (1999) $1150	$1,400	$1,125	$800

Level 3 Model # 6 - Bird's-eye maple forearm with black-bordered nickel silver rings above wrap, four ebony points, ebony butt sleeve with four ivory diamond-shaped inlays between nickel silver and black and ivory rings above and below.

MSR (1999) $400	$525	$400	$270

Level 2 Model # 6A - Bronze joint, rosewood forearm with mother-of-pearl dot and diamond-shaped inlays and black/white pearl rings, rosewood butt sleeve with mother-of-pearl dot-shaped inlays with metal rings and a personalized nameplate on white pearlized plastic beneath a clear acrylic ring above center.

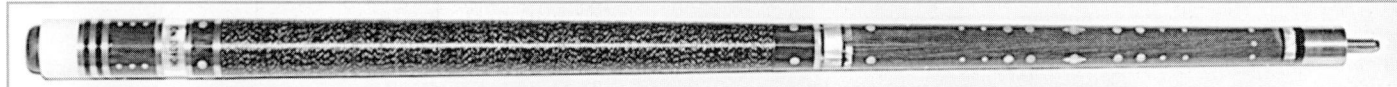

MSR (1999) $900	$1,250	$985	$650

GRADING	98%	90%	70%

Level 2 Model # 7 - Stained cherry forearm with a black pearlized plastic ring above wrap, stained cherry butt sleeve with black bordered silver rings above and below.

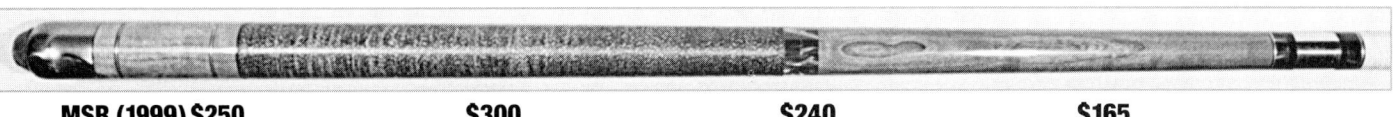

MSR (1999) $250	$300	$240	$165

SECONDARY MARKET MINIMUM VALUES

The following are minimum prices for other Don Doyon cues encountered on the secondary market. These prices are representative of cues utilizing basic materials and designs that may not be currently available. Don also offers one-of-a-kind cues that can command many times these prices due to the use of exotic materials and artistry.

Special construction note: There are many materials and construction techniques that can add value to Don Doyon cues. The following are the most important examples:

Add $150+ for each ivory point.

For all used Don Doyon cues, except where otherwise noted:

Add $100+ for each additional original straight playable shaft beyond one.
Deduct $150 for missing original straight playable shaft.
Add $150+ for ivory joint.
Add $65+ for each ivory ferrule.
Deduct 30% for obvious or improper refinish.

Level 2 - 0 points, 0-25 inlays.
Level 2 cues start at	$285	$220	$145

Level 3 - 2-6 points, 0-8 inlays.
Level 3 cues start at	$450	$350	$235

Level 4 - 4-10 points, 9-25 inlays.
Level 4 cues start at	$500	$390	$265

Level 5 - 0-12 points, 26-50 inlays.
Level 5 cues start at	$750	$575	$385

Level 6 - 0-12 points, 51-75 inlays.
Level 6 cues start at	$1,400	$1,050	$750

Level 7 - 0-12 points, 76-125 inlays.
Level 7 cues start at	$1,850	$1,425	$950

DP CUSTOM CUES

Maker of pool cues from 1987 to present in Orange Park, Florida, a suburb of Jacksonville.

Dale Perry began playing pool in high school. He became more involved in the game while pursuing a bachelor's degree in business administration, with an emphasis in accounting, at the University of North Florida. After graduation, Dale went into the banking field, working eight years as an auditor before becoming chief financial officer at a small Florida bank. Dale enjoyed woodworking as a hobby, and since he liked playing pool, he did cue repairs for several years. While still in the banking industry, Dale began making his own cues.

After becoming a CFO, Dale decided that banking was not for him and he began preparing to make cues full time. In 1990, he began marketing his cues nationwide, and made about 100 cues. In 1991, Dale built his state-of-the-art cuemaking shop. He purchased the finest, most modern equipment to suit his cuemaking needs. Although early cues were simple, and made entirely by hand, Dale now had the CNC capability to create limitless designs, leading to the unique look that DP cues have today. Strong geometric patterns against solid backgrounds are the most common themes. Dale prefers less "busy-looking" cues, so instead of filling a cue with many small inlays, he will start with a large pattern, and inlay the same pattern concentrically with many different materials. These patterns usually appear on the forearm and butt sleeve, being symmetrical except for length and width from the wrap. Although Dale has used the radial pin since 2003, standard joints such as 5/16-14, 3/8-10, or the Uni-Loc, which was his standard joint before 2003, are available at no extra charge. A gold leaf certificate is included with the purchase of any DP Custom cue.

Dale Perry

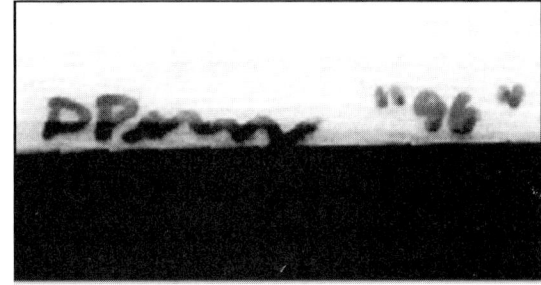

Limited Edition

Dale is proud that he is self-taught, never having worked with or for another cuemaker. Although the look is different, very little has changed in the specifications of DP cues since the first one was made. Dale did all work himself until 1997, when he hired craftsman and long-time friend Brian Mullins to help make cues. Now Brian is Dale's "right-hand man" in the two-man DP shop. They make everything except the joint pins and the rubber bumpers. In June of 1998, DP Custom Cues opened a new cuemaking facility, increasing the shop size from 900 square feet to 3,000 square feet. Dale maintains an extensive collection of hardwoods and other exotic materials, to which he is always adding new varieties.

Today Dale and Brian specialize in creating one-of-a-kind cues and limited editions of three cues, all of which are signed and numbered. They still make examples from the line that was available in 1999 as custom orders because those cues are so popular. Dale and Brian will be introducing a line of "Private Stock" cues which will be numbered "PS1" and up.

DP cues are easily recognizable by the DP logo on the butt cap, which has appeared on every cue Dale has ever made. On one-of-a-kind cues and limited edition cues, the number, and number of cues made of that design appears with the signature. For example, the identification on a one-of-a-kind example will appear "1 of 1". At times, 25 cues have been made of each limited edition original design. Now all DP cues are signed and numbered.

Dale guarantees DP cues indefinitely against manufacturing defects that are not the result of warpage or abuse. A DP Custom Cues catalog is available by sending a request with a self-addressed, stamped envelope. If you would like a catalog, have a DP cue that needs repair, or would like to talk to Dale about purchasing a new DP cue, please contact DP Custom Cues, listed in the Trademark Index.

SPECIFICATIONS

Butt material: hardwoods
Shaft material: rock maple
Standard length: 58 in.
Lengths available: 57 in. to 60 in.
Standard finish: UV synthetic
Joint screw: Uni-Loc/radial
Standard joint: stainless steel
Joint type: piloted/flat faced
Balance point: custom
Point construction: pantographed
Standard wrap: Irish linen
Standard butt cap: Ivorine 3
Standard number of shafts: two
Standard taper: 8 in. pro
Standard ferrules: Ivorine 3
Standard tip: Le Pro
Tip widths available: any
Annual production: approximately 250

OPTIONS (FOR NEW CUES ONLY)

Ivory joint: $200
Titanium joint: standard on light cues
Joint protectors: standard
Ivory butt cap: $300
Extra shaft: $100
Special length: no charge

REPAIRS

Repairs done on any fine cues.
Refinish (with linen wrap): $150
Rewrap (linen): $30
Replace shaft: $150
Replace ivory ferrule: $75
Replace Ivorine 3 butt cap: $50
Refinish shaft: $20

CURRENT DP CUES

DP two-piece bar cues start at $250. Basic DP cues with wraps and joints start at $400. DP cues with points start at $500. One-of-a-kind custom DP cues start at $800. The current delivery time is approximately three months.

CURRENT EXAMPLES

The following DP cues come with two shafts and joint protectors.

DP CUSTOM CUES, cont. 269

GRADING	100%	95%	70%

Level 2 Model 1 Ebony forearm with a white micarta ring above wrap and six upward-pointing intricate white micarta-bordered ebony floating spear-shaped inlays, ebony butt sleeve with six downward-pointing intricate white micarta-bordered ebony floating spear-shaped inlays below a white micarta ring below wrap.

MSR	$800	$750-900	$665	$550

Level 4 Model 2 - Cocobolo forearm, five long intricate bird's-eye maple floating points, cocobolo butt sleeve with five short intricate reverse bird's-eye maple floating points.

MSR	$900	$875-1,000	$775	$650

Level 4 Model 3 - Ebony forearm, five long spear-shaped curly maple floating points each inset with a kingwood spear-shaped inlay, ebony butt sleeve with five short spear-shaped curly maple reverse floating points each inset with a kingwood spear-shaped inlay.

MSR	$800	$750-900	$665	$550

Level 4 Model 4 - Bocote forearm, three long ebony points inlaid with an ivory spear shape and an ebony-bordered ivory diamond-shaped inlay at the tip of each alternating with three short ebony points inlaid with an ivory spear shape and an ebony bordered ivory diamond-shaped inlay at the tip of each, ebony butt sleeve with six bocote windows with an ebony-bordered ivory diamond-shaped inlay in each.

MSR	$1,200	$1,100-1,350	$950	$750

Level 4 Model 5 - Ebony forearm with a tulipwood ring set in ebony above wrap, three long tulipwood points inlaid with an ebony-bordered ivory spear shape and a tulipwood-bordered ivory diamond-shaped inlay at the tip of each alternating with three short tulipwood points inlaid with an ebony-bordered ivory spear shape and a tulipwood bordered ivory diamond-shaped inlay at the tip of each, ebony butt sleeve with a tulipwood ring set in ebony below wrap and six downward-pointing short tulipwood points inlaid with an ebony-bordered ivory spear shape and a tulipwood bordered ivory diamond-shaped inlay at the tip of each.

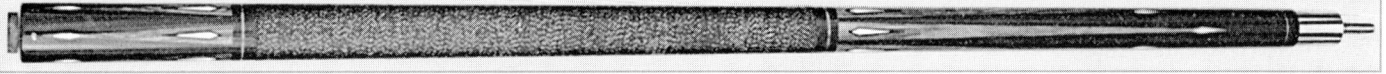

MSR	$1,650	$1,500-1,800	$1,300	$1,000

Level 5 Model 6 - Bird's-eye maple forearm with an ebony ring above wrap, three long ebony points inlaid with an ivory spear shape and an ebony-bordered ivory diamond-shaped inlay at the tip of each alternating with three short ebony points inlaid with an ivory spear shape and an ebony-bordered ivory diamond-shaped inlay at the tip of each, ebony butt sleeve with twelve ivory square-shaped inlays around center between twelve upward-pointing ivory spear-shaped inlays above and twelve downward-pointing ivory spear-shaped inlays below.

MSR	$2,500	$2,350-2,650	$2,000	$1,600

Level 2 Model 7 - Ebony forearm with red-stained curly maple and ebony and ivory checks within silver rings above wrap and six upward pointing intricate ivory-bordered, red-stained curly maple floating spear-shaped inlays, ebony butt sleeve with six downward-pointing intricate ivory-bordered red-stained curly maple floating spear-shaped inlays below red-stained curly maple and ebony and ivory checks within silver rings below wrap.

MSR	$1,800	$1,700-2,000	$1,500	$1,150

GRADING	100%	95%	70%

Level 4 Model 8 - Ebony forearm with ivory square-shaped inlays within pairs of silver rings above wrap, five long intricate pink ivory and ivory floating points, ebony butt sleeve with ivory square-shaped inlays within pairs of silver rings below wrap with five short intricate reverse pink ivory and ivory floating points.

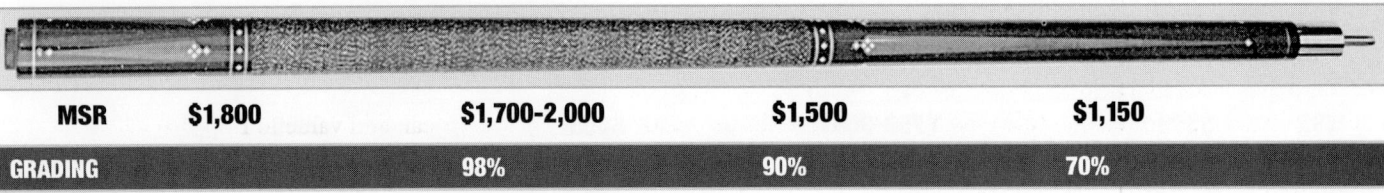

MSR	$1,800	$1,700-2,000	$1,500	$1,150
GRADING		98%	90%	70%

SECONDARY MARKET MINIMUM VALUES

The following are minimum prices for other DP cues encountered on the secondary market. These prices are representative of cues utilizing basic materials and designs that may not be currently available. currently specializes in limited edition cues that can command many times these prices do to the use of exotic materials and artistry.

Special construction note: There are many materials and construction techniques that can add value to DP custom cues.

For all used DP cues:
  Add $85+ for each additional original straight playable shaft (standard with two).
  Deduct $100 for each missing original straight playable shaft.
  Add $150+ for original leather wrap (no longer available).

Level 2 - 0 points, 0-25 inlays.
Level 2 cues start at	$465	$365	$240

Level 3 - 2-6 points, 0-8 inlays.
Level 3 cues start at	$650	$510	$345

Level 4 - 4-10 points, 9-25 inlays.
Level 4 cues start at	$800	$625	$425

Level 5 - 0-12 points, 26-50 inlays.
Level 5 cues start at	$1,275	$975	$650

Level 6 - 0-12 points, 51-75 inlays.
Level 6 cues start at	$1,450	$1,150	$800

Level 7 - 0-12 points, 76-125 inlays.
Level 7 cues start at	$1,850	$1,450	$1,000

PAUL DREXLER

Maker of pfd Studio Cues, for information refer to pfd Studio.

DUFFERIN CUES

Maker of pool cues from 1967, to 2005 in Toronto and Mississauga, Ontario Canada, and from 2005 to present in China.

The roots of Dufferin Games began when founders Al and Elizabeth Selinger purchased a small custom wood business called Dufferin Patterns & Wood Specialties in Toronto, Canada in 1967. Renaming it Dufferin Cue, the Selingers focused on producing the highest quality billiard cue at the best possible price, manufacturing 5,000 cues in the first year.

To produce the straightest cues, the Selingers hired expert wood craftsmen and built their own custom cue manufacturing equipment. As of January 2005, Dufferin Cue has been owned by Cue & Case Sales in Florida, and the cues are made by a technically advanced volume cue manufacturer in China, producing more than half a million Dufferin cues annually in 50 different models. Three-quarters of the Dufferin Games cue line are distributed on every continent worldwide, including the U.S., Europe, Australia, New Zealand, Central America, South America, and the Far East.

If you are interested in talking to Cue & Case Sales about a new Dufferin cue or a Dufferin cue that needs to be repaired, you can contact them at Cue & Case Sales, listed in the Trademark Index.

SPECIFICATIONS

Butt material: hardwoods
Shaft material: rock maple
Standard length: 58 in.
Point construction: full splice
Joint type: flat faced
Standard number of shafts: one
Standard taper: pro
Standard tip: Le Pro
Annual production: more than 500,000 cues

DUFFERIN CUES, cont.

GRADING	98%	90%	70%

CURRENT DUFFERIN CUES

Dufferin Sneaky Petes retail for $85. Over 50 other models of Dufferin cues are available for immediate delivery.

SECONDARY MARKET MINIMUM VALUES

The following are minimum values for Dufferin cues encountered on the secondary market. These prices are representative of cues utilizing basic materials and designs that are not necessarily available at present.

Special construction note: There are many materials and construction techniques that can add value to Dufferin cues.

For all used Dufferin cues, except where otherwise noted:
- Add $40+ for each additional original straight playable shaft beyond one.
- Deduct $50 for missing original straight playable shaft.
- Deduct 20% for obvious or improper refinish.

Level 1 - Hustler.
Level 1 cues start at	$60	$45	$30

Level 2 - 0 points, 0-25 inlays.
Level 2 cues start at	$90	$70	$40

Level 3 - 2-6 points, 0-8 inlays.
Level 3 cues start at	$100	$75	$45

Level 4 - 4-10 points, 9-25 inlays.
Level 4 cues start at	$125	$95	$60

DURBIN CUSTOM CUES

Maker of pool cues from 1995 to present in Sullivan, Illinois.

J. Michael Durbin grew up on a farm in Central Illinois, the seventh generation of his family to work this same area of rich farmland. During high school, Mike showed a lot of interest and talent in woodworking and the operation of milling equipment. During this time, he put these skills to work on the farm repairing equipment and building some furniture in the high school shop.

In 1985, after graduation, Mike attended Lake Land College, majoring in Agriculture Production and Management, and that is where he discovered the game of pool. It wasn't long until he was hooked on the game. In 1987, Mike transferred to Southern Illinois University in Carbondale, which is only about twenty minutes from Johnson City, the home of the great all-around tournaments of the 1960s and 1970s. While in Carbondale, Mike worked hard on his game and became one of the upper level players in the area. One day, while not satisfied with a repair job on his cue, Mike decided that he could do better. Soon Mike was doing most of the minor repair work in town, all by hand. In 1989 the players at the major pool room gave him a tenoning machine for replacing ferrules, which he still has today, but is no longer in use.

Present day

Identification

Mike Durbin

In 1995, after several years of doing shaft work, Mike decided to build his own cue. He bought a small lathe and started to make his first cue. It was an osage orange cue, made from the wood from the farm of one of his landowners, and is not for sale. Over the next year, Mike dissected a number of different cues from a variety of cuemakers to see what he liked and disliked about different construction methods. The early cues that he made are not visibly marked but all are signed under the wrap with the original specifications and the original owner (if custom ordered).

Mike believes in only using the finest materials. All white inlays are ivory and all work is done with no CNC machines. Mike enjoys making unique one-of-a-kind cues and uses very little maple in the forearm. He prefers to use ebony and other exotic hardwoods because of the value and beauty it adds and Mike believes it doesn't warp as easily as maple. Durbin Custom Cues are known for the playability first and the beauty second.

Farming is Mike's means of making a living, and therefore no cue leaves his shop that isn't up to the standards that his customers have come to expect. All work is done by Mike in his one-man shop and production is limited to fifty custom cues a year. Mike feels that making more than fifty cues in any one year will only hurt the value of the cues made in the past. Mike's cues are signed "J. Michael Durbin".

In 2001, Mike approached Mark Wilson, a professional pool player and top instructor, to make Mark a cue in order to have his input in building a better product. In 2002, during the "Dr. Cue 3-on-3 Team Tournament" Mark expressed in more detail what he would like to see in a custom cue. These things included G-10 joint pins, ivory joints and ferrules, and custom fitting. After a year of development, the first "Mark

272 DURBIN CUSTOM CUES, cont.

| GRADING | 100% | 95% | 70% |

Wilson Advanced Accuracy Cue" became available from Durbin's shop. These cues are available by custom order or from models in stock from Mike or from Mark at Advanced Accuracy Custom Cues. Production of Durbin Custom Cues is limited to fifty cues a year.

If you are interested in talking to J. Michael Durbin about a new cue or cue that needs to be repaired, you can contact him at Durbin Custom Cues, listed in the Trademark Index.

SPECIFICATIONS

- Butt material: hardwoods
- Shaft material: hard rock maple
- Standard length: 58 in.
- Lengths available: 55 in. to 61 in.
- Standard finish: urethane
- Standard butt cap: linen based
- Standard wrap: Irish linen
- Point construction: short splice or inlaid
- Standard joint: linen based
- Joint type: flat faced
- Joint screw threads: 3/8–11 stainless or G-10 glass epoxy
- Standard number of shafts: one
- Standard taper: 13 in. pro
- Standard ferrules: LBM
- Standard tip: Le Pro
- Tip widths available: any
- Annual production: 50 cues maximum

OPTIONS (FOR NEW CUES ONLY)

- Special length: no charge
- Layered tip: $15+
- Ivory butt cap: $240
- Ivory joint: $150
- Ivory ferrule: $75
- Ivory points: $120
- Leather wrap: $75
- Extra shaft: $100+

REPAIRS

Repairs done on all fine cues.
- Refinish (with Irish linen wrap): $150
- Refinish (with Leather wrap): $200
- Rewrap (Irish linen): $30
- Rewrap (leather): $75
- Clean and press linen wrap: $10
- Restore leather wrap: $10
- Replace shaft: $100+
- Replace Ivory ferrule: $75
- Replace butt cap: $50
- Replace ivory butt cap: $240
- Replace Le Pro/Triangle tip: $10
- Replaced layered tip: $15+
- Replace fiber/linen/Aegis ferrule: $25

CURRENT DURBIN CUES

Two-piece Durbin bar cues start at $400. Basic Durbin cues with wraps and joint rings start at $500. Four-point Durbin cues start at $750. Six-point Durbin cues start at $900. One-of-a-kind custom Durbin cues start at $2,000. The current delivery time for a Durbin cue is four to six months for custom orders.

CURRENT EXAMPLES

The following Durbin cues can be ordered as shown, modified to suit the desires of the customer, or new designs can be created.

Level 1 - Maple forearm, four full-spliced exotic hardwood points and handle.

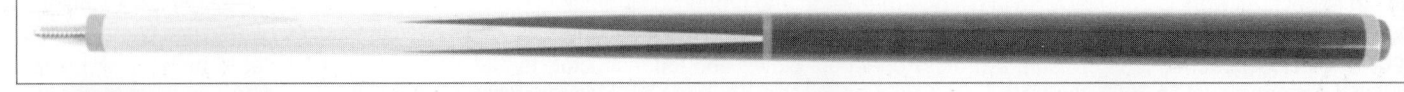

| MSR | $400 | $375-425 | $300 | $220 |

GRADING	100%	95%	70%

Level 2 - Exotic hardwood forearm with a dash ring above wrap, exotic hardwood butt sleeve with dash rings at top and bottom.

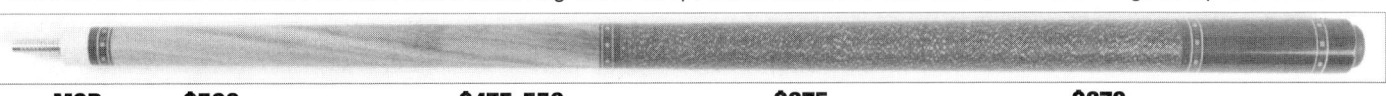

MSR	$500	$475-550	$375	$270

Level 3 - Exotic hardwood forearm with a dash ring above wrap, four exotic hardwood points with veneers, exotic hardwood butt sleeve with dash rings at top and bottom.

MSR	$750	$700-800	$550	$385

GRADING	98%	90%	70%

SECONDARY MARKET MINIMUM VALUES

The following are minimum values for other Durbin cues encountered on the secondary market. These prices are representative of cues utilizing basic materials and designs that are not necessarily available at present. Mike has offered one-of-a-kind cues that can command many times these prices due to the use of exotic materials and artistry.

Special construction note: There are many materials and construction techniques that can add value to Durbin cues. For all used Durbin cues, except where otherwise noted:

- Add $85 for each additional original straight playable shaft beyond one.
- Deduct $100+ for missing original straight playable shaft.
- Add $65 each for ivory ferrules.
- Add $50 for leather wrap.
- Deduct 20% for obvious or improper refinish.

Level 1 - Hustler.
Level 1 cues start at	$350	$270	$185

Level 2 - 0 points, 0-25 inlays.
Level 2 cues start at	$450	$350	$235

Level 3 - 2-6 points, 0-8 inlays.
Level 3 cues start at	$650	$505	$345

Level 4 - 4-10 points, 9-25 inlays.
Level 4 cues start at	$800	$620	$425

Level 5 - 0-12 points, 26-50 inlays.
Level 5 cues start at	$1,150	$900	$600

Level 6 - 0-12 points, 51-75 inlays.
Level 6 cues start at	$1,450	$1,125	$750

DZ CUSTOM CUES

Maker of pool cues from 1991 to present in Erie, Pennsylvania.

Bob Dzuricky has been a tool and die maker for over 30 years. He enjoyed playing pool and it was natural for him to decide to do his own cue repairs in the mid-1980s. Soon he was doing repairs for his friends as a hobby. By 1991, Bob made his first cue. Since then he has made over 500 cues, nearly half of which have been hustler cues. All but a few are easily recognizable by the stylized "DZ" logo on the buttcap. He has hand-signed his cues since 2000, and all work was done by hand until 1995, when Bob purchased CNC machinery. Before then, all points were short spliced. Now both short spliced or inlaid points are available. All cues made since 1998 have interchangeable shafts.

Bob makes every component of a DZ custom cue except for the joint screws, tips and bumpers. His wife, Gina, assists him in the shop, mainly with linen wraps, glue-up of veneers and points, and the clearcoat finishing, but she can fill in as a helping hand with just about everything. Basic DZ hustler cues are cut from select bar cues. Premium DZ hustler cues are available in a variety of exotic woods. Lately, Bob has been inlaying many of these cues. Custom cues are built to the customers' specifications with a variety of lengths, joints, weights, materials, and shaft tapers available. He prefers a cue with a stiff hit, and has developed his own 9 in. pro taper to help achieve this. Bob personally prefers a wood handle, but is more than happy to wrap a cue with Irish linen or leather.

1991 to Present Day — Bob Dzuricky

DZ CUSTOM CUES, cont.

GRADING	98%	90%	70%

DZ custom cues are guaranteed for life to the original owner against manufacturing defects that are not the result of warpage or abuse. If you have a DZ cue that needs further identification or repair, or would like to order a new DZ cue, contact DZ Custom Cues, listed in the Trademark Index.

SPECIFICATIONS:

- Butt material: exotic hardwoods
- Shaft material: rock maple
- Standard length: 58 in.
- Lengths available: 57 in. to 59 in.
- Standard finish: UV epoxy/catalyzed polyurethane
- Balance point: 18 in. to 19 in. from the butt
- Standard butt cap: linen phenolic
- Standard wrap: Irish linen
- Point construction: short spliced or inlaid
- Standard joints: stainless steel or linen based phenolic
- Joint type: flat faced
- Standard joint screw thread: 3/8-10
- Standard number of shafts: sne
- Standard taper: .005 growth over 10 in.
- Standard ferrules: linen phenolic
- Standard tip width: 13 mm
- Tip widths available: 12 mm to 13.5 mm
- Standard tips: Triangle or Triumph
- Annual production: approximately 40 cues

OPTIONS (FOR NEW CUES ONLY):

- Special length: $20
- Leather wrap: $75
- Clear over linen wrap: $25
- Extra shaft: $100
- Ivory ferrule: $55
- Ivory joint: $90
- Layered tip: $12+

REPAIRS:

Repairs done on all fine cues.
- Refinish with Irish linen wrap: $100
- Rewrap Irish linen: $35
- Rewrap Leather: $75+
- Replace butt cap: $25
- Replace joint screw: $20
- Replace shaft: $100
- Replace ivory ferrule: $55
- Replace fiber/linen ferrule: $22
- Replace tip: $8+
- Replace layered tip: $12+

CURRENT DZ CUES

Basic two-piece DZ bar cues start at $240. DZ cues with wraps and joint rings start at $325. DZ cues with points start at $425. One-of-a-kind custom DZ cues start at $500. The current delivery time for a DZ Cue is about 14 weeks.

SECONDARY MARKET MINIMUM VALUES

The following are minimum values for DZ custom cues encountered on the secondary market. These prices are representative of cues utilizing basic materials and designs that are not currently available. DZ has offered one-of-a-kind cues that can command many times these prices due to the use of exotic materials and artistry.

Special construction note: There are many materials and construction techniques that can add value to DZ cues.

For all used DZ cues, except where otherwise noted:
- Add $75 for each additional original straight playable shaft beyond one.
- Deduct $100 for missing original straight playable shaft.
- Add $50 each for ivory ferrules.
- Deduct 20% for obvious or improper refinish.

Level 1 - 4 points, hustler.

	98%	90%	70%
Level 1 cues start at	$200	$155	$105

GRADING	98%	90%	70%
Level 2 - 0 points, 0-25 inlays. Level 2 cues start at	$300	$235	$165
Level 3 - 2-6 points, 0-8 inlays. Level 3 cues start at	$375	$290	$195
Level 4 - 4-10 points, 9-25 inlays. Level 4 cues start at	$475	$365	$250
Level 5 - 0-12 points, 26-50 inlays. Level 5 cues start at	$750	$585	$400
Level 6 - 0-12 points, 51-75 inlays. Level 6 cues start at	$1,050	$850	$600

NOTES

E SECTION

ECKES CUES INC.

Maker of pool cues from 1965 to 1985 in Marshfield, Wisconsin.

Hubert "Hubs" Eckes was working in the roofing and siding business in Milwaukee, Wisconsin in the early sixties, when he bought a pool table for the family home. He was dissatisfied with the construction of the table, so he rebuilt it. When the project was finished, he realized that he could make a better product at a better price.

So in 1962 he started the Custom Craft Pool Table Co. in Milwaukee. After three successful years in the billiard industry, Eckes came to the conclusion that it would be much easier for him to make pool cues. In 1965, he returned to his hometown of Marshfield, Wisconsin to start Eckes Cue Inc. Although he had only an eighth grade education, he was very proficient at machine work, making his own machine, and patenting at least one of his cue construction techniques. The company soon became very successful. With his daughter and two teenage sons working for him, he was able to produce 7,000 cues in one year. He eventually was wholesaling cues to pool halls in all 50 states.

Although most Eckes cues are unmarked, they are easily identifiable to those who know what they look like. The most distinctive feature encountered will be a colored nylon wrap with rows of black stripes wound in. Maple, ebony, and rosewood were the woods primarily used, and Eckes cues were rarely inlaid. Some cues had pearlized plastic rings at the joints and butt caps. Those cues that were marked were from the Magnum line of cues and were marked "MAGNUM" on the butt caps.

In 1985, Eckes retired, and auctioned off the equipment from his shop. Although every cue he made sold for under $20 wholesale, Hubs Eckes was very influential in the development of Wisconsin cuemaking. His innovations in customizing machinery for cuemaking are in cuemakers' shops around the country. Today, Eckes and Magnum cues are encountered across the United States. If you have an Eckes cue that needs further identification or repair, contact Jacoby Custom Cues, listed in the Trademark Index.

SPECIFICATIONS

Butt material: hardwoods
Shaft material: rock maple
Standard joint: brass
Point construction: full splice
Standard wrap: nylon
Standard number of shafts: one
Total production: approx. 110,000

GRADING	98%	90%	70%

DISCONTINUED ECKES CUES

The following cues are from an Eckes catalogue, circa 1975.

Level 2 AM1 - Maple forearm, maple butt sleeve.

$110	$85	$55

Level 2 AM2 - Maple forearm with patterns of ebony notched diamond-shaped inlays and ebony dots, maple butt sleeve with a row of ebony notched diamond-shaped inlays and ebony dots.

$155	$120	$75

Level 2 AM3 - Maple forearm with patterns of intricate ebony inlays and ebony dots, maple butt sleeve with patterns of intricate ebony inlays and ebony dots.

$165	$125	$80

Level 3 AM4 - Maple forearm, four rosewood points, rosewood butt sleeve.

$120	$90	$55

GRADING	98%	90%	70%

Level 3 AM5 - Maple forearm with a row of ebony notched diamond-shaped inlays and ebony dots above points, four rosewood points, rosewood butt sleeve.

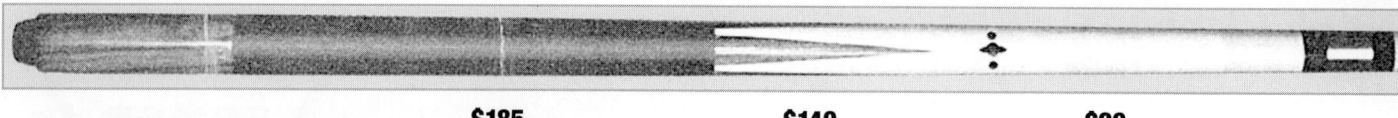

	$185	$140	$90

SECONDARY MARKET MINIMUM VALUES

The following are minimum prices for other Eckes or Magnum cues encountered on the secondary market. These prices are representative of cues utilizing the most basic materials and designs that were available. Hubert made a few one-of-a-kind cues that can command many times these prices due to the use of exotic materials and artistry. Eckes cues will be further covered in future editions.

For all used Eckes or Magnum cues:
   Add $20 for each additional original straight playable shaft (standard with one).
   Deduct $60% for missing original straight playable shaft.
   Deduct 30% for obvious or improper refinish.

Level 1 - 4 points, hustler.
Level 1 cues start at	$90	$70	$40

Level 2 - 0 points, 0-25 inlays.
Level 2 cues start at	$125	$95	$60

Level 3 - 2-6 points, 0-8 inlays.
Level 3 cues start at	$175	$135	$85

JERRY EICK

Maker of Black Heart Custom Cues. For information refer to Black Heart Custom Cues.

ELIMINATOR CUES

Line of pool cues distributed from Ontario, Canada.
Eliminator cues are easily identifiable by the "Eliminator" logo on the forearms and/or butt caps. If you have an Eliminator cue that needs further identification or repair, or you would like to order a new Eliminator cue, contact Mister Billiard, listed in the Trademark Index.

SPECIFICATIONS

Butt material: hardwoods
Shaft material: rock maple
Point construction: short splice
Standard joint: "Tru Lock" quick release
Standard length: 58 in.
Standard wrap: Irish linen
Standard number of shafts: one

CURRENT ELIMINATOR CUES

Mister Billiard currently has ten Eliminator models available for immediate delivery.

SECONDARY MARKET MINIMUM VALUES

The following are minimum prices for Eliminator cues encountered on the secondary market.
Special construction note: There are many materials and construction techniques that can add value to Eliminator cues.
For all used Eliminator cues:
   Deduct 60% for missing original straight playable shaft.

Level 1 - Hustler.
Level 1 cues start at	$65	$50	$30

Level 2 - 0 points, 0-25 inlays.
Level 2 cues start at	$70	$55	$35

Level 3 - 2-6 points, 0-8 inlays.
Level 3 cues start at	$100	$75	$45

Level 4 - 4-10 points, 9-25 inlays.
Level 4 cues start at	$135	$105	$65

GRADING	98%	90%	70%

ELITE CUSTOM CUES, INC.

Maker of pool cues from 1989 to about 2000 in Lincoln, Nebraska.

Dick Coons ran a pool room for years in Lincoln, Nebraska. He bought and sold cues and always dreamed of making cues of his own. In 1989, his wife started running the pool room and Dick was able to start Elite Custom Cues.

Elite cues are easily identifiable by the Elite logo on the butt cap. Diamond shapes, notched diamond shapes, and knight chess pieces were common inlay themes. Dick was opposed to the use of ivory, so it will not be found on Elite cues. Dick developed his own tips, which he had custom made for him. The Elite Ultra collection featured exotic hardwoods and intricate inlays. Each Elite Ultra cue featured a Uni-Loc joint and two shafts. Dick sold the business in about 2000. He died on April 5, 2003.

SPECIFICATIONS

Butt material: hardwoods
Shaft material: rock maple
Standard length: 58 in.
Lengths available: any
Joint screw: 5/16-14
Standard joint: stainless steel
Joint type: piloted
Balance point: 18 in. from butt
Point construction: inlaid
Standard wrap: Irish linen
Standard no. of shafts: one
Standard ferrules: Ivorine 3

SECONDARY MARKET MINIMUM VALUES

The following are minimum prices for Elite cues encountered on the secondary market.

Special construction note: There are many materials and construction techniques that can add value to Elite cues.

For all used Elite cues, except where otherwise noted:

Add $85 for each additional original straight playable shaft beyond one.
Deduct $100 for missing original straight playable shaft.

	98%	90%	70%
Level 2 - 0 points, 0-25 inlays.			
Level 2 cues start at	$225	$170	$110
Level 3 - 2-6 points, 0-8 inlays.			
Level 3 cues start at	$235	$180	$120
Level 4 - 4-10 points, 9-25 inlays.			
Level 4 cues start at	$285	$235	$140
Level 5 - 0-12 points, 26-50 inlays.			
Level 5 cues start at	$350	$270	$170
Level 6 - 0-12 points, 51-75 inlays.			
Level 6 cues start at	$450	$345	$220

TODD ELKINS

Maker of Parrot Cues, for information refer to Parrot Cue.

EMBASSY CUES

Line of pool cues distributed from Ontario, Canada.

Embassy cues are easily identifiable by the "Embassy" logo on the butt caps. If you have an Embassy cue that needs further identification or repair, or you would like to order a new Embassy cue, contact Mister Billiard, listed in the Trademark Index.

SPECIFICATIONS

Butt material: hardwoods
Shaft material: rock maple
Standard length: 58 in.
Standard wrap: Irish linen
Standard no. of shafts: one

CURRENT EMBASSY CUES

Mister Billiard currently has nineteen Embassy models available for immediate delivery.

SECONDARY MARKET MINIMUM VALUES

The following are minimum prices for Embassy cues encountered on the secondary market.

GRADING	98%	90%	70%

Special construction note: There are many materials and construction techniques that can add value to Embassy cues.
For all used Embassy cues:
  Deduct 60% for missing original straight playable shaft.

	98%	90%	70%
Level 2 - 0 points, 0-25 inlays.			
Level 2 cues start at	$75	$55	$35
Level 3 - 2-6 points, 0-8 inlays.			
Level 3 cues start at	$95	$70	$40
Level 4 - 4-10 points, 9-25 inlays.			
Level 4 cues start at	$135	$105	$65

ERWIN CUSTOM CUES

Maker of pool cues from the early 1990s to present in Sarah, Mississsippi.

Mike Erwin learned cue making from his fifteen years experience working with Meucci. He strives for color, quality, and playability in his cues. He does not use CNC. All cues are handmade using lathes and pantograph, and Mike signs all of his cues. His son Scott has been helping him since Scott was thirteen. Erwin cues are guaranteed for one year for manufacturing defects only.

If you are interested in talking to Mike Erwin about a new cue or cue that needs to be repaired, you can contact him at Erwin Custom Cues, listed in the Trademark Index.

SPECIFICATIONS

Butt material: hardwoods
Shaft material: maple and flat laminated maple
Standard length: 58 in.
Standard wrap: Irish linen
Standard ferrules: 1 in. capped phenolic
Standard tip: Triumph
Annual production: fewer than 100 cues

OPTIONS (FOR NEW CUES ONLY)

Ivory ferrules: $65 each
Moori tip: $30
Extra shaft: $90+

REPAIRS

Repairs done on all fine cues.
  Refinish (with Irish linen wrap): $95+
  Rewrap (Irish linen): $35
  Replace shaft: $90+
  Replace butt cap: $25+
  Replace tip: $10+

CURRENT ERWIN CUES

Erwin two-piece bar cues start at $200. Basic Erwin cues with wraps and joint rings start at $300. Erwin cues with points start at $400. One-of-a-kind Erwin custom cues start at $800. The current delivery time for one of Mike's custom cues is three to four months.

SECONDARY MARKET MINIMUM VALUES

The following are minimum values for Erwin cues encountered on the secondary market. These prices are representative of cues utilizing basic materials and designs that are not necessarily available at present. Mike has offered one-of-a-kind cues that can command many times these prices due to the use of exotic materials and artistry.

Special construction note: There are many materials and construction techniques that can add value to Erwin cues.
For all used Erwin cues, except where otherwise noted:
  Add $75 for each additional original straight playable shaft beyond two.
  Deduct $90 for missing original straight playable shaft under two.
  Add $50 each for ivory ferrules.
  Deduct 20% for obvious or improper refinish.

	98%	90%	70%
Level 1 - Hustler.			
Level 1 cues start at	$150	$120	$85
Level 2 - 0 points, 0-25 inlays.			
Level 2 cues start at	$250	$200	$135

GRADING	98%	90%	70%
Level 3 - 2-6 points, 0-8 inlays.			
Level 3 cues start at	$350	$270	$185
Level 4 - 4-10 points, 9-25 inlays.			
Level 4 cues start at	$445	$345	$235
Level 5 - 0-12 points, 26-50 inlays.			
Level 5 cues start at	$700	$550	$375

ESPIRITU HAND CRAFTED CUSTOM CUES

Maker of pool cues from 1984 to present in Brandon, Mississippi.

Russ Espiritu began playing pool at the age of 19. At the time, he was in college, working toward degrees in business and forestry. When he finished college, he bought the engraving business where he had been working part time since he was 16. It was there that he learned how to use a pantograph. He liked to work with wood and enjoyed the game of pool, so he started to do cue repairs as a hobby.

By 1984, he had made his first cue. He found that he loved the art of cuemaking and became more and more involved in it. Like most cuemakers, Russ did a lot of experimentation with design and construction methods on his early cues. Cues made between 1984 and 1990 were unmarked and had a 5/16-18 joint screw. Later cues had a variety of different identification marks and joint screws. In 1990, he switched to a 3/8-10 screw, which he used for about a year, changing to a 5/16-18 screw in 1991, when he started making cues full time. He used the 5/16-18 screw until 1993, when he settled on the current 5/16-14 joint screw. He also likes to use a radial pin on occasion. In 2002 he started making his points about one inch longer than before, so cues made since then will have points that come within two inches of the joint collar. Russ changed to a compound taper on the butts of his cues in 2004.

Russ makes every component on his cues except for the tips, bumpers and screws. He makes ferrules, collars, and butt caps that thread on for better durability. All white inlays in Espiritu cues are ivory, as opposed to synthetic substitutes. All silver rings are now sterling silver instead of nickel silver, which he had used in the past. Russ has a new system, like a triple press system, for smoothing his Irish linen wraps that makes them feel more like leather. Although he has a line of cues, Russ also is currently focusing on very intricate, one-of-a-kind cues, most of which go to Switzerland or Japan. Cues from his obsolete catalog are still available by special order. Now he is making very few hustler cues. Since 1994, Espiritu cues have been signed "Russ Espiritu" with the current year on the forearm. Cues that have the month after the signature were made before Russ changed to a UV finish.

Espiritu cues are indefinitely guaranteed for the original owner against construction defects that are not the result of warpage or abuse. If you have an Espiritu cue that needs repair, or would like to talk to Russ about ordering a new cue, contact Espiritu Handcrafted Custom Cues, listed in the Trademark Index.

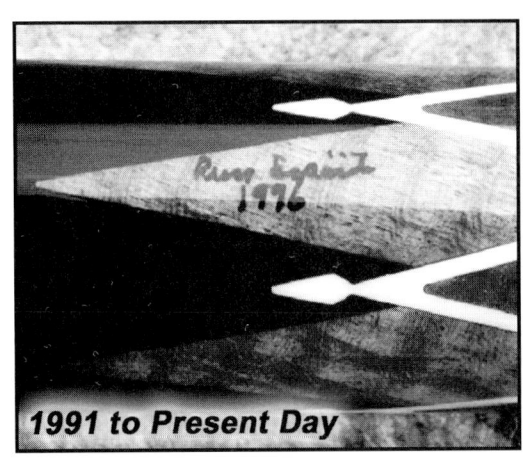

1991 to Present Day

Russ Espiritu

SPECIFICATIONS

- Butt material: hardwoods
- Shaft material: rock maple
- Standard length: 58 in.
- Lengths available: any under 61 in.
- Standard finish: UV polyurethane
- Joint screw: 5/16-14 or radial
- Standard joint: stainless steel
- Joint type: piloted or flat faced
- Balance point: 2 in. above wrap
- Point construction: short splice
- Standard wrap: Irish linen
- Standard butt cap: ABS
- Standard number of shafts: one
- Standard taper: two available
- Standard ferrules: linen phenolic
- Standard tip: water buffalo
- Tip widths available: any
- Annual production: fewer than 200 cues

282 ESPIRITU HAND CRAFTED CUSTOM CUES, cont.

GRADING	98%	90%	70%

OPTIONS (FOR NEW CUES ONLY)
Leather wrap: $100
Ivory joint: $220
Joint protectors: $25 per pair
Flat face joint: no charge
Extra shaft: $130

REPAIRS
Repairs done on most fine American cues.
Refinish (with leather wrap): $180
Refinish (with linen wrap): $150
Rewrap (leather): $100
Rewrap (linen): $50
Replace shaft: $130
Replace ivory ferrule: $80
Replace ABS butt cap: $50
Replace ivory butt cap: $200

CURRENT ESPIRITU CUES
Two-piece Espiritu bar cues start at $275. Basic Espiritu cues with wraps and joint rings start at $350. Espiritu cues with points start at $500. Espiritu cues over $1,500 come with two shafts. The current delivery time for an Espiritu cue is approximately twelve weeks to twelve months, depending on the intricacy of the cue.

PAST EXAMPLES
Russ currently specializes in one-of-a-kind custom cues. The following cues are from the late 1990s Russ Espiritu cue catalog. These cues can still be made as special orders as shown, modified to suit the desires of the customer, or new designs can be created.

Level 2 R-1 - Stained bird's-eye maple forearm, stained bird's-eye maple butt sleeve.

MSR (1999) $300	$400	$325	$225

Level 2 R-2 - Stained bird's-eye maple forearm, stained bird's-eye maple butt sleeve with nickel silver rings at top and bottom and four maple-bordered cocobolo diamond-shaped inlays set in stylized cocobolo windows within thick bocote rings above and below.

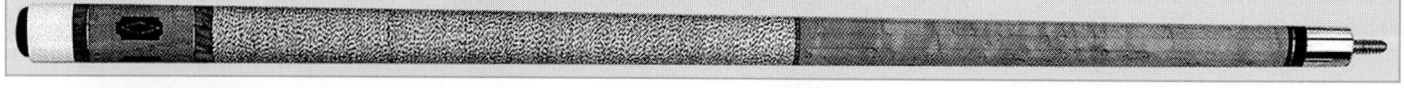

MSR (1999) $380	$475	$375	$250

Level 2 R-3 - Ebony forearm with six tulipwood arrowhead-shaped inlays with ebony dashes in each extending up from a tulipwood ring above wrap, ebony butt sleeve with six tulipwood arrowhead-shaped inlays with ebony dashes in each extending down from a tulipwood ring below wrap.

MSR (1999) $450	$600	$475	$325

Level 3 R-4 - Bird's-eye maple forearm with a nickel silver ring set in tulipwood above wrap, four tulipwood points, tulipwood butt sleeve.

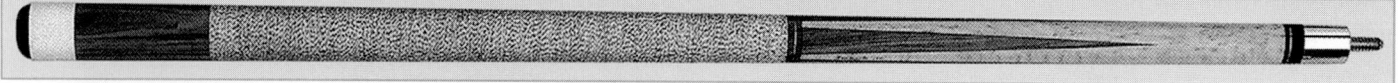

MSR (1999) $380	$485	$370	$245

Level 3 R-5 - Stained bird's-eye maple forearm with a nickel silver ring set in tulipwood above wrap, four tulipwood points, tulipwood butt sleeve with six long bird's-eye maple windows between nickel silver rings above and below.

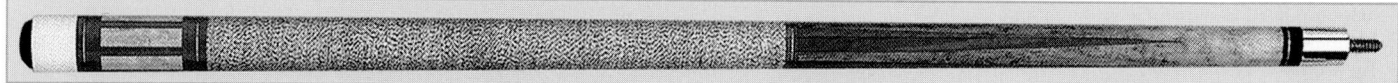

MSR (1999) $465	$615	$485	$335

ESPIRITU HAND CRAFTED CUSTOM CUES, cont. 283

GRADING	98%	90%	70%

Level 3 R-6 - Bird's-eye maple forearm with a nickel silver ring set in ebony above wrap, four ebony points with two veneers, ebony butt sleeve.

MSR (1999) $465	$615	$485	$335

Level 3 R-7 - Bird's-eye maple forearm with a nickel silver ring set in ebony above wrap, three long and three short ebony bordered bocote points, bocote butt sleeve with nickel silver rings set in ebony at top and bottom.

MSR (1999) $475	$625	$500	$340

Level 4 R-8 - Bird's-eye maple forearm with a nickel silver ring set in ebony above wrap, four ebony points with three colored veneers, ebony butt sleeve with six ivory-bordered bocote diamond-shaped inlays between nickel silver rings set in ebony at top and bottom.

MSR (1999) $630	$800	$625	$425

Level 4 R-9 - Stained bird's-eye maple forearm with a nickel silver ring set in tulipwood above wrap, six floating tulipwood points with an ivory diamond-shaped inlay in each, tulipwood butt sleeve with six large ivory diamond-shaped inlays alternating with six small ivory diamond-shaped inlays between nickel silver rings set in tulipwood at top and bottom.

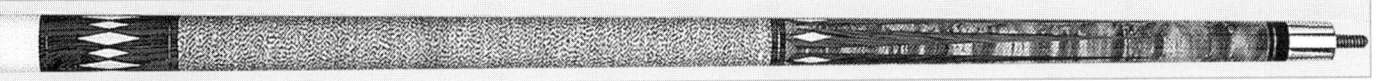

MSR (1999) $945	$1,150	$900	$600

Level 4 R-10 - Bird's-eye maple forearm with a nickel silver ring set in tulipwood above wrap, four tulipwood points with three colored veneers and a turquoise diamond-shaped inlay in each, tulipwood butt sleeve with six stylized ivory-bordered long turquoise ovals between pairs of nickel silver rings set in tulipwood at top and bottom.

MSR (1999) $790	$1,050	$825	$550

Level 4 R-11 - Bird's-eye maple forearm with ebony and ivory checks within nickel silver rings set in ebony above wrap, four ebony points with four colored veneers and an ivory diamond-shaped inlay in each, ebony butt sleeve with three large ivory diamond-shaped inlays alternating with three small ivory diamond-shaped inlays between ebony and ivory checks within nickel silver rings set in ebony at top and bottom.

MSR (1999) $850	$1,500	$1,200	$800

Level 4 R-12 - Bird's-eye maple forearm with a nickel silver ring set in ebony above wrap, four ebony points with three colored veneers and an upward pointing ivory spear with a turquoise square-shaped base in each, ebony butt sleeve with three upward-pointing ivory spears with turquoise square-shaped bases alternating with three downward-pointing ivory spears with turquoise square-shaped bases between nickel silver rings set in ebony at top and bottom.

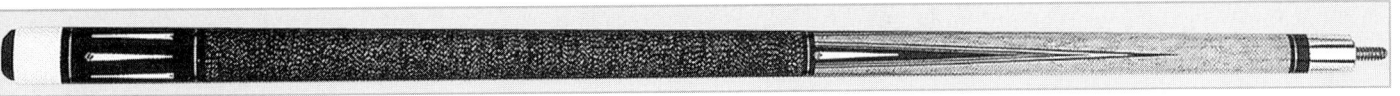

MSR (1999) $850	$1,200	$950	$650

| GRADING | 98% | 90% | 70% |

Level 4 R-13 - Bird's-eye maple forearm with a nickel silver ring set in ebony above wrap, four ebony points with three colored veneers and an ivory diamond-shaped inlay in each, ebony butt sleeve with six long ivory diamond-shaped inlays between nickel silver rings set in ebony at top and bottom.

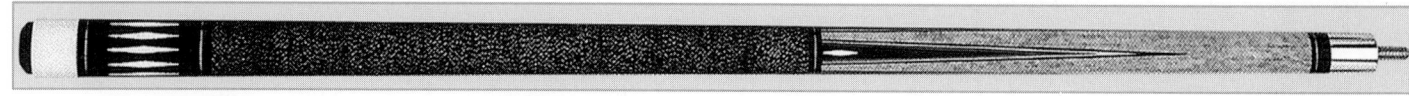

| MSR (1999) $850 | $1,250 | $975 | $675 |

Level 5 R-14 - Bird's-eye maple forearm with rosewood and ivory checks within nickel silver rings set in tulipwood above wrap, four rosewood points with three colored veneers and a long ivory spear-shaped inlay in each, rosewood butt sleeve with six ivory-bordered ebony diamond-shaped inlays alternating with six pairs of vertical ivory diamond-shaped inlays between rosewood and ivory checks within nickel silver rings set in rosewood at top and bottom.

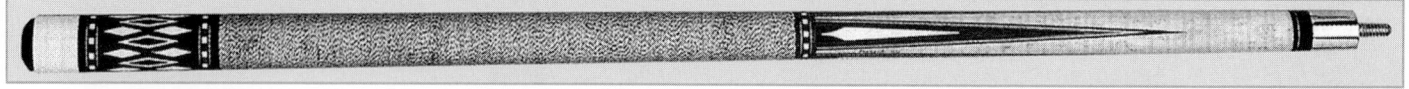

| MSR (1999) $1,590 | $2,000 | $1,600 | $1,100 |

Level 4 R-15 - Dark stained bird's-eye maple forearm with a nickel silver ring set in ebony above wrap, four stylized ebony-bordered floating ivory points, dark-stained bird's-eye maple butt sleeve with six turquoise patterns set in intricate ivory designs between nickel silver rings set in ebony at top and bottom.

| MSR (1999) $1,390 | $1,750 | $1,350 | $900 |

Level 5 R-16 - Bird's-eye maple forearm with a nickel silver ring set in ebony above wrap, six ebony-bordered bocote points with a long ivory diamond-shaped inlay in each and an ebony-bordered ivory spear-shaped inlay at the tip of each, bocote butt sleeve with six long ebony diamond-shaped inlays set in ivory windows alternating with six small ivory diamond-shaped inlays set in ebony windows that cut into the larger ivory windows between nickel silver rings set in ebony at top and bottom.

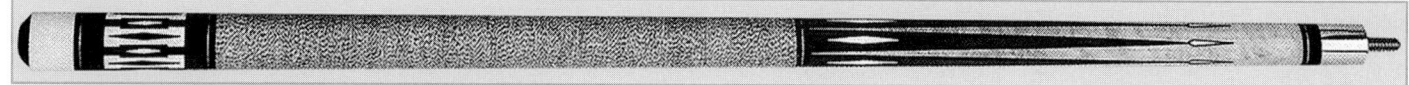

| MSR (1999) $1,390 | $1,800 | $1,400 | $950 |

SPECIAL INTEREST ESPIRITU CUES

Level 5 "Gambler" - Bird's-eye maple forearm, four ebony points with three veneers and an ivory diamond-shaped inlay in each, ebony butt sleeve with four intricate pairs of ivory dice inlays alternating with ivory diamond-shaped inlays.

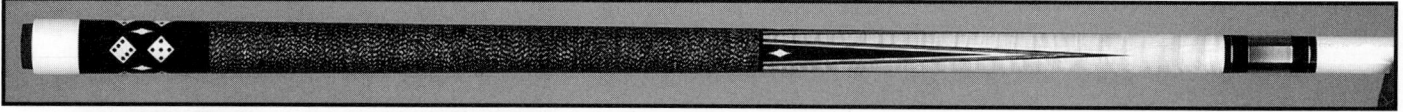

| MSR (1999) $800 | $1,250 | $975 | $650 |

Level 7 "USA #1" - Tiger maple forearm with a silver ring above wrap, four ebony points with red, white, and blue veneers and an ivory star-shaped inlay in each, ebony butt sleeve with intricate American flags made of inlays of red coral, blue dymondwood and ivory alternating with sterling silver star-shaped inlays between silver rings at top and bottom.

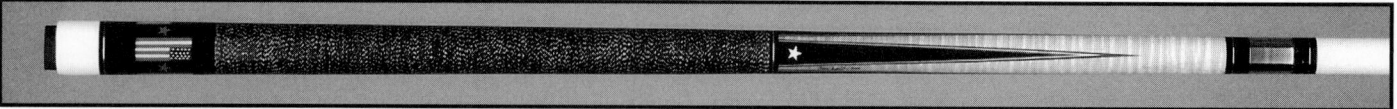

| MSR (2002) $1,500 | $2,250 | $1,800 | $1,250 |

Level 7 "Tuxedo" - Ivory joint, ebony forearm with intricate ivory inlays set in silver rings above wrap, four intricate sets of multi-piece floating ivory opposing points, leather wrap, ebony butt sleeve with four intricate sets of multi-piece floating ivory opposing point-shaped inlays set within intricate ivory inlays set in silver rings at top and bottom, ivory butt cap.

| MSR (2003) $3,000 | $3,500 | $2,650 | $1,750 |

GRADING	98%	90%	70%

SECONDARY MARKET MINIMUM VALUES

The following are minimum prices for other Espiritu cues encountered on the secondary market. These prices are representative of cues utilizing basic materials and designs that may not be currently available. Russ also offers one-of-a-kind cues that can command many times these prices due to the use of exotic materials and artistry. Certain discontinued models have also become collectible.

Special construction note: There are many materials and construction techniques that can add value to Espiritu cues. The following are the most important examples:
- Add $125+ for each ivory point.
- Add $350+ for ivory butt sleeve.

For all used Espiritu cues:
- Add $100+ for each additional original straight playable shaft beyond one.
- Deduct $130 for missing original straight playable shaft.
- Add $55+ for leather wrap.
- Add $200 for ivory joint.
- Add $60+ for each ivory ferrule.

	98%	90%	70%
Level 1 - 4 points, Hustler.			
Level 1 cues start at	$250	$195	$130
Level 2 - 0 points, 0-25 inlays.			
Level 2 cues start at	$325	$250	$165
Level 3 - 2-6 points, 0-8 inlays.			
Level 3 cues start at	$450	$345	$235
Level 4 - 4-10 points, 9-25 inlays.			
Level 4 cues start at	$700	$545	$375
Level 5 - 0-12 points, 26-50 inlays.			
Level 5 cues start at	$1,100	$875	$600
Level 6 - 0-12 points, 51-75 inlays.			
Level 6 cues start at	$2,000	$1,600	$1,150

MIKE ETHERIDGE

Maker of Showcase cues, for information refer to Showcase Custom Cues.

EUROWEST

Maker of pool cues from 1994 to present in Rodermark, Germany. Distributed in the United States from 1996 to 1997 by Joss West in Austin, Texas.

Andreas Stahl and Markus Funk

Present day

The Eurowest cue is the result of Bill Stroud's dream to manufacture cues to the specifications that he has found to be ideal over his almost thirty years of cuemaking. His Joss West cues had become very popular in Europe, and while on vacation there, he was approached by two German investors who wanted him to create a line of cues. A fan of German manufacturing quality in automobiles, machinery, and other fields, Bill saw this as the perfect opportunity to create a unique, superior quality cue.

Eurowest was opened in 1994 in Rodermark, Germany. Four employees were hired to make cues, all with professional technical training and experience in their respective backgrounds. For example, the man who applied finish to Eurowest cues used to apply finish on cars at BMW. Bill designed the cues, set up the facilities, and trained the cuemakers. Only new state-of-the-art cuemaking equipment was purchased, to ensure as near perfect tolerances as possible. All of the construction methods and components had been tried for at least ten years on Joss West cues, except for the then newly designed Uni-Loc Joint, which had been modified for Eurowest. With this joint, all

EUROWEST, cont.

GRADING	100%	95%	70%

butts and shafts were completely interchangeable. After two years of gaining popularity in Europe, Bill introduced Eurowest cues to the United States in 1996, and his involvement ended in 1997.

Production of Eurowest cues slowed from about 600 cues a year in 1996 to about 100 in 1999. In 2002 Eurowest introduced their new M-9 joint, which they developed themselves. They also developed their own custom shaft taper which is close to a European pro taper. The goal of Eurowest is to produce a good playing cue with typical German quality. All woods are of the finest grades. In 2005 Andreas Stahl and Markus Funk took over the company as sole owners. Andreas had been with the company since the beginning. Now production is back up to about 250 cues a year.

Most cues are custom orders, and almost all of the cues are one-of-a-kind. There is a series of Eurowest models that are available on their website (accessible in both Engilsh and German). Most Eurowest cues sold today stay in Europe, but many have made their way to the United States. Eurowest cues are easily identifiable by the Eurowest logo that appears on the butt caps. If you have a Eurowest cue that needs further identification or repair, contact Joss West, listed in the Trademark Index. Eurowest cues are guaranteed for life against construction defects that are not the result of warpage or abuse, and ferrules are guaranteed for life.

If you are interested in talking to Markus Funk or Andreas Stahl about a new cue or cue that needs to be repaired, you can contact them at Eurowest Cues, listed in the Trademark Index.

SPECIFICATIONS

Butt material: hardwoods
Shaft material: rock maple
Standard length: 58 in.
Lengths available: any
Standard finish: 3x3 layers of clear coat
Balance point: 1 in. above wrap
Standard butt cap: phenolic
Standard wrap: Irish linen
Point construction: inlaid
Standard joint: stainless steel m-9
Joint type: piloted
Joint screw thread: 9 mm diameter, 2 mm between threads
Joint protectors: standard
Standard number of shafts: one
Standard taper: Eurowest custom
Standard ferrules: Aegis II
Standard tip: Le Pro
Standard tip width: 13 mm
Tip widths available: any
Annual production: approximately 250 cues

OPTIONS (FOR NEW CUES ONLY)

Special length: $50
Layered tip: no charge
Ivory butt cap: $260
Ivory joint: $90
Ivory ferrule: $75
Leather wrap: $180
Extra shaft: $165

REPAIRS

Repairs done on all fine cues.
Refinish (with Irish linen wrap): $180
Refinish (with leather wrap): $220
Rewrap (Irish linen): $60
Replace shaft: $165

CURRENT EXAMPLES

The following cues are currently available from Eurowest Cues. They can be ordered as shown, or modified to suit the desires of the customer. Forearm and butt sleeve designs can be mixed, or new designs can be created.

Level 2 #98/01 - Stained bird's-eye maple forearm, ebony butt sleeve.

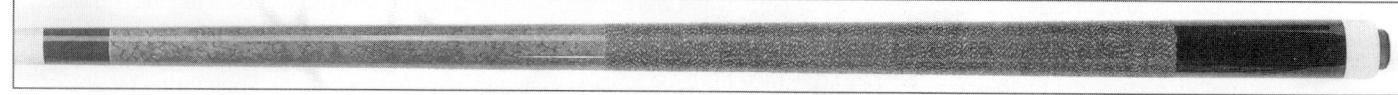

MSR	$293	$250-293	$205	$150

GRADING	100%	95%	70%

Level 2 #98/02 - Stained bird's-eye maple forearm, ebony butt sleeve with a stained maple ring at bottom.

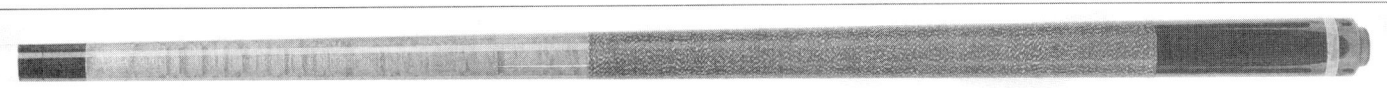

MSR	$319	$270-319	$220	$165

Level 3 #98/03 - Stained bird's-eye maple forearm, four ebony-bordered stained bird's-eye maple points, ebony butt sleeve.

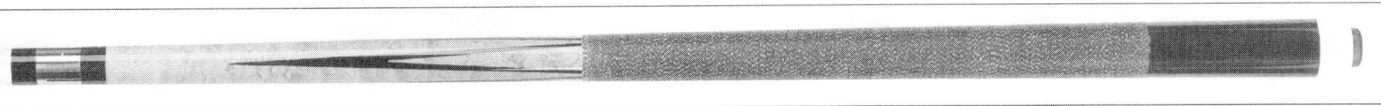

MSR	$371	$300-371	$250	$190

Level 3 #98/04 - Stained bird's-eye maple forearm, four ebony-bordered stained bird's-eye maple points, ebony butt sleeve with a stained maple ring at bottom.

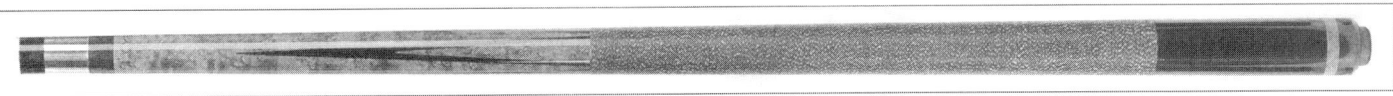

MSR	$384	$310-384	$255	$195

Level 3 #98/05 - Stained bird's-eye maple forearm, four ebony-bordered stained bird's-eye maple points, ebony butt sleeve with four stained maple diamond-shaped inlays.

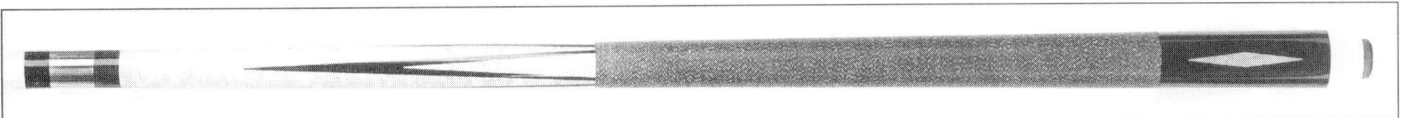

MSR	$423	$350-423	$285	$215

Level 3 #98/06 - Stained bird's-eye maple forearm, four ebony points with four veneers, ebony butt sleeve with a stained maple ring at bottom.

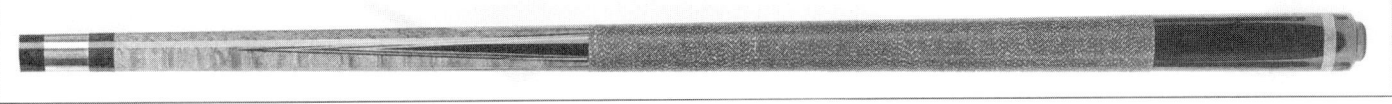

MSR	$449	$370-449	$310	$230

Level 3 #98/07 - Stained bird's-eye maple forearm, four ebony points with four veneers, ebony butt sleeve with micarta and ebony checks set in silver rings at top and bottom.

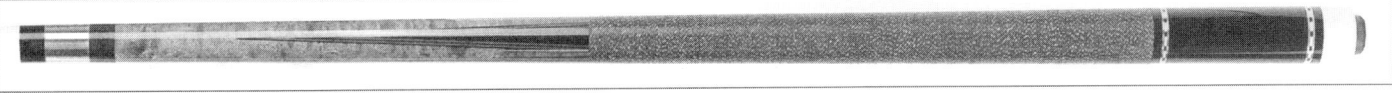

MSR	$519	$420-519	$345	$265

Level 3 #98/08 - Stained bird's-eye maple forearm with a stained maple ring set in silver rings above wrap, four ebony-bordered stained bird's-eye maple points, ebony butt sleeve with eight stained bird's-eye diamond-shaped inlays set between stained maple rings set in silver rings at top and bottom.

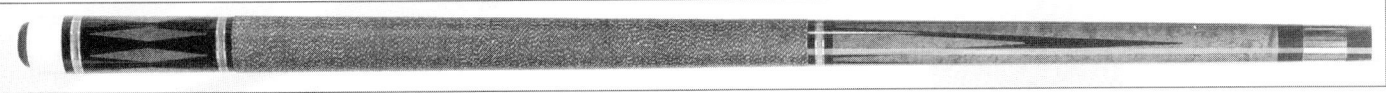

MSR	$553	$445-553	$365	$280

Level 3 #98/09 - Stained bird's-eye maple forearm with a stained maple ring set in silver rings above wrap, four ebony-bordered micarta points, ebony butt sleeve with a four-micarta bordered ebony diamond-shaped inlays set between stained maple rings set in silver rings at top and bottom.

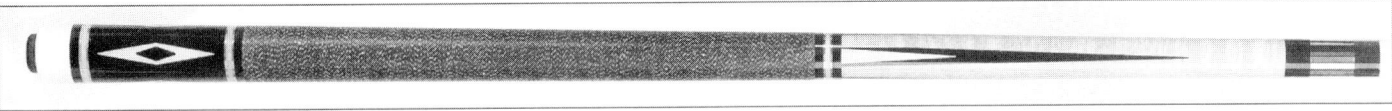

MSR	$644	$525-644	$435	$325

288 EUROWEST, cont.

GRADING	100%	95%	70%

Level 3 #98/11 - Stained bird's-eye maple forearm with a stained maple ring set in silver rings above wrap, six ebony-bordered stained bird's-eye maple points, stained bird's-eye maple butt sleeve with six reverse ebony-bordered stained bird's-eye maple points below a stained maple ring set in silver rings at top.

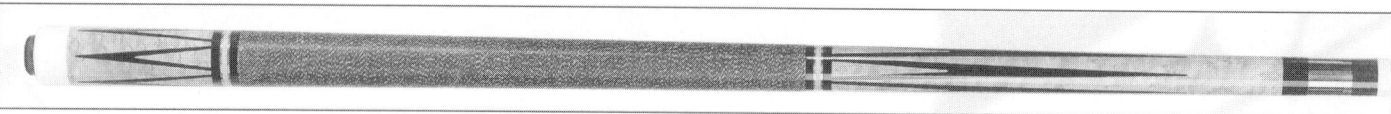

MSR	$689	$555-689	$455	$350

Level 3 #98/12 - Stained bird's-eye maple forearm, four ebony points with four colored veneers, ebony butt sleeve with four reverse ebony points with four colored veneers and a micarta spear-shaped inlay in each above a stained maple ring at bottom.

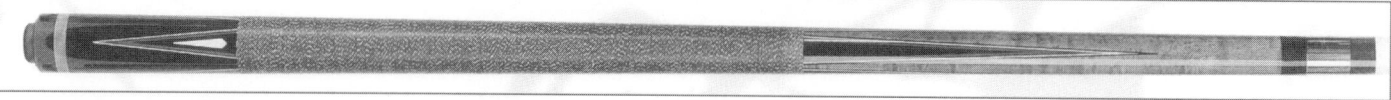

MSR	$793	$615-793	$510	$400

Level 4 #98/13 - Stained bird's-eye maple forearm, four ebony points with four colored veneers, ebony butt sleeve with four sets of four-piece micarta designs inlaid between silver rings at top and bottom.

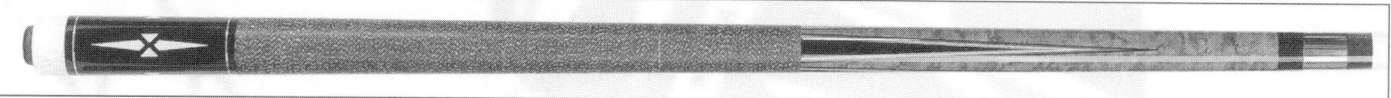

MSR	$852	$655-852	$550	$430

Level 3 #98/14 - Stained bird's-eye maple forearm with a maple dash ring set in ebony above wrap, four ebony points with four colored veneers and a micarta diamond-shaped inlay in each, ebony butt sleeve with four micarta diamond-shaped inlays set in colored veneer windows between ebony/micarta/stained maple checked rings at top and bottom.

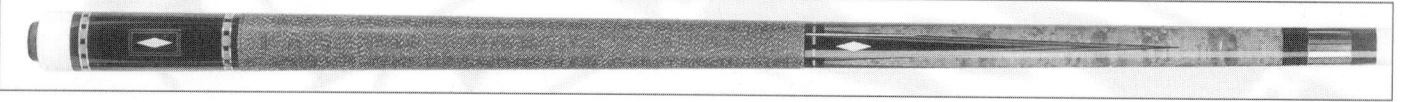

MSR	$982	$745-982	$630	$500

Level 3 #98/16 - Stained bird's-eye maple forearm with an ebony/micarta/stained maple checked ring set in ebony above wrap, six ebony-bordered micarta points, ebony butt sleeve with six micarta-bordered ebony diamond-shaped inlays between ebony/micarta/stained maple checked rings at top and bottom.

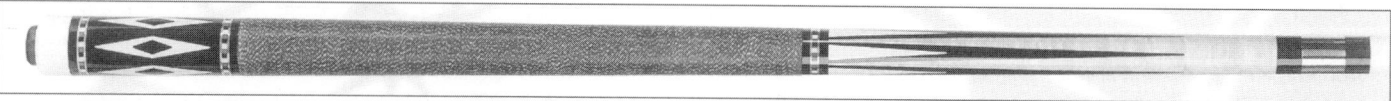

MSR	$1,138	$850-1,138	$725	$575

Level 4 #98/17 - Stained bird's-eye maple forearm with an ebony/micarta/stained maple checked ring set in ebony above wrap, four ebony-bordered ebony points with colored veneers and a micarta diamond-shaped inlay in each, ebony butt sleeve with intricate micarta inlays between ebony/micarta/stained maple checked rings at top and bottom.

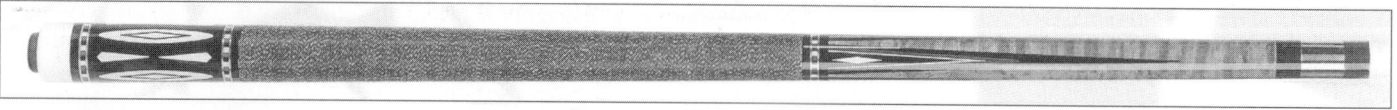

MSR	$1,169	$875-1,169	$740	$590

Level 4 #98/18 - Stained bird's-eye maple forearm with a maple dash ring set in ebony above wrap, four ebony points with four colored veneers and a micarta diamond-shaped inlay in each, ebony butt sleeve with four sets of four-piece micarta diamond-shaped inlays between maple dash rings above and below.

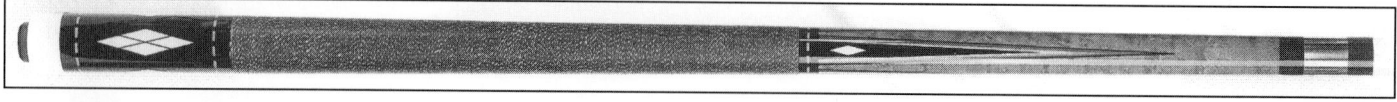

MSR	$1,260	$950-1,260	$815	$650

EUROWEST, cont. 289

GRADING	100%	95%	70%

Level 4 #98/19 - Stained bird's-eye maple forearm with a pair of silver rings set in ebony above wrap, four long ebony points alternating with four short ebony bordered micarta points, ebony butt sleeve with four sets of eight-piece micarta diamond-shaped inlays between pairs of silver rings set in ebony above and below.

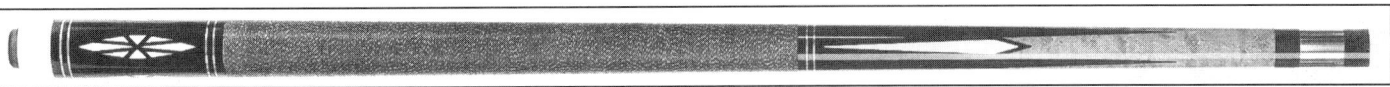

MSR	$1,429	$1,100-1,429	$925	$725

Level 4 #98/20 - Stained bird's-eye maple forearm with an ebony/micarta/pink ivory checked ring set in pink ivory above wrap, four pink ivory points with four colored veneers and a micarta diamond-shaped inlay in each, pink ivory butt sleeve with eight ebony-bordered micarta diamond-shaped inlays set over a thick ebony band between ebony/micarta/pink ivory checked rings at top and bottom.

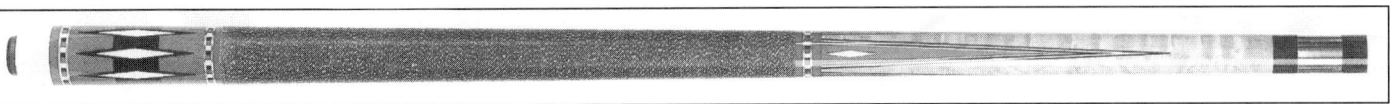

MSR	$1,547	$1,200-1,547	$1,025	$800

Level 5 #98/21 - Stained bird's-eye maple forearm with an ebony/micarta/pink ivory checked ring set in pink ivory above wrap, four long ebony and micarta four-piece points alternating with four short ebony-bordered micarta points, ebony butt sleeve with multiple intricate micarta inlays between ebony/micarta/pink ivory checked rings at top and bottom.

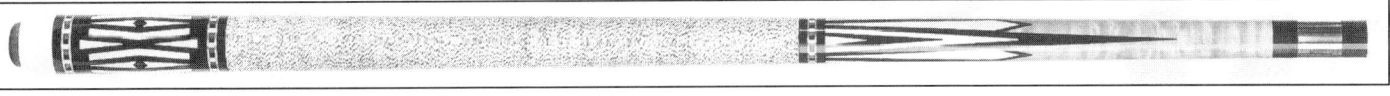

MSR	$1,606	$1,225-1,606	$1,040	$810

Level 4 #98/22 - Stained bird's-eye maple forearm with an ebony/micarta/pink ivory checked ring set in pink ivory above wrap, four long ebony points alternating with four short pink ivory bordered micarta points, pink ivory butt sleeve with eight pink ivory diamond-shaped inlays set in ebony-bordered, six-sided micarta windows set over a thick ebony band between ebony/micarta/pink ivory checked rings at top and bottom.

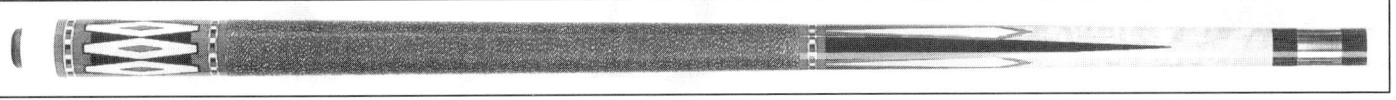

MSR	$1,754	$1,330-1,754	$1,120	$885

Level 5 #98/23 - Stained bird's-eye maple forearm with an ebony and pink ivory dash ring set in pink ivory above wrap, four ebony-bordered multi-piece micarta points, stained bird's-eye maple butt sleeve with four intricate ebony-bordered multi-piece micarta diamond-shaped inlays alternating with four micarta diamond-shaped inlays set in ebony-bordered pink ivory diamond windows between ebony and pink ivory dash rings set in pink ivory at top and bottom.

MSR	$2,079	$1,550-2,079	$1,315	$1,050

GRADING	98%	90%	70%

SECONDARY MARKET MINIMUM VALUES

The following are minimum values for other Eurowest cues encountered on the secondary market. These prices are representative of cues utilizing basic materials and designs that are not necessarily available at present. Eurowest has offered one-of-a-kind cues that can command many times these prices due to the use of exotic materials and artistry.

Special construction note: There are many materials and construction techniques that can add value to Eurowest cues.

For all used Eurowest cues, except where otherwise noted:
- Add $125 for each additional original straight playable shaft beyond one.
- Deduct $165 for missing original straight playable shaft.
- Add $60 each for ivory ferrules.
- Add $100 for leather wrap.
- Deduct 20% for obvious or improper refinish.

Level 2 - 0 points, 0-25 inlays.

Level 2 cues start at	$250	$200	$135

Level 3 - 2-6 points, 0-8 inlays.

Level 3 cues start at	$350	$270	$185

GRADING	98%	90%	70%
Level 4 - 4-10 points, 9-25 inlays.			
Level 4 cues start at	$500	$385	$260
Level 5 - 0-12 points, 26-50 inlays.			
Level 5 cues start at	$750	$590	$400

EYE CUE

Maker of pool cues from 1988 to the present in Defiance, Ohio.

Jeffrey Lipp was inspired by his grandfather, who owned and operated a machine shop for most of his life. He has since past on and is greatly missed. He built and restored antique high-wheeled bicycles in his shop. He would fabricate and design every part he needed. Jeffrey's grandmother, who is still living, helped Jeffrey's grandfather by making all of the leather seats needed for the bikes. It was a family operation. Jeffrey saw his grandparents' dedication to quality work and has tried to be a dedicated cue maker who strives for quality in his work. He started doing repair work on cues, starting with tips and ferrules. He slowly got into doing linen and leather wraps, and eventually progressed into making shafts and then the entire cue. Jeffrey learned about cue building from Chris Hightower, and has been inspired by Ray Schuler and Dennis Dieckman. Most of his learning was from trial and error. Early blanks were purchased from Dennis Dieckman, who had the first cuemaking shop Jeff ever visited.

Eye Cue is now a part-time business. Jeffrey is a heavy equipment operator with a background as a machinist and fabricator for several years. Jeffrey's cues can be identified by the symbol of an eye followed by the word "cue" in cursive. Early cues had the initials "JPL" (for Jeffrey Paul Lipp) on the butt caps. All Eye cues are guaranteed against manufacturer's defects that are not the result of warpage or abuse.

If you would like to talk to Jeff about a new Eye cue, or you have have an Eye cue that needs repair, contact Eye Cues, listed in the Trademark Index.

Jeff Lipp

Present day

SPECIFICATIONS

Butt material: hardwoods
Shaft material: rock maple
Standard length: 58 1/2 in.
Lengths available: any
Standard finish: custom
Balance point: 18 in. from butt
Standard butt cap: phenolic
Standard wrap: linen
Point construction: short spliced
Standard joint: stainless
Joint type: piloted
Joint screw thread: 5/16-14
Joint protectors: standard
Standard number of shafts: one
Standard taper: 9.5 in.
Standard ferrules: Aegis or Grice
Standard bumper: recessed bumper
Standard tip: Triangle
Standard tip width: 13 mm
Tip widths available: any
Annual production: under 15

OPTIONS (FOR NEW CUES ONLY)

Ivory ferrule: $75
Leather wrap: $75
Extra shaft: $90

REPAIRS

Repairs done on all fine cues.
Refinish (with linen wrap): $120
Refinish (with leather wrap): $175
Rewrap (linen): $40
Rewrap (leather): $75
Clean and press linen wrap: $15
Restore leather wrap: $15
Replace ivory ferrule: $75

GRADING	98%	90%	70%

Replace fibre/linen ferrule: $15+
Replace butt cap: $55
Replace shaft: $90

CURRENT EYE CUES

Two-piece Eye bar cues start at $200. Basic Eye cues with wraps and joint rings start at $300. Eye cues with points start at $450. The average order time for an Eye cue is currently five to six months, depending on the design of the cue.

SECONDARY MARKET MINIMUM VALUES

The following are minimum values for other Eye cues encountered on the secondary market. These prices are representative of cues utilizing basic materials and designs that are not necessarily available at present. Jeff has offered one-of-a-kind cues that can command many times these prices due to the use of exotic materials and artistry.

Special construction note: There are many materials and construction techniques that can add value to Eye cues.

For all used Eye cues, except where otherwise noted:
- Add $80 for each additional original straight playable shaft beyond one.
- Deduct $90 for missing original straight playable shaft.
- Add $60 each for ivory ferrules.
- Add $50 for leather wrap.
- Deduct 20% for obvious or improper refinish.

Level 1 - Hustler.
	98%	90%	70%
Level 1 cues start at	$175	$140	$95

Level 2 - 0 points, 0-25 inlays.
Level 2 cues start at	$250	$195	$130

Level 3 - 2-6 points, 0-8 inlays.
Level 3 cues start at	$400	$315	$220

Level 4 - 4-10 points, 9-25 inlays.
Level 4 cues start at	$550	$470	$285

Level 5 - 0-12 points, 26-50 inlays.
Level 5 cues start at	$800	$620	$425

NOTES

FALCON CUES LTD

Maker of pool cues from 1989 to present in Mississauga, Ontario, Canada.

Kathy Rohorek and Peter Chen started building Falcon cues in 1989 in Mississauga, Ontario Canada when the business was founded by Ernie Chen. Falcon cues are easily identifiable by the Falcon logo on the butt caps.

If you are interested in talking to Peter Chen or Kathy Rahorek about a new cue or cue that needs to be repaired, you can contact them at Falcon Cues Ltd, listed in the Trademark Index.

SPECIFICATIONS

Butt material: hardwoods
Shaft material: rock maple
Standard length: 58 in.
Standard wrap: Irish linen
Point construction: inlaid
Standard joint: stainless steel
Standard joint type: piloted
Standard joint screw: Uni-Loc
Joint protectors: standard
Standard number of shafts: one
Standard taper: pro
Standard ferrules: Aegis
Standard tip: Triangle
Standard tip width: 13 mm
Tip widths available: 12 mm, 12.5 mm, and 13 mm
Annual production: 9,000+ cues

OPTIONS (FOR NEW CUES ONLY)

Extra shaft: $45+

REPAIRS

Repairs done on Falcon, Predator, and Bear cues only.
Refinish (with Irish linen wrap): $140
Rewrap (Irish linen): $40
Replace shaft: $45+
Replace butt cap: $40
Replace tip: $15+
Replace Aegis ferrule: $15

CURRENT FALCON CUES

Falcon currently offers several lines of cues that are available for immediate delivery.

FALCON CUES

GRADING	98%	90%	70%

The following are minimum values for Falcon cues encountered on the secondary market. These prices are representative of cues utilizing basic materials and designs that are not necessarily available at present.

Special construction note: There are many materials and construction techniques that can add value to Falcon cues.

For all used Falcon cues, except where otherwise noted:
  Add $40+ for each additional original straight playable shaft beyond one.
  Deduct $45+ for missing original straight playable shaft.
  Deduct 20% for obvious or improper refinish.

	98%	90%	70%
Level 1 - Hustler.			
Level 1 cues start at	$100	$75	$45
Level 2 - 0 points, 0-25 inlays.			
Level 2 cues start at	$135	$105	$65
Level 3 - 2-6 points, 0-8 inlays.			
Level 3 cues start at	$165	$125	$80
Level 4 - 4-10 points, 9-25 inlays.			
Level 4 cues start at	$200	$150	$95

GRADING	98%	90%	70%

Level 5 - 0-12 points, 26-50 inlays.
Level 5 cues start at $250 $190 $120

FANELLI CUES

Maker of pool cues from 1982 to present in Clifton, New Jersey.

Paul Fanelli has always been interested in making and fixing things. His lifelong love of pool gave him the opportunity to start doing minor repairs on his friends' cues in 1980. As the repair business grew, so did Paul's capabilities. All proceeds went into the acquisition of machinery to further his ambitions to make his own cues. He made his first cue in 1982.

Paul Fanelli met Skip Weston in the mid-1990s. They would talk about cues, machines, and techniques. Paul's background in woodworking worked well with Skip's skills in machining. Paul benefited from sharing information and knowledge with Skip and this instilled his desire to always strive for excellence as the only "right" way to do things. In 2001 he tried his first butterfly splice as a way to stabilize the front of the butt where the points don't reach, creating a laminate effect that counteracts warping forces. Paul makes about half of his cues with some sort of butterfly splice.

Paul Fanelli

Cue making is part-time work for Paul, but since 2001 he has been devoting more and more time to it. He has made about 150 cues to date. He prefers not to take orders, but instead to make his own designs and then offer them for sale. Fanelli cues are guaranteed against any defects that are not the result of abuse.

If you are interested in talking to Paul Fanelli about a new cue or cue that needs to be repaired, you can contact him at Fanelli Cues, listed in the Trademark Index.

SPECIFICATIONS

Butt material: hardwoods
Shaft material: rock maple
Standard length: 58 in.
Lengths available: 55 in. to 60 in.
Standard finish: conversion varnish
Balance point: forward
Standard butt cap: phenolic
Standard wrap: Irish linen
Point construction: short splice
Standard joint: linen phenolic
Standard joint type: flat faced
Standard joint screw thread: 3/8-10
Joint protectors: standard
Standard number of shafts: two
Standard taper: custom modified pro
Standard ferrules: linen phenolic
Other ferrule options: ivory
Standard tip: Triangle
Standard tip width: 13 mm
Tip widths available: 9 mm to 14 mm
Annual production: fewer than 20 cues

OPTIONS (FOR NEW CUES ONLY)

Special length: no charge
Layered tip: $35
Ivory butt cap: $350
Ivory joint: $250
Ivory ferrule: $100
Leather wrap: $100
Joint protectors: no charge
Extra shaft: $125
Lizard or other exotic wraps: $250
Ivory Hoppe-style ring: $100

REPAIRS DONE ON ALL FINE CUES.

Refinish (with Irish linen wrap): $200
Refinish (with leather wrap): $300
Rewrap (Irish linen): $50

GRADING	100%	95%	70%

Rewrap (leather): $125
Clean and press linen wrap: $20
Replace shaft with fiber/linen ferrule: $125
Replace shaft with ivory ferrule: $225
Replace ivory ferrule: $100
Replace Delrin/phenolic butt cap: $50
Replace ivory butt cap: $300+
Replace tip: $15
Replaced layered tip: $35
Replace fibre/linen/composite ferrule: $35

CURRENT FANELLI CUES

Fanelli hustler cues start at $350. Basic Fanelli cues with wraps and joint rings start at $650. Fanelli cues with points start at $900. One-of-a-kind custom Fanelli cues start at $1,200. The current delivery time for a Fanelli cue is about four months.

CURRENT EXAMPLES

The following cue can be ordered as shown, modified to suit the desires of the customer, or new designs can be created.

Level 4 - Nara forearm with purpleheart and ebony ringword above wrap, four purpleheart points with four colored veneers alternating with multiple ebony and purpleheart butterfly splices with four veneers, leather wrap, purpleheart butt sleeve with multiple ebony and purpleheart butterfly splices with four veneers between purpleheart and ebony ringword at top and bottom.

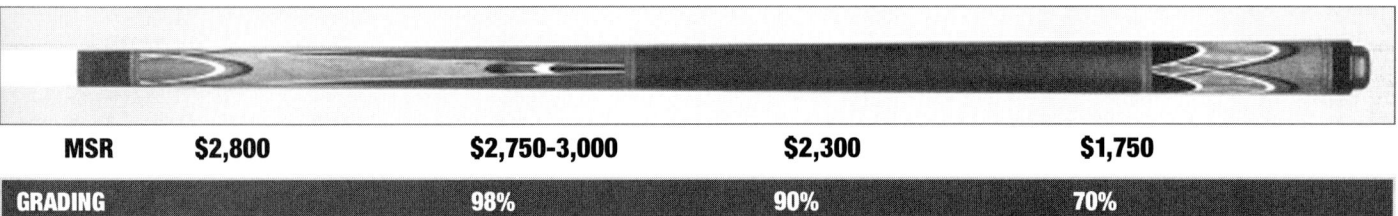

MSR			
$2,800	$2,750-3,000	$2,300	$1,750

GRADING	98%	90%	70%

FÁNELLI CUES

The following are minimum values for other Fanelli cues encountered on the secondary market. These prices are representative of cues utilizing basic materials and designs that are not necessarily available at present. Paul has offered one-of-a-kind cues that can command many times these prices due to the use of exotic materials and artistry.

Special construction note: There are many materials and construction techniques that can add value to Fanelli cues.

For all used Fanelli cues, except where otherwise noted:
  Add $100 for each additional original straight playable shaft beyond two.
  Deduct $125 for each missing original straight playable shaft under two.
  Add $75 each for ivory ferrules.
  Add $85 for leather wrap.
  Deduct 25% for obvious or improper refinish.

Level 1 – Hustler.
  Level 1 cues start at $300 $235 $165

Level 2 - 0 points, 0-25 inlays.
  Level 2 cues start at $600 $465 $315

Level 3 - 2-6 points, 0-8 inlays.
  Level 3 cues start at $900 $695 $475

Level 4 - 4-10 points, 9-25 inlays.
  Level 4 cues start at $1,100 $850 $575

Level 5 - 0-12 points, 26-50 inlays.
  Level 5 cues start at $1,500 $1,185 $800

Level 6 - 0-12 points, 51-75 inlays.
  Level 6 cues start at $2,000 $1,675 $1,200

| GRADING | 98% | 90% | 70% |

FARRIS CUES

Maker of pool cues from 1994 to present in Sapulpa, Oklahoma.

Ed Farris started playing pool at age 12 and enjoyed the game. He also collected cues for a time. His cue shop is located near Tulsa, in Sapulpa, Oklahoma. Ed has a one-man shop in his home, and all of his tools are manual operation. He uses a Groton inlay mill from the 1920s era. His other equipment is from the 1950s and 1960s. Ed enjoys working with older machinery.

Ed's goal is to make cues that are truly unique. His part-time cuemaking business began in 1994. He gives credit to Verl Horn for teaching him a lot about building cues. Another protégé is J. W. Petree. Ed usually makes from 5 to 20 custom cues per year.

Farris Cues are guaranteed against defects to the original owner. Repairs will be made, provided they are not the result of warpage or abuse.

If you are interested in talking to Eddie L. Farris about a new cue or cue that needs to be repaired, you can contact him at Ed Farris Cues, listed in the Trademark Index.

Eddie Farris

Present day

SPECIFICATIONS:

Butt material: Delrin
Shaft material: maple
Standard length: 58 in.
Standard wrap: Irish linen
Standard ferrules: Ivorine
Standard tip: Le Pro
Annual production: fewer than 20 cues

OPTIONS (FOR NEW CUES ONLY)

Ivory ferrule: $75
Leather wrap: $75
Extra shaft: $150

REPAIRS

Repairs done on Farris cues.
Refinish with Irish linen wrap: $150
Rewrap Irish linen: $40
Replace shaft: $150
Replace tip: $15 Le Pro

CURRENT FARRIS CUES

Two-piece Farris bar cues start at $200. Basic Farris cues with wraps and joint rings start at $500. Farris cues with points start at $700. One-of-a-kind custom Farris cues start at $1,000. The current delivery time for a Farris cue is two years.

FARRIS CUES

The following are minimum values for Farris cues encountered on the secondary market. These prices are representative of cues utilizing basic materials and designs that are not necessarily available at present. Ed has offered one-of-a-kind cues that can command many times these prices due to the use of exotic materials and artistry.

Special construction note: There are many materials and construction techniques that can add value to Farris cues.

For all used Farris cues, except where otherwise noted:

Add $100 for each additional original straight playable shaft beyond one.
Deduct $150 for missing original straight playable shaft.
Add $50 each for ivory ferrules.
Add $65 for leather wrap.
Deduct 20% for obvious or improper refinish.

	98%	90%	70%
Level 1 - Hustler.			
Level 1 cues start at	$200	$165	$125
Level 2 - 0 points, 0-25 inlays.			
Level 2 cues start at	$450	$350	$235
Level 3 - 2-6 points, 0-8 inlays.			
Level 3 cues start at	$600	$465	$320
Level 4 - 4-10 points, 9-25 inlays.			
Level 4 cues start at	$800	$625	$425
Level 5 - 0-12 points, 26-50 inlays.			
Level 5 cues start at	$1,200	$945	$650

FIERCE EAGLE CUES

Distributor of pool cues in Denver, Colorado.
Fierce Eagle cues are easily identifiable by the "Fierce Eagle" logo on the butt caps.
If you are interested in talking to someone about a new Fierce Eagle cue or cue that needs to be repaired, you can contact them at Fierce Eagle Cues, listed in the Trademark Index.

SPECIFICATIONS

Butt material: hardwoods
Shaft material: rock maple
Standard length: 58 in.
Standard number of shafts: one
Standard taper: 15 in. Pro
Standard tip: laminated pigskin

CURRENT FIERCE EAGLE CUES

Ten two-piece Fierce Eagle cue models are available for $29.95 each. The White Wolf Series from Fierce Eagle Cues consists of seven cue models priced at $39.95 each. Fierce Eagle cues are available for immediate delivery.

5280 CUES

Line of cues distributed from Lafayette, Colorado.
5280 Cues is the creation of the well-known distributor, CueStix International. Located 5,280 feet above sea level, 5280 Cues represents a bit of local pride for the Mile High City of Denver. These cues have unique inlay designs, an industry-first bumper, and come standard with a premium tip, Tiger's newest Red-Line® tip made exclusively for 5280 Cues.
3/8-8 flat-faced implex or 5/16-18 piloted stainless steel joints are offered. 5280 cues are easily identifiable by the 5280 logo on the butt caps and the new bumper design.
If you are interested in talking to 5280 Cues about a new cue or cue that needs to be repaired, you can contact CueStix International, listed in the Trademark Index.

SPECIFICATIONS

Butt material: hardwoods
Shaft material: Canadian hard rock maple
Standard length: 58 in.
Standard finish: polyurethane
Balance point: n/a
Standard butt cap: resin
Standard wrap: Irish linen
Point construction: inlaid
Standard joint: implex and stainless steel
Standard joint type: flat faced
Standard joint screw thread: 3/8-8
Joint protectors: standard
Standard number of shafts: one
Standard taper: 11 in. pro
Standard ferrules: Ivorene 3
Standard tip: Tiger Red-Line® Tip
Standard tip width: 13 mm
Tip widths available: 12 mm or 13 mm

OPTIONS (FOR NEW CUES ONLY)

Extra shaft: $140

CURRENT 5280 CUES

5280 Cues currently offers the Altitude Series, Apex Series, Cory Deuel Series, Mile High Series, Peak Series, and the RM Series. 5280 cues are available for immediate delivery.

5280 CUES

The following are minimum values for 5280 cues encountered on the secondary market. These prices are representative of cues utilizing basic materials and designs that are not necessarily available at present.
Special construction note: There are many materials and construction techniques that can add value to 5280 cues.
For all used 5280 cues, except where otherwise noted:
   Add $75 for each additional original straight playable shaft beyond one.
   Deduct $70% for missing original straight playable shaft.
   Deduct 15% for obvious or improper refinish.

GRADING	98%	90%	70%
Level 1 - Hustler.			
Level 1 cues start at	$65	$50	$30
Level 2 - 0 points, 0-25 inlays.			
Level 2 cues start at	$85	$65	$40
Level 3 - 2-6 points, 0-8 inlays.			
Level 3 cues start at	$100	$75	$45
Level 4 - 4-10 points, 9-25 inlays.			
Level 4 cues start at	$125	$95	$60
Level 5 - 0-12 points, 26-50 inlays.			
Level 5 cues start at	$150	$115	$70

FRANK FISHER CUSTOM CUES

Maker of pool cues in Johnson City, Tennessee.

If you have a Frank Fisher cue that needs further identification or repair, or would like to talk to Frank about ordering a new cue, contact Frank Fisher Custom Cues, listed in the Trademark Index.

RITCHIE FLORENCE CUES

Line of pool cues made by Dale Patten from 1975 to 1980 in Redondo Beach, California.

For more information, refer to Dale Patten Cues. If you have a Ritchie Florence cue that needs further identification or repair, contact Dale Patten Cues, listed in the Trademark Index.

TRAVIS FRAKES

Maker of Hammer Cues. For more information, refer to Hammer Cues.

JOSEPH FRANKE

Maker of Joseph Full Splice Cues. For more information, refer to Joseph Full Splice.

JERRY and LAURIE FRANKLIN

Makers of Southwest Cues. For more information, refer to Southwest.

ADAM FRANKS CUSTOM CUES

Maker of pool cues from 1986 in Corrales, New Mexico and presently in Albuquerque, New Mexico.

Adam Franks is a pool player and full-time cue maker located in Albuquerque, New Mexico. He began building cues in 1986, and his business was formerly known as OJO. Adam was not happy with the cues he saw in the marketplace and wanted to make something different. Having grown up in an art community, he was influenced by jewelers, painters, and potters. This is evident in his use of stones and precious metals in his inlay work. Shafts are made from old growth northern sugar maple. Adam uses tips that he makes himself.

Each Adam Franks Custom Cue is unique. Adam Franks cues are easily identifiable by the fingerprint Adam puts on each one. The average order time for an Adam Franks Custom Cue is one year.

If you are interested in talking to Adam C Franks about a new cue or cue that needs to be repaired, you can contact him at Adam Franks Custom Cues, listed in the Trademark Index.

Adam Franks

OJO CUES

SPECIFICATIONS

Butt material: hardwoods
Shaft material: sugar maple
Standard length: 58 in.
Lengths available: 56 ½ in. to 60 in.
Standard finish: urethane acrylic
Balance point: custom
Standard butt cap: wood
Standard wrap: Irish linen
Point construction: short splice
Standard joint: wood
Joint type: flat faced
Standard joint screw thread: 5/16-14
Joint protectors: standard
Standard number of shafts: two

GRADING	98%	90%	70%

Standard taper: medium stiff
Standard ferrules: Aegis
Standard tip: Adam Franks
Standard tip width: 12.85 mm
Tip widths available: any
Standard bumper: wood
Annual production: 20

OPTIONS (FOR NEW CUES ONLY)

Special length: no charge
Layered tip: $20+
Ivory butt cap: $300
Ivory joint: $175
Ivory ferrule: $100
Ivory points: $400+
Joint protectors: $50+
Extra shaft: $175+

REPAIRS

Repairs done on all fine cues. Prices quoted on a per cue basis.

ADAM FRANKS CUES

The following are minimum values for other Adam Franks cues encountered on the secondary market. These prices are representative of cues utilizing basic materials and designs that are not necessarily available at present. Adam has offered one-of-a-kind cues that can command many times these prices due to the use of exotic materials and artistry.

Special construction note: There are many materials and construction techniques that can add value to Adam Franks cues.

For all used Adam Franks cues, except where otherwise noted:
Add $125 for each additional original straight playable shaft beyond two.
Deduct $175 for each missing original straight playable shaft under two.
Add $65 each for ivory ferrules.
Deduct 20% for obvious or improper refinish.

	98%	90%	70%
Level 2 - 0 points, 0-25 inlays.			
Level 2 cues start at	$500	$385	$260
Level 3 - 2-6 points, 0-8 inlays.			
Level 3 cues start at	$650	$500	$335
Level 4 - 4-10 points, 9-25 inlays.			
Level 4 cues start at	$750	$585	$395
Level 5 - 0-12 points, 26-50 inlays.			
Level 5 cues start at	$1,100	$875	$600

DOC FRY

Maker of pool cues in the sixties and seventies in Feasterville, Pennsylvania, a suburb of Philadelphia.

Doc Fry was a cuemaker in the Philadelphia area. He was a pharmacist who owned his own pharmacy in Feasterville (hence the nickname "Doc") who played pool and made cues as a hobby. He is best known for inspiring Gus Szamboti, who was also from the Philadelphia area, to start making cues. Very few Doc Fry cues have points, and it is believed that all of those are made from Gus Szamboti blanks. Although Doc Fry cues are unmarked, they often will have a penny under the bumper. It is believed that Fry would go to the bank to get new pennies, so the years on these pennies indicate when the cues were made.

If you have a Doc Fry cue that needs further identification or repair, contact Szamboti Cues, listed in the Trademark Index.

SPECIFICATIONS

Butt material: hardwoods
Shaft material: rock maple
Standard length: 58 in.
Standard wrap: Irish linen
Standard joint: stainless steel
Joint screw: 5/16-14
Joint type: piloted
Point construction: short splice
Standard butt cap: Delrin
Standard ferrules: ivory

GRADING	98%	90%	70%

KNOWN EXAMPLES

The following cues are known examples of the work of Doc Fry. These cues can be encountered as shown, modified to suit the desires of the original customer, or entirely different designs can be encountered.

Level 2 - Hardwood forearm, butt sleeve usually of thick rings of marbled or glitter impregnated plastics.

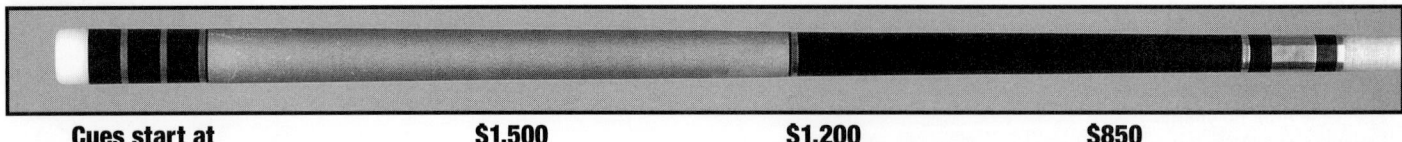

Cues start at	$1,500	$1,200	$850

Level 3 - Maple forearm, four ebony points with four colored veneers and possibly inlays of mother-of-pearl notched diamonds or dots, butt sleeve usually of thick rings of marbled or glitter impregnated plastics and possibly inlays of mother-of-pearl notched diamonds or dots set in black plastic.

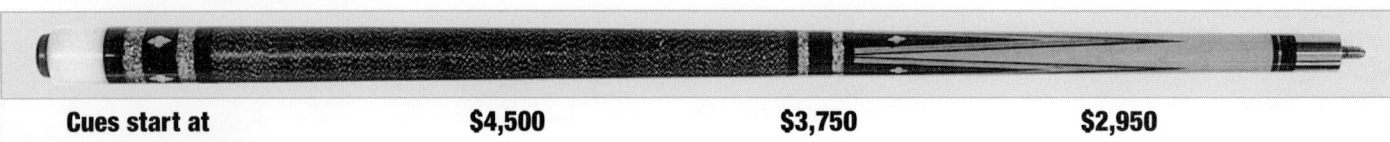

Cues start at	$4,500	$3,750	$2,950

DOC FRY CUES

The following are minimum prices for other Doc Fry cues encountered on the secondary market. These prices are representative of cues utilizing the most basic materials and designs that were available. Doc Fry offered one-of-a-kind cues that can command many times these prices due to the use of exotic materials and artistry. Doc Fry cues will be further covered in future editions.

Note: Due to the rarity of Doc Fry cues and increasing interest, prices are on the rise. Fewer original examples are surfacing, and collectors are holding on to the ones they have. Unique examples with pedigree are bringing the highest prices.

Special construction note: There are many materials and construction techniques that can add value to Doc Fry cues. The following are the most important examples:

Add $300+ for glitter rings.

For all used Doc Fry cues, except where otherwise noted:

Add $250 for each additional original straight playable shaft beyond one.
Deduct $350+ for missing original straight playable shaft.
Add $200+ for leather wrap.
Deduct 30% for obvious or improper refinish.

Level 2 - 0 points, 0-25 inlays.

Level 2 cues start at	$1,250	$1,000	$700

Level 3 - 2-6 points, 0-8 inlays.

Level 3 cues start at	$3,500	$2,850	$2,000

Level 4 - 4-10 points, 9-25 inlays.

Level 4 cues start at	$4,500	$3,700	$2,750

Level 5 - 0-12 points, 26-50 inlays.

Level 5 cues start at	$6,000	$4,850	$3,500

GARLAND "JUDD" FULLER

Maker of Judd's Custom Cues. For information refer to Judd's.

FURY CUES

Distributor of pool cues.

Fury cues are easily identifiable by the "Fury" logo on the butt caps.

If you are interested in talking to someone about a new Fury cue or cue that needs to be repaired, you can contact them at Fury Cues, listed in the Trademark Index.

SPECIFICATIONS

Butt material: hardwoods
Shaft material: rock maple
Standard length: 58 in.
Standard wrap: Irish linen
Point construction: short splice
Standard number of shafts: one
Standard ferrules: linen fiber
Standard tip: Le Pro

GRADING	98%	90%	70%

Standard tip width: 13 mm

CURRENT FURY CUES

Fury currently offers the DL Series, NR Series, and RP Series. Fury cues are available for immediate delivery.

FURY CUES

The following are minimum values for Fury cues encountered on the secondary market. These prices are representative of cues utilizing basic materials and designs that are not necessarily available at present.

Special construction note: There are many materials and construction techniques that can add value to Fury cues.

For all used Fury cues, except where otherwise noted:
- Add $40 for each additional original straight playable shaft beyond one.
- Deduct 60% for missing original straight playable shaft.
- Deduct 15% for obvious or improper refinish.

Level 2 - 0 points, 0-25 inlays.

	98%	90%	70%
Level 2 cues start at	$65	$45	$30

Level 3 - 2-6 points, 0-8 inlays.

	98%	90%	70%
Level 3 cues start at	$75	$55	$35

Level 4 - 4-10 points, 9-25 inlays.

	98%	90%	70%
Level 4 cues start at	$95	$75	$45

Level 5 - 0-12 points, 26-50 inlays.

	98%	90%	70%
Level 5 cues start at	$125	$95	$60

NOTES

G SECTION

GARDNER CUES

Maker of pool cues from 2001 to present in Mercer, Pennsylvania.

Mike Gardner noticed that there was a need for good repair work in his area, and from there he thought he would try his hand at building his own cue. In 2001, Gardner Cues was started. Cuemaking is a part-time job at present, but Mike would like it to become full time. He began in the basement of his house, with a small lathe in the corner. He did repairs for his local area. Because of increased traffic in and out of the house, Mike and his wife decided to open a Pro Shop to service the needs of players. He has since moved into a 1600 sq. ft. building, and has enlarged the Pro Shop. He has also added much more equipment, with room to expand.

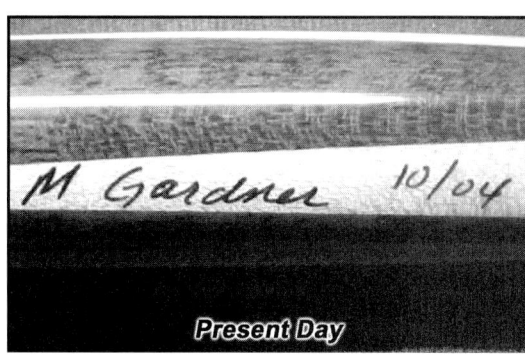
Present Day

Mike Gardner

Mike is a member of the International Cuemakers Association. He strives to make a cue with a unique look and great hit and feel. His cues are signed "M Gardner" on the forearm just above the wrap area. Mike's cues are guaranteed for life against defects in workmanship that are not the result of warpage or abuse.

If you would like to talk to Mike about a new cue or one that needs to be repaired, contact Gardner Cues, listed in the Trademark Index.

SPECIFICATIONS

Butt material: hardwoods
Shaft material: hard maple
Standard length: 58 in.
Standard wrap: Irish linen
Standard number of shafts: one
Standard ferrules: Grice
Standard tip: Le Pro
Annual production: fewer than 25 cues

OPTIONS (FOR NEW CUES ONLY)

Ivory ferrule: $60
Leather wrap: $60
Extra shaft: $80

REPAIRS

Repairs done on all fine cues.
Refinish (with Irish linen wrap): $100+
Rewrap (Irish linen): $40

CURRENT GARDNER CUES

Two-piece Gardner bar cues start at $200. Basic Gardner cues with wraps and joint rings start at $250. Gardner cues with points start at $300. One-of-a-kind custom Gardner cues start at $400.

GRADING	100%	95%	70%

CURRENT EXAMPLES

The following Gardner cues can be ordered as shown, modified to suit the desires of the customer, or new designs can be created.

Level 2 - Stained bird's-eye maple forearm with an ebony ring above wrap, stained bird's-eye maple butt sleeve with four ebony-bordered bird's-eye maple diamond-shaped inlays between brass rings set in ebony at top and bottom.

MSR	$250	$235-275	$190	$135

GRADING	100%	95%	70%

Level 3 - Maple forearm, four cocobolo points, ebony butt sleeve with a thick cocobolo ring above four zebrawood diamond-shaped inlays.

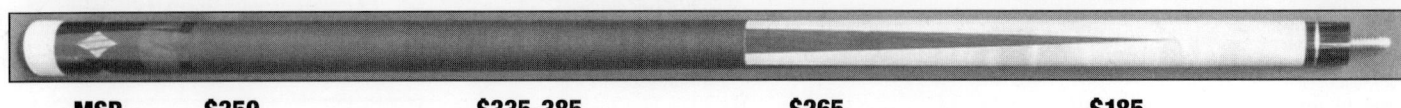

MSR	$350	$335-385	$265	$185

Level 4 - Ebony forearm, four floating turquoise points, ebony butt sleeve with four large turquoise diamond-shaped inlays alternating with pairs of ivory diamond-shaped inlays between ebony and turquoise stitches set in aluminum rings at top and bottom.

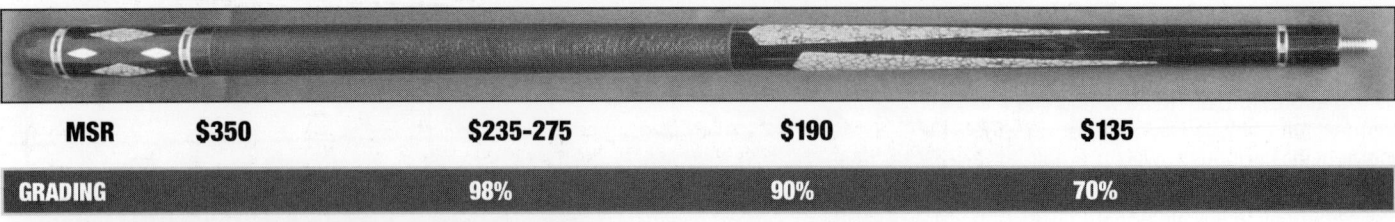

MSR	$350	$235-275	$190	$135

GRADING	98%	90%	70%

SECONDARY MARKET MINIMUM VALUES

The following are minimum values for other Gardner cues encountered on the secondary market. These prices are representative of cues utilizing basic materials and designs that are not necessarily available at present. Mike has offered one-of-a-kind cues that can command many times these prices due to the use of exotic materials and artistry.

Special construction note: There are many materials and construction techniques that can add value to Gardner cues.

For all used Gardner cues, except where otherwise noted:
- Add $65 for each additional original straight playable shaft beyond one.
- Deduct $80 for missing original straight playable shaft.
- Add $50 each for ivory ferrules.
- Add $50 for leather wrap.
- Deduct 20% for obvious or improper refinish.

Level 1 - Hustler.
Level 1 cues start at	$185	$145	$95

Level 2 - 0 points, 0-25 inlays.
Level 2 cues start at	$235	$180	$120

Level 3 - 2-6 points, 0-8 inlays.
Level 3 cues start at	$275	$215	$145

Level 4 - 4-10 points, 9-25 inlays.
Level 4 cues start at	$350	$270	$185

Level 5 - 0-12 points, 26-50 inlays.
Level 5 cues start at	$500	$385	$265

GATZKE'S CUSTOM CUES

Maker of pool cues from 1994 to present in Las Cruces, New Mexico.

Mike Gatzke was born and raised in Sidney, Montana. He moved to Las Cruces, New Mexico, at the age of 18. In 1994, Mike got a lathe and began doing repairs and building "sneaky petes." He eventually made his own taper bar for cutting butts and shafts. Gatzke currently has six lathes, with each one performing different functions. One is portable, allowing him to service cues for players at tournaments and on league nights.

In 2002, Mike purchased a CNC machine and taught himself how to operate it. Although he uses the CNC to design and create tighter-fitting inlays, he will still handcraft cues on request.

Gatzke has used at least five different two- and three-part car coat polyurethane finishes over the years. He is currently experimenting with UV polyester and polyurethane high-gloss finish. This allows him to be able to refinish a cue in a couple of days, as compared to weeks or months with the old finishes.

Mike only signs the cues he builds from scratch. Early cues had initials, but he feels the signature that appears on his current cues adds a more personal touch to his work.

If you are interested in talking to Mike Gatzke about a new cue or cue that needs to be repaired, you can contact him at Gatzke's Custom Cues, listed in the Trademark Index.

SPECIFICATIONS

Butt material: miscellaneous hardwoods, phenolics
Shaft material: maple
Standard length: 58 in.
Standard wrap: Irish linen

GRADING	98%	90%	70%

Standard finish: UV-activated polyurethane or polyester
Standard butt cap: phenolic
Standard ferrules: fiber
Standard tip: Le Pro and Moori
Joint screw thread: 3/8-10
Point construction: spliced or inlaid
Standard number of shafts: one
Annual production: fewer than 40 cues

OPTIONS PRICING FOR NEW CUES

Special lengths: $25 per extra inch
Ivory ferrule: $60
Ivory joint: $200
Ivory butt cap: $250
Extra shaft: $50+
Layered tip: $18+
Custom joint protectors: $35+

REPAIR COSTS FOR WORK DONE ON ALL FINE CUES

Refinish with Irish linen wrap: $140+
Rewrap with Irish linen: $45
Replace shaft: $50+
Replace tip: $6+
Replace ivory ferrule: $60
Replace ivory butt cap: $250

CURRENT GATZKE'S CUES

Mike Gatzke makes two-piece bar cues that start at $75. Basic two-piece Gatzke's cues with a wrap and joint rings start at $200. Cues with inlaid points start at $300. Gatzke's cues with spliced points start at at $350. One-of-a-kind custom Gatzke's cues start at $450. The average delivery time for a Gatzke Custom Cue is eight weeks to two years, depending on the intricacy of the cue.

SECONDARY MARKET MINIMUM VALUES

The following are minimum values for Gatzke's cues encountered on the secondary market. These prices are representative of cues utilizing basic materials and designs that are not necessarily available at present. Mike has offered one-of-a-kind cues that can command many times these prices due to the use of exotic materials and artistry.

Special construction note: There are many materials and construction techniques that can add value to Gatzke's cues.

For all used Gatzke's cues, except where otherwise noted:
- Add $50+ for each additional original straight playable shaft beyond one.
- Deduct $50+ for missing original straight playable shaft.
- Add $50 each for ivory ferrules.
- Add $150 for ivory joint.
- Deduct 20% for obvious or improper refinish.

	98%	90%	70%
Level 1 - Hustler.			
Level 1 cues start at	$65	$50	$35
Level 2 - 0 points, 0-25 inlays.			
Level 2 cues start at	$185	$145	$95
Level 3 - 2-6 points, 0-8 inlays.			
Level 3 cues start at	$285	$220	$150
Level 4 - 4-10 points, 9-25 inlays.			
Level 4 cues start at	$350	$270	$185
Level 5 - 0-12 points, 26-50 inlays.			
Level 5 cues start at	$550	$425	$290

DAN GAUDREAU

Maker of DG Cues. For information, refer to listing for DG Cues.

G.B. CUSTOM CUES

Maker of pool cues from 1993 to 1998 in Houston, Texas and from 1998 to present in Overland, Missouri, a suburb of St. Louis.
George Buss began playing pool when he was studying engineering in college in the late 1960s. An Iowa native, George moved to Santa Barbara, California after school, where he worked for many years as a quality control engineer. In the early 1990s, engineers were being

| GRADING | 98% | 90% | 70% |

laid off in large numbers, so George planned on making custom cues, like his brother Jim. He left his job in 1992 and, after spending a year in France, moved to Houston to make cues with his brother.

Although early cues were usually marked "G.B." on the butt sleeve, or on the forearm if the butt sleeve was a dark wood, George started signing "G.Buss" on the forearm soon after. General specifications have remained basically the same. G.B. Custom cues are made entirely by hand by George Buss, without the aid of CNC. George tries to create unique designs, but he will also make more traditional designs at the customer's request. No two cues are totally alike, and any length, taper, joint, or design can be ordered. George has created his own unique spliced floating points which are V-cut. He can inlay many of these points concentrically in different materials to create the effect of multiple veneers.

G. B. cues are becoming more and more popular in foreign markets, such as Europe and Asia. George and Jim moved into a larger shop outside of St. Louis in the summer of 1998. George works in the shop during the day while Jim comes in at night after working at Boeing. Both are there on weekends. Many repairs are done in the shop.

G.B. cues are guaranteed against construction defects that are not the result of warpage or abuse. If you have a G.B. cue that needs further identification or repair, or would like to talk to George about ordering a new cue, contact G.B. Custom Cues, listed in the Trademark Index.

SPECIFICATIONS

Butt material: hardwoods
Shaft material: rock maple
Standard length: 58 in.
Lengths available: any
Standard finish: acrylic polyurethane
Joint screw: 5/16-14
Standard joint: stainless
Joint type: piloted
Balance point: approximately 1 1/2 in. above the wrap
Point construction: short spliced
Standard wrap: Irish linen
Standard butt cap: black linen phenolic
Standard number of shafts: two
Standard taper: 10 in. pro
Standard ferrules: Ivorine-3
Standard tip: Le Pro
Tip widths available: any
Annual production: fewer than 50 cues

REPAIRS

Repairs done only on G.B. custom cues.

SECONDARY MARKET MINIMUM VALUES

The following are minimum prices for G.B. cues encountered on the secondary market. These prices are representative of cues utilizing basic materials and designs that may not be currently available. George also offers one-of-a-kind cues that can command many times these prices due to the use of exotic materials and artistry.

Special construction note: There are many materials and construction techniques that can add value to G.B. cues.

For all used G.B. cues:
Add $70+ for each additional original straight playable shaft beyond two.
Deduct $95 for each missing original straight playable shaft under two.
Add $50+ for each ivory ferrule.
Deduct 25% for obvious or improper refinish.

Level 2 - 0 points, 0-25 inlays.
| Level 2 cues start at | $375 | $285 | $190 |

Level 3 - 2-6 points, 0-8 inlays.
| Level 3 cues start at | $475 | $365 | $245 |

Level 4 - 4-10 points, 9-25 inlays.
| Level 4 cues start at | $800 | $625 | $420 |

Level 5 - 0-12 points, 26-50 inlays.
| Level 5 cues start at | $1,100 | $850 | $575 |

Level 6 - 0-12 points, 51-75 inlays.
| Level 6 cues start at | $1,400 | $1,100 | $750 |

| GRADING | 98% | 90% | 70% |

GCUE

Pool cues distributed by DMI Sports in Fort Washington, Pennsylvania.

Dart Mart Inc. is one of the largest distributors of pool and dart supplies in the United States. They have had licensing arrangements with Playboy, The Grateful Dead, Budweiser, Miller Lite, and other famous companies and organizations to market representative theme cues. These cues have been made for Dart Mart by cue manufacturers and have been distributed by the GCue division of Dart Mart. Secondary prices may be affected by the collector market for the organization represented and the number of cues manufactured. GCue introduced a series of graphite cues with images licensed by the likes of Playboy in the late 1990s. GCue is now DMI Sports, Inc. If you have a GCue cue that needs further identification or repair, contact DMI Sports, Inc., listed in the Trademark Index.

SPECIFICATIONS

Butt material: hardwoods
Shaft material: rock maple
Standard length: 58 in.
Standard number of shafts: one

SECONDARY MARKET MINIMUM VALUES

The following are minimum prices for GCue cues encountered on the secondary market.
For all used GCue cues:
Add $25 for graphite construction.
Deduct 20% for obvious or improper refinish.

Level 2 - 0 points, 0-25 inlays.

| Level 2 cues start at | $75 | $55 | $35 |

GD CUES

Maker of pool cues from 1995 to present in Augusta, Georgia.

Gary Dawkins was born in El Paso, Texas and raised in southern California. He served as a medic during the Vietnam conflict. He moved to Georgia in 1969 and became a licensed master plumber and general contractor. Gary always liked working with his hands and eventually decided to retire from construction. Since he loved to play pool and work with his hands, he became a cuemaker. His work is influenced by Paul Mottey, Bludworth, and Arnot.

Gary started out wanting to make his own cue, since he loved the game. He wanted a cue that would be different from everyone else's. He quickly learned that there is a lot more to building a cue than he thought at first. He bought a lathe and inlay pantograph machine and learned how to use them properly, and then he built his first cue and began playing with it.

As time went on, other players would ask Gary to fix cues they had. They would try Gary's cue, love the way it hit, and ask if Gary would build one for them. And so, GD Cues was born. GD cues is a one-man shop and Gary makes cues full time as of 2000, when Gary retired from another job. All inlays are done by hand with a pantograph. Gary does not have CNC. He is a gun stock engraver and he hand engraves the wood and steel joints in cues as well.

GD cues are guaranteed against construction defects that are not the result of warpage or abuse for life to the original owner. If you are interested in talking to Gary Dawkins about a new cue or cue that needs to be repaired, you can contact him at GD Cues, listed in the Trademark Index.

SPECIFICATIONS

Butt material: hardwoods
Shaft material: rock maple
Standard length: 58 in.
Lengths available: any up to 60 ½ in.
Standard finish: 6 to 8 clear coats
Balance point: varies, 1 to 2 in. above wrap
Standard butt cap: phenolic
Standard wrap: Irish linen
Point construction: short splice and inlaid
Standard joint: phenolic
Joint type: flat face
Joint screw thread: radial pin
Standard number of shafts: one
Standard taper: modified pro
Standard ferrules: Ivorine-3
Standard tip: Moori III
Standard tip width: 13 mm
Tip widths available: 10 to 14 mm
Annual production: fewer than 45 cues

GRADING	98%	90%	70%

OPTIONS (FOR NEW CUES ONLY)
Special length: $20
Layered tip: $25+
Ivory butt cap: $150
Ivory butt sleeve: $600
Ivory joint: $100
Engraved joint: $100+
Ivory ferrule: $50
Ivory points: $125 each
Ivory handle: $1500
Ivory Hoppe-style ring: $75
Leather wrap: $60
Lizard or other exotic wrap: $125
Joint protectors: $100
Quick-release joint: $25
Extra shaft: $100+
Extra rings (each): $10

REPAIRS
Repairs done on all fine cues.
Refinish (with Irish linen wrap): $125
Refinish (with leather wrap): $175
Rewrap (Irish linen): $35
Rewrap (leather): $60
Clean and press linen wrap: $25
Replace shaft with fiber/linen ferrule: $140
Replace shaft with ivory ferrule: $175
Replace ivory ferrule: $60
Replace butt cap (Delrin, linen): $50
Replace ivory butt cap: $160
Replace tip: $20
Replaced layered tip: $25+
Replace fiber/linen/composite ferrule: $25

CURRENT GD CUES

GD two-piece hustler cues start at $350. Basic two-piece GD cues with a wrap and joint rings start at $400. GD cues with veneered points start at $450. The current delivery time for a GD custom cue is at least two weeks depending on the intricacy of the design.

SECONDARY MARKET MINIMUM VALUES

The following are minimum values for other GD cues encountered on the secondary market. These prices are representative of cues utilizing basic materials and designs that are not necessarily available at present. Gary has offered one-of-a-kind cues that can command many times these prices due to the use of exotic materials and artistry.

Special construction note: There are many materials and construction techniques that can add value to GD cues.

For all used GD cues, except where otherwise noted:
Add $75 for each additional original straight playable shaft beyond one.
Deduct $100 for missing original straight playable shaft.
Add $50 each for ivory ferrules.
Add $50 for leather wrap.
Deduct 20% for obvious or improper refinish.

Level 1 - Hustler.

	98%	90%	70%
Level 1 cues start at	$300	$230	$155

Level 2 - 0 points, 0-25 inlays.

Level 2 cues start at	$350	$270	$180

Level 3 - 2-6 points, 0-8 inlays.

Level 3 cues start at	$400	$315	$220

Level 4 - 4-10 points, 9-25 inlays.

Level 4 cues start at	$500	$395	$265

Level 5 - 0-12 points, 26-50 inlays.

Level 5 cues start at	$650	$500	$325

GRADING	98%	90%	70%

GEM CUES

Maker of pool cues 1987 to present in Lake Charles, Louisiana.

Gary Medlin was an excellent pool player who started doing cue repairs in the mid-1970s. He opened a pool room with long-time friend Freddie Wherland in the 1980s, and worked on all kinds of cues there. Gary needed a new cue, and after reassembling so many of the top cues on the market he decided he would rather make his own cue than have someone else do it. Gary and Freddie decided to put a shop in the back of their room and make cues, and Gary went to machinist school at night and experimented with cuemaking during the day. Early Gem cues were simple hustlers, then they graduated to plain maple cues with wraps and stainless steel joints. Gary spent hours on the phone with cuemakers he respected. After a couple of years they sold the room and Gary chose to make Gem cues full time.

By 1990 Gary was making more complex custom cues that he was very proud of. Today he makes almost 100 cues a year by hand in his one-man shop. Gary makes everything in a Gem cue except for the tip and bumper. He prefers to use a 5/16-14 stainless steel joint but will make a 3/8-10 flat-faced joint if the customer chooses. Gem cues are easily identifiable by "Gem" in script engraved into the butt cap and can be encountered with "GEM" followed by the diamond logo under a clear plastic window in the butt sleeve.

Gem Cues are guaranteed for life against manufacturing defects that are not the result of warpage or abuse. If you have a Gem cue that needs further identification or repair, or would like to order a new Gem cue, contact Gem Cues, listed in the Trademark Index.

SPECIFICATIONS

Butt material: hardwoods
Shaft material: rock maple
Standard length: 58 in.
Lengths available: any
Standard finish: urethane
Balance point: 1 1/2 in. above wrap
Standard butt cap: Atlas MP
Standard wrap: Irish linen
Point construction: short splice
Standard joint: stainless steel
Joint type: piloted
Joint screw: 5/16-14
Standard number of shafts: one
Standard taper: 8 in. to 10 in. pro
Standard ferrules: melamine
Standard tip width: 13 mm
Standard tip: Le Pro
Annual production: fewer than 100 cues

REPAIRS

Repairs done on all fine cues.

SECONDARY MARKET MINIMUM VALUES

The following are minimum values for Gem cues encountered on the secondary market. These prices are representative of cues utilizing basic materials and designs that are not currently available. Gary has offered one-of-a-kind cues that can command many times these prices due to the use of exotic materials and artistry.

Special construction note: There are many materials and construction techniques that can add value to Gem cues. The following are the most important examples:

Add $750+ for ivory points.
Add $150+ for ivory joint.

For all used Gem cues, except where otherwise noted:

Add $85 for each additional original straight playable shaft beyond one.
Deduct $100 for missing original straight playable shaft.
Add $50 each for ivory ferrules.
Add $65 for leather wrap.
Deduct 25% for obvious or improper refinish.

Level 1 - 4 points, hustler.

	98%	90%	70%
Level 1 cues start at	$150	$120	$80

Level 2 - 0 points, 0-25 inlays.

Level 2 cues start at	$325	$250	$170

Level 3 - 2-6 points, 0-8 inlays.

Level 3 cues start at	$500	$385	$265

Level 4 - 4-10 points, 9-25 inlays.

Level 4 cues start at	$650	$515	$350

Level 5 - 0-12 points, 26-50 inlays.

Level 5 cues start at	$900	$695	$475

GEPPETTO CUSTOM CUES

Maker of pool cues in Glen Ellyn, Illinois.

If you have a Geppetto cue that needs further identification or repair, or would like to talk to Steven Hopper about ordering a new Geppetto cue, contact Geppetto Custom Cues, listed in the Trademark Index.

WILLIAM CHARLES GIBBS

Maker of Classic Custom Cues. For information, refer to Classic Custom Cues.

GILBERT CUSTOM CUES

Maker of pool cues from 1989 to 1994 in Traverse City, Michigan, and from 1994 to present in Frazier, Missouri.

Present Day

Vicki and Andy Gilbert

Andy Gilbert started playing pool as a young boy. At the age of 13, he started working in construction, which led to a lifelong woodworking hobby. He continued to play pool and, with his woodworking background, he learned to replace his own tips. Andy went into the glass business and enjoyed playing pool on the road when time allowed. He learned to repair his own cues and soon was doing minor repairs for others. Andy's repair work progressed and, by 1989, he made his first cue in Traverse City, Michigan. With the experimentation and the advice of a couple of cuemakers, Andy advanced his cuemaking skills. In 1994, after a severe cut to his hand that took Andy out of the glass business, he moved to Missouri to make cues full-time.

Gilbert cues are easily identifiable by the "G" logo that appears on the butt caps. Andy makes his cues one at a time, by hand, in his one-man shop, and is constantly making improvements in design and construction. He makes everything in his cues except for the tips and bumpers. He prefers a stiff hit, so he has developed his own taper, which starts to widen right from the thread on the ferrule. Andy likes to target league players, and tries to keep his prices very competitive. Gilbert cues were easily identifiable by a "G" in the butt cap until he recently started signing them on the forearm.

Gilbert cues are guaranteed indefinitely against construction defects that are not the result of warpage or abuse. If you have a Gilbert cue that needs further identification or repair, or would like to talk to Andy about ordering a new Gilbert cue, contact Gilbert Custom Cues, listed in the Trademark Index.

SPECIFICATIONS

Butt material: hardwoods
Shaft material: rock maple
Standard length: 58 in.
Lengths available: 57 to 60 in.
Standard finish: urethane
Joint type: 3/8-10 flat faced
Point construction: short spliced
Standard wrap: Irish linen
Standard butt caps: Delrin or phenolic
Standard number of shafts: two
Standard taper: custom
Standard ferrules: linen phenolic
Standard tip: Triangle
Tip widths available: any
Annual production: fewer than 200 cues

OPTIONS (FOR NEW CUES ONLY)

Leather wrap: $125
Ivory joint: $125
Ivory butt cap: $200
Ivory ferrules: $75
Extra shaft: $150

REPAIRS

Repairs done on all fine cues.
Refinish (with leather wrap): $225
Refinish (with Irish linen wrap): $125
Rewrap (leather): $100

GILBERT CUSTOM CUES, cont. 311

GRADING	100%	95%	70%

Rewrap (linen): $35
Replace shaft: $150
Replace phenolic ferrule: $30
Replace ivory ferrule: $75
Replace Triangle tip: $10

CURRENT GILBERT CUES

Two-piece Gilbert bar cues start at $375. Basic Gilbert cues with wraps and joint rings start at $600. Gilbert cues with points start at $700. One-of-a-kind custom Gilbert cues start at $2,000. The current delivery time for a Gilbert cue is approximately four to six months.

CURRENT EXAMPLES

The following Gilbert cues can be ordered as shown, modified to suit the desires of the customer, or new designs can be created.

Level 1 "Jump/Break" - Maple forearm with a jump break joint above handle, four cocobolo points, one-piece cocobolo handle and butt sleeve.

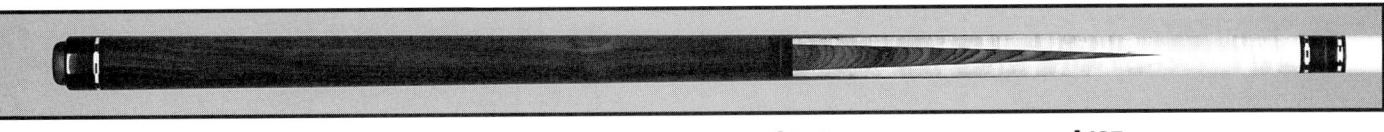

MSR	$350	$300-400	$250	$185

Level 4 "Sword Cue" - Maple forearm with a silver stitched ring above wrap, three long ebony points with a scrimshawed ivory sword-shaped inlay in each alternating with three short ebony points with a scrimshawed ivory shield-shaped inlay in each, ebony butt sleeve with three scrimshawed ivory sword-shaped inlays alternating with three scrimshawed ivory shield-shaped inlays within silver stitched rings at top and bottom.

MSR	$2,400	$2,400-3,275	$1,950	$1,400

Level 5 "TC Series #2 Butterfly Cue" - Ivory joint, maple forearm with a light blue and white stitched ring above wrap, three long ebony points with four colored veneers and an ivory diamond-shaped inlay in each alternating with three short ebony butterfly points with four colored veneers and an ivory-bordered purpleheart oval between opposing ivory triangle-shaped inlays in each point, ebony butt sleeve with three ivory diamond-shaped inlays alternating with three ivory-bordered purpleheart ovals between opposing ivory triangle-shaped inlays within light blue and white stitched rings at top and bottom.

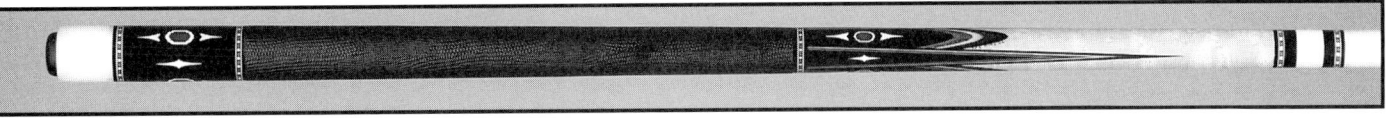

MSR	$2,500	$2,500-4,000	$2,050	$1,475

Level 5 - Ebony forearm with a green and white stitched ring above wrap, six floating ivory-bordered malachite points, ebony butt sleeve with four sets of four ivory-bordered malachite diamond-shaped inlays within green and white stitched rings at top and bottom.

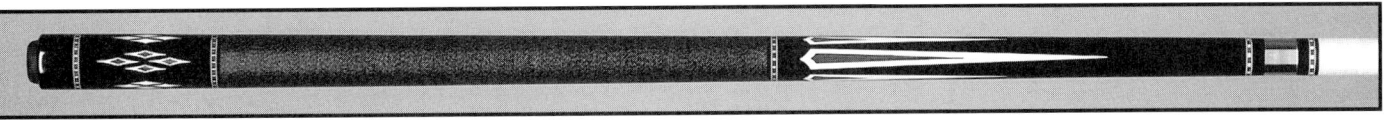

MSR	$2,840	$2,750-3,250	$2,450	$1,875

Level 4 - Maple forearm with a double silver ring above wrap, four ebony points with four colored veneers and an ivory diamond-shaped inlay above an ivory-bordered malachite diamond-shaped inlay in each, ebony butt sleeve with large ivory diamond-shaped inlays within double silver rings at top and bottom.

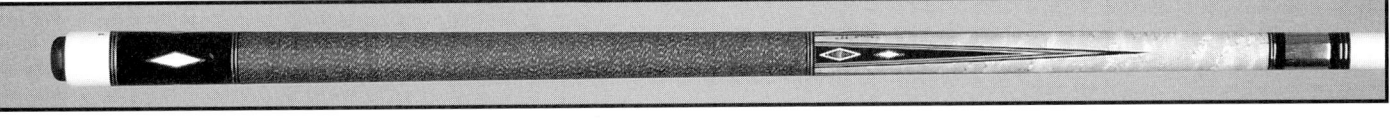

MSR (1997) $800	$1,350	$1,050	$700

GILBERT CUSTOM CUES, cont.

GRADING	98%	90%	70%

SECONDARY MARKET MINIMUM VALUES

The following are minimum prices for other Gilbert cues encountered on the secondary market. These prices are representative of cues utilizing basic materials and designs that may not be currently available. Andy also offers one-of-a-kind cues that can command many times these prices due to the use of exotic materials and artistry.

Special construction note: There are many materials and construction techniques that can add value to Gilbert cues.

For all used Gilbert cues, except where otherwise noted:
- Add $50+ for each additional original straight playable shaft (standard with one).
- Deduct $60 for missing original straight playable shaft.
- Deduct 25% for obvious or improper refinish.

Level 1 - 4 points, hustler.
Level 1 cues start at	$350	$275	$190

Level 2 - 0 points, 0-25 inlays.
Level 2 cues start at	$500	$390	$270

Level 3 - 2-6 points, 0-8 inlays.
Level 3 cues start at	$650	$500	$335

Level 4 - 4-10 points, 9-25 inlays.
Level 4 cues start at	$750	$585	$400

Level 5 - 0-12 points, 26-50 inlays.
Level 5 cues start at	$1,000	$785	$550

Level 6 - 0-12 points, 51-75 inlays.
Level 6 cues start at	$1,450	$1,150	$750

GINACUE

Maker of pool cues from 1961 to 1973 in Sherman Oaks, California, and from 1988 to present in North Hollywood, California.

Ernie Gutierrez has been exposed to fine custom woodworking since early childhood. His father was a woodworker who enjoyed making musical instruments as a hobby. Growing up with access to both woodworking knowledge and equipment enabled Ernie to meld his interest in pool with the art of woodworking.

Ernie worked on cue repair in the early 1960s and completed his first cue in 1962, just six days after the birth of his daughter, Gina. He chose to name his company after her and "Ginacue" became a source of custom cues for local players. That same year, Richie Florence won a tournament with his Ginacue and many orders started coming in.

Ernie Gutierrez

1961 to 1970

1988 to Present Day

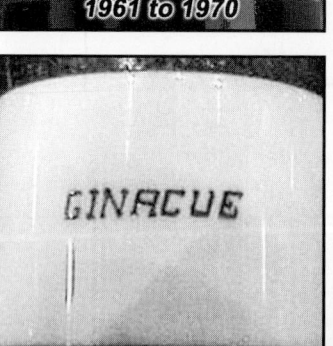

1970 to 1973

Pool was experiencing a resurgence from the film "The Hustler" and though Ernie was selling his cues at about $65 each, he had a vision of far greater things. The few well-known cuemakers of the time used exotic materials in some of their cues but tended toward simplicity in their designs. Ernie felt he could build a fancy cue, making use of exotic materials and artistic designs while preserving the finest characteristics of playability. In 1966, Ernie completed such a cue, fully reflecting this vision of functional art, which at that time had no equal. The cue was built with an ivory wrap section and joint. It had eight engraved silver points and a matching case. Ernie presented the cue at the tournament in Johnson City, Illinois, and within an hour, had so many requests for contact information that he ran out of business cards.

An interesting fact about Ernie's silver and ivory eight-point cue is that it did not sell for its initial asking price. In 1966, Ernie wanted $3500 yet there were no players or collectors who were willing, at that time, to purchase such a cue. Ernie held steadfast to his vision and continued offering extraordinary cues, often using lots of ivory, precious metals and gems. By the end of the 1960s, Ernie's cues commanded previously unheard-of prices, frequently selling for thousands of dollars each. His work was in demand by celebrities, athletes and top players. The early 1970s Johnson City tournaments saw many players using Ginacues and Ernie's work, and, at one point, the cues were being chosen by the majority of players in the tournament.

Ernie's creativity extended well beyond the boundaries of traditional cues. He was very original in each of his cue designs and, among other firsts, produced the earliest floating rectangle cue. Ernie recalled that the cue was constructed for player Ed Kelly. Another of Ernie's original creations was the oval tube case. Refined and made famous in later years by craftsmen like Bob Hempel, the tube case was an ingenious way to protect and store fine cues. Ernie looks upon the many design trends he has started with pride. While imitation may be seen as the highest form of flattery, Ernie has pointed out that it has helped him continue to innovate. Presently, new designs and one-of-a-kind cues make up about half of his annual production.

Ernie left cuemaking in 1973, and for 15 years, pursued other interests which included aircraft and racing car design. In 1988, Ernie returned to his former career and set up a new shop in North Hollywood, California. His creativity was as passionate as ever and his cue designs remained original and innovative. World-class players like Jose Parica and Jennifer Chen used fancy Ginacues and, with the enhanced precision of new customized equipment, Ernie was able to construct his best cues to date.

Ginacues from the 1990s to present are identified by the stylized "GC" which appears on the butt cap. Cues of the 1960s and 1970s were usually marked "Ginacue" on a ring just below the wrap. The logos of the 1960s era cues often yellowed since they were hand-scrolled on phenolic material cut from cue balls. In 1970, block lettering on Delrin became the norm.

Ginacue production is still less than 100 cues annually yet Ernie's work ethic is as regimented as ever. Each Ginacue is precious and represents the finest efforts of its maker. Few are produced so that no attention to detail is spared and so that the customer wait for delivery is minimal.

Ernie Gutierrez is known as an exotic cue designer and trendsetter to the cuemaking industry. He has been inducted into the American Cuemaker's Association Hall of Fame. He had the courage to pursue his vision and possessed both the talent and business acumen to recognize a new market niche. He has sold cues priced in the tens of thousands and his work remains in demand. Ernie still has his eight-point silver and ivory cue in its inscribed case: "Original by Ernie, Dec. 1966." Though it may not have brought the recognition he sought in 1966, it has become symbolic of his achievement since then. The collector who first refused the cue at its original $3500 asking price eventually offered $300,000 for it. In this way, it can be said that Ernie Gutierrez discovered and developed the market for high-end exotic custom cues

If you have questions about an older Ginacue, or would like to discuss the design of a new one, contact Ernie Gutierrez at Ginacue, listed in the Trademark Index.

SPECIFICATIONS

Butt material: hardwoods
Shaft material: rock maple
Standard length: 58 in.
Lengths available: any
Standard finish: secret
Standard joint screw: 5/16-18
Standard joint: stainless steel
Standard joint type: piloted
Balance point: custom
Point construction: short splice
Standard wrap: Irish linen
Standard butt cap: ivory substitute
Standard number of shafts: two
Standard taper: custom
Standard ferrules: ivory
Annual production: fewer than 100 cues

OPTIONS (FOR NEW CUES ONLY)

Leather/cork wrap: $125
Ivory joint: $175
Ivory butt cap: $400
Joint protectors: standard
Ivory joint protectors: $400
Extra shaft: $175+
Special length: no charge

REPAIRS

Repairs done only on Ginacues, Balabushkas, and Szambotis.
Refinish (with leather/cork wrap): $375
Refinish (with linen wrap): $285
Rewrap (leather): $125
Rewrap (linen): $35
Replace shaft: $175+
Replace ivory ferrule: $75
Replace ivory butt cap: $400
Replace tip: $10
Replace Moori tip
Replace bumper: $5

| GRADING | 100% | 95% | 70% |

CURRENT GINACUE CUES

Basic two-piece Ginacue cues with wraps and silver ringwork start at $2,000. One-of-a-kind custom Ginacue cues start at $15,000.

CURRENT EXAMPLES

The following cues are representations of the work of Ernie Gutierrez. These cues can be ordered as shown, modified to suit the desires of the customer, or new designs can be created. Ernie prefers to make a limited number of each design, so some of these examples may no longer be available. The current delivery time for a Ginacue cue is approximately ninety days to six months, depending on the intricacy of the cue.

Level 4 11c - Bird's-eye maple forearm, four long and four short Gabon ebony points crowned with mother-of-pearl clover leaves and dots with mother-of-pearl notched diamonds inlaid in each long point, bird's-eye maple butt sleeve with four veneered ebony windows inlaid with mother-of-pearl notched diamonds between two mother-of-pearl dots.

| MSR | $2,450 | $2,450-3,000 | $2,500 | $1,950 |

Level 5 11d - Bird's-eye maple forearm, four long and four short snakewood points crowned with ivory clover leaves and dots with ivory notched diamond-shaped inlays in each long point, bird's-eye maple butt sleeve with four ivory notched diamond-shaped inlays set in snakewood windows supported by snakewood pillars between snakewood rings inlaid with ivory dots at top and bottom.

| MSR | $2,500 | $2,500-3,100 | $2,600 | $2,000 |

Level 5 12a - Bird's-eye maple forearm with stitching above wrap and ivory inlays capped by rainbow-shaped colored veneers between the points, six Gabon ebony points crowned with ebony clover leaves, bird's-eye maple butt sleeve with six downward-pointing Gabon ebony points crowned with ebony clover leaves and ivory inlays capped by rainbow-shaped colored veneers between the points within stitched rings at top and bottom.

| MSR | $2,800 | $2,800-3,400 | $2,850 | $2,250 |

Level 5 12b - Bird's-eye maple forearm with stitching above wrap and ivory inlays capped by rainbow-shaped colored veneers between the points, six purple-red-grained tulipwood points with ebony veneers crowned with ebony clover leaves, bird's-eye maple butt sleeve with six downward-pointing purple-red-grained tulipwood points with ebony veneers and ivory inlays capped by rainbow-shaped colored veneers between the points within stitched rings at top and bottom.

| MSR | $2,900 | $2,900-3,500 | $3,000 | $2,300 |

Level 5 12c - Bird's-eye maple forearm with stitching above wrap and ivory inlays capped by rainbow-shaped colored veneers between the points, six snakewood points with ebony veneers crowned with ebony clover leaves, bird's-eye maple butt sleeve with six downward-pointing snakewood points with ebony veneers crowned with ebony clover leaves and ivory inlays capped by rainbow-shaped colored veneers between the points within stitched rings at top and bottom.

| MSR | $2,900 | $2,900-3,500 | $3,000 | $2,300 |

Level 5 12d - Bird's-eye maple forearm with stitching above wrap and ivory inlays capped by rainbow-shaped colored veneers between the points, six alternating snakewood and Gabon ebony points crowned with ebony clover leaves, bird's-eye maple butt sleeve with six downward-pointing alternating snakewood and Gabon ebony points crowned with ebony clover leaves and ivory inlays capped by rainbow-shaped colored veneers between the points within stitched rings at top and bottom.

| MSR | $2,900 | $2,900-3,500 | $3,000 | $2,300 |

GRADING	100%	95%	70%

Level 5 12e - Bird's-eye maple forearm with stitching above wrap and ivory inlays capped by rainbow-shaped colored veneers between the points, six snakewood points crowned with ebony clover leaves, bird's-eye maple butt sleeve with six downward-pointing snakewood points crowned with ebony clover leaves and ivory inlays capped by rainbow-shaped colored veneers between the points within stitched rings at top and bottom.

MSR	$2,900	$2,900-3,500	$3,000	$2,300

Level 5 13a - Gabon ebony forearm with ring pattern of alternating pure silver, ivory, and pink ivory squares above wrap and ivory inlays capped by rainbow-shaped colored veneers between the points, five sunset-hued pink ivory points, Gabon ebony butt sleeve with five downward-pointing sunset-hued pink ivory points with ivory inlays capped by rainbow-shaped colored veneers between the points within ring pattern of alternating pure silver, ivory, and pink ivory squares at top and bottom. (Ivory joint, and matching ivory and pink ivory joint protectors are standard on this cue.)

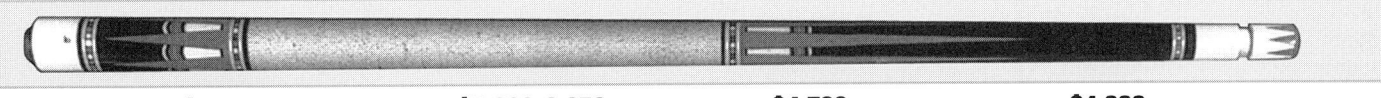

MSR	$5,200	$5,200-6,250	$4,700	$4,000

Level 5 13b - Gabon ebony forearm with ring pattern of alternating pure silver and ivory and snakewood squares above wrap and ivory inlays capped by rainbow-shaped colored veneers between the points, six snakewood points with pure silver veneers, Gabon ebony butt sleeve with six downward-pointing snakewood points with pure silver veneers with ivory inlays capped by rainbow-shaped colored veneers between the points within ring pattern of alternating pure silver, ivory, and snakewood squares at top and bottom. (Ivory joint, leather wrap, and matching ivory and snakewood joint protectors are standard on this cue.)

MSR	$7,500	$7,500-9,500	$7,500	$5,200

Level 5 13d - Bird's-eye maple forearm with ring pattern of alternating pure silver, ivory, and snakewood squares above wrap and ivory inlays with pure silver, ivory, and ebony veneers between the points, four snakewood points with pure silver, ivory, and ebony veneers, bird's-eye maple butt sleeve with four downward-pointing snakewood points with pure silver, ivory, and ebony veneers and ivory inlays with pure silver, ivory, and ebony veneers between the points within ring patterns of alternating pure silver, ivory, and snakewood squares at top and bottom. (Ivory joint, leather wrap, and matching ivory and snakewood joint protectors are standard on this cue.)

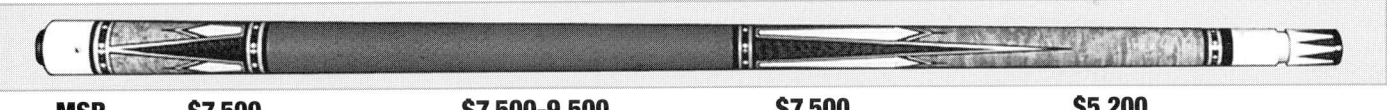

MSR	$7,500	$7,500-9,500	$7,500	$5,200

Level 5 13e - Gabon ebony forearm with ring pattern of alternating pure silver and ivory and ebony squares above wrap and ivory inlays capped by rainbow-shaped colored veneers between the points, six ivory points, Gabon ebony butt sleeve with six downward-pointing ivory points with ivory inlays capped by rainbow-shaped colored veneers between the points within ring pattern of alternating pure silver, ivory, and ebony squares at top and bottom. (Ivory joint, leather wrap, and matching ivory and ebony joint protectors are standard on this cue.)

MSR	$5,600	$5,600-6,750	$5,500	$4,000

Level 5 14a - Bird's-eye maple forearm with ring pattern of alternating pure silver, ivory, and pink ivory squares above wrap and sunset-hued pink ivory inlays with pure silver, ivory, and ebony veneers between the points, four ivory points with pure silver, ivory, and ebony veneers, bird's-eye maple butt sleeve with four downward-pointing ivory points with pure silver, ivory, and ebony veneers and pink ivory inlays with pure silver, ivory, and ebony veneers between the points within ring patterns of alternating pure silver, ivory, and pink ivory squares at top and bottom. (Ivory joint, leather wrap, and matching ivory and pink ivory joint protectors are standard on this cue.)

MSR	$7,500	$7,500-9,500	$7,500	$5,200

Level 5 14b - Gabon ebony forearm, four long and four short bird's-eye maple points crowned with cloverleaves highlighted with black Tahitian pearl, Gabon ebony butt sleeve with downward-pointing four long and four short bird's-eye maple points crowned with cloverleaves highlighted with black Tahitian pearl.

MSR	$2,800	$2,800-3,500	$2,450	$2,000

GRADING	100%	95%	70%

Level 5 14c - Gabon ebony forearm with ring pattern of alternating pure silver and ivory and ebony squares above wrap and ivory inlays capped by rainbow-shaped colored veneers between the points, six ivory points with pure silver veneers, Gabon ebony butt sleeve with six downward-pointing ivory points with pure silver veneers and ivory inlays capped by rainbow-shaped colored veneers between the points within ring pattern of alternating pure silver, ivory, and ebony squares at top and bottom. (Ivory joint, leather wrap, and matching ivory and ebony joint protectors are standard on this cue.)

MSR	$7,500	$7,500-9,500	$7,500	$5,200

Level 5 14e - Bird's-eye maple forearm with ring pattern of alternating pure silver, ivory, and pink ivory squares above wrap and ivory inlays with pure silver, ivory, and ebony veneers between the points, four sunset-hued pink ivory points with pure silver, ivory, and ebony veneers, bird's-eye maple butt sleeve with four downward-pointing sunset-hued pink ivory points with pure silver, ivory, and ebony veneers and ivory inlays with pure silver, ivory, and ebony veneers between the points within ring patterns of alternating pure silver, ivory, and pink ivory squares at top and bottom. (Ivory joint, leather wrap, and matching ivory and pink ivory joint protectors are standard on this cue.)

MSR	$7,500	$7,500-9,500	$7,500	$5,200

Level 5 16a - Bird's-eye maple forearm with ring pattern of alternating pure silver and ivory squares above wrap and snakewood inlays with five colored veneers between the points, four ivory points with five colored veneers, bird's-eye maple butt sleeve with four downward-pointing ivory points with five colored veneers and pink ivory inlays with five colored veneers between the points within ring patterns of alternating pure silver and ivory squares at top and bottom. (Ivory joint and leather wrap are standard on this cue.)

MSR	$5,200	$5,200-6,500	$5,300	$3,800

Level 5 16b - Bird's-eye maple forearm with ring pattern of alternating pure silver and ivory squares above wrap and ivory inlays capped by rainbow-shaped colored veneers between the points, six ivory points with ebony veneers, bird's-eye maple butt sleeve with six downward-pointing ivory points with ebony veneers and ivory inlays capped by rainbow-shaped colored veneers between the points within ring pattern of alternating pure silver and ivory squares at top and bottom. (Ivory joint and leather wrap are standard on this cue.)

MSR	$5,200	$5,200-6,500	$5,300	$3,800

Level 5 16c - Bird's-eye maple forearm with ring pattern of alternating pure silver and ivory squares above wrap and ivory inlays with pure silver and ivory and ebony veneers between the points, four ivory points with pure silver and ebony veneers, three-piece matching ivory handle separated by two ring patterns of alternating pure silver and ivory squares bird's-eye maple butt sleeve with four downward-pointing ivory points with pure silver and ebony veneers and ivory inlays with pure silver, ivory, and ebony veneers between the points within ring patterns of alternating pure silver and ivory squares at top and bottom. (Ivory joint and matching ivory and ebony joint protectors are standard on this cue.)

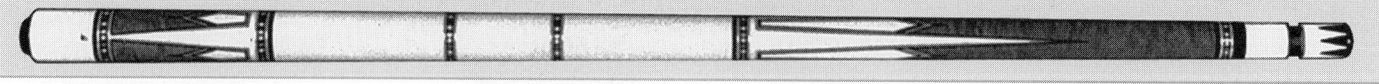

MSR	$N/A	$27,500-35,000	$28,000	$20,000

Level 3 17a - Bird's-eye maple forearm, five Gabon ebony points with five colored veneers, Gabon ebony butt sleeve.

MSR	$1,500	$1,500-2,000	$1,650	$1,200

Level 6 17b - Bird's-eye maple forearm, four long Gabon ebony points crowned with an ebony clover leaf highlighted with an ivory bordered abalone dot and inlaid with a long ivory lance above an abalone centered ivory rosette alternating with four short Gabon ebony points crowned with an ebony-bordered ivory arrowhead and inlaid with an ivory arrowhead above an ivory-bordered abalone dot, Gabon ebony butt sleeve with intricately inlaid ivory and abalone designs that mirror the inlays in the points between stitched rings of pure silver and ivory at top and bottom.

MSR	$3,600	$3,600-4,500	$3,125	$2,800

GRADING	100%	95%	70%

Level 4 17c - Bird's-eye maple forearm, five Gabon ebony points with five colored veneers, Gabon ebony butt sleeve with five intricate three-piece ivory inlays.

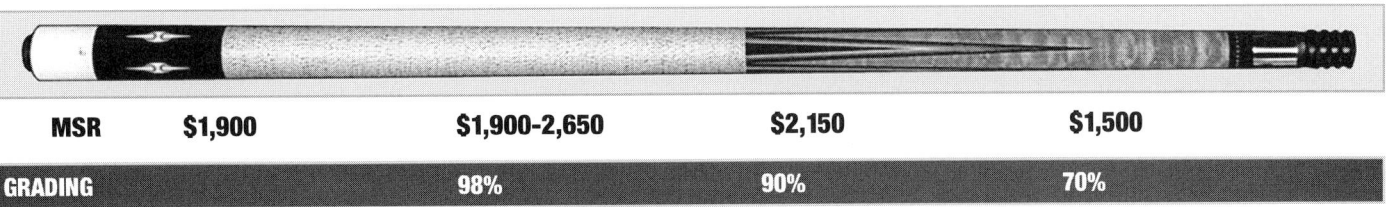

MSR	$1,900	$1,900-2,650	$2,150	$1,500

GRADING		98%	90%	70%

PAST EXAMPLES

The following cues represent examples of the work of Ernie Gutierrez during the late sixties and early seventies. All Ginacue cues at that time were one-of-a-kind.

Level 3 "Ginacue Titlist" - Maple forearm, four rosewood points with four colored veneers, black phenolic butt sleeve with a maple stitch ring set between silver rings below a white ring engraved "Ginacue" below wrap.

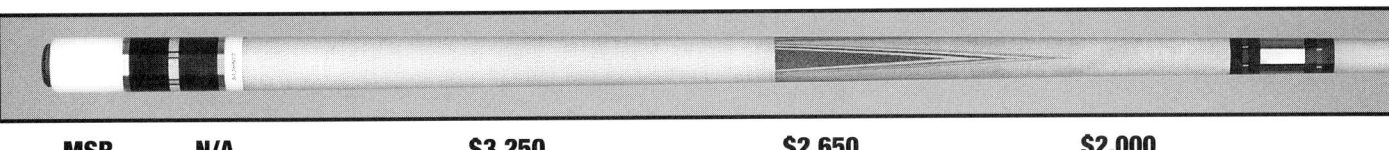

MSR	N/A	$3,250	$2,650	$2,000

Level 4 - Stained bird's-eye maple forearm with an ebony ring above wrap, long and short veneer line points with an ebony and ivory clover leaf-shaped inlay at the tip of each point, stained bird's-eye maple butt sleeve with stained maple windows inaid with veneer lines with an ebony and ivory clover leaf-shaped inlay at the tips of each within ebony rings below a white ring engraved "Ginacue" below wrap.

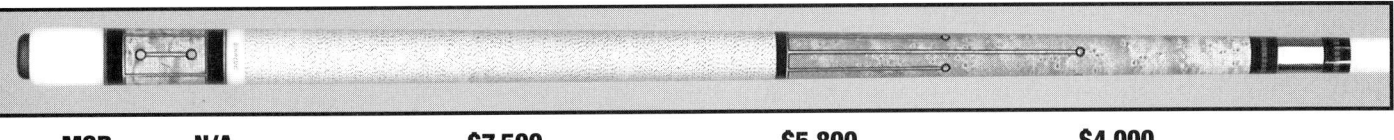

MSR	N/A	$7,500	$5,800	$4,000

Level 5 - Stained bird's-eye maple forearm with ivory inlays above an ebony ring above wrap, six ebony bordered ivory points, ebony butt sleeve with ivory and stained maple windows surrounded by ivory inlays below a white ring engraved "Ginacue" below wrap.

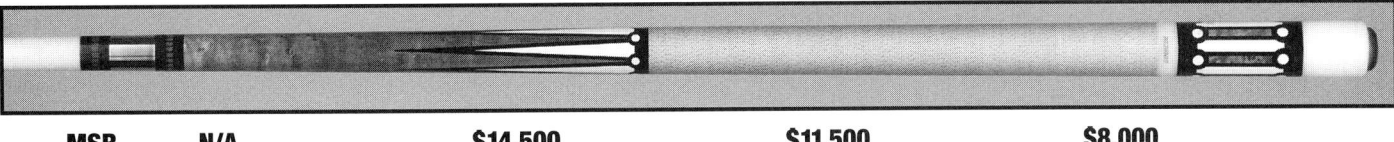

MSR	N/A	$14,500	$11,500	$8,000

Level 5 - Ivory joint with engraved sterling silver joint rings, bird's-eye maple forearm, four long and four short ebony points with opal ovals set in engraved sterling silver in each, two-piece ivory handle seperated engraved sterling silver rings, ebony butt sleeve with four opal ovals set in an engraved sterling silver ring.

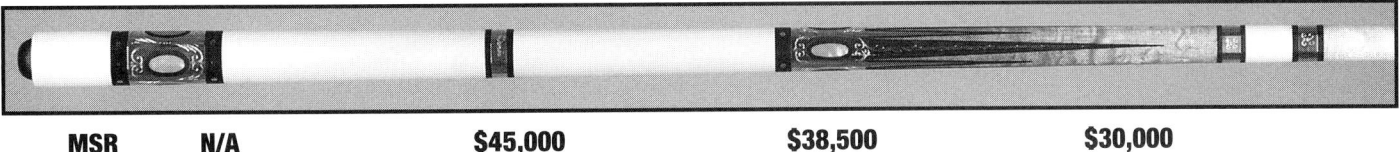

MSR	N/A	$45,000	$38,500	$30,000

SPECIAL INTEREST GINACUE CUES

Level 4 "30th Anniversary" - Stainless steel joint (add $1,000+ for two cues with ivory joints) bird's-eye maple forearm, five ebony points with two veneers alternating with five two-piece ivory columns below rainbow-shaped colored veneers between the points, ebony butt sleeve with five three-piece ivory columns. (30 made for 30-year Ginacue Anniversary with "# of 30" laser engraved on joint).

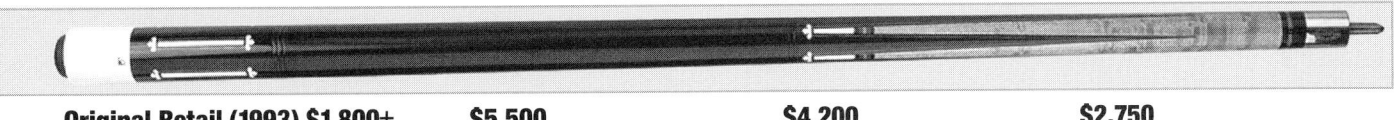

Original Retail (1993) $1,800+	$5,500	$4,200	$2,750

GRADING	98%	90%	70%

Level 6 "40th Anniversary" - Ivory joint ebony forearm with inricate ebony and ivory rings above wrap, intricate floating ivory points alternating with intricate ivory inlays, ebony butt sleeve with intricate ivory inlays matching the forearm between inricate ebony and ivory rings at top and bottom. (40 made for 40-year Ginacue Anniversary with "# of 40" laser engraved on joint).

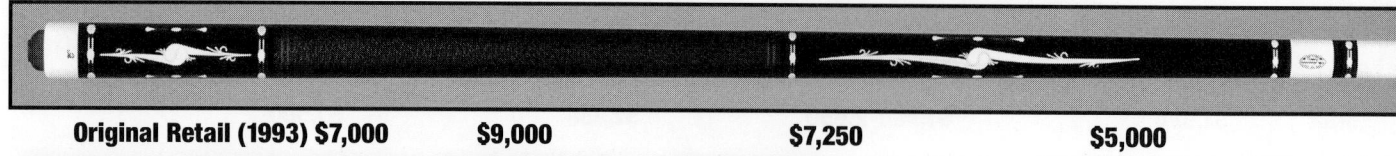

Original Retail (1993) $7,000	$9,000	$7,250	$5,000

SECONDARY MARKET MINIMUM VALUES (EARLY CUES)

The following are minimum values for other early Ginacue cues (made from 1962 to 1973, usually marked "Ginacue" on a white ring below the wrap) encountered on the secondary market. These prices are representative of cues utilizing basic materials and designs that may not be currently available. Ernie currently specializes in one-of-a-kind and limited edition cues that can command many times these prices due to the use of exotic materials and artistry.

Special construction note: There are many materials and construction techniques that can add value to early Ginacue cues. The following are the most important examples:

Add $15,500+ for ivory handle
Add $7,500+ for ivory points
Add $1,650+ for ivory butt sleeve
Add $750+ for ivory joint
Add 20%+ for 1962-1970 cues (identified by cursive "Ginacue" engraved on phenolic ring)
Add 100%+ for precious metals or stones
Add $950+ for excellent original Gina case

Level 2 - 0 points, 0-25 inlays.
Level 2 cues start at	$1,850	$1,550	$1,200

Level 3 - 2-6 points, 0-8 inlays.
Level 3 cues start at	$2,450	$2,000	$1,500

Level 4 - 4-10 points, 9-25 inlays.
Level 4 cues start at	$3,000	$2,500	$1,900

Level 5 - 0-12 points, 26-50 inlays.
Level 5 cues start at	$4,500	$3,750	$2,800

Level 6 - 0-12 points, 51-75 inlays.
Level 6 cues start at	$6,500	$5,450	$4,000

SECONDARY MARKET MINIMUM VALUES (LATER CUES)

The following are minimum values for later Ginacue cues (made from 1991 to present, marked "GC" on butt cap) encountered on the secondary market. These prices are representative of cues utilizing basic materials and designs that may not be currently available. Ernie currently specializes in one-of-a-kind and limited edition cues that can command many times these prices due to the use of exotic materials and artistry.

Special construction note: There are many materials and construction techniques that can add value to late Ginacue cues. The following are the most important examples:

Add $9,500+ for ivory handle.
Add $1,450+ for ivory butt sleeve.
Add $1,500+ for ivory points.
Add 100%+ for precious metals or stones.

For all used Ginacue cues, except where otherwise noted:

Add $155+ for each additional original straight playable shaft (standard with two).
Deduct $175+ for each missing original straight playable shaft.
Add $150+ for ivory joint.
Add $110+ for leather wrap.
Deduct 30% for obvious or improper refinish.

Level 2 - 0 points, 0-25 inlays.
Level 2 cues start at	$1,350	$1,125	$850

Level 3 - 2-6 points, 0-8 inlays.
Level 3 cues start at	$1,850	$1,445	$1,000

Level 4 - 4-10 points, 9-25 inlays.
Level 4 cues start at	$2,850	$2,300	$1,700

Level 5 - 0-12 points, 26-50 inlays.
Level 5 cues start at	$3,750	$3,150	$2,200

GRADING	98%	90%	70%
Level 6 - 0-12 points, 51-75 inlays.			
Level 6 cues start at	$6,000	$5,000	$3,800
Level 7 - 0-12 points, 76-125 inlays.			
Level 7 cues start at	$8,500	$6,750	$4,900

GIONNI POOL CUES

Maker of pool cues in Excelsior, Minnesota.

In 1996, Galen Golz approached acrylic experts with an idea for an ergonomically designed acrylic pool cue. Several prototypes were made and tested by players and technical experts. Six models were introduced at the 1997 BCA Trade Show in Las Vegas. Priced from $150 to $495, Gionni cues were available in three different weights and five different colors. The customer could have their name laser engraved inside the cue for an additional $150.

MICHAEL GIVENS

Maker of Michaelangelo Custom Cues, for more information refer to Michaelangelo Custom Cues.

JOE GOLD

Maker of Cognoscenti cues, for more information refer to Cognoscenti.

GOLDENROD CUES

Maker of pool cues in Lincoln, Illinois.

If you have a Goldenrod cue that needs further identification or repair, or would like to talk to Bill Hughes about ordering a new Goldenrod cue, contact Goldenrod Cues, listed in the Trademark Index.

MIKE "COSMO" GRAY

Maker of Bella Sera Cues. For more information, refer to Bella Sera.

NAT GREEN

Maker of Southeast Cues. For more information, refer to Southeast.

GREG'S KUES

Maker of pool cues from 1998 to present in Southington, Connecticut.

Greg Kucharski has been playing pool since 1966 competitively. After 30 years at his machinist job, he finally retired. He now produces Kucharski cues as a part time job and hobby. Only 10-15 GK cues are produced per year, enabling Greg to try to create top quality, one-of-a-kind cues.

All GK cues are constructed to the highest standards possible. These cues are structurally covered for life. Greg will not replace warped, bent, or visibly mistreated cues. Every measure has been taken so these cues will last a lifetime.

If you are interested in talking to Greg Kucharski about a new cue or cue that needs to be repaired, you can contact him at Greg's Kues, listed in the Trademark Index.

Greg Kucharski

SPECIFICATIONS

Butt material: hardwoods
Shaft material: rock maple
Standard length: 58 in.
Standard finish: dupont 7800
Balance point: 1 to 1 ½ in. above wrap
Standard butt cap: Delrin
Standard wrap: Irish linen
Point construction: short splice
Standard joint: stainless steel
Joint type: piloted
Joint screw thread: 5/16-14
Standard number of shafts: one
Standard taper: 12 in. straight
Standard ferrules: melamine
Annual production: fewer than 15 cues

OPTIONS (FOR NEW CUES ONLY)

Ivory joint: $80
Ivory ferrule: $80
Leather wrap: $100

GRADING	98%	90%	70%

REPAIRS

Repairs done on all fine cues.
- Refinish (with Irish linen wrap): $150
- Refinish (with leather wrap): $220
- Rewrap (Irish linen): $40
- Rewrap (leather): $100
- Replace shaft: $80
- Replace ferrule: $30

SECONDARY MARKET MINIMUM VALUES

The following are minimum values for other Greg's Kues cues encountered on the secondary market. These prices are representative of cues utilizing basic materials and designs that are not necessarily available at present. Greg has offered one-of-a-kind cues that can command many times these prices due to the use of exotic materials and artistry.

Special construction note: There are many materials and construction techniques that can add value to Greg's Kues cues.

For all used Greg's Kues cues, except where otherwise noted:
- Add $75 for each additional original straight playable shaft beyond one.
- Deduct $125 for missing original straight playable shaft.
- Add $50 each for ivory ferrules.
- Add $75 for leather wrap.
- Deduct 20% for obvious or improper refinish.

	98%	90%	70%
Level 2 - 0 points, 0-25 inlays.			
Level 2 cues start at	$300	$290	$165
Level 3 - 2-6 points, 0-8 inlays.			
Level 3 cues start at	$500	$395	$275
Level 4 - 4-10 points, 9-25 inlays.			
Level 4 cues start at	$600	$475	$325
Level 5 - 0-12 points, 26-50 inlays.			
Level 5 cues start at	$850	$675	$450

GRIFFIN and SON CUSTOM CUES

Maker of pool cues from 1996 to present in Deputy, Indiana.

Present Day

Present Day

Madison Bob Griffin and Wayne Griffin

"Madison" Bob Griffin began building cues in January of 1996. When he started, his cues were known as Madison Bob Custom Cues. Bob's son, Bobby Wayne Griffin, has been building cues with his father since May 1998. In January of 2004, their company name was changed to Griffin and Son Custom Cues.

Bob got interested in cue making when he could not find a cue to suit himself, so he decided to try to make one. He and his son strive for playability and workmanship in their finished products. Their shop has a CNC inlay machine, pantograph, modified Porper Model B cue lathes, plus band saws, milling machine, and other equipment. Griffin and Son cues are identified by either "MB" or "Griffin" on the bottom or on the forearm above the wrap.

Bob does scrimshaw work on his cues, if the customer wants it. Griffin and Son makes cues that are either half or full splice, with or without veneers, depending upon what the customer wants. They will build cues to be sent anywhere in the world. At present, Griffin and Son Custom Cues makes about 100 to 125 cues per year. Griffin and Son cues are guaranteed for a lifetime on workmanship and materials. There is no guarantee against warpage or abuse.

If you are interested in talking to "Madison" Bob Griffin about a new cue or cue that needs to be repaired, you can contact him at Griffin and Son Custom Cues, listed in the Trademark Index.

SPECIFICATIONS

- Butt material: hardwoods
- Shaft material: hard rock maple
- Standard length: 58 in.

GRADING	98%	90%	70%

Standard wrap: Irish linen
Standard finish: two-part sealer followed by UV curable clearcoat
Standard ferrules: melamine
Standard pin: radial pin
Standard tip: Le Pro or Triangle
Annual production: fewer than 125 cues

OPTIONS

For new cues only:
- Ivory ferrule: $75
- Leather wrap: $90
- Extra shaft: $90

REPAIRS

Repairs done on all fine cues.
- Refinish with Irish linen wrap: $150
- Rewrap with Irish linen: $40
- Replace shaft: $90+
- Replace tip: $10+

CURRENT GRIFFIN AND SON CUES

Basic Griffin and Son two-piece bar cues start at $350. Basic Griffin and Son cues cues with wraps and joint rings start at $400. Griffin and Son cues with points start at $525. One-of-a-kind custom Griffin and Son cues also start at $525. Griffin and Son keep a supply of cues ready for inlay work, so the average delivery time is four to eight weeks. If the customer wants a custom cue built from scratch, it will take three to six months.

SECONDARY MARKET MINIMUM VALUES

The following are minimum values for other Griffin and Son cues encountered on the secondary market. These prices are representative of cues utilizing basic materials and designs that are not necessarily available at present. Griffin and Son has offered one-of-a-kind cues that can command many times these prices due to the use of exotic materials and artistry.

Special construction note: There are many materials and construction techniques that can add value to Griffin and Son cues.

For all used Griffin and Son cues, except where otherwise noted:
- Add $75 for each additional original straight playable shaft beyond one.
- Deduct $90 for missing original straight playable shaft.
- Add $50 each for ivory ferrules.
- Add $60 for leather wrap.
- Deduct 20% for obvious or improper refinish.

	98%	90%	70%
Level 1 - Hustler.			
Level 1 cues start at	$300	$285	$160
Level 2 - 0 points, 0-25 inlays.			
Level 2 cues start at	$350	$270	$185
Level 3 - 2-6 points, 0-8 inlays.			
Level 3 cues start at	$450	$350	$235
Level 4 - 4-10 points, 9-25 inlays.			
Level 4 cues start at	$575	$445	$295
Level 5 - 0-12 points, 26-50 inlays.			
Level 5 cues start at	$750	$575	$390
Level 6 - 0-12 points, 51-75 inlays.			
Level 6 cues start at	$1,000	$795	$550

JIM GRIFFIN

Maker of Norwela Cues. For more information, refer to Norwela.

| GRADING | 100% | 95% | 70% |

GSCUE

Maker of pool cues from 1999 to present in Oakley, California.

Greg Sirca has been playing pool and working with hardwoods for over 25 years. He owned a woodshop and has worked in the framing business and in the building trades. A woodworking hobby would become a part-time business when, in 1999, a friend asked him to build a cue. Greg now builds about 50 custom cues a year as a full-time profession. He is pleased to be able to combine two enjoyable hobbies: playing the game of nine ball and building cues. Greg has added a CNC mill to his woodshop and loves designing and doing inlays in the custom cues he builds. He likes to put lots of inlays in his cues and he likes to use a lot of ivory. He tries to make a good-looking, good-hitting cue at a fair price.

GSCues are guaranteed for life against defects that are not the result of abuse or warpage.

If you are interested in talking to Greg Sirca about a new cue or cue that needs to be repaired, you can contact him at GSCUE, listed in the Trademark Index.

Greg Sirca

SPECIFICATIONS

Butt material: hardwoods
Shaft material: rock maple
Standard length: 58 in.
Lengths available: any
Standard finish: automotive
Balance point: 10 in. from joint
Point construction: CNC inlaid
Standard joint: phenolic or wood
Joint type: conical faced
Standard joint screw thread: 3/8-10
Standard number of shafts: one
Standard taper: pro taper
Standard ferrules: phenolic
Standard tip: Triangle
Standard tip width: 13 mm
Tip widths available: any
Annual production: approximately 50 cues

OPTIONS (FOR NEW CUES ONLY)

Layered tip: no charge
Ivory joint: $75
Ivory ferrule: $50
Extra shaft: $60

REPAIRS

Repairs done on GSCue cues only.
Refinish (with Irish linen wrap): $250
Rewrap (Irish linen): $25
Replace shaft: $65
Replace tip: $15
Replaced layered tip: $25
Replace fiber/linen ferrule: $25

CURRENT GSCUE CUES

Basic two-piece GSCue bar cues start at $200. Basic GSCues with wraps and joint rings start at $200. GSCue cues with points start at $250. One-of-a-kind custom GSCue cues start at $400. The current delivery time for a GSCue cue is about one month.

CURRENT EXAMPLES

The following GSCue cues can be ordered as shown, modified to suit the desires of the customer, or new designs can be created.

Level 5 - Ebony joint, bird's-eye maple forearm with an ebony and ivory ring set in brass rings above handle, four ebony-bordered dyed red alder boxwood burl floating points, bird's-eye maple handle with four five-piece ebony bordered dyed red alder boxwood burl inlays, bird's-eye maple butt sleeve with four three-piece ebony-bordered dyed red alder boxwood burl inlays alternating with four ebony-bordered dyed red alder boxwood burl diamond-shaped inlays below an ebony and ivory ring set in brass rings at top, ebony butt cap.

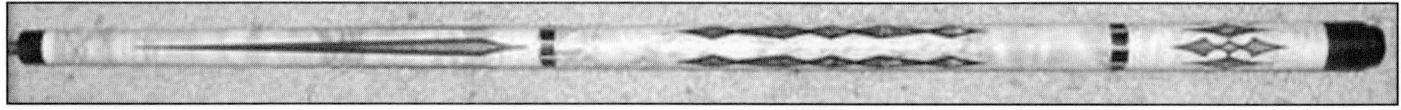

| MSR | $600 | $550-750 | $465 | $350 |

GSCUE, cont. 323

GRADING	100%	95%	70%

Level 5 - Ebony joint, bird's-eye maple forearm, four ebony-bordered floating ivory points, bird's-eye maple handle with four three-piece ebony-bordered ivory inlays between koa rings with sets of four inward pointing ebony points with an ivory diamond-shaped inlay in each at top and bottom, bird's-eye maple butt sleeve with four three-piece ebony-bordered ivory inlays alternating with four ebony-bordered ivory diamond-shaped inlays, koa butt cap.

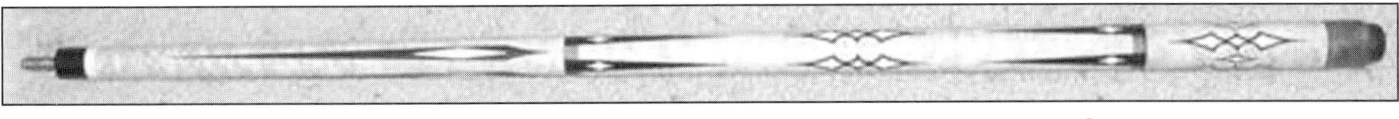

MSR	$1,000	$950-1,250	$765	$550

Level 6 - Ebony joint, bird's-eye maple forearm with a koa ring above handle, three long and three short ebony-bordered floating ivory points, ebony and koa handle with twelve sets of two ivory-bordered koa diamond-shaped inlays with an ivory diamond-shaped inlay in the center, bird's-eye maple butt sleeve with three three-piece ebony-bordered ivory inlays alternating with three ebony-bordered ivory diamond-shaped inlays between koa rings at top and bottom, ebony butt cap.

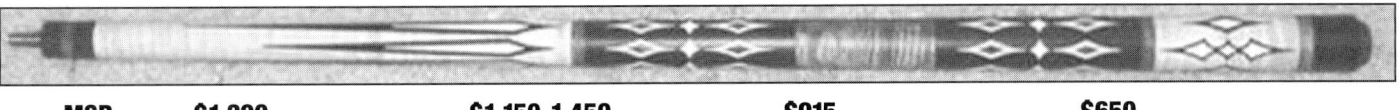

MSR	$1,200	$1,150-1,450	$915	$650

Level 4 - Ebony forearm with an ebony and ivory ring set in brass rings above handle, three long and three short ivory-bordered ebony floating aligator wrap handle, ebony butt sleeve with six intricate ivory inlays between ebony and ivory rings set in brass rings at top and bottom, ivory butt cap.

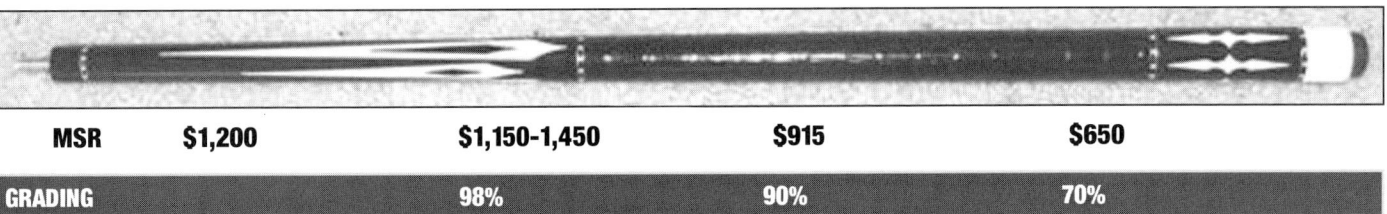

MSR	$1,200	$1,150-1,450	$915	$650

GRADING	98%	90%	70%

SECONDARY MARKET MINIMUM VALUES

The following are minimum values for other GSCue cues encountered on the secondary market. These prices are representative of cues utilizing basic materials and designs that are not necessarily available at present. Greg has offered one-of-a-kind cues that can command many times these prices due to the use of exotic materials and artistry.

Special construction note: There are many materials and construction techniques that can add value to GSCue cues.

For all used GSCue cues, except where otherwise noted:
- Add $50 for each additional original straight playable shaft beyond one.
- Deduct $60 for missing original straight playable shaft.
- Add $100 for ivory joint.
- Add $50 each for ivory ferrules.
- Deduct 20% for obvious or improper refinish.

Level 1 - Hustler.
Level 1 cues start at	$185	$145	$95

Level 2 - 0 points, 0-25 inlays.
Level 2 cues start at	$185	$145	$95

Level 3 - 2-6 points, 0-8 inlays.
Level 3 cues start at	$225	$175	$120

Level 4 - 4-10 points, 9-25 inlays.
Level 4 cues start at	$300	$235	$160

Level 5 - 0-12 points, 26-50 inlays.
Level 5 cues start at	$500	$390	$265

Level 6 - 0-12 points, 51-75 inlays.
Level 6 cues start at	$850	$665	$445

JOHN GUFFEY CUSTOM CUES/J.G. CUSTOM CUE

Maker of pool cues from 1981 to present in Edmond, Oklahoma.

JG Series

John Guffey

John Guffey learned to play pool while growing up in Oklahoma City. After high school, John became well-known in the Oklahoma area as a road and tournament player. John met a new cuemaker in 1975, while on the road in Texas, and spent some time with him learning the basics of the craft. After a few months, he left Texas to go on the road to Florida with "St. Louis" Louie Roberts. He loved the sport, but became tired of the player's lifestyle, so he decided to run a pool room for a while back home in Oklahoma City.

Approximately one year later, in 1979, John told Jimmy Ingram that he would be interested in buying out his cuemaking business when he chose to retire. Soon after that, Jimmy took him up on his offer, and taught John everything he needed to know about making cues as part of the deal.

John finished his first cue in 1981, and has been making cues ever since. The first seven cues John made had "John Guffey" burned into them, and the first three cues were numbered. John stopped doing both because he did not like the way it looked. Early John Guffey cues have six point blanks that were made by Burton Spain, and today John prefers to use eight point blanks on his own cues. John Guffey custom cues are all one-of-a-kind, and although the 3/8 in. joint is standard, he will make any common type joint the customer wants. John prefers engineering his cues to play well over the cosmetics aspect of cuemaking. His cues have been gaining popularity in Europe and Asia, as well as in the United States.

In 1986, John wrote to the Texas Billiard News about an article that he disagreed with, which led to his own column with the publication, titled "Trade Secrets." John has since written well over 100 articles which have appeared in The Snap, The National Billiard News, The American Cueist, The Player, etc. With all the articles that have appeared in these and other publications, John is one of the most widely read instructional writers in the sport. He is currently working on compiling and rewriting all of his articles into an instructional book. John still plays in tournaments when he can, and is a BCA-certified instructor.

Since 1997, John has been making John Guffey Custom Cues part time in a one-man shop behind his home. He has slowed down to about ten hustlers a year and about a half dozen custom cues a year. He also works full time in the furniture business. In the late nineties, he also marketed J.G. Custom Cues, which were made by Viking to his specifications. Although John's earlier custom cues are not marked, they now have "John Guffey" in script on the forearm, and the J.G. Custom Cues have a JG logo on the butt cap.

John offers a money-back guarantee, immediately after arrival, on new cues that the customer is not completely satisfied with, and John will indefinitely repair all construction defects that are not the result of warpage or abuse. If you have a John Guffey cue that needs identification or repair, or would like to talk to John about ordering a new custom cue, contact John Guffey Custom Cues, listed in the Trademark Index.

SPECIFICATIONS

Butt material: hardwoods
Shaft material: rock maple
Standard length: 58 in.
Lengths available: any
Standard finish: UV polyurethane
Joint screw: 3/8-10
Standard joint: high impact plastic
Joint type: flat faced
Balance point: 18-1/2 in. from butt
Point construction: short splice
Standard wrap: Irish linen
Standard butt cap: high impact black plastic
Standard number of shafts: two
Standard taper: 10 in. straight
Standard ferrules: fiber
Standard tip: Le Pro
Tip widths available: any
Annual production: under 20

OPTIONS (FOR NEW CUES ONLY)

Leather wrap: $125
Ivory joint: $100
Ivory butt cap: $250

GRADING	98%	90%	70%

Extra shaft: $100+
Ivory ferrules: $40 each

REPAIRS

Repairs done on all fine cues.
- Refinish (linen): $200
- Refinish (leather): $250
- Rewrap (leather): $125
- Rewrap (linen): $50
- Replace linen phenolic butt cap: $40
- Replace ivory butt cap: $250
- Replace shaft: $100+
- Replace ferrule: $20
- Replace Le Pro tip: $10

CURRENT JOHN GUFFEY CUES

John Guffey hustlers start at $160. John Guffey cues with points start at $695. One-of-a-kind custom John Guffey cues start at $850. The current delivery time for a John Guffey cue is approximately three to four months.

PAST EXAMPLES

The following were the cues in the J.G. custom cue line. Production of these cues stopped in the late nineties. Stained maple was available in six different colors.

Level 2 JG-1 - South American hardwood forearm, South American hardwood butt sleeve.

MSR	$189.95	$135-189.95	$120	$100

Level 3 JG-2 - Stained bird's-eye maple forearm, three South American hardwood points with single black veneers, South American hardwood butt sleeve.

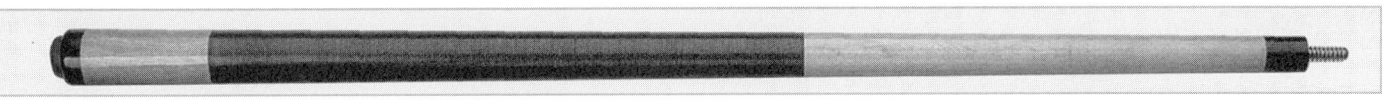

MSR	$239.95	$170-239.95	$155	$130

Level 2 JG-3 - Stained bird's-eye maple forearm, stained bird's-eye maple butt sleeve.

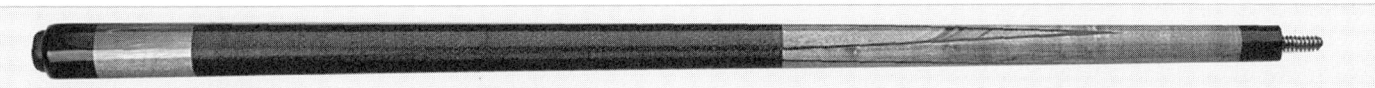

MSR	$259.95	$185-259.95	$165	$140

Level 3 JG-4 - Bird's-eye maple forearm, three rosewood points with four colored veneers, rosewood butt sleeve.

MSR	$309.95	$225-309.95	$200	$165

Level 3 JG-5 - Bird's-eye maple forearm, three ebony colored points with four colored veneers, ebony colored butt sleeve with six large bird's-eye maple windows.

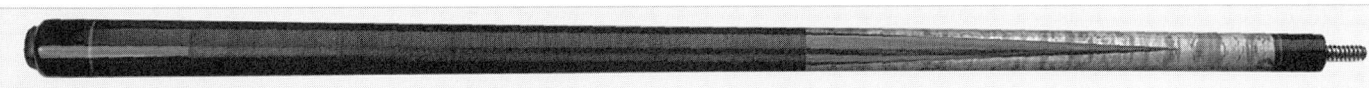

MSR	$359.95	$255-359.95	$225	$190

Level 3 JG-6 - Bird's-eye maple forearm, three rosewood points, bird's-eye maple butt sleeve.

MSR	$299.95	$215-299.95	$190	$160

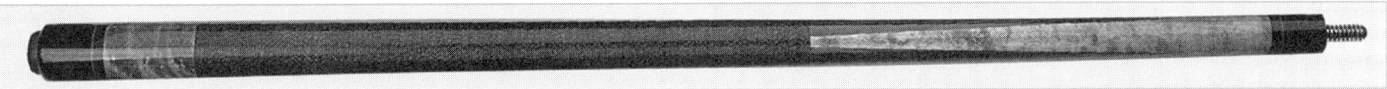

GRADING	100%	95%	70%

Level 3 JG-7 - Bird's-eye maple forearm, three rosewood points, rosewood butt sleeve.

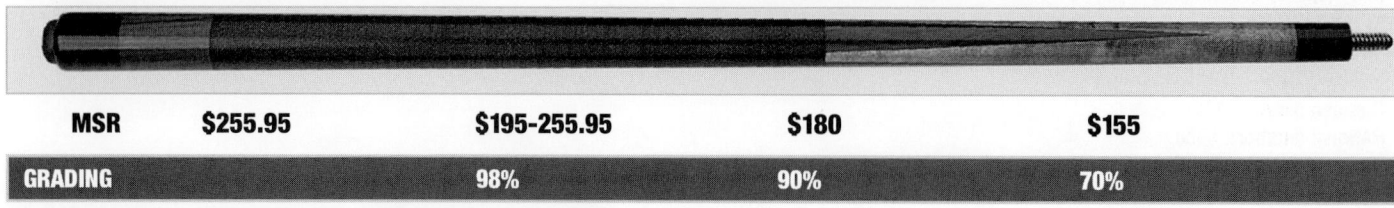

MSR	$255.95	$195-255.95	$180	$155

GRADING	98%	90%	70%

SECONDARY MARKET MINIMUM VALUES

The following are minimum prices for other John Guffey cues encountered on the secondary market. These prices are representative of cues utilizing basic materials and designs that may not be currently available. John also offers one-of-a-kind cues that can command many times these prices due to the use of exotic materials and artistry.

Special construction note: There are many materials and construction techniques that can add value to John Guffey cues.

For all used John Guffey cues, except where otherwise noted:
- Add $75+ for each additional original straight playable shaft beyond two.
- Deduct $100 for each missing original straight playable shaft under two.
- Add $75+ for ivory joint.
- Add $50+ for leather wrap.
- Deduct 20% for obvious or improper refinish.

Level 1 - 4 points, hustler.
Level 1 cues start at	$145	$115	$75

Level 2 - 0 points, 0-25 inlays.
Level 2 cues start at	$400	$310	$210

Level 3 - 2-6 points, 0-8 inlays.
Level 3 cues start at	$600	$485	$325

Level 4 - 4-10 points, 9-25 inlays.
Level 4 cues start at	$750	$585	$400

Level 5 - 0-12 points, 26-50 inlays.
Level 5 cues start at	$1,100	$950	$665

Level 6 - 0-12 points, 76-125 inlays.
Level 6 cues start at	$1,350	$1,100	$825

GUGINO'S CUSTOM CUES

Maker of pool cues from 1988 to present in Lemon Grove, California.

Tony Gugino is a full-time cue maker from Lemon Grove, California who grew up in Buffalo, New York. He made his first cue at the age of 17 on his father's wood lathe. Tony was also a gun stock carver and bar owner. He always loved billiards and the thought of cue making.

In 1988 Tony taught himself how to use all the machinery involved in cue making. He learned about inlay techniques, types of wood, and materials used in cue making. He then made his second cue and began to perfect his ability to build cues from scratch. Due to coaxing and support from his wife, Kathleen, inquiries and compliments from friends and fellow pool players, Tony decided to go full time into custom cue making and repairs.

Gugino's cues are diverse and unique. They can range anywhere from a sneaky-pete to a multi-point intricate inlay and special effects type artistic cue. Tony listens to what his customers want and then builds something that is a work of art, but also a good-playing cue. His cues are recognizable by the Gugino signature on the forearm and are also signed and dated underneath the wrap. His business comes mostly from word of mouth and referrals from customers. All work is performed by Tony himself. Depending on the type of cue ordered, the time frame is usually from one to three months.

If you are interested in talking to Tony Gugino about a new cue or cue that needs to be repaired, you can contact him at Gugino's Custom Cues, listed in the Trademark Index.

Present Day

Tony Gugino

SPECIFICATIONS

Butt material: hardwoods
Shaft material: rock maple

GRADING	98%	90%	70%

Standard length: 59 in.
Shaft lengths available: any up to 32 in.
Standard finish: two-part automotive
Balance point: 1 to 1 ½ in. above wrap
Standard butt cap: double black linen
Standard wrap: Irish linen
Point construction: short splice
Standard joint: brass
Standard joint type: flat faced or piloted
Joint screw threads: 3/8-10, 5/16-14, or 5/16-18
Standard number of shafts: one
Standard taper: pro
Standard ferrules: Aegis
Other ferrule options: ivory
Standard tip: Le Pro
Standard tip width: 13 mm
Tip widths available: any
Annual production: fewer than 20 cues
Options (for new cues only)
Special length: no charge
Layered tip: $25+
Ivory butt cap: $275
Ivory joint: $150
Ivory ferrule: $100
Ivory points: $150
Leather wrap: $100
Extra shaft: $125+

REPAIRS

Repairs done on all fine cues.
Refinish (with Irish linen wrap): $175
Refinish (with leather wrap): $225
Rewrap (Irish linen): $50
Rewrap (leather): $100
Clean and press linen wrap: $15
Replace shaft: $125+
Replace ivory ferrule: $100
Replace butt cap: $50+
Replace ivory butt cap: $275
Replace tip: $15+
Replaced layered tip: $25+
Replace fiber/linen ferrule: $35

CURRENT GUGINO'S CUES

Two-piece Gugino bar cues start at $250. Basic Gugino cues with wraps and joint rings start at $550. Gugino cues with points start at $750. One-of-a-kind Gugino custom cues start at $1,000. Two shafts are standard on Gugino cues over $700. The current delivery time for a Gugino custom cue is one to three months.

SECONDARY MARKET MINIMUM VALUES

The following are minimum values for other Gugino cues encountered on the secondary market. These prices are representative of cues utilizing basic materials and designs that are not necessarily available at present. Tony has offered one-of-a-kind cues that can command many times these prices due to the use of exotic materials and artistry.

Special construction note: There are many materials and construction techniques that can add value to Gugino cues.

For all used Gugino cues, except where otherwise noted:
Add $100 for each additional original straight playable shaft beyond one.
Deduct $125 for missing original straight playable shaft.
Add $75 each for ivory ferrules.
Deduct 20% for obvious or improper refinish.

Level 1 - Hustler.

	98%	90%	70%
Level 1 cues start at	$225	$175	$115

Level 2 - 0 points, 0-25 inlays.

	98%	90%	70%
Level 2 cues start at	$500	$390	$270

Level 3 - 2-6 points, 0-8 inlays.

GRADING	98%	90%	70%
Level 3 cues start at	$650	$510	$345
Level 4 - 4-10 points, 9-25 inlays.			
Level 4 cues start at	$750	$575	$390
Level 5 - 0-12 points, 26-50 inlays.			
Level 5 cues start at	$1,100	$875	$600
Level 6 - 0-12 points, 51-75 inlays.			
Level 6 cues start at	$1,450	$1,150	$800

GULYASSY CUES

Maker of pool cues from 1986 to present in Greenville, South Carolina.

Mike Gulyassy was a professional player who turned to making cues. He watched Leonard Bludworth repairing cues at a pro tournament where he was playing, and thought he would like to do the same. Mike tries to make a cue that fits the player's expectations and one that will last a lifetime. All butts are cored for extra stiffness and to prevent warpage.

Mike Gulyassy

Mike's shop contains two CNC lathes and a CNC mill for inlays. He also has five manual lathes and a mill, saws, polishing machines, and various cuemaking equipment. He also has a UV spray booth.

Mike has an MG logo and date that he puts on current playing cues. A Sledgehammer logo goes on his patent-pending break jump cues. Sledgehammer is a registered trademark with the U.S. Government.

All custom cues come with a lifetime warranty. The Sledgehammer II, made to Mike's specifications here in the United States, has a lifetime warranty. Mike's original Sledgehammer comes with the ferrule/tip guaranteed for life.

If you are interested in talking to Mike Gulyassy about a new cue or cue that needs to be repaired, you can contact him at Gulyassy Cues, listed in the Trademark Index.

SPECIFICATIONS

Butt material: hardwoods
Shaft material: hard rock maple
Standard length: 29 in. and 28 ½ in.
Standard wrap: Irish linen
Standard ferrules: melamine
Standard tip: Moori
Annual production (Mike Gulyassy Custom): approximately 50 cues
Annual production (Sledgehammer and Sledgehammer II): approximately 3,000 cues

OPTIONS (FOR NEW CUES ONLY)

Ivory ferrule: $100
Leather wrap: $100
Extra shaft: $100+

REPAIRS

Repairs done on all fine cues.
Refinish with Irish linen wrap: $125
Refinish shaft: $25
Rewrap with Irish linen: $40
Replace shaft: $100+
Replace tip: $10+

CURRENT GULYASSY CUES

Two-piece Gulyassy hustler cues start at $250. Gulyassy Sledgehammer II break/jump cues start $359. Basic Gulyassy custom cues with wraps and joint rings start at $500. Gulyassy cues with points start at $750. One-of-a-kind custom Gulyassy cues start at $1,000.

| GRADING | 98% | 90% | 70% |

SECONDARY MARKET MINIMUM VALUES

The following are minimum values for Gulyassy Custom cues encountered on the secondary market. These prices are representative of cues utilizing basic materials and designs that are not necessarily available at present. Mike has offered one-of-a-kind cues that can command many times these prices due to the use of exotic materials and artistry.

Special construction note: There are many materials and construction techniques that can add value to Gulyassy cues.

For all used Gulyassy cues, except where otherwise noted:
- Add $75 for each additional original straight playable shaft beyond two.
- Deduct $100+ for missing original straight playable shaft beyond two.
- Add $65 each for ivory ferrules.
- Add $75 for leather wrap.
- Deduct 20% for obvious or improper refinish.

Level 1 - Hustler.
Level 1 cues start at	$225	$180	$120

Level 2 - 0 points, 0-25 inlays.
Level 2 cues start at	$400	$310	$210

Level 3 - 2-6 points, 0-8 inlays.
Level 3 cues start at	$700	$535	$365

Level 4 - 4-10 points, 9-25 inlays.
Level 4 cues start at	$850	$655	$445

Level 5 - 0-12 points, 26-50 inlays.
Level 5 cues start at	$1,050	$825	$550

GUNN CUES

Maker of pool cues from 1972 to present in Thonotosassa, Florida.

Wayne Gunn and Terry McEniry share their talents in making Gunn Cues. Rocky Tillis gets the credit for getting them started, in Tampa, at Rocky's shop, in the late 1960s and early 1970s. Wayne is a certified welder with 40 years of experience. Terry's background is as a commercial fisherman and certified diver. Wayne was a player who could not find just the right cue for his game. He was looking for the right hit and has since discovered that in order to have the proper balance, the shaft of the cue needs to be tapered to fit the individual. Terry left commercial fishing in 1994, when they made gill net fishing illegal. Terry's nickname, Mullet Man, comes from his fishing background. Terry learned cuemaking from Rocky Tillis, and spent time in Rocky's shop from the age of twelve. Wayne started making cues in 1972, while Terry had started in 1967.

Wayne Gunn and Terry McEniry

Wayne and Terry make many hustler cues and two-piece cues with solid wood butts. Only about 25 to 50 custom Gunn cues are made a year. They will make custom cues to just about any specifications the customer wants. Terry also makes about fifteen to twenty custom walking canes a year. Gunn Cues stocks a large supply of wood and try not to use any of their wood until they have aged it at least ten years.

At present, the average order time for Gunn Cues is three to six months for simple cues. Custom cues with points can take about four years. If you are interested in talking to Wayne Gunn or Terry McEniry about a new cue or cue that needs to be repaired, you can contact them at Gunn Cues, listed in the Trademark Index.

SPECIFICATIONS

Butt material: hardwoods
Shaft material: Canadian hard rock maple
Standard length: 58 in.
Standard wrap: Irish linen
Standard finish: lacquer
Standard joint: black phenolic
Standard number of shafts: one
Standard ferrules: Ivorine III
Standard tip: Le Pro
Annual custom cue production: fewer than 50 cues

OPTIONS (FOR NEW CUES ONLY)

All options are available on Gunn Cues. Options are priced based on what the customer requests, and are quoted at that time.

GUNN CUES, cont.

GRADING	98%	90%	70%

REPAIRS
Repair prices are quoted based on what the customer requests.

CURRENT GUNN CUES
Two-piece Gunn hustler cues start at $175. Basic two-piece Gunn custom cues with solid wood butts start at $250. One-of-a-kind custom Gunn cues start at $3,000.

SECONDARY MARKET MINIMUM VALUES
The following are minimum values for other Gunn cues encountered on the secondary market. These prices are representative of cues utilizing basic materials and designs that are not necessarily available at present. Wayne and Terry have offered one-of-a-kind cues that can command many times these prices due to the use of exotic materials and artistry.

Special construction note: There are many materials and construction techniques that can add value to Gunn cues.

For all used Gunn cues, except where otherwise noted:
- Add $100 for each additional original straight playable shaft beyond two.
- Deduct $150 for missing original straight playable shaft under two.
- Add $50 each for ivory ferrules.
- Add $65 for leather wrap.
- Deduct 20% for obvious or improper refinish.

	98%	90%	70%
Level 1 - Hustler.			
Level 1 cues start at	$165	$130	$85
Level 2 - 0 points, 0-25 inlays.			
Level 2 cues start at	$235	$180	$120
Level 3 - 2-6 points, 0-8 inlays.			
Level 3 cues start at	$350	$270	$185
Level 4 - 4-10 points, 9-25 inlays.			
Level 4 cues start at	$450	$345	$230
Level 5 - 0-12 points, 26-50 inlays.			
Level 5 cues start at	$650	$510	$345
Level 6 - 0-12 points, 51-75 inlays.			
Level 6 cues start at	$950	$745	$500

RAY GURGALL
Maker of Northern Cues. For more information, refer to Northern.

ERNIE GUTIERREZ
Maker of Ginacues. For more information, refer to Ginacue.

HADRIANUS CUE COMPANY - HAND-MADE CUES BY ADRIAN VIGUERA

Maker of pool cues from 1992 to present, currently in Cicero, Illinois, a suburb of Chicago.

Adrian Viguera is a champion three-cushion and artistic billiards player, winning many national and international tournaments. In 1980, Adrian started working with a top cuemaker in Mexico (Rojelio) and six years later started working for Ray Schuler as a cue maker. Adrian started the Hadrianus Cue Company (derived from the Latin root of his first name) in 1992, after the birth of his first son. In the early 1990s, Adrian resided and built cues in El Paso, Texas. In 1995, Adrian returned to Cicero and established the cue shop where he builds cues today. Adrian also worked for Cognoscenti Cues for 18 months after his return to the Chicago area.

The name "Hadrianus" was burned into the forearm of his earlier cues. In early 1998 Adrian started signing the forearms of all of his cues with his full name. Adrian's cues are identifiable by their unique wood or G-10 glass epoxy joint screws. Adrain leaves the joint screw material decision to the player, because each has his own hit preference. He stopped using linen phenolic screws in 1996 because they had a greater tendency to break. Hadrianus cues most often feature solid wood forearms and hard rock maple shafts. As an option in his early cues, he would offer birch shafts for players who want a stiffer hit. He no longer offers birch as a shaft wood option. Playability is Adrian's main concern in a cue, and being a champion himself has helped him to understand what a good hitting cue should be. Inlaid points or butterfly splices are also available. Joint screws can be fixed in the butt or the shaft depending on player preference. Wound leather wraps are available and Adrian can dye them to match any color.

Adrian tries not to use artificial weights to adjust the balance or weight of Hadrianus cues. Adrian's early cues exhibited butt caps of natural materials, such as buck horn or exotic woods. Today, Adrian uses linen phenolic for joints and butt caps. Adrian makes everything that goes into a Hadrianus cue by hand in his one-man shop except for the tip and bumper. He manufactures his own screws from stock G-10 or raw woods.

If you have a Hadrianus cue that needs further identification or repair, or would like to talk to Adrian about ordering a new Hadrianus cue, contact the Hadrianus Cue Co., listed in the Trademark Index.

SPECIFICATIONS

- Butt material: exotic hardwoods
- Shaft material: hard rock maple
- Standard length: 58 in. (pool) to 56 in. (billiards)
- Lengths available: any up to 59 in.
- Standard finish: polyurethane
- Joint screw: G-10 glass epoxy or wood
- Standard joint: linen phenolic
- Joint type: flat faced
- Balance point: custom
- Point construction: inlaid
- Standard wrap: custom
- Standard butt cap: linen phenolic
- Standard number of shafts: one
- Standard taper: pro taper
- Standard ferrules: linen phenolic
- Standard tip: most available
- Tip widths available: any up to 13 mm
- Annual production: under 40

OPTIONS (FOR NEW CUES ONLY)

- Leather lace wrap: $100
- Extra shaft: $100
- Ivory joint: $150
- Ivory butt plate: $200
- Ivory ferrule: $50
- Joint protectors: $200

REPAIRS

Repairs done on most fine cues. Repair prices for Hadrianus cues only.

- Refinish: $120
- Refinish with linen wrap: $140
- Refinish with leather wrap: $200
- Rewrap (leather): $100
- Rewrap (linen): $50
- Replace shaft: $100
- Replace linen phenolic ferrule (includes Le Pro tip): $25
- Replace ivory ferrule: $50

GRADING	98%	90%	70%

CURRENT HADRIANUS CUES

The current delivery time for a custom Hadrianus cue is approximately 30 to 60 days.

SECONDARY MARKET MINIMUM VALUES

Note: The following are minimum prices for Hadrianus cues encountered on the secondary market. These prices are representative of cues utilizing basic materials and designs that may not be currently available. Adrian also offers one-of-a-kind cues that can command many times these prices due to the use of exotic materials and artistry.

Special construction note: There are many materials and construction techniques that can add value to Hadrianus cues. The following are the most important examples:

- Add $400+ for ivory points.
- Add $150+ for ivory joint.
- Add $250+ for "Hadrianus" burned into forearm.
- Add $250+ for exotic skin wrap.
- Add $200+ for original cork wrap.
- Add $100+ for original joint protectors.
- Add $200+ for each birch shaft.
- Add $250+ for experimental taper shaft.

For all used Hadrianus cues, except where otherwise noted:

- Add $85+ for each additional original straight playable shaft beyond.
- Deduct $100+ for missing original straight playable shaft.
- Deduct up to 40% for obvious or improper refinish.

Level 2 - 0 points, 0-25 inlays.

Level 2 cues start at	$800	$700	$450

Level 3 - 2-6 points, 0-8 inlays.

Level 3 cues start at	$950	$875	$500

Level 4 - 4-10 points, 9-25 inlays.

Level 4 cues start at	$1,100	$950	$600

HAGAN CUE

Maker of pool cues from 1987 in Gilbert, Arizona.

Bill Hagan started playing pool as a young boy. His older brother, Mike, taught him the finer points of the game. In 1987, while in the market for a new cue, Bill decided to use his engineering background to construct his own.

Bill made and designed each Hagan cue one at a time in his shop in Gilbert, Arizona. Hagan cues are easily identifiable by the letters "HC", usually engraved in the butt caps. Bill is rumored to have retired in recent years

SPECIFICATIONS

- Butt material: hardwoods
- Shaft material: rock maple
- Standard length: 58 in.
- Standard wrap: Irish linen
- Point construction: short splice

SECONDARY MARKET MINIMUM VALUES

The following are minimum values for Hagan cues encountered on the secondary market. These prices are representative of cues utilizing basic materials and designs that are not necessarily available at present. Bill offered one-of-a-kind cues that can command many times these prices due to the use of exotic materials and artistry.

Special construction note: There are many materials and construction techniques that can add value to Hagan cues.

For all used Hagan cues, except where otherwise noted:

- Add $100 for each additional original straight playable shaft beyond one.
- Deduct $175 for missing original straight playable shaft.
- Add $65 each for ivory ferrules.
- Add $75 for leather wrap.
- Deduct 25% for obvious or improper refinish.

Level 2 - 0 points, 0-25 inlays.

Level 2 cues start at	$500	$385	$255

Level 3 - 2-6 points, 0-8 inlays.

Level 3 cues start at	$700	$435	$360

Level 4 - 4-10 points, 9-25 inlays.

Level 4 cues start at	$900	$685	$460

GRADING	98%	90%	70%

Level 5 - 0-12 points, 26-50 inlays.
Level 5 cues start at $1,250 $975 $645

RON HALEY HANDMADE CUES

Maker of pool cues from 1990 to present in Springdale, Arkansas.

Ron Haley has been a pool enthusiast since 1965. In 1985, while attending a pro tournament, he became intrigued by a traveling cue repairman. Ron began doing repairs in his own area. This led to the purchase of more equipment, and in 1990 he built his first cue. From that point, it has been a non-stop learning process for Ron. He has been privileged to know and be advised by some very talented cue makers. He, in turn, has helped others along the way.

Ron is a part-time cue maker who prefers to make one-of-a-kind cues of his own design, but he will try to satisfy a customer's directives. Ron makes all of his own parts, so it takes about four months to complete a cue. Ron Haley only makes about fifteen cues per year so he does not advertise. Most of his cues are sold through a mailing list of prospective buyers. He prefers traditional designs and unusual techniques and does all of the work by hand, without the aid of CNC machinery. Ron's wife, Jaylon, signs all the cues with the Haley name. Each cue is numbered, dated, and photographed for future reference and identification.

Ron prefers natural materials for the artistic parts of a cue and manmade materials for the stressed areas. It is very important to him to do good quality work and in turn give the customer satisfaction for owning a Haley Cue.

Ron Haley cues are easily identifiable by the "Haley" signature and dates on the forearms. If you have a Ron Haley cue that needs further identification or repair, or would like to order a new cue, contact Ron Haley Custom Cues, listed in the Trademark Index.

Ron Haley

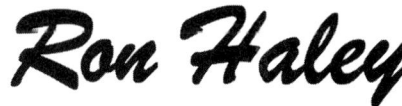
HANDMADE CUES

Present Day

SPECIFICATIONS

Butt material: hardwoods
Shaft material: hard rock maple
Standard length: 59 in.
Lengths available: 57 to 60 in.
Standard finish: acrylic urethane
Balance point: 1 to 2 in. above wrap
Standard butt cap: linen phenolic
Standard wrap: Irish linen
Point construction: structural short splice
Standard joint: stainless steel
Joint type: piloted
Joint screw: 5/16-14
Standard number of shafts: two
Standard taper: custom
Standard ferrules: melamine
Other ferrule options: ivory
Standard tip width: 13 mm
Tip widths available: 12 to 14 mm
Standard tip: Le Pro
Annual production: approximately 15 cues

OPTIONS (FOR NEW CUES ONLY)

Special length: no charge
Leather wrap: $100
Ivory ferrule: $75
Ivory butt cap: $200
Ivory joint: $150
Layered tip: $25
Extra shaft: $100

REPAIRS

Repairs done on Ron Haley cues only.
Refinish with linen wrap: $120
Refinish with leather wrap: $190
Rewrap linen: $30
Rewrap leather: $100
Clean and press linen wrap: $10

GRADING	98%	90%	70%

Restore leather wrap: $10+
Replace shaft: $125+
Replace fiber/linen ferrule: $20
Replace ivory ferrule: $75
Replace butt cap: $75
Replace ivory butt cap: $200+
Replace bumper: $3
Replace tip: $10
Replace layered tip: $25

CURRENT RON HALEY CUES:

The current delivery time for a Ron Haley custom cue is about eight to twelve months.

SECONDARY MARKET MINIMUM VALUES

The following are minimum values for Ron Haley cues encountered on the secondary market. These prices are representative of cues utilizing basic materials and designs that are not currently available. Ron has offered one-of-a-kind cues that can command many times these prices due to the use of exotic materials and artistry.

Special construction note: There are many materials and construction techniques that can add value to Ron Haley cues.

For all used cues, except where otherwise noted:

Add $100 for each additional original straight playable shaft beyond two.
Deduct $125+ for each missing original straight playable shaft under two.
Add $55 each for ivory ferrules.
Add $65 for leather wrap.
Deduct 20% for obvious or improper refinish.

	98%	90%	70%
Level 1 - 4 points, hustler.			
Level 1 cues start at	$200	$155	$105
Level 2 - 0 points, 0-25 inlays.			
Level 2 cues start at	$400	$315	$215
Level 3 - 2-6 points, 0-8 inlays.			
Level 3 cues start at	$650	$500	$335
Level 4 - 4-10 points, 9-25 inlays.			
Level 4 cues start at	$750	$575	$385
Level 5 - 0-12 points, 26-50 inlays.			
Level 5 cues start at	$1,250	$985	$655

HAMILTON CUE

Maker of pool cues from 1970 to the 1990s in Chicago, Illinois and from 1997 to present in Crystal River, Florida.

Al Hamilton began woodworking at age 17. In 1958 he began trap shooting, and made gun stocks with Russell Anton for eight years. He owned his own machine shop for 40 years, first in Chicago, then in Largo, Florida. He began to collect cues in the late 1960s. He has cues by Brunswick, Balabushka, Schon, and Kersenbrock, whom he particularly admires. Al made his own cues for fun, for himself and his friends and family in the 1970s, making a half dozen or so a year.

Al Hamilton is a pool player who has experience in doing cue repairs. He moved to Florida in the mid-1990s and began building cues once again in 1997. All Hamilton Cues are one-of-a-kind or limited editions.

If you are interested in talking to Al Hamilton about a new cue or cue that needs to be repaired, you can contact him at Hamilton Cue, listed in the Trademark Index.

SPECIFICATIONS

Butt material: hardwoods
Shaft material: Canadian white maple
Standard length: 58 in.
Lengths available: any up to 60 in.
Standard finish: proprietary
Balance point: 1½ to 2 in. above wrap
Standard butt cap: phenolic
Standard wrap: Irish linen
Point construction: short splice, full splice, or butterflies
Standard joint: phenolic
Joint type: flat faced
Standard joint screw thread: 3/8-10
Standard number of shafts: one
Standard taper: pro

GRADING	98%	90%	70%

- Standard ferrules: 1 in.
- Other ferrule options: ivory, ¾-1 in.
- Standard tip: Moori
- Standard tip width: 13 mm
- Tip widths available: 12 to 13 mm
- Standard bumper: 1x3/8 screw-in
- Annual production: fewer than 20 cues

OPTIONS (FOR NEW CUES ONLY)

- Special length: no charge
- Layered tip: no charge
- Ivory joint: $50
- Ivory ferrule: $40
- Joint protectors: $60
- Extra shaft: $120

REPAIRS

Repairs done on all fine cues.
- Replace shaft with fiber/linen ferrule: $120
- Replace shaft with ivory ferrule: $160
- Replace ivory ferrule: $40

CURRENT HAMILTON CUES

The average order time for a Hamilton cue is approximately one year.

SECONDARY MARKET MINIMUM VALUES

The following are minimum values for Hamilton cues encountered on the secondary market. These prices are representative of cues utilizing basic materials and designs that are not necessarily available at present. Al has offered one-of-a-kind cues that can command many times these prices due to the use of exotic materials and artistry.

Special construction note: There are many materials and construction techniques that can add value to Hamilton cues. For all used Hamilton cues, except where otherwise noted:
- Add $100 for each additional original straight playable shaft beyond one.
- Deduct $120 for missing original straight playable shaft.
- Add $40 each for ivory ferrules.
- Deduct 20% for obvious or improper refinish.

	98%	90%	70%
Level 2 - 0 points, 0-25 inlays.			
Level 2 cues start at	$450	$345	$235
Level 3 - 2-6 points, 0-8 inlays.			
Level 3 cues start at	$650	$495	$335
Level 4 - 4-10 points, 9-25 inlays.			
Level 4 cues start at	$750	$575	$395
Level 5 - 0-12 points, 26-50 inlays.			
Level 5 cues start at	$1,100	$850	$585

HAMMER CUSTOM CUES

Maker of pool cues from 1997 in Tulsa, Oklahoma.

Travis Frakes began building cues in 1997. He became addicted to the game of pool after meeting and becoming friends with one of the best players back in 1987. Along with the love of the game came the drive to find the best-playing cue.

Hammer Cues are built for structural integrity and unique but well-balanced designs. Playability is a dominating feature. Travis has a 500-square-foot shop that contains old-world equipment as well as state-of-the-art computer-controlled devices. Hammer Custom Cues are identified by the shape of Thor's Hammer, done in various inlay materials. Some cues may have just a signature or both the signature and the inlay of Thor's Hammer.

Hammer Cues are guaranteed for life against construction defects that are not the result of warpage or abuse. If you are interested in talking to Travis Frakes about a new cue or cue that needs to be repaired, you can contact him at Hammer Custom Cues, listed in the Trademark Index.

SPECIFICATIONS

- Butt material: hardwoods
- Shaft material: rock maple
- Standard length: 58 in.
- Standard wrap: Irish linen
- Standard ferrules: proprietary phenolic

GRADING	98%	90%	70%

Standard tip: Triangle
Annual production: approximately 100 cues

OPTIONS (FOR NEW CUES ONLY)

Ivory ferrule: $70
Leather wrap: $100
Extra shaft: $85

REPAIRS

Repairs done on all fine cues.
Refinish (with Irish linen wrap): $100
Rewrap (Irish linen): $35
Replace shaft: $85+
Replace tip: $10

CURRENT HAMMER CUES

Two-piece Hammer bar cues start at $200. Basic Hammer cues with wraps and joint rings start at $300. Hammer cues with points start at $400. One-of-a-kind custom Hammer cues start at $500.

SECONDARY MARKET MINIMUM VALUES

The following are minimum values for Hammer cues encountered on the secondary market. These prices are representative of cues utilizing basic materials and designs that are not necessarily available at present. Travis has offered one-of-a-kind cues that can command many times these prices due to the use of exotic materials and artistry.

There are many materials and construction techniques that can add value to Hammer cues.

For all used Hammer cues, except where otherwise noted:
Add $75 for each additional original straight playable shaft beyond one.
Deduct $85+ for missing original straight playable shaft.
Add $50 each for ivory ferrules.
Add $75 for leather wrap.
Deduct 20% for obvious or improper refinish.

Level 1 - Hustler.
Level 1 cues start at	$150	$120	$85

Level 2 - 0 points, 0-25 inlays.
Level 2 cues start at	$225	$175	$115

Level 3 - 2-6 points, 0-8 inlays.
Level 3 cues start at	$300	$245	$165

Level 4 - 4-10 points, 9-25 inlays.
Level 4 cues start at	$400	$315	$215

Level 5 - 0-12 points, 26-50 inlays.
Level 5 cues start at	$600	$475	$325

HARPER'S PERSONALIZED CUES

Maker of pool cues from 1960 to present in Creston, Iowa.

Bud Harper still lives in the small town of Creston, Iowa, where he was born. In his early years, Bud hunted and fished with his father, and he became interested in guns and building gun stocks. When he graduated from high school, he went to Kansas City school of Art and Design for two years, majoring in three-dimensional design. After school, he became an art director for Midwest Printing Company.

He was always interested in the game of pool. In 1960 he bought his first two-piece cue. Since he had been doing inlay work on gun stocks for years, he decided to do some inlay work on the Willie Hoppe shortly after he got it. Not too long after that, he got another Hoppe and proceeded to inlay it. Bud likes to use gold, silver, ivory, mother-of-pearl, abalone, and other exotic materials. He also will use lizard and snakeskin wrap, if the costomer wants it. He will also put the customer's name or monogram on a cue to give it a personal touch. Bud's inlays are usually either round dots, or diamond or rectangular shapes, but he also does intricate scroll designs on his cues.

Present Day

If you are interested in talking to Bud Harper about a new cue or cue that needs to be repaired, you can contact him at Harper's Personalized Cues, listed in the Trademark Index.

GRADING	98%	90%	70%

SPECIFICATIONS
Butt material: hardwoods
Shaft material: hard rock maple
Standard length: 58 in.
Standard wrap: Irish linen
Standard ferrules: Ivorine
Annual production: fewer than 35 cues

OPTIONS (FOR NEW CUES ONLY)
Ivory ferrule: $60
Leather wrap: $75
Extra shaft: $125+

REPAIRS
Repairs done on all fine cues.
    Rewrap (Irish linen): $35

CURRENT HARPER'S CUES
Two-piece Harper's bar cues start at $125. Basic Harper's cues with wraps and joint rings start at $185. Harper's cues with points start at $235. One-of-a-kind custom Harper's cues start at $450.

SECONDARY MARKET MINIMUM VALUES
The following are minimum values for Harper's cues encountered on the secondary market. These prices are representative of cues utilizing basic materials and designs that are not necessarily available at present. Bud has offered one-of-a-kind cues that can command many times these prices due to the use of exotic materials and artistry.

Special construction note: There are many materials and construction techniques that can add value to Harper's cues.

For all used Harper's cues, except where otherwise noted:
    Add $100 for each additional original straight playable shaft beyond one.
    Deduct $125+ for missing original straight playable shaft.
    Add $50 each for ivory ferrules.
    Add $65 for leather wrap.
    Deduct 15% for obvious or improper refinish.

Level 1 - Hustler.
    Level 1 cues start at $115 $90 $60

Level 2 - 0 points, 0-25 inlays.
    Level 2 cues start at $175 $135 $90

Level 3 - 2-6 points, 0-8 inlays.
    Level 3 cues start at $225 $175 $115

Level 4 - 4-10 points, 9-25 inlays.
    Level 4 cues start at $275 $215 $140

Level 5 - 0-12 points, 26-50 inlays.
    Level 5 cues start at $500 $390 $265

RICHARD HARRIS
Maker of Blue Grass Cues, for more information refer to Blue Grass Cues.

TED HARRIS CUSTOM CUES
Maker of pool cues from 1993, in Ocean City, Maryland, to present in Alto, Georgia.

As a kid, living in Florida, Ted Harris played pool at a friend's house. Later on, he discovered his real love for pool as a college student. By 1987, Ted had relocated to Ocean City, Maryland, and had taken a job as a "house man" at the only billiard establishment in town. He was determined to become the best pool player he could be.

In 1989, after visiting with cue maker Tim Scruggs, Ted decided to begin doing cue repairs. It wasn't long before he began to venture out to tournaments, both as a player and as a cue repairman with his cue repair equipment. Jerry and Laurie Franklin were instrumental in helping Ted decide to go on the road. Before long, the top players were counting on Ted to maximize the performance of their cues at the major tournaments.

Ted began making sneaky petes in 1993, in Los Angeles. In 1994, he started to purchase the equipment necessary to begin making his own custom pool cues. Ted's travels on the road slowed down as he became more interested in making his own cues and designing his own lathes and equipment. In 1997, he set up shop at Action Billiards in Salisbury, Maryland, and, with the help of his new wife, Kathy, began living his life's dream of building custom cues.

In July of 2000, Ted entered his cues for submission and admission to the ACA, and was accepted. Ted, for the most part, is a one-man shop, except for the wonderful help he gets from Kathy. She now does most of the wet sanding and polishing and adding the finish. All parts, except tips, joint screws, and the rubber bumpers, are made in-house from raw materials. All Ted Harris cues are one-of-a-kind, custom ordered to suit the customer. He cores his cues from the wrap to the joint with laminated maple rods, underneath short splice points or solid forearms for stability. Shafts are turned at least 24 times over a long period of time. Playability is the most important factor for Ted. If you visit Ted's shop, you will notice that the climate is controlled year round to maintain 75 degrees and 45-50% humidity. Ted feels that maintaining the climate is important to the cues he produces. He prefers to use wood-to-wood joints to get the best stable hit possible from his cues.

One of Ted's trademarks is to make wood joint collars from the same stock as the points. Ted Harris signs special cues with "Ted Harris" and the date of completion. All Ted Harris cues have his logo. If you are interested in talking to Ted Harris about a new cue or cue that needs to be repaired, you can contact him at Ted Harris Custom Cues, listed in the Trademark Index.

SPECIFICATIONS

Butt material: hardwoods
Shaft material: North American hard rock maple
Standard length: 58 in.
Lengths available: 54 to 62 in.
Standard finish: two-part catalyzed urethane automotive clear coat
Balance point: 18.5 in. from butt
Standard butt cap: phenolic
Standard wrap: Irish linen
Point construction: short splice
Standard joint: wood-to-wood
Standard joint type: flat faced
Joint screw thread: 3/8-7.5 radial pin
Joint protectors: standard
Standard number of shafts: two
Standard taper: custom stiff pro taper
Standard ferrules: ¾ in. melamine
Standard tip: Triangle or Le Pro
Standard tip width: 13 mm
Tip widths available: 10 to 15 mm
Standard bumper: 5/8 by 7/8 in. push-in
Annual production: approximately 100 cues

OPTIONS (FOR NEW CUES ONLY)

Special length: no charge
Layered tip: $25+
Ivory butt cap: $220+
Thin wall stainless steel joint: $75
Ivory joint: $165
Ivory ferrule: $75
Veneers: $25 per point
Ivory points: $150+
Exotic wood inlays: $15+ each
Ivory inlays: $20+ each
Leather wrap: $110
Printed leather wrap: $126
Stacked leather wrap: 150
Ring lizard or other exotic skin wrap: $250
Joint protectors: $100+
Extra shaft: $125
Predator 314 shaft: $225
Old growth shaft: $225

REPAIRS

Repairs done on all fine cues.

Refinish (with Irish linen wrap): $150+
Refinish (with leather wrap): $250+
Rewrap (Irish linen): $40+
Rewrap (leather): $100+
Clean and press linen wrap: $20
Restore leather wrap: $20
Replace shaft: $150+
Replace ivory ferrule: $75
Replace butt cap: $40+
Replace ivory butt cap: $200+
Replace tip: $10+

TED HARRIS CUSTOM CUES, cont. 339

GRADING	100%	95%	70%

Replaced layered tip: $25+
Replace fiber/linen ferrule: $35

CURRENT TED HARRIS CUES

A basic Ted Harris cue with a wrap and joint rings starts at $700. Ted Harris cues with points start at $920. The current dilivery time for a Ted Harris cue is about four months.

CURRENT EXAMPLES

The following cues are examples of the current work of Ted Harris. These cues can be ordered as shown, modified to suit the desires of the customer, or new designs can be created.

Level 2 - Cocobolo joint, figured cocobolo forearm with pairs of silver rings set in black phenolic above wrap, figured cocobolo butt sleeve with pairs of silver rings set in black phenolic rings at top and bottom.

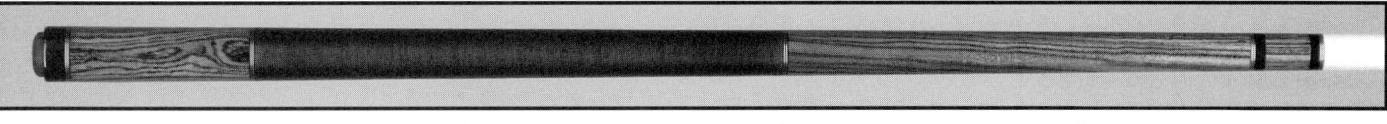

MSR	$600	$550-650	$475	$375

Level 2 - Figured cocobolo forearm with six ivory diamond-shaped inlays set in ebony bands within pairs of silver rings above wrap, figured cocobolo butt sleeve with six ivory diamond-shaped inlays set in ebony bands within pairs of silver rings below wrap.

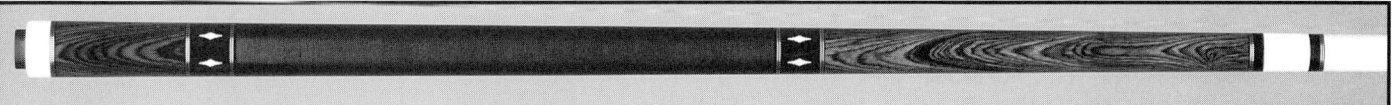

MSR	$1,010	$950-1,100	$825	$650

Level 3 "Play/Jump Special Edition" - Curly maple forearm with pairs of silver rings set in black phenolic above jump cue joint, four ebony points, one-piece ebony handle and butt sleeve.

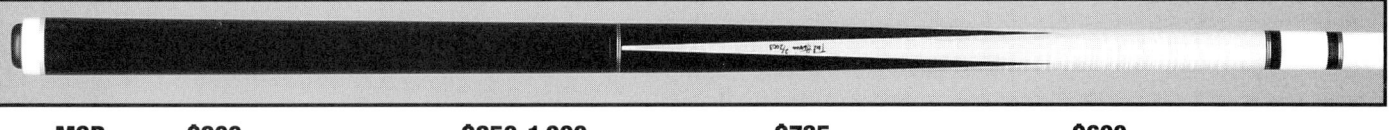

MSR	$900	$850-1,000	$735	$600

Level 3 - Cocobolo joint, ebony forearm with pairs of silver rings set in black phenolic above wrap, three long and three short cocobolo points with three colored veneers, cocobolo butt sleeve with pairs of silver rings set in black phenolic at top and bottom.

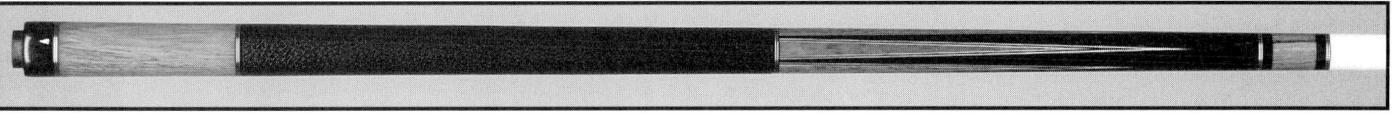

MSR	$1,040	$1,000-1,150	$850	$675

Level 3 - Ivory joint, curly maple forearm with pairs of silver rings set in black phenolic above wrap, four snakewood points with four colored veneers, snakewood butt sleeve with pairs of silver rings set in black phenolic at top and bottom, ivory butt cap.

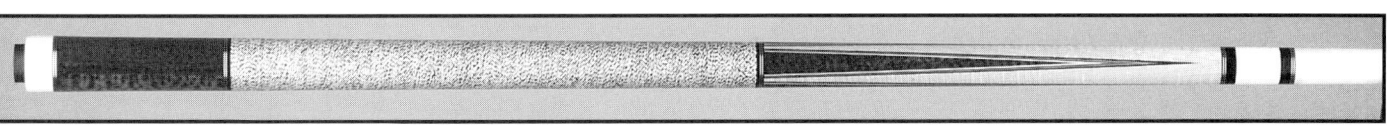

MSR	$1,645	$1,600-1,750	$1,300	$950

SPECIAL INTEREST TED HARRIS CUES

The following is an example of a Ted Harris US Open Signature Series Cue. These cues were made for the US Open, signed by all of the important players and participants, and offered for sale as Limited Editions.

Level 2 "1998 US Open Series Signature Cue" - One-piece maple butt with signatures of the major players that played or participated in the event, one of six cues of this kind.

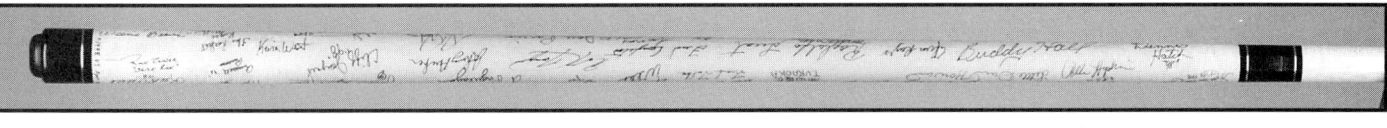

MSR	$1,000	$2,500	$1,950	$1,300

TED HARRIS CUSTOM CUES, cont.

GRADING	98%	90%	70%

SECONDARY MARKET MINIMUM VALUES

The following are minimum values for other Ted Harris cues encountered on the secondary market. These prices are representative of cues utilizing basic materials and designs that are not necessarily available at present. Ted has offered one-of-a-kind cues that can command many times these prices due to the use of exotic materials and artistry.

Special construction note: There are many materials and construction techniques that can add value to Ted Harris cues.

For all used Ted Harris cues, except where otherwise noted:
- Add $100 for each additional original straight playable shaft beyond two.
- Deduct $125+ for missing original straight playable shaft under two.
- Add $60 each for ivory ferrules.
- Add $75+ for leather wrap.
- Deduct 25% for obvious or improper refinish.

	98%	90%	70%
Level 1 - Hustler.			
Level 1 cues start at	$300	$235	$165
Level 2 - 0 points, 0-25 inlays.			
Level 2 cues start at	$600	$475	$325
Level 3 - 2-6 points, 0-8 inlays.			
Level 3 cues start at	$750	$585	$400
Level 4 - 4-10 points, 9-25 inlays.			
Level 4 cues start at	$900	$700	$475
Level 5 - 0-12 points, 26-50 inlays.			
Level 5 cues start at	$1,150	$900	$600

TOM HARRIS CUES

Maker of pool cues from 1976 to 1980 in Stamford, Connecticut and from 1997 to present in East Haven, Connecticut.

Tom Harris majored in mechanical engineering in college and went into the tool and die trade. A player in tournaments in the late sixties and early seventies, Tom met many pro players and learned a lot from them about what they wanted in their cues. He met many top cuemakers and visited many cuemaking shops including Palmer, Rich, Gus Szamboti, Richard Black, and others.

Tom decided to apply his engineering and machining background to cuemaking and made his first cue in April of 1976 in Stamford, Connecticut. Although most Harris cues were not marked, they do have some interesting identifiable characteristics. For example, Tom developed the 105-degree blank, which he cut on a table saw, and is the only cuemaker known to have used these. Cutting the points at 105 degrees instead of 90 degrees allowed the points to meet at the base of the forearm, while still leaving a wide core for the connecting bolt. Also, Harris cues had a 29 ½ in. butt and a 14 in. wrap section. Less than 500 Tom Harris cues were made from 1976 to 1980. Tom is proud of the developments he made during those years, when cuemaking was not as advanced as it is today.

Tom started repairing cues in 1995, in East Haven, Connecticut, after a fifteen-year break from the craft. He remained active in tournaments, and organized group instructional seminars for players. He returned to cuemaking in 1997. Tom makes all of his cues by hand, and signs most of them on the forearms. He now makes cues with 90-degree points, and uses a flat-faced joint with a brass insert. He designed these unique inserts which are available to other cuemakers. Tom is very proud of the playability of his cues and the resonance of their hit, and loves to prime cues for performance. He tries to make custom one-of-a-kind cues that are unique to the individual. He is constantly improving his construction techniques. Now most of his cues have linen phenolic or ivory joints, as opposed to the stainless steel joints that he used in the seventies. Tom prefers simple cues without much ring work or inlays, believing that simpler cues play better. He believes the more glue lines are in a cue, the worse the hit. And Tom no longer uses leather wraps, which may be encountered on his earlier works.

Tom Harris cues are guaranteed for life to the original owner against construction defects that are not the result of warpage or abuse. If you have a Tom Harris cue that needs further identification or repair, contact Tom Harris Cues, listed in the Trademark Index.

SPECIFICATIONS

Butt material: hardwoods
Shaft material: rock maple

GRADING	98%	90%	70%

Standard length: 58 3/8 in.
Joint screw: 5/16-14
Standard joint: stainless steel
Joint type: piloted
Point construction: short splice
Standard wrap: Irish linen
Standard butt cap: Delrin
Standard tip: water buffalo
Balance point: 18-3/4 in. from butt
Standard number of shafts: one
Standard taper: pro
Standard ferrules: linen-based melamine
Annual production: fewer than 40 cues

CURRENT TOM HARRIS CUES

Basic Tom Harris cues with wraps and black joint collars start at $800. Tom Harris cues with points start at $1,100. The current delivery time for a Tom Harris cue is at least eight months.

SECONDARY MARKET MINIMUM VALUES

The following are minimum values for recent Tom Harris cues encountered on the secondary market. These prices are representative of cues utilizing basic materials and designs that are not necessarily available now.

Level 2 - 0 points, 0-25 inlays.

Level 2 cues start at	$700	$545	$375

Level 3 - 2-6 points, 0-8 inlays.

Level 3 cues start at	$950	$750	$500

SECONDARY MARKET MINIMUM VALUES

The following are minimum prices for early Tom Harris cues encountered on the secondary market. They are identifiable by stainless steel piloted joints and 105 degree spliced points.

Special construction note: There are many materials and construction techniques that can add value to Tom Harris cues.

For all used Tom Harris cues, except where otherwise noted:
- Add $100+ for each additional original straight playable shaft (standard with two).
- Deduct $150 for each missing original straight playable shaft.
- Add $250+ for ivory joint.
- Deduct 30% for obvious or improper refinish.

Level 3 - 2-6 points, 0-8 inlays.

Level 3 cues start at	$1,400	$1,125	$800

Level 4 - 4-10 points, 9-25 inlays.

Level 4 cues start at	$1,950	$1,550	$1,100

TIM & JIM HASKIN

Makers of Cue Masters cues. For more information, refer to The Cue Masters.

STAN HAWKINS

Maker of Black Hawk Custom Cues. For more information, refer to Black Hawk.

HAWKINS CUES

Maker of pool cues in Eau Claire, Wisconsin.

If you have a Hawkins cue that needs further identification or repair, or would like to talk to Hal about ordering a new cue, contact Hawkins Cues, listed in the Trademark Index.

STEVE HEBERT

Maker of aBear Custom Cues. For more information, refer to aBear.

RICHARD HELMSTETTER

Founder of Adam cues. For more information see Adam Cues.

Richard Helmstetter is also famous for being one of the top makers of cues for billiard players. Original signed Helmstetter billiard cues are very collectible.

HERCEK FINE BILLIARD CUES

Maker of pool cues from 1993 to present in Mundelein, Illinois, a suburb of Chicago.

Joel Hercek was introduced to billiards at an early age. His father, a builder by trade, was an accomplished three-cushion and straight pool player. He taught Joel the intricacies of both billiard games. Growing up, Joel played a lot of pool and helped his father run tournaments by refereeing matches at local billiard rooms. The local American Legion hosted a large annual tournament which drew the best players from the greater Chicago-land area and bordering states. It was at these tournaments that Joel's interest in billiard cues was kindled. While watching matches, Joel would pay close attention to the cues that players were using and developed an interest in how they were constructed. During the late 1970s and 1980s, Joel's obsession with the game and its equipment grew. At the time, Joel was employed by Lake County (IL) as their Forestry Foreman, a position he held for 14 years. Along with his employment and schooling, Joel also owned two other businesses. One was a fitness equipment company called Healthware Inc. and the other was a tree care and removal company named Oakwood Enterprises. It was in the mid-1980s when Joel added cue dealing to his resume. Joel began dealing in investment grade cue sticks and bought and sold some of the most desirable cues on the market today. He concurrently built his own collection of fine billiard cues.

Joel Hercek

While dining with several other cue makers at a billiard related trade show, Joel met Burton Spain, a famed cue maker. The two formed an instant friendship and Joel soon added Burt's cues to his collection and inventory. Joel spent many days at Burt's shop and was always impressed by Burton's full splice construction techniques. To Joel, it made perfect sense to build a cue in this fashion considering some of Joel's favorite hitting cues were built on the full splice Titlist blank.

Joel left the Forest Preserve in 1992 to go into the billiard business full time. He planned to open his own billiard room in the town where he, and his very supportive wife Margaret, settled. Burton tried several times to talk Joel out of opening a billiard room by explaining the pitfalls of such a business. Joel was determined to go ahead with his plans despite Burton's advice. The only two obstacles to Joel's plan were approval from the village and the signing of the lease. The night before the lease was to be signed, Joel received a call from Burton. Burt wanted to meet Joel the next day to discuss some pressing news. The news was grim; Burton was dying of cancer. Burton offered to sell Joel his business and stay on to train him as long as possible. Joel accepted Burt's proposal and started his new career as a cuemaker. Burton passed away in 1994 at the young age of 54.

Joel built his first cue in 1993. That cue was one of seven built that year, all of which incorporated the full splice blank construction and the reverse joint that Burt made popular on his cues. As the years progressed Joel made many refinements to his cues. The first refinement was switching to a more conventional piloted joint using a 5/16-14 screw. Other changes including the taper and balance were implemented into Joel's construction throughout the years. Today, Joel only builds cues to order and enjoys challenging himself with new one-of-a-kind designs each and every batch. He works alone and all his designs and engravings are created and executed by himself. Although many Hercek designs look quite different from one another, they all share a common bond. They are all built on Joel's full splice blanks; he will not build a cue any other way. This construction method is time-consuming and quite costly. However, Joel believes this makes for the most sound and best hitting cue he can build. Joel's customers are players and collectors alike, from the U.S. and abroad. Each of Joel's cues are custom made, so he likes to deal directly with the customer. As a result of the one-on-one interaction, many of his customers have become friends throughout the years. Demand for Joel's work has far exceeded his output, so getting in Joel's order book could mean waiting nearly a decade before your name comes up on the list for a cue. Joel continues the tradition of building high quality cues in his one-man shop with the same care and diligence that he took on his very first cue. Considering Joel's pedigree and legacy of quality, it is no surprise that demand for his work is very high.

If you have a Hercek or Burton Spain cue that needs repair, or would like to talk to Joel about ordering a new cue, contact Hercek Fine Billiard Cues, listed in the Trademark Index.

SPECIFICATIONS

Butt material: hardwoods
Shaft material: rock maple
Standard length: 58 in.
Lengths available: 57 to 60 in.
Standard finish: automotive clear coat
Joint screw: 5/16-14
Standard joint: stainless steel
Joint type: piloted
Balance point: custom
Point construction: full splice
Standard wrap: Irish linen
Standard butt cap: Delrin
Standard number of shafts: two
Standard taper: Hercek
Standard ferrules: ivory
Standard tip: leather
Tip widths available: 11 to 15 mm
Annual production: fewer than 50 cues

HERCEK FINE BILLIARD CUES, cont.

GRADING	100%	95%	70%

OPTIONS (FOR NEW CUES ONLY)
- Leather wrap: $250
- Ivory joint: $250
- Ivory butt cap: $400
- Joint protectors: standard
- Custom joint protectors: por
- 3/8-10 flat face joint: no charge
- Extra shaft: $200+
- Ivory ferrule: $75
- Special length: no charge
- Layered tip: no charge

REPAIRS
Repairs done on Hercek and Burton Spain cues only.
- Refinish (with leather wrap): $550
- Refinish (with linen wrap): $350+
- Rewrap (leather): $250
- Rewrap (linen): $100
- Replace shaft: $200
- Replace ivory ferrule: $75
- Replace tip: $30

CURRENT HERCEK CUES
Hercek cues with full spliced points start at $2,000. There is about a seven-year wait to get on Joel's ordering list. Once a customer reaches the ordering point on the waiting list, the construction time is roughly eight months.

CURRENT EXAMPLES
Joel currently specializes in one-of-a-kind custom cues. The following cues are representations of the work of Joel Hercek. They can be ordered as shown, modified to suit the desires of the customer, or new designs can be created.

Level 3 - Bird's-eye nose with four points of cocobolo, black, mahogany, purple and white veneers. Cocobolo butt sleeve with ivory slotted trim ring. Ivory slotted trim ring on a flat face joint. Delrin butt cap. Irish linen wrap from Burton Spain's old stock.

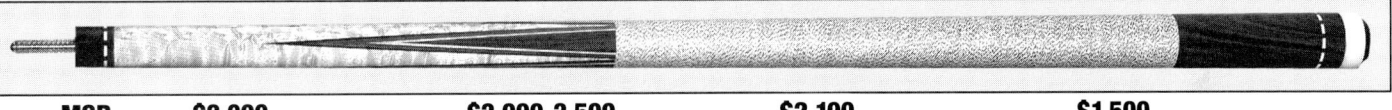

MSR	$2,000	$2,000-2,500	$2,100	$1,500

Level 4 Bird's-eye nose with four points of cocobolo, black, mahogany and white veneers. Notched ivory diamond in each point. Eight notched ivory diamonds with ivory dots separated by four fine ivory lines in the butt sleeve. Maple slotted trim rings below the wrap and at the joint. Stainless steel joint and Delrin butt cap.

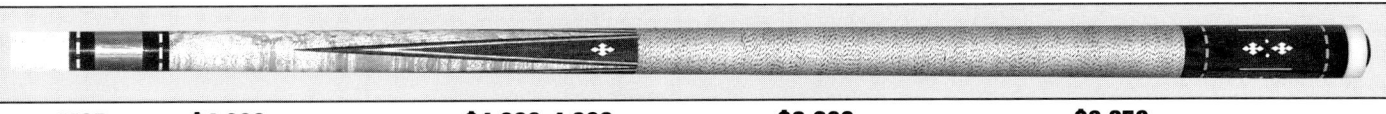

MSR	$4,000	$4,000-4,300	$3,800	$3,250

Level 7 - Ebony forearm with four rbony points, white, black, blue, white veneers. Ivory bars, squares and triangle make up the design in the points. The handle is made up of three sleeves of snakewood with two shorter sleeves of ivory. Below the handle is an ebony sleeve with a "Frank Lloyd Wright"-inspired ivory design. Ivory joint, butt cap and trim rings.

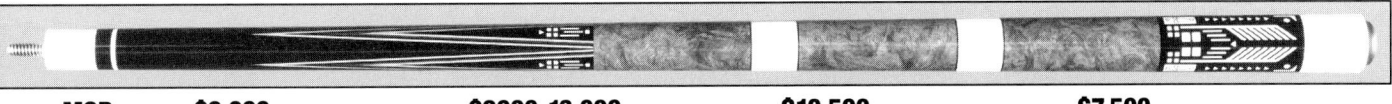

MSR	$9,000	$9000-13,000	$10,500	$7,500

Level 7 - Bloodwood nose with four points of Brazilian rosewood with white, red, white veneers. An ivory diamond/spade/club/heart is inlaid in the points. Two long sleeves of bloodwood with three ivory sleeves make up the handle. Two smaller ivory sleeves have a tumbling dice design engraving. The large ivory sleeve has the card suits with a larger number seven engraving. Below the handle is a Brazilian rosewood sleeve with two ivory cards inlaid. The cards are engraved with the queen of diamonds and the ace of spades. Between the cards are ivory and ebony three-dimensional inlaid dice. Ivory joint, butt cap and trim rings.

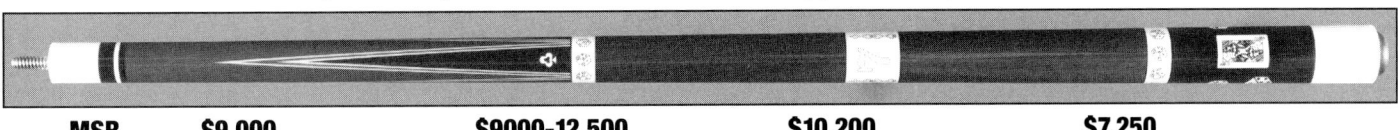

MSR	$9,000	$9000-12,500	$10,200	$7,250

HERCEK FINE BILLIARD CUES, cont.

GRADING	98%	90%	70%

PAST EXAMPLES

Level 3 - Bird's-eye nose with four points of ebony, black, red, blue and yellow veneers. Red, blue, and yellow veneer trim rings at the joint. Eight ivory dots in the butt sleeve separated by two sets of colored veneered trim rings. Stainless steel joint with a Delrin butt cap.

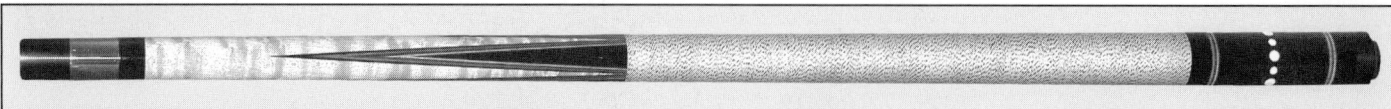

| MSR (1996) $2,000 | $3,200 | $2,750 | $2,175 |

Level 3 - Maple forearm, four rosewood points with four colored veneers, cork wrap, rosewood butt sleeve with four stacked veneers matching the veneers in points above butt cap.

| MSR (1999) $1,300 | $2,450 | $2,000 | $1,500 |

Level 3 - Bird's-eye maple forearm, four cocobolo points with four colored veneers, cocobolo butt sleeve with maple and colored veneer stitched rings towards bottom.

| MSR (1999) $1,200 | $2,350 | $1,950 | $1,450 |

Level 3 - Ivorine 3 joint, bird's-eye maple forearm, four ebony points with four colored veneers, ebony butt sleeve with a maple ring above butt cap.

| MSR (1999) $1,200 | $2,350 | $1,950 | $1,450 |

Level 3 - Ivory joint, bird's-eye maple forearm, four ebony points with four colored veneers, ebony butt sleeve with four ivory diamond-shaped inlays between maple and colored veneer stitched rings above and below.

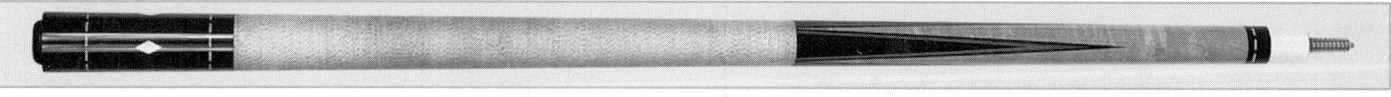

| MSR (1999) $1,500 | $2,750 | $2,300 | $1,775 |

Level 4 - Bird's-eye maple forearm, four ebony points with four colored veneers, ebony butt sleeve with four patterns of vertical pairs of ivory diamond-shaped inlays and a pair of horizontal ivory dots between maple checked rings above and below.

| MSR (1999) $1,450 | $2,700 | $2,275 | $1,750 |

Level 4 - Bird's-eye maple forearm, four ebony points with four colored veneers and an ivory diamond-shaped inlay in each, ebony butt sleeve with four patterns of vertical pairs of ivory diamond-shaped inlays and a pair of horizontal ivory dots alternating with four veneer lines between maple and colored veneer stitched rings above and below.

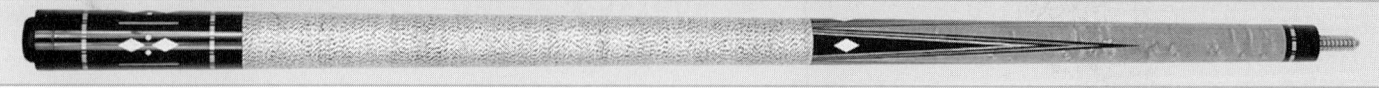

| MSR (1999) $1,550 | $2,800 | $2,365 | $1,825 |

Level 4 - Bird's-eye maple forearm, four ebony points with four colored veneers and an ivory spearhead-shaped inlay in each, leather wrap, ebony butt sleeve with four vertical pairs of opposing ivory spearhead-shaped inlays alternating with four long intricate ivory dished diamond-shaped inlays between maple checked rings above and below.

| MSR (1999) $1,750 | $2,950 | $2,550 | $2,075 |

HERCEK FINE BILLIARD CUES, cont. 345

GRADING	98%	90%	70%

Level 4 - Bird's-eye maple forearm, four cocobolo points with four colored veneers and an ivory diamond-shaped inlay in each and an ebony-bordered ivory dot at the tip of each, cocobolo butt sleeve with four patterns of vertical pairs of ivory diamond-shaped inlays and a pair of horizontal ivory dots alternating with four veneer lines between maple and colored veneer stitched rings above and below.

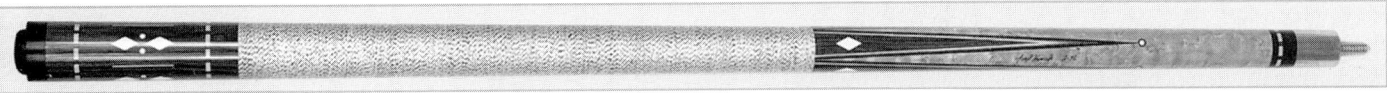

| MSR (1999) $1,600 | $2,800 | $2,375 | $1,875 |

Level 4 - Bird's-eye maple forearm, four ebony points with four colored veneers and an ivory spearhead-shaped inlay in each and an ebony bordered ivory dot at the tip of each, ebony butt sleeve with four patterns of a long intricate dished ivory diamond-shaped inlays within a pair of horizontal ivory dots alternating with four ivory lines between maple and colored veneer stitched rings above and below.

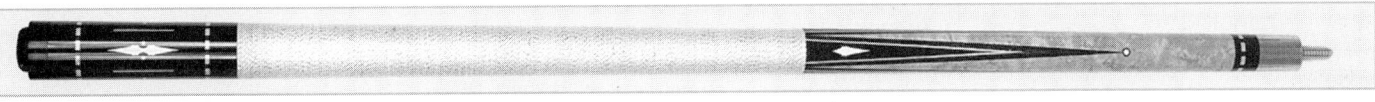

| MSR (1999) $1,700 | $2,900 | $1,475 | $1,975 |

Level 5 - Ivory joint, bird's-eye maple forearm, four cocobolo points with four colored veneers and a pattern of a veneer line within a pair of horizontal ivory dots in each, cocobolo butt sleeve with four patterns of vertical pairs of ivory diamond-shaped inlays and a pair of horizontal ivory dots alternating with four veneer lines between maple and colored veneer stitched rings above and below, ivory butt cap.

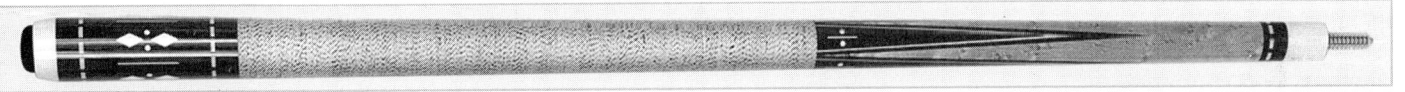

| MSR (1999) $2,000 | $3,250 | $2,775 | $2,250 |

Level 4 - Ivory joint, curly maple forearm, four ebony points with four colored veneers and an ivory diamond-shaped inlay in each, ebony butt sleeve with four patterns of vertical pairs of ivory diamond-shaped inlays and a pair of horizontal ivory dots alternating with four veneer lines between ebony and ivory checks within silver rings above and below.

| MSR (1999) $1,900 | $2,950 | $2,600 | $2,200 |

Level 6 - Fiddleback nose with eight ebony points, four long and four short. Long points have double black with white veneers. The short points are solid ebony. Ivory spears bordered in ebony above the points. Ivory diamonds in each long point with a turquoise diamond in each short point. Ebony butt sleeve with ivory tusk design with turquoise and ivory diamond accents. Ivory and turquoise trim rings, linen wrap. Ivory joint and butt cap. Only two eight-prongs have been build to date.

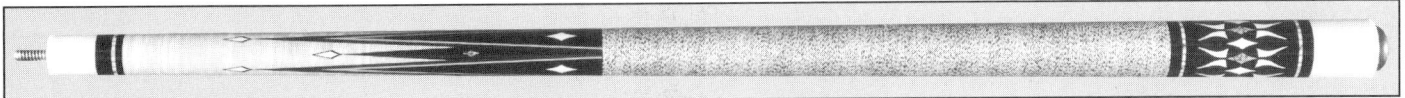

| MSR (2002) $7,000 | $10,500 | $9,250 | $7,500 |

Level 8 - Ebony forearm with long ivory-shaped vines with floral patterns. Ivory pillars with ivory-engraved ovals complete the nose. Three sleeves of ivory make up the handle. The top and bottom handle sleeve has pillar engravings with a wrap-around vine and twin sisters peering at each other. The middle sleeve has the prophet Joel with the Delphic Sibyl and the Erythraean Sibyl engraved into the ivory. The ebony butt sleeve is inlaid with ivory pillars with a different putto between each pillar. Between the putti are ivory-engraved ovals with ivory pillars above and below. The cue is finished off with ivory butt cap, joint and trim rings.

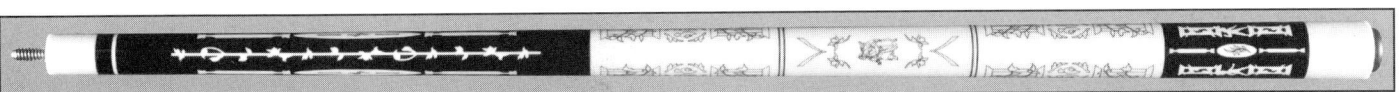

| MSR (2002) $18,000 | $30,000 | $26,000 | $20,000 |

SECONDARY MARKET MINIMUM VALUES

The following are minimum prices for other Hercek cues encountered on the secondary market. These prices are representative of cues utilizing basic materials and designs that may not be currently available. Joel also offers one-of-a-kind cues that can command many times these prices due to the use of exotic materials and artistry.

Special construction note: There are many materials and construction techniques that can add value to Hercek cues. Engraved Ivory handle can add up to $20,000 or more to the price of the cue. Ebony and other exotic wood noses can add up to $3000+ to the price of a cue. Gold inlays can add $5000 and up to the price of the cue. All cues are guaranteed indefinitely against construction defects that are not a result of warpage or abuse.

For all used Hercek cues, except where otherwise noted:

GRADING	98%	90%	70%

Add $200+ for each additional original straight playable shaft (standard with two).
Deduct $200 for each missing original straight playable shaft.
Add $250+ for ivory joint.
Add $400+ for ivory butt cap.
Add $250+ for leather wrap.
Add $50+ for each ivory ferrule.
Deduct up to 20% for obvious or improper refinish.

Level 3 - 2-6 points, 0-8 inlays.

Level 3 cues start at	$2,000	$1,650	$1,200

Level 4 - 4-10 points, 9-25 inlays.

Level 4 cues start at	$4,000	$3,300	$2,500

Level 5 - 0-12 points, 26-50 inlays.

Level 5 cues start at	$5,500	$5,225	$4,950

Level 6 - 0-12 points, 51-75 inlays.

Level 6 cues start at	$7,000	$6,650	$6,300

Level 7 - 0-12 points, 76-125 inlays.

Level 7 cues start at	$10,500	$9,500	$8,100

Level 8 - 0-12 points, 126+ inlays.

Level 8 cues start at	$13,000	$12,350	$11,700

HICKS STICKS

Maker of pool cues from 1981 to present in Stronghurst, Illinois.

Jeff Hicks has played pool since he was a young boy. His father, Wayne Hicks, was a player and pool room owner. Jeff started doing minor cue and table repairs in his father's room in the seventies. He made his first cue in his high school shop class. Jeff slowly acquired the equipment necessary for working on cues and did repairs as a hobby. When a divorce left him a single parent, he decided to make cues full-time as a means of staying home with his kids. He started Hicks Sticks from his home in Stronghurst, Illinois, in 1981. With the help of his father and some of the local players from the pool room, Jeff started to experiment with design and construction techniques in pursuit of the perfect playing cue. Early Hicks cues had brass 3/8-10 screws that Jeff made himself, and were stamped "Hicks Sticks." In 1988, Jeff started using stainless steel screws and changed the stamp to "H.S." All Hicks cues have been signed on the forearm since 1993. Currently, Jeff is concentrating on cue and table repairs and is not making as many cues as he has in the past

Hicks cues are guaranteed indefinitely against construction defects that are not the result of warpage or abuse. If you have a Hicks cue that needs further identification or repair, or would like to talk to Jeff about ordering a new Hicks cue, contact Hicks Sticks, listed in the Trademark Index.

Jeff Hicks

SPECIFICATIONS

Butt material: hardwoods
Shaft material: rock maple
Standard length: 58 in.
Lengths available: any
Standard finish: enamel clear coat
Joint screw: 3/8-10
Standard joint: linen phenolic
Joint type: flat faced
Balance point: custom
Point construction: short spliced
Standard wrap: Irish linen
Standard butt cap: linen phenolic
Standard no. of shafts: one
Standard taper: 10-1/2 in. pro
Standard ferrules: linen phenolic
Standard tip: Le Pro
Tip widths available: any

SECONDARY MARKET MINIMUM VALUES

The following are minimum prices for Hicks cues encountered on the secondary market. These prices are representative of cues utilizing basic materials and designs that may not be currently available. Jeff also offers one-of-a-kind cues that can command many times these prices due to the use of exotic materials and artistry.

HICKS STICKS, cont. 347

GRADING	98%	90%	70%

Special construction note: There are many materials and construction techniques that can add value to Hicks cues.
For all used Hicks cues:
- Add $60+ for each additional original straight playable shaft beyond one.
- Deduct $75 for missing original straight playable shaft.
- Deduct 25% for obvious or improper refinish.

Level 1 - 4 points, hustler.
Level 1 cues start at	$150	$120	$85

Level 2 - 0 points, 0-25 inlays.
Level 2 cues start at	$200	$155	$105

Level 3 - 2-6 points, 0-8 inlays.
Level 3 cues start at	$300	$235	$165

Level 4 - 4-10 points, 9-25 inlays.
Level 4 cues start at	$375	$295	$200

Level 5 - 0-12 points, 26-50 inlays.
Level 5 cues start at	$650	$515	$345

HIGHTOWER CUSTOM CUES

Maker of pool cues from 1988 to 1993 in Woodstock, Georgia, from 1993 to 2002 in Buffalo Missouri, and from 2002 to present in Aragon, Georgia.

Present Day

Chris Hightower began repairing cues in 1987. This led him into starting a cue sales and repair business, and got him the nickname "Cue Man." In 1988, Chris started modifying wood lathes into cue repair lathes and thus founded Cue Man Billiards. He set up at most of the pro tournaments in the Atlanta area, repairing and selling cues. He began building cues at that time. In 1989, Chris opened a pool room called Cue Man Billiards. In 1991, he used his cue building knowledge to develop the Cue Smith Lathe. At that point, the business really began to grow. Chris found out the drawbacks of building cues on wood and metal lathes and tried to eliminate the problems caused by using them. He has sold many hundreds of the Cue Smith Lathes and Inlay Machines since then.

Chris builds his cues with the same equipment he sells. He imports some of the highest quality exotic woods that can be found to use in his cues, and he supplies many other cue makers with their wood, as well as ivory, tooling, and other materials.

Some of Hightower Cue specialties are sterling silver stitch rings, ivory, abalone and turquoise inlays. His flat-faced 5/16 in. joint with phenolic or brass insert has given his cues a reputation for their solid feel and high action hit. He varies woods, inlay materials, and designs so that every cue he sells is a custom cue.

Chris sold his pool room in 1993, after moving to Buffalo, Missouri, where he started building lathes and cues full time. He moved his family and shop in 1999 to Goodson, Missouri, near Buffalo, and next to the church Chris ministered part time. In 2001, Chris authored the first edition of a complete "how to" cue building book entitled The Cue Building Book, From Tree to Tip to Tradeshow. In late 2002, Chris moved his family and business back to Georgia, settling in Aragon, a rural community. Today, Hightower Custom Cues and Cue Man Billiards is still a family business. Chris' son Isreal now makes up the other half of the Hightower Custom Cue building team.

Some early Hightower cues had no identification. From 1989 to 1992, they had eight "H's" inlaid in the joint ring. Then the cues were signed "Chightower" in the forearm. From 1994 to 2004, they have had a CH with the C going into the H in the butt plate. At present, they just have an H.

Hightower Custom Cues are guaranteed for life against manufacturing defects that are not the result of warpage or abuse. If you have a Hightower cue that needs further identification or repair, or would like to order a new cue, contact Hightower Custom Cues, listed in the Trademark Index.

SPECIFICATIONS

- Butt material: many exotic hardwoods
- Shaft material: maple
- Standard length: 58 in.
- Lengths available: any
- Standard finish: epoxy
- Balance point: approximately 18 in. from butt
- Standard butt cap: linen phenolic
- Standard wrap: Irish linen
- Point construction: short splice, full splice, or inlaid
- Standard joint: .850 in. diameter
- Joint type: flat faced
- Joint screw: 5/16-14 TPI
- Standard number of shafts: one
- Standard taper: 12 in. custom pro

GRADING	98%	90%	70%

Standard ferrules: white linen
Standard tip width: 13 mm
Standard tip: Triangle
Annual production: approximately 40 cues

OPTIONS (FOR NEW CUES ONLY)

Leather wrap: $75+
Special length: $50+
Ivory butt cap: $300+
Ivory joint: $200+
Custom joint protectors: $30+
Extra shaft: $150+
Ivory ferrule: $50
Ivory butt sleeve: $500+
Layered tip: $10+

REPAIRS

Repairs done on most fine cues.
Refinish (with linen wrap): $175+
Refinish (with leather wrap): $200+
Rewrap (Irish linen): $45+
Rewrap (leather): $95+
Rewrap lizard: $175+
Clean and press linen wrap: $20
Replace shaft: $150+
Replace ivory ferrule: $50
Replace tip: $10+
Replace fibre/linen ferrule: $25+
Replace butt cap: $50+ plus refinish
Replace ivory butt cap: $250+ plus refinish

CURRENT HIGHTOWER CUES

Basic two-piece Hightower cues with wraps and joint rings start at $500. Hightower cues with points start at $850. One-of-a-kind custom Hightower cues start at $1,000. The current delivery time for a Hightower custom cue is three to six months.

SECONDARY MARKET MINIMUM VALUES

The following are minimum values for Custom Cues encountered on the secondary market. These prices are representative of cues utilizing basic materials and designs that are not necessarily available at present. Chris has offered one-of-a-kind cues that can command many times these prices due to the use of exotic materials and artistry.

Special construction note: There are many materials and construction techniques that can add value to Hightower cues.

For all used Hightower cues, except where otherwise noted:
  Add $100 for each additional original straight playable shaft beyond two.
  Deduct $150 for each missing original straight playable shaft under two.
  Add $50 each for ivory ferrules.
  Add $65 for leather wrap.
  Deduct 25% for obvious or improper refinish.

Level 1 - 4 points, hustler.

	98%	90%	70%
Level 1 cues start at	$250	$195	$135

Level 2 - 0 points, 0-25 inlays.

Level 2 cues start at	$450	$350	$235

Level 3 - 2-6 points, 0-8 inlays.

Level 3 cues start at	$700	$545	$365

Level 4 - 4-10 points, 9-25 inlays.

Level 4 cues start at	$850	$675	$445

Level 5 - 0-12 points, 26-50 inlays.

Level 5 cues start at	$1,175	$925	$625

Level 6 - 0-12 points, 51-75 inlays.

Level 6 cues start at	$1,550	$1,225	$850

DAVID HODGES

Former maker of Parrot cues. For more information refer to Parrot Cue.

GRADING	98%	90%	70%

ORIE HOLMES CUSTOM CUES

Maker of pool cues from 1951 to 1994 in Baldwin Park, California.

Orie Holmes cues are identifiable by the letters "O.H." in the butt cap. If you have an Orie Holmes cue that needs further identification or repair, contact Wayne Custom Cues, listed in the Trademark Index.

SPECIFICATIONS

- Butt material: hardwoods
- Shaft material: rock maple
- Standard wrap: Irish linen
- Point construction: short splice

SECONDARY MARKET MINIMUM VALUES

The following are minimum values for other Orie Holmes cues encountered on the secondary market. These prices are representative of cues utilizing basic materials and designs that are not necessarily available at present. Orie Holmes has offered one-of-a-kind cues that can command many times these prices due to the use of exotic materials and artistry.

Special construction note: There are many materials and construction techniques that can add value to Orie Holmes cues.

For all used Orie Holmes cues, except where otherwise noted:

- Add $100 for each additional original straight playable shaft beyond one.
- Deduct $150 for missing original straight playable shaft.
- Add $65 each for ivory ferrules.
- Deduct 20% for obvious or improper refinish.

Level 2 - 0 points, 0-25 inlays.

Level 2 cues start at	$450	$350	$235

Level 3 - 2-6 points, 0-8 inlays.

Level 3 cues start at	$650	$510	$345

Level 4 - 4-10 points, 9-25 inlays.

Level 4 cues start at	$800	$625	$425

Level 5 - 0-12 points, 26-50 inlays.

Level 5 cues start at	$1,200	$945	$650

WAYNE HOLMES

Maker of Wayne Custom Cues. For more information, refer to Wayne Custom Cues.

VERL HORN CUES

Maker of pool cues from 1961 to 1999 in Mooreland, Oklahoma.

Verl Horn started playing snooker as a kid growing up in Oklahoma, becoming one of the better snooker players in the state. Then he joined the Army and fought in the infantry in the South Pacific during WWII. After returning from the war Verl opened an auto body shop and raised a family. He continued to play pool as a hobby. Verl could not find anyone locally to repair a cue for him, so he started doing repairs himself. By 1961, Verl made his first cue.

The first Verl Horn cues were identifiable by the name "-Horn-" branded into the butt caps. As time progressed, he improved his method of engraving his name into the butt caps. Early cues had green and white Irish linen wraps until the eighties when he started to use black and white Irish linen, which he stayed with. Cuemaking was a hobby for Verl until 1985, when he sold the auto body shop and began making cues full time.

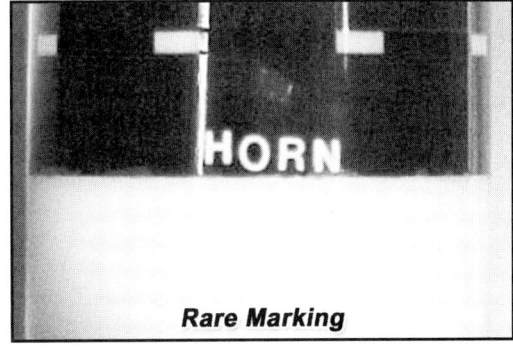

Rare Marking

Verl made fewer than 100 cues a year in his one-man shop in Mooreland, Oklahoma. He recently engraved the name "Horn" in gold on the third ring on the butt sleeve of his cues for identification. Verl was well known for applying Irish linen wraps that are very smooth and flush with the handles and butt sleeves of his cues. He loved making cues and was proud that he could play well with them. Verl died in May of 1999, after a long battle with cancer. He was 78 years old.

If you have a Verl Horn cue that needs further identification or repair, contact Prather Cues, listed in the Trademark Index.

SPECIFICATIONS

- Butt material: hardwoods
- Shaft material: rock maple
- Standard length: 58 in.
- Standard wrap: Irish linen
- Point construction: short splice
- Standard joint: ivory
- Joint type: flat faced

VERL HORN CUES, cont.

GRADING	98%	90%	70%

SECONDARY MARKET MINIMUM VALUES

The following are minimum prices for Verl Horn cues encountered on the secondary market. These prices are representative of cues utilizing basic materials and designs that were available. Verl also offered one-of-a-kind cues that can command many times these prices due to the use of exotic materials and artistry.

Special construction note: There are many materials and construction techniques that can add value to Verl Horn cues.

For all used Verl Horn cues:
- Add $125 for each additional original straight playable shaft beyond one.
- Deduct $175 for missing original straight playable shaft.
- Add $85 each for ivory ferrules.
- Deduct 25% for obvious or improper refinish.

Level 2 - 0 points, 0-25 inlays.

	98%	90%	70%
Level 2 cues start at	$700	$545	$365

Level 3 - 2-6 points, 0-8 inlays.

Level 3 cues start at	$1,000	$815	$600

Level 4 - 4-10 points, 9-25 inlays.

Level 4 cues start at	$1,400	$1,125	$800

Level 5 - 0-12 points, 26-50 inlays.

Level 5 cues start at	$2,000	$1,635	$1,200

HOWARD CUES

Maker of pool cues since 1989 in Bensenville, Illinois.

Bill Howard started playing pool at the age of seventeen. He learned woodworking as a commercial and residential contractor in the Chicago area, specializing in custom cabinets, room additions, and remodeling. Business was slow during the winters, and Bill would spend time in the machine shop in his basement. During the harsh winter of 1989, Bill decided to try making a pool cue. Starting with a 2 in. by 2 in. oak spindle, and some corian from a counter top, Bill made a four-point cue.

Since then, Bill constantly improved his design and construction methods in pursuit of the perfect playing cue. Bill experimented with several joint types, including wood screws. He settled on a 3/8-10 screw that he made himself. It is made of brass, with flat bottom threads for more wood contact, and a solid hit.

Bill made less than 20 cues a year, during the winters, in the basement of his Bensenville home. All of his cues are easily identifiable by the "BH" logo on the butt caps. Bill specialized in making one-of-a-kind cues to the designs and specifications of the individual customers. Diamonds, gold, sterling silver, and ivory were commonly used on Howard cues. All work was done by hand, and Bill made everything except for the bumpers and tips. Bill is believed to have retired from cuemaking a few years ago.

Bill Howard

SPECIFICATIONS

Butt material: hardwoods
Shaft material: rock maple
Standard length: 58 in.
Lengths available: any
Standard finish: two-part acrylic
Standard joint screw: 3/8-10
Standard joint: stainless steel
Standard joint type: flat faced
Balance point: 19 in. from butt
Point construction: inlaid and short spliced
Standard wrap: Irish linen
Standard butt cap: linen phenolic
Standard number of shafts: one
Standard taper: custom
Standard ferrules: fiber
Standard tip: Le Pro
Tip widths available: 10 to 14 mm
Total production: fewer than 250 cues

HOWARD CUES, cont. **351**

GRADING	98%	90%	70%

SECONDARY MARKET MINIMUM VALUES

Note: The following are minimum prices for Howard cues encountered on the secondary market. These prices are representative of cues utilizing basic materials and designs. Bill later specialized in one-of-a-kind cues that can command many times these prices due to the use of exotic materials and artistry.

Special construction note: There are many materials and construction techniques that can add value to Howard cues.

For all used Howard cues, except where otherwise noted:
- Add $100+ for each additional original straight playable shaft beyond one.
- Deduct $165 for missing original straight playable shaft.
- Deduct 30% for obvious or improper refinish.

	98%	90%	70%
Level 1 - 4 points, hustler.			
Level 1 cues start at	$250	$195	$140
Level 2 - 0 points, 0-25 inlays.			
Level 2 cues start at	$650	$520	$350
Level 3 - 2-6 points, 0-8 inlays.			
Level 3 cues start at	$800	$625	$435
Level 4 - 4-10 points, 9-25 inlays.			
Level 4 cues start at	$1,000	$815	$600
Level 5 - 0-12 points, 26-50 inlays.			
Level 5 cues start at	$1,650	$1,295	$850
Level 6 - 0-12 points, 51-75 inlays.			
Level 6 cues start at	$2,250	$1,785	$1,275

RICK HOWARD

Maker of Mace Custom Cues, for more information refer to Mace Custom Cues.

RICHARD HSU

Maker of RJH Cues. For more information, refer to RJH.

HUBBART CUES

Distributor of pool cues in the late seventies in Webster, New York.

Larry Hubbart was the 1977 World 8-Ball and 9-Ball champion. In the late seventies, he marketed a line of cues that were manufactured by Meucci Originals. Hubbart cues are easily identifiable by the Hubbart logo on the butt cap. Hubbart cues are now over 25 years old, and are fairly hard to find. They are being sought out by collectors of early Meucci cues, and fans of Larry Hubbart.

If you have a Hubbart cue that needs further identification or repair, contact Meucci Originals, listed in the Trademark Index.

SPECIFICATIONS

Butt material: hardwoods
Shaft material: rock maple
Standard length: 58 in.
Point construction: short splice
Standard joint: implex
Joint type: flat faced
Standard wrap: Irish linen
Standard butt cap: implex
Standard number of shafts: one
Standard tip width: 13 ¼ mm
Standard ferrules: synthetic
Standard tip: Le Pro

OPTIONS (FOR NEW CUES ONLY)

Flat-faced stainless steel joint

HUBBART CUES

The following cues are known examples of Hubbart cues.

For all used Hubbart cues, except where otherwise noted:
- Add $75 for each additional original straight playable shaft (standard with one).
- Deduct $100+ for missing original straight playable shaft.
- Add $150 for flat faced stainless steel joint.
- Deduct 30% for obvious or improper refinish.

HUBBART CUES, cont.

GRADING	98%	90%	70%

Level 2 LH-1 - Bird's-eye maple forearm, bird's-eye maple butt sleeve.

Original Retail (1977) $110	$325	$255	$170

Level 3 LH-2 - Bird's-eye maple forearm, two white points with three colored veneers, white butt sleeve with black and white checks within black rings at bottom.

Original Retail (1977) $125	$395	$305	$205

Level 2 LH-3 - Macassor ebony forearm, macassor ebony butt sleeve with a thick white ring inlaid with black rectangles over a black ring.

Original Retail (1977) $140	$450	$345	$235

Level 2 LH-4 - Vermilion forearm, four white points with two colored veneers, white butt sleeve with black and green barbell-shaped inlays alternating with black dots above black dashes within green rings.

Original Retail (1977) $170	$500	$395	$265

Level 2 LH-5 - Mayan rosewood forearm, four black points with two colored veneers, white butt sleeve with six black dots over black lines set in sunburst veneered windows between black chain links set in white rings above and below.

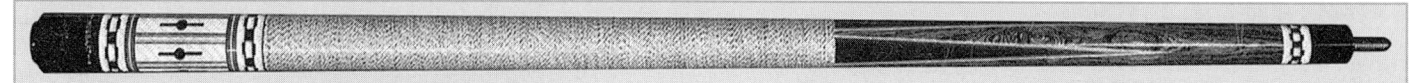

Original Retail (1977) $210	$600	$465	$320

HUEBLER INDUSTRIES, INC.

Maker of pool cues from 1974 to present in Linn, Missouri.

Paul Huebler comes from a family with a history of woodworking. Paul's grandfather was a cabinet maker in the Linn, Missouri area.

The youngest of eight children, Paul had an interest in billiards. Unfortunately, a serious auto accident at a young age kept him from becoming a player. However, it did not stop him from owning a room and sponsoring numerous tournaments.

Paul worked for the A.E. Schmidt Company, a manufacturer of billiard supplies in St. Louis, and became the national sales representative. He saw a market for quality cues, and started Huebler Industries in his home town of Linn, Missouri in the 1970s.

Huebler cues are usually marked on the butt cap. Those cues that are not marked are easily identifiable by a nylon insert in the shaft, which the joint screw threads into. Although several other cue manufacturers have switched to inlaid points, Huebler cues are still spliced. As Paul Huebler loves the game of chess, chess pieces have been common inlay themes. Various cross configurations are also common. Paul is proud that Huebler Industries makes all of the components that go into their cues. They even make the full splices for their hustler cues instead of just adding a joint to an existing one-piece, which allows them to offer these cues in rosewood or ebony.

Present Day

Now that Paul is in his late seventies he has slowed down production of Huebler cues. He sells only on his website and through established Huebler dealers. Paul is proud of the work of the cuemakers he has on his staff, many of whom have been working for him for many years. Paul still offers custom cues, and he personally overseas their construction. Huebler cues continues to sponsor the Valley National Youth Eight ball Tournament, which he has done for over fifteen years.

Huebler also sells a line of custom cases that range in price from $85 to $424.50. If you have a Huebler cue that needs repair, or would like to order a new cue, contact Huebler Industries Inc., listed in the Trademark Index.

HUEBLER INDUSTRIES, INC., cont. 353

GRADING	100%	95%	70%

SPECIFICATIONS
- Butt material: hardwoods
- Shaft material: rock maple
- Standard length: 58 in.
- Standard joint: stainless steel
- Joint type: flat faced
- Point construction: short splice and full splice
- Standard wrap: Irish linen
- Standard butt cap: white cyro
- Standard number of shafts: one
- Standard tip: Le Pro

OPTIONS (FOR NEW CUES ONLY)
Options prices available on a per cue basis.

REPAIRS
Repair prices available on a per-cue basis.

CURRENT HUEBLER CUES
Huebler cues now offers the "Mark V Laser Engraved Cues" which feature four point full splices and laser engraved butt sleeves, which are priced from $230 to $252. Also available are Huebler's "Anniversary Series Stained Maple" and "Anniversary Series Of The Hitters," which are shown following. One-of-a-kind custom cues by Paul Huebler start at $900. The current delivery time for a Huebler cue is a few weeks. One-of-a-kind custom Huebler cues take at least six weeks.

CURRENT EXAMPLES
The following cues are representations of the work of Huebler Industries, Inc. These cues can be ordered as shown, modified to suit the desires of the customer, or new designs can be created.

"STAINED MAPLE" SERIES
The following six cues all have had white synthetic joints in the past. Current examples have stainless steel joints.

Level 2 AS-E1 - Gold-stained maple forearm, gold-stained maple butt sleeve.

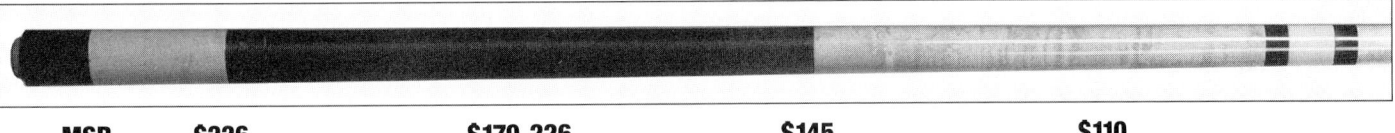

MSR	$226	$170-226	$145	$110

Level 2 AS-E2 - Red-stained maple forearm, red-stained maple butt sleeve with a black ring above butt cap.

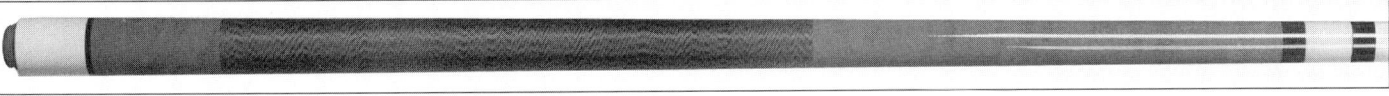

MSR	$233	$175-233	$150	$115

Level 2 AS-E3 - Emerald green-stained maple forearm, emerald green-stained maple butt sleeve with black and white rings above butt cap.

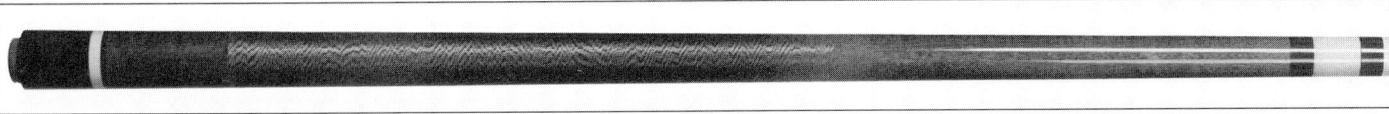

MSR	$240	$185-240	$155	$115

Level 2 AS-E4 - Sapphire blue-stained maple forearm, sapphire blue-stained maple butt sleeve with black and white rings above butt cap.

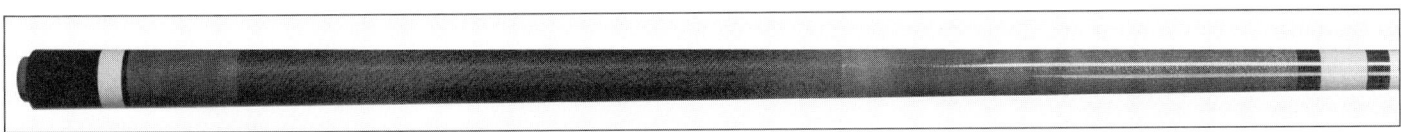

MSR	$246.50	$195-246.50	$165	$120

GRADING	100%	95%	70%

Level 2 AS-E5 - Brown-stained maple forearm, brown-stained maple butt sleeve with black and white rings above butt cap.

MSR	$253.50	$200-253.50	$165	$125

Level 2 AS-E6 - Grey-stained maple forearm, grey-stained maple butt sleeve with black and white rings above butt cap.

MSR	$260.50	$205-260.50	$170	$125

"ANNIVERSARY" SERIES

Level 1 AS-H1 - Maple forearm, dark hardwood points and butt sleeve (various hardwoods available).

MSR	$211	$160-211	$135	$105

Level 2 AS-H2 "Jump/Break Cue" - Hardwood forearm with quick-twist joint above wrap, hardwood butt sleeve (various hardwoods available).

MSR	$362.50	$285-362.50	$235	$175

Level 2 AS-H3 - One-piece hardwood butt (various hardwoods available).

MSR	$195.50	$155-195.50	$130	$95

Level 2 AS-H4 - Cocobolo forearm with maple and cocobolo checked rings above wrap and at joint, cocobolo butt sleeve with maple and cocobolo checked rings at top and bottom.

MSR	$417.50	$320-417.50	$270	$205

Level 3 AS-H5 - Maple forearm, four rosewood points with two colored veneers, butt sleeve of two large maple and two large rosewood windows with alternating maple and rosewood rings at top and bottom.

MSR	$577.50	$450-577.50	$375	$285

Level 3 AS-H6 - Maple forearm, four ebony points with two colored veneers, ebony butt sleeve with white/black/yellow stitched ring above butt cap.

MSR	$620.50	$485-620.50	$400	$300

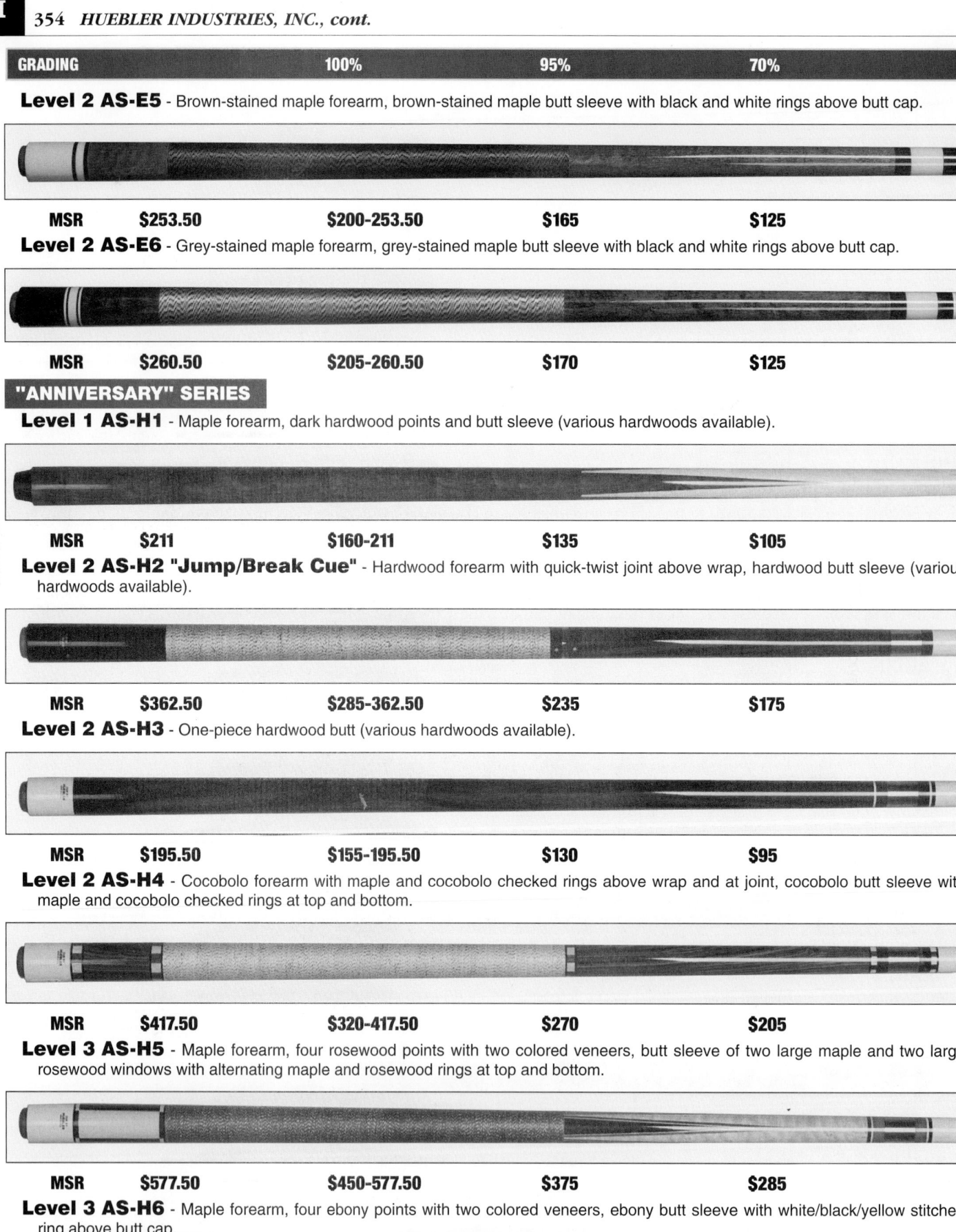

HUEBLER INDUSTRIES, INC., cont. 355

GRADING	100%	95%	70%

Level 3 AS-H7 - Maple forearm, four ebony points with four colored veneers, maple butt sleeve with four black-bordered red diamond-shaped inlays between red and black checked rings at top and bottom.

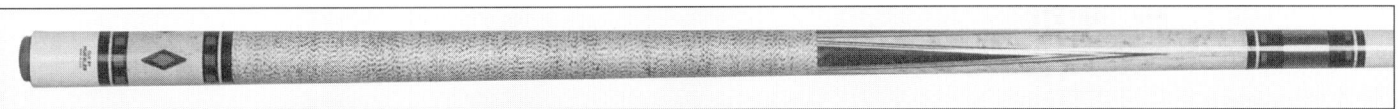

MSR	$707	$550-707	$455	$345

Level 3 AS-H8 - Maple forearm, four ebony points with four colored veneers and an ivory diamond-shaped inlay in each point, ebony butt sleeve with four ivory diamond-shaped inlays between red/black/white dash rings above and below.

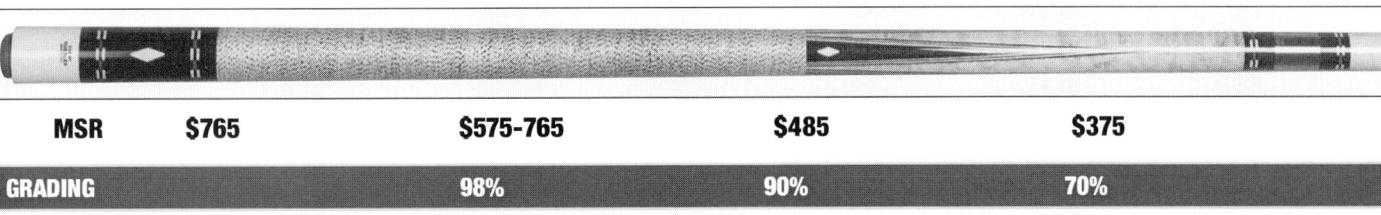

MSR	$765	$575-765	$485	$375

GRADING	98%	90%	70%

DISCONTINUED HUEBLER CUES

The following cues are from a custom line, circa 1980s. Extra shafts were available for these cues for $90.

Level 4 Custom #475 - Bird's-eye maple forearm, four ebony points with four colored veneers, ebony butt sleeve with six ebony inlays set in maple windows.

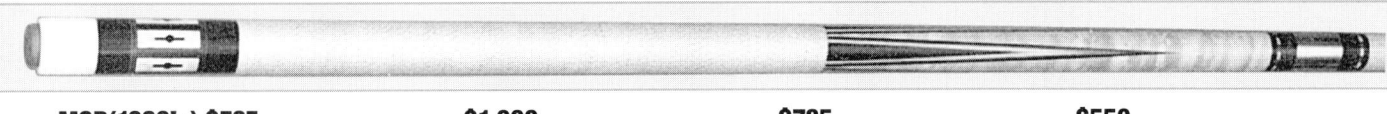

MSR(1980's) $525	$1,000	$785	$550

Level 4 Custom Arrow #50 - Bird's-eye maple forearm, four ebony points with four colored veneers and an ivory arrowhead-shaped inlay at the end of veneer inlays in each, ebony butt sleeve with opposing ivory arrowhead-shaped inlays at the ends of veneer inlays.

MSR(1980's) $550	$1,100	$875	$600

Level 4 Custom Diamond #550 - Bird's-eye maple forearm, four ebony points with four colored veneers and an ivory diamond-shaped inlay in each, ebony butt sleeve with ivory diamond-shaped inlays at the bottom of veneer inlays coming from top above a stitch ring at bottom.

MSR(1980's) $605	$1,260	$990	$650

Level 4 Custom Blue Ivory - Bird's-eye maple forearm with a stitch ring at bottom, four ebony points with four colored veneers and an ivory diamond-shaped inlay in each, ebony butt sleeve with ivory diamond-shaped inlays set in blue-stained maple windows alternating with ivory dots set in blue veneers within stitch rings at top and bottom.

MSR(1980's) $675	$1,500	$1,150	$775

Level 3 Cross #650 - Bird's-eye maple forearm, four ebony points with four colored veneers and an ivory cross-shaped inlay in each, ebony butt sleeve with four ivory cross-shaped inlays set in intricate blue windows.

MSR(1980's) $725	$1,650	$1,300	$850

GRADING	98%	90%	70%

Level 2 Custom Ivory Rectangle - Ebony forearm with floating ivory rectangles set in red veneer borders, ebony butt sleeve with ivory rectangles with red veneer borders set in red veneer framed ebony windows.

MSR(1980's) $800	$2,000	$1,560	$1,100

Level 4 Custom Teardrop #80 - Ebony forearm, four intricate ebony inlaid ivory teardrop-shaped floating points, ebony butt sleeve with four intricate ebony inlaid ivory teardrop-shaped inlays above stitched rings at bottom.

MSR(1980's) $900	$2,250	$1,750	$1,200

"FAST EDDIE PARKER SIGNATURE" SERIES

The following "Fast Eddie Parker Signature" Series cues came with one shaft. Extra shafts were available for $72 each for FE-1 through FE-3, and $82 each for FE-4 through FE-6.

Level 2 FE-1 - Cyro joint, gold-stained maple forearm with "Fast Eddie" below joint, gold-stained maple butt sleeve with a pair of ebony rings.

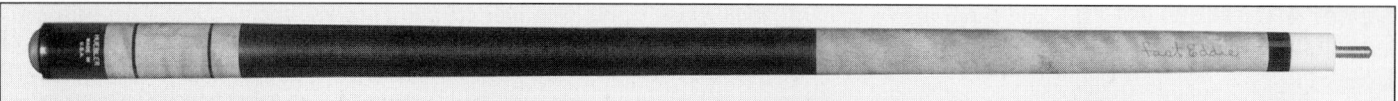

MSR (1999) $194.50	$175	$135	$90

Level 3 FE-2 - Maple forearm with "Fast Eddie" below joint, four ebony points, ebony butt sleeve with two alternative ivory rings.

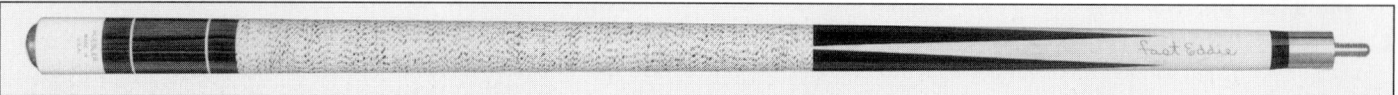

MSR (1999) $284.85	$245	$195	$135

Level 2 FE-3 - Maple forearm with "Fast Eddie" below joint and three floating ebony stylized chain link inlays, maple butt sleeve inlaid with three ebony stylized chain links.

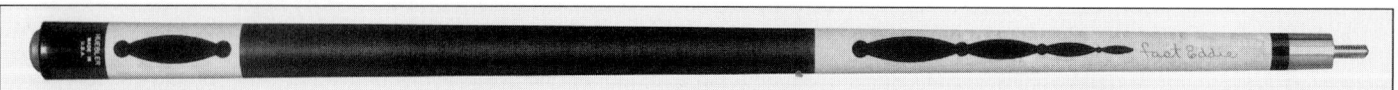

MSR (1999) $310	$275	$235	$145

Level 3 FE-4 - Maple forearm with "Fast Eddie" below joint, four tulipwood points with four colored veneers, tulipwood butt sleeve with two ebony rings.

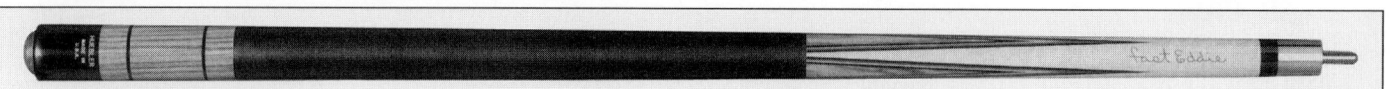

MSR (1999) $337.25	$285	$245	$155

Level 3 FE-5 - Sonokeling forearm with "Fast Eddie" below joint, four bird's-eye maple points with four colored veneers, bird's-eye maple butt sleeve with four redheart diamond-shaped inlays set in ebony ovals within three colored venners above and below and ebony rings at top and bottom.

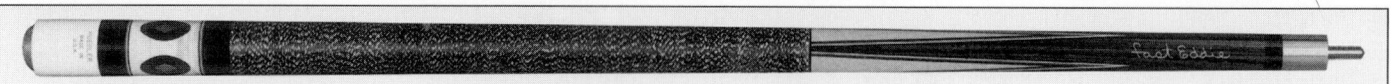

MSR (1999) $418	$360	$280	$185

Level 3 FE-6 - Ebony forearm with "Fast Eddie" below joint, two synthetic ivory split points hollowed in the "H" and eight ball designs, ebony butt sleeve inlaid with two synthetic ivory eight balls between two synthetic ivory rings.

MSR (1999) $496.85	$400	$315	$215

HUEBLER INDUSTRIES, INC., cont. 357

| GRADING | 98% | 90% | 70% |

"25TH ANNIVERSARY SILVER JUBILEE" SERIES

The following 25th Anniversary Silver Jubilee cues came with one shaft. Extra shafts were available for $72 each for SJ-1 and SJ-2, $77 each for SJ-3 and SJ-4, and $82 each for SJ-5 through SJ-7.

Level 2 SJ-1 - Stained maple forearm, stained maple butt sleeve with a silver ring at bottom, "Silver Jubilee 1995-1998" in black cyro butt cap, stain available in a variety of colors.

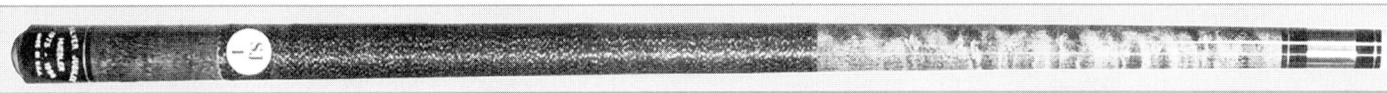

| MSR (1999) $200 | $185 | $145 | $95 |

Level 2 SJ-2 - Rosewood forearm, rosewood butt sleeve with black and white checks within silver rings at bottom, "Silver Jubilee 1995-1998" in black cyro butt cap.

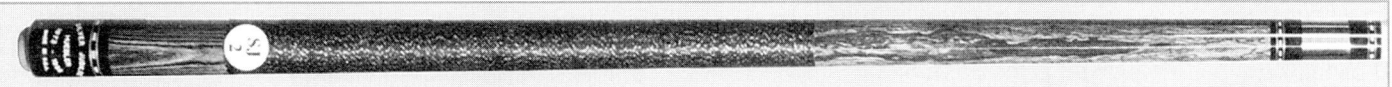

| MSR (1999) $224 | $200 | $155 | $105 |

Level 2 SJ-3 - Stained maple forearm, ebony butt sleeve with alternate ivory thin windows within silver rings at top and bottom, "Silver Jubilee 1995-1998" in white cyro butt cap, stain available in a variety of colors.

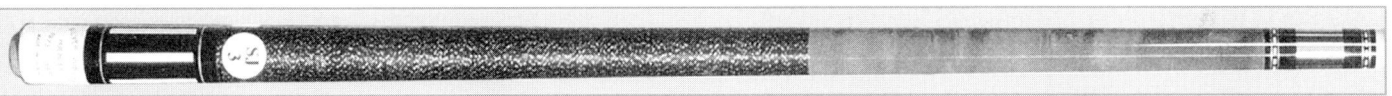

| MSR (1999) $260 | $230 | $180 | $120 |

Level 2 SJ-4 - Ebony colored forearm, ebony butt sleeve with large blue-stained maple oval shaped inlays alternating with alternate ivory columns, "Silver Jubilee 1995-1998" in black cyro butt cap.

| MSR (1999) $316 | $275 | $215 | $145 |

Level 3 SJ-5 - Stained maple forearm, four ebony points with three colored veneers, ebony butt sleeve with four alternate ivory bordered red-stained maple diamond-shaped inlays within black and red checks within silver rings at top and bottom, "Silver Jubilee 1995-1998" in white cyro butt cap.

| MSR (1999) $395 | $345 | $270 | $180 |

Level 3 SJ-6 - Rosewood forearm, four ebony-bordered redheart points with an ebony-bordered alternate ivory-shaped inlay in each, redheart butt sleeve with alternate ivory "25th" inlaid in palmwood within silver rings above and below, "Silver Jubilee 1995-1998" in black cyro butt cap.

| MSR (1999) $430 | $370 | $285 | $190 |

Level 3 SJ-7 - Ebony colored forearm, four ebony points with two colored veneers, ebony butt sleeve with alternate ivory-bordered ebony diamond-shaped inlays within tulipwood and silver pearlized plastic lace rings, "Silver Jubilee 1995-1998" in white cyro butt cap.

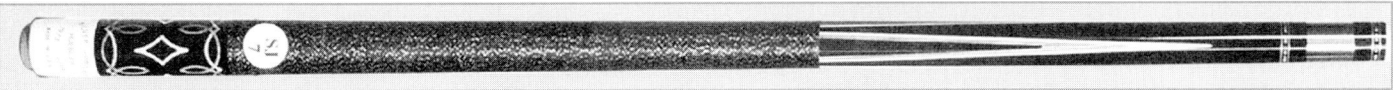

| MSR (1999) $550 | $500 | $390 | $260 |

"ELITE" SERIES

The following "Elite" Series cues came with one shaft. Extra shafts were available for $77 each for ES-1 through ES-3, and $82.00 each for ES-4 through ES-6.

GRADING	98%	90%	70%

Level 1 ES-1 - Maple forearm, stained bird's-eye maple points and butt sleeve each with a single ebony veneer.

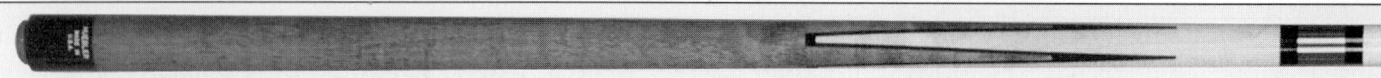

MSR (1999) $205	$180	$140	$95

Level 2 ES-2 - Stained bird's-eye maple forearm, ebony butt sleeve with four stained bird's-eye maple windows.

MSR (1999) $250	$215	$165	$110

Level 3 ES-3 - Maple forearm, four stained bird's-eye maple points each with a single veneer, stained bird's-eye maple butt sleeve.

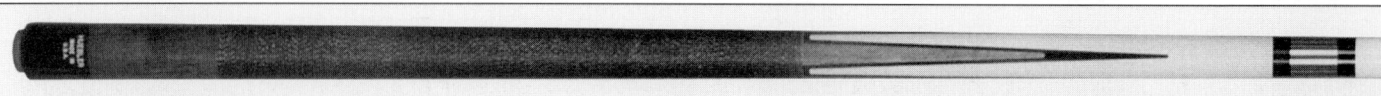

MSR (1999) $250	$215	$165	$110

Level 2 ES-4 - Stained bird's-eye maple forearm, stained bird's-eye maple butt sleeve with pearlized white squares set within an intricate ebony ring between pearlized white rings set in ebony at top and bottom.

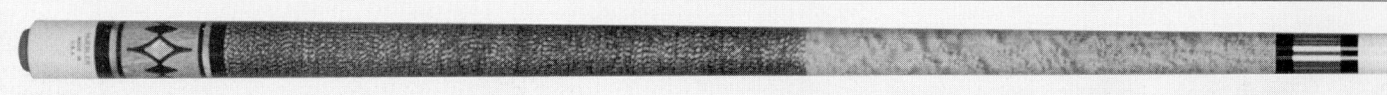

MSR (1999) $285	$245	$195	$130

Level 3 ES-5 - Stained bird's-eye maple forearm, four rosewood points each with a single ebony veneer, rosewood butt sleeve with a ring of maple squares set in ebony between stained bird's-eye maple and ebony rings above and below.

MSR (1999) $335	$295	$235	$160

Level 3 ES-6 - Stained bird's-eye maple forearm, four rosewood points each with a single ebony veneer and an ebony bordered pearlized white spear at the tip of each point, rosewood butt sleeve with a ring of maple squares set in ebony between stained bird's-eye maple and ebony rings above and below.

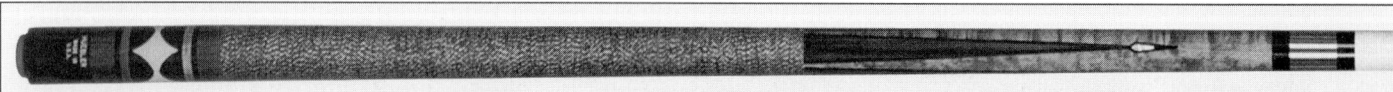

MSR (1999) $395	$350	$270	$185

THE JEAN BALUKAS SIGNATURE SERIES

Level 3 JB-1 - Bird's-eye maple forearm, four ebony points with four colored veneers, ebony butt sleeve.

MSR (1999) $300	$260	$210	$140

Level 3 JB-2 - Bird's-eye maple forearm, four redheart points with four colored veneers, redheart butt sleeve.

MSR (1999) $320	$275	$215	$145

Level 3 JB-3 - Macassor ebony forearm, four rosewood points with four colored veneers, rosewood and ebony checkered butt sleeve.

MSR (1999) $390	$350	$270	$185

GRADING	98%	90%	70%

Level 3 JB-4 - Macassor ebony forearm, four cocobolo points with four colored veneers, cocobolo butt sleeve with maple checks set in ebony between colored veneer rings at bottom.

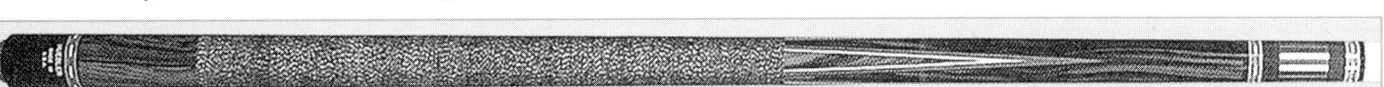

MSR (1999) $445	$400	$315	$215

"ANNIVERSARY" SERIES

The following "Anniversary" Series cues came with one shaft. Extra shafts were available for $70 each for AS-1 and AS-2, $77 each for AS-3 and AS-4, and $82 each for AS-5 and AS-6.

Level 2 AS-1 - Sonokoling forearm, sonokeling butt sleeve with two pearlized plastic rings above butt cap (available in a variety of other exotic hardwoods).

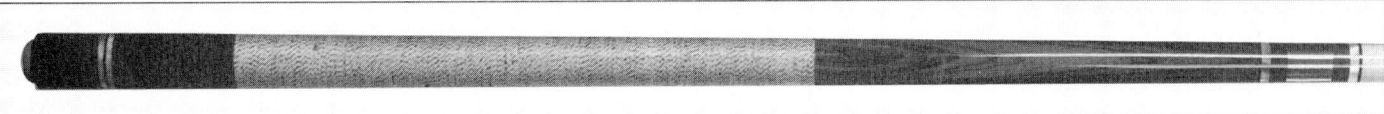

MSR (1999) $215	$185	$145	$95

Level 3 AS-2 - Maple forearm, four calon ebony points, calon ebony butt sleeve.

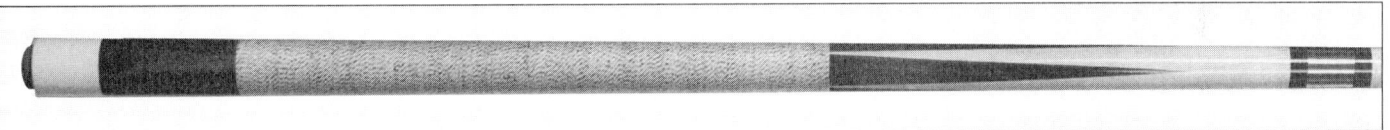

MSR (1999) $245	$210	$165	$110

Level 3 AS-3 - Maple forearm, four rosewood points with four colored veneers, cocobolo butt sleeve.

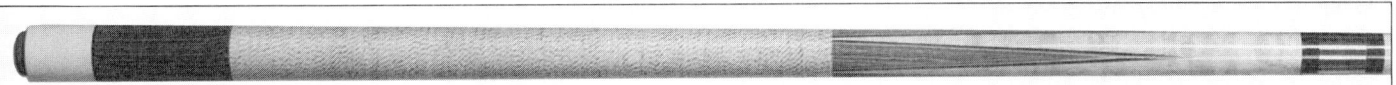

MSR (1999) $299	$270	$210	$145

Level 3 AS-4 The Iron Cross - Maple forearm, two ebony split points hollowed in an "H" and cross shape, maple butt sleeve with four ebony crosses.

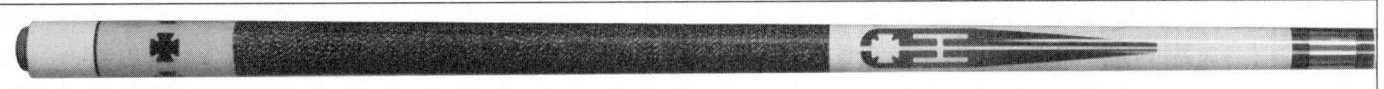

MSR (1999) $368	$320	$250	$170

Level 2 AS-5 Chain Point Front - Maple forearm with four floating ebony bordered red stylized chain link inlays, maple butt sleeve inlaid with four ebony-bordered red stylized chain links.

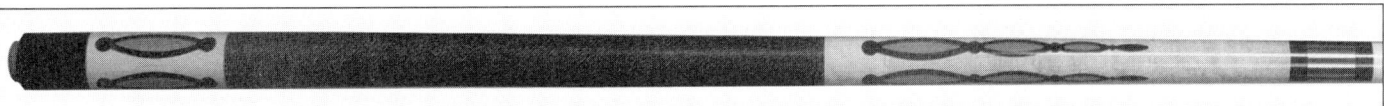

MSR (1999) $415	$360	$280	$185

Level 3 AS-6 - Ebony forearm, two synthetic ivory split points hollowed in the "H" and eight ball designs, ebony butt sleeve inlaid with two synthetic ivory eight balls.

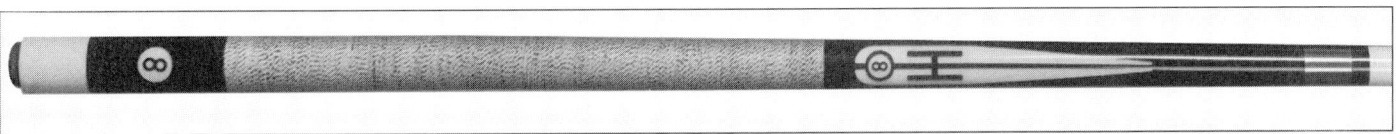

MSR (1999) $457	$400	$315	$215

"HS" SERIES

The following "HS" Series cues came with one shaft. Extra shafts were available for $77 each for HS-1 through HS-4, and $82 each for HS-5 and HS-6.

GRADING	98%	90%	70%

Level 3 HS-1 - Bird's-eye maple forearm, four redheart points with double black veneers, redheart butt sleeve.

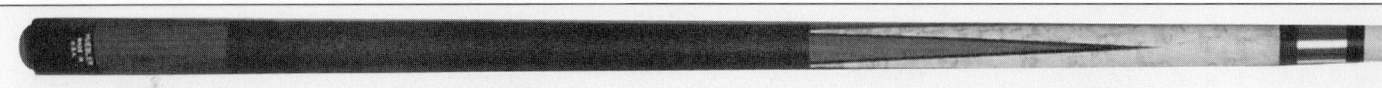

MSR (1999) $291	$260	$205	$145

Level 3 HS-2 - Bird's-eye maple forearm, four tulipwood points with four colored veneers, tulipwood butt sleeve.

MSR (1999) $299	$270	$215	$150

Level 3 HS-3 - Bird's-eye maple forearm, four ebony points with four colored veneers and an elongated ebony bordered blue diamond-shaped inlay at the end of each point, ebony butt sleeve.

MSR (1999) $368	$320	$250	$175

Level 3 HS-4 - Bird's-eye maple forearm, four ebony points with double black and triple blue veneers, ebony butt sleeve with maple/blue/ebony rings above butt cap.

MSR (1999) $389	$345	$275	$185

Level 3 HS-5 - Sonokeling forearm, four bird's-eye maple points with four colored veneers, bird's-eye maple butt sleeve with four redheart diamond-shaped inlays set in ebony ovals between black/red/white veneers and thick ebony rings at top and bottom.

MSR (1999) $393	$350	$280	$190

Level 3 HS-6 - Bird's-eye maple forearm, four redheart points with double black veneers, butt sleeve of a twelve-piece checkerboard pattern of African blackwood squares with a white diamond-shaped inlay in each and redheart squares with an ebony dot in each.

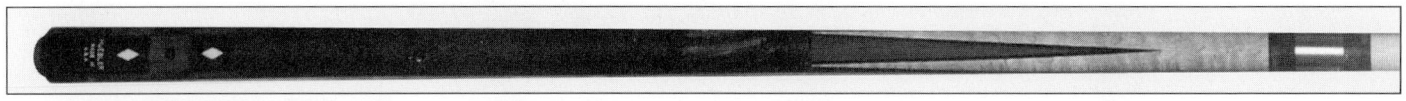

MSR (1999) $452	$405	$315	$215

HUEBLER CUSTOM SHOP

The following cues from the Huebler custom shop all came with two shafts with ivory ferrules, or buck horn ferrules where noted. They may still be custom ordered as shown, modified to suit the desires of the customer, or new designs can be created.

Level 4 Custom Chess Set - Bird's-eye maple forearm, four rosewood points with four colored veneers, bird's-eye maple butt sleeve with four chess pieces inlaid in ebony, tulipwood, pau ferro and cocobolo above a chess board ring design.

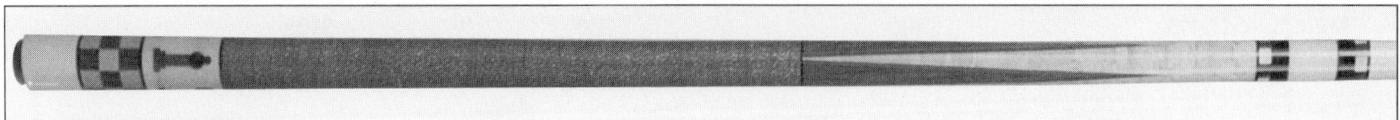

MSR (1999) $810	$750	$585	$400

Level 4 Custom Ebony - Bird's-eye maple forearm, four ebony points with four colored veneers, ebony butt sleeve with cross patterned inlays of tulipwood and Brazilian rosewood.

MSR (1999) $818	$760	$595	$405

GRADING	98%	90%	70%

Level 4 Custom Floral - African blackwood forearm, four fiddle back maple points with four colored veneers, fiddle back maple butt sleeve with an ivory and red veneer floral design inlaid in a thick ring of African blackwood.

MSR (1999) $888	$825	$645	$435

Level 4 Custom Ivory Queen - Bird's-eye maple forearm, four ebony points with four colored veneers and an ivory diamond-shaped inlay in each point, ebony butt sleeve with four maple windows with ivory dots at each corner and ivory diamond shapes set in ebony ovals in each.

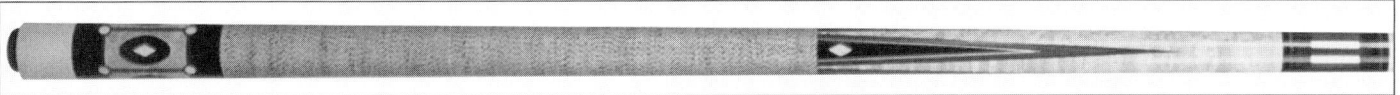

MSR (1999) $1,092	$950	$735	$490

Level 4 Custom Ebony King - Bird's-eye maple forearm with ivory joint, three long and three short ebony points with an ivory diamond-shaped inlay in each, ebony butt sleeve with six maple-bordered ebony windows inlaid with alternating ivory diamond shapes and long ivory hexagons pierced by red veneers at top and bottom.

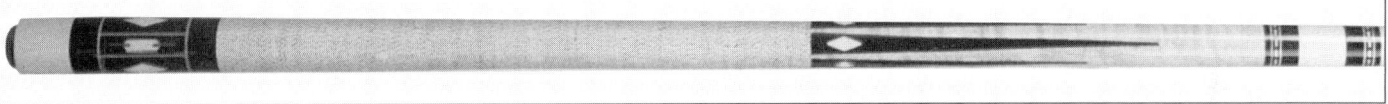

MSR (1999) $1,326	$1,200	$885	$700

Level 6 Custom Lacewood - Bird's-eye maple forearm with buckhorn joint and black leather wrap, two floating points of ebony and lacewood inlaid in a twist design, bird's-eye maple butt sleeve with two intricate ebony and lacewood inlays between rings of ebony and lacewood inlaid in a twist design above and below. (Comes with buckhorn ferrules instead of ivory.)

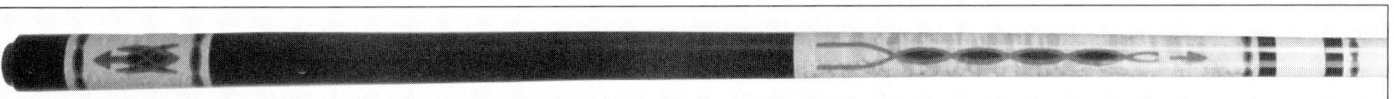

MSR (1999) $2,300	$2,000	$1,610	$1,175

Level 4 Custom Blue Mammoth - Bird's-eye maple forearm with colored dash ring between black trim rings above wrap, four ebony points with four colored veneers and a mammoth ivory triangle inlaid in each point, ebony butt sleeve with four mammoth ivory diamond-shaped inlays set in ovals of blue pearlized plastic with colored dash rings and black trim rings at top and bottom.

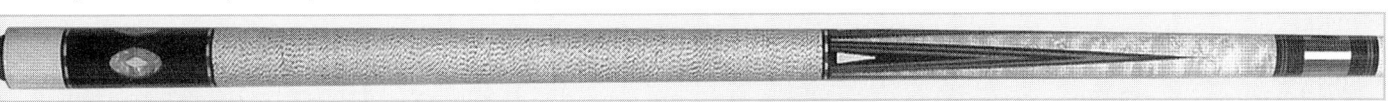

MSR (1999) $820	$775	$595	$400

Level 4 Custom Tulip - Fiddle-back maple forearm, four tulipwood points with single ebony veneers and an ebony-bordered ivory diamond-shaped inlay in each point, tulipwood butt sleeve with four ivory diamond-shaped inlays set in intricate ebony windows.

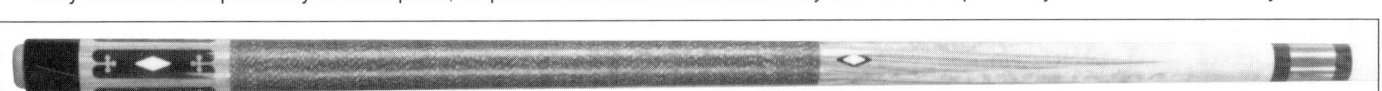

MSR (1999) $740	$700	$535	$360

Level 2 Custom Birdseye - Bird's-eye maple forearm with ivory joint and black leather wrap, bird's-eye maple butt sleeve with two rosewood inlaid cross patterns above a series of thin red and black trim rings.

MSR (1999) $690	$650	$505	$345

Level 4 Custom Rose - Bird's-eye maple forearm, four ebony points with four colored veneers, ebony butt sleeve with four green and red rose inlays set in intricate maple windows between maple dash rings at top and bottom.

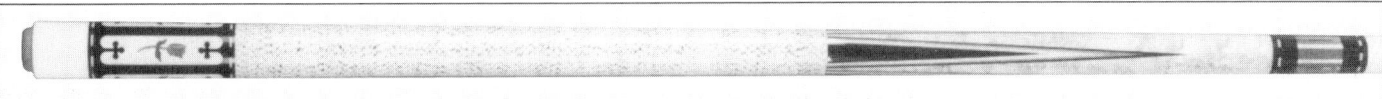

MSR (1999) $1,060	$950	$735	$490

| GRADING | 98% | 90% | 70% |

Level 4 Custom Ivory Cards - Bird's-eye maple forearm with maple dash rings above wrap, four ebony-bordered ivory points, ebony butt sleeve with symbols of four card suites each set in an ivory oval between opposing ivory triangles and maple dash rings at top and bottom.

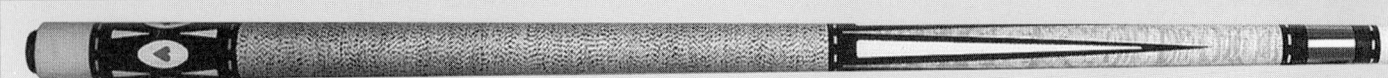

| MSR (1999) $1,600 | $1,450 | $1,150 | $750 |

Level 5 Custom U.S. Open - Bird's-eye maple forearm with buckhorn joint and black leather wrap with check rings of Brazilian rosewood and maple above wrap, four Brazilian rosewood points with intricate checked maple and Brazilian rosewood veneers, butt sleeve of intricate checked maple and Brazilian rosewood bordered maple and rosewood windows inlaid with alternating crosses and ivory patterns, ivory butt cap. (This cue has buckhorn ferrules instead of ivory.)

| MSR (1999) $1,980 | $1,775 | $1,400 | $950 |

Level 4 Custom Warrior - Forearm with redheart and maple rings above wrap, four floating ebony-bordered redheart points with ivory diamond-shaped inlays in the base of each point, butt sleeve with four small ivory diamond-shaped inlays each set in intricate redheart patterns inlaid in a thick ebony ring between rings of redheart and maple.

| MSR (1999) $898 | $800 | $615 | $425 |

Level 6 Custom Ivory Twist - Ebony forearm, two floating points of synthetic ivory-bordered ebony in a twist pattern, ebony butt sleeve with six inlays of synthetic ivory-bordered ebony in twist patterns between synthetic ivory-bordered ebony ovals in a ring pattern above and below.

| MSR (1999) $1,142.50 | $1,050 | $820 | $550 |

Level 4 Custom Ebony Spire - Bird's-eye maple forearm with an ebony geometrically patterned ring above wrap, six floating ebony points with an ivory diamond-shaped inlay below an ivory dot in each point, bird's-eye maple butt sleeve with six ebony rectangles each with two ivory diamond-shaped inlays above an ebony ring at bottom.

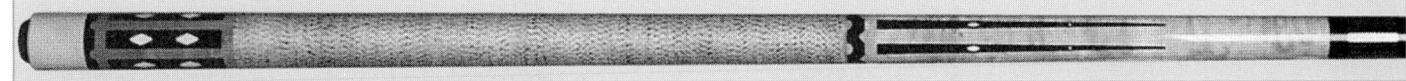

| MSR (1999) $1,195 | $1,000 | $765 | $525 |

Level 4 Custom Ebony Twist - Bird's-eye maple forearm, two floating points of ebony-bordered synthetic ivory in a twist pattern, bird's-eye maple butt sleeve with six inlays of ebony-bordered synthetic ivory in twist patterns between ebony-bordered synthetic ivory ovals in a ring pattern above and below.

| MSR (1999) $1,240 | $1,100 | $865 | $600 |

Level 4 Custom Crusader - Bird's-eye maple forearm, four ebony points with inlays of swords, shields and crosses, maple butt sleeve with pearlized plastic crosses set in ebony bordered redheart shields between ebony bordered redheart rings inlaid with ebony linked ovals at top and bottom.

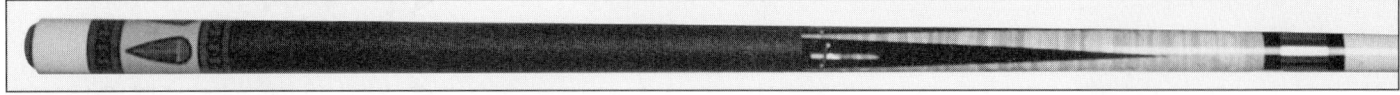

| MSR $1,320 | $1,150 | $920 | $645 |

GRADING	98%	90%	70%

SECONDARY MARKET MINIMUM VALUES

The following are minimum prices for other Huebler cues encountered on the secondary market. These prices are representative of cues utilizing basic materials and designs that are not currently available. Huebler also offers one-of-a-kind cues that can command many times these prices due to the use of exotic materials and artistry. Early models and limited editions are becoming collectible, and can also command many times these prices.

Special construction note: There are many materials and construction techniques that can add value to Huebler cues. The following are the most important examples:

- Add 400%+ for ivory inlaid custom cues by Paul Huebler.
- Add $500+ for ivory points.

For all used Huebler cues, unless otherwise noted:

- Add $75+ for each additional original straight playable shaft (standard with one).
- Deduct $90+ for missing original straight playable shaft.
- Add $50+each for ivory ferrules.
- Add $40+each for buckhorn ferrules.
- Deduct 20% for obvious or improper refinish.

	98%	90%	70%
Level 1 - 4 points, hustler.			
Level 1 cues start at	$135	$105	$70
Level 2 - 0 points, 0-25 inlays.			
Level 2 cues start at	$175	$135	$90
Level 3 - 2-6 points, 0-8 inlays.			
Level 3 cues start at	$255	$200	$135
Level 4 - 4-10 points, 9-25 inlays.			
Level 4 cues start at	$375	$290	$190
Level 5 - 0-12 points, 26-50 inlays.			
Level 5 cues start at	$600	$485	$325
Level 6 - 0-12 points, 51-75 inlays.			
Level 6 cues start at	$950	$735	$495

BILL HUGHES

Maker of Goldenrod pool cues in Lincoln, Illinois.

If you have a Goldenrod cue that needs further identification or repair, or would like to talk to Bill about ordering a new Goldenrod cue, contact Goldenrod Cues, listed in the Trademark Index.

HUNTER CLASSICS CUSTOM CUES

Maker of pool cues from 1989 to present in Alamagordo, New Mexico.

Wes Hunter has been playing pool since he was a kid. He has been in the construction business for years, specializing in custom wood and trim work. One day, he decided to open up a pool room on the side. After studying the new cues he was selling in his room, Wes decided that he could make cues as good or better than what he was selling. He soon started Hunter Classics Custom Cues, where he makes Hunter cues in his one-man shop to this day.

Hunter cues are easily identifiable by the "HC" logo on the butt sleeves. All cues, except for the hustler cues Wes makes, also have a serial number next to the logo. Wes likes his cues to have a different look, so he likes to make three-, five-, and six-point cues, with five points being the most popular. Although Wes does CNC inlay work, he prefers the sharpness and construction of spliced points. He stresses playability over cosmetics when crafting his cues. In 1996, Wes switched from a 3/8-10 joint screw to a 3/8-8 screw which he has custom made for him. A piloted stainless steel 5/16-14 joint is also available.

Present Day

Wes Hunter

HUNTER CLASSICS

| GRADING | 98% | 90% | 70% |

Wes uses a Uni-Loc joint above the wrap on his jump break cues and will use the Uni-Loc on the joint if the customer prefers.

Hunter cues are guaranteed indefinitely against construction defects that are not the result of warpage or abuse. If you have a Hunter cue that needs further identification or repair, or would like to talk to Wes about ordering a new Hunter cue, contact Hunter Classics Custom Cues, listed in the Trademark Index.

SPECIFICATIONS

Butt material: hardwoods
Shaft material: rock maple
Standard length: 58 in.
Lengths available: any
Standard finish: synthetic
Joint screw: 3/8-8
Standard joint: linen phenolic
Joint type: flat faced
Balance point: 1 1/2 in. above wrap
Point construction: short splice
Standard wrap: Irish linen
Standard butt cap: linen phenolic
Standard number of shafts: two
Standard taper: custom
Standard ferrules: linen phenolic
Standard tip: Triangle
Tip widths available: any up to 14 mm
Annual production: fewer than 100 cues

SECONDARY MARKET MINIMUM VALUES

The following are minimum prices for Hunter Classics cues encountered on the secondary market. These prices are representative of cues utilizing basic materials and designs that may not be currently available. Wes currently specializes in one-of-a-kind cues that can command many times these prices due to the use of exotic materials and artistry.

Special construction note: There are many materials and construction techniques that can add value to Hunter Classics cues.

For all used Hunter Classics cues:

Add $85+ for each additional original straight playable shaft beyond two.
Deduct $135 for each missing original straight playable shaft under two.
Deduct 20% for obvious or improper refinish.

	98%	90%	70%
Level 1 - 4 points, hustler.			
Level 1 cues start at	$300	$235	$165
Level 2 - 0 points, 0-25 inlays.			
Level 2 cues start at	$600	$460	$315
Level 3 - 2-6 points, 0-8 inlays.			
Level 3 cues start at	$850	$665	$445
Level 4 - 4-10 points, 9-25 inlays.			
Level 4 cues start at	$1,350	$1,050	$700
Level 5 - 0-12 points, 26-50 inlays.			
Level 5 cues start at	$1,950	$1,500	$1,000

HUNTER CUSTOM CUES

Maker of pool cues from 1992 to present in Carson City, Nevada.

Bobby Hunter is probably best known as the 1990 Straight Pool World Champion and as one of the top nine-ball players in the world. He fell in love with the game of pool as a teenager and was fascinated with the level of workmanship that went into the best custom cues of the day. At the age of nineteen, Bob traveled from his home town of Grand Rapids, Michigan to Brooklyn, New York to try to convince George Balabushka to build him a cue. He remembers George asking him about some of the players of the time such as Ritchie Ambrose and Jim Rempe. When George realized that Bob was a serious player, he agreed to make a cue for him.

Bob played on the road and in the occasional tournament throughout the 1970s. At a Burlington, Iowa tournament in 1974, he met cue maker Bill Stroud. He was impressed with the fine workmanship, and ended up ordering a Joss West cue from Bill. Bob played with Joss West cues for the next 18 years.

Bob decided to start doing some repair work on cues in 1980. He bought a lathe that was perfect for repairs but was not sufficient for making cues. After a short time, he closed his small shop to return to playing pool. In the eighties Bob was winning major tournaments leading up to his world championship victory in 1990.

HUNTER CUSTOM CUES, cont.

In 1992, Bob became interested in building cues again. He talked to Joe Gold (Cognoscenti), and decided to make cues on his own, and completed his first cue in 1992. Bob's first few cues were unmarked and about five had spliced points. Early cues had a screw above the wrap instead of the wood tenon he uses today. He constantly made improvements in design and construction, using his skill as a world class player to fine tune their playability. Bob developed some unique designs for floating points which have made his cues easily recognizable. In 1996, he started marking a stylized "H" on the butt caps.

Bob makes about 50 cues a year, by hand, in his one-man shop. He makes everything himself except for the tips, screws, and bumpers. Bob has won several tournaments with his cues, and even scored his high run with one (225 balls).

Hunter Custom Cues are guaranteed for life against manufacturing defects that are not the result of warpage or abuse. If you have a Bob Hunter cue that needs further identification or repair, or would like to order a new Bob Hunter cue, contact Hunter Custom Cues, listed in the Trademark Index.

SPECIFICATIONS

- Butt material: hardwoods
- Shaft material: maple
- Standard length: 57 1/2 in.
- Lengths available: any up to 60 in.
- Standard finish: Imron
- Balance point: 18 to 19 in. from butt
- Standard butt cap: linen phenolic
- Standard wrap: Irish linen
- Point construction: inlaid
- Standard joint: linen phenolic
- Joint type: flat faced
- Joint screw: 3/8-10
- Standard number of shafts: two
- Standard taper: custom
- Standard ferrules: ivory
- Standard tip width: 12.75 mm
- Standard tip: Le Pro
- Annual production: approximately 50 cues

OPTIONS (FOR NEW CUES ONLY)

- Leather wrap: $200
- Special length: $100
- Extra shaft: $275
- Ivory ferrule: no charge
- Ivory joint: $175
- Ivory butt cap: $375
- Layered tip: $30
- Steel joint: $50

REPAIRS

Certain Repairs done on select fine cues. Call for details.
- Refinish hunter cue (with Irish linen wrap): $300
- Rewrap (Irish linen): $50
- Clean and press linen wrap: $20
- Replace fiber/linen ferrule: $45
- Replace shaft: $275
- Replace ivory ferrule: $75
- Replace ivory butt cap: $375+
- Replace tip: $15
- Replace layered tip: $30

CURRENT HUNTER CUES

The current delivery time for a Hunter custom cue is about three months for most cues.

SECONDARY MARKET MINIMUM VALUES

The following are minimum values for Hunter Custom Cues encountered on the secondary market. These prices are representative of cues utilizing basic materials and designs that are not necessarily available at present. Bob has offered one-of-a-kind cues that can command many times these prices due to the use of exotic materials and artistry.

Special construction note: There are many materials and construction techniques that can add value to Bob Hunter cues. For all used cues, except where otherwise noted:

GRADING	98%	90%	70%

Add $150 for each additional original straight playable shaft beyond two.
Deduct $250 for each missing original straight playable shaft under two.
Add $150 for ivory joint.
Add $100 for leather wrap.
Deduct 25% for obvious or improper refinish.

	98%	90%	70%
Level 2 - 0 points, 0-25 inlays.			
Level 2 cues start at	$750	$575	$385
Level 3 - 2-6 points, 0-8 inlays.			
Level 3 cues start at	$1,000	$775	$520
Level 4 - 4-10 points, 9-25 inlays.			
Level 4 cues start at	$1,150	$895	$600
Level 5 - 0-12 points, 26-50 inlays.			
Level 5 cues start at	$1,450	$1,150	$750
Level 6 - 0-12 points, 51-75 inlays.			
Level 6 cues start at	$1,950	$1,495	$1,000

HURRICANE CUE CO.

Maker of pool cues since 1993 in Mount Pleasant, South Carolina.

James Spach was born in Illinois and grew up on a farm in Wisconsin. He had never even heard of pool until he joined the Navy in the early sixties. Working as a radio man, he played pool as often as he could. When he left the Navy, he settled in South Carolina and started servicing computers for NCR. James continued to play pool and also made custom furniture in his wood shop as a hobby. He was unable to find anyone that could do basic cue repair to his satisfaction, so he started doing his own. Soon, all of his pool-playing friends were asking him to do repairs for them, too. Before long he bought a lathe and, by 1980, he began making two-piece hustler cues out of one-piece house cues. His nickname was Whitey, and since these cues were unmarked, people started calling them Whitey Cues.

In 1988, after 23 years with the company, James left NCR to open a pool room and make hustler cues. James wanted to start making fancier cues, but he did not think Whitey was an appropriate name for the company. In 1993, he started the Hurricane Cue Company, named after the hurricanes that are common to South Carolina. James made fewer than 300 cues per year in his small shop with the help of two part-time workers. Most were jump/break cues. They made all components of the cues except for the tips, bumpers, and screws, with playability being the primary concern. James tried hard to keep the prices down, so ivory was never used. All Hurricane cues were marked with the Hurricane logo on the butt caps. A variety of designs, joint types, and specifications could be custom ordered. It is rumored that Hurricane is no longer in South Carolina.

James Spach

SPECIFICATIONS

Butt material: hardwoods
Shaft material: rock maple
Standard length: 58 in.
Lengths available: any
Standard finish: conversion varnish
Joint screw: 5/16-14
Standard joint: stainless steel
Joint type: flat faced
Balance point: custom
Point construction: short spliced or inlaid
Standard wrap: Irish linen
Standard butt cap: linen phenolic
Standard no. of shafts: one
Standard taper: 7 in. pro
Standard ferrules: Ivorine 3
Standard tip: Triangle
Tip widths available: any

SECONDARY MARKET MINIMUM VALUES

The following are minimum prices for Hurricane cues encountered on the secondary market. These prices are representative of cues utilizing basic materials and designs. James also offered one-of-a-kind cues that can command many times these prices due to the use of exotic materials and artistry.

Special construction note: There are many materials and construction techniques that can add value to Hurricane cues.

For all used Hurricane cues, except where otherwise noted:

GRADING	98%	90%	70%

Add $65+ for each additional original straight playable shaft beyond one.
Deduct $100 for missing original straight playable shaft.
Deduct 25% for obvious or improper refinish.

Level 1 - 4 points, hustler.

Level 1 cues start at	$150	$120	$80

Level 2 - 0 points, 0-25 inlays.

Level 2 cues start at	$240	$195	$130

Level 3 - 2-6 points, 0-8 inlays.

Level 3 cues start at	$275	$235	$145

Level 4 - 4-10 points, 9-25 inlays.

Level 4 cues start at	$350	$275	$185

Level 5 - 0-12 points, 26-50 inlays.

Level 5 cues start at	$550	$435	$290

Level 6 - 0-12 points, 51-75 inlays.

Level 6 cues start at	$850	$665	$445

MILT HYMAN

Maker of Miltonio Custom Cues. For more information, refer to Miltonio.

NOTES

I SECTION

IMPERIAL INTERNATIONAL

Distributor of Imperial pool cues in Hasbrouck Heights, New Jersey.

If you have an Imperial cue that needs further identification or repair, or would like to talk to someone about purchasing a new Imperial cue, contact Imperial International, listed in the Trademark Index.

INGRAM CUES

Maker of pool cues from 1975 to present in Oklahoma City, Oklahoma.

Jimmy Ingram began building cues in 1975 in Oklahoma City, Oklahoma. An army veteran, retired letter carrier, former drag racer, and great grandfather, Jimmy enjoys riding motorcycles and cheering for his team, the Sooners. Ingram has a Southbend lathe, made in August of 1936. His goal is now and always has been to build the best playing cue. Ingram Cues can be identified by the name "Ingram" in small letters branded between the points with a hot iron. Jimmy's work has been influenced by cue makers such as Balabushka, Szamboti and Horn. Jimmy prefers four point cues but sometimes makes five-, six-, or eight-point cues.

If you are interested in talking to Jimmy L. Ingram about a new cue or cue that needs to be repaired, you can contact him at Ingram Cues, listed in the Trademark Index.

SPECIFICATIONS

- Butt material: hardwoods
- Shaft material: maple
- Standard length: 58 in.
- Lengths available: any within reason
- Standard finish: catalyzed lacquer
- Balance point: approximately 17 in. from butt
- Standard butt cap: Delrin
- Standard wrap: Irish linen
- Point construction: short splice
- Standard joint: stainless steel
- Standard joint type: piloted
- Standard joint screw thread: 5/16-14
- Standard number of shafts: two
- Standard taper: .535 at midpoint
- Standard ferrules: linen base
- Standard tip: Triangle
- Standard tip width: 13 mm
- Tip widths available: 9 to 15 mm
- Annual production: fewer than 50 cues

OPTIONS (FOR NEW CUES ONLY)

- Special length: no charge
- Layered tip: no charge
- Ivory butt cap: $200
- Ivory joint: $125
- Ivory ferrule: $50
- Ivory points: $500
- Custom joint protectors: $50+
- Extra shaft: $150

REPAIRS

Repairs done on all fine cues.
- Refinish (with Irish linen wrap): $100
- Rewrap (Irish linen): $30
- Clean and press linen wrap: $15
- Replace shaft: $65+
- Replace ivory ferrule: $50
- Replace butt cap: $45
- Replace ivory butt cap: $200
- Replace tip: $10
- Replaced layered tip: $20+
- Replace fiber/linen ferrule: $20

CURRENT INGRAM CUES

Basic Ingram cues start at $500, with or without points. The current average delivery time for an Ingram Cue is about ten weeks.

GRADING	98%	90%	70%

SECONDARY MARKET MINIMUM VALUES

The following are minimum values for other Ingram cues encountered on the secondary market. These prices are representative of cues utilizing basic materials and designs that are not necessarily available at present. Jimmy has offered one-of-a-kind cues that can command many times these prices due to the use of exotic materials and artistry.

For special construction note: There are many materials and construction techniques that can add value to Ingram cues.

For all used Ingram cues, except where otherwise noted:
  Add $100 for each additional original straight playable shaft beyond two.
  Deduct $150 for each missing original straight playable shaft under two.
  Add $45 each for ivory ferrules.
  Deduct 20% for obvious or improper refinish.

Level 2 - 0 points, 0-25 inlays.

	98%	90%	70%
Level 2 cues start at	$400	$310	$210

Level 3 - 2-6 points, 0-8 inlays.

Level 3 cues start at	$450	$350	$235

Level 4 - 4-10 points, 9-25 inlays.

Level 4 cues start at	$525	$410	$275

Level 5 - 0-12 points, 26-50 inlays.

Level 5 cues start at	$700	$545	$375

IT'S GEORGE

Maker of pool cues from 1989 to 1998 in Shreveport, Louisiana.

Mike Roberts became involved in the billiard industry when he began making cue cases in the 1980s. He named the company for an old pool room expression from the 1920s: "It's George," was said to indicate that something was good, as opposed to, "It's Tom," which meant that something was bad.

After becoming successful in the cue case market, Mike knew he wanted to make cues next. Mike had one of the top cuemakers in the country help to set up his cuemaking operation, which started making cues in 1989. The cues were easily identifiable by the "It's George" logo on the but caps. The classic 5/16 in. piloted joint was standard on It's George cues, and a 3/8 in. flat-faced joint was also available. Shafts were interchangeable, so it was not necessary to send in the butt to replace them. In the mid-1990s, It's George introduced a new white linen phenolic for joints and ferrules, called I.V. Tech, which was more resistant to yellowing than other linen phenolics.

In 1997 Mike stopped making cues in order to concentrate on his case business. He made very few custom cues as a hobby until 1998.

SPECIFICATIONS

Butt material: hardwoods
Shaft material: rock maple
Standard length: 58 in.
Joint screw: 5/16-14
Joint type: piloted
Standard finish: polyurethane
Standard joint: stainless steel
Point construction: short splice
Balance point: 2 in. above wrap
Standard butt cap: Delrin
Standard wrap: Irish linen
Standard Ferrules: I.V. Tech

SECONDARY MARKET MINIMUM VALUES

The following are minimum prices for It's George cues encountered on the secondary market. These prices are representative of cues utilizing basic materials and designs. It's George also offered one-of-a-kind cues that can command many times these prices due to the use of exotic materials and artistry.

For special construction note: There are many materials and construction techniques that can add value to It's George cues.

For all used It's George cues, except where otherwise noted:
  Add $125+ for each additional original straight playable shaft beyond two.
  Deduct $175 for each missing original straight playable shaft under two.
  Deduct 25% for obvious or improper refinish.

Level 2 - 0 points, 0-25 inlays.

	98%	90%	70%
Level 2 cues start at	$500	$380	$255

Level 3 - 2-6 points, 0-8 inlays.

Level 3 cues start at	$750	$570	$385

Level 4 - 4-10 points, 9-25 inlays.

Level 4 cues start at	$1,150	$895	$600

Level 5 - 0-12 points, 26-50 inlays.

Level 5 cues start at	$1,650	$1,275	$850

J & J AMERICA

Distributor of pool cues from 1986 to present in Buena Park, California.

J & J cues are easily identifiable by the J & J logo that appears on the butt caps. If you have a J & J cue that needs repair, or would like to talk to someone about ordering a new J & J cue, contact J & J America, listed in the Trademark Index.

J & J AMERICA

SPECIFICATIONS

Butt material: hardwoods
Shaft material: rock maple
Standard length: 58 in.
Balance point: 9 to 10 in. from joint
Point construction: short splice
Standard wrap: nylon
Standard no. of shafts: one
Standard tip: Le Pro
Annual production: about 100,000

J & J CUES

J&J cues currently offer many cues ranging in price from $60 to $200. J&J Decal cues are $70. J&J jump/break cues start at $85. J&J also offers Kaiser cues for $200 and Panther cues for $300. Most J&J cues are available for immediate delivery.

GRADING	98%	90%	70%

SECONDARY MARKET MINIMUM VALUES

The following are minimum prices for J & J cues encountered on the secondary market.

Special construction note: There are many materials and construction techniques that can add value to J & J cues.

For all used J & J cues:

Add $25 for each additional original straight playable shaft beyond one.
Deduct 50% for missing original straight playable shaft.
Add $20 for Irish linen wrap.
Deduct 20% for obvious or improper refinish.

Level 2 - 0 points, 0-25 inlays.

Level 2 cues start at	$45	$35	$20

Level 3 - 2-6 points, 0-8 inlays.

Level 3 cues start at	$70	$55	$30

Level 4 - 4-10 points, 9-25 inlays.

Level 4 cues start at	$90	$70	$40

J.B. CUSTOM CUES

Maker of pool cues from 1988 to present in Lexington, Kentucky.

James Brumfield, an auto mechanic with a woodworking hobby, loved to play pool. He became friends with Leonard Bludworth while attending the pro tournaments in his home town of Lexington, Kentucky. This inspired him to combine his hobbies and start making pool cues.

James completed his first cue in 1988. He prefers making simple cues, with playability stressed as the most important factor. He turns the shafts on J.B. cues over a dozen times during the course of a year. Although Irish linen is available, he prefers to make cues with wood handles. Most J.B. cues have had identification marks, the first cues having "J.B. Cue" engraved on the forearms. In 1993, James started putting a 3/8 in. brass disc with the "J.B. Cue" logo on the butt caps. Other than that, the basic design has stayed primarily the same. In 1996, he switched from a lacquer finish to a much more durable synthetic finish. Today, James makes about a dozen cues a year by hand in his one-man shop part-time, while continuing to work as an auto mechanic full-time.

J.B. cues are guaranteed indefinitely against construction defects that are not the result of warpage or abuse. If you have a J.B. cue that needs further identification or repair, or would like to talk to James about ordering a new J.B. cue, contact J.B. Custom Cues, listed in the Trademark Index.

SPECIFICATIONS

Butt material: hardwoods
Shaft material: rock maple
Standard length: 58 in.
Lengths available: any
Standard finish: synthetic

J.B. CUSTOM CUES, cont.

GRADING	98%	90%	70%

Joint screw: 3/8-10 brass
Standard joint: linen phenolic
Joint type: flat faced
Balance point: varies
Point construction: butterfly splice
Standard wrap: Irish linen
Standard butt cap: linen phenolic
Standard number of shafts: one
Standard taper: 14 in. pro
Standard ferrules: Ivorine 3
Standard tip: Le Pro
Tip widths available: any
Annual production: fewer than 15 cues

SECONDARY MARKET MINIMUM VALUES

The following are minimum prices for J.B. cues encountered on the secondary market. These prices are representative of cues utilizing basic materials and designs that may not be currently available. James also offers one-of-a-kind cues that can command many times these prices due to the use of exotic materials and artistry.

Special construction note: There are many materials and construction techniques that can add value to J.B. cues.

For all used J.B. cues, except where otherwise noted:
Add $60+ for each additional original straight playable shaft beyond one.
Deduct $85 for missing original straight playable shaft.
Deduct 20% for obvious or improper refinish.

Level 1 - 4 points, hustler.

Level 1 cues start at	$150	$120	$80

Level 2 - 0 points, 0-25 inlays.

Level 2 cues start at	$250	$195	$135

Level 3 - 2-6 points, 0-8 inlays.

Level 3 cues start at	$385	$295	$195

Level 4 - 4-10 points, 9-25 inlays.

Level 4 cues start at	$600	$465	$315

JACKSON CUSTOM CUE

Maker of pool cues from 1992 to the present in several locations in Wisconsin.

Jackson Custom Cue was formed in 1992, when friends Tony Muesch and Mike Weyer joined forces to create a new cue for the billiard industry. Mike had spent 10+ years making cues at a large Wisconsin cue manufacturer. Tony was a well-known player in the area. Jackson Custom Cue started in the small town of Jackson, Wisconsin, thus the name of their company. They moved to West Bend, Wisconsin shortly after that, and remained there until July of 1997 when they moved to a larger 3,000 sq. ft. facility in Hartford, Wisconsin. In July 2001, Jackson Custom Cues moved one last time, to a 4800 sq. ft. building in Slinger, Wisconsin. The new facility provides greater visibility and room for a retail store.

In 1998, Jackson introduced a new 9/32-18 joint to replace the more familiar 5/16-14 joint. It is available in stainless steel or M.P. ivory substitute, and it allows all Jackson shafts of the same pin size to be interchangeable. In 2003, Jackson Cusom Cue reintroduced its interchangeable shaft feature in the original joint size 5/16-14.

Although Jackson Custom Cue only consists of two full-time cue makers/owners (Tony and Karen Muesch) and one part-time cue maker/owner (Mike Weyer), they can still produce about 400 cues a year, by hand, without the aid of computerized production machinery. They pick the best logs that are available from the sawmill to make their cues. Early Jackson Cues are easily identified by the vertical "J.C.C." logo within a rectangle on the butt caps. The current logo is more easily identified by the cursive

Tony Muesch

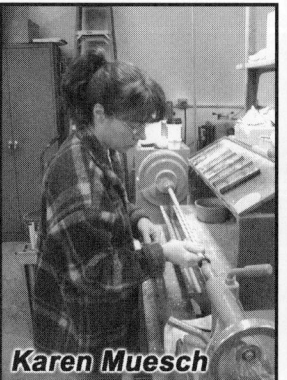
Karen Muesch

Mike Weyer

written "Jackson" in the butt cap. At the customer's request, the "Tony P. Muesch" signature in the forearm may be added. Jackson Custom Cues are guaranteed against construction defects that are not the result of warpage or abuse. If you have a Jackson Custom Cue that needs further identification or repair, or would like to talk to someone about ordering a new Jackson Custom Cue, contact Jackson Custom Cue, listed in the Trademark Index.

JACKSON CUSTOM CUE, cont.

GRADING	100%	95%	70%

SPECIFICATIONS
- Butt material: hardwoods
- Shaft material: rock maple
- Standard length: 58 in.
- Standard finish: two-part epoxy
- Joint screw: 5/16-14
- Standard joints: J.P. ivory substitute or stainless steel
- Joint type: flat faced
- Balance point: 1 1/2 in. above wrap
- Point construction: inlaid or spliced
- Standard wrap: Irish linen
- Standard butt cap: M.P. ivory substitute
- Standard number of shafts: one
- Standard taper: 8 in. pro
- Standard ferrules: Ivorine 3
- Standard tip: Le Pro
- Tip widths available: 11 to 15mm
- Annual production: about 400

OPTIONS (FOR NEW CUES ONLY)
- Leather wrap: $65
- Extra shaft: $75
- Custom joint protectors: $40
- Ivory joint: $140
- Ivory ferrule: $55
- Ivory butt cap: $230
- Black butt cap: $25
- Predator shaft: $175
- Predator 'z' shaft: $200

REPAIRS

Repairs done on all fine cues. Cues must be seen for an exact quote.
- Refinish (linen wrap): $150+
- Refinish (leather): $175
- Rewrap (linen): $55
- Rewrap (leather): $80
- Clean and press linen wrap: $25
- Replace shaft: $95+
- Replace ivory ferrule: $65
- Replace Le Pro tip: $12

CURRENT JACKSON CUES

Jackson manufactures a line of sixteen cues priced from $370 to $1,150. A basic two-piece hustler cue with a butt cap and stainless steel joint is $275. One-of-a-kind custom Jackson cues start at $450. The current average delivery time for a Jackson Custom Cue is three to twelve weeks, depending on the design of the cue.

CURRENT EXAMPLES

The following Jackson cues can be ordered as shown, modified to suit the desires of the customer, or new designs can be created.

Level 2 - Cocobolo forearm with tulipwood/maple/ebony rings set in nickel silver rings above wrap, cocobolo butt sleeve with tulipwood/maple/ebony rings set in nickel silver rings at top and bottom.

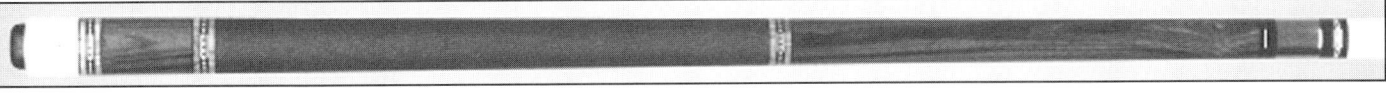

MSR	$650	$550-650	$440	$325

Level 3 - Bird's-eye maple forearm, four ebony points with four colored veneers, ebony butt sleeve with stitch rings above and below.

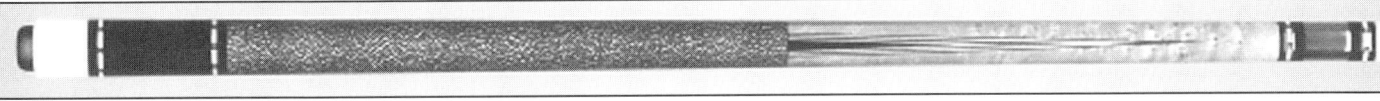

MSR	$800	$600-800	$510	$400

374 JACKSON CUSTOM CUE, cont.

GRADING	100%	95%	70%

Level 4 - Cocobolo forearm, four bird's-eye maple points with a cocobolo diamond-shaped inlay between cocobolo dots in each point, bird's-eye maple butt sleeve with four sets of two cocobolo diamond-shaped inlays around cocobolo dots.

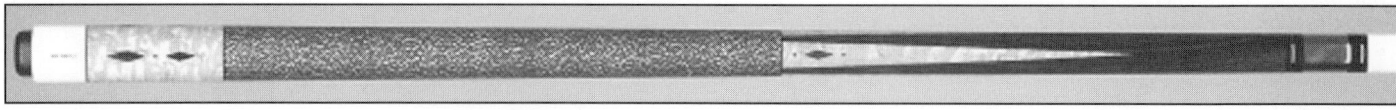

MSR	$850	$645-850	$540	$425

Level 4 - Redheart forearm with an ebony bordered blue Dymondwood ring above wrap, four ebony-bordered blue Dymondwood floating points, redheart butt sleeve with four pairs of ebony-bordered blue Dymondwood opposing spear-shaped inlays between ebony-bordered blue Dymondwood rings at top and bottom.

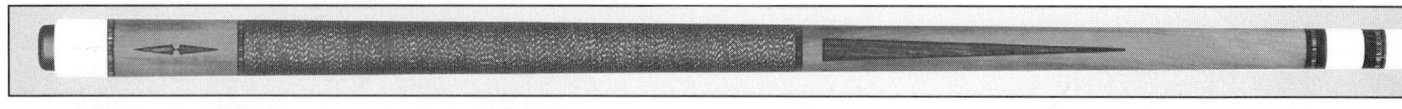

MSR	$850	$645-850	$540	$425

Level 4 - Bird's-eye maple forearm with an ebony ring set in tulipwood rings above wrap, four intricate five-piece green Dymondwood/tulipwood/ebony floating points, bird's-eye maple butt sleeve with four ebony-bordered tulipwood windows with green Dymondwood inlays between ebony rings set within tulipwood rings at top and bottom.

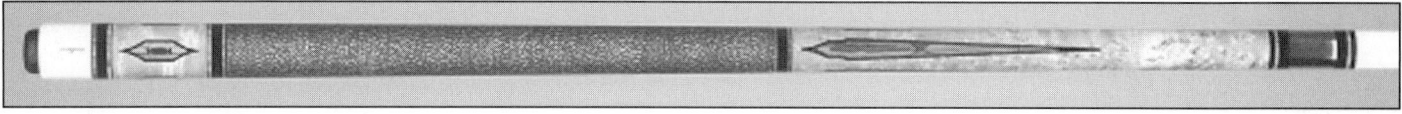

MSR	$900	$685-900	$575	$450

Level 4 - Bird's-eye maple forearm with a nickel silver ring above wrap, three long and three short floating ebony points with an ivory diamond-shaped inlay in each point, ebony butt sleeve with three pairs of facing ivory spear-shaped inlays alternating with three ivory diamond-shaped inlays between nickel silver and bird's-eye maple rings at top and bottom.

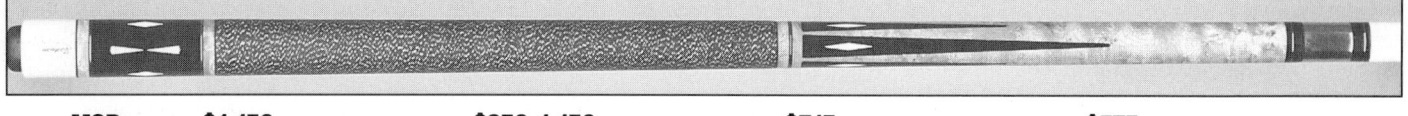

MSR	$1,150	$850-1,150	$715	$575

Level 4 - Ebony forearm with a green Dymondwood ring above wrap, four ebony points with green veneers and a mother-of-pearl notched diamond-shaped inlay between two mother-of-pearl dots in each point, green Dymondwood butt sleeve with four ebony windows with two mother-of-pearl notched diamond-shaped inlays around a mother-of-pearl dot in each window between ebony rings at top and bottom.

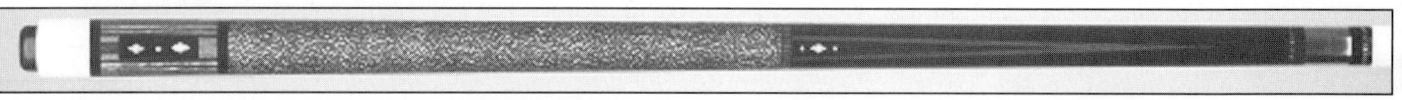

MSR	$1,400	$1,000-1,400	$865	$700

Level 5 - Bird's-eye maple forearm with four ebony bordered holly circles below joint, four intricate eleven-piece holly and ebony floating points, bird's-eye maple butt sleeve with four ebony and holly eight balls within ebony and holly dash rings between sets of four ebony bordered holly circles above and below.

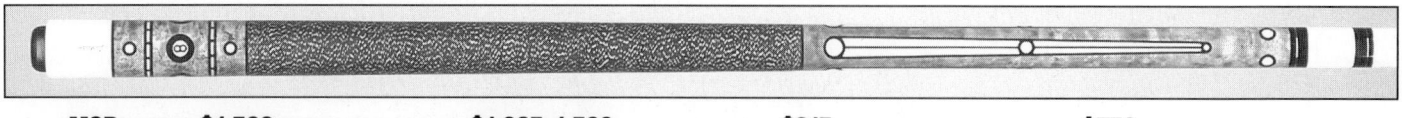

MSR	$1,500	$1,065-1,500	$915	$750

SECONDARY MARKET MINIMUM VALUES

The following are minimum prices for other Jackson cues encountered on the secondary market. These prices are representative of cues utilizing basic materials and designs that may not be currently available.

Special construction note: There are many materials and construction techniques that can add value to Jackson cues.

For all used Jackson cues, except where otherwise noted:
- Add $55+ for each additional original straight playable shaft beyond one.
- Deduct $75+ for missing original straight playable shaft.
- Add $50+ for leather wrap.
- Deduct 20% for obvious or improper refinish.

GRADING	98%	90%	70%
Level 1 - Hustler.			
Level 1 cues start at	$225	$175	$115
Level 2 - 0 points, 0-25 inlays.			
Level 2 cues start at	$300	$230	$155
Level 3 - 2-6 points, 0-8 inlays.			
Level 3 cues start at	$400	$305	$205
Level 4 - 4-10 points, 9-25 inlays.			
Level 4 cues start at	$550	$420	$285
Level 5 - 0-12 points, 26-50 inlays.			
Level 5 cues start at	$750	$570	$385

JACOBY CUSTOM CUES

Maker of pool cues from 1983 to 1998 in Wisconsin Rapids, Wisconsin and from 1998 to present in Nekoosa, Wisconsin.

In 1982, David Jacoby began doing cue repair and selling cues out of his home under the name "Dave's Cue Service." The following year, David and his son, Brandon, started making cues after visiting Viking Cue Manufacturing to pick up a lathe he bought from Gordon Hart.

During the early years, David made many trips to Marshfield, Wisconsin to visit Herbert Eckes, who was immensely important to Dave's cuemaking skills. In 1988, David changed the name of his business to Jacoby Custom Cues and began to attend billiard trade shows. David became a member of the American Cuemakers Association the year it was formed.

David's cues were easily identifiable by his signature on the forearm through 1996. They have undergone many improvements in design to arrive at their current specifications. For example, the very first few cues David made were identified by the Jacoby logo of the pool player chalking his cue decal on the butt sleeves. Cues made before 1991 had a lacquer finish instead of the polyurethane now used. In addition, cues made after 1995 feature a bumper with a threaded stem. These improvements have been geared towards players rather than collectors, as Jacoby cues are designed specifically to be used.

Brandon and David Jacoby

David prices his cues by starting with the basic design and construction of a cue and adding for each option and type of inlay. Jacoby Custom Cues makes everything that goes into their cues except for the tips and the joint screws. David also repairs all types of cues and will even fix cues that are broken into pieces.

In 1998, David and Brandon moved into a location that is triple the size of its predecessor, which they had occupied since 1992. The new facility includes a showroom for cues, tables, and accessories. Dave's wife, Peggy, handles the book work. Dave and Brandon have been taking several machine shop and CNC courses at a local technical college to boost their cuemaking skills. The instructor told them that Brandon had a talent for working with computers, so he concentrates on programming the inlay designs they create on their CNC machine.

On January 1, 1997, the company started engraving "Jacoby" in script for identification in the butt caps. David will still

Signed by request

1997 to Present Day

Early 1980s

sign a cue occasionally by request, and if he does he will include the date following the signature. In 2003, Jacoby Cues started threading all of their components and in 2004 they started using laminated tips. In late 2004 Jacoby Cues started producing limited editions consisting of six cues numbered "1-6" to "6-6".

Jacoby cues are guaranteed indefinitely against construction defects that are not the result of warpage or abuse. If you have a Jacoby cue that needs repair, or would like to talk to David about the design of a new custom cue, contact Jacoby Custom Cues, listed in the Trademark Index.

JACOBY CUSTOM CUES, cont.

GRADING	100%	95%	70%

SPECIFICATIONS
- Butt material: hardwoods
- Shaft material: rock maple
- Standard length: 58 in.
- Lengths available: 58 to 60 in.
- Standard finish: polyurethane and ultraviolet
- Joint screw: 5/16-14 and radial pin and custom
- Standard joint: stainless steel
- Joint type: piloted
- Balance point: 18 in. from butt
- Point construction: short splice and inlaid
- Standard wrap: Irish linen
- Standard butt cap: phenolic
- Standard number of shafts: one
- Standard taper: 10 in. pro
- Standard ferrules: melamine
- Standard tip: tiger
- Tip widths available: 12 to 14 mm
- Annual production: 1,200 cues

OPTIONS (FOR NEW CUES ONLY)
- Leather wrap: $85
- Ivory joint: $150
- Extra shaft: $100+
- Special length: $20+

REPAIRS
Repairs done on most fine cues.
- Refinish: $75
- Refinish with linen wrap: $115
- Rewrap (leather): $125
- Rewrap (linen): $45
- Replace shaft: $100+
- Replace ivory ferrule: $75
- Replace butt cap: $30
- Replace joint collar: $30+

CURRENT JACOBY CUSTOM CUES
Jacoby currently manufactures three lines of cues. The B Series, the C Series, and the Jesse James Bowman Series are all shown. Other lines and special editions are available from time to time on their website. The current delivery time for a Jacoby Custom Cue is approximately six to eight weeks. Special order cues will take a few weeks longer.

CURRENT EXAMPLES
The following Jacoby cues can be custom made in a variety of configurations.

THE B SERIES
Exra Jacoby B Series shafts are available for $130 each.

Level 3 "6PTJ4" - Bird's-eye maple forearm with a jump/break joint above handle, six cocobolo points, one-piece cocobolo handle and butt sleeve.

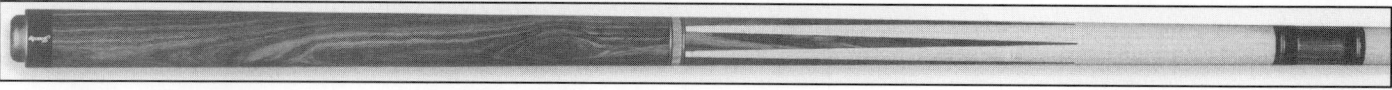

MSR	$425	$325-425	$275	$200

Level 3 "B-3" - Bird's-eye maple forearm, four ebony points with four colored veneers, ebony butt sleeve.

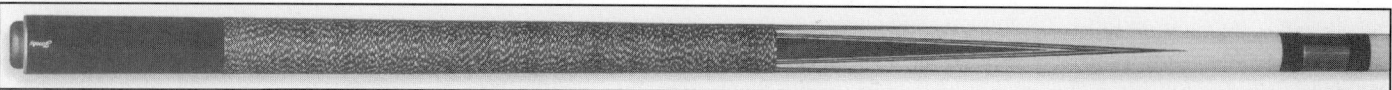

MSR	$475	$355-475	$295	$225

GRADING	100%	95%	70%

Level 3 "B-4" - Bird's-eye maple forearm, six ebony points with ebony spear-shaped tips, ebony butt sleeve with a white synthetic ring at bottom.

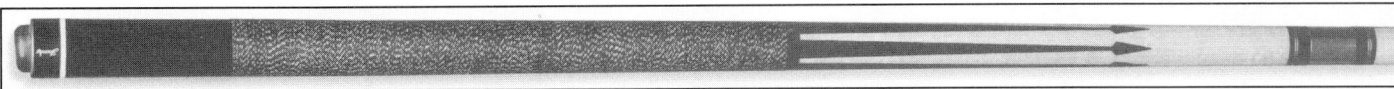

MSR	$495	$370-495	$320	$245

Level 4 "B-5" - Bird's-eye maple forearm with cocobolo set in metal rings at bottom, four three-piece cocobolo points with diamond-shaped center pieces, cocobolo butt sleeve with maple diamond-shaped inlays set between cocobolo set in metal rings at top and bottom.

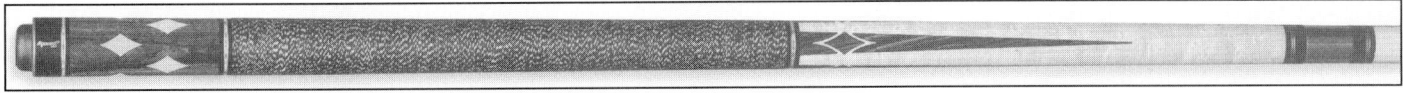

MSR	$550	$400-550	$335	$265

Level 4 "B-6" - Bird's-eye maple forearm, four ebony points with four colored veneers and a pearlized plastic diamond-shaped inlay in each, ebony butt sleeve with four pearlized plastic diamond-shaped inlays alternating with four pearlized plastic notched diamond-shaped inlays.

MSR	$575	$420-575	$355	$275

Level 3 "B-7" - Ebony forearm with a pair of metal rings at bottom, four ebony points with four colored veneers, leather wrap, ebony butt sleeve with pairs of metal rings at top and bottom.

MSR	$595	$435-595	$365	$285

Level 4 "B-8" - Ebony forearm with a pair of metal rings at bottom, four three-piece floating maple points with hollow diamond-shaped center pieces, ebony butt sleeve with four intricate multi-piece maple inlays between pairs of metal rings at top and bottom.

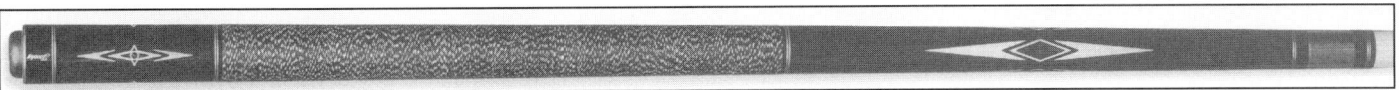

MSR	$625	$450-625	$385	$300

Level 4 "B-9" - Bird's-eye maple forearm with a metal ring at bottom, four ebony points with a white synthetic double-ended spear-shaped inlay in each, ebony butt sleeve with four maple windows with an ebony double-ended spear-shaped inlay in each alternating with four pearlized blue plastic windows with a white synthetic double-ended spear-shaped inlay in each between metal rings at top and bottom.

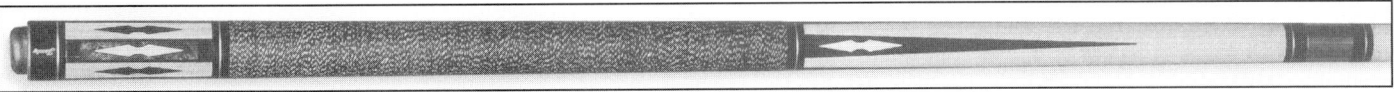

MSR	$650	$465-650	$395	$310

Level 5 "B-10" - Bird's-eye maple forearm with a pair of metal rings at bottom, four multi-piece floating ebony-bordered synthetic turquoise points with red diamond-shaped center pieces, maple butt sleeve with four multi-piece ebony bordered synthetic turquoise inlays with red diamond-shaped center pieces between pairs of metal rings at top and bottom.

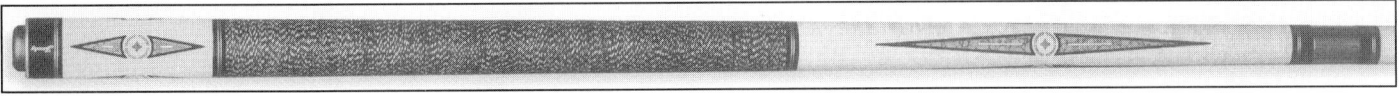

MSR	$695	$490-695	$415	$330

Level 4 "B-11" - Bird's-eye maple forearm with cocobolo stitched rings at bottom, six cocobolo points with a maple diamond-shaped inlay in each, maple butt sleeve six hollow cocobolo diamond-shaped inlays set between cocobolo stitched rings at top and bottom, cocobolo butt cap.

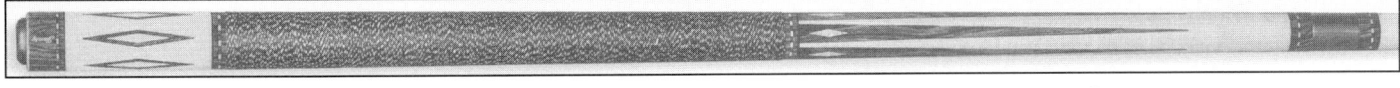

MSR	$725	$515-725	$435	$350

| GRADING | 100% | 95% | 70% |

Level 6 "B-12" - Rosewood forearm with six synthetic malachite diamond-shaped inlays set in white synthetic bordered stained maple ovals above a pair of metal rings at bottom, alligator textured brown leather wrap, rosewood butt sleeve with white synthetic bordered ebony diamond-shaped inlays set around six synthetic malachite diamond-shaped inlays set in white synthetic bordered stained maple ovals between pairs of metal rings at top and bottom.

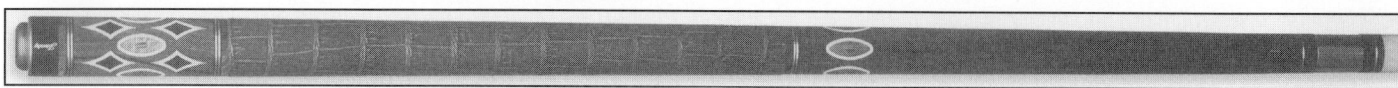

| MSR | $750 | $530-750 | $450 | $360 |

Level 5 "B-13" - Ebony forearm with ebony and white synthetic dashes within a pair of metal rings at bottom, four multi-piece floating white synthetic points with diamond-shaped center pieces, ebony butt sleeve with intricate multi-piece white synthetic inlays between ebony and white synthetic dashes set within pairs of metal rings at top and bottom.

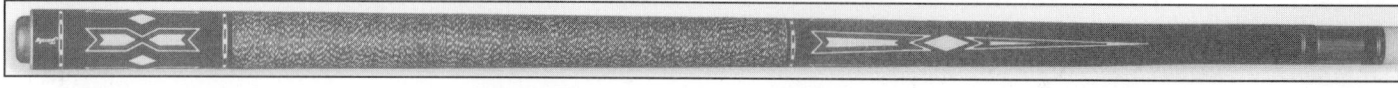

| MSR | $825 | $600-825 | $510 | $400 |

Level 4 "B-14" - Ebony forearm with synthetic turquoise dots set over a pair of metal rings at bottom, six maple-bordered floating rosewood points with a synthetic turquoise teardrop-shaped inlay in each, black leather wrap, ebony butt sleeve with six reverse maple-bordered floating rosewood points with a synthetic turquoise teardrop-shaped inlay in each between synthetic turquoise dots set over pairs of metal rings at top and bottom.

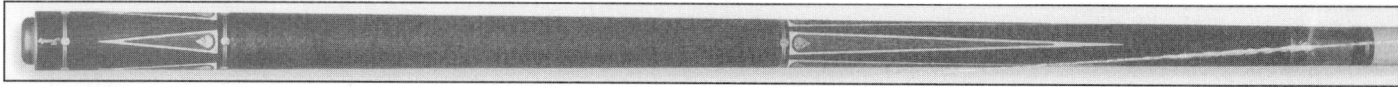

| MSR | $850 | $615-850 | $520 | $410 |

Level 5 "B-15" - Bird's-eye maple forearm with synthetic malachite blocks set in ebony within a pair of metal rings above a rosewood ring at bottom, four rosewood points with two colored veneers and pairs of white synthetic dashes and diamond-shaped inlays in each, rosewood butt sleeve with intricate multi-piece ebony and white synthetic inlayed patterns between synthetic malachite blocks set in ebony within pairs of metal rings within rosewood rings at top and bottom.

| MSR | $850 | $615-850 | $520 | $410 |

Level 3 "B-16" - Bird's-eye maple forearm with bocote blocks set in ebony within a pair of metal rings at bottom, six bocote points with two colored veneers, bird's-eye maple butt sleeve with six bocote windows bordered by four veneers between synthetic bocote blocks set in ebony within pairs of metal rings at top and bottom.

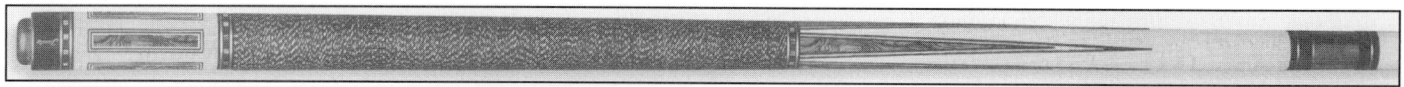

| MSR | $875 | $630-875 | $530 | $420 |

Level 3 "B-17" - Bird's-eye maple forearm with white synthetic dots and red ovals set over a pair of metal rings within ebony at bottom, three long and three short ebony points four colored veneers, three-piece bird's-eye maple handle divided by white synthetic dots and red ovals set over pairs of metal rings in ebony, ebony butt sleeve with white synthetic dots and red ovals set over pairs of metal rings at top and bottom.

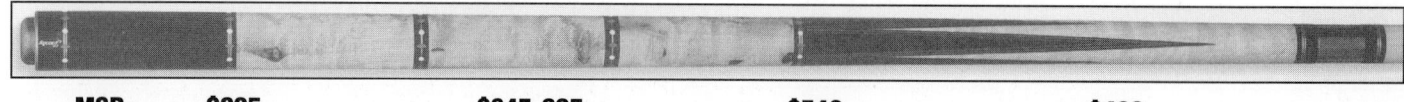

| MSR | $895 | $645-895 | $540 | $430 |

Level 2 "B-18" - Bird's-eye maple forearm with six ebony-bordered synthetic malachite spear-shaped inlays above synthetic malachite dots set over a pair of metal rings within ebony at bottom, three-piece ebony handle divided by synthetic malachite dots set over metal rings within ebony within pairs of six inward-pointing synthetic malachite spear-shaped inlays at top and bottom, bird's-eye maple butt sleeve with six ebony-bordered synthetic malachite spear-shaped inlays set within synthetic malachite dots set over pairs of metal rings at top and bottom.

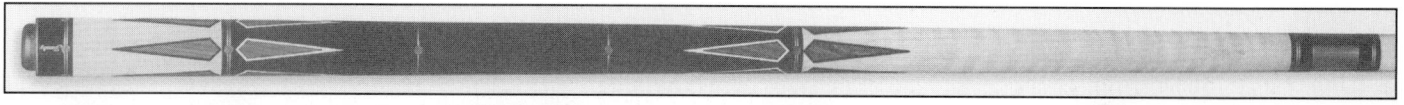

| MSR | $950 | $685-950 | $575 | $455 |

GRADING	100%	95%	70%

Level 6 "B-19" - Ebony forearm with a pair of metal rings at bottom, four intricate white synthetic bordered synthetic abalone points with a pearlized plastic dot-shaped inlay in each alternating with four white synthetic bordered synthetic abalone ovals with a pearlized plastic dot-shaped inlay in each, ebony butt sleeve with white synthetic bordered synthetic abalone diamond-shaped inlays set around four pearlized plastic diamond-shaped inlays set in white synthetic bordered synthetic abalone ovals between pairs of metal rings at top and bottom.

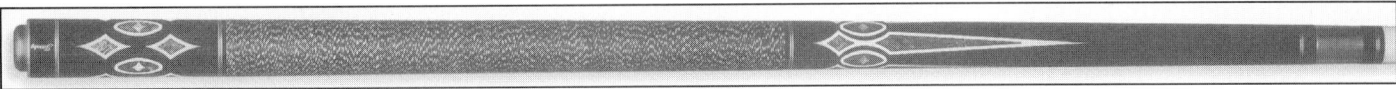

MSR	$950	$685-950	$575	$455

Level 6 "B-20" - Bird's-eye maple forearm with maple and ebony blocks set within a pair of metal rings at bottom, four ebony points with four colored veneers and a pearlized plastic notched diamond-shaped inlay in each, ebony butt sleeve with three rows of four pearlized plastic notched diamond-shaped inlays set within hollow maple diamond-shaped windows with synthetic malachite inlays at all corners within maple and ebony blocks set within pairs of metal rings at top and bottom.

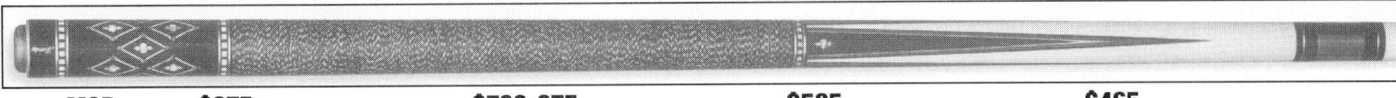

MSR	$975	$700-975	$585	$465

Level 6 "B-21" - Ebony forearm with a pair of metal rings at bottom, six white synthetic bordered floating stained maple points with a pearlized plastic diamond-shaped inlay in each alternating with six pearlized plastic cross-shaped inlays, ebony butt sleeve with six white synthetic bordered stained maple windows inlaid with pairs of pearlized plastic diamond-shaped inlays alternating with six intricate pearlized plastic inlays between pairs of metal rings at top and bottom.

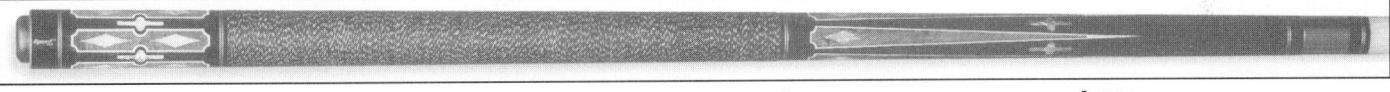

MSR	$995	$715-995	$600	$475

Level 6 "B-22" - Ebony forearm with a pair of metal rings at bottom, four ebony points with three veneers and a synthetic turquoise diamond-shaped inlay set in a maple border with opposing maple arrowhead tips in each point alternating with maple lines with opposing maple arrowhead tips, ebony butt sleeve with intricate patterns of maple and synthetic turquoise alternating with maple lines with opposing maple arrowhead tips between pairs of metal rings at top and bottom.

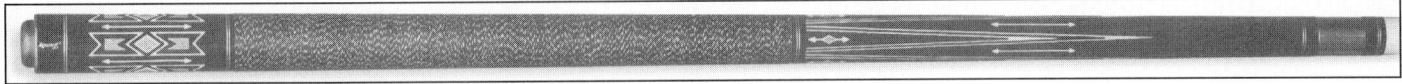

MSR	$1,050	$745-1,050	$625	$500

Level 6 "B-23" - Bocote joint, cocobolo forearm with intricate inlays of synthetic turquoise and red Dymondwood set in maple-bordered three-piece bocote windows alternating with maple-bordered ebony hourglass-shaped inlays above ebony within a pair of metal rings near bottom, cocobolo butt sleeve with intricate inlays of synthetic turquoise and red Dymondwood set in maple-bordered three-piece bocote windows alternating with maple bordered ebony hourglass-shaped inlays between ebony within pairs of metal rings near top and bottom.

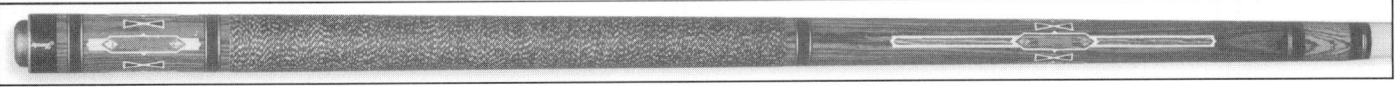

MSR	$1,095	$775-1,095	$655	$525

Level 6 "B-24" - Ebony forearm with intricate inlays of synthetic turquoise set in intricate maple patterns above a pair of metal rings near bottom, ebony butt sleeve with intricate inlays of synthetic turquoise set in maple inlays between within pairs of metal rings near top and bottom.

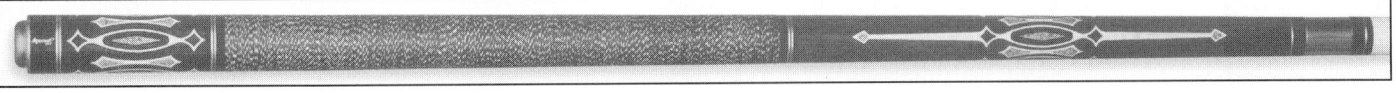

MSR	$1,250	$900-1,250	$775	$600

THE C SERIES

Exra Jacoby C Series shafts are available for $100 each.

Level 2 "C-1" - One-piece stained maple butt.

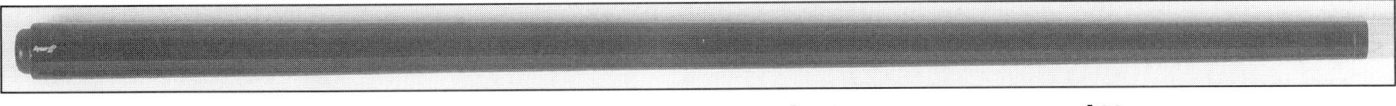

MSR	$180	$150-180	$120	$80

JACOBY CUSTOM CUES, cont.

GRADING	100%	95%	70%

Level 2 "C-2" - Stained maple forearm, stained maple butt sleeve.

MSR	$240	$200-240	$160	$110

Level 2 "C-3" - Stained maple forearm, ebony butt sleeve with synthetic malachite spear-shaped inlays set in intricate white synthetic windows.

MSR	$325	$280-325	$215	$140

Level 2 "C-4" - Stained maple forearm, ebony butt sleeve with synthetic turquoise diamond-shaped inlays set in intricate white synthetic windows.

MSR	$350	$300-350	$235	$155

Level 3 "C-5" - Bird's-eye maple forearm, four ebony points, ebony butt sleeve.

MSR	$375	$320-375	$255	$175

Level 4 "C-6" - Bird's-eye maple forearm, four ebony points with a synthetic turquoise diamond-shaped inlay in each, ebony butt sleeve with four large synthetic turquoise diamond-shaped inlays alternating with four short synthetic turquoise diamond-shaped inlays.

MSR	$450	$360-450	$285	$200

Level 4 "C-7" - Stained bird's-eye maple forearm, four intricate ebony-bordered maple points with an ebony diamond-shaped inlay in each, ebony butt sleeve with intricate stained maple inlaid patterns.

MSR	$475	$375-475	$300	$220

Level 4 "C-8" - Bird's-eye maple forearm, four ebony points with a white synthetic spear-shaped inlay in each, ebony butt sleeve with white synthetic spear-shaped inlays set in intricate white synthetic windows alternating with synthetic malachite elipses.

MSR	$525	$400-525	$335	$250

Level 4 "C-9" - Bird's-eye maple forearm, four ebony points with an intricate synthetic malachite-bordered white synthetic diamond-shaped inlay in each, ebony butt sleeve with intricate synthetic malachite-bordered white synthetic diamond-shaped inlays alternating with synthetic malachite hourglass-shaped inlays.

MSR	$550	$420-550	$355	$265

Level 4 "C-10" - Bird's-eye maple forearm, four ebony points with a pearlized plastic dot set in an intricate bocote inlay in each, ebony butt sleeve with pearlized plastic dots set in intricate hollow bocote windows alternating with pearlized plastic dots.

MSR	$595	$450-595	$375	$285

JACOBY CUSTOM CUES, cont.

GRADING	100%	95%	70%

THE JESSE JAMES BOWMAN SERIES

Exra Jacoby Jesse James Bowman Series shafts are available for $135 each.

Level 2 "JJB1" - Cocobolo forearm, tiger maple handle with "Jesse James Bowman" signature, cocobolo butt sleeve white synthetic pistol-shaped inlays.

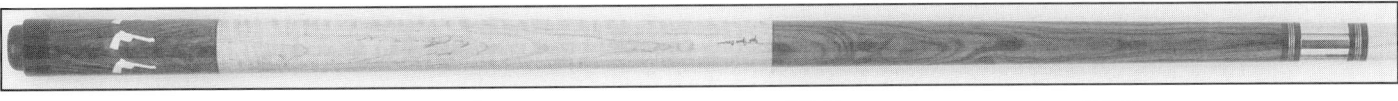

MSR	$365	$315-365	$255	$180

Level 3 "JJB2" - Tiger maple forearm with "Jesse James Bowman" signature between points and white synthetic dashes in an ebony ring at bottom, six cocobolo points, one-piece cocobolo handle and butt sleeve with stained maple pistol-shaped inlays at bottom.

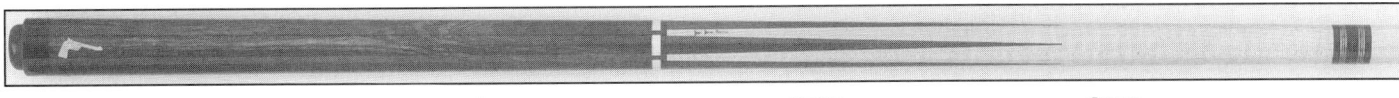

MSR	$425	$350-425	$285	$210

Level 3 "JJB3" - Ebony forearm with four short full-spliced reverse points with a white synthetic pistol-shaped inlay in each going into handle, tiger maple handle with "Jesse James Bowman" signature, ebony butt sleeve with four short full-spliced points with a white synthetic pistol-shaped inlay in each going into handle.

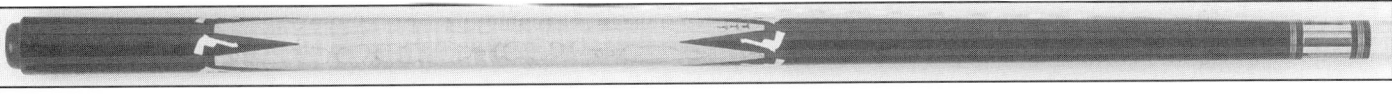

MSR	$450	$370-450	$300	$220

Level 5 "JJB4" - Ebony forearm, six short stained maple points with an ebony diamond-shaped inlay in each, tiger maple handle with "Jesse James Bowman" signature and six inward pointing short ebony points with a white synthetic diamond-shaped inlay in each at top and bottom, ebony butt sleeve with six short stained maple reverse points with an ebony diamond-shaped inlay in each above white synthetic pistol-shaped inlays at bottom.

MSR	$775	$600-775	$495	$375

Level 4 "JJB5" - One-piece stained maple butt with "Jesse James Bowman" signature, four pairs of intricate ebony-bordered three-piece opposing stained maple points with a white synthetic pistol-shaped inlay in each and a white synthetic base and a pearlized plastic oval-shaped middle section.

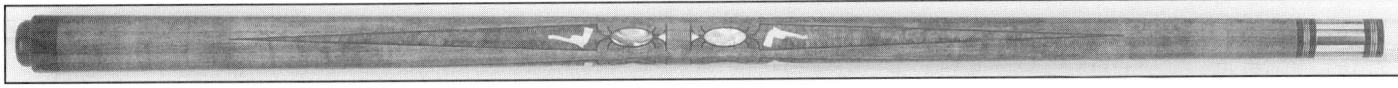

MSR	$795	$615-795	$505	$385

Level 4 "JJB6" - Tlipwood forearm with "Jesse James Bowman" signature between points, six ebony points with pairs of opposing white synthetic tear-shaped inlays set in synthetic malachite windows in each point, black leather wrap, tulipwood butt sleeve with six pairs of opposing white synthetic tear-shaped inlays set in synthetic malachite windows above white synthetic pistol-shaped inlays that cut into the butt cap.

MSR	$850	$650-850	$535	$415

Level 4 "JJB7" - Ebony forearm with a silver ring above wrap, four white synthetic-bordered three-piece opposing burl wood points with a "Jesse James Bowman" signature in one and a white synthetic pistol-shaped inlay in each and an ebony base and a pearlized plastic oval-shaped middle section, black leather wrap, ebony butt sleeve with four white synthetic-bordered burl wood oval windows with a white synthetic pistol-shaped inlay in each.

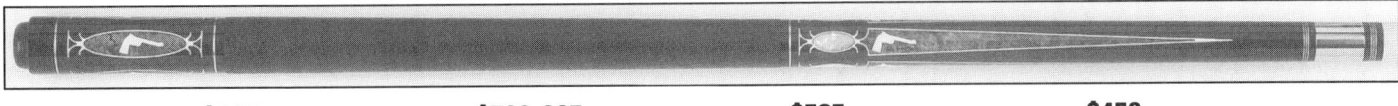

MSR	$925	$700-925	$585	$450

| GRADING | 98% | 90% | 70% |

DISCONTINUED JACOBY CUSTOM CUES

The following cues are from the 1999 Jacoby catalogue. They could be custom made in a variety of configurations. Exotic woods represent: bird's-eye maple, tiger maple, curly maple, ebony, bocote, purple heart, cocobolo, and other woods were available at that time. They can still be special ordered.

Level 2 J1 - Stained bird's-eye maple butt.

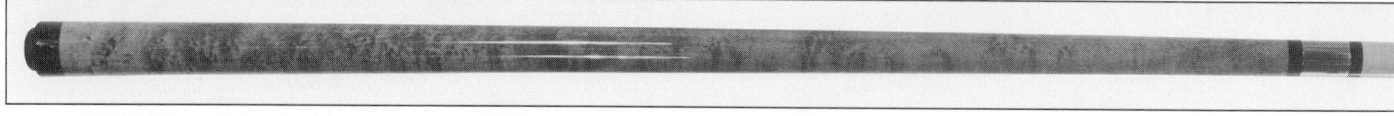

| MSR (1999) $240 | $220 | $180 | $105 |

Level 2 J2 - Hardwood forearm with silver rings at top and bottom, hardwood butt sleeve with silver rings at top and bottom (hardwoods available: bird's-eye maple, ebony, purple heart, bocote, and cocobolo).

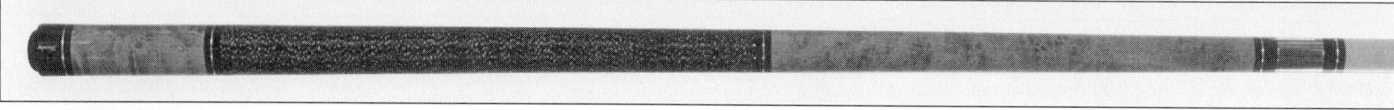

| MSR (1999) $295 | $275 | $205 | $130 |

Level 3 J3 - Maple forearm, six hardwood points, hardwood handle (hardwoods available: rosewood, purple heart, bocote, and cocobolo).

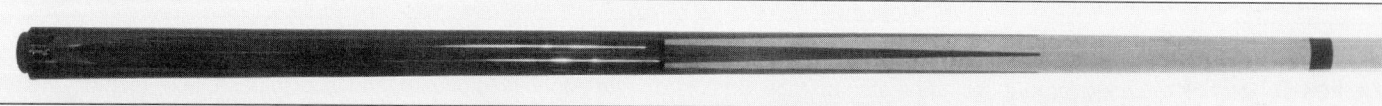

| MSR (1999) $330 | $295 | $245 | $145 |

Level 3 J4 - Bird's-eye or curly maple forearm with an exotic wood ring within silver rings above handle, four hardwood points, hardwood handle (hardwoods available: purple heart, bocote, and cocobolo).

| MSR (1999) $330 | $295 | $225 | $145 |

Level 2 J5 - Stained bird's-eye maple forearm, ebony butt sleeve with three large tulipwood diamond-shaped inlays alternating with three small maple diamond-shaped inlays within silver rings at top and bottom.

| MSR (1999) $340 | $305 | $230 | $150 |

Level 2 J6 - Stained bird's-eye maple forearm, ebony butt sleeve with intricate white cross-shaped inlays within silver rings at top and bottom.

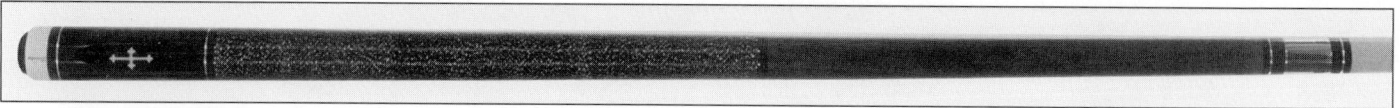

| MSR (1999) $355 | $325 | $245 | $160 |

Level 2 J7 - Stained bird's-eye maple forearm, ebony butt sleeve with intricate white inlays set in stained bird's-eye maple within silver rings at top and bottom.

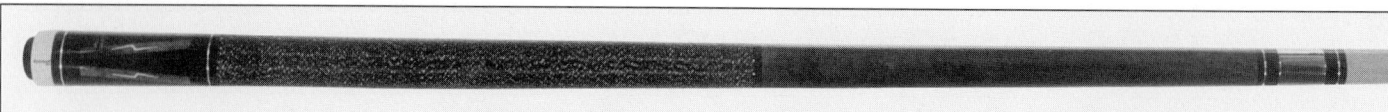

| MSR (1999) $365 | $335 | $255 | $165 |

JACOBY CUSTOM CUES, cont. **383**

GRADING	98%	90%	70%

Level 2 J8 - Stained bird's-eye maple forearm, ebony butt sleeve with white windows set in intricate stained bird's-eye maple windows alternating with stained bird's-eye maple windows set in intricate white windows within silver rings at top and bottom.

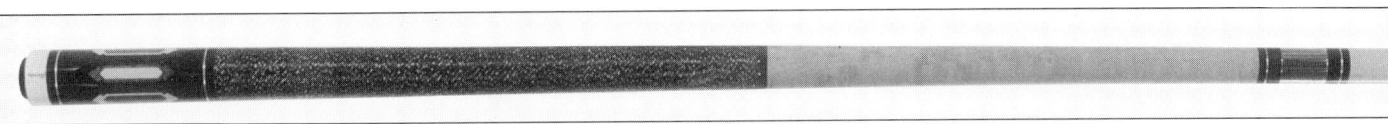

MSR (1999) $365	$335	$255	$165

Level 2 J9 - Stained bird's-eye maple forearm with triple brass rings at top and bottom, hardwood butt sleeve with sets of opposing hardwood windows alternating with sets of four white diamond-shaped inlays within triple brass rings at top and bottom (hardwoods available: ebony and cocobolo).

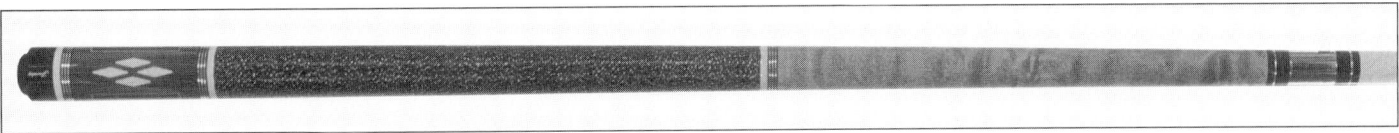

MSR (1999) $375	$345	$260	$170

Level 3 J10 - Stained bird's-eye maple forearm, six floating exotic wood points, ebony butt sleeve with silver rings at top and bottom.

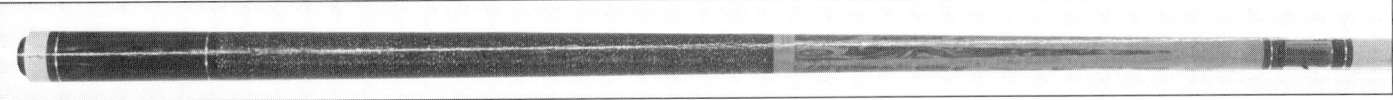

MSR (1999) $395	$355	$270	$175

Level 3 J11 - Stained bird's-eye maple forearm, four intricate black-bordered exotic wood floating points, matching exotic wood butt sleeve with silver rings at top and bottom.

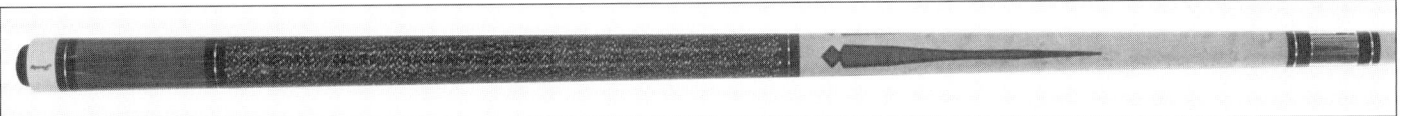

MSR (1999) $425	$375	$285	$185

Level 2 J12 - Stained bird's-eye maple forearm with black-bordered exotic wood arrowhead-shaped inlays pointing up from above wrap, exotic wood butt sleeve with black-bordered exotic wood arrowhead-shaped inlays pointing down from below wrap within silver rings at top and bottom.

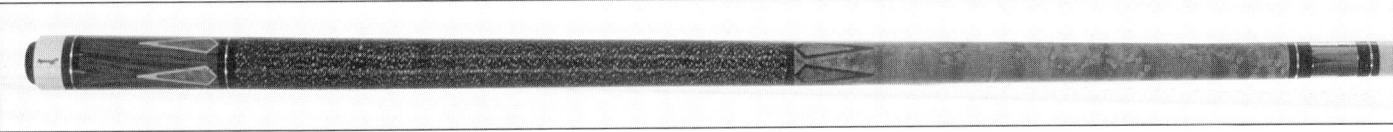

MSR (1999) $455	$400	$300	$195

Level 3 J13 - Hardwood forearm with triple brass rings above wrap, six curly maple points, hardwood butt sleeve six curly maple points coming down from wrap within triple brass rings at top and bottom (hardwoods available: ebony and cocobolo).

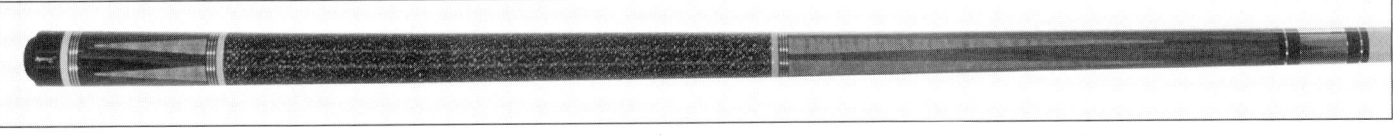

MSR (1999) $495	$435	$330	$215

Level 4 J14 - Curly maple forearm with an exotic wood ring above wrap, black-bordered white points with an exotic wood inlay at the base of each point, curly maple butt sleeve with exotic wood inlays and window borders.

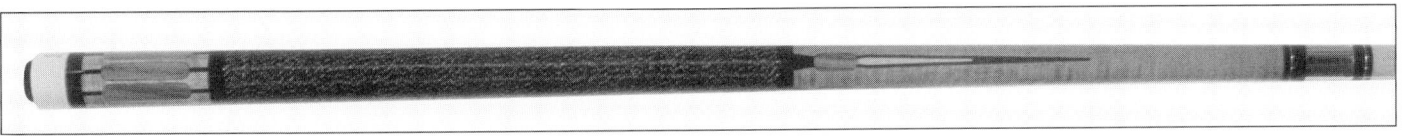

MSR (1999) $575	$525	$395	$260

| GRADING | 98% | 90% | 70% |

Level 4 J15 - Stained bird's-eye maple forearm with exotic wood rings within silver rings above wrap, ebony points with an exotic wood diamond-shaped inlay in each point, stained bird's-eye maple butt sleeve with white and ebony diamond-shaped inlays set in exotic wood windows between exotic wood rings within silver rings at top and bottom.

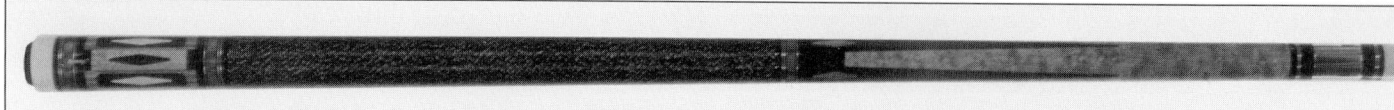

| MSR (1999) $595 | $535 | $415 | $265 |

Level 5 J16 - Stained bird's-eye maple forearm with exotic wood rings within silver rings above wrap, intricate black-bordered maple points with an exotic wood diamond-shaped inlay in each point, stained bird's-eye maple butt sleeve with concentric exotic wood diamond-shaped inlays set in exotic wood windows between exotic wood rings within silver rings at top and bottom.

| MSR (1999) $675 | $600 | $470 | $290 |

Level J17 - Curly maple forearm with black-bordered exotic wood arrowhead-shaped inlays coming up from handle and maple and ebony rings within silver rings above handle, exotic wood handle with black-bordered exotic wood arrowhead-shaped inlays coming down from forearm and up from butt sleeve, curly maple butt sleeve with black-bordered exotic wood arrowhead-shaped inlays coming down from handle within maple and ebony rings within silver rings at top and bottom.

| MSR (1999) $750 | $665 | $495 | $320 |

Level 5 J18 - Stained bird's-eye maple forearm with opposing black-bordered exotic wood spears above a silver ring above wrap, black-bordered exotic wood points, ebony butt sleeve with concentric white and exotic wood windows within silver rings at top and bottom.

| MSR (1999) $795 | $700 | $530 | $340 |

Level 5 J19 - Exotic wood forearm, six bordered exotic wood points with an exotic inlay in each point, exotic wood butt sleeve with intricate exotic inlays alternating with long bordered windows above a single brass ring at bottom.

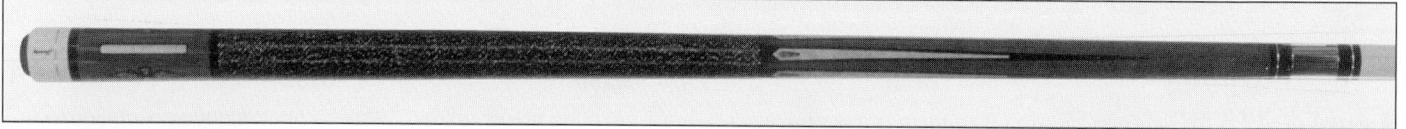

| MSR (1999) $835 | $735 | $555 | $360 |

Level 5 J20 - Exotic wood forearm with intricate cross-shaped inlays between the points and an exotic wood ring within brass rings above wrap, intricately bordered exotic wood floating points, exotic wood butt sleeve with white cross-shaped inlays alternating with white bordered exotic wood windows within exotic wood rings within brass rings at top and bottom.

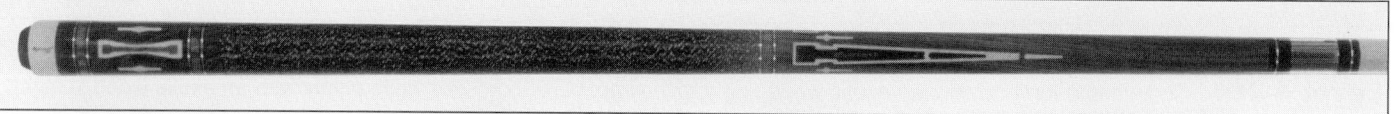

| MSR (1999) $865 | $755 | $570 | $370 |

Level 5 J21 - Curly maple forearm, intricately bordered points with intricate inlays in each, ebony butt sleeve with exotic wood diamond-shaped inlays alternating with intricate inlays matching those in the points.

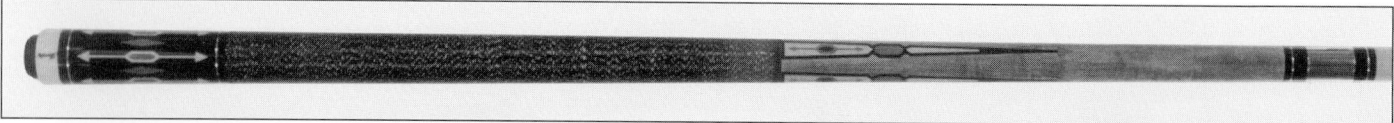

| MSR (1999) $865 | $755 | $570 | $370 |

JACOBY CUSTOM CUES, cont. 385

GRADING	98%	90%	70%

Level 6 J22 - Hardwood forearm with diamond-shaped inlays between the bases of the points and a silver ring above wrap, four double-bordered floating exotic wood points, exotic wood butt sleeve with intricate inlays set in exotic wood windows between diamond-shaped inlays above and below within silver rings at top and bottom (hardwoods available: stained tiger maple or ebony).

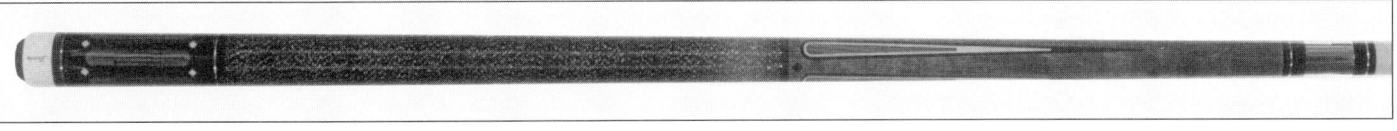

MSR (1999) $875	$765	$575	$375

Level 6 J23 - Hardwood forearm with dice-shaped inlays between the bases of the points and a silver ring above wrap, four bordered floating points, ebony butt sleeve with inlays of the four card suites set in bordered windows alternating with hollow bordered windows between rows of dice-shaped inlays above and below within silver rings at top and bottom (hardwoods available: stained tiger maple or ebony).

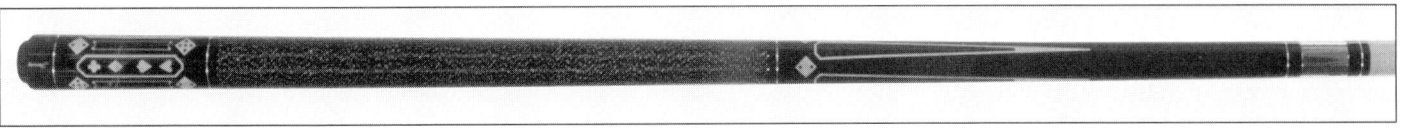

MSR (1999) $895	$780	$590	$385

Level 5 J24 - Stained bird's-eye maple forearm with windows set between the points and triple brass rings above wrap, four intricately bordered points, exotic wood butt sleeve with four intricately inlaid windows alternating with four smaller exotic windows within triple brass rings at top and bottom.

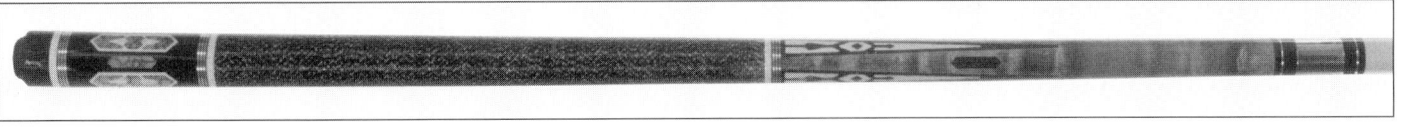

MSR (1999) $1,295	$1,100	$835	$535

SECONDARY MARKET MINIMUM VALUES

The following are minimum prices for other Jacoby cues encountered on the secondary market. These prices are representative of cues utilizing basic materials and designs that may not be currently available. David also offers one-of-a-kind cues that can command many times these prices due to the use of exotic materials and artistry.

Special construction note: There are many materials and construction techniques that can add value to Jacoby cues. The following are the most important examples:

- Add $450+ for ivory points.
- Add 100%+ for one-of-a-kind custom cues by David Jacoby.

For all used Jacoby cues, except where otherwise noted:

- Add $75+ for each additional original straight playable shaft beyond one.
- Deduct $100+ for missing original straight playable shaft.
- Add $120+ for ivory joint.
- Add $65+ for leather wrap.
- Deduct 20% for obvious or improper refinish.

Level 1 - 4 points, hustler.
Level 1 cues start at	$200	$150	$95

Level 2 - 0 points, 0-25 inlays.
Level 2 cues start at	$250	$190	$120

Level 3 - 2-6 points, 0-8 inlays.
Level 3 cues start at	$300	$230	$145

Level 4 - 4-10 points, 9-25 inlays.
Level 4 cues start at	$475	$380	$235

Level 5 - 0-12 points, 26-50 inlays.
Level 5 cues start at	$650	$495	$320

DAN JANES

Maker of Joss Cues. For information, refer to the listing for Joss.

JENSEN CUSTOM CUES

Maker of pool cues from 1969 to present in Baton Rouge, Louisiana.

Mike Johnson was born in New York, but he grew up traveling around the country. His father was an architect who worked on projects all over the United States. He also was an excellent straight pool player and taught Mike how to play when he was a young boy. One year, Mike got a pool cue as a birthday present. While playing with it one night, the cue broke into pieces. Mike was fascinated with the way the points were constructed, and he knew then that he wanted to make cues someday. Mike continued to play pool, and he started doing cue repairs and experimenting with basic construction in the late sixties. Although he got some advice from another maker, he was basically self taught. Later, he liked the way cues by Gus Szamboti played, and he bought two of them in the seventies. After this, Szamboti cues were Mike's benchmark.

Mike Johnson

Mike's ancestors were Swedish immigrants that made custom furniture. When they arrived in the United States, like many other immigrants, their name was changed. Mike named his cues after the original family name, "Jensen," in honor of the woodworking tradition they started, which he was about to carry on.

Mike started making Jensen cues in 1969, going full-time in 1985, when he retired from the nuclear plant he worked at in St. Francisville, Louisiana (near Baton Rouge).

Today, Mike makes under 200 cues a year in his one-man shop in Baton Rouge, Louisiana. Mike has been making more high-end cues with more complex inlays. Jensen cues made since 2003 are marked with "Jensen" and the year of completion. Although many early Jensen cues have no exterior markings, many have "Jensen" and the year of completion under the wrap. Early Jenson cues with "JC" on the Delrin butt caps are easy to identify. Mike prefers traditional designs, making spliced points, doing all inlay work by hand, and finishing the cues with lacquer as opposed to modern synthetics. He believes that playability and durability are the most important aspects of a fine cue. Most Jensen cues feature 5/16-14 piloted stainless steel joints, but Mike will make any style joint the customer prefers. Mike is well-known for his repair work, especially for fixing broken high-end custom cues that others have given up on. Jensen cues are guaranteed indefinitely against construction defects that are not the result of warpage or abuse. If you have a Jensen cue that needs further identification or repair, or would like to talk to Mike about ordering a new Jensen cue, contact Jensen Custom Cues, listed in the Trademark Index.

Sometimes marked

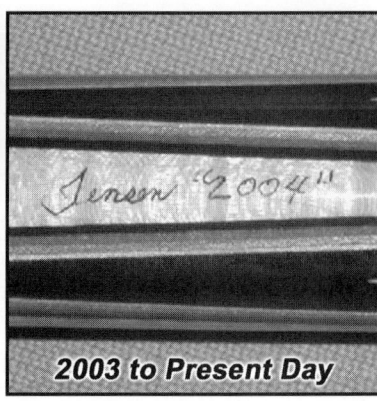
2003 to Present Day

SPECIFICATIONS

Butt material: hardwoods
Shaft material: rock maple
Standard length: 58 in.
Lengths available: any
Standard finish: lacquer
Joint screw: 5/16-14
Standard joint: stainless steel
Joint type: piloted
Balance point: 2 in. above
Point construction: short splice
Standard wrap: Irish linen
Standard butt cap: Delrin
Standard number of shafts: two
Standard taper: 12 in. pro
Standard ferrules: Ivorine 3
Standard tip: Le Pro
Tip widths available: any
Annual production: fewer than 200 cues

GRADING	98%	90%	70%

SECONDARY MARKET MINIMUM VALUES

The following are minimum prices for Jensen cues encountered on the secondary market. These prices are representative of cues utilizing basic materials and designs that may not be currently available. Mike also offers one-of-a-kind cues that can command many times these prices due to the use of exotic materials and artistry.

Special construction note: There are many materials and construction techniques that can add value to Jensen cues.

For all used Jensen cues:
  Add $125+ for each additional original straight playable shaft beyond two.
  Deduct $165 for each missing original straight playable.
  Deduct 20% for obvious or improper refinish.

	98%	90%	70%
Level 1 - 4 points, hustler.			
Level 1 cues start at	$250	$195	$135
Level 2 - 0 points, 0-25 inlays.			
Level 2 cues start at	$400	$320	$220
Level 3 - 2-6 points, 0-8 inlays.			
Level 3 cues start at	$900	$695	$475
Level 4 - 4-10 points, 9-25 inlays.			
Level 4 cues start at	$1,100	$875	$600
Level 5 - 0-12 points, 26-50 inlays.			
Level 5 cues start at	$1,600	$1,235	$850

JERICO CUES

Maker of pool cues from 1990 to present in Clyde, Texas.

Jerry Powers played pool on the road for about ten years, putting 487,000 miles on a van from the 1980s to the 1990s. He also helped start the Busch Pool League with Randy Goettlicher. But he could never find a cue he really liked. He likes physics and he knew what he wanted in a cue, so after retiring from owning several businesses, Jerry decided to start making cues for fun in 1990.

Today Jerry makes many one-of-a-kind Jerico cues, as well as his patented "Stinger" jump/break cue. He likes to come up with new designs and is always looking for new technological developments. Playability and performance are most important. Jerry is a master BCA instructor who helped start that program and he teaches at a pool school in Dallas. He sells CNC machines and cuemaking materials for cuemakers, and trains them how to use them. Jerry also makes videos to teach cuemakers how to use their equipment, and does a lot of cue repair work himself.

Jerico cues are easily identifiable by the "Jerico" marking that has appeared on all cues since the early nineties. A few early Jerico cues were signed "Jerry Powers." Since 2004, all Jerico cues have a patent number that applies to several patent claims in the cues.

Jerico cues are guaranteed for life against construction defects that are not the result of warpage or abuse. If you have a Jerico cue that needs further identification or repair, or would like to talk to Jerry Powers about ordering a new Jerico cue, contact Jerico Cues, listed in the Trademark Index.

Jerry Powers

SPECIFICATIONS

Butt material: hardwoods
Shaft material: Northern Canadian white hard rock maple
Standard length: 58 in.
Lengths available: 58 to 72 in.
Standard finish: UV custom formula
Point construction: spliced or inlaid
Standard joint: .860
Joint type: wood-to-wood
Joint screw thread: 3/8-10 radial
Standard number of shafts: two
Standard taper: Jerico
Standard tip: Jerico
Standard tip width: 13 mm
Annual stinger jump/break production: more than 1,000 cues
Annual custom cue production: more than 40 cues

OPTIONS (FOR NEW CUES ONLY)

Special length: no charge up to 60 in.

GRADING	98%	90%	70%

REPAIRS

Repairs done on all fine cues. Repair prices quoted on an individual basis.

CURRENT JERICO CUES

Basic two-piece Jerico bar cues start at $350. Basic Jerico cues with wraps and joint rings start at $375. Jerico cues with points start at $450. One-of-a-kind custom Jerico cues start at $875. The current delivery time for a Jerico custom cue is six to eight weeks.

SECONDARY MARKET MINIMUM VALUES

The following are minimum values for other Jerico cues encountered on the secondary market. These prices are representative of cues utilizing basic materials and designs that are not necessarily available at present. Jerry has offered one-of-a-kind cues that can command many times these prices due to the use of exotic materials and artistry.

Special construction note: There are many materials and construction techniques that can add value to Jerico cues.

For all used Jerico cues, except where otherwise noted:
- Add $85 for each additional original straight playable shaft beyond two.
- Deduct $125 for each missing original straight playable shaft under two.
- Add $50 each for ivory ferrules.
- Add $65 for leather wrap.
- Deduct 20% for obvious or improper refinish.

Level 1 - Hustler.
Level 1 cues start at	$300	$285	$160

Level 2 - 0 points, 0-25 inlays.
Level 2 cues start at	$325	$250	$170

Level 3 - 2-6 points, 0-8 inlays.
Level 3 cues start at	$400	$315	$220

Level 4 - 4-10 points, 9-25 inlays.
Level 4 cues start at	$500	$395	$270

Level 5 - 0-12 points, 26-50 inlays.
Level 5 cues start at	$750	$585	$395

JOBO CUES

Maker of pool cues from 2004 to present in Angeles City, Philippines.

"Jobo" cues is named after partners Joel Jose and Bong Nicdao. In mid-2004, Jose financed the opening of the cuemaking shop that Bong oversees. Jobo Cues specializes in one-of-a-kind original designs. Danny Aquino also works in the shop. If you have a Jobo cue that needs further identification or repair, or would like to talk to someone about ordering a new Jobo cue, contact Jobo Cues, listed in the Trademark Index.

SPECIFICATIONS

Butt material: hardwoods
Shaft material: rock maple

MIKE JOHNSON

Maker of Jensen Custom Cues. For more information, refer to the listing for Jensen.

CHRIS JONES CUSTOM CUES

Maker of pool cues in Yukon, Oklahoma.

If you are interested in talking to Chris Jones about a new cue or cue that needs to be repaired, you can contact him at Chris Jones Custom Cues, listed in the Trademark Index.

Chris Jones

DAVE JONES CUSTOM CUES

Maker of pool cues from 1998 to present in Lynnwood, Washington.

Dave Jones

Dave Jones started playing pool for kicks at his neighbor's house when he was just twelve, thus garnering a life-long love of the sport. During his formative years, Dave had the rare opportunity to work after school alongside his father. His father's little auto body shop turned out several show cars and was known for standards exceeding the competition. In his teen years, Dave was hired by the late Stan Baker, to work in his gun shop. A nationally known gunsmith, Stan was a perfectionist and had high expectations for the young teen. The relationship proved fruitful and Dave is forever grateful for the opportunity to work with such an innovator. Unlike his co-workers, Dave was not into the sport of shooting. Working as a gunsmith was simply a way to fund his budding interest in enduro, motorcycle racing. With several wins and high place finishes under his belt, it only made sense that he move on and work at A.J. Mazuko's Yamaha shop.

Dave's hobbies have always included building things. In the 1980s, he became involved in sprint car racing, becoming a crew chief. All of these accomplishments have contributed to Dave's knowledge and know-how.

In 1998, Dave and friend Bill Webb decided to try their hand at cuemaking. Bill had been making point blanks and collecting exotic woods for a while and together they decided to make a go of it. In 1999, Bill relocated to Arkansas, and their partnership dissolved. Dave then re-outfitted his shop. He designed and built a four-axis CNC just for the manufacturing of cues. He also designed and built two table saw machines, one for shafts and one for the handle of the cue. Thus, Dave Jones Custom Cues was born.

Present Day

The exposure Dave has had to local craftsmen has led him to be somewhat of an innovator himself. Through his lack of exposure to customary cue making methods, he unwittingly came up with what he thought were innovations. He later learned that these techniques were being used by other cue makers already. After having some enlightening conversations with friends, like Cole Dickson, Dave was able to apply new processes to the construction of his cues. He has developed techniques that he believes give his cues the balance and solid hit that complements the player.

Dave has been making cues for eight years and hopes to eventually retire from his municipality job to make cues full time. He has worked hard to build a reputation for customer satisfaction.

All Dave Jones Custom Cues are numbered and come with a complete specification sheet. They are guaranteed to the original buyer against warpage for one year, and workmanship defects that are not the results of warpage or abuse, indefinitely.

If you are interested in talking to Dave Jones about a new cue or cue that needs to be repaired, you can contact him at Dave Jones Custom Cues, listed in the Trademark Index.

SPECIFICATIONS

- Butt material: hardwoods
- Shaft material: rock maple
- Standard length: 58 in.
- Lengths available: 58 to 60 in.
- Standard finish: two-part urethane
- Balance point: 18.5 to 19 in. from the butt
- Standard butt cap: phenolic
- Standard wrap: Irish linen
- Point construction: short splice or inlaid
- Standard joint: phenolic
- Standard joint type: flat-faced wood-to-wood
- Standard joint screw thread: Uni-Loc
- Joint protectors: standard
- Standard number of shafts: two
- Standard taper: custom pro taper
- Standard ferrules: melamine
- Standard tip: Le Pro
- Standard tip width: 13 mm
- Annual production: approximately 20 cues

OPTIONS (FOR NEW CUES ONLY)

- Special length: no charge
- Ivory butt cap: $200
- Ivory butt sleeve: $550
- Ivory joint: $200
- Ivory ferrule: $85
- Ivory points: $800

DAVE JONES CUSTOM CUES, cont.

GRADING	98%	90%	70%

Ivory handle: $1500
Leather wrap: $100
Leather stack wrap: $150
Extra shaft: $140

REPAIRS

Repairs done only on Dave Jones cues.
Refinish (with Irish linen wrap): $140
Refinish (with leather wrap): $225
Rewrap (Irish linen): $45
Rewrap (leather): $100
Clean and press linen wrap: $10
Restore leather wrap: $20
Replace shaft: $140
Replace ivory ferrule: $110
Replace ivory butt cap: $270
Replace tip: $25
Replace fiber/linen ferrule: $55

CURRENT DAVE JONES CUES

Basic Dave Jones cues with wraps and joint rings start at $675. Dave Jones cues with points start at $775. One-of-a-kind Dave Jones cues start at $1,000. The average delivery time for a Dave Jones Custom Cue is one year.

SECONDARY MARKET MINIMUM VALUES

The following are minimum values for Dave Jones cues encountered on the secondary market. These prices are representative of cues utilizing basic materials and designs that are not necessarily available at present. Dave has offered one-of-a-kind cues that can command many times these prices due to the use of exotic materials and artistry.

Special construction note: There are many materials and construction techniques that can add value to Jerico cues.

For all used Jerico cues, except where otherwise noted:
Add $85 for each additional original straight playable shaft beyond two.
Deduct $125 for each missing original straight playable shaft under two.
Add $50 each for ivory ferrules.
Add $65 for leather wrap.
Deduct 20% for obvious or improper refinish.

Level 2 - 0 points, 0-25 inlays.

	98%	90%	70%
Level 2 cues start at	$500	$385	$260

Level 3 - 2-6 points, 0-8 inlays.

Level 3 cues start at	$650	$510	$345

Level 4 - 4-10 points, 9-25 inlays.

Level 4 cues start at	$750	$580	$390

Level 5 - 0-12 points, 26-50 inlays.

Level 5 cues start at	$1,000	$795	$575

Level 6 - 0-12 points, 51-75 inlays.

Level 6 cues start at	$1,250	$975	$650

JOSEPH FULL SPLICE CUES

Maker of pool cues from 1998 to present in Bayside, New York.

Born in 1969, son of Angela and Edward Franke, 6th generation born in the USA, Joseph Franke acquired his mechanical skills from his father, being not only a perfectionist, but truly enjoying his craft as well. He began to build and fly radio control aircraft in the 1980s. After learning to build extremely lightweight and precision aircraft, he began competing which led him to three national tournaments.

Joseph's father is an avid golfer earning a hole-in-one in 1996 at Clearview Golf Course. Joseph learned the game quickly from his dad. Being a natural athlete, he earned many medals and trophies during his school days and, with his excellent hand-to-eye coordination, Joseph continues excelling in this popular game of golf.

Joseph became acquainted with players at local pool halls and soon found himself engrossed in the game and became interested in the tournaments that were being held. However, one night in particular, when a big tournament was in progress, after studying the players and admiring the winner, Joseph finally found his true passion. He took the game extremely seriously and practiced very diligently on a continuous basis. Learning from local top players, he caught on relatively fast and displayed an enormous talent and love for the game.

Through the years he played with many different cues. While searching for the "perfect cue" he initially began doing repairs for himself as well as for other players. Finally, he stumbled upon a Brunswick-Willie Hoppe Titlist cue. After studying the design and the performance, he began to convert these one-piece house cues into beautiful two-piece custom cues.

His determination to devise a method to make a cue that hit like no other was to be the fulfillment of his dreams. He searched out and began purchasing exotic woods. Joseph believed the older the wood and the dryer the wood the more perfect the cue.

Realizing the full splice cue was extremely solid, he wanted to take on the challenge of making a full splice custom cue from scratch. Talking to many other custom cue builders, he could not gather much information about such a sophisticated splice. The cuts must be perfect in order to have the points the same length. Nevertheless, with this knowledge, he eagerly pursued his vision of achieving the best quality cue his God-given talents could provide until he reached the pinnacle and mastered his goal.

Joseph has admired the different cues he sees at tradeshows. The fancy inlays many custom cue makers use today are very impressive. However, he still prefers the simplicity and performance of the classics—Balabushka and Szamboti, etc.—and his love of the game continues to grow. He enjoys using the rails for position play as well as many other aspects of the game. His cues can be identified by his own design construction, 3/8-11 brass pin, and "JOSEPH" signed along the point. His shafts are hand selected, aged, and dipped, to be a great match along with his full splice cues.

Joseph Full Splice Cues are guaranteed for life against construction defects that are not the result of warpage or abuse to the original owner. If you are interested in talking to Joseph Franke about a new cue or cue that needs to be repaired, you can contact him at Joseph Full Splice Cues, listed in the Trademark Index.

Joseph Franke

Present Day

SPECIFICATIONS

Butt material: hardwoods
Shaft material: rock maple
Standard length: 58 in.
Standard finish: automotive clear coat
Balance point: approximately 1 3/8 in. above wrap
Standard butt cap: Delrin
Standard wrap: Irish linen
Point construction: full splice
Standard joint: flat faced
Joint type: flat faced
Joint screw thread: 3/8-11
Standard number of shafts: two
Standard taper: 9 in. straight
Standard ferrules: melamine
Standard tip: Le Pro
Standard tip width: 13 mm
Tip widths available: 12 3/4 to 13 mm
Annual production: approximately 12 cues

OPTIONS (FOR NEW CUES ONLY)

Special length: no charge
Ivory butt cap: $425
Ivory joint: $225
Ivory ferrule: $50
Extra shaft: standard $135+

REPAIRS

Repairs done on all fine cues.
Refinish (with Irish linen wrap): $150
Rewrap (Irish linen): $45
Clean and press linen wrap: $35
Replace shaft: $135
Replace ivory ferrule: $50
Replace butt cap: $60
Replace ivory butt cap: $425
Replace tip: $15+
Replaced layered tip: $35+
Replace fiber/linen/ferrule: $25+

CURRENT JOSEPH FULL SPLICE CUES

Two-piece Joseph Full Splice bar cues start at $300. Joseph Full Splice cues with points start at $1350. One-of-a-kind Joseph Full Splice cues with points start at $1550. The current delivery time for a Joseph Full Splice cue is about two years.

| GRADING | 98% | 90% | 70% |

SECONDARY MARKET MINIMUM VALUES

The following are minimum values for other Joseph cues encountered on the secondary market. These prices are representative of cues utilizing basic materials and designs that are not necessarily available at present. Joseph has offered one-of-a-kind cues that can command many times these prices due to the use of exotic materials and artistry.

There are many materials and construction techniques that can add value to Joseph Full Splice cues.

For all used Joseph cues, except where otherwise noted:
- Add $100 for each additional original straight playable shaft beyond two.
- Deduct $135 for each missing original straight playable shaft under two.
- Add $45 each for ivory ferrules.
- Deduct 25% for obvious or improper refinish.

Level 1 - Hustler.

	98%	90%	70%
Level 1 cues start at	$250	$195	$135

Level 3 - 2-6 points, 0-8 inlays.

	98%	90%	70%
Level 3 cues start at	$1,000	$825	$600

Level 4 - 4-10 points, 9-25 inlays.

	98%	90%	70%
Level 4 cues start at	$1,250	$975	$650

Level 5 - 0-12 points, 26-50 inlays.

	98%	90%	70%
Level 5 cues start at	$1,750	$1,400	$950

JOSEY CUSTOM CUES

Maker of pool cues from 1992 to present in Savannah, Georgia.

Keith Josey

JOSEY CUSTOM CUES
Savannah, GA

As a young boy, Keith Josey began his woodworking journey by helping out in his father's shop. His father started as a machinist and evolved into a custom home builder with a reputation for being a perfectionist. Keith is also a perfectionist in his cuemaking, after having grown up around this attitude about one's work performance. Keith, his father, and his four brothers would often play pool at a local billiard room after working all day. This is where Keith developed his passion for the game. His wife, Sherri, also enjoyed playing pool several times a week, for many years.

Keith went to the local pool hall repair shop for ferrule and tip replacement jobs. He was very disappointed in the work they did, as it was nowhere near the quality and service he was used to. Keith decided to start his own repair business, with quality service and high standards as his goal. It wasn't long before fellow league players were asking Keith to do their repairs. With the help of his father-in-law, he bought the necessary equipment in 1988 and started Josey Cue Repairs. Keith discovered that he really loved working on cues. His creativity began to develop, and in a couple of years, he made his first cue. Local players were very impressed with the quality of his first cue, and they insisted he build cues for them. In 1992, Josey Custom Cues was created. Keith has been making custom cues, one at a time, by hand, in his one-man shop ever since. Keith is the only person who touches each cue from start to finish.

All of Keith's cues have been hand-signed "Josey," sometimes followed by the year, for easy identification. Keith went to a slimmer joint and butt diameter in 1994 to improve playability, which is the most important aspect of his cues. Keith makes every component except for the tips, bumpers, and joint pins. Inlays were done on a small pantograph, until late 1998, when he purchased a CNC machine. This new CNC machine has allowed Keith to create more elaborate point and inlay designs. He is no longer limited to simple straight point cues. He likes to use exotic hardwoods as the base wood, as well as a variety of materials such as mother-of-pearl, ivory, stones, and contrasting exotic hardwoods for the points and inlays. Keith's capped ferrules used to be made from cut up phenolic resin cue balls until he was able to purchase the same phenolic material in rod form. He liked phenolic resin because of the hit, and because chalk stains wiped away easily. Sometime in 1999, he changed to linen phenolic (or melamine) instead because it provides a phenomenal hit as well as durability. In 2000, Keith switched from a 5/16-14 piloted stainless steel joint to his current flat-faced phenolic radial pin joint which threads into the shafts with precision. The ferrules, collars, and butt caps all thread on for more secure construction.

Keith's cues have a forward balance with a solid stiff hit which allows for less deflection. He turns his shafts many times over a six-month period, dipping them in a wood stabilizer after each turning. Spliced cues often sit for a month or more, to ensure stability and guard against warpage. Keith's attention to detail in the finishing and wrapping process are exceptional, and add that final touch to a real piece of functional artwork.

In 1996, Keith established his first dealer relationship with Jun Shimizu, who quickly spread Josey Custom Cues all over Japan. Since then, his cues have been very popular in other Asian countries as well. Keith is located near several military bases in Georgia, and Josey Cues have become popular with local servicemen. They have taken cues with them on different tours, generating orders for Josey Cues from around the world.

Keith currently specializes in floating point custom cues with a "medieval" motif as well as straight point custom designs. Josey Custom Cues are made to the customer's specifications. Keith is able to offer unlimited cue designs, thanks to Mr. Tim Lilik of Indiana, who has

| GRADING | 100% | 95% | 70% |

been a CNC machine code writer and point designer for Keith since 1999. Keith's wife, Sherri, handles all the business transactions for Josey Custom Cues.

Josey cues are guaranteed against construction defects that are not the result of warpage or abuse. If you have a Josey cue that needs further identification or repair, or would like to talk to Keith or Sherri about ordering a new Josey cue, contact Josey Custom Cues, listed in the Trademark Index.

SPECIFICATIONS

Butt material: exotic hardwoods
Shaft material: rock maple
Standard length: 58 in.
Lengths available: 58 to 60 in.
Standard finish: high gloss polyurethane
Joint screw: radial pin
Standard joint: phenolic
Joint type: flat face
Balance point: 3 in. above wrap
Point construction: flat bottom points and inlaid
Standard wrap: Irish linen
Standard butt cap: linen phenolic
Standard number of shafts: two
Standard taper: custom
Standard ferrules: linen phenolic
Standard tip: Triangle, Talisman
Tip widths available: 12 1/2 to 14 mm
Annual production: 150 to 175 cues

OPTIONS (FOR NEW CUES ONLY)

Leather wrap: $125
Ivory joint: $150
Joint protectors: no charge
Extra shaft: $150
Special length: $25
Ivory ferrules: $75 each
Ivory butt cap: $250

REPAIRS

Repairs done on most fine cues.
Refinish (with leather wrap): $225+
Refinish (with linen wrap): $150+
Rewrap (leather): $125
Rewrap (linen): $40
Replace shaft: $150+
Replace fiber ferrule: $25
Replace linen phenolic ferrule: $35
Replace ivory ferrule: $75
Replace linen phenolic butt cap: $50
Replace ivory butt cap: $250

CURRENT JOSEY CUES

Two-piece Josey bar cues with one shaft start at $240. Basic Josey cues with wraps and joint rings start at $650. Josey cues with points start at $1,100. One-of-a-kind custom Josey cues start at $3,000. The current delivery time for a Josey cue is approximately two to four months, depending on the intricacy of the cue.

CURRENT EXAMPLES

The following Josey cues can be ordered as shown, modified to suit the desires of the customer, or new designs can be created.

Level 1 - Bird's-eye maple forearm, four full-spliced cocobolo points and handle area with intricate maple inlays at the bases of the points and intricate cocobolo inlays at the tips of the points and a row of intricate maple inlays at bottom.

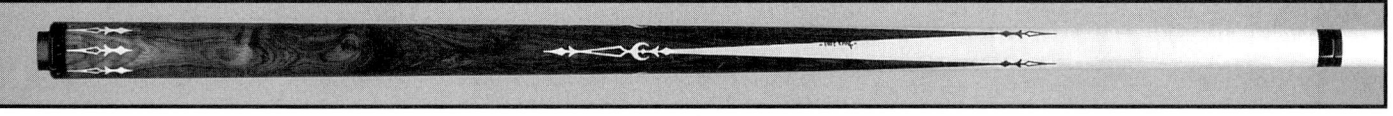

| MSR | $550 | $500-600 | $400 | $285 |

GRADING	100%	95%	70%

Level 2 - Big leaf maple forearm with a mother-of-pearl inlaid ebony ring above wrap, leather wrap, big leaf maple butt sleeve with a mother-of-pearl inlaid ebony ring below wrap.

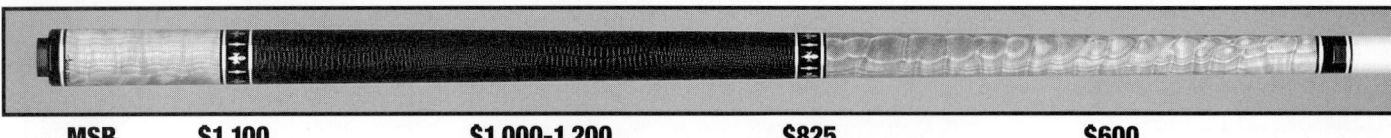

MSR	$1,100	$1,000-1,200	$825	$600

Level 5 - Ebony forearm with a mother-of-pearl and maple inlaid ebony ring above wrap, three long ebony and holly-bordered redwood points with an intricate maple diamond-shaped inlay in each alternating with three short ebony and holly-bordered redwood points, leather wrap, ebony butt sleeve with three long reverse ebony- and holly-bordered redwood points with an intricate maple diamond-shaped inlay in each alternating with three short reverse ebony- and holly-bordered redwood points below a mother-of-pearl and maple inlaid ebony ring below wrap.

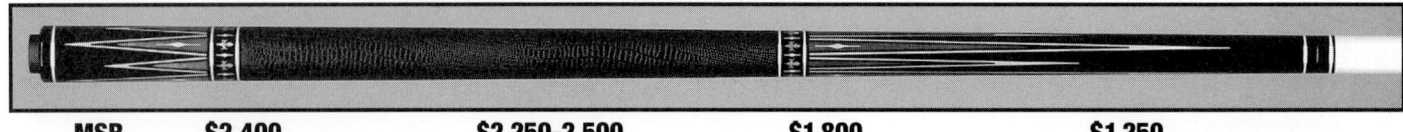

MSR	$2,400	$2,250-2,500	$1,800	$1,250

Level 6 "Blade" - Ebony forearm with a mother-of-pearl and turquoise inlaid ebony ring above wrap, five intricate three-piece holly points alternating with five intricate two-piece turquoise floating points, leather wrap, ebony butt sleeve with five intricate three-piece holly inlays alternating with five intricate two-piece turquoise inlays below a mother-of-pearl and turquoise inlaid ebony ring below wrap.

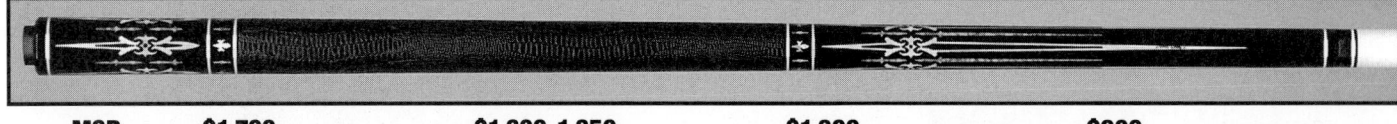

MSR	$1,700	$1,600-1,850	$1,300	$900

Level 7 "Gambler" - Ebony forearm with ebony and ivory dashes within silver rings above wrap, three intricate holly windows with inlaid ebony clubs and spades and redstone hearts and diamonds in each alternating with three pairs of intricate opposing holly floating points, leather wrap, ebony butt sleeve with three intricate holly windows with inlaid ebony clubs and spades and redstone hearts and diamonds in each alternating with three pairs of intricate opposing holly inlays within ebony and ivory dashes within silver rings at top and bottom above a mother-of-pearl and maple inlaid butt cap.

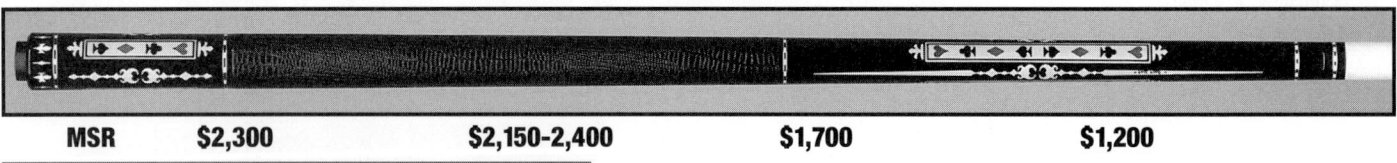

MSR	$2,300	$2,150-2,400	$1,700	$1,200

SECONDARY MARKET MINIMUM VALUES

The following are minimum prices for other Josey cues encountered on the secondary market. These prices are representative of cues utilizing basic materials and designs that may not be currently available. Keith also offers one-of-a-kind cues that can command many times these prices due to the use of exotic materials and artistry.

Special construction note: There are many materials and construction techniques that can add value to Josey cues.

For all used Josey cues, except where otherwise noted:
- Add $130+ for each additional original straight playable shaft beyond two.
- Deduct $150+ for each missing original straight playable shaft under two.
- Add $185+ for ivory joint.
- Add $100+ for leather wrap.
- Deduct 20% for obvious or improper refinish.

Level 1 - 4 points, hustler.
Level 1 cues start at	$225	$175	$120

Level 2 - 0 points, 0-25 inlays.
Level 2 cues start at	$575	$440	$290

Level 3 - 2-6 points, 0-8 inlays.
Level 3 cues start at	$950	$715	$445

Level 4 - 4-10 points, 9-25 inlays.
Level 4 cues start at	$1,150	$925	$650

Level 5 - 0-12 points, 26-50 inlays.
Level 5 cues start at	$1,750	$1,350	$900

Level 6 - 0-12 points, 51-75 inlays.
Level 6 cues start at	$2,250	$1,785	$1,250

JOSS CUES LTD.

Maker of pool cues from 1968 to present in Towson, Maryland.

Dan Janes

Dan Janes was running one of the top pool halls in Baltimore, Maryland in the mid-1960s. When road players came to Baltimore, he was the man to see to set up games. One of these road players was Bill Stroud. The two became friends, and before long, the two were on the road together. They spent three years traveling the country during warm weather seasons playing pool and selling cues. They found that good cues were very easy to sell, but very hard to come by. They believed that George Balabushka made the best playing cues, and he could not make them fast enough to keep up with the demand. Dan and Bill knew that there was an open market for great playing cues, and as players, they thought they were best suited to make them.

Tired of life on the road, in 1968, Dan and Bill set up shop in a two-car garage in Baltimore, Maryland. The two visited George Balabushka to try to learn how he was making cues, but he would not tell or show them anything, so they visited a few cuemakers in Chicago to learn some basics. With a manual lathe, a butcher shop band saw, a drill press, and a work bench, they set out to make cues that were better than what they had previously been playing with.

Although the first cue they made ended up in the trash, they sold the second one at a profit. Soon they were hand engraving the word "Joss" on the Delrin butt caps of the cues. The first one was for Ronnie Allen. They chose the word Joss from an oriental term that loosely translates to luck. It can mean good or bad fortune, depending on the individual.

Since their road experience introduced them to the best players in the country, they had a large market for cues. Soon these players were using Joss cues, and they quickly became known as one of the most popular player's cues of that time. Early Joss cues from that time period have become very desirable to collectors. They will have a very distinctive hand-carved Joss logo on Delrin or Implex butt caps, and will usually have a 5/16 in. joint screw, although they experimented with several other screws, settling on the 5/16 in. very late in their partnership.

The two worked together until 1972, when Dan bought out Bill's end of the company, and Bill began making his own cues under the name Joss West in Aspen, Colorado. Right after Bill left, Dan sent out pictures of his cues to all past Joss customers. The result was more orders than he could handle by himself. So, he called his friend, Tim Scruggs, who had worked for three months at Joss around 1970, and offered him a permanent full-time position. Immediately, they began filling the new orders.

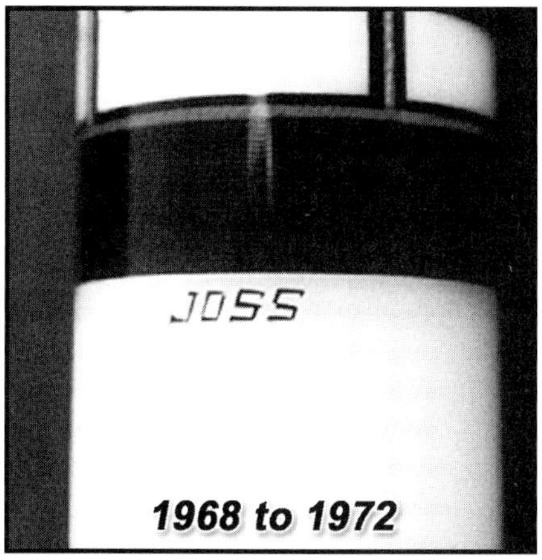

1968 to 1972

1970s

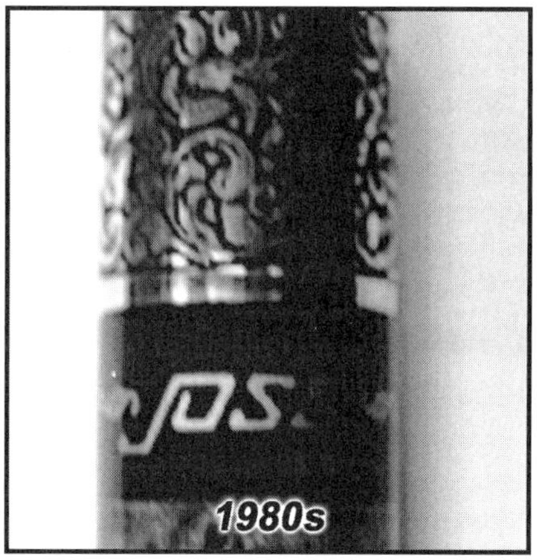

1980s

1990s

Present Day serial No. on joint

Present Day Bumper

Believing that a logo was an unnecessary, time-consuming cosmetic detail, Dan did not put any on these cues in an effort to complete these orders more quickly. Once these orders were completed, in 1973, Dan returned to hand engraving the word Joss on all cues as a result of customer demand. But the lettering would look different than on the early cues. The new lettering was more of a straight up and down block type which would continue to become more uniform over the next ten or so years. Some experimentation was done with logo markings during these years, and some cues will be seen with the Joss logo stamped into the butt cap, or signed with a pen or pencil.

Tim continued to work full-time at Joss until 1978, when he left to make cues on his own. In the summer of 1979, Dan's son, Stephen, began working for Joss cues full time. Mike Sigel also spent some time at Joss, when he was not playing in tournaments.

In the early 1980s, Joss cues saw some major construction changes. During this time, pantographed points replaced the short splice used on forearms. In 1981, Dan stopped using lacquer finish, in favor of a superior UV polyurethane. Later, Dan developed a finger joint as a means of attaching the forearm to the handle. This eliminated the potential for a rattle to develop from the screw which would otherwise be there. In 1983, Dan stopped engraving the Joss logo (which by then was very uniform) on the butt caps, and put the logo on the black joint collar rings on the butts. In 1986, Dan experimented with butt cap materials to replace Delrin, settling on cyro that same year. This was also the year that Joss provided the cues for the film "The Color of Money," including the "Balabushka," which was actually a standard model Joss that displayed the typical Balabushka style. In 1989, Dan trademarked the name "Aegis" for a new synthetic that has been used on Joss ferrules since. By the mid-1990s, a more stylized Joss logo was appearing on the butt cap. In 1995, the current logo appeared. It features the front of a cue within a bridge hand between "JOSS CUES" in a circular pattern above and below. In 1998, they started embossing a serial number into the joint of each cue that is randomly generated by a custom machine. At this time they also started molding the Joss logo into the bumper of every cue. In 2000, the letter "A" preceded the serial number. In 2001 the serial number was preceded by the letter "B", and so on up to the letter "E" in 2005, and so on.

In 2003, Dan was inducted into the American Cuemakers Association Hall of Fame. Today Stephen continues to improve the techniques used to make Joss cues. Dan's wife Debbie manages the operation, and Dan's daughter Amanda runs the office and is in charge of sales. Dan still personally makes about 10 to 15 one-of-a-kind custom cues a year, which, from 1995 to an unknown date, featured the name of the customer and the date of manufacture engraved on a silver ring. Today he signs his one-of-a-kind custom cues. He will also make limited edition cues for the shows they attend.

All Joss cues are guaranteed against construction defects that are not the result of warpage or abuse. Each comes with a numbered certificate of authenticity. If you have a Joss cue that needs repair or further identification, or would like to order a new Joss cue, contact Joss Cues Ltd., listed in the Trademark Index.

SPECIFICATIONS

Butt material: cored hardwood
Shaft material: rock maple
Standard length: 58 in.
Lengths available: any up to 60 in.
Standard finish: UV polyurethane
Joint screw: 5/16-14
Standard joint: stainless steel
Joint type: piloted
Balance point: varies
Point construction: inlaid
Standard wrap: Irish linen
Standard butt cap: cyro
Standard number of shafts: one
Standard taper: 10 in. straight
Standard ferrules: Aegis
Standard tip: Triangle
Standard tip width: 13 or 13 1/4 mm
Tip widths available: any up to 14 mm

OPTIONS (FOR NEW CUES ONLY)

Lettering on cue: price varies
Stain butt: $35
Extra shaft: $140
Special length: no charge

REPAIRS

Repairs done on all fine cues. (Add 10% to the prices listed below for cues not made by Joss.)

Refinish butt: $85
Rewrap (linen): $50
Replace Cyro or Delrin butt cap: $50
Replace tip: $16
Refinish shaft: $18
Retaper shaft: $20
Replace shaft: $140
Replace Aegis ferrule (with tip): $50

CURRENT EXAMPLES

There are many models currently available from Joss Cues Ltd. The Joss 2003 Series which is soon to be replaced consists of several models with prices starting at $220. Most are available for immediate delivery. Custom cues are also available on an individual order basis.

| GRADING | 98% | 90% | 70% |

DISCONTINUED JOSS CUES

The following cues are from a Joss catalogue, circa mid-1980s. These cues came with Irish linen wraps and ivory ferrules. The J-18 was the model used to portray the Balabushka in "The Color of Money" in 1986. These cues went through a number of price increases during the 1980s and original prices were not available for publication in this edition.

Level 2 J-1 - Bird's-eye maple forearm, bird's-eye maple butt sleeve.

$400	$305	$195

Level 2 J-2 - Stained bird's-eye maple forearm, stained bird's-eye maple butt sleeve.

$420	$315	$205

Level 2 J-3 - Bird's-eye maple forearm, bird's-eye maple butt sleeve with ebony-bordered slanted maple windows in a ring above center.

$430	$325	$210

Level 2 J-4 - Stained bird's-eye maple forearm, stained bird's-eye maple butt sleeve with intricate ebony windows between rings of ebony "S"-shaped inlays above and below.

$450	$345	$220

Level 2 J-5 - Black stained bird's-eye maple forearm, ebony butt sleeve with a row of mother-of-pearl notched diamond-shaped inlays between rings of maple-bordered ebony checks above and below.

$465	$355	$230

Level 3 J-6 - Bird's-eye maple forearm, four ebony points, ebony butt sleeve with mother-of-pearl diamond-shaped inlays around center.

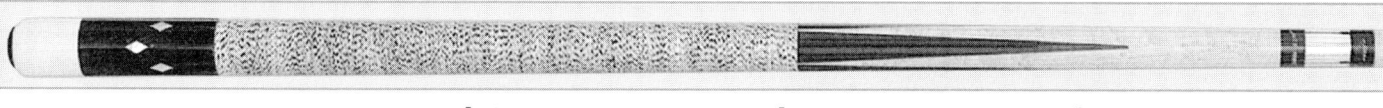

$495	$375	$240

Level 3 J-7 - Stained bird's-eye maple forearm, two ebony butterfly points with four veneers, ebony butt sleeve.

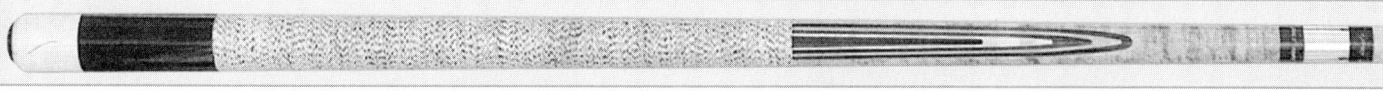

$525	$395	$255

Level 3 J-8 - Bird's-eye maple forearm, two ebony butterfly points with four veneers, ebony butt sleeve with maple-bordered slanted ebony windows in a ring above center.

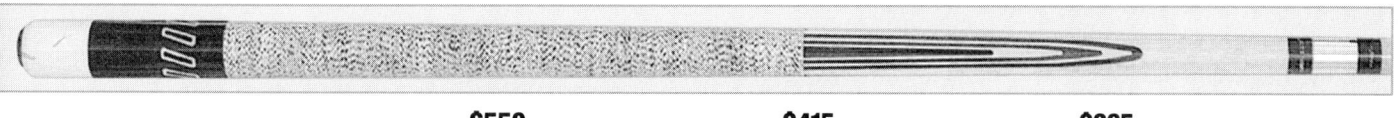

$550	$415	$265

JOSS CUES LTD., cont.

GRADING	98%	90%	70%

Level 4 J-9 - Bird's-eye maple forearm, two ebony butterfly points with four veneers, ebony butt sleeve with mother-of-pearl diamond-shaped inlays set in two-piece colored oval frames around center.

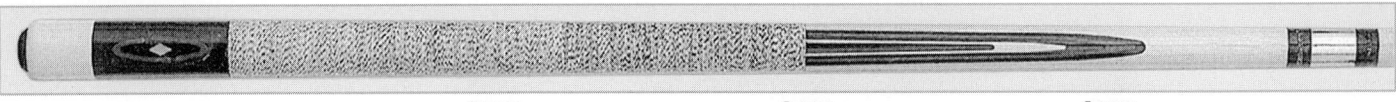

| $585 | $420 | $235 |

Level 4 J-10 - Stained bird's-eye maple forearm with ebony dashes above wrap, four ebony rectangles with intricate borders of colored veneers, ebony butt sleeve with four mother-of-pearl diamond-shaped inlays between pairs of mother-of-pearl dots within windows of two colored veneers between maple check rings above and below.

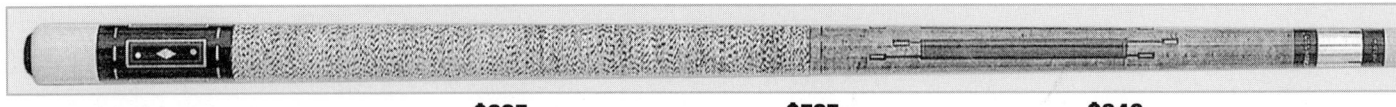

| $695 | $525 | $340 |

Level 4 J-11 - Bird's-eye maple forearm, four ebony points with four veneers, ebony butt sleeve with four mother-of-pearl notched diamond-shaped inlays between rings of maple-bordered ebony rectangles above and below.

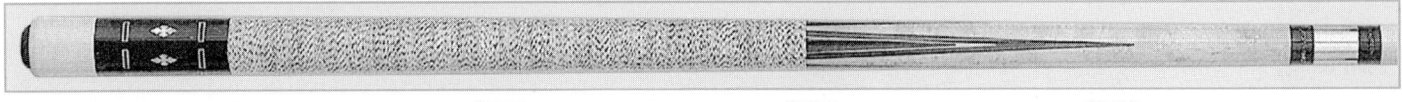

| $750 | $560 | $360 |

Level 5 J-12 - Stained bird's-eye maple forearm with intricate ebony inlays between and below the points, intricate three-piece ebony-bordered ivory points, ebony butt sleeve with ivory ovals alternating with intricate ebony centered ivory double ended spear-shaped inlays between double rows of maple dashes above and below.

| $1,395 | $1,050 | $680 |

Level 4 J-13 - Bird's-eye maple forearm, four ebony points with four colored veneers and a mother-of-pearl notched diamond-shaped inlay between two mother-of-pearl dots in each point, ebony butt sleeve with four mother-of-pearl notched diamond-shaped inlays set in colored veneer windows around center with rings of slanted maple-bordered ebony dashes above and below.

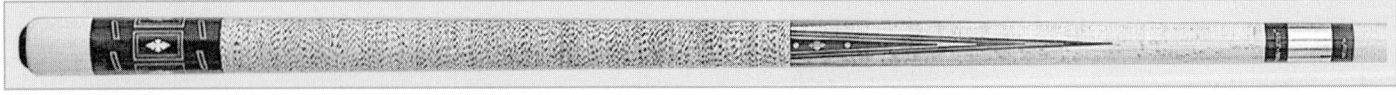

| $775 | $590 | $380 |

Level 5 J-14 - Bird's-eye maple forearm, four ebony points with four veneers and a mother-of-pearl notched diamond-shaped inlay between two mother-of-pearl dots in each point, ebony butt sleeve with four mother-of-pearl notched diamond-shaped inlays each set between two mother-of-pearl dots in a maple veneer ellipse alternating with sets of three mother-of-pearl dots between pairs of maple triangles below maple dashes above.

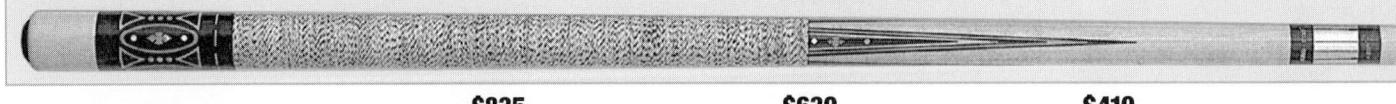

| $835 | $630 | $410 |

Level 4 J-15 - Stained bird's-eye maple forearm, four ebony points with four colored veneers and an ivory-bordered ebony spear-shaped inlay in each point, ebony butt sleeve with six intricate ivory blocks set in ebony within stained maple alternating with red veneers between maple dashes above and below.

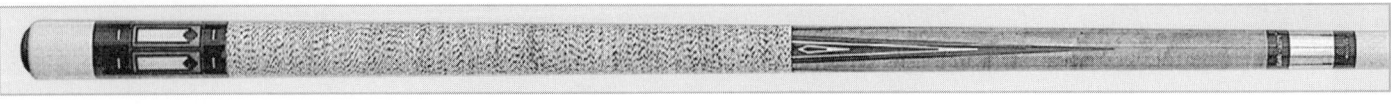

| $1,025 | $775 | $500 |

Level 4 J-16 - Stained bird's-eye maple forearm, four floating teardrop-shaped ebony points with maple and ebony borders, ebony butt sleeve with intricate maple ring design set below four mother-of-pearl dots.

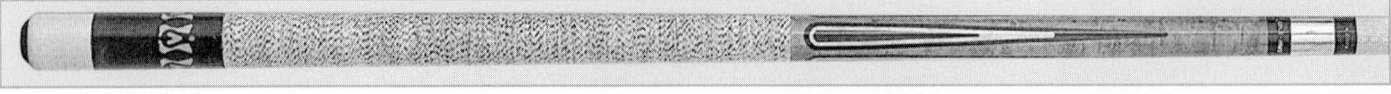

| $795 | $595 | $380 |

JOSS CUES LTD., cont. 399

| GRADING | 98% | 90% | 70% |

Level 5 J-17 - Stained bird's eye maple forearm with intricate maple and ebony inlays between the points, four floating ebony points with two color veneers and an intricate ivory spear-shaped inlay in each point, ebony butt sleeve with four intricate ivory inlays set in ebony with a red veneer border between maple-bordered ebony dashes above and below.

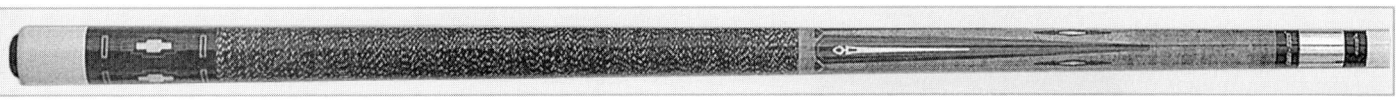

$1,250 $950 $630

Level 4 J-18 - Bird's-eye maple forearm, four ebony points with four colored veneers and a mother-of-pearl notched diamond-shaped inlay in each point, ebony butt sleeve with four mother-of-pearl notched diamond-shaped inlays set within two-piece maple bordered ebony triangle-shaped inlays.

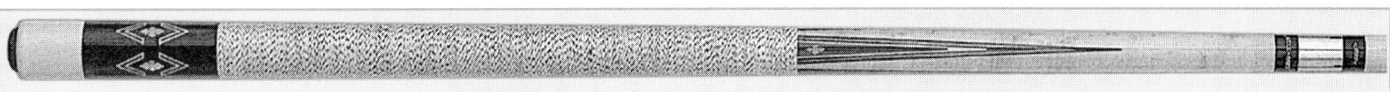

$1,350 $1,025 $650

Level 3 J-19 - Bird's-eye maple forearm, four ebony points with four veneers, ebony butt sleeve with four intricate maple blocks set between rings of maple S-shapes above and below.

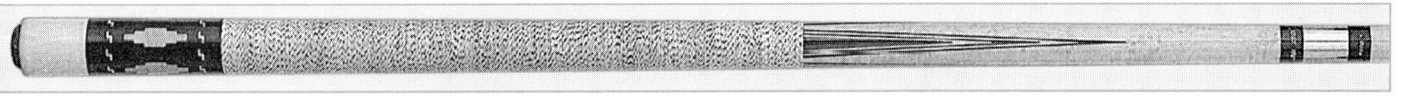

$665 $500 $320

Level 3 J-20 - Bird's-eye maple forearm, four bird's-eye points with three colored veneers, bird's-eye maple butt sleeve with four intricate ebony blocks set between rings of ebony S-shapes above and below.

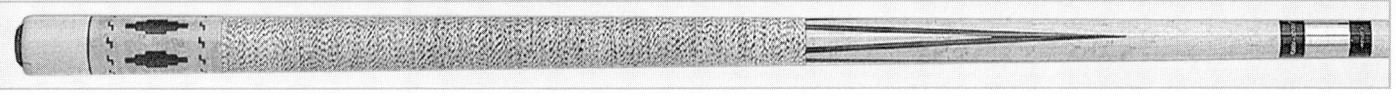

$700 $530 $340

Level 3 J-21 - Bird's-eye maple forearm, four ebony points with four veneers, ebony butt sleeve with a ring of maple-bordered ebony dashes above center.

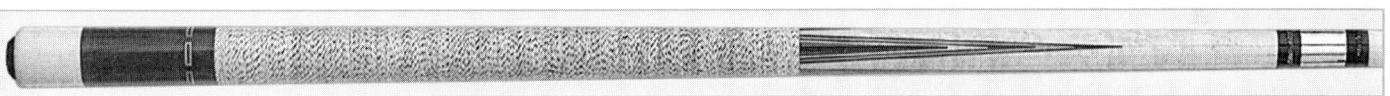

$650 $485 $315

Level 3 J-22 - Bird's-eye maple forearm, four bird's-eye maple points with three colored veneers, bird's-eye maple butt sleeve.

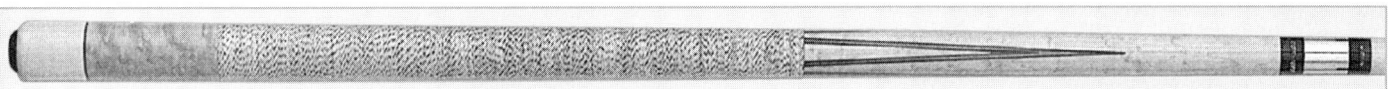

$545 $410 $255

Level 3 J-23 - Stained bird's-eye maple forearm, four ebony points, ebony butt sleeve.

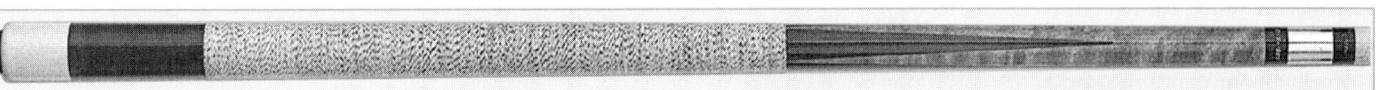

$460 $355 $225

Level 3 J-24 - Bird's-eye maple forearm, four ebony points with four colored veneers, ebony butt sleeve.

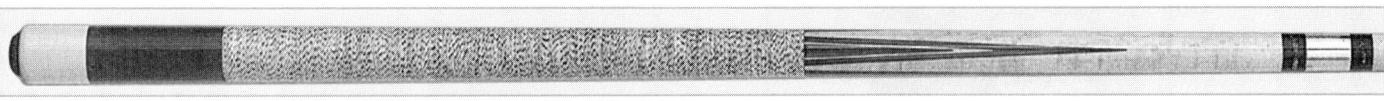

$510 $385 $245

2000 SERIES

The following 2000 Series Joss cues came with one shaft and featured a unique serial number embossed into the stainless steel joint.

JOSS CUES LTD., cont.

GRADING	98%	90%	70%

Level 2 2001 - Bird's-eye maple forearm, bird's-eye maple butt sleeve with ebony bordered pearlized plastic notched diamond-shaped inlays around center.

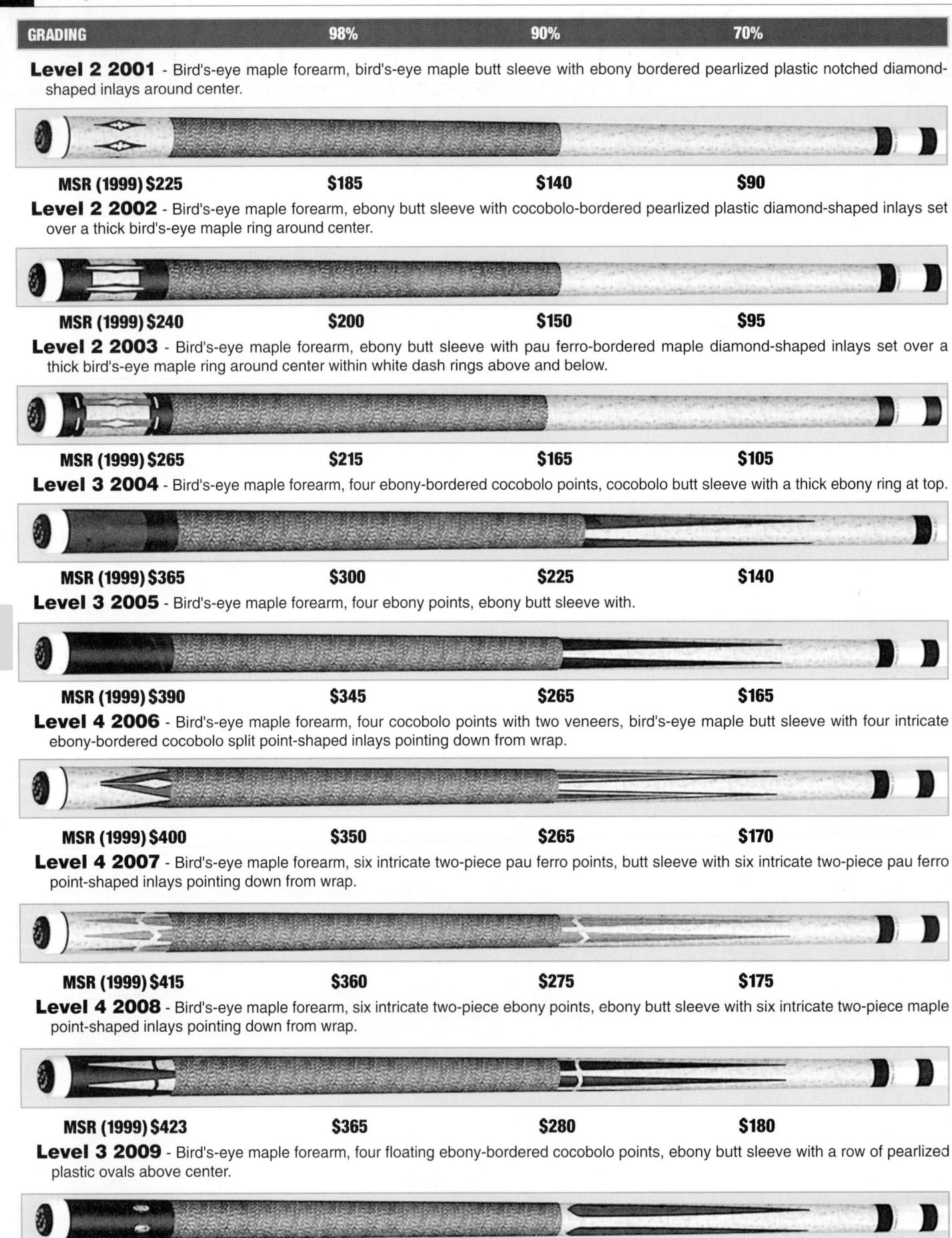

MSR (1999) $225	$185	$140	$90

Level 2 2002 - Bird's-eye maple forearm, ebony butt sleeve with cocobolo-bordered pearlized plastic diamond-shaped inlays set over a thick bird's-eye maple ring around center.

MSR (1999) $240	$200	$150	$95

Level 2 2003 - Bird's-eye maple forearm, ebony butt sleeve with pau ferro-bordered maple diamond-shaped inlays set over a thick bird's-eye maple ring around center within white dash rings above and below.

MSR (1999) $265	$215	$165	$105

Level 3 2004 - Bird's-eye maple forearm, four ebony-bordered cocobolo points, cocobolo butt sleeve with a thick ebony ring at top.

MSR (1999) $365	$300	$225	$140

Level 3 2005 - Bird's-eye maple forearm, four ebony points, ebony butt sleeve with.

MSR (1999) $390	$345	$265	$165

Level 4 2006 - Bird's-eye maple forearm, four cocobolo points with two veneers, bird's-eye maple butt sleeve with four intricate ebony-bordered cocobolo split point-shaped inlays pointing down from wrap.

MSR (1999) $400	$350	$265	$170

Level 4 2007 - Bird's-eye maple forearm, six intricate two-piece pau ferro points, butt sleeve with six intricate two-piece pau ferro point-shaped inlays pointing down from wrap.

MSR (1999) $415	$360	$275	$175

Level 4 2008 - Bird's-eye maple forearm, six intricate two-piece ebony points, ebony butt sleeve with six intricate two-piece maple point-shaped inlays pointing down from wrap.

MSR (1999) $423	$365	$280	$180

Level 3 2009 - Bird's-eye maple forearm, four floating ebony-bordered cocobolo points, ebony butt sleeve with a row of pearlized plastic ovals above center.

MSR (1999) $430	$370	$285	$180

JOSS CUES LTD., cont. 401

GRADING	98%	90%	70%

Level 3 2010 - Bird's-eye maple forearm, four ebony points with two colored veneers, ebony butt sleeve with pearlized plastic diamond-shaped inlays set within bird's-eye maple rings at top and bottom.

| MSR (1999) $440 | $380 | $290 | $185 |

Level 4 2011 - Bird's-eye maple forearm, four ebony points with two veneers and a white spear-shaped inlay in each point, ebony butt sleeve with white spear-shaped inlays pointing down from a bird's-eye maple ring at top.

| MSR (1999) $465 | $400 | $300 | $190 |

Level 3 2012 - Bird's-eye maple forearm, four ebony points with a pattern of three parallel green veneers running through each point, bird's-eye maple butt sleeve with intricate ebony hourglass-shaped inlays that create tall notched diamond shapes in the bird's-eye maple set within ebony rings at top and bottom.

| MSR (1999) $490 | $425 | $325 | $205 |

Level 3 2013 - Bird's-eye maple forearm, four ebony points with two colored veneers, bird's-eye maple butt sleeve with pearlized plastic oval-shaped inlays set in an intricate ebony ring at bottom.

| MSR (1999) $515 | $450 | $340 | $220 |

Level 3 2014 - Bird's-eye maple forearm, four ebony points with two veneers and a white spear-shaped inlay in each point, ebony butt sleeve with pearlized plastic spear-shaped inlays set below a row of white dashes.

| MSR (1999) $540 | $475 | $355 | $230 |

Level 4 2015 - Bird's-eye maple forearm, four ebony points with a pearlized plastic notched diamond-shaped inlay in each point, bird's-eye maple butt sleeve with four pearlized plastic notched diamond-shaped inlays alternating with two rows of white dashes set in an intricate ebony ring at top.

| MSR (1999) $550 | $480 | $360 | $235 |

Level 4 2016 - Bird's-eye maple forearm, four floating ebony points with a pearlized plastic diamond-shaped inlay in each point, bird's-eye maple butt sleeve with four pearlized plastic diamond-shaped inlays set in cocobolo spear-shaped inlays alternating with two rows of white dashes set in an ebony ring at top.

| MSR (1999) $565 | $490 | $370 | $240 |

Level 4 2017 - Bird's-eye maple forearm, four ebony points with two colored veneers, ebony butt sleeve with pearlized plastic diamond-shaped inlays set in an intricate pattern of bird's-eye maple windows and rings within rows of maple dashes above and below.

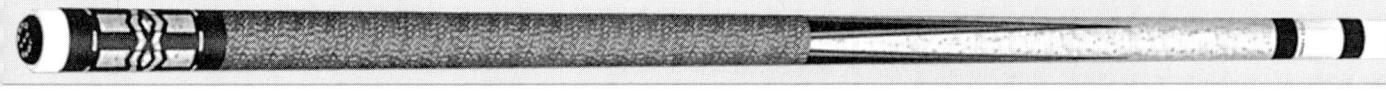

| MSR (1999) $590 | $510 | $385 | $250 |

GRADING	98%	90%	70%

Level 4 2018 - Bird's-eye maple forearm, three long and three short ebony points with a pearlized plastic oval-shaped inlay in each, bird's-eye maple butt sleeve with six pearlized plastic oval-shaped inlays set in ebony ovals within intricate ebony rings at top and bottom.

MSR (1999) $615	$525	$395	$255

Level 4 2019 - Bird's-eye maple forearm, four floating two-piece ebony-bordered bocote points with two ebony-bordered pearlized plastic oval-shaped inlays set in each, ebony butt sleeve with ebony-bordered pearlized plastic oval-shaped inlays set in a ring of bocote hexagonal windows in center.

MSR (1999) $690	$590	$440	$285

Level 4 2020 - Bird's-eye maple forearm, four two-piece cocobolo points with a pearlized plastic oval-shaped inlay set between the two pieces of each, cocobolo butt sleeve with two-piece bird's-eye maple windows with a pearlized plastic oval-shaped inlay set between the two pieces of each.

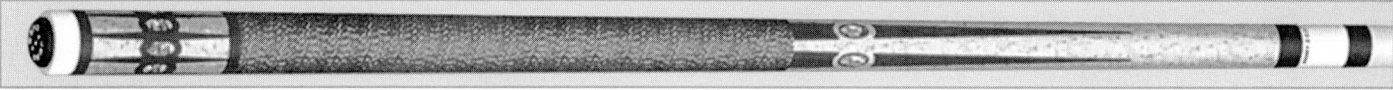

MSR (1999) $740	$635	$480	$310

"EDDIE TAYLOR SPECIAL EDITION" SERIES

The following "Eddie Taylor Special Edition" Series Joss cues came with one shaft and featured Eddie Taylor's name and a unique serial number embossed into the stainless steel joint.

Level 2 ET-01 - Stained bird's-eye maple forearm, stained bird's-eye maple butt sleeve with four ebony-bordered pearlized plastic diamond-shaped inlays set between ebony rings at top and bottom.

MSR (1999) $350	$310	$235	$150

Level 2 ET-02 - Stained bird's-eye maple forearm, ebony butt sleeve with four ebony-bordered pearlized plastic oval-shaped inlays set a ring of maple hexagonal windows.

MSR (1999) $400	$350	$265	$165

Level 4 ET-03 - Stained bird's-eye maple forearm, four ebony points with a white diamond-shaped inlay in each, ebony butt sleeve with white diamond-shaped inlays set between rows of white dashes above and below.

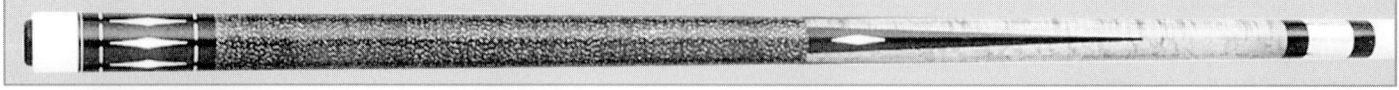

MSR (1999) $500	$435	$330	$215

Level 4 ET-04 - Stained bird's-eye maple forearm, four ebony points with two veneers, ebony butt sleeve with white diamond-shaped inlays alternating with white-bordered pearlized plastic windows set between double rows of white dashes above and below.

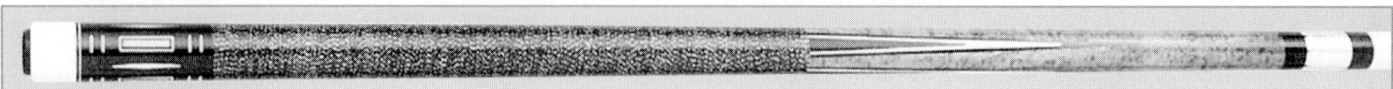

MSR (1999) $600	$500	$380	$245

Level 4 ET-05 - Stained bird's-eye maple forearm, four ebony points with two veneers and a white spear-shaped inlay in each, ebony butt sleeve with ebony diamond-shaped inlays set in maple windows alternating with maple diamond-shaped inlays between rows of white dashes above and below.

MSR (1999) $700	$585	$445	$285

GRADING	98%	90%	70%

Level 4 ET-06 - Stained bird's-eye maple forearm, three long ebony bordered stained bird's-eye maple points with a two-piece spear-shaped inlay in each alternating with three short ebony points with a two-piece spear-shaped inlay in each, hardwood butt sleeve with white oval-shaped inlays set in intricate ebony-bordered bocote windows between ebony rings at top and bottom.

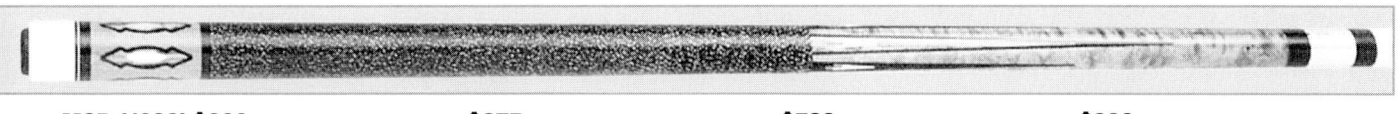

MSR (1999) $800	$675	$520	$330

SECONDARY MARKET MINIMUM VALUES (EARLY CUES)

The following are minimum values for other early Joss cues (1968-1972) encountered on the secondary market. These prices are representative of cues utilizing basic materials and designs that are not currently available. Joss also offers one-of-a-kind cues that can command many times these prices due to the use of exotic materials and artistry. Early models and limited editions are becoming collectible, and can also command many times these prices. Discontinued Joss cues will be further covered in future editions.

Level 2 - 0 points, 0-25 inlays.
Level 2 cues start at	$1,450	$1,175	$850

Level 3 - 2-6 points, 0-8 inlays.
Level 3 cues start at	$1,950	$1,575	$1,150

Level 4 - 4-10 points, 9-25 inlays.
Level 4 cues start at	$2,500	$2,050	$1,550

Level 5 - 0-12 points, 26-50 inlays.
Level 5 cues start at	$3,500	$2,950	$2,300

Level 6 - 0-12 points, 51-75 inlays.
Level 6 cues start at	$5,600	$4,800	$3,900

SECONDARY MARKET MINIMUM VALUES (1972-PRESENT CUES)

Special construction note: There are many materials and construction techniques that can add value to Joss cues. The following are the most important examples:

- Add 125%+ for seventies and early eighties era Joss cues with spliced points.
- Add $1,000+ for ivory points.
- Add $1,200+ for ivory butt sleeve.

For all used Joss cues:

- Add $110+ for each additional original straight playable shaft beyond one.
- Deduct $140+ for missing original straight playable shaft.
- Add $350+ for ivory joint.
- Add $175+ for original leather wrap.
- Deduct 30% for obvious or improper refinish.

Level 1 - 4 points, hustler.
Level 1 cues start at	$185	$145	$90

Level 2 - 0 points, 0-25 inlays.
Level 2 cues start at	$225	$175	$110

Level 3 - 2-6 points, 0-8 inlays.
Level 3 cues start at	$400	$305	$195

Level 4 - 4-10 points, 9-25 inlays.
Level 4 cues start at	$450	$335	$215

Level 5 - 0-12 points, 26-50 inlays.
Level 5 cues start at	$525	$380	$255

Level 6 - 0-12 points, 51-75 inlays.
Level 6 cues start at	$650	$495	$320

Level 7 - 0-12 points, 76-125 inlays.
Level 7 cues start at	$800	$615	$395

JOSSWEST

Maker of pool cues from 1968 to 1972 in Baltimore, Maryland as a partner in Joss Cues, from 1972 to 1974 in Aspen, Colorado, from 1974 to 1978 in Tulsa Oklahoma, from 1978 to 1989 in Colorado Springs, Colorado, from 1989 to 2000 just outside Austin, Texas, and from 2000 to present Josswest is located in Ruidoso Downs, New Mexico.

Bill Stroud learned to play pool while growing up on a farm in Missouri. At the age of fourteen, he moved to Dallas, Texas to live with his sister. It was there that he began to play pool more seriously. Bill spent his evenings in the pool room frequented by "Titanic Thompson," who was soon teaching Bill about pool, and about life. By the age of seventeen, Bill went on the road and began playing pool for a living. Starting in the late fifties, Bill covered the United States playing in virtually every part of the country. During this time, Bill traveled with, and learned from, Eddie Taylor and U.J. Pucket.

In the mid-1960s, Bill started a small ski business in Aspen, Colorado. For the next three years, Bill worked in Aspen during the winters and played on the road with his friend, Dan Janes, during the off-seasons. But eventually they found themselves dissatisfied with life on the road.

Believing there was a market for quality custom cues, the two founded Joss Cues in 1968 in Baltimore, Maryland. The name Joss was chosen from an oriental word that loosely translates to good luck. Although the two knew very little about making cues, they knew a lot about how great cues played. Soon, they were very successful in the custom cuemaking business.

In 1972, Dan Janes bought out Bill's share of Joss, and Bill returned to Aspen to make cues on his own under the name Joss West. He started hand-engraving a small stylized logo with an upright "J" connected to a "W" on its side on the butt caps of Joss West cues for identification. Over the next eight years, these marks gradually got larger.

In 1974, Bill moved to Tulsa, Oklahoma, where he made Joss West cues for the next four years. In 1978, Bill moved Joss West to Colorado Springs, Colorado. Here he began to experiment with CNC construction. Around 1980, Bill developed his current points which are cut out on a CNC mill but have mitred veneers. During this time, the logo changed a little, with the "W" being upright. Bill experimented more and more with computer-aided design and construction, executing designs with a precision that could not be attained entirely by hand. Bill felt that the design and execution of Joss West cues was so distinguishable that, in 1983, he stopped marking his cues. His customers seemed to prefer identification marks, so he started marking them again in 1985. But, knowing that his cues were starting to become collectible, he also added the date of manufacture.

Before leaving Colorado Springs, Bill was featured in an article which appeared in the November 1989 issue of Smithsonian Magazine. At this time, Bill moved again to Austin, Texas. In 1990, Bill changed the Joss West name to one word, Josswest, and again stopped putting visible marks on his cues. Instead he put "JW" followed by the date and a serial number under the bumper. It was that year that beautiful "his" and "hers" Josswest cues were offered in the Nieman Marcus Christmas Catalog. Around 1992, Bill started using the Uni-Loc joint, which has been available on his cues ever since.

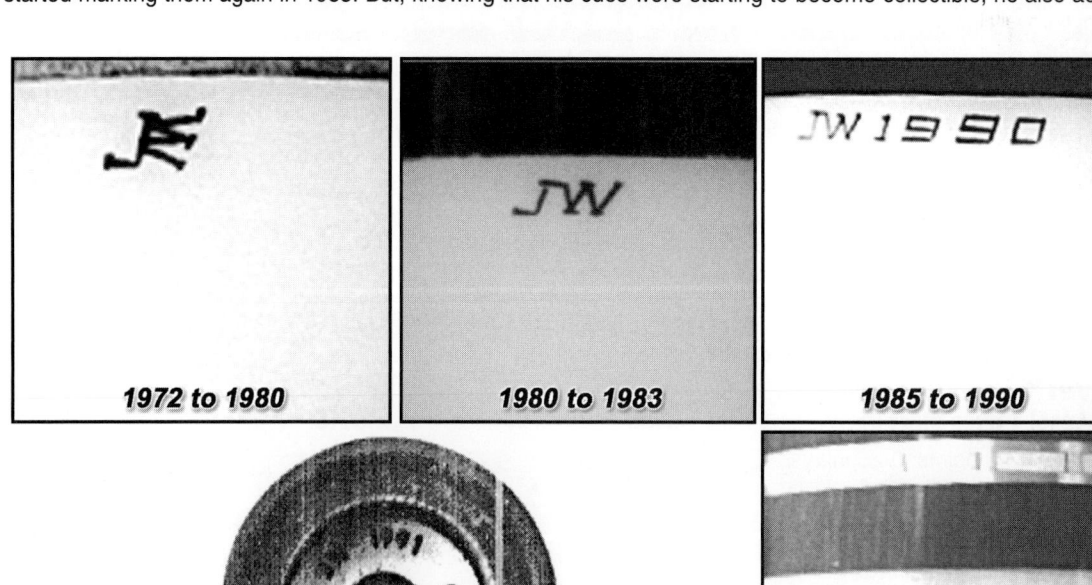

Customer demand for external markings brought them back again in 1995, when he settled on his current logo which reads "JW" right-side-up, or upside-down. Although the unmarked cues from the mid-1980s may be hard for the un-initiated to recognize, those who are familiar with Bill's work can easily identify them by their style, flawless execution, and playability. He is happy to identify his work when there is doubt. When Bill gets these cues back in the shop, he presently adds identification marks to avoid future confusion. Bill was the first cuemaker to begin using CNC technology on custom cues.

In early 1999, Bill won the first cuemakers' tournament ever held, at Magoo's in Tulsa, Oklahoma. All of the top cuemakers were invited, for a double elimination one-pocket tournament. Bill continues to play when he can, and should be a serious contender to win at future cuemakers' tournaments. In 2000, Bill moved Josswest to Ruidoso Downs, New Mexico. He held his first collector cue show there in 2003.

Bill has a state-of-the-art website which allows the customer to design their own cue and view it in three dimensions. Once the customer is satisfied with the design and materials, Bill will make it to their specifications. Bill feels that playability is the most important factor in a custom cue, and he believes that his road experience gives him an advantage over many other cuemakers in this area. He is willing to make virtually anything a customer desires, and will change any of the standard specifications if a customer desires. Bill believes that the great cues of the future will result from technology, and he is always experimenting with new ideas. He noticed that many players hold their cues on the butt sleeve, so he developed a new style of cue with the wrap above the butt cap and a much longer forearm. This design allows for a larger area to inlay. He also has an idea for a more ergonomic handle that would replace Irish linen and leather.

Bill has developed a website, www.cues.com, which helps a player to select the right cue for them. He stocks about three examples from each of about eight different makers to create a selection that will offer cues for most sizes and types of players. Bill personally tests each cue to determine their specifications and playing characteristics. Users answer a series of questions about their cue preferences, and the interactive program returns the three best cues for them that are currently in stock.

Currently Bill is not making as many cues as he did in the past. He has been a consultant for Taican in China, the largest manufacturer of cues in the world. Bill has designed new products for them including the new universal "Smart Shaft," patented by Bill and Paul Costane. This eight-piece radial laminated shaft features piezo electric material made from linear graphite in a viscus elastic medium that is wrapped around the shaft and covered with a maple sleeve. The piezo electric material converts mechanical energy into electrical energy. Bill claims it reduces vibration and quiets the hit, resulting in less abuse to the body and and more accurate striking of the cue ball. The Smart Shaft also features a new XTC ferrule with high modulus elasticity. This shaft is now standard on Josswest cues, and it is available seperately with universal adaptors that will allow it to fit any cue made. Traditional shafts are still available on Josswest cues if the customer prefers. Bill hopes to concentrate more on developing new state of the art products both inside and outside the billiard industry in the future.

Josswest cues are guaranteed against construction defects that are not the result of warpage or abuse. If you have a Josswest or an early Joss cue that needs identification or repair, or you would like to talk to Bill Stroud about the design of a new cue, contact Josswest, listed in the Trademark Index.

SPECIFICATIONS

- Butt material: hardwoods
- Standard shaft: smart shaft
- Standard length: 58 in.
- Lengths available: any
- Standard finish: polyurethane
- Standard joint screw: radial pin
- Standard joint: ivory
- Standard joint type: flat faced
- Standard wrap: Irish linen
- Standard point construction: inlaid
- Standard number of shafts: two
- Taper: custom
- Standard ferrules: XTC
- Annual production: approximately 35 cues

OPTIONS (FOR NEW CUES ONLY)

Option pricing depends entirely on the design and cost of the individual cue.

REPAIRS

Repairs done only on Joss West, early Joss (1968-1972), and Balabushka. Repair pricing depends entirely on the condition and make of the individual cue.

- Replace Shaft: $350

CURRENT JOSSWEST CUES

The current delivery time for a Joss West cue is at least six months, depending on the complexity of the cue. Bill currently specializes in one-of-a-kind cues starting at $3,500.

SECONDARY MARKET MINIMUM VALUES

The following are minimum prices for Joss West cues encountered on the secondary market. These prices are representative of cues utilizing basic materials and designs that are not currently available. Starting prices represent cues that will be encountered from when Bill made lines of cues in the seventies and eighties. Other Josswest cues can command many times the prices listed below, due to the use of exotic materials and artistry.

Special construction note: There are many materials and construction techniques that can add value to Josswest Cues. The following are the most important examples:

- Add 25%+ for early Joss West cues with horizontal "W" and spliced points.
- Add $1,000+ for ivory points.
- Add $1,200+ for ivory butt sleeve.

JOSSWEST, cont.

GRADING	98%	90%	70%

For all used Josswest cues, except where otherwise noted:
- Add $250+ for each additional original straight playable shaft (standard with two).
- Deduct $350 for each missing original straight playable shaft.
- Add $400+ for ivory joint.
- Add $175+ for leather wrap.
- Deduct 30% for obvious or improper refinish.

	98%	90%	70%
Level 2 - 0 points, 0-25 inlays.			
Level 2 cues start at	$1,000	$795	$550
Level 3 - 2-6 points, 0-8 inlays.			
Level 3 cues start at	$1,275	$1,000	$700
Level 4 - 4-10 points, 9-25 inlays.			
Level 4 cues start at	$1,650	$1,325	$950
Level 5 - 0-12 points, 26-50 inlays.			
Level 5 cues start at	$2,400	$1,800	$1,300
Level 6 - 0-12 points, 51-75 inlays.			
Level 6 cues start at	$3,500	$2,750	$1,850
Level 7 - 0-12 points, 76-125 inlays.			
Level 7 cues start at	$4,500	$3,650	$2,650
Level 8 - 4 or more points, 126 or more inlays.			
Level 8 cues start at	$6,000	$4,750	$3,350

JOUST GRAPHITE CUES

Maker of pool cues from 1994 to 1995 in Racial, Illinois.
The Joust Graphite Cue company was started in 1994 by a couple of partners in the Chicago area. The butts and shafts were made of graphite and medieval themes appeared on the cues.

SPECIFICATIONS

Butt material: graphite
Shaft material: graphite
Standard length: 58 in.
Balance point: 18 in. from butt

SECONDARY MARKET MINIMUM VALUES

For all used Joust cues, except where otherwise noted:
- Add $75 for each additional original straight playable graphite shaft (standard with one).
- Deduct 80% for missing original straight playable graphite shaft.

	98%	90%	70%
Level 2 - 0 points, 0-25 inlays.			
Level 2 cues start at	$145	$115	$70
Level 3 - 2-6 points, 0-8 inlays.			
Level 3 cues start at	$195	$150	$95

JUDD'S CUSTOM CUES

Maker of pool cues from 1989 to 1998 in Riverside, California and from 1998 to present in Yellow Jacket, Colorado.

Garland C. Fuller was born and raised in Marshall, Arkansas and moved to southern California at the age of 15. He played pool for most of his life, learning from his father, an Arkansas player nicknamed "Spot." After serving in the U.S. Army in Vietnam (where he acquired his nickname) Judd moved to Colorado to start logging. Eventually, he started a repair shop for logging trucks. During that time, Judd began doing cue repairs. He was in a small town and learned to work on his own cues by necessity, and soon he was doing work for others. Judd and Trudy met in 1988, and shortly put their lives on hold when Trudy's eldest son was involved in an auto accident and suffered a severe head injury. They moved to Riverside, California in the hopes of finding the best medical services for him. Judd started fooling with cues after hours at his place of employment while Trudy was busy in hospitals. Judd made his first cue on an old 1950s "brut" lathe at 600 RPMs. Judd was instantly hooked on cuemaking and purchased a lathe for their home. He began making cues for sale in 1989.

Trudy and Judd Fuller

Although his first cues are unmarked, Judd started engraving "Judd" in silver followed by the two-digit year of completion on custom cues starting in 1991. Early hustler cues had "Judd" branded on them until 1992, when he started engraving it on them. Recent cues are easily identified by the hand signature "Judd Fuller" followed by the two-digit date in black script on the forearm. One-of-a-kind and custom cues

JUDD'S Custom Cues

GRADING	100%	95%	70%

have various colors of script and placement or signature by request. Judd cues have a unique look, usually with long, thin, sharp points without veneers. Multicolored points are achieved with concentric splices. Inlay designs and wood combinations are tastefully chosen for their aesthetic appeal.

Judd introduced a line of cues in 1994 and uses these designs as a starting point for further creativity more than anything. In June of 1998, Judd and Trudy returned to Colorado to be closer to old friends and family. Judd now has a much bigger shop in which to work in Yellow Jacket, the place where he and Trudy met. Today, Judd makes 60-100 cues a year. All work is done by hand without the aid of computers, with playability stressed as the most important factor.

If not satisfied, Judd's Custom Cues offers a money-back guarantee minus shipping on any newly received Judd's cue that is returned in new condition. Judd's cues are guaranteed for life to the original owner against construction defects that are not the result of warpage or abuse. If you have a Judd cue that needs further identification or repair, or would like to talk to Judd about ordering a new cue, contact Judd's Custom Cues, listed in the Trademark Index.

SPECIFICATIONS

- Butt material: hardwoods
- Shaft material: rock maple
- Standard length: 58 in.
- Lengths available: any up to 60 in.
- Standard finish: synthetic
- Joint screw: 5/16-14 and 3/8-10
- Standard joint: phenolic
- Joint type: flat faced
- Balance point: 18 1/2 in. from butt
- Point construction: short splice
- Standard wrap: Irish linen
- Standard butt cap: linen-based fiber
- Standard number of shafts: two
- Standard taper: modified pro
- Standard ferrules: phenolic resin
- Standard tip: Le Pro
- Tip widths available: any
- Annual production: fewer than 100 cues

OPTIONS (FOR NEW CUES ONLY)

- Ivory joint: $150
- Joint protectors: $30+
- Extra shaft: $100+
- Ivory ferrules: $60 each

REPAIRS

Repairs done only on Judd's cues.
- Refinish: $150
- Rewrap (linen): $30
- Replace shaft: $100+
- Replace phenolic resin ferrule: $25
- Replace ivory ferrule: $60
- Replace linen-based fiber butt cap: $40

CURRENT JUDD CUES

Judd two-piece bar cues start at $300. Basic Judd's cues with wraps and joint rings start at $600. Judd's cues with points start at $850. One-of-a-kind custom Judd's cues start at $3,000. The current delivery time for a Judd's cue is about sixteen months.

CURRENT EXAMPLES

Judd currently specializes in one-of-a-kind custom cues. The following cues are representations of the work of Judd Fuller. These cues can be ordered as shown, modified to suit the desires of the customer, or new designs can be created.

Level 2 JT-1 - Bird's-eye maple forearm with a silver ring set in ebony above wrap, bird's-eye maple butt sleeve with ebony and ivory checks within silver rings set in ebony at top and bottom.

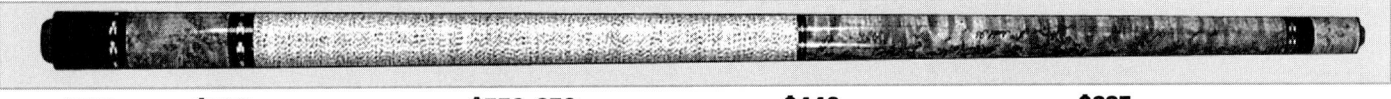

MSR	$600	$550-650	$440	$325

408 JUDD'S CUSTOM CUES, cont.

GRADING	100%	95%	70%

Level 4 JT-2 - Bird's-eye maple forearm, four long cocobolo points with a mother-of-pearl notched diamond-shaped inlay in each alternating with four short cocobolo points, cocobolo butt sleeve with four mother-of-pearl notched diamond-shaped inlays set in maple framed cocobolo windows between pairs of silver rings set in cocobolo above and below.

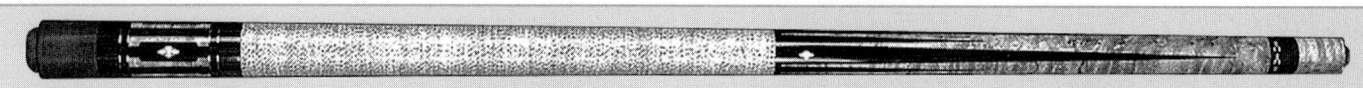

MSR	$1,190	$1,000-1,250	$825	$625

Level 3 JT-3 - Rosewood forearm, four long and four short bird's-eye maple points, rosewood butt sleeve with silver-bordered tulipwood checks set within pairs of silver rings above and below.

MSR	$850	$800-975	$635	$445

Level 4 JT-4 - Bird's-eye maple forearm, eight cocobolo points with an ivory six-point star-shaped inlay in every other point, cocobolo butt sleeve with four ivory six-point star-shaped inlays set in maple-framed cocobolo windows between maple and cocobolo and ebony checks within silver rings set in cocobolo above and below.

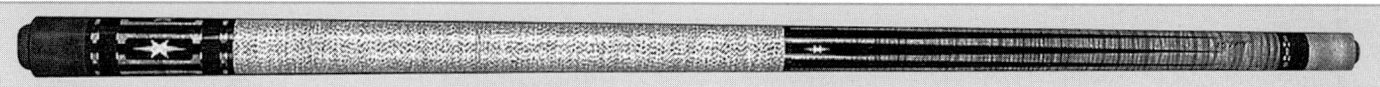

MSR	$1,375	$1,250-1,500	$1,000	$725

Level 4 JT-5 - Bird's-eye maple forearm with ebony and ivory checks within silver rings above wrap, eight ebony points with an ivory six-point star-shaped inlay in each, ebony butt sleeve with four large ivory six-point star-shaped inlays alternating with four vertical pairs of smaller ivory six-point star-shaped inlays between ebony and ivory checks within silver rings at top and bottom.

MSR	$1,400	$1,275-1,550	$1,025	$750

Level 5 JT-6 - Bocote forearm with cordia and ebony and ivory checks within silver rings set in ebony above wrap, four ebony points with a large ivory diamond-shaped inlay between a pair of smaller vertical ivory diamond-shaped inlays in each point alternating with four ebony points with a smaller ivory diamond-shaped inlay in each point, ebony butt sleeve with four large ebony and cordia-bordered ivory diamond-shaped inlays alternating with four smaller cordia-bordered ivory diamond-shaped inlays with horizontal pairs of smaller ivory diamond-shaped inlays above and below all between cordia, ebony, and ivory checks within silver rings set in ebony at top and bottom.

MSR	$1,560	$1,450-1,750	$1,150	$800

GRADING	98%	90%	70%

SECONDARY MARKET MINIMUM VALUES

The following are minimum prices for other Judd's cues encountered on the secondary market. These prices are representative of cues utilizing basic materials and designs that may not be currently available. Judd also offers one-of-a-kind cues that can command many times these prices due to the use of exotic materials and artistry.

Special construction note: There are many materials and construction techniques that can add value to Judd's cues.

For all used Judd's cues:
  Add $80+ for each additional original straight playable shaft beyond two.
  Deduct $100+ for each missing original straight playable shaft under two.
  Add $100+ for ivory joint.
  Add $50 for each ivory ferrule
  Deduct 25% for obvious or improper refinish.

Level 1 - 4 points, hustler.
  Level 1 cues start at $250 $195 $135
Level 2 - 0 points, 0-25 inlays.
  Level 2 cues start at $500 $335 $265

GRADING	98%	90%	70%
Level 3 - 2-6 points, 0-8 inlays.			
Level 3 cues start at	$750	$575	$390
Level 4 - 4-10 points, 9-25 inlays.			
Level 4 cues start at	$850	$665	$445
Level 5 - 0-12 points, 26-50 inlays.			
Level 5 cues start at	$1,250	$985	$675
Level 6 - 0-12 points, 51-76 inlays.			
Level 6 cues start at	$1,600	$1,275	$885

JUSTIS CUES

Maker of pool cues from 1991 to present in Coconut Creek, Florida.

Jack Justis has loved to play pool since he was a boy. Growing up in a small town, his parents did not want him in the local pool hall because they felt that it was kind of a seedy place. While he was there Jack always had an eye out for his father, and would sneak out the back door if he saw his father looking for him. The more they tried to keep him away, the more time he spent there.

As an adult, Jack went to work for Chris-Craft. He still liked to play pool, but spent more time fishing. He also spent a little time on woodworking projects. Jack left Chris-Craft after eighteen years, and started making fishing rods for enjoyment. Three years after starting, he entered an international fishing rod competition, sponsored by The American Fishing Tackle Association, in Las Vegas, Nevada. Jack won first place in the saltwater division, and first place in the freshwater division. He later gave seminars in rod building and became a master at thread art. Some of his wraps can be seen in the first edition of the Blue Book of Pool Cues.

Jack Justis

When he needed a new case for his pool cue, Jack decided to make one. A friend saw the case as it was being made, and started hounding Jack to sell it to him. Jack gave in, and ended up selling the next case before it was done too. Soon Jack was in the cue case business. Within that year he made his first cue as well. Jack has never done any inlay work on cues, but he has used thread art for the wraps. He has created pictures, designs, and even text from wraps of woven multi-colored threads.

Jack now makes about three batches of five cues a year, at his leisure. He starts with nice old full-spliced Brunswick one-piece cues. He adds joints and rings, threads on capped ferrules, tapers the shafts, sometimes adds wraps, signs and dates them, then finishes the cues. Jack spends more time making Jack Justis Custom Cue cases out of a variety of exotic skins and hand tooled hides. He got tired of making fishing rods, and has not made any since 1993.

Jack also notes that due to his cue case business taking up a majority of his time, he is no longer spending much time making cues.

Justis Cues are guaranteed for life against manufacturing defects that are not the result of warpage or abuse. If you have a Justis cue that needs further identification or repair, or would like to order a new Justis cue, contact Justis Cues, listed in the Trademark Index.

SPECIFICATIONS

Butt material: hardwoods
Shaft material: rock maple
Standard length: 58 in.
Lengths available: any
Standard finish: conversion varnish
Balance point: varies
Standard butt cap: Ivorine 3
Standard wrap: Irish linen
Point construction: short splice
Standard joint: Ivorine 3
Joint type: piloted
Joint screw: 3/8-10
Standard number of shafts: one
Standard taper: 12 in. straight
Standard ferrules: capped melamine
Tip widths available: any
Standard tip: Moori
Annual production: approximately 15 cues

OPTIONS (FOR NEW CUES ONLY)

Pigskin wrap: $75
Special length: no charge
Ivory butt cap: $250
Extra shaft: $200+
Ivory ferrule: $75

GRADING	98%	90%	70%

REPAIRS

Repairs done on all fine cues.
- Refinish (with Irish linen): $125
- Rewrap (Irish linen): $45
- Rewrap (pigskin): $75+
- Replace Moori tip: $45
- Replace shaft: $200+
- Replace melamine ferrule: $35

CURRENT JUSTIS CUES

Two piece Justis bar cues start at $350. One-of-a-kind Justis cues with or without points start at $450. The current delivery time for a Justis cue is one year.

SECONDARY MARKET MINIMUM VALUES

The following are minimum values for Justis Cues encountered on the secondary market. These prices are representative of cues utilizing basic materials and designs that are not currently available. Has offered one-of-a-kind cues that can command many times these prices due to the use of exotic materials and artistry.

Special construction note: There are many materials and construction techniques that can add value to Justis cues. The following are the most important examples:
- Add $650+ for thread art wrap.
- Add $250+ for veneers in points (Titlist blank).

For all used cues, except where otherwise noted:
- Add $165 for each additional original straight playable shaft beyond one.
- Deduct $200 for missing original straight playable shaft.
- Add $65 each for ivory ferrules.
- Add $75 for pigskin wrap.
- Deduct 25% for obvious or improper refinish.

Level 1 - 4 points, hustler.

Level 1 cues start at	$375	$295	$200

Level 2 - 0 points, 0-25 inlays.

Level 2 cues start at	$450	$370	$280

Level 3 - 2-6 points.

Level 3 cues start at	$500	$410	$295

K SECTION

RON KADEY

Maker of Syra Cues. For more information, refer to the listing for Syra Cues.

KAIZEN CUSTOM CUES

Maker of pool cues starting in 1997 in Lexington, Kentucky.

Greg Wilson and Matt Laughter became friends when Matt started working for Greg at Steepleton's Billiards in Lexington, Kentucky in 1992. Both had a background in billiards, liked to play pool, and had a love for fine cues. They bought and sold cues at Steepleton's, and both had cues of their own. They learned what they liked about the playability of different types of cues and the different makers that created them. Since they had a market for cues, and had strong opinions about how they should be made, Greg and Matt decided to make cues on their own.

They chose the name Kaizen, a Japanese word that describes when something is done right, and completed their first cue in 1997. Neither had a background in any type of woodworking, so they taught themselves with the help of many long phone conversations with cuemakers Mike Bender and Joe Gold. Playability was always their primary concern, so construction techniques that resulted in a solid hitting cue were more important than decoration. Kaizen cues had little or no inlay work and all work was done by hand. Most cues had no points, and they were so particular about the consistency of their spliced blanks, that they selected only the finest examples to use on their cues.

Early Kaizen cues had 3/8-10 stainless steel joint screws, and in 1998 they switched to a 3/8-11 titanium screw. The name Kaizen was laser cut into the base of the screw for identification. Although they had a linen phenolic joint, Kaizen cues tended to be forward balanced. Preferred woods included bird's-eye maple, fiddle-back maple, goncolo alves, and cocobolo. Each cue was crafted to the specifications of the individual customer, and then received at least eight coats of urethane finish. Greg and Matt were very proud of the appearance of the final product. The current status of Kaizen cues is unknown.

SPECIFICATIONS

Butt material: hardwoods
Shaft material: rock maple
Standard length: 58 in.
Lengths available: any
Standard finish: catelyzed urethane
Balance point: custom
Standard butt cap: linen phenolic
Standard wrap: Irish linen
Point construction: short splice
Standard joint: linen phenolic
Joint type: flat faced
Joint screw: 3/8-11 titanium
Standard number of shafts: two
Standard taper: custom
Standard ferrules: linen phenolic
Tip widths available: any
Standard tip: Moori

GRADING

	98%	90%	70%

SECONDARY MARKET MINIMUM VALUES

The following are minimum values for Kaizen custom cues encountered on the secondary market. These prices are representative of cues utilizing basic materials and designs that are not currently available.

Special construction note: There are many materials and construction techniques that can add value to Kaizen cues.

For all used Kaizen cues, except where otherwise noted:

Add $125 for each additional original straight playable shaft beyond two.
Deduct $175 for each missing original straight playable shaft under two.
Add $60 each for ivory ferrules.
Add $75 for leather wrap.
Deduct 30% for obvious or improper refinish.

	98%	90%	70%
Level 2 - 0 points, 0-25 inlays.			
Level 2 cues start at	$550	$395	$215
Level 3 - 2-6 points, 0-8 inlays.			
Level 3 cues start at	$800	$625	$390

| GRADING | 98% | 90% | 70% |

KARELLA CUES

Manufacturer of pool cues from 1993 to present in Thailand, imported by Competition Sports.

If you have a Karrella cue that needs repair, or would like to talk to someone about ordering a new cue, contact Competition Sports listed in the Trademark Index.

Present Day

SPECIFICATIONS

Butt material: hardwoods
Shaft material: rock maple
Standard length: 58 in.
Balance point: 1 1/2 in. above wrap
Standard wrap: Irish linen
Standard number of shafts: one

CURRENT KARELLA CUES

As of 2005, Karella cues have been temporarily discontinued by Competition Sports.

SECONDARY MARKET MINIMUM VALUES

The following are minimum prices for Karella cues encountered on the secondary market.
Special construction note: There are many materials and construction techniques that can add value to Karella cues.
For all used Karella cues:

Deduct 50% for missing original straight playable shaft.
Deduct 20% for obvious or improper refinish.

Level 2 - 0 points, 0-25 inlays.
   Level 2 cues start at $95 $75 $45

Level 3 - 2-6 points, 0-8 inlays.
   Level 3 cues start at $135 $105 $65

Level 4 - 4-10 points, 9-25 inlays.
   Level 4 cues start at $165 $125 $80

Level 5 - 0-12 points, 26-50 inlays.
   Level 5 cues start at $200 $155 $95

KEITH KUSTOM KUES

Maker of pool cues from 1989 to 1997 in Sioux Falls, South Dakota.

Keith Holcomb was a retired machinist from San Jose, California. He began making cues as a hobby in the mid-1960s, going full-time in 1986. He hired Keith Hanssen as his apprentice the following year. In 1989, Keith Hanssen purchased the business, and made Keith cues until closing the shop in March of 1997.

 **KEITH KUSTOM KUES**

Keith made every component of his cues, including the tips and bumpers, by hand in his one-man shop. Keith cues were signed, dated, and serial numbered for easy identification. 45 of the 60 cues Keith made each year were available for immediate delivery to customers. The rest were custom orders built to the designs and specifications of the individual customer.

SPECIFICATIONS

Butt material: hardwoods
Shaft material: rock maple
Standard length: 58 in.
Lengths available: any
Joint screw: 3/8-10
Joint type: flat faced
Point construction: short splice
Standard wrap: Irish linen
Standard number of shafts: two
Standard tip: black widow
Tip widths available: any
Total production: approximately 500 cues

GRADING	98%	90%	70%

SECONDARY MARKET MINIMUM VALUES

The following are minimum values for Keith cues encountered on the secondary market. These prices are representative of cues utilizing basic materials and designs that were available. Keith offered one-of-a-kind cues that can command many times these prices due to the use of exotic materials and artistry. More information on Keith cues will be covered in future editions. Special construction note: There are many materials and construction techniques that can add value to Keith cues. The following are the most important examples:

Add for 50%+ for use of 14-karat gold inlays.

For all used Keith cues, except where otherwise noted:

Add $150 for each additional original straight playable shaft beyond two.
Deduct $250 for each missing original straight playable shaft under two.
Add $100 each for original ivory ferrules.
Add $175 for original leather wrap.
Deduct 30% for obvious or improper refinish.

Level 2 - 0 points, 0-25 inlays.

	98%	90%	70%
Level 2 cues start at	$1,350	$1,025	$650

Level 3 - 2-6 points, 0-8 inlays.

Level 3 cues start at	$1,800	$1,350	$850

Level 4 - 4-10 points, 9-25 inlays.

Level 4 cues start at	$2,250	$1,650	$1,050

Level 5 - 0-12 points, 26-50 inlays.

Level 5 cues start at	$3,000	$2,775	$1,450

Level 6 - 0-12 points, 51-75 inlays.

Level 6 cues start at	$3,500	$2,800	$1,950

Level 7 - 0-12 points, 76-125 inlays.

Level 7 cues start at	$4,500	$3,600	$2,400

Level 8 - 4 or more points, 126 or more inlays.

Level 8 cues start at	$6,000	$4,750	$3,200

KELLY CUES

Maker of pool cues in Indianapolis, Indiana.
For more information, please contact Kelly Cues, listed in the Trademark Index.

DAVID PAUL KERSENBROCK

Maker of pool cues from 1972 to 1990 primarily on his own, from 1990 to 1996 with Omega/dpk, and from 1993 to present in Chicago, Illinois.

David Paul Kersenbrock has had a fascination with physics for as long as he can remember. He learned to play pool, and became an excellent player, while growing up in a small town in Wyoming. After serving in Vietnam, David settled in Las Vegas, Nevada. In 1972, David decided to use his knowledge of physics to try to create the perfect pool cue. He experimented with different designs and construction techniques before settling on what he believed was

Very rare signature

David Paul Kersenbrock

best. He started the Kersenbrock Cue Service later that year. Instead of following the trend of stainless steel piloted joints with stainless screws, David designed a flat-faced phenolic joint with a longer brass 3/8-11 screw. David's joint was thinner and lighter than other cues, which meant that the cue was not as forward heavy as other cues. His taper was a parabolic curve from the tip to the butt, making for a very stiff hit, with minimal cue deflection. For inlay work, David developed an optical pantograph, which allows him to artistically freehand his inlays instead of tracing them from a pattern.

In 1976, David made a cue for Jerry Franklin, an accounting student at U.N.L.V., in exchange for repairs to David's car. Soon the two were making cues together based on David's cuemaking philosophy. In 1978 David relocated briefly to Arizona and then to Caliente, Nevada. He worked alone in a stone walled structure he built himself. By 1981, when Jerry Franklin opened his shop as South West Cues in Las Vegas, David began sending fancy inlayed cues for shafts and finish work. David's engineering genius contributed to the

GRADING	98%	90%	70%

setup of the South West shop. Many of the Kersenbrock visual traits were incorporated by South West as well. As a result, many South West cues over the years have been sold as Kersenbrock cues. After David left South West in 1988, he moved around the west coast, making cues in Van Nuys, Caliente, Phoenix, and even in L.A. working for Bert Schrager. He was in none of these locations for more than a year, and eventually settled in Chicago where he currently lives and works.

David's innovations have inspired many of the current generation of cuemakers. He can be credited with reinventing the cuemaking process and some of his machine designs and jigs are ubiquitous in the cuemaking industry. His cues have also become very desirable by collectors and bring top dollar in the market. Although Kersenbrock cues can be difficult to identify, except for the cues David has signed, David believes he can identify virtually every cue he ever made if he can look at it. He has written a manual on cuemaking, which is rather difficult to obtain and has become sought after by many cuemakers and cue collectors. In 1990, David joined Omega/dpk, and built a handful of one-of-a-kind custom Omega cues every year until 1996.

Since 1993, David has been teaching his techniques to Chicago cuemaker Ed Young, and making about six to ten very fancy cues a year. Each cue comes with a certificate of authenticity, and many include a photo of David working on the cue. If you have a Kersenbrock cue that needs further identification or repair, contact Ed Young Custom Cues, listed in the Trademark Index.

SPECIFICATIONS

Butt material: hardwoods
Shaft material: rock maple
Standard length: 58 in.
Standard joint screw: 3/8-11
Standard joint: custom
Joint type: flat faced
Point construction: custom
Standard wrap: Irish linen
Standard butt cap: custom

CURRENT EXAMPLES

David currently specializes in one-of-a-kind custom cues. He is only making six to ten cues annually and starting at $25,000. The following cues are representations of the work of David Kersenbrock. Many South West cues are mistakenly believed to be Kersenbrock cues. Thus, authentic Kersenbrock cues with provenance and original finish are most sought after. Also, cues that belonged to players of note are in high demand.

Level 7 - Ebony nose with six points (three high and three low) of ivory detailed with intricate engravings. Each point tip embellished with fancy inlaid designs. Wrap is Irish linen. Butt sleeve of ivory and ebony inlaid with ivory windows and fancy designs. Each ivory window engraved with alternating designs. Large ivory ring below wrap is engraved. Joint is ivory and phenolic, and the ivory is engraved with a miniture design found alternating in the butt cap windows.

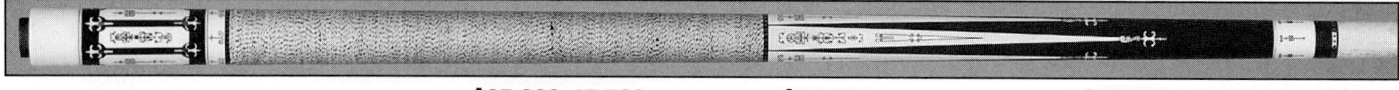

	$35,000-45,500	$30,100	$17,000

Level 8 - Forearm is cocobolo with six curly maple points (three high and three low). The long points feature a semi-oval void which are inlaid with ivory and white sapphires in a free-form design. At the base of the points are ivory inlays. Wrap is Irish linen. Butt sleeve is cocobolo with several curly maple windows which create the illusion that the cocobolo is inlaid. Between each window are ivory inlays masking the edges of the maple inlays. In the cocobolo are several inlays of ivory and white sapphires in free-form designs. Joint is ivory and is heavily engraved with original designs. Butt cap is ivory. Cue is one of the fanciest cues made by David.

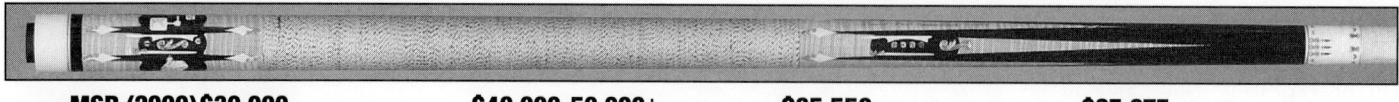

MSR (2000) $30,000	$40,000-50,000+	$35,550	$25,075

PAST EXAMPLES

Level 2 - Bird's-eye maple nose, Irish linen wrap and bird's-eye maple butt sleeve. Phenolic joint with fancy ringwork. Joint engraved and includes initials "DPK."

MSR (1970s) $75	$3,700	$3,000	$1,875

Level 3 - Bird's-eye maple forearm, four rosewood points no veneers, Irish linen wrap, rosewood butt sleeve. Joint is micarta with phenolic collars. Butt cap is phenolic.

MSR (1980s) $100	$4,250	$3,800	$2,000

DAVID PAUL KERSENBROCK, cont. **415**

GRADING	98%	90%	70%

Level 3 - Brunswick Titlist conversion cue with four rosewood points, each with four veneers and an inlay, into a straight grain maple forearm. Wrap is black leather. Butt sleeve is rosewood inlayed with engraved windows, and straight grain maple seperated by white phenolic ring. Joint and butt cap are home-made white linen phenolic. Fancy box-type rings are on each side of the joint and in the maple butt sleeve.

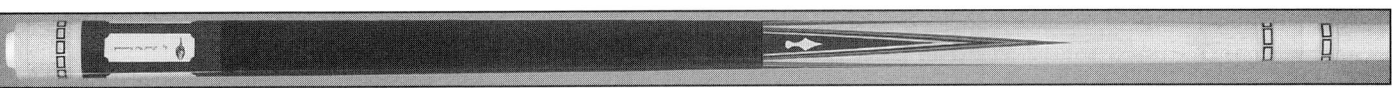

MSR (1970s) $100	$6,000	$5,550	$2,900

Level 4 -Forearm is ebony with unique inlaid curly maple pitchfork point designs. Handle is curly maple. Butt sleeve is ebony with curly maple inlay designs, between which are red lines topped with circular inlays. Joint and butt cap are black phenolic embellished with fancy white box-type rings.

MSR (1980s) $1000	$5,850	$5,250	$2,800

Level 4 - Rosewood forearm, with four floating inlaid points of curly maple, ebony, and white inlays. Irish linen wrap. Butt sleeve is rosewood with maple inlay work. Joint and butt cap are white phenolic with fancy ringwork. Rings and butt cap are omega-style, and butt cap is signed "Kersenbrock."

	$10,000	$6,500	$4,275

Level 5 - Brazilian rosewood forearm, inlaid with elongated musical notes. Handle is curly maple. Butt sleeve is tulipwood and is inlaid with long windows which are re-inlaid with a violin. Rings are stacked solids of black and white. Joint and butt cap are micarta. Cue was made for a well-known violinist and received much press.

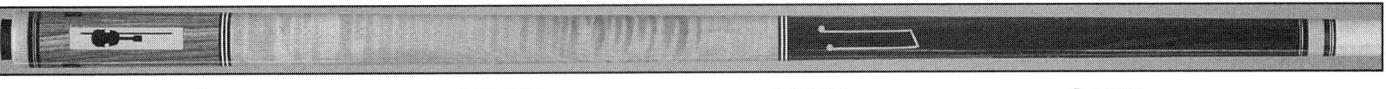

MSR (1970s) $300	$10,000	$6,200	$4,000

Level 8 - Forearm is ebony with four unique floating silver points. Handle is white linen. Butt sleve is ebony with fancy silver inlay work inlcuding large torches. Joint and butt cap are black phenolic. There are no rings, though the joint is heavily inlaid with free-form grape-leaf designs mimicking fancy ringwork. All silver in cue is sterling silver.

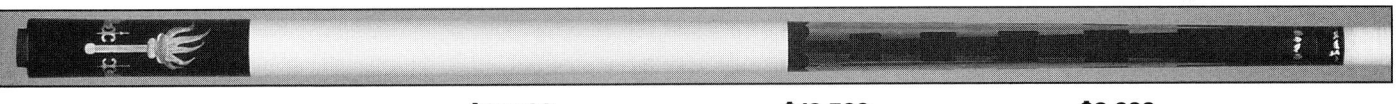

	$17,500	$13,500	$8,000

SECONDARY MARKET MINIMUM VALUES

Note: The following are minimum prices for Kersenbrock cues encountered on the secondary market. These prices are representative of cues utilizing basic materials and designs. David has made many one-of-a-kind cues that can command many times these prices due to the use of exotic materials and artistry.

Special construction note: There are many materials and construction techniques that can add value to Kersenbrock cues.

For all used Kersenbrock cues:

Deduct up to 30% for obvious or improper refinish.
Add $950+ for an original ivory joint.
Add $1,500+ for original ivory butt cap.
Add $1,500+ for "k" logo, or signature.
Add $450+ for each additional original straight playable shaft.
Deduct $450 for each missing original straight playable shaft with owner's initials under two.
Add $400 for original leather wrap.
Add $400+ for original white rubber bumper.
Add $650+ for use of in-house made white linen phenolic.

Level 2 - 0 points, 0-25 inlays.

Level 2 cues start at	$2,000	$1,800	$1,100

Level 3 - 2-6 points, 0-8 inlays.

Level 3 cues start at	$3,000	$2,700	$1,800

Level 4 - 4-10 points, 9-25 inlays.

Level 4 cues start at	$5,000	$4,500	$2,900

GRADING	98%	90%	70%
Level 5 - 0-12 points, 26-50 inlays.			
Level 5 cues start at	$8,000	$7,200	$4,650
Level 6 - 0-12 points, 51-75 inlays.			
Level 6 cues start at	$9,500	$8,700	$5,100
Level 7 - 0-12 points, 76-125 inlays.			
Level 7 cues start at	$15,500	$14,000	$8,800
Level 8 - 0-12 points, 126+ inlays.			
Level 8 cues start at	$19,000	$17,000	$11,100

KIKEL CUSTOM CUES

Maker of pool cues from 1987 to 2001 to Colorado Springs and 2001 to present in Pueblo, Colorado.

David Kikel started woodworking at the age of five, when he made a crude birdhouse. He has played pool since the age of seven, when his father put a pool table in the basement of the family home in Pueblo, Colorado. He furthered his interest in woodworking while still in school. He later worked in the custom framing business, advancing to custom woodworking in high-end homes and restoring antique furniture. David continued to play pool, winning the Colorado Springs city championships many times, and placing fourth in a BCA national eight-ball tournament.

During this time, Bill Stroud was living in Colorado Springs, and the two became friends. David played with a Joss West cue that Bill had custom made for him, and David became interested in cuemaking. During a very bad winter, which slowed down his home construction work, David bought a lathe and started doing cue repairs. His first cues were one-piece house cues that he cut down into hustler cues. He then made eight or nine custom cues using blanks that were given to him by Bill. Soon, he was making his own cues from scratch, even making his own hustler cues, with inlaid points.

Dave Kikel

Since then, David has changed his shaft taper six times, and the butt taper four times, for better playability, which is his primary concern. He has developed his own wood-to-wood joint that softens the hit. David tries to make his two-piece cues hit like one-piece cues. Kikel cues are easily identifiable by the stylized "KQ" logo with a square san sarif "Q" that has been rotated 45 degrees, which appears on all of David's cues. Early logos were cut by hand, but now he uses a pantograph. Today, David makes less than 100 cues per year in his shop in Colorado Springs, with one every year being for his own collection.

He prides himself on execution, with extremely clean inlays, finish, and wraps being very important to him. David's cue, "Imperial Inspiration" with over 1,200 inlays won the silver medal at the 1998 Gallery of American Cue Art in New York City. David says it was one of the most difficult cues he has ever done. Other examples of David's high end work have appeared in magazines like Playboy and Maxim.

His most basic cue has four points, as cues without points are no longer available. Three-point cues were available in the past. David makes everything except for the bumpers, tips, and screws, and all work is done by hand, without the aid of CNC. He finishes the cues with a conversion varnish, which is safer than many of the commonly used synthetic finishes. All high end Kikel cues feature ivory ferrules as standard.

1987 to Present Day

At present, David prefers to use the radial pin or the 5/16-14 piloted joint. In the past, David has used a standard 3/8-10, and a 5/16-18 joint. In 1998, David developed a unique flat faced 3/8-10 Stub ACME joint which he used and with only 25 thousandths of an inch in depth to the thread pattern, it has virtually complete surface contact between the screw and the shaft. This joint was available without collars for even more wood-to-wood contact. Now he no longer uses that joint at all. Resin-impregnated wood ferrules are available on request, and the standard ferrule is melamine.

Kikel cues are guaranteed indefinitely against construction defects that are not the result of warpage or abuse. If you have a Kikel cue that needs further identification or repair, or would like to talk to David about the design of a new cue, contact Kikel Custom Cues, listed in the Trademark Index.

SPECIFICATIONS

Butt material: hardwoods
Shaft material: rock maple
Standard length: 58 in.
Lengths available: any
Standard finish: conversion varnish
Standard joint screw: radial pin
Standard joint: linen phenolic
Standard joint type: flat faced

| GRADING | 98% | 90% | 70% |

Balance point: approximately 2 in. above wrap
Point construction: inlaid
Standard wrap: Irish linen
Standard butt cap: linen phenolic
Standard number of shafts: two
Standard taper: modified pro
Standard ferrules: melamine
Standard tip: sumo
Tip widths available: any
Annual production: fewer than 100 cues

OPTIONS (FOR NEW CUES ONLY)

Leather wrap: $100
Ivory joint: $150
Stainless steel joint: $75
3/8-10 flat-faced joint: no charge
Ivory butt cap: $250
Special length: no charge
Veneers: $25 per point
Ivory ferrules: $50 each
Extra shaft: $115

REPAIRS

Repairs done only on Kikel cues or cues by past masters.
Refinish (with leather wrap): $300
Refinish (with linen wrap): $200
Rewrap (leather): $100
Rewrap (linen): $50
Replace shaft: $115+
Replace ivory ferrule: $50
Replace Delrin butt cap: $35
Replace ivory butt cap: $250

KIKEL CUES

Basic Kikel cues with four points start at $700. Basic six-point Kikel cues start at $770. Eight-point Kikel cues start at $950. One-of-a-kind custom Kikel start at $2,000. The current delivery time for a cue is approximately five to six months depending on the intricacy of the cue.

SECONDARY MARKET MINIMUM VALUES

The following are minimum prices for Kikel cues encountered on the secondary market. These prices are representative of cues utilizing basic materials and designs that may not be currently available. David currently specializes in one-of-a-kind cues that can command many times these prices due to the use of exotic materials and artistry.

Special construction note: There are many materials and construction techniques that can add value to Kikel cues. The following are the most important examples:

Add $150+ for each ivory point.
Add $3,000+ for an ivory handle.

For all used Kikel cues:

Add $100+ for each additional original straight playable shaft beyond two.
Deduct $115+ for each missing original straight playable shaft under two.
Deduct 25% for obvious or improper refinish.

Level 1 - 4 points, hustler.

	98%	90%	70%
Level 1 cues start at	$300	$230	$155

Level 2 - 0 points, 0-25 inlays.

Level 2 cues start at	$550	$425	$285

Level 3 - 3-6 points, 0-8 inlays.

Level 3 cues start at	$750	$575	$385

Level 4 - 4-10 points, 9-25 inlays.

Level 4 cues start at	$900	$715	$475

Level 5 - 0-12 points, 26-50 inlays.

Level 5 cues start at	$1,500	$1,175	$800

KIKEL CUSTOM CUES, cont.

GRADING	98%	90%	70%
Level 6 - 4-12 points, 51-75 inlays.			
Level 6 cues start at	$2,000	$1,650	$1,200
Level 7 - 4-12 points, 76-125 inlays.			
Level 7 cues start at	$2,650	$2,085	$1,350

RONALD KILBY CUES

Maker of pool cues from 1987 to present in Medford, Oregon.

Ron Kilby started making sneaky petes and jump-break cues in 1985. Since 1987 Ron has created cues for players of every level. Cue building was a natural transition for him, since he had been a woodworking hobbyist and had done cue repairs. In 1995 he began to focus on carom cues, with their traditional wood-thread joint and characteristics distinct from pool cues. His designs span a wide range, from traditional butterfly points to avant garde cues including precious stones, scrimshaw ivory exotic inlays, and eight-segment laminated and graphite shafts. Pool and three-cushion players prefer wood shafts, while balkline and straight rail players sometimes prefer the graphite shafts. The graphite shafts are only 2.5 ounces, resulting in cues that can weigh under 15 ounces. They are also very stiff. He builds cues for playability first, with classical designs being prominent in his work.

Ron has a relatively small and rather crowded shop. He produces cues and guitars at the same time. His work, particularly in the carom world, has become instantly recognizable. All Kilby cues since 1993 have a small mylar decal on the buttcap, "RK", for identification. Cues before 1993 were hand-etched under the rubber bumper.

Ron Kilby

Kilby sells custom-designed cues as well as those displayed in his catalog. He still makes pool cues using a wood-thread joint. There are usually one or two in the current inventory. Ron Kilby also makes a three-piece cue for traveling.

Kilby Cues are warrantied for workmanship for life. Warping and obvious abuse are not covered.

If you are interested in talking to Ron about a new cue or cue that needs to be repaired, you can contact him at Kilby Cues, listed in the Trademark Index.

SPECIFICATIONS

- Butt material: hardwoods
- Shaft material: hard maple or graphite
- Standard length: 58 in.
- Standard carom length: 56 in.
- Standard wrap: Irish linen
- Standard ferrules: Atlas MPI
- Standard tip: Talisman
- Annual production: fewer than 100 cues

OPTIONS (FOR NEW CUES ONLY)

- Carom shaft ivory ferrule: $35
- Pool shaft ivory ferrule: $50
- Leather wrap: $50
- Extra shaft: $100
- Extra segmented or graphite shaft: $175

REPAIRS

Repairs done only on Kilby Cues. Repairs priced on an individual basis. Contact Ron Kilby for repair pricing.

CURRENT RONALD KILBY CUES

Two-piece Ronald Kilby bar cues start at $240, including US delivery. Basic Ronald Kilby cues with wraps and joint rings start at $425. Ronald Kilby Cues with four sharp or butterfly points with two veneers start at $525. One-of-a-kind custom Ronald Kilby cues start at $595. The current delivery time for a Ronald Kilby cue is three to four months.

SECONDARY MARKET MINIMUM VALUES

The following are minimum values for Ronald Kilby cues encountered on the secondary market. These prices are representative of cues utilizing basic materials and designs that are not necessarily available at present. Ron has offered one-of-a-kind cues that can command many times these prices due to the use of exotic materials and artistry.

Special construction note: There are many materials and construction techniques that can add value to Ronald Kilby cues.

GRADING	98%	90%	70%

For all used Ronald Kilby cues, except where otherwise noted:
- Add $75+ for each additional original straight playable shaft beyond one.
- Deduct $100+ for missing original straight playable shaft.
- Add $40+ each for ivory ferrules.
- Add $40 for leather wrap.
- Deduct 15% for obvious or improper refinish.

Level 1 - Hustler.
Level 1 cues start at	$225	$175	$120

Level 2 - 0 points, 0-25 inlays.
Level 2 cues start at	$400	$310	$215

Level 3 - 2-6 points, 0-8 inlays.
Level 3 cues start at	$500	$390	$265

Level 4 - 4-10 points, 9-25 inlays.
Level 4 cues start at	$600	$475	$325

Level 5 - 0-12 points, 26-50 inlays.
Level 5 cues start at	$850	$675	$450

Level 6 - 0-12 points, 51-75 inlays.
Level 6 cues start at	$1,150	$900	$600

RON KITZMILLER CUES

Maker of pool cues in Hixson, Tennessee.

Ron Kitzmiller has been building cues since the late eighties out of Hixson, Tennessee. His cues are all completely handmade using traditional construction methods. He is known locally for his great playing cues, replacement shafts, and repair work. His cue designs are very original and unique. All inlay work is hand cut and fitted using a manual pantograph, with no CNC. From "sneaky Petes" to fancy one-of-a-kind inlaid cues, Ron's prices are very reasonable and he takes great pride in producing fine playing cues.

SPECIFICATIONS

Butt material: hardwoods
Shaft material: rock maple

SECONDARY MARKET MINIMUM VALUES

The following are minimum values for other Ron Kitzmiller cues encountered on the secondary market. These prices are representative of cues utilizing basic materials and designs that are not necessarily available at present. Ron has offered one-of-a-kind cues that can command many times these prices due to the use of exotic materials and artistry.

Special construction note: There are many materials and construction techniques that can add value to Ron Kitzmiller cues.

For all used Ron Kitzmiller cues, except where otherwise noted:
- Add $65 for each additional original straight playable shaft beyond one.
- Deduct $100 for missing original straight playable shaft.
- Add $40 each for ivory ferrules.
- Add $50 for leather wrap.
- Deduct 15% for obvious or improper refinish.

Level 1 - Hustler.
Level 1 cues start at	$125	$100	$65

Level 2 - 0 points, 0-25 inlays.
Level 2 cues start at	$200	$160	$110

Level 3 - 2-6 points, 0-8 inlays.
Level 3 cues start at	$300	$235	$160

Level 4 - 4-10 points, 9-25 inlays.
Level 4 cues start at	$400	$315	$220

Level 5 - 0-12 points, 26-50 inlays.
Level 5 cues start at	$650	$510	$345

KLEIN CUSTOM CUES

Maker of pool cues from 1998 to present in Flower Mound, Texas.

Steve Klein decided to become a cuemaker in 1998. He started playing pool as a youngster in Pennsylvania with his cousin who would come and visit for the summer. They would play for hours at end all summer long. His pool playing was put into hibernation by an appointment to the Naval Academy and subsequent career as a Navy Fighter Pilot, only getting to play and be around the game infrequently. His interest in the game was rekindled when his son took up an interest in the game and they purchased a table. Not being around the game for quite a while, he was amazed at the quantity and quality of cues available. Contacting his cousin who had originally gotten him started, he was introduced to the world of custom cues. His cousin had once owned a Balabushka and he became intrigued with the lore and workmanship of these cues.

1997 saw the start of Steve's quest for cue knowledge. While shopping around for custom cues, he contacted Chester Krick. Originally planning on making some decorative cues, Chester spent immeasurable time on the phone and through emails, telling him about how, and more importantly, why, cues are made in particular ways. The more they communicated and interacted, the more Steve became hooked on cuemaking. He decided decorative cues weren't going to be enough. Chester and Steve still discuss cuemaking on a regular basis. Both are always striving to make a better cue.

1998 was the official beginning of Klein Custom Cues. Having already accumulated some of the necessary equipment, Steve contacted Leonard Bludworth and purchased one of Leonard's professional cuemaking machines. Along with the machine he also received the benefit of Leonard's many years of cuemaking, and still continues to talk cuemaking with him to this day.

Preferring to make short spliced as opposed to inlaid point cues, Steve does both veneered and remachined points. Being influenced by both Balabushka and Szamboti, the majority of his cues are of classic design, emphasizing maple, ebony and ivory. That being said, he occasionally will produce a CNC artistic cue. His cues are either signed or have the Klein Cues logo of an "S" superimposed over a "K" engraved in the butt sleeve. All cues are finished with a hand-rubbed, three-part urethane finish.

Currently, Steve makes around 50 cues a year and will continue to do so until retiring from his airline career, when he envisions production peaking at around 100 cues a year.

If you are interested in contacting Steven Klein about a new cue or cue that needs to be repaired, you can contact him at his website, listed in the Trademark Index.

SPECIFICATIONS

Butt material: assorted
Shaft material: maple
Standard length: 58 in.
Lengths available: 61 in. maximum
Standard finish: three-part urethane
Standard butt cap: phenolic
Standard wrap: Irish linen
Point construction: short splice
Standard joint: wood-to-wood
Joint type: piloted
Joint screw thread: 3/8-11 modified
Standard number of shafts: two
Standard taper: custom
Standard ferrules: melamine
Standard tip: triangle
Standard tip width: 13 mm
Tip widths available: 12.25 to 13.5 mm
Annual production: approximately 50 cues

OPTIONS (FOR NEW CUES ONLY)

Ivory butt cap: $350
Ivory joint: $150
Ivory ferrule: $75
Leather wrap: $100
Extra shaft: $125
Old growth shaft: $220

REPAIRS

Repairs done only on Klein cues.
Refinish (with Irish linen wrap): $125
Refinish (keeping original leather wrap): $125
Rewrap (linen): $35
Rewrap (leather): $100
Clean and press linen wrap: $35
Replace shaft: $125+
Replace ivory ferrule: $75
Replace butt cap: $35
Replace ivory butt cap: $175
Replace tip: $15+
Replace fiber/linen/melamine ferrule: $25+

CURRENT KLEIN CUSTOM CUES

Two-piece Klein bar cues start at $275. Basic Klein cues with wraps and joint rings start at $450. Klein cues with points start at $600. One-of-a-kind custom Klein cues start at $650. The current delivery time for a Klein cue is about six months.

GRADING	98%	90%	70%

SECONDARY MARKET MINIMUM VALUES

The following are minimum values for other Klein cues encountered on the secondary market. These prices are representative of cues utilizing basic materials and designs that are not necessarily available at present. Steve has offered one-of-a-kind cues that can command many times these prices due to the use of exotic materials and artistry.

Special construction note: There are many materials and construction techniques that can add value to Klein cues.

For all used Klein cues, except where otherwise noted:
- Add $100 for each additional original straight playable shaft beyond two.
- Deduct $125 for each missing original straight playable shaft under two.
- Add $60 each for ivory ferrules.
- Add $75 for leather wrap.
- Deduct 15% for obvious or improper refinish.

Level 1 - Hustler.
	98%	90%	70%
Level 1 cues start at	$200	$160	$110

Level 2 - 0 points, 0-25 inlays.
Level 2 cues start at	$350	$270	$180

Level 3 - 2-6 points, 0-8 inlays.
Level 3 cues start at	$500	$385	$260

Level 4 - 4-10 points, 9-25 inlays.
Level 4 cues start at	$600	$465	$310

Level 5 - 0-12 points, 26-50 inlays.
Level 5 cues start at	$800	$615	$420

Level 6 - 0-12 points, 51-75 inlays.
Level 6 cues start at	$1,100	$865	$595

KLICKCUE CUES

Maker of pool cues from 1992, in Olathe, Kansas, to the present in Lawrence, Kansas.

Chris Klindt is a full-time cuemaker from Kansas. He has been making cues since 1992. He was inspired by makers Prather and Burton Spain. He learned the trade from Mike Kinder. Klindt's background includes industrial instrumentation and as an electronic technician. He worked for Mike Kinder—Tunder and MWK Cues.

If you are interested in talking to Chris Klindt about a new cue or cue that needs to be repaired, you can contact him at Klickcue Cues, listed in the Trademark Index.

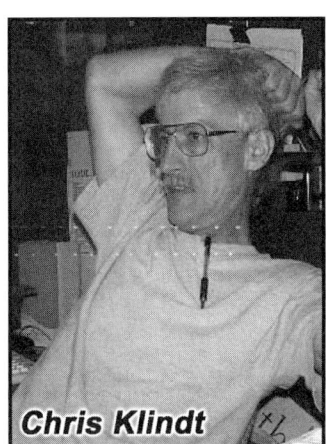
Chris Klindt

SPECIFICATIONS

Butt material: hardwoods
Shaft material: rock maple
Standard length: 58 in.
Lengths available: any
Standard finish: acrylic urethane
Standard butt cap: ABS
Standard wrap: Irish linen
Point construction: short spliced or inlaid
Standard joint: stainless steel
Joint type: piloted
Joint screw thread: 5/16-14
Standard number of shafts: one
Standard taper: 12 in. pro
Standard ferrules: linen
Standard tip: hercules hard
Standard tip width: 13 mm
Tip widths available: any
Annual production: fewer than 100 cues

OPTIONS (FOR NEW CUES ONLY)

Special length: no charge
Layered tip: no charge
Ivory butt cap: $150
Ivory joint: $75
Ivory ferrule: $50
Leather wrap: $100
Joint protectors: $50+
Extra shaft: $55+

1987 to Present Day

GRADING	98%	90%	70%

REPAIRS

Repairs done on all fine cues.
- Refinish (with Irish linen wrap): $100
- Rewrap (Irish linen): $35
- Replace ivory ferrule: $50
- Replace butt cap: $40+
- Replace tip: $10
- Replaced layered tip: $18+
- Replace fiber/linen ferrule: $20

CURRENT KLICKCUE CUES

Two-piece Klickcue bar cues start at $200. Basic Klickcue cues with wraps and joint rings start at $300. Klickcue cues with points start at $400. The current delivery time for a Klickcue cue is about one year.

SECONDARY MARKET MINIMUM VALUES

The following are minimum values for other Klickcue cues encountered on the secondary market. These prices are representative of cues utilizing basic materials and designs that are not necessarily available at present. Chris has offered one-of-a-kind cues that can command many times these prices due to the use of exotic materials and artistry.

Special construction note: There are many materials and construction techniques that can add value to Klickcue cues.

For all used Klickcue cues, except where otherwise noted:
- Add $45 for each additional original straight playable shaft beyond one.
- Deduct $55 for missing original straight playable shaft.
- Add $40 each for ivory ferrules.
- Add $45 for leather wrap.
- Deduct 20% for obvious or improper refinish.

Level 1 - Hustler.

	98%	90%	70%
Level 1 cues start at	$175	$135	$90

Level 2 - 0 points, 0-25 inlays.

Level 2 cues start at	$250	$195	$135

Level 3 - 2-6 points, 0-8 inlays.

Level 3 cues start at	$350	$270	$185

Level 4 - 4-10 points, 9-25 inlays.

Level 4 cues start at	$450	$350	$240

Level 5 - 0-12 points, 26-50 inlays.

Level 5 cues start at	$700	$550	$385

TAD KOHARA

Maker of Tad's Custom Cues. For more information, refer to Tad's.

KORNELE CUSTOM CUES

Maker of pool cues from 2000 to present in Mooreland, Oklahoma.

Steve Kornele

Steve Kornele grew up in the small town of Mooreland, Oklahoma with only 1000 residents. However, it was also the home of some great cuemakers, including Verl Horn and Dan, Jeff, and Daniel Prather. Steve developed a major interest in cues at the age of 16. He began spending most of his spare time in both of these cuemakers' shops and learning all about cues over the years. At the age of only 17, he built his first personal cue. He worked on it in both cuemakers' shops and finished it with the ivory that Verl had given him. It was a great ebony and ivory cue with elaborate decorative ringwork, ivory inlays, points, joint and ferrules. Steve continued his interest in cues while he went to college, coming home every weekend just to learn more about cuemaking. He would take his custom cue with him to the pool halls at college and was amazed at how the other players admired the cue. In 2001, Steve moved to Hot Springs, Arkansas where he teamed up with Greg Willingham, who had worked with Verl Horn for several years. They began building cues bearing the name WW Cues. After a year and a half, Steve moved back to his hometown. Not long after his move, he realized that his love for building cues would never fade. He built a new shop and began building his own custom cues with the signature or "KORNELE" and the year of completion handwritten on the forearm of his cues. Steve builds a variety of styles in his cues. He uses traditional hand-milled, short-spliced points in all of his cues. Most of his cues have intricate CNC inlays or hand-milled windows in the butt sleeve. The standard cue has a 3/8-10 flat-faced joint. Steve also builds cues with a piloted stainless steel joint, on

KORNELE CUSTOM CUES, cont. 423

equest. His high end cues incorporate ivory joints, points, inlays, dash rings, ferrules and buttcaps. Steve feels very fortunate to make a ving at what he loves to do.

 you are interested in talking to Steve about a new cue or cue that needs to be repaired, you can contact him at Kornele Custom Cues, sted in the Trademark Index.

SPECIFICATIONS

Butt material: hardwoods
Shaft material: rock maple
Standard length: 58 in.
Lengths available: 57 to 60 in.
Standard finish: two-part urethane
Balance point: 1 to 2 in. above wrap
Standard butt cap: Ivorine
Standard wrap: Irish linen
Point construction: short splice
Standard joint: Ivorine
Standard joint type: flat face
Standard joint screw thread: 3/8-10
Standard number of shafts: two
Standard taper: custom
Standard ferrules: ivory
Standard tip: Le Pro
Standard tip width: 13 mm
Tip widths available: 12.5 to 14mm
Annual production: approximately 60 cues

OPTIONS (FOR NEW CUES ONLY)

Special length: $50+
Layered tip: $20+
Ivory butt cap: $250
Ivory butt sleeve: $450+
Ivory joint: $100
Ivory ferrule: $40
Ivory points: $200+
Ivory dash rings: $15+ each
Joint protectors: $25+
Extra shaft: $100+

REPAIRS

Repairs done on Kornele cues, Verl Horn Cues, and WW Cues

Refinish (with Irish linen wrap): $150+
Rewrap (Irish linen): $40+
Replace shaft: $100 and up
Replace ivory ferrule: $50+
Replace butt cap: $50+
Replace ivory butt cap: $250+
Replace tip: $20
Replaced layered tip: $25+
Replace Ivorine ferrule: $30
Replace ivory ferrule: $50

CURRENT KORNELE CUES

Basic Kornele cues with wraps and joint rings start at $350, with or without points. One-of-a-kind custom Kornele cues start at $1250 The average delivery time for a Kornele cue is fourteen weeks.

SECONDARY MARKET MINIMUM VALUES

The following are minimum values for other Kornele cues encountered on the secondary market. These prices are representative of cues utilizing basic materials and designs that are not necessarily available at present. Steve has offered one-of-a-kind cues that can command many times these prices due to the use of exotic materials and artistry.

Special construction note: There are many materials and construction techniques that can add value to Kornele cues.

For all used Kornele cues, except where otherwise noted:

Add $100 for each additional original straight playable shaft beyond two.
Deduct $80 for each missing original straight playable shaft under two.
Add $40 each for ivory ferrules.
Deduct 20% for obvious or improper refinish.

GRADING	98%	90%	70%
Level 2 - 0 points, 0-25 inlays.			
Level 2 cues start at	$275	$215	$145
Level 3 - 2-6 points, 0-8 inlays.			
Level 3 cues start at	$300	$285	$160
Level 4 - 4-10 points, 9-25 inlays.			
Level 4 cues start at	$375	$295	$195
Level 5 - 0-12 points, 26-50 inlays.			
Level 5 cues start at	$600	$465	$315

MICHAEL KRATOCHVILL
Maker of Michael's cues. For more information see Michael's Custom Cues.

CHESTER KRICK
Maker of CK Custom Cues. For more information see CK Custom Cues.

GREG KUCHARSKI
Maker of Greg's Kues. For more information see Greg's Kues.

L SECTION

LAMBROS CUES, INC.

Maker of pool cues from 1990 to present in Baltimore, Maryland.

Mike Lambros was a successful engineer in the late 1980s. He was also an avid pool player. But he was dissatisfied with the pool cues that were available, and he felt he could make better cues than what he was able to buy.

In 1990, he made the commitment to utilize his engineering skills to create Lambros Cues. The cues made in the first year are identifiable by the letters "ML," for Mike Lambros, on the Delrin butt cap. Cues made from 1991 to the present will have the name "Lambros" there instead. In 1995, Mike started making the points much longer and changed the dimensions of the butt cap. Cues made from 1990 to 1995 will have points that usually come to within 2 1/2 in. of the joint collar, and will have a 1 1/4 in. Delrin butt cap. Cues made from 1995 to 1999 feature 10 in. points which come to within 1 in. of the joint collar and have a 1 1/2 in. Delrin butt cap. From 1999 to the present, all cues feature the longer points but have a 5/8 in. phenolic butt cap. All cues are designed for playability, and the motto of Lambros Cues is "The Hit."

Mike makes less than 200 cues per year and cues are made to the design and specifications of the customer. In the summer of 1996, Mike introduced a new joint design for which a patent had been issued in 1998, called the Ultra-Joint. It features a 3/8-10 joint screw with an innovative, new concave face on the butt that joins with a convex face on the shaft. This joint is now the standard joint on all cues.

Lambros cues are guaranteed indefinitely against manufacturing defects that are not the result of abuse. If you have a Lambros cue that needs further identification or repair, or would like to talk to Mike about the design and specifications you have in mind for a custom-made cue, contact Lambros Cues Inc., listed in the Trademark Index.

Mike Lambros

1991 to Present Day

SPECIFICATIONS

Butt material: hardwoods
Shaft material: rock maple
Standard length: 58 in.
Lengths available: 57 to 61 in.
Standard finish: proprietary
Joint screw: 3/8-10
Standard joint: phenolic
Joint type: ultra
Balance point: 1 1/2 in. above wrap
Point construction: short splice
Standard wrap: Irish linen
Standard butt cap: phenolic
Standard number of shafts: two
Annual production: fewer than 200 cues

OPTIONS (FOR NEW CUES ONLY)

Special length: $50
Leather wrap: $150
Ivory joint: $200
Ivory ferrules: $75 each
Extra shaft: $200
Ivory points: $200 each
Ivory butt cap: $400
Layered tip: $45

REPAIRS

Repairs done on most fine cues.

Refinish (with leather wrap): $450
Refinish (with linen wrap): $300
Rewrap (leather): $150
Rewrap (linen): $75
Clean and press linen wrap: $25
Replace butt cap: $200
Replace shaft: $200
Replace fiber/linen ferrule: $75
Replace ivory ferrule: $100
Replace ivory butt cap: $400
Replace tip: $25

| GRADING | 98% | 90% | 70% |

CURRENT LAMBROS CUES

Basic Lambros cues with wraps and joint rings start at $1,000. Lambros cues with points start at $1,550. One-of-a-kind custom Lambros cues start at $5,000. The current delivery time for a Lambros cue is about four months to one year, depending on the design of the cue.

PAST EXAMPLES

The following cues are representations of older work of Lambros Cues Inc., All cues came with two shafts, and feature the new Lambros "Ultra" joint. These cues could be ordered as shown, or modified to suit the desires of the customer. Note: Since mid-2004, Lambros Cues no longer makes four-point cues. The current designs are based on five-, six-, eight-, and ten-point cues.

Level 2 #1 - Hardwood forearm with nickel silver rings above wrap, hardwood butt sleeve with nickel silver rings at top and bottom.

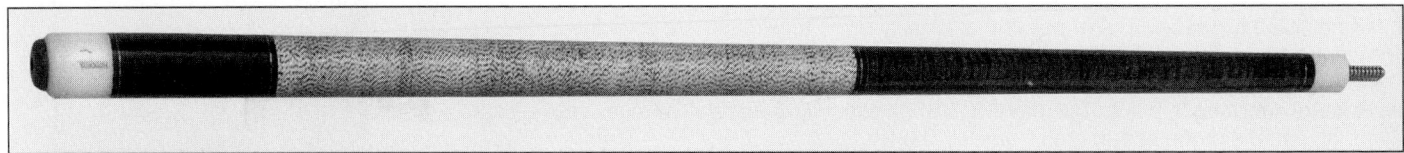

| MSR (1999) $750 | $950 | $800 | $440 |

Level 3 #2 - Hardwood forearm with alternating hardwood and ivory checks within nickel silver rings above wrap, four hardwood points, hardwood butt sleeve with alternating hardwood and ivory checks within nickel silver rings at top and bottom.

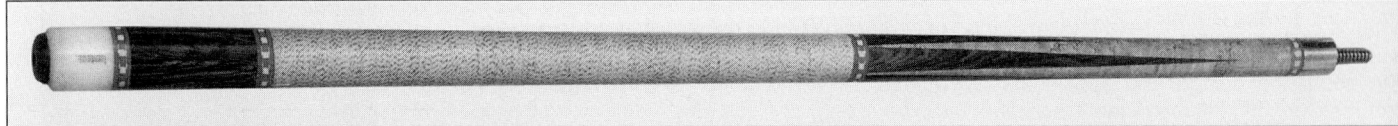

| MSR (1999) $1,200 | $1,450 | $1,125 | $750 |

Level 3 #3 - Hardwood forearm with hardwood rings above wrap, four hardwood points with multiple hardwood veneers, hardwood butt sleeve with hardwood rings at top and bottom.

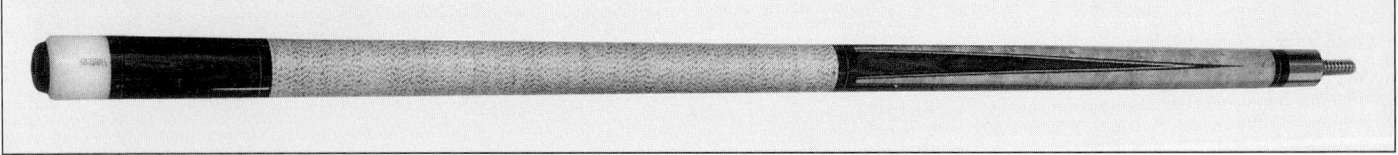

| MSR (1999) $1,000 | $1,200 | $935 | $625 |

Level 4 #4 - Hardwood forearm with hardwood set within nickel silver rings above wrap, three long hardwood points with an ivory diamond-shaped inlay in each alternating with three short contrasting hardwood points, hardwood butt sleeve with three large ivory diamond-shaped inlays alternating with three small ivory diamond-shaped inlays between hardwood set within nickel silver rings at top and bottom.

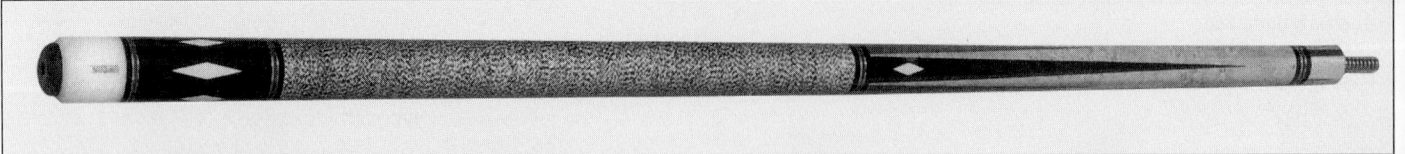

| MSR (1999) $1,550 | $1,850 | $1,435 | $950 |

Level 4 #5 - Ivory joint, hardwood forearm with alternating hardwood and ivory checks within nickel silver rings above wrap, four hardwood points with multiple hardwood veneers and a hardwood diamond-shaped inlay set in an ivory oval within each point, hardwood butt sleeve with four hardwood diamond-shaped inlays set in ivory ovals alternating with four long ivory-dished diamond-shaped inlays between alternating hardwood and ivory checks within nickel silver rings at top and bottom.

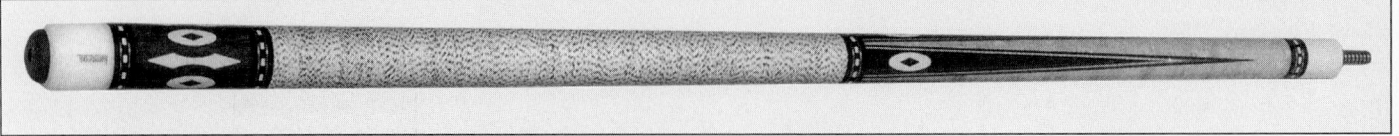

| MSR (1999) $2,150 | $2,500 | $1,950 | $1,300 |

LAMBROS CUES, INC., cont. 427

GRADING	98%	90%	70%

Level 4 #6 - Ivory joint, hardwood forearm with alternating hardwood and ivory checks within nickel silver rings above wrap, three long hardwood points with multiple hardwood veneers and an ivory spear-shaped inlay in each alternating with three short hardwood points with multiple hardwood veneers, hardwood butt sleeve with six pairs of opposing ivory spear-shaped inlays between alternating hardwood and ivory checks within nickel silver rings at top and bottom.

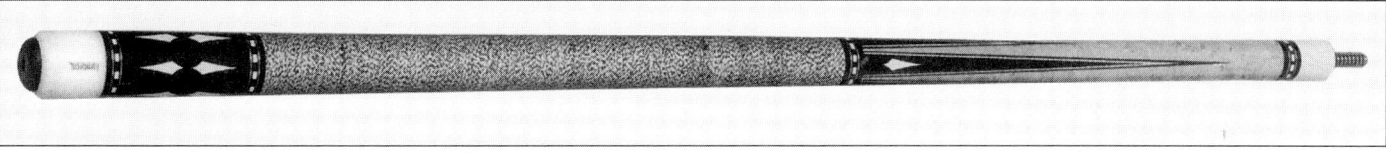

MSR (1999) $2,000	$2,400	$1,850	$1,275

Level 3 #7 - Hardwood forearm with hardwood set within nickel silver rings above wrap, four hardwood points with a single hardwood veneer, hardwood butt sleeve with four reverse hardwood points with a single hardwood veneer between hardwood set within nickel silver rings at top and bottom.

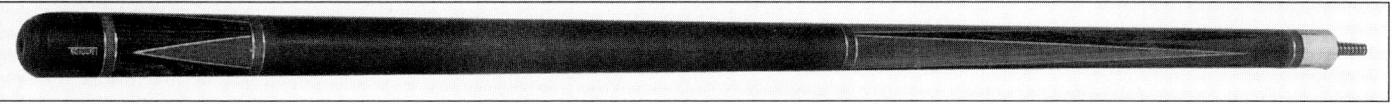

MSR (1999) $1,250	$1,450	$1,150	$750

Level 3 #8 - Hardwood forearm with a pair of nickel silver rings set in hardwood above wrap, four hardwood points with multiple veneers and an ivory clock-hand-shaped inlay in each, hardwood butt sleeve with four ivory diamond-shaped inlays between pairs of nickel silver rings set in hardwood rings at top and bottom.

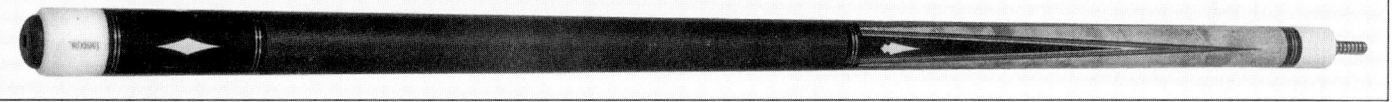

MSR (1999) $1,400	$1,650	$1,275	$850

Level 4 #9 - Ivory joint, hardwood forearm with alternating hardwood and ivory checks within nickel silver rings above wrap, four hardwood points with multiple veneers and an ivory diamond-shaped inlay in each, hardwood butt sleeve with four vertical pairs of ivory diamond-shaped inlays alternating with four single ivory diamond-shaped inlays between alternating hardwood and ivory checks within nickel silver rings at top and bottom.

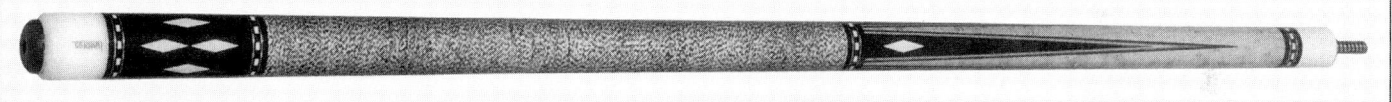

MSR (1999) $1,700	$2,000	$1,550	$1,050

Level 4 #10 - Hardwood forearm with nickel silver ring above wrap, six hardwood points with an ivory Tiffany diamond-shaped inlay in each, hardwood butt sleeve with six long ivory Tiffany diamond-shaped inlays between nickel silver rings at top and bottom.

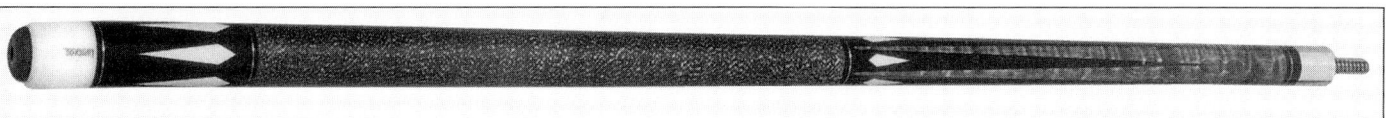

MSR (1999) $1,550	$1,800	$1,425	$975

Level 4 #11 - Hardwood forearm with alternating hardwood and ivory checks within nickel silver rings above wrap, four hardwood points with multiple veneers and an ivory diamond-shaped inlay in each, hardwood butt sleeve with four large ivory diamond-shaped inlays alternating with four smaller ivory diamond-shaped inlays between alternating hardwood and ivory checks within nickel silver rings at top and bottom.

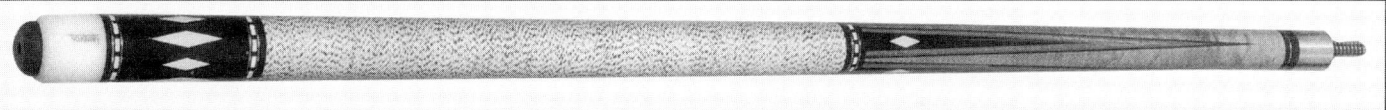

MSR (1999) $1,650	$1,925	$1,485	$1,000

Level 3 #12 - Hardwood forearm, six hardwood points, hardwood butt sleeve with six hardwood windows.

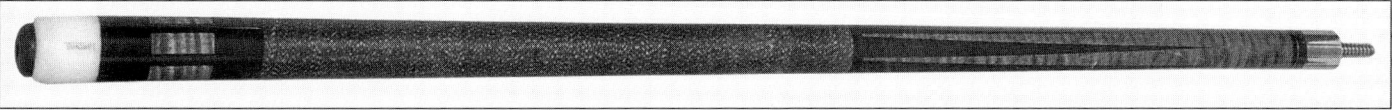

MSR (1999) $1,250	$1,500	$1,165	$785

428 LAMBROS CUES, INC., cont.

GRADING	98%	90%	70%

Level 3 #13 - Ivory joint, hardwood forearm with alternating hardwood and ivory checks within nickel silver rings above wrap, four hardwood points, hardwood butt sleeve with alternating hardwood and ivory checks within nickel silver rings at top and bottom, hardwood butt cap.

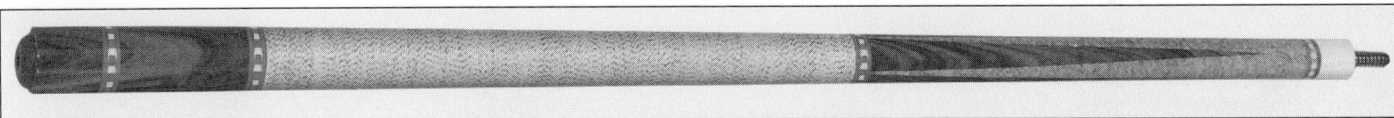

MSR (1999) $1,300	$1,650	$1,275	$845

Level 3 #14 - Hardwood forearm with nickel silver ring above wrap, four hardwood points with an ivory diamond-shaped inlay in each, hardwood butt sleeve with four large ivory diamond-shaped inlays between nickel silver rings at top and bottom.

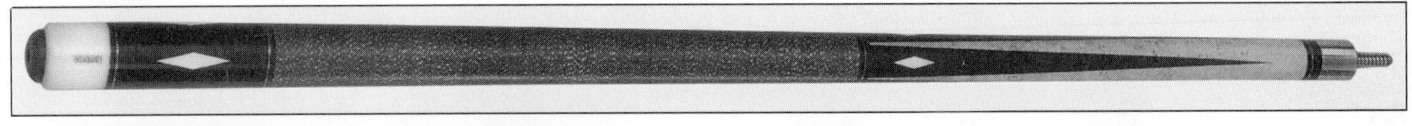

MSR (1999) $1,200	$1,475	$1,165	$800

SECONDARY MARKET MINIMUM VALUES

The following are minimum prices for other Lambros cues encountered on the secondary market. These prices are representative of cues utilizing basic materials and designs that may not be currently available. Mike also offers one-of-a-kind cues that can command many times these prices due to the use of exotic materials and artistry.

Special construction note: There are many materials and construction techniques that can add value to Lambros cues. The following are the most important examples:

- Add $750+ for ivory points.
- Add $950+ for ivory butt sleeve.

For all used Lambros cues, except where otherwise noted:
- Add $125 for each additional original straight playable shaft beyond two.
- Deduct $200 for missing original straight playable shaft.
- Add $200+ for ivory joint.
- Add $100+ for leather wrap.
- Deduct 20% for obvious or improper refinish.

	98%	90%	70%
Level 2 - 0 points, 0-25 inlays. Level 2 cues start at	$800	$620	$420
Level 3 - 2-6 points, 0-8 inlays. Level 3 cues start at	$1,150	$900	$600
Level 4 - 4-10 points, 9-25 inlays. Level 4 cues start at	$1,350	$1,150	$700
Level 5 - 0-12 points, 26-50 inlays. Level 5 cues start at	$1,850	$1,445	$950
Level 6 - 0-12 points, 51-75 inlays. Level 6 cues start at	$2,450	$1,900	$1,300
Level 7 - 0-12 points, 76-125 inlays. Level 7 cues start at	$3,000	$2,600	$1,600

LANZ CUSTOM CUES

Maker of pool cues since 1998 in Toledo, Ohio.

Richard Lanz has played pool since the age of sixteen. After retiring from working as a boilermaker for 34 years, he decided to try his hand at cuemaking. He works out of his two-and-a-half-car garage. His shop equipment includes a taper-shaper machine and a four-axis CNC, both from Unique Products out of Indiana. Richard strives for a high quality finish and workmanship and enjoys using exotic woods.

Lanz cues are guaranteed against defects in material and workmanship. If you have a Lanz cue that needs further identification or repair, or would like to order a new Lanz cue, contact Lanz Custom Cues, listed in the Trademark Index.

SPECIFICATIONS

Butt material: domestic and exotic hardwoods
Shaft material: hard rock maple
Standard length: 58 to 60 in.

LANZ CUSTOM CUES, cont.

GRADING	100%	95%	70%

Standard wrap: Irish linen
Standard finish: UV-cured urethane
Standard ferrules: PVC
Joint screws: 3/8-10 or 5/16-18, piloted or flat faced
Point construction: short spliced or inlaid
Standard tip: Le Pro
Annual production: approximately 30 cues

OPTIONS (FOR NEW CUES ONLY)

Ivory ferrule: $80
1 in. ivory butt cap: $300
Ivory joint collars: $250
Leather wrap: $75
Extra shaft: $100+

REPAIRS

Repairs done on all fine cues.
Refinish (with Irish linen wrap): $100
Rewrap (Irish linen): $35
Replace shaft: $100+
Replace tip: $10 standard Le Pro

CURRENT LANZ CUES

Two-piece Lanz bar cues start at $100. Basic Lanz cues with wraps and joint rings start at $250. Lanz cues with points start at $350. One-of-a-kind custom Lanz cues start at $450. The average delivery time for a Lanz cue is three to six weeks, depending on the amount of inlays, points and veneers.

CURRENT EXAMPLES

The following Lanz cues can be ordered as shown, modified to suit the desires of the customer, or new designs can be created.

Level 3 - Stained burl maple forearm with a colored trim ring above handle, four tulipwood points with colored veneers, bird's-eye maple handle, stained burl maple butt sleeve with four tulipwood reverse points with colored veneers between colored tirm rings at top and bottom.

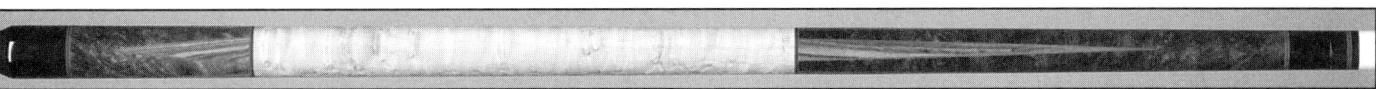

MSR	$600	$550-650	$445	$320

Level 4 - Black joint with pairs of large and small mother-of-pearl notched diamond-shaped inlays, white synthetic pearl forearm with black ring above handle, four black points with a large and small mother-of-pearl notched diamond-shaped inlay in each point, black butt sleeve with rows of large and small mother-of-pearl notched diamond-shaped inlays between white synthetic pearl at top and bottom.

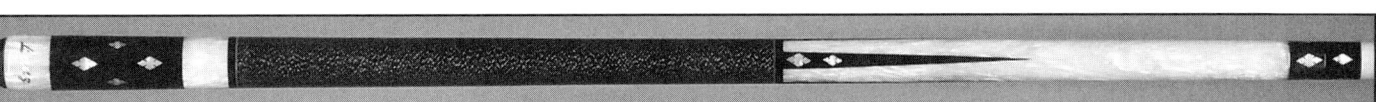

MSR	$900	$850-1,000	$675	$475

Level 3 - Stained bird's-eye maple forearm with sterling silver tirm ring above wrap, four synthetic ivory points with four colored veneers, stained bird's-eye maple butt sleeve with four synthetic ivory reverse points with four colored veneers between sterling silver tirm rings at top and bottom.

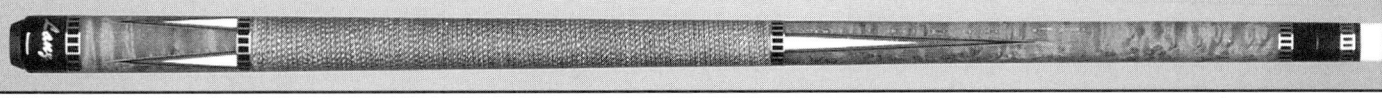

MSR	$1,200	$1,100-1,250	$895	$650

Level 5 - Black joint with pairs of large and small mother-of-pearl notched diamond-shaped inlays, white synthetic pearl forearm with a thick black ring with four white synthetic pearl points above handle, four short black points, black handle with rows of large and small mother-of-pearl notched diamond-shaped inlays, white synthetic pearl butt sleeve.

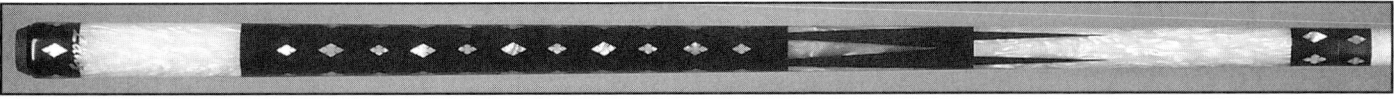

MSR	$1,200	$1,100-1,250	$895	$650

GRADING	100%	95%	70%

Level 3 - Ivory joint, snakewood forearm, three snakewood butterfly points with three colored veneers, segmented three-piece highly figured burl handle seperated by ivory rings, snakewood butt sleeve with three reverse snakewood butterfly points with three colored veneers, ivory butt cap.

	MSR	$3,200	$2,500-3,250	$2,100	$1,650
GRADING			98%	90%	70%

SECONDARY MARKET MINIMUM VALUES

The following are minimum values for other Lanz cues encountered on the secondary market. These prices are representative of cues utilizing basic materials and designs that are not necessarily available at present. Richard has offered one-of-a-kind cues that can command many times these prices due to the use of exotic materials and artistry.

Special construction note: There are many materials and construction techniques that can add value to Lanz cues.

For all used Lanz cues, except where otherwise noted:
  Add $75 for each additional original straight playable shaft beyond one.
  Deduct $100+ for missing original straight playable shaft.
  Add $60 each for ivory ferrules.
  Add $50 for leather wrap.
  Deduct 20% for obvious or improper refinish.

Level 1 - Hustler.
  Level 1 cues start at $85 $65 $45
Level 2 - 0 points, 0-25 inlays.
  Level 2 cues start at $200 $160 $110
Level 3 - 2-6 points, 0-8 inlays.
  Level 3 cues start at $300 $235 $160
Level 4 - 4-10 points, 9-25 inlays.
  Level 4 cues start at $400 $315 $210
Level 5 - 0-12 points, 26-50 inlays.
  Level 5 cues start at $650 $510 $345

CUES BY LARUE

Maker of pool cues in Tampa, Florida.

If you have a LaRue cue that needs further identification or repair, or would like to order a new LaRue cue, contact Cues by LaRue, listed in the Trademark Index.

EDDIE LAUBE CUES

Maker of pool cues from the late sixties to the early seventies, in Chicago, Illinois.

Eddie Laube was a tool and die maker who also enjoyed the game of pool. He started making cues in the sixties, and made his own full-spliced blanks, usually with five veneers. He patented a unique brass-to-brass joint, which he used exclusively for his pool cues.

Eddie Laube cues are easily identifiable by the "Eddie Laube" trademark with the patent number, which will appear under a plastic window in the butt sleeve. Eddie also patented an original design for adjusting the balance point. This involved a brass weight in the hollow forearm, which was threaded onto a screw that could be turned from the butt. People that visited Eddie remember the talking parakeet that he had in his shop and was very proud of.

About 1973, Eddie sold his equipment to Frank Stellman, known as "Sailor," and retired to Arizona. If you have an Eddie Laube cue that needs further identification or repair, contact Deno Andrews, listed in the Buy, Sell, Trade Index.

SPECIFICATIONS

Butt material: hardwoods
Shaft material: rock maple
Point construction: full splice
Standard number of shafts: one

KNOWN EDDIE LAUBE EXAMPLES

The following cues are a representation of the work of Eddie Laube. Eddie Laube cues can be encountered as shown, or modified to suit the desires of the original customer, or entirely different designs can be encountered.

EDDIE LAUBE CUES, cont. 431 **L**

GRADING	98%	90%	70%

Level 4 - Brazilian rosewood forearm with four full-spliced points and handle of bird's-eye maple. The tip of each point inlaid with an ivory dot, and the base of each point inlaid with a red dot. The base of the handle is inlaid with four smaller red dots. The sub-handle area has a Brazilian rosewood sleeve inlaid with four ivory windows. The butt area consists of the name window framed by two ivory rings, a pearlized plastic ring, and an ivory butt cap. The joint is brass.

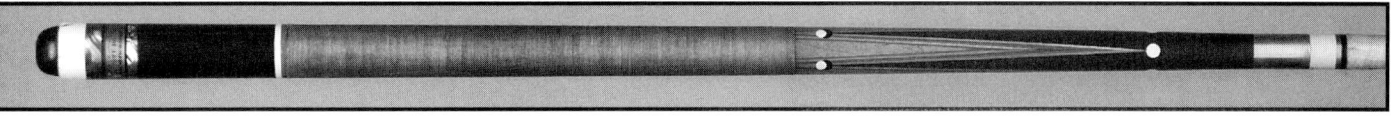

MSRP (1970) $95	$3,750	$3,250	$1,850

Level 2 - Forearm is straight grained maple and Brazilian rosewood inlaid with nine ivory dots. Wrap is Cortland linen. Butt sleeve is Brazilian rosewood inlaid with six ivory dots. Butt cap has white and red rings, and a white butt cap which all appear to be made from billiard ball plastic.

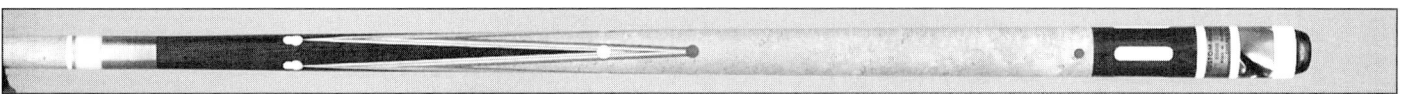

MSRP (1967) N/A	$1,750	$1,500	$935

Level 2 - Forearm is Brazilian rosewood. Wrap is Irish linen. Butt sleeve is bird's-eye maple. Name window is framed by two pearlized plastic rings. Butt cap is plastic which appears to be from a billiard ball.

MSRP (1972) N/A	$1,150	$1,000	$635

SECONDARY MARKET MINIMUM VALUES

The following are minimum prices for other Eddie Laube cues encountered on the secondary market. These prices are representative of cues utilizing basic materials and designs. Eddie also made a few one-of-a-kind cues that can command many times these prices due to the use of exotic materials and artistry.

Special construction note: There are many materials and construction techniques that can add value to Eddie Laube cues.

For all used Eddie Laube cues, except where otherwise noted:

Add $300 for each additional original straight playable shaft (standard with one).
Deduct $300 for missing original straight playable shaft.
Deduct 30% for obvious or improper refinish.

Level 2 - 0 points, 0-25 inlays.
Level 2 cues start at	$1,500	$1,350	$800

Level 3 - 2-6 points, 0-8 inlays.
Level 3 cues start at	$2,150	$1,900	$1,200

Level 4 - 4-10 points, 9-25 inlays.
Level 4 cues start at	$2,600	$2,300	$1,500

Level 5 - 0-12 points, 26-50 inlays.
Level 5 cues start at	$3,250	$2,650	$2,000

LAWHEAD CUES

Maker of pool cues in Winter Haven, Florida.

If you have a Lawhead cue that needs further identification or repair, or would like to order a new Lawhead cue, contact Lawhead Cues, listed in the Trademark Index.

LAYANI CUES

Maker of pool cues from 1989 in Sherbrooke, Canada, to present in Quebec, Canada.

Layani Cues first began with Alain Gendron in 1988. As a fine woodworker and a true lover of pool and snooker, he shifted his interest and talent toward the making of cues. With the help of pro players, he developed a cue with a distinctive feel and energy transfer. Alain met Thierry Layani in 1996. Thierry was working as a philosophy professor in a Montreal college, but was also a pool player. In 2001, they decided to join efforts and build cues based on their extensive knowledge and research.

Their first innovation, and what is now the signature of cues, is what they call the conical joint. The conical tapered joint was invented and patented by Alain in 1996. The idea behind this

Alain Gendron and Thierry Layani

new joint configuration was to increase the surface area of contact between the shaft and the butt, and to provide a radial consistency that no other type of joint could provide. Indeed, the conical joint provides a hit that is solid, quiet and smooth.

To joint the forearm to the handle in the butt section, they also use a cone. This one is done in maple because of its vibratory characteristics. These construction elements have an impact on the way the cue feels and plays. Layani cues have a distinctive hit.

Cuemaking is a challenge similar to making a musical instrument for Alain and Thierry. They believe that the performance of a pool player is mostly determined by the pleasure provided by the use of his cue. For them, cuemaking is not only a matter of knowledge and techniques, it mostly requires imagination and intuition.

If you are interested in talking to Alain Gendron and Thierry Layani about a new cue or cue that needs to be repaired, you can contact them at Layani Cues, listed in the Trademark Index.

SPECIFICATIONS

Butt material: hardwoods
Shaft material: Canadian hard rock maple
Standard length: 58 in.
Lengths available: 54 to 60 in.
Standard finish: Dupont two-part urethane
Balance point: about 19 in. from butt
Standard butt cap: phenolic
Standard wrap: Irish linen
Point construction: inlaid
Standard joint: patented conical joint
Joint screw thread: 5/16-18
Standard number of shafts: one
Standard taper: progressive pro taper
Standard ferrules: LBM
Standard tip: tiger laminated
Standard tip width: 12.75 mm
Tip widths available: 9 to 14 mm
Annual production: approximately 100 cues

OPTIONS (FOR NEW CUES ONLY)

Special length: no charge
Layered tip: $15
Leather wrap: $75
Joint protectors: $60
Extra shaft: $150

REPAIRS

Repairs done on all fine cues.
Refinish (with Irish linen wrap): $200
Refinish (with leather wrap): $250
Rewrap (Irish linen): $50
Rewrap (leather): $75
Clean and press linen wrap: $15
Replace shaft: Layani only: $150
Replace tip: $10
Replaced layered tip: $30
Replace fiber/linen ferrule: $30

CURRENT LAYANI CUES

Basic cue Layani cues with wraps and joint rings start at $500. Layani cues with points start at $800. One-of-a-kind custom Layani cues start at $1,000. The current delivery time for a Layani custom cue is about six months.

CURRENT EXAMPLES

The following are examples of Layani cues. They can be ordered as shown, modified to suit the desires of the customer, or new designs can be created.

LAYANI CUES, cont. 433

GRADING	100%	95%	70%

Level 2 - Cocobolo forearm with a cocobolo- and maple-stitched ring above handle, tiger maple handle, cocobolo butt sleeve with cocobolo and maple stitched rings at top and bottom.

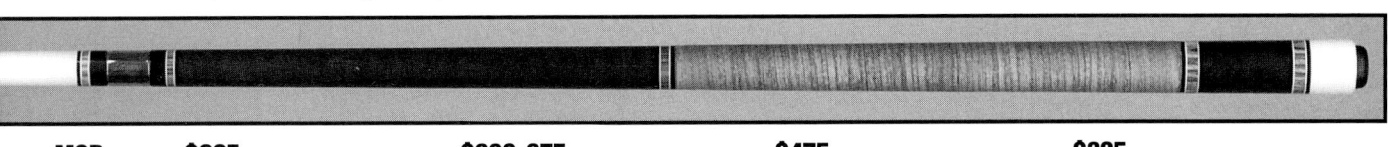

MSR	$625	$600-675	$475	$325

Level 3 - Cocobolo forearm with a micarta ring above wrap, six micarta points with a micarta diamond-shaped inlay at the tip of each, cocobolo butt sleeve with twelve reverse micarta points with a micarta diamond-shaped inlay at the tip of each below a micarta ring at top.

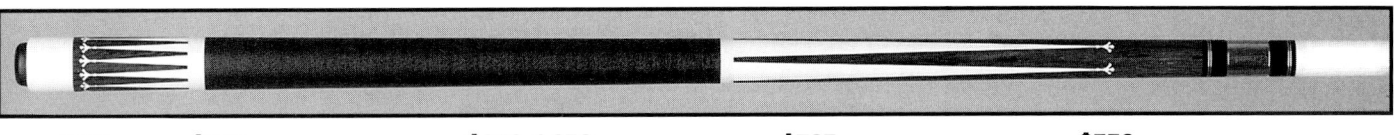

MSR	$975	$950-1,050	$765	$550

Level 5 - Bird's-eye maple forearm with a purpleheart and ebony ring above wrap, six multi-piece floating purpleheart points, maple butt sleeve with six sets of multi-piece intricate purpleheart inlays above a purpleheart and ebony ring at bottom.

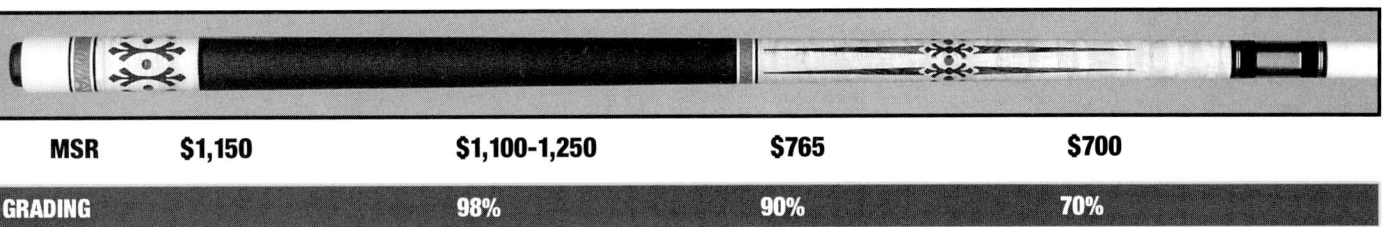

MSR	$1,150	$1,100-1,250	$765	$700

GRADING	98%	90%	70%

SECONDARY MARKET MINIMUM VALUES

The following are minimum values for other Layani cues encountered on the secondary market. These prices are representative of cues utilizing basic materials and designs that are not necessarily available at present. Layani has offered one-of-a-kind cues that can command many times these prices due to the use of exotic materials and artistry.

Special construction note: There are many materials and construction techniques that can add value to Layani cues.

For all used Layani cues, except where otherwise noted:
- Add $100 for each additional original straight playable shaft beyond one.
- Deduct $150 for missing original straight playable shaft.
- Add $50 for leather wrap.
- Deduct 20% for obvious or improper refinish.

Level 2 - 0 points, 0-25 inlays.
Level 2 cues start at	$400	$315	$215

Level 3 - 2-6 points, 0-8 inlays.
Level 3 cues start at	$700	$540	$365

Level 4 - 4-10 points, 9-25 inlays.
Level 4 cues start at	$850	$655	$445

Level 5 - 0-12 points, 26-50 inlays.
Level 5 cues start at	$1,150	$895	$600

LEBOW CUSTOM CUES

Maker of pool cues from 1999 to present in Springfield, Oregon.

Sheldon Lebow's background is in construction. He also likes to play pool, and still plays in the local pool league. He learned cuemaking from Clark Smith and was inspired by Dave Jones, McWorter and Wayne. He started by doing simple repairs. In 1999 he bought the shop and supplies of a beginning cuemaker, and started making his own cues. Lebow Custom Cues are typically signed "Lebow" in very small letters. Sometimes the identification markings are engraved. Sheldon's cues are all custom made in a one-man shop. He makes everything except for the tips, bumpers, and joint pins. He specializes in veneers of gold, silver, ivory, and exotic stones. He uses these materials for inlays as well. He likes to be able to execute unique and creative designs.

Lebow cues are guaranteed for life to the original owner against construction defects that are not the result of abuse. If you are interested in talking to Sheldon Lebow about a new cue or cue that needs to be repaired, you can contact him at Lebow Custom Cues, listed in the Trademark Index.

Sheldon Lebow

SPECIFICATIONS

Butt material: hardwoods
Shaft material: premium hard rock maple
Standard length: 59 in.
Lengths available: any
Balance point: custom
Standard butt cap: phenolic
Standard wrap: linen
Point construction: inlay
Joint type: flat faced phenolic
Joint screw thread: radial pin
Standard number of shafts: one
Standard taper: custom
Standard ferrules: melamine
Standard tip: Talisman
Standard tip width: custom
Annual production: fewer than 30 cues

OPTIONS (FOR NEW CUES ONLY)

Special length: no charge
Layered tip: $15+
Ivory butt cap: $150
Ivory butt sleeve: $450
Ivory joint: $100
Ivory ferrule: $50
Ivory handle: $1500
Leather wrap: $120
Joint protectors: $30+
Extra shaft: $100+

REPAIRS

Repairs done on all fine cues.

Refinish (with Irish linen wrap): $125
Refinish (with leather wrap): $210
Rewrap (Irish linen): $35
Rewrap (leather): $120
Clean and press linen wrap: $10
Restore leather wrap: $20
Replace shaft: $100+
Replace ivory ferrule: $50
Replace butt cap: $35
Replace ivory butt cap: $150
Replace tip: $10+
Replaced layered tip: $15+
Replace fiber/linen ferrule: $20

CURRENT LEBOW CUES

Two-piece Lebow bar cues start at $250. Basic Lebow cues with wraps and joint rings start at $500. Lebow cues with points start at $600. The current delivery time for a Lebow cue is four months.

LEBOW CUSTOM CUES, cont. 435

GRADING	98%	90%	70%

SECONDARY MARKET MINIMUM VALUES

The following are minimum values for other Lebow cues encountered on the secondary market. These prices are representative of cues utilizing basic materials and designs that are not necessarily available at present. Sheldon has offered one-of-a-kind cues that can command many times these prices due to the use of exotic materials and artistry.

Special construction note: There are many materials and construction techniques that can add value to Lebow cues.

For all used Lebow cues, except where otherwise noted:
- Add $80 for each additional original straight playable shaft beyond one.
- Deduct $100 for missing original straight playable shaft.
- Add $40 each for ivory ferrules.
- Add $85 for leather wrap.
- Deduct 20% for obvious or improper refinish.

Level 1 - Hustler.
Level 1 cues start at	$225	$185	$120

Level 2 - 0 points, 0-25 inlays.
Level 2 cues start at	$400	$310	$210

Level 3 - 2-6 points, 0-8 inlays.
Level 3 cues start at	$500	$390	$270

Level 4 - 4-10 points, 9-25 inlays.
Level 4 cues start at	$650	$515	$345

Level 5 - 0-12 points, 26-50 inlays.
Level 5 cues start at	$900	$700	$485

WILLIAM LEE

Maker of WilleeCue, for information refer to listing for Willee Cue.

LEGACY CUES

Maker of pool cues from 1991 before being purchased by A.M.F., from 1994 to 1995 in Memphis, Tennessee, and for a few years beginning in 1995 in Bland, Missouri.

The Legacy Cue Company had been in business making cues in the United States for approximately three years, when A.M.F. Playmaster bought the company. They moved cuemaking operations to Memphis, Tennessee in 1994 and, about a year later, they moved to Bland, Missouri. They made cues for a short time before closing operations.

A.M.F. has been in business since 1901 and, for a while, they were the only company making tables, pockets, and cues.

Legacy cues are easily identifiable by the "A.M.F. Legacy" logo on the butt caps.

SPECIFICATIONS

Butt material: hardwoods
Shaft material: rock maple
Standard length: 58 in.
Lengths available: 58 in.
Standard joint: Implex
Joint type: piloted
Standard wrap: Irish linen
Point construction: short spliced
Standard number of shafts: one
Standard tip width: 13 mm
Standard ferrules: fiber
Standard tip: Le Pro

SECONDARY MARKET MINIMUM VALUES

The following are minimum prices for Legacy cues encountered on the secondary market. These prices are representative of cues utilizing basic materials and designs that may not be currently available.

For all used Legacy cues, except where otherwise noted:
- Add $35+ for each additional original straight playable shaft (standard with one).
- Deduct 60% for missing original straight playable shaft.
- Deduct 30% for obvious or improper refinish.

Level 1 - 4 points, hustler.
Level 1 cues start at	$65	$50	$30

Level 2 - 0 points, 0-25 inlays.
Level 2 cues start at	$85	$65	$40

GRADING	98%	90%	70%
Level 3 - 2-6 points, 0-8 inlays.			
Level 3 cues start at	$100	$75	$45

LEGEND CUES

Line of pool cues distributed by DMI Sports.

Legend cues are manufactured in southern China using hand selected wood from climate controlled vaults and inlay materials that are imported to China from the US, Canada, and around the world. Legend cues are easily identifiable by the Legend trademark. All Legend cues are guaranteed for one year.

If you are interested in talking to DMI Sports about a new Legend cue, you can contact them at DMI Sports, Inc, listed in the Trademark Index.

SPECIFICATIONS

Butt material: hardwoods
Shaft material: rock maple
Standard length: 58 in.
Standard wrap (Legend): Irish linen

CURRENT LEGEND CUES

DMI Sports offers several models of legends cues priced from $60 to $500.

SECONDARY MARKET MINIMUM VALUES

The following are minimum values for Legend cues encountered on the secondary market. These prices are representative of cues utilizing basic materials and designs that are not necessarily available at present.

Special construction note: There are many materials and construction techniques that can add value to Legend cues.

For all used Legend cues, except where otherwise noted:

Add $150+ for each predator shaft.
Deduct 60% for missing original straight playable shaft.
Deduct 15% for obvious or improper refinish.

	98%	90%	70%
Level 1 - Hustler.			
Level 1 cues start at	$50	$35	$20
Level 2 - 0 points, 0-25 inlays.			
Level 2 cues start at	$65	$50	$30
Level 3 - 2-6 points, 0-8 inlays.			
Level 3 cues start at	$80	$60	$35
Level 4 - 4-10 points, 9-25 inlays.			
Level 4 cues start at	$100	$75	$45
Level 5 - 0-12 points, 26-50 inlays.			
Level 5 cues start at	$135	$100	$60

LIBRA CUES

Maker of cues in Dallas, Texas from 1988 to 1990.

Libra Cues were one-of-a-kind custom cues, made by Johnny Sanchez and Jack Potter in Dallas, Texas in the late 1980s.

LINEAR Q

Pool cues manufactured in China, and distributed by Hyper-designs in Simi Valley, California.

The linear cue is a unique stainless steel cue with a slider for the bridge hand that was introduced in 2005. The Linear cue complies with BCA guidelines for tournament use. It was developed over the course of seven years in the United States, and it has received a U.S. Patent.

If you are interested in talking to someone about a new Linear cue, you can contact them at Linear Q, listed in the Trademark Index.

SPECIFICATIONS

Butt material: stainless steel
Shaft material: stainless steel
Standard length: 57 in.
Joint type: quick release
Weights available: 18 to 25 ounces

OPTIONS (FOR NEW CUES ONLY)

Custom color: $75

| GRADING | 100% | 95% | 70% |

CURRENT EXAMPLES

The following Linear cues is available in red, gold, teal, purple, or silver.

Level 2 - Stainless steel butt and shaft.

| MSR | $299.95 | $250-299.95 | $185 | $100 |

JEFF LIPP

Maker of Eye Cues. For more information refer to the listing for Eye Cues.

LOMAX CUSTOM CUES

Maker of pool cues from 2003 to present in Cornelia, Georgia.

Steve Lomax has been around the game of pool since the early 1970s. In 2000, he started doing cue repairs for himself and friends from local pool rooms. This business began to grow and Steve ended up doing cue repairs and refinishing for players all over the country. In about 2003, he started making his own jump cues and break-jump cues. In late 2003, he started building a few playing cues and has been building about a dozen each year during his spare time. He appreciates the help he has gotten from other cuemakers.

Steve takes orders for custom cues to the customer's specifications. Within the last year, he has become part owner of Bunjee Billiards. He has redesigned their jump-break cues and currently builds a custom line for Bunjee.

If you are interested in talking to Steve Lomax about a new cue or cue that needs to be repaired, you can contact him at Lomax Custom Cues, listed in the Trademark Index.

Steve Lomax

SPECIFICATIONS

- Butt material: hardwoods
- Shaft material: rock maple
- Standard length: 58 in.
- Standard wrap: Irish linen
- Standard ferrules: LBM or phenolic
- Standard tip: Le Pro
- Annual production: more than 20 cues

OPTIONS (FOR NEW CUES ONLY)

- Ivory ferrule: $75
- Leather wrap: $100+
- Extra shaft: $125

REPAIRS

Repairs done on all fine cues.
- Refinish (with Irish linen wrap): $150
- Rewrap (Irish linen): $45
- Replace shaft: $125
- Replace tip: $15+

CURRENT LOMAX CUES

Two-piece Lomax bar cues start at $250. Basic Lomax cues with wraps and joint rings start at $450. Lomax cues with points start at $600.

SECONDARY MARKET MINIMUM VALUES

The following are minimum values for other Lomax cues encountered on the secondary market. These prices are representative of cues utilizing basic materials and designs that are not necessarily available at present. Steve has offered one-of-a-kind cues that can command many times these prices due to the use of exotic materials and artistry.

Present Day

Special construction note: There are many materials and construction techniques that can add value to Lomax cues.

For all used Lomax cues, except where otherwise noted:
- Add $100 for each additional original straight playable shaft beyond one.
- Deduct $125 for missing original straight playable shaft.
- Add $50 each for ivory ferrules.
- Add $65 for leather wrap.
- Deduct 20% for obvious or improper refinish.

GRADING	98%	90%	70%
Level 2 - 0 points, 0-25 inlays.			
Level 2 cues start at	$300	$235	$160
Level 3 - 2-6 points, 0-8 inlays.			
Level 3 cues start at	$450	$350	$235
Level 4 - 4-10 points, 9-25 inlays.			
Level 4 cues start at	$525	$405	$270
Level 5 - 0-12 points, 26-50 inlays.			
Level 5 cues start at	$700	$550	$385

LONGONI CUSTOM CUES

Maker of pool cues since the 1950s in Mariano Comense, Italy.

Alessandro Longoni started Longoni in 1945, soon after World War II. He had learned about the billiard industry while working at a famous Italian billard manufacturer. His wife Maria and his sons Emilio and Renzo helped to build the small business in Mariano Comense into a successful company. Longoni started manufacturing cues in the 1950s. About ten years later they began to export cues to the United States.

In the 1970s, Renzo Longoni took over cue development for the company. The company founder, Alessandro Longoni, died in 1978. Longoni later experimented with new materials such as Kewlar, Ergal, and graphite for shafts. Cues and shafts have been developed specifically for the disciplines of pool, carom, three cushion, Russian pyramid, Carolina, five skittles, Goriziana, and Italiana.

Longoni cues have been imported to the USA in the past by companies such as J-S Sales and D & R Industries. Today they manufacture four different types of cues and five different lines of pool cues. Longoni cues are easily recognizable by the "Longoni" logo in the butt caps.

If you have a Longoni cue that needs further identification or repair, or would like to talk to someone about ordering a new Longoni cue, contact Longoni Cues, listed in the Trademark Index.

SPECIFICATIONS

Butt material: hardwoods
Shaft material: rock maple
Point construction: inlaid
Standard number of shafts: one
Standard ferrules: CBR
Standard tips: Le Pro

CURRENT LONGONI CUES

Longoni currently offers eight pool cues in the "Classica" Line, three pool cues in the "Niels Feijen" Line, eleven pool cues in the "Revolution" Line, four pool cues in the "M" Line, and six pool cues in the "E" Line. High end Longoni cues come with two shafts and a certificate of authenticity.

Present Day

GRADING	100%	95%	70%

CURRENT EXAMPLES

The following cues were formerly imported by D&R Industries and are still available from Longoni. Current retail prices in US Dollars were not available.

Level 3 E/10 - Briar forearm, floating stained maple points with an intricate ebony border that forms a diamond in the center of each point, briar butt sleeve with pairs of opposing ebony-bordered triangles.

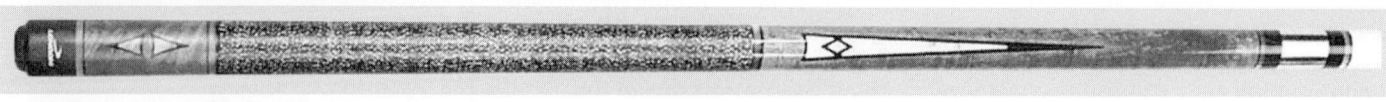

| MSR | N/A | $380 | $285 | $180 |

Level 4 97/2 - Stained bird's-eye maple forearm with an opposing stained ring above wrap, four floating ebony-bordered violetto points, ebony butt sleeve with a stained maple ring below wrap and intricate pearlized plastic-bordered violetto inlays.

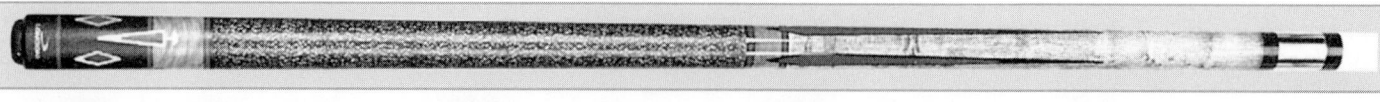

| MSR | N/A | $535 | $400 | $260 |

LONGONI CUSTOM CUES, cont. 439

GRADING	100%	95%	70%

Level 4 97/3 - Ebony forearm, floating violetto points with an alternate pearl border and a turquoise ellipse-shaped inlay in each point, ebony butt sleeve with violetto windows with an alternate pearl border and a turquoise ellipse-shaped inlay in each.

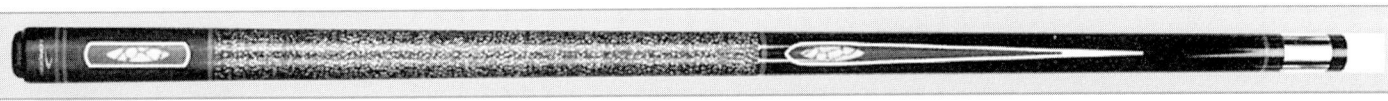

MSR	N/A	$555	$425	$275

Level 3 LV4 - Stained bird's-eye maple forearm with ebony columns, octagonal handle with thick rings of zebra/cocobolo/ebony/maple/briar down to buttcap.

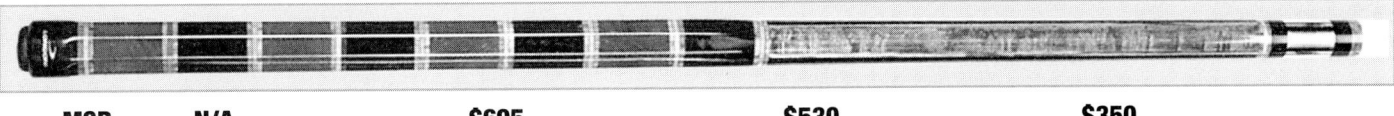

MSR	N/A	$695	$530	$350

Level 4 LV8B - Stained bird's-eye maple forearm with ebony-bordered Ivorine ovals above handle, ebony-bordered two-piece Ivorine points, ebony handle with stitched leather columns, briar butt sleeve with ebony-bordered opposing Ivorine triangles alternating with ebony-bordered Ivorine ellipse-shaped inlays.

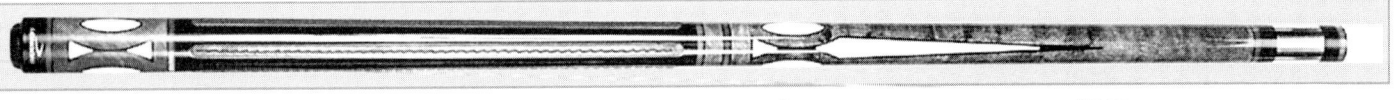

MSR	N/A	$745	$565	$365

Level 8 LV10 - Bird's-eye maple forearm with intricate ebony-bordered Ivorine rectangles alternating with ebony columns, ebony handle with an intricate picture of an ancient warrior hand inlaid in colored maple, briar butt sleeve with ebony-bordered Ivorine diamond-shaped inlays.

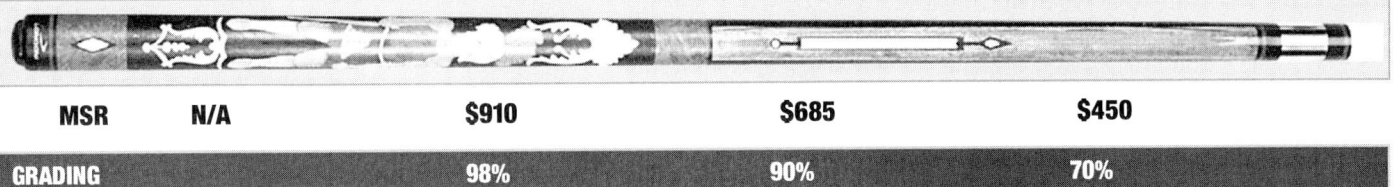

MSR	N/A	$910	$685	$450

GRADING	98%	90%	70%

SECONDARY MARKET MINIMUM VALUES

The following are minimum values for other Longoni cues encountered on the secondary market. These prices are representative of cues utilizing basic materials and designs that are not currently available. Longoni has offered one-of-a-kind cues that can command many times these prices due to the use of exotic materials and artistry. Early models and limited editions are becoming collectible, and can also command many times these prices. Discontinued Longoni cues will be further covered in future editions.

Special construction note: There are many materials and construction techniques that can add value to Longoni cues.

For all used cues, except where otherwise noted:
Add $125 for each additional original straight playable shaft beyond one.
Deduct $150+ for missing original straight playable shaft.
Deduct 20% for obvious or improper refinish.

Level 2 - 0 points, 0-25 inlays.
Level 2 cues start at	$275	$210	$135

Level 3 - 2-6 points, 0-8 inlays.
Level 3 cues start at	$350	$255	$145

Level 4 - 4-10 points, 9-25 inlays.
Level 4 cues start at	$395	$300	$190

Level 5 - 0-12 points, 26-50 inlays.
Level 5 cues start at	$575	$435	$275

Level 6 - 0-12 points, 51-75 inlays.
Level 6 cues start at	$700	$535	$340

L.T.D. CUES

GRADING	98%	90%	70%

L.T.D. CUES

Maker of pool cues in Sultan, Washington.

Dale Teague has been making cues for over 25 years, by hand in his one-man shop. Recently he has been going by the name L.T.D. Cues. Although L.T.D. cues are not marked, they are easily recognizable to those familiar with his work. Dale currently specializes in one-of-a-kind custom cues, with playability being the most important factor.

L.T.D. Cues are guaranteed for life against manufacturing defects that are not the result of warpage or abuse. If you have an L.T.D. cue that needs further identification or repair, or would like to order a new L.T.D. cue, contact L.T.D.Cues, listed in the Trademark Index.

Dale Teague

SPECIFICATIONS

Butt material: hardwoods
Shaft material: rock maple
Standard length: 58 1/2 in.
Lengths available: any
Balance point: custom
Standard wrap: Irish linen
Joint type: flat faced
Joint screw: 3/8-10
Standard number of shafts: two
Standard taper: custom
Standard tip: Triangle
Tip widths available: any

SECONDARY MARKET MINIMUM VALUES

The following are minimum values for other L.T.D. cues encountered on the secondary market. These prices are representative of cues utilizing basic materials and designs that are not necessarily available at present. Dale has offered one-of-a-kind cues that can command many times these prices due to the use of exotic materials and artistry.

Special construction note: There are many materials and construction techniques that can add value to L.T.D. cues.

For all used L.T.D. cues, except where otherwise noted:

Add $85 for each additional original straight playable shaft beyond one.
Deduct $125 for missing original straight playable shaft.
Add $45 each for ivory ferrules.
Add $65 for leather wrap.
Deduct 20% for obvious or improper refinish.

	98%	90%	70%
Level 2 - 0 points, 0-25 inlays.			
Level 2 cues start at	$400	$315	$215
Level 3 - 2-6 points, 0-8 inlays.			
Level 3 cues start at	$550	$420	$285
Level 4 - 4-10 points, 9-25 inlays.			
Level 4 cues start at	$650	$505	$345
Level 5 - 0-12 points, 26-50 inlays.			
Level 5 cues start at	$900	$700	$480

LUCASI CUE

Line of pool cues imported by Cue & Case Sales, Inc.

Lucasi cues are easily identifiable by the "Lucasi" marking on the butt caps. If you have a Lucasi cue that needs further identification or repair, or would like to order a new Lucasi cue, contact Cue & Case Sales, listed in the Trademark Index.

Present Day

SPECIFICATIONS

Butt material: hardwoods
Shaft material: hard rock maple
Standard length: 58 in.
Standard finish: UV
Standard butt cap: Implex
Standard wrap: Irish linen
Standard joints: Uni-Loc or Accu-Loc 5/16-18
Standard number of shafts: one
Standard taper: pro
Standard ferrules: XTC

LUCASI CUE, cont. 441

GRADING	98%	90%	70%

Standard tip: Triangle
Standard tip width: 13 mm

OPTIONS (FOR NEW CUES ONLY)

Joint protectors: $29
Extra shaft: $110

CURRENT LUCASI CUES

Many current models of Lucasi cues are available, priced from $159 to $460. Lucasi cues are usually available for immediate delivery.

SECONDARY MARKET MINIMUM VALUES

The following are minimum values for Custom Cues encountered on the secondary market. These prices are representative of cues utilizing basic materials and designs that are not necessarily available at present.

Special construction note: There are many materials and construction techniques that can add value to Lucasi cues.

For all used Lucasi cues, except where otherwise noted:
   Add $85 for each additional original straight playable shaft beyond one.
   Deduct $110 for missing original straight playable shaft.
   Deduct 15% for obvious or improper refinish.

Level 2 - 0 points, 0-25 inlays.
   Level 2 cues start at $95 $75 $45
Level 3 - 2-6 points, 0-8 inlays.
   Level 3 cues start at $110 $85 $50
Level 4 - 4-10 points, 9-25 inlays.
   Level 4 cues start at $145 $210 $70
Level 5 - 0-12 points, 26-50 inlays.
   Level 5 cues start at $185 $140 $90

LUDWIG CUSTOM CUES

Maker of pool cues from 2002 to present in Scottsdale, Arizona.

Todd Ludwig began building cues in 2002. His part-time business is located in Scottsdale, Arizona. He worked in the grocery business before getting into the computer industry. He purchased a high-end Scruggs cue and appreciated the beauty and playability of it. It inspired him to try his hand at making his own cues.

If you are interested in talking to Todd Ludwig about a new cue or cue that needs to be repaired, you can contact him at Ludwig Custom Cues, listed in the Trademark Index.

SPECIFICATIONS

Butt material: hardwoods
Shaft material: rock maple
Standard length: 58 in.
Lengths available: 57 to 60 in.
Standard finish: auto clear coat
Standard butt cap: phenolic
Standard wrap: Irish linen
Point construction: short splice
Standard joint: phenolic
Standard number of shafts: two
Standard taper: custom
Standard ferrules: LBM
Standard tip: Le Pro
Standard tip width: 13 mm
Tip widths available: any
Annual production: approximately 20 cues

OPTIONS (FOR NEW CUES ONLY)

Special length: no charge
Layered tip: $10+
Ivory butt cap: $150
Ivory joint: $100
Ivory ferrule: $50
Leather wrap: $75
Joint protectors: $50+

GRADING	98%	90%	70%

Extra shaft: $100

REPAIRS

Repairs done on all fine cues.
- Refinish (with Irish linen wrap): $125
- Refinish (with leather wrap): $175
- Rewrap (Irish linen): $25
- Rewrap (leather): $75
- Clean and press linen wrap: $20
- Replace shaft: $100
- Replace ivory ferrule: $45
- Replace butt cap: $50
- Replace ivory butt cap: $150
- Replace tip: $10+
- Replaced layered tip: $15+
- Replace fiber/linen ferrule: $20

CURRENT LUDWIG CUES

The current delivery time for a Ludwig cue is about four months.

SECONDARY MARKET MINIMUM VALUES

The following are minimum values for other Ludwig cues encountered on the secondary market. These prices are representative of cues utilizing basic materials and designs that are not necessarily available at present. Todd has offered one-of-a-kind cues that can command many times these prices due to the use of exotic materials and artistry.

Special construction note: There are many materials and construction techniques that can add value to Ludwig cues.

For all used Ludwig cues, except where otherwise noted:
- Add $75 for each additional original straight playable shaft beyond two.
- Deduct $100 for each missing original straight playable shaft under two.
- Add $40 each for ivory ferrules.
- Add $65 for leather wrap.
- Deduct 15% for obvious or improper refinish.

Level 2 - 0 points, 0-25 inlays.

	98%	90%	70%
Level 2 cues start at	$300	$285	$160

Level 3 - 2-6 points, 0-8 inlays.

Level 3 cues start at	$450	$350	$240

Level 4 - 4-10 points, 9-25 inlays.

Level 4 cues start at	$550	$425	$290

Level 5 - 0-12 points, 26-50 inlays.

Level 5 cues start at	$750	$575	$390

M SECTION

MACE CUES BY RICK HOWARD

Maker of pool cues from 1987 to present in Navarre, Florida.

As a teenager growing up in Indiana, Rick Howard dreamed of being a professional bowler. He spent most of his free time in the local bowling alley. Soon after high school, Rick started playing pool at the bowling alley instead. He seemed to have a talent for the game and, before long, he was beating most of the local players. He hooked up with a top player, and soon the two were on the road together. They spent some time in Chicago in the early seventies, where Rick got to meet the top cuemakers in town at the time. It was then that he realized he wanted to make cues someday. Rick continued to play pool and eventually became an upper rank pro player.

In 1980, Rick moved to Florida and opened up a jet ski and para-sail business. The tourists kept him busy during the summer months and he kept playing pool during the winter. After a few years of this, Rick started accumulating some equipment and doing some cue repairs at the tournaments he played in.

Before long, Rick was out of the jet ski and para-sail business, and by 1987 he had made his first cue. The cues Rick made in the first year are all marked "Mace," a term he chose because it represents both a billiard implement and a medieval weapon. One year later, Rick introduced the Mace break-jump cue that has given him worldwide recognition. This 58 in. cue has a 5/16-18 screw, and breaks down to 45 in. for jumping balls. It was one of the first cues of its kind and is still available for $275 with one shaft. When he started producing this cue, Rick put the "Mace" logo on it and started signing all of his custom cues "R. Howard" on the forearms. Rick should not be confused with another Rick Howard, pro player David Howard's brother, who has just begun making cues.

Today, Rick makes about 400 break-jump cues a year, with the help of a part-time worker. He also makes about 120 custom cues, entirely on his own. He makes all of the components of his cues except for the tips, bumpers, and screws. Mace Custom Cues usually have six points, with veneers offered as an option at $25 each. In 1998, Rick replaced the old 3/8-10 stainless screw with a 3/8-11 brass screw. All work is done by hand and inlays are done with a manual pantograph. Shafts are turned six times over the course of a year. Playability is stressed as the most important aspect of all Mace cues.

All Mace cues are guaranteed indefinitely against construction defects that are not the result of wrapage or abuse. If you have a Mace cue that needs further identification or repair, or would like to talk to Rick about ordering a new Mace cue, contact Mace Custom Cues by Rick Howard, listed in the Trademark Index.

Rick Howard

1989 to Present Day, custom cues

1989 to Present Day, break/jump

SPECIFICATIONS

Butt material: phenolic
Shaft material: hard rock maple
Standard length: 58 in.
Lengths available: up to 60 in.
Standard finish: three-part urethane
Joint screw: 3/8-11 and 5/16-18 (Mace)
Standard joint: phenolic
Joint type: flat face
Point construction: v bottom or short splice
Standard wrap: Irish linen
Standard butt cap: phenolic
Standard number of shafts: two (custom)
Standard ferrules: melamine
Standard tip width: 13 mm
Standard bumper: 1 in. x 5/8 rubber
Annual production: 30 custom cues, 120 Mace break jump cues

GRADING	98%	90%	70%

OPTIONS (FOR NEW CUES ONLY)
Special lengths: no charge
Extra shaft: $100+
Ivory joint: $140
Ivory ferrule: $60
Ivory butt cap: $220
Layered tip: $10
Custom joint protectors: $125
Leather wrap: $100

Repairs done on most fine cues.
Refinish (with linen wrap): $125
Refinish (with leather wrap): $175
Rewrap linen: $35
Rewrap leather: $100
Clean and press linen wrap: $15
Replace shaft: $125+
Replace ivory ferrule: $75
Replace fiber/linen ferrule: $25
Replace butt cap: $35+
Replace ivory butt cap: $225
Replace tip: $10
Replace layered tip: $35

PAST EXAMPLES

The first three Mace cues shown came with one shaft, and the last four came with two shafts.

Level 1 "Mace Hustler" - Maple forearm, four full-spliced rosewood points and butt sleeve.

| MSR (1999) $185 | $235 | $185 | $120 |

Level 2 "Mace Break/Jump Cue" - Bird's-eye maple forearm with a joint above wrap to break down into a 42-inch jump cue, maple butt sleeve.

| MSR (1999) $275 | $350 | $270 | $180 |

Level 2 "Mace Break/Jump Cue" - Stained bird's-eye maple forearm with a joint above wrap to break down into a 42-inch jump cue, stained maple butt sleeve.

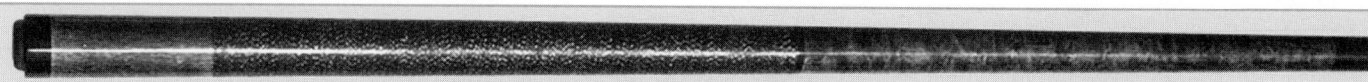

| MSR (1999) $275 | $350 | $270 | $180 |

Level 2 - Bird's-eye maple forearm, bird's-eye maple butt sleeve with maple dash rings at bottom.

| MSR (1999) $450 | $550 | $420 | $285 |

Level 3 - Bird's-eye maple forearm, four cocobolo points with two veneers, cocobolo butt sleeve with cocobolo dash rings at bottom.

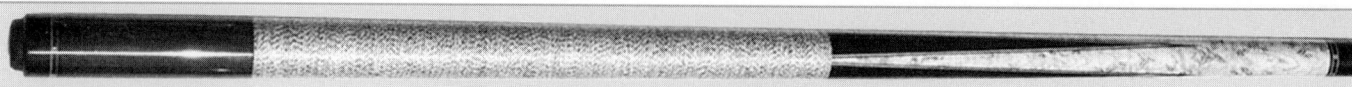

| MSR (1999) $550 | $700 | $545 | $365 |

Level 3 - Bird's-eye maple forearm, three long and three short ebony points with two colored veneers, ebony butt sleeve with maple dash rings at bottom.

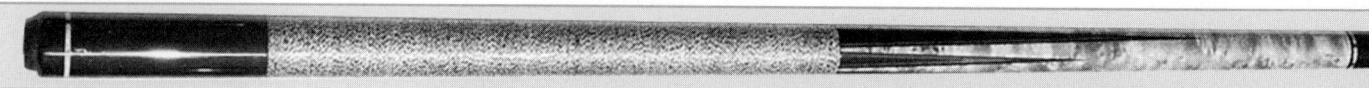

| MSR (1999) $675 | $800 | $625 | $425 |

GRADING	98%	90%	70%

Level 3 - Ebony forearm, three long and three short tulip wood points, ebony butt sleeve with six tulipwood windows above tulipwood set in nickel silver rings at bottom.

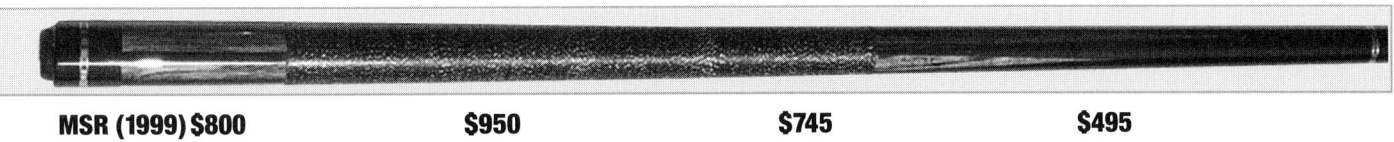

MSR (1999) $800	$950	$745	$495

SECONDARY MARKET MINIMUM VALUES

The following are minimum values for other Mace cues encountered on the secondary market. These prices are representative of cues utilizing basic materials and designs that are not necessarily available at present. Rick has offered one-of-a-kind cues that can command many times these prices due to the use of exotic materials and artistry.

Special construction note: There are many materials and construction techniques that can add value to Mace cues.

For all used Mace cues, except where otherwise noted:
- Add $100 for each additional original straight playable shaft beyond two.
- Deduct $150 for each missing original straight playable shaft under two.
- Add $60 each for ivory ferrules.
- Add $75 for leather wrap.
- Deduct 20% for obvious or improper refinish.

Level 1 - Hustler.
Level 1 cues start at	$225	$175	$120

Level 2 - 0 points, 0-25 inlays.
Level 2 cues start at	$500	$390	$270

Level 3 - 2-6 points, 0-8 inlays.
Level 3 cues start at	$700	$545	$375

Level 4 - 4-10 points, 9-25 inlays.
Level 4 cues start at	$850	$665	$450

Level 5 - 0-12 points, 26-50 inlays.
Level 5 cues start at	$1,150	$900	$600

Level 6 - 0-12 points, 51-75 inlays.
Level 6 cues start at	$1,600	$1,315	$900

THE MACE

Implement used to play lawn and table billiards from the 1100s to the early 1900s, primarily in Europe.

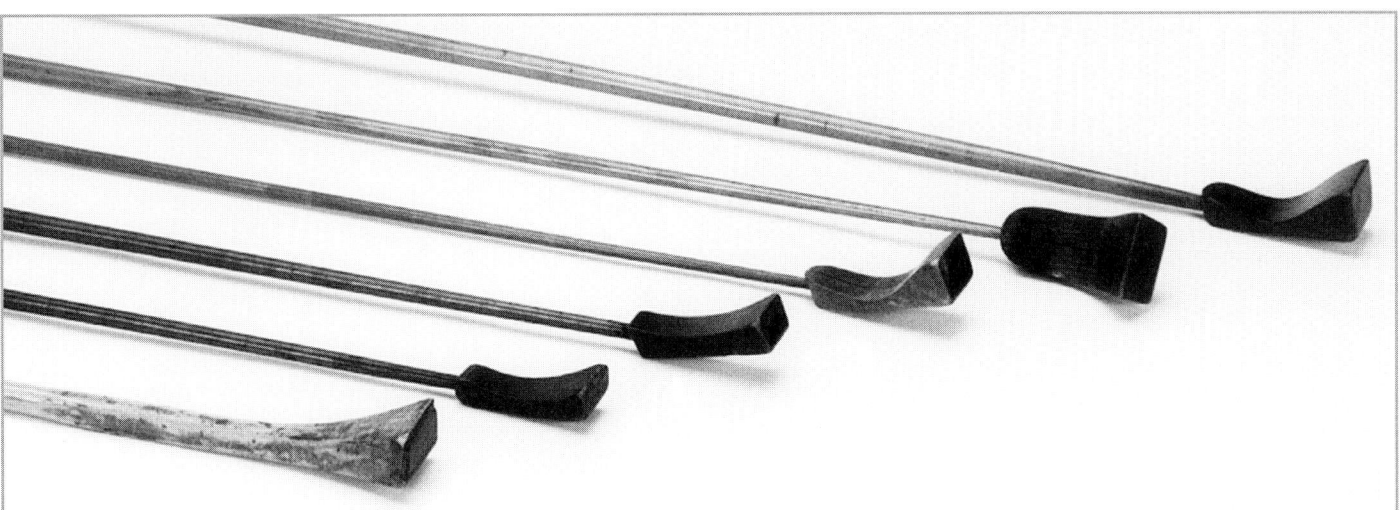

The mace was the predecessor to both the cue and the mechanical bridge stick. Based on portrayals in engravings, cues were thought to have evolved in the mid-1600s from curved mallets used in lawn games comparable to croquet. The word "mace" originates from the French word "masse," a term that, when translated, means "hammer." In England, they were labeled "masts" or in simple terms, "sticks." For the most part maces had solid wooden heads affixed to wooden handles, while some were carved from one solid piece of wood. The head was normally set at a slope to allow the end of the mace to rest comfortably on the player's shoulder (see illustration). An aiming line was often cut or inlaid into the midpoint of the head to aid in sighting the ball. As a rule, maces were nearly four feet in length, though several longer maces were implemented. Maces were occasionally capped with ivory on the front end, and later on maces frequently boasted leather pads on the front edge, an enhancement that was translated to the cue in the early 1800s.

The mace and ball were glided concurrently across the table with an extended, sweeping reach. But, keeping the mace in contact with the ball for a prolonged time was regarded as dishonest and was penalized as a foul, in the same way the "push shot" foul rule is present in contemporary billiard games. Given that it was challenging to drive a ball resting near a cushion, the mace would be reversed and the competitor would use the tip of the handle to make the shot. This handle was frequently alluded to as the "tail" - or, in French, the "queue." By 1680 the "cue" was being utilized exclusive of the mace head and advanced on its own as an independent apparatus. Prior to the conception of the leather tip, only proficient players were permitted usage of the cue, because of the possibility of damaging the table cloth by mis-cues from an untipped stick. The mace gradually descended into disuse. By the late 1700s it was put into application as a mechanical bridge. Throughout the 19th century the mace was used predominantly by ladies, for whom it was not only "improper" to bend over to make a shot, but physically challenging due to the corsets that were mainstays in apparel at the time. The mace became archaic by 1900. As they are undeniably dissimilar from pool cues, the grading procedures in this text do not pertain to the mace. Antique maces commonly trade from several hundred to thousands of dollars, contingent on age, features, condition, originality, and rarity.

JOHN MADDEN CUES

Maker of pool cues, originally in Phoenix, Arizona, and from 2003 to present in St. Ignatius, Montana.

John "Jack" Madden began his first cue building project at the age of 12. He wanted his own cue when playing at the Boys Club because he felt he would win if he had his cue, and he did. That original cue has been lost over time, but playing pool and working with wood has endured for the last 40+ years.

Playing pool was the overriding passion in Jack's life, having played in the local rooms in Phoenix, Arizona. One of the most interesting people Jack had played in Phoenix was U. J. Puckett. Twenty-five years later, U. J. saw Jack at a tournament in Reno and said, "Jack Madden, Phoenix, Arizona, 1968."

Jack worked in construction in most of the western United States and found time to travel around and play pool. Jack placed in the World Nine Ball Championship held at Terry Stonier's Jointed Cue in Sacramento, California, when it was invitation only. He was dubbed "The Sacramento Surprise." Jack placed third, behind Keith McCready and Larry Hubbard. Jack also competed and placed in several other tournaments including the US Open 9 Ball and One Pocket Championship tournaments at Barry Behrman's in Virginia.

Beverly and Jack Madden

In the 1960s, Gus Szamboti built Jack a beautiful and playable custom cue with a heart inlay. Jack got the desire to build such fantastic cues himself. His cuemaking started by using a drill motor mounted to the dining room table, for putting on tips and cleaning his shafts. Jack could not find anyone to replace his tips to his satisfaction. In the 1990s, he was at a point in his life that gave him the opportunity to really pursue this long-held desire. He received bonus money from his employer and used it to purchase a 1953 Cincinnati engine lathe. Since then, he has not looked back. He has continued to acquire the equipment, specialized tooling, and materials needed to build cues. Jack worked evenings and weekends learning to build cues. He turned his obsession into a full-time vocation, and in March 2003 he was accepted as a voting member of the American Cuemakers Association.

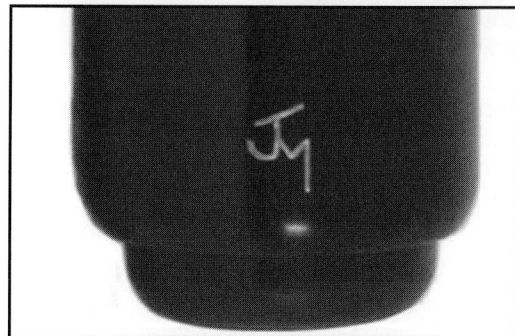

In May of 2003, Jack and his wife Beverly moved to western Montana. Jack built his dream one-man shop in the middle of a hay field. He has metal lathes, mill, CNC, dust collection system, spray booth, and the special tooling needed to build custom cues. It gives him more time to design and make one-of-a-kind cues. Jack makes his cues using the finest woods and materials available. Madden cues started with pantographed points, but have evolved to the short spliced recut points that Jack prefers to build. The cues meet the highest standards for quality construction and workmanship, as required for membership in the American Cuemakers Association. The cues also meet another standard, that of the player. Jack's goal is to be the "cuemaker of choice" for anyone buying a stick, by providing his customers with a handmade cue that is customized to their needs and desires and that plays well. Jack was a "player" before becoming a cuemaker, so he knows what a player needs and wants in a cue. John Madden Custom Cues have the "hit." The average order time for a Madden Custom cue is about four months.

Present Day

Madden cues have a "JM" logo in the butt cap. More recently, Jack has been hand signing his cues.

Madden cues are guaranted against defects that are not the result of warpage or abuse. Customers with concerns are urged to give Jack a call.

If you have a Madden cue needing further identification or repair, or would like to order a new Madden custom cue, contact Jack at John Madden Cues, listed in the Trademark Index.

SPECIFICATIONS

Butt material: hardwoods
Shaft material: hard rock maple
Standard length: 58 in.

GRADING	98%	90%	70%

Standard wrap: Irish linen
Standard ferrules: Aegis
Standard tip: Triangle
Annual production: 50 to 70 cues

OPTIONS (FOR NEW CUES ONLY)

Ivory ferrule: $75
Ivory joint: $150
Leather wrap: $150
Extra shaft: $125

REPAIRS

Repairs done on all fine cues.
Refinish (with Irish linen wrap): $200
Rewrap (Irish linen): $40
Replace shaft: $125
Replace tip: $15

CURRENT MADDEN CUES

Two-piece John Madden bar cues start at $250. Basic John Madden cues with wraps and joint rings start at $400. John Madden cues with points start at $520.

SECONDARY MARKET MINIMUM VALUES

The following are minimum values for other John Madden cues encountered on the secondary market. These prices are representative of cues utilizing basic materials and designs that are not necessarily available at present. John has offered one-of-a-kind cues that can command many times these prices due to the use of exotic materials and artistry.

Special construction note: There are many materials and construction techniques that can add value to John Madden cues.
For all used John Madden cues, except where otherwise noted:
Add $100 for each additional original straight playable shaft beyond one.
Deduct $125 for missing original straight playable shaft.
Add $65 each for ivory ferrules.
Add $85 for leather wrap.
Deduct 20% for obvious or improper refinish.

	98%	90%	70%
Level 1 - Hustler.			
Level 1 cues start at	$225	$175	$115
Level 2 - 0 points, 0-25 inlays.			
Level 2 cues start at	$350	$270	$180
Level 3 - 2-6 points, 0-8 inlays.			
Level 3 cues start at	$500	$385	$260
Level 4 - 4-10 points, 9-25 inlays.			
Level 4 cues start at	$600	$465	$320
Level 5 - 0-12 points, 26-50 inlays.			
Level 5 cues start at	$850	$665	$450
Level 6 - 0-12 points, 51-75 inlays.			
Level 6 cues start at	$1,200	$950	$650

MADISON BOB'S CUSTOM CUES

Name for Griffin & Son Custom Cues. For more information, refer to Griffin & Son Custom Cues.

MALI CUES

Maker of pool cues from 1961 to 2001 in Sheffield, Massachusetts, now distributing imported cues, headquartered in New York, New York.

The Henry W.T. Mali & Co., Inc. was founded by Henry Williams Theodore Mali, a young immigrant from Verviers, Belgium. He had learned the billiard cloth business while working for the Iwan Simonis Company (founded in 1680). He was commissioned by Simonis to market their billiard cloth in the United States, and sailed 31 days to arrive in New York. He soon started The Henry W.T. Mali & Co., Inc. in 1826. Later, he was joined by his much younger brother, Charles. They conducted business until around 1878. In 1898, they were joined by Pierre Mali, a young nephew whose father was the manager of the Simonis plant in Verviers. Mali eventually became one of the largest distributors of billiard cloth in the U.S. The company never made cues until 1961, when Fred Mali started cuemaking operations as an offshoot of the company.

GRADING	100%	95%	70%

Fred was the fifth generation of the Mali family to be involved in the business. He was exposed to woodworking as a boy in the shop at home where his father made things as a hobby. Fred attended Yale, where he majored in anthropology and history. He then went to Harvard Business School as a graduate student. After a year at Harvard, Fred was drafted into the U.S. Army, in 1953. Fred served his time in the U.S. and Paris, and, after being discharged, returned home to the family business. One of his first assignments was to go to Belgium to train at Simonis. He returned to apply his training to The Henry W.T. Mali & Co., Inc.

The Mali family spent much of their free time at a farm in Connecticut. It was there that Fred met Berkley Marchione, a farmer next door. Berkley was very mechanically inclined and was always fixing or improving the tractors or other farm equipment. Berkley also had a wood shop in his barn where he made odds and ends as a hobby. When one of Mali's closest competitors stopped making wooden triangles, a large distributor asked Fred if he could produce them. Fred contacted Marchione, and soon the two were producing wooden triangles in Marchione's barn. Soon afterwards, Bud Schmidt asked Fred if Mali could produce a line of cues. Before long, a line of cues was also being made under the supervision of Fred Mali and Berkley Marchione for the A.E. Schmidt Company in St. Louis. The cuemaking company was named Cuesport in 1965.

It was not long before Mali was marketing cues on his own. Constant improvements were made in the design and construction of Mali cues. In 1998, Peter Balner, formerly of Palmer in the sixties and seventies bought a stake in the company. Peter and Fred introduced a new line of Mali cues in 1999.

After closing Cuesport production, Mali began importing and distributing new lines of Mali cues in 2001. Fred Mali's philosophy has always been to make a good cue at a good price. Mali cues are easily identifiable by the Mali emblem on the butt cap.

If you would like to order a new Mali cue, contact The Henry W.T. Mali & Co., Inc., listed in the Trademark Index.

SPECIFICATIONS

- Butt material: hardwoods
- Shaft material: rock maple
- Standard length: 58 in.
- Lengths available: 58 in.
- Standard finish: catalyzed urethane
- Joint screw: 5/16-14
- Standard joint: stainless steel
- Joint type: piloted
- Balance point: 1 in. above wrap
- Point construction: inlaid
- Standard wrap: Irish linen
- Standard butt cap: cyro
- Standard number of shafts: one
- Standard taper: 10 in. pro
- Standard ferrules: Ivorine
- Standard tip: Le Pro
- Tip widths available: 11.5 to 14 mm
- Weights available: 18 to 20 oz.

OPTIONS (FOR NEW CUES ONLY)

- Extra shaft: $55
- Flat face joint: standard on some cues

CURRENT MALI CUES

Mali currently offers the Vintage Series and the F Series. The current delivery time for a Mali cue is approximately 1 week.

CURRENT EXAMPLES

The following 2005 Mali F Series cue is available in burgundy as the "F-2", green as the "F-3", blue as the "F-4", purple as the "F-5", and charcoal as the "F-6".

Level 2 "F-1" - Red stained maple forearm, red-stained maple butt sleeve with a thick maple ring set in metal rings at bottom.

MSR	$99	$70-99	$60	$45

2005 MALI VINTAGE

The following 2005 Mali Vintage Series cues have a piloted stainless steel joint with a 5/16-14 screw, except for the V-1 which has a flat faced Implex wood-to-wood joint, with a 3/8-10 screw.

MALI CUES, cont.

GRADING	100%	95%	70%

Level 1 "V-1" - Maple forearm, four full-spliced ebony points and handle with a synthetic ivory ring at bottom.

MSR	$140	$100-140	$85	$65

Level 3 "V-2" - Maple forearm, four rosewood points, rosewood butt sleeve.

MSR	$150	$105-150	$90	$70

Level 3 "V-3" - Maple forearm, four ebony points, ebony butt sleeve.

MSR	$170	$115-170	$100	$80

Level 3 "V-4" - Maple forearm with metal ringwork above wrap, four ebony points with four colored veneers, ebony butt sleeve with metal ringwork at top and bottom.

MSR	$190	$130-190	$115	$90

Level 3 "V-5" - Maple forearm, four ebony points with four colored veneers, ebony butt sleeve with a synthetic ivory ring at bottom.

MSR	$205	$140-205	$125	$100

Level 4 "V-6" - Maple forearm, four rosewood points with four veneers and a four point mother-of-pearl star shaped inlay between a pair of mother-of-pearl dots in each point, rosewood butt sleeve with four sets of four-pointed mother-of-pearl star-shaped inlays beteen pairs of mother-of-pearl dots alternating with mother-of-pearl dots.

MSR	$225	$155-225	$135	$110

Level 4 "V-7" - Maple forearm, four ebony points with four veneers and a four point mother-of-pearl star-shaped inlay between a pair of mother-of-pearl dots in each point, ebony butt sleeve with four sets of four pointed mother-of-pearl star-shaped inlays beteen pairs of mother-of-pearl dots alternating with mother-of-pearl dots.

MSR	$225	$155-225	$135	$110

Level 4 "V-8" - Maple forearm with metal ringwork above wrap, four ebony points with four colored veneers and an intricate four-piece synthetic ivory spear shape inlaid in each point, ebony butt sleeve with four intricate four-piece synthetic ivory diamond-shaped inlays alternating with synthetic ivory dots between metal ringwork at top and bottom.

MSR	$250	$170-250	$150	$120

Level 4 "V-9" - Ebony forearm, five intricate synthetic ivory bordered floating crushed turquoise and ebony four piece points, ebony butt sleeve with five intricate synthetic ivory bordered floating crushed turquoise and ebony four piece reverse point shaped inlays.

MSR	$250	$170-250	$150	$120

| GRADING | 98% | 90% | 70% |

DISCONTINUED EXAMPLES

1996 "SPECTRUM SERIES"

The following "Spectrum" Series cues were available in a variety of stain colors. The Implex joint was flat faced wood-to-wood, with a 3/8-10 screw. The stainless steel joint was piloted, with a 5/16-14 screw.

Level 2 Spectrum Implex - Implex joint, stained maple forearm, stained maple butt sleeve.

Orig. Retail (1996) $120 $100 $85 $45

Level 2 Spectrum Stainless Steel - Stainless steel joint, stained maple forearm, stained maple butt sleeve.

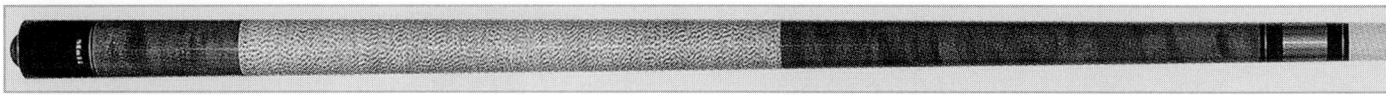

Orig. Retail (1996) $139 $115 $95 $55

"386" SERIES

The following "386" Series cues featured piloted stainless steel 5/16-14 joints or 3/8-10 Implex wood-to-wood flat faced joints where noted. Models 10 and 14 were available in a number of stain and wrap colors.

Level 2 386-1 - One-piece charcoal-stained maple butt with flat face joint.

Orig. Retail (1996) $99 $85 $75 $35

Level 2 386-2 - Natural maple forearm with flat face joint, natural maple butt sleeve.

Orig. Retail (1996) $120 $100 $80 $40

Level 2 386-3 - Green-stained maple forearm with flat-face joint, green-stained maple butt sleeve.

Orig. Retail (1996) $125 $105 $85 $45

Level 1 386-4 - Maple forearm, four dark hardwood points and butt sleeve.

Orig. Retail (1996) $130 $110 $90 $50

Level 2 386-5 - Bird's-eye maple forearm, bird's-eye maple butt sleeve with black Greek-Key motif ring above butt cap.

Orig. Retail (1996) $160 $125 $110 $60

Level 2 386-6 - Ebony forearm, ebony butt sleeve with six white diamond-shaped inlays between double rings above and below.

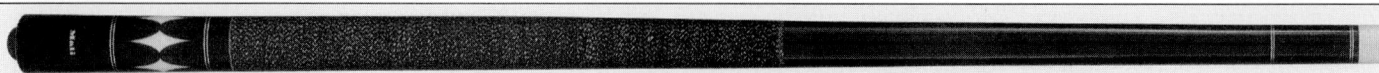

Orig. Retail (1996) $170 $135 $115 $65

MALI CUES, cont. 451

GRADING	98%	90%	70%

Level 3 386-7 - Bird's-eye maple forearm, four ebony-stained points bird's-eye maple butt sleeve with inward-pointing ebony-stained rings at top and bottom.

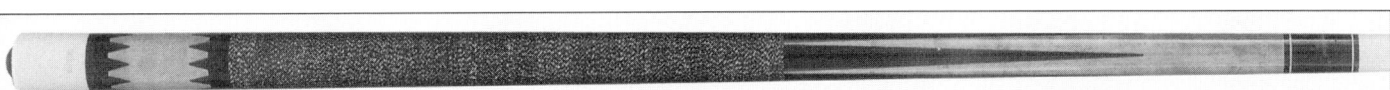

Orig. Retail (1996) $175	$145	$125	$70

Level 4 386-8 - Maple forearm, four floating blue, black, and white points, ebony-stained butt sleeve with four white four-piece diamond-shaped inlays between thin white rings above and below.

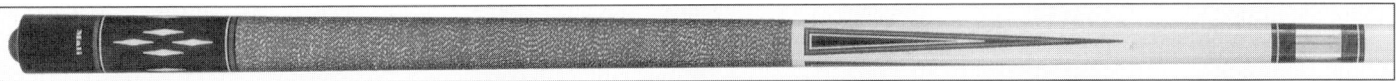

Orig. Retail (1996) $190	$160	$125	$75

Level 4 386-9 - Charcoal-stained bird's-eye maple forearm, four black points with black and white veneers, black butt sleeve with white chain link rings at top and bottom.

Orig. Retail (1996) $199	$165	$140	$80

Level 4 386-10 - Lightly stained bird's-eye maple forearm, four intricate three-piece black and white floating points, lightly stained bird's-eye maple butt sleeve with four intricate black and white "X"-shaped inlays alternating with four black-bordered white diamond-shaped inlays between black and white rings at top and bottom.

Orig. Retail (1996) $225	$185	$155	$85

Level 4 386-11 - Charcoal-stained maple forearm, four floating white and black-bordered ebony points with white and black-bordered ebony diamond-shaped inlays at the tip of each point and between the base of the points, Macassar ebony butt sleeve with four white-bordered windows inlaid with three vertical white diamond-shaped inlays in each between thin white rings at top and bottom.

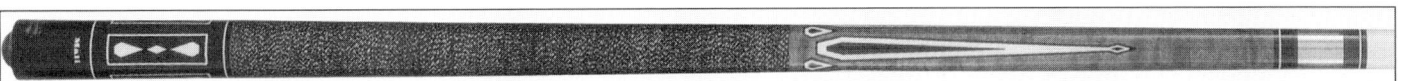

Orig. Retail (1996) $260	$215	$185	$100

Level 4 386-12 - Maple forearm, four floating white-bordered ebony points inlaid with white opposing arrowhead-shaped designs in each, Macassar ebony butt sleeve with four white-bordered windows inlaid with white opposing arrowhead-shaped designs in each.

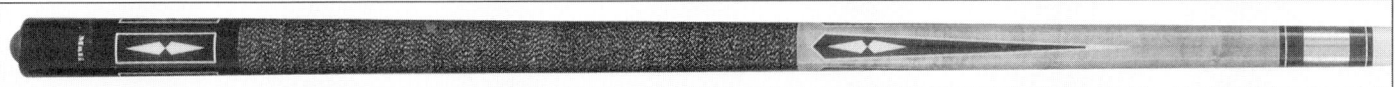

Orig. Retail (1996) $260	$200	$170	$90

Level 4 386-13 - Bird's-eye maple forearm, four Macassar ebony points with four colored veneers, Macassar ebony butt sleeve with four mother-of-pearl notched diamond-shaped inlays set in red and white rectangles between intricate rings of angled white diamond-shaped inlays above and below.

Orig. Retail (1996) $260	$205	$175	$95

Level 4 386-14 - Burgundy-stained bird's-eye maple forearm with four black-bordered white stylized triangles inlaid between the bases of the points, four floating black-bordered white points, burgundy-stained bird's-eye maple butt sleeve with four black-bordered white ovals inlaid with black opposing one-piece stylized triangles alternating with inward-pointing black-bordered white stylized triangles.

Orig. Retail (1996) $285	$240	$195	$115

| GRADING | 98% | 90% | 70% |

Level 4 386-15 - Charcoal-stained bird's-eye maple forearm, four floating black-bordered white points each inlaid with a black vertical four point star, Macassar ebony butt sleeve with four white diamond-shaped inlays alternating with ebony and white ovals inlaid with a black vertical four-point star in each.

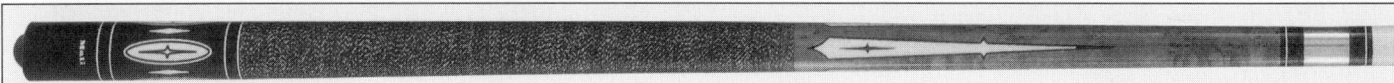

| Orig. Retail (1996) $285 | $225 | $185 | $105 |

"CLASSIC" SERIES

The following "Classic" Series cue was available in a variety of different stain and wrap colors. It had a 3/8-10 flat faced wood-to-wood Implex joint.

Level 4 Classic - Stained maple forearm, four white points with black veneers, white butt sleeve with four matching stained ovals set in black-bordered windows between double black rings at top and bottom.

| Orig. Retail (1996) $199 | $160 | $140 | $75 |

"REGALIA" SERIES

The following "Regalia" Series cues all featured piloted stainless steel joints.

Level 4 R1 - Charcoal-stained bird's-eye maple forearm, six white points with colored veneers, charcoal-stained bird's-eye maple butt sleeve with multi-colored veneered white diamond-shaped inlays alternating with pairs of opposing multi-colored veneered white triangle-shaped inlays between black and white rings at top and bottom.

| Orig. Retail (1996) $340 | $255 | $225 | $125 |

Level 4 R2 - Bird's-eye maple forearm, four ebony points with long white diamond-shaped inlays in each, ebony butt sleeve with four long white diamond-shaped inlays alternating with four short white diamond-shaped inlays between thin white rings at top and bottom.

| Orig. Retail (1996) $360 | $280 | $235 | $135 |

Level 4 R3 - Bird's-eye maple forearm, four ebony points with long white diamond-shaped inlays in each, ebony butt sleeve with four long white diamond-shaped inlays alternating with four opposing pairs of large tiger maple hexagons.

| Orig. Retail (1996) $380 | $295 | $245 | $145 |

Level 5 R4 - Bird's-eye maple forearm, four three-piece white points with black and white veneers, Macassar ebony butt sleeve with four long three-piece white diamond-shaped inlays alternating with four long three-piece black diamond-shaped inlays set in white windows.

| Orig. Retail (1996) $395 | $340 | $265 | $165 |

Level 5 R5 - Bird's-eye maple forearm, six floating tiger maple points with black-bordered white diamond-shaped inlays at the base of each, ebony butt sleeve with six three-piece long white and tiger maple diamond-shaped inlays alternating with six opposing pairs of small two white piece spears.

| Orig. Retail (1996) $430 | $355 | $290 | $170 |

MALI CUES, cont. **453**

GRADING	98%	90%	70%

Level 5 R5a - Charcoal-stained bird's-eye maple forearm, six floating tiger maple points with black-bordered white diamond-shaped inlays at the base of each, ebony butt sleeve with six three-piece long white and tiger maple diamond-shaped inlays alternating with six opposing pairs of small white two-piece spears.

Orig. Retail (1996) $430	$350	$285	$165

1999 SERIES"

The following 1999 Mali cues had a piloted stainless steel joint with a 5/16-14 screw, except for M-3 and M-4 which had flat faced Implex wood-to-wood joints, with 3/8-10 screws. M-3, M-4, and M-5 were available in five different stain colors.

Level 2 M-1 - Grey stained maple forearm, handle with joint to break down into a jump cue, short grey stained maple butt sleeve.

Orig. Retail (1999) $190	$135	$100	$60

Level 1 M-2 - Maple forearm and four rosewood points and butt sleve.

Orig. Retail (1999) $90	$80	$60	$35

Level 2 M-3 - One-piece stained maple butt.

Orig. Retail (1999) $110	$90	$70	$40

Level 2 M-4 - Stained maple forearm, stained maple butt sleeve.

Orig. Retail (1999) $140	$115	$90	$55

Level 2 M-5 - Stained maple forearm, stained maple butt sleeve.

Orig. Retail (1999) $165	$125	$95	$60

Level 2 M-6 - Brown stained bird's-eye maple forearm, brown-stained maple butt sleeve.

Orig. Retail (1999) $190	$145	$115	$75

Level 3 M-7 - Rock maple forearm, three ebony points, ebony butt sleeve.

Orig. Retail (1999) $210	$165	$125	$80

Level 2 M-8 - Cherry-stained bird's-eye maple forearm with an intricate Greek key motif ring above wrap, cherry-stained maple butt sleeve with ivory-bordered blocks in an ebony ring around center with Greek key motif rings above and below.

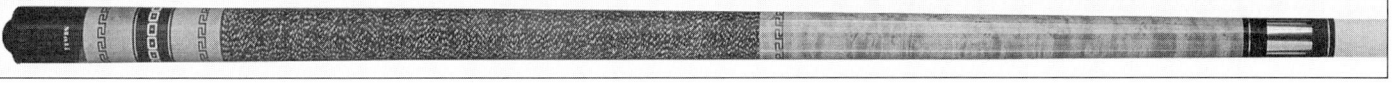

Orig. Retail (1999) $225	$175	$135	$85

| GRADING | 98% | 90% | 70% |

Level 3 M-9 - Stained bird's-eye maple forearm, four cocobolo points with four colored veneers, cocobolo butt sleeve.

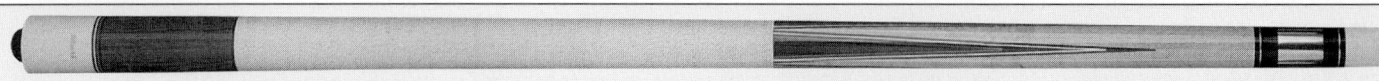

| Orig. Retail (1999) $250 | $185 | $145 | $90 |

Level 3 M-10 - Cherry-stained bird's-eye maple forearm, five cocobolo points, cocobolo butt sleeve with scalloped maple slanted blocks in a ring of ebony around center.

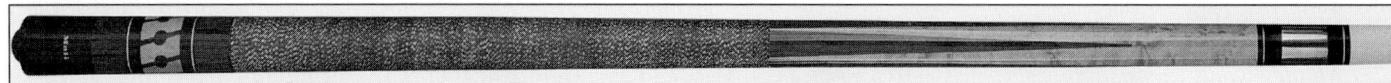

| Orig. Retail (1999) $275 | $235 | $180 | $115 |

Level 4 M-11 - Stained bird's-eye maple forearm, five cocobolo points, stained bird's-eye maple butt sleeve with large white acrylic diamond-shaped inlays alternating with small white acrylic diamond-shaped inlays around center.

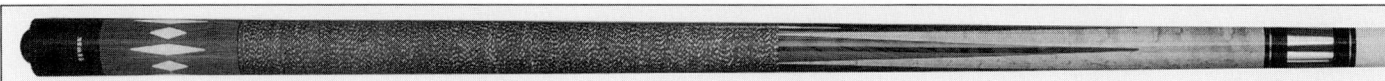

| Orig. Retail (1999) $300 | $250 | $190 | $120 |

Level 4 M-12 - Cherry stained bird's-eye maple forearm, four ebony points with two veneers, cherry stained bird's-eye maple butt sleeve with a ring of white acrylic squares set in ebony between rings of rosewood at top and bottom.

| Orig. Retail (1999) $325 | $265 | $200 | $130 |

Level 4 M-13 - Plum-stained bird's-eye maple forearm, five white acrylic points with a black border and a black acrylic diamond-shaped inlay in each point, plum-stained bird's-eye maple butt sleeve with four black acrylic diamond-shaped inlays set in black-bordered white acrylic ovals.

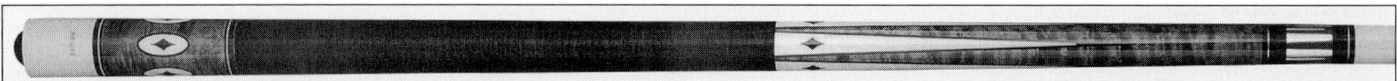

| Orig. Retail (1999) $350 | $285 | $220 | $140 |

Level 4 M-14 - Grey stained bird's-eye maple forearm, four ebony points with two veneers and a pair of white acrylic diamond-shaped inlays in each point, ebony butt sleeve with four cocobolo windows with black and white acrylic borders and pairs of white acrylic diamond-shaped inlays in each.

| Orig. Retail (1999) $375 | $315 | $240 | $150 |

Level 4 M-15 - Grey-stained bird's-eye maple forearm with four black- and white-bordered ebony spear-shaped inlays above wrap, four intricate white- and black-bordered floating ebony points, grey-stained bird's-eye maple butt sleeve with four ebony windows with black and white borders and three intricate white acrylic inlays in each.

| Orig. Retail (1999) $400 | $330 | $250 | $160 |

Level 4 M-16 - Mauve stained bird's-eye maple forearm, six white acrylic points with three veneers, mauve-stained bird's-eye maple butt sleeve with intricate three-piece black and white diamond-shaped inlays.

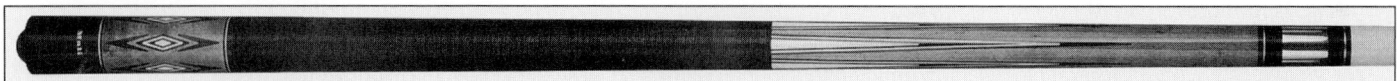

| Orig. Retail (1999) $450 | $385 | $285 | $175 |

MALI CUES, cont. 455

GRADING	98%	90%	70%

Level 4 M-17 - Pale brown-stained bird's-eye maple forearm, four intricate black-bordered white acrylic floating points with a four point black acrylic star-shaped inlay in each, pale brown-stained bird's-eye maple butt sleeve with four black dagger-shaped inlays set in black-bordered white acrylic shields between black and white checked rings at top and bottom.

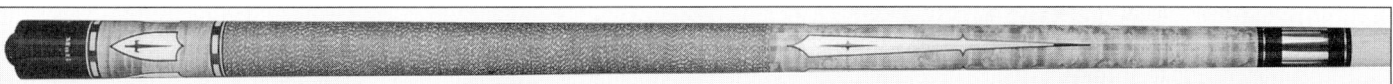

Orig. Retail (1999) $500	$425	$325	$205

Level 5 M-18 - Grey-stained bird's-eye maple forearm with four-point white acrylic stars set in ebony and purpleheart ovals, pairs of opposing ebony floating split points with a purpleheart oval in each, grey stained bird's-eye maple butt sleeve with four-point white acrylic star-shaped inlays set in ebony and purpleheart inlays between rings of purpleheart ovals above and below.

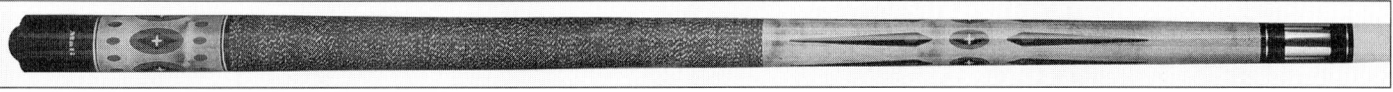

Orig. Retail (1999) $550	$455	$345	$220

Level 6 M-19 - Cherry stained bird's-eye maple forearm, six two-piece ebony points with two veneers split by black-bordered white acrylic squares, cherry-stained bird's-eye maple butt sleeve with a very intricate pattern of ebony and black-bordered white acrylic inlays.

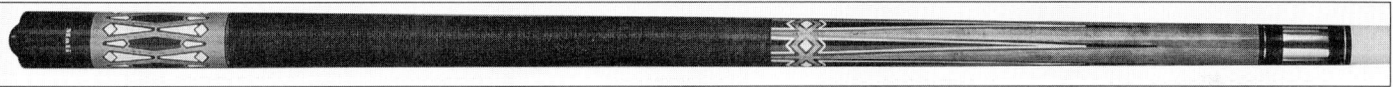

Orig. Retail (1999) $600	$535	$410	$260

Level 6 M-20 - Sienna-stained bird's-eye maple forearm, four intricate three-piece ebony floating points with two veneers and intricate pattern of white acrylic inlays in each, sienna-stained bird's-eye maple butt sleeve with four ebony windows with black and white borders and a very intricate pattern of white acrylic inlays in each.

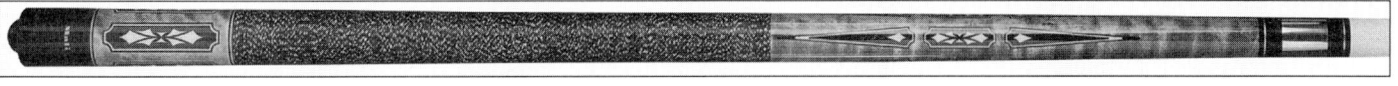

Orig. Retail (1999) $750	$615	$465	$300

SECONDARY MARKET MINIMUM VALUES

The following are minimum prices for older American-made Mali cues encountered on the secondary market. These prices are representative of cues utilizing basic materials and designs that are not currently available. Early models and limited editions are becoming collectible, and can also command many times these prices. Discontinued Mali cues will be further covered in future editions.

Special construction note: There are many materials and construction techniques that can add value to Mali cues.

For all used Mali cues, except where otherwise noted:
- Add $50+ for each additional original straight playable shaft beyond one.
- Deduct $60 for missing original straight playable shaft.
- Deduct 25% for obvious or improper refinish.

Level 1 - 4 points, hustler.
Level 1 cues start at	$75	$50	$30

Level 2 - 0 points, 0-25 inlays.
Level 2 cues start at	$95	$75	$55

Level 3 - 2-6 points, 0-8 inlays.
Level 3 cues start at	$175	$95	$70

Level 4 - 4-10 points, 9-25 inlays.
Level 4 cues start at	$225	$115	$90

Level 5 - 0-12 points, 26-50 inlays.
Level 5 cues start at	$325	$225	$165

Level 6 - 0-12 points, 51-75 inlays.
Level 6 cues start at	$450	$195	$150

MANZINO CUSTOM POOL CUES

Maker of pool cues from 1994 to present in Boca Raton, Florida.

Growing up in the New York City area in the 1960s and 1970s gave Robert Manzino the opportunity to watch some of the great players of that era. Bob was very observant of playing styles and also the cues that were popular. By the age of twenty, he was addicted to the game and started collecting pool cues.

While working as a machinist, Bob often thought of learning more about cue construction. His interest was side tracked as he pursued a career in the marine industry. Several years ago, Bob began doing cue repairs for some of the local pool halls in South Florida where he lives. Working with a small lathe and tooling skills acquired early on, he learned about fine cue construction. In 1994, Bob invested in a larger lathe more suitable for cue building, a manual pantograph, and enough woodworking machinery to construct his first high quality cue. It played well, so Bob was encouraged by friends and local players.

Bob initially was able to deliver up to 40 one-of-a-kind cues per year even while constantly expanding the shop which now includes several lathes, a precision milling machine, and a spray booth. As the inlay patterns got more elaborate, he enlisted his wife, Dany, to help with new designs. Bob now finds he can only produce 12 to 20 new cues each year.

In the past five years they've been building some unique triple-milled point blanks, which have proven to yield a more solid forearm than the traditional veneer blank. Bob prefers bird's-eye maple and ebony for their consistency in balance and beauty. He also enjoys working with pure (.999) silver, ivory, exotic burls, and Madagascar rosewood. Only top grade rock maple is used for shaft wood, well-seasoned between turns. Inlays are done by hand on a pantograph. Manzino cues often feature intricate rings using scroll or chain motifs created from materials such as pure silver, 14-karat gold, ebony, and ivory. Early Manzino cues were hand-signed, usually on the forearm. Since 1999 he has identified his cues by marking the top of his custom pins with "MANZINO".

Manzino cues are guaranteed for life for the original owner against manufacturing defects that are not the result of warpage or abuse. If you have a Manzino cue that needs further identification or repair, or would like to order a new Manzino cue, contact Manzino Custom Pool Cues, listed in the Trademark Index.

SPECIFICATIONS

Butt material: hardwoods
Shaft material: rock maple
Standard length: 58 in.
Lengths available: any up to 60 in.
Standard finish: hand polished urethane (Imron)
Balance point: 18 1/2 to 19 in. from butt
Standard butt cap: custom
Standard wrap: linen
Point construction: inlaid or short splice
Standard joint: flat face
Joint screw: 3/8-12 flat trough thread
Standard number of shafts: two
Standard taper: custom
Standard ferrules: ivory
Tip widths available: any up to 14 mm
Standard tip: Triangle
Annual production: fewer than 20 cues

OPTIONS (FOR NEW CUES ONLY)

Leather wrap: $200
Special length: no charge
Ivory points: call for quote
Ivory joint: $150
Ivory handle: $10,000+
Extra shaft: $200

REPAIRS

Repairs done on Manzino cues only. Repair prices quoted individually depending on the cue.

CURRENT EXAMPLES

The current delivery time for a Manzino cue is approximately one year.

MANZINO CUSTOM POOL CUES, cont. 457

GRADING	100%	95%	70%

CURRENT EXAMPLES

The following cues are representations of the work of Manzino Custom Cues, and come with two shafts with ivory ferrules and custom joint protectors. They can be ordered as shown, modified to suit the desires of the customer, or new designs can be created.

Level 5 – amboyna burl forearm, four points ivory with ebony/silver/ebony veneers and abalone inlays, ivory butt sleeve with four veneered amboyna windows to match forearm. Pure silver and ebony ringwork in chain design. Flat trough thread anodized aluminum pin, flat-faced ivory joint, butt cap. Custom amboyna, abalone and ivory joint protectors. Black leather wrap.

MSR	$5,500	$5,500-7,500	$6,000	$4,500

Level 5 - Amboyna burl forearm with four triple-milled points of ebony/maple/ebony, small ivory diamonds in each point, four ivory skirts with ebony veneer and spear tips between main points, amboyna butt sleeve with matching points and ivory skirts between 14-karat gold rosary rings with mother-of-pearl inserts, black calfskin wrap.

MSR	$4,500	$4,500-5,000	$4,000	$3,750

Level 6 "Tuxedo Collection" – Ebony forearm, five floating ivory points with pure silver veneer and silver medallion tips, five silver medallions between points, fancy scroll work with ebony and silver inlays in center. Ebony butt sleeve with five fancy ivory rectangle shapes, scroll and inlays to match points, five silver medallions between rectangles, crown-shaped ivory rings with silver bands and inlays at ABCD. Black monitor lizard wrap engraved joint protectors.

MSR	$6,500	$6,500-7,500	$6,000	$3,950

Level 7 – Ebony forearm, five stylized sabre-shaped points of ivory with inlays of black Tahitian pearl, pure silver filigree and 14-karat gold bands, five four-point star inlays of ivory and 14-karat gold between each point, pure silver bars above and below. Ebony butt sleeve, 10 matching fleur-de-lis ivory inlays of ivory (mirrored effect) with silver, gold and Tahitian pearl inlays, five four-point stars between the sets silver bars above and below, ivory bands inlayed with ebony scroll work and 14-karat gold stars bordered by sterling bands. Three-section ivory handle laced with pure silver inlays. Over 400 inlays, one of one.

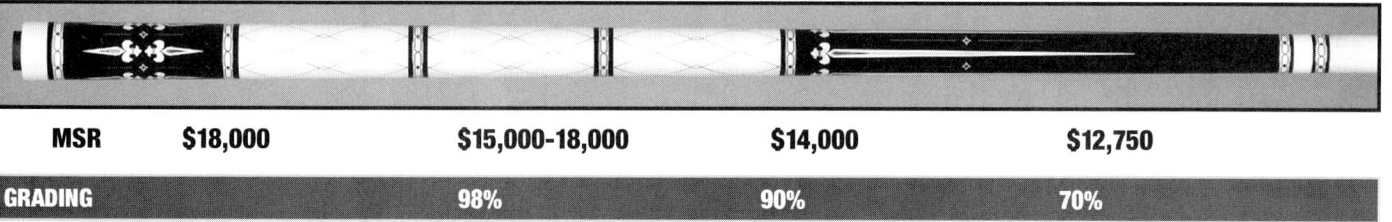

MSR	$18,000	$15,000-18,000	$14,000	$12,750

GRADING	98%	90%	70%

SECONDARY MARKET MINIMUM VALUES

The following are minimum values for Manzino cues encountered on the secondary market. These prices are representative of cues utilizing basic materials and designs that are not currently available. Bob Manzino has offered one-of-a-kind cues that can command many times these prices due to the use of exotic materials and artistry.

Special construction note: There are many materials and construction techniques that can add value to Manzino cues. (Please refer to listing and articles in the front of this text.)

For all used Manzino cues, except where otherwise noted:
- Add $85+ for each additional original straight playable shaft beyond two.
- Deduct $100 for each missing original straight playable shaft under two.
- Add $50 each for ivory ferrules.
- Add $150 for leather wrap.
- Deduct 20% for obvious or improper refinish.

Level 3 - 2-6 points, 0-8 inlays.

Level 3 cues start at	$1,200	$950	$650

Level 4 - 4-10 points, 9-25 inlays.

Level 4 cues start at	$1,600	$1,275	$1,000

GRADING	98%	90%	70%
Level 5 - 0-12 points, 26-50 inlays.			
Level 5 cues start at	$2,300	$1,900	$1,600
Level 6 - 0-12 points, 51-75 inlays.			
Level 6 cues start at	$3,500	$2,800	$2,400
Level 7 - 0-12 points, 76-125 inlays.			
Level 7 cues start at	$4,000	$3,500	$2,850
Level 8 - 0-12 points, 126-200 inlays.			
Level 8 cues start at	$4,850	$4,000	$3,500
Level 9 - 4 or more points, 201+ inlays.			
Level 9 cues start at	$7,000	$6,000	$4,800

JOE MARCHANT

Maker of pool cues until the early 1970s in the Detroit, Michigan area.

Hailing from the Detroit area, Joe Marchant was a cue craftsman during the 1960s and 1970s. Richard Chudy was an apprentice at Saffron Billiard Supply when he met Marchant there in the early 1970s. Existing representations of Marchant cues were fashioned in the style accredited to George Britner, the foremost ivory turner at Brunswick-Balke-Collender in Chicago in the late 1800s through the early 1900s. (Britner operated the ivory lathe, producing balls. It was purported that Britner completed a number of cues for Brunswick, as well as his own cues.)

Numerous identified exemplars of Marchant's cues introduce intarsia bands of petite offset stacked (1/10 by 1/2 in.) squares of fair and brunette woods. Marchant's cues can be identified by the piloted brass joint imprinted with the name "Marchant" in script. He used a 14-thread flat-topped brass pin. His cues accentuated a smooth-bottomed solid ivory butt cap with no bumper. During that era, bumpers were not as fashionable on custom cues as they are today. Billiard enthusiasts of the time were partial to the cue butts tap on the floor to signal the opponent's shot, over a bumper. Many principal Detroit players such as Tom Collins, stroked with a Marchant cue. Joe Marchant departed us a few years ago, living well into his 90s.

SPECIFICATIONS

Butt material: hardwoods
Shaft material: maple
Standard length: 58 in.
Standard finish: lacquer
Joint screw: 14-thread brass
Standard joint: piloted brass
Standard butt cap: ivory
Standard number of shafts: one
Standard ferrules: ivory

KNOWN EXAMPLES

Level 8 - Forearm consists of six 1/2 in. wide rectangular pieces of wood, ebony alternating with one of each of the three woods used in the inlays (satinwood, padauk, and rosewood). Center (wrap) section consists of seven wide bands of figured dark rosewood alternating with six 1/2 in. wide inlaid bands of 35 offset stacked pieces of a variety of light and dark woods. Each piece is 1/10 in. x 1/2 in. Ebony butt sleeve, 1.25 in. ivory butt cap with ebony and ivory rings above, no bumper. Piloted brass joint with "Marchant" engraved in script. Ivory ferrule, black linen shaft collar with ivory ring.

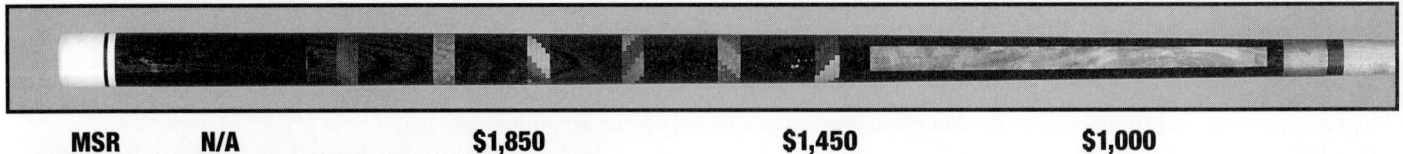

MSR	N/A	$1,850	$1,450	$1,000

SECONDARY MARKET MINIMUM VALUES

The following are minimum values for other Marchant cues encountered on the secondary market. These prices are representative of cues utilizing basic materials and designs that were available. Joe offered one-of-a-kind cues that can command many times these prices due to the use of exotic materials and artistry.

Special construction note: There are many materials and construction techniques that can add value to Marchant cues.

For all used Marchant cues, except where otherwise noted:

Add $150+ for each additional original straight playable shaft beyond one.
Deduct 50% for missing original straight playable shaft.
Add $100 for leather wrap.
Deduct 30% for obvious or improper refinish.

Level 2 - 0 points, 0-25 inlays.
    Level 2 cues start at $400 $300 $190

GRADING	98%	90%	70%
Level 3 - 2-6 points, 0-8 inlays.			
Level 3 cues start at	$600	$450	$290
Level 4 - 4-10 points, 9-25 inlays.			
Level 4 cues start at	$850	$650	$400
Level 5 - 0-12 points, 26-50 inlays.			
Level 5 cues start at	$1,050	$800	$500
Level 6 - 0-12 points, 51-75 inlays.			
Level 6 cues start at	$1,350	$1,000	$600

MARIPOSA CUE CO.

Maker of pool cues from 1994 to 1996 in Chicago, Illinois.

Kyle Van den Bosch has been involved with pool since he was a young child. His father was the owner of the Chicago Billiard Cafe, (now run by his brother) which exposed Kyle to the world's best cues and players for many years. A semi-pro for about ten years, he dreamt of making a living as a pro player, but knew that he would not like the lifestyle.

As a result of his woodworking hobby, Kyle became an apprentice for a Chicago-area cuemaker. During his first day on the job, he knew that cuemaking was what he wanted to pursue. Cuemaking allowed him to work within the sport he loved, while only being on the road for the tournaments he wanted to go to. After a year-and-a-half of learning cuemaking skills, he set out to make cues on his own. This was in 1994, when he started Mariposa Cue Co.

Although they were not marked, Mariposa cues are easily recognizable by their 15/32 in. diameter wooden joint screws. Approximately 40% of Kyle's cues (60-65) featured rounded "flame" butterfly points with beautifully colored veneers. He made fewer than 30 "Two Flame" cues, approximately 25 "Four Flame" versions, a dozen or so "Six Flame" and only one with eight butterfly splices. Usually three or five veneers were used. The cues with six butterflies were often referred to as the "Carter Cue" as the first one was made for pro Jeff Carter. Ten Carter cues were made, several for Jeff, the rest for other Chicago players who liked the design. Most had a maple screw, and some of the earlier ones had nickel silver rings.

Kyle Van den Bosch

Mariposa cues have no inlays, as Kyle felt they weakened the integrity of a cue. KyLe Proudly referred to his cues as "environmentally sane." He refused to use ebony or ivory, and only environmentally safe, non-toxic glues and finishes were used. It took over a year of experimentation for Kyle to perfect this type of construction to his satisfaction. All of the wood Kyle used was harvested through sustainable yield forestry. Instead of using a steel bolt between the forearm and the handle to add weight to a cue, Kyle used denser and heavier woods under the wrap. For plain wood forearms and butt sleeves, Kyle would usually laminate two pieces of wood together, sometimes with a veneer between them. This made the cue stiffer, prevented warping, and allowed more wood grain to be visible. Most cues had solid maple handles under the linen wrap, but some of the later cues were made with laminated handles.

Kyle could often be seen at tournaments in the Midwest playing competitively and offering his cues for sale. He made Mariposa cues in his shop in the basement of the Chicago Billiard Café until 1996, when he left cuemaking.

Now, at age 30, Kyle is gearing up to get back into cuemaking. He still has most of his equipment, including a lathe and some blanks, and he is doing minor repair work. He is now looking for a permanent workshop space and is saving money to buy wood to start turning down. He has a lot of ideas for cue designs he'd like to make.

For information or authentication of a Mariposa cue, contact Kyle Van den Bosch, listed under Mariposa Cue Co. in the Trademark Index.

SPECIFICATIONS

Butt material: hardwoods
Shaft material: rock maple
Standard length: 59 in.
Lengths available: 55 to 60 in.
Standard finish: water-based polyurethane
Joint screw thread: 15/32-10
Joint type: flat-faced wood-to-wood
Joint and pin material: wood
Balance point: 20 in. from butt
Point construction: butterfly splice
Standard wrap: Irish linen
Standard butt cap: black phenolic
Standard number of shafts: two
Standard taper: pro
Standard ferrules: linen melamine
Standard tip: Le Pro
Tip widths available: 9 to 16 mm
Total production (1994-96): approximately 150 cues

GRADING	98%	90%	70%

REPAIRS
Repairs done on most fine cues.
- Rewrap linen: $50
- Clean and press linen wrap: $15
- Replace fiber/linen composite ferrule: $25
- Replace tip: $15+

PAST EXAMPLES

The following cues could be ordered in a variety of hardwoods, the most popular being bocote, cocobolo, purpleheart, chocte kok, chechen, zircote, and hard maples. Wood pins were usually maple, but six cues were made with bacote or cocobolo screws to match the forearm, and approximately 25% of his cues had wood wraps.

Level 2 "Plain Cue" - Hardwood forearm, maple joint pin, hardwood butt sleeve, linen wrap.

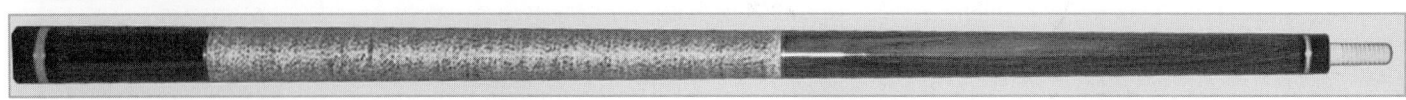

MSR(1996) $395	$500	$400	$300

Level 3 "Two Flame" Bird's-eye maple forearm, maple joint pin, two butterfly-spliced cocobolo points with five veneers, bird's-eye maple butt sleeve, maple veneer slot rings CDE, custom flat-face wood-to-wood joint, linen wrap.

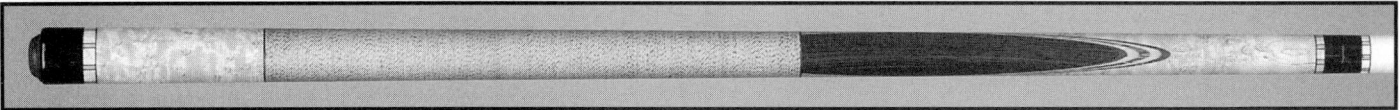

MSR(1996) $595	$850	$700	$450

Level 3 "Four Flame" 1996 Bocote forearm with maple joint pin, four butterfly-spliced bocote points with five veneers (green, black, yellow, black, green), bocote butt sleeve, maple underwrap, with Irish linen wrap. Twice-cut rings (green and yellow into maple) at BCDE., flat-face wood-to-wood joint, black linen phenolic joint, shaft collars and butt cap.

MSR(1996) $695	$900	$750	$550

Level 3 "Six Flame" c. 1995 - "Jeff Carter" design; first Carter Cue (1st of 10) - Zircote nose with four butterfly-spliced bocote points with three maple veneers (white, black, white; black is dyed maple). Laminated two–piece bird's-eye maple handle. Zircote butt sleeve with two bocote butterfly points to match forearm, black and maple block rings in between nickel silver rings at CDE. Thin black and nickel silver rings above and below handle (A&B). Flat-face wood-to-wood joint with proprietary 10-thread bocote joint screw (one of only three made). White linen phenolic joint and black linen phenolic shaft collars and butt cap.

MSR(1995) $795	$1,200	$1,000	$800

SECONDARY MARKET MINIMUM VALUES

The following are minimum prices for other Mariposa cues encountered on the secondary market. These prices are representative of cues utilizing basic materials and designs that were available. Kyle also offered one-of-a-kind cues that can command many times these prices due to the use of exotic materials and artistry.

Special construction note: There are many materials and construction techniques that can add value to Mariposa cues.

For all used Mariposa cues, except where otherwise noted:
- Add $100+ for each additional original straight playable shaft (standard with two).
- Deduct $100 for each missing original straight playable shaft.
- Add $75 for set of original custom joint caps.
- Deduct 25% for obvious or improper refinish.

Level 2 - 0 points, 0-25 inlays.

Level 2 cues start at	$500	$350	$300

Level 3 - 2-6 points, 0-8 inlays.

Level 3 cues start at	$800	$600	$400

MARQUETRY BILLIARD CUES

Type of decorated billiard cue made predominately in the 1700s and 1800s in Europe.

Marquetry is the art of inlaying various colored woods to form pictures or patterns. Marquetry furniture has been crafted for over 500 years, and the technique has been applied to embellish European billiard cues since at least the 1700s. The word "marquetry" derives from the French "marqueter" meaning "inlaid work." Once an image has been designed, the marqueter selects contrasting colors, wood grains and shapes of veneers to create the composition. These veneers are then cut out, carefully fitted and glued to a base wood. The veneers themselves are generally thin sheets of wood, and sometimes metals.

During the Renaissance, new marquetry techniques were developed and the designs themselves became highly sophisticated, creating landscapes, figures, and other complex scenes, often making full use of architectural perspective. Polychrome marquetry was invented, using natural or stained woods. This new advance in marquetry technique became known as "intarsia" or "tarsia," from the Italian words "intarsiare" (to inlay) and "tarsiare" (an inlay or incrustation). It was Italian marqueters working in southern Germany in the Augsburg region around 1620 who saw the potential of the recently invented fret saw, and who developed the next important marquetry technique: "tarsia a incastro." Tarsia a Incastro is more commonly known as Boulle (or Boule) marquetry, from its association with the work of the French royal cabinet maker Andre-Charles Boulle (1642-1732). Probably the most famous of all the marqueters and cabinet makers in history, Boulle popularized the use of this technique using predominately brass and tortoiseshell.

Marquetry cues were crafted in Europe for playing billiards, and reached their heyday in the 19th century. They were expensive objects even then, ordered primarily by the nobility for use in their private billiard rooms. In the 1800s a fancy marquetry cue would sometimes be presented to the winner of a tournament as a trophy. Fine antique examples are rare and command many thousands and even tens of thousands of dollars, depending on intricacy, quality, originality, and condition.

A few marquetry and intarsia cues are still being produced today. The Italian pool and billiard cuemaker Longoni makes several models of marquetry cues, and American custom cuemaker Samsara is particularly known for their unique intarsia cues. Richard Black, pfd Studios, and Thomas Wayne are among the contemporary makers who have created cues using intarsia.

HARVEY MARTIN

Maker of pool cues from the 1920s to 1984, primarily in Los Angeles, California.

At the age of nineteen, Harvey Martin was a talented billiard player who thought he could build a better cue than those that were available. He was working at a Seattle pool hall when he constructed his own woodworking lathe and built his first cue. Harvey let another player try his cue and a short time later, that player offered to buy it. Harvey's second cue sold in similar fashion, and in time, he had created a new profession: custom cuemaking.

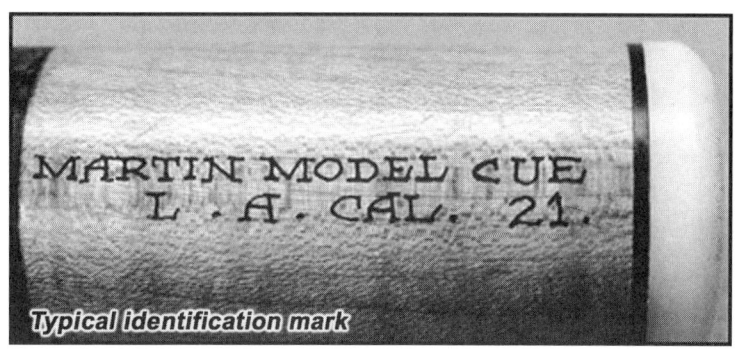

Harvey's background lent itself favorably to cuemaking. He had experience harvesting wood, working with metals as a welder and toolmaker, and possessed the meticulous attention to detail required of a cabinetmaker. He also had experience with leather and ivory. When combined, his experiences and talents formed a nearly ideal skill set for a cuemaker. By the late 1920s, some of the world's best players were using Harvey Martin cues and, in terms of custom cuemaking, his only real competitor at the time was Herman Rambow in Chicago.

Harvey provided a rare service to his customers, even by today's standards, by tailoring the cue to the individual. He would watch his customer play, studying dimensions like stance and stroke, arm length and grip position. Harvey would take all the information, combined with any customer requests, and construct a cue specifically dedicated to that person, from the finest materials available.

Favoring product integrity over aesthetics, Harvey rarely did inlay work in his cues. Though his designs were fairly simple, Harvey's construction methods were ingenious and, in some cases, well ahead of their time. He experimented with innovative solutions to current day performance issues such as deflection. Use of the spliced shaft, for instance, an idea recently promoted as new, was tried decades ago by Harvey Martin. Harvey designed shaft weight inserts that were located behind the ferrule to help the tip stay on the ball longer during a shot. He also experimented with interchangeable metal inserts located above and below the wrap so that the cue's balance point could be adjusted.

Harvey Martin cues through the 1960s are most simply identified by the name and date stamped into the fiber ring just above the butt cap. Later cues are identified by handwritten markings of identification and weight that were inked onto the butt sleeve. The owner's name might also be stamped or printed in ink on the butt sleeve. Almost all Harvey Martin cues had bird's-eye maple forearms and butt sleeves. His joints were often ivory with 3/8 in. joint screws made of brass or aluminum. Wraps on Martin cues were typically leather or cork with butt caps of ivory or white Delrin. Harvey would sometimes stain the cue to bring out the natural figure of the wood; some examples of cues with two stains are also known. A few Harvey Martin cues were made with points and were full spliced from Brunswick blanks. Harvey also made cues with ivory handles. This was accomplished by using nine segments of ivory, each turned down from a billiard ball then stacked to form the handle. The lightest weight among the eight known examples of this style of Martin cue is 20-3/8 ounces.

Another practice Harvey is known for his case making. His creations are often as recognizable as his cues. He used a leather tube-style design and usually stamped his name and the date inside the case: "Martin Cues & Cases, LA, Cal."

Harvey Martin's contribution to cuemaking is largely unrivaled. For three-fourths of a century his cues have been used by the world's best players and prized by collectors. For his contributions, insight and innovations, Harvey Martin has been admitted into the American Cuemaker's Association "Hall of Fame."

If you have questions about a Harvey Martin cue, or have one needing shafts or restoration, Bert Schrager knew Harvey and his cues well and has worked with more of these cues than anyone. Please contact Bert Schrager, listed in the Trademark Index.

| GRADING | 98% | 90% | 70% |

SPECIFICATIONS

Butt materials: bird's-eye maple or ivory
Shaft material: rock maple
Standard length: custom
Standard wrap: leather or cork
Standard taper: custom
Balance point: custom
Standard joint: flat face ivory
Standard ferrules: ivory
Standard finish: oil

KNOWN EXAMPLES

Level 2 "Joe Procita 1944" Bird's-eye maple forearm, bird's-eye maple butt sleeve with handwritten "Joe Procita MARTIN MODEL CUE L.A. CAL. 19 ½ Oz. 1944", ivory butt cap with black linen ring above, ivory joint, leather wrap.

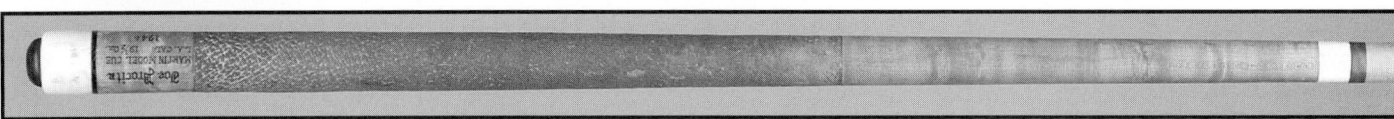

| $4,100 | $2,750 | $2,250 |

Level 2 "1968" – Natural bird's-eye maple forearm, bird's-eye maple butt sleeve with handwritten initials "S.S." and "MARTIN CUE LA CAL 1-2-68 in. on veneered collar at bottom, 19 ½ embossed on the other side, flat-faced ivory joint, brown linen shaft collar, shaft stamped "SS2", white Delrin butt cap with two brown fiber rings above, rubber bumper, leather wrap, ivory ferrules.

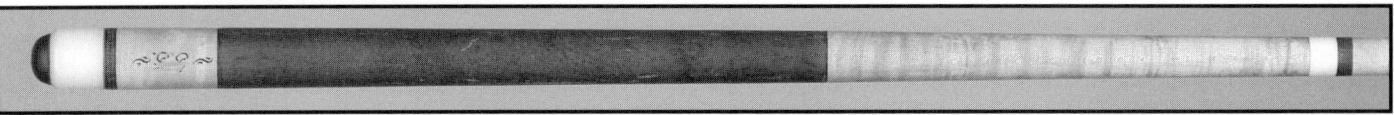

| $3,750 | $2,300 | $1,800 |

Level 2 "1967" - Bird's-eye maple forearm, two-color stain to highlight figuring. Matching bird's-eye buttsleeve with brown and black fiber rings above Delrin butt cap. Ring stamped: "MARTIN CUE LA CAL 11.30.67 SL". Three shafts, stamped "SL 1" with micarta ferrule, "SL 2" with ivory ferrule, and "SL 3" with ivory ferrule. Flat-faced ivory joint with 3/8 in. brass joint screw, original wood joint pin protector, dark brown leather wrap. With original brown alligator leather case, stamped inside: "MARTIN CUES & CASES, LA CAL 12 1 1967".

| $6,250 | $5,750 | $3,550 |

Level 2 "PASTOR" - Bird's-eye maple forearm, handle, and butt sleeve with no wrap, smoke gray stain, ivory butt cap with red fiber ring above, ivory joint. Red phenolic and ivory dot inlays. Stamped above butt cap: "PASTOR".

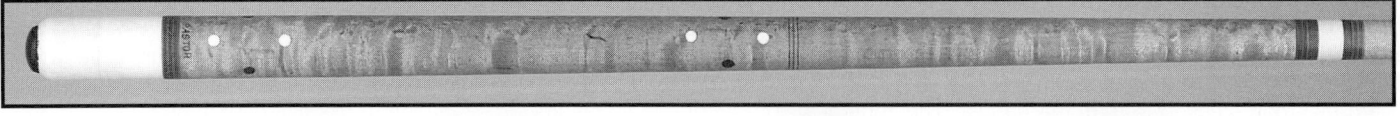

| $4,800 | $4,000 | $2,800 |

Level 2 "Ivory Handle" - Bird's-eye maple forearm, nine-section ivory handle, bird's-eye maple butt sleeve, black and brown fiber rings ABCDE, ivory butt cap and joint.

| $25,000 | $15,000 | $12,000 |

Level 3 "Full Splice Ivory Handle" - Bird's-eye maple forearm, four full splice ebony points with veneers, nine-section ivory handle, bird's-eye maple butt sleeve, ivory butt cap and joint.

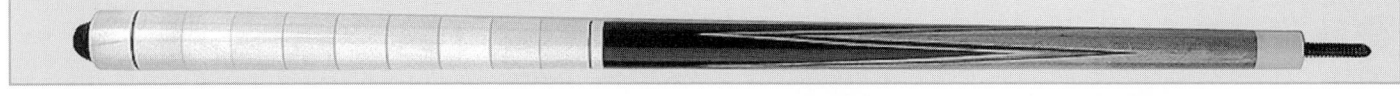

| $30,000 | $20,000 | $12,000 |

GRADING	98%	90%	70%

SECONDARY MARKET MINIMUM VALUES

The following are minimum prices for other Martin cues encountered on the secondary market. These prices are representative of cues utilizing the most basic materials and designs that were available. Harvey also offered one-of-a-kind cues that can command many times these prices due to the use of exotic materials and artistry. Early examples are very collectible, and can also command many times these prices.

Due to the rarity of Harvey Martin cues and increasing interest, prices are on the rise. Fewer original examples are surfacing, and collectors are holding on to the ones they have. Unique examples with pedigree, and cues made for top professional players are bringing the highest prices.

Special construction note: There are many features which can add value to Martin cues. The following are the most important examples:
- Add $500+ for each spliced shaft.
- Add $500+ for weighted shaft (metal rod under ferrule).
- Add $400 for each additional straight playable shaft (standard with two).
- Deduct $500 for each missing straight playable shaft.
- Add $1,250+ for good condition original martin case.

Level 2 - 0 points, 0-25 inlays.
Level 2 cues start at	$4,600	$4,000	$2,500

Level 3 - 2-6 points, 0-8 inlays.
Level 3 cues start at	$6,000	$4,500	$3,200

Level 4 - 4-10 points, 9-25 inlays.
Level 4 cues start at	$6,500	$5,000	$3,750

MIKE MARTIN CUSTOM CUES

Maker of pool cues from 2001 to present in Austintown, Ohio.

Mike Martin began playing pool at the age of 15 at "The Q-Club" in Austintown, Ohio. The owner of the club, Michael Steiner, also did cue repairs. This is where Mike learned how to do minor cue work. This is also where he developed a love of the game and an interest in cues.

Mike had his first band saw at about the age of 9 or 10. He always enjoyed working with wood. He was always building just about anything he could. After high school, Mike tried a number of jobs, including roofing, plumbing, carpentry, and construction. Then he started building cabinets, bookcases and hutches and really enjoyed it. In the spring of 2001, he started building pool cues. He opened Mahoning Valley Billiards in Youngstown, Ohio, where he did some repair work, and soon after, he bought his first lathe. It was just a matter of time before he was living his dream of building beautiful and great hitting cues. He loves turning an exotic piece of wood into a functional piece of artwork.

Mike has three lathes in his shop. One of them is a CNC, which is used to turn round stock only. A hand pantograph is used for points and smaller work.

Mike's cues can be identified by his signature and the date the cue was finished. Some earlier cues had a real diamond inlaid into the butt of the cue. Later cues have his signature in the butt cap.

If you are interested in talking to Mike Martin about a new cue or cue that needs to be repaired, you can contact him at Mike Martin Custom Cues, listed in the Trademark Index.

SPECIFICATIONS

Butt material: hardwoods
Shaft material: maple
Standard finish: UV since 2005
Standard length: 58 in.
Standard number of shafts: one
Standard ferrules: linen phenolic
Standard joint screw: 3/8-10 stainless
Standard taper: 10 in. pro
Standard tip: Talisman medium
Annual production: approximately 100 cues

OPTIONS (FOR NEW CUES ONLY)

Ivory ferrule: $75
Leather wrap: $95
Stack leather: $165
Joint protectors: $45
Special length: $25
Stainless steel joint: $85
Ivory butt cap: $375
Ivory joint: $250
Extra shaft: $100

| GRADING | 98% | 90% | 70% |

REPAIRS

Repairs done on all fine cues.
- Refinish (with Irish linen wrap): $130
- Rewrap (Irish linen): $40
- Rewrap (leather): $95
- Replace butt cap (linen phenolic): $75
- Replace ferrule (linen phenolic): $35 plus tip
- Replace shaft: $100+
- Replace tip: $10+

CURRENT MARTIN CUES

Basic two-piece Mike Martin cues start at $300. Mike Martin cues with wraps and joint rings start at $410. Mike Martin cues with points start at $570. One-of-a-kind custom Mike Martin cues start at $750.

SECONDARY MARKET MINIMUM VALUES

The following are minimum values for Mike Martin cues encountered on the secondary market. These prices are representative of cues utilizing basic materials and designs that are not necessarily available at present. Mike has offered one-of-a-kind cues that can command many times these prices due to the use of exotic materials and artistry.

Special construction note: There are many materials and construction techniques that can add value to Mike Martin cues.

For all used Mike Martin cues, except where otherwise noted:
- Add $85 for each additional original straight playable shaft beyond one.
- Deduct $100 for missing original straight playable shaft.
- Add $60 each for ivory ferrules.
- Add $65 for leather wrap.
- Deduct 20% for obvious or improper refinish.

Level 2 - 0 points, 0-25 inlays.
| Level 2 cues start at | $275 | $225 | $145 |

Level 3 - 2-6 points, 0-8 inlays.
| Level 3 cues start at | $500 | $335 | $265 |

Level 4 - 4-10 points, 9-25 inlays.
| Level 4 cues start at | $650 | $510 | $345 |

Level 5 - 0-12 points, 26-50 inlays.
| Level 5 cues start at | $950 | $850 | $500 |

ERNIE MARTINEZ CUSTOM CUES

Maker of pool cues from 1988 to 1999, and from 2003 to present in Denver, Colorado.

Ernie Martinez was born in 1965 and learned to play pool as a young boy. He and his father would play pool on the table in Ernie's uncle's basement. When Ernie was about 14, he and his father, who had a woodworking hobby, built a pool table for the family home. They went to Showcase Billiards, in Westminster, Colorado for pockets, cloth and other table components. There, Ernie became fascinated with the assortment of custom cues and became friends with the owner.

Ernie made his first cue on a lathe in high school in 1985. Even as a freshmen, Ernie excelled in machine work in shop class. He landed a job right out of high school at a custom machine shop, doing full-time metal work, primarily for small government contracts. While working as a machinist, Ernie started doing cue repairs and building two-piece house cues under the supervision of Clay Etheridge at Showcase Billiards. In the early nineties, Ernie left the machine shop to work for Showcase Billiards full-time. He made a majority of the Showcase custom cues during this time, most of which are identifiable by a stylized "S" logo on the butt caps, and/or a diamond with an "S" in the center engraved on the tip of the metric 1.5 by 10 joint screw. He used this pin on most of his custom cues from 1989 until 1994, although cues with piloted 5/16-14 stainless steel joints would be made at a customer's request.

1995 to Present Day

Ernie noted Bob Meucci as another early influence, and also admired the craftsmanship of Bill Stroud, David Kikel, Ernie, Gutierrez, and David Kersenbrock.

In the winter of 1995, Ernie started his own custom cue shop in Commerce City, Colorado. In his one-man shop he built approximately 40 cues per year, making every component in his cues except the tips and bumpers. All work was done by hand, without the aid of CNC. Most of his screws were custom-made to his specs. He preferred to use a flat-face wood-to-wood joint with linen phenolic ringwork. Early cues had metric 1.5 by 10 pins. Most Martinez cues made from 1995 to present have a unique 3/8-12 joint pin which Ernie spent a lot of time developing for his cues. The thread on these screws begins at about a quarter of an inch forward of the joint, allowing for the base of the joint to seat tighter. Ernie's "EM" logo and serial number of the individual cue appears on this joint screw. The "EM" logo also appears on the butt cap of every Ernie Martinez cue made since he started his own shop in 1995.

ERNIE MARTINEZ CUSTOM CUES, cont.

GRADING	98%	90%	70%

Ernie specialized in one-of-a-kind custom cues made of hardwoods, ivories, metals, and stones. He refused to use any plastics or alternate substances. A two-piece hustler cue is also available, which Ernie initially used to make from scratch. Later he started making them from Valley one-piece cues to allow himself more time for high-end custom work. He would do true custom work, tailoring a cue to any specifications a player might require. Ernie Martinez cues are regarded as exceptionallly playable, with a slight forward balance and "soft" hit.

Ernie's artistic designs are also much admired. In February of 1993 he placed in the design category at the 1st American Cuemakers Association show in Houston, Texas. Ernie exhibited at the 1995 Showcase of American Cue Art in Los Angeles and the 1998 Gallery of American Cue Art in New York. Five of his cues were featured in the 1995 "Hand of the Masters" Cue Calendar. Among these were his two "Escher" design cues, inspired by the graphic artist known for repeating geometric patterns and spacial illusions requiring a "second look." As in Escher's work, with Ernie Martinez's cues what you see the first time is not all there is to see.

Because his shop was far from Denver, and many customers had trouble finding it, in June of 1999 he moved to a location close to downtown Denver. Then he took a break from cuemaking for a few years. Ernie started making cues again at a new location in 2003. He is still making cues by hand in a one man shop, with all inlay work being done with a manual pantograph. Ernie started using a brass 3/8-12 joint screw in 2005.

If you have an Ernie Martinez cue that needs further identification or repair, or would like to talk to Ernie about a new custom cue, contact Ernie Martinez Custom Cues, listed in the Trademark Index.

SPECIFICATIONS

- Butt material: hardwoods
- Shaft material: rock maple
- Standard length: 58 in.
- Standard finish: catalyzed urethane
- Joint screw: 3/8-12
- Standard joint: linen phenolic
- Joint type: flat-faced wood-to-wood
- Balance point: 18 to 19 in. from the butt
- Point construction: short splice
- Standard wrap: Irish linen
- Standard butt cap: linen phenolic
- Standard number of shafts: two
- Standard taper: custom
- Standard ferrules: melamine
- Standard tip: water buffalo
- Annual production: fewer than 60 cues

OPTIONS (FOR NEW CUES ONLY)

- Special length: no charge up to 60 in.
- Leather wrap: $75
- Ivory ferrule: $50
- Ivory butt cap: $250
- Ivory joint: $150
- Joint protectors: standard
- Extra shaft: $150+

REPAIRS

Repairs done on all fine cues.
- Refinish (with Irish linen wrap): $150
- Refinish (with leather wrap): $225
- Rewrap (Irish linen): $50
- Rewrap (leather): $150
- Replace water buffalo tip: $20
- Replace ivory ferrule: $75

CURRENT ERNIE MARTINEZ CUES

Basic two-piece Ernie Martinez hustler cues start at $190. Basic two-piece Ernie Martinez cues with wraps and joint rings start at $450. Ernie Martinez cues with points start at $900. One-of-a-kind Ernie Martinez custom cues start at $1,800. Delivery time for an Ernie Martinez cue is four to six months depending on the intrcacy of the cue.

PAST EXAMPLES

Level 3 "Circa 1997" - Curly maple forearm, six points (three long alternating three short) short-splice Gabon ebony points, Gabon ebony butt sleeve with a thick maple band at base, black and white ringwork above black linen phenolic butt cap with "EM" logo, 3/8-12 flat-face linen phenolic joint, joint collar with black and white ringwork, Irish linen wrap, melamine ferrules.

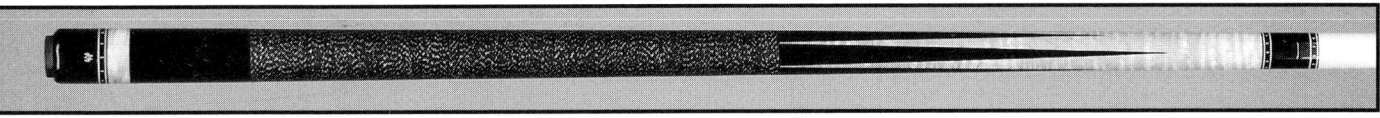

$2,050	$1,700	$1,350

466 ERNIE MARTINEZ CUSTOM CUES, cont.

GRADING	98%	90%	70%

Level 3 – stained bird's-eye maple forearm, four short-splice ebony points with four colored veneers ans an ivory peacock inlay in each point, black and ivory check "Bushka" ringwork above leather wrap, ebony butt sleeve with Gus Szamboti-style ivory inlays: two inlaid ivory windows alternating with two four-piece exploding diamonds, separated by ivory dots, large ivory stitch rings at top and bottom. Piloted 5/16-14 stainless steel joint with black phenolicand ivory dash rings, black linen phenolic butt cap with "EM" logo.

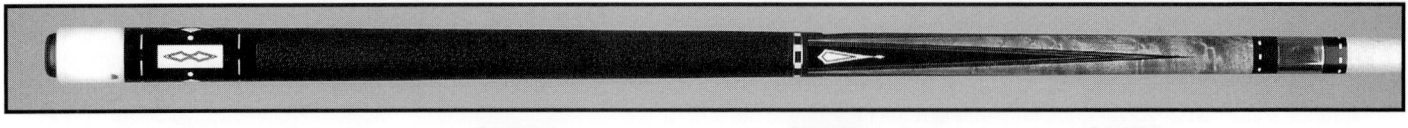

	$2,850	$2,400	$2,050

Level 3 – 1993 "Escher" – first Escher design cue, made at Showcase; alternating curly maple and Macassar ebony forearm with eight split points (four curly maple and four ebony), ebony and curly maple butt sleeve with matching points echoing design, black phenolic collars with gold wire chain ringwork at ABCDE, flat-faced wood-to-wood joint with stainless steel metric 1.5 x 10 flat-top pin with "S' logo, ivory-colored phenolic joint rings and butt cap, melamine ferrules, linen wrap, 1 of 1, signed on forearm "Ernie Martinez 2-3-93".

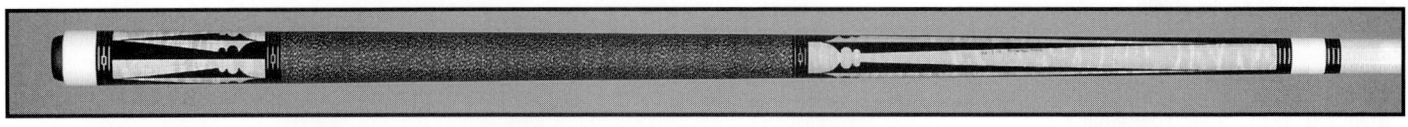

	$4,800	$4.350	$3,300

Level 3 – 1995 "Hollywood" – second one-of-a-kind Escher design cue made for 1995 Showcase of American Cue Art; alternating holly and Macassar ebony forearm with six split points of holly and ebony and split dot inlays, ebony and holly butt sleeve with matching inlays echoing the positive-negative design, silver dots at ovals, black phenolic collars with three silver rings at ABCDE, flat-faced wood-to-wood joint with stainless steel metric 3/8-12 custom pin with "EM" logo and serial number 3395 on base of pin, black phenolic joint rings and butt cap with "EM" logo, leather wrap, ivory ferrules.

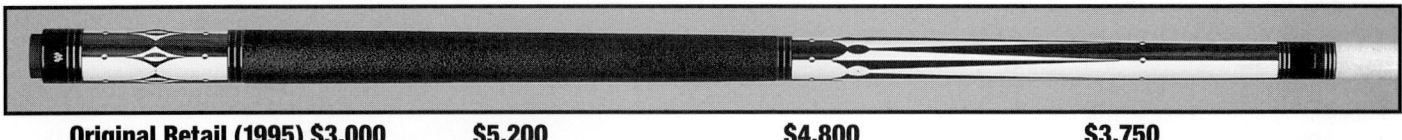

Original Retail (1995) $3,000	$5,200	$4,800	$3,750

SECONDARY MARKET MINIMUM VALUES

The following are minimum prices for Ernie Martinez cues encountered on the secondary market. These prices are representative of cues utilizing basic materials and designs that may not be currently available. Ernie specialized in one-of-a-kind cues that can command many times these prices due to the use of exotic materials and artistry.

Special construction note: There are many materials and construction techniques that can add value to Ernie Martinez cues.

For all used Ernie Martinez cues, except where otherwise noted:

- Add $300 for ivory butt cap.
- Add $1250 for ivory joint.
- Add $125 for leather wrap.
- Add $125 for each additional original straight playable shaft (standard with two).
- Deduct $150 for each missing original straight playable shaft.
- Add $75 for each ivory ferrule.
- Deduct 25% for obvious or improper refinish.

	98%	90%	70%
Level 1 - 4 points, hustler.			
Level 1 cues start at	$300	$200	$150
Level 2 - 0 points, 0-25 inlays.			
Level 2 cues start at	$650	$450	$375
Level 3 - 2-6 points, 0-8 inlays.			
Level 3 cues start at	$1,500	$1,350	$950
Level 4 - 4-10 points, 9-25 inlays.			
Level 4 cues start at	$1,700	$1,500	$1,100
Level 5 - 0-12 points, 26-50 inlays.			
Level 5 cues start at	$2,000	$1,600	$1,250
Level 6 - 0-12 points, 51-75 inlays.			
Level 6 cues start at	$2,500	$2,000	$1,475
Level 7 - 0-12 points, 76-125 inlays.			
Level 7 cues start at	$4,500	$3,500	$2,350

| GRADING | 98% | 90% | 70% |

ANNIE MAYES

Maker of AO Cues. For more information, refer to the listing for AO Custom Cues.

MAXIMUM CUE

Maker of pool cues from 1995 to 1998 in Olive Branch, Mississippi.

Maximum Cue was a company started by Bob Meucci as a complement to his Meucci line of cues. His objective was to create a more competitively priced American-made cue that would utilize the design and construction methods that he had perfected with Meucci Originals.

Maximum cues are easily identifiable by the "Maximum" logo that appears on the butt caps. If you have a Maximum cue that needs repair, contact Meucci Originals, Inc., listed in the Trademark Index.

SPECIFICATIONS

Butt material: hardwoods
Shaft material: rock maple
Standard length: 58 in.
Lengths available: 50 in., 54 in., 57 in., 58 in.
Standard finish: fireproof urethane
Joint screw: 5/16-18
Standard joint: meucci synthetic
Joint type: flat faced
Balance point: 17-1/2 in. from butt
Point construction: short splice
Standard wrap: Irish linen
Standard butt cap: Meucci synthetic
Standard number of shafts: one
Standard taper: 14 in. straight
Standard ferrules: Meucci synthetic
Standard tip: Le Pro

SECONDARY MARKET MINIMUM VALUES

Note: The following are minimum prices for Maximum cues encountered on the secondary market. These prices are representative of cues utilizing basic materials and designs that were available.

For all used Maximum Cues:

Deduct 20% for obvious or improper refinish.

	98%	90%	70%
Level 2 - 0 points, 0-25 inlays.			
Level 2 cues start at	$110	$85	$50
Level 3 - 2-6 points, 0-8 inlays.			
Level 3 cues start at	$145	$120	$70
Level 4 - 4-10 points, 9-25 inlays.			
Level 4 cues start at	$175	$140	$85

JOE MAZLEWSKI

Maker of Cadillac Custom Cues. For more information, refer to Cadillac.

KARL MEYER CUE

Maker of pool cues in North Plainfield, New Jersey until 2003.

Karl Meyer made Merry Widow-type cues, either plain or with inlays of dots and diamonds, in North Plainfield, New Jersey for many years. Karl and his wife traveled around the East Coast selling them to pool rooms, and Mrs. Meyer handled the cue sales. The cues retailed for $60-80 apiece. Karl is believed to have worked for Frank Paradise or Palmer at one time. He passed on in 2003.

SPECIFICATIONS

Butt material: hardwoods
Shaft material: maple
Standard length: 58 in.
Standard wrap: Irish linen

SECONDARY MARKET MINIMUM VALUES

The following are minimum values for Karl Mayer cues encountered on the secondary market. These prices are representative of cues utilizing basic materials and designs that were available. Karl offered one-of-a-kind cues that can command many times these prices due to the use of exotic materials and artistry.

Special construction note: There are many materials and construction techniques that can add value to Karl Mayer cues.

GRADING	98%	90%	70%

For all used Karl Mayer cues, except where otherwise noted:
- Add $125 for each additional original straight playable shaft beyond one.
- Deduct 50% for missing original straight playable shaft.
- Add $50 each for ivory ferrules.
- Add $100 for leather wrap.
- Deduct 30% for obvious or improper refinish.

Level 2 - 0 points, 0-25 inlays.

Level 2 cues start at	$250	$200	$115

BILL MCDANIEL CUES

Maker of pool cues from 1974 to present in Jackson, Tennessee.

Bill McDaniel grew up around the game of pool. His family owned McDaniel Amusements, a vending company that owned many pool tables in various establishments around Bill's hometown of Jackson, Tennessee. Bill went with his father to check on the tables and machines.

While his father was working, Bill would play pool. He was so small when he started, he had to surround the table with pop bottle boxes in order to stand and reach the table. Before long, he became one of the better players in the area, and became a regular at tournaments such as the famous Johnston City tournaments in the sixties and early seventies. During his years as a player, Bill paid constant attention to what type of cues other players were using. He became friends with many cuemakers of the time. Although he owned virtually every kind of cue that was available, he was never able to find a cue that completely suited him. At this time, Bill decided to set out on a mission to master the art of cuemaking and make the perfect cue.

Bill McDaniel

Bill continued his education, earning a business degree. When an astigmatism affected his eyesight to the point that he was no longer as competitive at pool, Bill decided to combine his business knowledge, artistic ability, and love for pool to start making cues. He got to know George Balabushka through several phone conversations. George gave Bill some advice to help him get started in the right direction. Bill later became friends with Tim Scruggs, eventually becoming a partner in Tim's shop.

Bill's early cues were inspired by the work of George Balabushka, and Bill has been making constant design improvements ever since. Bill's very early cues were mostly four-point short spliced cues with veneers and were not marked with any type of identification. Soon Bill originated a shark logo and a stylized MC logo. Both logos have been used throughout most of his cuemaking career, and are still being used today. He has also hand-signed special cues at the customer's request. Bill has always used the same 5/16-14 piloted joint that Balabushka used since he started making cues. In 1993 he invented a shock absorbing ring that is placed under the stainless steel joints. The wood does not touch the stainless steel and Bill believes this gives an unequaled hit that compares to the feel and playability of an ivory joint. As an option, he offers a 3/8-11 flat face joint in steel, phenolic, and ivory.

Mid-90s to Present Day

In 1994 Bill started using a CNC for his inlaid points and inlays. He has fourth-axis machining capability, which allows him to execute virtually any type of inlay or inlaid point a customer desires. Inlaid points are available in any number, though he prefers multiples of four. He will also make short or full spliced forearms if the customer desires, although most of his cues with veneers are V-groove short splice. Bill still makes a small number of hustler cues with his own full splices, which are available in rosewood, cocobolo, or ebony, with a bird's-eye maple forearm. If you need an extra shaft for your Bill McDaniel cue, it is not necessary to send in the butt, as all McDaniel shafts are designed to be interchangeable.

Bill is justifiably proud of the quality of his leather wraps, and offers a large selection of exotic skins, including lizard and snakeskin. He believes that some of the changes he has made in the construction of his cues in the past three or four years make his cues among the best constructed cues available today. A number of top pro players have won championships with their McDaniel cues, including Karen Corr, Julie Kelly, Ismael "Morro" Paez, and Nick Varner, Alex Pagulayn, Jose Parika, and Santos Sambajon.

All Bill McDaniel cues are guaranteed indefinitely against construction defects that are not the result of warping or abuse. If you have a Bill McDaniel cue that needs further identification or repair, or would like to talk to Bill about ordering a new cue, contact Bill McDaniel Cues, listed in the Trademark Index.

SPECIFICATIONS

Butt material: hardwoods
Shaft material: rock maple
Standard length: 58 in.
Lengths available: any
Standard finish: UV-cured polyurethane

BILL MCDANIEL CUES, cont.

GRADING	100%	95%	70%

Joint screw: 5/16-14 or 3/8-11
Standard joint: piloted stainless steel
Balance point: 18 3/4 in. from butt
Point construction: inlaid, short splice, or full splice
Standard wrap: linen
Standard butt cap: ivory substitute
Standard number of shafts: two
Standard taper: 12 in. pro taper
Standard ferrules: phenolic
Standard tip: Triangle
Tip widths available: any

OPTIONS (FOR NEW CUES ONLY)

Leather and exotic skin wrap: $100+
Phenolic joint: no extra charge
Ivory joint: $125+ depending on length
Joint protectors: standard
Ivory butt cap: $250+ depending on length
Extra shaft: $125+
Ivory ferrules: $65 each

REPAIRS

Repairs done on most fine cues.
Lacquer refinish (for restoration of older cues) call for quote
UV polyurethane refinish (linen $150
UV polyurethane refinish (leather) $250+
Rewrap (leather): $100
Rewrap (linen): $50
Replace Ivorine-3 butt cap: $45
Replace ivory butt cap: $250+ depending on length
Replace shaft: $125 and up
Replace phenolic ferrule and tip: $35
Replace ivory ferrule: $75
Replace Triangle tip: $10

CURRENT EXAMPLES

The following cues come standard with two shafts and joint protectors. They can be ordered as shown, modified to suit the desires of the customer, or new designs can be created.

Level 1 "Hustler" Bird's-eye maple forearm, four full splice rosewood points, ivory substitute ring at bottom of butt, white phenolic joint, black phenolic collar with silver ring.

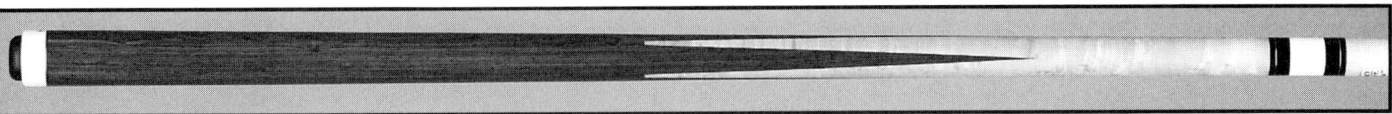

MSR (2004) $500	$400-500	$335	$255

Level 2 "Merry Widow" Stained bird's-eye forearm, handle and butt sleeve, ivory substitute ring at bottom, black phenolic joint collar with silver ring.

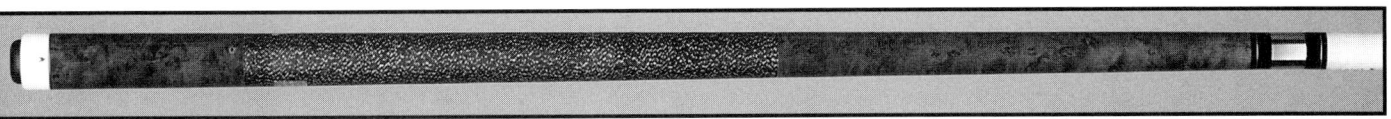

MSR (2004) $650	$575-650	$465	$350

Level 4 - Gabon ebony forearm, 12 ivory inlays of large floating ivory windows and notched diamonds, ebony butt sleeve with ivory notched diamonds and smaller ivory windows, thin black phenolic and nickel silver rings separate three-segment bird's-eye maple wrap, also at ABCDE; piloted ivory joint, ivory substitute butt cap with "MC" logo, leather wrap, ivory ferrules.

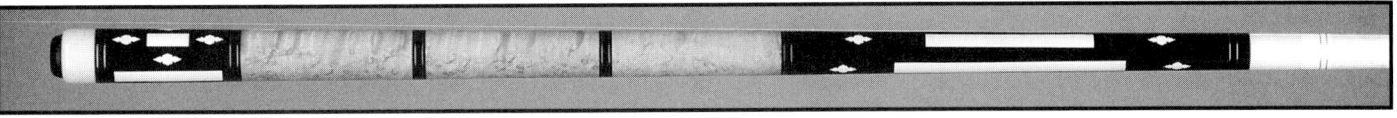

MSR(2003) $2,950	$2,550-2,950	$2,150	$1,550

GRADING	100%	95%	70%

Level 4 - Gabon ebony forearm, five ivory floating dagger points with maple and cocobolo veneers, ivory spearheads at tips, separated by ivory Tiffany diamonds, Gabon ebony butt sleeve has reverse matching points and inlays, piloted stainless steel joint, leather wrap, ivory ferrules.

MSR(2003) $2150	$1,850-2,150	$1,525	$1,150

Level 5 - Bird's-eye maple forearm, eight floating cocobolo points, cocobolo spearheads at tips, joined by eight silver veneered ivory dots, butt sleeve with reverse matching points and inlays, total of 48 inlays consisting of silver outlined ivory dots and the floating points; an additional 32 inlays of ivory dots in the black phenolic rings above and below the wrap, piloted stainless steel joint, black phenolic joint collar with silver ring, alternate ivory butt cap with "MC" logo, linen wrap.

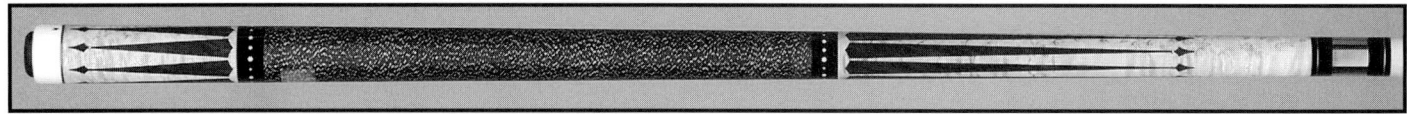

MSR(2003) $1950	$1,750-1,950	$1,475	$1,150

Level 7 "Starburst" - Gabon ebony forearm, 16 floating ivory points separated by ivory dots and dismonds, Gabon ebony butt sleeve with matching ivory points and inlays, ivory Tiffany diamonds and dots in black phenolic rings at A/B/D/E, piloted stainless steel joint, alternate ivory butt cap with "MC" logo, linen wrap.

MSR(2003) $3,450	$3,150-3,450	$2,500	$1,800

Level 7 "Tuxedo" - Ebony forearm, four long altrnating with four short ivory points, silver circles at the front and base of the points, ivory spear inlays at the tips, ivory ringwork with ebony veneered ivory diamonds, ebony butt sleeve with eight reverse matching points and inlays, ivory joint and butt cap with "MC" logo, lizard wrap.

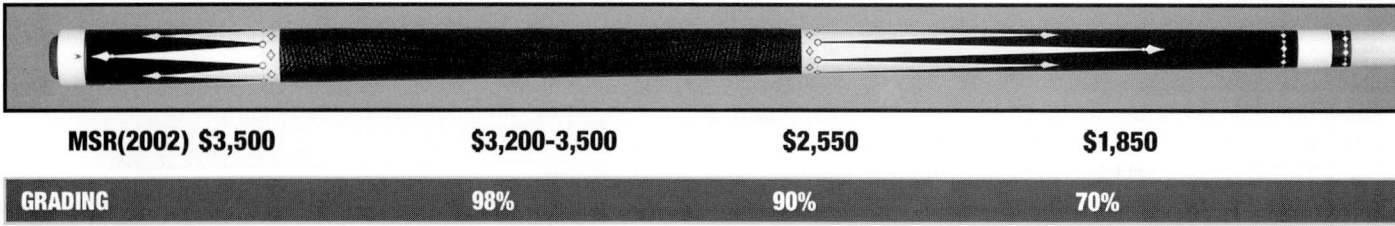

MSR(2002) $3,500	$3,200-3,500	$2,550	$1,850
GRADING	98%	90%	70%

SECONDARY MARKET MINIMUM VALUES

The following are minimum prices for Bill McDaniel cues encountered on the secondary market. These prices are representative of cues utilizing basic materials and designs that may not be currently available. Bill also offers one-of-a-kind and limited edition cues that can command many times these prices due to the use of exotic materials and artistry.

Special construction note: There are many materials and construction techniques that can add value to Bill McDaniel cues, including gold and silver ringwork and diamond inlays. The following are the most important examples:

Add $300+ for ivory points.
Add $500+ for ivory butt sleeve.
Add 30%+ for ivory inlays.
For all used bill mcdaniel cues:
Add $100 for each additional original straight playable shaft (standard with two).
Deduct $100 for each missing original straight playable shaft.
Add $150+ for ivory joint.
Add $100+ for leather wrap.
Add $40 for each ivory ferrule.
Deduct 25% for obvious or improper refinish.

Level 1 - 4 points, hustler.

Level 1 cues start at	$350	$250	$175

Level 2 - 0 points, 0-25 inlays.

Level 2 cues start at	$475	$350	$275

BILL MCDANIEL CUES, cont. 471

GRADING	98%	90%	70%
Level 3 - 2-6 points, 0-8 inlays.			
Level 3 cues start at	$725	$600	$475
Level 4 - 4-10 points, 9-25 inlays.			
Level 4 cues start at	$945	$765	$550
Level 5 - 0-12 points, 26-50 inlays.			
Level 5 cues start at	$1,175	$800	$750
Level 6 - 0-12 points, 51-75 inlays.			
Level 6 cues start at	$1,550	$1,250	$975
Level 7 - 0-12 points, 76-125 inlays.			
Level 7 cues start at	$2,200	$1,750	$1,250
Level 8 - 4 or More points, 125-200 inlays.			
Level 8 cues start at $3,200	$2,650	$1,900	

MCDERMOTT CUE MANUFACTURING INC.

Maker of pool cues from 1975 to present in Menomonee Falls, Wisconsin, a suburb of Milwaukee.

McDermott has become one of the most recognized and respected names in the billiard world. It all started when Jim McDermott was repairing cues in the mid-1960s at home in the Milwaukee area. Jim would regularly travel to all of the local bars and pool rooms, picking up and delivering the cues he repaired. It was in 1966 that Jim met master cuemaker Rollie Welch and worked with him for several years.

The first official line of McDermott cues was introduced in 1975, all ten of which featured the now-famous McDermott interchangeable weight bolt system that has appeared on almost all McDermott cues produced since then. Although many collectors and players refer to these as the A-line due to the later alphabetical progression, they were actually called the M/R Line at the time. These cues all featured the McDermott flat-faced, wood-to-wood joint, and had color coordinated bumpers.

One year later, in 1976, the B-line was introduced. The line consisted of the original ten M/R cues with some minor changes, plus six new cues, all of which had black bumpers. The six new cues were the first McDermott cues with points.

Jesse and Jim McDermott

In 1980, McDermott introduced the C-line that was made up of 21 all new cues. In this collection was the C-1, the only two-piece hustler cue that McDermott ever made and, today, examples are being sought by collectors. All of the C-Line cues are desirable today, especially the more intricate examples. The C-21 is arguably the most sought after standard production cue McDermott ever made.

The D-line came out in 1984, featuring 26 new cues. The line started with the D-1, a simple cue without points or inlays, and progressed to the D-25 and D-26, both of which had floating inlays in the forearm instead of points. Now that these cues have been discontinued, they are being purchased by collectors. In the past, it had been possible to order early cues as custom models. But now that McDermott no longer uses splices for points, B-, C-, or D-line cues with points can no longer be made. Other discontinued collectible McDermotts include the original Harley Davidson series from the 1980s, which are now sought after by cue collectors and fans of Harley Davidson memorabilia. There was also the Wildlife Collection, made from 1987 to 1988, which featured six cues that had intricate wildlife scenes depicted in wood inlays. Very few Wildlife cues were made. The Legend Cues featured images of Elvis Presley or Marilyn Monroe in the mid-1990s. The Masterpiece Series utilized the most intricate designs ever done on McDermott cues and featured the patented "centric" joint. The Revival Series, introduced to commemorate the company's 20th anniversary, brought back some of the basic wood inlays and joint rings which made McDermott famous. The Commemorative Series included the 1996 limited edition Founder's Cue. Only 1,000 of these cues were made, and each was numbered. They were individually signed on the forearm by Jim McDermott.

In 1988, McDermott moved to its new state-of-the-art production facility, custom designed for the art of cuemaking. It features several climate-controlled rooms individually designed for their different cuemaking steps. Jim McDermott sold the company in 1994 to his son Jesse, and Larry Johns. Today the company has new owners. McDermott is now making several different series of cues. The 2001, 2002, and 2003 series cues feature designs introduced in those years. The Legacy cue series is a collection of some of the more popular designs going back into the 1990s. The Transfer series include images of the art of Frank Mittelstadt, a Wisconsin native famous for his depictions of wild animals. New Harley Davidson cues, Jack Daniels Limited Editions, Metal X Series cues, E and M lines, Prestige series cues, a new design every month, etc., are also available.

In 2004, McDermott launched the following: Intimidator shafts, a series of high-performance shafts that fit any cue; Shooter's Collection Cases, a series of seven cue cases; Lifestyle Collection Clothing line, an exclusive line of apparel for the McDermott enthusiast; V2 Series of cues, cases and clothing for women players and designed by Vivian Villarreal; M2 Series of cues designed by Mike Massey; Lifetime Maintenance (free lifetime maintenance of your McDermott cue for life).

McDermott also offers a number of billiard items including cue care products, cases, chalk, racks, etc., for distribution around the world.

McDermott cues have become collectible for a number of reasons. Each of the individual lines have been made up of cues that were well-designed and well-marketed. The success of McDermott has resulted in familiarity with many of the C- and D-line cues by players that were active when these cues were available. All McDermott cues are guaranteed for life, for the original owner, against construction defects, including warpage, that are not the result of abuse. For further information, or a free catalog, contact McDermott Cue Manufacturing Company Incorporated, listed in the Trademark Index.

SPECIFICATIONS

- Butt material: hardwoods
- Shaft material: rock maple
- Standard length: 58 in.
- Lengths available: 54 to 62 in.
- Standard weights 18 to 21 oz.
- Standard wrap: Irish linen
- Standard finish: urethane
- Standard taper: 10 to 12 in.
- Balance point: variable
- Standard ferrules: Ivorine-3
- Standard butt cap: urethane
- Standard tip: Triangle
- Standard tip widths: 10 to 15 mm
- Standard joint: urethane
- Joint type: flat-faced wood-to-wood
- Standard number of shafts: one
- Standard joint screws: 3/8-10
- Point construction: inlaid

OPTIONS (FOR NEW CUES ONLY)

- Extra shaft (standard joint): $75+
- Extra shaft (Uni-Loc joint): $105
- Extra shaft (quick release joint): $105
- 31 in. shaft: +$15
- Leather wrap: $30
- Ivory ferrule: +$50
- Intimidator shaft (3/8-10 joint): $236
- Intimidator shaft (quick release joint): $242
- Intimidator shaft (Uni-Loc joint): $249
- Predator 314 shaft (3/8-10 joint): $220
- Predator 314 shaft (quick release joint): $240
- Predator 314 shaft (Uni-Loc joint): $240
- Predator 314 shaft (discontinued model shaft): add $50
- Finish over wrap: +$50
- Pearl /metallic paint: +$30
- Engraving on butt cap: $20 per line

REPAIRS (FOR MCDERMOTT CUES ONLY)

Repairs require 2-3 weeks in house plus shipping time.

- Refinish (requires rewrap): $120
- Refinish with leather wrap: $120
- Rewrap (Irish linen): $40
- Rewrap leather: $50
- Rewrap (leather): $60
- Mcdermott tip and ferrule: $25
- Mcdermott shaft clean: no charge
- Mcdermott tip and shaft clean: no charge
- Replace standard 29 in. shaft: $75+
- Replace quick release joint 29 in. shaft: $105
- Replace Uni-Loc joint 29 in. shaft: $105
- Replace discontinued 29 in. shaft: $120
- Turn down shaft: $25
- Rethread shaft: $40
- Replace buttcap: $40

CURRENT CUES

McDermott currently offers the Prestige Series, the Elite Series, the Professional Series, the Competitor Series, the Licensed Series, and the Signature Series, all of which are shown following, except for the Signature Series. The current delivery time to dealers for a new McDermott cue is approximately two weeks. Custom cues are also available but will take longer, depending on the design.

MCDERMOTT CUE MANUFACTURING INC., cont. 473

GRADING	100%	95%	70%

"PRESTIGE" SERIES

The following Prestige Series cues are limited editions that feature McDermott's quick release joint. Each Prestige Series cue is limited to production of 100.

Level 7 #M8PR-1 "Prestige I" - Ebony forearm with brass rings above wrap, four intricate bone-bordered purpleheart floating points featuring inlays of bocote and mother-of-pearl, leather wrap, ebony butt sleeve with four brass-bordered widows inlaid with intricate patterns of bocote and bone and purpleheart and mother-of-pearl between brass rings at top and bottom, black butt cap with 24-karat gold engraved ring and "Prestige Cue" medallion.

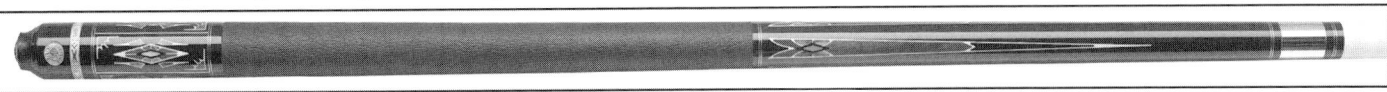

| MSR | $2,575 | $2,000-2,575 | $1,550 | $1,000 |

Level 6 #M8PR-2 "Prestige II" - Bird's-eye maple forearm with a wavy double-bordered purpleheart ring above wrap, six intricate ebony- and maple-bordered purpleheart floating points featuring inlays of brass crosses in each, leather wrap, ebony butt sleeve with six intricate maple-bordered widows inlaid with a brass cross in each between brass rings within purpleheart and black urethane at top and bottom, black butt cap with 24-karat gold engraved ring and "Prestige Cue" medallion.

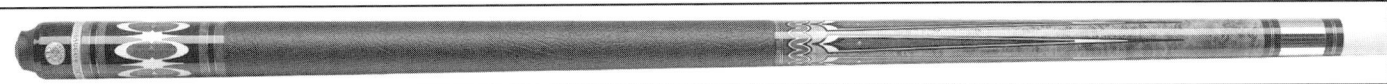

| MSR | $2,575 | $2,000-2,575 | $1,550 | $1,000 |

Level 6 #M8PR-3 "Prestige III" - Bird's-eye maple forearm with a metal-bordered bocote ring set within ebony rings above wrap and three multi-piece floating bocote and ebony points coming down from joint, three intricate multi-piece criss-crossing bocote and ebony and silver and stone inlaid floating points, leather wrap, bird's-eye maple butt sleeve with three intricate maple inlaid ebony bullet-shaped windows inlaid with a silver medallion marked "XXV" for McDermott's 25th Anniversary between metal-bordered bocote rings set within ebony rings at top and bottom, black butt cap with white gold engraved ring and "Prestige Cue" medallion.

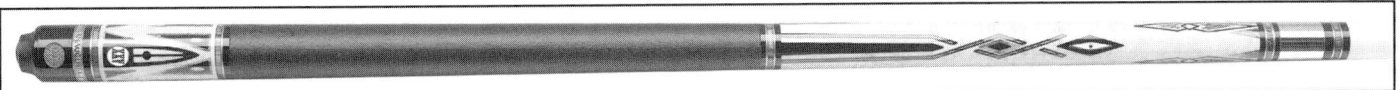

| MSR | $2,575 | $2,000-2,575 | $1,550 | $1,000 |

Level 6 #M8PR-4 "Prestige IV" - Curly maple forearm, three long ebony-bordered box elder burl points with a mother-of-pearl notched diamond-shaped inlay and four mother-of-pearl dots set in an ebony butterfly alternating with three short ebony-bordered box elder burl points, leather wrap, box elder burl butt sleeve with a mother-of-pearl notched diamond-shaped inlay set between two mother-of-pearl dots set in ebony and maple-bordered ebony windows set between bocote set in brass rings at top and bottom, black butt cap with 24-karat gold engraved ring and "Prestige Cue" medallion.

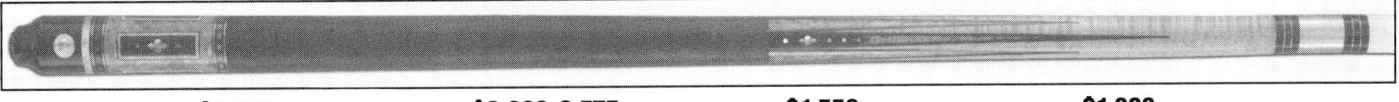

| MSR | $2,575 | $2,000-2,575 | $1,550 | $1,000 |

"ELITE" SERIES

Level 8 #M2-9B "Bridgeport" - Cocobolo forearm with a brass ring above handle, six intricate multi-piece ebony-bordered white urethane floating points with pairs of synthetic turquoise diamond-shaped inlays, stained bird's-eye maple handle with intricate multi-piece ebony-bordered white urethane and turquoise diamond-shaped inlays within cocobolo above and below, cocobolo butt sleeve with six intricate multi-piece ebony-bordered white urethane windows with a turquoise diamond-shaped inlay in each below a brass ring below handle.

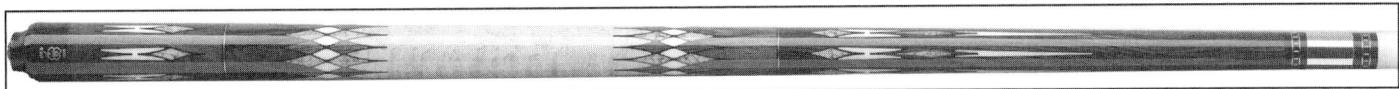

| MSR | $1,239 | $900-1,239 | $765 | $600 |

Level 5 #M2-9C "Sexton" - Stained bird's-eye maple forearm with pewter checks set in black urethane within pewter rings above wrap, three long ebony points with maple and ebony borders and an abalone dot set between a pair of abalone diamond-shaped inlays in each alternating with three short ebony points with maple and ebony borders and a pewter-bordered abalone diamond-shaped inlay in each, leather wrap, ebony butt sleeve with abalone dots set between pairs of abalone diamond-shaped inlays alternating with pewter-bordered abalone diamond-shaped inlays between pewter checks set in ebony within pewter rings at top and bottom.

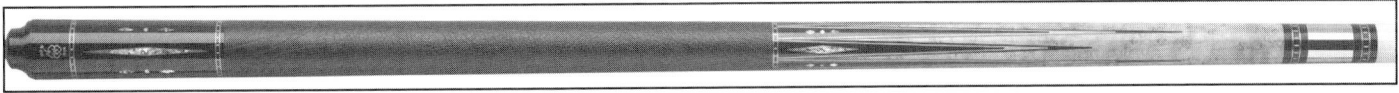

| MSR | $1,239 | $900-1,239 | $765 | $600 |

GRADING	100%	95%	70%

Level 6 #M2-9A "Knight" - Ebony forearm with a bordered bubinga wave ring above a pewter ring above wrap, four intricate bordered bubinga split floating points inlaid with intricate pieces of pewter and turquoise with pewter-bordered turquoise diamond-shaped inlays in the centers, leather wrap, ebony butt sleeve with intricate bordered bubinga split windows inlaid with intricate pieces of pewter and turquoise alternating with pewter-bordered turquoise diamond-shaped inlays between bordered bubinga wave rings within pewter rings at top and bottom.

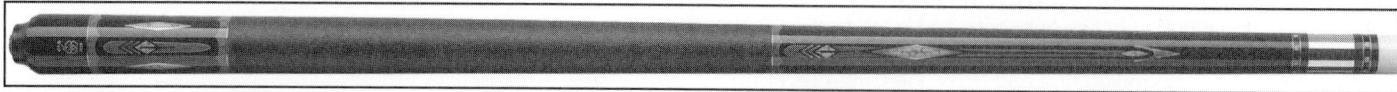

| MSR | $1,139 | $850-1,139 | $700 | $525 |

Level 4 #M1-6A "Sedona" - Stained bird's-eye maple forearm with an ebony-bordered cocobolo ring above a brass ring above wrap, four intricate ebony-bordered hollow cocobolo floating points inlaid with intricate pieces of ebony-bordered turquoise, leather wrap, stained bird's-eye maple butt sleeve with four ebony and cocobolo-bordered maple windows inlaid with intricate pieces of ebony-bordered turquoise and cocobolo between ebony-bordered cocobolo rings above brass rings at top and bottom.

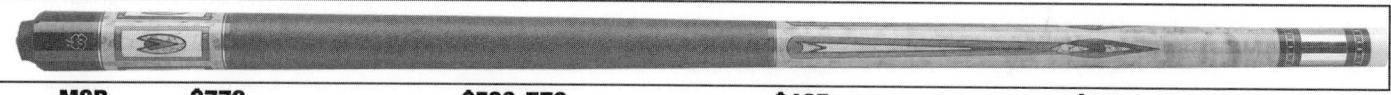

| MSR | $779 | $590-779 | $485 | $375 |

Level 4 #M1-4D "Portico" - Stained bird's-eye maple forearm, four black and white urethane-bordered green stained box elder burl points with an ebony point shaped inlay at the base of each, stained bird's-eye maple butt sleeve with four black and white urethane-bordered green stained box elder burl windows set in ebony inlaid with intricate pieces of mother-of-pearl between pairs of metal rings set in black urethane at top and bottom.

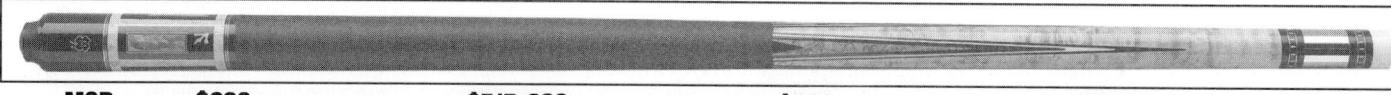

| MSR | $699 | $515-699 | $430 | $335 |

Level 5 M7QR-6 "Voyager" - Stained bird's-eye maple forearm with a staggered ebony ring above metal checks set in ebony between brass rings above wrap, six intricate floating ebony-bordered intricate white urethane and maple points, ebony butt sleeve with very intricate five-piece maple and white urethane patterns inlaid between metal checks set in ebony between brass rings at top and bottom.

| MSR | $699 | $520-899 | $430 | $330 |

Level 6 #M3-9A "Bridgeport C" - Cocobolo forearm with a brass ring above wrap, six intricate multi-piece black urethane-bordered white urethane floating points with pairs of turquoise diamond-shaped inlays, leather wrap, cocobolo butt sleeve with six intricate multi-piece black urethane-bordered white urethane windows with a turquoise diamond-shaped inlay in each below a brass ring below wrap.

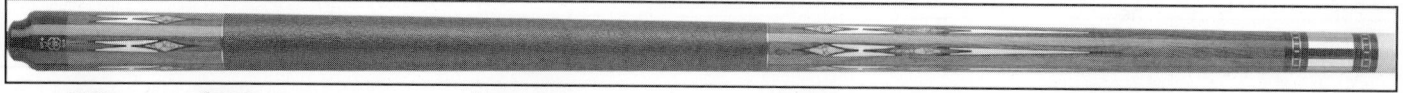

| MSR | $689 | $515-689 | $425 | $325 |

Level 6 #M1-5B "Navigator II" - Ebony forearm with nickel silver checks set in black urethane between nickel silver rings above wrap, four intricate white urethane-bordered hollow bocote floating points inlaid with intricate pieces of white urethane-bordered ebony and bocote, leather wrap, ebony butt sleeve with four white urethane and bocote partially bordered ebony windows inlaid with intricate pieces of white urethane-bordered ebony and bocote between nickel silver checks set in black urethane between nickel silver rings at top and bottom.

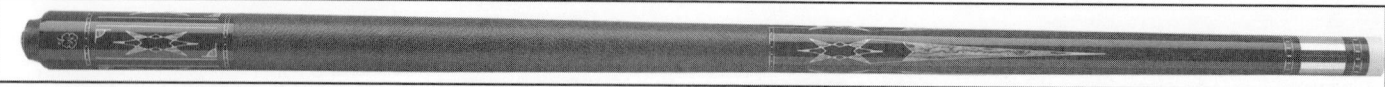

| MSR | $679 | $500-679 | $410 | $330 |

Level 6 #M2-4C "Emerald Warrior" - Stained bird's-eye maple forearm with four black urethane-bordered brown box elder diamond-shaped inlays above brass checks set in black urethane between brass rings above wrap, four black urethane-bordered brown box elder floating points with intricate black urethane-bordered synthetic green stone and brown box elder inlays at the base of each, stained bird's-eye maple butt sleeve with four intricate black urethane-bordered synthetic green stone and brown box elder inlays between brass checks set in black urethane between brass rings at top and bottom.

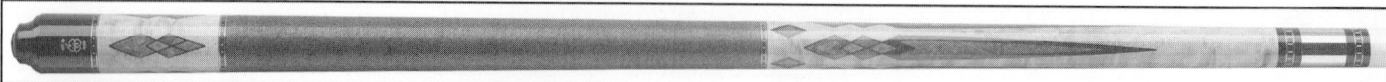

| MSR | $679 | $500-679 | $420 | $330 |

MCDERMOTT CUE MANUFACTURING INC., cont. 475

GRADING	100%	95%	70%

Level 6 #M1-5A "Navigator" - Stained bird's-eye maple forearm with a black urethane-bordered cocobolo ring above wrap, four intricate black urethane-bordered hollow cocobolo floating points inlaid with intricate pieces of black urethane-bordered cocobolo and malachite, leather wrap, stained bird's-eye maple butt sleeve with four black urethane and malachite partially bordered stained bird's-eye maple windows inlaid with intricate pieces of black urethane-bordered cocobolo and malachite between black urethane-bordered cocobolo rings at top and bottom.

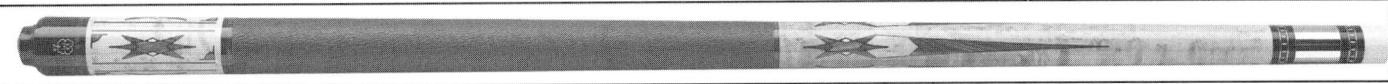

MSR	$669	$495-669	$415	$325

Level 5 #M3-9B "Bridgeport E" - Ebony forearm with a pair of metal rings above wrap, six intricate multi-piece black urethane-bordered white urethane floating points with pairs of Blue River agate diamond-shaped inlays, leather wrap, ebony butt sleeve with six intricate multi-piece black urethane-bordered white urethane windows with a Blue River agate diamond-shaped inlay in each between pairs of metal rings at top and bottom.

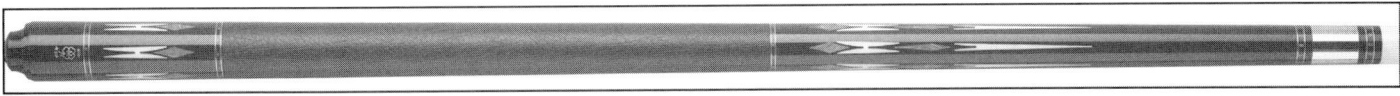

MSR	$659	$490-659	$410	$320

Level 4 #M1-4A "Sentinel" - Stained bird's-eye maple forearm with an ebony ring above wrap, four intricate black and white urethane-bordered split bocote floating points inlaid with an ebony diamond-shaped inlay in each, stained bird's-eye maple butt sleeve with four black urethane-bordered oval bocote windows with an ebony diamond-shaped inlay in each between bocote checks set in black urethane between maple rings at top and bottom.

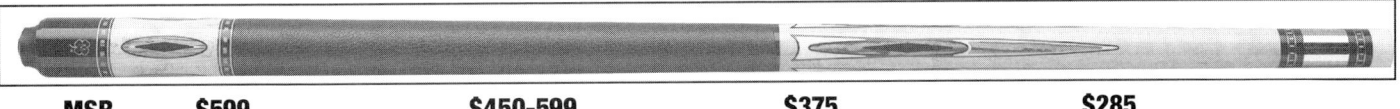

MSR	$599	$450-599	$375	$285

"PROFESSIONAL" SERIES

Level 4 M7QR-5 "Defender" - Stained bird's-eye maple forearm, intricate floating hardwood points with intricate black and white urethane borders and black urethane-bordered white pearlescent inlay work at bottom, stained bird's-eye maple butt sleeve with intricate pearlized plastic patterns inlaid in an ebony ring around center.

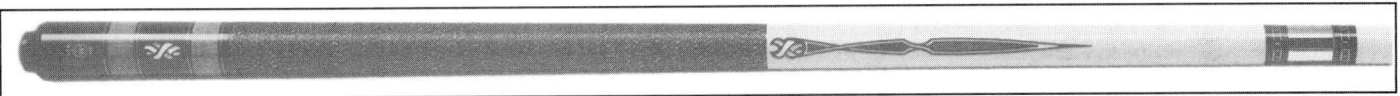

MSR	$589	$440-589	$365	$280

Level 2 #M2-9D "Sierra" - Stained bird's-eye maple forearm with jagged black urethane and bocote and maple rings at top and bottom, black stained maple handle, stained bird's-eye maple butt sleeve with jagged black urethane and bocote and maple rings at top and bottom.

MSR	$579	$435-579	$360	$275

Level 3 #M1-4B "Silhouette" - Stained bird's-eye maple forearm, four black and white urethane-bordered black urethane points, black urethane butt sleeve with four white urethane razor blade shaped windows inlaid with a white urethane pool hustler in each between pewter checks set above and below pairs of metal rings at top and bottom.

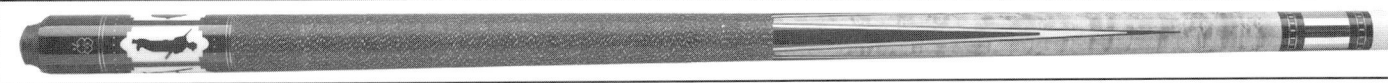

MSR	$539	$410-539	$340	$255

Level 4 #M3-4A "Symphony" - Stained bird's-eye maple forearm, four ebony points with cocobolo and colored urethane borders, ebony butt sleeve with pairs of black urethane-bordered synthetic mother-of-pearl dots set in white urethane windows within intricate cocobolo inlay patterns.

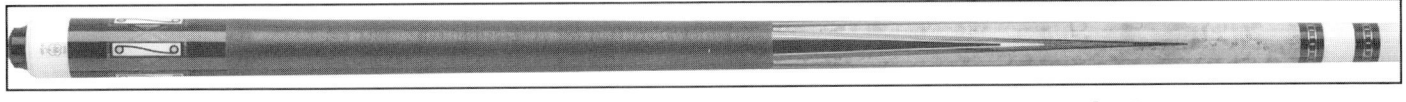

MSR	$519	$400-519	$335	$250

MCDERMOTT CUE MANUFACTURING INC., cont.

GRADING	100%	95%	70%

Level 5 M7QR-3 "Lucky 7" - Stained bird's-eye maple forearm, intricate white and black urethane floating points with inlays of white dice in each point, stained bird's-eye maple butt sleeve with inlays of white dice set in an ebony-colored ring with brass rings at bottom.

MSR	$509	$395-509	$230	$245

Level 4 #M1-3C "Bristlecone II" - Walnut forearm, four intricate black urethane-bordered white urethane floating points with black urethane-bordered paduuk and white urethane inlays at the base of each, walnut butt sleeve with four black urethane-bordered padauk and white urethane reverse spear-shaped inlays.

MSR	$489	$365-489	$300	$230

Level 4 #M3-4D "Edinburgh" - Stained bird's-eye maple forearm, four black urethane points with colored urethane borders and a turquoise point inlay at the base of each, black urethane butt sleeve with an intricate ring of white urethane-bordered turquoise inlays between pairs of nickel silver rings at top and bottom.

MSR	$489	$370-489	$305	$230

Level 3 #M3-5B "Torch" - Stained bird's-eye maple forearm, four black urethane points with colored urethane borders and a red-bordered white pearlescent point inlay at the base of each, black urethane butt sleeve with red-bordered white pearlescent torch flame inlays set into a notched maple ring below.

MSR	$479	$355-479	$295	$225

Level 4 #M3-4B "Biltmore" - Stained bird's-eye maple forearm, four black urethane points with colored urethane borders and a synthetic turquoise point inlay at the base of each, black urethane butt sleeve with an intricate ring of synthetic turquoise inlays between pairs of blue rings at top and bottom.

MSR	$469	$345-469	$285	$220

Level 3 #M3-5A "Guardian" - Stained bird's-eye maple forearm, four black urethane points with colored urethane borders and a pearlescent blue point inlay at the base of each, black urethane butt sleeve with maple bordered pearlescent blue inlays between blue dash rings at top and bottom.

MSR	$459	$335-459	$275	$210

Level 4 #M1-3B "Bristlecone" - Walnut forearm with a brass ring within black urethane above wrap, four intricate black urethane-bordered white urethane floating points with black urethane-bordered bubinga and white urethane inlays at the base of each, walnut butt sleeve with four black urethane-bordered bubinga and white urethane inlays between brass rings set in black urethane at top and bottom.

MSR	$459	$345-459	$290	$220

Level 4 M8-2 "Blaze" - Stained bird's-eye maple forearm, intricate black urethane points with white urethane and hardwood bordered hardwood inlays, black urethane butt sleeve with intricate hardwood and white urethane rings.

MSR	$449	$325-449	$270	$205

| GRADING | 100% | 95% | 70% |

Level 3 #M3-3B "Rail" - Stained bird's-eye maple forearm, four black urethane points with colored urethane borders and a box elder burl point inlay at the base of each, black urethane butt sleeve with intricate maple-bordered box elder burl maple inlays between bubinga rings at top and bottom.

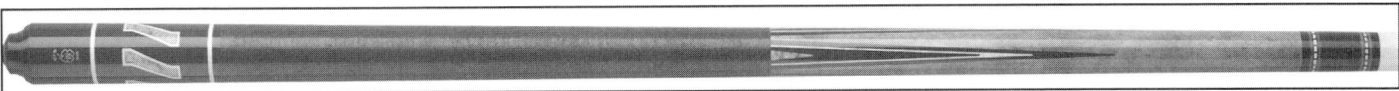

| MSR | $449 | $325-449 | $270 | $205 |

Level 3 #M3-3A "Classic" - Stained bird's-eye maple forearm, four ebony points with exotic hardwood and colored urethane borders, ebony butt sleeve with pairs of metal rings at top and bottom.

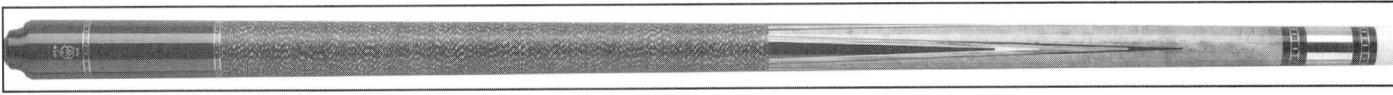

| MSR | $439 | $320-439 | $265 | $200 |

Level 4 #M3-4C "Windsor" - Stained bird's-eye maple forearm, four cocobolo points with exotic wood and colored urethane borders, cocobolo butt sleeve with an intricate ring of black urethane-bordered turquoise inlays between stained maple rings at top and bottom.

| MSR | $429 | $315-429 | $260 | $195 |

Level 2 #M3-2R "Victorian E" - Ebony forearm with an intricate ring of white urethane and pearlescent inlays above a metal ring above wrap, ebony butt sleeve with intricate rings of white urethane and pearlescent inlays between metal rings at top and bottom.

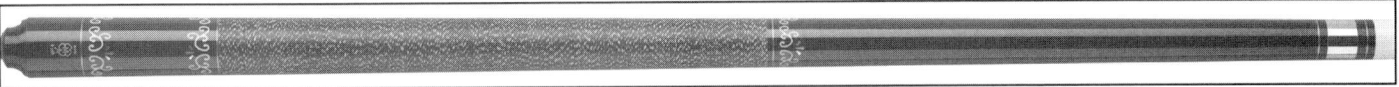

| MSR | $429 | $320-429 | $270 | $205 |

Level 4 #M3-3G "Masquerade" - Stained bird's-eye maple forearm, six black urethane points with a Blue River agate diamond-shaped inlay in each point, black urethane butt sleeve with intricate pairs of hollow Blue River agate diamond-shaped inlays.

| MSR | $419 | $310-419 | $360 | $200 |

Level 3 #M8-F5 "Sword" - Rosewood forearm, four intricate criss-crossing hollow maple points, rosewood butt sleeve.

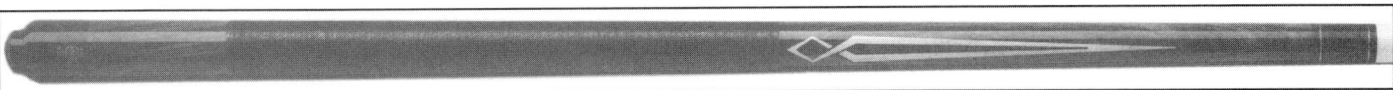

| MSR | $399 | $300-399 | $250 | $190 |

Level 2 #M1-2R "Victorian" - Stained bird's-eye maple forearm with an intricate ring of black urethane inlays above a nickel silver ring above wrap, stained bird's-eye maple butt sleeve with intricate rings of black urethane inlays above and below nickel silver rings at top and bottom.

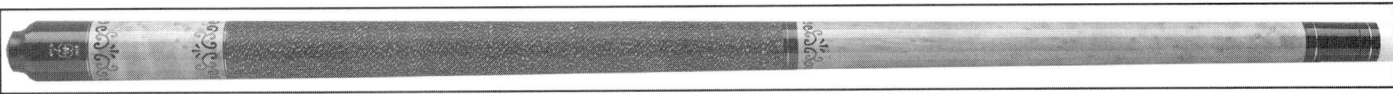

| MSR | $399 | $300-399 | $250 | $185 |

Level 3 #M1-2P "Spectrum" - Stained bird's-eye maple forearm, four black urethane-bordered laminated "Rainbow Color-Ply" floating points, laminated "Rainbow Color-Ply" butt sleeve with black urethane rings at top and bottom.

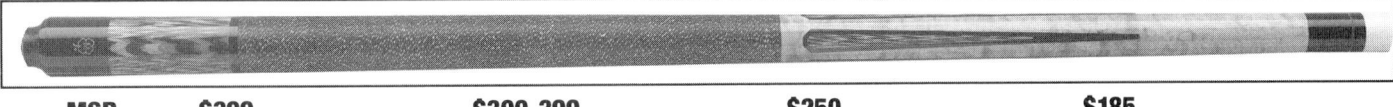

| MSR | $399 | $300-399 | $250 | $185 |

GRADING	100%	95%	70%

Level 2 #M7-6 "Peak" - Stained bird's-eye maple forearm with intricate jagged black urethane and bocote and maple rings at bottom, stained bird's-eye maple butt sleeve with intricate jagged black urethane and bocote and maple rings at bottom.

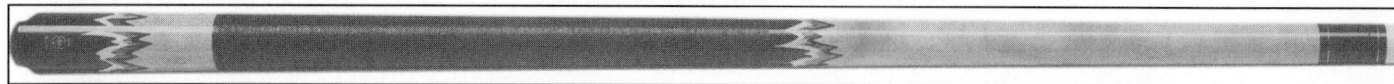

MSR	$389	$295-389	$245	$175

Level 4 #M3-4F "Rose" - Stained bird's-eye maple forearm, six black urethane points with a green Dymondwood spear-shaped inlay at the tip of each, black urethane butt sleeve with intricate rose inlays of red and green stained burled wood.

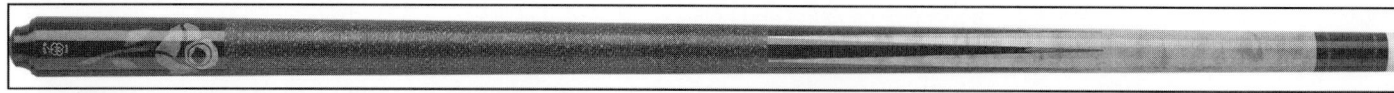

MSR	$389	$290-389	$240	$180

Level 3 M2K-5 "Pulse" - Cocobolo forearm, maple points with an intricate jagged "pulse" hardwood inlay in each, cocobolo butt sleeve with an intricate jagged maple and black urethane "pulse" ring between jagged maple rings at top and bottom.

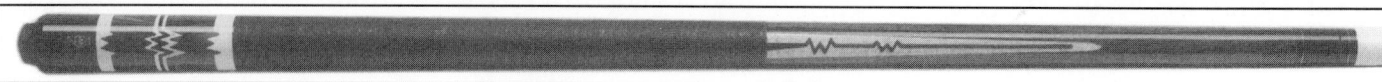

MSR	$389	$290-389	$240	$180

Level 3 #M1-2O "Odyssey" - Stained bird's-eye maple forearm, four black urethane-bordered laminated "Santa Fe Color-Ply" floating points, laminated "Santa Fe Color-Ply" butt sleeve with black urethane rings at top and bottom.

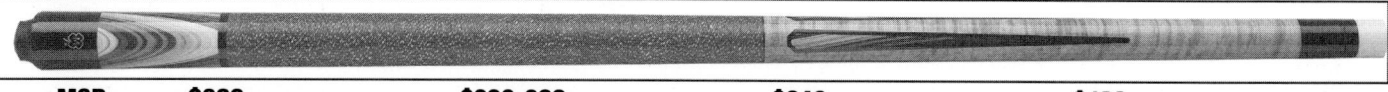

MSR	$389	$290-389	$240	$180

Level 2 #M1-2Q "Shadow" - Black painted maple forearm, black urethane butt sleeve with four white urethane razor blade-shaped windows inlaid with a black urethane lady pool player in each between white urethane checks set above and below pairs of nickel silver rings at top and bottom.

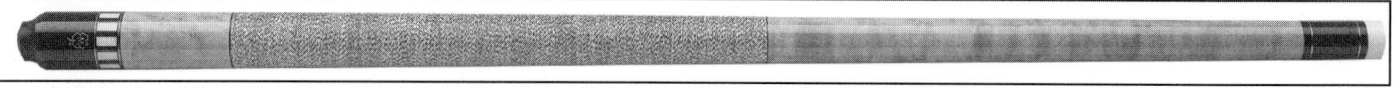

MSR	$379	$285-379	$235	$175

Level 4 #M4-4A "Bishop" - Morada forearm, four intricate bird's-eye maple maple floating points, morada butt sleeve with four intricate four-piece hollow star-shaped inlays.

MSR	$359	$275-359	$225	$160

Level 4 #M4-4B "Saphire" - Stained rock maple forearm, six synthetic ebony points with blue synthetic tips, synthetic ebony butt sleeve with six blue synthetic diamond-shaped inlays.

MSR	$359	$275-359	$225	$160

Level 2 #M2-3A "Spalted Gecko" - Spalted maple forearm with bubinga gecko-shaped inlays, lizard embossed leather wrap, spalted maple butt sleeve with bubinga gecko-shaped inlays.

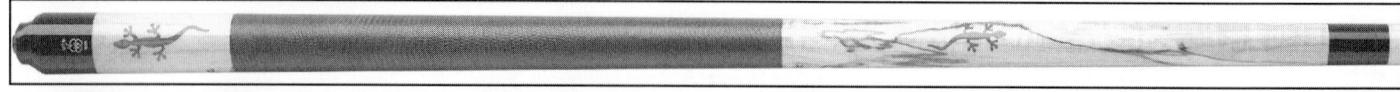

MSR	$359	$275-359	$225	$160

Level 3 #M3-4E "Lil Guy" - Stained bird's-eye maple forearm, four black urethane points with a green four-leaf clover-shaped inlay in each, black urethane butt sleeve with images of a leprechaun.

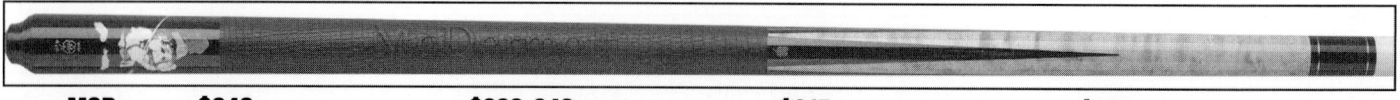

MSR	$349	$260-349	$215	$165

GRADING	100%	95%	70%

Level 3 #M3-3E "Lance" - Rosewood forearm, four intricate criss-crossing hollow maple points, rosewood butt sleeve with intricate hollow open diamond-shaped inlays.

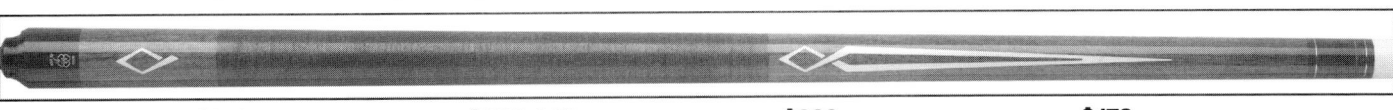

MSR	$349	$265-349	$220	$170

"TOURNAMENT" SERIES

Level 2 #M3-3F "Arizona" - Stained bird's-eye maple forearm with a cocobolo ring within intricate black and white urethane rings above wrap, stained bird's-eye maple butt sleeve with cocobolo rings within intricate black and white urethane rings at top and bottom.

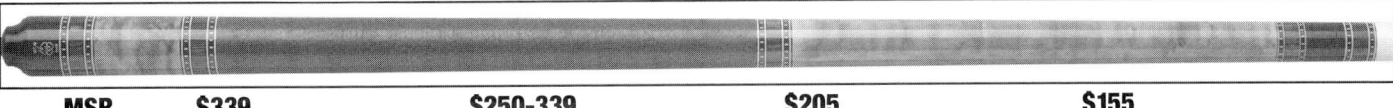

MSR	$339	$250-339	$205	$155

Level 2 #M1-2N "Gecko" - Stained maple forearm with black urethane gecko-shaped inlays, stained maple butt sleeve with black urethane gecko-shaped inlays.

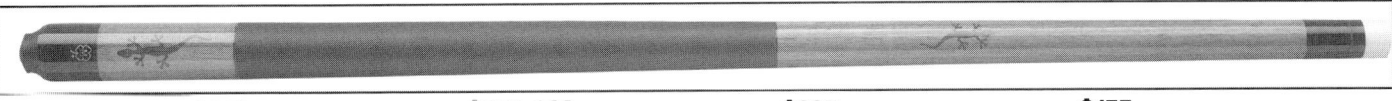

MSR	$339	$250-339	$205	$155

Level 2 M8P-6 "Heartbreaker" - Black painted maple forearm with "heart breaker" written above and below a broken red heart-shaped inlay and a joint above wrap for breaking/jumping, black painted maple butt sleeve with red broken hearts above center.

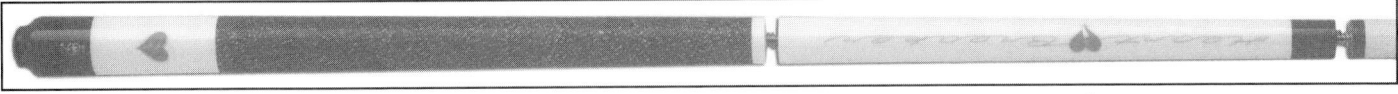

MSR	$329	$245-329	$200	$150

Level 2 #M1-2L "Corona" - Black painted maple forearm, black urethane butt sleeve with cocobolo windows alternating with hollow white urethane windows inlaid over a paduuk ring between white urethane rings above and below cocobolo rings at top and bottom.

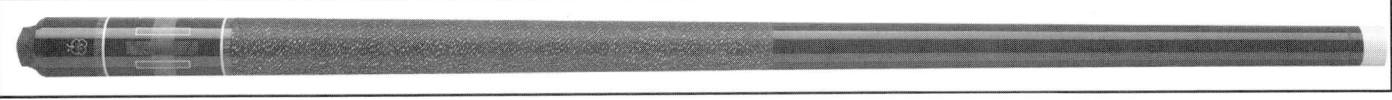

MSR	$329	$245-329	$200	$150

Level 2 #M1-2J "Mohave" - Spalted maple forearm, leather wrap, spalted maple butt sleeve.

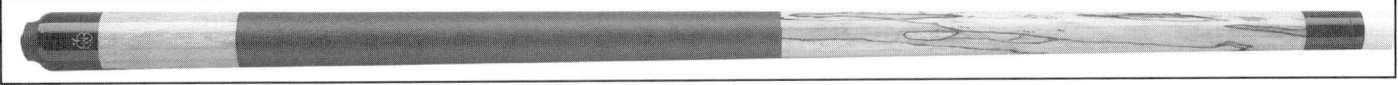

MSR	$319	$240-319	$200	$150

Level 2 #M1-2B "Bat" - Black stained bird's-eye maple forearm, black stained bird's-eye maple butt sleeve with white urethane-bordered laminated "Eclipse Color-Ply" rings above and below black urethane rings at top and bottom.

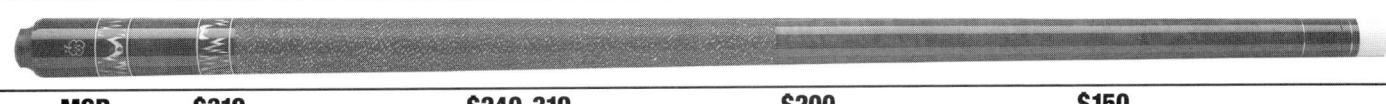

MSR	$319	$240-319	$200	$150

Level 2 #M2K-1 "Ring" - Stained bird's-eye maple forearm, zebrawood butt sleeve with pairs of cocobolo rings set within pairs of maple rings above and below.

MSR	$309	$230-309	$190	$145

Level 2 #M4-3A "Tucson" - Stained bird's-eye maple forearm with a brass ring set in bocote and synthetic ebony rings above wrap, stained bird's-eye maple butt sleeve with brass rings set in bocote and synthetic ebony rings at top and bottom.

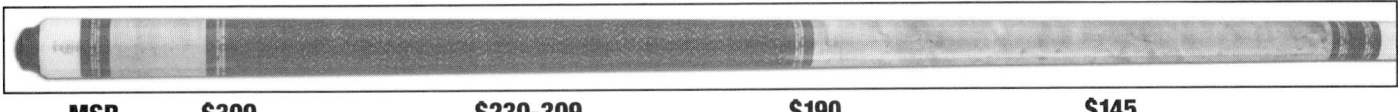

MSR	$309	$230-309	$190	$145

MCDERMOTT CUE MANUFACTURING INC., cont.

GRADING	100%	95%	70%

Level 2 #M4-3B "Tempe" - Morada forearm with a tulipwood ring set in padauk and synthetic ebony rings above wrap, morada butt sleeve with tulipwood rings set in padauk and synthetic ebony rings at top and bottom.

MSR	$309	$230-309	$190	$145

Level 2 EB7-JW "Jump-Break" - Black painted maple forearm jointed above wrap for breaking/jumping, black painted maple butt sleeve.

MSR	$309	$230-309	$190	$145

Level 2 EB6-JW "Jump-Break" - Black painted maple forearm jointed above handle for breaking/jumping, black painted maple handle.

MSR	$299	$225-299	$185	$140

Level 2 EF-19 "Heritage" - High figure bird's-eye maple forearm, high figure bird's-eye maple butt sleeve.

MSR	$299	$225-299	$185	$140

Level 2 #M3-3C "Twilight" - Ebony-painted maple forearm with Blue River agate checks in synthetic ebony set within a pair of nickel silver rings above wrap, ebony painted maple butt sleeve with Blue River agate checks in synthetic ebony set within pairs of nickel silver rings at top and bottom.

MSR	$299	$230-299	$180	$140

Level 2 #M1-2A "Montana" - Stained bird's-eye maple forearm with a black urethane-bordered laminated "Adobe Color-Ply" ring above wrap, laminated "Adobe Color-Ply" butt sleeve with black urethane rings at top and bottom.

MSR	$299	$225-299	$185	$140

Level 2 #M1-2K "Gentry" - Rosewood forearm with rosewood and maple blocks set within maple rings above wrap, rosewood butt sleeve with rosewood and maple blocks set within maple rings at top and bottom.

MSR	$299	$225-299	$185	$140

Level 2 #M1-1A "Warden" - Stained bird's-eye maple forearm, stained bird's-eye maple butt sleeve with maple blocks set in black urethane between brass rings at bottom.

MSR	$299	$225-299	$185	$140

Level 2 EF-1 "Blade" - Bocote forearm, bocote butt sleeve.

MSR	$289	$220-289	$180	$130

MCDERMOTT CUE MANUFACTURING INC., cont. 481

GRADING	100%	95%	70%

Level 2 EF-3 "Cutlass" - Cocobolo forearm, cocobolo butt sleeve.

MSR	$289	$220-289	$180	$130

Level 2 #M3-3D "Sunrise" - Ebony-painted maple forearm with a thin padauk ring between a pair of brass rings above wrap, ebony-painted maple butt sleeve with a thick padauk ring within a pair of brass rings at bottom.

MSR	$279	$210-279	$175	$130

Level 1 #M1-1B "The Hustler" - Maple forearm, four full-spliced exotic hardwood points and handle with the gold McDermott logo at bottom and brass insert in shaft joint.

MSR	$279	$210-279	$175	$135

Level 2 #MG-31 "Mystic Blue" - Metallic blue-painted maple forearm, metallic blue-painted maple butt sleeve with white dashes set in black urethane between pairs of metal rings at top and bottom.

MSR	$249	$185-249	$155	$115

Level 2 #MG-32 "Meteor Silver" - Metallic silver-painted maple forearm, metallic silver-painted maple butt sleeve with white dashes set in black urethane between pairs of metal rings at top and bottom.

MSR	$249	$185-249	$155	$115

Level 2 #MG-33 "Bordeaux Red" - Metallic red-painted maple forearm, metallic red-painted maple butt sleeve with white dashes set in black urethane between pairs of metal rings at top and bottom.

MSR	$249	$185-249	$155	$115

Level 2 #MG-34 "Classic Pewter" - Metallic blue-painted maple forearm, metallic pewter-painted maple butt sleeve with white dashes set in black urethane between pairs of metal rings at top and bottom.

MSR	$249	$185-249	$155	$115

Level 2 #MT-2 "White Rose" - White-painted maple forearm with black and white transfer points, white-painted maple butt sleeve with a transfer image of a red rose.

MSR	$249	$185-249	$155	$115

Level 2 #MT-5 "Spider" - White-painted maple forearm with black and white transfer points, white-painted maple butt sleeve with a transfer image of an 8-ball caught in a spider's web.

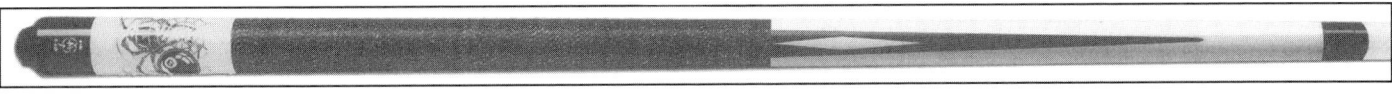

MSR	$249	$185-249	$155	$115

GRADING	100%	95%	70%

Level 2 #M2WW "Wolf" - White-painted maple forearm with image of an arctic wolf in the snow, white-painted maple butt sleeve with image of an arctic with her cubs.

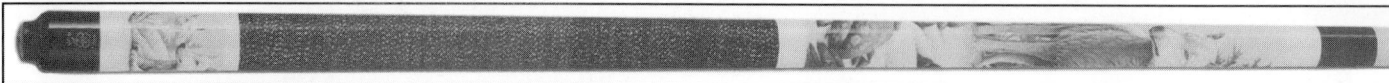

MSR	$249	$185-249	$155	$115

Level 2 #M2WP "Panther" - Black-painted maple forearm with image of a black panther ready to pounce, black-painted maple butt sleeve with image of head of a black panther.

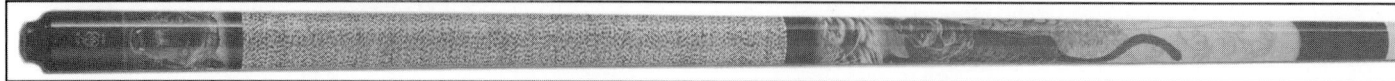

MSR	$249	$185-249	$155	$115

Level 2 #M2WL "Leopard" - Black-painted maple forearm with image of a snow leopard coming down a frozen waterfall, black-painted maple butt sleeve with image of reclining snow leopard.

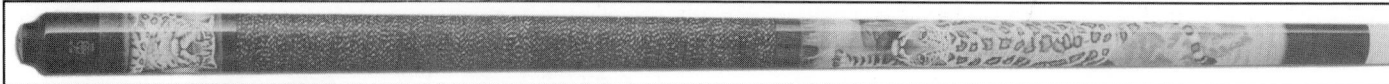

MSR	$249	$185-249	$155	$115

Level 2 #M2WE "Eagle" - White-painted maple forearm with image of a bald eagle pulling a fish out of the water, white-painted maple butt sleeve with image of a bald eagle in its nest.

MSR	$249	$185-249	$155	$115

Level 2 #M2-2A "Mano" - White-painted maple forearm with a transfer image of sharks swimming under the tip of a cue striking the moon, white-painted maple butt sleeve with a transfer image of a shark with an 8-ball in its mouth swimming under the tip of a cue striking the moon.

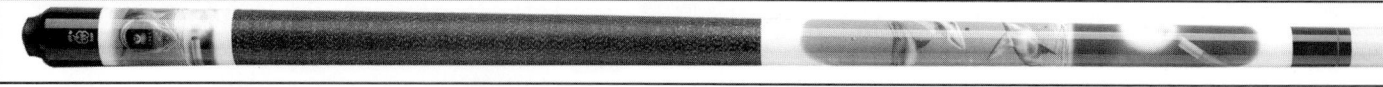

MSR	$249	$185-249	$155	$115

Level 2 #M2-2B "Spirit of America" - White-painted maple forearm with a transfer image of an eagle flying under the American flag, white-painted maple butt sleeve with a transfer image of an eagle flying in front of the American flag.

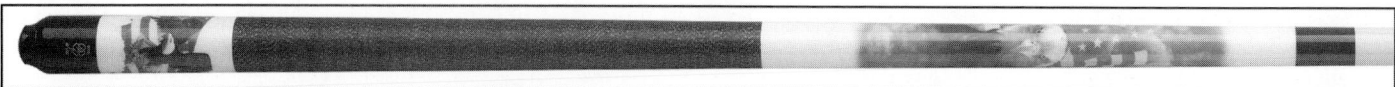

MSR	$249	$185-249	$155	$115

Level 2 #M2-2C "Sentry" - White-painted maple forearm with a transfer image of an eagle perched on the tip of a cue, white-painted maple butt sleeve with a transfer image of an eagle flying clutching a cue.

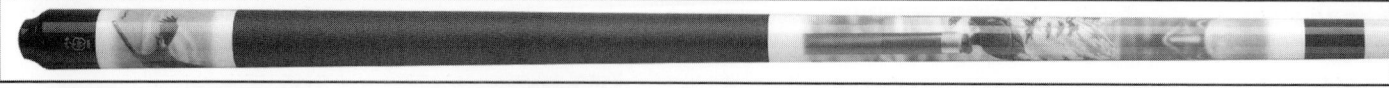

MSR	$249	$185-249	$155	$115

Level 2 #M2-2D "Moon Dance" - White-painted maple forearm with a transfer image of a wolf standing under the moon, white-painted maple butt sleeve with a transfer image of a wolf running over a rack of pool balls.

MSR	$249	$185-249	$155	$115

Level 2 #M3-3I "Intimidator" - Ebony-painted maple forearm with a transfer image of a warrior on a horse approaching a snake, ebony-painted maple butt sleeve with a transfer image of a warrior on a horse spearing a snake.

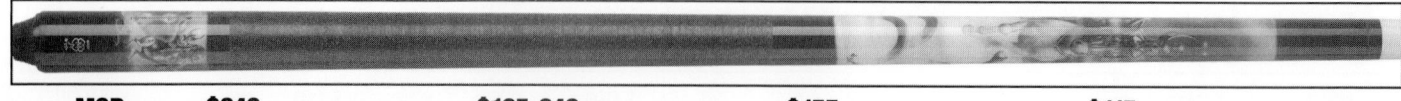

MSR	$249	$185-249	$155	$115

MCDERMOTT CUE MANUFACTURING INC., cont.

GRADING	100%	95%	70%

Level 2 #M3-2E "Lil Guy II" - Ebony-painted maple forearm, ebony-painted maple butt sleeve with images of a leprechaun.

MSR	$249	$185-249	$155	$115

Level 2 #M3-2D "Panther 03" - Ebony-painted maple forearm with a transfer image of a panther climbing pool balls, ebony-painted maple butt sleeve with a transfer image of a panther climbing down a 9-ball.

MSR	$249	$185-249	$155	$115

Level 3 #M4-3I "8-Ball" - Stained bird's-eye maple forearm with transfer images of points with a diamond in the center of each, stained bird's-eye maple butt sleeve with a transfer image of an eight-ball.

MSR	$249	$185-249	$155	$115

Level 3 #M4-3J "9-Ball" - Stained bird's-eye maple forearm with transfer images of points with a diamond in the center of each, stained bird's-eye maple butt sleeve with a transfer image of a nine-ball.

MSR	$249	$185-249	$155	$115

Level 2 #MT-1 "Pool Shark" - Stained bird's-eye maple forearm, stained bird's-eye maple butt sleeve with a transfer image of a shark in sunglasses holding an eight-ball and a cue.

MSR	$249	$185-249	$155	$115

"COMPETITOR" SERIES

Level 2 #MG-21 "Mystic Blue" - Pearlescent gunmetal blue-painted maple forearm, pearlescent gunmetal blue-painted maple butt sleeve. Also available: MG-22 is "Meteor Silver," MG-23 is "Venetion Gold," MG-24 is "Deep Purple," MG-25 is "Bordeaux Red," MG-26 is "Classic Pewter," and MG-28 is "B. R. Green."

MSR	$209	$155-209	$130	$95

Level 2 #C-251 "Arctic Blue" - Blue-stained maple forearm, blue-stained maple butt sleeve. Also available: C-252 is "White Opal," C-254 is "Orchid Purple," C-255 is "Mars Red," C-256 is "Bolero Gold," C-257 is "Black Opal," and C-259 is "Aztec Bronze."

MSR	$209	$155-209	$130	$95

Level 2 #MG-1 "Pacific Blue" - Royal blue-stained bird's-eye maple forearm, royal blue-stained bird's-eye maple butt sleeve. Also available: MG-2 is "Titanium Gray," MG-3 is "Dark English," MG-4 is "Royal Purple," MG-5 is "Colorado Red," MG-7 is "Nighthawk Black," MG-8 is "Oxford Green," and MG-9 is "American Cherry."

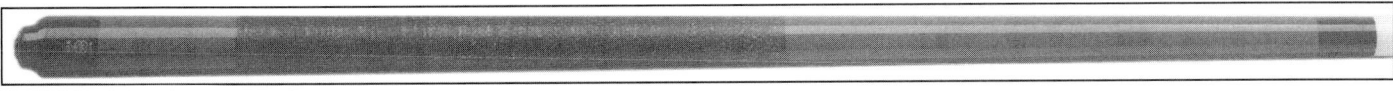

MSR	$189	$140-189	$115	$80

MCDERMOTT CUE MANUFACTURING INC., cont.

GRADING	100%	95%	70%

Level 2 #C-151 "Pacific Blue" - Royal blue-stained bird's-eye maple one-piece butt. Also available: C-152 is "Titanium Gray," C-153 is "Dark English," C-155 is "Colorado Red," C-157 is "Nighthawk Black," and C-158 is "Oxford Green."

MSR	$159	$120-159	$100	$70

Level 2 #C-100 "Natural Walnut" - Natural walnut one-piece butt.

MSR	$149	$115-149	$95	$65

Level 2 #C-110 "American Cherry" - American cherry one-piece butt.

MSR	$149	$115-149	$95	$65

"LICENSED" SERIES

Level 4 #HD-30 "Inlay" - Stained bird's-eye maple forearm, four cocobolo-bordered synthetic ebony points with a bird's-eye maple "Harley Davidson" shield inlay in each point, ebony butt sleeve with bird's-eye maple "Harley Davidson" script inlays between pairs of brass rings above and below.

MSR	$450	$350-450	$285	$215

Level 2 #HD-24 "Flames" - Metallic gold-painted maple forearm with a transfer image of "Harley Davidson" in orange flames, leather wrap, metallic gold-painted maple butt sleeve with a transfer image of "Harley Davidson" in orange flames over the Harley Davidson shield.

MSR	$250	$185-250	$155	$120

Level 2 #HD-25 "Stars & Stripes" - Black-painted maple forearm with a transfer image of "Harley Davidson" in red over red and white and blue stars and stripes, black painted maple butt sleeve with a transfer image of "Harley Davidson" in red under a red and white and blue stars and stripes eagle silhouette.

MSR	$230	$155-230	$135	$110

Level 2 #M9HD-5 "Streamline Eagle" - Black-painted maple forearm with a transfer image of "Harley Davidson" in white over a blue eagle, black-painted maple butt sleeve with a transfer image of an eagle over the Harley Davidson shield.

MSR	$195	$150-195	$125	$95

Level 6 #JD-30 "Collectors" - "Jack Daniel's" engraved joint, morada forearm with a morada ring set in brass rings above wrap, four intricate multi-piece maple floating points, "Jack Daniel's" embossed leather wrap, morada butt sleeve with intricate bird's-eye maple inlays surrounding two brass "Jack Daniel's" medallion inlays between morada rings set in brass rings above and below.

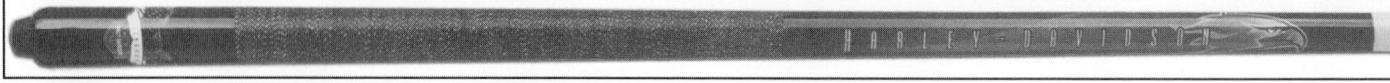

MSR	$750	$600-750	$485	$365

GRADING	100%	95%	70%

Level 2 #JD-04 "Old No. 7" - Black-painted maple forearm with a transfer image of "Jack Daniel's" portrait and logo over orange background, black-painted maple butt sleeve with a transfer image of "Jack Daniel's" logo in white.

MSR	$229	$155-229	$135	$110

GRADING	98%	90%	70%

DISCONTINUED CUES

A-LINE SERIES

The MR-Line (nicknamed the A-Line) was introduced in 1975 and was produced until 1976. They are identifiable by colored bumpers that match the color schemes of the cues. The standard wrap was nylon; leather or Irish linen was available as an option. Original MR cues are very difficult to find.

Level 2 MR-1 - Walnut forearm, butt sleeve with black and white rings at top and bottom (center ring of butt sleeve available in a variety of different colors).

Orig. Retail $40	$435	$360	$265

Level 2 MR-2 - Maple forearm, butt sleeve with pearlized plastic ring (available in a variety of colors) between two maple rings.

Orig. Retail $50	$465	$395	$285

Level 2 MR-3 - Rosewood forearm, butt sleeve with series of small rosewood squares and rosewood and pearlized plastic rings with matching plastic rings at joint (center ring of butt sleeve available in a variety of different colors).

Orig. Retail $60	$520	$425	$300

Level 2 MR-4 - Bird's-eye maple forearm with bird's-eye maple butt sleeve with same checked rings at bottom.

Orig. Retail $70	$550	$450	$315

Level 2 MR-5 - Nickel silver joint collar, rosewood forearm with wood joint rings, butt sleeve with ring of maple rectangles between a series of wood rings.

Orig. Retail $80	$600	$485	$340

Level 2 MR-6 - Rosewood forearm with maple ring above wrap and at joint, rosewood butt sleeve with maple rings at top and bottom.

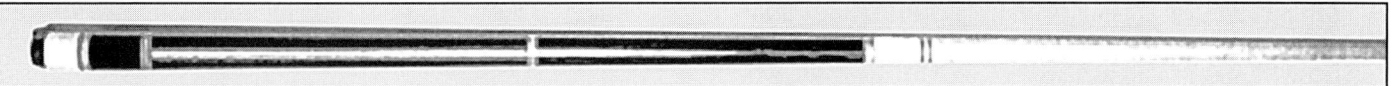

Orig. Retail $90	$640	$500	$360

GRADING	98%	90%	70%

Level 2 MR-7 - Rosewood forearm, rosewood butt sleeve with black-bordered maple rectangles inlaid in a ring pattern at top and bottom and at joint.

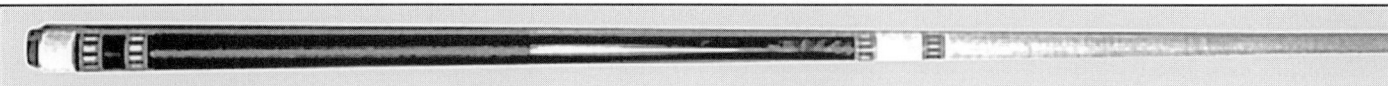

Orig. Retail $100	$685	$555	$380

Level 2 MR-8 - Bird's-eye maple forearm with black-bordered maple checks above wrap and at joint, bird's-eye maple butt sleeve with a large ring of black-bordered windows between smaller rings of the same (this cue was also available with a black butt cap and joint).

Orig. Retail $110	$715	$570	$400

Level 2 MR-9 - Nickel silver joint collar, rosewood forearm with intricate checked ring design above wrap and at joint, rosewood butt sleeve with same ring design at top and bottom of thick wood rings.

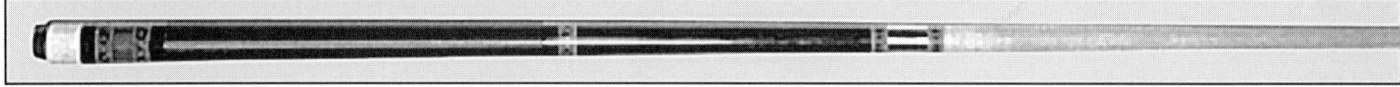

Orig. Retail $120	$755	$600	$415

Level 2 MR-10 - Bird's-eye maple forearm with brown wood rings between pairs of intricate checked rings above wrap and at joint, the same rings are at top and bottom of butt sleeve with ring pattern of black-bordered maple windows in between.

Orig. Retail $130	$795	$635	$435

B-LINE SERIES

The following B-Line cues were produced from 1976 to 1979. Nylon wraps were standard on B1-10, leather or Irish linen wraps were an option available on all these cues and were no extra charge on B11-16.

Level 2 B-1 - Walnut forearm, butt sleeve with black and white rings at top and bottom (center ring of butt sleeve available in a variety of different colors).

Orig. Retail $40	$385	$325	$255

Level 2 B-2 - Maple forearm, butt sleeve with pearlized plastic ring (available in a variety of colors) between two maple rings.

Orig. Retail $50	$440	$365	$270

Level 2 B-3 - Rosewood forearm, butt sleeve with series of small rosewood squares and rosewood and pearlized plastic rings with matching pearlized plastic rings at joint (center ring of butt sleeve available in a variety of different colors).

Orig. Retail $60	$465	$385	$280

Level 2 B-4 - Bird's-eye maple forearm with checked ring above wrap and at joint, bird's-eye maple butt sleeve with same checked rings at top and bottom.

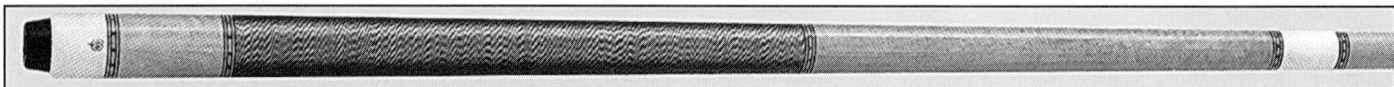

Orig. Retail $70	$485	$405	$300

MCDERMOTT CUE MANUFACTURING INC., cont.

GRADING	98%	90%	70%

Level 2 B-5 - Rosewood forearm with zebrawood joint rings, butt sleeve with ring of maple rectangles between a series of wood rings.

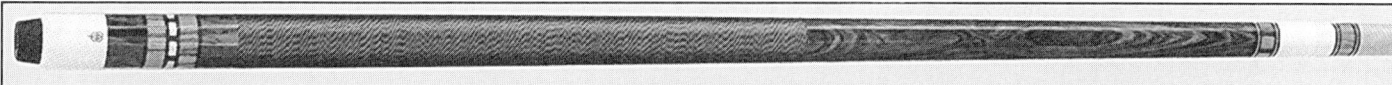

Orig. Retail $80	$525	$425	$315

Level 2 B-6 - Rosewood forearm with maple ring above wrap and at joint, rosewood butt sleeve with maple rings at top and bottom.

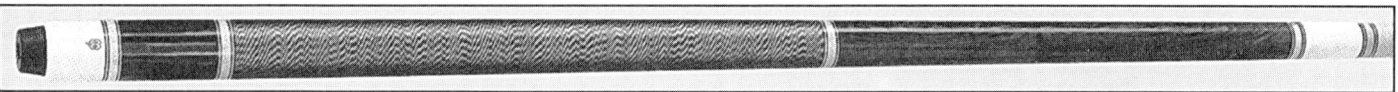

Orig. Retail $90	$555	$465	$340

Level 2 B-7 - Rosewood forearm, rosewood butt sleeve with black-bordered maple rectangles inlaid in a ring pattern at top and bottom and at joint.

Orig. Retail $100	$580	$485	$355

Level 2 B-8 - Bird's-eye maple forearm with black-bordered maple checks above wrap and at joint, bird's-eye maple butt sleeve with a large ring of black-bordered windows between smaller rings of the same.

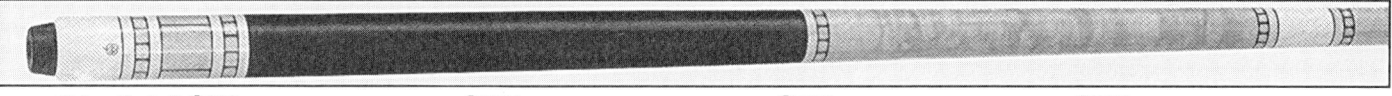

Orig. Retail $110	$625	$500	$360

Level 2 B-9 - Rosewood forearm with intricate checked ring design above wrap and at joint, rosewood butt sleeve with same ring design at top and bottom of thick wood ring.

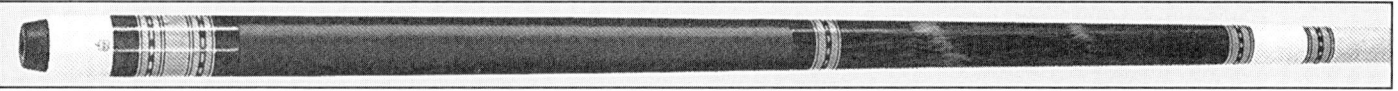

Orig. Retail $120	$645	$525	$375

Level 2 B-10 - Bird's-eye maple forearm with colored wood rings between pairs of intricate checked rings above wrap and at joint, the same rings are at top and bottom of butt sleeve with ring pattern of black-bordered maple windows in between (available in a variety of different colors of wood rings).

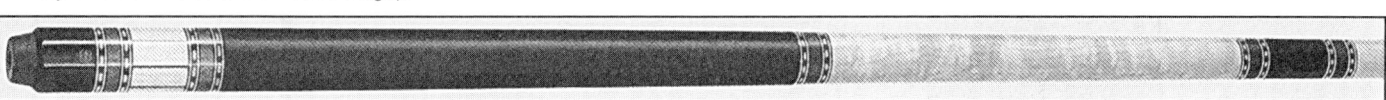

Orig. Retail $130	$685	$560	$390

Level 3 B-11 - Bird's-eye maple forearm with pairs of intricate checked rings at joint, four maple points with colored veneers, maple butt sleeve with four large matching colored diamond-shaped inlays split by a pair of black rings.

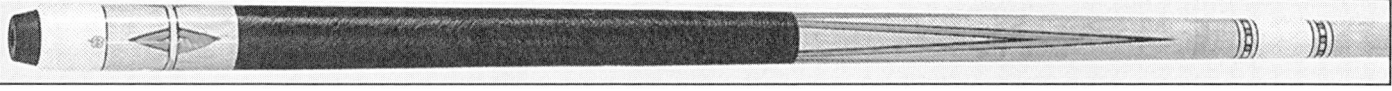

Orig. Retail $160	$765	$630	$425

Level 3 B-12 - Rosewood forearm, four points with colored veneers, rosewood butt sleeve with a series of three vertical hollow maple circles alternating with vertical lines set between pairs of thin white rings above and below.

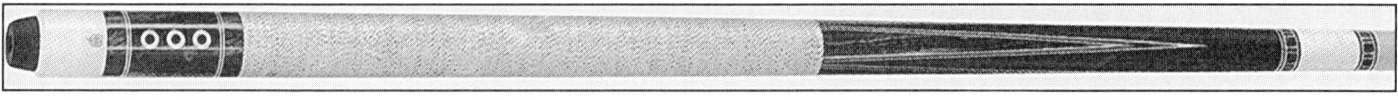

Orig. Retail $170	$795	$645	$450

Level 3 B-13 - Bird's-eye maple forearm with intricate checked ring above wrap and different maple rectangle rings at joint, four ebony points with veneers, ebony butt sleeve with ring pattern of maple veneers in a rectangular pattern between maple checks at top and bottom.

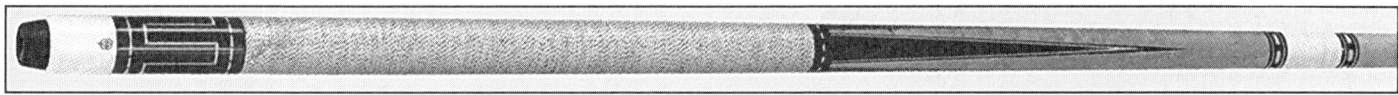

Orig. Retail $180	$835	$675	$475

GRADING	98%	90%	70%

Level 4 B-14 - Bird's-eye maple forearm with intricate maple checked rings at joint, four maple points with colored veneers, maple butt sleeve with long bordered rectangles set between maple checked rings at top and bottom.

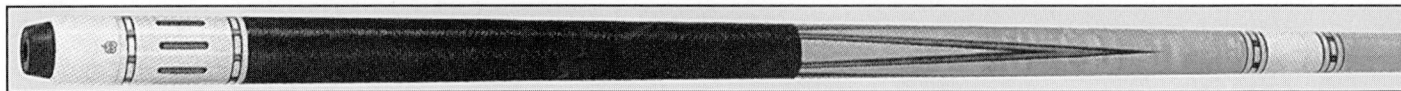

Orig. Retail $190	$850	$695	$500

Level 4 B-15 - Rosewood forearm with intricate pattern of three maple checked rings at joint, four rosewood points with colored veneers, rosewood butt sleeve with a pair of maple veneers in a triangular ring pattern split by a maple-bordered ring of ebony.

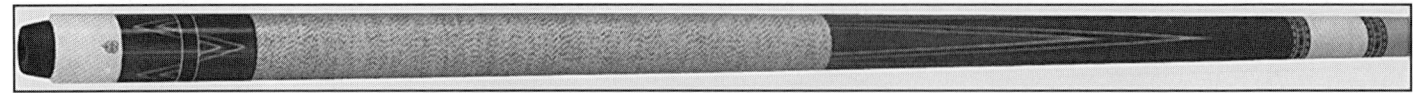

Orig. Retail $200	$880	$700	$500

Level 4 B-16 - Bird's-eye maple forearm with intricate checked rings above wrap, four ebony points with colored veneers, ebony butt sleeve with maple windows framed by colored veneers between rings of maple checks at top and bottom.

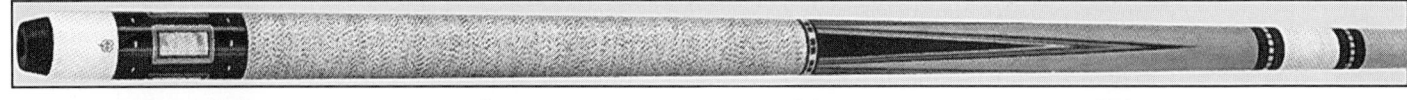

Orig. Retail $220	$1,100	$855	$635

C-LINE SERIES

The following C-line cues were produced from 1980 to 1984. Nylon wrap was standard. Leather, Irish linen, or cork wraps were available for $25 extra.

Level 1 C-1 "McDermott Hustler" - Maple forearm, four full-spliced points and handle of various dark hardwoods and the McDermott logo stamped at the bottom. (Not to be confused with the 2001 "M1-1B" which has the McDermott logo in gold, and has a brass insert in the shaft joint.)

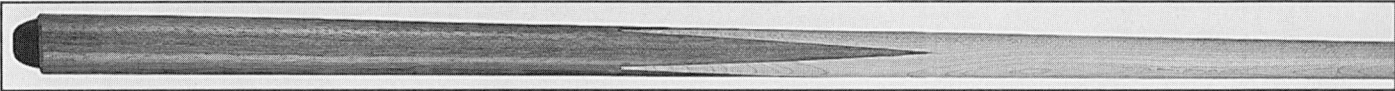

Orig. Retail (1980) $50	$500	$315	$210

Level 2 C-2 - Walnut forearm, walnut butt sleeve with black-bordered zebrawood ring at bottom.

Orig. Retail (1980) $60	$300	$265	$185

Level 2 C-3 - Bird's-eye maple forearm, butt sleeve with ring of black-bordered maple rectangles between thick wood rings above and below.

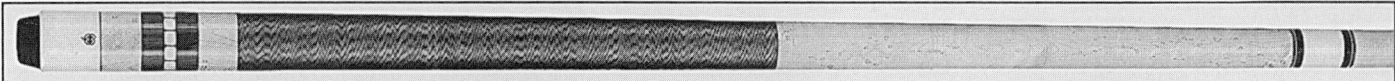

Orig. Retail (1980) $70	$355	$295	$200

Level 2 C-4 - Rosewood forearm, rosewood butt sleeve with six long thin maple inlays.

Orig. Retail (1980) $80	$380	$315	$220

Level 2 C-5 - Bird's-eye maple forearm, bird's-eye maple butt sleeve with four pearl notched diamond inlays set in rosewood windows between rosewood check rings at top and bottom.

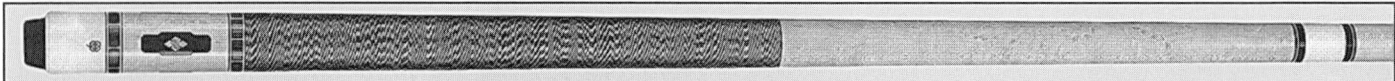

Orig. Retail (1980) $90	$395	$320	$215

GRADING	98%	90%	70%

Level 3 C-6 - Bird's-eye maple forearm, four rosewood points with colored veneers, solid rosewood butt sleeve.

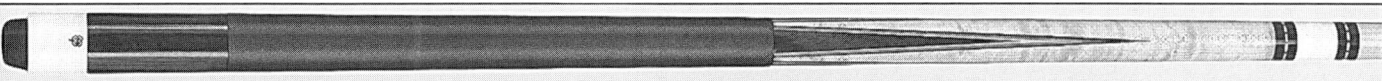

Orig. Retail (1980) $110	$600	$450	$275

Level 3 C-7 - Bird's-eye maple forearm with black rings above wrap, four maple points with black veneers, bird's-eye maple butt sleeve with black rings at top and bottom.

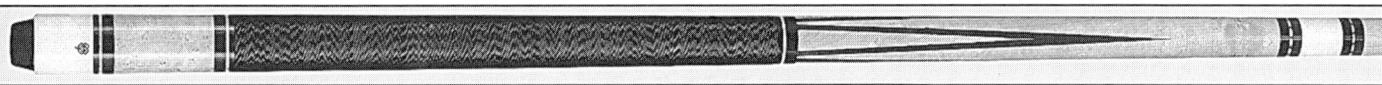

Orig. Retail (1980) $120	$650	$500	$300

Level 3 C-8 - East Indian rosewood forearm, four bird's-eye maple points with colored veneers, bird's-eye maple butt sleeve with eight long thin wood inlays between maple squares set in black rings at top and bottom.

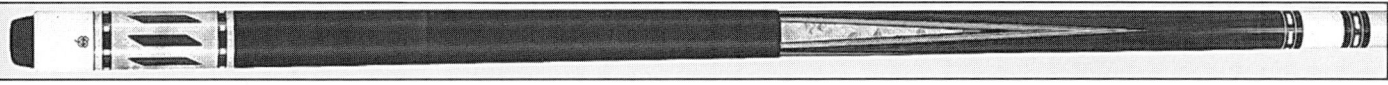

Orig. Retail (1980) $130	$675	$525	$325

Level 3 C-9 - Bird's-eye maple forearm, four cocobolo points with colored veneers, butt sleeve with six black oval inlays set in maple windows between thin tulipwood rings at top and bottom.

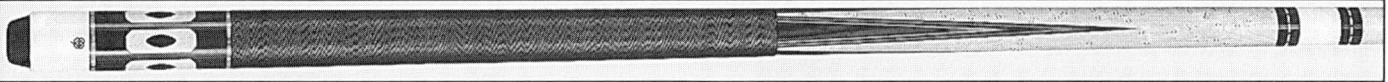

Orig. Retail (1980) $140	$685	$535	$335

Level 3 C-10 - Bird's-eye maple forearm, four ebony points with colored veneers, ebony butt sleeve with three maple long thin designs alternating with three bubinga long thin designs inlaid between thin triple rings at top and bottom.

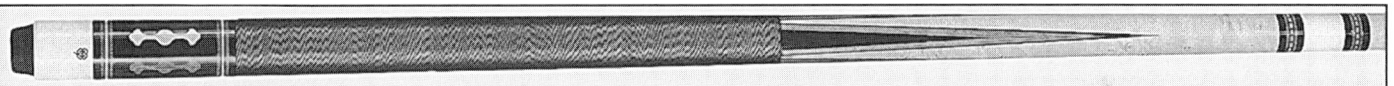

Orig. Retail (1980) $150	$750	$565	$350

Level 3 C-11 - Rosewood forearm, four bird's-eye maple points with colored veneers, bird's-eye maple butt sleeve with six pearl notched diamond-shaped inlays set in long thin patterned windows between thin triple rings at top and bottom.

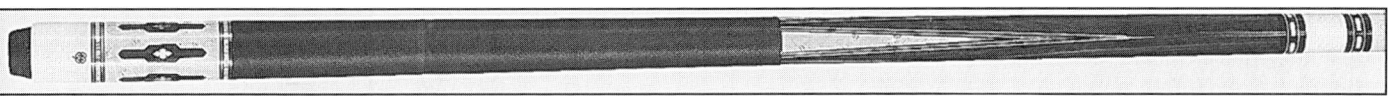

Orig. Retail (1980) $160	$785	$595	$375

Level 4 C-12 - Rosewood forearm with checked ring above wrap, four floating winding scroll designs, rosewood butt sleeve with pearl and maple inlays between checked rings at top and bottom.

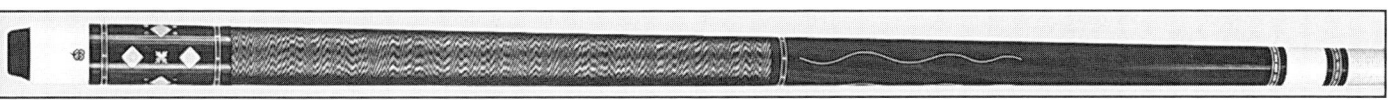

Orig. Retail (1980) $180	$800	$625	$385

Level 4 C-13 - Bird's-eye maple forearm with a black ring above wrap, two long, four medium, and two short floating black lines, bird's-eye maple butt sleeve with pearl designs set in six ebony patterned windows between black rings at top and bottom.

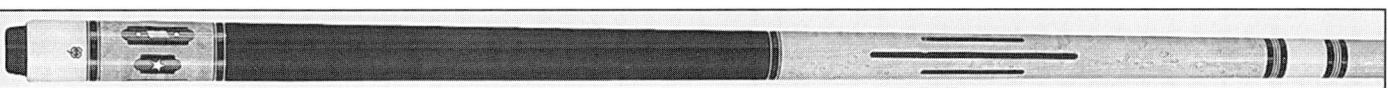

Orig. Retail (1980) $200	$850	$650	$400

Level 4 C-14 - Bird's-eye maple forearm, four ebony points with black, orange, and red veneers, ebony butt sleeve with six long thin maple diamond-shaped inlays split by smaller tulipwood diamond-shaped inlays between thin tulipwood rings at top and bottom.

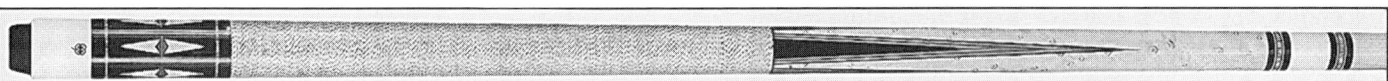

Orig. Retail (1980) $220	$900	$675	$425

GRADING	98%	90%	70%

Level 4 C-15 - Bird's-eye maple forearm, four ebony points with colored veneers, ebony butt sleeve with a pattern of small white intricate inlays between maple checked rings at top and bottom.

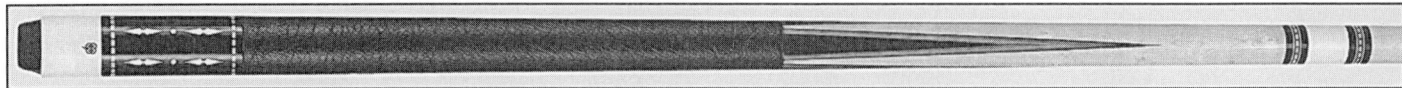

Orig. Retail (1980) $240	$925	$750	$450

Level 4 C-16 - Bird's-eye maple forearm, four ebony points with colored veneers and a pearl square-shaped inlay between two pearl dots in each point, ebony butt sleeve with pearl squares between a pattern of small white intricate inlays between maple checked ring designs at top and bottom.

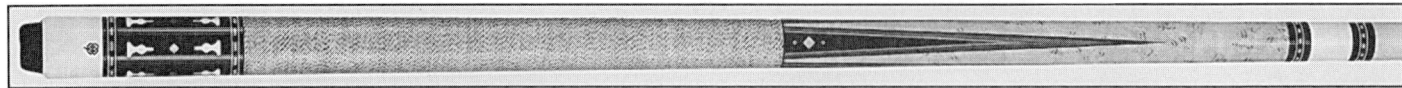

Orig. Retail (1980) $260	$1,050	$800	$500

Level 4 C-17 - Bird's-eye maple forearm, four ebony points with veneers and a pearl star-shaped inlay between two pearl dots in each point, ebony butt sleeve with pearl dots between a pattern of hollow white opposing triangular patterned inlays between pairs of thin maple rings at top and bottom.

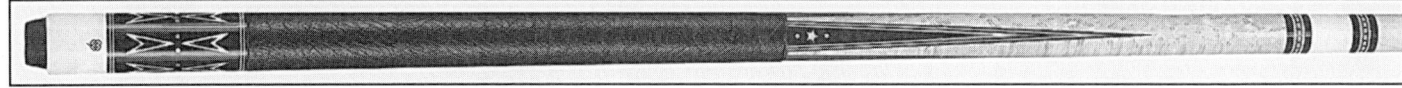

Orig. Retail (1980) $300	$1,150	$895	$550

Level 4 C-18 - Bird's-eye maple forearm, four ebony points with green and black veneers and a pearl oval-shaped inlay between two pearl dots in each point, ebony butt sleeve with six intricate hollow white inlays creating a green shamrock in the center between pearl dots and thin pairs of green rings at top and bottom.

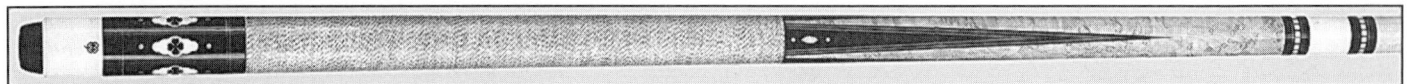

Orig. Retail (1980) $340	$1,200	$925	$575

Level 4 C-19 - Bird's-eye maple forearm, four ebony points with blue and black veneers and a pearl rectangular-shaped inlay between two pearl dots in each point, ebony butt sleeve with six long thin hollow white double triangles inlaid between two pearl dots on each side and maple check patterned rings at top and bottom.

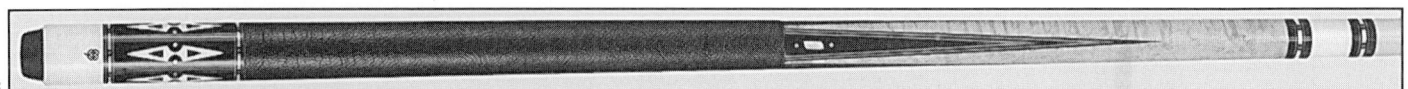

Orig. Retail (1980) $380	$1,400	$1,075	$650

Level 4 C-20 - Bird's-eye maple forearm, four ebony points with red and black veneers and a single waving scroll in each point, ebony butt sleeve with white squares inlaid with the symbols for hearts, diamonds, spades, and clubs inlaid in red and black between red and black checked rings at top and bottom.

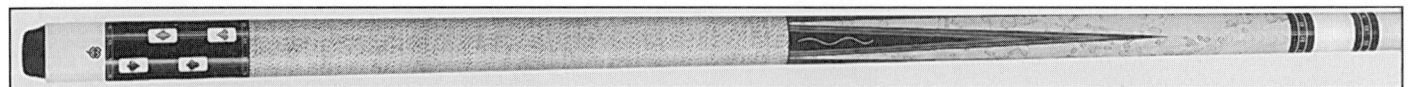

Orig. Retail (1980) $440	$1,600	$1,200	$750

Level 5 C-21 - Bird's-eye maple forearm with a checked ring above wrap, six ebony points with four pearl dots between two opposing pearl triangles above and below in each point, ebony butt sleeve with six long thin hollow intricate white patterns inlaid between checked rings at top and bottom.

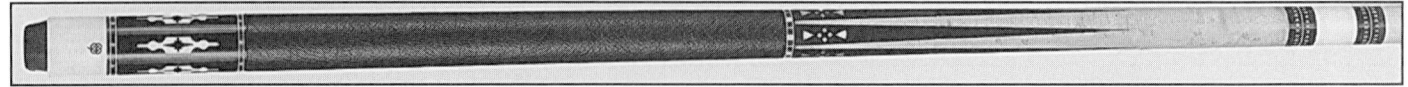

Orig. Retail (1980) $500	$1,850	$1,400	$900

D-LINE SERIES

The following D-line cues were manufactured from 1984 to 1990. Cork, leather, or Irish linen wraps were standard on Models D-14 through D-26, and were an option on the other models which came standard with nylon wrap. Wrap was not available on the D-5, which had an oak handle. All D-line cues with maple forearms were available in five different stain colors at no extra charge.

MCDERMOTT CUE MANUFACTURING INC., cont. 491

GRADING	98%	90%	70%

Level 2 D-1 - Maple forearm, maple butt sleeve.

Orig. Retail (1984) $100	$135	$110	$60

Level 2 D-2 - Walnut forearm, walnut butt sleeve with black-bordered maple ring.

Orig. Retail (1984) $105	$145	$115	$70

Level 2 D-3 - Bubinga forearm, bubinga butt sleeve with maple checked rings at top and bottom.

Orig. Retail (1984) $110	$145	$115	$70

Level 2 D-4 - Bird's-eye maple forearm, bird's-eye maple butt sleeve with bubinga-bordered rosewood rectangles in a ring pattern at bottom.

Orig. Retail (1984) $115	$150	$125	$75

Level 2 D-5 - Congo alves forearm, oak handle, Congo alves butt sleeve with central pointing rings at top and bottom.

Orig. Retail (1984) $120	$155	$130	$70

Level 2 D-6 - Bird's-eye maple forearm, bird's-eye maple butt sleeve with four black patterns with white insets inlaid between thin white rings set in thick black bands at top and bottom.

Orig. Retail (1984) $135	$160	$135	$75

Level 2 D-7 - Bird's-eye maple forearm, butt sleeve with a ring of maple diamonds in ebony between thick brown rings.

Orig. Retail (1984) $135	$165	$130	$80

Level 2 D-8 - Bird's-eye maple forearm, bird's-eye maple butt sleeve with a white waving band between ebony and maple rings bordered by ebony checked rings.

Orig. Retail (1984) $135	$170	$135	$75

Level 2 D-9 - Bird's-eye maple forearm, bird's-eye maple butt sleeve with a maple zig-zag ring in ebony between black-bordered maple checks.

Orig. Retail (1984) $135	$175	$140	$70

GRADING	98%	90%	70%

Level 2 D-10 - Rosewood forearm, rosewood butt sleeve with four black diamond-shaped inlays set in maple windows between black-bordered maple checked rings at top and bottom.

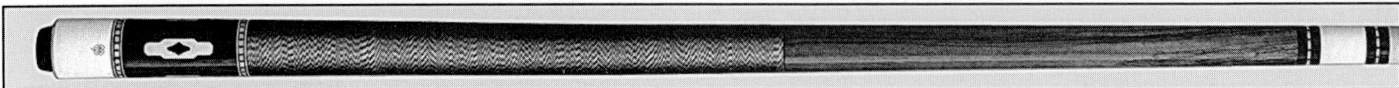

Orig. Retail (1984) $145	$185	$140	$80

Level 3 D-11 - Bird's-eye maple forearm, four walnut points with black veneers, walnut butt sleeve with an ebony hexagon ring pattern set in black-bordered maple rings.

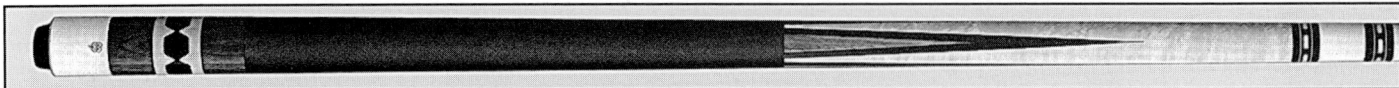

Orig. Retail (1984) $175	$445	$335	$200

Level 3 D-12 - Bird's-eye maple forearm, four bird's-eye maple points with colored veneers, bird's-eye maple butt sleeve with intricate colored checked ring.

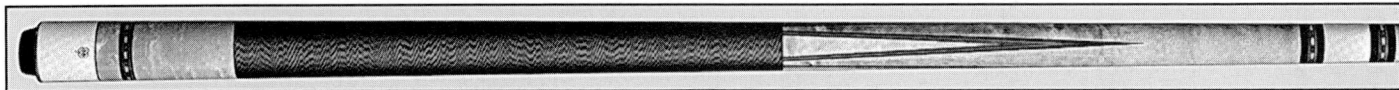

Orig. Retail (1984) $190	$475	$365	$225

Level 3 D-13 - Bird's-eye maple forearm, four cocobolo points with colored veneers, cocobolo butt sleeve with thin black-bordered maple ring between two colored rings.

Orig. Retail (1984) $200	$500	$375	$230

Level 3 D-14 - Bird's-eye maple forearm, four bird's-eye maple points with red and black veneers, bird's-eye maple butt sleeve with black-bordered thin red veneers in a figure-eight pattern between thin black-bordered red rings at top and bottom.

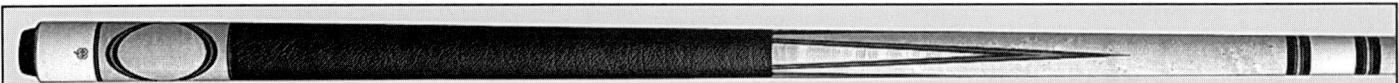

Orig. Retail (1984) $230	$575	$420	$220

Level 3 D-15 - Bird's-eye maple forearm, four cocobolo points with colored veneers, cocobolo butt sleeve with black-bordered maple check rings at top and bottom.

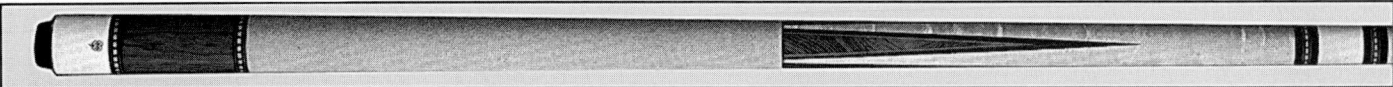

Orig. Retail (1984)$245	$550	$415	$250

Level 4 D-16 - Rosewood forearm, four rosewood points with colored veneers, rosewood butt sleeve with thin colored rings set between colored veneers in opposing double arches between colored rings at top and bottom.

Orig. Retail (1984) $265	$600	$445	$275

Level 4 D-17 - Bird's-eye maple forearm, four ebony points with colored veneers, ebony butt sleeve with four white-bordered green windows inset with white three-piece diamond shapes between thin white-bordered green rings above and below.

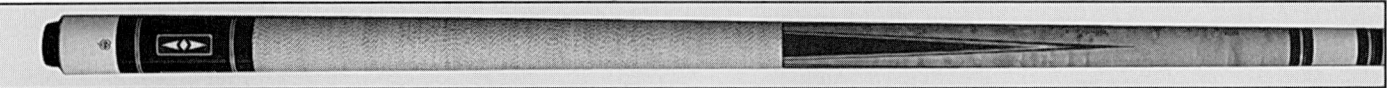

Orig. Retail (1984) $290	$585	$435	$270

MCDERMOTT CUE MANUFACTURING INC., cont. 493

GRADING	98%	90%	70%

Level 4 D-18 - Bird's-eye maple forearm, four tulipwood points with black veneers, ebony butt sleeve with four tulipwood-bordered ebony windows inlaid with five-piece tulipwood designs.

Orig. Retail (1984) $310	$600	$450	$275

Level 4 D-19 - Bird's-eye maple forearm, three long and three short ebony points with veneers, ebony butt sleeve with pairs of three-piece dice inlays between white-bordered black rings above and below.

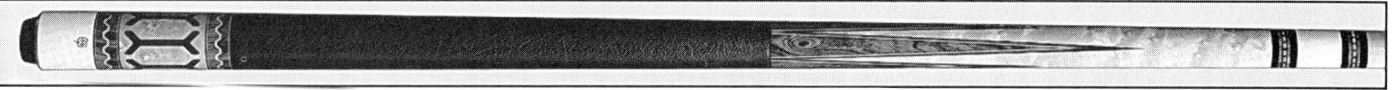

Orig. Retail (1984) $340	$975	$725	$450

Level 4 D-20 - Bird's-eye maple forearm, three long and three short cocobolo points with veneers, bird's-eye maple butt sleeve with "Y"-ended ebony inlays between pairs of thick patterned cocbolo rings at top and bottom.

Orig. Retail (1984) $340	$700	$550	$335

Level 4 D-21 - Bird's-eye maple forearm, three long and three short ebony points with red and black veneers, butt sleeve with four white diamond-shaped inlays connected by thin red lines in black rectangles set in black and red bordered maple windows between pairs of thick patterned black rings at top and bottom.

Orig. Retail (1984) $340	$685	$530	$330

Level 4 D-22 - Bird's-eye maple forearm, three long and three short tulipwood points with colored veneers, butt sleeve with four blue-bordered maple windows inlaid with five-piece multi-colored designs between pairs of thick patterned tulipwood rings at top and bottom.

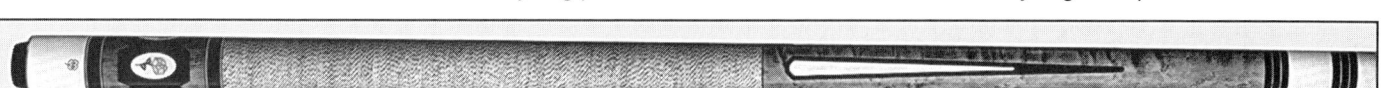

Orig. Retail (1984) $340	$675	$525	$325

Level 4 D-23 - Bird's-eye maple forearm, four floating ebony-bordered white points, maple butt sleeve with green and red images of roses set in four white ovals inlaid in an ebony ring pattern between white-bordered thick ebony rings at top and bottom.

Orig. Retail (1984) $340	$725	$550	$350

Level 4 D-24 - Bird's-eye maple forearm inlaid with a series of floating black-bordered tulipwood patterned windows, maple butt sleeve with black-bordered tulipwood patterned windows set in four ebony and tulipwood-bordered maple rectangles.

Orig. Retail (1984) $340	$600	$450	$285

Level 5 D-25 - Bird's-eye maple forearm inlaid with a series of red-bordered white and ebony rectangles of varying sizes, bird's-eye maple butt sleeve with four black- and red-bordered bird's-eye maple windows inlaid with a pattern of large red-bordered ebony rectangles overlaid with two small red-bordered white rectangles at top and bottom.

Orig. Retail (1984) $560	$850	$650	$400

GRADING	98%	90%	70%

Level 5 D-26 - Bird's-eye maple forearm, four floating ebony inlays with short red lines running to the center of small white circles at top and bottom, black butt sleeve with four white-bordered black windows inlaid with three small white circles that appear to be pierced by a red line with thin white solid and checked rings at top and bottom.

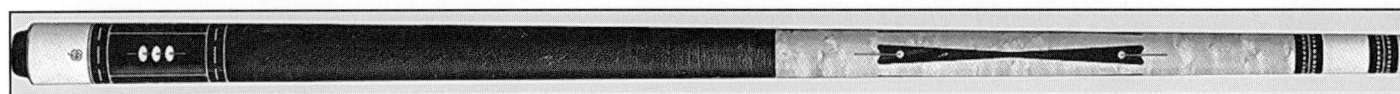

Orig. Retail (1984) $560	$675	$495	$315

"WILDLIFE SERIES"

The following "Wildlife Series" cues were manufactured from 1987 to 1988. Cork, leather, or Irish linen wraps were standard.

Level 2 WL-1 - Maple forearm with the image of grass inlaid in multi-colored dymond wood, maple butt sleeve with the image of fish jumping inlaid in multi-colored dymond wood.

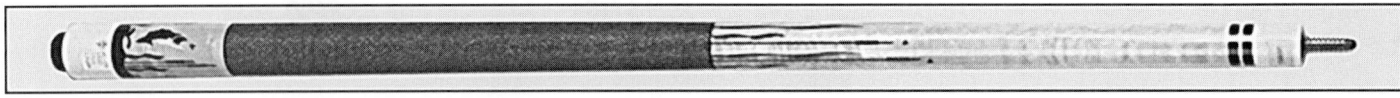

	$855	$650	$410

Level 2 WL-2 - Maple forearm with the image of a whitetail doe in trees inlaid in multi-colored dymond wood, maple butt sleeve with the image of a white tail buck in trees inlaid in multi-colored dymond wood.

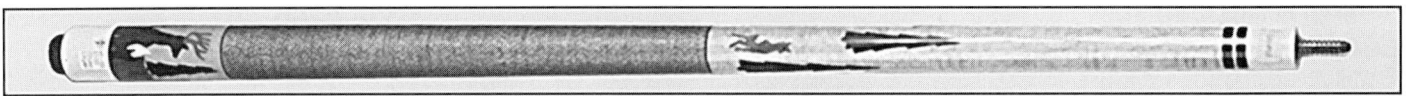

	$860	$645	$400

Level 2 WL-3 - Maple forearm with the image of geese inlaid in multi-colored dymond wood, maple butt sleeve with the image of geese flying over barbed-wire fence inlaid in multi-colored dymond wood.

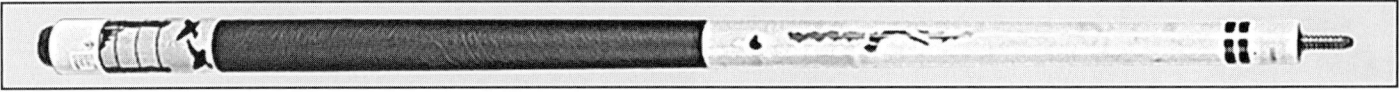

	$845	$635	$415

Level 2 WL-4 - Maple forearm with the image of a duck flying over grass inlaid in multi-colored dymond wood, maple butt sleeve with the image of duck flying over hunting dog inlaid in multi-colored dymond wood.

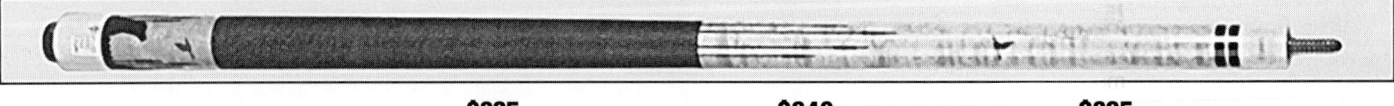

	$825	$640	$395

Level 2 WL-5 - Maple forearm with the image of a flock of geese inlaid in multi-colored dymond wood, maple butt sleeve with the image of a flock of geese inlaid in multi-colored dymond wood.

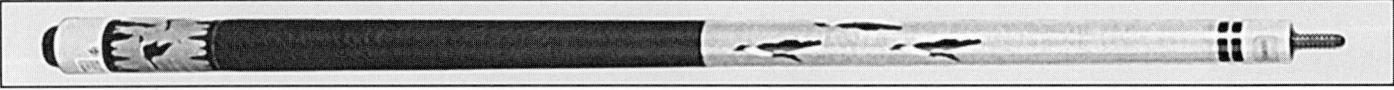

	$865	$650	$400

Level 2 WL-6 - Maple forearm with the image of bear cubs climbing trees inlaid in multi-colored dymond wood, maple butt sleeve with the image of bears and mountains inlaid in multi-colored dymond wood.

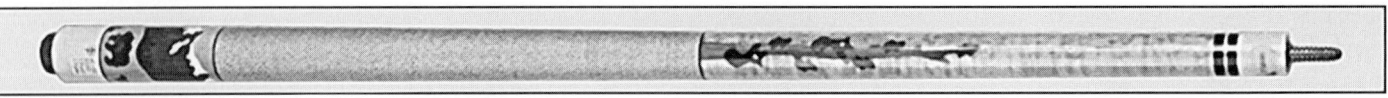

	$850	$645	$405

HD-LINE (HARLEY DAVIDSON SERIES)

The following HD-line (Harley Davidson Series) cues were produced under license from 1988 to 1993. Leather, Irish linen, or cork wraps were standard on Models HD-2 and HD-3, and were available as options on the other cues, which came standard with nylon wrap. Red, blue, or black stains were available on the HD-4 through HD-7 cues. Models HD-4 through HD-7 featured reproductions of the art of Blaine Heilman.

GRADING	98%	90%	70%

Level 2 HD-1 The Classic - Grey-stained bird's-eye maple forearm, ebony butt sleeve with the Harley Davidson bar and shield emblem between double orange rings at top and bottom.

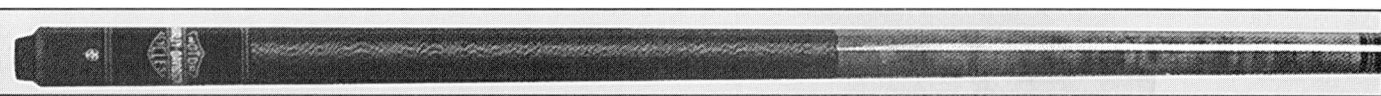

| Orig. Retail (1988) $190 | $655 | $500 | $320 |

Level 3 HD-2 The Script - Red stained bird's-eye maple forearm, four ebony points with colored veneers, ebony butt sleeve with the updated Harley Davidson script emblem inlaid between double red rings at top and bottom.

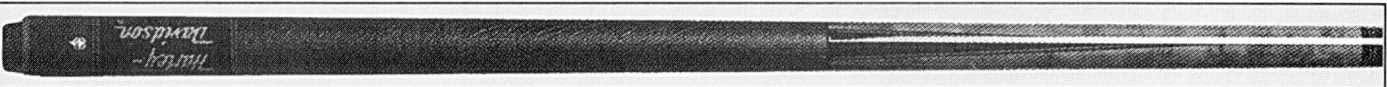

| Orig. Retail (1988) $290 | $900 | $675 | $425 |

Level 3 HD-3 The Eagle - Grey-stained bird's-eye maple forearm, three long and three short cocobolo points with veneers, cocobolo butt sleeve with eagle's head and Harley Davidson bar and shield logo inlaid between white-bordered thin black rings at top and bottom.

| Orig. Retail (1988) $390 | $1,200 | $900 | $550 |

Level 2 HD-4 - Maple forearm with applied image of a wolf above a motorcycle and rider, maple butt sleeve with applied image of the Harley Davidson bar and shield emblem.

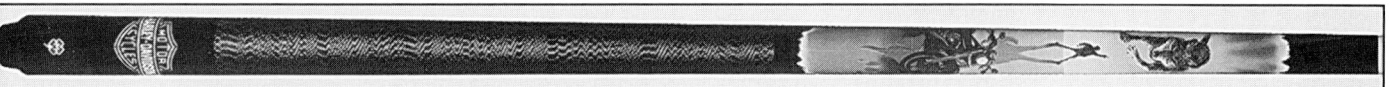

| Orig. Retail (1992) $250 | $325 | $250 | $150 |

Level 2 HD-5 - Maple forearm with applied image of an eagle's head leading "Harley Davidson" in red white and blue letters, maple butt sleeve with applied image of an eagle breaking through an eight-ball rack.

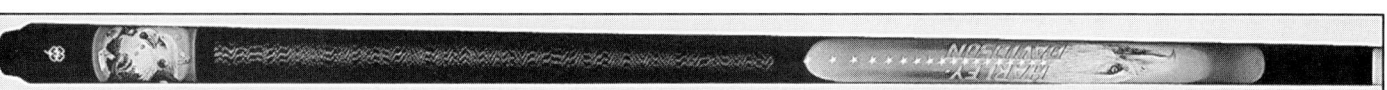

| Orig. Retail (1992) $250 | $330 | $260 | $160 |

Level 2 HD-6 - Maple forearm with applied image of an eagle and wolf over a Harley rider traveling a road at night with "Harley Davidson" above wrap, maple butt sleeve with applied image of a forward view of a Harley Davidson rider traveling a road at night.

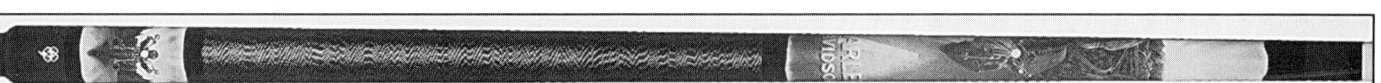

| Orig. Retail (1992) $250 | $320 | $255 | $155 |

Level 2 HD-7 - Maple forearm with applied image of an eagle projecting from the headlight beam of a Harley Davidson rider going by a billiards parlor in the desert, maple butt sleeve with applied image of an eight-ball rack in front of the earth with lightning bolts projecting from the sides.

| Orig. Retail (1992) $250 | $335 | $255 | $150 |

E-A SERIES

The following E-line cues were introduced in 1990 and have since been discontinued. Aside from the E-D series cues and E-A1 and E-A3, which were cues without wraps, all came with standard nylon wrap except for the E-F5 and E-J4 through E-J6, which came with leather, Irish linen, or cork wraps.

GRADING	98%	90%	70%

Level 2 E-A1 - Solid mahogany butt.

Orig. Retail (1990) $95 $100 $85 $50

Level 2 E-A2 - Solid mahogany butt, cut for wrap.

Orig. Retail (1990) $105 $125 $95 $60

Level 2 E-A3 - Solid mahogany butt with a three-piece dymond wood spear-shaped inlay around an oval.

Orig. Retail (1990) $120 $135 $100 $60

Level 2 E-A4 - Solid mahogany butt cut for wrap, with a six-piece duck inlaid in dymond wood.

Orig. Retail (1990) $135 $150 $105 $70

Level 2 E-A5 - Solid mahogany butt cut for wrap, with black and red dymond wood inlays which create images of the four-card suites in the mahogany between them.

Orig. Retail (1990) $135 $155 $110 $65

Level 2 E-A6 - Solid mahogany butt cut for wrap, with four green dymond wood points with black veneers, with two-piece dragon shaped green dymond wood inlays.

Orig. Retail (1990) $155 $165 $115 $75

"E-B" SERIES

Nylon wraps were standard on the following E-B Series cues, until 1998 when Irish linen was standard. These E-B series cues were discontinued in 1999 for new versions with stainless steel joints.

Level 2 E-B1 - Royal navy-stained maple forearm and butt sleeve.

MSR(1998) $185 $175 $140 $90

Level 2 E-B2 - Charcoal grey-stained maple forearm and butt sleeve.

MSR(1998) $185 $160 $135 $95

Level 2 E-B3 - Dark English-stained maple forearm and butt sleeve.

MSR(1998) $185 $170 $140 $90

MCDERMOTT CUE MANUFACTURING INC., cont. **497**

GRADING	98%	90%	70%

Level 2 E-B4 - Deep violet-stained maple forearm and butt sleeve.

MSR(1998) $185	$165	$135	$85

Level 2 E-B5 - Ruby red-stained maple forearm and butt sleeve.

MSR(1998) $185	$160	$135	$90

Level 2 E-B6 - Black onyx-stained maple butt, no wrap.

MSR(1998) $185	$170	$145	$95

Level 2 E-B6JW - Same as above, except butt is jointed and breaks down into a jump cue.

MSR(1998) $215	$175	$155	$110

Level 2 E-B7 - Black onyx-stained maple forearm and butt sleeve (with Irish linen wrap).

MSR(1998) $185	$160	$135	$90

Level 2 E-B7JW - Same as above, except butt is jointed and breaks down into a jump cue.

MSR(1998) $215	$175	$150	$105

Level 2 E-B8 - Teal-stained maple forearm and butt sleeve.

MSR(1998) $185	$170	$145	$90

Level 2 E-B9 - Emerald green-stained maple forearm and butt sleeve.

MSR(1998) $185	$160	$135	$85

Level 2 E-B10 - Rich maple-stained forearm and butt sleeve.

MSR(1998) $185	$165	$140	$95

Level 2 E-B11 - Amethyst-stained maple forearm and butt sleeve.

MSR(1998) $185	$160	$135	$90

MCDERMOTT CUE MANUFACTURING INC., cont.

GRADING	98%	90%	70%

Level 2 E-B12 - Pearl white-stained maple forearm and butt sleeve.

MSR(1998) $215	$185	$155	$105

"E-C" SERIES

Level 2 E-C1 - Neon green-painted maple forearm, neon green-painted maple butt sleeve.

Orig. Retail (1990) $165	$170	$120	$85

Level 2 E-C2 - Neon pink-painted maple forearm, neon pink-painted maple butt sleeve.

Orig. Retail (1990) $165	$180	$120	$80

Level 2 E-C3 - Neon yellow-painted maple forearm, neon yellow-painted maple butt sleeve.

Orig. Retail (1990) $165	$175	$125	$85

Level 2 E-C4 - Neon red-painted maple forearm, neon red-painted maple butt sleeve.

Orig. Retail (1990) $165	$185	$130	$80

Level 2 E-C5 - Neon orange-painted maple forearm, neon orange-painted maple butt sleeve.

Orig. Retail (1990) $165	$185	$125	$80

"E-D" SERIES

Level 1 E-D1 - Maple forearm, grey dymond wood butt with three long and three short spliced points.

Orig. Retail (1990) $150	$170	$125	$75

Level 1 E-D2 - Maple forearm, bocote butt with three long and three short spliced points.

Orig. Retail (1990) $150	$165	$130	$80

Level 1 E-D3 - Maple forearm, cocobolo butt with three long and three short spliced points.

Orig. Retail (1990) $150	$160	$125	$65

MCDERMOTT CUE MANUFACTURING INC., cont. 499

GRADING	98%	90%	70%

Level 1 E-D4 - Maple forearm, green dymond wood butt with three long and three short spliced points.

Orig. Retail (1990) $150	$160	$135	$75

Level 1 E-D5 - Maple forearm, blue dymond wood butt with three long and three short spliced points.

Orig. Retail (1990) $150	$170	$130	$70

Level 1 E-D6 - Maple forearm, red dymond wood butt with three long and three short spliced points.

Orig. Retail (1990) $150	$165	$135	$75

"E-F" SERIES

Level 3 E-F5 - Maple forearm with six black onyx colored points, black onyx colored butt sleeve.

Orig. Retail (1990) $275	$290	$230	$140

Level 3 E-F6 - Maple forearm with three long and three short rosewood points, intricate rings at top and bottom of butt sleeve.

MSR(1996) $325	$295	$255	$185

Level 3 E-F7 - Maple forearm with six black onyx colored points, black onyx colored butt sleeve with two images of roses.

MSR(1996) $325	$275	$255	$175

Level 3 E-F8 - Maple forearm with four black ebony points with veneers, black ebony butt sleeve with white stars and checked rings.

MSR(1996) $359	$310	$275	$200

"E-G" SERIES

All "E-G" series cues had a single checked joint ring on both butt and shaft.

Level 2 E-G1 - Bird's-eye maple forearm, cocobolo butt sleeve with solid rings.

MSR(1996) $175	$165	$125	$90

Level 2 E-G2 - Bird's-eye maple forearm, red-stained butt sleeve with a checked index ring between solid rings.

MSR(1996) $195	$175	$140	$95

| GRADING | 98% | 90% | 70% |

Level 2 E-G3 - Bird's-eye maple forearm, butt sleeve with a checked index ring between solid rings.

| MSR(1996) $195 | $180 | $145 | $100 |

Level 2 E-G4 - Bird's-eye maple forearm, maple butt sleeve with a pair of checked rings, both between solid rings.

| MSR(1996) $205 | $195 | $155 | $105 |

Level 2 E-G5 - Bird's-eye maple forearm, maple butt sleeve with a pair of stitched rings between blue-stained solid rings.

| MSR(1996) $230 | $225 | $185 | $120 |

Level 2 E-G6 - Bird's-eye maple forearm, maple windows between solid rings in butt sleeve.

| MSR(1996) $235 | $210 | $175 | $105 |

Level 2 E-G7 - Bird's-eye maple forearm, maple butt sleeve with a ring of ruby red hearts between two checked index rings.

| MSR(1996) $235 | $225 | $185 | $110 |

"E-H" SERIES

Level 2 E-H3 - Maple forearm, cocobolo butt sleeve with a pair of six-piece eagle inlays between black-bordered thin maple rings at top and bottom.

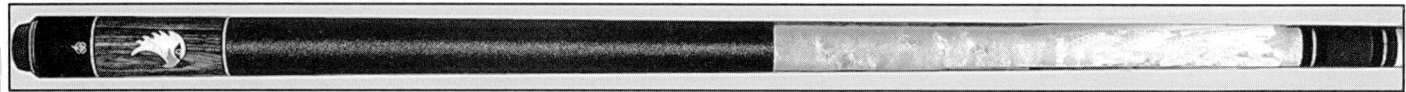

| Orig. Retail (1990) $190 | $220 | $155 | $100 |

Level 2 E-H4 - Maple forearm, maple butt sleeve with cocobolo steer head inlays arranged in a pair of opposing ring patterns between black-bordered maple checks and cocobolo rings at top and bottom.

| Orig. Retail (1990) $195 | $235 | $160 | $105 |

Level 2 E-H5 - Maple forearm, maple butt sleeve with black elephant inlays arranged in a ring pattern between black-bordered maple checks and thick black rings at top and bottom.

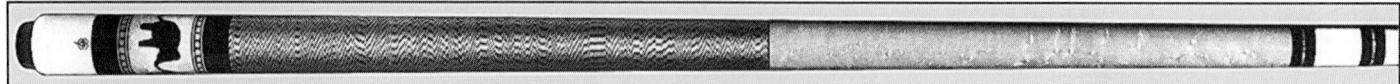

| Orig. Retail (1990) $195 | $225 | $165 | $100 |

Level 2 E-H6 - Maple forearm, maple butt sleeve with a pair of six-piece penguin inlays between inward-pointing black patterned rings at top and bottom.

| Orig. Retail (1990) $225 | $245 | $185 | $115 |

| GRADING | 98% | 90% | 70% |

"E-I" SERIES

The following "E-I" Series cues featured reproductions of the art of Wisconsin native, Wes Spencer.

Level 2 E-I3 - Maple forearm with image of a cue ball being struck by a cue, maple butt sleeve with image of an eight-ball rack on one side and a nine-ball rack on the other.

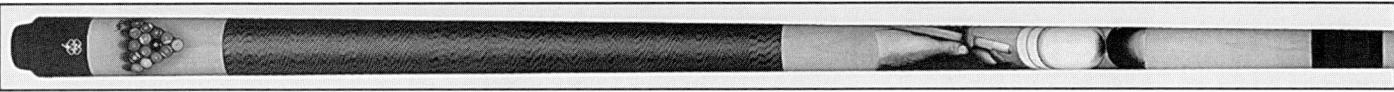

| MSR(1996) $235 | $235 | $180 | $110 |

Level 2 E-I4 - Maple forearm with image of an eagle landing on a tree stump, maple butt sleeve with image of an eagle flying over a stream.

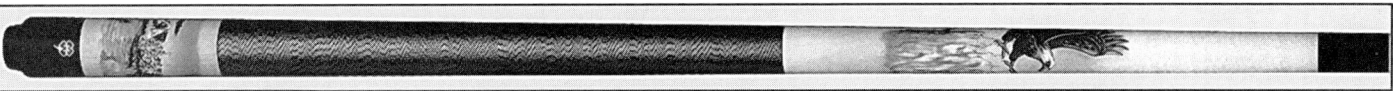

| Orig. Retail (1990) $235 | $245 | $190 | $110 |

Level 2 E-I6 - Maple forearm with battle scene showing soldiers, tanks, ships, and aircraft, maple butt sleeve with image of American eagle clutching two U.S. flags.

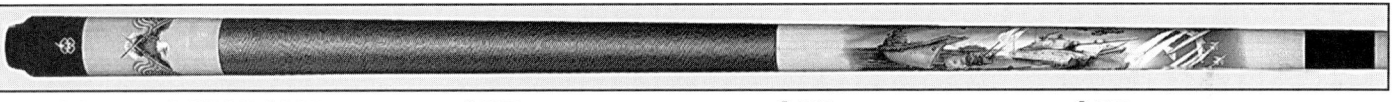

| Orig. Retail (1990) $235 | $255 | $195 | $120 |

"E-J" SERIES

Level 2 E-J2 - Bird's-eye maple forearm with multiple colored butterflies inlaid around three green dymond wood blades of grass, maple butt sleeve with multiple colored butterflies inlaid between black-bordered tulipwood rings at top and bottom.

| Orig. Retail (1990) $295 | $325 | $235 | $155 |

Level 2 E-J3 - Bird's-eye maple forearm inlaid with multiple colored hot air balloons, maple butt sleeve with multiple colored hot air balloon inlays over a green dymond wood landscape between thin black rings at top and bottom.

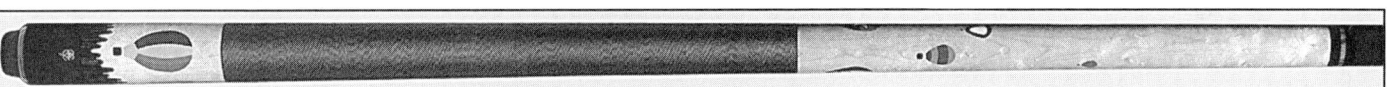

| Orig. Retail (1990) $350 | $365 | $295 | $180 |

Level 3 E-J4 - Bird's-eye maple forearm, three floating blue dymond wood-bordered white floating points with an ebony black cat inlaid below each, blue dymond wood butt sleeve with four ebony black cat inlays set in thick white base with block border at top between thin white rings at top and bottom.

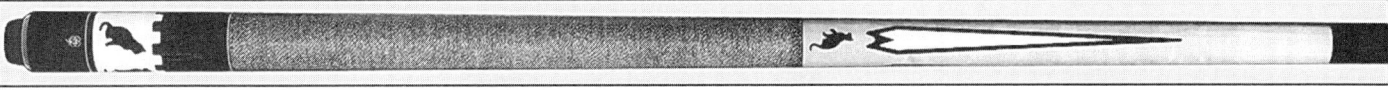

| Orig. Retail (1990) $395 | $425 | $325 | $200 |

Level 4 E-J5 - Bird's-eye maple forearm, three floating cocobolo-bordered white points, cocobolo butt sleeve with three different multiple-piece Teddy Bear inlays set in connected white ovals between thin white rings at top and bottom.

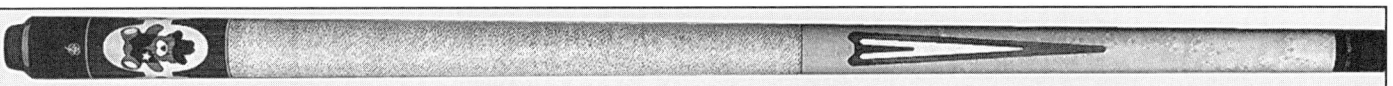

| Orig. Retail (1990) $450 | $485 | $380 | $230 |

Level 5 E-J6 - Bird's-eye maple forearm, three floating ebony-bordered white points with three different multiple-piece bird inlays below each, ebony butt sleeve with three different multiple-piece birds inlaid in large white rounded top windows between thin white rings at top and bottom.

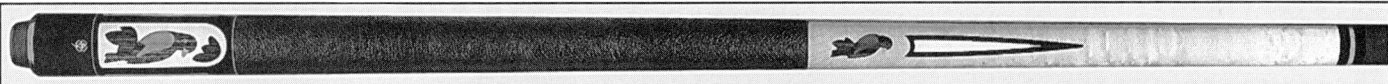

| Orig. Retail (1990) $495 | $535 | $395 | $245 |

| GRADING | 98% | 90% | 70% |

"E-K" SERIES

All "E-K" series cues featured standard traditional stainless steel joints and Irish linen wraps.

Level 3 E-K1 - Bird's-eye maple forearm, four floating intricate black split points, black onyx butt sleeve with four intricate split inlays.

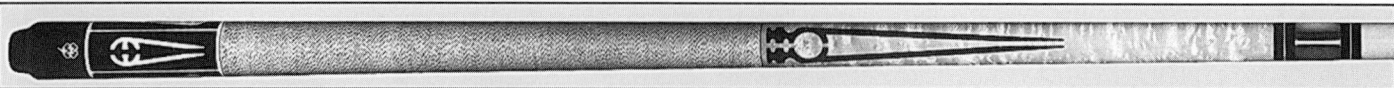

| Orig. Retail (1996) $360 | $325 | $265 | $175 |

Level 4 E-K2 - Bird's-eye maple forearm, four floating split points, cocobolo and black onyx butt sleeve with white ovals and checked rings at top and bottom.

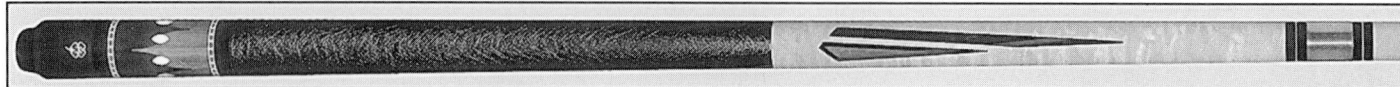

| Orig. Retail (1996) $395 | $365 | $285 | $205 |

Level 4 E-K3 - Bird's-eye maple forearm, four intricate black floating split points, butt sleeve with four intricate black inlay chess pieces within split maple windows and checked rings at top and bottom.

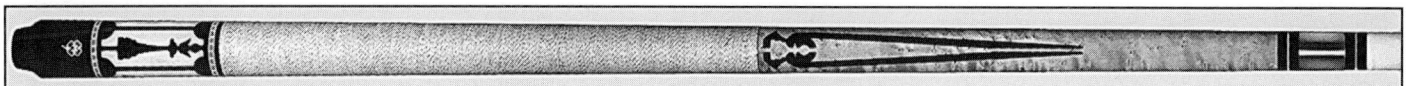

| Orig. Retail (1996) $480 | $425 | $345 | $275 |

Level 4 E-K4 - Bird's-eye maple forearm, four black floating split points with single pearl inlays in each piece, butt sleeve with six notched pearl squares within black-white design.

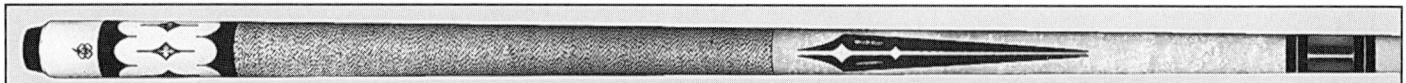

| Orig. Retail (1996) $545 | $455 | $385 | $300 |

Level 4 E-K5 - Bird's-eye maple forearm, three long and three short floating points, black onyx butt sleeve with intricate pattern of red and pearl inlays.

| Orig. Retail (1996) $600 | $495 | $410 | $315 |

Level 4 E-K6 - Bird's-eye maple forearm, four small dark blue floating spears between intricate black split points, butt sleeve with intricate black-white and dark blue pattern of inlays.

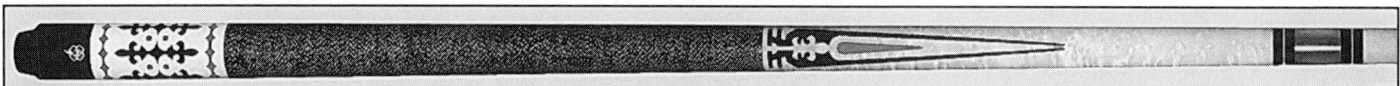

| Orig. Retail (1996) $665 | $550 | $445 | $365 |

"E-L" SERIES

The following "E-L" series cues featured reproductions of the art of Wisconsin native, Terry Doughty.

Level 2 E-L2 - Maple forearm with image of stalking tiger, maple butt sleeve with image of tiger's head.

| Orig. Retail (1996) $235 | $190 | $165 | $130 |

Level 2 E-L3 - Maple forearm with image of two American eagles, maple butt sleeve with image of eagle's head.

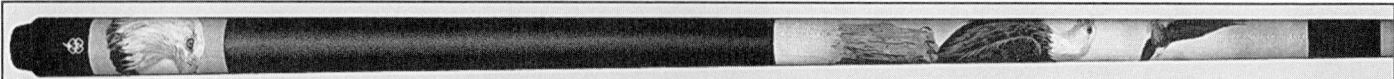

| Orig. Retail (1996) $235 | $200 | $170 | $130 |

MCDERMOTT CUE MANUFACTURING INC., cont. 503

GRADING	98%	90%	70%

Level 2 E-L4 - Maple forearm with image of whitetail deer and elk, maple butt sleeve with image of moose head.

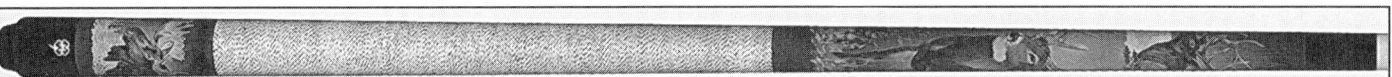

Orig. Retail (1996) $235	$195	$165	$125

Level 2 E-L5 - Maple forearm with image of two great horned owls, maple butt sleeve with image of owl's head.

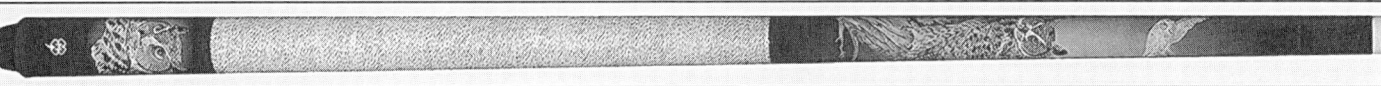

Orig. Retail (1996) $235	$190	$170	$130

"E-M" (MASTERPIECE SERIES)

All "E-M" (Masterpiece Series) Cues featured the patented stainless steel "Centric" joint, came with two shafts and joint protectors, came with Irish linen or leather wrap at no extra charge, and included a "Super Mac" tube case with the Masterpiece logo engraved on the solid wood end of the cap.

Level 6 E-M 1a - Bird's-eye maple forearm, six multicolored, intricately inlaid points with small spears at tip of each and floating inlays between them, multicolored intricate inlays featuring six hollow inlaid windows between winding scroll ring patterns in a black onyx butt sleeve and butt cap. The b & c variations are the different color schemes available for the inlays on this cue.

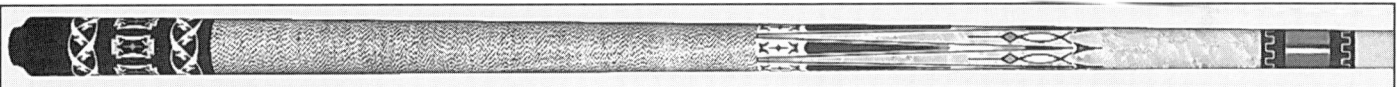

Orig. Retail (1996) $2,000	$1,200	$900	$550

Level 6 E-M 2b - Bird's-eye maple forearm, six floating multicolored concentrically inlaid points just above and between six hollow inlaid windows, multicolored intricate inlays featuring large inlaid hollow windows between smaller inlaid hollow windows above and below in a black onyx butt sleeve and butt cap. The a & c variations are the different color schemes available for the inlays on this cue.

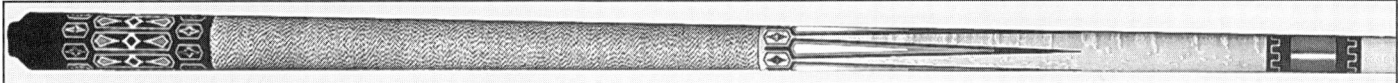

Orig. Retail (1996) $2,000	$1,250	$950	$600

Level 6 E-M 3b - Bird's-eye maple forearm, six multicolored intricately inlaid points with small spears at tips of each and floating curl inlays between them, multicolored intricate inlays featuring long inlaid hollow upward pointing triangles above intricate scroll and below a pattern of intricate circles and diamond shapes in a ring pattern in a black onyx butt sleeve above a short white butt cap. The a & c variations are the different color schemes available for the inlays on this cue.

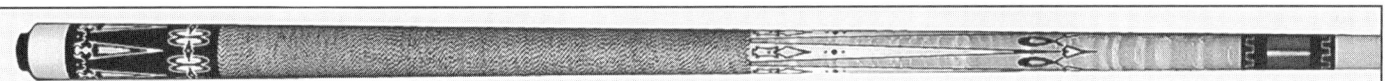

Orig. Retail (1996) $2,000	$1,100	$925	$525

Level 6 E-M 4c - Bird's-eye maple forearm, three long floating and three short standard multicolored intricately inlaid points, multicolored intricate inlays in ring patterns in a black onyx butt sleeve and butt cap. The a & b variations are the different color schemes available for the inlays on this cue.

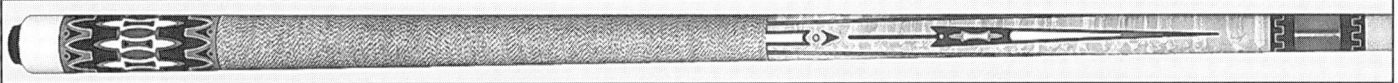

Orig. Retail (1996) $2,000	$1,150	$875	$575

Level 6 E-M 5a - Bird's-eye maple forearm, three long and three short multicolored intricately inlaid points with concentric diamond-shaped inlays above and between two very small circles at the tips of each, long and short alternating hollow multicolored intricate inlays between dots in a cornered veneer ring pattern in a black onyx butt sleeve and butt cap. The b & c variations are the different color schemes available for the inlays on this cue.

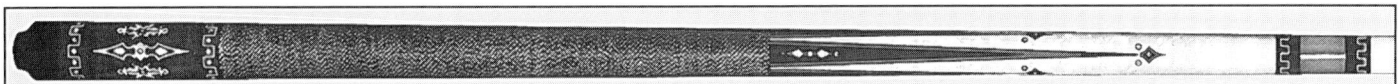

Orig. Retail (1996) $2,000	$1,200	$900	$550

| GRADING | 98% | 90% | 70% |

Level 6 E-M 6a - Bird's-eye maple forearm, six multicolored intricately inlaid points with three points that come down from joint and meet every other upward point at a diamond-shaped hollow inlay, hollow inlaid rectangular multicolored intricate inlays in a ring pattern between ring patterns of "X" shapes and diamond shapes in the black onyx butt sleeve and butt cap. The b & c variations are the different color schemes available for the inlays on this cue.

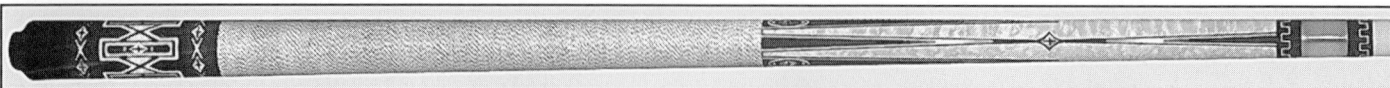

| Orig. Retail (1996) $2,000 | $1,200 | $900 | $575 |

"E-N" SERIES

All "E-N" Series cues were available with Irish linen or leather wrap at no extra charge.

Level 3 E-N1 - Bird's-eye maple forearm, four jet black points with red veneers, black onyx butt sleeve with four V-shaped white inlays with red inserts in the Vs.

| Orig. Retail (1996) $325 | $285 | $230 | $170 |

Level 4 E-N2 - Bird's-eye maple forearm, four jet black points with white veneers, black onyx butt sleeve with series of white long "S" scrolls inlaid in an upward ring pattern.

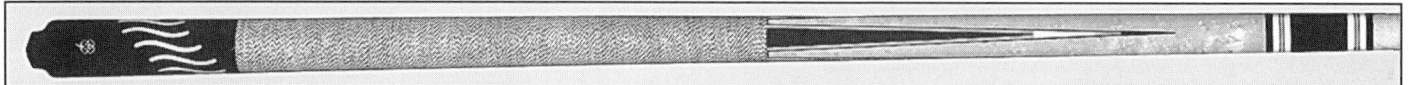

| Orig. Retail (1996) $325 | $270 | $225 | $165 |

Level 3 E-N3 - Bird's-eye maple forearm, four jet black points with white veneers, black onyx butt sleeve with hollow white diamond-shaped inlays with V-shaped red inserts.

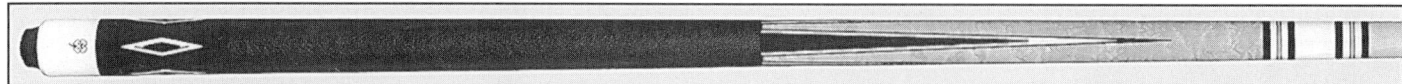

| Orig. Retail (1996) $325 | $280 | $235 | $165 |

Level 3 E-N4 - Bird's-eye maple forearm, four jet black points with white veneers, black onyx butt sleeve with white waving ring with black onyx triangles inlaid in and above with pairs of thin white rings at top and bottom.

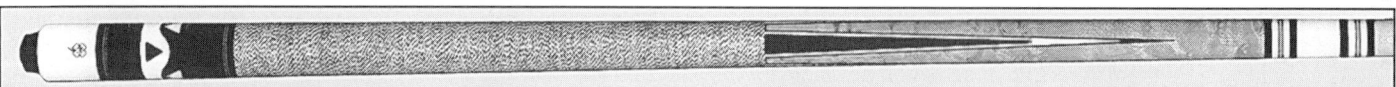

| Orig. Retail (1996) $325 | $275 | $225 | $170 |

Level 3 E-N5 - Bird's-eye maple forearm, four jet black points with red veneers, black onyx butt sleeve with four hollow red double diamond-shaped inlays with white double diamond-shaped inserts.

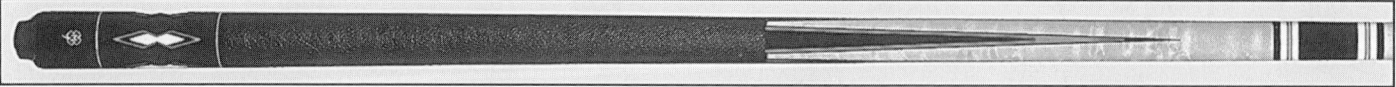

| Orig. Retail (1996) $325 | $270 | $230 | $165 |

Level 4 E-N6 - Bird's-eye maple forearm, four jet black points with white veneers and hollow white spear shapes inlaid in each point, black onyx butt sleeve with hollow white spear-shaped inlays above and below a ring of white semi-circles.

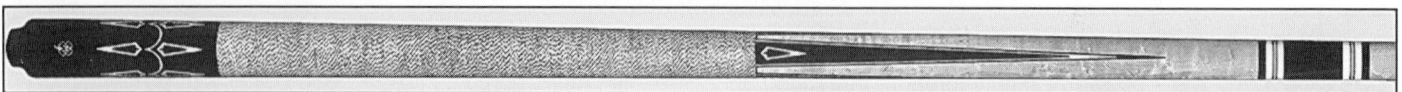

| Orig. Retail (1996) $450 | $390 | $325 | $240 |

Level 4 E-N7 - Bird's-eye maple forearm, three long jet black points with red veneers and three short jet black points with white veneers, black onyx butt sleeve with white diamond-shaped inlays between intricate red patterns and white checks in a ring pattern at top and bottom.

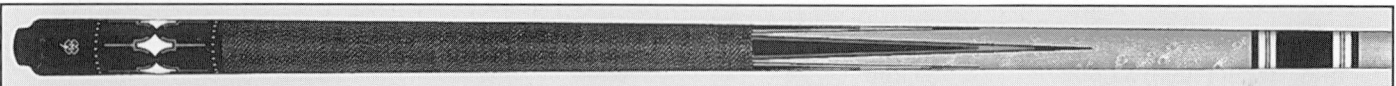

| Orig. Retail (1996) $450 | $380 | $345 | $245 |

MCDERMOTT CUE MANUFACTURING INC., cont. 505

GRADING	98%	90%	70%

Level 4 E-N8 - Bird's-eye maple forearm, three long and three short jet black points with white veneers, black onyx butt sleeve with a series of white hollow rectangular inlays.

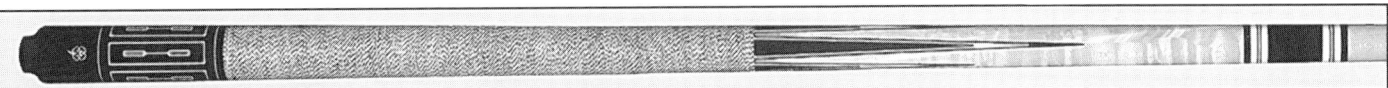

| Orig. Retail (1996) $495 | $385 | $340 | $265 |

Level 4 E-N9 - Bird's-eye maple forearm, four jet black points with white veneers and red diamond-shaped inlays with white borders in each point, white butt sleeve with six red diamond-shaped inlays with white borders in black ovals and between a series of white and black rings.

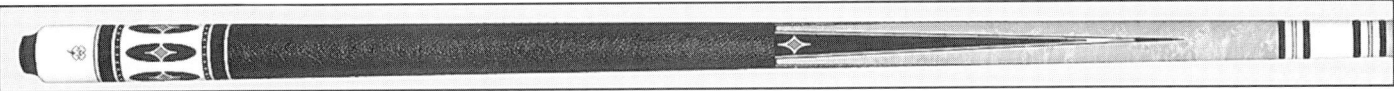

| Orig. Retail (1996) $495 | $375 | $335 | $275 |

Level 4 E-N10 - Bird's-eye maple forearm, four jet black points with bone colored veneers and red diamond-shaped inlays with bone colored borders in each point, bone colored butt sleeve with six red diamond-shaped inlays with bone colored borders in black ovals and between a series of red and black rings.

| Orig. Retail (1996) $495 | $395 | $340 | $265 |

Level 2 MW-02 - Maple forearm with image of flaming eight ball and "POOL'S HOT," maple butt sleeve with image of an eight ball.

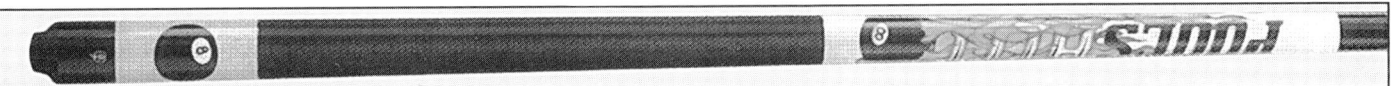

| Orig. Retail (1996) $235 | $185 | $150 | $120 |

Level 2 MW-03 - Maple forearm with image of rose and "I LOVE POOL," maple butt sleeve with image of an eight-ball rack on one side and a nine-ball rack on the other.

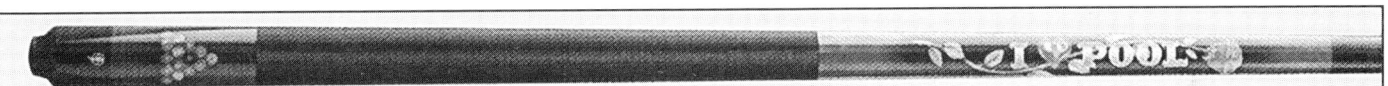

| Orig. Retail (1996) $235 | $195 | $165 | $115 |

"M7" COLLEGIATE SERIES

The following "M7" Collegiate series cues were officially licensed, and featured the logos of seven different colleges. The forearms were stained in coordinating colors.

Level 2 M7-DK - Royal navy-stained maple forearm, maple butt sleeve with an applied image of the Duke logo.

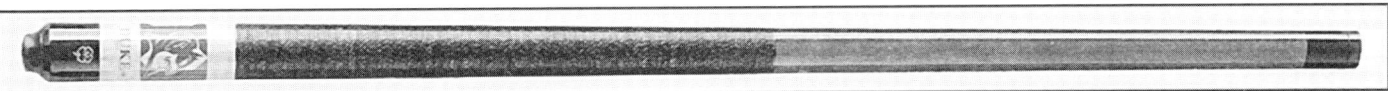

| Orig. Retail (1998) $225 | $190 | $160 | $115 |

Level 2 M7-FS - American cherry-stained maple forearm, maple butt sleeve with an applied image of the Florida State Seminoles logo.

| Orig. Retail (1998) $225 | $185 | $155 | $120 |

Level 2 M7-KT - Royal navy-stained maple forearm, maple butt sleeve with an applied image of the University of Kentucky Wildcats logo.

| Orig. Retail (1998) $225 | $195 | $160 | $120 |

GRADING	98%	90%	70%

Level 2 M7-MI - Black onyx-stained maple forearm, maple butt sleeve with an applied image of the Michigan Wolverines logo.

Orig. Retail (1998) $225	$180	$165	$115

Level 2 M7-NC - Black onyx-stained maple forearm, maple butt sleeve with an applied image of the North Carolina Tar Heels logo.

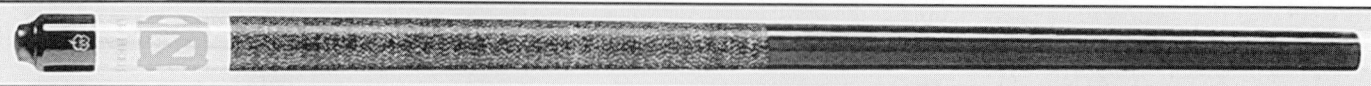

Orig. Retail (1998) $225	$190	$165	$120

Level 2 M7-NE - Ruby red-stained maple forearm, maple butt sleeve with an applied image of the Nebraska Huskers logo.

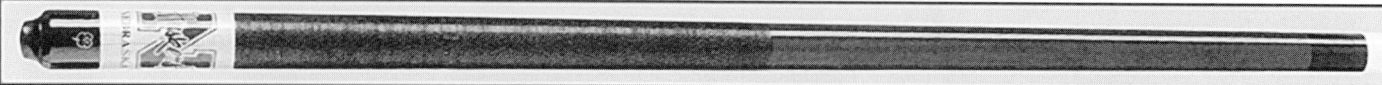

Orig. Retail (1998) $225	$190	$160	$115

Level 2 M7(1998)-WI - Ruby red-stained maple forearm, maple butt sleeve with an applied image of the Wisconsin Badgers logo.

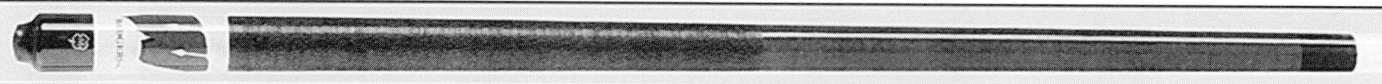

Orig. Retail (1998) $225	$185	$155	$120

"RS" (REVIVAL SERIES)

All of the following "RS" (Revival Series) cues were available with Irish linen or leather wraps at no additional charge.

Level 3 RS-01 - Bird's-eye maple forearm, four white points with wood veneers, butt sleeve with four long diamond-shaped inlays over hollow white hexagons.

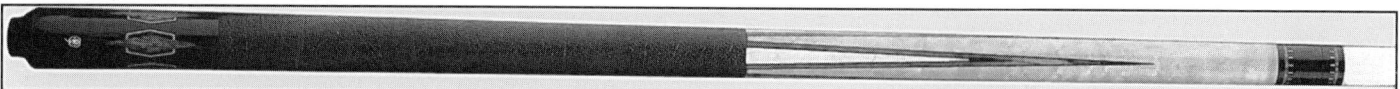

Orig. Retail (1998) $375	$400	$300	$185

Level 3 RS-02 - Bird's-eye maple forearm, four points with wood veneers, butt sleeve with four long maple diamond-shaped inlays between expanded rings.

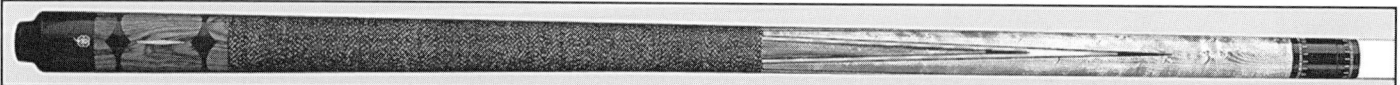

Orig. Retail (1998) $375	$400	$300	$185

Level 3 RS-03 - Bird's-eye maple forearm, four points with wood veneers, black onyx butt sleeve with four large diamond-shaped inlays over a thick ring of tulipwood.

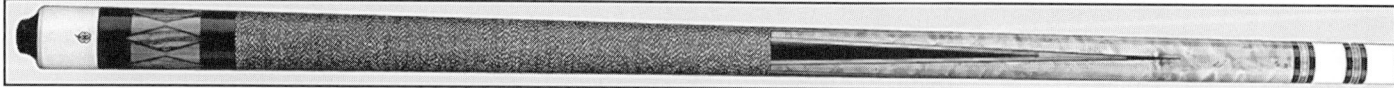

Orig. Retail (1998) $425	$450	$345	$215

Level 3 RS-04 - Bird's-eye maple forearm, four points with wood veneers, butt sleeve with six inlays in a thick black ring.

Orig. Retail (1998) $450	$460	$350	$220

Level 3 RS-05 - Bird's-eye maple forearm, four points with wood veneers, butt sleeve with six large bordered diamond-shaped inlays in a thick black ring.

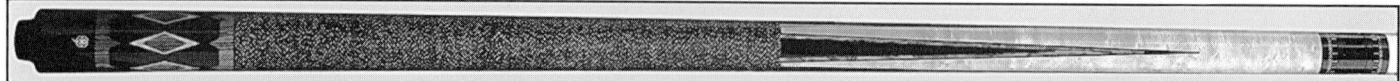

Orig. Retail (1998) $450	$460	$350	$220

MCDERMOTT CUE MANUFACTURING INC., cont.   507

GRADING	98%	90%	70%

Level 3 RS-06 - Bird's-eye maple forearm, four tulipwood points with bone-colored veneers, butt sleeve with rings of tulipwood and maple and a center ring inlaid with six three-piece oval inlays.

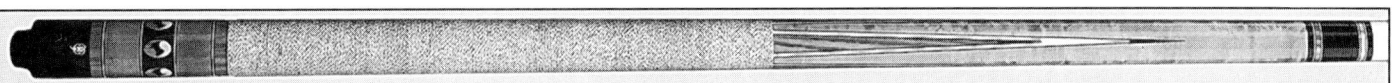

Orig. Retail (1998) $495	$550	$425	$285

Level 3 RS-07 - Bird's-eye maple forearm, four cocobolo points with bone colored veneers, cocobolo butt sleeve with six five-piece inlays centered in a thick ring between thin bone-colored rings.

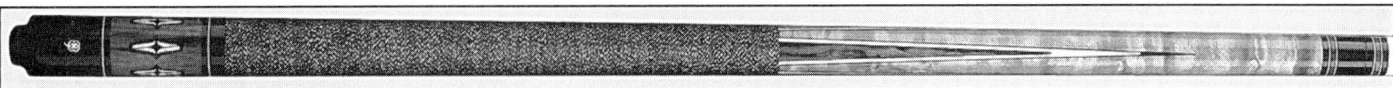

Orig. Retail (1998) $550	$600	$450	$285

Level 3 RS-08 - Bird's-eye maple forearm, four points with wood veneers, butt sleeve with long thin oval inlays inset with four point designs in a thick ring between pairs of thin bone-colored rings and short vertical lines in ring patterns.

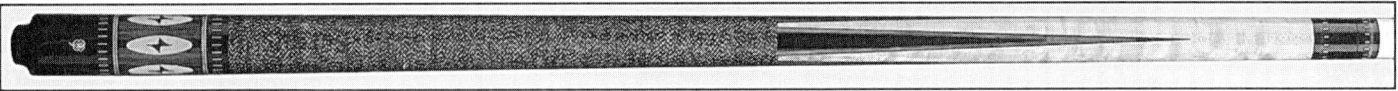

Orig. Retail (1998) $625	$700	$525	$325

Level 3 RS-09 - Cocobolo forearm, four cocobolo points with bone colored veneers, butt sleeve with six long black diamond-shaped inlays set in between several cocobolo rings.

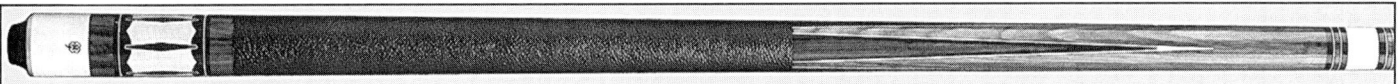

Orig. Retail (1998) $625	$700	$525	$325

Level 3 RS-10 - Rosewood forearm, four cocobolo points with bone colored veneers, butt sleeve with six long white diamond-shaped inlays set in between several rings.

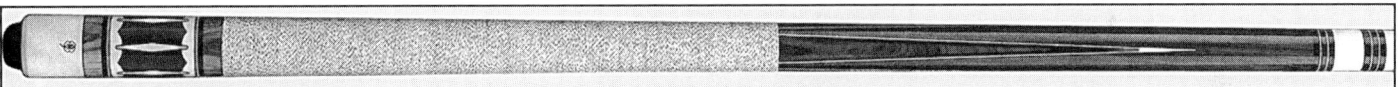

Orig. Retail (1998) $625	$700	$525	$325

Level 3 RS-11 - Bird's-eye maple forearm, four rosewood points with bone colored veneers and intricate bone colored scroll inlays in each point, rosewood butt sleeve with six bone-colored and wood designs set between a series of rings with pairs of nickel silver rings at top and bottom.

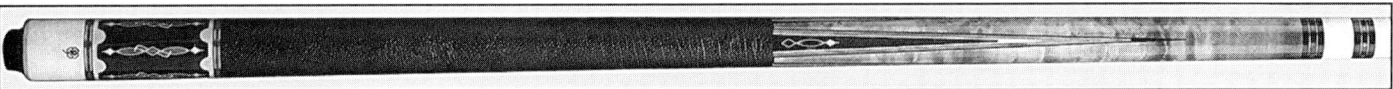

Orig. Retail (1998) $725	$800	$600	$385

Level 3 RS-12 - Masterpiece Joint, bird's-eye maple forearm, four cocobolo points with wood and bone-colored veneers, butt sleeve with six white long designs set between a series of rings with nickel silver rings at top and bottom.

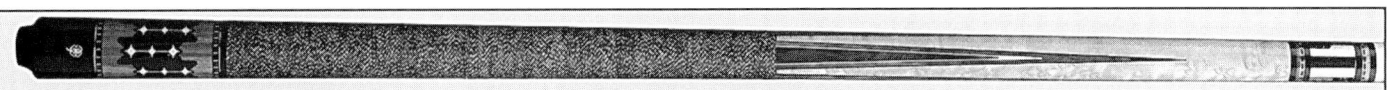

Orig. Retail (1998) $825	$950	$725	$450

Level 3 RS-13 - Masterpiece Joint, bird's-eye maple forearm, four black points with tulipwood and bone-colored veneers and small diamond-shaped bone colored inlays in each point, black onyx butt sleeve with intricate hollow design set between a series of rings with pairs of nickel silver rings at top and bottom.

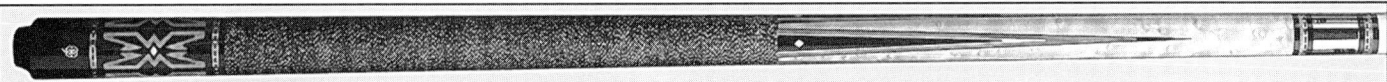

Orig. Retail (1998) $895	$1,000	$750	$475

| GRADING | 98% | 90% | 70% |

GENESIS SERIES CUES

The following "M7 Quick Release" series cues featured McDermott's 3/8-10 quick release joint. They were available in a variety of different stain colors.

Level 2 M7-QR1 - Stained bird's-eye maple forearm with checked ring above wrap, stained bird's-eye maple butt sleeve with checked rings at top and bottom.

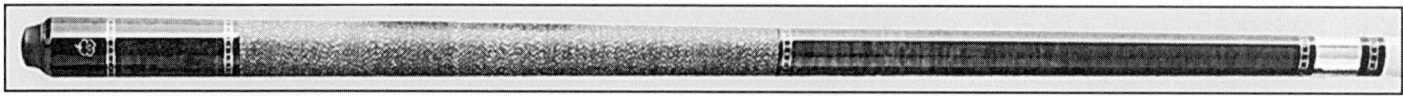

| Orig. Retail (1999) $395 | $325 | $245 | $155 |

Level 3 M7-QR2 - Stained bird's-eye maple forearm, intricate black-bordered floating hardwood points, stained bird's-eye maple butt sleeve with rings of woven hardwoods at top and bottom.

| Orig. Retail (1999) $475 | $375 | $285 | $175 |

Level 4 M7-QR4 - Stained bird's-eye maple forearm, floating ebony points with a four-point star next to a long thin line in each point, ebony-colored butt sleeve with four-point stars next to single lines between checked rings at top and bottom.

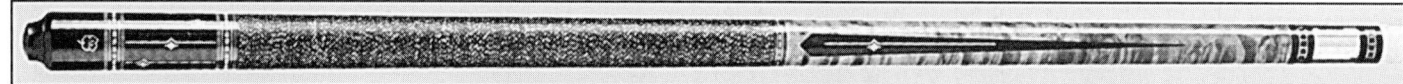

| Orig. Retail (1999) $495 | $400 | $300 | $185 |

"M-8" SERIES

The following seven "M-8" Series cues come with Irish linen wraps and stainless steel joints.

Level 3 M8-01 - Stained bird's-eye maple forearm, intricate black-bordered cocobolo floating points, stained bird's-eye maple butt sleeve with intricate black-colored and cocobolo rings towards bottom.

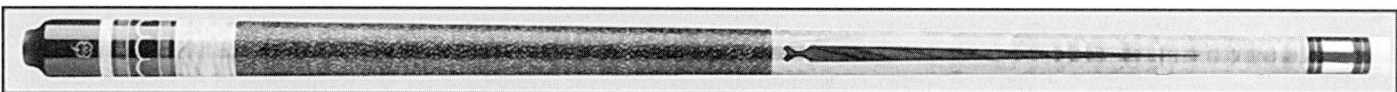

| Orig. Retail (1999) $295 | $220 | $165 | $105 |

Level 4 M8-03 - Stained bird's-eye maple forearm, intricate two-piece hardwood points with double borders, ebony-colored butt sleeve with intricate three-piece "Z" shaped inlays alternating with stained bird's-eye maple windows.

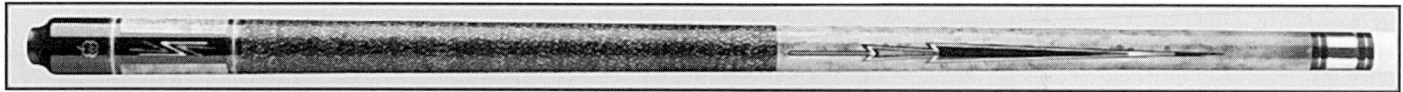

| Orig. Retail (1999) $375 | $275 | $210 | $130 |

Level 4 M8-04 - Stained bird's-eye maple forearm, floating double-bordered points with a zigzag patterned center, ebony-colored butt sleeve with zigzag patterned inlays between zigzag rings above and below.

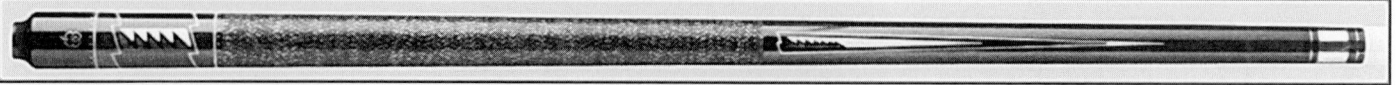

| Orig. Retail (1999) $395 | $280 | $210 | $125 |

Level 5 M8-05 - Stained bird's-eye maple forearm, ebony-colored points with two veneers and an intricate three-piece tulipwood inlay in each point, stained bird's-eye maple butt sleeve with intricate black-bordered tulipwood three-piece inlays between intricate colored and hardwood rings at top and bottom.

| Orig. Retail (1999) $425 | $295 | $225 | $140 |

| GRADING | 98% | 90% | 70% |

"M-7" SERIES

The following seven "M-7" Series cues offer Irish linen or leather wraps and a variety of stain colors at no extra charge. Stainless steel joints are available for an extra $30.

Level 2 M7-01 - Stained bird's-eye maple forearm, stained bird's-eye maple butt sleeve with a ring of stylized "M"s in an ebony-colored ring around bottom.

| Orig. Retail (1999) $235 | $180 | $135 | $85 |

Level 2 M7-02 - Stained bird's-eye maple forearm, stained bird's-eye maple butt sleeve with checked rings at top and a ring of bone-shaped inlays between checked rings at bottom.

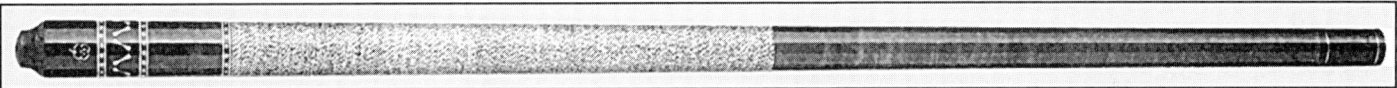

| Orig. Retail (1999) $245 | $185 | $145 | $90 |

Level 2 M7-03 - Stained bird's-eye maple forearm, stained bird's-eye maple butt sleeve with intricate black-bordered hardwood propeller-shaped inlays between intricate colored rings above and below.

| Orig. Retail (1999) $265 | $190 | $140 | $85 |

Level 2 M7-04 - Stained bird's-eye maple forearm, ebony-colored butt sleeve with intricate patterns below hardwood rings at top.

| Orig. Retail (1999) $275 | $200 | $150 | $95 |

Level 2 M7-05 - Stained bird's-eye maple forearm, stained bird's-eye maple butt sleeve with intricate hardwood rings at bottom.

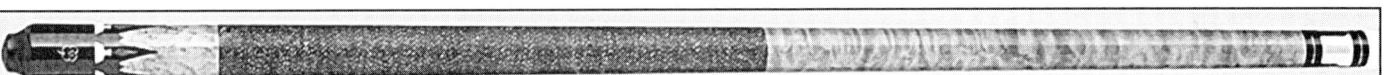

| Orig. Retail (1999) $290 | $215 | $165 | $100 |

Level 2 M7-07 - Stained bird's-eye maple forearm inlaid with a golf ball next to the #1 hole and flag, maple butt sleeve with golfers inlaid in windows alternating with flags inlaid into windows between nickel silver rings in ebony rings at top and bottom.

| Orig. Retail (1999) $425 | $315 | $240 | $145 |

"M8 PROFESSIONAL" SERIES

The following "M8 Professional" series cues feature Irish linen wraps and are available in many different stain colors.

Level 2 M8-PS1 - Stained bird's-eye maple forearm, ebony-colored butt sleeve with intricate red and white inlays between checked rings at top and bottom. Add $50 for early versions with names of pro players on them.

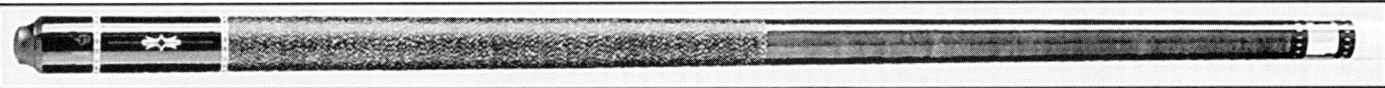

| Orig. Retail (1999) $315 | $245 | $185 | $120 |

Level 4 M8-PS2 - Stained bird's-eye maple forearm, four ebony points with a stack of crescent moons inlaid in each point, ebony-colored butt sleeve with yin and yang symbols above center.

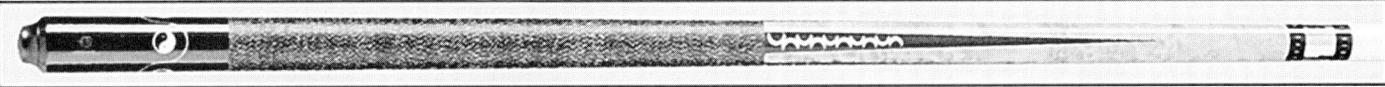

| Orig. Retail (1999) $400 | $300 | $225 | $140 |

GRADING	98%	90%	70%

Level 3 M8-PS3 - Stained bird's-eye maple forearm, black-bordered cocobolo floating points, cocobolo butt sleeve with very intricate woven symbols in ebony-colored rings above and below.

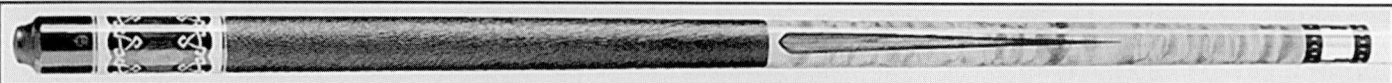

Orig. Retail (1999) $425 $325 $245 $155

Level 3 M8-PS4 "The Nighthawk" - Stained bird's-eye maple forearm, six ebony points, ebony-colored butt sleeve with white-bordered hardwood nighthawk-shaped inlays.

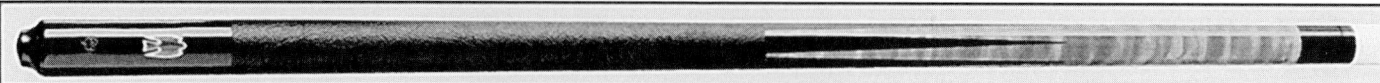

Orig. Retail (1999) $275 $200 $150 $95

Level 4 M8-PS5 "The Guardian Spirit" - Stained bird's-eye maple forearm, intricate black-bordered floating tulipwood points, tulip wood butt sleeve with intricate black-bordered white guardian spirits around center.

Orig. Retail (1999) $315 $235 $175 $105

Level 2 M8-PS7 - Stained bird's-eye maple forearm, stained bird's-eye maple sleeve with an image of an eight ball stuck in a spider web.

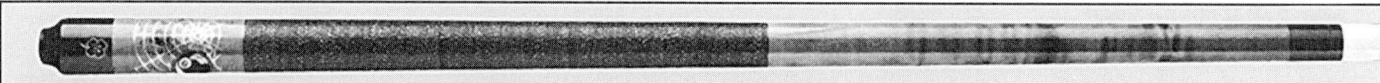

Orig. Retail (1999) $235 $175 $130 $80

Level 2 M8-PS8 - Cocobolo forearm, cocobolo butt sleeve with intricate six-point star-shaped inlays around center.

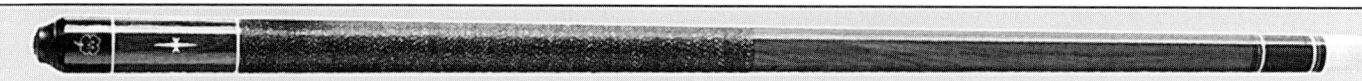

Orig. Retail (1999) $245 $180 $135 $85

Level 2 M8-PS9 - Stained bird's-eye maple forearm, ebony-colored butt sleeve with intricate inlays alternating with stained maple columns.

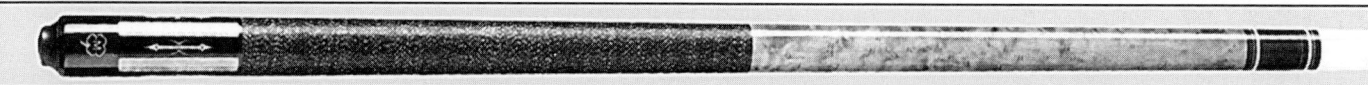

Orig. Retail (1999) $250 $195 $145 $90

Level 2 M8-PS10 - Stained bird's-eye maple forearm, ebony-colored points with an ivory-colored spear-shaped inlay in each point, ebony-colored butt sleeve with ivory-colored spear-shaped inlays at the tips of the points on an intricate tulipwood ring above.

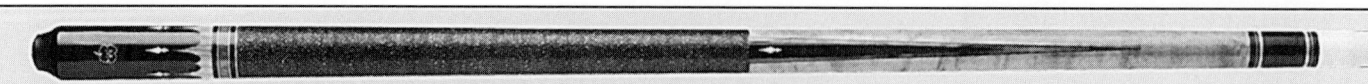

Orig. Retail (1999) $325 $245 $185 $115

Level 3 M8-PS11 - Stained bird's-eye maple forearm, ebony-colored points with two veneers, stained bird's-eye maple butt sleeve with fleur-de-lis inlays in an intricate ebony-colored ring above center.

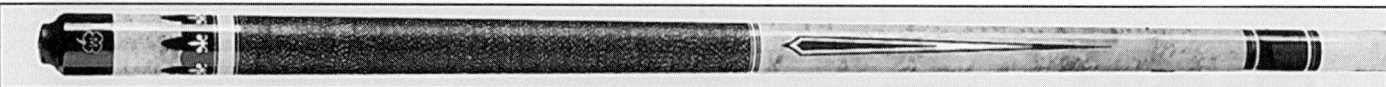

Orig. Retail (1999) $355 $265 $210 $125

"E-I" SERIES

The "E-I" Series cue features reproductions of the art of Wisconsin native, Wes Spencer.

MCDERMOTT CUE MANUFACTURING INC., cont. 511

GRADING	98%	90%	70%

Level 2 E-I5 - Maple forearm with image of a black panther, maple butt sleeve with image of two black panthers fighting.

| Orig. Retail (1999) $275 | $215 | $165 | $105 |

"E-L" SERIES

Both "E-L" series cues feature reproductions of the art of Wisconsin native, Terry Doughty.

Level 2 E-L1 - Maple forearm with image of a prowling timber wolf, maple butt sleeve with image of wolf's head.

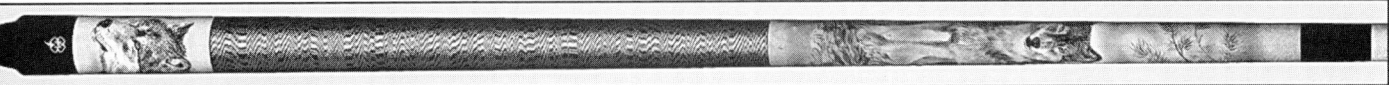

| Orig. Retail (1999) $275 | $210 | $155 | $95 |

Level 2 E-L6 - Maple forearm with image of coiled cobra, maple butt sleeve with image of cobra's head.

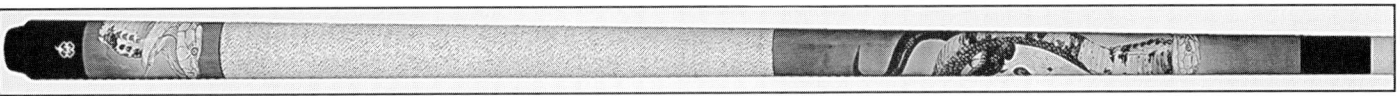

| Orig. Retail (1999) $275 | $215 | $165 | 100 |

HARLEY DAVIDSON SERIES

The following Harley Davidson cue offered Irish linen or leather wraps at no extra charge. It was part of the Road House Collection, officially licensed by Ace Product Management Group, Inc. Cases with the Harley Davidson logo were also available.

Level 2 HD-08 - Maple forearm with image of "Harley Davidson" in red next to a bald eagle and the American flag, maple butt sleeve with image of a bald eagle and the American flag over the Harley Davidson shield.

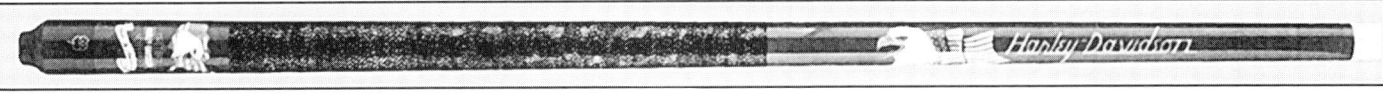

| Orig. Retail (1999) $295 | $225 | $175 | $105 |

"E-F" SERIES

"E-F" Series cues offer Irish linen or leather wraps at no extra charge.

Level 2 E-F2 - Ziricote forearm and butt sleeve.

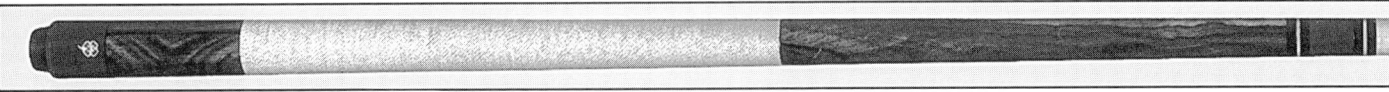

| Orig. Retail (1999) $229 | $195 | $145 | $90 |

Level 3 E-F4 - Maple forearm with four floating tulipwood points, tulipwood butt sleeve.

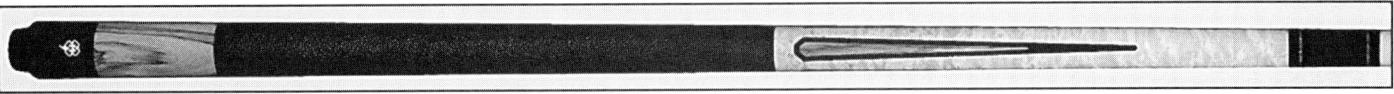

| Orig. Retail (1999) $289 | $250 | $190 | $120 |

"E-H" SERIES

"E-H" Series cues come with Irish linen wraps.

Level 2 E-H1 - Stained bird's-eye maple forearm, maple butt sleeve with image of an eight ball.

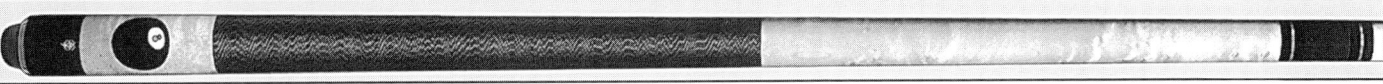

| Orig. Retail (1999) $235 | $175 | $130 | $80 |

Level 2 E-H2 - Stained bird's-eye maple forearm, black onyx-colored butt sleeve with image of a nine ball.

| Orig. Retail (1999) $235 | $170 | $130 | $80 |

GRADING	98%	90%	70%

Level 2 M7-H4 - Stained bird's-eye maple forearm, stained bird's-eye maple butt sleeve with image of a boy juggling pool balls.

Orig. Retail (1999) $235	$175	$135	$85

"E-B" SERIES

The following "E-B" Series cues had Irish linen wraps.

Level 2 E-B8 - Teal-stained maple forearm and butt sleeve.

Orig. Retail (1999) $195	$155	$120	$75

Level 2 E-B10 - Rich maple-stained forearm and butt sleeve.

Orig. Retail (1999) $195	$155	$115	$70

Level 2 E-B11 - Amethyst-stained maple forearm and butt sleeve.

Orig. Retail (1999) $195	$155	$120	$75

Level 2 E-B12 - Pearlescent white-painted maple forearm and butt sleeve.

Orig. Retail (1999) $225	$180	$135	$85

HARLEY DAVIDSON SERIES

The following Harley Davidson cues featured McDermott's standard 3/8-10 joint. They were part of the Road House Collection, officially licensed by Ace Product Management Group, Inc. Harley Davidson cases were also available.

Level 2 M8HD-3 - Pearlescent white-painted maple forearm with a transfer image of "Harley Davidson" in blue over orange flames, lizard-embossed leather wrap, pearlescent white-painted maple butt sleeve with a transfer image of a bald eagle over the Harley Davidson shield.

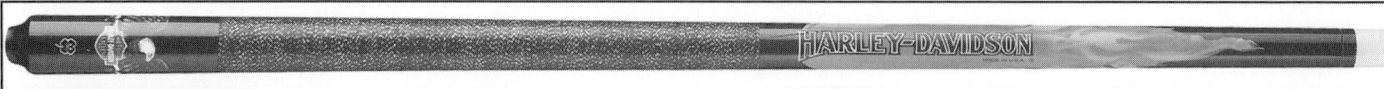

MSR (2004) $295	$225	$185	$140

Level 2 HD-26 - Black-painted maple forearm with a transfer image of "Harley Davidson" in orange over a blue background, black-painted maple butt sleeve with a transfer image of "Harley Davidson" in orange over a blue background above the Harley Davidson shield.

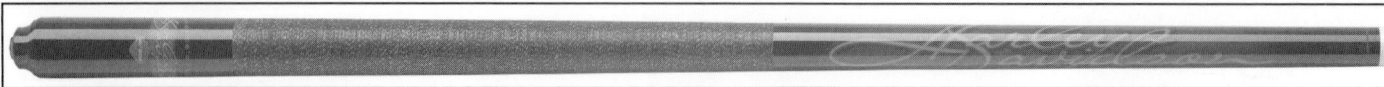

MSR (2004) $230	$155	$135	$110

SPECIAL INTEREST MCDERMOTT CUES

Both of the following "LGD" (Legend Series) cues were available with Irish linen or leather wrap at no additional charge.

MCDERMOTT CUE MANUFACTURING INC., cont.

GRADING	98%	90%	70%

Level 2 LGD-01 - Black forearm and butt sleeve with images of Elvis Presley.

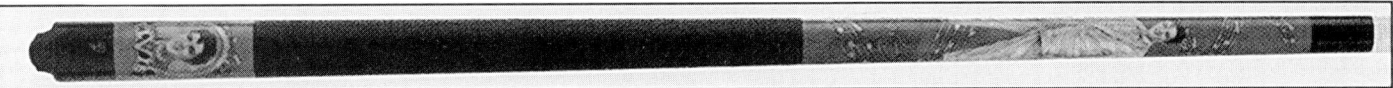

Orig. Retail (1993) $295	$385	$320	$240

Level 2 LGD-02 - Black forearm and butt sleeve with images of Marilyn Monroe.

Orig. Retail (1993) $295	$375	$320	$240

COMMEMORATIVE SERIES

The following CS (Commemorative Series) cue was limited to a production run of 1,000. Each cue was serial numbered and personally signed by Jim McDermott.

Level 4 CS-01 "Founder's Cue" - Bird's-eye maple forearm with "James D. McDermott" original signature below joint, three long and three short black- and green-bordered white points with a green shamrock between two black dots inlaid in each point, black butt sleeve with six white oval windows inlaid with a green shamrock between two black dots in each, serial numbered 001 through 1000 on butt cap.

Orig. Retail (1994) $1,000	$1,500	$1,200	$900

SECONDARY MARKET MINIMUM VALUES

One-of-a-kind cues have been available from the McDermott custom shop since 1975. The following are minimum values for custom McDermott cues encountered on the secondary market. These prices are representative of cues utilizing basic materials and designs. These cues can command many times these prices due to the use of exotic materials and artistry.

Special construction note: There are many materials and construction techniques that can add value to Custom McDermott cues. For all used McDermott Cues, except where otherwise noted:

- Add $50+ for each additional original straight playable shaft.
- Deduct $60 for missing original straight playable shaft.
- Add $40+ for leather, Irish linen, or cork wrap (only on cues with standard nylon wrap).
- Add $55+ for each additional custom inlay (available on MR-line through D-line).
- Add $50+ for each ivory ferrule.
- Deduct 25% for obvious or improper refinish.

Level 2 - 0 points, 0-25 inlays.
Level 2 cues start at	$350	$265	$185

Level 3 - 2-6 points, 0-8 inlays.
Level 3 cues start at	$475	$365	$250

Level 4 - 4-10 points, 9-25 inlays.
Level 4 cues start at	$585	$450	$300

Level 5 - 0-12 points, 26-50 inlays.
Level 5 cues start at	$900	$695	$475

Level 6 - 0-12 points, 51-75 inlays.
Level 6 cues start at	$1,250	$985	$650

CHAD MCLENNAN

Maker of CAM Custom Cues. For more information, refer to the listing for CAM.

MCWORTER CUES

Maker of pool cues from 1989 to present, currently in Ventura, California.

Jerry McWorter started playing pool when he was very young. He always had a fascination with cues and built his first cue in his high school wood shop class. When he finished high school, Jerry worked for another cuemaker for about three months. After this, he served a two-year mission in South Carolina for the Church of Jesus Christ of Latter Day Saints. When he returned, Jerry worked in the concrete and excavation business with his father for a few years. In the late eighties, after the southern California real estate crash, the business slowed down considerably. Jerry was still playing pool and decided that there was a market for custom cues.

By 1989, he had made the first McWorter cue. Although the early cues are not easily identifiable, they are signed in ink under the wrap. Many were done in the "South West" style, which he still offers for his basic six-point cue. In 1990, Jerry started making cues with shafts that are completely interchangeable. From 1994 on, all cues carry the "McWorter" name and serial number engraved in white on the butt cap of his cues. In early 1996, Jerry changed to an improved bumper.

With the assistance of Brent Harding, Jerry makes between 90 and 100 custom cues per year in his shop in Ventura, California, (northwest of Los Angeles). He molds his own bumpers, makes his own screws, and makes all of the other components except for the tips. He likes to build cues to his own designs and then offer them for sale. He prefers making cues in small groups of four or five, rather than batches, to ensure the highest quality construction. Ivory ferrules and leather wraps are standard features on high-end McWorter cues. Jerry cites his friend Thomas Wayne as a major inspiration and teacher for his work with CNC-aided designs.

Jerry is well-known as a good player on the West Coast, and his wife, Jan, has played for many years on the Women's Professional Billiard tour. Jerry's cues have become very popular with players and collectors both in the U.S. and in Japan. Jerry travels to Japan and plays in pro tournaments there to help promote his cues. His playing experience has helped him to develop his own shaft taper, which is medium-stiff. He has exhibited at all the major cue shows in recent years. In February of 1999, Jerry won the bronze medal at the Gallery of American Cue Art. Among his innovations is a 2004 special edition of cues, featuring ivory joint pins, which he sold as a five-cue retrospective set in their own custom presentation case.

McWorter cues are guaranteed indefinitely against construction defects that are not the result of warping or abuse. If you have a McWorter cue that needs identification or repair, or would like to talk to Jerry about the design of a new custom cue, contact McWorter Cues, listed in the Trademark Index.

SPECIFICATIONS

Butt material: hardwoods
Shaft material: rock maple
Standard length: 58 in.
Lengths available: 58 in.
Standard finish: imron
Standard joint screw: 3/8-10 radial
Standard joint and pin material: stainless steel
Joint type: flat-faced wood-to-wood
Balance point: 19 in. from butt
Point construction: inlaid and short splice
Standard wrap: leather
Standard butt cap: black linen phenolic 1.275 in.
Standard number of shafts: two
Standard taper: custom straight
Standard ferrules: ivory
Standard tip: Le Pro
Tip widths available: any
Annual production: fewer than 100 cues

OPTIONS (FOR NEW CUES ONLY)

Special length: no charge
Extra shaft: $200

REPAIRS

Repairs done only on McWorter cues.
Refinish (with leather wrap): $250
Refinish (with linen wrap): $250
Replace shaft with fiber/linen ferrule: $200
Replace shaft with ivory ferrule: $200
Replace ivory ferrule: $75
Replace layered tip: $40+

CURRENT MCWORTER CUES

The current delivery time for a McWorter cue is approximately six months depending on the intricacy of the cue.

CURRENT EXAMPLES

The following cues represent designs currently available from McWorter Custom Cues. They come with leather wrap, two shafts, and joint protectors standard. The "McWorter" name and the unique four-digit serial number are engraved in the butt cap or at the base of each butt sleeve.

MCWORTER CUES, cont. 515

GRADING	100%	95%	70%

Level 5 # "Ivory Deco" - Ebony forearm, five ivory points split by pairs of double silver feathers with interior abalone points and an abalone spear-shaped inlay in each alternating with sets of three silver lines between the points, ebony butt sleeve with five reverse ivory points split by pairs of double silver feathers with interior abalone points and an abalone spear-shaped inlay in each alternating with sets of three silver lines between the points, black phenolic joint collar with silver ring.

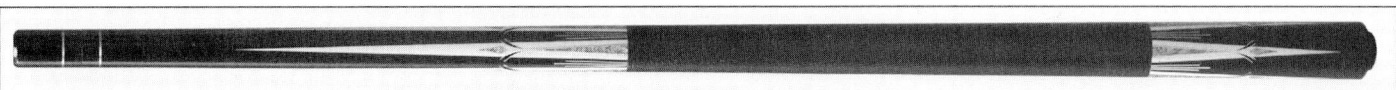

MSR	$5,500	$5,500-8,000	$5,350	$4,200

Level 5 Ebony forearm, five long and five short ivory points with ivory inlays at base of each point and silver inlays in between, ebony butt sleeve with ten reverse ivory points and silver inlays in a smaller mirrored version of the forearm, "McWorter" logo and serial number above ivory butt cap, black phenolic joint collar with silver ring, leather wrap

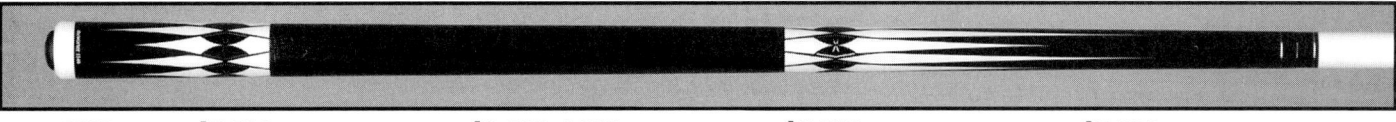

MSR	$3,500	$3,500-4,200	$3,300	$2,800

Level 8 "Pinnacle" Ebony forearm, six brown wildwood points in hourglass design trimmed in silver with inlays of ivory diamonds and silver bowties, tipped by ivory diamond inlays, brown wildwood butt sleeve with six silver veneered ebony elipses with silver starburst diamonds and ivory diamonds above and in between echoing the point design, black phenolic joint collar with silver ring.

MSR	$5,000	$5,000-7,000	$4,500	$4,000

Level 8 "Spaniard" - Ebony forearm, six bird's-eye maple split maple points with abalone spears at tips and ivory veneered spears in-between, and ebony Tiffany diamond and ivory spear inlays at bottom of each point., ebony butt sleeve has reverse points with same inlays, no butt cap, black phenolic joint collar with silver ring.

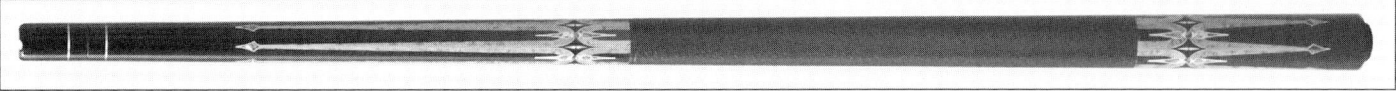

MSR	$5,200	$5,200-7,500	$4,600	$4,100

Level 6 "Ivory Twist" Ebony forearm, five twisting ivory points interlaced with ten anboyna burl-crowned points trimmed in silver, ivory rings above and below leather wrap, amboyna burl butt sleeve has ten ivory and ebony elipses with silver veneers, ivory butt cap, black phenolic joint collar with silver ring.

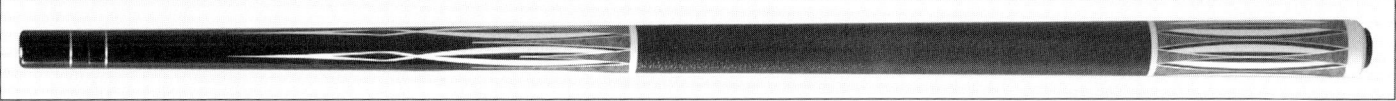

MSR	$4,300	$4,300-6,000	$3,800	$3,300

Level 7 "Victorian" - Ebony forearm, six red wildwood points trimmed in sterling silver veneers, tipped by ivory diamond inlays, with ivory, ebony, and bird's-eye maple "cat's-eyes" at base of points, bird's-eye maple teardrops in-between, doble silver rings above and below leather wrap, ebony butt sleeve with six matching silver veneered red wildwood points with same ivory, ebony and bird's-eye maple inlays, black phenolic joint collar with silver ring.

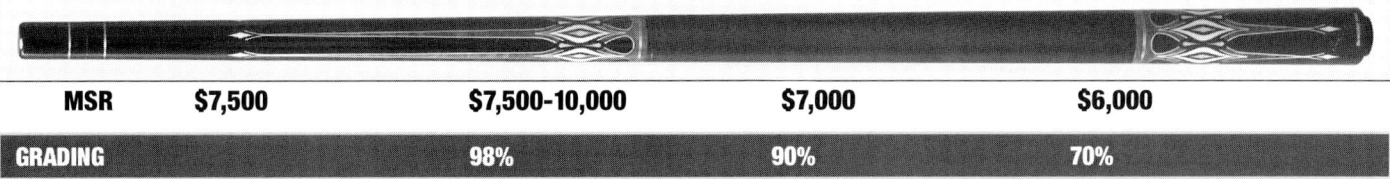

MSR	$7,500	$7,500-10,000	$7,000	$6,000

GRADING	98%	90%	70%

PAST EXAMPLES

Level 5 - Cocobolo forearm, three long and three short floating maple burl points with four blocks of ivory and maple burl below the bases of each, cocobolo forearm with three long and three short reverse floating maple burl points with four blocks of ivory and maple burl above the bases of each, small black butt cap with "McWorter" and serial number, silver ring above, linen wrap.

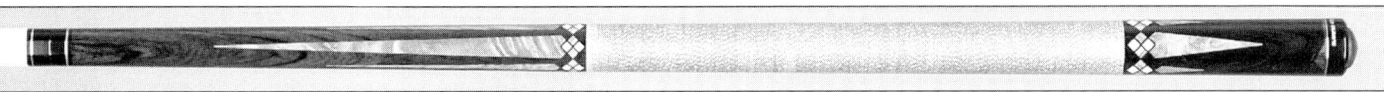

MSR (1998) $2,250	$2,400	$1,650	$1,250

MCWORTER CUES, cont.

GRADING	98%	90%	70%

Level 6 - Ebony forearm, three long and three short floating "broken spear" curly maple points with four inlays of ivory and silver Tiffany diamonds creating medallions between the bases of each, ebony forearm with three long and three short reverse floating curly maple points with matching inlays in the bases of each, black phenolic joint collar with silver ring, black phenolic butt cap with "McWorter" and serial number, leather wrap.

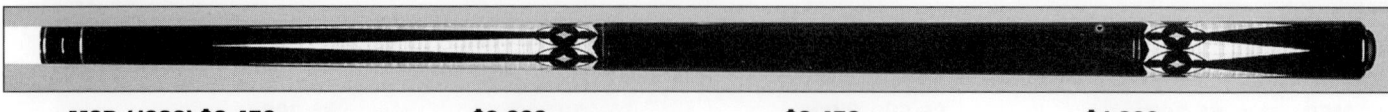

MSR (1999) $2,450	$3,000	$2,450	$1,800

SECONDARY MARKET MINIMUM VALUES

The following are minimum prices for other McWorter cues encountered on the secondary market. These prices are representative of cues utilizing basic materials and designs that may not be currently available. Jerry currently specializes in one-of-a-kind cues that can command many times these prices due to the use of exotic materials and artistry.

Special construction note: There are many materials and construction techniques that can add value to McWorter cues, including gold and gemstone inlays.

For all used McWorter cues:
- Add $150 for each additional original straight playable shaft (standard with two).
- Deduct $150 for each missing original straight playable shaft.
- Deduct 20% for obvious or improper refinish.

Level 2 - 0 points, 0-25 inlays.

Level 2 cues start at	$850	$600	$475

Level 3 - 2-6 points, 0-8 inlays.

Level 3 cues start at	$1,400	$1,000	$750

Level 4 - 4-10 points, 9-25 inlays.

Level 4 cues start at	$1,800	$1,450	$950

Level 5 - 0-12 points, 26-50 inlays.

Level 5 cues start at	$2,700	$2,150	$1,650

Level 6 - 0-12 points, 51-75 inlays.

Level 6 cues start at	$3,200	$2,700	$2,250

Level 7 - 0-12 points, 76-125 inlays.

Level 7 cues start at	$3,800	$3,500	$2,800

Level 8 - 4 or More points, 126 + inlays.

Level 8 cues start at	$4,300	$3,850	$3,100

GARY MEDLIN

Maker of Gem Cues. For more information, refer to the listing for Gem Cues.

MEISTER CUES

Maker of pool cues from 1995 to present in Jupiter, Florida.

Fred C. Meister began making cues after a forty-year career as a boat builder. The attention to detail, creative design skills, and experience in working with exotic woods has made the move to fabricating cues a fairly smooth one. In the early 1990s he began repairing cues, and by 1995 Fred was building cues on a part-time basis. His career change has been facilitated by learning from Florida cuemakers Paul Dayton and Dennis Searing. All cues are one-of-a-kind, and approximately half are made to order. Playability is most important to Fred.

Fred makes all cue components except the bumpers and tips in his one-man shop. He makes his own custom radial pins for his joints. Butts are cored with four-piece double laminated radial spliced rods with opposing grains from the joint to the butt cap so that the butt will not warp.

Fred C. Meister

A Fred C. Meister cue can be readily identified by the "FCM" initials on the butt cap. Fred's cues come with a lifetime guarantee. For more information or to order a custom cue, please contact Fred C. Meister Cues, listed in the Trademark Index

GRADING	98%	90%	70%

SPECIFICATIONS

- Butt material: hardwoods
- Shaft material: rock maple
- Standard length: 58 in.
- Lengths available: up tp 62 in.
- Standard finish: urethane
- Standard joint screw: radial
- Standard joint: linen phenolic
- Joint type: flat face
- Standard wrap: linen
- Standard butt cap: linen phenolic 1 in.
- Standard number of shafts: one
- Standard taper: pro custom
- Standard ferrules: Aegis
- Standard tip: Le Pro
- Tip widths available: any up to 14 mm
- Annual production: approximately 12 cues
- Options (for new cues only)
- Extra shaft: $100
- Custom joint protectors: $40
- Ivory ferrule: $50
- Leather wrap: $85

CURRENT FRED MEISTER CUES

Fred Meister hustler cues start at $200. Fred Meister cues with points start at $400. Custom orders take ten to sixteen weeks.

SECONDARY MARKET MINIMUM VALUES

The following are minimum prices for Meister cues encountered on the secondary market. These prices are representative of cues utilizing basic materials and designs that may not be currently available. Fred currently specializes in one-of-a-kind cues that can command many times these prices due to the use of exotic materials and rare woods.

For all used Meister cues:
- Add $100 for each additional original straight playable shaft beyond one.
- Deduct $75 for each missing original straight playable shaft.
- Add $50 for each ivory ferrule.
- Deduct 20% for obvious or improper refinish.

Level 1 - 4 points, hustler.

	98%	90%	70%
Level 1 cues start at	$200	$160	$110

Level 2 - 0 points, 0-25 inlays.

Level 2 cues start at	$300	$235	$160

Level 3 - 2-6 points, 0-8 inlays.

Level 3 cues start at	$400	$315	$220

Level 4 - 4-10 points, 9-25 inlays.

Level 4 cues start at	$500	$335	$260

MEUCCI ORIGINALS INC.

Maker of pool cues from 1975 to 1998 in Olive Branch, Mississippi, and from 1998 to present in Sledge, Mississippi.

Bob Meucci was born in Glenview, Illinois, the son of William "Red" Meucci, an Industrial Engineer. "Red" worked as a freelance designer and die maker and holds three patents. The most successful being for the Mutone Duck Call, which Red designed, produced, and marketed in the late 1940s. He also designed the Nydar gun sight, which was used by the U.S. military in World War II, and a weedless fishing lure. Bob was raised around his father's equipment and his creativity. He learned how to operate the machines in his father's tool and die shop as a preteen.

By the mid-1960s, Bob was making a few cues and experimenting with new types of construction. He founded B.M.C. to make cues in Glenview around this time. In 1968, he took over management of the cue department at National Chalk Co. One year later, National Chalk moved to Georgia and Bob chose to stay in Chicago. During this time, Bob helped to set up other cuemaking operations such as WICO, the company that made the first blanks for Gus Szamboti. He quickly gained recognition as a talented and creative cuemaker. In the early seventies, Bob was making cues in Memphis, Tennessee.

Bob Meucci

On March 24, 1975, Bob founded Meucci Originals in Olive Branch, Mississippi, in a newly designed cuemaking facility. The company has grown to become one of the most successful and recognized names in the cuemaking industry. His understanding of woodworking equipment allowed him to make his own machines, capable of turning out very unique cues. For instance, he is one of few cuemakers ever to make cues with mother-of-pearl points. And, he was one of the first to inlay pictures in 14-karat gold. When Bob started making cues, most had points or traditional inlays in the forearm. He was the first modern cuemaker to use the forearm as a canvas, creating theme cues with intricate inlaid scenes on the forearms. In 1998, Bob moved production to a more modern facility in Sledge, Mississippi, about 70 miles from Olive Branch.

Recent Meucci cues are easily identifiable by the Meucci trademark on the butt cap. Cues made before 1990 will have "Meucci Originals" instead. Although Meucci has tried a number of different joints, the 5/16-18 flat-face Implex joint is the one most frequently encountered. Chain links and checkered rings are common on Meucci cues, especially on the joints and butt sleeves. New cues come with finish over the Irish Linen for protection, which players can sand off if they choose to feel the wrap.

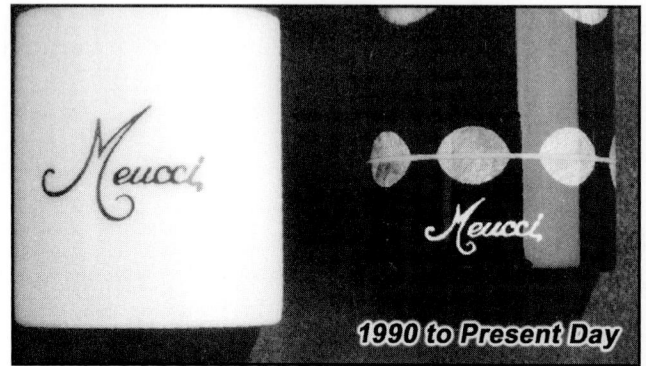

Bob was one of the first cuemakers to foresee cues as becoming collectible, and was one of the first to market limited edition cues, and for a time offered special edition cues each month. Limited edition cues can be marked such as SE 1-7, for "Summer Edition," and may also have serial numbers and/or dates on the butt caps. In the early eighties, Meucci made a "Roadrunner" cue featuring inlays of the Roadrunner cartoon character. About a half a dozen of these cues were made at a retail price of approximately $600. Today, a Meucci Roadrunner cue can easily bring thousands.

Meucci has also made some of the most intricate and ornate cues ever built. The Taj Mahal cue featured a bird's-eye maple forearm with a scene depicting scrimshawed ivory elephants carrying treasures up an Indian ebony winding road. The cue was inlaid with lapis lazuli, bloodstone, and over 3 1/2 ounces of 14-karat gold. The cue took over 350 man-hours of labor to complete. Another famous Meucci cue was "The King James." Originally made for Jim Rempe, this cue was inlaid with gold, ivory, emeralds, rubies, and diamonds. It sold new for $22,000, but has sold several times since, each time for more money. It is known to have sold for $40,000 and is rumored to have brought $75,000.

Bob is very proud that Meucci makes all parts except for the Le Pro tips, as opposed to buying them from suppliers. Meucci cues still feature spliced forearms, while many of his competitors now inlay their points with CNC machines. Most of the inlay work on Meucci cues is still done by hand. His wood is processed in his own sawmills and kilns which allows him more control over quality. He prefers to make lighter cues that are balanced further to the rear than most other cues, as he believes they play better.

In 1998, Bob built the "Myth Destroyer," a robot to test deflection in cues. He used this device to develop his "Red Dot" shafts, which are now standard for Meucci and are available for other manufacturers' cues. Bob has developed a new taper designed to reduce deflection, which he believes to be a primary concern among players. A video that explains the "Myth Destroyer" and the results Bob achieved in testing his Red Dot shafts is available from Meucci Originals, Inc. Now Meucci offers the Black Dot Bullseye Flat Laminated Shaft with 35 laminations of Northern hard rock maple. Meucci Laminated Tips are also an option.

Although Bob also owns a large ranch where he raises champion Appaloosa horses and cattle, he still crafts custom numbered and dated cues to the customer's designs and specifications in his own private workshop. In the past, Meucci Originals has offered a line of clothing including hats, jackets, shirts, sweaters, shoes, and warm up suits, all of which featured the Meucci trademark.

The current Meucci line includes a variety of cues ranging from a simple two-piece hustler to some very ornate high end cues. New limited edition cues are often made available. Power Piston Accelerator Cues feature Meucci's new Black Dot Bullseye Shafts. Metallic Series cues and other lines are also available. Meucci also offers educational video tapes for free on their website.

Meucci cues come with a full year guarantee against manufacturing defects and material flaws that are not the result of warpage or abuse, except cues purchased on Internet auctions from non-authorized sellers. This warranty applies indefinitely to cues that are in new, unplayed condition. If you have questions about identifying or repairing an old Meucci cue, or if you are interested in purchasing a new one through the dealer nearest you, please contact Meucci Originals Inc., listed in the Trademark Index.

SPECIFICATIONS

Butt material: hardwoods
Shaft material: rock maple
Standard length: 58 in.
Lengths available: any up to 62 in.
Standard finish: fireproof urethane
Joint screw: 5/16-18
Standard joint: Meucci synthetic
Joint type: flat faced

MEUCCI ORIGINALS INC., cont. 519

GRADING	100%	95%	70%

Balance point: 16-1/2 in. from butt
Point construction: short splice
Standard wrap: Irish linen
Standard butt cap: Meucci synthetic
Standard number of shafts: one "Red Dot"
Standard taper: Meucci custom
Standard ferrules: Meucci synthetic
Standard tip: Le Pro
Standard tip width: 12 3/4 mm

OPTIONS

For option availability and pricing, please contact Meucci Originals Inc., listed in the Trademark Index.

REPAIRS

For repair services and pricing, please contact Meucci Originals Inc., listed in the Trademark Index.

CURRENT EXAMPLES

The following are some of the cues available from Meucci Originals. New Limited Edition Meucci Cues, and other lines are also offered. Cues costing $690 or more come with two shafts. These cues are available for immediate delivery.

Level 1 M1 - Maple forearm, rosewood points and butt sleeve.

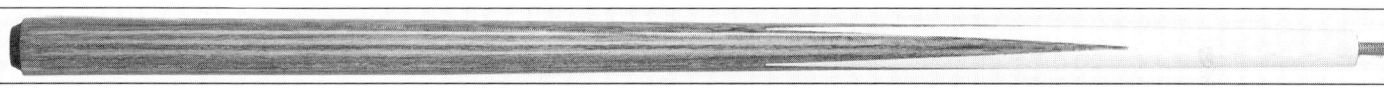

MSR	$275	$200-275	$165	$125

Level 3 97-9 - Grey stained bird's-eye maple forearm, four ivory-colored points with three veneers, ivory-colored butt sleeve with purple blocks within green outlines.

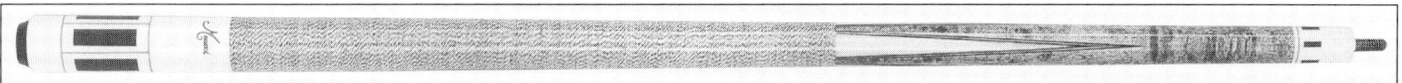

MSR	$415	$325-415	$265	$200

Level 4 97-10 - Stained bird's-eye maple forearm, four ebony-colored points with ebony-colored butt sleeve with patterns of pearlized plastic blocks connected by red lines.

MSR	$440	$340-440	$280	$210

Level 3 97-11 - Stained bird's-eye maple joint, stained bird's-eye maple forearm, four ebony-colored points with three colored veneers, ebony-colored butt sleeve with stained bird's-eye blocks between blue-colored checks and dashes above and below.

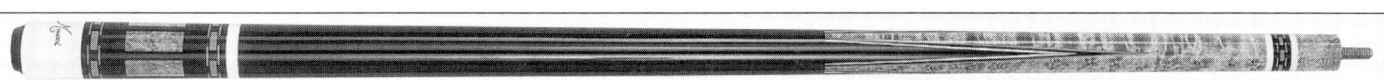

MSR	$440	$350-440	$285	$215

Level 3 97-12 - Grey-stained bird's-eye maple forearm, four ivory-colored points with three colored veneers and a colored diamond-shaped inlay atop a thin line in each point, grey-stained bird's-eye butt sleeve with multi-colored blocks in ivory-colored rings at top and bottom.

MSR	$440	$345-440	$275	$200

Level 5 97-15 - Stained bird's-eye maple forearm, four ebony-colored points with three colored veneers and intricate pearlized plastic inlay between two pearlized plastic dots in each point, ebony-colored butt sleeve with four red-bordered windows with two intricate pearlized plastic inlays between two pearlized plastic dots in each.

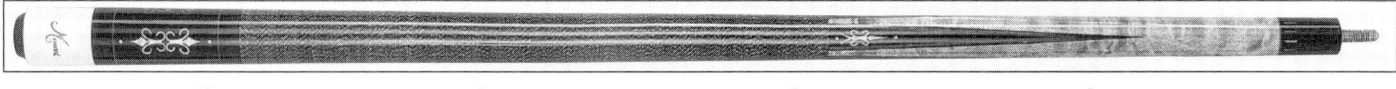

MSR	$515	$395-515	$330	$245

GRADING	100%	95%	70%

Level 4 95-16 - Stained bird's-eye maple forearm, four stained bird's-eye maple points with three colored veneers and a scene depicting the end of a cue and three balls inlaid into each point, stained bird's-eye maple butt sleeve with four white fish hooks set within red- and black-bordered ebony-colored diamond-shaped inlays between thin red and black rings at top and bottom.

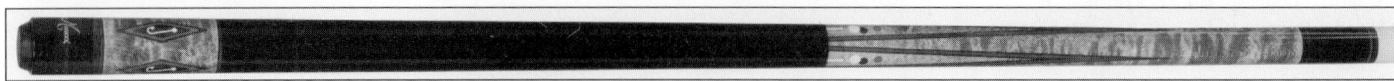

MSR	$490	$400-490	$315	$225

Level 4 97-21 - Ivory-colored forearm, six ebony-colored points with an intricate pearlized plastic and ebony-colored design in each, ivory-colored butt sleeve with six ebony-colored notched diamond-shaped inlays with lines extending above and below set in pearlized plastic and ebony-colored ovals.

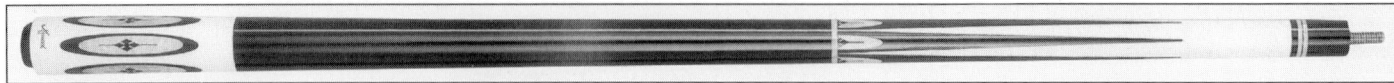

MSR	$690	$520-690	$430	$325

Level 4 97-22 - Grey-stained bird's-eye maple forearm, four ebony-colored points with two colored veneers and a pearlized plastic notched diamond-shaped inlay below a pearlized plastic dot set in ebony at bottom, ebony-colored butt sleeve with four pearlized plastic notched diamond-shaped inlays between pearlized plastic dots above and below set in stained bird's-eye ovals.

MSR	$690	$525-690	$425	$320

Level 4 97-28 - Cocobolo forearm, ivory-colored points with a cameo inlaid within intricate designs in each point alternating with ivory-colored diamond shapes atop white lines, cocobolo butt sleeve with four ivory-colored windows with cameos inlaid between intricate patterns set in the corners of each.

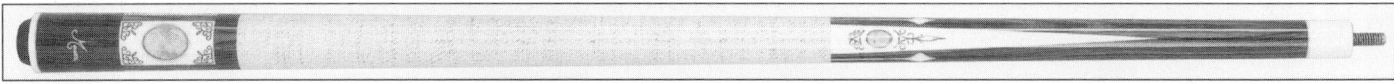

MSR	$940	$700-940	$590	$465

Level 3 HOF-1 - Stained bird's-eye maple forearm, four ebony-colored points with four colored veneers, ebony-colored butt sleeve with six long ivory-colored windows between ivory-colored chain link rings at top and bottom.

MSR	$415	$295-415	$250	$190

Level 3 HOF-2 - Stained bird's-eye maple forearm, four ivory-colored points with four colored veneers, ebony-colored butt sleeve with a thick ring of stained bird's-eye maple between maple and blue-stained maple checks within ivory-colored rings above and below.

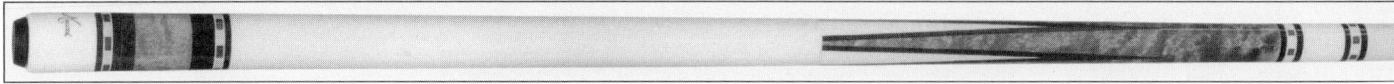

MSR	$415	$305-415	$255	$195

Level 4 HOF-3 - Stained bird's-eye maple forearm, two ebony-colored points with two colored veneers and a white pearlescent dot at the end of a white pearlescent line extending from the base of each alternating with two cocobolo points with two colored veneers and a white pearlescent dot at the end of a white pearlescent line extending from the base of each, stained bird's-eye maple butt sleeve with six white pearlescent-bordered ebony-colored ovals set in a thick cocobolo ring within thin yellow and ebony-colored rings.

MSR	$480	$375-480	$300	$220

Level 5 HOF-4 - Ebony-colored forearm, four ivory-colored points with four colored veneers, ebony-colored butt sleeve with four playing cards set within a pair of thin white rings between six dice inlaid in a ring above and below.

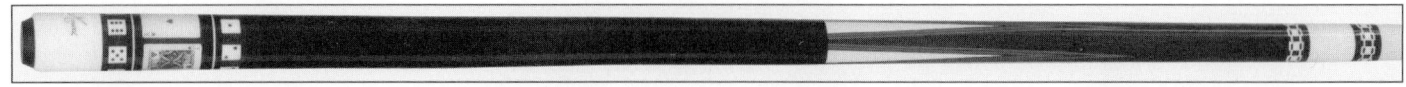

MSR	$540	$365-454	$315	$255

MEUCCI ORIGINALS INC., cont. 521

GRADING	100%	95%	70%

Level 2 HOF-5 - Ebony-colored forearm with red and green inlays representing roses on stems, ebony-colored butt sleeve with red and green inlays representing roses on stems between thin yellow rings above and below.

MSR	$690	$485-690	$430	$340

Level 8 HOF-6 - Stained bird's-eye maple forearm, four ebony-colored points with inlays representing a car and a center line going up from the base to an ebony-colored inlay of a city skyline at the tip of each point, stained bird's-eye maple butt sleeve with an ebony-colored inlay of a city skyline with inlaid windows an antennas above an ebony-colored road with an inlaid center line.

MSR	$740	$565-740	$475	$365

Level 6 HOF-7 - Stained bird's-eye maple forearm, two ebony-colored points with two colored veneers and a two-piece sword-shaped inlay in each alternating with two ebony-colored points with two colored veneers and a two-piece mace-shaped inlay in each, stained bird's-eye maple butt sleeve with medieval swords, maces, shields, and helmets inlaid into a thick ebony-colored ring between thin red rings set in ebony-colored rings at top and bottom, stained bird's-eye maple butt cap.

MSR	$815	$625-815	$515	$395

HI-PRO SERIES

Level 4 HP-1 - Bird's-eye maple forearm, four ebony points with four colored veneers and a synthetic mother-of-pearl dot above a synthetic mother-of-pearl notched diamond-shaped inlay in each point, black composite butt sleeve with four pairs of synthetic mother-of-pearl dot above and below a synthetic mother-of-pearl notched diamond-shaped inlays set in veneered black composite windows.

MSR	$340	$265-340	$215	$160

Level 3 HP-2 - Bloodwood forearm with bloodwood blocks set in white composite within nickel silver rings above wrap, four floating white composite ellipses inlaid with bronze acrylic mirror, bloodwood butt sleeve with four floating white composite ellipses inlaid with bronze acrylic mirror set between bloodwood blocks set in white composite within nickel silver rings at top and bottom.

MSR	$340	$265-340	$215	$160

Level 4 HP-3 - Bird's-eye maple forearm, six black composite points with a blue acrylic dot within a black and white composite inlay within each and a blue acrylic dot within a black composite spear at the tip of each point, bird's-eye maple butt sleeve with black composite point-shaped inlays with a blue acrylic dot in each.

MSR	$340	$265-340	$215	$160

GRADING	98%	90%	70%

DISCONTINUED MEUCCI CUES

The following cues are from Meucci's first catalogue, circa 1975, just before the company moved from Memphis, Tennessee to Olive Branch, Mississippi. These cues were available with flat-faced Implex, wood, or metal joints. Extra shafts were $21 each, and a leather wrap was a $30 option. Prices represent values for this series only, not later similar-looking cues.

Level 2 MO-1 - One-piece bocote butt.

Orig. Retail (1975) $48	$265	$200	$125

Level 2 MO-2 - Bocote forearm, bocote butt sleeve with a black-bordered white ring at bottom.

Orig. Retail (1975) $70	$295	$225	$135

Level 2 MO-3 - Cocobolo forearm, ebony butt sleeve with black squares in white rings at top and bottom.

Orig. Retail (1975) $90	$340	$265	$160

MEUCCI ORIGINALS INC., cont.

GRADING	98%	90%	70%

Level 3 MO-4 - Maple forearm, four rosewood points with four colored veneers, ebony butt sleeve with white checks in a black ring at bottom.

Orig. Retail (1975) $115	$500	$365	$210

Level 3 MO-5 - Maple forearm, four ebony points with four colored veneers, cocobolo butt sleeve.

Orig. Retail (1975) $135	$535	$405	$255

Level 2 MO-6 - Cocobolo forearm, white butt sleeve with cocobolo rectangles alternating with black dots within white chain link rings set in black at top and bottom.

Orig. Retail (1975) $150	$625	$445	$245

Level 3 MO-7 - Maple forearm, four ebony points with four colored veneers, black butt sleeve with white rectangles within white chain link rings set in black at top and bottom.

Orig. Retail (1975) $170	$800	$595	$365

Level 3 MO-8 - Bocote forearm, four white points with four colored veneers, white butt sleeve with a row of black chess pieces above a black and white chess board pattern.

Orig. Retail (1975) $190	$1,225	$920	$575

Level 4 MO-10 - Maple forearm, four ebony points with four colored veneers, green- or ivory-colored butt sleeve with images of the king, queen, jack, and ace of spades set between white chain link rings set in black at top and bottom.

Orig. Retail (1975) $240	$1,200	$900	$550

Level 4 MO-11 - Ebony forearm, four rosewood points with four colored veneers, ebony butt sleeve with figures inlaid in 14-karat gold within black chain link rings set in white at top and bottom.

Orig. Retail (1975) $275	$1,900	$1,400	$800

Level 4 MO-12 - Ebony forearm, four maple points with four colored veneers, white butt sleeve with the queens of hearts, clubs, spades and diamonds within dice set in black at top and bottom.

Orig. Retail (1975) $300	$1,650	$1,200	$700

1990'S CUES

The following cues represent discontinued models the 1996 and 1999 line available from Meucci Originals. Cues costing $600 or more in 1996 or $650 or more in 1999 came with two shafts. Some of these cues are still available as special orders.

MEUCCI ORIGINALS INC., cont. 523

GRADING	98%	90%	70%

Level 1 95-1 - Maple forearm with black ring marked "Meucci" at base of points, rosewood points and butt sleeve.

Orig. Retail (1996) $180	$165	$135	$80

Level 2 95-2 - Maple forearm, maple butt sleeve.

Orig. Retail (1996) $190	$160	$125	$70

Level 2 95-3 - Purple-stained maple forearm, purple-stained maple butt sleeve with black-bordered white ring at bottom.

Orig. Retail (1996) $210	$180	$135	$75

Level 2 95-4 - Grey-stained maple forearm, grey-stained maple butt sleeve with black-bordered white ring at bottom.

Orig. Retail (1996) $210	$165	$130	$75

Level 2 95-5 - Blue-stained maple forearm, blue-stained maple butt sleeve with black-bordered white ring at bottom.

Orig. Retail (1996) $210	$175	$135	$80

Level 3 95-6 - Stained bird's-eye maple forearm, two cocobolo points with thick ebony-colored veneers, ebony-colored butt sleeve with cocobolo ring at bottom.

Orig. Retail (1996) $235	$185	$145	$90

Level 3 95-7 - Stained bird's-eye maple forearm, two stained bird's-eye maple points with thick ebony-colored veneers, ivory-colored butt sleeve with white pearlescent checks set in an ebony-colored ring within very thin ebony-colored rings at bottom.

Orig. Retail (1996) $260	$205	$155	$100

Level 3 95-8 - Stained bird's-eye maple forearm, two ebony-colored points with two colored veneers, ebony-colored butt sleeve with ivory-colored checks set in an ebony-colored ring within two ivory-colored rings.

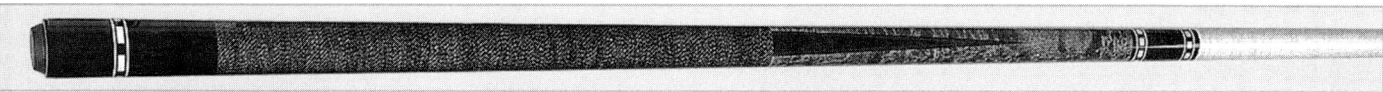

Orig. Retail (1996) $265	$295	$220	$135

Level 3 95-9 - Stained bird's-eye maple forearm, four ebony-colored points with two colored veneers, ebony-colored butt sleeve with long white pearlescent windows above a red ring.

Orig. Retail (1996) $315	$265	$205	$125

MEUCCI ORIGINALS INC., cont.

GRADING	98%	90%	70%

Level 3 95-10 - Stained bird's-eye maple forearm, four ebony-colored points with four colored veneers, ebony-colored butt sleeve with purple squares between thin yellow rings at bottom.

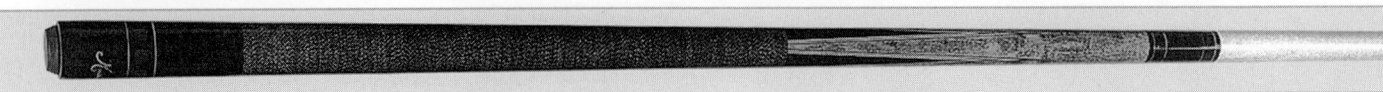

| Orig. Retail (1996) $320 | $265 | $195 | $130 |

Level 3 97-13 - Stained bird's-eye maple forearm, four ebony-colored points with three colored veneers, ebony butt sleeve with red blocks alternating with white lines.

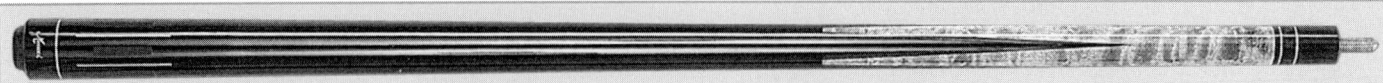

| Orig. Retail (1999) $400 | $350 | $265 | $165 |

Level 4 95-14 - Stained bird's-eye maple forearm, six ebony-colored points with a black-bordered white pearlescent dot at the end of each, ebony-colored butt sleeve with six white pearlescent diamond-shaped inlays set within large stained bird's-eye maple diamond-shaped inlays.

| Orig. Retail (1996) $375 | $420 | $365 | $190 |

Level 4 95-17 - Bird's-eye maple forearm, four ebony-colored points with four colored veneers and a white pearlescent notched diamond-shaped inlay in each, ebony-colored butt sleeve with four white pearlescent notched diamond-shaped inlays with a white pearlescent dot above and below each.

| Orig. Retail (1996) $415 | $515 | $375 | $225 |

Level 5 95-18 - Stained bird's-eye maple forearm, four ivory-colored points with a thick blue veneer and a white pearlescent dot above a white pearlescent diamond-shaped inlay set in a blue-colored window in each point, ivory-colored butt sleeve with six white pearlescent diamond-shaped inlays with a white pearlescent dot above and below each set in a blue-colored window inside thin blue-colored veneers.

| Orig. Retail (1996) $450 | $565 | $415 | $235 |

Level 4 95-19 - Bird's-eye maple forearm, four ebony-colored points with four colored veneers and a white pearlescent dot above a white pearlescent spear-shaped inlay in each point, ebony-colored butt sleeve with four pairs of opposing white-bordered white pearlescent spear-shaped inlays alternating with four white pearlescent dots between thin nickel silver rings above and below.

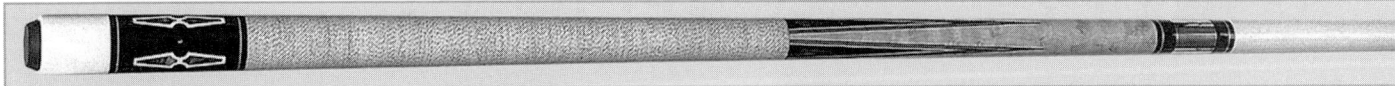

| Orig. Retail (1996) $430 | $535 | $395 | $250 |

Level 5 97-19 - Ebony-colored forearm, four four-piece grey bird's-eye maple and ivory-colored points alternating with four four-piece ivory-colored and grey-stained bird's-eye maple blocks atop red lines, ivory-colored butt sleeve with four intricate nine-piece ivory-colored and grey-stained bird's-eye maple windows.

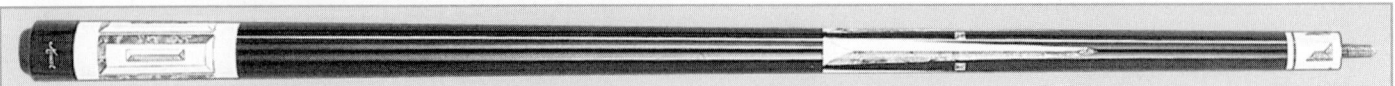

| Orig. Retail (1999) $590 | $465 | $365 | $220 |

Level 4 97-20 - Cocobolo joint, grey-stained bird's-eye maple forearm, four ivory-colored points with a cocobolo triangle inlaid with a pearlized plastic design in each, ivory-colored butt sleeve with a ring of cocobolo triangles inlaid with pearlized plastic designs.

| Orig. Retail (1999) $590 | $460 | $355 | $220 |

MEUCCI ORIGINALS INC., cont. **525**

GRADING	98%	90%	70%

Level 2 95-21 - Stained bird's-eye maple forearm with inlays of cues over racks with cue balls, green-stained bird's-eye maple butt sleeve representing a table with inlays of cues striking balls towards a pocket at the top, above a cocobolo ring at bottom with white pearlescent dots representing the table rail.

| Orig. Retail (1996) $425 | $525 | $375 | $220 |

Level 5 95-23 - Stained bird's-eye maple forearm with four red six-point asterisks set in ivory-colored ovals above wrap and over the points, four ebony-colored points with two colored veneers, stained bird's-eye maple butt sleeve with four red six-point asterisks set in ivory-colored ovals alternating with tall red-bordered maple windows each inlaid with four vertical ebony-colored block designs all set within a red-bordered thick ebony-colored ring.

| Orig. Retail (1996) $535 | $565 | $425 | $265 |

Level 5 97-23 - Stained bird's-eye maple forearm with billiard-related images, stained bird's-eye maple butt sleeve with billiard balls and a cue below a cocobolo ring representing the rail of a table.

| Orig. Retail (1999) $750 | $585 | $435 | $280 |

Level 4 97-25 - Grey-stained bird's-eye maple forearm, four ivory-colored points with a red-bordered ivory-colored dot at the tip of each point alternating with four ebony-colored ovals with intricate white patterns, ivory-colored butt sleeve with a crown-shaped bottom and intricate white patterns in an ebony-colored ring.

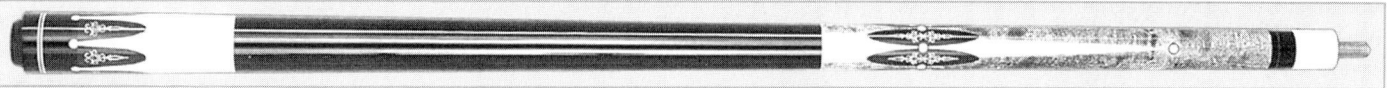

| Orig. Retail (1999) $750 | $625 | $470 | $300 |

Level 4 97-26 - Grey-stained bird's-eye maple forearm, four cocobolo points with three colored veneers and an intricate ivory-colored inlay in each point, cocobolo butt sleeve with four intricate ivory-colored windows with intricate colored designs in each.

| Orig. Retail (1999) $800 | $650 | $490 | $315 |

Level 5 97-27 - Stained bird's-eye maple forearm, four ivory-colored points with three colored veneers and multi-colored inlays surrounding pearlized plastic and cocobolo ovals in each point, ivory-colored butt sleeve with four red-bordered windows with multi-colored inlays surrounding pearlized plastic and cocobolo ovals in each.

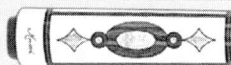

| Orig. Retail (1999) $850 | $655 | $500 | $320 |

Level 5 97-29 - Stained bird's-eye maple forearm, intricate multi-colored hardwood and ivory-colored floating points, stained bird's-eye maple butt sleeve with intricate hardwood and ivory-colored designs within metal rings at top and bottom.

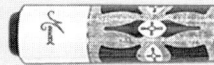

| Orig. Retail (1999) $900 | $685 | $515 | $325 |

Level 6 95-30 - Stained bird's-eye maple forearm with four ivory-colored dots set in floating ebony-colored four point stars alternating with the points, four black-bordered ivory-colored points with a black line extending up from a black dot in each and an ivory-colored dot set in the bottom of each black border, stained bird's-eye maple butt sleeve with four intricate black-bordered ivory-colored windows with a black line extending up from a black dot in each and a white pearlescent dot set in the top and bottom of each black border alternating with four black-bordered ivory-colored barbell-shaped inlays.

| Orig. Retail (1996) $800 | $750 | $565 | $365 |

| GRADING | 98% | 90% | 70% |

Level 7 95-31 - Ebony-colored forearm with two tall ivory-colored torch-shaped inlays with red flames set on a red line alternating with two shorter ivory-colored torch-shaped inlays with red flames set on a red line, four intricate floating ivory-colored Roman pillar-shaped inlays, ebony-colored butt sleeve with four intricate torch-shaped inlays with red flames alternating with four intricate ivory-colored Roman pillar-shaped inlays between rings of ivory-colored blocks at top and bottom.

| Orig. Retail (1996) $1,100 | $1,000 | $750 | $475 |

Level 8 95-32 - Stained bird's-eye maple forearm, two floating intricate ivory-colored designs with an intricately inlaid sword set in purple-stained maple in each alternating above two floating intricate ivory-colored designs with an intricately inlaid ivory-colored medieval design set in purple-stained maple, purple-stained maple butt sleeve with two intricately inlaid purple and ivory-colored crowns set in a five-sided stained bird's-eye maple window alternating with two intricate ivory-colored Roman pillar-shaped inlays between rings of purple- and ivory-colored blocks at top and bottom.

| Orig. Retail (1996) $2,000 | $1,750 | $1,355 | $800 |

Level 8 HOF-8 - Ebony-colored forearm, two floating intricate ivory-colored designs with an intricately inlaid sword set in red-stained maple in each alternating above two floating intricate ivory-colored designs with an intricately inlaid ivory-colored medieval design set in red-stained maple, red-stained maple butt sleeve with two intricately inlaid red- and ivory-colored crowns set in a five-sided stained bird's-eye maple window alternating with two intricate ivory-colored Roman pillar-shaped inlays between rings of red and ivory-colored blocks at top and bottom.

| Orig. Retail (1999) $2,200 | $1,550 | $1,155 | $700 |

SPECIAL INTEREST MEUCCI CUES

About six of the following Road Runner cues were custom made by Bob Meucci in the late 1970s/early 1980s. He also made other custom cues using real ivory and other exotic materials. One-of-a-kind custom Bob Meucci cues sell for thousands of dollars.

Level 5 "Custom Road Runner" - Stained bird's-eye maple forearm with inlaid rock formations made of stacked multi-colored veneers, two ivory points shaped like winding roads, stained bird's-eye maple butt sleeve with inlaid rock formations made of stacked multi-colored veneers and an ebony road runner standing on a rock formation under an ivory crescent moon, black synthetic butt sleeve with a brass coyote running up a white-striped road that leads towards the road runner.

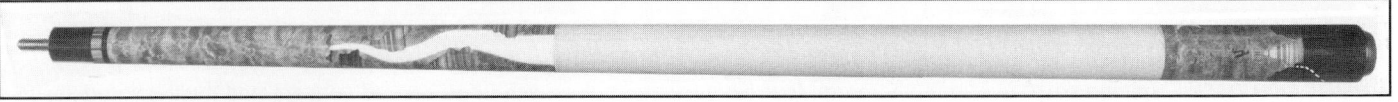

| MSR (early 1980's) $600 | $5,000 | $3,950 | $2,750 |

SECONDARY MARKET MINIMUM VALUES

The following are minimum prices for other Meucci cues encountered on the secondary market. These prices are representative of cues utilizing basic materials and designs that are not currently available. Bob Meucci has made many one-of-a-kind cues that can command many times these prices due to the use of exotic materials and artistry. Early models and limited editions are becoming collectible, and can also command many times these prices. Other discontinued Meucci cues will be further covered in future editions.

Special construction note: There are many materials and construction techniques that can add value to Meucci cues. The following are the most important examples:

- Add 20%+ for "meucci originals" on butt cap (made before 1990).
- Add 500%+ for early one-of-a-kind custom cues by Bob Meucci.

For all used Meucci cues, except where otherwise noted:

- Add $60+ for each additional original straight playable shaft (standard with one).
- Deduct $80+ for missing original straight playable shaft.
- Deduct 30% for obvious or improper refinish.

Level 1 - 4 points, hustler

| Level 1 cues start at | $135 | $95 | $50 |

Level 2 - 0 points, 0-25 inlays.

| Level 2 cues start at | $150 | $110 | $65 |

Level 3 - 2-6 points, 0-8 inlays.

| Level 3 cues start at | $250 | $185 | $115 |

GRADING	98%	90%	70%
Level 4 - 4-10 points, 9-25 inlays.			
Level 4 cues start at	$285	$265	$140
Level 5 - 0-12 points, 26-50 inlays.			
Level 5 cues start at	$375	$275	$165
Level 6 - 0-12 points, 51-75 inlays.			
Level 6 cues start at	$500	$380	$245

MEZZ CUES

Line of pool cues made by Miki Co., a maker of pool cues in Tomioka-City, Japan from 1963 to present.

Yuji Miki, founder of Miki Company, was brought up in his father's workshop. His father made traditional Japanese wooden products. Yuji became familiar with the various types and properties of wood at a young age. In 1960 he started making unfinished one-piece cues using a machine that he had constructed himself. He then sold the cues to another company to be finished. By 1963 he was making finished cues to be sold to a trading company doing business in the United States. Demand for his cues grew quickly. In order to keep up with the demand, Miki moved the factory to a larger building in the same city. Miki Company was producing 240,000 one-piece cues annually by this time.

In 1971 Miki Company signed a contract to produce cues exclusively for an American company. By the terms of the agreement, Miki could not sell any cues under its own name in Japan. In the late 1970s Miki was producing wood-screw carom billiard cues and snooker cues.

In the early 1990s the Japanese yen became very strong against other currencies and orders dropped off sharply. Miki and its American distributor severed their contract agreement.

In 1994 Yuki's son joined Miki and started a campaign to take the company on a new path. Kazunori Miki recruited a network of distributors both in Japan and abroad. He developed unique designs and continued to develop methods of creating cues with excellent playability. Since then, the Mezz name has spread worldwide.

Mezz translates from Japanese to mean "something that is loved, something that is treasured." The Miki Company's goal is to make cues that are treasured by players and collectors everywhere.

If you are interested in talking to someone about a new Mezz cue or cue that needs to be repaired, you can contact them at Mezz Cues, listed in the Trademark Index. J&J America is the major distributor of Mezz cues in the USA; see Trademark Index for further information.

SPECIFICATIONS

Butt material: hardwoods
Shaft material: rock maple
Standard length: 58 in.
Standard wrap: Irish linen
Joint screw: 5/16-14
Standard joint: Ivorine 3
Joint type: flat faced
Ferrules: Ivorine 3
Standard number of shafts: one

SECONDARY MARKET MINIMUM VALUES

The following are minimum values for Mezz Cues encountered on the secondary market. These prices are representative of cues utilizing basic materials and designs that are not necessarily available at present.

Special construction note: There are many materials and construction techniques that can add value to Mezz cues. The following are the most important examples:

Add 20% for cues with stainless steel piloted joints.

For all used Mezz cues, except where otherwise noted:

Add $75 for each additional original straight playable shaft.
Deduct $90 for missing original straight playable shaft.
Deduct 15% for obvious or improper refinish.

	98%	90%	70%
Level 2 - 0 points, 0-25 inlays.			
Level 2 cues start at	$160	$100	$85
Level 3 - 2-6 points, 0-8 inlays.			
Level 3 cues start at	$150	$120	$95
Level 4 - 4-10 points, 9-25 inlays.			
Level 4 cues start at	$195	$155	$105
Level 5 - 0-12 points, 26-50 inlays.			
Level 5 cues start at	$250	$195	$125
Level 6 - 0-12 points, 51-75 inlays.			
Level 6 cues start at	$400	$300	$200

MICHAELANGELO CUSTOM CUES

Maker of pool cues from 1993 in Boise, Idaho, presently in Carrollton, Texas.

Michael Givens has loved to play pool since he was in high school. After getting a degree in civil engineering, Michael worked a couple of years in that field. He then started making custom knives in 1974. Michael studied under Robert Loveless and Kuzan Oda, two of the top names in the custom knife business. He made Michael Givens knives for over twenty years. By the early nineties he was getting tired of breathing metal dust and making knives. He had seen pictures of custom cues in magazines, and thought they would be fun to make.

One day in 1993 his son Doug needed a tip replaced on his cue. Doug had a local cue repairman replace the tip for him. When Michael saw the poor quality of the work, he knew that he could do a much better job himself. Although he was in the middle of making a custom knife, Michael stopped to figure out how to properly repair his son's cue. He quickly started doing repairs, bought a lathe, and started making cues. And to this day, he still has not finished that knife.

Michael Givens

Michael knew that he could not just start making cues full time and expect to support himself right away, so he opened a billiard pro shop in Boise, Idaho with Doug as his partner. By selling custom cues he quickly learned what he did and didn't like about their designs and playability characteristics. He took many cues apart to learn about their internal construction. Michael befriended a few of the top cuemakers, and asked them questions during many long phone conversations. He knew how to work with many exotic materials such as "oosic" (dried walrus penis) from his experience as a custom knife maker, and he now uses such materials on his cues. About a half dozen of the first cues he made were unmarked, but all of them since have been signed "Michael Givens" and most of those have a date of completion after the signature. He used engineering formulas to develop his own custom parabolic shaft taper which is surprisingly stiff even with thin shafts, and he is experimenting with carbon fiber reinforced shafts.

Michael likes to use as many exotic materials as possible, and likes natural joints of ivory, elk horn, India stag, horn, bone, and water buffalo. He prefers to use purpleheart shafts on his break/jump cues, believing that it has less flex and more power. He has tried every type of joint design, and has even made cues with wood screws. Michael helped patent the "Kinetic Cue" with friend Frank Jordan. It is a training aid for developing a better stroke. Michael sold his interest in the Kinetic Cue in 1998 to concentrate on building one-of-a-kind custom cues. All work has been done by hand on a manual pantograph.

Michael is constantly experimenting with improvements in design, and has developed his own full splice blanks. All parts are threaded together, and he uses a wood tenon instead of a metal screw to join the handle to the forearm. He is very proud of his repair work, and can exactly copy the taper of an existing shaft. He tries to help beginning cuemakers with the same types of questions he asked when he started. Michaelangelo cues are easily identifiable by "Michael Givens", "Michaelangelo", "Michaelangelo Givens," or "Michaelangelo Customs" signatures, or by Michaelangelo's "Creative Excellence" logo. Matching custom knives and cases are also available. Michaelangelo produces 25 to 70 cues per year.

Michaelangelo Custom Cues are guaranteed for life against manufacturing defects that are not the result of warpage or abuse. If you have a Michaelangelo cue that needs further identification or repair, or would like to order a new Michaelangelo cue, contact Michaelangelo Custom Cues, listed in the Trademark Index.

SPECIFICATIONS

Butt material: hardwoods
Shaft material: rock maple and purpleheart
Standard length: 58 in.
Lengths available: 40 in. to 64 in.
Standard finishes: automotive urethane or UV
Balance point: 19 1/2 in. from butt
Standard butt cap: linen phenolic
Standard wrap: Irish linen
Point construction: short splice, full splice, inlaid, or Michaelangelo full splice
Standard joint: wood-to-wood
Joint type: flat faced
Standard number of shafts: two
Standard taper: Michaelangelo parabolic taper
Standard ferrules: Aegis 2
Standard tip width: 13 1/8 mm
Standard tip: Triangle
Annual production: 50 to 70

OPTIONS (FOR NEW CUES ONLY)

Leather wrap: $125
Extra length: $25 per extra inch
Custom joint protectors: $35+

GRADING	98%	90%	70%

Ivory butt cap: $250
Ivory joint: $150
Ivory ferrule: $75
Ivory butt sleeve: $600
Ivory points: $250 each
Ivory handle: $1,000
Extra shaft: $100
Layered tip: $50

REPAIRS

Repairs done on all custom cues.
   Refinish (with Irish linen wrap): $150
   Refinish (with leather wrap): $225
   Rewrap (Irish linen): $50
   Rewrap (leather): $125
   Clean and press linen wrap: $25
   Restore leather wrap: $35
   Replace butt cap: $50
   Replace ivory butt cap: $300
   Replace joint (ivory): $175
   Replace shaft: $100+
   Replace fiber/linen ferrule: $30
   Replace ivory ferrule: $85
   Replace tip: $20
   Replace layered tip: $50

CURRENT MICHAELANGELO CUES

Two-piece Michaelangelo bar cues start at $250. Basic Michaelangelo cues with wraps and joint rings start at $500. Michaelangelo cues with points start at $750. One-of-a-kind custom Michaelangelo cues start at $1,000. The current delivery time for a Michaelangelo custom cue is six months.

SECONDARY MARKET MINIMUM VALUES

The following are minimum values for Michaelangelo custom cues encountered on the secondary market. These prices are representative of cues utilizing basic materials and designs that are not currently available. Michaelangelo has offered one-of-a-kind cues that can command many times these prices due to the use of exotic materials and artistry.

Special construction note: There are many materials and construction techniques that can add value to Michaelangelo cues. For all used Michaelangelo cues, except where otherwise noted:
   Add $85 for each additional original straight playable shaft beyond two.
   Deduct $100 for each missing original straight playable shaft under two.
   Add $500 for ivory butt sleeve
   Add $200 for each ivory point.
   Add $65 each for ivory ferrules.
   Add $100 for leather wrap.
   Deduct 20% for obvious or improper refinish.

	98%	90%	70%
Level 1 - 4 points, (Hustler)			
Level 1 cues start at	$225	$175	$120
Level 2 - 0 points, 0-25 inlays.			
Level 2 cues start at	$450	$350	$235
Level 3 - 2-6 points, 0-8 inlays.			
Level 3 cues start at	$650	$510	$340
Level 4 - 4-10 points, 9-25 inlays.			
Level 4 cues start at	$775	$595	$395
Level 5 - 0-12 points, 26-50 inlays.			
Level 5 cues start at	$1,000	$775	$525
Level 6 - 0-12 points, 51-75 inlays.			
Level 6 cues start at	$1,500	$1,175	$800

MICHAEL MORGAN CUES

Maker of pool cues from 1992 to present in North Massapequa, New York.

Michael Miller

Michael Miller restored antique pool tables many years ago in the greater New York area for Jackie Grimaldi. It was then that he became acquainted with cuemakers such as George Balabushka and Eugene Balner of Palmer. As a teenager, he often watched Eugene Balner work. Later, Michael owned a pool room, and became a fairly good player. He became friends with master machinist Harry Stower of Deer Park, Long Island. Harry used his years of machining experience to help teach Michael how to make cues. Michael named his cue business after his son, Michael, and his daughter, Morgan.

Michael Morgan cues are easily identifiable by an "MM" logo on the forearm or the butt cap that he has hand-signed. The first 25 cues had a serial number following the logo, while later cues have the year of completion. Two joint styles are available, a 3/8-10 flat faced, and a 5/16-14 piloted. Michael experimented in the late nineties with ferrules of impregnated holly, but now uses linen micarta. With his assistant, Mario Carasa, he makes everything by hand on a manual pantograph, except for the tips, screws, inserts, and bumpers. Michael carefully selects his woods and allows time for long aging to maximize the stability of the wood. He does a lot of repair work, and especially likes to work on older cues. Michael Morgan cues are guaranteed for five years to the original owner with proper care. If you have a Michael Morgan cue needing further identification or repair, or would like to talk to Michael about ordering a new cue, contact Michael Morgan Cues, listed in the Trademark Index.

SPECIFICATIONS

Butt material: hardwoods
Shaft material: rock maple
Standard length: 58 in.
Lengths available: up to 62 in.
Joint screw: 3/8-10 or 5/16-14
Standard finish: urethane
Balance point: 18 1/2 in. from butt
Point construction: short splice
Standard wrap: Irish linen
Standard number of shafts: two
Standard ferrules: linen micarta
Stanard tip: Le Pro
Tip widths available: 11 to 14 mm
Annual production: 20

OPTIONS (FOR NEW CUES ONLY)

Leather wrap: $125
Special length: no charge
Ivory butt cap: $125
Ivory joint: $100
Nickel silver joint: $50
Wood joint: no charge
Custom joint protectors: $30 to $100
Extra shaft: $150
Ivory ferrule: $50
Layered tip: $20

REPAIRS

Repairs done on all fine cues.

Refinish: $150 and up
Rewrap (Irish linen): $35
Rewrap (leather): $125
Restore leather wrap: $25
Replace Delrin butt cap: $30
Replace shaft: $150
Replace ivory ferrule: $60

CURRENT EXAMPLES

The following cues are currently available from Michael Morgan Custom Cues. They can be ordered as shown, or modified to suit the desires of the customer. The current delivery time for a custom cue is approximately one year.

MICHAEL MORGAN CUES, cont. 531

GRADING	100%	95%	70%

Level 1 - Maple forearm with mother-of-pearl dots at bases of points, four full-spliced purpleheart points and handle, mother-of-pearl ringwork above butt cap.

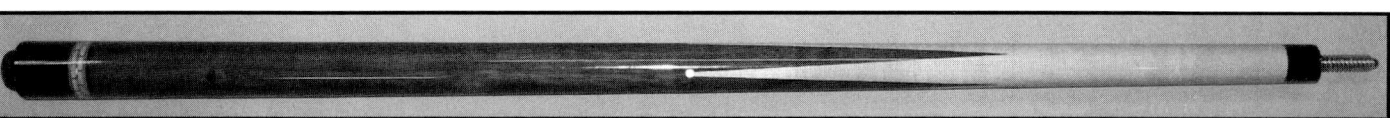

MSR	$400	$365-425	$295	$220

Level 4 - Cocobolo forearm with rings above wrap, four ebony points with four veneers and an abalone notched diamond-shaped inlay in each and at the tip of each point, lizard wrap, cocobolo butt sleeve with twelve abalone oval-shaped inlays between rings above and below.

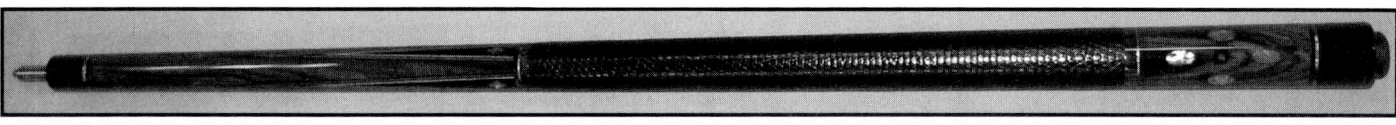

MSR	$1,200	$1,100-1,250	$885	$650

Level 4 - Maple forearm with mother-of-pearl dots at bases of points, four full-spliced purpleheart points with four colored veneers and a purpleheart-bordered micarta spear-shaped inlay at the tip of each point, stacked leather wrap, purpleheart butt sleeve with four long and four short reverse micarta points with micarta and purpleheart veneers.

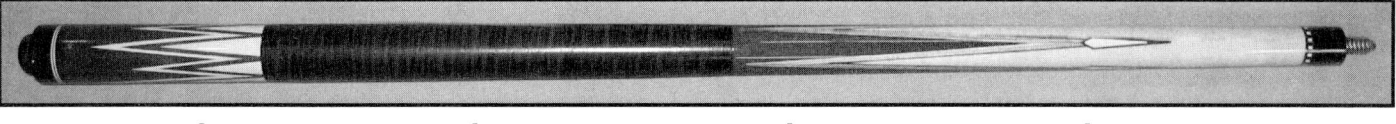

MSR	$1,600	$1,500-1,650	$1,200	$850

Level 5 "Titlist" - Maple forearm, four full-spliced rosewood points with four colored veneers and a mother-of-pearl notched diamond-shaped inlay surrounded by three mother-of-pearl dots in each point, Cortland Irish linen wrap, rosewood butt sleeve with four sets of mother-of-pearl notched diamond-shaped inlays surrounded by mother-of-pearl dots.

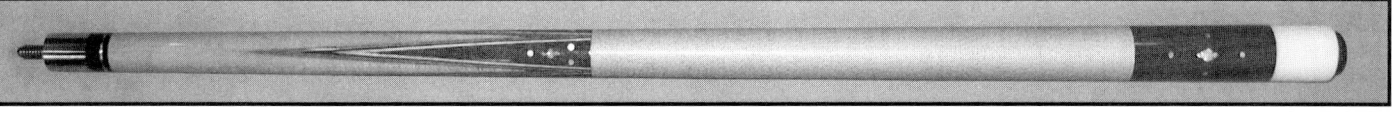

MSR	$2,400	$2,100-2,500	$1,750	$1,350

Level 5 - Ebony forearm with ivory blocks set in an ebony ring above wrap, four long and four short holly-bordered burl wood points with an ivory spear-shaped inlay at the tip of each point, lizard wrap, ebony butt sleeve with four sets of four-piece ivory diamond-shaped inlays surrounded by ivory dots between ivory blocks set in ebony rings at top and bottom.

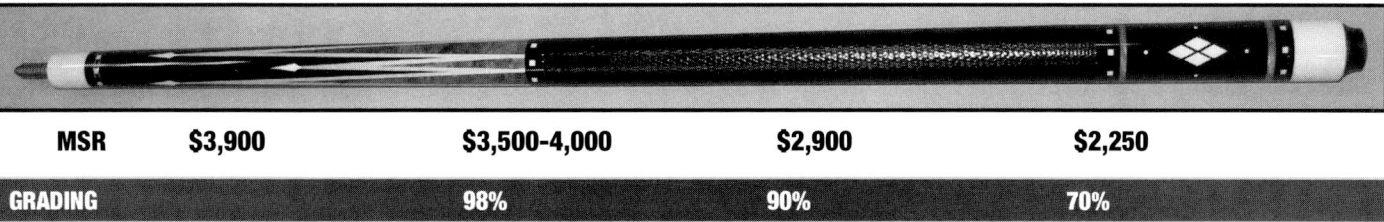

MSR	$3,900	$3,500-4,000	$2,900	$2,250

GRADING	98%	90%	70%

PAST EXAMPLES

The following cues are custom examples available from Michael Morgan Cues. The following Series cues under $900 came with one shaft. Cues at $900 or more came with two shafts.

Level 3 Ebony forearm, three long and three short bird's-eye maple points with two veneers and a pink ivory diamond-shaped inlay at the tip of each point, bird's-eye maple butt sleeve with three ebony spears pointing down from top alternating with three ebony spears pointing up from bottom.

MSR (1999) $900	$1,075	$835	$560

Level 3 - Ebony forearm, three long and three short quilted maple points, ebony butt sleeve with three large ivory diamond-shaped inlays alternating with three smaller ivory diamond-shaped inlays.

MSR (1999) $900	$1,050	$825	$550

SECONDARY MARKET MINIMUM VALUES

GRADING	98%	90%	70%

Special construction note: There are many materials and construction techniques that can add value to Michael Morgan cues. For all used cues, except where otherwise noted:

- Add $115 for each additional original straight playable shaft beyond two.
- Deduct $150 for each missing original straight playable shaft under two.
- Add $45 each for ivory ferrules.
- Add $85 for leather wrap.
- Deduct 20% for obvious or improper refinish.

Level 1 - 4 points, (Hustler)

	98%	90%	70%
Level 1 cues start at	$250	$200	$135

Level 2 - 0 points, 0-25 inlays.

Level 2 cues start at	$350	$275	$185

Level 3 - 2-6 points, 0-8 inlays.

Level 3 cues start at	$495	$385	$265

Level 4 - 4-10 points, 9-25 inlays.

Level 4 cues start at	$650	$515	$350

Level 5 - 0-12 points, 26-50 inlays.

Level 5 cues start at	$1,100	$865	$595

MICHAEL'S CUSTOM CUES

Maker of pool cues from 1994 to present in Racine, Wisconsin.

Mike Kratochvill grew up in Glenview, Illinois, never playing pool until the age of 21. Before long, he became interested in pool leagues and was doing minor cue repairs for league friends by the mid-1970s. Although Mike worked as a full-time auto mechanic for many years, he was never satisfied with that field.

He eventually gave up on being a mechanic and started making Michael's Custom Cues full time in 1994. Since then, Michael's cues have undergone numerous improvements. Most of Mike's cues have been easily identifiable by the "Michael's" logo burned into the butt caps. All Michael's cues are hand-made in Mike's one-man shop. Mike makes everything, except the bumpers, tips, and screws, without the aid of CNC. All collars, ferrules, and butt caps are threaded on. Shafts are turned six to ten times over a period of at least three months, and all but the shafts with custom rings are interchangeable. In 1997, Michael changed his joint and butt cap material from high impact styrene to ABS. That same year he started using ivory for inlays.

Michael retired in 2000 and continues to make cues part time as a hobby.

Michael's cues are guaranteed for one year against construction defects that are not the result of warpage or abuse to the original owner. If you have a Michael's cue that needs further identification or repair, or would like to talk to Mike about ordering a new custom cue, contact Michael's Custom Cues, listed in the Trademark Index.

Mike Kratochvill

SPECIFICATIONS

Butt material: hardwoods
Shaft material: rock maple
Standard length: 59 in.
Lengths available: any
Standard finish: epoxy
Joint screw: 3/8-10
Standard joint: ABS
Joint type: flat faced
Balance point: 2 in. above wrap
Point construction: inlaid
Standard wrap: Irish linen
Standard butt cap: ABS
Standard number of shafts: one
Standard taper: custom
Standard ferrules: Ivorine 3
Standard tip: Le Pro
Tip widths available: any
Annual production: fewer than 50 cues

OPTIONS

Options priced on an individual basis depending on the cue.

GRADING	98%	90%	70%

REPAIRS
Repairs done on most fine cues. Repairs priced on an individual basis depending on the cue.

CURRENT MICHAEL'S CUES
Michael's two-piece bar cues start at $175. Basic Michael's cues with wraps and joint rings start at $400. Michael's cues with points start at $500. The current delivery time for a Michael's cue is at least one month depending on the intricacy of the cue.

SECONDARY MARKET MINIMUM VALUES
The following are minimum prices for Michael's cues encountered on the secondary market. These prices are representative of cues utilizing basic materials and designs that may not be currently available. Mike also offers one-of-a-kind cues that can command many times these prices due to the use of exotic materials and artistry.

Special construction note: There are many materials and construction techniques that can add value to Michael's cues.

For all used Michael's cues, except where otherwise noted:
- Add $75+ for each additional original straight playable shaft (standard with one).
- Deduct $85 for each missing original straight playable shaft.
- Deduct 25% for obvious or improper refinish.

Level 1 - 4 points, hustler.
Level 1 cues start at	$165	$135	$95

Level 2 - 0 points, 0-25 inlays.
Level 2 cues start at	$325	$350	$175

Level 3 - 2-6 points, 0-8 inlays.
Level 3 cues start at	$650	$500	$350

Level 4 - 4-10 points, 9-25 inlays.
Level 4 cues start at	$750	$575	$395

Level 5 - 0-12 points, 26-50 inlays.
Level 5 cues start at	$1,100	$875	$625

Level 6 - 0-12 points, 51-75 inlays.
Level 6 cues start at	$1,450	$1,200	$875

MID WEST CUSTOM CUES

Maker of pool cues from 1993 to present in South St. Paul, Minnesota.

Steve Morris began playing snooker in 1963, when his father bought a table for the family home. Growing up playing pool, he owned many different cues and started to learn what features and specifications he preferred. After graduating from college, Steve worked as a chemical engineer, and began to collect custom cues. He accumulated quite a few cues, and eventually had five or six that needed refinishing.

In May of 1993, he bought a lathe to do ferrule work and began to do his own refinishing. Immediately, one of his friends wanted Steve to make a cue for him, and he has been making cues ever since.

Mid West cues are easily identifiable by a logo on the butt cap which was embossed up to January of 1996, and printed ever since. The first Mid West cues featured a 3/8-10 joint screw, but in April of 1994, Steve changed to the current radial pin. In September of 1995, Steve started using Moori tips.

Steve does all of the inlay work on a pantograph he acquired. He handcrafts the cues by himself, hence the phrase, "From My Hands to Yours," which has become Steve's motto, and he prefers linen phenolics and micartas over plastics. He makes everything except for the tips, bumpers, and screws. All ferrules and collars are threaded on.

Steve is well-known as one of the better players in the Minneapolis/St. Paul area, and he tries to use this ability to make cues that play well. A feature that improves the hit is Mid West's tight/intimate joint that provides more surface contact than traditional joints. Steve uses laminated shafts on his jump/break cues to increase the transmission of power. His "Hollow Hopper" jump cue won a jump cue contest among the eleven cues tested by Chalk Talk magazine several years ago. Currently Steve makes more high end cues. He has been working with exotic hand cut stones such as malachite, red jasper, turquoise, tiger eye, opals, and lapis set in sterling silver. Exotic wraps of python and lizard have become popular for Steve, and he even makes a jump cue with a lizard wrap called the "Leaping Lizard."

Steve will repair any manufacturing defects that are not the result of warpage or abuse indefinitely for the original purchaser. He is so confident in the performance of his jump/break cues that they can be returned (in excellent condition) for up to two weeks after purchase, if not

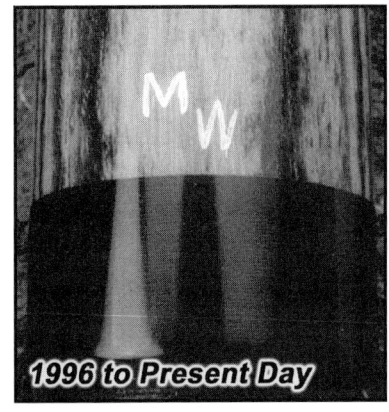

MID WEST CUSTOM CUES, cont.

GRADING	98%	90%	70%

completely satisfied with their playability. If you have a Mid West custom cue that needs repair, or would like to talk to Steve about the purchase of a new custom cue, contact Mid West Custom Cues, listed in the Trademark Index.

SPECIFICATIONS

Butt material: hardwoods
Shaft material: rock maple
Standard length: 58 in.
Lengths available: 40 to 62 in.
Standard finish: PPG
Joint screw: radial pin
Standard joint: black linen phenolic
Joint type: flat faced
Balance point: 9-1/2 to 10 in. from joint
Point construction: short splice
Standard wrap: Irish linen
Standard butt cap: black linen phenolic
Standard number of shafts: one
Standard taper: custom
Standard ferrules: Ivorine 3
Standard tip: Moori medium
Tip widths available: 10 to 14 mm
Annual production: approximately 20

OPTIONS (FOR NEW CUES ONLY)

Special length: no charge
Leather wrap: $20
Ostrich/lizard/python wrap: $120
Ivory ferrule: $40
Ivory butt cap: $250
Ivory joint: $150
Joint protectors: standard
Extra shaft: $100+
Extra flat laminated shaft: $125+
Extra radial laminated shaft: $150+

REPAIRS

Repairs done on all fine cues.
Refinish (with Irish linen wrap): $125+
Refinish (with leather wrap): $150+
Rewrap (Irish linen): $40
Rewrap (leather): $100+
Replace Moori tip: $20
Replace ivory ferrule: $60

CURRENT CUES

Basic two-piece Mid West hustler cues start at $330. Basic two-piece Mid West cues with wraps and joint rings start at $400. Mid West cues with points start at $600. One-of-a-kind custom Mid West cues start at $750. The current delivery time for a Mid West cue is four weeks to one year, depending on the intricacy of the cue.

SECONDARY MARKET MINIMUM VALUES

The following are minimum prices for Mid West cues encountered on the secondary market. These prices are representative of cues utilizing basic materials and designs that may not be currently available. Steve also offers one-of-a-kind cues that can command many times these prices due to the use of exotic materials and artistry.

Special construction note: There are many materials and construction techniques that can add value to Mid West cues.

For all used Mid West cues, except where otherwise noted:

Add $85+ for each additional original straight playable shaft (standard with one).
Deduct $100 for missing original straight playable shaft.
Add $100+ for ivory joint.
Add $20+ for leather wrap.
Deduct 30% for obvious or improper refinish.

Level 1 - 4 points, hustler.

	98%	90%	70%
Level 1 cues start at	$275	$200	$150

MID WEST CUSTOM CUES, cont.

GRADING	98%	90%	70%
Level 2 - 0 points, 0-25 inlays.			
Level 2 cues start at	$350	$250	$175
Level 3 - 2-6 points, 0-8 inlays.			
Level 3 cues start at	$500	$450	$250
Level 4 - 4-10 points, 9-25 inlays.			
Level 4 cues start at	$650	$500	$350
Level 5 - 0-12 points, 26-50 inlays.			
Level 5 cues start at	$1,200	$900	$650
Level 6 - 0-12 points, 51-75 inlays.			
Level 6 cues start at	$1,650	$1,250	$850

TOMMY MIGLIORE

Maker of TNS Cues. For more information, refer to the listing for TNS.

MIKI CO. LTD.

Maker of pool cues in Japan; for more information refer to listing for "Mezz Cues."

S.C. MILLER CUSTOM CUES

Maker of pool cues from 1984 to 1995 in Racine, Wisconsin.

Steve Miller started playing pool as a young boy. He developed an interest in woodworking in his high school shop class and later worked in a custom cabinet shop. Within six months after graduating from high school, Steve made his first pool cue. He named his one-man cuemaking operation "S.C. Miller Custom Cues." Steve constantly improved his design and construction methods toward better playability.

The first few S.C. Miller cues had 5/16-18 joint screws, but Steve soon switched to a 5/16-14 screw. About ten of the early cues he made for his friends were marked "ICKY," Steve's nickname in the local pool rooms. All other cues were marked "S.C. Miller" or "S.C.M." In 1993, Steve stopped using short spliced blanks and started inlaying his points. One year later, he started using an epoxy finish instead of the lacquer he had used previously.

In 1995, Steve joined Nova cues, and stopped making S.C. Miller cues. Only one of his cues had ivory inlays, and it was extremely fancy. Other S.C. Miller cues were usually simple, with inlays of wood, synthetics or pearl.

For more information, please see listing for "Nova Cues".

Steve Miller

SPECIFICATIONS

Butt material: hardwoods
Shaft material: rock maple
Standard length: 58 in.
Standard finish: lacquer
Joint screw: 5/16-14
Standard joint: stainless steel
Point construction: inlaid and short splice
Standard wrap: Irish linen
Standard butt cap: Delrin
Standard number of shafts: one
Standard taper: 12 in. pro
Standard ferrules: Ivorine 3
Standard tip: Le Pro
Total production: fewer than 150 cues

S.C.MILLER
Late 80s to 1995

SECONDARY MARKET MINIMUM VALUES

The following are minimum prices for S.C. Miller cues encountered on the secondary market. These prices are representative of cues utilizing basic materials and designs. Steve also made a few one-of-a-kind cues that can command many times these prices due to the use of exotic materials and artistry.

Special construction note: There are many materials and construction techniques that can add value to S.C. Miller cues.

For all used S.C. Miller cues:

Add 25%+ for cues marked "icky".
Add $85+ for each additional original straight playable shaft.
Deduct $100 for missing original straight playable shaft.
Deduct 25% for obvious or improper refinish.

S.C. MILLER CUSTOM CUES, cont.

GRADING	98%	90%	70%
Level 2 - 0 points, 0-25 inlays.			
Level 2 cues start at	$400	$325	$250
Level 3 - 2-6 points, 0-8 inlays.			
Level 3 cues start at	$625	$550	$425
Level 4 - 4-10 points, 9-25 inlays.			
Level 4 cues start at	$800	$675	$525
Level 5 - 0-12 points, 26-50 inlays.			
Level 5 cues start at	$1,200	$950	$725

MICHAEL MILLER

Maker of Michael Morgan Custom Cues. For more information, refer to listing for Michael Morgan.

MILTONIO CUSTOM CUES

Maker of pool cues from 1990 to present in Vista, California.

Milt Hyman was drawn to working with wood as a youngster. By age seven, he had built his first model airplane, one of many to come. Even before junior high school, he was taking woodshop classes where he made a model sailboat and a bow and arrow set.

Much later, after joining the Navy and flying combat missions in Korea, Milt graduated from the Art Center School for professional artists, designers, and photographers in Los Angeles, which led to a successful career in commercial photography. During this time, Milt fell in love with the game of pool. He moved to SanDiego County, upon retirement from his photography career. He bought a house and a pool table. He wanted to buy a cue but could not find one to his liking, so he looked at a large billiard supply showroom and was disappointed that nothing appealed to him. Given Milt's love of pool, his experience with tools and woodworking, and his formal art training, he decided to try his hand at making his own cue.

In 1990, Milt started building custom machines for cuemaking, and he made his first cues under the name "Miltonio." The first four Miltonio cues were entered in a woodworking contest at the San Diego County Fair, and each one won a blue ribbon.

Milt has since taken some furniture making classes to help hone his woodworking skills. He now makes between 15 and 25 cues per year. All of his work is done by hand. Milt does not do inlay work. Instead, his fancier Miltonio cues rely on a variety of complicated splices and joints. He decided to use only normal woodworking tools, plus jigs and fixtures that he could make himself. Milt makes cues which are quite unique. "Saturn Rings" and "Super points" are names he uses to describe some of his original design elements. Milt sometimes uses butterfly points to add color to a cue. The "Saturn Rings" are parallel layers of exotic woods, placed at an angle to the long axis, to creat elliptical rings. He sees no limits to creating unique designs, using different woods, splices, points, and rings.

Milt personally likes an unwrapped handle, because it gives him more room to be creative. But when a wrapped cue is called for, he sometimes uses a double strand of two complementary colors of Irish linen. This gives him many more wrap colors to play with.

Milt prefers not to use ivory for environmental reasons and because he believes there are plenty of alternative materials that offer superior playability. He hand-selects every piece of wood he will use to make a cue. Every Miltonio cue is a one-of-a-kind original. It is both an object of art and a tool that works well. Style is important, but playability is paramount. Miltonio cues are well known for their solid hitting quality.

Milt enjoys customizing a cue to the individual taste of the client, whenever practical. Clients are encouraged to talk about their likes and dislikes, concerning construction and design, before the cue is made. Each cue can be easily identified by the "Miltonio" signature, followed by the month and year of completion.

Milt specializes in custom orders for longer cues over 58 in. Although he is not tall, Milt plays with a 61 in. cue himself. He has also made a 64 in. cue, with a joint below the wrap, for those tall players with an extra long wingspan. Since such a cue is prone to hitting obstructions behind the shooter, the butt sleeve on long cues can be removed, if necessary, shortening the cue to 58 in. and making it lighter by only an ounce or so.

Miltonio custom cues are guaranteed for life against manufacturing defects that are not the result of warpage or abuse. If, for any reason, a client is not happy with a new Miltonio cue, within 30 days, Miltonio will buy it back or build the client another cue.

If you have a Miltonio cue that needs further identification or repair, or would like to order a new one, contact Miltonio Custom Cues, listed in the Trademark Index.

SPECIFICATIONS

Butt material: hardwoods
Shaft material: sugar maple
Standard length: custom
Lengths available: custom
Standard finish: two-part automotive clear coat
Balance point: custom
Standard wrap: Irish linen
Point construction: short splice
Standard joint: linen phenolic, wood
Joint type: flat face
Joint screw thread: 3/8-10, 5/16-14, 5/16-18
Standard number of shafts: two
Standard taper: 13 to 15 in.

MILTONIO CUSTOM CUES, cont. 537

GRADING	100%	95%	70%

Standard ferrules: linen phenolic
Standard tip: Le Pro
Annual production: 15 to 25 cues

OPTIONS (FOR NEW CUES ONLY)

Special length: no charge
Layered tip: $25
Custom joint protectors: $30 each
Extra shaft: $100+

REPAIRS

Repairs done on all fine cues.
Refinish with linen wrap: $100
Rewrap Irish linen: $45+
Rewrap double Irish linen: $60
Clean and press linen wrap: $15
Replace shaft: $100+
Replace ferrule: $25
Replace butt cap: $20+
Replace tip: $15+

CURRENT MILTONIO CUES

Basic Miltonio cues with wraps and joint rings start at $700. Miltonio cues with points and one-of-a-kind custom Miltonio cues start at $850. The current delivery time for a Miltonio cue is six to eight weeks.

CURRENT EXAMPLES

Level 1 "Three-Piece Travel Cue" - Solid quilted maple forearm/wrap/butt three-piece cue with two invisible wood-to-wood joints, faux joint in center section, invisble joint in shaft, extra joint in handle creating three equal pieces which fit in its own custom tube case. Maple stitch ringwork on butt sleeve above white butt cap and on faux joint collar, white rubber bumper, signed on butt sleeve: 'Miltonio 4/02', custom wood joint protectors.

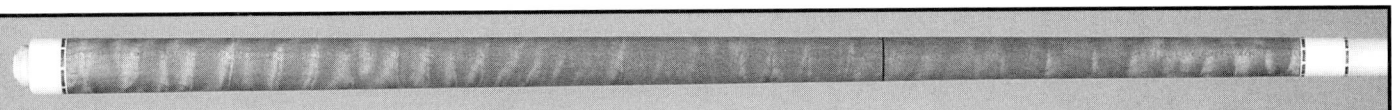

MSR	$650	$650-850	$750	$550

Level 2 "Merry Widow with Extension" - Cocobolo forearm and butt sleeve, bloodwood, maple and orange veneer ringwork above and below the linen wrap and at the base of the butt sleeve, ebony butt cap with a screw-in rubber bumper which removes to attach a 10 in. extension made of Douglas Fir, Miltonio signature in black on the butt sleeve.. Wood-to-wood joint with stainless steel 3/8-10 pin and brown linen phenolic joint collar with a brass ring. Two shafts with custom cocobolo joint protectors.

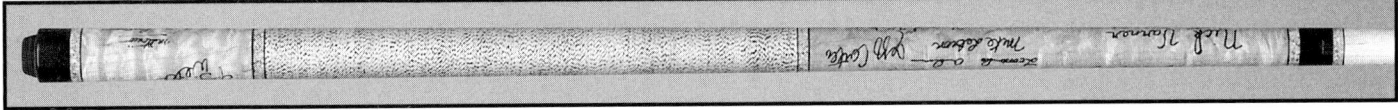

MSR	$900	$900-1050	$800	$600

Level 5 - Orange Dymondwood joint, quarter sectioned ebony and snow white holly forearm seperated by single orange veneers with blocks of ebony and snow white holly seperated by single orange veneers above wrap, quarter sectioned ebony and snow white holly butt sleeve seperated by single orange veneers with blocks of ebony and snow white holly seperated by single orange veneers below wrap and snow white holly checks set in ebony at bottom.

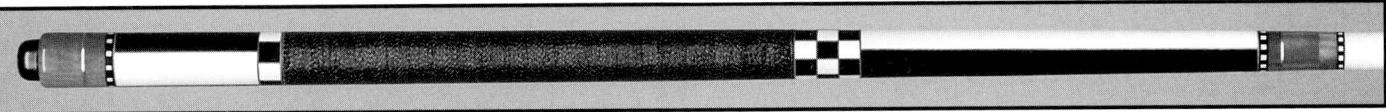

MSR	$3,000	$2,500-3,250	$2,050	$1,650

Level 3 - Long one-piece rosewood forearm and handle, four 18 1/2 in. maple-bordered bloodwood points, ebony butt sleeve with four bloodwood-bordered maple points below a brass-bordered white ring below handle.

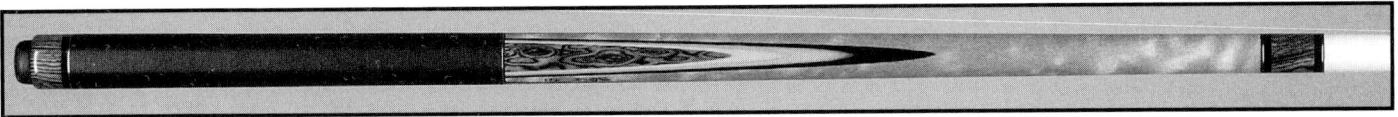

MSR	$1,500	$1,300-1,650	$1,100	$850

MILTONIO CUSTOM CUES, cont.

GRADING	100%	95%	70%

Level 3 - Corian joint, rosewood forearm, two full-spliced tiger maple points and handle with five colored veneers, rosewood butt sleeve with three purpleheart butterfly points with four colored veneers between a veneer-bordered angled bloodwood ring below handle and a corian ring at bottom.

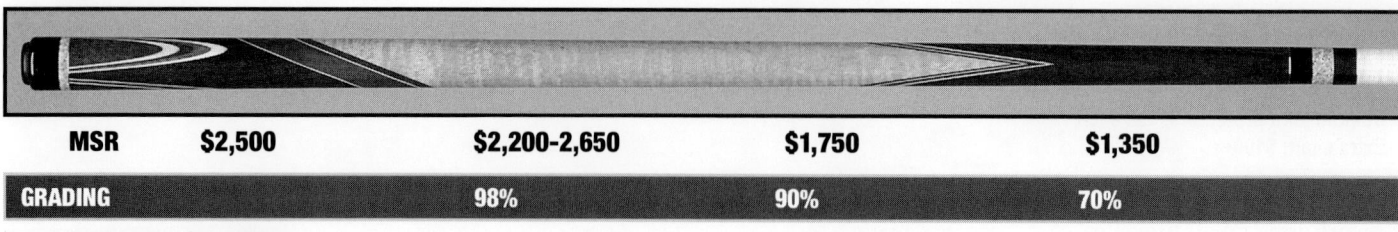

MSR	$2,500	$2,200-2,650	$1,750	$1,350
GRADING		98%	90%	70%

PAST EXAMPLES

Level 3 - Satinwood forearm, four points Kingwood with three veneers, with four purpleheart reverse points at top, satinwood butt with matching purpleheart points and purpleheart ring at base of butt sleeve. Ebony ringwork with white/magenta/white dash inlays at ABCDE, two shafts with custom turned wood custom joint protectors, double-wrapped burgundy/white/burgundy/black linen. 1 of 1. Signed: "Miltonio 9.98" on butt sleeve. 60 in.

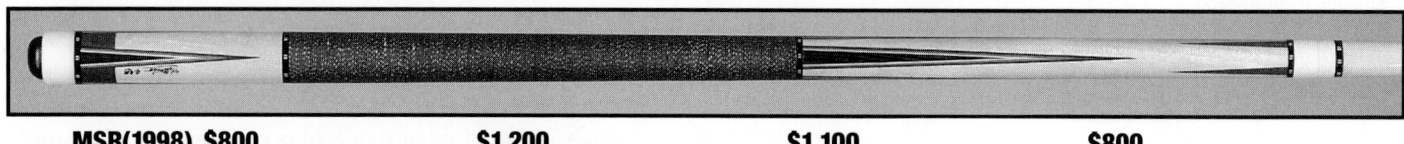

MSR(1998) $800	$1,200	$1,100	$800

SECONDARY MARKET MINIMUM VALUES

The following are minimum values for Miltonio Custom Cues encountered on the secondary market. These prices are representative of cues utilizing basic materials and designs that are not currently available. Miltonio makes one-of-a-kind cues that can command many times these prices due to the use of exotic or rare woods, or complicated construction techiques.

Special construction note: There are many materials and construction techniques that can add value to Miltonio cues. The following are the most important examples:

- Add $300+ for "saturn rings."

For all used Miltonio cues, except where otherwise noted:

- Add $100 for each additional original straight playable shaft beyond two.
- Deduct $100 for each missing original straight playable shaft under two.
- Deduct 25% for obvious or improper refinish.

Level 2 - 0 points, 0-25 inlays.
Level 2 cues start at	$500	$385	$260

Level 3 - 2-6 points, 0-8 inlays.
Level 3 cues start at	$650	$510	$350

Level 4 - 4-10 points, 9-25 inlays.
Level 4 cues start at	$850	$665	$450

Level 5 - 0-12 points, 26-50 inlays.
Level 5 cues start at	$1,200	$950	$650

MINNESOTA FATS CUES

Line of pool cues distributed by DMI Sports since 1990.

DMI Sports, Inc. introduced its first full line of cues under the Minnesota Fats brand in 1990. The company was initially known as Dart Mart, Inc., a small dart specialty company, focused on importing and producing high quality dart products.

DMI cues are manufactured in southern China using wood and inlay materials that are imported to China from the US, Canada, and around the world. Minnesota Fats cues are marked with the Minnesota Fats trademark and materials used range from hardwoods to graphites to professional grade maples. All Minnesota Fats cues are guaranteed for one year.

If you are interested in talking to someone about a new Minnesota Fats cue, you can contact them at DMI Sports, Inc, listed in the Trademark Index.

SPECIFICATIONS

Butt material: hardwoods
Shaft material: rock maple
Standard lengths: 57 to 58 in.
Standard wraps: nylon, matte paint, or Irish linen

CURRENT MINNESOTA FATS CUES

Retail prices on current Minnesota Fats cues range from $12 to $150.

GRADING	98%	90%	70%

MISTER BILLIARD CUES

Line of pool cues distributed by Mister Billiard in Ontario, Canada.
Mister Billiard cues are easily identifiable by the "Mr. Billiard" logo on the butt caps.
If you are interested in talking to someone about a new Mister Billiard cue, you can contact them at Mister Billiard, listed in the Trademark Index.

RANDY MOBLEY

Maker of pool cues in Largo, Florida.

MOHAWK CUES

Importer of pool cues in Gloucester City, New Jersey in the mid-1990s.
Mohawk cues are identifiable by the "Mohawk" logo on a wood ring just above the butt cap.

SPECIFICATIONS

Butt material: hardwoods
Shaft material: rock maple
Standard length: 58 in.
Point construction: short splice
Standard wrap: Irish linen
Standard number of shafts: one

MOHAWK CUES

The following are minimum prices for Mohawk cues encountered on the secondary market. These prices are representative of cues utilizing the most basic materials and designs that were available.
Special construction note: There are many materials and construction techniques that can add value to Mohawk cues.
For all used Mohawk cues:
Add $50+ for each additional original straight playable shaft beyond one.
Deduct $75 for missing original straight playable shaft.
Deduct 20% for obvious or improper refinish.

Level 1 - 4 points, hustler.

	98%	90%	70%
Level 1 cues start at	$90	$75	$40

Level 2 - 0 points, 0-25 inlays.

Level 2 cues start at	$110	$85	$50

Level 3 - 2-6 points, 0-8 inlays.

Level 3 cues start at	$185	$135	$95

BRYAN MORDT

Maker of BCM Cues. For more information, refer to the listing for BCM.

HAROLD MOREY CUES

Maker of pool cues from 1989 until 2003 in Alpena, Michigan.
Harold Morey is a precision machinist who discovered cue manufacturing by restoring Gus Szamboti and George Balabushka cues in 1985. Having restored over 40 Szamboti cues and a number of Balabushka cues, Morey became familiar with Szamboti's techniques and materials and in 1989 began creating cues in the Szamboti method. Given that Morey was only able to produce a few cues per year, there was typically an extensive wait for his cues. Although the cues were few in quantity, the materials and craftsmanship of Morey cues were extraordinary in quality. Morey employed a stunning calfskin leather wrap (which was used on nearly half of his cues), sections of elephant tusk (cut out by hand with a pantograph) for the inlays, the butt cap was traditionally white Delrin, and the black rubber bumpers were affixed with aluminum hex screws. Morey has completed a number of cues utilizing Burton Spain blanks exclusively, until Spain's death in 1994. For the most part Spain blanks were four-point, although he crafted a handful of cues with eight-point blanks. Morey's cues can be identified by the "MOREY" signature among the points, accompanied by the year of its crafting and the number of the cue sequence (eg: "94-014 in.). Morey currently abstains from procuring orders for cues; however, he will repair his own cues. Harold Morey's concentration is presently on music and expending his leisure time fabricating electric guitars.
If you have a Harold Morey cue that needs further identification or repair, contact Harold Morey, listed in the Trademark Index.

SPECIFICATIONS

Butt material: hardwoods
Shaft material: rock maple
Standard length: 58 1/2 in.
Lengths available: 57 to 59 in.
Standard finish: lacquer
Point construction: short splice

Standard joint: piloted 5/16-14 stainless steel or ivory
Joint protectors: standard with ivory joint
Standard butt cap: Delrin
Standard number of shafts: two
Standard taper: szamboti-type 8 to 10 in. straight
Balance point: forward weighted
Standard wrap: Irish linen or calfskin leather
Standard ferrules: ivory
Standard tip: water buffalo
Total production: approximately 50 cues

PAST EXAMPLES

Level 3 "1994 #14 Burton Spain Blank" – Bird's-eye maple forearm, four points ebony with four veneers (black, light blue, orange, white). Signed on forearm "MOREY 94 – 014". Piloted stainless steel joint 5/16-14, black joint collars with ring of ivory and ebony squares. Ebony butt sleeve, white Delrin butt cap, calfskin leather wrap. Burton Spain blank, Morey's 14th cue.

GRADING	98%	90%	70%
MSR (1994) $1,500	$1,850	$1,475	$1,050

SECONDARY MARKET MINIMUM VALUES

The following are minimum prices for other Morey cues encountered on the secondary market. These prices are representative of cues utilizing basic materials and designs that are not currently available. Harold Morey cues can command many times these prices due to the use of rare materials and limited availability.

For all used Morey cues:
Add $100 for each additional original straight playable shaft beyond two.
Deduct $150 for each missing original straight playable shaft under two.
Add $650 for Burton Spain blanks.
Add $125 for ivory joint.
Add $100 for calfskin leather wrap.
Subtract 25% for inappropriate (non-lacquer) refinishing.

Level 2 - 0 points, 0-25 inlays.

	98%	90%	70%
Level 2 cues start at	$600	$450	$275

Level 3 - 2-6 points, 0-8 inlays.

	98%	90%	70%
Level 3 cues start at	$1,000	$835	$650

Level 4 - 4-10 points, 9-25 inlays.

	98%	90%	70%
Level 4 cues start at	$1,200	$985	$750

MORRIS CUSTOM CUES

Maker of pool cues from 1992 to present in Desert Hot Springs, California.

Ned Morris and Mark Schwenson were luthiers for twelve years before they made their first pool cue together, while working for a guitar company. They have been building cues full-time since 1992 in Desert Hot Springs, California. Morris cues feature a flat-faced joint with a solid high-grade bronze pin, as they believe it provides a softer and more sensitive hit than stainless steel. All points are V-cut or channel cut, and woods are seasoned for a minimum of one year to assure stability. They make all their cue components.

From 1992 until 2003 Morris cues were marked with an "MC." In the autumn of 2003 they started engraving the year on the butt cap as well; eg. "Morris 03".

For more information or to order a cue, contact Morris Custom Cue, listed in the Trademark Index.

Ned Morris and Mark Schwenson

SPECIFICATIONS

Butt material: hardwoods
Shaft material: North American maple
Standard length: 58 in.
Standard finish: four-part automotive
Point construction: short spliced or inlaid
Standard joint: flat face
Joint protectors: standard
Standard number of shafts: two
Balance point: 17 ½ in. from the butt end
Standard wrap: Irish linen
Standard ferrules: Ivorine 3
Standard tip: layered

MORRIS CUSTOM CUES, cont. **541**

GRADING	100%	95%	70%

OPTIONS (FOR NEW CUES ONLY)
Special lengths: $200
Extra shaft: $85+
Ivory ferrule: $70
Ivory joint: $150
Ivory butt cap: $200+
Ivory points or butt sleeve: $400+
Leather wrap: $125
Custom joint protectors: $25+
Layered tip: $35+
Annual production: fewer than 125 cues

CURRENT EXAMPLES

The following Morris Cues come standard with two shafts. Current order time is two to six months depending on the cue design.

Level 2 - Cocobolo forearm and butt sleeve, maple and cocobolo ringwork at bottom of butt, brown linen joint collar, linen wrap.

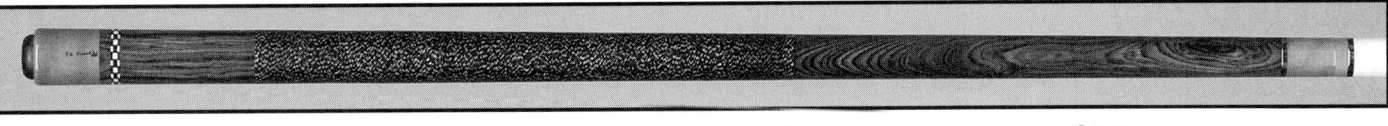

MSR	$650	$600-700	$550	$400

Level 4 - Bird's-eye maple forearm, four ebony points, four veneers and three mother-of-pearl inlays, ebony butt sleeve with eight ivory notched diamonds, 24 silver dots, silver ring top and bottom, phenolic joint with silver ring, Delrin butt cap with "MC" logo, linen wrap.

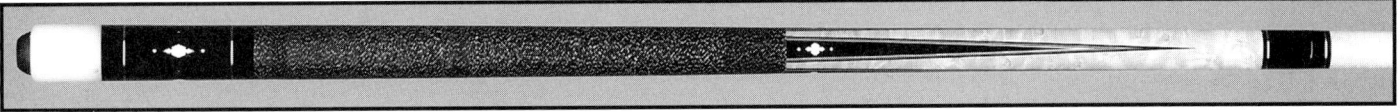

MSR	$1,800	$1,450-1,800	$1,250	$1,000

Level 6 - Ebony forearm, floating ivory and pink ivory points, ebony butt sleeve, pink ivory and ivory inlays, flat face ivory joint, ivory butt cap and ferrules, linen wrap.

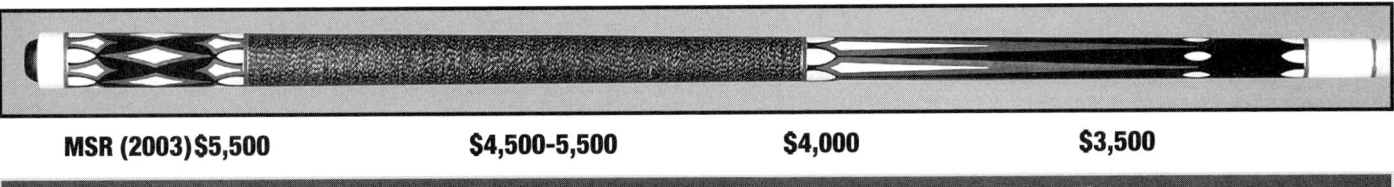

MSR (2003)	$5,500	$4,500-5,500	$4,000	$3,500

GRADING	98%	90%	70%

SECONDARY MARKET MINIMUM VALUES

The following are minimum values for other Morris cues encountered on the secondary market. These prices are representative of cues utilizing basic materials and designs that are not necessarily available at present. Ned has offered one-of-a-kind cues that can command many times these prices due to the use of exotic materials and artistry.

Special construction note: There are many materials and construction techniques that can add value to Morris cues.

For all used Morris cues, except where otherwise noted:
- Add $65 for each additional original straight playable shaft beyond two.
- Deduct $85+ for each missing original straight playable shaft under two.
- Add $50 each for ivory ferrules.
- Add $70 for leather wrap.
- Deduct 20% for obvious or improper refinish.

Level 2 - 0 points, 0-25 inlays.
Level 2 cues start at	$500	$390	$265

Level 3 - 2-6 points, 0-8 inlays.
Level 3 cues start at	$650	$510	$345

Level 4 - 4-10 points, 9-25 inlays.
Level 4 cues start at	$750	$580	$395

Level 5 - 0-12 points, 26-50 inlays.
Level 5 cues start at	$900	$765	$495

STEVE MORRIS

Refer to listing for Mid West Custom Cues.

STU MORTENSON

Inlayer of pool cues in Los Angeles and Chicago.

Kenneth "Stu" Mortenson is a very talented designer and artist with a manual pantograph. He has worked for cuemakers such as Bert Schrager and Ray Schuler, doing inlay work on very elaborate one-of-a-kind creations. While at these shops, Stu has inlaid many one-of-a-kind cues for his own collection. All of the inlay work in these extremely complex designs has been executed by Stu from the finest materials available. They are identifiable by a backwards "S" inlaid somewhere on the cue. Stu rarely offers these cues for sale.

SPECIFICATIONS

Butt material: hardwoods
Shaft material: rock maple
Standard length: 58 in.
Standard wrap: Irish linen
Total production: approximately 80 cues

Kenneth "Stu" Mortenson

MOSCONI CUES

Maker of pool cues from 1977 to present in Evansville, Indiana.

Escalade sports was founded in 1927 as the Indian Archery and Toy Company. Today they distribute Mosconi cues and three other brands.

If you are interested in talking to Randy Beckum about a new Mosconi cue or cue that needs to be repaired, you can contact him at Escalade Sports, listed in the Trademark Index.

SPECIFICATIONS

Butt material: hardwoods
Shaft material: rock maple
Standard length: 58 in.
Standard finish: lacquer
Standard wrap: Irish linen
Standard joint: stainless steel pin
Joint protectors: standard
Standard number of shafts: one
Standard taper: pro taper
Standard ferrules: fiber
Standard tip width: 12.875 mm
Tip widths available: 12 to 13 mm

CURRENT MOSCONI CUES

Escalade Sports has several models of Mosconi cues available. The current delivery time for a Mosconi cue is four to six weeks.

MOTTEY CUSTOM CUES

Maker of pool cues from 1983 to present in Pittsburgh, Pennsylvania.

In the early 1980s, Paul Mottey was working as a public accountant from his own tax office. During the slow summer months, he worked as a construction contractor. Most evenings were reserved for his first love: playing pool. As Paul was one of the best players in the Pittsburgh area, he played in the pro tournaments when they were in the region.

One night in 1983 while playing pool after work, Paul decided that he could make a cue that was better than the one he was using. That year, he purchased the necessary equipment and started making cues as a hobby. He visited Gus Szamboti several times, and credits Gus and Dan Janes of Joss for their influences on his work. By 1984, Paul gave up construction work to start making cues full-time, while still doing accounting work during tax season.

Most of Paul's cues, including the two-piece hustler cues he used to make, are easily recognizable by the "Paul F. Mottey" signature on the forearm along with the month and year, something he started in 1988. Cues made before this time are not signed, and some recent cues have "MOTTEY" on ivory butt caps instead. In 1995, four high-end custom cues had "PM" engraved on them. His one-of-a-kind high-end cues have had engraved ivory butt caps with "PM" in front of the Pittsburgh skyline since 1991, when the same logo appeared on his business card.

Paul Mottey

Several of Paul's designs have been inspired by the late Gus Szamboti, with ivory inlaid propellers being a common theme. No confusion has been intended, however, as the designs are not exact copies. As a sure means of identification on an unsigned Mottey versus a Szamboti, the screw that holds the butt cap on a Mottey will be a 3/8-16, and on a Szamboti it will be a 5/16-18.

Paul's first 15 or 20 cues had a 5/16-18 joint pin. Since then he has mostly stuck with a 5/16-14 piloted joint. A few cues have been made with Uni-Loc pins, and he will make a flat-faced 3/9-10 joint if the customer requests it.

Among Paul's best known designs are the scrimshawed ivory cues he has collaborated on with artist Salman Rashidi. Many feature ivory handles serving as "canvases" for elaborate designs, such as "Sea World," "Butterflies and Flowers," "Samurai Warrior," and "Kwan Yin." He was one of the first cuemakers to do segmented leather wraps, and also to use lizard.

As a player, Paul believes that the feel of a cue is very important. He tries to make his cues feel like a solid piece of wood, with as smooth of a surface as possible from tip to butt. Paul makes all of the components in Mottey cues except for the tips, bumpers, and screws, which he has custom-made to his specifications.

Today, Paul wears yet another hat, as the proprietor of his own billiard room, "Breakers," since October of 2003. He plays on the Senior Tour when he can; he's known by as many top pros as "Pittsburgh Paul" the pool player, and he is a highly regarded cuemaker. Paul currently spends most of his time making one-of-a-kind custom cues to the

One-of-a-kind cues

design and specifications of the customer. James White has been working with Paul since 1992; for the past several years he has also been making cues on his own.

Mottey cues are guaranteed indefinitely against manufacturing defects that are not the result of warpage or abuse. If you have a Paul Mottey cue that needs repair or further identification, or if you would like to talk to Paul about the design of a new one-of-a-kind custom cue, contact Mottey Custom Cues, listed in the Trademark Index.

High-end One-of-a-kind cues

SPECIFICATIONS

Butt material: hardwoods
Shaft material: rock maple
Lengths available: any
Standard finish: urethane
Standard joint screw: 5/16-14
Standard joint: stainless steel
Joint type: piloted
Balance point: 18 1/2 in. from butt
Point construction: short splice or inlaid
Standard wrap: Irish linen
Standard butt cap: wood
Standard number of shafts: two
Standard taper: 9 in. straight
Standard ferrules: ivory
Standard tip: water buffalo
Tip widths available: 9 to 15 mm
Annual production: fewer than 40 cues

OPTIONS (FOR NEW CUES ONLY)

Leather wrap: $100+
Ivory joint: $250
Custom joint protectors: $50+
Flat face 3/8-10 joint: no charge
Extra shaft: $200+
Special length: no charge
Ivory butt cap: $225+
Ivory points: $600+
Ivory butt sleeve: $1,000+
Ivory handle: $3,000+

MOTTEY CUSTOM CUES, cont.

GRADING	100%	95%	70%

REPAIRS
Repairs done on Mottey cues only.
- Refinish (linen wrap): $150
- Refinish (leather wrap): $200
- Refinish (lizard wrap): $350
- Rewrap (leather): $100
- Rewrap (lizard): $250
- Rewrap (linen): $50
- Replace Delrin butt cap: $40
- Replace ivory butt cap: $225+
- Replace tip (Le Pro): $10
- Replace tip (layered): $25
- Replace shaft: $200 to $350
- Replace ivory ferrule: $75

CURRENT MOTTEY CUES
The current delivery time for a Paul Mottey cue is ten months.

CURRENT EXAMPLES
The following cues are representations of the work of Paul Mottey. These cues can be ordered as shown, modified to suit the desires of the customer, or new designs can be created. The majority of Paul's work is custom. Prices include two shafts with ivory ferrules. They are available with non-ivory ferrules for $100 less.

Level 3 - Curly maple forearm, four ebony points with four colored veneers, ebony butt sleeve.

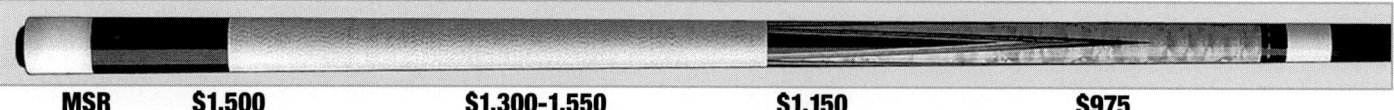

MSR	$1,500	$1,300-1,550	$1,150	$975

Level 3 - Ivory joint, ebony forearm, four ivory points with ebony and holly veneers alternating over four ebony points with holly veneers, ebony butt sleeve with a thin ivory ring at bottom.

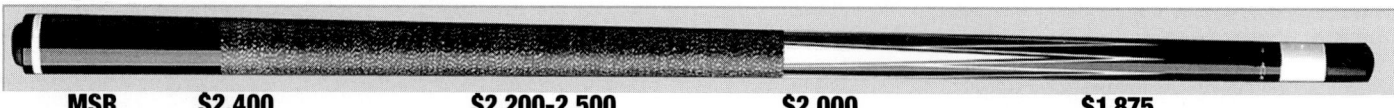

MSR	$2,400	$2,200-2,500	$2,000	$1,875

Level 4 - Bird's-eye maple forearm, four ebony points with four veneers and abalone inlay in each point, maple and ebony Bushka ring above lizard wrap, ebony butt sleeve with four notched mother-of-pearl diamonds with four dots in-between, Delrin butt cap, stainless steel joint with silver ring.

MSR	$2,250	$1,950-2,350	$1,850	$1,600

Level 3 - Ebony forearm with ebony points with three colored veneers, ivory rung above lizard wrap, ebony butt sleeve with a Hoppe-style ring at bottom, ivory joint with ivory dash ring in joint collar.

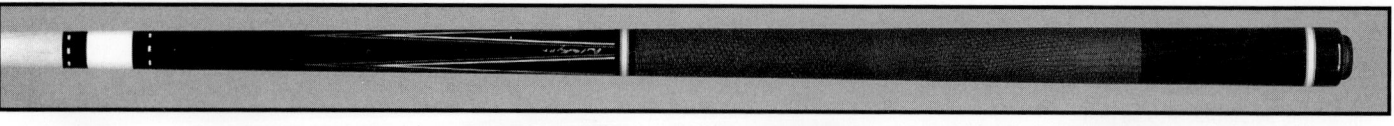

MSR	$2,350	$2,000-2,450	$1,900	$1,650

Level 6- Curly maple forearm, four points of Gabon ebony with four veneers, base of each point inlaid with a sterling silver spear, Gabon ebony butt sleeve has four large rectangular "windows" of turquoise veneered in sterling silver, alternating with four sterling silver diamond inlays. Fancy ringwork of turquoise diamonds set in black linen fiber and stainless steel rings at joint and shaft collars and above the wrap, matching rings of turquoise, ebony, and stainless steel at the top and bottom of the butt sleeve, piloted polished stainless steel joint, 5/16-14 joint pin, linen wrap.

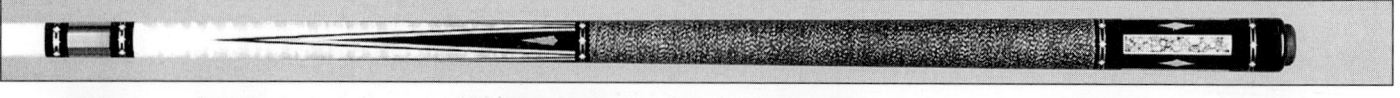

MSR	$3,500	$3,500-4,200	$3,200	$2,000

MOTTEY CUSTOM CUES, cont. 545

GRADING	100%	95%	70%

Level 6 "Szamboti Style" - Bird's-eye maple forearm, eight points ebony, four long and four short, with ebony-veneered ivory diamonds at tips and ivory peacock inlays in points, ebony butt sleeve with ivory Szanboti-style inlays: two engraved ivory windows, triple arrows, spears and dimonds, ebony ring with ivory dot inlays above lizard wrap, ivory butt cap and joint, ebony and ivory ringwork at joint and shaft collars with eight inlaid ivory diamonds in each ring.

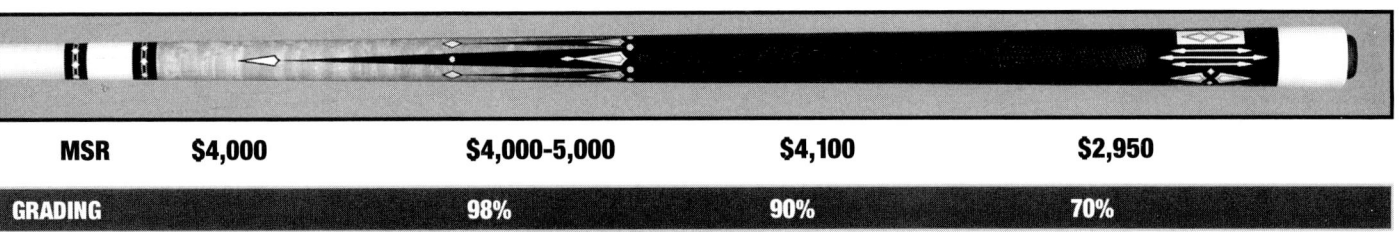

MSR	$4,000	$4,000-5,000	$4,100	$2,950

GRADING	98%	90%	70%

PAST EXAMPLES

Level 7 "1999 'Ginky' for George San Souci" Bird's-eye maple forearm, six points, three long ivory points with ebony and pink ivorywood veneers alternating with three shorter points of pink ivorywood with ebony veneers; pink ivorywood butt sleeve has six ebony-veneered pink ivorywood windows with ivory ovals: five are scrimshawed with G-I-N-K-Y and the 6th is engraved with Mottey's special 'PM' logo used on only his most select cues. Segmented black lizard wrap featuring ivory, pink ivorywood and ebony fancy ringwork. Piloted ivory joint and butt cap. Six shafts, second Mottey custom cue for Ginky.

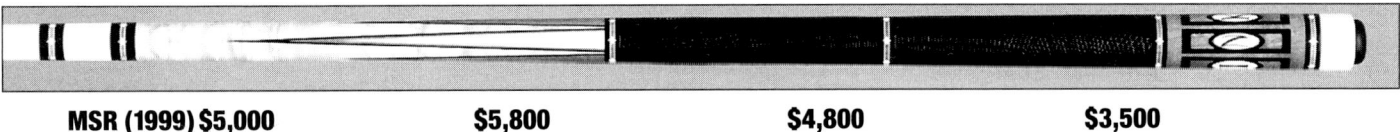

MSR (1999) $5,000	$5,800	$4,800	$3,500

SECONDARY MARKET MINIMUM VALUES

The following are minimum prices for other Mottey cues encountered on the secondary market. These prices are representative of cues utilizing basic materials and designs that may not be currently available. Paul currently specializes in one-of-a-kind cues that can command many times these prices due to the use of exotic materials and artistry.

Special construction note: There are many materials and construction techniques that can add value to Paul Mottey cues. The following are the most important examples:

Add $600+ for ivory points.
Add $600+ for ivory butt sleeve.

For all used Mottey cues:
Add $125+ for each additional original straight playable shaft (standard with two).
Deduct $160 for each missing original straight playable shaft.
Add $125+ for ivory joint.
Add $250+ for ivory butt cap.

Level 1 - 4 points, hustler.
Level 1 cues start at	$325	$250	$200

Level 2 - 0 points, 0-25 inlays.
Level 2 cues start at	$750	$600	$400

Level 3 - 2-6 points, 0-8 inlays.
Level 3 cues start at	$1,200	$950	$800

Level 4 - 4-10 points, 9-25 inlays.
Level 4 cues start at	$1,850	$1,550	$1,350

Level 5 - 0-12 points, 26-50 inlays.
Level 5 cues start at	$2,350	$1,895	$1,500

Level 6 - 0-12 points, 51-75 inlays.
Level 6 cues start at	$2,850	$2,400	$1,900

Level 7 - 0-12 points, 76-125 inlays.
Level 7 cues start at	$4,000	$3,000	2,350

DON MOYER

Maker of Quest ASP Custom Cues. For more information, refer to Quest.

GRADING	98%	90%	70%

RAY MUDDER

Maker of pool cues in Brownsburg, Indiana.
Ray Mudder makes all the components for his custom cues except the 3/8-10 joint pin.

SPECIFICATIONS

Butt material: hardwoods
Shaft material: rock maple
Standard joint screw: 3/8-10
Standard joint: flat face
Standard number of shafts: two
Standard ferrules: melamine

CURRENT RAY MUDDER CUES

Basic two-piece Ray Mudder cues with wraps and joint rings start at $350. Ray Mudder cues with points start at $600.

SECONDARY MARKET MINIMUM VALUES

The following are minimum values for Ray Mudder cues encountered on the secondary market. These prices are representative of cues utilizing basic materials and designs that are not necessarily available at present. Ray has offered one-of-a-kind cues that can command many times these prices due to the use of exotic materials and artistry.

Special construction note: There are many materials and construction techniques that can add value to Ray Mudder cues.

For all used Ray Mudder cues, except where otherwise noted:

Add $100 for each additional original straight playable shaft beyond one.
Deduct $150 for missing original straight playable shaft.
Add $50 each for ivory ferrules.
Add $75 for leather wrap.
Deduct 20% for obvious or improper refinish.

Level 2 - 0 points, 0-25 inlays.

	98%	90%	70%
Level 2 cues start at	$300	$240	$160

Level 3 - 2-6 points, 0-8 inlays.

	98%	90%	70%
Level 3 cues start at	$500	$390	$270

Level 4 - 4-10 points, 9-25 inlays.

	98%	90%	70%
Level 4 cues start at	$600	$470	$320

MUELLER SPORTING GOODS

Maker of pool cues from 1992 to present in Lincoln, Nebraska. Also home of Troy Downey, for more information refer to listing for Troy Downey. Rory Mueller started making cues out of his Mueller Sporting Goods warehouse in 1992 when he hired Troy Downey to run the cue shop. Now Troy makes custom cues, as does Ryan Theewen who makes "Rat" cues. The cue shop still turns out about 400 Mueller hustler cues. If you have a Mueller Sporting Goods cue that needs further identification or repair, or would like to talk to Troy or Ryan about a new Mueller cue, contact Mueller Sporting Goods, listed in the Trademark Index.

SPECIFICATIONS

Butt material: hardwoods
Shaft material: rock maple
Standard length: 58 in.
Lengths available: any
Standard finish: polyurethane acrylic
Balance point: 17 in. from butt
Point construction: full splice
Joint type: flat faced
Joint screw: 3/8-10
Standard number of shafts: one
Standard taper: 12 1/2 in. pro
Standard ferrules: linen based
Standard tip: Le Pro
Annual production: approximately 400 cues

OPTIONS (FOR NEW CUES ONLY)

Extra shaft: $55

GRADING	100%	95%	70%

CURRENT EXAMPLES – MUELLER SPORTING GOODS

The following cue is a representation of the hustler cues made by Mueller Sporting Goods. These cues can be ordered as shown or modified to suit the desires of the customer. The current delivery time for a custom Mueller hustler cue is approximately three to four weeks.

For all used Mueller cues, except where otherwise noted:
- Add $45 for each additional original straight playable shaft beyond one.
- Deduct $55 for missing original straight playable shaft.
- Add $50 each for ivory ferrules.
- Deduct 20% for obvious or improper refinish.

Level 1 - Maple forearm, four dark hardwood points and butt sleeve.

MSR	$160	$100-160	$85	$70

KENNETH MURRELL CUSTOM CUES

Maker of pool cues from 2002 to 2003 in Newport, Rhode Island, and from 2003 to present in Swansea, Illinois.

Kenneth Murrell spent two years at the University of Southern Mississippi, after which he joined the U. S. Navy. He spent 21 years as a Navy Machinist, honorably retiring in 2002. His wife, Laura, has played an integral part in all design work and the choosing of wraps for his cues, based on color, design, and texture. Laura remains on active duty in the Navy.

An avid nine-ball player with a wood turning hobby and machinist background, Kenneth did refurbishment and repair of cues. Curiosity, and a love of billiards, ignited a personal challenge within him. Possessing a strong desire for creativity in his woodturning, and utilizing sound engineering practices, he designed and built his first cue. Since that first cue, many changes have taken place, but the basic construction of his cues remains the same. He continues to strive for perfection and continually searches for better materials to use in the building of his cues. He prefers to stick to the familiar, and having worked with manual lathes for years, builds all cues without the aid of CNC. All inlays are done with a manual pantomill or hand milled. No two Kenneth Murrell Custom Cues are alike.

Kenneth Murrell cues are guaranteed for life to the original owner against construction defects that are not the result of warpage or abuse. If you are interested in talking to Kenneth Murrell about a new cue or cue that needs to be repaired, you can contact him at Kenneth Murrell Custom Cues, listed in the Trademark Index.

SPECIFICATIONS

Butt material: hardwoods
Shaft material: rock maple
Standard length: 58.250 in.
Lengths available: any
Standard finish: polymer
Balance point: 19.0 to 19.5 in. from butt
Standard butt cap: linen phenolic
Standard wrap: leather
Point construction: short splice
Standard joint: linen phenolic
Joint type: flat faced
Joint screw thread: 3/8 x 10
Standard number of shafts: one
Standard taper: custom
Standard ferrules: melamine
Other ferrule options: ivory
Standard tip: Moori
Standard tip width: 13 mm
Tip widths available: any under 14 mm
Annual production: approximately 65 cues

OPTIONS (FOR NEW CUES ONLY)

Special length: no charge
Layered tip: standard
Ivory butt cap: $235
Ivory joint: $165
Ivory ferrule: $75
Joint protectors: $70+
Lizard or ostrich wrap: $210
Alligator or elephant wrap: $300
Extra shaft: $125+
Laminated shaft: $145+

548 KENNETH MURRELL CUSTOM CUES, cont.

GRADING	100%	95%	70%

REPAIRS
Repairs done on all fine cues.
- Refinish (with leather wrap): $160
- Rewrap (leather): $125
- Replace shaft: $125 plus ringwork
- Replace ivory ferrule: $75
- Replace melamine ferrule: $35
- Replace butt cap: $65 (linen)
- Replace ivory butt cap: $235
- Replace Moori tip: $40 (Moori)
- Replaced hercules/tiger tip: $35

CURRENT MURRELL CUES
Basic Murrell cues with wraps and joint rings start at $400. Murrell cues with points start at $650. One-of-a-kind custom Murrell cues start at $1,000. Delivery time for a Kenneth Murrell Custom Cue is six months to one year, depending on complexity of design.

CURRENT EXAMPLES
The following cues are currently available from Murrell Cues. They can be ordered as shown, or modified to suit the desires of the customer.

Level 2 - Three shafts (one break shaft), bird's-eye maple forearm, one-piece bloodwood handle and butt with a bloodwood and ebony chain link ring above a bird's-eye maple butt cap.

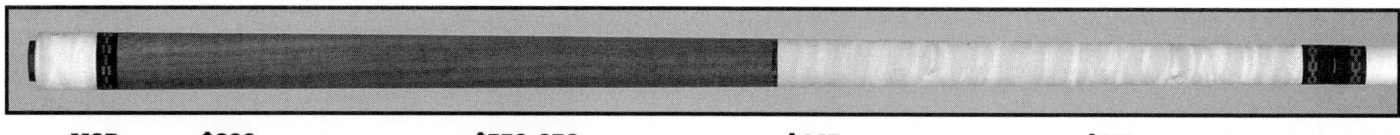

MSR	$600	$550-650	$445	$325

Level 3 - Ebony forearm with a colored veneer check ring above wrap, four purpleheart points with four colored veneers, lizard wrap, purpleheart butt sleeve with colored veneer check rings at top and bottom.

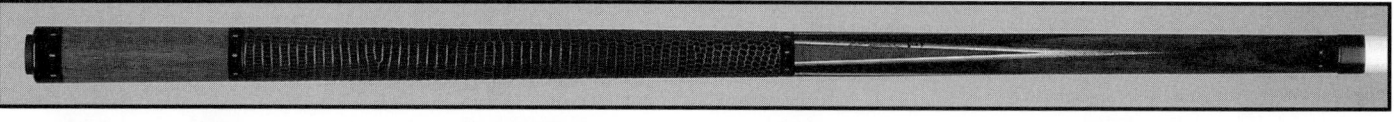

MSR	$875	$775-1,000	$625	$445

Level 3 - Ivory joint, bird's-eye maple forearm with a bird's-eye maple and ebony veneer check ring above handle, four long zircote points alternating with four short zircote points, bird's-eye maple handle, zircote butt sleeve with bird's-eye maple and ebony veneer check rings at top and bottom, ivory butt cap.

MSR	$1,100	$975-1,250	$815	$625

Level 3 - Bird's-eye maple forearm with satinwood and ebony checks within satinwood rings above handle, six long ebony points with two colored veneers alternating with six short satinwood points with a black veneer, three sectioned satinwood handle seperated by satinwood and ebony checks within satinwood rings between sections, ebony butt sleeve with satinwood and ebony checks within satinwood rings at top and bottom.

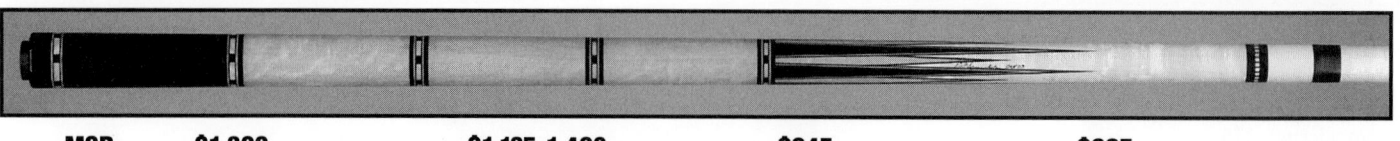

MSR	$1,300	$1,125-1,400	$945	$685

GRADING	100%	95%	70%

Level 3 - Ivory joint, bird's-eye maple forearm with a colored veneer check ring above wrap, four snakewood points with two colored veneers in an ebony border with an ivory spear-shaped inlay in each, lizard wrap, snakewood butt sleeve with four reverse ivory spear-shaped inlays above an ivory ring and snakewood butt cap.

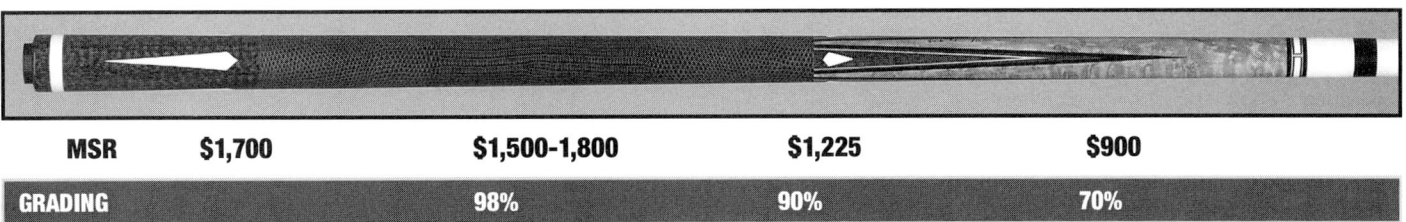

MSR			
$1,700	$1,500-1,800	$1,225	$900

GRADING	98%	90%	70%

SECONDARY MARKET MINIMUM VALUES

The following are minimum values for other Murrell cues encountered on the secondary market. These prices are representative of cues utilizing basic materials and designs that are not necessarily available at present. Ken has offered one-of-a-kind cues that can command many times these prices due to the use of exotic materials and artistry.

Special construction note: There are many materials and construction techniques that can add value to Murrell cues.

For all used Murrell cues, except where otherwise noted:
- Add $100 for each additional original straight playable shaft beyond one.
- Deduct $125 for missing original straight playable shaft.
- Add $60 each for ivory ferrules.
- Deduct 20% for obvious or improper refinish.

Level 2 - 0 points, 0-25 inlays.
  Level 2 cues start at $350 $275 $185

Level 3 - 2-6 points, 0-8 inlays.
  Level 3 cues start at $600 $475 $325

Level 4 - 4-10 points, 9-25 inlays.
  Level 4 cues start at $750 $575 $385

Level 5 - 0-12 points, 26-50 inlays.
  Level 5 cues start at $1,100 $875 $600

Level 6 - 0-12 points, 51-75 inlays.
  Level 6 cues start at $1,650 $1,275 $850

MYSTYQUE

Maker of pool cues from 1988 to present in the Chicago, Illinois area.

Brad Zaccone learned cuemaking from some of the best: Mike Bender (his brother-in-law), David Kersenbrock (a neighbor who came by regularly and gave him pointers), and Joe Gold, for whom Brad fabricates templates for the Cognoscenti cues. He started cuemaking in 1988, calling his company "Mystyque." Brad is a machinist by profession, and only makes cues on a part-time basis, at the most producing ten cues per year.

Brad makes his own polished aluminum joint pins, similar to the one used by Bender Cues, but with a slightly different thread. Most shafts are 30 inches long and the cues measure 59 inches in total length, although some cues have been made with standard 29 inch shafts. The inlay designs in Mystyque cues run the gamut from large ivory diamonds to the most delicate curls of ivory. Mystyque cues are unmarked, but can be identified by their proprietary joint pins and their silver ladder design ringwork.

Because Brad is a family man with a full-time job, he has not had much time for cue building in the past two years, and is not currently taking new cue orders.

SPECIFICATIONS

Butt material: hardwoods
Shaft material: rock maple
Standard length: 59 in.
Standard joint screw: custom
Standard joint: flat faced
Point construction: inlaid
Standard wrap: linen
Standard butt cap: linen phenolic
Standard number of shafts: two
Standard ferrules: Aegis
Standard tip width: 13 mm
Total production: fewer than 150 cues

GRADING	98%	90%	70%

PAST EXAMPLES

Level 5 Ebony forearm, five ivory ellipses and five floating ivory points, five silver veneers in between, ebony butt sleeve with five ivory elipses alternating with five silver veneer lines, silver and ebony ladder ringwork at A/B/C/D/E, proprietary polished aluminum joint pin, linen wrap.

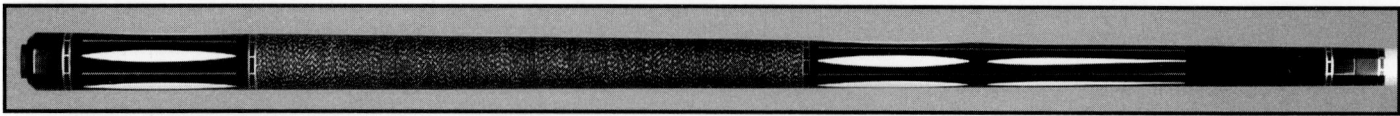

MSR (1999) $1,750	$1,800	$1,500	$1,350

Level 6 "Curly-Qs" Ebony forearm and butt sleeve, 64 delicate ivory "curly-que" inlays, silver and ebony ladder ringwork at ABCDE, proprietary polished aluminum joint pin, linen wrap, 59 in.

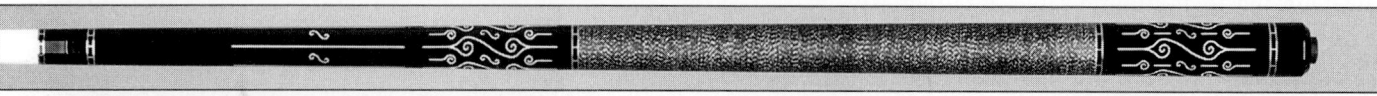

MSR (1999) $2200	$2,600	$2,250	$2,000

SECONDARY MARKET MINIMUM VALUES

The following are minimum values for other Mystique cues encountered on the secondary market. These prices are representative of cues utilizing basic materials and designs that are not necessarily available at present. Brad has offered one-of-a-kind cues that can command many times these prices due to the use of exotic materials and artistry.

Special construction note: There are many materials and construction techniques that can add value to Mystique cues.

For all used Mystique cues, except where otherwise noted:
- Add $100 for each additional original straight playable shaft beyond one.
- Deduct $125 for missing original straight playable shaft.
- Add $55 each for ivory ferrules.
- Add $65 for leather wrap.
- Deduct 25% for obvious or improper refinish.

Level 2 - 0 points, 0-25 inlays.

Level 2 cues start at	$400	$310	$210

Level 3 - 2-6 points, 0-8 inlays.

Level 3 cues start at	$600	$465	$320

Level 4 - 4-10 points, 9-25 inlays.

Level 4 cues start at	$700	$545	$370

Level 5 - 0-12 points, 26-50 inlays.

Level 5 cues start at	$900	$700	$485

N SECTION

NATIONAL CUES

Maker of pool cues in the late 1960s in Chicago, Illinois.

In 1968 the National Tournament Chalk Company decided to start making a line of cues. They set up a cue manufacturing facility in Chicago. Several cuemakers who later went on to start major cuemaking companies of their own were hired. Bob Meucci and Richard Helmstetter, among others, made cues and ran the operation. After about a year the facility moved to Georgia, and was closed not long after. Most National cues are easily identified by the "National" name engraved on the butt caps.

SPECIFICATIONS

Butt material: hardwoods
Shaft material: rock maple
Standard length: 58 in.
Standard wrap: Irish linen

SECONDARY MARKET MINIMUM VALUES

The following are minimum values for other National cues encountered on the secondary market. These prices are representative of cues utilizing the most basic materials and designs that were available at the time.

Special construction note: There are many materials and construction techniques that can add value to National cues.

For all used National cues, except where otherwise noted:
- Add $100 for each additional original straight playable shaft beyond one.
- Deduct 50% for missing original straight playable shaft.
- Deduct 30% for obvious or improper refinish.

GRADING	98%	90%	70%
Level 2 - 0 points, 0-25 inlays.			
Level 2 cues start at	$200	$150	$90
Level 3 - 2-6 points, 0-8 inlays.			
Level 3 cues start at	$350	$260	$160
Level 4 - 4-10 points, 9-25 inlays.			
Level 4 cues start at	$500	$375	$230
Level 5 - 0-12 points, 26-50 inlays.			
Level 5 cues start at	$700	$550	$330

MIKE NEAL CUSTOM CUES

Maker of pool cues from 1992 to present in Lincoln, Nebraska.

In 1991, Mike Neal was working for Dick Coons, who had just recently started his own line of cues (Elite Custom Cues). Dick needed someone to do repair work for his customers. Mike went with Dick to the BCA Trade Show and bought everything he needed to begin doing cue repairs. After replacing tips and ferrules on numerous house cues, he started repairing cues part time. He learned other aspects of cue repair as he went along.

Mike played in pool leagues three nights a week. He noticed a need for a good portable cue rack. In 1992, he began to manufacture and market the Black Max line of portable cue racks. For the next few years, Mike traveled to tournaments and trade shows doing cue repairs and talking with different cuemakers. He learned everything he could about the art, techniques, and principles of building a high quality pool cue.

In 1997 at the World Nine-Ball Championships in Chicago, Mike Neal had a booth next to Bill Schick. He visited with Bill extensively throughout the tournament. In fact, Bill went out of his way to teach Mike things that would have taken years to learn. Mike feels that he owes Bill Schick a debt of gratitude for this.

Today Mike takes pride in building one-of-a-kind custom cues, by hand, one at a time, in the style of the cues made in the early 1900s.

If you are interested in talking to Mike about a new cue or cue that needs to be repaired, you can contact him at Mike Neal's Custom Cues, listed in the Trademark Index.

MIKE NEAL CUSTOM CUES, cont.

GRADING	100%	95%	70%

SPECIFICATIONS
Butt material: hardwoods
Shaft material: hard rock maple
Standard length: 58 in.
Standard wrap: Irish linen
Standard ferrules: Ivorine-3
Standard tip: Tiger Everest
Annual production: 40 to 50 cues

OPTIONS (FOR NEW CUES ONLY)
Ivory ferrule: $65
Leather wrap (one piece): $100
Stack leather wrap: $150+
Extra shaft: $100+

REPAIRS
Repairs done on all fine cues.
Refinish (with Irish linen wrap): $175
Rewrap (Irish linen): $45+
Replace shaft: $100+
Replace Tiger X shaft: $150+
Predator shaft: $230+
Universal Smart Shaft: $200+
Replace tip: $10+

CURRENT MIKE NEAL CUES
Two-piece Mike neal bar cues start at $250. Basic Mike Neal cues with wraps and joint rings start at $350. Mike Neal cues with points start at $450. One-of-a-kind custom Mike Neal cues start at $600.

CURRENT EXAMPLES
The following current and past Mike Neal cues can be ordered as shown, modified to suit the desires of the customer, or new designs can be created.

Level 7 "Zipper" - Chechen forearm, two full-spliced short ebony butterfly points and handle with intricate zipper inlays of maple between red veneers running down to the butt cap.

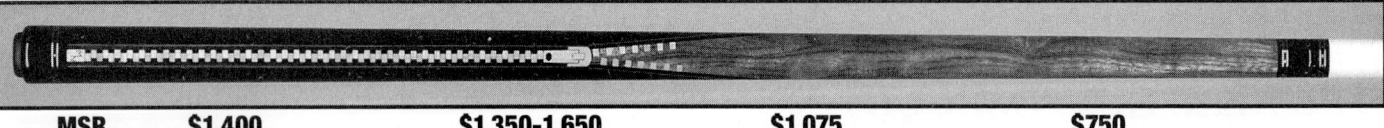

| MSR | $1,400 | $1,350-1,650 | $1,075 | $750 |

PAST EXAMPLES

Level 3 - Maple forearm, two full-spliced short cocobolo butterfly points, ebony handle and butt with two butterfly splices with ebony/maple/cocobolo butterfly veneers.

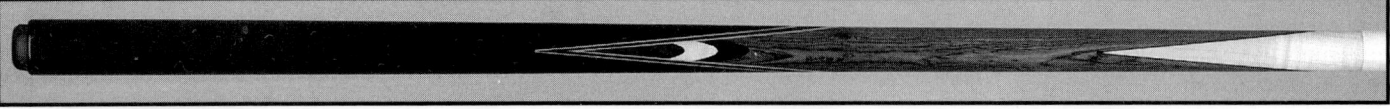

| MSR (1997) $450 | $850 | $675 | $450 |

Level 3 "Hoppe" - Ivory joint, bird's-eye maple forearm, four ebony points with four veneers, stacked leather wrap, ebony butt sleeve with an ivory ring at bottom.

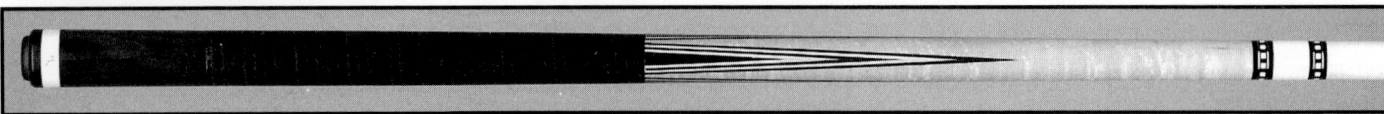

| MSR (2002) $650 | $800 | $625 | $425 |

Level 3 - Redheart forearm, butterfly-spliced bird's-eye maple handle with bird's-eye maple butterfly splices with redheart/maple/ebony veneers towards bottom above a bird's-eye maple ring set between redheart/maple/ebony stitch rings at bottom.

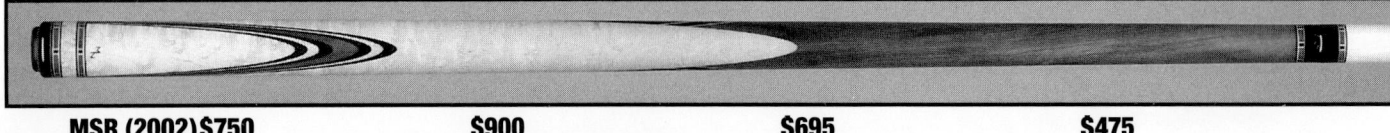

| MSR (2002) $750 | $900 | $695 | $475 |

GRADING	98%	90%	70%

SECONDARY MARKET MINIMUM VALUES

The following are minimum values for other Mike Neal cues encountered on the secondary market. These prices are representative of cues utilizing basic materials and designs that are not necessarily available at present. Mike has offered one-of-a-kind cues that can command many times these prices due to the use of exotic materials and artistry.

Special construction note: There are many materials and construction techniques that can add value to Mike Neal cues. For all used Mike Neal cues, except where otherwise noted:
- Add $80 for each additional original straight playable shaft beyond one.
- Deduct $100 for missing original straight playable shaft.
- Add $45 each for ivory ferrules.
- Add $65 for leather wrap.
- Deduct 20% for obvious or improper refinish.

Level 1 - Hustler.

	98%	90%	70%
Level 1 cues start at	$230	$180	$120

Level 2 - 0 points, 0-25 inlays.

Level 2 cues start at	$325	$250	$170

Level 3 - 2-6 points, 0-8 inlays.

Level 3 cues start at	$400	$315	$210

Level 4 - 4-10 points, 9-25 inlays.

Level 4 cues start at	$600	$470	$325

Level 5 - 0-12 points, 26-50 inlays.

Level 5 cues start at	$850	$660	$445

RICHARD H. NEIGHBORS

Maker of R.H.N. Cues. For more information, refer to the listing for R.H.N.

JESSI NESTER

Maker of Todd Cues. For more information, refer to the listing for Todd Cues.

NEWPORT CUSTOM CUES

Maker of pool cues since 1975 in Edgewater, Maryland.

Gothern "Gene" Newport has played pool for most of his life. He started a fishing lure business part time in the 1950s. In 1965 he retired from 22 years as a government electrical engineer, also having worked in metalurgy and chemistry. In 1975 he sold his fishing lure business, which had 40 employees. That same year he decided to start making pool cues.

At one time he was making over 500 cues a year, but he has since slowed down to a fraction of that number. Gene has been married for over 65 years and is ready to enjoy more free time. He has a large one-man shop with a large supply of wood that is aged and waiting. All materials are natural as he won't use any dies or painted colors. Gene makes everything in his cues except for the tips, bumpers, and screws. He can make a cue with whatever wrap, joint, or tip the customer desires.

All of Gene's cues are one-of-a-kind and custom made. At nearly 90 years of age, he is still making cues, but would like to sell his business. Gene will take orders by email and will quote prices once he knows what his customer would like in a cue. Newport Custom Cues are guaranteed against construction defects that are not the result of warpage or abuse. If you are interested in talking to Gene about a new cue or cue that needs to be repaired, you can contact him at Gene Newport Cues, listed in the Trademark Index.

SPECIFICATIONS

Butt material: hardwoods
Shaft material: rock maple
Standard length: 58 in.
Standard handle: exotic woods
Standard number of shafts: one
Annual production: fewer than 50 cues

OPTIONS (FOR NEW CUES ONLY)

Option prices given on a per cue basis, depending on the cue.

REPAIRS

Repair prices given on a per cue basis, depending on the cue.

CURRENT GENE NEWPORT CUES

Two-piece Newport bar cues start at $300. Basic Newport cues with wraps and joint rings start at $400. Newport cues with points start at $600. The current delivery time for a Newport cue is about two weeks.

GRADING	98%	90%	70%

SECONDARY MARKET MINIMUM VALUES

The following are minimum values for other Newport cues encountered on the secondary market. These prices are representative of cues utilizing basic materials and designs that are not necessarily available at present. Gene has offered one-of-a-kind cues that can command many times these prices due to the use of exotic materials and artistry.

Special construction note: There are many materials and construction techniques that can add value to Newport cues.

For all used Newport cues, except where otherwise noted:
- Add $65 for each additional original straight playable shaft beyond one.
- Deduct $100 for missing original straight playable shaft.
- Add $50 each for ivory ferrules.
- Add $75 for leather wrap.
- Deduct 25% for obvious or improper refinish.

Level 1 - Hustler.

	98%	90%	70%
Level 1 cues start at	$250	$195	$130

Level 2 - 0 points, 0-25 inlays.

Level 2 cues start at	$350	$275	$190

Level 3 - 2-6 points, 0-8 inlays.

Level 3 cues start at	$500	$390	$260

Level 4 - 4-10 points, 9-25 inlays.

Level 4 cues start at	$600	$470	$320

Level 5 - 0-12 points, 26-50 inlays.

Level 5 cues start at	$850	$665	$445

NEW YORK BILLIARD TABLE CO.

Maker of pool cues in New York City, founded by Isadore Rutzisky in 1912. For further information, refer to the listings for Blatt Billiards and Star Cue Mfg.

TRAVIS NIKLICH

Maker of Blackcreek Custom Cues. For more information, refer to Blackcreek.

NITTI CUES

Maker of pool cues from 1992 to present in Orlando, Florida.

Chris Nitti has loved the game of pool for as long as he can remember. He thought about opening a pool room and playing in tournaments. However, after having his cue repaired, the idea to build cues occurred to him. Chris already knew how to use a lathe. He was turning armatures at an automotive alternator-starter rebuilding shop at age 16. With that experience and over 20 years as an auto technician, it was easy to find a lathe and start to experiment.

In April of 1992, Chris made his first cue. His first five cues were made from blanks that he bought. All of his cues since then have been built entirely by him. Chris attended the Houston Cue Show in February 1993. While there, Chris picked the brains of Burton Spain, Bill Stroud, and Leonard Bludworth. He also met Ron Haley, an Arkansas cuemaker, who invited Chris to his shop. After a week with Ron, the way to build quality cues became much clearer. Chris then enrolled in a metal machining class at night. The knowledge he gained in that class made building cues much easier, and it enabled him to make the necessary jigs and fixtures for cue building.

Chris has hand signed "Nitti" on the forearm of his cues since the beginning, adding the last two digits of the year in 1996. Since 2002, he has added the year and production number. All inlay work is done on a manual pantagraph, and Chris prefers traditional cue designs with mitred veneers and sharp inlays. High quality work and customer satisfaction are very important to him. Chris's love for building cues shows in each and every cue he produces.

Nitti cues are guaranteed for life against manufacturing defects that are not the result of warpage or abuse. If you have a Nitti cue that needs further identification or repair, or would like to order a new Nitti cue, please contact Nitti Cues, listed in the Trademark Index.

SPECIFICATIONS

- Butt material: exotic hardwoods
- Shaft material: hard rock maple
- Standard length: 58 in.
- Lengths available: 57 to 59 in.
- Standard finish: three part urethane
- Balance point: 19 in. from bottom of cue

NITTI CUES, cont.

GRADING	100%	95%	70%

Standard butt cap: phenolic
Standard wrap: Irish linen
Point construction: short splice
Standard joint type: flat-faced wood-to-wood
Standard joint pins: radial pin or piloted Uni-Loc
Standard number of shafts: two
Standard taper: 13 in. pro
Standard ferrules: linen-based melamine (LBM)
Standard tip: WB water buffalo
Annual production: 75 to 100 cues

OPTIONS (FOR NEW CUES ONLY)

Special length: no charge
Extra shaft: $150
Ivory butt cap: $250
Ivory joint: $100
Ivory ferrule: $50
Custom joint protectors: $50+
Leather wrap: $100

REPAIRS

Repairs done on most fine cues.
Refinish (with linen wrap): $150
Refinish (with leather wrap): $250
Rewrap (Irish linen): $40
Rewrap (leather): $100
Clean and press linen wrap: $10
Replace shaft: $100+
Replace butt cap: $60+
Replace tip: $15+

CURRENT NITTI CUES

Basic Nitti cues with wraps and joint rings start at $700. Nitti cues with points start at $900. One-of-a-kind custom Nitti cues start at $2,500. The current delivery time for a Nitti cue is about four to six months.

CURRENT EXAMPLES

The following Nitti cues can be ordered as shown, modified to suit the desires of the customer, or new designs can be created.

Level 4 - Phenolic joint, bird's-eye maple forearm with an ebony and ivory checked ring above wrap, four ebony points with four veneers and an ivory diamond-shaped inlay in each, ebony butt sleeve with four red dymondwood dots set in ivory diamond-shaped inlays between ebony and ivory checked rings at top and bottom.

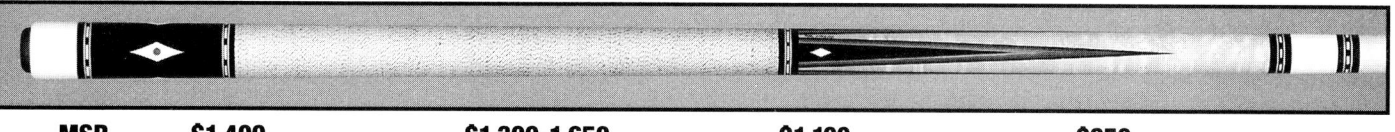

| MSR | $1,400 | $1,300-1,650 | $1,100 | $850 |

Level 4 - Phenolic joint, bird's-eye maple forearm with an ebony and ivory checked ring above wrap, four ebony points with four veneers and an ivory spear-shaped inlay in each, ebony butt sleeve with patterns of ivory dots and ivory spear-shaped inlays between ebony and ivory checked rings at top and bottom.

| MSR | $2,000 | $1,800-2,250 | $1,500 | $1,250 |

Level 4 - Phenolic joint, bird's-eye maple forearm with an ebony and ivory checked ring above wrap, four ebony points with four veneers and an ivory diamond-shaped inlay between two ivory dots in each, ebony butt sleeve with patterns of ivory dots and ivory diamond-shaped inlays set in windows between ebony and ivory checked rings at top and bottom.

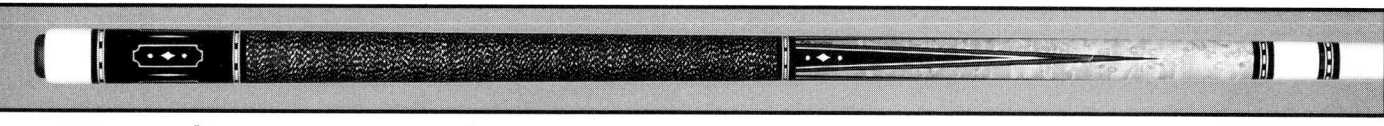

| MSR | $2,000 | $1,800-2,250 | $1,500 | $1,250 |

GRADING	100%	95%	70%

Level 6 - Ivory joint, ebony forearm with an ebony and ivory checked ring above wrap, four multi-piece floating ivory points, leather wrap, ebony butt sleeve eight multi-piece ivory inlays between ebony and ivory checked rings at top and bottom.

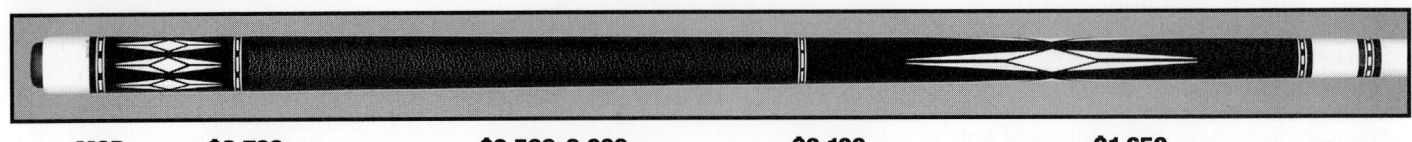

MSR	$2,700	$2,500-3,000	$2,100	$1,650

Level 6 - Ivory joint, bird's-eye maple forearm with an ebony and ivory checked ring above wrap, four ebony points with colored veneers and an abalone diamond-shaped inlay between two abalone dots in each alternating with four short ivory points with veneers, leather wrap, ebony butt sleeve with patterns of abalone dots and abalone diamond-shaped inlays set in ivory windows alternating with ivory inlays between ebony and ivory checked rings at top and bottom.

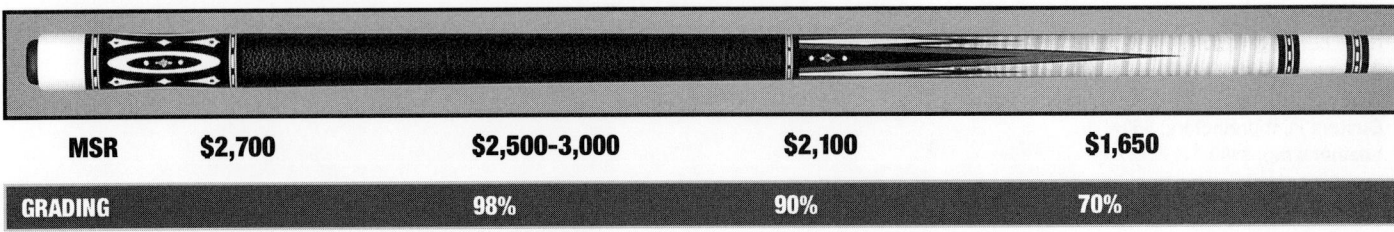

MSR	$2,700	$2,500-3,000	$2,100	$1,650
GRADING	98%	90%	70%	

SECONDARY MARKET MINIMUM VALUES

The following are minimum values for Nitti Cues encountered on the secondary market. These prices are representative of cues utilizing basic materials and designs that are not currently available. Nitti Cues has offered one-of-a-kind cues that can command many times these prices due to the use of exotic materials and artistry.

Special construction note: There are many materials and construction techniques that can add value to Nitti cues. The following are the most important examples:
  Add $400+ for ivory points.
For all used Nitti cues, except where otherwise noted:
  Add $100 for each additional original straight playable shaft beyond two.
  Deduct $150 for each missing original straight playable shaft under two.
  Add $45 each for ivory ferrules.
  Add $85 for ivory joint.
  Deduct 25% for obvious or improper refinish.

Level 1 - 4 points, hustler.
Level 1 cues start at	$300	$245	$170

Level 2 - 0 points, 0-25 inlays.
Level 2 cues start at	$650	$500	$335

Level 3 - 2-6 points, 0-8 inlays.
Level 3 cues start at	$800	$625	$420

Level 4 - 4-10 points, 9-25 inlays.
Level 4 cues start at	$1,000	$765	$550

Level 5 - 0-12 points, 26-50 inlays.
Level 5 cues start at	$1,250	$985	$650

Level 6 - 0-12 points, 51-75 inlays.
Level 6 cues start at	$1,750	$1,395	$950

NORTHERN CUE

Maker of pool cues starting in Norway, Michigan, now in Hermansville, Michigan.
Ray Gurgall is making cues in Hermansville, Michigan. He is a part-time cuemaker. His full-time occupation is in cabinet making and building log homes. He got interested in making cues and selling cue parts from talking with other cuemakers.
If you are interested in talking to Ray Gurgall about a new cue or cue that needs to be repaired, you can contact him at Northern Cue, listed in the Trademark Index.

SPECIFICATIONS

Butt material: hardwoods
Shaft material: maple
Standard length: 30 in.
Lengths available: any
Standard finish: clear car lacquer

GRADING	98%	90%	70%

Standard wrap: Irish linen
Standard number of shafts: one
Annual production: approximately 50 cues

OPTIONS (FOR NEW CUES ONLY)

Special length: no charge
Layered tip: no charge
Extra shaft: $70

REPAIRS

Repairs done on all fine cues.
  Refinish (with Irish linen wrap): $80
  Rewrap (Irish linen): $30
  Clean and press linen wrap: $40
  Replace shaft: $70
  Replace butt cap: $15
  Replace tip: $6
  Replace fiber/linen ferrule: $15

CURRENT NORTHERN CUES

The current delivery time for a Northern cue is about one year.

SECONDARY MARKET MINIMUM VALUES

The following are minimum values for other Northern cues encountered on the secondary market. These prices are representative of cues utilizing basic materials and designs that are not necessarily available at present. Ray has offered one-of-a-kind cues that can command many times these prices due to the use of exotic materials and artistry.

Special construction note: There are many materials and construction techniques that can add value to Northern cues.

For all used Northern cues, except where otherwise noted:
  Add $75 for each additional original straight playable shaft beyond one.
  Deduct $100 for missing original straight playable shaft.
  Add $45 each for ivory ferrules.
  Add $65 for leather wrap.
  Deduct 20% for obvious or improper refinish.

Level 2 - 0 points, 0-25 inlays.
Level 2 cues start at	$300	$290	$160

Level 3 - 2-6 points, 0-8 inlays.
Level 3 cues start at	$500	$395	$270

Level 4 - 4-10 points, 9-25 inlays.
Level 4 cues start at	$650	$510	$345

Level 5 - 0-12 points, 26-50 inlays.
Level 5 cues start at	$850	$665	$450

NORWELA CUES

Maker of pool cues from 1993 to present in Shreveport, Louisiana.

Jim Griffin started playing pool at the age of 12 at the old "Spot Club" in Shreveport, Louisiana. Eight years later, he joined the Marines, serving his country for 12 years. In 1991 he opened a lounge and resumed playing pool once again to keep his "bar box" (3 ½ by 7 ft. coin-operated table) busy. Eventually, Jim had eight "bar box" tables and one 4 ½ by 9 ft. table in his establishment, along with 30+ teams playing in various leagues.

Jim met an out-of-work cue builder who suggested that he buy a lathe and learn cuemaking. Jim's appreciation for wood and woodworking made him think that he just might enjoy building cues. In 1993, he purchased a lathe and began learning the craft from a cuemaker who had been trained under both Richard Black and Bill Schick, and started Norwela Cues. The name Norwela (Nor-we-la) is a derivitive of North West Louisiana.

In 1999, Jim purchased all of the cuemaking equipment from what was once called "Its George" and set up a full-blown shop. He now has eight lathes, a pantograph, table saw, chop saw, scroll saw, two hand saws, buffer, rod sander, grinder, drill press, etc. No CNC! He has made several changes to the manner in which he was taught to make cues, which he believes have given his cues a superior hit. His "Dominoe Cue," or "The True Gamblers Cue" as he calls it, was built because Jim was told he could not do it!

Jim retired from his lounge/pool room business a few years ago and has been building cues full time since then. He has time to be more creative with his work, which keeps him active and out of his wife's way.

Jim's cues can be identified by the Norwela logo, the year it was finished, and "Jim Griffin" signature. He is a member of the International Cuemakers Association.

Jim will replace a defective shaft or cue as long as there is no evidence of abuse.

GRADING	98%	90%	70%

If you are interested in talking to Jim about a new Norwela cue or cue that needs to be repaired, you can contact him at Norwela Cues, listed in the Trademark Index.

SPECIFICATIONS

Butt material: hardwoods
Shaft material: rock maple
Standard length: 58 in.
Standard finish: PPG automotive urethane
Standard wrap: Irish linen
Standard number of shafts: two
Joint screws: 3/8-10 or radial
Joint type: flat faced
Standard joint: stainless steel
Standard ferrules: LBM
Standard butt cap: Delrin
Standard tips: Triangle or Talisman
Annual production: approximately 120 cues

OPTIONS (FOR NEW CUES ONLY)

Ivory ferrule: $60
Ivory joint: $125
Ivory butt cap: $200
Leather wrap: $75
Extra shaft: $100

REPAIRS

Repairs done on all fine cues.
Refinish (with Irish linen wrap): $150
Rewrap (Irish linen): $40
Rewrap (leather): $100
Replace shaft: $100+
Replace tip: $10+
Replace butt cap (Delrin): $40
Replace ivory ferrule: $75
Replace standard ferrule: $40

CURRENT NORWELA CUES

Two-piece Norwela bar cues start at $175. Basic Norwela cues with wraps and joint rings start at $250. Four-point Norwela cues start at $350. Six-point Norwela cues start at $450. One-of-a-kind custom Norwela cues start at $800.

SECONDARY MARKET MINIMUM VALUES

The following are minimum values for other Norwela cues encountered on the secondary market. These prices are representative of cues utilizing basic materials and designs that are not necessarily available at present. Jim has offered one-of-a-kind cues that can command many times these prices due to the use of exotic materials and artistry.

Special construction note: There are many materials and construction techniques that can add value to Norwela cues.

For all used Norwela cues, except where otherwise noted:
Add $75 for each additional original straight playable shaft beyond two.
Deduct $100 for each missing original straight playable shaft under two.
Add $50 each for ivory ferrules.
Add $60 for leather wrap.
Deduct 20% for obvious or improper refinish.

Level 1 - Hustler.
	98%	90%	70%
Level 1 cues start at	$165	$130	$85

Level 2 - 0 points, 0-25 inlays.
Level 2 cues start at	$225	$175	$120

Level 3 - 2-6 points, 0-8 inlays.
Level 3 cues start at	$300	$235	$160

Level 4 - 4-10 points, 9-25 inlays.
Level 4 cues start at	$400	$315	$220

Level 5 - 0-12 points, 26-50 inlays.
Level 5 cues start at	$600	$475	$320

NOVA CUES INC.

Maker of pool cues starting in 1994 in West Bend, Wisconsin.

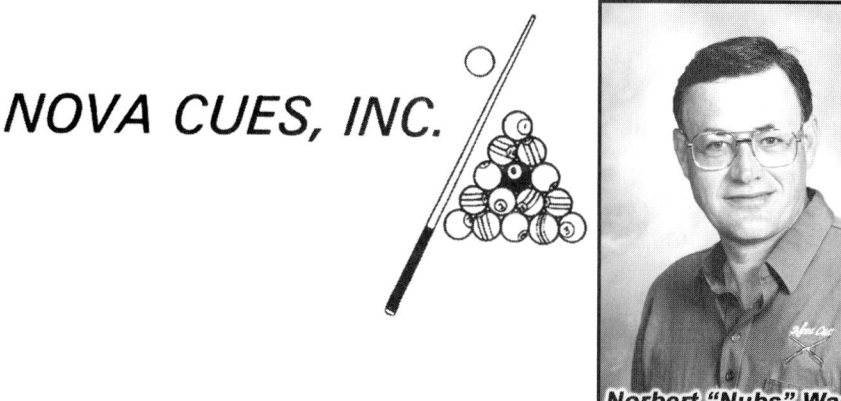

Norbert "Nubs" Wagner has enjoyed playing the game of pool for over 35 years. A tool and die maker by trade, Nubs became interested in cuemaking in the 1970s. He visited and befriended a couple of the top Wisconsin area cuemakers, and was Jim McDermott's first full-time employee in the mid-1970s.

In 1977, Nubs started Pro-Line Custom Cues in Milwaukee, working out of Romine's pool room. It was a short-lived endeavor, and he returned to tool making, progressing into CNC machining and programming. This experience was instrumental in developing his ability to work to the very close tolerances required for making cues.

Nubs kept involved in the cue industry. He continued to do repair work, sold a few cues in his retail shop, and played in leagues and tournaments. He always listened to the praise and criticism other players had for their cues. He helped start a small cue company in 1990, which increased his desire to start a cuemaking company of his own. The dream was realized in March of 1994, when Nubs founded Nova Cues Inc.

Nova made around 750 cues per year in West Bend, Wisconsin. Twelve different popular designs could be custom ordered in a variety of stains, wraps, weights, and lengths. No cues were kept in stock—all were custom made to order. All Nova cues are easily identifiable by the Nova logo on the butt caps, which has appeared there since 1994, even on the few hustler cues they made.

1994 to 1997

1997 to Present Day

Present Day custom cues

Nova Cues was a small shop, and they made everything that went into their cues except the tips, bumpers, and screws. To prevent warping, the butt sections were turned nine times and the shafts were turned twelve times over a two-month period. Nova cues tended to be forward balanced, with shafts that weighed around four ounces and were interchangeable. Depending on the woods used, Nova cues usually weighed in at 19 to 19 1/2 oz. without the addition of weights. Nova stressed the use of exotic woods, and beautifully dyed exotic woods, ivory, and pink ivory were also available. Nubs was very particular about attention to detail. For example, he spent a lot of time developing the finish that was used on Nova cues. It was applied entirely by hand (no spraying) over the course of four days. The result was a very thick, shiny, clear coat that is very resistant to dings and scratches. Nova cues became very popular in Europe, especially in Germany.

The Nova shop closed sometime after 2000. All of the equipment and materials are still there, and Nubs may reopen the Nova shop sometime in the future.

SPECIFICATIONS

Butt material: hardwoods
Shaft material: rock maple
Standard length: 58 1/2 in.
Lengths available: any up to 61 in.
Standard finish: proprietary
Joint screw: 5/16-14
Standard joint: stainless steel
Joint type: piloted
Balance point: varies
Point construction: inlaid
Standard wrap: Irish linen
Standard butt cap: MP ivory substitute
Standard number of shafts: one
Standard taper: 11 in. pro
Standard ferrules: Ivorine-3

| GRADING | 98% | 90% | 70% |

Standard tip: Le Pro
Tip widths available: any up to 15 mm

SECONDARY MARKET MINIMUM VALUES

The following are minimum prices for Nova cues encountered on the secondary market. These prices are representative of cues utilizing the most basic materials and designs that were available. Nova also offered one-of-a-kind cues that can command many times these prices due to the use of exotic materials and artistry.

Special construction note: There are many materials and construction techniques that can add value to Nova cues.

The following are the most important examples:

- Add $650+ for ivory points.
- Add $450+ for pink ivory butt sleeve.
- Add $350+ for pink ivory points.

For all used Nova cues:

- Add $85+ for each additional original straight playable shaft beyond one.
- Deduct $135 for missing original straight playable shaft.
- Add $95+ for ivory joint.
- Add $70+ for leather wrap.
- Add $65+ for each ivory ferrule.
- Deduct 30% for obvious or improper refinish.

Level	Description	98%	90%	70%
Level 1 - 4 points, hustler.	Level 1 cues start at	$250	$200	$115
Level 2 - 0 points, 0-25 inlays.	Level 2 cues start at	$375	$285	$175
Level 3 - 2-6 points, 0-8 inlays.	Level 3 cues start at	$450	$350	$215
Level 4 - 4-10 points, 9-25 inlays.	Level 4 cues start at	$600	$450	$275
Level 5 - 0-12 points, 26-50 inlays.	Level 5 cues start at	$850	$650	$400
Level 6 - 0-12 points, 51-75 inlays.	Level 6 cues start at	$1,150	$875	$550
Level 7 - 0-12 points, 76-125 inlays.	Level 7 cues start at	$1,500	$1,150	$700

O SECTION

ODOM CUES

Maker of pool cues from 1998 to present in Ft. Worth, Texas.

Jim Odom is a part-time cuemaker in Fort Worth, Texas. His work is influenced by Herman Rambow and David Paul Kersenbrock. Jim's full-time job is a semi-retired trick driver. He bought a Paradise Cue in 1964 and had been thinking about making cues since then.

If you are interested in talking to Jim Odom about a new cue or cue that needs to be repaired, you can contact him at Odom Cues, listed in the Trademark Index.

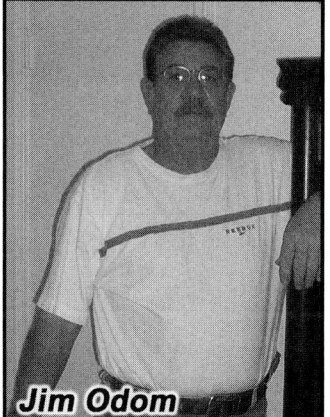
Jim Odom

SPECIFICATIONS

Butt material: hardwoods
Shaft material: premium maple
Standard length: 58 in.
Lengths available: any within reason
Standard finish: Dupont Hyper-Cure
Standard butt cap: Delrin
Standard wrap: Irish linen
Point construction: short splice
Standard joint: stainless steel
Standard joint type: piloted
Standard joint screw thread: 5/16-14
Standard number of shafts: two
Standard taper: custom
Standard ferrules: Aegis II
Standard tip: Le Pro
Standard tip width: 13 mm
Annual production: approximately 50 cues

OPTIONS (FOR NEW CUES ONLY)

Special length: no charge

REPAIRS

Repairs done on all fine cues.
- Refinish (with Irish linen wrap): $140
- Refinish (with leather wrap): $200
- Rewrap (Irish linen): $45
- Rewrap (leather): $100
- Clean and press linen wrap: $15
- Replace shaft: $90
- Replace ivory ferrule: $60
- Replace butt cap: $50
- Replace ivory butt cap: $200
- Replace tip: $15+
- Replace fiber/linen ferrule: $25

CURRENT ODOM CUES

The current delivery time for an Odom cue is about six to twelve weeks.

SECONDARY MARKET MINIMUM VALUES

The following are minimum values for other Odom cues encountered on the secondary market. These prices are representative of cues utilizing basic materials and designs that are not necessarily available at present. Jim has offered one-of-a-kind cues that can command many times these prices due to the use of exotic materials and artistry.

Special construction note: There are many materials and construction techniques that can add value to Odom cues.

For all used Odom cues, except where otherwise noted:
- Add $100 for each additional original straight playable shaft beyond two.
- Deduct $150 for missing original straight playable shaft.
- Add $50 each for ivory ferrules.
- Add $65 for leather wrap.
- Deduct 20% for obvious or improper refinish.

GRADING	98%	90%	70%
Level 2 - 0 points, 0-25 inlays.			
Level 2 cues start at	$200	$160	$110
Level 3 - 2-6 points, 0-8 inlays.			
Level 3 cues start at	$350	$270	$185
Level 4 - 4-10 points, 9-25 inlays.			
Level 4 cues start at	$450	$295	$235
Level 5 - 0-12 points, 26-50 inlays.			
Level 5 cues start at	$650	$500	$340

OJO CUES

Former name of Adam Franks Cues. Please refer to Adam Franks Cues.

JERRY OLIVIER HAND CRAFTED CUSTOM CUES

Maker of pool cues from 1995 to present in Pearland, Texas.

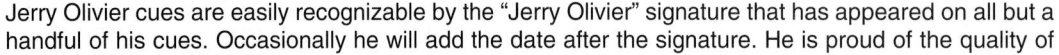

Jerry Olivier has been obsessed with the game of pool since he was a kid. Growing up, he played as often as he could for as long as he could. He liked to play in local amateur tournaments, and won many of the events he entered. After finishing school, Jerry went to work for Dow Chemical, working with chemical formulas and computer programs. He worked four days on and four days off, giving him plenty of time to play pool. He liked cues and started doing cue repairs in his garage as a hobby. Soon cues were his new obsession and by 1995 Jerry made his first one.

Jerry enjoyed cuemaking much better than his job with Dow, so when the time was right he took an early retirement package after 13 years with the company. 1n 1997, he invested everything he received into a new 1500-square-foot shop with all-new equipment. Jerry now makes about 150 to 200 cues per year. He has produced a catalogue with a line of twelve cues, but these cues are mainly used as a starting point for custom orders. Jerry is always creating new designs, and makes many one-of-a-kind custom cues in his one-man shop. Jerry likes to use ivory, and will not use any substitutes. Aside from linen fiber ferrules on cues under $1,200, if it's white on a Jerry Olivier cue, it is ivory. This is true for the inlays, joints, and butt caps as well.

Jerry Olivier cues are easily recognizable by the "Jerry Olivier" signature that has appeared on all but a handful of his cues. Occasionally he will add the date after the signature. He is proud of the quality of his leather wraps and takes great care in selecting the hides and applying them to the cues. Jerry strives to make the best cue he can, and will stand behind any problems that are not the fault of the customer.

In 2005 Jerry designed and built a new UV paint booth so he could start applying a UV finish to his cues. The new finish is more durable and has a more brilliant shine than the PPG finish he was using before.

Jerry tries to attend every major tournament and billiard event in the U.S. that he can. He usually makes cues for about a month and then attends tournaments and trade shows for about a month. He has a website that he keeps tabs on, and will e-mail pictures of individual cues that customers are interested in.

Jerry Olivier Hand Crafted Custom Cues are guaranteed for life against manufacturing defects that are not the result of warpage or abuse. If you have a Jerry Olivier cue that needs further identification or repair, or would like to order a new Jerry Olivier cue, contact Jerry Olivier Hand Made Custom Cues, listed in the Trademark Index.

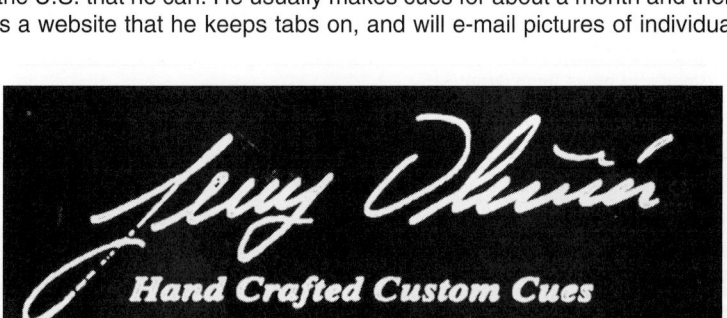

SPECIFICATIONS

Butt material: hardwoods
Shaft material: rock maple
Standard length: 58 1/4 in.
Lengths available: any up to 60 in.
Standard finish: UV finish
Balance point: 1 1/4 in. above wrap
Standard butt cap: linen phenolic
Standard wrap: Irish linen
Point construction: short splice or inlaid
Standard joint: linen-based fiber
Joint type: flat faced
Joint screw: 3/8-10
Standard number of shafts: one
Standard taper: 10 1/2 in. pro
Standard ferrules: linen-based fiber
Tip widths available: 12.5 to 13.5 mm
Standard tip: eleven-layered pigskin tip
Annual production: fewer than 250 cues

JERRY OLIVIER HAND CRAFTED CUSTOM CUES, cont.

GRADING	100%	95%	70%

OPTIONS (FOR NEW CUES ONLY)
- Leather wrap: $150+
- Special length: $50
- Ivory butt sleeve: $240
- Ivory joint: $220
- Joint protectors: $20+
- Extra shaft: $150
- Ivory ferrule: $100

REPAIRS
Repairs done on all fine cues.
- Refinish: $150
- Rewrap (Irish linen): $40
- Rewrap (leather): $150
- Replace phenolic butt cap: $50
- Replace shaft: $150
- Replace ivory ferrule: $100
- Replace standard tip: $15
- Replace Moori tip: $35

CURRENT JERRY OLIVIER CUES
Two-piece Jerry Olivier bar cues start at $225. Basic Jerry Olivier cues with wraps and joint rings start at $350. Jerry Olivier cues with points start at $400. One-of-a-kind custom Jerry Olivier cues start at $1,200. Cues starting at $1,200 come with two shafts with ivory ferrules. The current delivery time for a custom Jerry Olivier cue is six to eight months.

CURRENT EXAMPLES
The following Jerry Olivier cues can be ordered as shown, modified to suit the desires of the customer, or new designs can be created.

Level 4 - Bird's-eye maple forearm with a silver ring set in ebony above wrap, four ebony-bordered snakewood floating points alternating with four ivory diamond-shaped inlays set in snakewood ovals, bird's-eye maple butt sleeve with four ebony-bordered snakewood double spear-shaped inlays alternating with four ivory diamond-shaped inlays set in snakewood ovals between silver rings set in ebony at top and bottom.

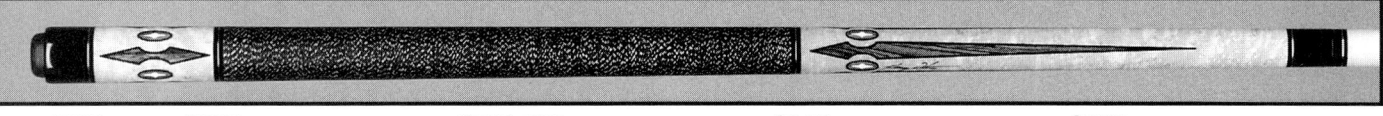

MSR	$850	$800-950	$645	$450

Level 4 - Bird's-eye maple forearm with a silver ring set in ebony above wrap, four ebony points with veneers and an ivory diamond-shaped inlay in each, ebony butt sleeve with four ivory windows alternating with four ivory diamond-shaped inlays between silver rings at top and bottom.

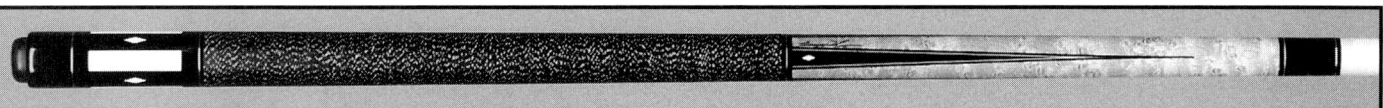

MSR	$1,100	$1,000-1,250	$825	$600

Level 5 in.DS#1 in. - Ebony forearm with a silver ring above wrap, four ivory-bordered turquoise floating points above intricate ivory and turquoise inlays, ebony butt sleeve with intricate ivory and turquoise inlays between silver rings at top and bottom.

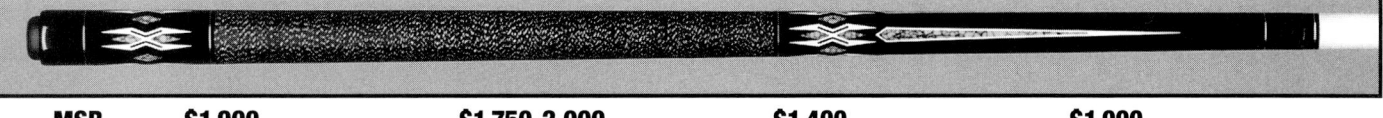

MSR	$1,900	$1,750-2,000	$1,400	$1,000

Level 4 - Ivory joint, bird's-eye maple forearm with a scrimshawed ivory ring set in silver above wrap, four ebony-bordered scrimshawed ivory points, leather wrap, ebony butt sleeve with four scrimshawed ivory windows alternating with four lightning bolt-shaped inlays between scrimshawed ivory rings set in silver at top and bottom.

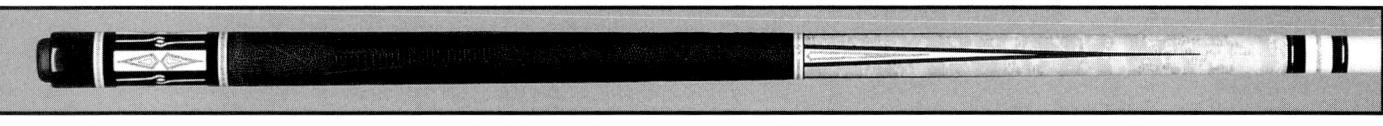

MSR	$2,100	$2,000-2,250	$1,650	$1,100

| GRADING | 98% | 90% | 70% |

PAST EXAMPLES

The following cues were available from Jerry Olivier Hand Crafted Custom Cues in the past. They are still available by special order. Hardwoods include bird's-eye maple, cocobolo, bocote, ebony, and other exotic woods that the customer can specify.

Level 2 #1 - Stained bird's-eye maple forearm with a nickel silver ring above wrap, stained bird's-eye maple butt sleeve with nickel silver rings at top and bottom.

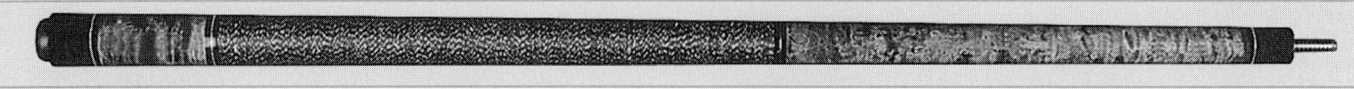

| MSR (1999) $320 | $350 | $270 | $185 |

Level 3 #2 - Hardwood forearm with a nickel silver ring above wrap, four floating hardwood points, hardwood butt sleeve with nickel silver rings at top and bottom.

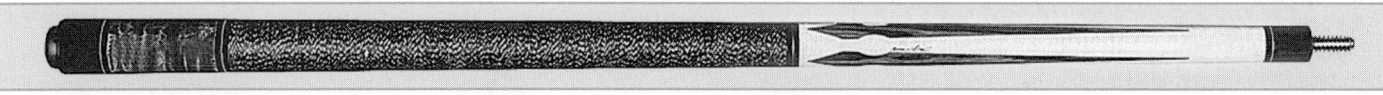

| MSR (1999) $400 | $450 | $350 | $235 |

Level 3 #3 - Hardwood forearm with a nickel silver ring above wrap, four floating hardwood points, hardwood butt sleeve with four hardwood diamond-shaped inlays between nickel silver rings at top and bottom.

| MSR (1999) $450 | $500 | $385 | $265 |

Level 4 #4 - Hardwood forearm with a nickel silver ring above wrap, four floating hardwood points with a hardwood diamond-shaped inlay in each, hardwood butt sleeve with four hardwood windows alternating with four hardwood diamond-shaped inlays between nickel silver rings at top and bottom.

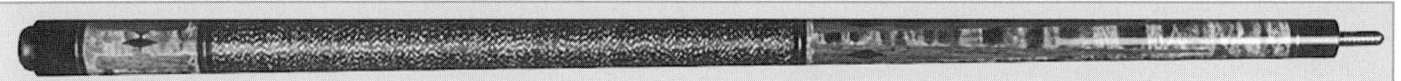

| MSR (1999) $600 | $650 | $500 | $335 |

Level 4 #5 - Hardwood forearm with a nickel silver ring above wrap, five double-ended floating hardwood points with an ivory diamond-shaped inlay in each, hardwood butt sleeve with five ivory diamond-shaped inlays set in four-point hardwood windows between nickel silver rings at top and bottom.

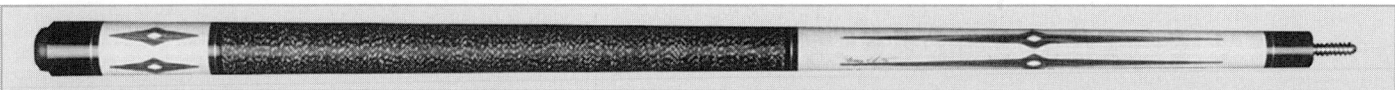

| MSR (1999) $650 | $700 | $540 | $370 |

Level 3 #6 - Hardwood forearm with a nickel silver ring above wrap, four hardwood points with an ivory diamond-shaped inlay in each, hardwood butt sleeve with four large ivory diamond-shaped inlays between nickel silver rings at top and bottom.

| MSR (1999) $700 | $750 | $575 | $390 |

Level 4 #7 - Hardwood forearm with a nickel silver ring above wrap, six floating hardwood points with a hardwood scalloped diamond-shaped inlay in each, hardwood butt sleeve with six hardwood windows with a hardwood scalloped diamond-shaped inlay in each between nickel silver rings at top and bottom.

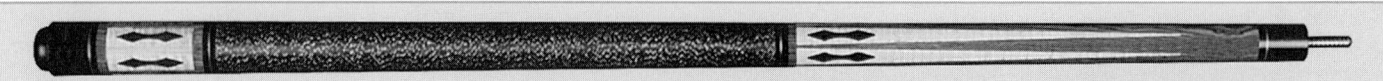

| MSR (1999) $800 | $875 | $675 | $450 |

JERRY OLIVIER HAND CRAFTED CUSTOM CUES, cont.

GRADING	98%	90%	70%

Level 4 #8 - Hardwood forearm with a nickel silver ring above wrap, four hardwood points with an ivory diamond-shaped inlay in each alternating with four hardwood bars with a bordered ivory diamond-shaped inlay at the tip of each, hardwood butt sleeve with four large ivory diamond-shaped inlays between nickel silver rings at top and bottom.

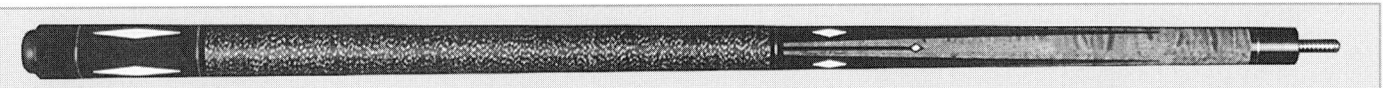

MSR (1999) $900	$1,000	$785	$550

Level 4 #9 - Ivory joint, hardwood forearm with a nickel silver ring above wrap, four bordered floating hardwood points with an intricate three-piece ivory diamond-shaped inlay in each, hardwood butt sleeve with four bordered hardwood windows with an intricate three-piece ivory diamond-shaped inlay in each between nickel silver rings at top and bottom, ivory butt cap.

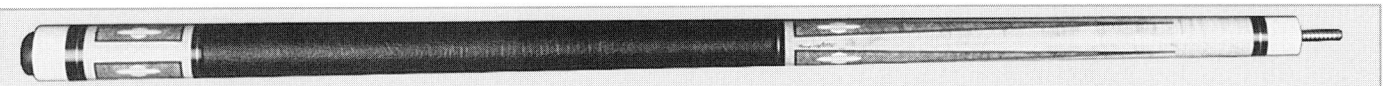

MSR (1999) $1,500	$1,550	$1,200	$800

Level 4 #10 - Ivory joint, hardwood forearm with a brass-bordered cocobolo ring above wrap, six floating hardwood points with a hardwood scalloped diamond-shaped inlay in each, hardwood butt sleeve with six hardwood windows with a hardwood scalloped diamond-shaped inlay in each between brass-bordered cocobolo rings at top and bottom, ivory butt cap.

MSR (1999) $1,700	$1,700	$1,350	$900

Level 5 #11 - Ivory joint, hardwood forearm with a nickel silver ring above wrap, four ivory-bordered hardwood points with four intricate ivory inlays in each, hardwood butt sleeve with four ivory-bordered hardwood windows with five intricate ivory inlays in each between nickel silver rings at top and bottom, ivory butt cap.

MSR (1999) $1,900	$1,800	$1,450	$1,000

Level 5 #12 - Ivory joint, hardwood forearm with a nickel silver ring above wrap and a series of ebony-bordered ivory inlays, four ebony-bordered ivory points with an ebony-bordered ivory diamond-shaped inlay in each, hardwood butt sleeve with a series of ebony-bordered ivory inlays and four ebony-bordered ivory diamond-shaped inlays between nickel silver rings at top and bottom, ivory butt cap.

MSR (1999) $3,450	$2,750	$2,250	$1,550

SECONDARY MARKET MINIMUM VALUES

The following are minimum values for other Jerry Olivier cues encountered on the secondary market. These prices are representative of cues utilizing basic materials and designs that are not necessarily available at present. Jerry has offered one-of-a-kind cues that can command many times these prices due to the use of exotic materials and artistry.

Special construction note: There are many materials and construction techniques that can add value to Jerry Olivier cues. The following are the most important examples:

Add $150 for ivory joint.

For all used Jerry Olivier cues, except where otherwise noted:

Add $115 for each additional original straight playable shaft beyond one.
Deduct $150 for missing original straight playable shaft.
Add $75 each for ivory ferrules.
Add $85 for leather wrap.
Deduct 20% for obvious or improper refinish.

Level 1 - 4 points, hustler.
Level 1 cues start at	$200	$160	$115

Level 2 - 0 points, 0-25 inlays.
Level 2 cues start at	$300	$235	$160

GRADING	98%	90%	70%
Level 3 - 2-6 points, 0-8 inlays.			
Level 3 cues start at	$350	$270	$185
Level 4 - 4-10 points, 9-25 inlays.			
Level 4 cues start at	$500	$390	$265
Level 5 - 0-12 points, 26-50 inlays.			
Level 5 cues start at	$750	$575	$385
Level 6 - 0-12 points, 51-75 inlays.			
Level 6 cues start at	$1,200	$935	$645

JIM OLMS CUES

Maker of pool cues from 1993 to present in Genoa, Ohio.

Jim Olms has repaired and crafted custom cues since 1993 when J.O.B.E. (Jim Olms Billiard Equipment) opened its doors in Genoa, Ohio. Jim was introduced to billiards before he was 10 years old, and played on a 3 ft. by 6 ft. table his father purchased for the basement recreation room. Olms spent his adolescence dividing his time between billiards, hockey, and baseball. After completing high school, Olms pursued his pitching ability to the Detroit Tigers farm system where he stayed three years as a long relief pitcher. During those years in Florida and North Carolina in the minor leagues, Olms spent his days playing baseball and his evenings playing billiards with his fellow teammates until a shoulder injury ended his chances of a big league career. After an occupation at Toledo Edison, Olms' interest sparked in the cue repair business. He met Bill Connelly at a Toledo area tournament and observed his cue repair techniques. Olms found his passion and, at Connelly's encouragement, acquired his first cue lathe and instructional video from Chris Hightower. Olms relocated to central Michigan, which placed him in the hub of numerous local and regional tournaments and he has consistently turned out cues from that time on. Reminiscent of several cue craftsmen who started out in refurbishing, Olms concentrated on "Sneaky Petes" (constructed by severing bar cues in half). Nevertheless, he has evolved into a master wood finisher. Lacking the tools and technique to fabricate points and inlays, Olms' attention was centered on finding the finest woods and cultivating exclusive finishing processes, which place his cues among the most remarkable worldwide. It is not uncommon for Olms to spend a week in northern Michigan cataloging mountains of rough wood searching for the precise grain. Experimenting with his own proprietary stains over the years, Olms perfected an irridescent finish that transforms spectacularly under the lights. To add further ornamentation to his cues, Olms exchanges his superior grained shaft wood for stunning pointed forearms with Dave Barenbrugge, a great influence on Olms' cue crafting expertise. Having never replicated the same design twice, each Jim Olms cue is an exclusive. The amalgamation of the premium obtainable maples, accents in dozens of exotic hardwoods, and the distinctive staining methods Olms has developed, make Jim Olms cues a standout.

Jim Olms

If you are interested in talking to Jim about a new cue or cue that needs to be repaired, you can contact him at Jim Olms Cues, listed in the Trademark Index.

SPECIFICATIONS

Butt material: hardwoods
Shaft material: rock maple
Standard length: 58 in.
Standard wrap: Irish linen

SECONDARY MARKET MINIMUM VALUES

The following are minimum values for other Jim Olms cues encountered on the secondary market. These prices are representative of cues utilizing basic materials and designs that are not necessarily available at present. Jim has offered one-of-a-kind cues that can command many times these prices due to the use of exotic materials and artistry.

Special construction note: There are many materials and construction techniques that can add value to Jim Olms cues.

For all used Jim Olms cues, except where otherwise noted:

Add $60 for each additional original straight playable shaft beyond one.
Deduct $90 for missing original straight playable shaft.
Add $40 each for ivory ferrules.
Deduct 20% for obvious or improper refinish.

Level 2 - 0 points, 0-25 inlays.			
Level 2 cues start at	$200	$160	$110
Level 3 - 2-6 points, 0-8 inlays.			
Level 3 cues start at	$300	$240	$160
Level 4 - 4-10 points, 9-25 inlays.			
Level 4 cues start at	$400	$310	$210
Level 5 - 0-12 points, 26-50 inlays.			
Level 5 cues start at	$600	$470	$320

OLNEY CUSTOM CUES

Maker of pool cues from 1992 to present in Boone, Iowa.

Jeff Olney started playing pool in the early 1970s at the local pool hall. The better players preferred snooker. As a young boy, he also enjoyed the challenge of snooker, watching and learning from the older players. Jeff noticed right away that the house cues were not the greatest, and at age 15, he made his first two pool cues in woodworking class.

Jeff also liked playing baseball. By the time he was 15, he had developed a strong throwing arm and a powerful pool stroke. Jeff soon began running a lot of 50-point runs at snooker and had one run of 70. The pool hall closed when Jeff was 16, but he continued playing a little.

In 1978, Jeff joined the Navy and was stationed in San Diego. He discovered the Billiard Tavern downtown. It became his favorite hangout after work and on weekends. It was a 40-table room and one of the finest in the USA. Jeff enjoyed watching players such as Erving Crane and Steve Mizerak. Jeff got tips from the city's top players and practiced hard to take his game up a notch or two. He had a strong stroke and became known as the "Gunner."

Jeff began looking for the perfect playing cue. He bought some collectable custom cues also. Jeff was a mechanical engineer in the Navy, and sometimes worked in tolerances into the 1-10 thousands of an inch. He was aware that some cues had too much flex in the shaft and others not enough. He realized the butt, joint, ferrule and tip were very important parts of the cue, but it was the shaft that was the main factor in the playability. Jeff uses a gradual taper of .002 of an inch for the first 14 inches, providing good action with maximum accuracy and a smooth feel.

Jeff's game was at its best from 1988 to 1991. He played in tournaments and made cues at the same time. In 1992, he got out of the Navy and started making cues full time. He started getting orders from all over the world from his website and is busy as ever in his one-man shop.

Jeff makes his cues one at a time. Custom orders can take years. He makes all his own parts, except for the tips and bumpers. Jeff likes to make 6-point cues but also makes 4-, 5-, 8-, 10-, 12-, and even one 16-point splice cue.

If you are interested in talking to Jeff Olney about a new cue or cue that needs to be repaired, you can contact him at Olney Custom Cues, listed in the Trademark Index.

Jeff Olney

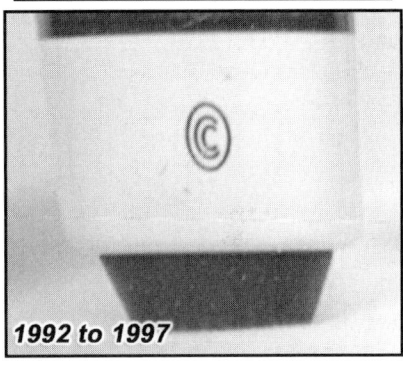

1992 to 1997

1998 to Present Day

SPECIFICATIONS

- Butt material: linen base
- Shaft material: hard maple
- Standard length: 58 in.
- Lengths available: 56 to 59 ½ in.
- Standard finish: Dupont Clearcoat
- Balance point: 1 ½ in. above wrap
- Standard butt cap: linen base
- Standard wrap: Irish linen
- Point construction: short splice
- Standard joint: linen based
- Other joints offered: ivory
- Joint type: flat face
- Joint screw thread: 3/8-10
- Standard number of shafts: one
- Standard taper: custom
- Standard ferrules: linen based
- Standard tip: Triangle
- Standard tip width: 13 mm
- Annual production: approximately 60 cues

OPTIONS (FOR NEW CUES ONLY)

- Special length: n/c
- Layered tip: $35
- Ivory butt cap: $250
- Ivory joint: $150
- Ivory ferrule: $50
- Joint protectors: $20 for two
- Extra shaft: $150+

REPAIRS

Repairs done on all fine cues.
- Clean and press linen wrap: $10
- Replace ivory ferrule: $50
- Replace Triangle tip: $15
- Replaced Moori tip: $35
- Replace fiber/linen/ferrule: $25

568 OLNEY CUSTOM CUES, cont.

GRADING	98%	90%	70%

CURRENT OLNEY CUES

Two-piece Olney bar cues start at $275. Basic Olney cues with wraps and joint rings start at $350. Olney cues with points start at $525. One-of-a-kind Olney custom cues start at $800. The current delivery time for an Olney cue is three years.

SECONDARY MARKET MINIMUM VALUES

The following are minimum values for other Olney cues encountered on the secondary market. These prices are representative of cues utilizing basic materials and designs that are not necessarily available at present. Jeff has offered one-of-a-kind cues that can command many times these prices due to the use of exotic materials and artistry.

Special construction note: There are many materials and construction techniques that can add value to Olney cues.

For all used Olney cues, except where otherwise noted:
- Add $100 for each additional original straight playable shaft beyond one.
- Deduct $150 for missing original straight playable shaft.
- Add $40 each for ivory ferrules.
- Deduct 20% for obvious or improper refinish.

Level 1 - Hustler.

	98%	90%	70%
Level 1 cues start at	$250	$195	$130

Level 2 - 0 points, 0-25 inlays.

Level 2 cues start at	$300	$240	$160

Level 3 - 2-6 points, 0-8 inlays.

Level 3 cues start at	$500	$385	$260

Level 4 - 4-10 points, 9-25 inlays.

Level 4 cues start at	$600	$470	$320

Level 5 - 0-12 points, 26-50 inlays.

Level 5 cues start at	$900	$700	$480

OMEGA CUES

Distributor of pool cues from 2003 to present in Forth Worth, Texas.

Omega cues are the result of years of traveling on the pro circuit, learning what qualities make a pool cue "play" great. After years of doing extensive research, the first Omega cues were made in 2003 with emphasis on performance, quality, and affordability. All inlays are done by hand. All materials and components are hand selected for best quality.

Omega cues are designed in the US and have a lifetime warranty on construction. They are easily identified by the name "Omega" engraved on the butt sleeve.

If you are interested in talking to Mike Hoang about a new cue or cue that needs to be repaired, you can contact him at Omega Cues, listed in the Trademark Index.

SPECIFICATIONS

Butt material: exotic hardwoods
Shaft material: Canadian maple
Point construction: hand-spliced
Standard ferrules: melamine
Standard tip: multi-layered Everest

OPTIONS (FOR NEW CUES ONLY)

Extra shaft: $100

CURRENT OMEGA CUES

Omega currently offers the "OM-Series" of 14 cues priced from $175 to $245, three jump/break cues from $95 to $175, and eight jump cues that are available for $79 each. Most Omega cues are available for immediate delivery.

SECONDARY MARKET MINIMUM VALUES

The following are minimum values for Omega cues encountered on the secondary market. These prices are representative of cues utilizing basic materials and designs that are not necessarily available at present.

Special construction note: There are many materials and construction techniques that can add value to Omega cues.

For all used Omega cues, except where otherwise noted:
- Add $70 for each additional original straight playable shaft beyond two.
- Deduct $100 for missing original straight playable shaft.
- Deduct 15% for obvious or improper refinish.

OMEGA CUES, cont. 569

GRADING	98%	90%	70%
Level 1 - Hustler.			
Level 1 cues start at	$65	$50	$30
Level 2 - 0 points, 0-25 inlays.			
Level 2 cues start at	$100	$75	$45
Level 3 - 2-6 points, 0-8 inlays.			
Level 3 cues start at	$125	$95	$60

OMEGA CUE COMPANY, LATER OMEGA/DPK

Maker of pool cues from 1989 to 1996 in Wauconda, Illinois, a suburb of Chicago.

The Omega Cue Company was founded in 1989 by Edward Boado, an entrepreneur and cue collector, and Mike Bender, a very skilled mechanical engineer who enjoyed working on cues. Ed was very happy with the cue repair Mike had done for him in the past, and Ed knew that they had the ability to become successful making cues together. Soon after Omega started, Ed and Mike were joined by David Paul Kersenbrock, at which time the letters "dpk" were added to the company name. David was a highly respected and innovative cuemaker who had written a book on the science of cuemaking and was involved in the creation of the South West cue.

In 1991, Mike Bender moved to Alaska to start making custom cues on his own and he was later replaced at Omega by his brother, Matt Bender. Although they were never marked, Omega/dpk cues are easily identifiable by their unique flared butt caps and long stainless steel joint pins with thin collars. In 1996, Ed stopped making Omega cues in order to pursue other interests

If you have an Omega cue that needs further identification or repair, contact Ed Young Custom Cues, listed in the Trademark Index.

SPECIFICATIONS

- Butt material: hardwoods
- Shaft material: rock maple
- Standard length: 58 in.
- Joint type: flat faced
- Point construction: short splice
- Standard wrap: Irish linen

OMEGA CUES

The following are minimum prices for Omega cues encountered on the secondary market. These prices are representative of cues utilizing basic materials and designs that were available. Omega also offered one-of-a-kind cues that can command many times these prices due to the use of exotic materials and artistry.

PAST EXAMPLES

Level 3 Bird's-eye nose with four ebony points, black leather wrap, and ebony butt sleeve.

| MSR (1991) N/A | $2,000 | $1,650 | $1,275 |

Level 4 - Bird's-eye nose with four ebony points with black and white veneers. Each point inlaid with ivory which is engraved with geometric patterns. Wrap is Irish linen. Butt sleeve is ebony with large ivory windows engraved with geometric patterns. Fancy box-type ringwork. Black leather wrap and ebony butt sleeve.

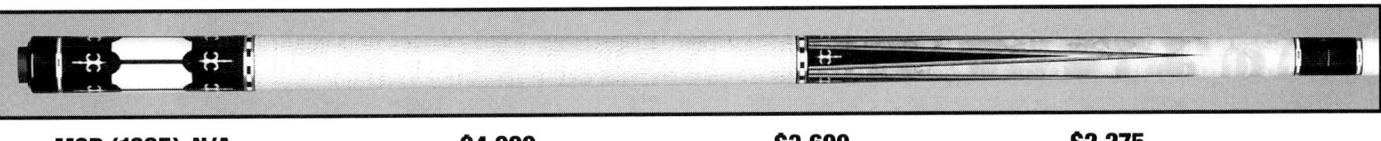

| MSR (1995) N/A | $4,000 | $3,600 | $2,275 |

Level 5 - Bird's-eye nose with six ebony points (three high and three low) with no veneers. Each point tip inlaid with sharp ebony and ivory diamonds. Each point inlaid with ivory, in which the tall point inlays are engraved with a floral-type design and the short points a geometric shape. Wrap is Irish linen. Butt sleeve is ebony with large ivory geometric shape inlays and ivory windows which are engraved with floray-type patterns. Fancy box-type and architectural ringwork.

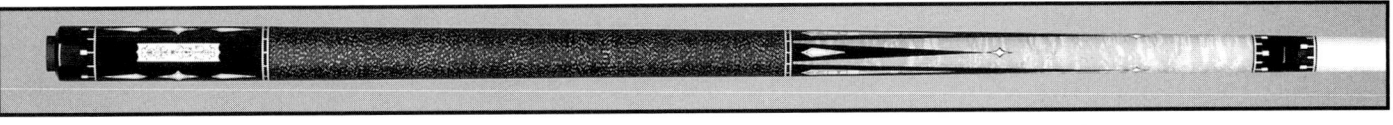

| MSR (1990s) N/A | $5,500 | $4,900 | $2,575 |

GRADING	98%	90%	70%

Level 5 - Ebony nose with ivory points. Each point inlaid with precious metal geometric shapes and lines. Between each point are inlaid precious stones. Wrap is black leather. Butt sleeve is ebony with ivory points mimicking tall points and inlaid with the same pattern as above the wrap. Precious stones inlaid between the points. Fancy box-type ringwork. Joint and butt plate are ivory.

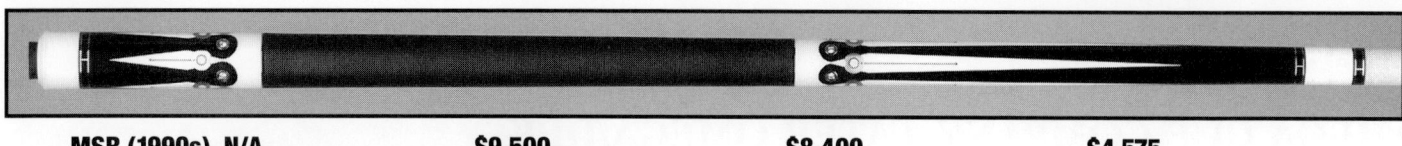

MSR (1990s) N/A	$9,500	$8,400	$4,575

SECONDARY MARKET MINIMUM VALUES

The following are minimum prices for other Omega cues encountered on the secondary market. These prices are representative of cues utilizing basic materials and designs that may not be currently available.

Special construction note: There are many materials and construction techniques that can add value to Omega cues.

For all used Omega cues, except where otherwise noted:

Add $300+ for each additional original straight playable shaft (standard with two).
Deduct $300 for each missing original straight playable shaft.
Add $250+ for ivory joint.
Add $350+ for ivory butt cap.
Add $200+ for leather wrap.
Add $50+ for each ivory ferrule.
Deduct up to 30% for obvious or improper refinish.

Level 3 - 2-6 points, 0-8 inlays.
Level 3 cues start at	$2,000	$1,650	$1,200

Level 4 - 4-10 points, 9-25 inlays.
Level 4 cues start at	$2,800	$2,400	$1,600

Level 5 - 0-12 points, 26-50 inlays.
Level 5 cues start at	$3,500	$3,150	$1,800

Level 6 - 0-12 points, 51-75 inlays.
Level 6 cues start at	$4,800	$4,250	$2,400

Level 7 - 0-12 points, 76-125 inlays.
Level 7 cues start at	$6,100	$5,550	$3,100

Level 8 - 0-12 points, 126+ inlays.
Level 8 cues start at	$8,100	$7,350	$4,500

OMEN CUSTOM CUES

Maker of pool cues since 1979 in Melbourne, Florida.

Peter Ohman began building cues in 1979. He had owned a pool room for 24 years and found it was necessary to be able to repair his equipment. This eventually got him into cuemaking. Peter strives to make cues that people enjoy using and will rave about. As a pool player for a number of years, Ohman feels that he knows how a cue should play and feel.

Peter's one-man shop has four lathes, one with a digital readout. He has two computerized mills, an internal spray booth, and also a photo "set" for taking pictures of his work. Peter makes everything in Omen cues except for the tips, bumpers, and screws.

Omen Custom Cues are easily recognizable by the Peter Ohman signature followed by the year of completion on the forearms. His standard joint is a brass pin with an "Omen" insignia that has been engraved on the flat of the pin since the mid-1990s.

Omen Cues come with an unlimited warranty under reasonable usage.

If you have a cue that needs further identification or repair, or would like to order a new cue, contact Omen Custom Cues, listed in the Trademark Index.

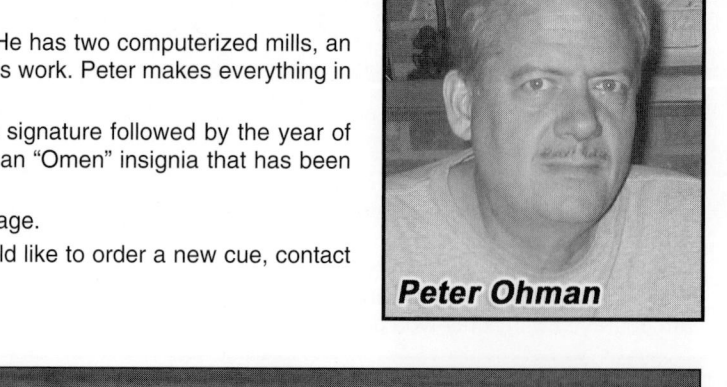

Peter Ohman

SPECIFICATIONS

Butt material: hardwoods
Shaft material: rock maple
Standard length: 58 in.
Lengths available: 58 to 60 in.
Standard finish: acrylic urethane
Standard butt cap: black linen fiber
Standard wrap: Irish linen
Point construction: short splice
Standard joint: brass pin with "Omen" insignia

Present Day

GRADING	100%	95%	70%

Joint type: flat-faced wood-to-wood
Joint screw thread: 11
Standard number of shafts: two
Standard ferrules: melamine
Standard tip: Triangle
Standard tip width: 13 mm+
Annual production: 75 to 100 cues

OPTIONS (FOR NEW CUES ONLY)

Special length: $25
Layered tip: $25
Ivory butt cap: $175
Ivory ferrule: $150
Leather wrap: $100+
Joint protectors: $30 per set of three
Extra shaft: $95

REPAIRS

Repairs done on all fine cues.
Refinish (with Irish linen wrap): $115
Rewrap (Irish linen): $40
Clean and press linen wrap: $15
Replace shaft: $115
Replace butt cap: $40+
Replace tip: $10+

CURRENT OMEN CUES

Basic Omen cues with wraps and ringwork start at $675. Four-point Omen cues start at $1,096. Six-point Omen cues start at $1,195. Eight-point Omen cues start at $1,295. The current delivery time for an Omen cue is four months.

CURRENT EXAMPLES

The following Omen cue can be ordered as shown, modified to suit the desires of the customer, or new designs can be created.

Level 2 - Bloodwood forearm, three long bloodwood points with holly veneers alternating with three bloodwood points with ebony veneers, bloodwood butt sleeve with a stitch ring at bottom.

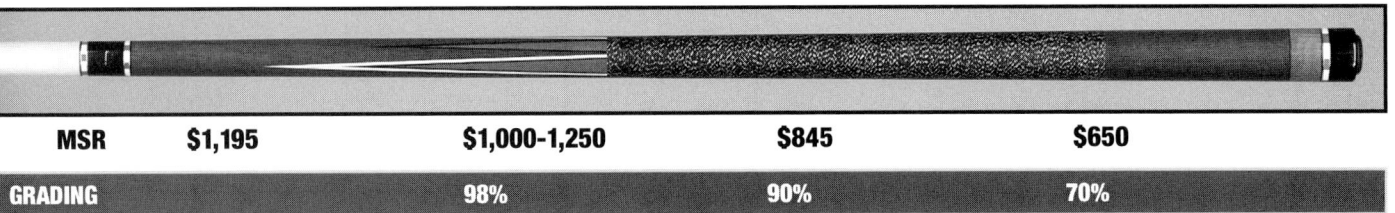

MSR	$1,195	$1,000-1,250	$845	$650
GRADING		98%	90%	70%

SECONDARY MARKET MINIMUM VALUES

The following are minimum values for other Omen cues encountered on the secondary market. These prices are representative of cues utilizing basic materials and designs that are not necessarily available at present. Peter has offered one-of-a-kind cues that can command many times these prices due to the use of exotic materials and artistry.

Special construction note: There are many materials and construction techniques that can add value to Omen cues.

For all used Omen cues, except where otherwise noted:
Add $85 for each additional original straight playable shaft beyond two.
Deduct $115 for each missing original straight playable shaft under two.
Add $75 each for ivory ferrules.
Add $75 for leather wrap.
Deduct 20% for obvious or improper refinish.

Level 2 - 0 points, 0-25 inlays.
Level 2 cues start at	$500	$390	$260

Level 3 - 2-6 points, 0-8 inlays.
Level 3 cues start at	$850	$655	$445

Level 4 - 4-10 points, 9-25 inlays.
Level 4 cues start at	$1,000	$785	$540

Level 5 - 0-12 points, 26-50 inlays.
Level 5 cues start at	$1,400	$1,000	$750

ONE ON ONE CUE STICKS

Maker of pool cues from 1994 to present in Cary, North Carolina.

Bill Stelzenmuller began playing pool in the mid-1980s, when age-related injuries drove him out of other sports he enjoyed. Because of his long-time hobbies of woodworking and furniture design, it didn't take long before he got interested in cue repair and fabrication. Bill has a Master's Degree in Electrical Engineering from the New Jersey Institute of Technology. He worked for IBM for 32 years before retiring in 1997.

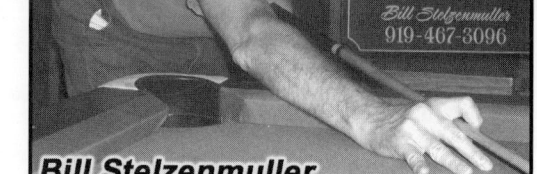
Bill Stelzenmuller

Bill's woodworking hobby took him into an unusual direction: that of designing and building magic illusions when his son had a 10-year fling with stage magic. Like pool cues, constructing magic illusions is tricky because the mechanisms must be smooth, reliable, silent and be activated by the slight bump of a knee or elbow. Also, like building a good pool cue, the feeling of accomplishment can be very rewarding when your creation performs flawlessly and the customer is pleased. Pool cues bring their own unique list of interesting design challenges. Vibrations, rattles, stability, balance, stiffness, and that ill-defined "feel of the hit" bring with them a myriad of design constraints that make every day interesting and unique.

Bill says the best part of the cuemaking business is meeting and working with the players who can be as colorful as the magicians who once frequented this same shop with their wish list of miracles. Evenings are spent playing pool and socializing with potential customers (marketing research).

Bill's company name, One On One Cue Sticks, refers to "One craftsman building one cue at a time." All of Bill's cues are made to order. All different types of popular joints, ferrules, tips, handles, etc. are available. Bill prefers a balance point that is 30% to 33% of the length of the cue from the butt. All cues are made by hand in Bill's one-man shop without the aid of CNC.

The cue design is a two-part process. It begins with determining the physical characteristics of the cue. This is usually accomplished by hitting balls with a variety of demo cues. The customer is invited to play with cues of varying length, shaft and butt diameter, weight, balance point, shaft stiffness, and tip hardness. An alternative approach is to measure the size and characteristics of a cue that the customer already likes to play with. The second part of the design process is the artistic implementation of the physical design. A large variety of exotic woods and materials are available for the customer to design a look that suits his or her personality.

All One On One cues have Bill's signature, the date of purchase, and the serial number engraved into the butt cap under the rubber bumper. All cues have a lifetime guarantee against defects that are not the result of abuse.

If you are interested in talking to Bill Stelzenmuller about a new cue or cue that needs to be repaired, you can contact him at One On One Cue Sticks, listed in the Trademark Index.

SPECIFICATIONS

Butt material: hardwoods
Shaft material: rock maple
Standard length: 57 to 60 in.
Lengths available: any under 62 in.
Standard finish: catalyzed polyurethane
Recommended balance point: 17 to 18 in. from butt
Standard butt cap: linen phenolic
Standard wrap: linen
Point construction: short spliced
Standard joints: double black linen phenolic
Standars joint type: flat faced
Standard joint screw thread: 5/16-18
Standard number of shafts: one
Standard taper: pro taper
Standard ferrules: fiber
Standard tip width: less than 14 mm
Standard bumper: beveled 1 x .5
Annual production: fewer than 50 cues

OPTIONS (FOR NEW CUES ONLY)

Special length: no charge
Layered tip: $3+
Moori tip: $12
Ivory butt cap: $200
Ivory joint: $150
Ivory ferrule: $50
Leather wrap: $70
Custom joint protectors: $25
Extra shaft: $90

ONE ON ONE CUE STICKS, cont. 573

GRADING	98%	90%	70%

REPAIRS

Repairs done on most popular brand cues.
- Refinish with Irish linen wrap: $90
- Refinish with leather wrap: $120
- Rewrap Irish linen: $45
- Rewrap leather: $70
- Replace shaft: $90
- Replace ivory ferrule: $60
- Replace butt cap: $40
- Replace tip: $10
- Replaced layered tip: $10+ cost of tip
- Replace fiber/linen ferrule: $30

CURRENT ONE ON ONE CUES

One On One two-piece bar cues start at $150. Basic One On One cues with wraps and joint rings start at $200. One On One cues with points start at $275. The current delivery time for a One On One cue can vary from several weeks to a month or more, especially during the Christmas season.

SECONDARY MARKET MINIMUM VALUES

The following are minimum values for One On One cues encountered on the secondary market. These prices are representative of cues utilizing basic materials and designs that are not necessarily available at present. Bill has offered one-of-a-kind cues that can command many times these prices due to the use of exotic materials and artistry.

Special construction note: There are many materials and construction techniques that can add value to One On One cues.

For all used One On One cues, except where otherwise noted:
- Add $75 for each additional original straight playable shaft beyond one.
- Deduct $90 for missing original straight playable shaft.
- Add $40 each for ivory ferrules.
- Add $50 for leather wrap.
- Deduct 20% for obvious or improper refinish.

Level 1 - Hustler.
Level 1 cues start at	$135	$105	$70

Level 2 - 0 points, 0-25 inlays.
Level 2 cues start at	$180	$145	$100

Level 3 - 2-6 points, 0-8 inlays.
Level 3 cues start at	$250	$200	$140

Level 4 - 4-10 points, 9-25 inlays.
Level 4 cues start at	$400	$315	$220

Level 5 - 0-12 points, 26-50 inlays.
Level 5 cues start at	$475	$385	$250

ORCHID U.S.A.

Importer of pool cues in Lynbrook, New York.

Orchid cues are easily identifiable by the Orchid logo on the butt caps. If you have an Orchid cue that needs further identification or repair, or would like to talk to someone about ordering a new Orchid cue, contact Orchid U.S.A., listed in the Trademark Index.

SPECIFICATIONS

- Butt material: hardwoods
- Shaft material: rock maple
- Standard length: 58 in.
- Standard wrap: Irish linen

ORCHID CUES

The following are minimum prices for Orchid cues encountered on the secondary market.

Special construction note: There are many materials and construction techniques that can add value to Orchid cues.

For all used Orchid cues:
- Deduct 20% for obvious or improper refinish.

Level 2 - 0 points, 0-25 inlays.
Level 2 cues start at	$75	$55	$35

GRADING	98%	90%	70%
Level 3 - 2-6 points, 0-8 inlays.			
Level 3 cues start at	$95	$75	$45
Level 4 - 4-10 points, 9-25 inlays.			
Level 4 cues start at	$115	$90	$55

GUIDO ORLANDI CUSTOM CUES

Maker of pool cues, formerly in Van Nuys, California, currently in Channing, MI.
If you have a Guido Orlandi cue that needs further identification or repair, or would like to order a new Guido Orlandi cue, contact Guido Orlandi Custom Cues, listed in the Trademark Index.

P SECTION

PADGETT CUSTOM CUES

Maker of pool cues from 1986 to present in Duarte, California.

Tim Padgett became interested in pool as a teenager. He would watch the game being played in the local room where he played pinball and video games. By the age of eighteen, Tim started to play the game, and eventually he was playing pool professionally.

In 1982, Tim visited Bert Schrager to have a shaft made. While Tim was admiring the work Bert was doing, Bert had mentioned the employee he had lost that same week. By the end of their conversation, Tim agreed to start working for Schrager. This led to an apprenticeship which lasted three years.

After learning the art of cuemaking from Schrager, Tim left to work at a machine shop. In 1986, while still working at the machine shop, a Japanese cue buyer approached Tim with a business offer. The gentleman had seen some of the work Tim had done for Schrager and told Tim that if he started making cues, he would place an order for the first hundred.

That year, Tim founded Padgett Custom Cues. Since then, Tim has been making less than 50 cues per year, by hand, without the use of CNC. Tim takes a great degree of pride in his work, making every component except for the tips, bumpers, and screws. Every Padgett cue is marked "Padgett" on the butt cap, and no two cues have been identical. Tim likes to use a lot of ivory, and he also makes some of his own templates for the pantograph.

Padgett cues are guaranteed indefinitely against construction defects that are not the result of warpage or abuse. If you have a Padgett cue that needs further identification or repair, or would like to talk to Tim about ordering a new Padgett cue, contact Padgett Custom Cues, listed in the Trademark Index.

SPECIFICATIONS

- Butt material: hardwoods
- Shaft material: rock maple
- Standard length: 58 in.
- Lengths available: any
- Joint screw: 3/8-10
- Standard finish: urethane
- Standard joint: ivory
- Joint type: flat faced
- Point construction: short splice
- Standard butt cap: linen phenolic
- Balance point: 17 1/2 in. from butt
- Standard wrap: Irish linen
- Standard butt cap: ivory
- Standard number of shafts: two
- Standard ferrules: ivory
- Standard tip: Triangle
- Annual production: approximately 40 cues

OPTIONS (FOR NEW CUES ONLY)

- Leather wrap: $125
- Ivory joint: $150
- Joint protectors: $150 a set
- Ivory butt cap: $200+
- Extra shaft: $175

REPAIRS

Repairs done on all fine cues. Repair prices are for Padgett cues only.

- Refinish (with leather wrap): $275
- Refinish (with Irish linen wrap): $225
- Rewrap (leather): $125
- Rewrap (linen): $50
- Replace linen phenolic butt cap: $30
- Replace ivory butt cap: $200+
- Replace shaft: $175
- Replace ivory ferrule: $60
- Replace fiber ferrule: $20
- Replace Triangle tip: $15

CURRENT PADGETT CUES

Two-piece Padgett bar cues start at $300. Basic Padgett cues with wraps and joint rings start at $800. Padgett cues with points start at $1,000. One-of-a-kind custom Padgett cues start at $2,500. The current delivery time for a Padgett cue is approximately fourteen months, depending on the intricacy of the cue.

GRADING	98%	90%	70%

SECONDARY MARKET MINIMUM VALUES

The following are minimum prices for Padgett cues encountered on the secondary market. These prices are representative of cues utilizing basic materials and designs that may not be currently available. Tim currently specializes in one-of-a-kind cues that can command many times these prices due to the use of exotic materials and artistry.

Special construction note: There are many materials and construction techniques that can add value to Padgett cues.

For all used Padgett cues:
- Add $140+ for each additional original straight playable shaft beyond two.
- Deduct $175 for each missing original straight playable shaft under two.
- Add $135+ for ivory joint.
- Add $85+ for leather wrap.
- Deduct 25% for obvious or improper refinish.

Level 1 - 4 points, hustler.

	98%	90%	70%
Level 1 cues start at	$285	$240	$145

Level 2 - 0 points, 0-25 inlays.

Level 2 cues start at	$750	$585	$400

Level 3 - 2-6 points, 0-8 inlays.

Level 3 cues start at	$950	$745	$500

Level 4 - 4-10 points, 9-25 inlays.

Level 4 cues start at	$1,100	$885	$600

Level 5 - 0-12 points, 26-50 inlays.

Level 5 cues start at	$1,850	$1,450	$1,000

Level 6 - 0-12 points, 51-75 inlays.

Level 6 cues start at	$2,500	$2,000	$1,450

PADISHAN INTERNATIONAL

Maker of pool cues from 1987 to present in Taiwan.

Padishan has made hundreds of different models of Padishan cues since 1987. Padishan cues are sometimes identifiable by the Padishan marking on the butt cap.

If you would like to talk to Padishan about ordering cues, contact Padishan International Inc., listed in the Trademark Index.

SPECIFICATIONS

Butt material: maple
Shaft material: rock maple
Standard length: 58 in.
Lengths available: 57 to 58 in.
Standard wrap: Irish linen
Standard number of shafts: one
Standard ferrules: fiber
Standard tip: Le Pro
Standard tip width: 13 mm
Annual production: many thousands of cues

SECONDARY MARKET MINIMUM VALUES

The following are minimum prices for Padishan cues encountered on the secondary market.

For all used Padishan cues:
- Deduct 75% for missing original straight playable shaft.

Level 1 - 4 points, hustler.

	98%	90%	70%
Level 1 cues start at	$50	$35	$20

Level 2 - 0 points, 0-25 inlays.

Level 2 cues start at	$55	$35	$25

Level 3 - 2-6 points, 0-8 inlays.

Level 3 cues start at	$65	$50	$30

PALMER CUSTOM CUES COMPANY

Maker of pool cues from 1964 to 1994 in Elizabeth, New Jersey.

The Palmer Custom Cues Company was founded in 1964, by Eugene Balner and his son, Peter, after ending a partnership with Frank Paradise the same year. Balner had escaped from Hungary with his wife and children in 1956, during the country's communist revolution. A wood turner in Hungary, he was soon working in the United States at a company that made pool cues.

By 1961, Eugene Balner was a partner with Frank Paradise. Three years later, Balner was making cues right across the street. The name "Palmer" was inspired by Arnold Palmer, one of the most recognized names in sports at the time. Eugene felt the name Balner was not recognizable enough to be appropriate for the new company. Eventually, Eugene was more widely known as Gene Palmer.

The first Palmer catalog was introduced in 1965, and featured eleven cues and two cases. All of the cues were available with either a nickel silver or brass joint. The Paradise influence was obvious on these cues, especially on the ones with the Palmer name under clear plastic windows in the butt sleeves. Another feature influenced by Paradise was the availability of screw-off ferrules. None of the cues had bumpers, as Balner believed these to be features of lesser quality cues, and ten of the eleven had points.

Late 70s

The first line of cues proved to be very successful, and within a few years a new catalog was introduced. The second Palmer catalog featured thirteen new cues with letters for model designations ranging from Model A to Model M. The most visible change in these cues was that the butt caps were twice as long, but they still were without bumpers. The new cues also used a thicker joint that seated more securely, and Irish linen was being used more for the wrap. The most sought after cue from this line is the Model J, which has an ebony forearm and four maple points. Some of the blanks for this model were made by Gus Szamboti or Burton Spain, specifically for Palmer. This cue can give a collector the opportunity to own and appreciate the quality of a Gus Szamboti splice. The Model M was the most expensive and elaborate cue from this line. With winding veneers running down an ebony forearm, inlaid with mother-of-pearl dots and notched diamonds, this cue is one of the most recognizable production cues ever made.

Pete Margo Series

Although these were production cues, Balner was able to make each one to the specifications of the individual customer. The company became so proficient at this that by the early seventies they were making approximately 200 cues per week.

In January of 1972, Eugene Balner passed away. His widow, Ilona, and son, Peter, were left to lead the company during its most productive years. At this time, the company's only serious competitor in cue manufacturing was Viking, in Wisconsin, but by the early 1970s, several new companies such as McDermott, Meucci, Joss, and Adam were entering the market.

The next Palmer catalog met the competition with twenty new cues, now with bumpers and most with stainless steel joints. On these cues, less plastic was used, while exotic hardwoods were becoming more prevalent. The first eight-point cue was introduced and cues with blanks by Gus Szamboti were still available. Most of these blanks had bird's-eye maple forearms, four ebony points, and black, orange, chartreuse, and maple veneers.

For Christmas of 1975, Palmer made 100 cues with Szamboti blanks that had black, red, blue, and white veneers to commemorate the upcoming bicentennial. The points on the Szamboti blank cues are much sharper and a little longer than on other Palmers, sometimes coming within 2 1/4 in. of the joint collar.

During the late 1970s and the 1980s, Palmer expanded its line of billiard supplies and increased its foreign markets. The company stopped making cues in 1994. Today, Peter Balner is CEO of the Palmer Video chain, which he started out of the Palmer billiard showroom in 1981.

Collectors are now acquiring Palmer cues, especially the ones from the first two catalogs. The early models with inlay work on the shafts seem to be the most popular. Many Palmer cues will have the original customer's name under a clear plastic window in the butt sleeve. Palmer cues made for famous players such as Minnesota Fats are prized pieces in any collection, and are hard to evaluate because of their historical significance. In 1998, Peter Balner bought a percentage of CueSport, a cue manufacturing company in Sheffield, Massachusetts. There is talk of reintroducing the Palmer name with an all new line of American-made cues.

If you have questions about a Palmer cue that is in need of repair, contact Paul Rubino, listed in the Trademark Index.

Note: Palmer's first and second catalogs are shown in color in the 2nd Edition Blue Book of Pool Cues.

SPECIFICATIONS

Butt material: hardwoods
Shaft material: rock maple
Standard joint: stainless steel
Joint type: piloted
Point construction: short splice
Standard wrap: Irish linen
Standard number of shafts: two
Total production: many thousands

OPTIONS

Leather wrap
Ivory joint
Joint protectors
Flat face joint

578 PALMER CUSTOM CUES COMPANY, cont.

| GRADING | 98% | 90% | 70% |

KNOWN PALMER EXAMPLES

The following cues are representations of the more desirable known models of Palmer cues. These cues can be encountered as shown, modified to suit the desires of the original customer, or entirely different designs can be encountered.

FIRST PALMER CATAOLOG (1965)

Palmer's first catalog in 1965 featured 11 models of cues numbered 1 through 11. Almost all early Palmers had wide pearlized plastic joint collars and no rubber bumpers.

Level 4 Model 3 - Maple forearm, four rosewood points with four colored veneers, ebony butt sleeve with four mother-of-pearl notched diamond-shaped inlays in the center within rows of mother-of pearl dots in ebony above and below between metal rings at top and bottom.

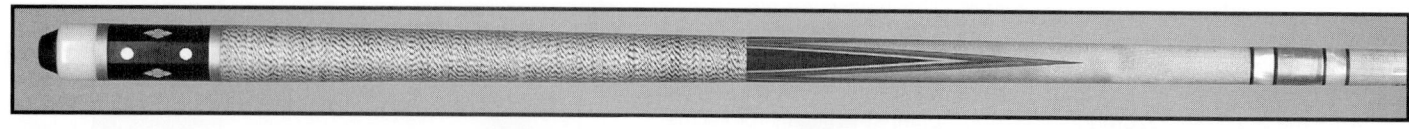

$1,250 $785 $650

Level 5 Model 5 - Maple forearm, four ebony points with four colored veneers and a pattern consisting of a mother-of-pearl notched diamond-shaped inlay with two vertical mother-of pearl dots above and two horizontal mother-of-pearl dots below in each point, ebony butt sleeve with four mother-of-pearl notched diamond-shaped inlays in the center within rows of mother-of pearl dots in ebony at top and bottom.

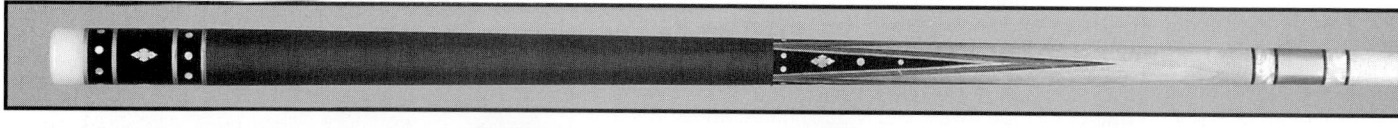

$1,350 $1,050 $700

Level 5 Model 5 (Custom) - Maple forearm, four ebony points with four colored veneers and a pattern consisting of a mother-of-pearl notched diamond-shaped inlay with two vertical mother-of pearl dots above and two horizontal mother-of-pearl dots below in each point, ebony butt sleeve with "Original by Palmer" and sometimes the original owner's name on silver foil under a clear plastic window in the center within pattern of mother-of-pearl notched diamond-shaped inlays and mother-of pearl dots in ebony at top and bottom.

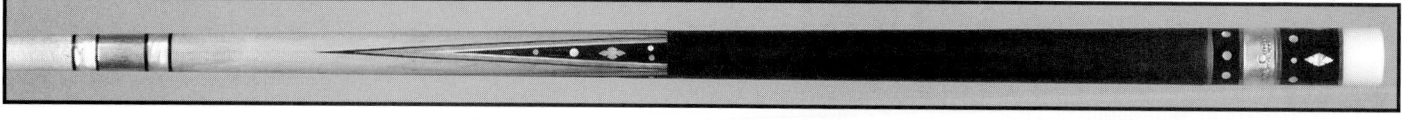

$1,550 $1,250 $850

Level 3 Model 6 - Maple forearm, four rosewood points with four colored veneers, butt sleeve with "Original by Palmer" and sometimes the original owner's name on gold foil between colored plastic rings under a clear plastic window.

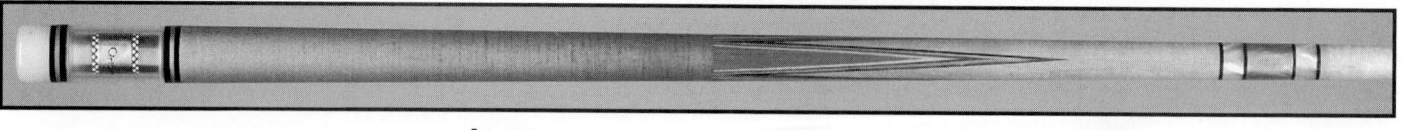

$1,150 $900 $600

Level 4 Model 10 - Maple forearm, four rosewood points with four colored veneers and a pattern consisting of a mother-of-pearl notched diamond-shaped inlay with two vertical mother-of pearl dots above and two horizontal mother-of-pearl dots below in each point, colored plastic butt sleeve with "Original by Palmer" and sometimes the original owner's name on silver foil under a clear plastic window in the center.

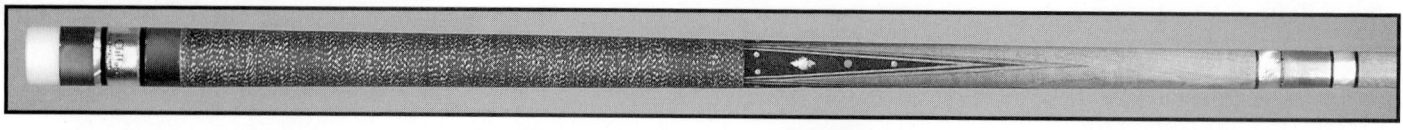

$1,350 $1,050 $700

SECOND PALMER CATAOLOG

Palmer's second catalog from the early 1970s featured 13 models of cues lettered A through M. Almost all early 1970s Palmers had joint collars of white plastic or pearlized plastic. Later examples have rubber bumpers.

PALMER CUSTOM CUES COMPANY, cont.

GRADING	98%	90%	70%

Level 3 Model B - Maple forearm, four short rosewood points, two-tone nylon wrap, red plastic butt sleeve with "Original by Palmer" and usually original owner's name on silver foil under a clear plastic window at bottom.

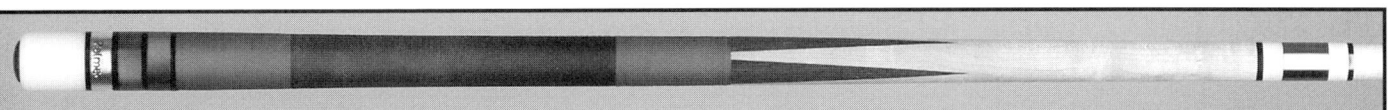

| Original Retail (Early 1970s) N/A | $750 | $600 | $400 |

Level 5 Model K - Bird's-eye maple forearm with a thick ebony-bordered white pearlescent ring above wrap, four ebony points with four colored veneers and a mother-of-pearl notched diamond-shaped inlay set within a vertical line of mother-of-pearl dots in each point, ebony butt sleeve with "Original by Palmer" and usually original owner's name on silver foil under a clear plastic window within four vertical lines of mother-of-pearl dots.

| Original Retail (Early 1970s) $140 | $1,850 | $1,520 | $1,150 |

Level 5 Model J - Ebony forearm with four mother-of-pearl notched diamond-shaped inlays set within vertical lines of mother-of-pearl dots between points, four maple points with four colored veneers, ebony butt sleeve with four vertical lines of mother-of-pearl dots above "Original by Palmer" and usually original owner's name on silver foil under a clear plastic window at bottom (shown with custom solid ebony butt sleeve).

| Original Retail (Early 1970s) $150 | $2,850 | $2,250 | $1,550 |

Level 2 Model L - Ebony forearm with white pearlescent rings above wrap and mother-of-pearl notched diamond-shaped inlays and mother-of-pearl dots, ebony butt sleeve with "Original by Palmer" and usually original owner's name on silver foil under a clear plastic window.

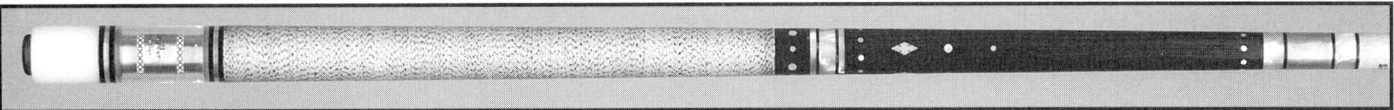

| Original Retail (Early 1970s) N/A | $3,000 | $2,500 | $1,850 |

Level 2 Model M - Ebony forearm with white pearlescent rings above wrap and mother-of-pearl notched diamond-shaped inlays set within vertical lines of mother-of-pearl dots between long-winding maple veneers, ebony butt sleeve with "Original by Palmer" and usually original owner's name on silver foil under a clear plastic window within vertical lines of mother-of-pearl notched diamond-shaped inlays set within vertical lines of mother-of-pearl dots between winding maple veneers.

| Original Retail (Early 1970s) $195 | $4,000 | $3,250 | $2,400 |

LATER PALMER CATAOLOGS

The following cues were featured in later catalogs.

Level 3 - Maple forearm, four ebony points with four colored veneers, ebony butt sleeve with "Original by Palmer" and sometimes the original owner's name on silver foil under a clear plastic window.

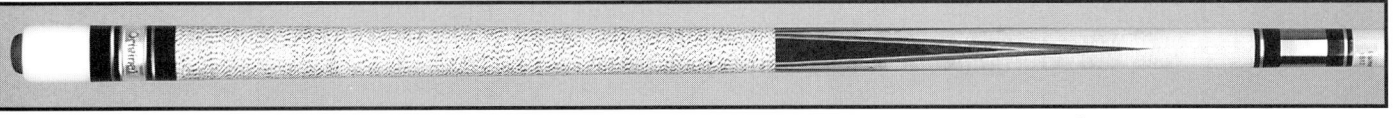

| | $1,450 | $1,125 | $750 |

Level 5 Model 18 - Maple forearm with tall maple windows set in ebony within maple rings within ebony above wrap, four ebony points with four colored veneers and a pattern consisting of a mother-of-pearl rectangle with a mother-of pearl dot above and two mother-of-pearl dots below in each point, butt sleeve with tall maple windows set in ebony within maple rings within ebony rings with mother-of-pearl rectangles alternating with patterns consisting of four mother-of-pearl dots at top and bottom.

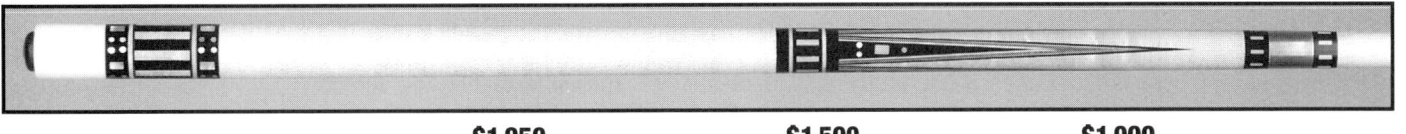

| | $1,950 | $1,500 | $1,000 |

GRADING	98%	90%	70%

Level 5 - Maple forearm ringwork above wrap, four ebony points with four veneers and a pattern consisting of a mother-of-pearl notched diamond-shaped inlay with a mother-of pearl dot above and two mother-of-pearl dots below in each point, ebony butt sleeve with a pattern consisting of four mother-of-pearl notched diamond-shaped inlays connected by rows of vertical and diagonal mother-of pearl dots between ringwork below wrap and "Original by Palmer" and sometimes the original owner's name on silver foil under a clear plastic window at bottom.

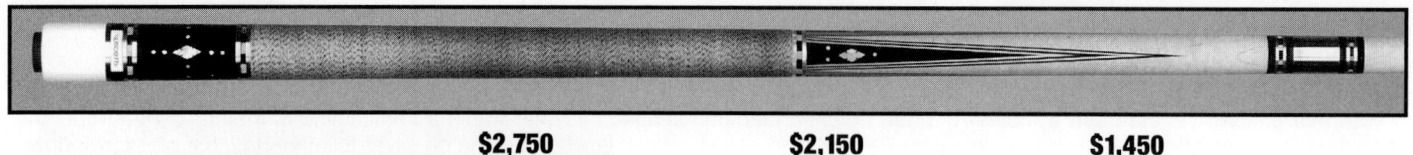

	$2,750	$2,150	$1,450

SECONDARY MARKET MINIMUM VALUES

(Not to be confused with cues marked "Palmer Industries")

The following are minimum prices for other Palmer cues encountered on the secondary market. These prices are representative of cues utilizing the most basic materials and designs that were available. Palmer offered one-of-a-Kind cues that can command many times these prices due to the use of exotic materials and artistry. Early variations are becoming very collectible, and can also command many times these prices. Palmer cues will be further covered in future editions.

Due to the rarity of early Palmer cues (mid-1970s and earlier) and increasing interest, prices are on the rise. Fewer original examples are surfacing, and collectors are holding on to the ones they have. Unique examples with pedigree, and cues made for top professional players are bringing the highest prices.

Special construction note: There are many materials and construction techniques that can add value to Palmer cues. The following are the most important examples:

Add 100%+ for "Original by Palmer" on silver foil under clear plastic window (25% more for gold foil).

For all used Palmer cues, except where otherwise noted:

Add $1,250+ for Gus Szamboti blank.
Add $125+ for each additional original straight playable shaft (standard with two).
Deduct $175 for each missing original straight playable shaft under two.
Add $500+ for ivory joint.
Add $250+ for original leather wrap.
Deduct 35% for obvious or improper refinish.

Level 1 - 4 points, hustler.

Level 1 cues start at	$300	$225	$140

Level 2 - 0 points, 0-25 inlays.

Level 2 cues start at	$400	$300	$185

Level 3 - 2-6 points, 0-8 inlays.

Level 3 cues start at	$600	$450	$275

Level 4 - 4-10 points, 9-25 inlays.

Level 4 cues start at	$1,200	$900	$500

Level 5 - 0-12 points, 26-50 inlays.

Level 5 cues start at	$1,500	$1,150	$700

Level 6 - 0-12 points, 51-75 inlays.

Level 6 cues start at	$2,500	$1,950	$1,100

PANCERNY CUSTOM CUES

Maker of pool cues from 1997 in Windsor Ontario to present in Chesterfield, Michigan.

Pancerny Custom Cues
"Custom Cue Building and Professional Cue Repair"

Mike Pancerny has a background in communications, and currently works full-time for Corporate Television Broadcasting. He is a part-time cuemaker whose work has been influenced by Burton Spain, Gus Szamboti, and Schon Cues. Mike did minor cue repairs for friends, and his experience at Dufferin Cues led to the purchase of better cue repair equipment and the ability to make sneaky-pete cues. Eventually, he wanted to make a cue with playability comparable to the higher end cues he was used to using in his game.

Mike signs his cues next to the points or else puts MP in the butt. The month and year the cue is completed appear next to the signature. There is no serial number used for identification. Cues are guaranteed 100% against manufacturing defects.

GRADING	100%	95%	70%

If you are interested in talking to Mike Pancerny about a new cue or cue that needs to be repaired, you can contact him at Pancerny Custom Cues, listed in the Trademark Index.

SPECIFICATIONS

Butt material: exotic hardwoods
Shaft material: maple
Standard length: 58.5 in.
Lengths available: 58.5 to 60 in.
Standard finish: automotive urethane
Balance point: 18 in. from butt cap
Standard butt cap: Delrin
Standard wrap: Irish linen
Point construction: spliced or inlaid
Standard joint: stainless steel
Joint type: piloted
Joint screw thread: 5/16-14
Standard number of shafts: one
Standard taper: custom
Standard ferrules: Aegis II
Other ferrule options: ivory
Standard tip: Le Pro
Standard tip width: 12.75 mm
Tip widths available: any
Annual production: 15 to 20 cues

Mike Pancerny

OPTIONS (FOR NEW CUES ONLY)

Special length: no charge
Layered tip: $20
Ivory butt cap: $120
Ivory joint: $80
Ivory ferrule: $40
Extra shaft: $85

Present Day

REPAIRS

Repairs done on all fine cues.
Refinish (with Irish linen wrap): $100
Refinish (with leather wrap): $160
Rewrap (Irish linen): $45
Rewrap leather: $100
Clean and press linen wrap: $15
Restore leather wrap: $10
Replace shaft with fiber/linen ferrule: $85
Replace shaft with ivory ferrule: $135
Replace ivory ferrule: $50
Replace Delrin/linen butt cap: $45
Replace ivory butt cap: $125
Replace tip: $12
Replaced layered tip: $30
Replace fiber/linen ferrule: $20

CURRENT PANCERNY CUES

Two-piece Pancerny bar cues start at $175. Basic Pancerny cues with wraps and joint rings start at $350. Pancerny cues with points start at $425. One-of-a-kind custom Pancerny custom cues start at $650. Pancerny cues costing $700 or more come with two shafts. The current delivery time for a Pancerny custom cue is six to eight weeks.

CURRENT EXAMPLES

The following Pancerny cues can be ordered as shown, modified to suit the desires of the customer, or new designs can be created.

Level 1 - Maple forearm, four full-spliced cocobolo points and handle with four ivory diamond-shaped inlays above butt cap.

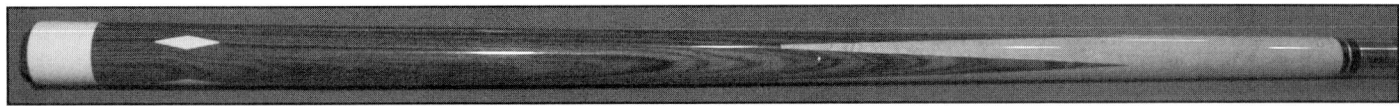

MSR	$250	$235-275	$190	$135

582 PANCERNY CUSTOM CUES, cont.

GRADING	100%	95%	70%

Level 1 - Maple forearm, four full-spliced purpleheart points and handle with a ring of mother-of-pearl diamond-shaped inlays above butt cap.

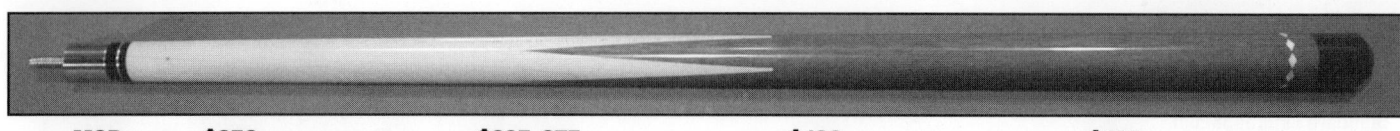

MSR	$250	$235-275	$190	$135

Level 2 - Cocobolo forearm with four ivory diamond-shaped inlays above handle, curly maple handle, cocobolo butt sleeve with four ivory diamond-shaped inlays around center.

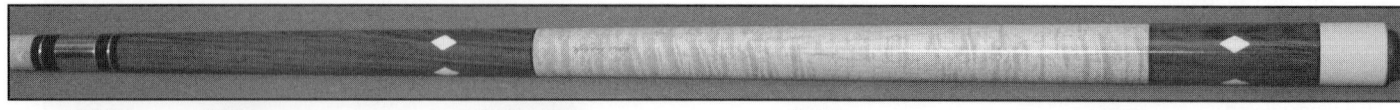

MSR	$450	$425-500	$335	$235

Level 4 "White Lightning" - Bird's-eye maple forearm with a silver ring set in ebony above wrap, four ebony floating points with an ivory lightning bolt-shaped inlay in each and an ebony-bordered ivory spear-shaped inlay at the tip of each point, ebony butt sleeve with four large ivory lightning bolt-shaped inlays alternating with four smaller ivory lightning bolt-shaped inlays between silver rings above and below.

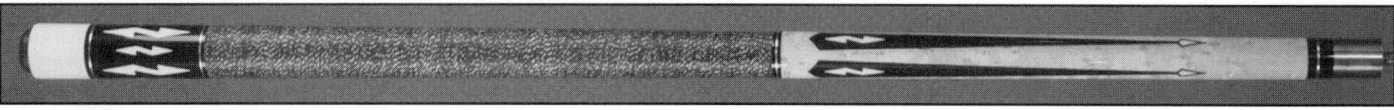

MSR	$700	$675-850	$545	$400

Level 4 "Tribal" - Bird's-eye maple forearm with a silver ring set in ebony above wrap, four ebony floating points with an engraved ivory spear-shaped inlay in each and an ebony-bordered ivory spear-shaped inlay at the tip of each point, ebony butt sleeve with four engraved ivory windows alternating with sets of three mother-of-pearl diamond-shaped inlays between silver rings above and below.

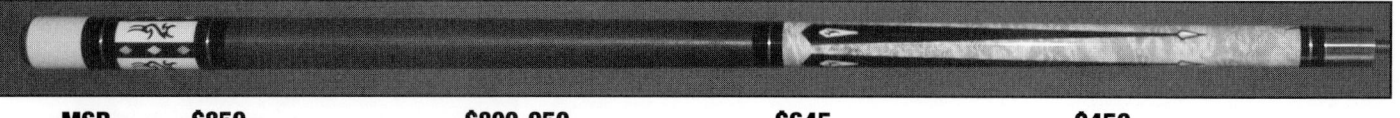

MSR	$850	$800-950	$645	$450

Level 5 - Ebony forearm with a silver ring set in ebony above wrap, four bubinga floating points with an ivory spear-shaped inlay and two mother-of-pearl dots in each and a bubinga-bordered ivory spear-shaped inlay at the tip of each point, ebony butt sleeve with four ivory diamond-shaped inlays surrounded by sets of intricate mother-of-pearl/ivory/bubinga inlays between silver rings above and below.

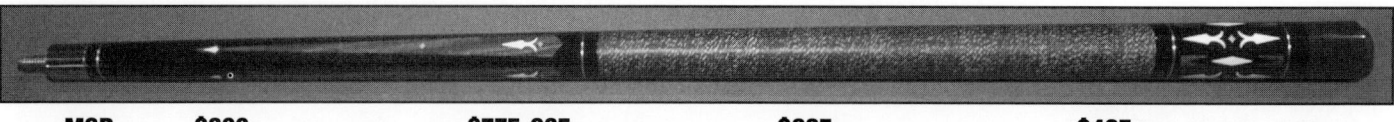

MSR	$800	$775-925	$625	$425

Level 5 - Amboyna burl forearm with a silver ring set in ebony above wrap, three long ebony-bordered bubinga points with a scrimshawed ivory double spear-shaped inlay in ebony at bottom and an ebony-bordered ivory spear-shaped inlay at the tip of each point alternating with three short ebony points with an ivory diamond-shaped inlay in each point, ebony butt sleeve with three scrimshawed ivory double spear-shaped inlays alternating with three ivory diamond-shaped inlays set in amboyna burl windows between silver rings above and below.

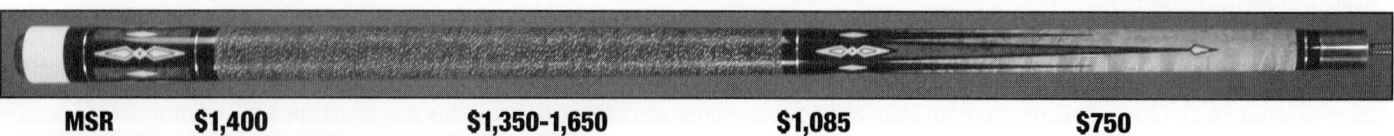

MSR	$1,400	$1,350-1,650	$1,085	$750

SECONDARY MARKET MINIMUM VALUES

The following are minimum values for other Pancerny cues encountered on the secondary market. These prices are representative of cues utilizing basic materials and designs that are not necessarily available at present. Mike has offered one-of-a-kind cues that can command many times these prices due to the use of exotic materials and artistry.

Special construction note: There are many materials and construction techniques that can add value to Pancerny cues.

For all used Pancerny cues, except where otherwise noted:

Add $75 for each additional original straight playable shaft beyond one.
Deduct 85 for missing original straight playable shaft.
Add $40 each for ivory ferrules.
Deduct 20% for obvious or improper refinish.

GRADING	98%	90%	70%
Level 1 - Hustler.			
Level 1 cues start at	$150	$120	$80
Level 2 - 0 points, 0-25 inlays.			
Level 2 cues start at	$300	$235	$160
Level 3 - 2-6 points, 0-8 inlays.			
Level 3 cues start at	$400	$310	$210
Level 4 - 4-10 points, 9-25 inlays.			
Level 4 cues start at	$500	$385	$260
Level 5 - 0-12 points, 26-50 inlays.			
Level 5 cues start at	$750	$575	$385

PANTHER CUSTOM CUES

Line of pool cues imported by J & J America.

Panther cues are easily identifiable by the Panther logo on the butt cap. If you have a Panther cue that needs further identification or repair, or would like to order a new cue, contact J & J America, listed in the Trademark Index.

SPECIFICATIONS

Butt material: hardwoods
Shaft material: rock maple
Standard length: 58 in.
Standard wrap: Irish linen

CURRENT PANTHER CUES

Panther Series 1 cues are priced from $80 to $350. Panther Series 2 cues are priced from $220 to $300. Most Panther cues are available for immediate delivery.

SECONDARY MARKET MINIMUM VALUES

The following are minimum values for Panther Custom Cues encountered on the secondary market.

For all used Panther cues, except where otherwise noted:
Add $50 for each additional original straight playable shaft beyond one.
Deduct 50% for missing original straight playable shaft.
Deduct 20% for obvious or improper refinish.

Level 2 - 0 points, 0-25 inlays.			
Level 2 cues start at	$60	$45	$25
Level 3 - 2-6 points, 0-8 inlays.			
Level 3 cues start at	$90	$70	$40
Level 4 - 4-10 points, 9-25 inlays.			
Level 4 cues start at	$120	$90	$55

FRANK PARADISE

Maker of pool cues from 1948-1958 in Brooklyn, New York, and from 1958-1968 in Little Falls, New Jersey.

Frank Paradise was born Frank Thomas, but changed his last name to Paradise during a musical stint in the late 1930s. He felt that Thomas was a boring name and Paradise better reflected the mood of the music he was playing. Frank had been a pool player since he was younger, and after giving up music during World War II, went back to playing the game. During this time, most potential players had been drafted, so Frank got a job driving a bus for Greyhound to help make ends meet.

In 1948, after winning a Herman Rambow cue in a game, he was inspired to try to make custom cues. Frank liked the playability of Rambow cues, but felt that they were not very attractive. He knew that if he could make a better looking cue that played just as well, he would be successful. That year, he purchased a lathe and other equipment, and started making cues in his basement.

Frank's early cues were very similar to Rambow's, with a brass pin running through the center of the joints, and no bumpers. Soon, Paradise began experimenting with plastic, which after World War II was a state-of-the-art synthetic material that was being produced in a variety of colors and styles. Frank even made one cue, "The Space Age," which had a clear, solid plastic forearm. Although this cue was never popular, it was very innovative at the time. Along with plastic, Frank used hardwoods, brass, nickel silver, mother-of-pearl, ivory, and other materials in the construction of his cues. One of Frank's trademark features was the interchangeable screw-off ferrule. If a player lost or damaged a tip, they could replace the ferrule instead of replacing the entire shaft. Of course, it was much easier to carry a couple of extra ferrules in one's pocket than to carry extra shafts.

Although many Paradise cues can be difficult to identify, in the late 1950s Frank started marking many of them. These cues will usually have a gold foil label under a clear plastic ring in the butt sleeve. These labels may be seen in a number of different configurations, but will always include the name Paradise. Frank's first name or the name of the person for whom the cue was made will also be commonly encountered.

GRADING	98%	90%	70%

In 1958, Frank moved from Brooklyn, New York to Little Falls, New Jersey. Although his new shop was larger, it still remained in the basement of his home.

At this time, during the late fifties and early sixties, a Paradise cue was the one to have for players on the East Coast. Some players had not heard of Harvey Martin, Rambow cues were fairly rare, and George Balabushka was not well-known until years later. Players would routinely go to Frank's shop to go over the designs and specifications of their cues. When their cues were finished, they would go back to his shop to get them. He also was a regular face at the major tournaments, where he sold many cues. Paradise employed a few men as helpers over the years, at times when he could not keep up with orders by himself. These men included Harry King, Jack Colavita, Mike Fudunka, and Eugene Balner. Balner worked for Frank from 1961 to 1964, when he left to start Palmer Cues.

Today, original Paradise cues are sought after by collectors. Paradise was an innovator, especially in the areas of using plastics, and made some of the fanciest cues of his era. Collectors are primarily searching out the cues with names, extremely fancy cues, and cues made for well-known players or celebrities.

If you have a Paradise cue that needs further identification or repair, contact Rubino cues, listed in the Trademark Index.

SPECIFICATIONS
- Butt material: hardwoods or plastics
- Shaft material: rock maple
- Standard length: 57 in.
- Standard wrap: nylon
- Standard joint: brass
- Joint type: piloted
- Standard ferrules: ivory

OPTIONS ENCOUNTERED
- Nickel silver joint
- Irish linen wrap
- Screw-off ferrules
- Owner's name on foil under clear plastic window

KNOWN PARDISE EXAMPLES

The following seven cues are from the 1965 Paradise catalog. Paradise cues were almost all one-of-a-kind, and examples usually differ slightly from the cues shown.

Level 3 Model "A" The Collegiate - Titlist maple forearm with Paradise label under clear plastic between colored plastic rings above wrap, four rosewood points with four colored veneers, butt sleeve of pearlized plastic rings.

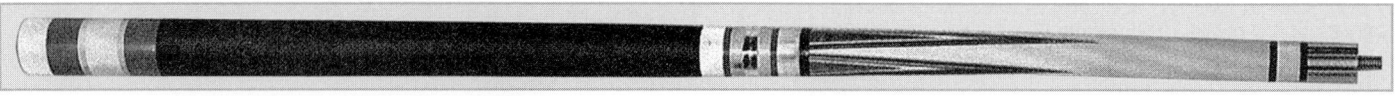

	$4,500	$3,600	$2,500

Level 4 Model "B" Diamond King - Burton Spain maple forearm with pearlized plastic and nickel silver rings above wrap, four ebony points with five colored veneers and single mother-of-pearl notched diamonds within a triangular pattern of mother-of-pearl dots in each point, butt sleeve with Paradise label under clear plastic between colored plastic rings.

Orig. Retail (1965) $125	$5,000	$4,250	$3,000

Level 3 Model "C" House Special - Maple forearm made from house cue, four rosewood points, butt sleeve of pearlized plastic rings.

Orig. Retail (1965) $32.50	$3,000	$2,500	$1,800

Level 3 Model "D" Black Zephyr - Ebony forearm by Burton Spain, four maple points with five colored veneers, butt sleeve with Paradise label under clear plastic between colored plastic rings.

Orig. Retail (1965) $100	$3,500	$2,850	$2,000

FRANK PARADISE, cont. 585

GRADING	98%	90%	70%

Level 2 Model "E" The Space Age - Clear acrylic plastic forearm, butt sleeve with Paradise label under clear plastic between colored plastic rings.

	$10,000	$8,500	$6,500

Level 3 Model "F" The Aristocrat - Titlist maple forearm with rings of brass and plastic above wrap, four rosewood points with four colored veneers, butt sleeve with Paradise label under clear plastic between colored plastic rings.

Orig. Retail (1965) $85	$4,000	$3,350	$2,450

Level 3 Model "G" The Hustler's Pride - Rosewood forearm, four maple points with a white dot at the end of each, butt sleeve of pearlized plastic rings.

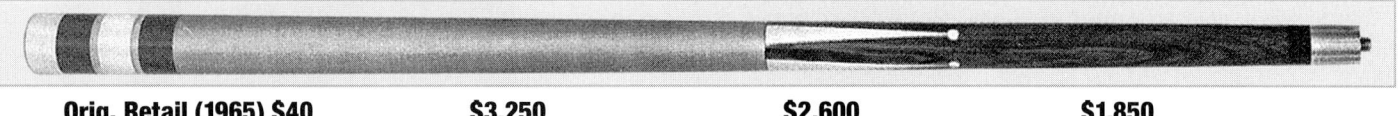

Orig. Retail (1965) $40	$3,250	$2,600	$1,850

HIGH-END CUSTOM PARADISE CUE

The following cue is an example of a high-end custom Paradise cue. Similar Paradise cues have been encountered, and examples usually differ slightly from the cue shown.

Level 6 - Bird's-eye maple forearm with a thick ebony-bordered white pearlescent ring above wrap, four ebony points with four colored veneers and a mother-of-pearl notched diamond-shaped inlay set next to a diagonal line of mother-of-pearl dots in each point, ebony butt sleeve with "Paradise" and sometimes original owner's name on silver foil under a clear plastic window below wrap above intricate patterns of mother-of-pearl inlays.

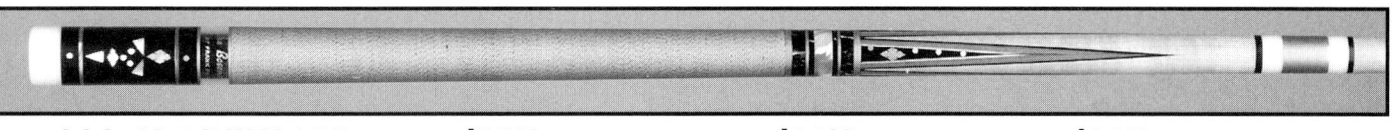

Original Retail (1960s) N/A	$5,500	$4,400	$3,000

SECONDARY MARKET MINIMUM VALUES

The following are minimum prices for other Paradise cues encountered on the secondary market. These prices are representative of cues utilizing the most basic materials and designs that were available. Frank also offered one-of-a-kind cues that can command many times these prices due to the use of exotic materials and artistry. Early variations are becoming very collectible, and can also command many times these prices. Frank Paradise cues will be further covered in future editions.

Due to the rarity of Frank Paradise cues and increasing interest, prices are on the rise. Fewer original examples are surfacing, and collectors are holding on to the ones they have. Unique examples with pedigree, and cues made for top professional players are bringing the highest prices.

Special construction note: There are many materials and construction techniques that can add value to Paradise cues. The following are the most important examples:

Add $500+ for Paradise logo under clear plastic ring in butt sleeve.

For all used Paradise cues:
Add $275+ for each additional original straight playable shaft beyond two.
Deduct $450 for each missing original straight playable shaft under two.
Add $600+ for ivory joint.
Deduct 35% for obvious or improper refinish.
Add 20%+ for totally original finish, wrap, shafts, and ferrules.

Level 2 - 0 points, 0-25 inlays.

Level 2 cues start at	$2,000	$1,655	$1,200

Level 3 - 2-6 points, 0-8 inlays.

Level 3 cues start at	$2,500	$2,000	$1,450

Level 4 - 4-10 points, 9-25 inlays.

Level 4 cues start at	$3,000	$2,450	$1,700

Level 5 - 0-12 points, 26-50 inlays.

Level 5 cues start at	$5,000	$4,000	$2,850

ANDREW PARK

Maker of AP Cues. For more information, see listing for AP Cues.

JOHN PARKER

Maker of Auerbach Custom Cues. For more information, see listing for Auerbach.

PARROT CUES

Maker of pool cues from 1980 to present in Richmond, Virginia.

David Hodges took a craftsman's approach to his hobbies. A fishing enthusiast, he built his own custom rods and sold his work locally. It comes as no surprise that as a pool player, his fascination with design and workmanship led him to cuemaking. He began doing repair work for his friends in 1978 and within a year had built his first cue. By 1980, David was performing inlay work and improving the playability of his cues. He drew upon his rod building experience to develop a custom polymer finish and worked to establish a cue with the playability characteristics he sought.

In 1990, with more than a decade of cuemaking experience, David Hodges bought Parrot Cues from its founder, Charlie Flemming. Flemming had made only eight cues under the Parrot name but each is distinctly identifiable by its left-facing parrot logo. When David Hodges took over, the parrot was turned to face the right and serves as the best means of identification for his cues. The cues that David made prior to 1990 are signed on the forearm or bear "DH" on their butt cap. Also, between 1990 and 2001, David marked some of his cues that were offered for less than $1000 with "DH" on their butt caps.

Todd Elkins

Todd Elkins became interested in recreational pool while in his 20s. He began playing competitively in a local pool league and his curiosity in cuemaking began to grow. In 1996, he became an apprentice cuemaker to Parrot Cues. He worked closely with David Hodges and after five years of apprenticeship, bought Parrot Cues in 2001. David moved on to develop and market a revolutionary new pool table cloth cleaner known as Quick-Clean. David recalls with fondness his scrimshaw work done in the last years that he owned Parrot Cues; he engraved fewer than 100 cues.

Todd Elkins has continued in the tradition of quality cue building at Parrot and, under his craftsmanship, recent demand has been high. To meet his customer's needs, Todd has recruited long-time friend Jeff Martin as a business partner. This has allowed him more time to spend on cue design and custom cue making. Parrot cues made by Todd Elkins after 2001 are distinct because of the date and his signature between the points or, as in the case of the hustler cues he makes today, the "TE" on the butt section.

If you have a Parrot cue that needs further identification or repair or would like to talk to Todd about ordering a new cue, contact Parrot Cues, listed in the trademark index.

SPECIFICATIONS

Butt material: hardwoods
Shaft material: rock maple
Standard length: 58 in.
Lengths available: up to 33 in.
Standard finish: polymer
Standard joint screws: 5/16-14 or 3/8-10
Standard joints: stainless steel or Implex
Other joints offered: ivory
Balance point: 1 in. above wrap
Point construction: short splice or inlaid
Standard wrap: Irish linen
Standard butt cap: linen base
Standard number of shafts: two
Standard taper: pro
Standard ferrules: Corian
Other ferrule options: Aegis and ivory
Standard tip: Triumph
Standard tip width: 13 mm
Tip widths available: up to 14 mm
Annual production: fewer than 100 cues

OPTIONS (FOR NEW CUES ONLY)

Leather wrap: $250
Ivory joint: $150
Joint protectors: $25+
Ivory butt cap: $250

GRADING	98%	90%	70%

Ivory ferrule: $80
Extra shaft: $125
Layered tip: $30
Lizard or other exotic wraps: $150
Extra rings (each): $40

REPAIRS

Repairs done on all fine cues.
Refinish with linen wrap: $140
Refinish with leather wrap: $300
Rewrap (linen): $40
Rewrap (leather): $250
Clean and press linen wrap: $20
Restore leather wrap: $50
Replace shaft: $125+
Replace Delrin/linen butt cap: $40
Replace ivory butt cap: $250
Replace fiber/linen/composite ferrule: $15+
Replace ivory ferrule: $80
Replace layered tip: $35
Replace tip: $15+

CURRENT PARROT CUES

Two-piece Parrot bar cues start at $300. Basic Parrot cues with or without points start at $500. One-of-a-kind custom Parrot cues start at $700. The current delivery time for a Parrot custom cue is approximately three to six months.

SECONDARY MARKET MINIMUM VALUES

The following are minimum prices for Parrot cues encountered on the secondary market. These prices are representative of cues utilizing basic materials and designs that may not be currently available. Todd currently specializes in one-of-a-kind cues that can command many times these prices due to the use of exotic materials and artistry.

Special construction note: There are many materials and construction techniques that can add value to Parrot cues.

For all used Parrot cues:
Add $100+ for each additional original straight playable shaft beyond two.
Deduct $125 for each missing original straight playable shaft under two.
Add $135+ for ivory joint.
Add $70+ for each ivory ferrule.
Add $100 for leather wrap.
Deduct 20% for obvious or improper refinish.

	98%	90%	70%
Level 1 - 4 points, hustler.			
Level 1 cues start at	$275	$225	$140
Level 2 - 0 points, 0-25 inlays.			
Level 2 cues start at	$450	$260	$235
Level 3 - 2-6 points, 0-8 inlays.			
Level 3 cues start at	$475	$365	$245
Level 4 - 4-10 points, 9-25 inlays.			
Level 4 cues start at	$650	$500	$340
Level 5 - 0-12 points, 26-50 inlays.			
Level 5 cues start at	$1,150	$900	$600
Level 6 - 0-12 points, 51-75 inlays.			
Level 6 cues start at	$1,650	$1,300	$900

ROBERT PARSONS

Maker of Bob's Cues. For more information, see listing for Bob's Cues.

PATRICK CUSTOM CUES

Maker of pool cues from 1994 to 2005 in Granite City, Illinois, and from 2005 to present in Hazelwood, Missouri (a suburb of St. Louis).

Doug Patrick became interested in pool right out of high school. He had a best friend who was an excellent player, and Doug would go with him to the different rooms in the St. Louis area. Soon Doug was playing the game as well.

He grew tired of paying a lot of money for mass manufactured cues, and asked a local cuemaker to make a cue to his specifications. When he failed to provide the cue Doug wanted, Doug set out to make cues on his own. Doug bought a small lathe for repair work, and three months later he was able to buy a lathe suitable for cuemaking.

PATRICK CUSTOM CUES, cont.

In 1994, Doug started to make his own cues under the name of Patrick Custom Cues. Since then, Doug has made constant improvements in Patrick cues for the sake of better playability. In 1998, he started doing inlay work on a manual pantograph. In 1999, Doug redesigned the construction of his butts for better weight distribution. Doug now makes Patrick Custom Cues with the aid of a helper one at a time, by hand, in his two-man shop. They make everything except the tips, bumpers, and screws. He specializes in building custom cues to the specifications of the individual player. All collars, ferrules, and butt caps are threaded on Patrick cues. Doug personally applies his urethane finish three times on every cue. The short-spliced blanks are joined to the handle by a unique threaded tenon. Shafts are turned a minimum of three to four times, ten days apart.

Patrick cues are easily identifiable by the "Patrick Custom Cues" logo, which was laser imprinted into the forearm or butt sleeve until the end of 1998, or by the "Patrick" signature followed by the year of completion on cues made since. One-of-a-kind cues will have "1 of 1" following the date. Doug's goal is to create a top-quality custom cue, at a reasonable price. In 1999, Doug started providing cuemaking supplies for other cuemakers. He sells all types of wood and other cuemaking materials including screws and components.

Patrick cues are guaranteed against warpage for two months, and are indefinitely guaranteed against any construction defects that are not the result of warpage or abuse. If you have a Patrick cue that needs further identification or repair, or would like to talk to Doug about ordering a new cue, contact Patrick Custom Cues, listed in the Trademark Index.

SPECIFICATIONS

- Butt material: hardwoods
- Shaft material: rock maple
- Standard length: 58 in.
- Lengths available: any up to 61 1/2 in.
- Standard finish: urethane
- Joint screw: 5/16-14
- Standard joint: stainless steel
- Joint type: flat faced
- Balance point: 1 in. above wrap
- Point construction: short splice
- Standard wrap: Irish linen
- Standard butt cap: MP ivory substitute
- Standard number of shafts: one
- Standard taper: 13 in. pro
- Standard ferrules: linen phenolic
- Standard tip: Le Pro
- Tip widths available: any
- Annual production: fewer than 200 cues

OPTIONS (FOR NEW CUES ONLY)

- Leather wrap: $125
- Ivory joint: $100
- 3/8-10 flat faced joint: no charge
- G-10 glass epoxy joint screw: no charge
- Joint protectors: $35
- Ivory butt cap: $200
- Ivory ferrules: $75 each
- Extra shaft: $100

REPAIRS

Repairs done on all fine cues.

- Refinish (with leather wrap): $250
- Refinish (with Irish linen wrap): $125+
- Rewrap (leather): $125
- Rewrap (linen): $45
- Replace mp butt cap: $50
- Replace ivory butt cap: $200
- Replace shaft: $100
- Replace linen phenolic ferrule: $35
- Replace ivory ferrule: $60
- Replace Le Pro tip: $10

CURRENT PATRICK CUES

Two-piece Patrick bar cues start at $175. Basic Patrick cues with wraps and joint rings start at $375. Patrick cues with points start at $550. One-of-a-kind custom Patrick cues start at $1,750. The current delivery time for a Patrick custom cue is three to four weeks.

SECONDARY MARKET MINIMUM VALUES

The following are minimum prices for Patrick cues encountered on the secondary market. These prices are representative of cues utilizing basic materials and designs that may not be currently available. Doug also offers one-of-a-kind cues that can command many times these prices due to the use of exotic materials and artistry.

Special construction note: There are many materials and construction techniques that can add value to Patrick cues.

GRADING	98%	90%	70%

For all used Patrick cues, except where otherwise noted:
- Add $85+ for each additional original straight playable shaft beyond one.
- Deduct $100 for missing original straight playable shaft.
- Add $85+ for ivory joint.
- Add $75+ for leather wrap.
- Add $50+ for each ivory ferrule.
- Deduct 20% for obvious or improper refinish.

Level 1 - 4 points, hustler.

Level 1 cues start at	$165	$130	$85

Level 2 - 0 points, 0-25 inlays.

Level 2 cues start at	$350	$475	$185

Level 3 - 2-6 points, 0-8 inlays.

Level 3 cues start at	$500	$390	$270

Level 4 - 4-10 points, 9-25 inlays.

Level 4 cues start at	$650	$515	$350

Level 5 - 0-12 points, 26-50 inlays.

Level 5 cues start at	$950	$745	$500

Level 6 - 0-12 points, 51-75 inlays.

Level 6 cues start at	$1,400	$1,100	$750

CUSTOM CUES BY DALE PATTEN

Maker of pool cues from 1975 to present in Redondo Beach, California.

Dale Patten was a successful prototype machine maker in southern California when his brother-in-law, Ritchie Florence, urged him to start making cues. Dale liked to build things as a hobby, so he knew he could learn how to make cues. After studying cues by Balabushka and Szamboti, Dale developed his own design, and Ritchie Florence helped fine tune the cue's playability. Dale learned how to do inlay work with a manual pantograph. The cues were marketed at tournaments as "Ritchie Florence" cues, by Ritchie Florence himself. In about 1980, Dale stopped making the Ritchie Florence line. He continued to custom make cues, one at a time, for individual customers. In the meantime, Dale still worked as a custom machinist and restored cars, making custom parts for them.

Although most Dale Patten cues are unmarked, they are easily identifiable to those people who know his work. He has put identification marks on cues at customers' requests, and all of the Ritchie Florence cues were marked "R.F." on the butt caps. The 5/16-18 piloted stainless steel joint is Dale's preference, but he has also made some cues with 5/16-18 flat-faced ivory joints. Some Dale Patten cues with points feature blanks by Gus Szamboti, while most of the other blanks with points were made by Burton Spain. Although the two never met in person, Dale and Gus talked at length about machining techniques many times. Dale has always enjoyed designing and building the machinery for making cues, and he has built a one-of-a-kind machine specifically for tapering shafts.

Dale planned on spending more time making cues when he retired in 1997, but has been busy with other activities. He spends most of his time machining parts for 1950s era T-Birds. Dale makes a custom cue every month or two, as a hobby in his spare time.

If you have a Dale Patten cue that needs further identification or repair, or would like to talk to Dale about ordering a new Dale Patten cue, contact Dale Patten, listed in the Trademark Index.

SPECIFICATIONS

Butt material: hardwoods
Shaft material: rock maple
Standard length: 58 in.
Joint screw: 5/16-18
Standard joint: stainless steel
Joint type: piloted
Point construction: short splice
Standard wrap: Irish linen
Standard number of shafts: one
Standard taper: 11 in. straight
Standard ferrules: Ivorine
Standard tip: Triangle
Annual production: fewer than 20 cues

OPTIONS (FOR NEW CUES ONLY)

Options are priced on an individual basis, depending on the cue.

REPAIRS

Repairs are priced on an individual basis, depending on the cue.

CURRENT DALE PATTEN CUES

The current delivery time for a Dale Patten cue depends entirely on the intricacy of the cue.

GRADING	98%	90%	70%

SECONDARY MARKET MINIMUM VALUES

The following are minimum prices for Dale Patten cues encountered on the secondary market. These prices are representative of cues utilizing basic materials and designs that may not be currently available. Dale currently specializes in one-of-a-kind cues that can command many times these prices due to the use of exotic materials and artistry.

Special construction note: There are many materials and construction techniques that can add value to Dale Patten cues. The following are the most important examples:

Add $1,000+ for Gus Szamboti blank.

For all used Dale Patten cues, except where otherwise noted:

Add 40%+ for Ritchie Florence cues (marked "R.F.").
Add $140+ for each additional original straight playable shaft beyond one.
Deduct $200 for missing original straight playable shaft.
Add $150+ for ivory joint.
Deduct 30% for obvious or improper refinish.

	98%	90%	70%
Level 2 - 0 points, 0-25 inlays.			
Level 2 cues start at	$500	$385	$260
Level 3 - 2-6 points, 0-8 inlays.			
Level 3 cues start at	$1,000	$790	$550
Level 4 - 4-10 points, 9-25 inlays.			
Level 4 cues start at	$1,200	$945	$650
Level 5 - 0-12 points, 26-50 inlays.			
Level 5 cues start at	$1,650	$1,300	$900
Level 6 - 0-12 points, 51-75 inlays.			
Level 6 cues start at	$2,150	$1,750	$1,250

J. PECHAUER CUSTOM CUES

Maker of pool cues from 1975 to present in Green Bay, Wisconsin.

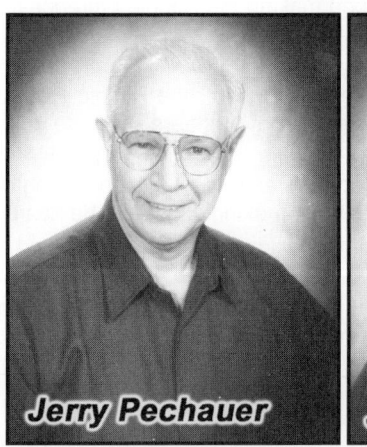
Jerry Pechauer

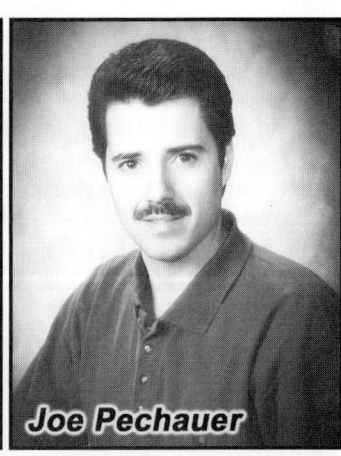
Joe Pechauer

Jerry Pechauer began playing pool at the age of seventeen. He quickly became known as one of the better pool players in his hometown of Green Bay, Wisconsin. In 1960, he began working for the International Harvester Company, and started to learn about the business world. Jerry spent four years there as an apprentice truck mechanic, where he learned many of his mechanical skills. He repaired a Willie Hoppe cue in the basement of his home in 1963, and began making cues as a hobby in 1965. His son, Joseph, made his first cue at the age of 12, and soon they were both taking evening and weekend shop classes to perfect their skills and equipment. Cuemaking was a hobby that began to take over Jerry's basement and two-car garage with machinery and cue parts.

In 1975, Jerry left his sales job at International Harvester to found J. Pechauer Custom Cues. Jerry and Joe began designing much of the equipment they use to make cues, including one of the most sophisticated tapering machines in the industry. This machine allows them to custom taper shafts to suit each customer's preference, and store the dimensions in memory so they can be used again. Because of these machining skills, all parts are made in house, including stainless steel and duralite joints, ferrules, weight screws, joint screws, inserts, butt caps, etc. All parts on J. Pechauer cues are threaded on, and the only metal screws are the joint screw and weight screw. The three sections of the butt are joined by threaded wood tenons.

The "snow white" shaft wood used on J. Pechauer cues is recognized as among the best in the industry. In the past, Jerry has sold excess wood to many of the top custom cuemakers. The quality of this wood is dependant on the way it is selected, cut, dried, stored, machined, and finished. Jerry makes at least a half a dozen trips to forests in the U.S. and Canada to pick out high grade veneer, bird's-eye, and curly maple logs from log yards. He will not buy from sawmills, because they don't have the best wood, and they are not properly cut for cuemaking purposes. They start with logs, cut them on their own saw mill, then dry the lumber in their own special kiln.

It would be impossible for the two of them to do all of this work on their own, so they developed a custom shop. Now, employees machine parts, cut logs, and rough cut blanks, allowing Jerry and Joe the time necessary to be more creative and do the final detail work. Jerry's wife, Karen, also plays a major role in the day-to-day operations of the business.

Today, there are two lines of J. Pechauer cues. The less expensive J.P. Series cues had 3/8-10 flat-faced Implex joints until 1996, when the joints were changed to 5/16-14, and are marked "JP" on the butt cap. The more expensive Pro Series cues had 5/16-14 piloted stainless steel joints and are hand-signed with "J. Pechauer" on the forearm. In 2003, the patented "Pechauer Precision Self Aligning Speed Joint" (Patent Number 6-582-317) became standard on both series of cues. Custom designed cues are also available by special order.

Jerry has designed very nice cue display racks for cue dealers made by a top cabinet maker. These are lighted and ventilated with a fan to release heat to protect the cues. They hold 12 cues behind glass sliding doors, and have extra room for cases and accessories behind glass. More cues can be stored in lower drawers. These custom furniture-quality display racks are beautiful for displaying cue collections, and are available in oak- or mahogany-stained maple.

JP Series

Pro Series

J. Pechauer cues are guaranteed indefinitely against construction defects that are not the result of abuse. If you have a J. Pechauer cue that needs repair, or you would like to talk to Jerry or Joseph about ordering a new cue, contact J. Pechauer Custom Cues, listed in the Trademark Index.

SPECIFICATIONS

Butt material: hardwoods
Shaft material: rock maple
Standard length: 58 in.
Lengths available: any
Standard finish: hi-tech poly
Standard wrap: Irish linen
Standard joint screw: patented precision self aligning speed joint
JP series joint: Implex-Duralite
Pro series joint: stainless steel
JP series joint type: flat faced
Pro series joint type: piloted
Balance point: approx. 1 1/2 in. above wrap
Point construction: inlaid or short splice
Standard butt cap: Duralite
Standard ferrules: CT
Standard number of shafts: one
Standard taper: custom
Standard tip: French with padded base
Tip widths available: any

OPTIONS (NEW CUES ONLY)

Leather wrap: $90
Ivory joint: by quote
Joint protectors: $8 each
Ivory ferrules: $50+
Extra shaft: $150
Special length: by quote

REPAIRS

Repairs done on most cues, all makes.
Refinish (with leather wrap): $170
Refinish (with linen wrap): $120
Rewrap (leather): $90
Rewrap (linen): $40
Replace shaft: $150
Replace ivory ferrule: $50+
Replace Duralite butt cap: $35
Replace ivory butt cap: by quote

CURRENT J PECHAUER CUES

J. Pechauer currently manufactuers the JP Series and the Professional Series. Limited editions and one-of-a-kind J. Pechaur cues are also available. Most J. Pechaur cues are available for immediate delivery.

CURRENT EXAMPLES

The following cues are representations of the work of J Pechauer Custom Cues. These cues can encountered as shown, or modified to suit the desires of the customer.

GRADING	100%	95%	70%

"JP" SERIES

The following "JP" Series cues all feature J. Pechauer's new patented Precision Self Aligning Speed Joint with Implex-Duralite flat faced collars. Several different stain colors are available at no extra charge.

Level 2 "JP01" - Stained bird's-eye maple forearm with a dash ring above wrap, stained bird's-eye maple butt sleeve with dash rings at top and bottom.

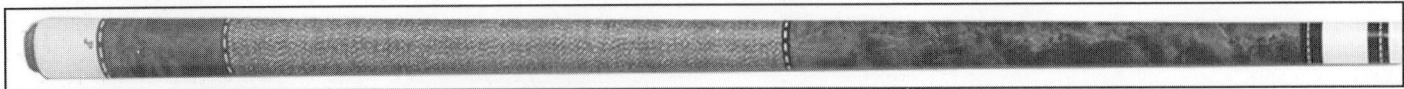

| MSR | $230 | $175-230 | $145 | $110 |

Level 2 "JP02" - Stained bird's-eye maple forearm with a dash ring above wrap, stained bird's-eye maple butt sleeve with three-piece ebony-bordered pearlized plastic diamond-shaped inlays between dash rings above and below.

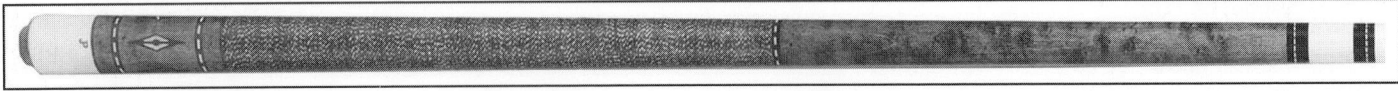

| MSR | $260 | $200-260 | $165 | $125 |

Level 2 "JP03" - Stained bird's-eye maple forearm with ebony-bordered pearlized plastic starburst-shaped inlays above a dash ring above wrap, stained bird's-eye maple butt sleeve with ebony-bordered pearlized plastic starburst-shaped inlays between dash rings at top and bottom.

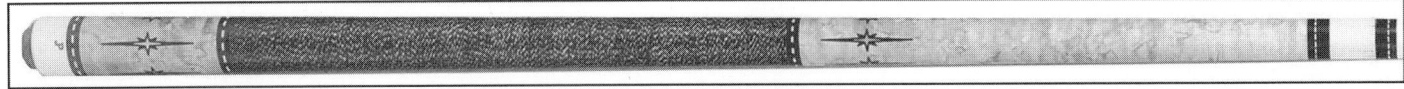

| MSR | $280 | $215-280 | $180 | $135 |

Level 3 "JP04" - Stained bird's-eye maple forearm with a dash ring above wrap, four ebony-bordered bird's-eye maple points with an ebony-bordered synthetic ivory diamond-shaped inlay in each, bird's-eye maple butt sleeve with ebony-bordered synthetic ivory diamond-shaped inlays between dash rings above and below.

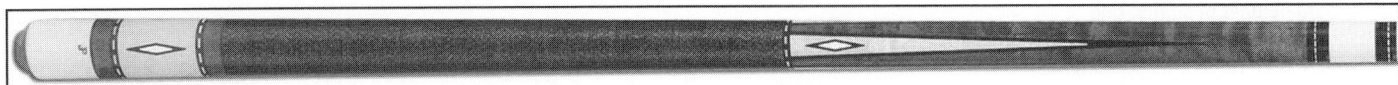

| MSR | $300 | $225-300 | $190 | $145 |

Level 3 "JP05" - Stained bird's-eye maple forearm with a dash ring above wrap, four ebony-bordered bird's-eye maple points with an ebony-bordered pearlized plastic diamond-shaped inlay in each, bird's-eye maple butt sleeve with ebony-bordered pearlized plastic diamond-shaped inlays between dash rings above and below.

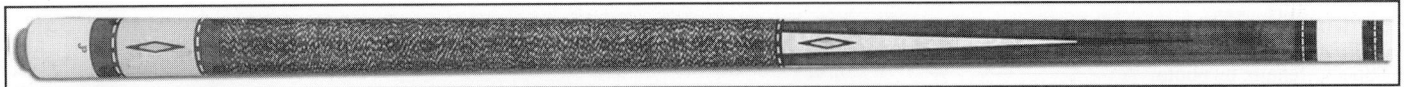

| MSR | $300 | $225-300 | $190 | $145 |

Level 4 "JP06" - Bird's-eye maple forearm with a maple and rosewood dash ring set in ebony above wrap, four rosewood-bordered floating bird's-eye maple diamond-shaped points alternating with four rosewood diamond-shaped inlays, bird's-eye maple butt sleeve with four rosewood-bordered bird's-eye maple diamond-shaped inlays alternating with four rosewood diamond-shaped inlays between maple and rosewood dash rings set in ebony at top and bottom.

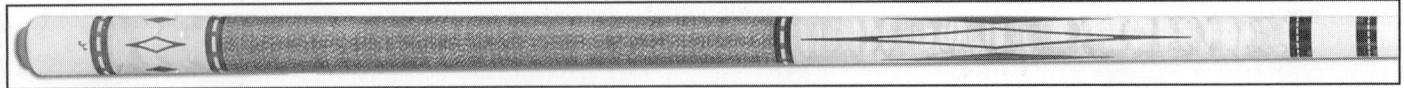

| MSR | $320 | $240-320 | $200 | $155 |

Level 4 "JP07" - Stained bird's-eye maple forearm with double a metal ring set in ebony below a thick maple ring above wrap, four ebony-bordered bird's-eye maple points with an ebony-bordered pearlized plastic spear-shaped inlay in each, stained bird's-eye maple butt sleeve with ebony-bordered pearlized plastic spear-shaped inlays between metal rings outside thick bird's-eye maple rings at top and bottom

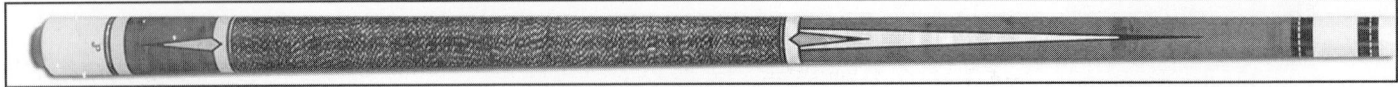

| MSR | $340 | $255-340 | $215 | $165 |

GRADING	100%	95%	70%

J. PECHAUER CUSTOM CUES, cont.

Level 4 "JP08" - Stained bird's-eye maple forearm with a dash ring above wrap, four intricate ebony-bordered three-piece maple floating points with an ebony-bordered pearlized plastic diamond-shaped inlay in the center of each, stained bird's-eye maple butt sleeve with four intricate ebony-bordered maple windows with ebony-bordered pearlized plastic diamond-shaped inlays in the centers between dash rings at top and bottom.

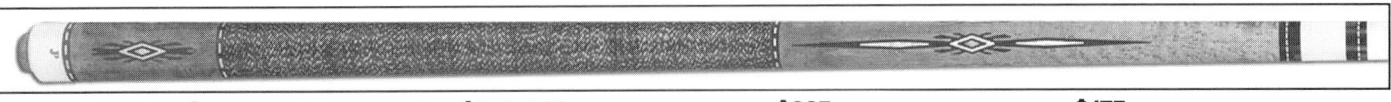

MSR	$360	$270-360	$225	$175

Level 4 "JP09" - Stained bird's-eye maple forearm with a dash ring set in trim rings above wrap, four intricate ebony-bordered two-piece maple floating points with three ebony-bordered synthetic ivory diamond-shaped inlays in the center of each, stained bird's-eye maple butt sleeve with four intricate ebony-bordered two-piece maple windows with three ebony-bordered synthetic ivory diamond-shaped inlays in the center of each between dash rings set in trim rings at top and bottom.

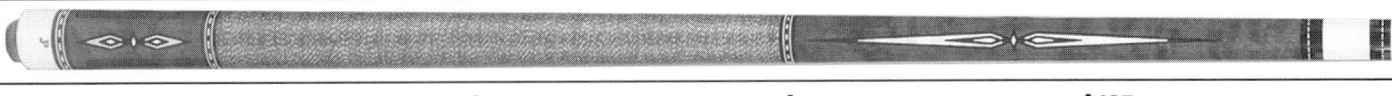

MSR	$380	$285-380	$240	$185

Level 4 "JP10" - Stained bird's-eye maple forearm with a dash ring above wrap, four intricate ebony-bordered three-piece maple floating points with an ebony-bordered pearlized plastic long spear-shaped inlay in the center of each, stained bird's-eye maple butt sleeve with four intricate ebony-bordered two-piece maple windows with an ebony-bordered pearlized plastic spear-shaped inlays in the centers between dash rings at top and bottom.

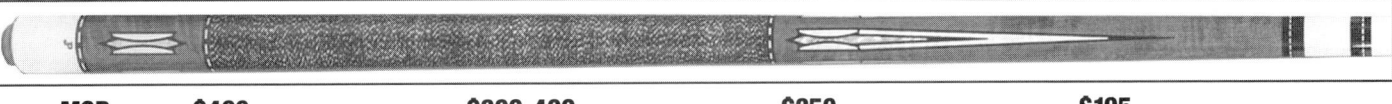

MSR	$400	$300-400	$250	$195

Level 4 "JP11" - Bird's-eye maple forearm with a dash ring above wrap, four ebony points with a synthetic ivory diamond-shaped inlay in each, ebony butt sleeve with four ebony windows alternating four synthetic ivory diamond-shaped inlays between dash rings at top and bottom.

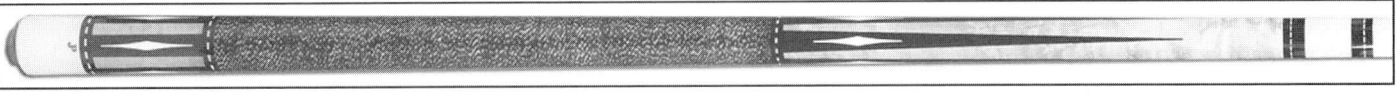

MSR	$420	$315-420	$265	$205

Level 4 "JP12" - Stained bird's-eye maple forearm with double metal rings set in ebony above wrap, four intricate ebony-bordered four-piece maple floating points with an ebony-bordered pearlized plastic diamond-shaped inlay in the center of each, bird's-eye maple handle, stained bird's-eye maple butt sleeve with four intricate ebony-bordered four-piece maple windows with an ebony-bordered pearlized plastic diamond-shaped inlays in the centers between double metal rings set in ebony above and below.

MSR	$440	$325-440	$275	$215

Level 4 "JP13" - Bird's-eye maple forearm with a checked ring above wrap, four intricate ebony-bordered three-piece maple floating points with an ebony-bordered synthetic ivory diamond-shaped inlay in the center of each alternating with four intricate ebony-bordered two-piece maple ovals with an ebony-bordered synthetic ivory diamond-shaped inlay in the center of each, bird's-eye maple butt sleeve with four intricate ebony-bordered two-piece maple inlays alternating with four intricate ebony-bordered two-piece maple ovals with an ebony-bordered synthetic ivory diamond-shaped inlay in the center of each between checked rings above and below.

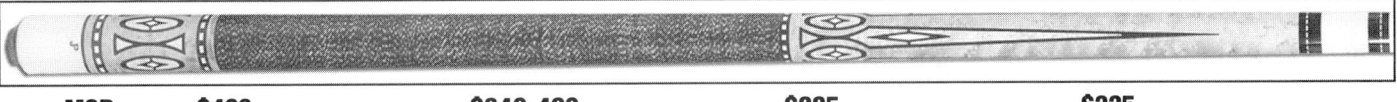

MSR	$460	$340-460	$285	$225

Level 4 "JP14" - Rosewood forearm with a checked ring set in metal rings above wrap, four intricate synthetic ivory-bordered three-piece rosewood floating points with a synthetic ivory-bordered blue lapis diamond-shaped inlay in the center of each above a synthetic ivory-bordered two-piece blue lapis bowtie-shaped inlay towards the base of each point, rosewood butt sleeve with four intricate synthetic ivory-bordered two-piece rosewood windows with a synthetic ivory-bordered blue lapis bowtie-shaped inlay in the center of each between checked rings set in metal rings at top and bottom.

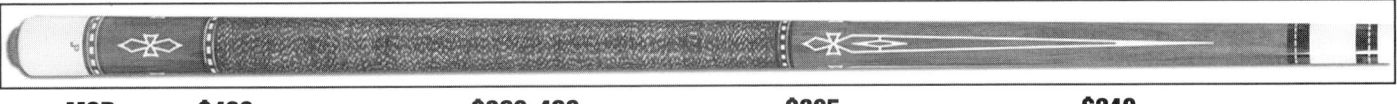

MSR	$490	$360-490	$305	$240

J. PECHAUER CUSTOM CUES, cont.

GRADING	100%	95%	70%

Level 4 "JP15" - Ebony forearm with a dash ring above wrap, four intricate synthetic ivory-bordered two-piece ebony floating points with a synthetic ivory-bordered coral lapis diamond-shaped inlay in the center of each, ebony butt sleeve with four intricate synthetic ivory-bordered two-piece ebony windows with a synthetic ivory-bordered coral lapis diamond-shaped inlay in the center of each between dash rings at top and bottom.

MSR	$490	$360-490	$305	$240

PROFESSIONAL SERIES

The following Professional Series cues all feature J. Pechauer's new patented Precision Self Aligning Speed Joint with stainless steel piloted collars. Several different stain colors are available at no extra charge.

Level 1 "Pro-H" - Curly maple forearm, four full-spliced ebony-bordered rosewood points and handle.

MSR	$280	$225-280	$185	$135

Level 1 "PS02" - Stained curly maple forearm, three long and three short full-spliced ebony-bordered curly maple points and handle.

MSR	$300	$240-300	$195	$145

Level 2 "PS03" - Stained bird's-eye maple forearm with dashes set in metal rings above wrap, stained bird's-eye maple butt sleeve with dashes set in metal rings at top and bottom.

MSR	$380	$300-380	$245	$185

Level 2 "PS04" - Cocobolo forearm with dashes set in metal rings above handle, bird's-eye maple handle, cocobolo butt sleeve with dashes set in metal rings at top and bottom.

MSR	$430	$340-430	$280	$210

Level 2 "BJC" - Stained bird's-eye maple forearm with a dash ring above a break/jump joint above wrap, stained bird's-eye maple butt sleeve with a dash ring at top and bottom.

MSR	$480	$380-480	$310	$235

Level 3 "PS06" - Stained bird's-eye maple forearm, three long and three short full-spliced ebony-bordered bird's-eye maple points and handle, stained bird's-eye maple butt with three long and three short full-spliced ebony-bordered bird's-eye maple reverse points coming out of handle.

MSR	$450	$360-450	$295	$220

Level 3 "PS07" - Stained bird's-eye maple forearm with double metal rings above wrap, four ebony-bordered bird's-eye maple points with an ebony-bordered pearlized plastic diamond-shaped inlay in each, bird's-eye maple butt sleeve with ebony-bordered pearlized plastic diamond-shaped inlays between double metal rings within stained bird's-eye maple rings at top and bottom.

MSR	$460	$370-460	$300	$225

J. PECHAUER CUSTOM CUES, cont.

GRADING	100%	95%	70%

Level 3 "PS08" - Bird's-eye maple forearm, four ebony- and maple-bordered ebony points, ebony butt sleeve with a synthetic ivory ring at bottom.

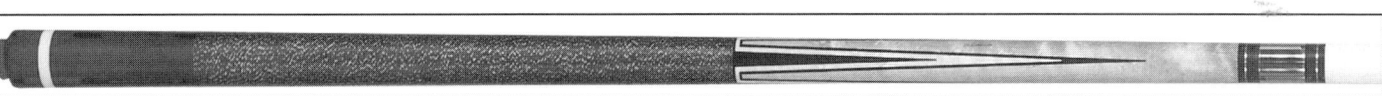

MSR	$500	$400-500	$325	$240

Level 4 "PS09" - Cocobolo forearm with dashes set in metal rings above handle, four ebony-bordered bird's-eye maple points with an ebony-bordered synthetic ivory diamond-shaped inlay in each, cocobolo butt sleeve with four ebony-bordered bird's-eye maple windows with an ebony-bordered synthetic ivory diamond-shaped inlay in each between dashes set in metal rings at top and bottom.

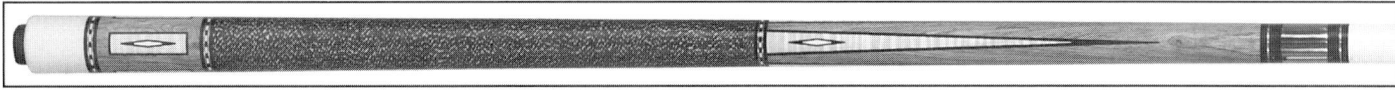

MSR	$550	$440-550	$360	$270

Level 3 "PS10" - Ebony forearm with maple and ebony rings above handle, four maple-bordered ebony points, bird's-eye maple handle, ebony butt sleeve with four maple-bordered reverse ebony points between maple and ebony rings at top and bottom.

MSR	$580	$460-580	$375	$280

Level 4 "PS11" - Bird's-eye maple forearm with dashes set in metal rings above wrap, five intricate ebony-bordered cocobolo three-piece floating points with synthetic ivory diamond-shaped centers, bird's-eye maple butt sleeve with five intricate ebony-bordered cocobolo three-piece inlays with synthetic ivory diamond-shaped centers between dashes set in metal rings at top and bottom.

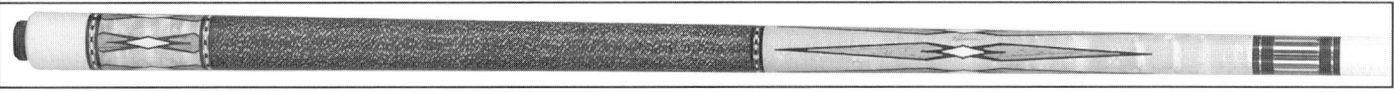

MSR	$580	$460-580	$375	$280

Level 4 "PS12" - Bird's-eye maple forearm with dashes set in metal rings above wrap, four floating palm wood points with a synthetic ivory diamond-shaped inlay in each, stained bird's-eye maple handle, bird's-eye maple butt sleeve with four palm wood windows with a synthetic ivory diamond-shaped inlay in each between dashes set in metal rings at top and bottom.

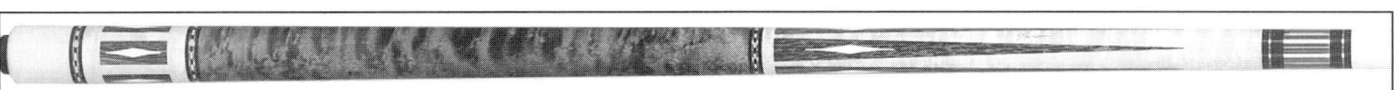

MSR	$600	$475-600	$385	$290

Level 4 "PS13" - Bird's-eye maple forearm, four ebony points with four colored veneers and a synthetic ivory diamond-shaped inlay in each, ebony butt sleeve with four synthetic ivory diamond-shaped inlays alternating with four smaller synthetic ivory diamond-shaped inlays between dashes set in metal rings above and below.

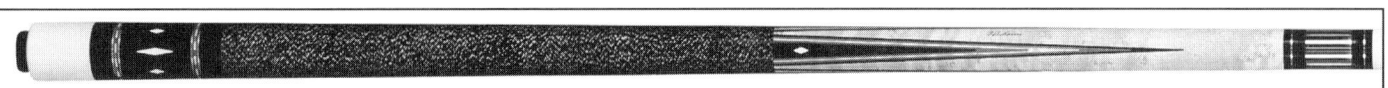

MSR	$600	$475-600	$385	$290

Level 4 "PS14" - Bird's-eye maple forearm with bocote set in double metal rings above wrap, four ebony-bordered floating bocote points with an ebony-bordered pearlized plastic spear-shaped inlay in each alternating with four ebony-bordered bocote diamond-shaped inlays with an ebony-bordered pearlized plastic spear-shaped inlay in each, bocote handle, bird's-eye maple butt sleeve with four ebony-bordered floating bocote reverse point-shaped windows with an ebony-bordered pearlized plastic spear-shaped inlay in each alternating with four ebony-bordered bocote diamond-shaped inlays with an ebony-bordered pearlized plastic spear-shaped inlay in each within stained bird's-eye maple rings at top and bottom.

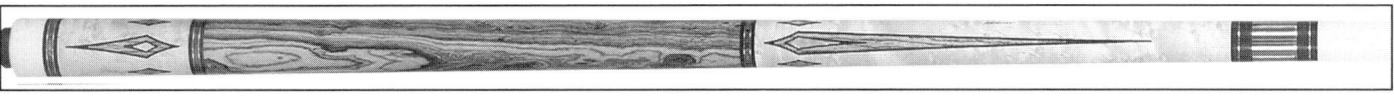

MSR	$600	$475-600	$385	$290

GRADING	100%	95%	70%

Level 4 "PS15" - Bird's-eye maple forearm with dashes set in metal rings above handle, four ebony- and maple-bordered floating bird's-eye maple points with an ebony-bordered synthetic ivory diamond-shaped inlay in each, stained bird's-eye maple butt sleeve with four ebony-bordered bird's-eye maple windows with an ebony-bordered synthetic ivory diamond-shaped inlay in each between dashes set in metal rings at top and bottom.

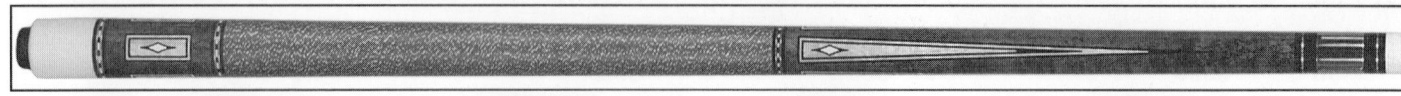

MSR	$600	$475-600	$385	$290

Level 4 "PS16" - Bird's-eye maple forearm, four ebony points with four colored veneers and a pearlized plastic notched diamond-shaped inlay in each, ebony butt sleeve with four pairs of pearlized plastic notched diamond-shaped inlays alternating with four pearlized plastic dot-shaped inlays between pairs of metal rings above and below.

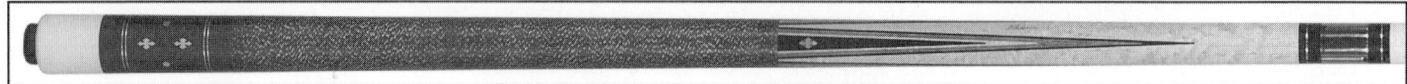

MSR	$620	$490-620	$400	$300

Level 4 "PS17" - Bird's-eye maple forearm, three long and three short intricate maple and ebony points, ebony handle with sets of three long and three short intricate maple and ebony points pointing inward from top and bottom, maple butt sleeve with three long and three short intricate maple and ebony points pointing down from top.

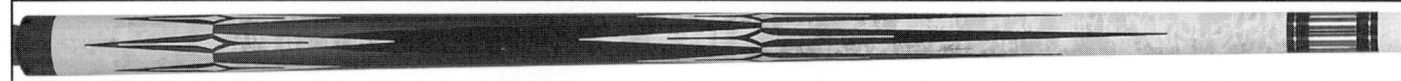

MSR	$650	$510-650	$415	$315

Level 4 "PS18" - Bird's-eye maple forearm with dashes set in metal rings above handle, six ebony points with a cocobolo-bordered synthetic ivory diamond-shaped inlay in each, ebony butt sleeve with six cocobolo-bordered synthetic ivory diamond-shaped inlays between dashes set in metal rings above and below.

MSR	$700	$550-700	$450	$340

Level 4 "PS19" - Bird's-eye maple forearm with ebony and synthetic ivory rings above wrap, five intricate maple and ebony points with synthetic ivory lines and pairs of synthetic ivory diamond-shaped inlays in each, maple butt sleeve with five intricate maple and ebony patterns with pairs of synthetic ivory diamond-shaped inlays in each between ebony and synthetic ivory rings at top and bottom.

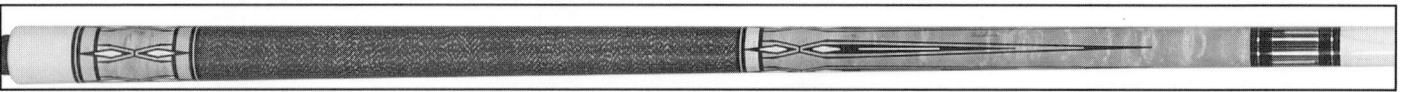

MSR	$750	$580-750	$480	$365

Level 4 "PS20" - Bird's-eye maple forearm with dashes set in metal rings above wrap, five long and five short ebony points with an ebony-bordered synthetic ivory spear-shaped inlay at the tip of each, bird's-eye maple butt sleeve with five synthetic ivory diamond-shaped inlays set in ebony windows alternating with five smaller synthetic ivory diamond-shaped inlays set in ebony windows between dashes set in metal rings at top and bottom.

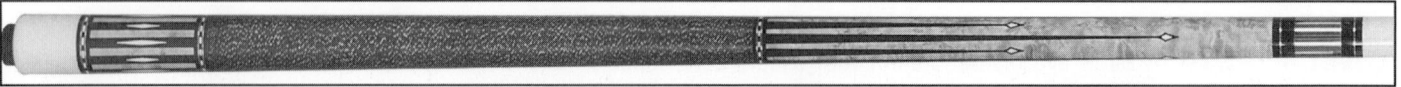

MSR	$750	$580-750	$480	$365

Level 5 "PS21" - Bird's-eye maple forearm with dashes set in metal rings above wrap, five ebony points with pairs of synthetic ivory diamond-shaped inlays set within turquoise spear- and diamond-shaped inlays in each, bird's-eye maple butt sleeve with five pairs of synthetic ivory diamond-shaped inlays set within turquoise diamond-shaped inlays between dashes set in metal rings at top and bottom.

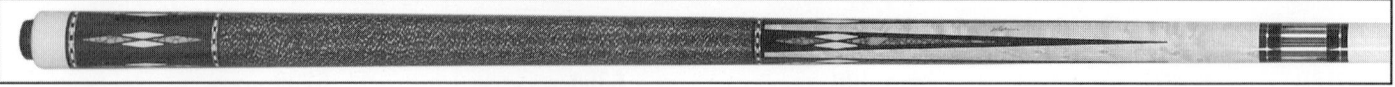

MSR	$800	$600-800	$500	$395

J. PECHAUER CUSTOM CUES, cont.

GRADING	100%	95%	70%

Level 5 "PS22" - Bird's-eye maple forearm, five intricate ebony-bordered curly maple points alternating with intricate maple and ebony ovals, bird's-eye maple handle with sets of five intricate ebony-bordered curly maple points pointing inward from top and bottom, bird's-eye maple butt sleeve with five intricate ebony-bordered curly maple points alternating with intricate maple and ebony ovals pointing down from top.

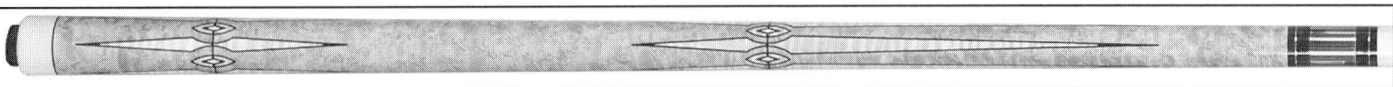

MSR	$850	$640-850	$535	$420

Level 4 "PS23" - Bird's-eye maple forearm with a thick intricate ebony ring above wrap, six intricate ebony-bordered bloodwood points alternating with six ebony-bordered synthetic ivory diamond-shaped inlays, ebony butt sleeve with ebony-bordered synthetic ivory diamond-shaped inlays set in ebony-bordered bird's-eye maple hexagonal windows between thick intricate ebony rings at top and bottom.

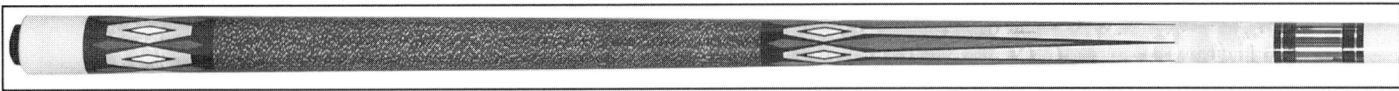

MSR	$850	$640-850	$535	$420

Level 5 "PS24" - Cocobolo forearm, five intricate ebony-bordered curly maple points alternating with intricate maple/cocobolo/ebony ovals, bird's-eye maple handle with sets of five intricate ebony-bordered cocobolo points pointing inward from top and bottom, cocobolo butt sleeve with five intricate ebony-bordered curly maple points alternating with intricate maple/cocobolo/ebony ovals pointing down from top.

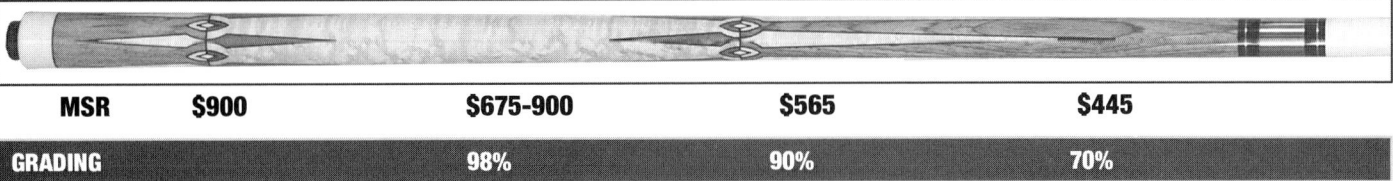

MSR	$900	$675-900	$565	$445

GRADING	98%	90%	70%

DISCONTINUED EXAMPLES

1980'S "JP" SERIES

The following 1980s era "JP" Series cues all featured 3/8-10 flat-faced Duralite joints with maple stitching in the joint collars. Stain was available on most cues at no extra charge.

Level 2 #1 - One-piece stained bird's-eye maple butt.

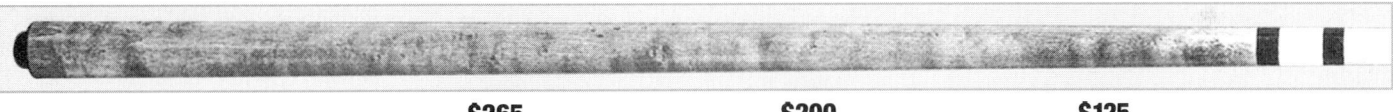

	$265	$200	$125

Level 2 #2 - Stained bird's-eye maple forearm, stained bird's-eye maple butt sleeve.

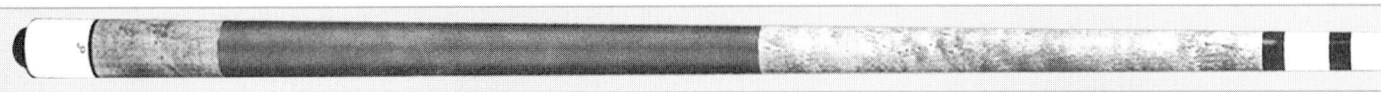

	$225	$170	$110

Level 2 #3 - Stained bird's-eye maple forearm, stained bird's-eye maple butt sleeve with a white ring around bottom.

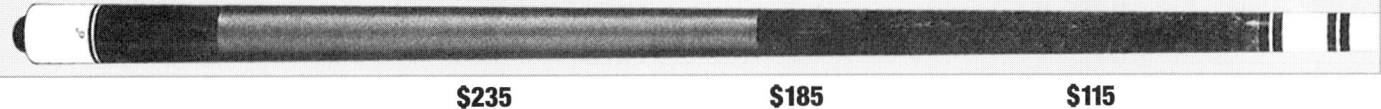

	$235	$185	$115

Level 2 #4 - Stained bird's-eye maple forearm, stained bird's-eye maple butt sleeve with a maple checked ring around bottom.

	$260	$195	$125

Level 2 #5 - Stained bird's-eye maple forearm, stained bird's-eye maple butt sleeve with maple blocks set in a hardwood ring at bottom.

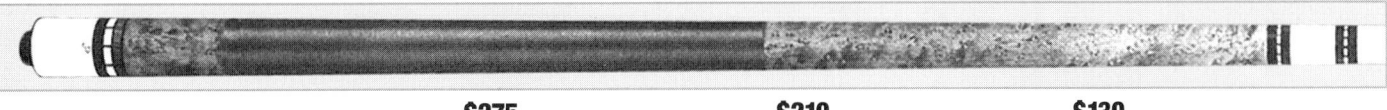

	$275	$210	$130

GRADING	98%	90%	70%

Level 2 #6 - Stained bird's-eye maple forearm, stained bird's-eye maple butt sleeve with a thick hardwood ring around center.

	$280	$215	$135

Level 2 #7 - Stained bird's-eye maple forearm, stained bird's-eye maple butt sleeve with mother-of-pearl dots set in an ebony ring below center.

	$285	$220	$140

Level 2 #8 - Stained bird's-eye maple forearm, stained bird's-eye maple butt sleeve with mother-of-pearl notched dot-shaped inlays set in an ebony ring around center with maple checks at top and bottom.

	$300	$230	$145

Level 2 #9 - Stained bird's-eye maple forearm, stained bird's-eye maple butt sleeve with four mother-of-pearl notched diamond-shaped inlays set in ebony blocks between maple checks at top and bottom.

	$335	$250	$160

Level 3 #10 - Stained bird's-eye maple forearm, four maple points with three colored veneers, ebony butt sleeve with maple windows alternating with pairs of mother-of-pearl dots.

	$525	$395	$260

Level 3 #11 - Stained bird's-eye maple forearm, four maple points with three colored veneers, ebony butt sleeve with four maple windows alternating with four mother-of-pearl notched diamond-shaped inlays between ebony checks set in white rings above and below.

	$615	$465	$305

Level 4 #12 - Stained bird's-eye maple forearm, four stained maple points with three colored veneers, ebony butt sleeve with four mother-of-pearl notched diamond-shaped inlays with mother-of-pearl dots above and below alternating with pairs of stained bird's-eye maple blocks around center.

	$665	$505	$330

1992 "JP" SERIES

The following 1992 "JP" Series cues all featured 3/8-10 flat-faced Duralite joints with maple stitching in the joint collars. Stain was available on most cues at no extra charge.

Level 2 JP01 - Stained bird's-eye maple forearm, stained bird's-eye maple butt sleeve.

MSR (1992) $210	$245	$185	$120

J. PECHAUER CUSTOM CUES, cont.

GRADING	98%	90%	70%

Level 2 JP02 - Stained bird's-eye maple forearm, stained bird's-eye maple butt sleeve with a dark hardwood ring around center.

MSR (1992) $210 $245 $185 $120

Level 2 JP03 - Stained bird's-eye maple forearm, stained bird's-eye maple butt sleeve with mother-of-pearl dots in ebony diamond-shaped inlays between ebony rings at top and bottom.

MSR (1992) $240 $285 $215 $140

Level 2 JP04 - Stained bird's-eye maple forearm, ebony butt sleeve with mother-of-pearl notched dot-shaped inlays within maple stitches between ivory-colored rings above and below.

MSR (1992) $260 $310 $235 $150

Level 3 JP05 - Stained bird's-eye maple forearm, four maple points with two colored veneers, stained bird's-eye maple butt sleeve with maple stitches within ivory-colored rings at top and bottom.

MSR (1992) $280 $335 $245 $160

Level 3 JP06 - Stained bird's-eye maple forearm, four floating ebony-bordered, ivory-colored points, stained bird's-eye maple butt sleeve with ebony-bordered, ivory-colored windows between ebony rings at top and bottom.

MSR (1992) $300 $365 $275 $175

Level 3 JP07 - Stained bird's-eye maple forearm, four ebony-bordered, ivory-colored points, stained bird's-eye maple butt sleeve with pearlized plastic ovals set in ebony windows within an ivory-colored ring with maple stitches at top and bottom.

MSR (1992) $350 $420 $320 $200

Level 3 JP08 - Stained bird's-eye maple forearm, four ebony points with three colored veneers, ebony butt sleeve with pearlized plastic diamond-shaped inlays around center.

MSR (1992) $400 $465 $350 $225

Level 4 JP09 - Stained bird's-eye maple forearm, four ebony floating points with a large ivory-colored diamond-shaped inlay in each point, stained bird's-eye maple butt sleeve with four ivory-colored diamond-shaped inlays set in ebony windows alternating with four large ebony diamond-shaped inlays between maple stitch rings above and below.

MSR (1992) $450 $515 $395 $250

Level 3 JP10 - Stained bird's-eye maple forearm, four ivory-colored points with two colored veneers, ebony butt sleeve with four ivory-colored diamond-shaped inlays set in red veneer windows between stitch rings above and below.

MSR (1992) $500 $575 $440 $280

J. PECHAUER CUSTOM CUES, cont.

GRADING	98%	90%	70%

Level 4 JP11 - Stained bird's-eye maple forearm, four floating ebony points with three colored veneers and a pearlized plastic oval-shaped inlay in each point, ebony butt sleeve with four pearlized plastic ovals set in colored veneer windows between metal rings above and below.

MSR (1992) $550	$650	$495	$320

Level 4 JP12 - Stained bird's-eye maple forearm, four ebony points with three colored veneers and a pearlized plastic diamond-shaped inlay in each point, ebony butt sleeve with four pearlized plastic diamond-shaped inlays alternating with maple windows between rings of metal and maple checks.

MSR (1992) $600	$715	$545	$350

1995 "JP" SERIES

The following 1995 "JP" Series cues all featured 5/16-14 flat-faced Implex joints with maple stitching in the joint collars. Stain was available on most cues at no extra charge.

Level 2 J1 - Black-stained bird's-eye maple forearm, black-stained bird's-eye maple butt sleeve.

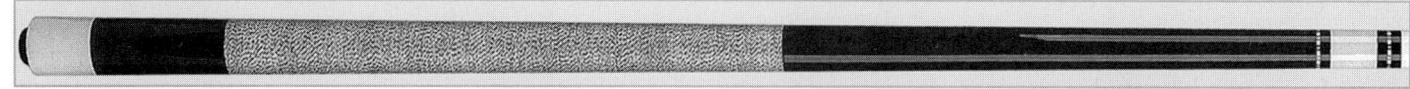

MSR (1996) $210	$225	$175	$110

Level 2 J2 - Wine-stained bird's-eye maple forearm, cherry-stained bird's-eye maple butt sleeve with thick ebony ring in middle.

MSR (1996) $220	$235	$180	$115

Level 2 J3 - Natural (very light stain) -stained bird's-eye maple forearm, stained bird's-eye maple butt sleeve with ebony propellers inlaid with a mother-of-pearl dot between black-bordered dark-stained maple rings at top and bottom.

MSR (1996) $240	$260	$200	$125

Level 2 J4 - Emerald green-stained bird's-eye maple forearm, emerald green stained bird's-eye maple butt sleeve with intricate mother-of-pearl diamond-shaped inlays set in a thick ebony ring between nickel silver and white rings above and below.

MSR (1996) $260	$285	$225	$140

Level 3 J5 - Burgundy wine-stained bird's-eye maple forearm, two maple points with two colored veneers, maple butt sleeve with a thick wine-stained bird's-eye maple ring bordered by maple and red stitching at top and bottom.

MSR (1996) $280	$310	$235	$150

Level 3 J6 - Ebony-stained bird's-eye maple forearm, two maple points with two colored veneers, maple butt sleeve with bocote-bordered thick black-stained maple ring in middle.

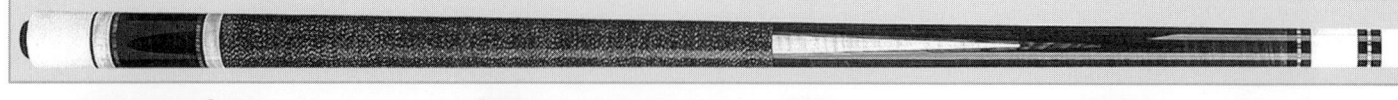

MSR (1996) $280	$310	$235	$150

J. PECHAUER CUSTOM CUES, cont.

GRADING	98%	90%	70%

Level 3 J7 - Wine-stained bird's-eye maple forearm, four floating ebony points with a long white spear inlaid in each, cherry-stained bird's-eye maple butt sleeve with four thick ebony-bordered long white hexagons between ebony rings at top and bottom.

MSR (1996) $310	$335	$255	$165

Level 3 J8 - Danish-stained bird's-eye maple forearm, four ebony points with long white diamond-shaped inlays in each, Danish-stained bird's-eye maple butt sleeve with four downward-pointing ebony points with white diamond-shaped inlays in each.

MSR (1996) $340	$375	$285	$185

Level 3 J9 - Bocote-stained bird's-eye maple forearm, four ebony-bordered bocote points, bocote butt sleeve with four mother-of-pearl diamond-shaped inlays set in ebony windows between stitching above and below.

MSR (1996) $360	$400	$300	$190

Level 3 J10 - Natural-stained bird's-eye maple forearm, four ebony-bordered cocobolo points, natural-stained maple butt sleeve with four mother-of-pearl diamond-shaped inlays set in ebony windows in a thick ring of cocobolo.

MSR (1996) $360	$400	$300	$190

Level 3 J11 - Coco dark-stained bird's-eye maple forearm, four ebony-bordered white points, coco dark-stained bird's-eye maple butt sleeve with four mother-of-pearl diamond-shaped inlays set in ebony windows in a thick ring of white.

MSR (1996) $360	$400	$300	$190

Level 3 J12 - Natural-stained bird's-eye maple forearm, four ebony points with three colored veneers of ebony, cocobolo, maple, and a mother-of-pearl diamond-shaped inlay set in each, ebony butt sleeve with four long mother-of-pearl diamond-shaped inlays.

MSR (1996) $410	$450	$345	$215

Level 3 J13 - Coco dark-stained bird's-eye maple forearm, four ebony points with three colored veneers of ebony, purpleheart, maple, and a mother-of-pearl diamond-shaped inlay set in each, ebony butt sleeve with four long mother-of-pearl diamond-shaped inlays.

MSR (1996) $410	$450	$345	$215

Level 4 J14 - Natural-stained bird's-eye maple forearm, four floating ebony points with three colored veneers of ebony, maple, choc de koke, and a mother-of-pearl oval set in each, ebony butt sleeve with four mother-of-pearl oval set in windows of colored veneers.

MSR (1996) $500	$550	$340	$210

GRADING	98%	90%	70%

Level 4 J15 - Natural stained bird's-eye maple forearm with four long ebony diamond-shaped inlays between each point, four floating ebony points with a long white diamond-shaped inlay in each and a black-bordered white stylized arrowhead at each base, stained bird's-eye maple butt sleeve with four black-bordered white stylized arrowheads alternating with four long ebony diamond-shaped inlays between ebony rings inlaid with white checks above and below.

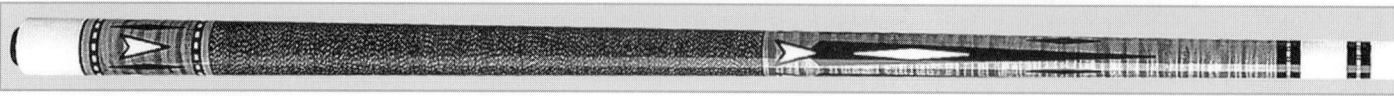

MSR (1996) $600	$665	$500	$325

"PROFESSIONAL" SERIES

Except for the Pro Hustler, the following "Pro" Series cues all featured 5/16-14 piloted stainless steel joints with nickel silver rings in the joint collars.

Level 1 Pro Hustler - Wine-stained curly maple butt (various color stains available), maple forearm, four ebony veneered points.

MSR (1996) $260	$285	$215	$140

Level 2 P2 - Ebony-stained bird's-eye maple forearm with nickel silver ring above wrap, black-stained bird's-eye maple butt sleeve with nickel silver rings above and below.

MSR (1996) $360	$400	$300	$195

Level 3 P3 - Wine-stained bird's-eye maple forearm, four ebony-bordered maple points, maple butt sleeve with a thick ring of wine-stained bird's-eye maple.

MSR (1996) $400	$460	$345	$220

Level 3 P4 - Wine-stained bird's-eye maple forearm, four ebony-bordered maple points, maple butt sleeve with a thick ring of ebony-stained bird's-eye maple.

MSR (1996) $400	$460	$345	$220

Level 3 P5 - Rose-stained bird's-eye maple forearm, four floating maple points with three veneers of ebony, maple, and rosewood, stained bird's-eye maple butt sleeve with four black-bordered mother-of-pearl diamond-shaped inlays between nickel silver rings set in ebony at top and bottom.

MSR (1996) $450	$515	$395	$250

Level 3 P6 - Coco brown-stained bird's-eye maple forearm, four floating maple points with three colored veneers of ebony, maple, and ebony, bird's-eye maple handle, stained bird's-eye maple butt sleeve with four black-bordered mother-of-pearl diamond-shaped inlays between nickel silver rings set in ebony at top and bottom.

MSR (1996) $500	$575	$435	$280

Level 3 P7 - Natural-stained bird's-eye maple forearm, four stained bird's-eye maple points with three colored veneers of ebony, maple, and purpleheart, stained bird's-eye maple butt sleeve with four dark-bordered maple diamond-shaped inlays set in ebony-bordered maple windows between stitched rings above and below.

MSR (1996) $500	$575	$435	$280

J. PECHAUER CUSTOM CUES, cont.

GRADING	98%	90%	70%

Level 4 P8 - Natural-stained bird's-eye maple forearm, four cocobolo points with three colored veneers of ebony, bocote, and maple, and a white diamond-shaped inlay in each, ebony butt sleeve with four large white diamond-shaped inlays alternating with four small white diamond-shaped inlays.

MSR (1996) $550	$630	$475	$310

Level 4 P9 - Natural-stained bird's-eye maple forearm, four cocobolo points with three colored veneers of ebony, cocobolo, and maple, and a white diamond-shaped inlay in each, cocobolo butt sleeve with four large white diamond-shaped inlays alternating with four small white diamond-shaped inlays.

MSR (1996) $550	$630	$475	$310

Level 4 P10 - Natural bird's-eye maple forearm, four ebony points with three colored veneers of ebony, cocobolo, and maple, and a mother-of-pearl diamond-shaped inlay in each, ebony butt sleeve with four large mother-of-pearl diamond-shaped inlays alternating with four small mother-of-pearl diamond-shaped inlays.

MSR (1996) $550	$630	$475	$310

Level 4 P11 - Natural-stained bird's-eye maple forearm, four floating white points with two colored veneers of ebony and rosewood, and an ebony-bordered mother-of-pearl diamond-shaped inlay in each, ebony butt sleeve with four small mother-of-pearl bordered ebony diamond-shaped inlays between nickel silver rings above and below.

MSR (1996) $650	$745	$565	$360

Level 4 P12 - Natural-stained bird's-eye maple forearm, six tulipwood points with a long ebony diamond-shaped inlay in each, tulipwood butt sleeve with six long ebony diamond-shaped inlays.

MSR (1996) $700	$785	$595	$380

Level 4 P13 - Natural-stained bird's-eye maple forearm, six cocobolo points with a long white diamond-shaped inlay in each, cocobolo butt sleeve with six long white diamond-shaped inlays.

MSR (1996) $700	$785	$595	$380

Level 4 P14 - Natural-stained bird's-eye maple forearm, six rosewood points with a long cocobolo diamond-shaped inlay in each, ebony sleeve with six long cocobolo diamond-shaped inlays.

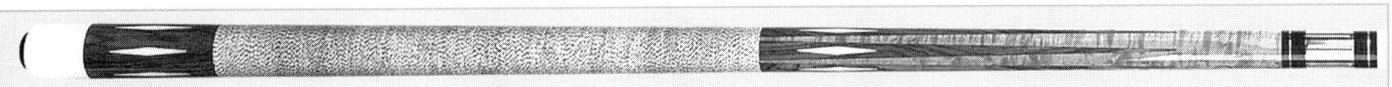

MSR (1996) $700	$785	$595	$380

Level 4 P15 - Non-stained bird's-eye maple forearm, four chac de koke points with a long ebony-bordered mother-of-pearl diamond-shaped inlay in each, chac de koke butt sleeve with four long ebony-bordered mother-of-pearl diamond-shaped inlays.

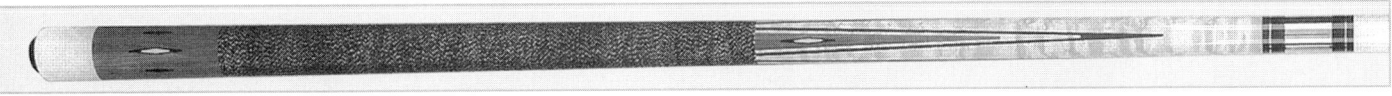

MSR (1996) $750	$845	$640	$410

J. PECHAUER CUSTOM CUES, cont.

GRADING	98%	90%	70%

Level 4 P16 - Natural-stained bird's-eye maple forearm, four ebony points with ebony-bordered cocobolo veneers and a long mother-of-pearl-bordered cocobolo diamond-shaped inlay in each, ebony butt sleeve with four long mother-of-pearl-bordered cocobolo diamond-shaped inlays alternating with four small mother-of-pearl diamond-shaped inlays between nickel silver rings set in cocobolo above and below.

MSR (1996) $800	$900	$650	$380

Level 4 P17 - Natural-stained bird's-eye maple forearm, four ebony points with black-bordered purpleheart veneers and a long mother-of-pearl-bordered purpleheart diamond-shaped inlay in each, ebony butt sleeve with four long mother-of-pearl bordered purpleheart diamond-shaped inlays alternating with four small mother-of-pearl diamond-shaped inlays between nickel silver rings set in purpleheart above and below.

MSR (1996) $800	$900	$650	$380

Level 4 P18 - Natural-stained bird's-eye maple forearm, four ebony points with ebony-bordered bocote veneers and a long mother-of-pearl-bordered bocote diamond-shaped inlay in each, ebony butt sleeve with four long mother-of-pearl-bordered bocote diamond-shaped inlays alternating with four small mother-of-pearl diamond-shaped inlays between nickel silver rings set in bocote above and below.

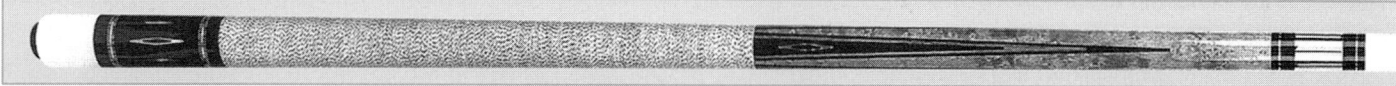

MSR (1996) $800	$900	$650	$380

Level 4 P19 - Ebony-stained bird's-eye maple forearm, four chac de koke points with long ebony-bordered maple diamond-shaped inlays in each, ebony butt sleeve with four long black-bordered maple diamond-shaped inlays set in chac de koke windows.

MSR (1996) $800	$900	$650	$380

Level 4 P20 - Tulipwood forearm, four floating ebony-bordered tulipwood points with a long ebony-bordered white diamond-shaped inlay in each, tulipwood butt sleeve with four long ebony-bordered white diamond-shaped inlays.

MSR (1996) $800	$900	$650	$380

Level 4 P21 - Natural bird's-eye maple forearm with ebony and white checks within nickel silver rings above wrap, six ebony points with a long white diamond-shaped inlay in each, ebony butt sleeve with four long white diamond-shaped inlays between ebony and white checks within nickel silver rings above and below.

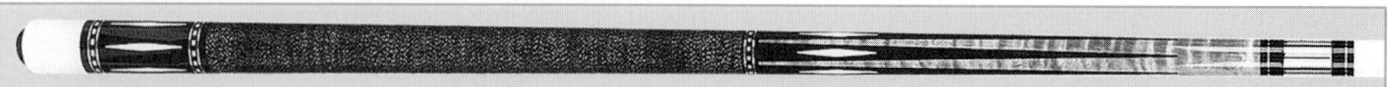

MSR (1996) $800	$900	$650	$380

Level 4 P22 - Natural-stained curly maple forearm with ebony within nickel silver rings set in ebony above wrap, four floating cocobolo points with two veneers, ebony and maple, and an ebony-bordered mother-of-pearl diamond-shaped inlay in each, stained cocobolo maple butt sleeve with four ebony-bordered mother-of-pearl diamond-shaped inlays set in cocobolo windows with two veneers with ebony within nickel silver rings set in ebony above and cocobolo within nickel silver rings set in ebony below.

MSR (1996) $800	$900	$650	$380

J. PECHAUER CUSTOM CUES, cont.

GRADING	98%	90%	70%

Level 4 P23 - Rosewood-stained bird's-eye maple forearm with ebony and white checks within nickel silver rings set in ebony above wrap, four floating rosewood points with two veneers, ebony and maple, and an ebony-bordered mother-of-pearl diamond-shaped inlay in each rosewood-stained bird's-eye maple butt sleeve with four mother-of-pearl-bordered ebony diamond-shaped inlays set in ebony windows with two veneers, ebony and maple, between ebony and white checks within nickel silver rings set in ebony above and below.

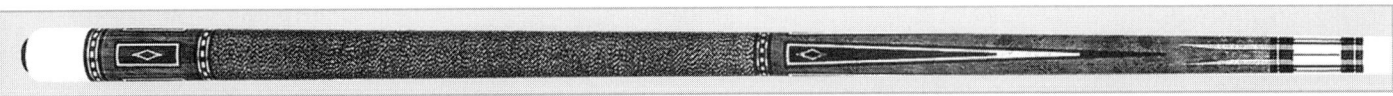

MSR (1996) $900	$1,025	$775	$500

Level 4 P24 - Natural-stained bird's-eye maple forearm, three ebony points with a cocobolo-bordered white diamond-shaped inlay in each alternating with three cocobolo points with an ebony-bordered white diamond-shaped inlay in each, stained bird's-eye maple butt sleeve with six white diamond-shaped inlays set in windows of alternating ebony and cocobolo between black-bordered cocobolo rings above and below.

MSR (1996) $900	$1,025	$775	$500

Level 4 P25 - Natural-stained bird's-eye maple forearm with cocobolo rings within two rings of nickel silver set in ebony above wrap, three ebony points with a cocobolo diamond-shaped inlay in each alternating with three ebony-bordered cocobolo points, stained bird's-eye maple butt sleeve with three downward pointing ebony-bordered cocobolo points alternating with three ebony-bordered cocobolo diamond-shaped inlays between cocobolo rings within two rings of nickel silver set in ebony at top and bottom.

MSR (1996) $900	$1,025	$775	$500

Level 4 P26 - Natural-stained bird's-eye maple forearm with cocobolo rings within two rings of nickel silver set in ebony above wrap, three short ebony points with a cocobolo-bordered mother-of-pearl diamond-shaped inlay in each alternating with three long ebony-bordered cocobolo points, stained bird's-eye maple butt sleeve with three downward-pointing ebony-bordered cocobolo points alternating with three downward-pointing short ebony points with a small cocobolo-bordered mother-of-pearl diamond-shaped inlay in each between cocobolo rings within two rings of nickel silver set in ebony at top and bottom.

MSR (1996) $900	$1,025	$775	$500

Level 5 P27 - Danish-stained bird's-eye maple forearm with a nickel silver ring set in ebony above wrap and curving ebony lines between points, four floating ebony points with a long six-point star between lines all of mother-of-pearl, Danish-stained bird's-eye maple butt sleeve with four long mother-of-pearl six-point stars set in ebony windows alternating with curving ebony lines between nickel silver rings set in ebony at top and bottom.

MSR (1996) $950	$1,075	$810	$520

Level 5 P28 - Natural-stained curly maple forearm with purpleheart diamond-shaped inlays and dashes between the points, four ebony points with three colored veneers, ebony, bocote, and purpleheart, ebony butt sleeve with four purpleheart diamond-shaped inlays set in bocote windows alternating with four mother-of-pearl diamond-shaped inlays between nickel silver rings and maple dash rings above and below.

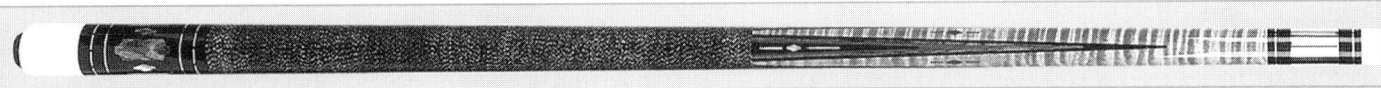

MSR (1996) $950	$1,075	$810	$520

Level 4 P29 - Natural-stained bird's-eye maple forearm with ebony and white checks within nickel silver rings set in ebony above wrap, six ebony-bordered cocobolo points with a long ebony-bordered diamond-shaped inlay in each, cocobolo butt sleeve with six long ebony-bordered diamond-shaped inlays between ebony and white checks within nickel silver rings set in ebony at top and bottom.

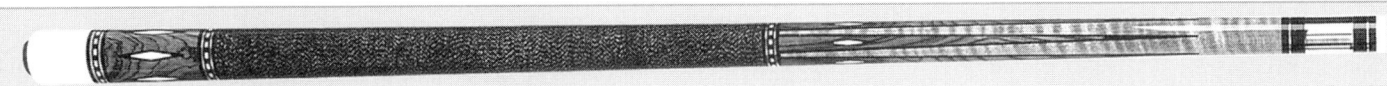

MSR (1996) $1,000	$1,150	$875	$550

GRADING	98%	90%	70%

Level 4 P30 - Ebony-stained bird's-eye maple forearm with ebony and white checks within nickel silver rings set in ebony above wrap, six tulipwood points with an ebony-bordered diamond-shaped inlay in each, tulipwood butt sleeve with six long ebony-bordered diamond-shaped inlays between ebony and white checks within nickel silver rings set in ebony at top and bottom.

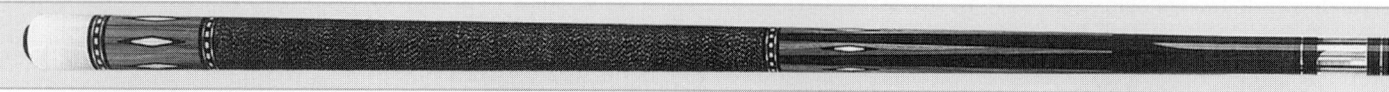

MSR (1996) $1,000	$1,150	$875	$550

Level 4 P31 - Bocote-stained bird's-eye maple forearm with ebony and white checks within nickel silver rings set in ebony above wrap, six ebony-bordered bocote points with a long ebony-bordered diamond-shaped inlay in each, bocote butt sleeve with six long ebony-bordered diamond-shaped inlays between ebony and white checks within nickel silver rings set in ebony at top and bottom.

MSR (1996) $1,000	$1,150	$875	$550

Level 5 P32 - Natural-stained bird's-eye maple forearm with a nickel silver ring set in cocobolo within ebony above wrap and ebony-bordered white diamond-shaped inlays between the points, four floating ebony-bordered cocobolo points each inlaid with a spear and two diamond-shaped inlays in white, ebony butt sleeve with four white-bordered cocobolo windows inlaid with two white diamond-shaped inlays alternating with four white-bordered ebony diamond-shaped inlays between nickel silver rings set in cocobolo above and below.

MSR (1996) $1,200	$1,365	$1,025	$650

Level 5 P33 - Dark English-stained bird's-eye maple forearm with a nickel silver ring set in purpleheart within ebony above wrap and ebony-bordered mother-of-pearl diamond-shaped inlays between the points, four floating ebony-bordered white points each inlaid with a spear and two diamond-shaped inlays of purpleheart, ebony butt sleeve with four purpleheart bordered white windows inlaid with two purpleheart diamond-shaped inlays alternating with four white-bordered purpleheart diamond-shaped inlays between nickel silver rings set in purpleheart above and below.

MSR (1996) $1,200	$1,365	$1,025	$650

Level 5 P34 - Natural-stained curly maple forearm with ebony and white checks within nickel silver rings set in ebony above wrap, six ebony points inlaid with a pattern of a diamond-shaped inlay between two opposing arrowhead-shaped inlays all of mother-of-pearl set within a white border design in each point, ebony butt sleeve with six patterns of diamond-shaped inlays between two opposing arrowhead shaped inlays all of mother-of-pearl set within white border designs between ebony and white checks within nickel silver rings set in ebony above and below.

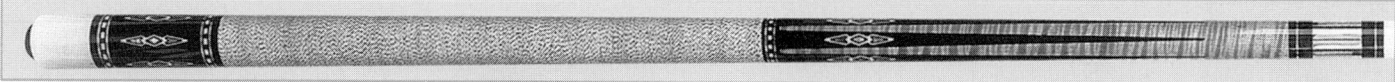

MSR (1996) $1,300	$1,475	$1,100	$700

Level 4 P35 - Wine-stained curly maple forearm with long ebony-bordered white diamond-shaped inlays between the points, six ebony-bordered white points with an ebony-bordered mother-of-pearl diamond-shaped inlay in each, wine-stained curly maple butt sleeve with six downward-pointing ebony-bordered white points with an ebony-bordered mother-of-pearl diamond-shaped inlay in each alternating with six long ebony-bordered white diamond-shaped inlays between the points.

MSR (1996) $1,300	$1,475	$1,100	$700

Level 4 P36 - Natural-stained curly maple forearm with long ebony-bordered white diamond-shaped inlays between the points, six ebony-bordered cocobolo points with an ebony-bordered white diamond-shaped inlay in each, natural-stained curly maple butt sleeve with six downward-pointing ebony-bordered cocobolo points with an ebony-bordered white diamond-shaped inlay in each alternating with six long ebony-bordered white diamond-shaped inlays between the points.

MSR (1996) $1,300	$1,475	$1,100	$700

J. PECHAUER CUSTOM CUES, cont. 607

| GRADING | 98% | 90% | 70% |

Level 4 P37 - Tulipwood forearm with a nickel silver ring set in ebony above the wrap, four ebony-bordered stylized bois de rose points inlaid with opposing ebony-bordered mother-of-pearl triangles at the base of each and a long ebony-bordered mother-of-pearl diamond-shaped inlay in each, tulipwood butt sleeve with four ebony-bordered cocobolo designs with opposing ebony-bordered mother-of-pearl triangles through the middle of each between nickel silver rings set in ebony at top and bottom.

MSR (1996) $1,400 $1,600 $1,225 $775

Level 4 P38 - Ebony forearm with white checks set in purpleheart within nickel silver rings above the wrap, four purpleheart-bordered stylized ebony points inlaid with opposing purpleheart-bordered mother-of-pearl triangles at the base of each and a long purpleheart-bordered mother-of-pearl diamond-shaped inlay in each, ebony butt sleeve with four purpleheart-bordered ebony designs with opposing purpleheart-bordered mother-of-pearl triangles through the middle of each between white checks set in purpleheart within nickel silver rings at top and bottom.

MSR (1996) $1,400 $1,600 $1,225 $775

Level 5 P39 - Natural-stained bird's-eye maple forearm with ebony and white checks within nickel silver rings set in ebony above the wrap, six intricate ebony-bordered white points with an ebony- and white-bordered mother-of-pearl diamond-shaped inlay towards the base of each and an ebony line between two opposing ebony triangles within each point, stained bird's-eye maple butt sleeve with six patterns of an ebony- and white-bordered mother-of-pearl diamond-shaped inlay within two inward-pointing ebony-bordered white triangles between ebony and white checks within nickel silver rings set in ebony at top and bottom.

MSR (1996) $1,500 $1,725 $1,300 $850

Level 5 P40 - Cocobolo forearm with ebony and white checks within nickel silver rings set in ebony above the wrap, six intricate ebony-bordered white points with an ebony- and white-bordered mother-of-pearl diamond-shaped inlay towards the base of each and an ebony line between two opposing ebony arrowheads within each point, cocobolo butt sleeve with six patterns of an ebony- and white-bordered mother-of-pearl diamond-shaped inlay within two inward-pointing ebony-bordered white triangles between ebony- and white-checks within nickel silver rings above and below.

MSR (1996) $1,800 $2,050 $1,550 $1,000

Level 5 P41 - Ebony forearm with ebony and white checks within nickel silver rings above the wrap, six intricate holly-bordered bois-de-rose points with an ebony-bordered mother-of-pearl diamond-shaped inlay towards the base of each and a holly line between two opposing mother-of-pearl arrowheads within each point, ebony butt sleeve with six patterns of a bois-de-rose and holly-bordered mother-of-pearl diamond-shaped inlay within two inward-pointing holly bordered bois-de-rose triangles between ebony and white checks within nickel silver rings above and below.

MSR (1996) $2,000 $2,250 $1,700 $1,100

Level 5 P42 - Cocobolo forearm with long cocobolo-bordered mother-of-pearl diamond-shaped inlays set in maple-bordered ebony ovals between the points and ebony and white checks within nickel silver rings set in ebony above the wrap, four intricate floating maple-bordered ebony points with a long cocobolo-bordered mother-of-pearl diamond-shaped inlay in each point, cocobolo butt sleeve with four long cocobolo-bordered mother-of-pearl diamond-shaped inlays set in maple-bordered ebony ovals alternating with four patterns of two inward-pointing ebony triangles within a single long maple border between ebony and white checks within nickel silver rings set in ebony at top and bottom.

MSR (1996) $2,000 $2,250 $1,700 $1,100

GRADING	98%	90%	70%

"JP USA" SERIES

The following "JP USA" Series cue all featured J. Pechauer's Speed Joint. Stain was available in several different colors at no extra charge.

Level 2 JP USA - Stained bird's-eye maple forearm, stained bird's-eye maple butt sleeve.

MSR (1999) $200	$175	$135	$85

"JP" SERIES

The following "JP" Series cues all featured 5/16-14 flat-faced Implex joints with maple stitching in the joint collars. Stain was available on most cues at no extra charge.

Level 2 JP1 - Stained bird's-eye maple forearm with a checked ring above wrap, stained bird's-eye maple butt sleeve with checked ring at top and bottom.

MSR (1999) $220	$195	$145	$90

Level 2 JP2 - Stained bird's-eye maple forearm with a stained bird's-eye maple ring below a checked ring above wrap, stained bird's-eye maple butt sleeve with a thick stained bird's-eye maple ring bordered by checked rings at top and bottom.

MSR (1999) $230	$200	$150	$95

Level 2 JP3 - Stained bird's-eye maple forearm with a checked ring towards bottom, stained bird's-eye maple butt sleeve with pearlized plastic diamond-shaped inlays set in ebony oval borders within checked rings above and below.

MSR (1999) $250	$215	$165	$105

Level 2 JP4 - Stained bird's-eye maple forearm with a black-bordered white ring towards bottom, ebony butt sleeve with intricate pearlized plastic inlays set between metal white and stained bird's-eye maple rings at top and bottom.

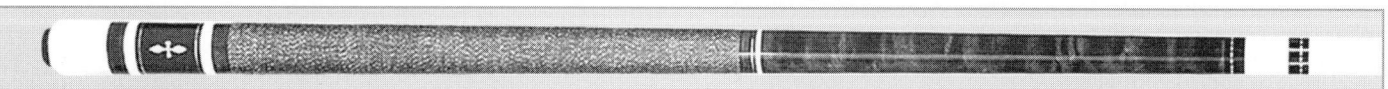

MSR (1999) $270	$225	$170	$110

Level 3 JP5 - Stained bird's-eye maple forearm, maple points with two veneers, maple butt sleeve with cocobolo-bordered maple diamond-shaped inlays between cocobolo and stained bird's-eye maple rings at top and bottom.

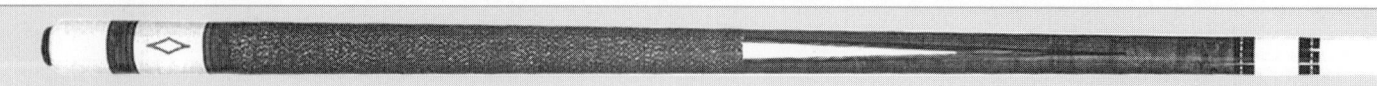

MSR (1999) $290	$240	$180	$115

Level 3 JP6 - Stained bird's-eye maple forearm, maple points with two veneers, maple butt sleeve with cocobolo-bordered diamond-shaped inlays between checked rings and stained bird's-eye maple rings at top and bottom.

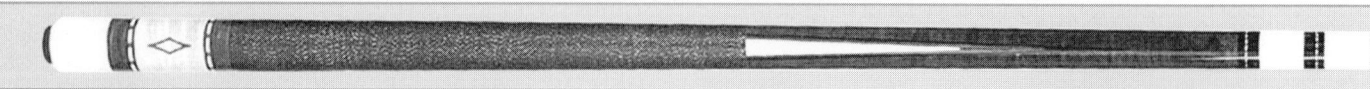

MSR (1999) $290	$240	$180	$115

Level 3 JP7 - Stained bird's-eye maple forearm, ebony-bordered long maple floating points alternating with short ebony floating points, stained maple butt sleeve with ebony-bordered maple diamond-shaped inlays alternating with ebony diamond-shaped inlays between intricate maple checked rings at top and bottom.

MSR (1999) $320	$265	$200	$130

J. PECHAUER CUSTOM CUES, cont.

GRADING	98%	90%	70%

Level 4 JP8 - Stained bird's-eye maple forearm, four ebony-bordered scalloped ivory-colored points alternating with four ebony diamond-shaped inlays, stained bird's-eye maple butt sleeve with four ebony-bordered scalloped ivory-colored reverse pointing inlays alternating with ebony diamond-shaped inlays.

| MSR (1999) $340 | $285 | $220 | $140 |

Level 3 JP9 - Stained bird's-eye maple forearm, four ivory-colored points with ebony veneers, stained bird's-eye maple butt sleeve with four ivory-colored diamond-shaped inlays set in intricate ebony windows between checked rings at top and bottom.

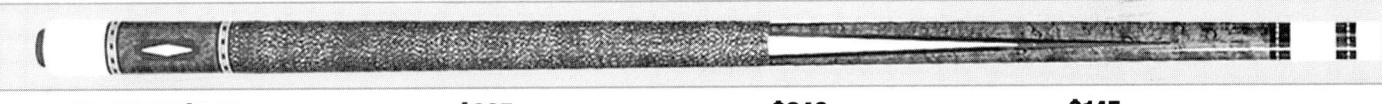

| MSR (1999) $360 | $295 | $240 | $145 |

Level 3 JP10 - Stained bird's-eye maple forearm, four bocote points with ebony veneers, bocote butt sleeve with four pearlized plastic diamond-shaped inlays set in intricate ebony windows between checked rings and stained bird's-eye maple rings at top and bottom.

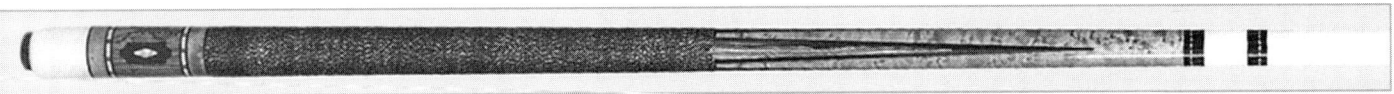

| MSR (1999) $360 | $295 | $240 | $145 |

Level 4 JP11 - Stained bird's-eye maple forearm with a checked ring above wrap, four ivory-colored points with ebony veneers and an ebony spear-shaped inlay in each point, stained bird's-eye maple butt sleeve with four ivory-colored reverse point-shaped inlays with an ebony spear-shaped inlay in each between checked rings at top and bottom.

| MSR (1999) $400 | $325 | $245 | $155 |

Level 3 JP12 - Stained bird's-eye maple forearm with a checked ring above wrap, four ebony points with an ivory diamond-shaped inlay in each, ebony butt sleeve with four ivory-colored diamond-shaped inlays between checked rings at top and bottom.

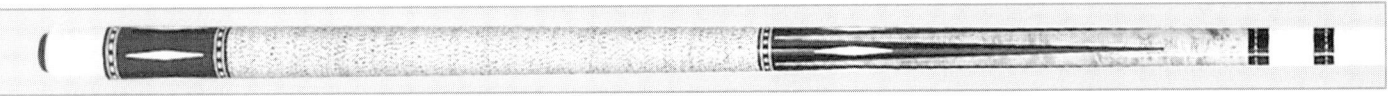

| MSR (1999) $400 | $325 | $245 | $155 |

Level 4 JP13 - Stained bird's-eye maple forearm with checked ring towards bottom, four two-piece ebony-bordered ivory-colored floating points alternating with four ebony diamond-shaped inlays, stained bird's-eye maple butt sleeve with four ebony-bordered ivory-colored arrowhead-shaped inlays alternating with four ebony diamond-shaped inlays between checked rings above and below.

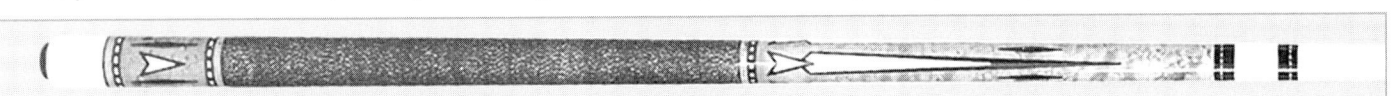

| MSR (1999) $400 | $325 | $245 | $155 |

Level 4 JP14 - Stained bird's-eye maple forearm with a checked ring above wrap, pairs of opposing ebony-bordered ivory-colored floating points alternating with ebony-bordered ivory-colored diamond-shaped inlays, stained bird's-eye maple butt sleeve with pairs of opposing ebony-bordered ivory-colored point-shaped inlays alternating with ebony-bordered ivory-colored diamond-shaped inlays.

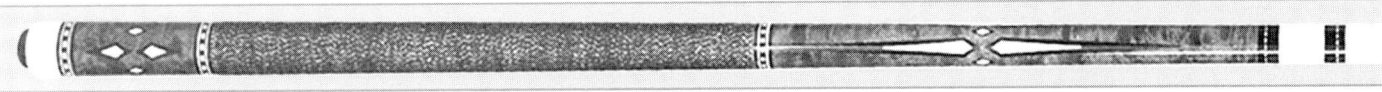

| MSR (1999) $400 | $325 | $245 | $155 |

Level 4 JP15 - Stained bird's-eye maple forearm, four ebony points with three veneers and a pearlized plastic diamond-shaped inlay in each point, ebony butt sleeve with pearlized plastic diamond-shaped inlays in bocote-bordered windows between bocote and metal rings above and below.

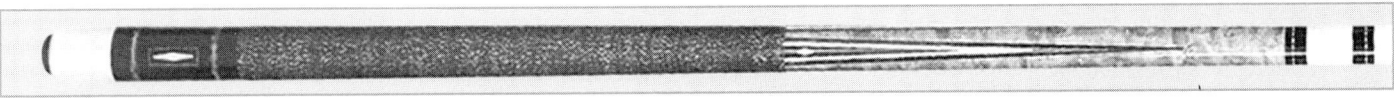

| MSR (1999) $450 | $365 | $275 | $175 |

GRADING	98%	90%	70%

Level 4 JP16 - Stained bird's-eye maple forearm with an intricate checked ring above wrap, intricate five-piece floating points with pearlized plastic four-point spear-shaped inlay in center of each, stained bird's-eye maple butt sleeve with four ebony-bordered pearlized plastic four-point star-shaped inlays set in split ebony windows between intricate checked rings at top and bottom.

MSR (1999) $450	$365	$275	$175

"J. PECHAUER PROFESSIONAL" SERIES

The following "J. Pechauer Professional" Series cues all featured J. Pechauer's Speed-Joint. Stain was available in several different colors at no extra charge.

Level 1 Pro Hustler - Maple forearm, four stained bird's-eye maple points and butt sleeve with black veneers.

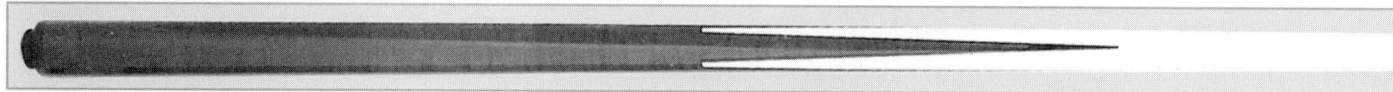

MSR (1999) $260	$220	$165	$105

Level 2 Break Jump - Stained bird's-eye maple forearm with checked ring above wrap, stained bird's-eye maple butt sleeve with checked rings at top and bottom.

MSR (1999) $450	$385	$295	$185

Level 2 PR3 - Stained bird's-eye maple forearm with black and white checks set in metal rings above wrap, stained bird's-eye maple butt sleeve with black and white checks set in metal rings at top and bottom.

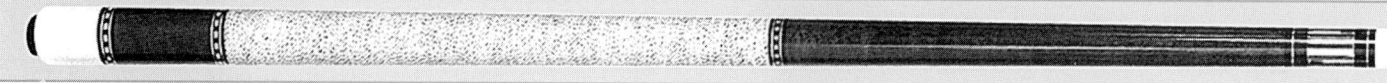

MSR (1999) $360	$315	$240	$155

Level 3 PR4 - Stained bird's-eye maple forearm, four bocote points, bocote butt sleeve.

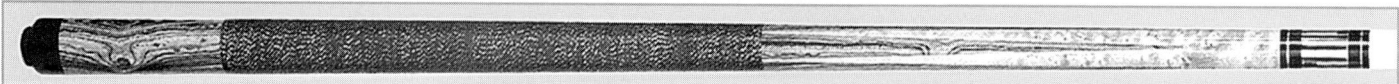

MSR (1999) $380	$335	$245	$160

Level 3 PR5 - Stained bird's-eye maple forearm with a metal ring above wrap, four maple points with black veneers, stained bird's-eye maple butt sleeve with metal rings above and below.

MSR (1999) $400	$350	$265	$170

Level 3 PR6 - Stained bird's-eye maple forearm, four stained bird's-eye maple points with black veneers and an ebony-bordered ivory diamond-shaped inlay in each point, stained bird's-eye maple butt sleeve with ebony-bordered ivory diamond-shaped inlays between checked rings at top and bottom.

MSR (1999) $450	$385	$295	$185

Level 4 PR7 - Stained bird's-eye maple forearm with metal ring above wrap, four intricate floating points with mother-of-pearl diamond-shaped inlay in center, stained bird's-eye maple butt sleeve with four intricate windows with mother-of-pearl diamond-shaped inlays in the center between metal rings at top and bottom.

MSR (1999) $500	$430	$330	$210

J. PECHAUER CUSTOM CUES, cont.

GRADING	98%	90%	70%

Level 4 PR8 - Stained bird's-eye maple forearm with metal rings above wrap, stained bird's-eye maple points with three veneers, ebony handle, stained bird's-eye maple butt sleeve with four reverse stained bird's-eye maple point shaped inlays with three veneers between metal rings at top and bottom.

MSR (1999) $530	$450	$345	$220

Level 4 PR9 - Stained bird's-eye maple forearm, four ebony points with three veneers and an ivory diamond-shaped inlay in each point, ebony butt sleeve with four large ivory diamond-shaped inlays alternating with four small ivory diamond-shaped inlays between checks above and below.

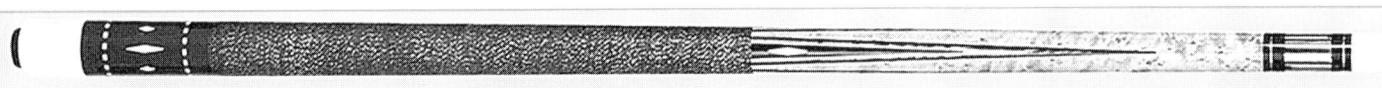

MSR (1999) $550	$465	$355	$225

Level 4 PR10 - Stained bird's-eye maple forearm with checks between metal rings above handle, four bird's-eye maple floating points with three veneers and an ebony-bordered ivory diamond-shaped inlay in each point, bird's-eye maple handle, stained bird's-eye maple butt sleeve with four ebony-bordered ivory diamond-shaped inlays set in maple windows with three veneers between checks set in maple rings at top and bottom.

MSR (1999) $600	$500	$375	$240

Level 4 PR11 - Stained bird's-eye maple forearm with checks within metal rings above wrap, four floating ebony points with three veneers and an ivory diamond-shaped inlay in each point, ebony butt sleeve with four ivory diamond-shaped inlays set in intricate red borders between checks set in metal rings above and below.

MSR (1999) $600	$500	$375	$240

Level 4 PR12 - Exotic hardwood forearm with checks set in metal rings above wrap, four intricate ebony floating points with an ivory spear-shaped inlay in the center of each alternating with four ebony-bordered ivory diamond-shaped inlays, exotic hardwood butt sleeve with four large ivory diamond-shaped inlays with intricate two-piece ebony borders alternating with ebony-bordered ivory diamond-shaped inlays between checks set in metal rings at top and bottom.

MSR (1999) $650	$540	$415	$260

Level 4 PR13 - Stained bird's-eye maple forearm with bocote set in metal rings above handle, four floating maple points with three veneers and a bocote-bordered mother-of-pearl diamond-shaped inlay in each point, bocote handle, stained bird's-eye maple butt sleeve with four bocote-bordered mother-of-pearl diamond-shaped inlays set in maple windows with three veneers between bocote set in metal rings at top and bottom.

MSR (1999) $700	$585	$445	$285

Level 4 PR14 - Stained bird's-eye maple forearm with checks set in metal rings above wrap, six ebony points with an exotic hardwood bordered ivory diamond-shaped inlay in each point, ebony butt sleeve with six exotic hardwood-bordered diamond-shaped inlays between checks set in metal rings above and below.

MSR (1999) $800	$650	$490	$315

GRADING	98%	90%	70%

Level 4 PR15 - Stained bird's-eye maple forearm with checks set in metal rings above wrap, six ebony-bordered hardwood points with an ebony-bordered ivory diamond-shaped inlay in each point, stained bird's-eye maple butt sleeve with six ebony-bordered ivory diamond-shaped inlays set in ebony-bordered exotic hardwood windows between checks set in metal rings at top and bottom.

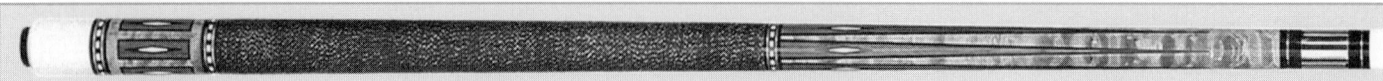

MSR (1999) $900	$735	$550	$350

Level 5 PR16 - Stained bird's-eye maple forearm with checks set in maple rings above wrap, four floating ebony-bordered two-piece maple split floating points with a bordered ivory diamond-shaped inlay in each point alternating with four bordered ivory diamond-shaped inlays set in ebony-bordered maple ovals, stained bird's-eye maple butt sleeve with two ebony-bordered maple triangular barbells alternating with bordered ivory diamond-shaped inlays set in ebony-bordered maple ovals between checks set in metal rings at top and bottom.

MSR (1999) $900	$735	$550	$350

Level 4 PR17 - Cocobolo forearm with checks set in metal rings above wrap, six floating ebony-bordered maple points with an ebony-bordered ivory diamond-shaped inlay in each point, cocobolo butt sleeve with six ebony-bordered ivory diamond-shaped inlays set in ebony-bordered maple windows between checks set in metal rings above and below.

MSR (1999) $950	$775	$585	$380

Level 4 PR18 - Stained bird's-eye maple forearm with checks set in metal rings above wrap, four intricate two-piece floating points with a pair of opposing ivory spear-shaped inlays in each point alternating with four short ivory floating points with two veneers, stained bird's-eye maple butt sleeve with four ivory spear-shaped inlays set in ebony-bordered windows alternating with four ivory spear-shaped inlays with two veneers between checks set in metal rings at top and bottom.

MSR (1999) $1,000	$815	$615	$400

Level 5 PR19 - Stained bird's-eye maple forearm with checks set in metal rings above wrap, six ivory points with ebony veneers and an ebony-bordered turquoise diamond-shaped inlay in each point alternating with six ebony-bordered mother-of-pearl diamond-shaped inlays towards top, stained bird's-eye maple butt sleeve with six ivory reverse point-shaped inlays with ebony veneers and an ebony-bordered turquoise diamond-shaped inlay in each alternating with six ebony-bordered mother-of-pearl diamond-shaped inlays between checks set in metal rings at top and bottom.

MSR (1999) $1,500	$1,150	$875	$550

Level 5 PR20 - Stained bird's-eye maple forearm with checks set in metal rings above wrap, four floating ebony-bordered hardwood points with a pair of opposing ivory spear-shaped inlays around a turquoise dot in the center of each point alternating with ebony-bordered ivory hour-glass-shaped inlays, stained bird's-eye maple butt sleeve with exotic hardwood windows with pairs of opposing ivory spear-shaped inlays with a turquoise dot in center alternating with ebony-bordered ivory hourglass-shaped inlays between checks set in metal rings at top and bottom.

MSR (1999) $1,500	$1,150	$875	$550

Level 4 PR21 - Cocobolo forearm with checks set in metal rings above wrap, six ebony-bordered ivory floating points with turquoise and ivory diamond-shaped inlays in each point, cocobolo butt sleeve with six ivory windows with turquoise and ivory diamond-shaped inlays in each between checks set in metal rings at top and bottom.

MSR (1999) $1,800	$1,350	$1,025	$650

J. PECHAUER CUSTOM CUES, cont.

GRADING	98%	90%	70%

Level 5 PR22 - Ebony forearm with ivory checks above wrap, six ivory-bordered two-piece purpleheart floating points with intricate mother-of-pearl inlays in each point, ebony butt sleeve with ivory and ebony and purpleheart diamond-shaped inlays between ivory checks above and below.

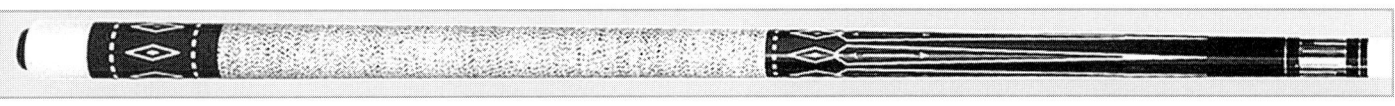

MSR (1999) $2,000	$1,500	$1,150	$700

Level 5 PR23 - Ebony forearm with ivory diamond-shaped inlays set in metal rings above wrap, four super-intricate floating ebony and ivory points, ebony butt sleeve with intricate ivory diamond-shaped inlays in a woven pattern between the ivory diamond-shaped inlays set in metal rings at top and bottom.

MSR (1999) $2,500	$1,950	$1,500	$950

Level 5 PR24 - Cocobolo forearm with checks set in metal rings above wrap, super-intricate ebony and ivory long and short floating points with mother-of-pearl diamond-shaped inlays in centers, cocobolo butt sleeve with an intricate design of ivory, ebony, and mother-of-pearl inlays between checks set in metal rings at top and bottom.

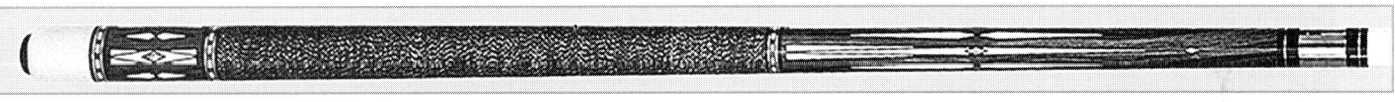

MSR (1999) $3,000	$2,250	$1,725	$1,100

SECONDARY MARKET MINIMUM VALUES (JP SERIES)

The following are minimum values for other J. Pechauer cues encountered on the secondary market. These prices are representative of cues utilizing basic materials and designs that are not currently available. J. Pechauer also offers one-of-a-kind cues that can command many times these prices due to the use of exotic materials and artistry. Early models and limited editions are becoming collectible, and can also command many times these prices. Discontinued J. Pechauer cues will be further covered in future editions.

Special construction note: There are many materials and construction techniques that can add value to J. Pechauer custom cues. The following are the most important examples:

- Add 650+ for ivory points.
- Add 100%+ for precious metals or stones.

For all used J. Pechauer cues:

- Add $100 for each additional original straight playable shaft beyond one.
- Deduct $150 for missing original straight playable shaft.
- Add $60 each for ivory ferrules.
- Deduct 20% for obvious or improper refinish.

Level 2 - 0 points, 0-25 inlays.
Level 2 cues start at	$175	$135	$85

Level 3 - 2-6 points, 0-25 inlays.
Level 3 cues start at	$225	$170	$110

Level 4 - 4-10 points, 0-8 inlays.
Level 4 cues start at	$390	$295	$190

Level 5 - 0-12 points, 9-25 inlays.
Level 5 cues start at	$510	$385	$250

SECONDARY MARKET MINIMUM VALUES (PROFESSIONAL SERIES)

Level 1 - 4 points, hustler.
Level 1 cues start at	$200	$150	$95

Level 2 - 0 points, 0-25 inlays.
Level 2 cues start at	$285	$215	$135

Level 3 - 2-6 points, 0-8 inlays.
Level 3 cues start at	$325	$250	$160

Level 4 - 4-10 points, 9-25 inlays.
Level 4 cues start at	$430	$325	$210

Level 5 - 0-12 points, 26-50 inlays.
Level 5 cues start at	$750	$565	$365

| GRADING | 98% | 90% | 70% |

JOSEPH PECHAUER CUSTOM CUES

Maker of pool cues from 2004 to present in Green Bay, Wisconsin.

Joseph Pechauer learned cuemaking from, and was inspired by, his father Jerry Pechauer. He made his first cue at the age of 12 and started working in the family business at the age of 16. He took numerous classes in machining at technical school.

Pechauer began by watching his dad, and then experimenting with bar cues, adding a joint or wrap and expanding from there.

In 2004, after many years of experience in the cue industry, Joseph started making a few high end custom cues of his own in the J. Pechauer shop. All Joseph Pechauer cues are one-of-a-kind, constructed from the most exotic materials available. Joseph puts his signature on the butt plate and numbers each of his custom made cues. His cues are guaranteed for life against construction defects that are not the result of warpage or abuse.

If you are interested in talking to Joseph Pechauer about a new one-of-a-kind cue or a Joseph Pechauer cue that needs to be repaired, you can contact Joseph at J. Pechauer Custom Cues, listed in the Trademark Index.

SPECIFICATIONS

Butt material: hardwoods
Shaft material: hard rock maple
Standard length: 58 in.
Lengths available: any up to 62 in.
Standard finish: four-part urethane
Standard wrap: leather
Point construction: inlaid
Standard joint: stainless steel
Joint type: piloted
Joint screw thread: patented Pechauer speed joint
Standard number of shafts: two
Standard taper: 12 ½" pro taper
Standard ferrules: ivory
Standard tip: Moori
Tip widths available: any
Other tips available: Triangle
Annual production: fewer than 15 cues

OPTIONS (FOR NEW CUES ONLY)

Layered tip: no charge
Ivory butt cap: $250
Ivory joint: $125
Ivory ferrule: no charge
Leather wrap: no charge
Lizard or other exotic wraps: no charge

REPAIRS

Repairs prices for Joseph Pechauer cues only. For basic repair work, refer to J. Pechauer Custom Cues.
Replace Shaft With ivory ferrule: $200
Replace ivory ferrule: $50
Replace ivory butt cap: $250

CURRENT JOSEPH PECHAER CUES

One-of-a-kind Joseph Pechauer cues start at $4,400. The current delivery time for a Joseph Pechauer cue is several months.

SECONDARY MARKET MINIMUM VALUES

The following are minimum values for Joseph Pechauer cues encountered on the secondary market. Joseph has offered one-of-a-kind cues that can command many times these prices due to the use of exotic materials and artistry.

Special construction note: There are many materials and construction techniques that can add value to Joseph Pechauer cues.

For all used Joseph Pechauer cues, except where otherwise noted:
Add $135 for each additional original straight playable shaft beyond two.
Deduct $200 for each missing original straight playable shaft under two.
Deduct 25% for obvious or improper refinish.

Level 6 - 0-12 points, 51-75 inlays.

	98%	90%	70%
Level 6 cues start at	$4,000	$3,350	$2,400

Level 7 - 0-12 points, 76-125 inlays.

	98%	90%	70%
Level 7 cues start at	$4,500	$3,650	$2,500

Level 8 - 4-20 points, 126+ inlays.

	98%	90%	70%
Level 8 cues start at	$5,000	$4,100	$2,950

PENROSE CUES

Maker of pool cues from 2000 to present in Tilburg, the Netherlands, Europe.

Tom Penrose is an Englishman, living in the Netherlands. His background is in marketing, management, communication and languages. He has been playing billiards since 1992. He started out changing tips as it was too expensive for him to pay to have it done. After a while, Tom began doing cue work for other people, and in 1999 he proved to a friend, as a bet, that he was able to make a cue. He began making cues full time in 2001. He learned from cuemakers including Arnot, Paul Drexler, Dick Neighbors and Dennis Searing. Tom Penrose hand signs his cues, and they can also be identified by his logo in the butt cap of ithe highest end cues. He makes all compunents except bumpers and pins.

If you are interested in talking to Tom Penrose about a new cue or cue that needs to be repaired, you can contact him at Penrose Cues, listed in the Trademark Index.

SPECIFICATIONS

- Butt material: hardwoods
- Shaft material: rock maple
- Standard length: 59 in.
- Lengths available: up to 63 in.
- Standard finish: flexible automotive finish
- Balance point: about 17 in. from butt cap
- Standard butt cap: black fiber
- Standard wrap: Irish linen
- Point construction: full splice
- Standard joint: black fiber
- Joint type: wood-to-wood
- Joint screw thread: Uni-Loc radial pin
- Matching joint protectors: standard
- Standard number of shafts: two
- Standard taper: custom
- Standard ferrules: melamine
- Standard tip: Moori
- Standard tip width: 13 mm
- Tip widths available: any up to 14 mm
- Annual production: fewer than 60 cues

OPTIONS (FOR NEW CUES ONLY)

- Special length: no charge
- Layered tip: Moori only
- Ivory butt cap: $220+
- Ivory butt sleeve: $500+
- Ivory joint: $130+
- Ivory ferrule: $80+
- Ivory points: $150+ each
- Ivory handle: $1200+
- Leather wrap: $100+
- Custom joint protectors: $100+
- Extra shaft: $100

REPAIRS

Repairs can be done on all fine cues. Pricing on request.

CURRENT PENROSE CUES

Two-piece Penrose bar cues, Penrose cues with wraps and joint rings, and one-of-a-kind cuestom Penrose cues start at $850. Penrose cues with points start at $1,100. The current delivery time for a Penrose cue is at least three months, depending on the intricacy of the cue.

SECONDARY MARKET MINIMUM VALUES

The following are minimum values for Penrose cues encountered on the secondary market. These prices are representative of cues utilizing basic materials and designs that are not necessarily available at present. Tom has offered one-of-a-kind cues that can command many times these prices due to the use of exotic materials and artistry.

Special construction note: There are many materials and construction techniques that can add value to Penrose cues.

For all used Penrose cues, except where otherwise noted:

GRADING	98%	90%	70%

Add $85 for each additional original straight playable shaft beyond two.
Deduct $115 for each missing original straight playable shaft under two.
Add $50 each for ivory ferrules.
Add $65 for leather wrap.
Deduct 20% for obvious or improper refinish

	98%	90%	70%
Level 1 - Hustler.			
Level 1 cues start at	$400	$315	$220
Level 2 - 0 points, 0-25 inlays.			
Level 2 cues start at	$600	$470	$325
Level 3 - 2-6 points, 0-8 inlays.			
Level 3 cues start at	$900	$700	$475
Level 4 - 4-10 points, 9-25 inlays.			
Level 4 cues start at	$1,150	$900	$600
Level 5 - 0-12 points, 26-50 inlays.			
Level 5 cues start at	$1,450	$1,150	$800

DALE PERRY

Maker of D.P. Custom Cues. For more information, refer to listing for D.P. Cues.

CRAIG PETERSEN

Maker of pool cues from the early sixties to 1992 in the Chicago, Illinois area.

Craig Petersen started making cues as a teenager around 1963. He had learned to play pool at the YMCA in Evanston, Illinois, a suburb of Chicago. He soon became fascinated with cues, and started doing repairs in a local pool room. Soon, he had a full service shop in that room, but later ended up working in the cue department at Brunswick.

In 1967, Craig got married and moved to California. He was away from cuemaking for the next eight years, returning to Chicago in 1975. For the next ten years, Craig worked off and on for some of the top Chicago area cuemakers.

In 1985, he opened a shop of his own in Bartlett, Illinois. This shop relocated to Addison, Illinois in 1988, and to Fort Wayne, Indiana in 1990. Craig died unexpectedly in 1992, at the age of 46, having made less than one thousand cues. At the time of his death, Craig was in the process of completing his first five-point cue.

Today, Craig Petersen cues are sought after by cue collectors around the world. Later cues are easily identifiable by a "C.P." logo on their butt caps. Craig was famous for extremely sharp and even points. Also, he had a talent for getting inlays, rings, and points to line up perfectly. This was amazing, considering that all work was done by hand with very little equipment. Cues with piloted joints have very thick joints, usually of stainless steel, with very thin pilots.

Craig was a very influential cuemaker whose designs bridged the gap between traditional cues and cutting edge contemporary inlay patterns. Craig's design and construction influence can be seen in many of today's cues and he had a profound direct influence on the early work of Joe Gold of Cognoscenti Cues because of his having trained Joe in the late 1980s.

If you have a Craig Petersen cue that needs further identification or repair, contact Deno Andrews in the Buy, Sell, Trade Index, or Joe Gold of Cognoscenti Cues, listed in the Trademark Index.

SPECIFICATIONS

Butt material: hardwoods
Shaft material: rock maple
Standard length: varies
Lengths encountered: 56 to 64 in.
Standard finish: lacquer
Joint screw: several used
Standard joint: stainless steel
Standard joint type: piloted
Point construction: short splice
Standard butt cap: Delrin
Standard wrap: Irish linen
Standard number of shafts: one
Standard ferrules: ivory
Total production: fewer than 1,000 cues

OPTIONS ENCOUNTERED

Leather wrap
Ivory joint
Joint protectors
Ivory butt cap
Ivory ferrules
Ivory points

| GRADING | 98% | 90% | 70% |

CRAIG PETERSEN CUES

The following cues are representations of the work of Craig Petersen. These cues can be encountered as shown, modified to suit the desires of the original customer, or entirely different designs can be encountered. Petersen specialized in one-of-a-kind cues.

Level 3 Full-splice cue with five veneers, no wrap, brass joint, large ringwork at butt.

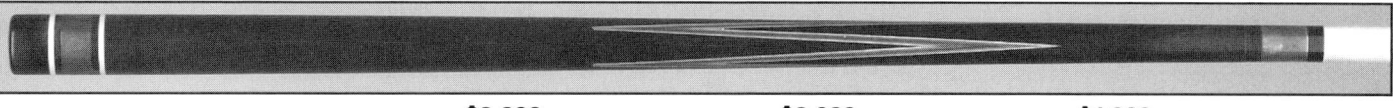

| $3,300 | $2,900 | $1,800 |

Level 3 - Bird's-eye maple nose with four rosewood points and two veneers, Irish linen wrap, ivory joint, Hoppe-style ivory disk at butt. Fancy notched ringwork.

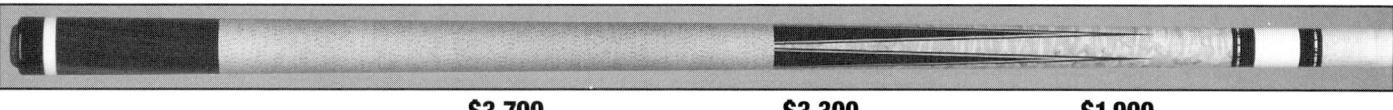

| $3,700 | $3,300 | $1,900 |

Level 4 - Bird's-eye maple forearm with four points of rosewood with black, orange, green, and white veneers. Inlaid dots into maple above points. Butt sleeve is rosewood with six inlaid dots and veneer rings matching those on the prongs. Joint is piloted stainless steel and wrap is Cortland.

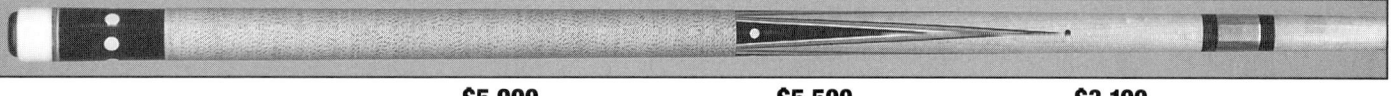

| $5,900 | $5,500 | $3,100 |

Level 4 - Bird's-eye maple forearm with six ivory points (three high and three low). Wrap is Irish linen. Butt sleeve is maple with large ivory windows. Fancy ringwork. Joint is stainless steel.

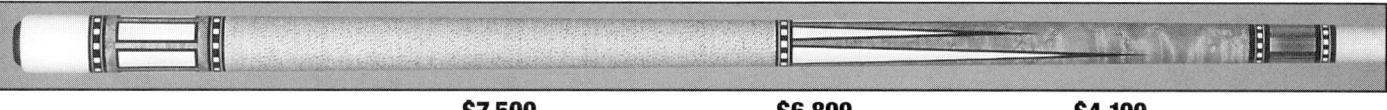

| $7,500 | $6,800 | $4,100 |

Level 4 - Bird's-eye maple forearm with six ebony and veneered points (three high and three low). Wrap is Irish linen. Butt sleeve is ebony with large framed ivory windows. Fancy ringwork. Joint is phenolic. Initials "CP" on butt cap.

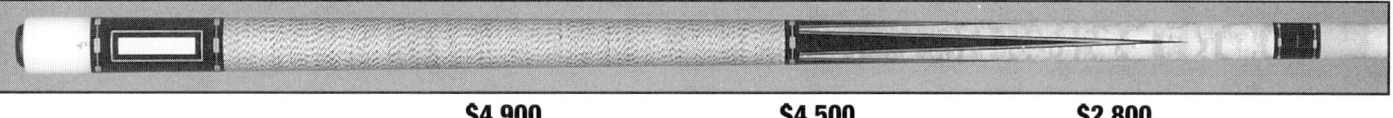

| $4,900 | $4,500 | $2,800 |

Level 4 - Bird's-eye maple forearm with four ebony points and four veneers. Each point inlaid with mother-of-pearl notched dimonds. Wrap is leather. Butt sleeve is ebony with maple windows and inlaid mother-of-pearl notched diamonds. Joint is piloted stainless steel.

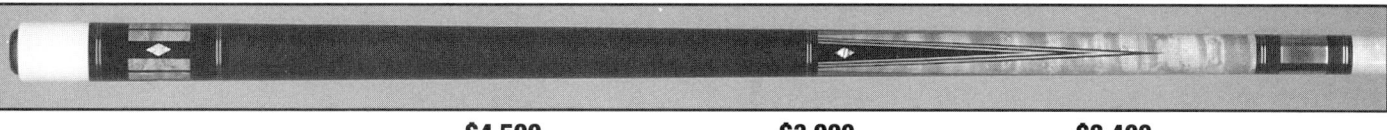

| $4,500 | $3,900 | $2,400 |

Level 4 - Bird's-eye maple forearm with eight ivory points (four high and four low). Wrap is Irish linen. Butt sleeve is ebony with many ivory diamond inlays in window frames. Fancy box-type ringwork. Joint and Hoppe-style disk are ivory.

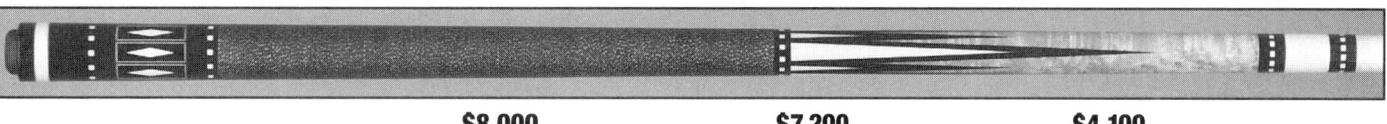

| $8,000 | $7,200 | $4,100 |

Level 5 - Highly figured bird's-eye maple forearm with six spliced ebony points (three high and three low), recut with floating ivory points. The tips of each short point inlaid with ebony and ivory circles, and the long point tips inlaid with a floral design. Wrap is Irish linen. Butt sleeve is ebony with large framed ivory windows and Art-Deco-style ivory inlays between the windows. Fancy ringwork. Joint is phenolic. Butt sleeve is Delrin, where the initials "CP" appear.

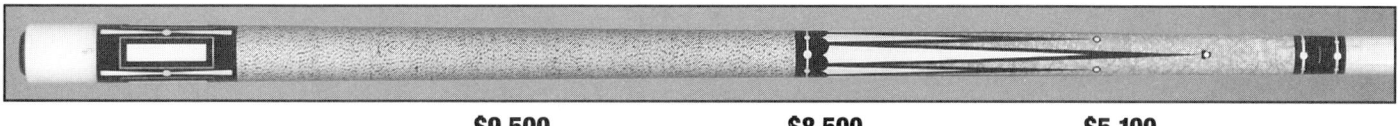

| $9,500 | $8,500 | $5,100 |

GRADING	98%	90%	70%

Level 6 - Bird's-eye maple forearm with eight ebony points (four high and four low). The tips of each short point inlaid with ebony and ivory circles, and the long point tips inlaid with a floral design. Wrap is leather. Butt sleeve is ebony with Art-Deco style ivory inlay work and fancy ringwork. Joint is stainless steel. Butt cap is Delrin, where the initials "CP" appear.

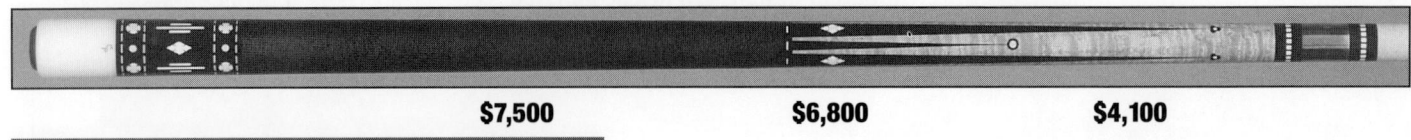

	$7,500	$6,800	$4,100

SECONDARY MARKET MINIMUM VALUES

The following are minimum prices for Craig Petersen cues encountered on the secondary market. These prices are representative of cues utilizing the most basic materials and designs that were available. Craig made many one-of-a-kind cues that can command many times these prices due to the use of exotic materials and artistry. Early variations are becoming very collectible, and can also command many times these prices. Craig Petersen cues will be further covered in future editions.

Due to the rarity of Craig Petersen cues and increasing interest, prices are on the rise. Fewer original examples are surfacing, and collectors are holding on to the ones they have. Unique examples with pedigree, and cues made for top professional players are bringing the highest prices.

Special construction note: There are many materials and construction techniques that can add value to Craig Petersen cues. The following are the most important examples:

- Add $2,500+ for ivory points.
- Add $1,850+ for ivory butt sleeve.

For all Craig Petersen cues:
- Add $450 for each additional original straight playable shaft (standard with one).
- Deduct $450+ for missing original straight playable shaft.
- Add $700 for original ivory joint.
- Add $1000 for original ivory butt plate.
- Add $400 for original leather wrap.
- Add $500 for initials or signature.

Level 1 - 4 points, hustler.

Level 1 cues start at	$1,650	$1,500	$900

Level 2 - 0 points, 0-25 inlays.

Level 2 cues start at	$2,000	$1,800	$1,200

Level 3 - 2-6 points, 0-8 inlays.

Level 3 cues start at	$3,000	$2,750	$1,700

Level 4 - 4-10 points, 9-25 inlays.

Level 4 cues start at	$4,500	$4,000	$2,600

Level 5 - 4-10 points, 26-50 inlays.

Level 5 cues start at	$5,850	$5,100	$3,000

Level 6 - 0-12 points, 51-75 inlays.

Level 6 cues start at	$6,900	$6,450	$3,750

PETREE CUSTOM CUES

Maker of pool cues from 2001 to present in Tulsa, Oklahoma.

J. W. Petree is a full time cuemaker in Tulsa, Oklahoma. He is about 90% self-taught, but picked up tips from various cuemakers. Petree's background is in computers and Internet programming and he has always liked to play pool. He was a custom pen maker who happened to make a joint protector for a friend. That led to making more joint protecters, making shafts, doing cue repairs, and then on to making cues. He makes a lot of points and butt sleeves for other cuemakers. He has always liked working with wood and playing pool. Petree's shop, which started in Edmond, Oklahoma, is now located inside the Tulsa Billiard Palace in Tulsa. As of 2005, J.W. is now making cues full time.

All Petree cues are one-of-a-kind, and are made by J. W. in his one-man shop. J. W. makes his own short-spliced blanks and has CNC capabilities for inlays.

Every Petree cue is signed with "J W Petree" and the year of completion, usually under the joint. Petree Custom Cues are guaranteed for life to the original owner against construction defects that are not the result of warpage or abuse.

If you are interested in talking to J. W. Petree about a new cue or cue that needs to be repaired, you can contact him at Petree Custom Cues, listed in the Trademark Index.

SPECIFICATIONS

Butt material: hardwoods
Shaft material: premium maple
Standard length: 58.5 in.
Lengths available: any

PETREE CUSTOM CUES, cont. 619

GRADING	98%	90%	70%

Standard finish: auto clear urethane
Balance point: varies
Standard butt cap: phenolic
Standard wrap: Irish linen
Point construction: short splice
Standard joint: radial
Joint type: wood-to-wood
Joint screw thread: Uni-Loc Radial
Joint protectors: standard
Standard number of shafts: two
Standard taper: 12 to 14 in. pro
Standard ferrules: Ivorine-3
Standard tip: Hercules
Standard tip width: 13.25 mm
Tip widths available: any
Annual production: fewer than 200 cues

OPTIONS (FOR NEW CUES ONLY)

Special length: no charge
Layered tip: no charge
Ivory butt cap: $125
Ivory joint: $100
Ivory ferrule: $60
Leather wrap: $100
Extra shaft: $100

REPAIRS

Repairs done on all fine cues, but refinishing is available on Petree cues only.
Refinish Petree cue (with Irish linen wrap): $100
Refinish Petree cue (with leather wrap): $200
Rewrap (Irish linen): $50
Rewrap (leather): $100
Clean and press linen wrap: $20
Replace shaft: $125
Replace ivory ferrule: $60
Replace butt cap: $50
Replace ivory butt cap: $125
Replace tip: $10 + cost of tip
Replaced layered tip: $10 + cost of tip
Replace fiber/linen ferrule: $20

CURRENT PETREE CUES

Basic two-piece Petree hustler cues start at $300. Basic two-piece Petree cues with wraps and joint rings start at $450. Petree cues with points start at $600. The current delivery time for a Petree cue is six months.

SECONDARY MARKET MINIMUM VALUES

The following are minimum values for other Petree cues encountered on the secondary market. These prices are representative of cues utilizing basic materials and designs that are not necessarily available at present. JW has offered one-of-a-kind cues that can command many times these prices due to the use of exotic materials and artistry.

Special construction note: There are many materials and construction techniques that can add value to Petree cues.

For all used Petree cues, except where otherwise noted:
    Add $85 for each additional original straight playable shaft beyond two.
    Deduct $100 for each missing original straight playable shaft under two.
    Add $50 each for ivory ferrules.
    Add $80 for leather wrap.
    Deduct 20% for obvious or improper refinish.

Level 1 - Hustler.
	98%	90%	70%
Level 1 cues start at	$275	$235	$145

Level 2 - 0 points, 0-25 inlays.
	98%	90%	70%
Level 2 cues start at	$400	$310	$210

Level 3 - 2-6 points, 0-8 inlays.
	98%	90%	70%
Level 3 cues start at	$500	$385	$260

GRADING	98%	90%	70%
Level 4 - 4-10 points, 9-25 inlays.			
Level 4 cues start at	$650	$500	$335
Level 5 - 0-12 points, 26-50 inlays.			
Level 5 cues start at	$950	$715	$445

pfd STUDIOS

Maker of pool cues from 1989 to present in Marlborough, Connecticut.

Paul and Ellen Drexler

Present Day

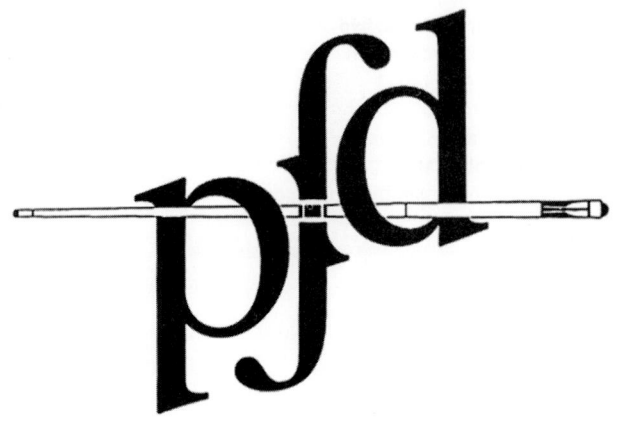

As a young boy, Paul Drexler spent much of his time at his grandfather's workshop. His grandfather, Jeremias Van Neil, was a master cabinetmaker who immigrated to the U.S. from Holland in 1920. He taught his grandson much about woodworking, and helped Paul develop the fundamental skills necessary to become a master craftsman in his own right.

While growing up in New York, Paul saw some of the best players in the world, including Mike Sigel, Irving Crane, and Arthur "Babe" Cranfield in the local halls where he liked to play. Pool was always a part of his life, and while attending Syracuse University, he worked for a billiards company. At the same time, as manager of an art gallery that specialized in custom framing, he also did frame work for many of the University's galleries and private art galleries in central New York, utilizing much of the woodworking skills he learned from his grandfather.

Woodworking remained an interest, but his father, a Harvard Business School graduate working for Eastman Kodak, convinced Paul that his brightest future awaited him in the business world. Paul continued to play pool as a hobby, and one day, after refinishing the pool table in the home he had just built, he decided that he was not satisfied with the cues that he owned. This was in 1989, and Paul set out to combine his woodworking knowledge and his love for pool by making cues while still maintaining his corporate job.

After eight years working in the investment business (four years in the insurance industry, four years selling computer software) Paul set out to do something he really loved.

Two years later, at the 1991 BCA Show, he met and talked to many of the top makers. Paul was especially intrigued with Bert Schrager. In November of 1991, he was invited to visit Bert's shop in California and get some hands-on knowledge about making cues. This trip was such an inspiration that Paul decided to leave the corporate world and devote his full attention to cuemaking.

Paul's cues are easily identified by the "pfd" logo on the butt cap, and he has signed several of his cues on the forearm. In 1994, Paul started to note the month and year of manufacture on the butt cap on many of his more notable creations, and also includes the number of similar cues. Paul significantly improved his equipment in 1998 to some of the most advanced CNC and fourth axis machinery in the industry. Custom software had to be written for Paul's applications. It took about six months to attain peak performance out of this new equipment, which he started using in 1999.

Paul specializes in making one-of-a-kind custom cues to the designs and specifications of individual customers. His wife, Ellen, has become more involved in designing and inlaying the cues. They are among the leaders in creating original, intricate, and artistic cues that also play very well. Paul also makes three simple cues a month with one shaft for $650 to $750 specifically for entry level players. Paul's motto is "different by design," which relates to the uniqueness of his cues.

He guarantees his cues against construction defects that are not the result of warpage or abuse. If you have a pfd cue that needs repair, or would like to talk to Paul about the design of a new custom cue, contact pfd Studios, listed in the Trademark Index.

SPECIFICATIONS

Butt material: exotic hardwoods
Shaft material: rock maple
Standard length: 58 in.
Lengths available: up to 64 in.
Standard finish: urethane
Standard joint screw: Uni-Loc, radial pins
Standard joint: phenolic
Balance point: 18+ in. from butt
Point construction: mitered, inlayed, floating

pfd STUDIOS, cont.

GRADING	100%	95%	70%

Standard wrap: linen
Standard butt cap: phenolic
Standard number of shafts: two
Standard taper: modified European
Standard ferrules: Ivorx, Ivorine
Standard tip: Le Pro, Triangle
Standard tip width: 13 mm
Tip widths available: up to 14.5 mm
Annual production: approximately 100 cues

OPTIONS (FOR NEW CUES ONLY)

Leather wrap: $85
Lizard or other exotic wrap: $250
Ivory ferrule: $65
Ivory butt cap: $300
Ivory butt sleeve: $800
Ivory points: $200 each
Ivory joint: $200
Ivory handle: $3000+
Custom joint protectors: $150+
Extra shaft: $100+
Special length: no charge
Replace Moori tip: $35

REPAIRS

Repairs done only on fine American made cues.
 Refinish (with leather wrap): $350
 Refinish (with linen wrap): $250
 Rewrap (leather): $85
 Rewrap (linen): $35
 Clean and press linen wrap: $20
 Restore leather wrap: $35
 Replace shaft (with fiber/linen ferrule): $125
 Replace shaft (with ivory ferrule): $165+
 Replace fiber/linen/composite ferrule: $100+
 Replace ivory ferrule: $65
 Replace Delrin butt cap: $65
 Replace ivory butt cap: $300
 Replace tip: $10
 Replace layered tip (Moori): $35

CURRENT PFD CUES

Basic two-piece pfd cues with wraps and joint rings start at $650 with one shaft. Four-point pfd cues start at $800, five-point pfd cues start at $1,000, and six-point pfd cues start at $1,200. Eight-point pfd cues start at $1,600. One-of-a-kind custom ordered cues start at $3,000 and include a Whitten case. The current delivery time for a pfd cue is approximately three to six months.

CURRENT EXAMPLES

The following pfd cues can be ordered as shown, modified to suit the desires of the customer or new designs can be created.

Level 2 - Purpleheart forearm with six long ivory lightning bolt-shaped inlays, leather wrap, purpleheart butt sleeve with six long ivory lightning bolt-shaped inlays.

MSR	$1,800	$1,750-2,000	$1,400	$1,000

Level 3 - Ivory joint, bird's-eye maple forearm, four full-spliced purpleheart points with four colored veneers (full-spliced Burton Spain blank), leather wrap, purpleheart butt sleeve with an ivory "Hoppe" ring at bottom.

MSR	$1,800	$1,750-2,000	$1,400	$1,000

GRADING	100%	95%	70%

Level 4 - Ebony forearm with double ivory rings above wrap, five madrone burl points with a madrone burl-bordered ivory spear-shaped inlay at the tip of each point, ebony butt sleeve with five madrone burl reverse points with a madrone burl-bordered ivory spear-shaped inlay at the tip of each point over double ivory rings below wrap.

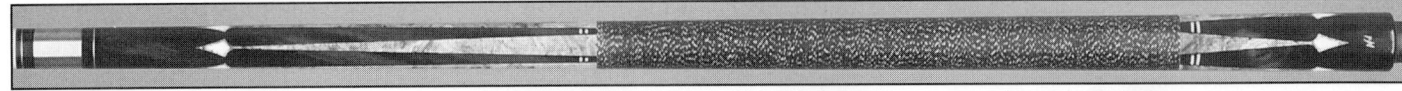

MSR	$1,800	$1,750-2,000	$1,400	$1,000

Level 4 - Ivory joint, purpleheart forearm, five intricate ivory-bordered paua shell points alternating with ivory arched triangle-shaped inlays below ivory dots, leather wrap, purpleheart butt sleeve with five intricate ivory-bordered paua shell windows alternating with pairs of ivory arched triangle-shaped inlays outside pairs of ivory dots.

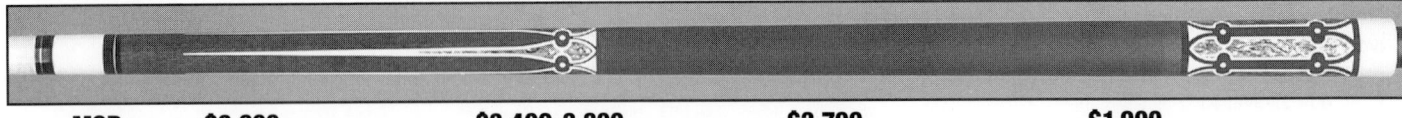

MSR	$3,600	$3,400-3,800	$2,700	$1,900

Level 4 - Bird's-eye maple forearm, four three-piece ivory points with veneers and an ebony inlay in each point, leather wrap, ebony butt sleeve with two veneer-bordered ivory windows alternating with two sets of four hollow ivory diamond-shaped inlays, ivory butt cap.

MSR	$3,800	$3,500-4,000	$2,750	$2,000

Level 5 - Ivory joint, bird's-eye maple forearm with ivory-bordered ebony dots in an arched ebony ring above wrap, three long ebony points with four veneers and a scrimshawed ivory peacock inlay in each point and an ebony-bordered ivory diamond-shaped inlay at the tip of each point alternating with three short ebony points with four veneers and an ivory spear-shaped inlay in each point and an ebony and ivory clover leaf-shaped inlay at the tip of each point, leather wrap, ebony butt sleeve with three ivory double spear-shaped inlays and pairs of scrimshawed ivory dots alternating with three sets of ivory lines between ivory segmented ringwork at top and bottom, ivory butt cap.

MSR	$4,200	$3,950-4,500	$3,100	$2,200

Level 5 "Study In Black and White" - Ivory joint, ebony forearm, six long ivory two-piece points, ebony handle with six intricate ivory-bordered two-piece ebony columns, ebony butt sleeve with six reverse ivory two-piece points, ivory butt cap.

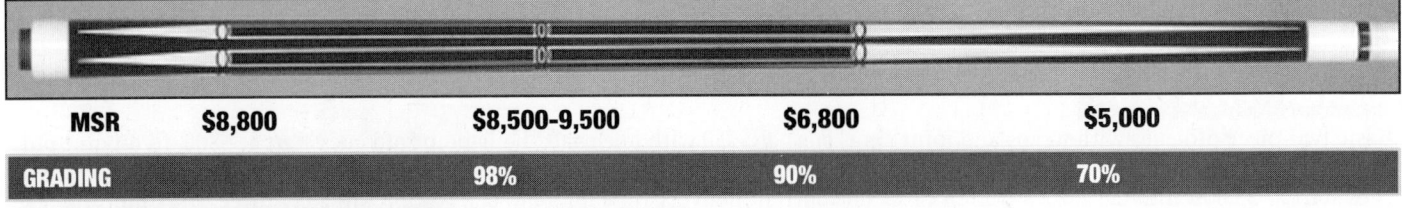

MSR	$8,800	$8,500-9,500	$6,800	$5,000

GRADING	98%	90%	70%

SPECIAL INTEREST PFD CUES

The following limited edition pfd cues were created to comemmorate the 10th and 15th anniversaries of pfd Studios.

Level 5 "10th Anniversary Ebony Artist's Proof" - Ivory joint, ebony forearm with a ring of ivory triangles above wrap, six intricate floating ivory five-piece points, leather wrap, ebony butt sleeve with six intricate reverse ivory four-piece points between rings of ivory triangles at top and bottom, ivory butt cap. (Seven were made in ebony, ten in snakewood.)

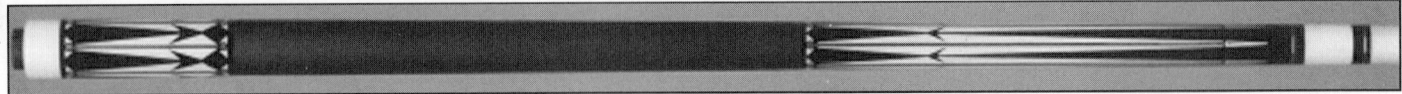

MSR (1999) $2,650	$5,000	$4,000	$2,750

Level 5 "15th Anniversary in Snakewood" - Ivory joint, snakewood forearm with silver and ivory ringwork above wrap, three long and three short two-piece ivory points with a silver spear-shaped inlay at the tip of each, pigskin wrap, snakewood butt sleeve with six two-piece silver circles alternating with pairs of opposing two-piece ivory points between silver and ivory ringwork at top and bottom, ivory butt cap. (Also was available in ebony.)

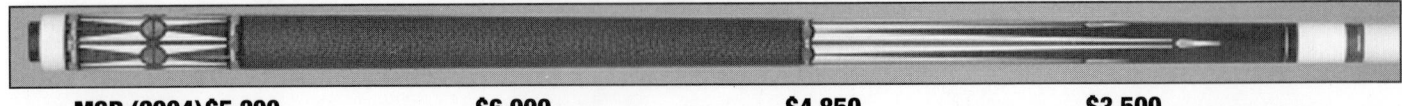

MSR (2004) $5,200	$6,000	$4,850	$3,500

pfd STUDIOS, cont.

GRADING	98%	90%	70%

SECONDARY MARKET MINIMUM VALUES

The following are minimum prices for pfd cues encountered on the secondary market. These prices are representative of cues utilizing basic materials and designs that may not be currently available. Paul currently specializes in one-of-a-kind cues that can command many times these prices due to the use of exotic materials and artistry.

Special construction note: There are many materials and construction techniques that can add value to pfd cues. The following are the most important examples:
- Add $1,200+ for ivory points.
- Add $1,500+ for ivory butt sleeve.

For all used pfd cues:
- Add $95+ for each additional original straight playable shaft beyond two.
- Deduct $100+ for each missing original straight playable shaft under two.
- Add $175+ for ivory joint.
- Add $65+ for leather wrap.
- Deduct 25% for obvious or improper refinish.

	98%	90%	70%
Level 1 - 4 points, hustler.			
Level 1 cues start at	$325	$250	$175
Level 2 - 0 points, 0-25 inlays.			
Level 2 cues start at	$600	$470	$320
Level 3 - 2-6 points, 0-8 inlays.			
Level 3 cues start at	$750	$620	$450
Level 4 - 4-10 points, 9-25 inlays.			
Level 4 cues start at	$1,200	$950	$650
Level 5 - 0-12 points, 26-50 inlays.			
Level 5 cues start at	$2,000	$1,650	$1,150
Level 6 - 0-12 points, 51-75 inlays.			
Level 6 cues start at	$2,500	$2,100	$1,500

PHILLIPPI CUSTOM CUES

Maker of pool cues from 1973 to present in Pasadena, Maryland.

Richard Phillippi made his first pool cue by turning down a broomstick in his high school shop class at the age of 16. Of course, this experiment did not turn out well, but it reflected an interest that would manifest itself into a profession many years later.

At the age of 17, Richard joined the Navy, and spent the next four years traveling and playing pool. It was during this time, while stationed in Norfolk, Virginia, that Richard became friends with Luther "Wimpy" Lassiter. The two would regularly practice together in one of the local pool halls, and later, Richard made a shaft for Lassiter's Balabushka.

Once out of the Navy, Richard went on the road playing pool, and competing in tournaments. Although he was exposed to virtually every cue available, he never found a cue that hit the way he wanted.

1973 to Present Day

Rick and Richard Phillippi

In 1973, at the age of 32, he married and settled in the town of Pasadena, Maryland. Working as a machinist and custom cabinetmaker, Richard started to make custom cues part time.

Phillippi cues are easily identified by Richard's signature on the forearm, a means of identification that has been on every Phillippi cue since he started in 1973. Only if the cue has been poorly refinished will the signature be gone. Richard has constantly been improving his cues to play better and has completely re-engineered the Phillippi cue four times in the last twenty years. The 5/16-14 piloted joint is most often encountered, and a flat-face radial pin joint is also currently available. Although it is very difficult to tell the age of a Phillippi cue, Richard can tell by the construction, which may necessitate removing the wrap.

In the late 1980s, Richard started making cues full-time, and his son, Rick, started in the shop as his apprentice, and has been working full time ever since. When Richard retires, Rick will continue to make cues. Today, Rick and Richard specialize in one-of-a-kind custom cues, costing thousands of dollars. Rick got married to his new wife, Terri Phillippi, in 2005.

Phillippi cues are guaranteed against all construction defects that are not the result of warpage or abuse. If you have a Phillippi cue that needs repair, or would like to talk to Richard about the design of a one-of-a-kind custom cue, contact Phillippi Custom Cues, listed in the Trademark Index.

PHILLIPPI CUSTOM CUES, cont.

| GRADING | 100% | 95% | 70% |

SPECIFICATIONS
Butt material: hardwoods
Shaft material: rock maple
Standard length: 58 in.
Lengths available: 57 to 60 in.
Standard finish: UV cured
Standard joint screws: 5/16-14
Standard joint: stainless steel
Standard joint type: piloted
Balance point: custom
Point construction: short spliced
Standard wrap: Irish linen
Standard butt cap: Delrin
Standard number of shafts: two
Standard taper: custom
Standard ferrules: Aegis
Standard tip: Le Pro
Tip widths available: any
Annual production: approximately 50 cues

OPTIONS (FOR NEW CUES ONLY)
Leather wrap: $100
Ivory joint: $200
Ivory ferrule: $100
Ivory butt cap: $300
Radial pin joint: no charge
Extra shaft: $175
Special length: $25

REPAIRS: (DONE ON ALL CUES)
Refinish cue and shafts: $150
Rewrap (linen): $45
Replace Aegis ferrule: $40
Fit Predator shaft to your cue: $75+
Replace ivory ferrule: $95
Replace shaft: $175+
Replace ivory butt cap: $400

CURRENT PHILLIPPI CUES

Two-piece Phillipi bar cues start at $300. Basic Phillippi cues with wraps and joint rings start at $600. Phillippi cues with points start at $1,000. One-of-a-kind custom Phillippi cues start at $2,000. The current delivery time for a Phillippi cue is approximately six to eight months.

CURRENT EXAMPLES

The following Phillippi cues can be ordered as shown, modified to suit the desires of the customer, or new designs can be created.

Level 2 - Stained bird's-eye maple forearm, stained bird's-eye maple butt sleeve with maple blocks in a ring around bottom.

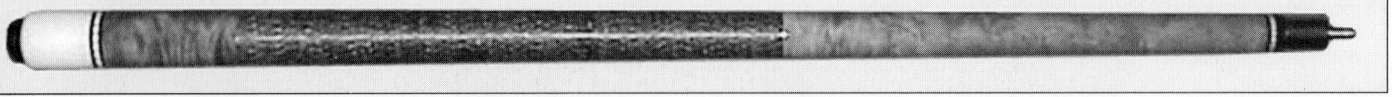

| MSR | $600 | $575-700 | $475 | $350 |

Level 3 - Bird's-eye maple forearm, four ebony points with four colored veneers, ebony butt sleeve.

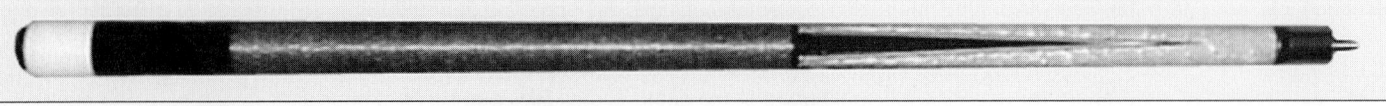

| MSR | $800 | $750-950 | $625 | $450 |

GRADING	100%	95%	70%

Level 4 - Bird's-eye maple forearm with ivory ringwork above wrap, four ebony points with four colored veneers and ivory inlays in each point, ebony butt sleeve with ivory inlays between ivory ringwork at top and bottom.

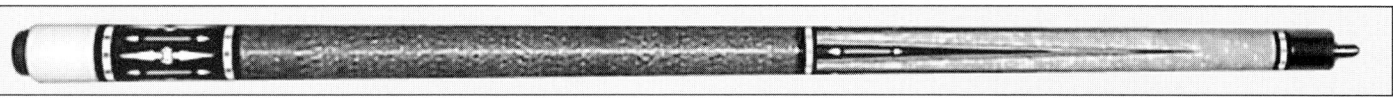

MSR	$2,000	$1,900-2,150	$1,585	$1,200

Level 5 - Bird's-eye maple forearm with pink ivory and ivory ringwork set in ebony above wrap, three long and three short ebony-bordered pink ivory and ivory points, ebony butt sleeve with itricate ivory and pink ivory inlays around center between pink ivory and ivory ringwork at top and bottom.

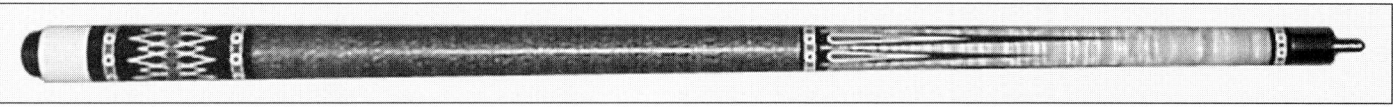

MSR	$3,500	$3,250-3,750	$2,600	$1,800

Level 6 - Ivory joint, bird's-eye maple forearm with pink ivory and ebony ringwork set above ivory above handle, redwood burl handle with ebony-bordered ivory ovals, three long and three short ebony-bordered ivory points, ivory butt sleeve with ebony windows around center between pink ivory and ebony ringwork set in ivory at top and bottom, ivory butt cap.

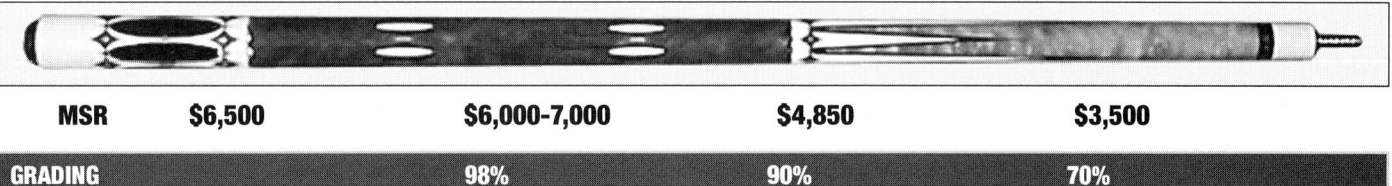

MSR	$6,500	$6,000-7,000	$4,850	$3,500

GRADING		98%	90%	70%

SECONDARY MARKET MINIMUM VALUES

The following are minimum prices for other Phillippi cues encountered on the secondary market. These prices are representative of cues utilizing basic materials and designs that may not be currently available. Richard and Rick currently specialize in one-of-a-kind cues that can command many times these prices due to the use of exotic materials and artistry.

Special construction note: There are many materials and construction techniques that can add value to Phillippi cues. The following are the most important examples:

- Add $1,200+ for ivory points.
- Add $850+ for ivory butt sleeve.
- Add $250+ for ivory joint.
- Add $250+ for ivory butt cap.

For all used Phillippi cues:

- Add $130+ for each additional original straight playable shaft beyond two.
- Deduct $175 for each missing original straight playable shaft under two.
- Add $65+ for each ivory ferrule.
- Add $65+ for leather wrap.
- Deduct 25% for obvious or improper refinish.

Level 1 - 4 points, hustler.

Level 1 cues start at	$250	$195	$130

Level 2 - 0 points, 0-25 inlays.

Level 2 cues start at	$650	$500	$335

Level 3 - 2-6 points, 0-8 inlays.

Level 3 cues start at	$900	$700	$475

Level 4 - 4-10 points, 9-25 inlays.

Level 4 cues start at	$1,350	$1,050	$700

Level 5 - 0-12 points, 26-50 inlays.

Level 5 cues start at	$1,850	$1,450	$950

Level 6 - 0-12 points, 51-75 inlays.

Level 6 cues start at	$2,500	$2,000	$1,350

Level 7 - 0-12 points, 76-125 inlays.

Level 7 cues start at	$3,000	$2,475	$1,875

Level 8 - 4 or more points, 126 or more inlays.

Level 8 cues start at	$4,000	$3,250	$2,400

| GRADING | 98% | 90% | 70% |

ALBERT PICK COMPANY

Maker of pool cues in the 1920s and 1930s in Chicago, Illinois.

After the turn of the century, in the early 1900s, pool was extremely popular in the U.S. Brunswick cues dominated the market. Usually rosewood or ebony was used, and cues either had pointed or butterfly splices in a variety of configurations. The Albert Pick Company in Chicago introduced a very unique line of cues in the 1920s. Colored woods were used, and patented checkered rings and box rings were featured. At the time they were revolutionary, and became very popular in Chicago and the midwest. One-piece and two-piece cues were available, all identifiable by the circular "Albert Pick Co." decal at the bottoms. Some later cues, circa 1929, did not have labels.

Today these cues are sought after by serious collectors. One can see the influence they had on the cues to follow. Many of the rings and designs can be found in similar variations on the custom cues of today. Totally original examples with the original oil or French polish finishes are extremely rare and are quickly appreciating in value.

SPECIFICATIONS

Butt material: hardwoods
Shaft material: rock maple
Standard finish: oil
Standard wrap: Irish linen
Point construction: full splice
Standard number of shafts: one
Standard ferrules: ivory

DISCONTINUED CUES

The following one piece cues are from an Albert Pick catalogue, circa 1920s. They originally had Albert Pick Company stickers on the bottoms and one shaft.

Level 3 "Wallace" - Maple forearm, four full-spliced hardwood points, hardwood handle with veneered checker rings at top and bottom.

| Original Retail (1920s) $1.65 | $1,750 | $1,200 | $750 |

Level 2 "Berkeley" - Maple forearm, carved handle with veneered checker rings at top and bottom.

| Original Retail (1920s) $2.15 | $3,000 | $1,800 | $1,000 |

Level 2 "Coronado" - Maple forearm, hardwood handle with four alternating hardwood checker rings.

| Original Retail (1920s) $2.35 | $3,400 | $1,900 | $1,050 |

Level 2 "Belmont" - Maple forearm, handle of alternating hardwood rings with hardwood checker rings at top and bottom.

| Original Retail (1920s) $2.60 | $3,800 | $2,000 | $1,100 |

Level 3 "Vincent" - Maple forearm, four full-spliced hardwood points, linen wrapped handle with hardwood checker rings at top and bottom.

| Original Retail (1920s) $2.85 | $3,200 | $1,600 | $900 |

Level 3 "Alcazar" - Maple forearm, hardwood handle with three hardwood checker rings at top, bottom, and in center.

| Original Retail (1920s) $3.00 | $3,700 | $2,000 | $1,000 |

ALBERT PICK COMPANY, cont. 627

GRADING	98%	90%	70%

Level 3 - Maple forearm, two pairs of butterfly spliced hardwood points with two veneers, carved hardwood handle.

Original Retail (1920s) $2.25	$2,250	$1,000	$800

Level 3 - Maple forearm, two hardwood butterfly spliced points with two veneers, linen-wrapped handle.

Original Retail (1920s) $1.50	$950	$550	$425

Level 3 - Maple forearm with ebony splice towards tip, four full-spliced hardwood points and handle.

Original Retail (1920s) $3.00	$1,200	$700	$575

SECONDARY MARKET MINIMUM VALUES

The following are minimum values for other Albert Pick cues encountered on the secondary market. These prices are representative of cues utilizing the most basic materials and designs that were available.

Special construction note: There are many materials and construction techniques that can add value to cues.

For all used Albert Pick cues, except where otherwise noted:
- Add $220 for each additional original straight playable shaft beyond one.
- Deduct 55% for missing original straight playable shaft.
- Deduct $100 each for non ivory ferrules.
- Deduct 30% for obvious or improper refinish.

PICONE CUES

Maker of pool cues from 1984 to present in Fort Lauderdale, Florida.

Joseph Picone's first exposure to the game of pool came at the age of twelve. While attending a birthday party that was being held at a local bowling alley, he wandered into the billiard room. The next two hours were spent sitting in a chair watching a number of men playing pool. Not long after that experience, he learned that a nextdoor neighbor, an old woman about eighty years old, had a pool table in her basement. It had belonged to her deceased husband. The table was a nine-foot Susser and Gramaldy, made in the 1920s. After asking a few times, she agreed to let him come over and use it. The table had torn cloth and the cues had no tips. Joe taped down the torn cloth and made tips for the cues by cutting up an old belt. Even as a beginning player, he always felt that using the right cue was important. His first two-piece cue was a Brunswick "Willie Hoppe." He used the cue for a short time before deciding the butt was too fat for his fourteen-year-old hands. He took off the leather wrap and sanded down the entire butt by hand. He played with that cue for two years, turning down many offers to buy it. Most of his teenage years he worked in different poolrooms and was called upon by players to work on their cues, putting on tips, ferrules, wraps and refinishing. All of the work was done by hand.

Joe Picone

During these years, and until it closed, Joseph was a regular customer at a poolroom in Miami called Abes Congress Billiards. Abes Congress Billiards was one of the top action poolrooms in the country. The Congress was open twenty-four hours and it wasn't unusual to stay there for days at a time when things were going on. Players came from all over the country to play at the Congress and with them they brought their cues: Balabushka, Palmer, Paradise, Gina, Martin, Joss, etc. This exposure to fine cues started a fascination with custom cues. It was not long before he was ordering cues from every cuemaker. When he heard about a new cuemaker, he would order a cue. If he got his hands on a broken cue, he would cut it apart to see how the cue was made. This process taught him a lot about what makes a good cue. In 1976 he bought the Gold Crown Billiards in Hollywood, Florida. It wasn't until 1983, when he sold the Gold Crown, that with the encouragement of his wife, Tanya, he began to think seriously about doing cue work. This was before "The Color of Money" and the big pool boom. There were not many cuemakers, and suppliers of cue components and machines to build cues were expensive.

In 1984, while searching for cuemaking equipment, Joseph called Bert Schrager, having heard that he had some equipment for sale. It was already sold, but in the course of the conversation, Bert Schrager said, "If you want to see firsthand what it takes to build a cue, come out here and I'll show you." Joseph jumped at the offer and in a few days flew from Florida to California. The time spent at Bert Schrager's shop saved him many months of frustration. Tim Scruggs was also a big help in getting materials by sharing sources.

After using several kinds of joint designs, Joseph settled on wood to wood with a 3/8-10 screw. This joint went unchanged until 1997 when a radial screw was offered as an option. Butts are built using the short splice with the wrap section made of special hardwood for more natural weight. Joseph's points are longer than most. The standard is five or six points. Joseph likes to build cues of his own design, but he will work with a customer who has something special in mind. Unique designs are produced by selecting rare exotic highly figured hardwoods as well as inlay.

Although some early cues are not signed, starting in about 1986, cues are signed Joseph Picone and dated in front of the wrap. Joseph casts his own bumpers, and tints the rubber to match the color scheme of the cue. Joseph makes all parts except tips and screws. All woods are kept in a climate-controlled environment. Picone cues have a solid, quiet type of play. Joseph feels that with careful material selection and consistent construction methods, it is possible to build cues that reflect the same quality of play from one cue to the next.

Joseph Picone cues are guaranteed against construction defects that are not the result of warpage or abuse. If you have a Picone cue that needs further identification or repair, or would like to order a new Picone cue, contact Picone Cues, listed in the Trademark Index.

SPECIFICATIONS

- Butt material: exotic hardwoods
- Shaft material: rock maple, laminated shafts since 2003
- Standard length: 58 in.
- Lengths available: up to 61 in.
- Balance point: 18.5 to 19 in. from the butt
- Standard finish: catalyzed urethane
- Standard butt cap: linen phenolic
- Standard wrap: Irish linen
- Point construction: short splice
- Joint protectors standard: Delrin
- Standard joint: linen phenolic
- Joint type: flat face
- Joint screw thread: radial
- Standard number of shafts: one
- Standard taper: custom
- Standard ferrules: linen phenolic
- Standard tip: Le Pro, Triangle
- Annual production: approximately 120 cues

OPTIONS

- Special lengths: no charge
- Leather wrap: $60
- Ivory joint: $90
- Extra shaft: $120
- Ivory ferrule: $60
- Ivory butt cap: $110

REPAIRS

- Refinish with linen wrap: $120 (Picone cues only)
- Refinish with leather wrap: $145 (Picone cues only)
- Rewrap linen: $35
- Rewrap leather: $60
- Clean and press linen wrap: $15
- Replace shaft: $120
- Replace ivory ferrule: $60
- Replace Le Pro or Triangle tip: $10
- Replace fiber/linen ferrule: $35
- Replace butt cap: $35
- Replace ivory butt cap: $110
- Replace layered tip: $30

CURRENT PICONE CUES

Two-piece Picone bar cues start at $225. Basic Picone cues with wraps and joint rings start at $450. Basic Picone cues with points start at $650. One-of-a-kind custom Picone cues start at $1,000. The current delivery time for a custom Picone cue is approximately six months.

SECONDARY MARKET MINIMUM VALUES

The following are minimum values for Picone cues encountered on the secondary market. These prices are representative of cues utilizing basic materials and designs that are not necessarily available at present. Joseph Picone has offered one-of-a-kind cues that can command many times these prices due to the use of exotic materials and artistry.

Special construction note: There are many materials and construction techniques that can add value to cues.

For all used cues, except where otherwise noted:

PICONE CUES, cont.

GRADING	98%	90%	70%

Add $100 for each additional original straight playable shaft beyond one.
Deduct $120 for missing original straight playable shaft.
Deduct 20% for obvious or improper refinish.

	98%	90%	70%
Level 1 - 4 points, hustler.			
Level 1 cues start at	$200	$160	$110
Level 2 - 0 points, 0-25 inlays.			
Level 2 cues start at	$400	$320	$220
Level 3 - 2-6 points, 0-8 inlays.			
Level 3 cues start at	$600	$475	$330
Level 4 - 4-10 points, 9-25 inlays.			
Level 4 cues start at	$750	$580	$395
Level 5 - 0-12 points, 26-50 inlays.			
Level 5 cues start at	$1,150	$850	$610
Level 6 - 0-12 points, 51-75 inlays.			
Level 6 cues start at	$1,750	$1,395	$950

PIERCE CUES

Maker of pool cues starting in 1989 in Missoula, Montana.

AUGUSTO "GUS" PINCA

Maker of Ting Cues. For more information, refer to the listing for Ting.

PLAYER'S CUES

Line of pool cues imported from 1991 to present by Cue & Case Sales Corp. in Jacksonville, Florida.
Player's cues are easily identifiable by the "Player's" logo that appears on the butt caps. If you have a Player's cue that needs repair, or would like to talk to someone about ordering a new Player's cue, contact Cue & Case Sales Corp. listed in the Trademark Index.

SPECIFICATIONS

Butt material: hardwoods
Shaft material: rock maple
Standard length: 58 in.
Lengths available: 58 in.
Balance point: 18 in. from butt
Point construction: short splice
Standard wrap: Irish linen
Standard number of shafts: one

REPAIRS

Repairs are not available. Replacements are provided as necessary.

CURRENT PLAYER'S CUES

Current Player's cues retail for $39.99 to $170. The current delivery time is immediate for in-stock models.

SECONDARY MARKET MINIMUM VALUES

The following are minimum prices for Player's cues encountered on the secondary market. These prices are representative of cues utilizing basic materials and designs that may not be currently available.
Special construction note: There are many materials and construction techniques that can add value to Player's cues.
For all used Player's cues:

Add $20+ for each additional original straight playable shaft beyond one.
Deduct 50%+ for missing original straight playable shaft.
Deduct 15% for obvious or improper refinish.

	98%	90%	70%
Level 2 - 0 points, 0-25 inlays.			
Level 2 cues start at	$35	$30	$15
Level 3 - 2-6 points, 0-8 inlays.			
Level 3 cues start at	$50	$35	$20
Level 4 - 4-10 points, 9-25 inlays.			
Level 4 cues start at	$75	$55	$35
Level 5 - 0-12 points, 26-50 inlays.			
Level 5 cues start at	$90	$70	$40

GRADING	100%	95%	70%

PORCUPINE CUES

Distributor of pool cues from 1995 to present in Meridianville, Alabama.

Glen Sadler has been playing pool since he was a kid. While working as a plumbing contractor in the home and commercial construction business, Glen became intrigued with a tip tapper that a friend invented. Glen thought it was a great product, but the inventor never seemed to have enough to sell, and Glen thought it could be marketed better.

So, in 1988, Glen bought the patent rights, and started Porcupine, Inc. Glen's goal with Porcupine, Inc. has been to introduce a new billiard product every year. Although some products have been successful and some have not, every year there has been a new Porcupine product. In 1995, the new product was a line of cues. Glen teamed up with Ken Lane, a cuemaker in Canada, to create a line of Porcupine cues. Ken assembled the cues in Canada, and Glen distributes the cues in the United States. Although production ended in 1997, Glen still has every model in stock.

Porcupine cues are easily identifiable by the Porcupine logo on the butt caps. They feature a stainless steel joint that is thicker than most joints, for a stiffer hit. In 1996, the 5/16-18 flat faced joint was changed to a 5/16-14 piloted joint. Porcupine still offers the Ken Lane series, which were assembled in Canada. The Redstone series, which was assembled in the United States is no longer available.

Porcupine cues are guaranteed for one year against construction defects that are not the result of warpage or abuse. If you have a Porcupine cue that needs further identification or warranty repair, or would like to talk to Glen about ordering a new Porcupine cue, contact Porcupine, Inc., listed in the Trademark Index.

1995 to Present Day

SPECIFICATIONS

Butt material: hardwoods
Shaft material: rock maple
Standard length: 58 in.
Lengths available: 58 in. only
Standard finish: lacquer
Joint screw: 5/16-14
Standard joint: stainless steel
Joint type: piloted
Balance point: approximately 2 in. above wrap
Point construction: short splice
Standard wrap: Irish linen
Standard butt cap: nylon
Standard number of shafts: one
Standard ferrules: fiber
Standard tip: Le Pro
Total production: approximately 1,500 cues

OPTIONS (FOR NEW CUES ONLY)

Extra shaft: $60

REPAIRS

Repairs available for warranty work on Porcupine cues only.

CURRENT EXAMPLES

The following cues are representations of the "Ken Lane" series from Porcupine Inc. These cues are marked "Ken Lane" on the butt caps, on the reverse side of the Porcupine logo. The current delivery time for a Porcupine cue is immediate.

For all used Porcupine cues:
Add $45+ for each additional original straight playable shaft (standard with one).
Deduct $60 for missing original straight playable shaft.

Level 1 KL1 - Maple forearm, four dark hardwood points and butt sleeve.

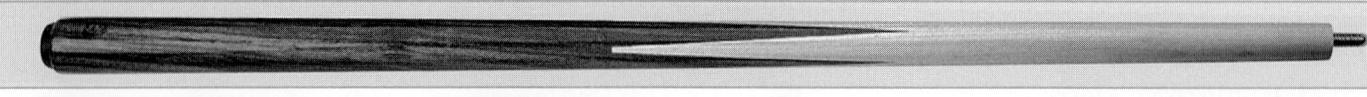

MSR	$120	$95-120	$85	$75

PORCUPINE CUES, cont. 631

GRADING	100%	95%	70%

Level 1 KL1r - Maple forearm, four rosewood points and butt sleeve.

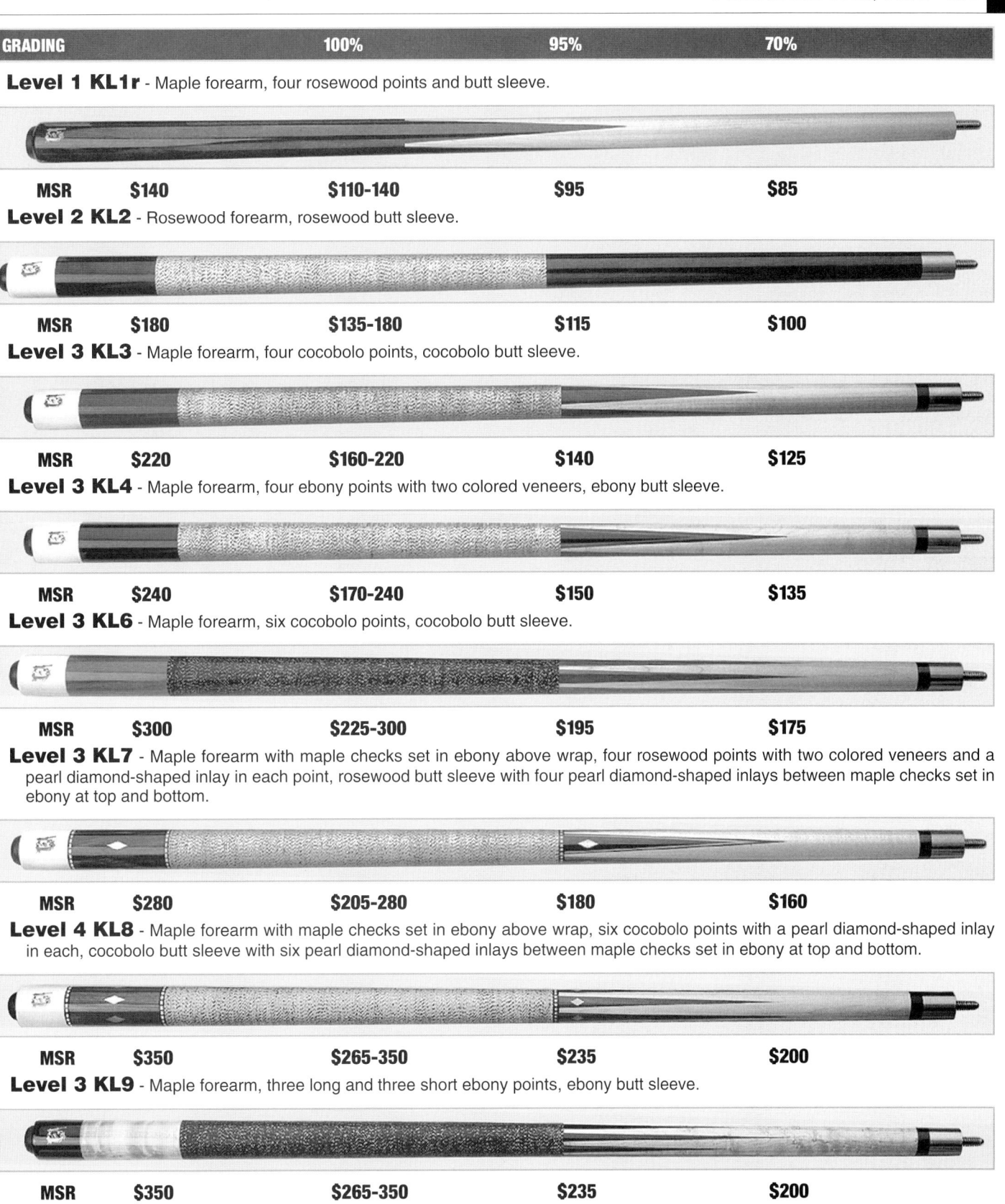

MSR	$140	$110-140	$95	$85

Level 2 KL2 - Rosewood forearm, rosewood butt sleeve.

MSR	$180	$135-180	$115	$100

Level 3 KL3 - Maple forearm, four cocobolo points, cocobolo butt sleeve.

MSR	$220	$160-220	$140	$125

Level 3 KL4 - Maple forearm, four ebony points with two colored veneers, ebony butt sleeve.

MSR	$240	$170-240	$150	$135

Level 3 KL6 - Maple forearm, six cocobolo points, cocobolo butt sleeve.

MSR	$300	$225-300	$195	$175

Level 3 KL7 - Maple forearm with maple checks set in ebony above wrap, four rosewood points with two colored veneers and a pearl diamond-shaped inlay in each point, rosewood butt sleeve with four pearl diamond-shaped inlays between maple checks set in ebony at top and bottom.

MSR	$280	$205-280	$180	$160

Level 4 KL8 - Maple forearm with maple checks set in ebony above wrap, six cocobolo points with a pearl diamond-shaped inlay in each, cocobolo butt sleeve with six pearl diamond-shaped inlays between maple checks set in ebony at top and bottom.

MSR	$350	$265-350	$235	$200

Level 3 KL9 - Maple forearm, three long and three short ebony points, ebony butt sleeve.

MSR	$350	$265-350	$235	$200

JOE PORPER'S CREATIVE INVENTIONS

Maker of pool cues from 1985 to present in Canoga Park, California.

Joe Porper

CREATIVE INVENTIONS

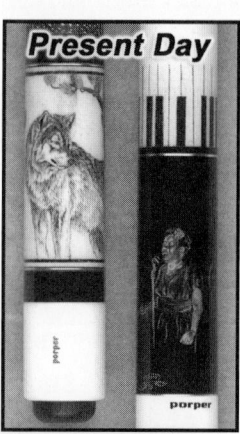
Present Day

Joe Porper grew up around a machine shop. With a father who was a machinist, Joe learned how to build things at a very early age. He also liked to play pool. As an adult, Joe continued to make things. He restored cars and built props for magicians, among other things. He also continued to play pool, and he eventually purchased a beautiful custom cue from Bert Schrager. He wanted a special case for this cue, but could not find what he wanted. So, he designed and built his own case for the cue. Whenever he went into pool halls, other players would try to buy that case. Soon, he was building other examples for his friends.

Before long, the Porper cue case became one of the hottest selling products in the billiard industry. Unfortunately, Joe never patented the design, so the market became flooded with cheap, imported copies. Always coming up with new ideas, Joe designed a new piloted pool cue joint with the step in the butt instead of in the shaft. He had his friend, Jerry Franklin, build him a cue with this joint

1994 to Present Day

design. He liked it so much that he decided to start using the joint in cues that he would make himself.

The Joe Porper cue was introduced in 1985. From the beginning, Joe stressed playability in his cues. To this day, Joe believes that cuemakers should be good players, so they at least know how a good cue should hit. He also believes that designs are limitless, so no one should have to copy other people's work. Joe is always coming up with new ideas for original designs, of which he makes only one, or occasionally two examples. He strives for all Porper cues to have a unique look. All inlay work is done by hand on a pantograph, without the aid of a CNC mill. Although most of his points are floating, so they must be pantographed, Joe also makes short-spliced forearms, if the customer desires.

Joe Porper cues made between 1985 and 1994 are easily identifiable by the "Porper" logo on the butt cap. In 1994, Joe started using a stylized "J.P." instead, which remains to the present. In the summer of 1996, Joe started marking a completion date and serial number on an identification plate under the bumper of all subsequently made Joe Porper cues. A year later he moved into a bigger and more modern facility. He changed his joint from a silver plated 5/16-18 thread screw to a radial pin in 1999.

Recently Joe has been experimenting with a new technique for creating points from exotic stones such as jasper, agate, tiger iron, and lapis. He has also been using exotic hides from snakes and lizards for points and inlays. Most cues are one-of-a-kind and Joe is always coming up with new and different ideas. His scrimshawed buffalo horn, ivory, and sterling silver "Ballad of Blues" cue won the People's Choice Award at the 1999 Gallery of American Cue Art in New York.

Porper cues still feature the softer hitting reverse piloted concave cone joint that screws into a linen phenolic insert in the shaft. Another one of Joe's new developments is his laminated "Lama" tip that is standard on all of his cues, or can be purchased separately. Laminated leather wraps, a Joe Porper original, is available on Joe Porper cues only. He also markets a line of lathes specifically designed for cuemakers. Lately Joe has slowed down on making cues to further persue the design and construction of magicians' props.

Joe Porper cues are guaranteed indefinitely to the original owner against construction defects that are not the result of warpage or abuse. If you have a Joe Porper cue that needs further identification or repair, or would like to talk to Joe about ordering a new Joe Porper cue, contact Joe Porper's Creative Inventions listed in the Trademark Index.

SPECIFICATIONS

Butt material: hardwoods
Shaft material: rock maple
Standard length: 58 in.
Lengths available: any
Standard finish: two-part urethane
Joint screw: custom radial pin
Standard joint: linen phenolic
Joint type: flat faced
Balance point: approximately 1 1/2 in. above wrap

JOE PORPER'S CREATIVE INVENTIONS, cont.

GRADING	98%	90%	70%

Point construction: pantographed
Standard wrap: Irish linen
Standard butt cap: linen phenolic
Standard number of shafts: two
Standard taper: 11 in. pro
Standard ferrules: melamine
Standard tip: laminated buffalo
Tip widths available: any
Annual production: approximately 100 cues

OPTIONS (FOR NEW CUES ONLY)

Joe Porper offers almost every option imaginable, the price of which depends on the design and price of the individual cue.

REPAIRS

Repairs done only on Joe Porper cues.
Refinish (with leather wrap): $300
Refinish (with linen wrap): $150
Rewrap (leather): $125
Rewrap (linen): $40
Replace linen phenolic butt cap: $30
Replace ivory butt cap: $140
Replace shaft: $90
Replace melamine ferrule: $20
Replace ivory ferrule: $65

CURRENT JOE PORPER CUES

Basic Porper cues with wraps and joint rings start at $700. Porper cues with points start at $1,200. One-of-a-kind Joe Porper cues start at $3,500. The current delivery time for a custom Joe Porper cue is approximately six months.

SECONDARY MARKET MINIMUM VALUES

The following are minimum prices for Joe Porper cues encountered on the secondary market. These prices are representative of cues utilizing basic materials and designs that may not be currently available. Joe also offers one-of-a-kind cues that can command many times these prices due to the use of exotic materials and artistry.

Special construction note: There are many materials and construction techniques that can add value to Joe Porper cues.

For all used Joe Porper cues:
Add $75+ for each additional original straight playable shaft beyond.
Deduct $90 for each missing original straight playable shaft under two.

	98%	90%	70%
Level 1 - 4 points, hustler. Level 1 cues start at	$350	$275	$185
Level 2 - 0 points, 0-25 inlays. Level 2 cues start at	$650	$510	$345
Level 3 - 2-6 points, 0-8 inlays. Level 3 cues start at	$1,000	$785	$550
Level 4 - 4-10 points, 9-25 inlays. Level 4 cues start at	$1,350	$1,050	$700
Level 5 - 0-12 points, 26-50 inlays. Level 5 cues start at	$1,850	$1,450	$1,000
Level 6 - 0-12 points, 51-75 inlays. Level 6 cues start at	$2,450	$1,950	$1,350
Level 7 - 0-12 points, 76-125 inlays. Level 7 cues start at	$3,000	$2,400	$1,750

JERRY POWERS

Maker of Jerico Cues. For more information, refer to listing for Jerico.

PRATHER CUE

Maker of pool cues from 1975 to present in Mooreland, Oklahoma.

Dan Prather was a pilot and building contractor in Mooreland, Oklahoma in the early 1970s. He loved the game of pool, and enjoyed a woodworking hobby. Verl Horn, long time cuemaker and friend, came to Dan and asked him to cut and construct some cue materials. Dan discovered then how high priced cue components really were. By the late 1970s, Dan could see that there was a market for someone to supply quality cuemaking components to cuemakers at a reasonable price. From peddling parts out of a suitcase to a showroom at the BCA Show, Prather's has become one of the leading suppliers of cue components, and the largest source for Irish linen in the United States. Although Prather's is probably best known for making components for custom cuemakers, they also make custom cues themselves.

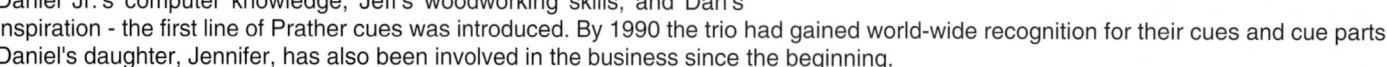
Jeff, Dan, Jennifer, and Daniel Prather

Daniel's two sons, Daniel Jr. and Jeff, moved to Mooreland in the mid-1980s to form the business "by PRATHER, inc.," with subsidiaries Prather cues and Prather parts. Using their combined unique talents - Daniel Jr.'s computer knowledge, Jeff's woodworking skills, and Dan's inspiration - the first line of Prather cues was introduced. By 1990 the trio had gained world-wide recognition for their cues and cue parts. Daniel's daughter, Jennifer, has also been involved in the business since the beginning.

Prather cues are identifiable by a signature on the forearm, and also have "PRATHER" along with the year etched on the butt cap screw. Most Prather cues were custom made for individuals to their design and specifications until 1993, when the first line was introduced. Now Prather no longer makes a line of cues, just one-of-a-kinds. Because of this, their production has been reduced significantly. Six-point Prather cues are very rare, as only one or two are made a year. Prather makes every component in all of their cues.

Many unique one-of-a-kind Prather cues have been made for tournaments, gallery showings, and cue shows. In 2004, five of these cues were stolen from a gallery in Oklahoma. The stolen cues, which were pictured in color in the First or Second Editions of the Blue Book of Pool Cues, consist of the "Bomber Cue," "Zeus' Abacus," "Golden Avenue," "Floral Tapestry," and "Marscessant Pearl." A custom case was also stolen. The cues are pictured on the Prather website. Jeff will custom build a beautiful one-of-a-kind custom cue for the person whose information leads to the recovery of the five stolen cues.

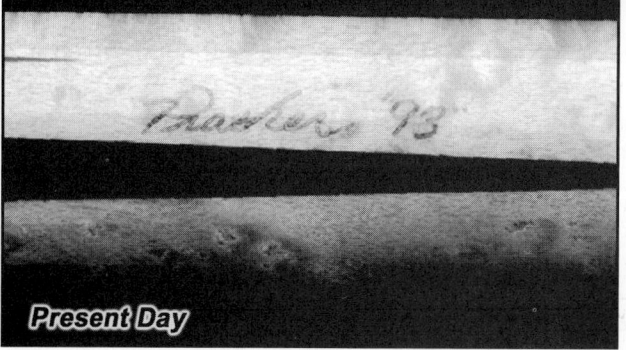
One-of-a-kind / Present Day

Weight bolt under bumper

Dan is still involved in the business, and he also enjoys fishing, flying, building planes, traveling to Thailand, and collecting cues. Daniel Jr. is a musician and has mastered several instruments; also, he enjoys creating graphic art images, designing exotic cue art, and listening to music. They all feel very lucky to be able to make a living at what they do.

The company moved into a new 9,000-square-foot facility on Main street in Mooreland, Oklahoma, just four blocks from the original shop, in 2000, and continues to grow. They now are involved in selling, installing, and repairing pool tables as well.

Prather Cue insists on 100% customer satisfaction, and will indefinitely repair any defects in workmanship that are not the result of abuse. If you have a Prather cue that needs further identification or repair, would like to order one of the following cues, or would like to talk to Jeff about your idea for a one-of-a-kind cue, contact Prather Cues, listed in the Trademark Index.

SPECIFICATIONS

Butt material: hardwoods
Shaft material: rock maple
Standard length: 58 in.
Lengths available: 57 to 62 in.
Standard finish: automotive clear coat
Joint screw: 3/8-11
Standard joint: flat faced
Joint type: flat faced
Balance point: custom
Point construction: short splice and inlaid

GRADING	100%	95%	70%

Standard Wrap: Irish linen (optional wood handle)
Standard butt cap: linen base fiber
Standard number of shafts: one
Standard taper: custom
Standard ferrules: linen base fiber
Standard tip: custom
Tip widths available: 11 to 15 mm
Annual production: less than 150 cues

OPTIONS (FOR NEW CUES ONLY)

Leather wrap: $150
Joint protectors: $45+
Extra shaft: $120+
Special length: $50
Ivory ferrule: $100

REPAIRS

Repairs done only on Prather's cues
Refinish: $100
Replace butt cap: $40+
Rewrap (leather): $150
Rewrap (linen): $45
Replace shaft: $120+

CURRENT PRATHER CUES

Two-piece Prather bar cues start at $350. Basic Prather cues with wraps and joint rings start at $450. Prather cues with points start at $550. One-of-a-kind custom Prather cues start at $500. The current delivery time for a Prather cue is eight to twelve weeks.

CURRENT EXAMPLES

The following Prather cues can be ordered as shown, modified to suit the desires of the customer, or new designs can be created. Prather Cue currently specializes in one-of-a-kind custom cues.

Level 3 - Bocote forearm, three long and three short holly-bordered tulipwood points, bocote butt sleeve with holly dashes set in tulipwood rings at top and bottom.

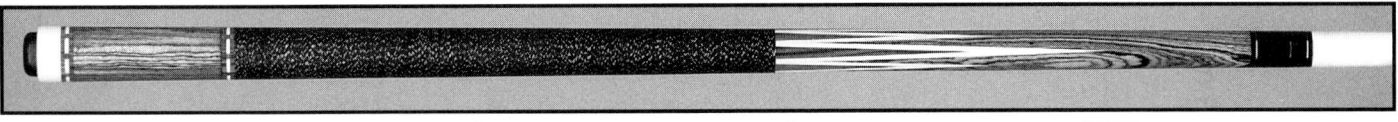

| MSR | $900 | $850-1,000 | $685 | $495 |

Level 3 - Ebony forearm with four reverse holly points coming down from joint above a holly-checked ring above wrap, four holly points, ebony butt sleeve, four holly windows with holly and ebony veneers and a holly checked ring below wrap.

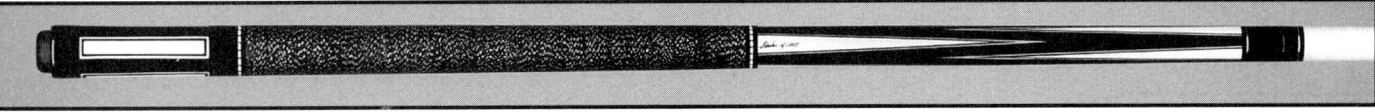

| MSR | $1,200 | $1,100-1,350 | $925 | $700 |

Level 4 - Bird's-eye maple forearm with ringwork above wrap, four long ebony points with four colored veneers alternating with four short ebony points with a mother-of-pearl dot in each, ebony butt sleeve with mother-of-pearl notched diamond-shaped inlays and mother-of-pearl dots within ringwork at top and bottom.

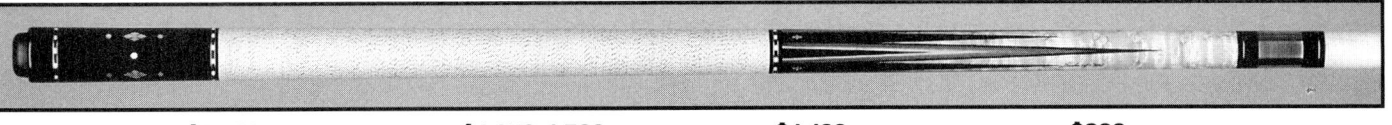

| MSR | $1,400 | $1,350-1,500 | $1,100 | $800 |

Level 4 - Ebony forearm with a pink ivory and ivory stitch ring set in ebony above wrap, four long buck-eye burl points alternating with four short pink ivory points, pink ivory butt sleeve with four intricately inlayed ivory diamond-shaped inlays below a pink ivory and ivory stitch ring below wrap.

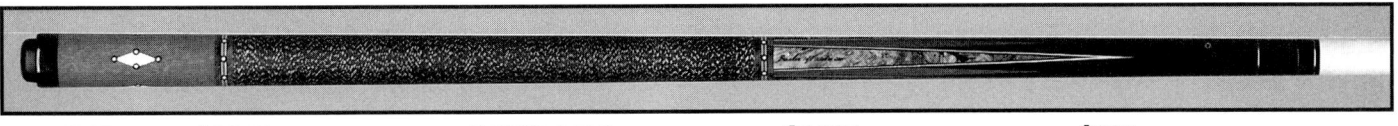

| MSR | $1,600 | $1,500-1,750 | $1,225 | $900 |

GRADING	98%	90%	70%

DISCONTINUED EXAMPLES
The following cues are representations of lines available from Prather's Custom Cues. These cues could be ordered as shown, modified to suit the desires of the customer, or new designs could be created. These designs can still be ordered as custom cues.

P-SERIES
The following P-Series cues had stainless steel joints, nickel silver joint rings, and Irish linen wraps.

Level 3 P-1 - Stained curly maple forearm, three long and three short ebony points, ebony butt sleeve.

MSR (1996) $465	$500	$390	$270

Level 3 P-2 - Ebony forearm, four tulipwood points, tulipwood butt sleeve with an ebony crown-patterned ring at bottom.

MSR(1996) $500	$550	$375	$295

Level 3 P-3 - Bird's-eye maple forearm, four ebony points with colored veneers and single mother-of-pearl diamond in each point, bird's-eye maple butt sleeve with four mother-of-pearl diamonds set in ebony rectangles coming down from wrap.

MSR (1996) $674	$750	$580	$395

Level 4 P-4 - Lightly stained bird's-eye maple forearm, three long and three short floating ebony points each inlaid with large or small ivory diamonds, lightly stained bird's-eye maple butt sleeve with three small ebony lines between three large ebony-bordered ivory diamonds.

MSR(1996) $759	$850	$665	$445

Level 4 P-5 - Bird's-eye maple forearm, four long and four short ebony points with colored veneers and short bodark lines inlaid in each long point, ebony butt sleeve with four hollow pink ivory windows that are pierced by bodark lines coming down from wrap.

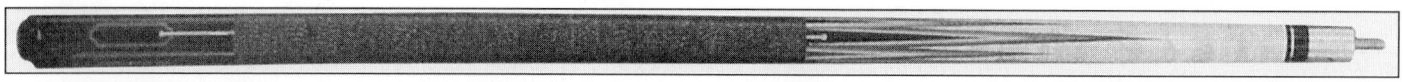

MSR(1996) $720	$800	$615	$420

Level 4 P-6 - Bird's-eye maple forearm, four lacewood points with colored veneers, lacewood butt sleeve with eight ebony-bordered ivory diamonds with ebony rectangles between them set in a ring pattern.

MSR(1996) $754	$845	$660	$440

Level 4 P-7 - Lightly stained bird's-eye maple forearm, four ebony points with colored veneers and short bird's-eye maple lines inlaid in each point and longer ebony lines inlaid between each point, ebony butt sleeve with four long thin bird's-eye maple inlays coming down from wrap each inlaid with a line of ebony with shorter maple lines coming down from wrap in between.

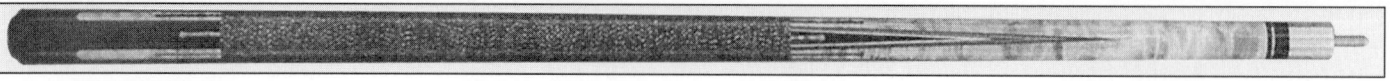

MSR(1996) $709	$800	$610	$410

Level 4 P-8 - Ebony forearm, six lightly stained curly maple points with lightly stained curly maple-bordered ebony spears at the end of each, lightly stained curly maple butt sleeve with six ebony-bordered lightly stained curly maple spears.

MSR(1996) $741	$840	$635	$415

GRADING	98%	90%	70%

Level 4 P-9 - Bird's-eye maple forearm, four long and four short cocobolo points with an ivory diamond in each long point, bird's-eye maple butt sleeve with four downward-pointing cocobolo points with cocobolo rectangles between them inlaid with two ivory diamonds in each.

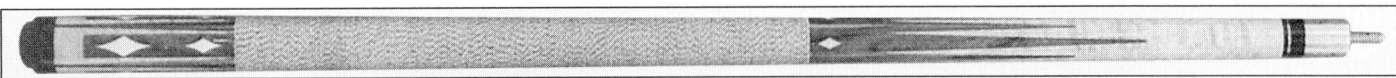

MSR(1996) $988	$1,100	$865	$595

Level 5 P-10 - Lightly stained bird's-eye maple forearm, with four long and four reversed short ebony points with an ivory diamond in each, lightly stained bird's-eye maple butt sleeve with four upward-pointing and four downward-pointing ebony points with an ivory diamond in each.

MSR(1996) $1,043	$1,200	$945	$650

Level 4 P-11 - Darkly stained bird's-eye maple forearm, for pink ivory points with ebony veneers and ebony-bordered pink ivory spears at the ends of each point, ebony butt sleeve with four spear patterns and four spider patterns inlaid in pink ivory.

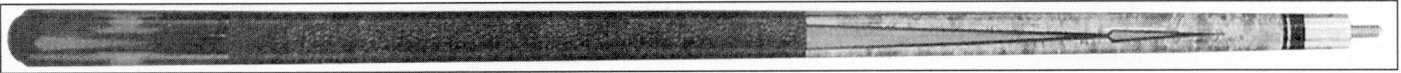

MSR(1996) $1,067	$1,225	$965	$660

Level 5 P-12 - Cocobolo forearm, three long and three short bird's-eye maple points with colored veneers and bodark-bordered pink ivory spears at the end of each point, bird's-eye maple butt sleeve with six cocobolo rectangles inlaid with a total of 30 bird's-eye maple triangles above a ring pattern of twelve bodark and twelve pink ivory inlays.

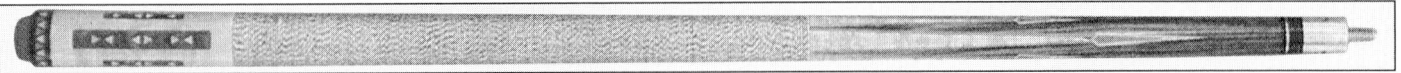

MSR(1996) $1,123	$1,250	$975	$670

Level 4 P-13 - Dark-stained bird's-eye maple forearm, four long and four short ebony points with colored veneers and ebony-bordered snakewood diamonds at the end of each point and snakewood diamonds inlaid in each point, darkly stained bird's-eye maple butt sleeve with eight snakewood diamonds inlaid between ring patterns of 16 ebony inlays above and below.

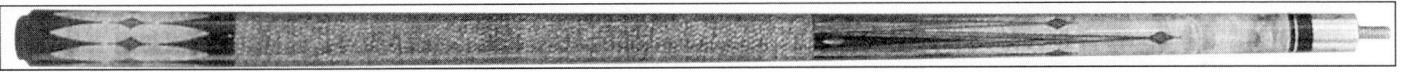

MSR(1996) $1,143	$1,275	$985	$680

Level 4 P-14 - Bird's-eye maple forearm, four pink ivory points with purpleheart and ebony veneers, ebony butt sleeve with four purpleheart-bordered pink ivory ovals with ivory diamonds between them and slotted pink ivory ring patterns above and below.

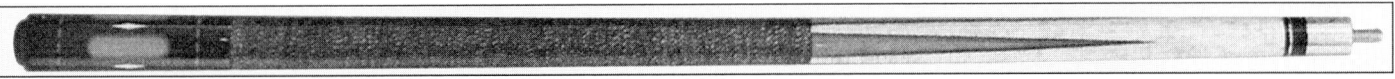

MSR(1996) $1,240	$1,400	$1,095	$750

201, 301, AND 401 SERIES

The following Prather cues had 5/16-14 piloted joints. The 201 Series and 301 Series cues came with one shaft. The 401 Series cues came with two shafts.

Level 2 201a - Cordia forearm, bird's-eye maple handle and butt sleeve.

MSR (1999) $250	$295	$235	$160

Level 2 201b - Cocobolo forearm, bird's-eye maple handle and butt sleeve.

MSR (1999) $300	$350	$270	$185

GRADING	98%	90%	70%

Level 4 201c - Bird's-eye maple forearm, three floating purpleheart points, purpleheart handle and butt sleeve with three floating bird's-eye maple points and sets of six ebony-bordered abalone ovals at top and bottom.

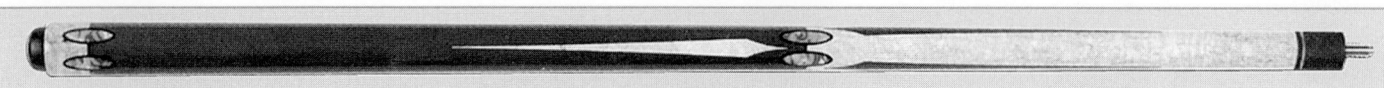

MSR (1999) $780	$865	$670	$455

Level 4 201d - Cocobolo forearm, four curly maple floating points with four ebony-bordered marble diamond-shaped inlays at the base of each point, curly maple handle and butt sleeve with four ebony-bordered marble diamond-shaped inlays at bottom.

MSR (1999) $475	$550	$420	$285

Level 2 201e - Cocobolo forearm, bird's-eye maple handle and butt sleeve with two ebony-bordered marble dots surrounded by cocobolo lines.

MSR (1999) $460	$510	$345	$265

Level 3 201f - Ebony forearm, six full-spliced red heart points extending to butt with six ivory dots between the points.

MSR (1999) $430	$500	$390	$270

Level 5 201g - Cocobolo forearm, three curly maple floating points alternating with woven curly maple designs, curly maple handle and butt sleeve with three cocobolo floating points alternating with woven cocobolo designs.

MSR (1999) $395	$435	$340	$225

Level 4 201h - Ebony forearm, three bird's-eye maple floating points, bird's-eye maple handle and butt sleeve with three floating ebony reversed points and six ebony-bordered amboyna burl ovals at top and bottom.

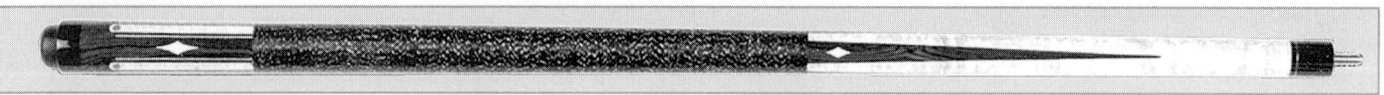

MSR (1999) $730	$825	$640	$435

Level 4 301a - Bird's-eye maple forearm, four cocobolo points with an ivory diamond-shaped inlay in each point, cocobolo butt sleeve with four ivory diamond-shaped inlays alternating with four bird's-eye maple slots with a marble dot at the bottom of each.

MSR (1999) $870	$950	$715	$450

Level 4 301b - Cocobolo forearm, three bird's-eye maple floating points with an ebony dot in the center of a cordia diamond-shaped inlay in each point, cocobolo butt sleeve with three ebony dots in cordia diamond-shaped inlays.

MSR (1999) $535	$595	$460	$310

Level 4 301c - Cordia forearm, four bird's-eye maple floating points with an ebony-bordered ivory diamond-shaped inlay in each point, cordia butt sleeve with four ebony-bordered ivory diamond-shaped inlays atop bird's-eye maple windows.

MSR (1999) $712	$820	$635	$430

PRATHER CUE, cont. 639

GRADING	98%	90%	70%

Level 4 301d - Cocobolo forearm, six bird's-eye maple points with a bird's-eye maple bordered cocobolo spear-shaped inlay at the tip of each point, cocobolo butt sleeve with six bird's-eye maple reverse point-shaped inlays with bird's-eye maple bordered cocobolo spear-shaped inlays at the tip of each.

MSR (1999) $554	$615	$465	$300

Level 4 301e - Ebony forearm with an ivory dash ring towards bottom, three cocobolo floating points with curly maple borders, ebony butt sleeve with an ivory dash ring towards top above three curly maple-bordered cocobolo reverse point-shaped inlays.

MSR (1999) $740	$800	$620	$420

Level 4 301f - Bird's-eye maple forearm, four ebony points with an ivory diamond-shaped inlay in each point, ebony butt sleeve with two ebony diamond-shaped inlays set in ivory windows alternating with two ivory diamond-shaped inlays.

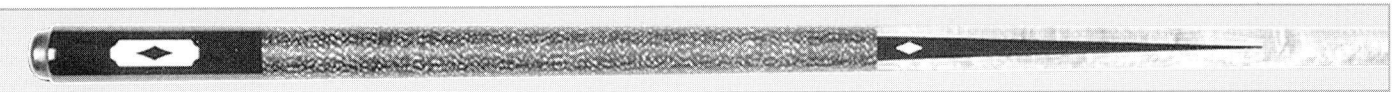

MSR (1999) $540	$600	$465	$315

Level 4 301g - Cocobolo forearm with bird's-eye maple dashes towards bottom, four floating bird's-eye maple points with an ebony-bordered ivory diamond-shaped inlay towards the tip of each, cocobolo butt sleeve with curly maple dash rings towards top above four ebony-bordered ivory diamond-shaped inlays over bird's-eye maple windows.

MSR (1999) $760	$800	$625	$425

Level 3 301h - Ebony forearm, three curly maple floating points alternating with three curly maple-bordered marble diamond-shaped inlays, ebony butt sleeve with three curly maple reverse point-shaped inlays alternating with three curly maple-bordered marble diamond-shaped inlays.

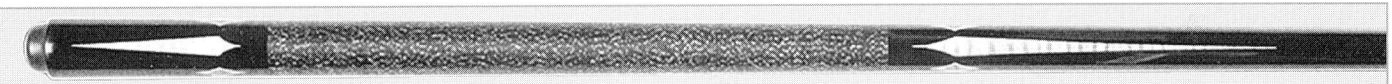

MSR (1999) $570	$600	$465	$320

Level 4 401a - Cocobolo forearm with six ebony-bordered bird's-eye maple dots, three floating bird's-eye maple points, bird's-eye maple handle with six cocobolo floating point-shaped inlays, cocobolo butt sleeve with six floating bird's-eye maple point-shaped inlays between rows of six ebony-bordered maple dot-shaped inlays at top and bottom.

MSR (1999) $1,225	$1,300	$1,000	$685

Level 4 401b - Bird's-eye maple forearm with ivory dashes above wrap, four ebony points with an ivory diamond-shaped inlay in each point, ebony butt sleeve with four sets of four ivory diamond-shaped inlays between ivory dashes above and below.

MSR (1999) $1,325	$1,385	$1,170	$725

Level 4 401c - Cocobolo forearm with a nickel silver ring above wrap, six floating curly maple points alternating with six abalone crosses set in curly maple-bordered amboyna burl ovals, cocobolo butt sleeve with six abalone crosses set in curly maple-bordered amboyna burl ovals alternating with six abalone lines between nickel silver rings at top and bottom.

MSR (1999) $1,350	$1,400	$10,35	$745

GRADING	98%	90%	70%

Level 7 401d - Ebony forearm with a ring of ivory arrowhead shapes towards bottom, five two-piece maple burl floating points with five ivory caps inlaid around each and two cocobolo inlays around each, ebony butt sleeve with seventy intricate inlays of maple burl and cocobolo and ivory.

MSR (1999) $1,500	$1,550	$1,200	$800

Level 7 401e - Cocobolo forearm, five olivewood floating points surrounded by eight intricate ivory and amboyna burl and olivewood inlays, cocobolo butt sleeve with five intricate olivewood inlays surrounded by twelve intricate ivory and amboyna burl and olivewood inlays.

MSR (1999) $1,575	$1,600	$1,245	$850

SECONDARY MARKET MINIMUM VALUES

The following are minimum prices for other Prather's cues encountered on the secondary market. These prices are representative of cues utilizing basic materials and designs that may not be currently available. Dan and Jeff also offer one-of-a-kind cues that can command many times these prices due to the use of exotic materials and artistry.

Special construction note: There are many materials and construction techniques that can add value to Prather's cues.

For all used Prather cues, except where otherwise noted:
- Add $100+ for each additional original straight playable shaft beyond one.
- Deduct $120 for each missing original straight playable shaft.
- Deduct 25% for obvious or improper refinish.

Level 1 - Hustler.

Level 1 cues start at	$275	$235	$145

Level 2 - 0 points, 0-25 inlays.

Level 2 cues start at	$400	$315	$215

Level 3 - 2-6 points, 0-8 inlays.

Level 3 cues start at	$500	$385	$265

Level 4 - 4-10 points, 9-25 inlays.

Level 4 cues start at	$650	$505	$340

Level 5 - 0-12 points, 26-50 inlays.

Level 5 cues start at	$850	$660	$440

Level 6 - 0-12 points, 51-75 inlays.

Level 6 cues start at	$1,250	$975	$650

PRECISION CUE DESIGN

For more information refer to Barenbrugge cues.

PREDATOR CUES

Maker of pool cues distributed from 1994 to present by Predator Cue in Jacksonville, Florida.

Predator cues are the result of the collaboration of two men using scientific research for the first time to develop the best hitting cue they could. Allan McCarty, the president of Clawson Cues in Michigan, teamed up with cuemaker Steve Titus, in 1992, to create a cue with minimal deflection.

Allan had experimented with spliced shafts in the past, but he had never seen one as well executed as the one Steve was playing with when they met. Allan immediately hired Steve as a technician to head up the necessary scientific testing on cues. Allan had been planning on creating a robot to test cues, and he knew that Steve had the technical ability to pull it off. They designed and built a robot, which they named "Iron Willie," to stroke shots with perfect consistency. With the cue being the only variable in the testing, they began to determine what factors reduced deflection and increased power. They found that the ferrule was the one variable that had the most effect on deflection, so they concentrated their efforts on the first ten inches of the cue. By scientifically developing a special ferrule and a hollow cavity inside the first five inches of the shaft, they were able to get the front of the cue to deflect off of the ball instead of the ball deflecting off the cue. This meant that the tip actually stayed on the ball longer on contact, resulting in more power. According to tests using Iron Willie, the Predator cues had 25% less deflection than any other cue tested. To increase radial consistency and decrease the likelihood of warpage, they developed spliced shafts. Although many people believe that the spliced shafts are the secret behind the Predator's playability, the engineering at the front of the shaft is the real secret. Jim Lucas later joined the team to provide manufacturers for the butts and to offer his distribution channels. Clawson developed the Predator Cat logo in 1994, with the Cat comprising features of several different predatory felines.

Since 1995, Clawson Cue has gone by the name Predator Cue to avoid confusion. They manufacture the shafts, and the butts are made elsewhere, to their specifications. Early spliced shafts were six- or twelve-piece, but they soon settled on a ten-piece, centrally aligned, radial-spliced shaft. Very early examples of Predator cues had the special ferrules and inserts without the spliced shafts. The early experimental shafts are quickly becoming collectible, with twelve-piece shafts now bringing $350 or more. Generally, the earlier the Predator shaft, the longer the ferrule will be. The Predator Cat logo started to appear on 314 shafts in 2001.

1994 to Present Day

1994 to 2001

The Predator 2 was introduced in May of 1999. It featured a 10-piece radially spliced butt with a Uni-Loc joint. Predator set out to develop the most accurate cue that modern technology would allow, and used that technology to develop the Predator 2. A high-speed camera capable of taking 12,000 frames a second was used to determine what really happens when a tip hits a ball. This information was used to design a cue from tip to bumper that would minimize squirt and deflection. The butts and shafts on every Predator 2 were weighed and matched to help provide a variety of weights and balance points, and each cue had a serial number on a metal ring at the bottom. A new urethane wrap

2003 to Present Day

2001 to Present Day

similar to leather was developed for the handle. The Predator 2 has been redone and improved upon, and is now available in eight different models.

In 2002 Predator changed from its original 5/16-14 piloted stainless steel joint to the Uni-Loc joint. In 2003 Predator introduced the Z shaft. Like the 314 shaft, the Z shaft is hollow for the first five inches. But the Z shaft has a shorter ferrule, is thinner at 11.75 mm, and it has a lower deflection European taper.

Predator shafts are available for most fine cues. Predator Cue is presently using scientific research to develop a superior tip.

All Predator cues are easily identifiable by the Predator Cat logo on the butt cap, and the shafts are marked with a Cat logo and "314" or "Z" above the joint rings.

Predator shafts are guaranteed indefinitely against manufacturing defects that are not the result of warpage or abuse. If you have a Predator cue or shaft that needs replacement, or would like to order a new cue or new shaft for your existing cue, contact Predator Cue, listed in the Trademark Index.

SPECIFICATIONS

Butt material: hardwoods
Shaft material: spliced rock maple
Standard length: 58 in.
Lengths available: 58 to 59 in.
Standard finish: UV urethane
Joint screw: 5/16-14
Standard joint: Uni-Loc
Point construction: inlaid
Standard butt cap: linen phenolic
Standard wrap: Irish linen
Standard taper: 15 in. pro
Standard number of shafts: one
Standard tip: water buffalo
314 tip width available: 12 3/4 mm only
Z tip width available: 11.75 mm only
Annual production: approximately 8,000 shafts

PREDATOR CUES, cont.

GRADING	100%	95%	70%

OPTIONS (FOR NEW CUES ONLY)
Extra 314 shaft: $250+
Extra Z shaft: $275+
Special length: $10 for 30 in. shaft
Joint protectors: $25
Moori tip: $25

REPAIRS
In case of manufacturing defects, Predator cues and shafts will be replaced while still under the warranty period.
314 shaft: $230+
Z shaft: $255+

CURRENT EXAMPLES
The following cues are currently available from Predator Cue. The current delivery time for most Predator cues is three to five days.

PREDATOR BREAK CUES
The following Predator BK break cues all come standard with one Predator Strong Taper 314 shaft with a hard tip. Predator BK break cues have Uni-Loc joints standard. Irish linen wrap is a $20 option. There currently is a several month delivery time for Predator BK break cues.

Level 2 BK - Black-finished maple forearm with "Predator BK" and the Predator cat logo on the forearm, black-finished maple butt sleeve.

MSR	$375	$325-400	$370	$210

PREDATOR SNEAKY PETES
The following Predator Sneaky Petes cues all come standard with one Predator 314 shaft. A Predator Z Shaft is a $25 upgrade. All cues shown have Uni-Loc joints and all except for the SPWU have stainless steel joints.

Level 1 SPWU - Maple forearm, four full-spliced rosewood points and handle with four black- and green-colored veneers.

MSR	$355	$300-355	$250	$195

Level 1 SPJU - Maple forearm, four full-spliced rosewood points and handle with four black- and green-colored veneers.

MSR	$405	$345-405	$295	$225

Level 1 SPJLW - Maple forearm, four full-spliced rosewood points and handle with four black- and green-colored veneers, Irish linen wrap, rosewood butt sleeve.

MSR	$445	$375-445	$315	$250

PREDATOR 4K SERIES
The following Predator 4K Series cues all come with one Predator 314 shaft. A Predator Z Shaft is a $25 upgrade. All cues shown have stainless steel Uni-Loc joints and German nickel silver rings on the joint collars.

Level 2 4K1 - Black-stained maple forearm with double silver rings above wrap, black-stained maple butt sleeve with double silver rings at top and bottom.

MSR	$545	$450-545	$370	$275

GRADING	100%	95%	70%

Level 2 4K2 - Burgundy-stained bird's-eye maple forearm with double silver rings above wrap, burgundy-stained bird's-eye maple butt sleeve with double silver rings at top and bottom.

MSR	$585	$480-585	$400	$305

Level 3 4K3 - Curly maple forearm with double silver rings above wrap, four floating ebony points with two veneers, curly maple butt sleeve with double silver rings at top and bottom.

MSR	$695	$570-695	$485	$385

Level 4 4K4 - Burgundy-stained bird's-eye maple forearm with double silver rings above wrap, four ebony-bordered curly maple floating two-piece points with an ebony-bordered abalone diamond-shaped inlay in the center of each point, burgundy-stained bird's-eye maple butt sleeve with four ebony-bordered curly maple two-piece windows with an ebony-bordered abalone diamond-shaped inlay in the center of each window between double silver rings at top and bottom.

MSR	$865	$700-865	$615	$500

Level 4 4K5 - Bird's-eye maple forearm with double silver rings above wrap, four intricate ebony and synthetic ivory-bordered ebony two-piece floating points with an ebony-bordered mother-of-pearl diamond-shaped inlay in the center of each point, bird's-eye maple butt sleeve with four intricate ebony and synthetic ivory-bordered ebony two-piece windows with an ebony-bordered mother-of-pearl diamond-shaped inlay in the center of each window between double silver rings at top and bottom.

MSR	$915	$740-915	$640	$530

Level 4 4K6 - Rosewood forearm with double silver rings above wrap, four intricate synthetic ivory-bordered three-piece rosewood floating points with a turquoise diamond-shaped inlay between two opposing turquoise spear-shaped inlays in each point, rosewood butt sleeve with four intricate synthetic ivory-bordered two-piece rosewood windows with a turquoise diamond-shaped inlay between two opposing turquoise spear-shaped inlays in each window between double silver rings at top and bottom.

MSR	$965	$775-965	$675	$565

Level 4 4K7 - Bird's-eye maple forearm with double silver rings above wrap, four intricate ebony and synthetic ivory-bordered ebony multi-piece floating points with an ebony-bordered mother-of-pearl diamond-shaped inlay in the center of each point, bird's-eye maple butt sleeve with four intricate ebony and synthetic ivory-bordered ebony multi-piece windows with an ebony-bordered mother-of-pearl diamond-shaped inlay in the center of each window between double silver rings at top and bottom.

MSR	$1,145	$925-1,145	$825	$700

PREDATOR P2 CUES

The following Predator P2 cues all come standard with one Predator 314 shaft. A Predator Z shaft is a $25 upgrade. Predator P2 cues have stainless steel Uni-Loc joints and numbered stainless steel butt caps. Irish linen wrap is a $50 option. Leather wrap is a $150 option. Weights are adjustable from 18.5 to 20.5 ounces. Predator P2 cues are made to order with a three- to five-week delivery time. Three of the eight different current models are shown.

Level 2 P2B - Ten-piece radially spliced ebony-colored butt.

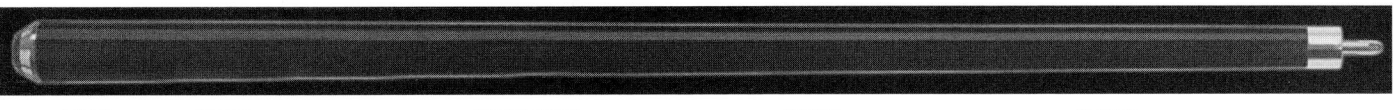

MSR	$695	$635-695	$525	$400

GRADING	100%	95%	70%

Level 2 P2LC - Ten-piece radially spliced leopard wood and curly maple butt.

MSR	$895	$800-895	$665	$500

Level 2 P2C - Ten-piece radially spliced curly maple butt.

MSR	$995	$885-995	$745	$575

PREDATOR P2 "10TH ANNIVERSARY"

The following Predator P2 10th Anniversary cue comes standard with a choice of a Predator 314 shaft or a Predator Z shaft. A Moori tip is standard. These cues have stainless steel Uni-Loc joints and stainless steel butt caps numbered one to sixty.

Level 2 P2 10th Anniversary - Stained highly figured bird's-eye maple butt with a ten-piece radially spliced curly maple core.

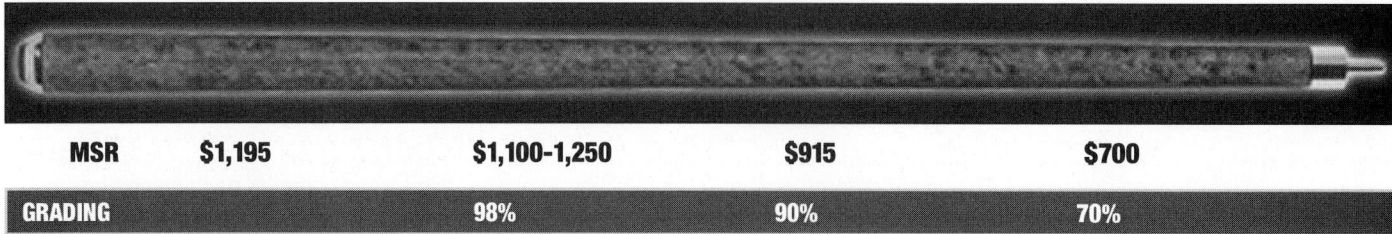

MSR	$1,195	$1,100-1,250	$915	$700

GRADING	98%	90%	70%

DISCONTINUED EXAMPLES

PREDATOR 1996 SERIES

The following Predator 1996 series cues all came with one 314 shaft, except for the 314-6, which came with two 314 shafts. All six cues had piloted stainless steel joints with 5/16-14 pins and 314-2 through 314-6 had German nickel silver rings on the joint collars. They are shown with early "Predator First Edition" butt cap markings without the Predator Cat logo.

Level 2 314-1 - High gloss black-stained maple forearm, high gloss black-stained maple butt sleeve.

MSR (1996) $420	$450	$350	$235

Level 2 314-2 - Golden-stained bird's-eye maple forearm with a German nickel silver ring set in black above wrap, golden-stained bird's-eye maple butt sleeve with German nickel silver rings set in black at top and bottom.

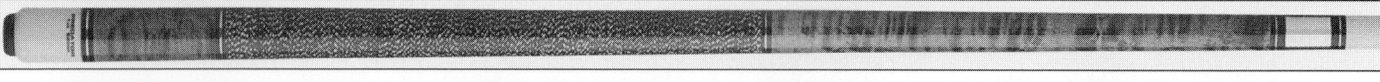

MSR (1996) $500	$550	$425	$285

Level 3 314-3 - Dark walnut-stained bird's-eye maple forearm with a German nickel silver ring set in black above wrap, four ebony points with four colored veneers, ebony butt sleeve with German nickel silver rings set in black at top and bottom.

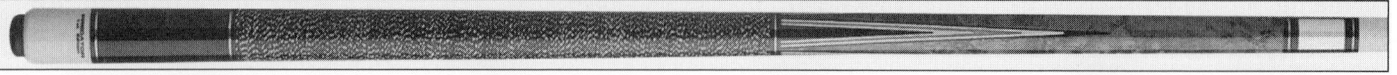

MSR (1996) $650	$700	$540	$365

Level 4 314-4 - Dark walnut-stained bird's-eye maple forearm with a German nickel silver ring set in black above wrap, four ebony points with a large bone diamond-shaped inlay in each, ebony butt sleeve with four large bone diamond-shaped inlays alternating with four smaller mother-of-pearl diamond-shaped inlays between German nickel silver rings set in black at top and bottom.

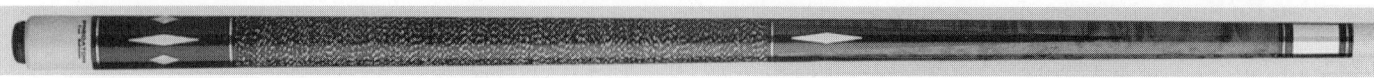

MSR (1996) $775	$850	$665	$435

GRADING	98%	90%	70%

Level 4 314-5 - Dark walnut-stained bird's-eye maple forearm with a pair of German nickel silver rings set in black above wrap, four large black-bordered bone ovals within floating two-piece ebony-bordered maple points, ebony butt sleeve with four large bone ovals alternating with four pairs of opposing bone inlays between German nickel silver rings set in black at top and bottom.

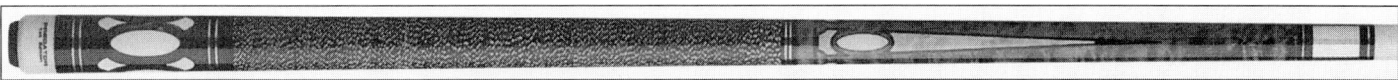

MSR (1996) $950	$1,100	$875	$600

Level 4 314-6 - Dark walnut-stained bird's-eye maple forearm, four long ebony points with two colored veneers and a bone diamond-shaped inlay in each alternating with four short ebony points with four small black-bordered bone diamond-shaped inlays at the tip of each, ebony butt sleeve with four large bone diamond-shaped inlays alternating with four pairs of opposing dark walnut-stained bird's-eye maple hexagons (comes with two shafts).

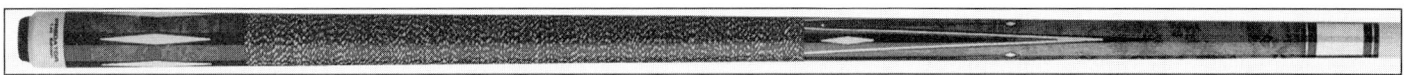

MSR (1996) $1,250	$1,350	$1,050	$700

1999 PREDATOR 2

The following Predator 2 cue was available in any 1/10 oz. weight increment from 18 to 20.5 ounces, and any balance point from 17 in. to 19 in. from the butt. One matched Predator shaft was included, and an extra matched 314 shaft was available at the time of purchase for $175. An Irish linen wrap was $40 extra, and a leather wrap was $70 extra, which affects the values accordingly.

Level 2 "PREDATOR 2" - Ten-piece radially spliced ebony-colored butt.

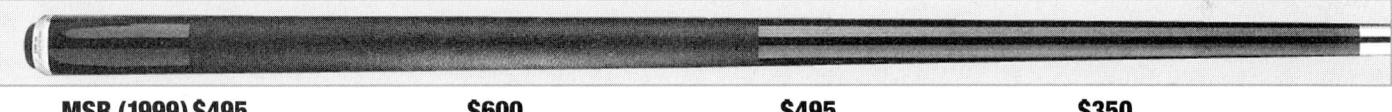

MSR (1999) $495	$600	$495	$350

PREDATOR 1999 SERIES

The following Predator 1999 Series cues all came with one Predator shaft. All cues but the SPW had stainless steel piloted joints with 5/16-14 pins and 99-2 through 99-6 had German nickel silver rings on the joint collars.

Level 1 SPW - Maple forearm, four full-spliced rosewood points with four black- and green-colored veneers.

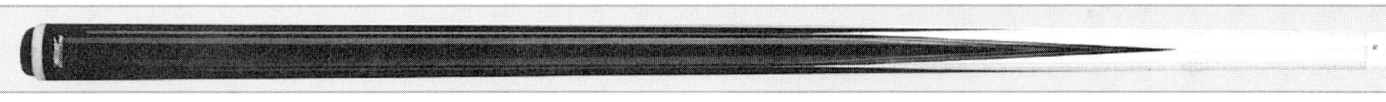

MSR (1999) $295	$275	$240	$190

Level 1 SPJ - Maple forearm, four full-spliced rosewood points with four black- and green-colored veneers.

MSR (1999) $345	$325	$260	$175

Level 2 99-1 - Black-stained maple forearm, black-stained maple butt sleeve.

MSR (1999) $420	$400	$315	$215

Level 2 99-2 - Burgandy-stained maple forearm with a German nickel silver ring above wrap, burgandy-stained maple butt sleeve with German nickel silver rings at top and bottom.

MSR (1999) $495	$450	$350	$235

Level 3 99-3 - Rosewood forearm with a German nickel silver ring above wrap, four ebony points with three colored veneers, ebony butt sleeve with German nickel silver rings at top and bottom.

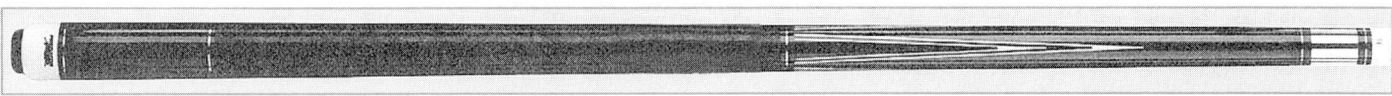

MSR (1999) $575	$550	$425	$285

GRADING	98%	90%	70%

Level 4 99-4 - Brown-stained maple forearm with a German nickel silver ring above wrap, four ebony points with a mother-of-pearl notched diamond-shaped inlay in each, brown-stained maple butt sleeve with four mother-of-pearl notched diamond-shaped inlays set in ebony windows between German nickel silver rings at top and bottom.

MSR (1999) $845	$800	$625	$425

Level 4 99-5 - Brown-stained maple forearm with a German nickel silver ring above wrap, six intricate ebony-bordered floating points with an ebony-bordered white diamond-shaped inlay at the top and bottom of each, brown-stained maple butt sleeve with six intricate ebony-bordered windows with an ebony-bordered white diamond-shaped inlay at the top and bottom of each between German nickel silver rings at top and bottom.

MSR (1999) $845	$800	$625	$425

Level 4 99-6 - Maple forearm with a pair of German nickel silver rings above wrap, four long ebony points with two veneers and a white diamond-shaped inlay in each alternating with four short ebony points with an ebony-bordered white diamond-shaped inlay at the tip of each, ebony butt sleeve with eight tall white diamond-shaped inlays alternating with pairs of intricate octagonal maple windows between a pair of German nickel silver rings at top and bottom.

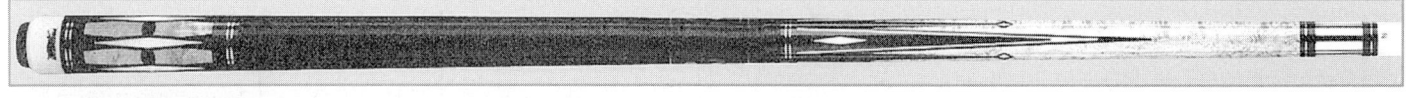

MSR (1999) $995	$925	$715	$475

2000 2K SERIES

The following Predator 2K Series cues all came with one Predator shaft. All cues shown had piloted stainless steel joints with 5/16-14 pins and German nickel silver rings on the joint collars. The 2K Series was discontinued in November of 2002.

Level 2 2K2 - Brown-stained bird's-eye maple forearm with double silver rings above wrap, brown-stained bird's-eye maple butt sleeve with double silver rings at top and bottom.

MSR (2000) $545	$495	$400	$295

Level 3 2K3 - Maple forearm with double silver rings above wrap, four ebony points with two veneers, ebony butt sleeve with double silver rings at top and bottom.

MSR (2002) $675	$575	$485	$385

Level 4 2K4 - Rosewood forearm with double silver rings above wrap, six curly maple floating points, rosewood butt sleeve with six hexagonal curly maple windows between double silver rings at top and bottom.

MSR (2000) $825	$710	$600	$465

Level 4 2K5 - Brown-stained bird's-eye maple forearm with double silver rings above wrap, four ebony points with a mother-of-pearl notched diamond-shaped inlay in the center of each point, ebony butt sleeve with eight mother-of-pearl notched diamond-shaped inlays between double silver rings at top and bottom.

MSR (2000) $925	$800	$675	$500

PREDATOR CUES, cont. 647

GRADING	98%	90%	70%

Level 4 2K6 - Brown-stained bird's-eye maple forearm with double silver rings above wrap, four intricate ebony and synthetic ivory-bordered ebony two-piece floating points with an ebony-bordered mother-of-pearl diamond-shaped inlay in the center of each point, brown-stained bird's-eye maple butt sleeve with four intricate ebony and synthetic ivory-bordered ebony two-piece windows with an ebony-bordered mother-of-pearl diamond-shaped inlay in the center of each window between double silver rings at top and bottom.

MSR (2000)$1,050	$875	$720	$550

2002 3K SERIES

The following Predator 3K Series cues all came with one Predator shaft. All cues shown had stainless steel Uni-Loc joints and German nickel silver rings on the joint collars. The 3K Series was discontinued in April of 2004.

Level 2 3K2 - Grey-stained bird's-eye maple forearm with double silver rings above wrap, grey-stained bird's-eye maple butt sleeve with double silver rings at top and bottom.

MSR (2002)$575	$500	$405	$300

Level 3 3K3 - Rosewood forearm with double silver rings above wrap, four floating ebony points with two veneers, rosewood butt sleeve with double silver rings at top and bottom.

MSR (2002)$695	$600	$495	$375

Level 4 3K4 - Brown-stained bird's-eye maple forearm with double silver rings above wrap, four ebony-bordered curly maple floating two-piece points with an ebony-bordered synthetic ivory oval-shaped inlay in the center of each point, brown-stained bird's-eye maple butt sleeve with four ebony-bordered curly maple two-piece windows with an ebony-bordered synthetic ivory oval-shaped inlay in the center of each window between double silver rings at top and bottom.

MSR (2002)$845	$700	$615	$495

Level 5 3K5 - Bird's-eye maple forearm with double silver rings above wrap, four ebony points with a synthetic ivory diamond-shaped inlay in the center of each point surrounded by three smaller synthetic ivory diamond-shaped inlays above and below, ebony butt sleeve with four synthetic ivory diamond-shaped inlays surrounded by three smaller synthetic ivory diamond-shaped inlays above and below between double silver rings at top and bottom.

MSR (2002)$895	$735	$635	$525

Level 4 3K6 - Burgundy-stained bird's-eye maple forearm with double silver rings above wrap, four floating ebony points with two veneers and a synthetic ivory diamond-shaped inlay in each point, burgundystained bird's-eye maple butt sleeve with four hexagonal ebony windows with two veneers and a synthetic ivory diamond-shaped inlay in each window between double silver rings at top and bottom.

MSR (2002)$945	$765	$670	$560

Level 4 3K7 - Bird's-eye maple forearm with double silver rings above wrap, four intricate ebony and synthetic ivory-bordered ebony two-piece floating points with an ebony-bordered mother-of-pearl diamond-shaped inlay in the center of each point, bird's-eye maple butt sleeve with four intricate ebony and synthetic ivory-bordered ebony two-piece windows with an ebony-bordered mother-of-pearl diamond-shaped inlay in the center of each window between double silver rings at top and bottom.

MSR (2002)$1,125	$900	$785	$650

GRADING	98%	90%	70%

SPECIAL INTEREST PREDATOR CUES

The following "LE3" limited edition Predator cue featured a butt made by Joss Cues Ltd. A total of 300 of these cues were made.

Level 2 LE3 - Red-stained bird's-eye maple forearm with six pearl notched diamond-shaped inlays set in ebony ovals above wrap, red-stained bird's-eye maple butt sleeve with six pearl notched diamond-shaped inlays set in ebony ovals in center.

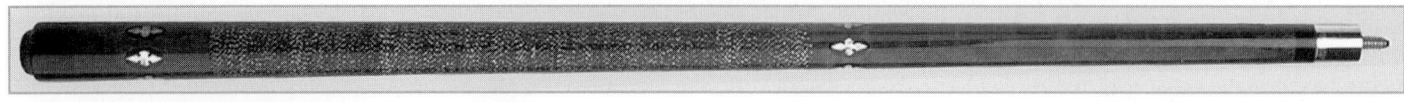

Original Retail (1996)$495	$650	$520	$350

LE4 LIMITED EDITION

The following "LE4" limited edition Predator cues were numbered 1 to 150 on the stainless steel joints. Each cue came with two Predator 314 shafts.

Level 4 LE4 - Stained bird's-eye maple forearm with a nickel silver ring above wrap, six ebony points with a mother-of-pearl notched diamond-shaped inlay in each point, stained bird's-eye maple butt sleeve with six ebony windows with a mother-of-pearl notched diamond-shaped inlay in each between nickel silver rings at top and bottom.

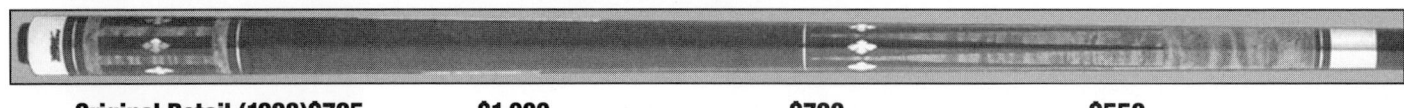

Original Retail (1998)$795	$1,000	$790	$550

LE5 LIMITED EDITION

The following "LE5" limited edition Predator cues were numbered 1 to 250 on the stainless steel joints. Each cue came with one Predator 314 shaft.

Level 3 LE5 - Purpleheart forearm, four maple-bordered snakewood points with a maple diamond-shaped inlay at the tip of each point, purpleheart butt sleeve with four intricate maple-bordered snakewood windows.

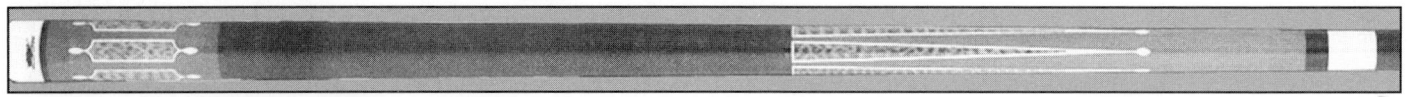

Original Retail (1999)$745	$900	$715	$500

SE1 AND SE2 SPECIAL EDITION

The following "SE1" and "SE2" special edition Predator cues featured butts made by J. Pechauer Custom Cues. Each featured stainless steel Uni-Loc Joints and joint protectors. A total of 55 of each of these cues were made. All were signed and numbered by Jerry Pechauer. Each came with one Predator 314 shaft with a Moori tip.

Level 5 SE1 - Bird's-eye maple forearm with a ring of five synthetic ivory diamond-shaped inlays above a nickel silver ring above wrap, five ebony points with a cocobolo-bordered synthetic ivory diamond-shaped inlay in each point, ebony butt sleeve with five bird's-eye maple windows alternating with five cocobolo-bordered synthetic ivory diamond-shaped inlays between rings of five synthetic ivory diamond-shaped inlays within nickel silver rings at top and bottom.

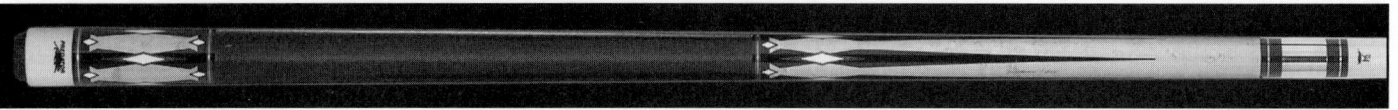

Original Retail$1,495	$1,500	$1,195	$800

Level 5 SE2 - Stained bird's-eye maple forearm with a ring of six synthetic ivory diamond-shaped inlays set in an ebony ring above handle, six ebony-bordered micarta points, bird's eye maple handle with sets of six ebony inward-pointing points at top and bottom with diamond-shaped ebony tips and a synthetic ivory diamond-shaped inlay at the base of each point, bird's-eye maple butt sleeve with six ebony-bordered micarta reverse points below a ring of six synthetic ivory diamond-shaped inlays set in an ebony ring below handle.

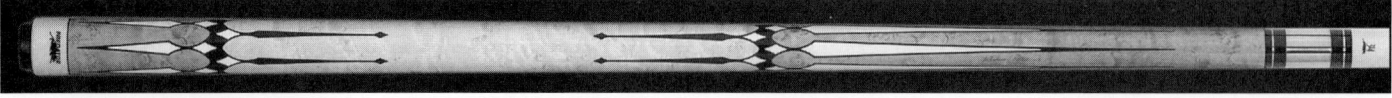

Original Retail$1,495	$1,500	$1,195	$800

SE3 SPECIAL EDITION

The following "SE3" and "SE3" special edition Predator cues featured butts made by J. Pechauer Custom Cues. Each featured stainless steel Uni-Loc Joints and joint protectors. A total of 100 of each of these cues were made. All were signed and numbered by Jerry Pechauer. Each came with one Predator 314 shaft with a Moori tip.

PREDATOR CUES, cont. 649

GRADING	98%	90%	70%

Level 5 SE3 - Bird's-eye maple forearm with an ebony ring above handle, five long and five short ebony points with diamond-shaped tips, bird's-eye maple handle with sets of five short ebony inward-pointing points at top and bottom with diamond-shaped tips alternating with five long ebony inward-pointing points at top and bottom that meet at five ebony-bordered abalone diamond-shaped inlays in the center, bird's-eye maple butt sleeve with five long and five short ebony reverse points with diamond-shaped tips below an ebony ring below handle.

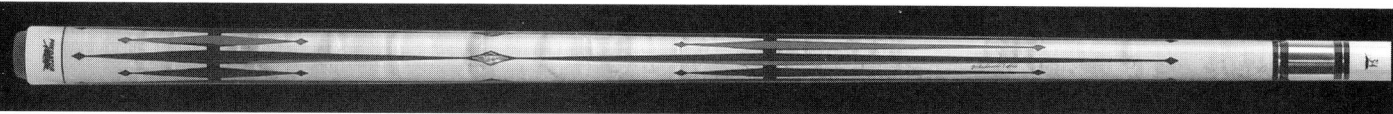

Original Retail $1,595	$1,600	$1,195	$875

Level 5 SE4 - Burgundy-stained bird's-eye maple forearm with six synthetic ivory squares set in ebony above handle, six ebony-bordered micarta points, ebony handle with sets of six inward-pointing micarta points at top and bottom, burgundy-stained bird's-eye maple butt sleeve with six ebony-bordered micarta reverse points below six synthetic ivory squares set in ebony above handle.

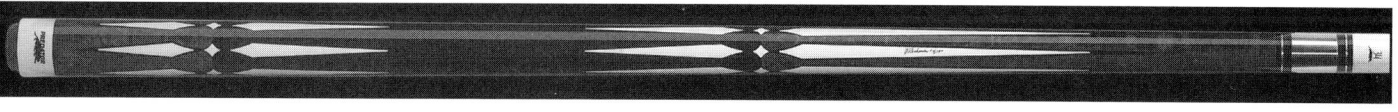

Original Retail $1,595	$1,600	$1,195	$875

SE5 SPECIAL EDITION

The following "SE5" special edition Predator cue featured a butt made by Samsara Custom Cues. Each featured a stainless steel Uni-Loc Joint and joint protectors. A total of 100 of each of these cues were made. All were signed and numbered by the craftsmen at Samsara. Each came with one Predator 314 shaft or Predator Z shaft with a Moori tip.

Level 5 SE5 - Ebony forearm with silver rings above wrap, three long and three short holly points with two veneers, leather wrap, ebony butt sleeve with intricate ebony-bordered holly woven inlays set between silver rings at top and bottom.

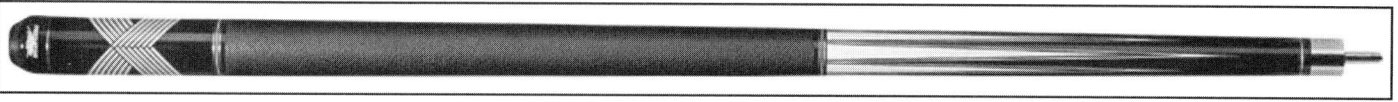

Original Retail $1,695	$1,750	$1,395	$975

SECONDARY MARKET MINIMUM VALUES

The following are minimum values for other Predator cues encountered on the secondary market. These prices are representative of cues utilizing basic materials and designs that are not necessarily available at present. Predator has offered limited and special edition cues that can command many times these prices due to the use of exotic materials and artistry.

Special construction note: There are many materials and construction techniques that can add value to Predator cues. The following are the most important examples.

- Add $100+ for "Predator First Edition" on butt cap.
- Add 100%+ Limited or Special Editions.

For all used Predator cues, except where otherwise noted:
- Add $150+ for each additional original straight playable Predator 314 shaft.
- Add $200+ for each additional original straight playable predator Z shaft.
- Deduct $230+ for missing original straight playable Predator shaft.
- Deduct 20% for obvious or improper refinish.

Level 3 - 2-6 points, 0-8 inlays.

Level 3 cues start at	$300	$250	$185

Level 4 - 4-10 points, 9-25 inlays.

Level 4 cues start at	$400	$335	$250

Level 5 - 0-12 points, 26-50 inlays.

Level 5 cues start at	$600	$500	$385

PREWITT CUSTOM CUES

Maker of pool cues in Santa Monica, California.

If you are interested in talking to Ed Prewitt about a new cue or cue that needs to be repaired, you can contact him at Prewitt Custom Cues, listed in the Trademark Index.

PRINCE CUES

Maker of pool cues from 1998, in Hanover Park, Illinois, to present in Glendale Heights, Illinois.

Tim Prince was born and raised in the suburbs just outside Chicago. He began playing pool in his early teens, and fell in love with the game and played whenever he could. After graduating high school, he attended college to become a mechanical engineer. It didn't take long for him to realize that he wanted a career that enabled him to work with his hands and not sit behind a desk or computer all day. Tim joined the carpenter's union and served his apprenticeship building upper class homes in the area. Once his apprenticeship was over as a carpenter, he again decided to switch careers. Tim became a tool and die maker like his father and served his apprenticeship under his father. As a tool maker, he learned about close tolerance machining and building progressive dies and tools. Tim completed the Tooling and Manufacturing Associations (TMA) four-year apprenticeship program and was nominated for apprentice of the year.

Tim went to have a cue repaired by a local cuemaker and knew immediately that he could do a better job if he had the machinery. Tim was already a very skilled tool and die maker and an excellent machinist so he started purchasing the machines he needed. He started doing repairs for a local pool hall, while experimenting with different cue constructions, until he devised the method he uses today. Prince cues have a very solid hit and feel to them. Playability is his main concern when building a cue. Each cue is made with great pride and attention to detail. All materials for Prince cues are hand selected and machined slowly over time to ensure straightness. Tim's motto is: "Made by a Prince, fit for a King." Prior to 2000, the logo was a crown with T.Prince engraved under it. The current logo is engraved under the bumper: "T. Prince" with the year of production.

If you are interested in talking to Tim Prince about a new cue or cue that needs to be repaired, you can contact him at Prince Cues, listed in the Trademark Index.

SPECIFICATIONS

Butt material: hardwoods
Shaft material: rock maple
Standard length: 58 in.
Standard finish: dupont
Balance point: 18.5 in. from butt
Standard butt cap: phenolic
Standard wrap: Irish linen
Point construction: spliced
Standard joint: phenolic
Joint type: flat faced
Joint screw thread: 3/8-10
Joint protectors: standard
Standard number of shafts: two
Standard taper: modified pro
Standard ferrules: Ivorine-3
Standard tip: Triangle
Standard tip width: 13 mm
Annual production: fewer than 30 cues

OPTIONS (FOR NEW CUES ONLY)

Ivory butt cap: $200
Ivory joint: $150
Ivory ferrule: $70
Extra shaft: $150

REPAIRS

Repairs done on all fine cues.
Rewrap (Irish linen): $45
Clean and press linen wrap: $25
Replace shaft: $140
Replace tip: $15+
Replace fiber/linen ferrule: $30+

CURRENT PRINCE CUES

Two-piece Prince bar cues start at $250. Basic Prince cues with wraps and joint rings start at $350. Prince cues with points start at $550. One-of-a-kind custom Prince cues start at $750. The current delivery time for a Prince cue is four to six months.

GRADING	98%	90%	70%

SECONDARY MARKET MINIMUM VALUES

The following are minimum values for other Prince cues encountered on the secondary market. These prices are representative of cues utilizing basic materials and designs that are not necessarily available at present. Tim has offered one-of-a-kind cues that can command many times these prices due to the use of exotic materials and artistry.

Special construction note: There are many materials and construction techniques that can add value to Prince cues.

For all used Prince cues, except where otherwise noted:
- Add $100 for each additional original straight playable shaft beyond two.
- Deduct $150 for each missing original straight playable shaft under two.
- Add $50 each for ivory ferrules.
- Add $60 for leather wrap.
- Deduct 20% for obvious or improper refinish.

Level 1 - Hustler.
	98%	90%	70%
Level 1 cues start at	$200	$155	$110

Level 2 - 0 points, 0-25 inlays.
Level 2 cues start at	$300	$235	$160

Level 3 - 2-6 points, 0-8 inlays.
Level 3 cues start at	$500	$390	$270

Level 4 - 4-10 points, 9-25 inlays.
Level 4 cues start at	$650	$510	$345

Level 5 - 0-12 points, 26-50 inlays.
Level 5 cues start at	$900	$695	$475

PROFICIENT BILLIARDS

Another name for Scot Sherbine Cues in Ephrate, Pennsylvania. Please refer to Scot Sherbine Cues.

SHAWN PUTNAM CUES

Maker of pool cues in Youngstown, Ohio.

If you are interested in talking to Shawn Putnam about a new cue or cue that needs to be repaired, you can contact him at Shawn Putnam Cues, listed in the Trademark Index.

Shawn Putnam

NOTES

QUEST ASP CUSTOM CUES

Maker of pool cues from 1998 to present in Harrisburg, Pennsylvania.

Donald Moyer developed a skill for playing first. He started working on cues when local players showed disdain when having to drive for hours to get even the simplest of repairs done on their cues. Starting with repairs, the building of cues was only a short step away. In 1984, his first cue was completed. Eighteen months later, he began production. In 1987, five cues were built. In 1997, 65 cues were built, not counting about 100 custom hammer break cues. Don's cues were either marked with initials "DM" or signed with the year of production.

In 1998, Don started Quest ASP (Artistic Spherical Projectors). Although CNC is being integrated into the Quest ASP shop, the majority of work is still done one part at a time. All components, with the exception of tips, bumpers and screws, are made in shop. Ninety percent of weighting is done by natural weighting, using computers with custom programs. No weight bolts are used. Weights of cues are determined for the most part before cue construction actually begins. Quest will continue to make the famous hammer break cue produced by Don for so many years.

Quest ASP Custom Cues are guaranteed for life against manufacturing defects that are not the result of warpage or abuse. If you have a Quest ASP cue that needs further identification or repair, or would like to order a new Quest ASP cue, contact Quest ASP Custom Cues, listed in the Trademark Index.

SPECIFICATIONS

Butt material: hardwoods
Shaft material: rock maple
Standard length: 58 in.
Lengths available: any up to 64 in.
Standard finish: UV polyurethane
Balance point: 2 in. above wrap
Standard butt cap: linen phenolic
Standard wrap: Irish linen
Point construction: short splice
Standard joint: stainless steel
Joint type: piloted
Joint screw: 5/16-14
Standard number of shafts: one
Standard taper: two available
Standard ferrules: linen phenolic
Tip widths available: 10 to 15 mm
Standard tip: Moori
Annual production: more than 100 cues

GRADING

	98%	90%	70%

SECONDARY MARKET MINIMUM VALUES

The following are minimum values for Quest ASP custom cues encountered on the secondary market. These prices are representative of cues utilizing basic materials and designs that are not necessarily available at present. Don has offered one-of-a-kind cues that can command many times these prices due to the use of exotic materials and artistry.

Special construction note: There are many materials and construction techniques that can add value to Quest ASP cues.

For all used Quest ASP cues, except where otherwise noted:

- Add $75 for each additional original straight playable shaft beyond one.
- Deduct $100 for missing original straight playable shaft.
- Add $55 each for ivory ferrules.
- Add $45 for leather wrap.
- Deduct 20% for obvious or improper refinish.

Level 2
	98%	90%	70%
Level 2 cues start at	$250	$195	$135

Level 3
Level 3 cues start at	$450	$350	$235

Level 4
Level 4 cues start at	$600	$470	$320

Level 5
Level 5 cues start at	$1,000	$785	$545

GRADING	98%	90%	70%

Q-WORKS

Maker of pool cues from 1991 to present in Chico, California

Bob Burgoyne started playing pool at the young age of 16. He became a welder and excelled in designing and fabricating. He dabbled in woodworking, making furniture in his spare time. In 1994, Bob became more serious about playing pool. He played in pool tournaments around town. Bob wanted to play with a better cue, and used his design and fabrication knowledge to make his first cue. Bob is presently incorporating designs from the past and exotic woods into his cues. All cue sticks are made by hand in his one man shop, and many feature points in the shafts. Bob makes cues part time while working full time in the vending and billiards business.

Q-Works cues are guaranteed for life against manufacturing defects that are not the result of warpage or abuse to the original owner. If you have a Q-Works cue that needs further identification or repair, or would like to order a new cue, contact Q-Works, listed in the Trademark Index.

Robert Burgoyne

SPECIFICATIONS

Butt material: hardwoods
Shaft material: rock maple
Standard length: 58 in.
Balance point: custom
Standard wrap: Irish linen
Standard finish: polyurethane clear
Point construction: short splice
Standard joint: linen phenolic
Joint screws: 3/8-10
Standard number of shafts: two
Standard taper: custom
Standard ferrules: linen phenolic
Standard tip: Triangle
Annual production: fewer than 100 cues

OPTIONS (FOR NEW CUES ONLY)

Leather wrap: $120
Ivory joint: $140
Ivory ferrule: $65
Extra shaft: $110+

REPAIRS

Repairs done on most custom cues. Repairs priced on an individual basis.

CURRENT Q-WORKS CUES

Basic two-piece Q-Works cues with wraps and joint rings start at $250. Q-Works cues with points start at $600. Q-Works cues over $600 come with Uni-Loc joints. The current delivery time for a Q-Works cue is about two months.

SECONDARY MARKET MINIMUM VALUES

The following are minimum values for other Q-Works cues encountered on the secondary market. These prices are representative of cues utilizing basic materials and designs that are not necessarily available at present. Bob has offered one-of-a-kind cues that can command many times these prices due to the use of exotic materials and artistry.

Special construction note: There are many materials and construction techniques that can add value to Q-Works cues.

For all used Q-Works cues, except where otherwise noted:

Add $75 for each additional original straight playable shaft beyond two.
Deduct $110 for each missing original straight playable shaft under two.
Add $50 each for ivory ferrules.
Add $75 for leather wrap.
Deduct 20% for obvious or improper refinish.

Level 2 - 0 points, 0-25 inlays.

Level 2 cues start at	$200	$160	$110

Level 3 - 2-6 points, 0-8 inlays.

Level 3 cues start at	$500	$390	$265

Level 4 - 4-10 points, 9-25 inlays.

Level 4 cues start at	$650	$510	$350

Level 5 - 0-12 points, 26-50 inlays.

Level 5 cues start at	$900	$715	$500

R SECTION

HERMAN RAMBOW

Maker of pool cues from approximately 1915 to 1967 in Chicago, Illinois.

Born in Chicago in 1880, Herman Rambow began working for Brunswick as a mail boy at the age of fourteen. Not long after joining Brunswick, Herman was attracted to cuemaking and began working in the cuemaking operation. Herman learned the diverse aspects of cue construction and quickly proved his aptitude as a cuemaker. In the repair department, Herman would customize cues to suit their owners. Eventually, his talents at customizing cues became so well known that he began making custom Brunswick cues for many of the top professionals at the time.

In 1921, Herman left Brunswick to start his own company, the Superior Cue Co. It was during this time that he was awarded a patent for his new balancing system that involved cutting a cue in half near the balance point and inserting a threaded rod of brass or steel. The length and weight of this rod were calculated to ensure the proper weight and balance of the finished cue. Unfortunately, the Superior Cue Co. did not last long. It is commonly believed that the professional players Rambow was counting on to use his cues and services were unable to do business with him because of endorsement contracts with Brunswick.

In 1925, Herman signed over his patent rights to Brunswick. By 1927, Herman was again working for Brunswick, this time as head foreman of cuemaking operations. Brunswick used Herman's balancing system on a model called the "Hub" cue, which was popular for several years. In the late 1930s, Brunswick and Rambow were developing a full-splice cue that incorporated veneers between the points and the forearm. Despite not being a new concept for Brunswick, this new full-splice cue blank, named the Titlist, became the basis for nearly every Rambow cue made until his death in 1967. Rambow continued to oversee the cuemaking operations at Brunswick while concurrently making a line of his custom cues for the best Brunswick players and customers. It is widely believed that Rambow also built the more exclusive, ebony "Willie Hoppe" model, though there is little evidence to support this belief.

Titlist cues were first introduced to the public in the 1940-1941 Brunswick catalog. Demand for Rambow cues using the Titlist blank increased quickly; Herman began filling orders. These first generation prototypes of Rambow's cues which used the Titlist blank exhibited ivory joints with black collars, and joint screws (mostly aluminum or steel) that protruded from the shaft and screwed into the butt. Brass was Herman's material of choice for the joint and screw. However, brass was in limited supply as a result of the second World War. It is not known how many of these original Titlist/Rambow cues were produced, but only a few remain in existence today.

As brass became more widely available, Herman used it for joint screws. He also reconfigured the joint to a piloted mechanism in which the screw protruded from the butt section and screwed into a brass receiver machined into the shaft. Some of these early examples were built using a brown fibrous material as the joint collar, which was quickly replaced by brass. Since that time in the mid- to late 1940s, Herman exclusively used brass for joint collars, pins, and receivers, with few exceptions. In 1950, Rambow was forced to retire from Brunswick. The company offered to let him take some of his cuemaking equipment and materials home with him, as they had no future plans to use them, and he accepted. Once again, Rambow began making cues on his own, only this time his reputation as a great cuemaker drove his business. Rambow established a humble shop at the Keefe & Hamer Co. in downtown Chicago, and soon had so many orders that he needed help. In 1956, Herman hired Steve Bihun as his apprentice and started him on simple tasks.

Many famous players used Herman Rambow cues during the fifties and sixties. The most notable were Willie Hoppe and Willie Mosconi. Hoppe at that time was regarded as the greatest cue man to have ever lived, after having dominated billiards for a half-century. Mosconi was recognized as Hoppe's counterpart in the pocket billiard world. Mosconi's favorite cue was a Rambow. Mosconi's Rambow cue was one of the fanciest cues Herman ever made. It was very similar to the Rambow he used when he ran a record 526 balls in a row in Springfield, Ohio in 1956. In contrast, Hoppe's cue was simple with no inlay or writing on the cue. Hoppe's last cue also had a modified joint (per Hoppe's specifications) with a more shallow depth for the shaft pilot than usual. Rambow also made the cues used by Paul Newman and Jackie Gleason in "The Hustler." By the mid-1960s, Keefe & Hamer was a very busy place. In the final years of Rambow's career, his cues were so sought after that he and Bihun were years behind filling all their orders. In 1967, Herman Rambow died at home after complaining of stomach pains and lying down to rest. He left behind the longest legacy of custom cuemaking known to this day. One year later, in 1968, Herman Rambow became the only cuemaker ever inducted into the Billiard Congress of America's Hall of Fame.

Today, cues by Herman Rambow are rare and sought after by collectors. Although most are not easily identifiable, except by experts, some cues will have Rambow's name penciled on the forearm. Many Rambow cues have a four-point Titlist blank with little or no inlay work. Brunswick "Willie Hoppe" model cues are commonly sold as Rambows because of their similarity in style. Since many of these Brunswick cues are difficult to differentiate from Rambow's work, it is important to consult an expert on Rambow's work when purchasing one. Rambow cues with inlays will usually have a few dots of ivory or other materials. Most joints were piloted, almost always of brass or stainless steel, although ivory was also available. Sometimes the owner's name is penciled on the forearm, and when so, their initials should be near the joint rings on the shafts. Although Rambow made many cues for decades, few seem to have survived in excellent original condition. (Referenced from The Billiard Encyclopedia.)

If you would like to have a Rambow cue authenticated or appraised, or have questions regarding Rambow cues, their restoration or conservation, contact Deno J. Andrews who is listed in the Buy, Sell, Trade Index.

SPECIFICATIONS

Butt material: hardwoods
Shaft material: maple
Standard length: 56 in.
Standard joint: brass
Joint type: piloted
Point construction: full splice
Standard wrap: leather or Irish linen

GRADING	98%	90%	70%

Standard number of shafts: two
Standard ferrules: ivory
Total production: a few thousand cues

OPTIONS ENCOUNTERED
Ivory dots
Ivory joint
Ivory butt cap
Signed by Rambow
Player's name on forearm and initials on shafts

COMMON RAMBOW EXAMPLES
The following cues represent the work of Herman Rambow. These cues can be encountered as shown, or with slight variations.

Level 3 "Prototype Titlist" - Reversed ivory joint, maple forearm with important player's name (and initials on shaft), four oak (rare) full-splice points with four colored veneers, no wrap (rare), no butt plate, rubber bumper. Was the playing cue of Ernie Presto, a student of Jake Schaefer Jr.

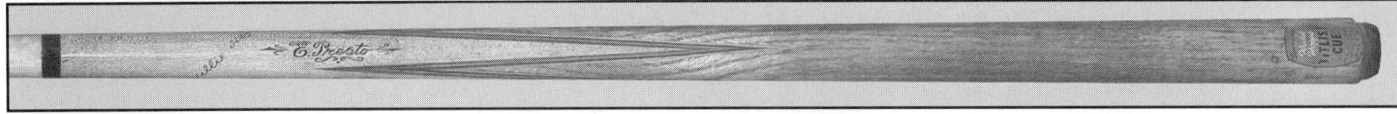

| MSR (1940) $65 | $9,000 | $8,250 | $4,800 |

Level 3 "War-time Titlist" Brown fiber joint, maple forearm, four ebony full-splice points with four colored veneers, leather wrap, Hoppe-style ivory disk butt cap design. Approximate value considering additions $4,500.

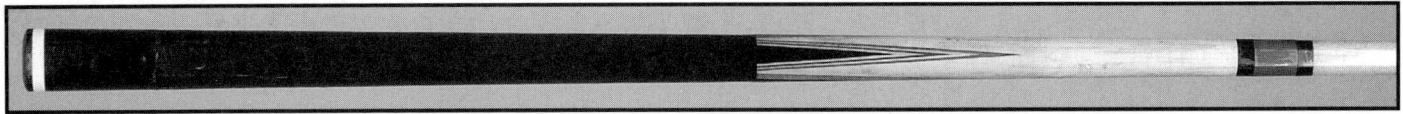

| MSR (c.1944) $85 | $4,500 | $3,750 | $2,500 |

Level 3 "Titlist" Brass joint, maple forearm, four rosewood full-splice points with four colored veneers, leather wrap, Hoppe-style ivory disk butt cap design. Cue was one of Willie Hoppe's personal playing cues and was designed per Hoppe's specifications for a nearly flat-faced piloted joint that is thinner than other Rambow cues.

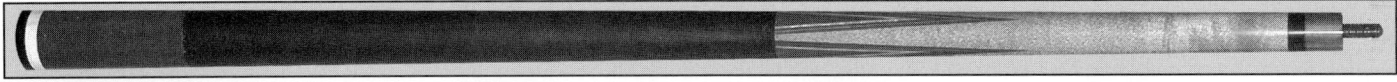

| MSR (c. 1950) N/A | $25,500+ | $23,750 | $15,500 |

Level 3 "Titlist" Brass joint, maple forearm with customer's name (and initials on shaft) and "by Rambow," four rosewood points with four colored veneers, Irish linen wrap, rosewood butt with late-style butt cap design.

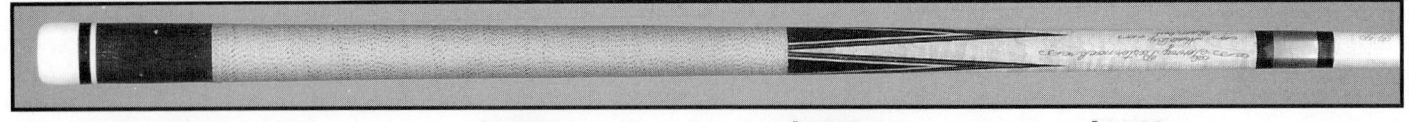

| | $4,700 | $4,250 | $2,500 |

Level 5 "Titlist" Brass joint, maple forearm with customer's name (and initials on shaft), four rosewood points with four colored veneers, Irish linen wrap, rosewood butt with late-style butt cap design. Three black dots inlaid between tips of points. Black and ivory dots at the top of each point. Area below wrap adorned with ivory and black and ivory dots in repeated circular design. Artisan pentimento also exhibited on butt area below wrap. Approximate value considering additions $15,500.

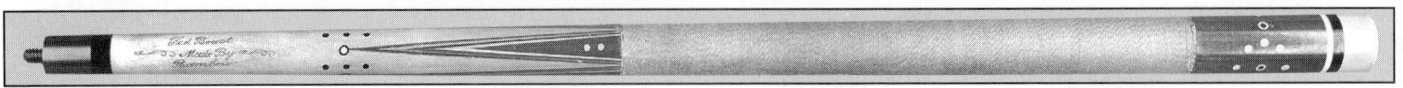

| | $14,500+ | $13,000 | $9,000 |

SECONDARY MARKET MINIMUM VALUES
The following are minimum prices for Rambow cues, with authentication or provenance, encountered on the secondary market. These prices are representative of cues utilizing the most basic materials and designs that were available. Many Brunswick model cues are passed off as Rambow cues. Cues with provenance or authentication from a Rambow expert will command higher prices. Herman also offered one-of-a-kind cues that can command many times these prices due to the use of exotic materials and artistry. Early variations are becoming extremely collectible, and can also command many times these prices. Rambow was not known for his diversity in cue making, thus, the construction notes and corresponding values play a large role in valuing a Rambow cue.

GRADING	98%	90%	70%

Note: Due to the rarity of Herman Rambow cues and increasing interest, prices are on the rise. Fewer original examples are surfacing, and collectors are holding on to the ones they have. Unique examples with pedigree, and cues made for top professional and important players are demand the highest prices.

Special construction note: There are many materials and construction techniques that can add value to Rambow cues.

For all Rambow cues:
- Add $1,500+ for ivory joint.
- Add $1,000+ for brown fiber joint.
- Add $1000+ for ivory butt cap (not ivory "Hoppe" ring).
- Add $1,500+ for "By Rambow" penciled on forearm.
- Add $500 for customer's name penciled on forearm.
- Add $2500+ for important player's name on forearm.
- Add $1000+ for butt wood other than rosewood.
- Add $450+ for each additional original straight playable shaft with owner's initials beyond two.
- Deduct $450 for each missing original straight playable shaft with owner's initials under two.
- Add $1000 for all-wood handle (no wrap).
- Add $500 for original leather wrap.
- Add $500 for original joint pin that is not brass.
- Add $500 for each original bell-shaped ferrule.
- Deduct up to 40% for obvious or improper refinish.

Level 2 - 0 points, 0-25 inlays.
Level 2 cues start at	$3,000	$2,500	$1,500

Level 3 - 2-6 points, 0-8 inlays.
Level 3 cues start at	$3,700	$3,250	$1,900

Level 4 - 4-10 points, 9-25 inlays.
Level 4 cues start at	$8,000	$7,200	$4,150

Level 5 - 0-12 points, 26-50 inlays.
Level 5 cues start at	$14,500	$13,000	$9,000

RAT CUES

Maker of pool cues from 1996 to present in Lincoln, Nebraska.

Ryan Theewen started working for Mueller Recreational Products while attending the University of Nebraska-Lincoln, studying biochemistry. He began by doing repairs and then started making bar cues. He then had the opportunity to train under Troy Downey and could not pass it up. Ryan soon realized that building cues was what he wanted to do, not become a biochemist. Also, Ryan's grandfather owned a car repair business, so he knew his way around a machine shop.

A pool lover for many years, Ryan appreciated the playability of well-made cues and knew what he liked and did not like about them. He has tried to incorporate this knowledge in his RAT cues. The name RAT comes from a family nickname given to Ryan since very early childhood.

Ryan likes straightforward designs that do not get "too busy." He prefers to build traditional and simple cues. He wants his buyers to have confidence in the performance of the RAT cue they purchase. Ryan works within the Mueller building, alongside Troy Downey, and they share several lathes and CNC machines. They also use the machines in the Mueller woodshop.

RAT cues are hand-signed with "RAT" on the butt cap. Cues made prior to 1999 will not be marked unless it was one-of-a-kind or made for someone special, in which case the writing was in gold.

RAT cues are guaranteed for life against everything except warpage and/or abuse, to the original buyer.

If you are interested in talking to Ryan Theewen about a new cue or cue that needs repaired, you can contact him at RAT Cues, listed in the Trademark Index.

SPECIFICATIONS

Butt material: hardwoods
Shaft material: hard rock maple
Standard finish: polyurethane
Standard length: 58 in.
Standard wrap: Irish linen
Standard joint screw: 5/16-14
Standard joint type: piloted
Standard taper: 12.5 in. modified
Standard ferrules: linen based
Standard tip: laminated boar's hide
Annual production: 200 To 250

OPTIONS (FOR NEW CUES ONLY)

Ivory ferrule: $55
Leather wrap: $30
Extra shaft: $70

RAT CUES, cont.

GRADING	98%	90%	70%

REPAIRS

Repairs done on all fine cues.
- Refinish with Irish linen wrap: $120
- Rewrap with Irish linen: $35
- Rewrap with leather: $65
- Rewrap with stack leather: $95
- Rewrap with cork: $100
- Replace shaft: $65+
- Replace tip: $10+

CURRENT RAT CUES

Two-piece Rat bar cues start at $125. Basic Rat cues with wraps and joint rings start at $190. Rat cues with points start at $300.

SECONDARY MARKET MINIMUM VALUES

The following are minimum values for other Rat cues encountered on the secondary market. These prices are representative of cues utilizing basic materials and designs that are not necessarily available at present. Ryan has offered one-of-a-kind cues that can command many times these prices due to the use of exotic materials and artistry.

Special construction note: There are many materials and construction techniques that can add value to Rat cues.

For all used Rat cues, except where otherwise noted:
- Add $50 for each additional original straight playable shaft beyond one.
- Deduct $70 for missing original straight playable shaft.
- Add $45 each for ivory ferrules.
- Add $20 for leather wrap.
- Deduct 20% for obvious or improper refinish.

Level 1 - Hustler.

	98%	90%	70%
Level 1 cues start at	$110	$90	$60

Level 2 - 0 points, 0-25 inlays.

	98%	90%	70%
Level 2 cues start at	$175	$145	$95

Level 3 - 2-6 points, 0-8 inlays.

	98%	90%	70%
Level 3 cues start at	$250	$200	$140

Level 4 - 4-10 points, 9-25 inlays.

	98%	90%	70%
Level 4 cues start at	$325	$250	$170

RATHBUN CUES

Maker of pool cues from 1993 to present in Deltona, Florida.

William Rathbun has always enjoyed working with exotic woods. His 24 ft. by 30 ft. shop contains a 60-year old South Bend machinist lathe, saws, planer, jointer, and handmade pantograph. He builds his cues for players who want a good hit and sound construction. Rathbun cues can be identified by his "William Rathbun" signature, plus date if the customer requests it. Cues are unconditionally guaranteed on parts and workmanship. There is a one-year warranty against shaft warpage.

If you are interested in talking to William Rathbun about a new cue or cue that needs to be repaired, you can contact him at Rathbun Cues, listed in the Trademark Index.

William Rathbun

SPECIFICATION

- Butt material: hardwoods
- Shaft material: 4-A rock hard maple
- Standard length: 58 in.
- Standard wrap: Irish linen
- Standard ferrules: Implex
- Standard tip: pressed Triangle
- Annual production: 25 to 35 cues

OPTIONS (FOR NEW CUES ONLY)

- Ivory ferrule: $45
- Leather wrap: $75
- Extra shaft: $65+

GRADING	98%	90%	70%

REPAIRS

Repairs done on all fine cues.
- Rewrap (Irish linen): $35
- Replace shaft: $65
- Replace tip: $7
- Replace layered tip: $25

CURRENT RATHBUN CUES

Basic Rathbun cues with wraps and joint rings start at $145. Rathbun cues with points start at $285. The current delivery time for a Rathbun cue is about six weeks.

SECONDARY MARKET MINIMUM VALUES

The following are minimum values for other Rathbun cues encountered on the secondary market. These prices are representative of cues utilizing basic materials and designs that are not necessarily available at present. Bill has offered one-of-a-kind cues that can command many times these prices due to the use of exotic materials and artistry.

Special construction note: There are many materials and construction techniques that can add value to Rathbun cues.

For all used Rathbun cues, except where otherwise noted:
- Add $50 for each additional original straight playable shaft beyond one.
- Deduct $65 for missing original straight playable shaft.
- Add $40 each for ivory ferrules.
- Add $50 for leather wrap.
- Deduct 205% for obvious or improper refinish.

	98%	90%	70%
Level 2 - 0 points, 0-25 inlays.			
Level 2 cues start at	$140	$110	$75
Level 3 - 2-6 points, 0-8 inlays.			
Level 3 cues start at	$250	$200	$135
Level 4 - 4-10 points, 9-25 inlays.			
Level 4 cues start at	$350	$270	$185
Level 5 - 0-12 points, 26-50 inlays.			
Level 5 cues start at	$700	$545	$370

RAUENZAHN CUSTOM CUES

Maker of pool cues from 1986 to present in Warren, Pennsylvania.

Jerry Rauenzahn (pronounced Ronzon) was born and raised in Reading, Pennsylvania. As a teen, he developed a love for the game. He was fortunate to have spent approximately 10 years as a road partner to a professional player, Jimmy Matz, who is now deceased. In 1972, Jerry became frustrated and discouraged with the fact that there was no one around to do general repairs, such as rewraps, tips, etc. So, he bought a lathe. With the knowledge he had gained in high school about the equipment, he made a few "Sneaky Petes" from house cues. In the years to follow, he learned to machine his own shafts and to cut in his own points. Whereas his "prime" business was home improvements, he worked on his cuemaking during the winter months. In 1986, a serious shoulder injury abruptly halted his home improvement business. That is when he became serious about a career in the pool cue business.

Rauenzahn's point construction is short splice, using a 5/8 tenon at the base of the points, similar to McDermott. His veneer points are V-grooved. Floating points are flat bottomed.

Rauenzahn Cues can be identified by the "R" on the butt plate. This insignia was first used in 1988. Before 1988, all Rauenzahn Cues had a blue 1 in. by 2 in. paper folded under the bumper describing the cue, date of manufacture, and his signature. Since 2000, Jerry has put his signature on all cues. Today, Jerry does extensive pantograph work and can do customized work which is handmade and unique to the owner of the cue.

If you have a Rauenzahn cue that needs further identification or repair, or would like to talk to Jerry about ordering a new Rauenzahn cue, contact Rauenzahn Custom Cues, listed in the Trademark Index.

GRADING	100%	95%	70%

SPECIFICATIONS
Butt material: hard maple
Shaft material: rock maple
Standard length: 58 in.
Lengths available: any up to 61 in.
Standard wrap: linen
Standard finish: PPG
Balance point: custom
Point construction: short splice
Standard joint: stainless steel piloted
Joint screw: 5/16-14
Standard butt cap: Delrin 1 1/8 in.
Standard number of shafts: one
Standard taper: 10 in. pro
Standard ferrules: melamine
Standard tip: Triangle
Standard tip width: 13 mm

OPTIONS & PRICING (FOR NEW CUES ONLY)
Ivory joint: $125
Ivory ferrule: $65
Ivory butt cap: $160
Custom joint protectors: $50 per set
Leather wrap: $75
Lizard and exotic wraps: $125
Layered tip: $40

REPAIR PRICING (RAUENZAHN, MEUCCI, MCDERMOTT ONLY)
Refinish with Irish linen: $110
Refinish with leather wrap: $150
Rewrap linen: $35
Rewrap leather: $75
Replace fiber ferrule: $25
Replace linen ferrule: $35
Replace ivory ferrule: $65
Replace shaft with fiber/melamine ferrule: $95
Replace shaft with ivory ferrule: $130
Replace butt cap (Delrin/linen): $35
Replace ivory butt cap: $160
Replace tip: $15
Replace layered tip: $45

CURRENT RAUENZAHN CUES
Basic two-piece Rauenzahn cues with wraps and joint rings start at $200. Rauenzahn cues with points start at $375. Rauenzahn cues with veneered points start at $475. One-of-a-kind custom Rauenzahn cues start at $775. The current delivery time for a Rauenzahn cue is five to ten weeks.

CURRENT EXAMPLES
The following Rauenzahn cues can be ordered as shown, modified to suit the desires of the customer, or new designs can be created.

Level 2 - Ivory joint, ebony forearm with ivory ringwork above wrap, leather wrap, ebony butt sleeve with ivory ringwork at top and bottom, ivory butt cap.

MSR	$850	$800-950	$650	$450

Level 3 - Ebony forearm with an ebony/snakewood/maple stitch ring above wrap, three long and three short snakewood points, leather wrap, snakewood butt sleeve with an ebony/snakewood/maple stitch ring below wrap above a thick ebony ring with ebony/snakewood/maple stitch rings at top and bottom.

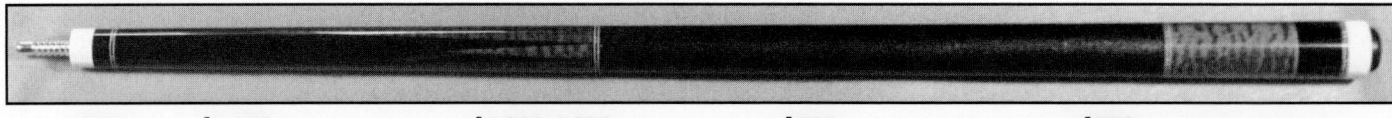

MSR	$1,250	$1,200-1,350	$985	$750

RAUENZAHN CUSTOM CUES, cont.

GRADING	100%	95%	70%

Level 4 - Ivory joint, bird's-eye maple forearm, four ebony points with four colored veneers and an ivory spear-shaped inlay in each point, leather wrap, ebony butt sleeve with two ivory windows with four colored veneers alternating with two four-piece diamond-shaped inlays, ivory butt cap.

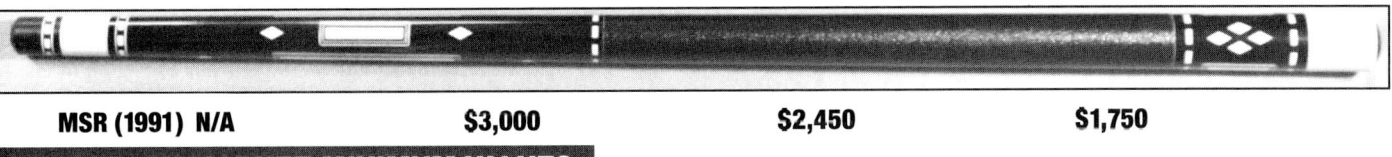

MSR	$1,400	$1,300-1,500	$1,095	$850

GRADING	98%	90%	70%

DISCONTINUED EXAMPLES

Level 4 - Ivory joint, ebony forearm with a ring of ivory blocks above wrap, two long ivory windows with four colored veneers between ivory diamond-shaped inlays above and below alternating with two short ivory windows with four colored veneers between ivory diamond-shaped inlays above and below, leather wrap, ebony butt sleeve with two ivory windows with four colored veneers alternating with two four-piece diamond-shaped inlays between rings of ivory blocks above and below, ivory butt cap.

MSR (1991) N/A	$3,000	$2,450	$1,750

SECONDARY MARKET MINIMUM VALUES

The following are minimum values for other Rauenzahn cues encountered on the secondary market. These prices are representative of cues utilizing basic materials and designs that are not necessarily available at present. Jerry has offered one-of-a-kind cues that can command many times these prices due to the use of exotic materials and artistry.

Special construction note: There are many materials and construction techniques that can add value to Rauenzahn cues. For all used Rauenzahn cues, except where otherwise noted:

- Add $80 for each additional original straight playable shaft beyond one.
- Deduct $95 for missing original straight playable shaft.
- Add $55 each for ivory ferrules.
- Add $65 for leather wrap.
- Deduct 20% for obvious or improper refinish.

Level 2 - 0 points, 0-25 inlays.
Level 2 cues start at	$185	$145	$95

Level 3 - 2-6 points, 0-8 inlays.
Level 3 cues start at	$350	$270	$185

Level 4 - 4-10 points, 9-25 inlays.
Level 4 cues start at	$450	$350	$240

Level 5 - 0-12 points, 26-50 inlays.
Level 5 cues start at	$750	$575	$390

Level 6 - 0-12 points, 51-75 inlays.
Level 6 cues start at	$1,100	$865	$595

RAVEN CUSTOM CUES

Maker of pool cues from 2000 to present in Marion, Iowa.

Michael Wagner, cuemaker and owner of Raven Custom Cues, has varied interests and aptitudes. From an early age, he immersed himself in the things that interested him. At age sixteen, he began to work at a local bowling alley that had a large poolroom. That is when his interest in pool playing really got started. While in college, Michael started playing golf and learned to scuba dive. Later, he owned a successful scuba diving business.

Michael was exposed to building as an art form while working on building sailing yachts in Galveston, Texas. He was an apprentice to men who had been woodworking since before Michael was born. Their use of tools and techniques, as well as the quality aspects of the work they were doing, would become part of the foundation for Michael's cue building.

Michael was a golfer who built and repaired golf clubs for 27 years. That is where he honed his art of craftsmanship. There are far more similarities between golf clubs and pool cues than one might initially think. Each club has a look, a feel, a specific length, a specific weight and its own playing characteristics. It is one of a set and has to be matched to the others in the set as far as performance is concerned. By building golf clubs that fit his hands, physical build, swing and style of play, Michael significantly lowered his own handicap. He found he could do that for others as well.

Michael's other passion was pool. He started to experiment with cues and found that he could make them play better, just as he had with golf clubs. He started RAVEN Custom Cues with the same goals in mind. Michael builds cues to fit the physical characteristics of the individual client. He tries to determine as much as he can about the client, taking into account their tastes as far as style is concerned.

He tries to determine their style of play, what games they play, their strengths and weaknesses as a player, and the areas they want to improve. Michael builds cues to fit the physique and preferences of different players. He uses different woods, different construction techniques, and different joint configurations to produce cues with a range of playing characteristics to choose from. Raven Custom Cues is a voting member of the American Cuemakers Association.

If you are interested in talking to Michael Wagner about a new cue or cue that needs to be repaired, you can contact him at Raven Custom Cues, listed in the Trademark Index.

Michael Wagner

Present Day

SPECIFICATIONS

Butt material: hardwoods
Shaft material: hard rock maple
Standard length: 58.5 in.
Lengths available: up to 64 in.
Standard finish: automotive clear coat
Balance point: 18 to 18.5 in. from butt
Standard butt cap: linen phenolic
Standard wrap: Irish linen
Point construction: short splice or inlaid
Standard joint: phenolic
Standard joint type: flat faced
Standard number of shafts: one
Standard taper: Raven proprietary
Standard ferrules: fiber
Standard tip: Le Pro
Standard tip width: 13 mm
Tip widths available: 9 mm to 14 mm
Annual production: fewer than 50 cues

OPTIONS (FOR NEW CUES ONLY)

Special length: no charge
Layered tip: $5+
Ivory butt cap: $225
Ivory butt sleeve: $700+
Ivory joint: $150
Ivory ferrule: $50
Inlaid ivory points: $150 each
Leather wrap: $175+
Joint protectors: $40+
Extra shaft: $59+

REPAIRS

Repairs done on all fine cues.
Refinish (with Irish linen wrap): $175
Refinish (with leather wrap): $275+
Rewrap (Irish linen): $35
Rewrap (leather): $175+
Clean and press linen wrap: $15
Restore leather wrap: $25+
Replace shaft: $125+
Replace ivory ferrule: $55
Replace butt cap: $35+
Replace ivory butt cap: $240+
Replace tip: $10 + tip
Replace fiber/linen ferrule: $25

CURRENT RAVEN CUES

Two-piece Raven bar cues start at $269. Basic Raven cues with wraps and joint rings start at $299. Raven cues with points start at $479. One-of-a-kind custom Raven cues start at $649. The current delivery time for a Raven cue is about one year.

CURRENT EXAMPLES

The following Raven cues can be ordered as shown, modified to suit the desires of the customer, or new designs can be created.

GRADING	100%	95%	70%

Level 1 - Maple forearm, four full-spliced rosewood points and handle with a yellowheart/ebony/purpleheart butterfly splice coming up from the butt cap.

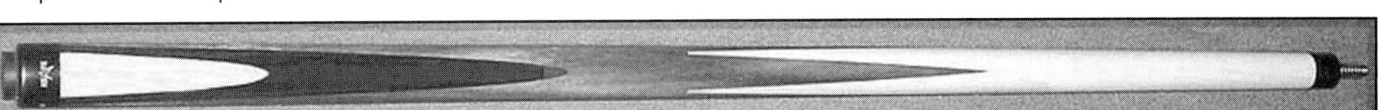

MSR	$329	$300-350	$245	$185

Level 2 - Hickory forearm, hickory butt sleeve.

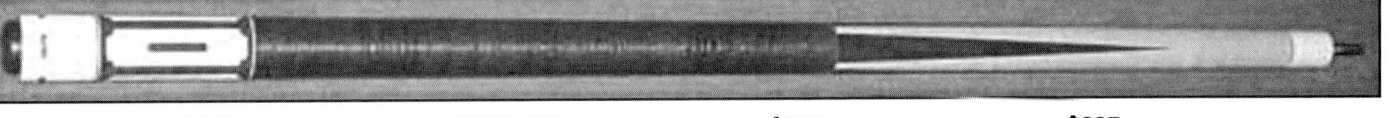

MSR	$359	$340-395	$275	$200

Level 3 - Curly maple forearm with a blue and white ring above handle, four purpleheart points, purpleheart butt sleeve with four hollow synthetic ivory razor blade-shaped windows between blue and white rings at top and bottom.

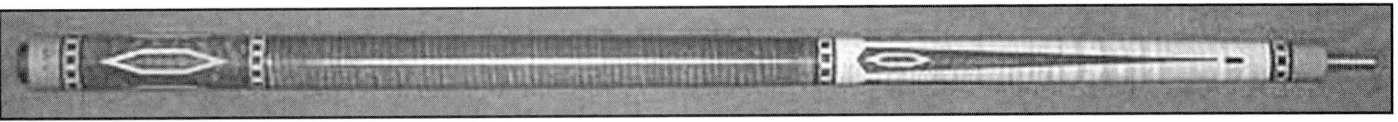

MSR	$425	$400-475	$325	$235

Level 4 - Stained curly maple forearm with an ebony/maple/yellowheart/cocobolo block ring above wrap, four floating snakewood points with a hollow hexagonal yellowheart diamond-shaped inlay in each point and an ebony spear-shaped inlay above the tip of each point, stacked leather wrap, snakewood butt sleeve with four hollow hexagonal yellowheart diamond-shaped inlays between ebony/maple/yellowheart/cocobolo block rings at top and bottom.

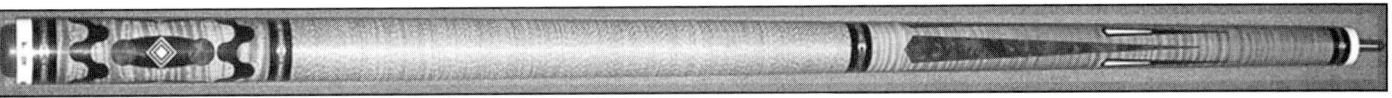

MSR	$1,350	$1,300-1,450	$1,045	$750

Level 5 - Stained curly maple forearm with double nickel silver rings above wrap, four long floating amboyna burl points alternating below four short floating ebony-bordered ivory points, stained curly maple butt sleeve with four intricate ivory/ebony/amboyna burl windows within wavy ebony rings between double nickel silver rings at top and bottom.

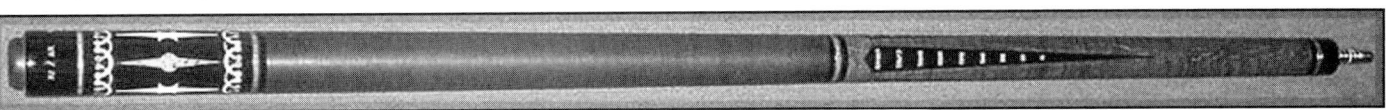

MSR	$1,869	$1,750-2,000	$1,445	$1,050

Level 6 - Stained curly maple forearm with a maple and silver stich ring above wrap, four floating ebony points with nine rectangular web turquoise inlays in each point, ebony butt sleeve with three intricate web turquoise augmented diamond-shaped inlays alternating with three intricate ivory augmented diamond-shaped inlays within rings of overlapping intricate web turquoise horseshoe-shaped inlays alternating with intricate ivory horseshoe-shaped inlays between maple and silver stich rings at top and bottom.

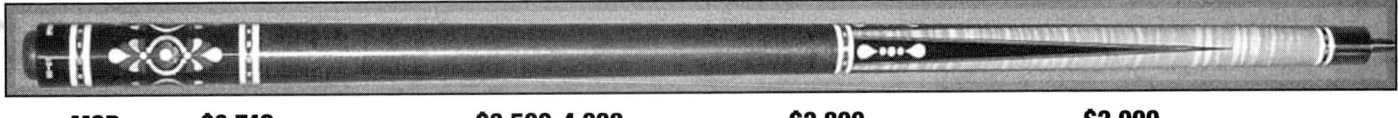

MSR	$2,549	$2,400-2,750	$2,000	$1,500

Level 7 - Stained curly maple forearm with a maple and cocobolo stitch ring set in brass rings above wrap, four ebony points with veneers and five-piece ivory inlay in each point, ebony butt sleeve with four ivory/bloody basin jasper/yellowheart/amboyna burl mosaic inlaid patterns between maple and cocobolo stich rings set in brass rings at top and bottom.

MSR	$3,749	$3,500-4,000	$2,800	$2,000

GRADING	98%	90%	70%

SECONDARY MARKET MINIMUM VALUES

The following are minimum values for other Raven cues encountered on the secondary market. These prices are representative of cues utilizing basic materials and designs that are not necessarily available at present. Raven has offered one-of-a-kind cues that can command many times these prices due to the use of exotic materials and artistry.

Special construction note: There are many materials and construction techniques that can add value to Raven cues.

For all used Raven cues, except where otherwise noted:
- Add $50+ for each additional original straight playable shaft beyond one.
- Deduct $60+ for missing original straight playable shaft.
- Add $45 each for ivory ferrules.
- Add $75 for leather wrap.
- Deduct 20% for obvious or improper refinish.

Level 1 - Hustler.

	98%	90%	70%
Level 1 cues start at	$225	$175	$115

Level 2 - 0 points, 0-25 inlays.

Level 2 cues start at	$250	$195	$130

Level 3 - 2-6 points, 0-8 inlays.

Level 3 cues start at	$400	$315	$215

Level 4 - 4-10 points, 9-25 inlays.

Level 4 cues start at	$500	$390	$265

Level 5 - 0-12 points, 26-50 inlays.

Level 5 cues start at	$800	$620	$420

Level 6 - 0-12 points, 51-75 inlays.

Level 6 cues start at	$1,100	$860	$585

REEVES CUSTOM CUES

Maker of pool cues from 2003 to present in Easley, South Carolina.

Jimmy Reeves has always worked with his hands. He is a tool and die maker by trade and Jimmy has always been fascinated with playing pool. Jimmy built tooling for another cuemaker, and decided to start making his own cues part time in 2003. Jimmy continues to do tool and die work full time while making one-of-a-kind handmade cues in his spare time with partner Larry Nevel. They make everything except for the tips, bumpers, and screws in their two-man shop. Playability is the most important factor in the construction of Reeves cues. Short-spliced blanks are made in-house.

Reeves cues are easily identified by the "Reeves" name engraved in the butt caps. If you are interested in talking to Jimmy about a new cue or cue that needs to be repaired, you can contact him at Reeves Custom Cues, listed in the Trademark Index.

SPECIFICATIONS

- Butt material: hardwoods
- Shaft material: rock maple
- Standard length: 58 in.
- Standard wrap: Irish linen

SECONDARY MARKET MINIMUM VALUES

The following are minimum values for Reeves cues encountered on the secondary market. These prices are representative of cues utilizing basic materials and designs that are not necessarily available at present. Jimmy has offered one-of-a-kind cues that can command many times these prices due to the use of exotic materials and artistry.

Special construction note: There are many materials and construction techniques that can add value to Reeves cues.

For all used Reeves cues, except where otherwise noted:
- Add $75 for each additional original straight playable shaft beyond one.
- Deduct $100 for missing original straight playable shaft.
- Add $50 each for ivory ferrules.
- Add $65 for leather wrap.
- Deduct 20% for obvious or improper refinish.

Level 1 - Hustler.

	98%	90%	70%
Level 1 cues start at	$250	$195	$135

Level 2 - 0 points, 0-25 inlays.

Level 2 cues start at	$350	$275	$190

Level 3 - 2-6 points, 0-8 inlays.

Level 3 cues start at	$450	$345	$230

Level 4 - 4-10 points, 9-25 inlays.

Level 4 cues start at	$600	$565	$315

GRADING	98%	90%	70%
Level 5 - 0-12 points, 26-50 inlays.			
Level 5 cues start at	$900	$700	$480

BOB RENIS

Maker of pool cues in San Diego, California.

EDWIN REYES CUSTOM HANDCRAFTED CUES

Maker of pool cues from 1988, in Yucca Valley, California, to present in Quezon City, Philippines.

Edwin Reyes has a background in engineering technology, advertising, and radiologic technology. He got into cuemaking by starting with repairs. He started repairing cues in 1986 and was inspired to create his own cue after beholding, for the first time, an ebony and ivory Schrager and Ron Rosas rosewood Gina cue at a national tournament in Las Vegas. There is a minimum order time of six months, depending on intricacy of design, for a Reyes Custom Cue. Edwin Reyes cues are easily identifiable by the Edwin Reyes logo on the bumpers. If you are interested in talking to Edwin Reyes about a new cue or cue that needs to be repaired, you can contact him at Edwin Reyes Custom Handcrafted Cues, listed in the Trademark Index.

SPECIFICATIONS

- Butt material: hardwoods
- Shaft material: North American hard maple
- Standard length: 58 in.
- Lengths available: any
- Standard finish: proprietary
- Balance point: custom
- Standard butt cap: double black linen
- Standard wrap: Irish linen
- Point construction: short splice or inlaid
- Standard joint: double black linen
- Joint type: flat faced
- Standard joint screw thread: 5/16-14
- Joint protectors: standard
- Standard number of shafts: two
- Standard taper: parabolic to shoulder
- Standard ferrules: ivory
- Standard tip: proprietary
- Standard tip width: 13 mm
- Tip widths available: 10 to 14 mm
- Annual production: fewer than 40 cues

OPTIONS (FOR NEW CUES ONLY)

- Ivory butt cap: $350+
- Ivory joint: $250+
- Joint protectors: $200+
- Extra shaft: $250+

SECONDARY MARKET MINIMUM VALUES

The following are minimum values for other Reyes cues encountered on the secondary market. These prices are representative of cues utilizing basic materials and designs that are not necessarily available at present. Edwin has offered one-of-a-kind cues that can command many times these prices due to the use of exotic materials and artistry.

Special construction note: There are many materials and construction techniques that can add value to Reyes cues.

For all used Reyes cues, except where otherwise noted:

- Add $85 for each additional original straight playable shaft beyond two.
- Deduct $100 for each missing original straight playable shaft under two.
- Add $50 each for ivory ferrules.
- Add $60 for leather wrap.
- Deduct 20% for obvious or improper refinish.

	98%	90%	70%
Level 2 - 0 points, 0-25 inlays.			
Level 2 cues start at	$300	$235	$160
Level 3 - 2-6 points, 0-8 inlays.			
Level 3 cues start at	$450	$350	$235
Level 4 - 4-10 points, 9-25 inlays.			
Level 4 cues start at	$525	$405	$270
Level 5 - 0-12 points, 26-50 inlays.			
Level 5 cues start at	$800	$615	$420

RHINO CUES

GRADING	98%	90%	70%

Maker of pool cues from 1992 to present in Danbury, Texas.

Charlie Wilhite began building Rhino cues in 1992. His wife, Debbie, helped him come up with the cue name. They were looking for a name that exuded toughness. "Rhino" seemed perfect. Charlie credits Kim Van Zandt with his development as a cuemaker. Dennis Dieckman, Gary Medlin, Jim and George Buss and Richard Black also offered encouragement and advice along the way. Rhino cues have been featured several times in the American Cueist, including once on its cover.

Most Rhino cues are built with a wood-to-wood flat-face joint and a 3/8-10 stainless pin. Charlie builds other types of joints (customer's preference) but believes that Harvey Martin's joint style is hard to beat! Having built many pieces of custom jewelry, Charlie can work with precious metals, scrimshaw and gems to create an elaborate or unusual cue. However, his primary concern has always been to build well-balanced cues that hit solidly and feel "just right" in the player's hands. Don't look for CNC equipment in Charlie's shop. "I have no quarrel with the guys who utilize computers. I just truly enjoy building cues in the time-honored fashion of cuemakers of yesteryear." He wants to build cues of your design or his design. Cue inlays range from simple diamonds to other geometric designs, animals, and even angels.

Rhino cues are guaranteed for life against manufacturing defects that are not the result of warpage or abuse. If you have a Rhino cue that needs further identification or repair, or would like to order a new Rhino cue, contact Rhino Cues, listed in the Trademark Index.

Charlie Wilhite

Present Day

SPECIFICATIONS

Butt material: hardwoods
Shaft material: hard maple
Standard length: 58 in.
Lengths available: any
Standard finish: polyurethane
Point construction: short splice
Standard butt cap: linen phenolic
Standard wrap: Irish linen
Joint type: flat faced
Joint screw: 3/8-10
Standard taper: 10 in. straight

SECONDARY MARKET MINIMUM VALUES

The following are minimum prices for Rhino cues encountered on the secondary market. These prices are representative of cues utilizing basic materials and designs that may not be currently available. Charlie also offers one-of-a-kind cues that can command many times these prices due to the use of exotic materials and artistry.

Special construction note: There are many materials and construction techniques that can add value to Rhino cues.

For all used Rhino cues, except where otherwise noted:
- Add $95+ for each additional original straight playable shaft beyond one.
- Deduct $120 for missing original straight playable shaft.
- Add $85+ for ivory joint.
- Add $60+ for leather wrap.
- Deduct 20% for obvious or improper refinish.

Level 1 - 4 points, hustler.

	98%	90%	70%
Level 1 cues start at	$275	$200	$150

Level 2 - 0 points, 0-25 inlays.

Level 2 cues start at	$350	$250	$175

Level 3 - 2-6 points, 0-8 inlays.

Level 3 cues start at	$500	$380	$250

Level 4 - 4-10 points, 9-25 inlays.

Level 4 cues start at	$650	$510	$350

Level 5 - 0-12 points, 26-50 inlays.

Level 5 cues start at	$1,000	$785	$550

| GRADING | 98% | 90% | 70% |

R.H.N. CUSTOM CUES

Maker of pool cues from 1994 to present in Cincinnati, Ohio.

Richard Neighbors grew up with a pool table in his parents' home and has played the game since the age of seven. He started working on cues when he left the service in 1966, and even made a few hustler cues during that time. He later became a partner with his cuemaking friend, Sherm Adamson, in 1992. In 1994, the two split up the partnership and Richard started making cues on his own. The two remain the best of friends, and often spend time in each other's shops.

Richard now makes about one cue a week in his one-man shop. He makes everything himself, except for the tips, screws, and bumpers. Custom-designed inlays and points are available, and Richard uses the latest in CNC technology. He can also make short-spliced cues if the customer prefers. Most R.H.N. cues are easily identifiable by the "Richard H. Neighbors" signature that is usually followed by the date of completion on the cues.

R.H.N. custom cues are guaranteed for life against manufacturing defects that are not the result of warpage or abuse. If you have an R.H.N. cue that needs further identification or repair, or would like to order a new R.H.N. cue, contact R.H.N. Custom Cues, listed in the Trademark Index.

Richard Neighbors

SPECIFICATIONS

Butt material: hardwoods
Shaft material: rock maple
Standard length: 58 in.
Balance point: 18 1/2 in. from the butt
Standard finish: three-part urethane
Standard wrap: Irish linen
Point construction: inlaid or short splice
Standard joint: short stainless steel
Joint type: flat faced
Joint screw: 3/8-10
Standard number of shafts: one
Standard ferrules: melamine
Standard tip: water buffalo
Annual production: fewer than 60 cues

CURRENT R.H.N. CUES

The current delivery time for an R.H.N. cue is five to eight weeks.

SECONDARY MARKET MINIMUM VALUES

The following are minimum values for R.H.N. custom cues encountered on the secondary market. These prices are representative of cues utilizing basic materials and designs that are not necessarily available at present. Richard has offered one-of-a-kind cues that can command many times these prices due to the use of exotic materials and artistry.

Special construction note: There are many materials and construction techniques that can add value to R.H.N. cues.

For all used R.H.N. cues, except where otherwise noted:
Add $75 for each additional original straight playable shaft beyond one.
Deduct $95 for missing original straight playable shaft.
Add $55 each for ivory ferrules.
Deduct 20% for obvious or improper refinish.

Level 2 - 0 points, 0-25 inlays.
| Level 2 cues start at | $325 | $250 | $170 |

Level 3 - 2-6 points, 0-8 inlays.
| Level 3 cues start at | $450 | $355 | $245 |

Level 4 - 4-10 points, 9-25 inlays.
| Level 4 cues start at | $600 | $465 | $315 |

Level 5 - 0-12 points, 26-50 inlays.
| Level 5 cues start at | $850 | $655 | $440 |

Level 6 - 0-12 points, 51-75 inlays.
| Level 6 cues start at | $1,200 | $945 | $650 |

GRADING	98%	90%	70%

RICCO CUSTOM CUES

Maker of pool cues from 1967 to 1995, primarily in Tampa, Florida, currently in Glen Ellyn, Illinois.

Rigoberto "Ricco" Cervantes immigrated to the United States from Mexico at the age of eighteen. His interest in billiards led to a job at National Tournament Cues in Chicago. He was introduced to cuemaking by Richard Helmstetter. Ricco worked with other cuemakers, such as Wayne Gunn and Craig Peterson, who have had an influence on his work. He worked at making cues from 1967 to 1969, and then moved to Macon, Georgia and continued to work for National until 1971. From 1971 to 1973, he worked for Gandy Billiards.

Ricco eventually returned to Chicago to continue his original tool and die career. From 1973 to 1984 he made cues part time out of his home. After a five-year return to his home country, Mexico, he moved to Tampa in 1989, where he worked full time making cues for Robertson Billiards until 1993. Ricco then made cues part time in a small wood shop behind Baker's Billiards (the oldest pool hall in Florida) in Tampa, until his retirement in 1995.

In 2002, Ricco spent one year living in Glen Ellyn, Illinois, teaching his son, Marco Cervantes, how to make cues. Marco continues the family tradition to this day. Ricco has returned to Mexico.

Ricco made more than 100 cues per year, entirely by hand, in his one man-shop in Tampa, Florida. Ivory points, precious metals and stones, and rare coins were commonly featured on high end Ricco cues. All Ricco cues are easily identifiable by the "Ricco" logo which appears on the butt caps. Today, Marco Cervantes marks the cues with "Ricco Cues" with a small mustache. He is building about a dozen cues per year, part time, while working full time as a facility manager for a large consulting firm.

Rigoberto "Ricco" Cervantes

Ricco cues are guaranteed indefinitely against construction defects that are not the result of warpage or abuse. If you have a Ricco cue that needs further identification or repair, contact Ricco Custom Cues, listed in the Trademark Index.

SPECIFICATIONS

Butt material: exotic woods
Shaft material: Canadian hard maple
Standard length: 58 in.
Lengths available: 57 to 59 in.
Standard finish: clear lacquer
Standard joint type: wood
Standard ferrules: fiber
Standard wrap: Irish linen
Standard tip: 13 mm Le Pro

OPTIONS (FOR NEW CUES ONLY)

Ivory ferrule: $45+
Leather wrap: $85+
Extra shaft: $85+
Lizard and other exotic wraps: $95+
Custom joint protectors: $40

REPAIRS

Repairs are not offered.

CURRENT RICCO CUES

The current delivery time for a Ricco custom cue is eight to twelve weeks.

SECONDARY MARKET MINIMUM VALUES

The following are minimum prices for Ricco cues encountered on the secondary market. These prices are representative of cues utilizing basic materials and designs. Ricco made many one-of-a-kind cues that can command many times these prices due to the use of exotic materials and artistry.

Special construction note: There are many materials and construction techniques that can add value to Ricco cues.

For all used Ricco cues:
Add $75 for each extra straight playable shaft beyond one.
Deduct $85 for missing original straight playable shaft.
Deduct 25% for obvious or improper refinish.

Level 2 - 0 points, 0-25 inlays.
	98%	90%	70%
Level 2 cues start at	$500	$390	$265

Level 3 - 2-6 points, 0-8 inlays.
Level 3 cues start at	$650	$515	$345

Level 4 - 4-10 points, 9-25 inlays.
Level 4 cues start at	$950	$735	$500

Level 5 - 0-12 points, 26-50 inlays.
Level 5 cues start at	$1,550	$1,200	$800

| GRADING | 98% | 90% | 70% |

ABE RICH

Maker of cues for Star Cue Company. For information, refer to the listing for Star Cue.

RICH CUE

Maker of pool cues from 1912 to 1982 in Freeport, New York.

The Rich Cue Company was founded in 1912 in Freeport, New York. The company made many thousands of cues over seven decades. Saul Rich operated the family business in its heyday with the assistance of two of his relatives who were both talented cuemakers in their own right: his uncle, Isadore Rutzisky, and cousin, Abe Rich. It remained a family business until Saul sold the company to Ike Algaze in 1970. Ike then ran the business until he sold it to Imperial Billiards in the mid-1970s. In 1982, Imperial ceased production of Rich cues. Most Rich cues are unmarked, but those with "Rich Q" under a clear plastic window are easy to identify. Some Rich cues from the 1960s bear a strong resemblance to those made by Doc Fry which were being made at the same time from similar materials such as marbled plastic rings in the butt sleeve. If you have a Rich cue that needs further identification or repair, contact Mark Kulungian at Pool Table Magic, listed in the Buy, Sell, Trade Index, or Rubino Cues, listed in the Trademark Index.

SPECIFICATIONS

Butt material: hardwoods
Shaft material: rock maple
Standard wrap: nylon
Point construction: full or short splice
Standard number of shafts: one

DISCONTINUED CUES

The following cues are from the 1976 Rich Cue catalogue. They were easily identifiable by the "Rich Q" logo under a clear plastic window above the butt cap. They were originally available from $17 to $50 wholesale, with the retail prices to be determined by the seller.

Level 2 5-E - One-piece rosewood butt with "Rich Q" on gold foil under a clear plastic window at bottom.

$385 $285 $175

Level 2 5-F - Rosewood forearm, multi-colored nylon wrap, rosewood butt sleeve with "Rich Q" on gold foil under a clear plastic window at bottom.

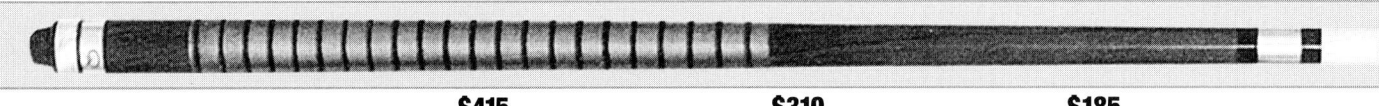

$415 $310 $185

Level 2 5-G - Rosewood forearm, multi-colored nylon handle, butt sleeve with three rings of multi-colored plastic with "Rich Q" on gold foil under a clear plastic window at bottom.

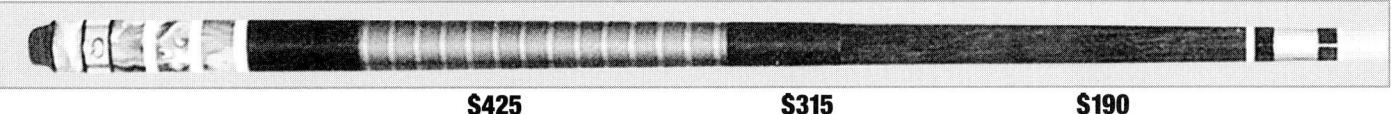

$425 $315 $190

Level 3 5-H - Maple forearm, four rosewood points with four colored veneers, rosewood butt sleeve with "Rich Q" on gold foil under a clear plastic window at bottom.

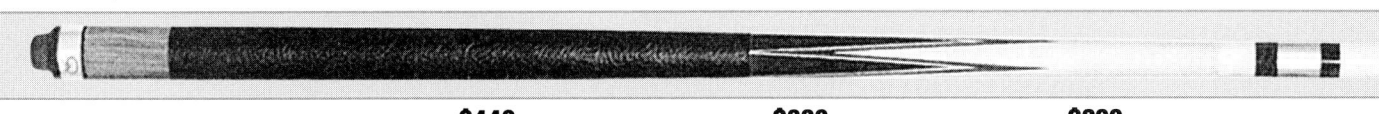

$440 $330 $200

Level 2 5-I - Rosewood forearm with pairs of mother-of-pearl dots above and below mother-of-pearl notched diamond-shaped inlays towards bottom, butt sleeve with plastic rings above "Rich Q" on gold foil under a clear plastic window at bottom.

$455 $340 $210

GRADING	98%	90%	70%

Level 3 5-J - Maple forearm with pearlized plastic rings at bottom, four rosewood points with four colored veneers, butt sleeve of pearlized plastic rings with "Rich Q" on gold foil under a clear plastic window in center.

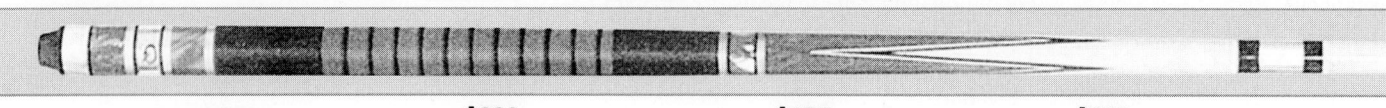

	$660	$495	$300

Level 4 5-K - Maple forearm with a plastic ring at bottom, four rosewood points with four colored veneers, butt sleeve of hardwood blocks inlaid above "Rich Q" on gold foil under a clear plastic window at bottom.

	$510	$385	$240

Level 2 5-L - Rosewood forearm with a series of mother-of-pearl dots and notched diamond-shaped inlays above pearlized plastic rings at bottom, maple butt sleeve with pearlized plastic notched diamond-shaped inlays set in ebony windows between ebony dots and rings above "Rich Q" on gold foil under a clear plastic window at bottom.

	$820	$615	$395

Level 4 5-M - Maple forearm with plastic rings at bottom, three long and three short rosewood points with four colored veneers, ebony butt sleeve with white plastic dots above "Rich Q" on gold foil under a clear plastic window at bottom.

	$700	$515	$315

Level 4 5-N - Maple forearm with pearlized plastic rings at bottom, four rosewood points with mother-of-pearl dots in each point, ebony butt sleeve with mother-of-pearl dots above "Rich Q" on gold foil under a clear plastic window at bottom.

	$765	$565	$350

Level 4 5-O - Maple forearm with a ring of hardwood blocks at bottom, four rosewood points with four colored veneers and a pair of pearlized plastic dots above and below an ivory-colored diamond-shaped inlay in each point, butt sleeve with rings of hardwood blocks above "Rich Q" on gold foil under a clear plastic window at bottom.

	$950	$695	$425

Level 5 5-P - Maple forearm with pearlized plastic rings at bottom, three long and three short rosewood points with four colored veneers and a mother-of-pearl diamond-shaped inlay between three mother-of-pearl dots above and two mother-of-pearl dots below in each long point, rosewood butt sleeve with three mother-of-pearl diamond-shaped inlays between white plastic rings above "Rich Q" on gold foil under a clear plastic window at bottom.

	$725	$540	$340

Level 5 5-Q - Maple forearm, three long and three short ebony points with four colored veneers and a mother-of-pearl notched diamond-shaped inlay between three mother-of-pearl dots above and two mother-of-pearl dots below in each long point, ebony butt sleeve with four mother-of-pearl notched diamond-shaped inlays set in veneer-bordered ebony windows between checked rings above "Rich Q" on gold foil under a clear plastic window at bottom.

	$1,200	$895	$550

GRADING	98%	90%	70%

Level 5 5-R - Maple forearm with patterns of ebony dots towards top and pearlized plastic rings at bottom, three long and three short ebony points with pearlized plastic notched diamond-shaped inlays between pairs of mother-of-pearl dots in each long point, maple butt sleeve with four mother-of-pearl notched diamond-shaped inlays set in veneer-bordered ebony windows above "Rich Q" on gold foil under a clear plastic window at bottom.

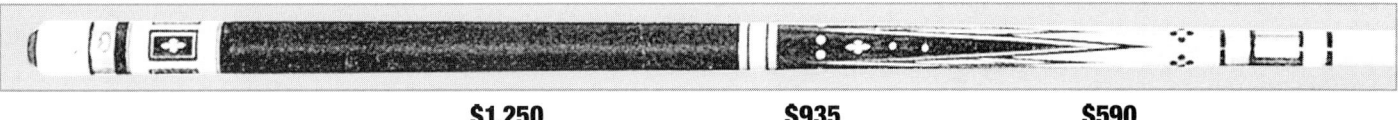

	$1,250	$935	$590

SECONDARY MARKET MINIMUM VALUES

The following are minimum values for other Rich cues encountered on the secondary market. These prices are representative of cues utilizing basic materials and designs that were available at the time the cues were made. Early models and limited editions are becoming collectible, and can also command many times these prices. Rich cues will be further covered in future editions.

Special construction note: There are many materials and construction techniques that can add value to Rich cues. The following are the most important examples:

Add 25% for identification marks such as "Rich Q" under a clear plastic window.

For all used Rich cues, except where otherwise noted:

Add $95 for each additional original straight playable shaft beyond one.
Deduct 50% for missing original straight playable shaft.
Add $60 each for ivory ferrules.
Add $125 for leather wrap.
Deduct 30% for obvious or improper refinish.

Level 2 - 0 points, 0-25 inlays.
Level 2 cues start at	$255	$190	$115

Level 3 - 2-6 points, 0-8 inlays.
Level 3 cues start at	$335	$250	$150

Level 4 - 4-10 points, 9-25 inlays.
Level 4 cues start at	$450	$290	$220

Level 5 - 0-12 points, 26-50 inlays.
Level 5 cues start at	$675	$510	$320

Level 6 - 0-12 points, 51-75 inlays.
Level 6 cues start at	$900	$685	$430

HARRY RICHARDS CUSTOM CUES

Maker of pool cues from 1989 to present in Daytona Beach, Florida.

Harry Richards' cuemaking experience started in Tampa, Florida, in the late 1980s. He was trying to find someone who knew how to put a tip on a cue and do it properly. It was there that he met Wayne Gunn, who had made cues and had the know-how for doing a good job. Harry decided that cuemaking would be something he might enjoy. Wayne took him under his wing and began the slow process of learning how to work on pool cues.

In 1989 Harry made his first sneaky pete, a great playing cue. He made sneaky petes, break jump cues, and merry widows for two years, learning, experimenting, and trying to find the secret ingredient that makes for an excellent playing cue. Every time he put a cue together, Harry was looking for something that could be done to make it even better than what it was. During this same time, Harry started doing cue work at pool tournaments around Florida. This was a valuable experience for him, learning what needed to be done to make a cue play better.

In about 1994, Harry met another cuemaker, Dennis Searing, from Ft Lauderdale. He had been making cues for quite some time. They became friends and swapped trade secrets. In 1999, Harry went to work for Dennis and gained an immense amount of education, for which Harry is thankful. Commuting became a major problem, and now Harry is back in Daytona, Florida in his own shop.

If you are interested in talking to Harry Richards about a new cue or cue that needs to be repaired, you can contact him at Harry Richards Custom Cues, listed in the Trademark Index.

Present Day

SPECIFICATIONS

Butt material: hardwoods
Shaft material: Canadian maple
Standard length: 58 in.
Lengths available: any up to 60 in.
Standard finish: PPG
Balance point: 18 to 18 ½ in.
Standard butt cap: phenolic, 1.250 in.

GRADING	98%	90%	70%

Standard wrap: Irish linen
Point construction: short splice
Standard joint: phenolic
Standard joint type: flat faced
Standard joint screw thread: radial pin
Joint protectors: standard
Standard number of shafts: two
Standard taper: conical
Standard ferrules: linen based
Other ferrule options: ivory
Standard tip: Triangle
Standard tip width: 13 mm
Annual production: approximately 50 cues

OPTIONS (FOR NEW CUES ONLY)

Special length: no charge
Layered tip: $20+
Ivory butt cap: $175
Ivory joint: $100
Ivory ferrule: $60
Leather wrap: $80
Extra shaft: $115+

REPAIRS

Repairs done on all fine cues.
Refinish (with Irish linen wrap): $135
Refinish (with leather wrap): $200
Rewrap (Irish linen): $45
Rewrap (leather): $80
Clean and press linen wrap: $15
Replace shaft (fiber/linen ferrule): $115+
Replace shaft (ivory ferrule): $175+
Replace ivory ferrule: $60
Replace butt cap: $50+
Replace ivory butt cap: $175
Replace tip: $10+
Replaced layered tip: $20+
Replace fiber/linen ferrule: $40

SECONDARY MARKET MINIMUM VALUES

The following are minimum values for Harry Richards cues encountered on the secondary market. These prices are representative of cues utilizing basic materials and designs that are not necessarily available at present. Harry has offered one-of-a-kind cues that can command many times these prices due to the use of exotic materials and artistry.

Special construction note: There are many materials and construction techniques that can add value to Harry Richards cues.

For all used Harry Richards cues, except where otherwise noted:

Add $90 for each additional original straight playable shaft beyond two.
Deduct $115 for each missing original straight playable shaft under two.
Add $50 each for ivory ferrules.
Add $65 for leather wrap.
Deduct 25% for obvious or improper refinish.

	98%	90%	70%
Level 1 - Hustler.			
Level 1 cues start at	$250	$195	$130
Level 2 - 0 points, 0-25 inlays.			
Level 2 cues start at	$400	$315	$210
Level 3 - 2-6 points, 0-8 inlays.			
Level 3 cues start at	$650	$500	$340
Level 4 - 4-10 points, 9-25 inlays.			
Level 4 cues start at	$750	$570	$385
Level 5 - 0-12 points, 26-50 inlays.			
Level 5 cues start at	$1,100	$870	$600
Level 6 - 0-12 points, 51-75 inlays.			
Level 6 cues start at	$1,450	$1,150	$800

| GRADING | 98% | 90% | 70% |

RIEPER MANUFACTURING CO.

Maker of pool cues from the 1870s to 1930s in New York.

Rieper Manufacturing was launched in the late 1800s and, at the turn of the century, was the leading American business committed solely to cue production. Rieper's total output never reached Brunswick's; however, the array and variety of cues that Rieper made accessible unquestionably rivaled Bruswick and perhaps exceeded it. Rieper's catalogs presented multiple design variations and an assortment of styles. In excess of twenty inscribed butt designs were depicted and the corporation was able to produce an infinite quantity of patterns.

From a quality perspective, Rieper's high end cues were considered to be top of the line. In an era when manufacturing procedures had reached a point where products could be produced mechanically in vast amounts, Rieper maintained use of traditional hand fashioning to adorn their cues. Rieper concentrated in custom pieces and was renowned for their "Trophy Cues" and additional distinctive creations for customers desiring an exceptionally unique product. Although Brunswick was more prominent and was unquestionably proficient in satisfying a customer request, Rieper specialized in it and elevated it further. During a period when cues lacked distinguishing marks or labels, one has to scrutinize these cues meticulously to differentiate them from Brunswick and other European manufacturers. After seeing a reasonable quantity of them, certain cues allude to the proper course. Some of the identifiers are the manner in which the base of the cue is finished and formed, bumper varieties, color, and thickness of veneers. Catalogs are usually beneficial; however, the central element is physical contact by handling several and evaluating them with recognized models. Since Brunswick published numerous catalogs and over an extended duration, don't presume that every model 360 or nameless "Prize Cue" is a Brunswick. It may well be a Rieper.

SPECIFICATIONS

Butt material: hardwoods
Shaft material: rock maple
Standard finish: oil
Point construction: full splice
Standard number of shafts: one
Standard ferrules: ivory

DISCONTINUED CUES

The following cues are from a Rieper catalogue, circa 1920s.

Level 3 - Maple forearm, two butterfly spliced hardwood points, woven engraved handle, hardwood butt sleeve.

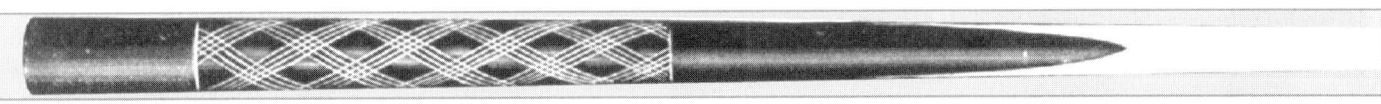

| $950 | $700 | $420 |

Level 3 - Maple forearm, two butterfly spliced hardwood points, floral engraved hardwood handle, hardwood butt sleeve.

| $1,650 | $1,200 | $700 |

Level 3 - Maple forearm, two butterfly spliced hardwood points, floral engraved hardwood handle, hardwood butt sleeve.

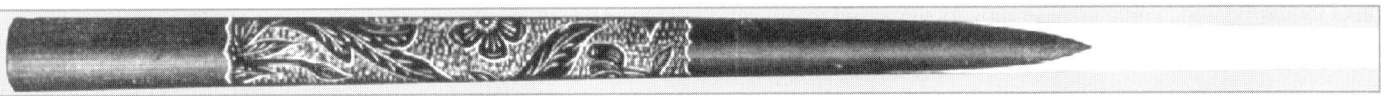

| $1,650 | $1,200 | $700 |

Level 3 - Maple forearm, two butterfly spliced hardwood points, floral engraved hardwood handle, hardwood butt sleeve.

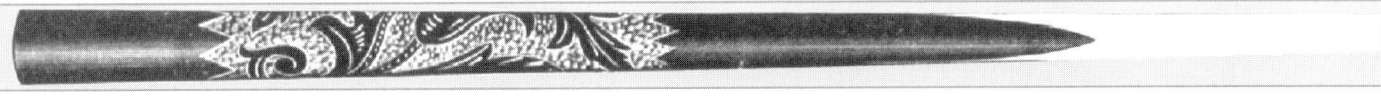

| $1,650 | $1,200 | $700 |

Level 3 - Maple forearm, two butterfly spliced hardwood points with two veneers, engraved handle, hardwood butt sleeve.

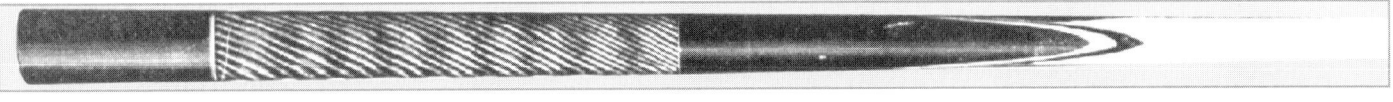

| $1,100 | $800 | $460 |

| GRADING | 98% | 90% | 70% |

Level 3 - Maple forearm, two butterfly spliced hardwood points with two veneers, floral engraved hardwood handle, hardwood butt sleeve with beveled triangle.

| | $2,300 | $1,700 | $995 |

Level 3 - Maple forearm, four full-spliced hardwood points, hand-hammered hardwood handle, hardwood butt sleeve.

| | $1,050 | $785 | $475 |

Level 3 - Maple forearm, four full-spliced hardwood points, engraved hardwood handle, hardwood butt sleeve.

| | $1,750 | $1,300 | $800 |

Level 3 - Maple forearm, four full-spliced hardwood points, engraved hardwood handle, hardwood butt sleeve.

| | $1,775 | $1,315 | $800 |

Level 3 - Maple forearm, four full-spliced hardwood points, engraved handle, hardwood butt sleeve.

| | $2,350 | $1,715 | $1,000 |

Level 3 - Maple forearm, four full-spliced hardwood points, engraved hardwood handle, hardwood butt sleeve with mother-of-pearl beveled triangle with two veneers.

| | $2,000 | $1,500 | $950 |

Level 3 - Maple forearm, four full-spliced hardwood points, floral engraved handle and points, hardwood butt sleeve with mother-of-pearl beveled triangle with two veneers.

| | $2,800 | $2,100 | $1,300 |

Level 3 - Maple forearm, four full-spliced hardwood points with four veneers, engraved hardwood handle, hardwood butt sleeve with mother-of-pearl beveled triangle with two veneers.

| | $2,400 | $1,800 | $1,100 |

Level 3 - Maple forearm, four full-spliced hardwood points with four veneers alternating with four butterfly spliced points with two veneers, engraved hardwood handle, hardwood butt sleeve with mother-of-pearl beveled triangle with two veneers.

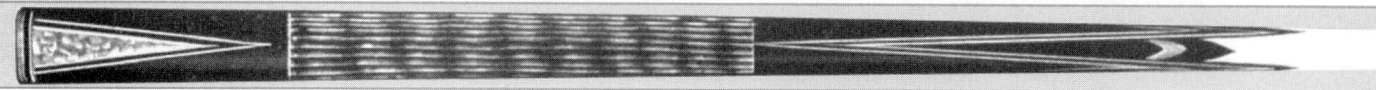

| | $3,850 | $2,850 | $1,750 |

GRADING	98%	90%	70%

Level 3 - Maple forearm, four full-spliced hardwood points with four veneers alternating with two hardwood butterfly points with two veneers, floral engraved handle and points, hardwood butt sleeve with mother-of-pearl beveled rectangle.

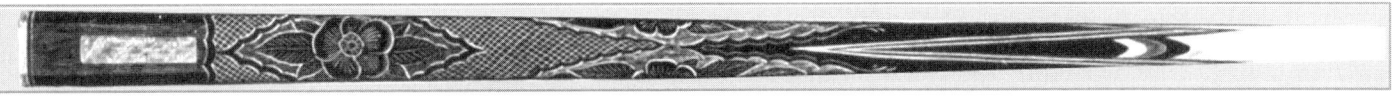

	$5,600	$4,200	$2,600

Level 3 - Maple forearm, two butterfly spliced points with two veneers above four full-spliced hardwood points with four veneers, hand hammered handle, hardwood butt sleeve.

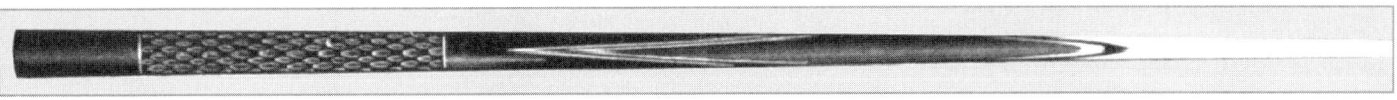

	$5,000	$3,750	$2,200

Level 3 - Maple forearm, four full-spliced hardwood points with veneers alternating with butterfly spliced points with two veneers above two butterfly spliced points with two veneers, hand-hammered hardwood handle, hardwood butt sleeve with mother-of-pearl beveled triangle with two veneers.

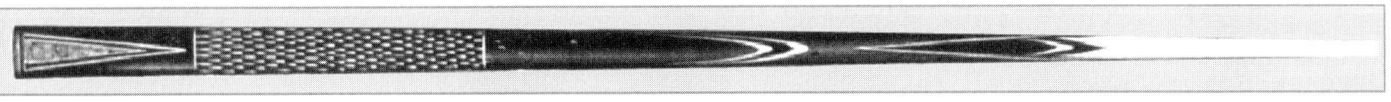

	$5,500	$3,900	$2,100

Level 3 - Maple forearm, four hardwood full-spliced points with four veneers between pairs of butterfly-spliced points with two veneers above and below, engraved hardwood handle, butt sleeve with mother-of-pearl beveled triangle with two veneers.

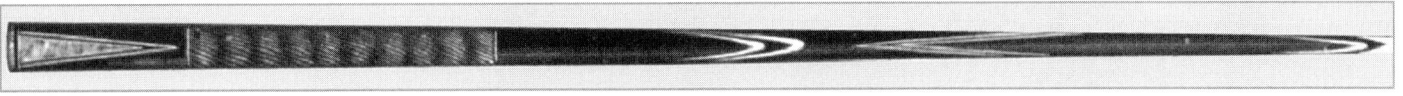

	$6,800	$5,000	$3,000

Level 3 - Maple forearm, two sets of four full-spliced hardwood points with veneers alternating with four hardwood butterfly spliced points with two veneers, stippled hardwood handle, hardwood butt sleeve with mother-of-pearl beveled triangle with two veneers.

	$6,850	$5,000	$3,200

Level 3 - Maple forearm, two sets of four full-spliced hardwood points with veneers alternating with sets of four butterfly spliced points with two veneers around two butterfly spliced points with two veneers, hand hammered handle, hardwood butt sleeve with mother-of-pearl beveled triangle with two veneers.

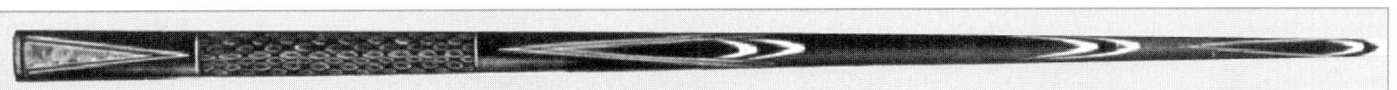

	$9,500	$7,000	$4,350

SECONDARY MARKET MINIMUM VALUES

The following are minimum values for other cues encountered on the secondary market. These prices are representative of cues utilizing basic materials and designs that are not currently available. has offered one-of-a-kind cues that can command many times these prices due to the use of exotic materials and artistry. Early models and limited editions are becoming collectible, and can also command many times these prices. Discontinued Reiper cues will be further covered in future editions.
Special construction note: There are many materials and construction techniques that can add value to Rieper cues.
For all Rieper cues, except where otherwise noted:
   Add $175+ for each additional original straight playable shaft beyond one.
   Deduct 50% for missing original straight playable shaft.
   Deduct 40% for missing original ivory ferrule.
   Deduct 35% for obvious or improper refinish.

| GRADING | 98% | 90% | 70% |

RIKARD CUSTOM CUES

Maker of pool cues from 1982 to present in Galena Park, Texas.

William Rikard started playing pool at the age of eighteen, when some of his friends took him to a pool hall. He has been hooked on the game ever since, and is now on a league team that has placed in the top half dozen in the nation several times. A pipe fitter by trade, William began selling cues in the late 1970s. By 1982, William bought an old lathe and started making cues of his own.

Rikard cues are easily identifiable by the "William Rikard" signature, usually on maple, on the forearms or butt sleeves. Some are signed instead with "Toeboy", William's nickname since he was a kid. William makes everything by hand in his one-man shop. He doesn't stock many cues, instead building them to fill custom orders.

If you have a Rikard cue that needs further identification or repair, or would like to talk to someone about ordering a new Rikard cue, contact Rikard Custom Cues, listed in the Trademark Index.

SPECIFICATIONS

Butt material: hardwoods
Shaft material: rock maple
Standard length: 58 in.
Lengths available: any
Standard finish: acrylic urethane
Balance point: varies
Standard butt cap: linen phenolic
Standard wrap: Irish linen
Point construction: short splice
Standard joint: linen phenolic
Joint type: flat faced
Joint screw: 3/8-10
Standard number of shafts: two
Standard taper: pro
Standard ferrules: melamine
Standard tip width: 13 mm
Standard tip: Le Pro
Annual production: approximately 70 cues

The current delivery time for a Rikard custom cue is eight to twelve weeks.

SECONDARY MARKET MINIMUM VALUES

The following are minimum values for Rikard custom cues encountered on the secondary market. These prices are representative of cues utilizing basic materials and designs that are not necessarily available at present. William Rikard has offered one-of-a-kind cues that can command many times these prices due to the use of exotic materials and artistry.

Special construction note: There are many materials and construction techniques that can add value to Rikard cues. The following are the most important examples:

Add 450+ for ivory points.

For all used Rikard cues, except where otherwise noted:

Add $85 for each additional original straight playable shaft beyond two.
Deduct $110 for each missing original straight playable shaft under two.
Add $60 each for ivory ferrules.
Add $75 for leather wrap.
Deduct 20% for obvious or improper refinish.

Level 1 - 4 points, hustler.
| Level 1 cues start at | $175 | $140 | $95 |

Level 2 - 0 points, 0-25 inlays.
| Level 2 cues start at | $350 | $275 | $185 |

Level 3 - 2-6 points, 0-8 inlays.
| Level 3 cues start at | $450 | $350 | $240 |

Level 4 - 4-10 points, 9-25 inlays.
| Level 4 cues start at | $565 | $435 | $295 |

Level 5 - 0-12 points, 26-50 inlays.
| Level 5 cues start at | $850 | $655 | $445 |

RJH CUSTOM CUES

Maker of pool cues from 1996 to present in Brooklyn, New York.

Having played pool since the age of 17, Richard Hsu quickly fell in love with the game. He had won numerous local tournaments by the age of 21. His passion for the game grew more and more as he played. When he was 18, he came across a BCA instructor, retired cuemaker Bob Neil. Mr. Neil taught Richard the art of cuemaking. Richard began doing minor cue repair work for a pool room in Brooklyn, New York, while he learned the art of cuemaking.

At age 19, Richard worked for his family-owned retail business and began saving his earnings to purchase his own cue building equipment. In 1996, with a single lathe, he turned out his very first cue. Richard has been building custom cues for local players ever since, but only as a hobby. In January of 2002, Richard became a full-time cuemaker. He turns out less than 50 cues a year in his shop. He now has some high quality exotic woods and cue building machinery. Richard pays close attention to design, detail, and playability in his custom cues, and he rarely duplicates a design, so most cues are one-of-a-kind. RJH cues are identified by a signature in the forearm, or "RJH Custom Cues" engraved in the butt cap.

RJH Custom Cues are guaranteed for life against defects that are not the result of warpage or abuse.

If you are interested in talking to Richard about a new cue or cue that needs to be repaired, you can contact him at RJH Custom Cues, listed in the Trademark Index.

Richard Hsu

Present Day

Present Day

SPECIFICATIONS

- Butt material: exotic hardwoods
- Shaft material: hard maple
- Standard length: 58 in.
- Lengths available: up to 64 in.
- Standard finish: clearcoat
- Balance point: 1 to 1.5 in. above wrap
- Standard butt cap: phenolic
- Standard wrap: Irish linen
- Point construction: short spliced or inlaid
- Standard joints: phenolic or stainless steel
- Joint type: flat-faced wood-to-wood
- Joint screw threads: 3/8-10, 5/16-14, 5/16-18, or Uni-Loc radial
- Standard number of shafts: one
- Standard taper: 15 in. pro
- Standard ferrules: melamine
- Standard tip: Le Pro
- Standard tip width: 13 mm
- Tip widths available: any up to 14 mm
- Annual production: fewer than 50 cues

OPTIONS (FOR NEW CUES ONLY)

- Special length: no charge
- Layered tip: $15+
- Ivory butt cap: $200
- Ivory joint: $150
- Ivory ferrule: $50
- Ivory points: $200+
- Leather wrap: $75
- Stack leather: $150
- Exotic prints: $125
- Joint protectors: $25+
- Extra shaft: $100+

CURRENT RJH CUES

Two-piece RJH bar cues start at $150. Basic RJH cues with wraps and joint rings start at $250. RJH cues with points start at $350. RJH cues over $1,000 come with two shafts. The current delivery time for an RJH cue is four to six months.

SECONDARY MARKET MINIMUM VALUES

The following are minimum values for other RJH cues encountered on the secondary market. These prices are representative of cues utilizing basic materials and designs that are not necessarily available at present. Richard has offered one-of-a-kind cues that can command many times these prices due to the use of exotic materials and artistry.

Special construction note: There are many materials and construction techniques that can add value to RJH cues.

For all used RJH cues, except where otherwise noted:

GRADING	98%	90%	70%

Add $80 for each additional original straight playable shaft beyond one.
Deduct $100+ for missing original straight playable shaft.
Add $100 for ivory joint.
Add $45 each for ivory ferrules.
Add $60 for leather wrap.
Deduct 15% for obvious or improper refinish.

	98%	90%	70%
Level 1 - Hustler.			
Level 1 cues start at	$135	$105	$70
Level 2 - 0 points, 0-25 inlays.			
Level 2 cues start at	$225	$175	$115
Level 3 - 2-6 points, 0-8 inlays.			
Level 3 cues start at	$300	$235	$160
Level 4 - 4-10 points, 9-25 inlays.			
Level 4 cues start at	$400	$315	$215
Level 5 - 0-12 points, 26-50 inlays.			
Level 5 cues start at	$750	$575	$390
Level 6 - 0-12 points, 51-75 inlays.			
Level 6 cues start at	$1,200	$945	$650

ROBINSON CUES

Maker of pool cues from 1960 to 1973 in Hayward, California, from 1973 to 1991 in Santa Barbara, California, and from 1991 to present in Scottsdale, Arizona.

John Robinson was born in Arkansas, but his family moved to California when he was four. He grew up around the Oakland area. John had an interest in hand-carving wooden toys that began around the time he moved to California. When he found a piece of billiard cloth in a park at about twelve years old, he decided to use it on a miniature table that he then hand-carved. He used marbles for the balls, and his interest in playing pool developed.

Although the local pool halls were not supposed to allow minors, John had a friend that would let him in before he was eighteen. By the time John was 27, he had made his first cue. He took it into an Oakland pool hall and sold it for $20 and two theater tickets. John gained a good reputation as a cuemaker, and made about 1,000 cues while he was in the bay area. During those years, John visited and got cuemaking advice from Harvey Martin and Tex Zimmerman.

The first cues had a Delrin joint, which was changed to brass in the early 1960s. It was during this time that John started to develop his own style, and started putting the joint screws in the shafts, a feature which continues to this day. The joint is so strong that John can set a cue on two blocks about 14 inches apart and stand on it. Although about half of the early cues had leather wraps, they rarely are done today. Early Robinson cues were all 57 inches, and changed to 58 inches in the late 1960s.

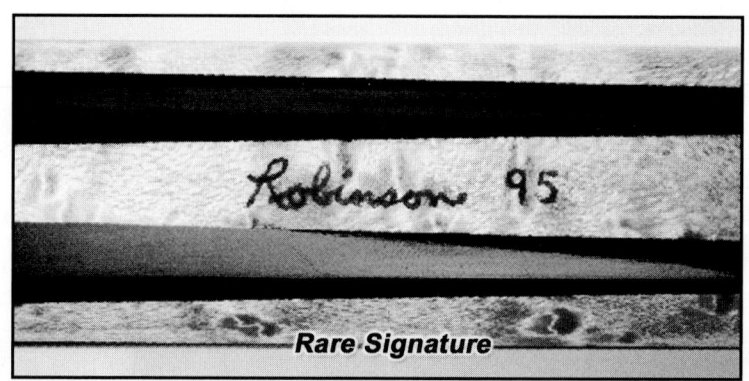

Rare Signature

In 1973, John moved to Santa Barbara, California, where he worked full-time in the flooring business, making cues in his spare time. In 1977, John's son, Greg, started to help with Robinson Cues, helping out for the next few years. About a year after Greg joined, the standard brass joint was replaced with stainless steel. In 1986, with the increased demand for custom cues brought about by "The Color of Money," John started making cues full-time, and Greg joined the business full-time soon after.

Robinson Cues makes fewer than 60 cues per year, by hand, without the aid of CNC machines. Inlays are done on a manual pantograph, as are the points, as John has never made spliced blanks. Greg inlays the points, which are cut by hand at the ends, to make the tips razor sharp. He is very particular about the extremely close tolerances of his inlay work, and stresses original designs which have inspired other makers. Among the unique features of Robinson cues are the ivory inlays, which Greg can dye to any color. Greg also applies the finish on Robinson cues which requires an average of 10 to 15 hand-rubbed coats. John and Greg make every component of Robinson cues, except for the bumpers and tips, which John treats and compresses, using a process he developed himself. Although very few Robinson cues have ever been signed, they are easily identifiable by their joint and unique style. Playability is an important factor, and John and Greg try to build a low-deflection, two-piece cue that feels like a one-piece. In 1999, John began to core the butts in his cues with rock maple for a more solid hit, and to prevent warping.

In his spare time, Greg is a self-taught musician who writes music, makes custom guitars for his own use, and pursues other forms of art. John is always trying to make constant improvements to Robinson cues, and is constantly searching for the finest materials. Ivory ferrules are standard on the higher-end cues. The Robinsons also market the "Perfex" tip tapper, which John designed and patented. In 1999, they opened a website which has pictures of the cues and products they have for sale at a given time.

| GRADING | 98% | 90% | 70% |

Robinson cues are guaranteed indefinitely against construction defects that are not the result of warpage or abuse. If you have a Robinson cue that needs further identification or repair, or would like to talk to John or Greg about ordering a new cue, contact Robinson Cues, listed in the Trademark Index.

SPECIFICATIONS

Butt material: hardwoods
Shaft material: rock maple
Standard length: 58 in.
Lengths available: any
Standard finish: PPG
Standard joint screw: 5/16-18
Standard joint: stainless steel
Joint type: custom piloted
Balance point: approximately 19 in. from butt
Point construction: pantographed
Standard wrap: Irish linen
Standard butt cap: alternate ivory
Standard number of shafts: one
Standard taper: custom 12 in. pro
Standard ferrules: ivory
Standard tip: Elk Master
Tip widths available: any
Annual production: fewer than 100 cues

OPTIONS (FOR NEW CUES ONLY)

Leather wrap: $100
Cork wrap: $100
Delrin joint protectors: $45 per set
Ivory butt cap: $200
Extra shaft: $125
Extra shaft (with ivory ferrules): $150

REPAIRS

Repairs done on all fine cues.

Refinish (with Irish linen wrap): $150
Rewrap (linen): $40
Replace Delrin butt cap: $40
Replace ivory butt cap: $200
Replace shaft: $150+
Replace Ivorine-3 ferrule: $35
Replace ivory ferrule: $50
Replace Elk Master or Le Pro tip: $10
Add joint to bar cue: $50

CURRENT ROBINSON CUES

Basic Robinson cues with wraps and joint rings start at $550. Robinson cues with points start at $650. The current delivery time for a Robinson custom cue is under two months.

SECONDARY MARKET MINIMUM VALUES

The following are minimum prices for Robinson cues encountered on the secondary market. These prices are representative of cues utilizing basic materials and designs that may not be currently available. John and Greg currently specialize in one-of-a-kind and limited edition cues that can command many times these prices due to the use of exotic materials and artistry.

Special construction note: There are many materials and construction techniques that can add value to Robinson cues. The following are the most important examples:

Add $1,200+ for ebony butt with ivory points.

For all used Robinson cues, except where otherwise noted:

Add $100+ for each additional original straight playable shaft (standard with two).
Deduct $125 for each missing original straight playable shaft.
Add $85+ for leather wrap.
Deduct 25% for obvious or improper refinish.

Level 2 - 0 points, 0-25 inlays.
    Level 2 cues start at $500 $395 $285

Level 3 - 2-6 points, 0-8 inlays.
    Level 3 cues start at $600 $470 $325

GRADING	98%	90%	70%
Level 4 - 4-10 points, 9-25 inlays.			
Level 4 cues start at	$850	$655	$445
Level 5 - 0-12 points, 26-50 inlays.			
Level 5 cues start at	$1,500	$1,195	$800
Level 6 - 0-12 points, 51-75 inlays.			
Level 6 cues start at	$2,000	$1,655	$1,200

ROMERO CUES

Maker of pool cues from 1979 to 1988 in Norwalk, California, and from 1988 to present at Hard Times Billiards in Bellflower, California.

Al Romero was a pool player for over ten years before he decided to start making cues. He visited his friend Tad Kohara many times and learned a lot from him about making cues. He started making cues in 1979 in Norwalk, California. In 1988 Al had the opportunity to move his shop into an upstairs 15 ft. by 30 ft. room at the famous Hard Times Billiards in Bellflower, California. Today he is making cues by hand in that shop, which has one lathe and a manual pantograph. Al makes everything in his cues except for the tips, bumpers, and screws, with the occasional help of his son.

Playability is most important to Al, and he believes that finding the best materials is the key. He has even driven to Michigan in search of sawmills that have the best shaft wood. Being above the pool room, Al does a lot of repairs, and he also makes a lot of two-piece bar cues. Al's Sneaky Petes are easily identifiable by the "Al Romero" stamp that is burned into them. He also makes a few custom cues which are not marked.

If you are interested in talking to Al about a new cue or cue that needs to be repaired, you can contact him at Romero Cues, listed in the Trademark Index.

SPECIFICATIONS

Butt material: hardwoods
Shaft material: rock maple
Standard length: 58 in.
Lengths available: any
Standard finish: lacquer
Standard butt cap: linen phenolic
Standard wrap: Irish linen
Point construction: short splice
Standard joint: linen phenolic
Standard joint type: flat faced
Joint screw: 5/16-18
Standard number of shafts: one
Standard ferrules: Aegis
Annual production: fewer than 150 cues

OPTIONS (FOR NEW CUES ONLY)

Special length: no charge
Extra shaft: $110+

REPAIRS

Repairs done on all fine cues.
Rewrap (Irish linen): $50
Put joint in a house cue: $40
Replace tip: $10+
Replace melamine ferrule: $40

CURRENT ROMERO CUES

Basic two-piece hustler cues start at $220. Basic two-piece cues with wraps and joint rings start at $600. Cues with points start at $1,500. The current delivery time is at least two weeks, depending on the cue.

SECONDARY MARKET MINIMUM VALUES

The following are minimum values for Romero cues encountered on the secondary market. These prices are representative of cues utilizing basic materials and designs that are not necessarily available at present. Al has offered one-of-a-kind cues that can command many times these prices due to the use of exotic materials and artistry.

Special construction note: There are many materials and construction techniques that can add value to Romero cues.

For all used Romero cues, except where otherwise noted:

Add $100 for each additional original straight playable shaft beyond one.
Deduct $110+ for missing original straight playable shaft.
Deduct 20% for obvious or improper refinish.

GRADING	98%	90%	70%
Level 1 - Hustler.			
Level 1 cues start at	$200	$165	$115
Level 2 - 0 points, 0-25 inlays.			
Level 2 cues start at	$500	$335	$260
Level 3 - 2-6 points, 0-8 inlays.			
Level 3 cues start at	$900	$745	$465
Level 4 - 4-10 points, 9-25 inlays.			
Level 4 cues start at	$1,000	$775	$525
Level 5 - 0-12 points, 26-50 inlays.			
Level 5 cues start at	$1,350	$1,050	$700

RUBINO CUES

Maker of pool cues from 1983 to present in New Windsor, New York.

Paul Rubino

Paul Rubino is well-known as the co-author of The Billiard Encyclopedia, and it is important to understand his involvement in that project to appreciate his approach to cuemaking. A player since the age of thirteen, Paul began keeping a journal of the finest cues that he saw in the mid-1970s. He noted the designs and specifications of all the Balabushkas, Paradises, Palmers and other fine cues that he came across.

Paul began doing repairs on cues in 1980, and during that year, he made his first two-piece house cue. By 1983, he had made his first cue from scratch. The early cues were very plain, as he did not start doing inlay work until later. His construction techniques were inspired by cues he studied up to that time. Previously a full-time machinist, Paul made cues part time until 2004 when he became a full-time cuemaker.

While working on The Billiard Encyclopedia, Paul was exposed to cues, construction techniques, and patents, going back over two hundred years. Now that the project is finished, Paul can spend more time perfecting his craft, and research billiard history at his leisure, studying the very old material. This has made him one of the best at restoring and identifying antique cues. Paul was fortunate enough to acquire Herman Rambow's lathe and materials. In addition, he has original Palmer and Paradise material.

Today, Paul enjoys making one-of-a-kind custom cues to the designs and specifications of his customers. Most of his cues are unsigned. They are usually finished with lacquer or oils, depending upon the type of cue. He prefers the feel and natural beauty of wood, as opposed to covering the cue with a wrap and heavy finish. Paul likes the hit of ivory joints, and prefers to match them up with ivory butt caps instead of Delrin. He believes that the most important aspect of a cue is the way it plays, and his cues are crafted for a very solid hit.

Many of his designs reflect that Old World tradition, yet many of his latest works incorporate the artistic diversity his one-of-a-kind cues demand. Precious metals and other exotic materials are used, and his commitment to excellence and delivering exactly what the customer requests has made his cues popular in Germany and Japan, as well as other parts of the world.

Paul guarantees his cues indefinitely, and will fix any construction defects that are not the result of warpage or abuse. If you have a Rubino cue or a cue by a past master that needs repair, or if you would like to talk to Paul about the design of a one-of-a-kind custom cue, contact Paul Rubino, listed in the Trademark Index.

SPECIFICATIONS

Butt material: hardwoods
Shaft material: hard maple
Standard length: 58 in.
Lengths available: any
Joint screws: any
Preferred joint: piloted
Preferred joint type: ivory
Balance point: custom
Point construction: short splice and butterfly splice
Standard handles: wood or Irish linen
Standard number of shafts: two
Standard taper: custom
Standard tip: modified Triangle
Tip widths available: any
Annual production: fewer than 100 cues

OPTIONS (FOR NEW CUES ONLY)

Leather wrap: $150
Ivory joint: $150
Flat face joint: no charge
Ivory butt cap: $300
Extra shaft: $125
Special length: no charge

GRADING	98%	90%	70%

REPAIRS

Repairs done on most fine cues and antique cues. (Paul prefers that cues be repaired by the original maker, if possible.)
- Rewrap (leather): $200+
- Rewrap (linen): $50
- Replace phenolic ferrule: $40
- Replace ivory ferrule: $75
- Replace Delrin butt cap: $50
- Replace ivory butt cap: $300+
- Replace shaft: $125+

CURRENT RUBINO CUES

Two-piece Rubino bar cues start at $200. Basic Rubino cues with wraps and joint rings start at $650. Rubino cues with points start at $850. One-of-a-kind custom Rubino cues start at $2,500.

PAST EXAMPLES

Paul specializes in one-of-a-kind custom cues, and proper restorations of the works of legendary cuemakers. The following cues are representations of the work of Paul Rubino. These cues can still be ordered as shown, modified to suit the desires of the customer, or new designs can be created.

Level 2 - One-piece rosewood butt, ivory joint, short ivory butt cap.

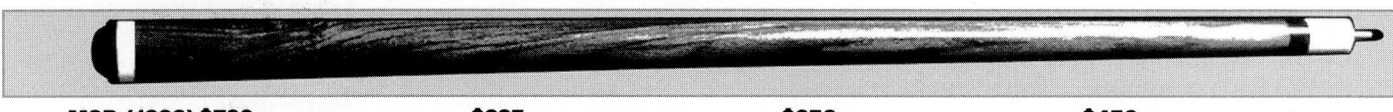

MSR (1999) $700	$825	$650	$450

Level 3 - Paduak forearm, two rosewood butterfly points with colored veneers, rosewood handle and butt sleeve.

MSR (1999) $900	$1,045	$810	$550

Level 3 - Bird's-eye maple forearm, two bubinga butterfly points with colored veneers, bubinga handle and butt sleeve with ebony ring between two ivory rings, bubinga butt cap.

MSR (1999) $1,200	$1,375	$1,085	$750

SECONDARY MARKET MINIMUM VALUES

The following are minimum prices for Rubino cues encountered on the secondary market. These prices are representative of cues utilizing basic materials and designs that may not be currently available. Paul also offers one-of-a-kind cues that can command many times these prices due to the use of exotic materials and artistry.

Special construction note: There are many materials and construction techniques that can add value to Rubino cues. The following are the most important examples:
- Add $1,750+ for ivory points.
- Add $1,000+ for ivory butt sleeve.
- Add $650+ for abalone inlays.

For all used Rubino cues:
- Add $100 for each additional original straight playable shaft beyond two.
- Deduct $125 for each missing original straight playable shaft under two.
- Add $150+ for ivory joint.
- Add $75 for each ivory ferrule.
- Add $125+ for leather wrap.
- Deduct 25% for obvious or improper refinish.

Level 1 - Hustler.

Level 1 cues start at	$250	$200	$135

Level 2 - 0 points, 0-25 inlays.

Level 2 cues start at	$700	$550	$385

Level 3 - 2-6 points, 0-8 inlays.

Level 3 cues start at	$950	$515	$445

GRADING	98%	90%	70%
Level 4 - 4-10 points, 9-25 inlays.			
Level 4 cues start at	$1,150	$900	$600
Level 5 - 0-12 points, 26-50 inlays.			
Level 5 cues start at	$1,950	$1,545	$1,050
Level 6 - 0-12 points, 51-75 inlays.			
Level 6 cues start at	$3,000	$2,400	$1,750

BOB RUNDE CUES

Maker of pool cues from 1994 to present in Bristol, Wisconsin.

Bob Runde started playing pool at the age of 15. He started making cues in the early 1970s, while working as the head engineer of a company in Wisconsin that made musical instruments. In 1975, he started working with a large Wisconsin cue manufacturer. After 2 1/2 years of 65-mile one-way drives to get there, Bob decided to return to making cues on his own. In 1981, Bob founded Schon Custom Cues with partner Terry Romine. Bob was involved with every Schon cue made during the twelve years he was there.

In late 1992, Bob sold his interest in Schon and retired. A little more than a year later, he started making a few cues every year as a hobby.

Bob now makes a few cues a year in the winter months, and plays golf during the warmer seasons. His cues are of a totally new construction design which he personally developed. All work is done by hand, and all inlays are of exotic woods or ivory. He does not accept any custom orders. Bob enjoys creating his own one-of-a-kind designs and offering them for sale. Bob Runde cues are easily identifiable by "Bob Runde" followed by a number and the year of completion, which appears on every cue he makes. About a half a dozen or so cues a year have ivory joints. All of his cues tend to have more of a forward balance than most other cues. In 2002, Bob started making short-spliced blanks instead of inlaying the points, as he had done previously.

Bob guarantees his cues indefinitely against defects that are not the result of warpage or abuse. If you have a Bob Runde cue that needs further identification or repair, or would like to talk to Bob about obtaining a new cue, contact Bob Runde Cues, listed in the Trademark Index.

SPECIFICATIONS

Butt material: hardwoods
Shaft material: rock maple
Standard length: 58 in.
Point construction: short splice
Joint screw: 5/16-14
Standard joint: stainless steel
Joint type: piloted
Standard finish: epoxy
Standard wrap: Irish linen
Standard number of shafts: two
Standard taper: 10 in. pro
Standard ferrules: ivory
Standard tip: Le Pro
Annual production: fewer than 20 cues

OPTIONS (FOR NEW CUES ONLY)

Option prices are incorporated into the final price of each cue.

REPAIRS

Repairs done only on Bob Runde cues. Repairs priced on a per cue basis.

BOB RUNDE CUES

Two-piece Bob Runde hustler cues made from scratch start at $500. Basic Bob Runde cues with points start at $1,000. One-of-a-kind custom Bob Runde cues start at $1,500. The current delivery time for a Bob Runde cue is six to nine months.

SECONDARY MARKET MINIMUM VALUES

The following are minimum prices for Bob Runde cues encountered on the secondary market. These prices are representative of cues utilizing basic materials and designs that may not be currently available. Bob currently specializes in one-of-a-kind cues that can command many times these prices due to the use of exotic materials and artistry.

Special construction note: There are many materials and construction techniques that can add value to Bob Runde cues.

For all used Bob Runde cues:

Add $150+ for each additional original straight playable shaft beyond two.
Deduct $200 for each missing original straight playable shaft.
Add $325+ for ivory joint.
Deduct 30% for obvious or improper refinish.

	98%	90%	70%
Level 1 - Hustler.			
Level 1 cues start at	$400	$315	$215

GRADING	98%	90%	70%
Level 3 - 2-6 points, 0-8 inlays.			
Level 3 cues start at	$1,150	$900	$600
Level 4 - 4-10 points, 9-25 inlays.			
Level 4 cues start at	$1,350	$1,045	$700
Level 5 - 0-12 points, 26-50 inlays.			
Level 5 cues start at	$1,850	$1,450	$1,000
Level 6 - 0-12 points, 51-75 inlays.			
Level 6 cues start at	$2,350	$1,850	$1,250
Level 7 - 0-12 points, 76-125 inlays.			
Level 7 cues start at	$3,000	$2,375	$1,650

RUTZISKY, ISADORE

Maker of pool cues starting in 1912 for many years in New York City, New York.

When Isadore Rutzisky came to New York City from Lithuania in 1911 he was already a talented wood turner. Settling in the Jewish ghetto in the Bowery, he opened the doors to the New York Billiard Table Co. in 1912. The company was known for the quality of its ivory turning as well as its wood turning. Despite the name, no tables were made there. Rather, it was the place in New York to buy both the finest ivory billiard balls and some of the best custom two-piece cues available. The celebrities of the day flocked to the store to have "the professor" make them a beautiful cue to impress their famous friends. Among the stars who ordered cues from Isadore were Fred Astaire, Milton Berle, Tony Curtis, Sammy Davis, Jr., Jack Lemmon, and Kim Novak. For a picture of Isadore Rutzisky, refer to the listing for Blatt Billiards. If you have an Isadore Rutzisky cue that needs further identification or repair, contact Paul Rubino at Rubino Cues, listed in the Trademark Index.

SPECIFICATIONS

Butt material: hardwoods
Shaft material: rock maple
Standard finish: oil
Point construction: full splice
Standard number of shafts: one
Standard ferrules: ivory

SECONDARY MARKET MINIMUM VALUES

The following are minimum values for other Rutzisky cues encountered on the secondary market. These prices are representative of cues that utilized the most basic materials and designs that were available. Isadore offered one-of-a-kind cues that can command many times these prices due to the use of exotic materials and artistry.

Special construction note: There are many materials and construction techniques that can add value to Rutzisky cues.

For all Rutzisky cues, except where otherwise noted:

Add $150+ for each additional original straight playable shaft beyond one.
Deduct 40% for missing original straight playable shaft.
Deduct $75 for missing original ivory ferrule.
Deduct 35% for obvious or improper refinish.

Level 2 - 0 points, 0-25 inlays.			
Level 2 cues start at	$500	$375	$220
Level 3 - 2-6 points, 0-8 inlays.			
Level 3 cues start at	$800	$600	$350
Level 4 - 4-10 points, 9-25 inlays.			
Level 4 cues start at	$1,400	$1,065	$600

S SECTION

SAILOR CUES

Maker of pool cues from the early 1970s to present in Racine, Wisconsin.

Frank Stellman was a top straight pool player, establishing prominence in the Chicago area during the 1950s and 1960s. He earned the nickname "Sailor" from a tour in the Navy. In the early 1970s, Frank purchased Eddie Laube's lathe and the Laube patent rights, and started making his own cues in his hometown of Racine, Wisconsin.

Sailor cues are identifiable by the name "Sailor" usually stamped into the forearms. They also can be identified by their unique flared butt caps, which may be black or white. (Frank refers to his cues as "the cue with the flair.") Most Sailor cues have a solid forearm, and most cues with points are made from full-spliced house cues, to accommodate the regional economy. He also made some cues with blanks by Burton Spain, which today demand a premium. Buck horn and mother-of-pearl are common materials for inlays. Boxed ringwork in maple and ebony is very common in the butt sleeves, with colored synthetic pearls being very common also. The use of ivory in Sailor cues is extremely rare. A few Sailor cues have been made by his son, Kelly.

Frank liked to take measurements, watch a player play, and make them a custom cue based on their size and playing style. He is also one of the best teachers in the game, with students that have become top professionals. He loves the game of pool, and he has a way of motivating and inspiring players to obtain peak performance. After making cues for over 25 years, Frank slowed down his cuemaking in the late 1990s. If you have a Sailor cue that needs further identification or repair, contact Sailor Cues, listed in the Trademark Index.

Frank Stellman

SPECIFICATIONS

Butt material: hardwoods
Shaft material: rock maple
Standard length: custom
Lengths available: any
Joint type: flat faced
Point construction: short-splice and full-splice conversions (most cues have solid forearms)
Standard wrap: Irish linen
Standard number of shafts: one

GRADING	98%	90%	70%

PAST EXAMPLES

Level 4 Bird's-eye maple forearm, four ebony points with two veneers, mother-of-pearl notched diamond and two dots in each point, ebony butt sleeve with maple box veneer windows, four dot inlays, and ringwork at top and bottom with pearlized plastic rings above and below, stainless steel joint with black joint collar with thin maple and pearlized rings, flared ivory-colored butt cap with large rubber bumper, linen wrap.

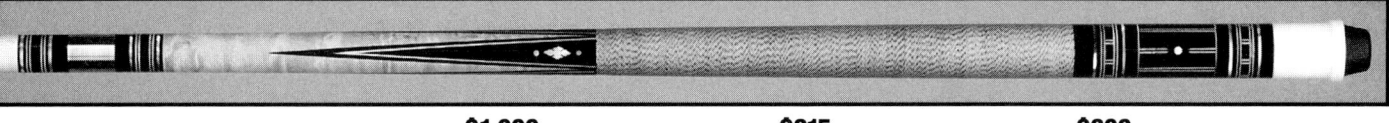

	$1,000	$815	$600

SECONDARY MARKET MINIMUM VALUES

The following are minimum prices for Sailor cues encountered on the secondary market. These prices are representative of cues utilizing basic materials and designs that may not be currently available. Sailor also offers one-of-a-kind cues that can command many times these prices due to the use of exotic materials and artistry.

Special construction note: There are many materials and construction techniques that can add value to Sailor cues.

For all used Sailor cues, except where otherwise noted:
  Add $500+ for a Burton Spain blank.
  Add $100+ for each additional original straight playable shaft beyond one.
  Deduct $125 for missing original straight playable shaft.
  Deduct 25% for obvious or improper refinish.

Level 2 - 0 points, 0-25 inlays.
  Level 2 cues start at $400 $350 $250
Level 3 - 2-6 points, 0-8 inlays.
  Level 3 cues start at $600 $500 $375
Level 4 - 4-10 points, 9-25 inlays.
  Level 4 cues start at $850 $700 $550

| GRADING | 98% | 90% | 70% |

SAMPAIO BILLIARD CUES

Maker of pool cues from 1880 to the mid-1970s in Lisbon, Portugal.

Sampaio was founded in Portugal in 1880. A family-owned and operated business run by meticulous old-world craftsmen, the company rose to prominence throughout Europe by the early 1900s. Their expertise was in three-cushion billiard cues and their reputation for quality and playability was well deserved. Their early cues (1880-1930) were on par with anything being made in Europe at the time. Exotic hardwoods gathered from the four corners of the world and quality craftsmanship combined to make the company world-famous by 1940. A wide assortment of designs was offered and, although they primarily made a line of cues, they also offered custom work to their clients. All of their cues were hand-carved and hand-polished rosewood with real mother-of-pearl inlays, and genuine ivory and ebony trim. Shafts were available in a variety of lengths and tapers for the assorted billiard games that were popular at the time. At different periods they were stamped with the "Sampaio" logo. Somewhere along the line, this logo was moved to the forearm and the word "Portugal" remained stamped on the shafts. Early cues featured a wooden pin billiards joint which continued to be popular in European carom players into the 1960s. Most cues had ivory ferrules.

Ben Shimel, the founder and then-owner of J-S Sales, was impressed with the quality of the Sampaio cues and visited the Sampaio family in 1962. A joint venture resulted and a new line of cues meeting American standards were developed. Shimel invested in and guided the redesign from billiard to pool cues as pocket billiards was unknown in Portugal. Pool cues with longer ferrules, pro tapers, brass joints and colorful nylon wraps were added to the line. Both billiard and pool cues were now available and proved to be very successful in America, and the Sampaio family struggled to keep up with the orders pouring in from the U.S. J-S Sales imported up to 60,000 cues annually. Though quite different in appearance from American cues of the time, both lines had solid old-world craftsmanship built into them. Today, the billiard cues are much more popular than the pool cues with collectors because of the hand craftsmanship, exotic hand-carving and use of ivory and mother-of-pearl. Among the Sampaio cues popular with collectors are the carved handle Sampaio cues The Premier, The Zenith, The Astro, The Navarro, The Lisbon, and also The Princess, with its intricate floral design. Sampaio ceased production in the 1970s after over 90 years in business.

SPECIFICATIONS

Butt material: rosewood and other hardwoods
Shaft material: maple
Standard length: varies
Joint type: brass or wood-to-wood
Standard finish: oil
Standard wrap: nylon
Point construction: full splice
Standard number of shafts: one

DISCONTINUED CUES

The following cues are from the Sampaio catalogue, circa 1964. They were imported and distributed by J-S Sales Co. Inc., in Mount Vernon, New York.

Level 2 "The Premier" - One-piece hand-carved hardwood butt with mother-of-pearl dots and shield-shaped inlays throughout.

Original Retail (1964) $50 $800 $400 $325

Level 4 "The Astro" - Maple forearm, four full-spliced hand-engraved hardwood points, floral engraved hardwood handle with mother-of-pearl dots in the center of the flowers between mother-of-pearl dots in hardwood rings at top and bottom, hand engraved hardwood butt sleeve with large mother-of-pearl dots.

Original Retail (1964) $45 $775 $375 $290

Level 2 "The Lisbon" - One-piece hardwood butt with floral carved handle with mother-of-pearl dots above and below.

Original Retail (1964) $40 $600 $325 $275

Level 2 "The Duke" - One-piece black hardwood butt, knurled handle with mother-of-pearl dots below.

Original Retail (1964) $30 $550 $300 $225

SAMPAIO BILLIARD CUES, cont. 687

GRADING	98%	90%	70%

Level 2 "The Princess" - One-piece hornbeam butt, floral engraved handle with black mother-of-pearl dots in the centers of the flowers between ebony and ivory rings at top and bottom.

Original Retail (1964) $60 $1,200 $950 $700

Level 3 "The Plaza" - Maple forearm, four full-spliced hardwood points and butt sleeve with mother-of-pearl dots towards bottom.

Original Retail (1964) $25 $400 $275 $200

Level 3 "The Navarro" - Maple forearm, four full-spliced hand engraved hardwood points, leaf pattern carved hardwood handle, hardwood butt sleeve with mother-of-pearl dots around center.

Original Retail (1964) $35 $600 $375 $300

Level 2 "Mark VII" - Maple forearm, knurled hardwood handle with mother-of-pearl dots set in contrasting hardwood rings above and below.

Original Retail (1964) $35 $550 $325 $250

Level 2 "The Monaco" - Maple forearm with mother-of-pearl dots set in hardwood above handle, leaf pattern hand carved handle, hardwood butt sleeve with mother-of -pearl dots.

Original Retail (1964) $40 $700 $350 $285

Level 3 "The Squire" - Maple forearm, four full-spliced hardwood points and butt sleeve with large mother-of-pearl dots at bottom.

Original Retail (1964) $20 $375 $275 $185

Level 3"The Viscount" - Maple forearm, four full-spliced hardwood points with large mother-of-pearl dots at bottom.

Original Retail (1964) $10 $365 $265 $175

Level 2 "The Sportsman" - One-piece mahogany butt with knurled handle.

Original Retail (1964) $8 $300 $225 $135

Level 2 "The Challenger" - One-piece mahogany butt with knurled handle (same as "The Sportsman" but 5 in. shorter).

Original Retail (1964) $6 $300 $225 $135

688 SAMPAIO BILLIARD CUES, cont.

GRADING	98%	90%	70%

Level 2 "The Kent" - Maple forearm, knurled mahogany handle and butt sleeve with mother-of-pearl dots above and below.

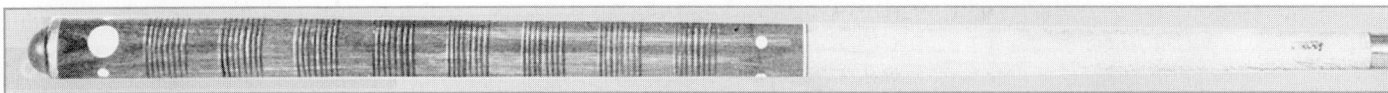

Original Retail (1964) $18	$375	$275	$200

Level 2 "The Lido" - Maple forearm, knurled mahogany handle and butt sleeve with mother-of-pearl dots above and below (same as "The Kent" but not jointed).

Original Retail (1964) $10	$285	$195	$150

Level 2 "The Baron" - One-piece mahogany butt with a knurled handle.

Original Retail (1964) $13	$325	$250	$165

Level 2 "The Lancer" - One-piece mahogany butt with mother-of-pearl dots at bottom.

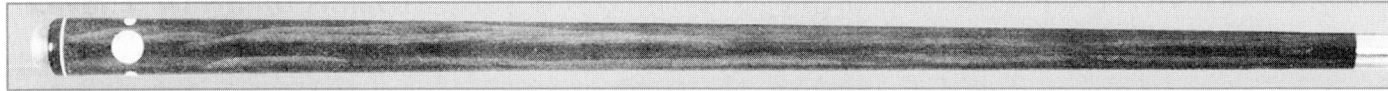

Original Retail (1964) $28	$400	$300	$195

Level 2 "The Apex" - Maple forearm, hardwood handle and butt sleeve with mother-of-pearl dots above and below.

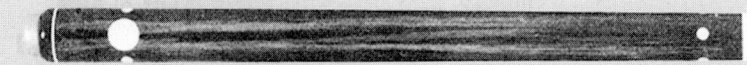

Original Retail (1964) $25	$385	$265	$175

SECONDARY MARKET MINIMUM VALUES

The following are minimum values for other Sampaio cues encountered on the secondary market. These prices are representative of cues utilizing the most basic materials and designs that were available.

Special construction note: There are many materials and construction techniques that can add value to Sampaio cues. Pre-1960s cues with wooden pins are of particular interest to collectors.

For all used Sampaio cues, except where otherwise noted:
- Add 25% for pre-1960s cues in original condition.
- Add $100 for each additional original straight playable shaft beyond one.
- Deduct 40% for missing original straight playable shaft.
- Add $50 each for ivory ferrules.
- Deduct 30% for obvious or improper refinish.

Level 2 - 0 points, 0-25 inlays.
Level 2 cues start at	$270	$195	$135

Level 3 - 2-6 points, 0-8 inlays.
Level 3 cues start at	$360	$265	$195

Level 4 - 4-10 points, 9-25 inlays.
Level 4 cues start at	$700	$385	$275

Level 5 - 0-12 points, 26-50 inlays.
Level 5 cues start at	$950	$550	$385

SAMSARA CUES

Maker of pool cues from 1991 until 2000 in Nashua, New Hampshire, and 2001 to present in Rugby, North Dakota.

Dave Doucette made his first cue when he was 12 years old. Growing up in a house with a pool table and a woodworking shop, he decided to make his own cue rather than buy one. As an adult, he gained experience as a master cabinet maker, machinist, and design engineer. By age 26, he had built his own pool table. In 1990, he met Jim Stadum when Jim commissioned him to build a cue. From that first collaboration was born both a friendship and a partnership. Jim was a second generation carpenter with a background in sales and marketing. They combined their mutual interest in pool with the challenge of creating functional art by combining fine woodworking with machining.

Samsara is derived from a Native American word that means "looking for the best." Jim and Dave started their quest on a part-time basis, creating their first cue in 1991. They were inspired by cuemakers Thomas Wayne, Ernie Gutierrez of Ginacue, and Richard Black. By 1993 they were successfully building cues full time. Their cues are very unique in appearance, with diamond-patterned ring designs and polychromatic intarsia inlays being typical features. Some of their design motifs, such as the spider web, the braid, the swirl and the fantail, have become instantly recognizable to the Samsara cue. Dave and Jim are very proud of the way that Samsara cues are constructed, with an emphasis on natural materials. No dyes or stains are used on the woods, and even the butt caps are often made of exotic hardwoods. All the work, even the most intricate inlays, is done by hand or on machines that they have designed and built themselves.

Samsara cues can be identified by the "Samsara" name engraved on a ring just below the wrap, prior to 1996, or on the butt cap, more recently. In 1996, Samsara started using a stylized "S" logo, which appears on the butt caps of most of their cues made from 1996 to 2003. Samsara cues had serial numbers stamped on their joint faces throughout most of the 1990s, but now the serial number is under the bumper. Cues made from 2003 on had their logo on the bottom of the rubber bumper. An important change made to Samsara cues in 1997 was coring the butts with rock maple rods, to prevent warping, stiffen the hit, and make the cues play more consistently. The standard joint was changed from a 5/16-18 screw to the Uni-Loc for a short time around 1997, but in recent years most cues have been built with flat-faced joints using radial pins. Both radial and Uni-Loc are available, at the customer's choice.

Samsara produces some of the most original designs in cuemaking. Their cues won the first place award at the 1993 Baltimore A.C.A. Cue Expo for "Best Design of Show," and the third place award for "Best Execution of Show." This was quite an accomplishment for a company that had been in business for only three years at that time. Samsara won the Bronze Award for "Best Design of Show" at the 1998 Gallery of American Cue Art, and has exhibited at every major cue show in the past ten years. Samsara is a founding member of the Gallery, and Jim served for six years on the board of the American Cuemakers Association. Their cue "Illusions" is one of the cues in the permanent collection at the Smithsonian Institute.

Samsara cues are available in a variety of styles and price ranges. They have recently introduced the "Barcue" line of basic playing cues that range in price from $400 to $850. They are all marked "Barcue" and they have Samsara on the bumpers. At least a half dozen Samsara cues costing over $5,000 are made each year. Every new Samsara cue comes with a certificate of authenticity, and a guarantee to the original buyer against warpage for one year, and workmanship defects that are not the result of warpage or abuse indefinitely.

If you would like to talk to Dave Doucette, Jim Stadum, or Laurie Stadum about purchasing a new Samsara cue, or if you have a cue in need of repair, contact Samsara Cues, listed in the Trademark Index.

SPECIFICATIONS

Butt material: hardwoods
Shaft material: rock maple
Standard length: 58 in.
Lengths available: 57 to 60 in.
Standard finish: polyester acrylic
Joint screw: radial or Uni-Loc
Standard joint: linen phenolic
Joint type: flat-face or piloted wood-to-wood
Balance point: forward of wrap
Point construction: short splice
Standard wrap: Irish linen
Standard butt cap: black linen phenolic
Standard number of shafts: two
Standard taper: modified pro taper
Standard ferrules: LBM linen-based melamine
Standard tip: Triangle
Standard tip width: 13 mm
Annual production: 300 to 400 cues

OPTIONS (FOR NEW CUES ONLY)

Leather wrap: $100
Ivory joint: $200
Ivory butt cap: $300
Ivory points: $1000
Ivory ferrule: $75
Extra shaft: $150+
Upgrade to Predator 314 shafts: $175
Upgrade to Predator Z shafts: $225
Layered tip: $50
Custom joint protectors: call for quote

GRADING	100%	95%	70%

REPAIRS

Repairs done on most fine cues.
- Refinish: $200 to $250
- Replace phenolic butt cap: $100 + refinish
- Rewrap (leather): $150
- Rewrap (linen): $50
- Replace shaft: $150+
- Replace LBM ferrule: $25
- Replace ivory ferrule: $75

CURRENT SAMSARA CUES

Two-piece "Barcue" bar cues by Samsara start at $400. Basic two-piece Samsara cues with wraps and joint rings start at $850. Samsara cues with points start at $1,000. One-of-a-kind custom Samsara cues made to order start at $10,000. The current delivery time for most Samsara cues is twelve to fourteen weeks.

CURRENT EXAMPLES

The following are representations of Samsara cues. These cues can be ordered as shown, modified to suit the desires of the customer, or new designs can be created. Some cues may be in stock, custom orders are usually available within ten weeks.

Level 3 - Bird's-eye maple forearm, bird's-eye maple butt sleeve.

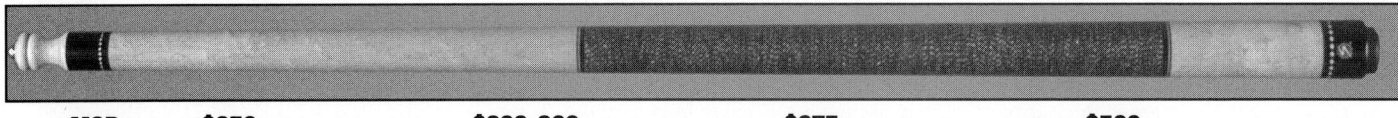

MSR	$850	$800-900	$675	$500

Level 3 - Bird's-eye maple forearm with an ebony ring above wrap, four ebony points, ebony butt sleeve.

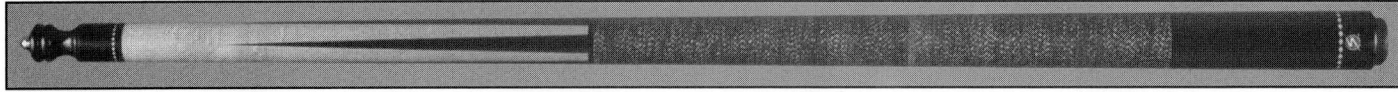

MSR	$1,100	$1,050-1,200	$875	$650

Level 3 - Bird's-eye maple forearm, four cocobolo points with mahogany veneers, cocobolo handle with intricate cocobolo and mahogany woven ringwork at bottom.

MSR	$1,400	$1,350-1,500	$1,100	$800

Level 3 - Purpleheart forearm with a purpleheart and maple zig-zag ring above handle, three long and three short bird's-eye maple points with paduak and purpleheart veneers, bird's-eye maple handle, purpleheart butt sleeve with a purpleheart and maple zig-zag ring below handle and a purpleheart zig-zag ring at bottom.

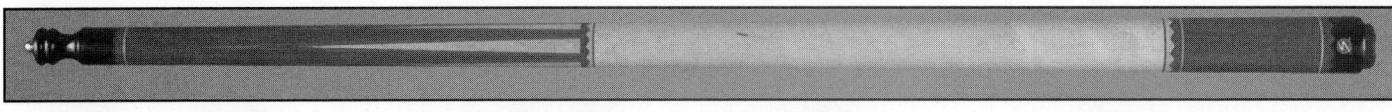

MSR	$1,600	$1,550-1,750	$1,225	$925

Level 3 - Ebony forearm with intricate pink ivory and holly triple diamond ringwork set in ebony above wrap, three long and three short pink ivory points with holly veneers, leather wrap, ebony butt sleeve with three long and three short pink ivory reverse points with holly veneers below intricate pink ivory and holly triple diamond ringwork set in ebony below wrap.

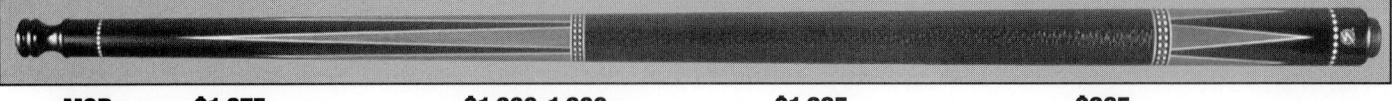

MSR	$1,675	$1,600-1,800	$1,295	$965

Level 3 - Ebony forearm with intricate snakewood and holly triple diamond ringwork set in ebony above wrap, three long and three short snakewood points with holly veneers, leather wrap, ebony butt sleeve with three long and three short snakewood reverse points with holly veneers below intricate snakewood and holly triple diamond ringwork set in ebony below wrap.

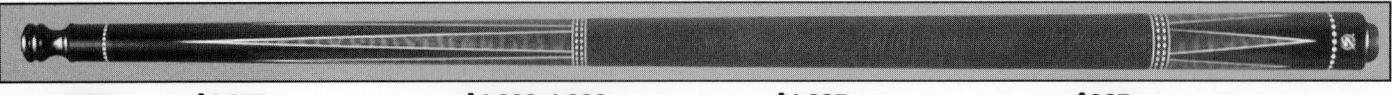

MSR	$1,675	$1,600-1,800	$1,295	$965

SAMSARA CUES, cont.

GRADING	100%	95%	70%

Level 6 - Cocobolo forearm with intricate cocobolo and pink ivory fantail ringwork above wrap, three long and three short holly points with pink ivory veneers, pigskin wrap, cocobolo butt sleeve with an intricate inlaid holly and pink ivory fantail pattern between intricate cocobolo and pink ivory fantail ringwork at top and bottom.

MSR	$3,375	$3,300-3,750	$2,650	$1,900

Level 6 - Ebony forearm with intricate ebony and holly ringwork above wrap, three long and three short holly points with holly and ebony veneers, pigskin wrap, ebony butt sleeve with an intricate inlaid holly and ebony woven pattern between intricate ebony and holly ringwork at top and bottom.

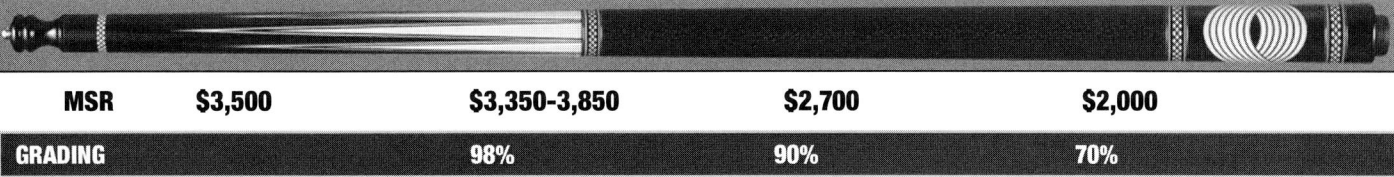

MSR	$3,500	$3,350-3,850	$2,700	$2,000

GRADING	98%	90%	70%

DISCONTINUED EXAMPLES

The following Samsara cues may be encountered as shown, or modified to suit the desires of the original customer. They are identifiable by the "Samsara" name on a ring below wrap.

Level 2 #1 - Cocobolo forearm and butt sleeve.

MSR (1996) $500	$900	$700	$485

Level 2 #2 - Rosewood forearm with two small ivory oval inlays, rosewood butt sleeve with two large ivory oval inlays.

MSR (1996) $650	$1,100	$875	$600

Level 3 #3 - Zerecote forearm, six ebony points with veneers, zerecote butt sleeve.

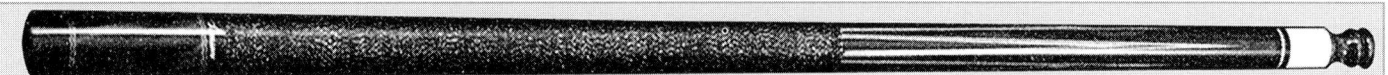

MSR (1996) $825	$1,450	$1,115	$750

Level 3 #4 - Curly maple forearm, six cocobolo points with veneers, cocobolo butt sleeve.

MSR (1996) $950	$1,500	$1,150	$785

Level 3 #6 - Curly maple forearm with double diamond ring design above wrap, six camatilla points with veneers, curly maple butt sleeve with double diamond ring designs at top and bottom.

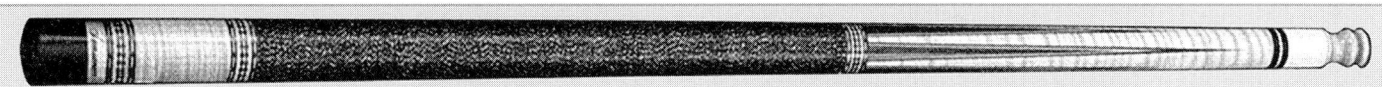

MSR (1996) $1,075	$1,650	$1,000	$875

Level 4 #7 - Curly maple forearm, six purpleheart points with veneers and single ivory ovals in each, purpleheart butt sleeve with four small and two large inlaid ivory ovals.

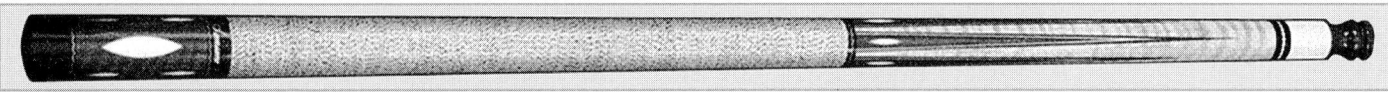

MSR (1996) $1,150	$1,700	$1,350	$900

GRADING	98%	90%	70%

Level 3 #8 - Walnut forearm with ebony double diamond ring design above wrap, six tulipwood points with veneers, tulipwood butt sleeve with ebony double diamond ring designs at top and bottom.

MSR (1996) $1,175	$1,725	$1,375	$925

Level 3 #9 - Walnut forearm with padauk single diamond ring design above wrap, six bird's-eye maple points with veneers, hardwoods inlaid in a polychromatic swirl pattern in the butt sleeve with padauk single diamond ring designs at top and bottom.

MSR (1996) $1,440	$2,150	$1,720	$1,225

Level 3 #10 - Curly maple forearm with triple diamond ring design above wrap, six ebony points with veneers, hardwoods inlaid in a polychromatic fan tail pattern in the butt sleeve with triple diamond ring designs at top and bottom, black leather wrap.

MSR (1996) $1,650	$2,300	$1,850	$1,325

Level 3 #11 - Ebony forearm with silver triple diamond ring design above wrap, six pink ivory points with single veneers, ebony butt sleeve with six downward-pointing pink ivory points with single veneers and triple diamond ring designs at top and bottom, ostrich leather wrap.

MSR (1996) $2,100	$2,900	$2,300	$1,650

Level 5 #12 - Bird's-eye maple forearm with ivory double diamond ring design above wrap, six purpleheart points with veneers, butt sleeve with inlaid ivory pool tables inlaid with racks of balls with money balls of gold.

MSR (1996) $2,200	$3,000	$2,400	$1,700

Level 3 #13 - Bird's-eye maple forearm with ivory triple diamond ring design above wrap, six snakewood points with veneers, bird's-eye maple butt sleeve with six downward-pointing snakewood points with veneers and ivory triple diamond ring designs at top and bottom, calfskin leather wrap.

MSR (1996) $2,400	$3,150	$2,500	$1,800

Level 4 #14 - Bird's-eye maple forearm, six snakewood points with veneers and single ivory ovals in each, bird's-eye maple butt sleeve with six downward-pointing snakewood points with veneers and single ivory ovals in and between each, calfskin leather wrap.

MSR (1996) $2,500	$3,250	$2,600	$1,850

Level 4 #15 - Curly maple forearm, six pink ivory points with veneers and single ivory ovals in each, pink ivory butt sleeve with twelve small and six large inlaid ivory ovals, ostrich leather wrap.

MSR (1996) $2,600	$3,300	$2,650	$1,900

GRADING	98%	90%	70%

Level 3 Snakewood forearm with amboyna and red veneer zig-zag ring design above wrap, six amboyna burl points with two veneers, snakewood butt sleeve with six reverse aboyna burl points with two veneers and snakewood and amboyna zig-zag ring designs at bottom, snakewood butt cap with "S" logo, Uni-Loc joint with brown linen joint collar, amboyna burl wrap with snakewood and amboyna zig-zag designs at top and bottom.

MSR (1997) $2,800	$3,350	$2,700	$2,000

DISCONTINUED EXAMPLES

The following Samsara cues may be encountered as shown, or modified to suit the desires of the original customer. They are identifiable by the Samsara "S" logo on the butt caps.

Level 2 - Cocobolo forearm, cocobolo butt sleeve.

MSR (1999) $750	$800	$620	$420

Level 3 - Curly maple forearm, three long and three short kingwood or bloodwood points, curly maple butt sleeve with three long and three short reverse kingwood or bloodwood points.

MSR (1999) $1000	$1,100	$850	$575

Level 3 - Curly maple forearm, three long and three short exotic wood points with two veneers, curly maple butt sleeve with three long and three short exotic wood reverse points with two veneers.

MSR (1999) $1,250	$1,350	$1,050	$700

Level 3 - Ebony forearm, three long and three short exotic wood points with a single veneer, ebony butt sleeve with three long and three short exotic wood reverse point-shaped inlays.

MSR (1999) $1,350	$1,450	$1,150	$750

Level 3 Ebony forearm with triple zigzag rings above wrap, three long and three short cherry burl points with two veneers, cherry burl butt sleeve with triple zigzag rings at top and bottom.

MSR (1999) $1,450	$1,550	$1,200	$800

Level 4 "Braid" - Curly maple forearm with intricate cocobolo double diamond-shaped rings at bottom, three long and three short cocobolo points with two veneers, butt sleeve of braided cocobolo and curly maple between cocobolo double diamond-shaped rings at top and bottom.

MSR (1999) $1,700	$1,825	$1,400	$950

Level 5 "Braid" - Cocobolo forearm with maple double diamond-shaped rings at bottom, three long and three short ebony points with three veneers, butt sleeve of braided ebony and cocobolo between maple double diamond-shaped rings at top and bottom.

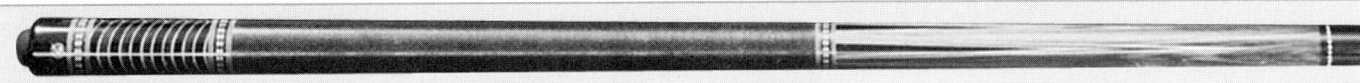

MSR (1999) $1,850	$2,000	$1,575	$1,100

694 SAMSARA CUES, cont.

GRADING	98%	90%	70%

Level 4 - Ebony forearm with malachite triple diamond-shaped rings at bottom, three long and three short curly maple points with two veneers with a malachite diamond-shaped inlay in each point, ebony butt sleeve with three long and three short curly maple reverse point-shaped inlays with a malachite diamond-shaped inlay in each between malachite triple diamond-shaped rings at top and bottom.

| MSR (1999) $2,400 | $2,550 | $1,950 | $1,300 |

Level 4 "Swirl" - Cocobolo forearm with a mahogany triple diamond-shaped ring at bottom, three long and three short cocobolo points with two veneers, exotic hardwood swirled butt sleeve between mahogany triple diamond-shaped rings at top and bottom.

| MSR (1999) $2,500 | $2,650 | $2,050 | $1,350 |

Level 8 "Spider Web" - Curly maple forearm with holly triple diamond-shaped rings at bottom, three long and three short ebony points with four veneers, holly and ebony spider web-patterned butt sleeve between holly triple diamond-shaped rings at top and bottom.

| MSR (1999) $3,000 | $3,250 | $2,500 | $1,650 |

Level 5 "White Barrel" - Ebony forearm with holly triple diamond-shaped rings at bottom, three long and three short holly points with two veneers, ebony butt sleeve with holly barrel stave-shaped inlays between holly triple diamond-shaped rings at top and bottom.

| MSR (1999) $3,500 | $3,750 | $2,850 | $1,900 |

Level 7 "Fantail" - Ebony forearm with mahogany triple diamond-shaped rings at bottom, three long and three short snakewood points with two veneers, exotic wood fantail-patterned intarsia inlaid butt sleeve with mahogany triple diamond-shaped rings at top and bottom.

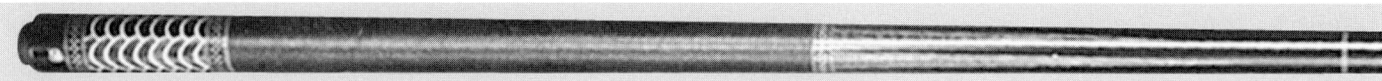

| MSR (1999) $4,500 | $4,850 | $3,800 | $2,500 |

Level 6 "Tuxedo" - Ebony forearm with four ivory double-ellipse floating points with ivory and ebony veneers with ivory X-shaped inlays at the base of each, ebony butt sleeve with four pairs of ebony and ivory veneered ivory ellipses linked by ivory X-shaped inlays, triple diamond ivory and ebony ringwork at bottom and also at joint collar, ivory butt cap with engraved "Samsara" script logo, leather wrap with ivory and ebony rings above and below.

| MSR (2003) $3,500 | $3,800 | $2,950 | $2,000 |

Level 5 "Ivory Swirl" - Snakewood forearm with ivory triple diamond-shaped ringwork at ABCDE, six long ivory points with two veneers, six large ivory spears between the points, snakewood butt sleeve with three bands of ivory inlays in a swirl pattern, ivory butt cap with engraved "Samsara" script logo, three-segment ivory wrap with inlaid rings of ivory spears and dots.

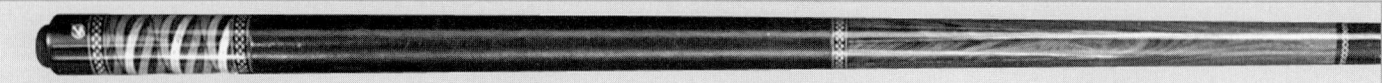

| MSR (2003) $14,000 | $15,000 | $11,750 | $8,000 |

SECONDARY MARKET MINIMUM VALUES

The following are minimum prices for other Samsara cues encountered on the secondary market. These prices are representative of cues utilizing basic materials and designs that may not be currently available. Samsara also offers one-of-a-kind cues that can command many times these prices due to the use of exotic materials and construction techniques.

Special construction note: There are many materials and construction techniques that can add value to Samsara cues. The following are the most important examples:

GRADING	98%	90%	70%

Add $1000+ for ivory points.
Add $2,000+ for polychromatic wood handle.
Add $350+ for polychromatic wood butt sleeve.
Deduct 50% for "Barcue"-marked cues.

For all used Samsara cues, except where otherwise noted:

Add $125+ for each additional original straight playable shaft beyond two.
Deduct $150 for missing original straight playable shaft.
Add $150+ for ivory joint.
Add $100 for leather wrap.
Add $50 for each ivory ferrule.
Deduct 25% for obvious or improper refinish.

	98%	90%	70%
Level 2 - 0 points, 0-25 inlays. Level 2 cues start at	$800	$620	$425
Level 3 - 2-6 points, 0-8 inlays. Level 3 cues start at	$900	$700	$475
Level 4 - 4-10 points, 9-25 inlays. Level 4 cues start at	$1,300	$1,000	$800
Level 5 - 0-12 points, 26-50 inlays. Level 5 cues start at	$1,750	$1,450	$950
Level 6 - 0-12 points, 51-75 inlays. Level 6 cues start at	$2,350	$1,850	$1,250
Level 7 - 0-12 points, 76-125 inlays. Level 7 cues start at	$2,750	$2,250	$1,500

SANKO CUSTOM CUES

Maker of pool cues from 1994 to present in Naples, Florida.

Born and raised in Minnesota, Joe Sanko worked for several years as a mechanical draftsman and doing custom marine canvas before moving to Florida in 1989. Joe had been building custom canvas boat tops when he joined a BCA pool league and started doing cue repairs for the players. By 1994 he began making "Sneaky Petes." With a background as a design engineer and a general do-it-yourselfer, he started getting more interested in the design of pool cues. Joe set up a small shop with two wood lathes and some woodworking tools, and started building some basic cues: bird's-eye maple forearm with four ebony points, usually with white and black or red and black veneers and an ebony butt. He built about two dozen cues during the first two years and all of them sold as soon as they were completed. The early cues had a 5/16-18 flat-faced joint. As playability became more of a factor, he switched to a 3/8-10 flat-faced joint, which he still uses today on his entry level cues.

Joe builds one-of-a-kind custom cues on a part-time basis in his pro shop, which is on the main street of Naples, Florida. In his Pro Shop he has some manufactured cues, cases and maintainence items, including the "Q-Wiz" which was invented by his best friend. But mainly Joe promotes his own cues that he builds on speculation. Tips and minor repairs can be done while you wait.

Joe purchases the forearms and metal components for his cues, but takes special pride in turning his own shafts. Every month he takes another cut on a group of shaft blanks. The complete process takes about 24 months, only removing about .040 at a time. One of the first things you see when you enter his shop are barrels of shaft blanks in line to be turned and several hundred shafts hanging from ceiling racks. Joe offers buck horn ferrules as an option and custom joint protectors made from materials such as antler. Many cues feature exotic wood in the handle area. Also, the use of antler for the handle, joints and butt caps is available.

Sanko cues are easily identifiable by the "Sanko" signature which will appear somewhere on the cue. Most of the early cues were signed, although the signatures may have faded or worn off because some were signed on top of the finish. Early cues were signed after completion, but after a learning process, the signature now is under the finish. Joe builds approximately 60 cues a year, along with running his custom marine canvas shop. Every Tuesday night, as he has for many years, he shows up to play in his BCA league at Art's Place in Naples, Florida, and Wednesday in a Valley league, where he enjoys seeing a number of his cues being used.

If you have a Sanko cue that needs further identification or repair, or would like to order a new Sanko cue, contact Joe at Sanko Custom Cues, listed in the Trademark Index.

SPECIFICATIONS

Butt material: hardwoods
Shaft material: rock maple
Standard length: 58 1/2 in.
Standard finish: proprietary
Balance point: 17 to 18 in. from butt
Standard butt cap: linen phenolic
Standard wrap: Irish linen
Standard joint: linen phenolic

SANKO CUSTOM CUES, cont.

GRADING	100%	95%	70%

Joint type: flat faced
Joint screw: 3/8-10
Standard number of shafts: one
Standard taper: custom
Standard ferrules: linen phenolic
Tip widths available: any
Standard tip: Le Pro
Annual production: approximately 60 cues

OPTIONS (FOR NEW CUES ONLY)

Leather wrap: $100
Ivory butt cap: $200
Ivory joint: $130
Custom joint protectors: $75
Extra shaft: $100
Ivory ferrule: $100

REPAIRS

Repairs done on all fine cues.
Refinish (with Irish linen wrap): $140
Refinish (with leather wrap): $200
Rewrap (Irish linen): $40
Rewrap (leather): $100
Replace linen phenolic butt cap: $65
Replace shaft: $100
Replace linen phenolic ferrule: $35
Replace Le Pro tip: $10
Replace layered tip: $26

CURRENT SANKO CUES

Basic two-piece cues with wraps and joint rings start at $300. Cues with points start at $395. One-of-a-kind custom cues start at $395. The current delivery time for a Sanko cue is about eighteen months.

CURRENT EXAMPLES

The following cues are currently available from Sanko Custom Cues. All cues come with one shaft standard. They can be ordered as shown, modified to suit the desires of the customer, or new designs can be created.

Level 2 - Quilted maple forearm, quilted maple butt sleeve.

MSR	$380	$365-400	$290	$200

Level 3 - Bird's-eye maple forearm, four cocobolo points with two colored veneers, cocobolo butt sleeve.

MSR	$395	$385-435	$300	$210

Level 3 - Cocobolo forearm, four long and four short maple points with colored veneers, cocobolo butt sleeve with four synthetic ivory spear-shaped inlays alternating with four turquoise double spearhead-shaped inlays between cocobolo stitch rings above and below.

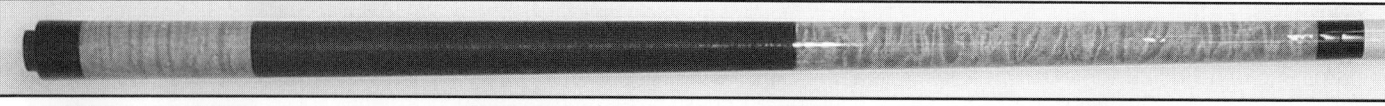

MSR	$595	$580-650	$460	$320

Level 4 - Bird's-eye maple forearm with a nickel silver ring set in black linen phenolic above wrap, four long ebony-bordered burl wood points alternating with four short ebony-bordered pink ivory points, bird's-eye maple butt sleeve with four black linen phenolic spears pointing down from a black linen phenolic ring inlaid with eight ivory diamond-shaped inlays between nickel silver rings set in black linen phenolic at top and bottom.

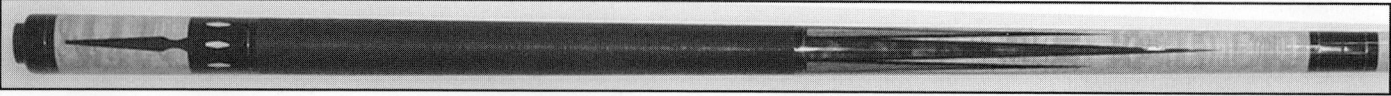

MSR	$825	$800-895	$650	$450

SANKO CUSTOM CUES, cont.

GRADING	100%	95%	70%

Level 4 - Ebony forearm, four long and four short pink ivory-bordered ebony points, alternating rings of bone ivory/pink ivory/ebony in handle, ebony butt sleeve with a pink ivory ring at bottom.

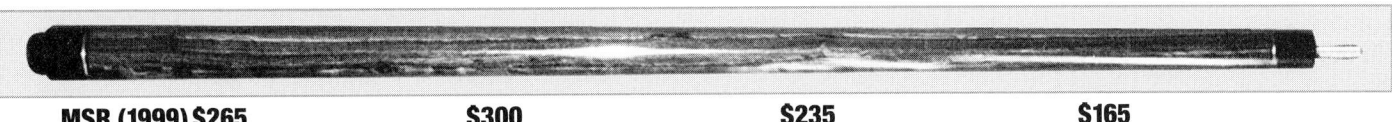

MSR	$1,895	$1,800-1,895	$1,450	$1,000

GRADING	98%	90%	70%

PAST EXAMPLES

The following Sanko cues came with one shaft standard. They can be encountered as shown, or modified to suit the desires of the original customers.

Level 2 - One-piece bocote butt with brass or silver rings at top and bottom. Also available in bird's-eye maple.

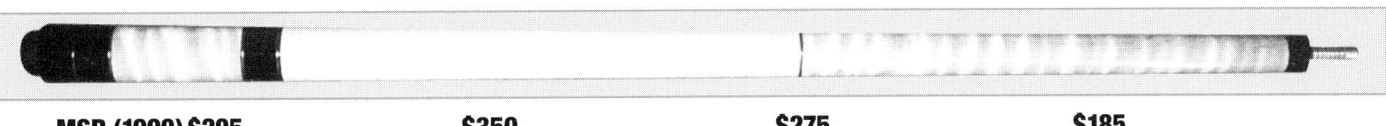

MSR (1999) $265	$300	$235	$165

Level 2 - Curly maple forearm with a silver ring at bottom, curly maple butt sleeve with thick ebony rings set within silver rings at top and bottom.

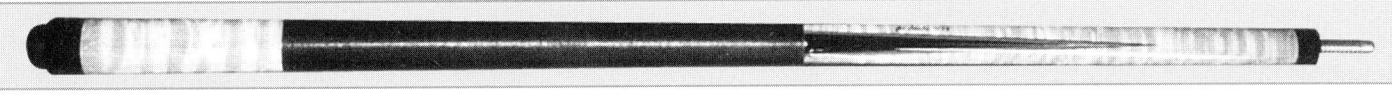

MSR (1999) $295	$350	$275	$185

Level 3 - Bird's-eye maple forearm, four ebony points with two colored veneers, bird's-eye maple butt sleeve.

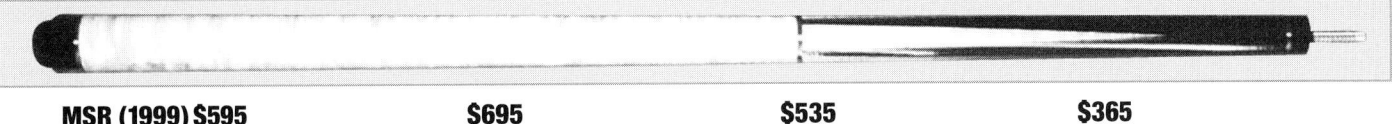

MSR (1999) $390	$465	$365	$240

Level 3 - Ebony forearm, four bird's-eye maple points, one-piece bird's-eye maple handle and butt sleeve with silver rings at top and bottom.

MSR (1999) $595	$695	$535	$365

SECONDARY MARKET MINIMUM VALUES

The following are minimum values for other Sanko cues encountered on the secondary market. These prices are representative of cues utilizing basic materials and designs that are not currently available. Joe offers one-of-a-kind cues that can command many times these prices due to the use of exotic materials, such as horn and antler, and special construction techniques, such as re-cut veneers.

Special construction note: There are many materials that can add value to Sanko cues, such as horn and antler, and special construction techniques such as re-cut veneers.

For all used cues, except where otherwise noted:
- Add $85+ for each additional original straight playable shaft beyond one.
- Deduct $100 for missing original straight playable shaft.
- Add $1,000 for bone ivory handle.
- Add $65 each for ivory or buck horn ferrules.
- Add $45 for leather wrap.
- Deduct 20% for obvious or improper refinish.

Level 2 - 0 points, 0-25 inlays.
Level 2 cues start at	$275	$215	$145

Level 3 - 2-6 points, 0-8 inlays.
Level 3 cues start at	$375	$290	$195

Level 4 - 4-10 points, 9-25 inlays.
Level 4 cues start at	$550	$425	$290

GRADING	98%	90%	70%
Level 5 - 0-12 points, 26-50 inlays.			
Level 5 cues start at	$950	$745	$495
Level 6 - 0-12 points, 51-75 inlays.			
Level 6 cues start at	$1,350	$1,045	$700

BILL SCHICK ORIGINALS

Maker of pool cues from 1970 to present in Shreveport, Louisiana.

Bill Schick started playing pool as a young boy. In the late 1960s, Buddy Hall moved to Bill's hometown of Shreveport, Louisiana. Buddy spent many hours a day practicing at the pool room where Bill liked to play, and before long, the two became good friends. One day, Jersey Red came into the room, and was showing off a custom cue he had just acquired. Buddy and Bill both played with Balabushkas, but they liked Red's cue so much that they each decided to order one.

When their cues arrived, they were both disappointed. Bill made the comment that he could make better cues himself, and Buddy dared him to actually do it. Soon, Bill had bought the necessary equipment, including a lathe, drill press, and band saw. Bill had never worked with machines before, so he had to find a local machinist to show him how to use the stuff. After about a year of experimentation, Bill completed his first cue. He used Balabushkas as patterns, dissecting a few of them to learn how they were constructed. Although he talked to George Balabushka many times while ordering cues, Bill regrets that they never actually discussed cuemaking. Bill inventoried the Balabushka workshop after George passed on, and hoped to buy the equipment and other contents, but the deal fell through. Due to his experience in dissecting and restoring Balabushka cues, he is one of the most knowledgable cuemakers in regards to these cues.

Early Bill Schick cues were 57 inches long, with piloted 5/16-14 stainless steel joints, and they were unmarked. After several customers requested that their cues be marked, Bill decided that he should get the butt caps engraved. It just so happened that one of the pool room regulars was one of a handful of master engravers in the world at that time. He refused to engrave the cues, offering to teach Bill how to do it instead. In 1977, Bill started engraving "Schick" in block letters on the butt caps, and started adding the last two digits of the year soon after. It was around this time that the standard cue length increased to 58 inches. In the early 1980s, Bill started marking all four digits of the year on his cues, since some customers were confusing the earlier two-digit style for serial numbers. Engraving continues to be a common feature on Schick cues to this day. Many of Bill's most elaborate cues feature intricate engraving. The work is so tiring to his eyes that he can only work on it for a few hours at a time.

About twenty years ago, Bill was unhappy with the quality of tips he was purchasing, so he set out to make his own. He found a source in France for water buffalo hides, and learned how to cut and treat them. He has been using his own tips ever since.

Bill has created a number of "signature" designs over the years. Among the best known are his "Chicago-style" cues, which got their name from the place in which they made their debut at a Willard's tournament in Chicago in the early 1990s. Bill wanted to make a few cues to pay for the trip, and his wife suggested that the forearm design would look good turned around on the butt sleeve. They turned out so well that he built six variations in different materials to display at the tournament. They sold instantly. From that time on Bill started getting orders for "Chicago-style" cues.

Bill took time off from cuemaking from 1994 to 1995 to open his new pool room in Shreveport called "Bill Schick Billiards". It is decorated with antiques, including antique fixtures and decor. These furnishings have come from Bill's younger brother, who salvages architectural antiques from old buildings. All of the tables in the room are antique, except for the bar tables.

Bill now makes only about 12 cues per year. Although he spends more time than ever making cues, he makes fewer than before he opened his room. This is because most of his cues are elaborate works of art requiring many weeks of work. Bill makes every component of Schick cues except for the screws, which he has custom made for him, and the rubber bumpers. Little has changed in design except for the ferrules, which were improved with the help of an aerospace engineer. Playability is stressed as the most important factor. Bill likes to put a small ivory cap, scrimmed with a stylized "S" logo, at the tip of his 3/8-10 joint screws, which is done strictly for aesthetics. Bill says he just doesn't like the way they look without them. Although he used Imron from the late 1970s to the beginning of the 1990s, he switched to the clear coat that Mercedes Benz uses, and is much happier with it. Bill's cues often feature scrimmed ivory, engraving, and gold and silver ringwork. He will only make solid forearm cues out of exotic woods that are less likely to warp than maple. Often Schick cues will have a solid wood butt sleeve of exotic wood or ivory instead of having a butt cap. He still makes the "traditional" player cues with Delrin butt caps and 5/16-14 piloted joints, although most of his cues now have 3/8-10 flat-faced joints.

Schick cues are guaranteed indefinitely against construction defects that are not the result of warpage or abuse, or, as Bill phrases his warranty, "to do the best I can." If you have a Schick cue that needs further identification or repair, or would like to talk to Bill about ordering a new Schick cue, contact Bill Schick Originals, listed in the Trademark Index.

SPECIFICATIONS

Butt material: hardwoods
Shaft material: rock maple
Standard length: 58 in.
Lengths available: custom
Standard finish: automotive clear coat
Joint screws: 5/16-14 or 3/8-10

GRADING	98%	90%	70%

Standard joint: custom
Joint type: custom
Balance point: custom
Point construction: custom
Standard wrap: Irish linen
Standard butt cap: custom
Standard number of shafts: two
Standard taper: modified Balabushka
Standard ferrules: ivory
Standard tip: Bill Schick
Tip widths available: 12 to 14 mm
Annual production: fewer than 25 cues

OPTIONS (FOR NEW CUES ONLY)

Joint protectors: standard
3/8-10 flat-face joint: no charge
Extra shaft: $300+
Ivory ferrule: standard
Special length: no charge
Layered tip: no charge

REPAIRS

Repairs done on Schick Originals and cues from deceased cuemakers. Repair prices available by request.

CURRENT BILL SCHICK CUES

Bill currently specializes in one-of-a-kind custom cues with points and ivory inlays starting at $3,000. Schick cues priced over $7,500 come with custom joint protectors standard. The current delivery time for a Bill Schick cue is at least two years.

PAST EXAMPLES

The following cues are representations of the recent work of Bill Schick. All are one-of-a-kind cues that will not be duplicated. Many came with one-of-a-kind cases. Similar cues can be ordered and modified to suit the desires of the customer, or new designs can be created.

Level 5 - Curly maple nose with six points of ebony and ivory inlays inside and at the tips of the points. Butt sleeve is ebony with ivory inlay patterns. Cue has leather wrap, ivory joint, and fancy ringwork.

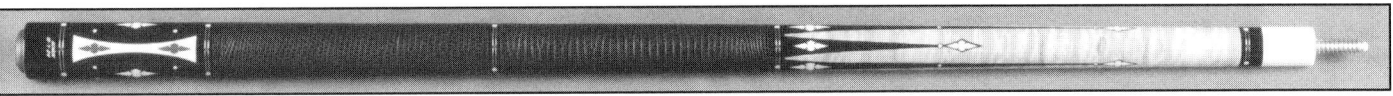

$4,400	$4,000	$2,500

Level 5 Bird's-eye nose with ebony points and engraved ivory inlays inside and at tips of points. Wrap is Irish linen. Butt sleeve is ebony with engraved ivory inlays. Cue has fancy box-type rings, ivory joint and butt cap.

$6,000	$5,500	$3,250

Level 5 Maple nose with eight ebony points and engraved ivory inlays inside and at tips of points. Wrap is Irish linen. Butt sleeve is ebony with engraved ivory inlays. Cue has fancy box-type rings, ivory joint and butt cap.

$6,500	$6,000	$3,400

Level 6- "Gargoyle Cue" - Cue butt is amboyna burl wood inlaid with fancy floating ivory points high and low. Between points are large ivory shapes featuring art engravings. Other engravings throughout ivory inlays. Cue has ivory joint and butt cap.

$15,000	$13,500	$8,000

700 BILL SCHICK ORIGINALS, cont.

GRADING	98%	90%	70%

Level 6- "Panda" - Ebony cue with large inlaid ivory windows throughout featuring art engravings of panda bear scenes. Cue has ivory joint and butt cap.

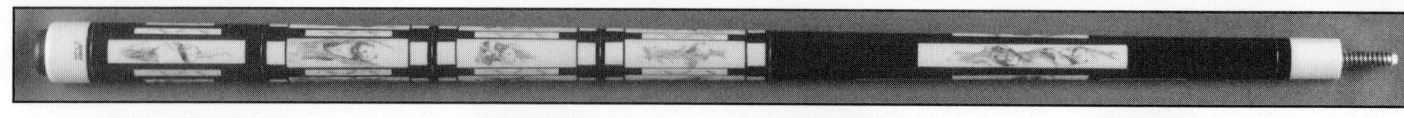

	$24,000	$22,000	$13,400

Level 6- "Chicago Bar Split" - Bird's-eye and ivory nose with four points of ebony. Each point has original ivory inlay patterns that are duplicated in the butt section of ebony. Cue has ivory joint and butt cap and an Irish linen wrap.

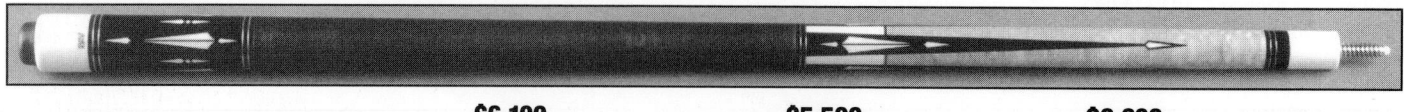

	$6,100	$5,500	$3,200

Level 7 - Spalted buckeye burl wood butt with ebony points inlaid with ivory designs. Handle area is three sections of ebony inlaid with Deco-style ivory inlays. Butt sleeve is spalted buckeye burl wood with downward-facing points and ivory inlays. Cue has ivory joint and butt cap and stacked ringwork.

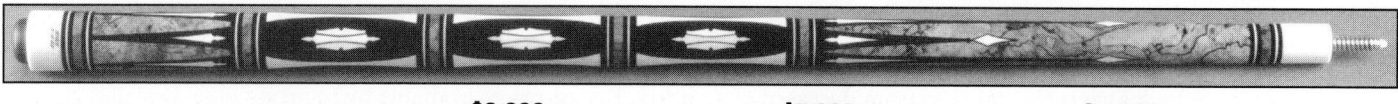

	$8,000	$7,200	$4,700

Level 8 - "The Art of Medicine" - Koa wood nose with eight points of engraved ivory. Handle is spalted sapota wood with Deco-style inlays and engraved ivory windows. Butt sleeve has large ivory windows engraved with medical imagery. Cue has ivory joint and butt cap and fancy rings.

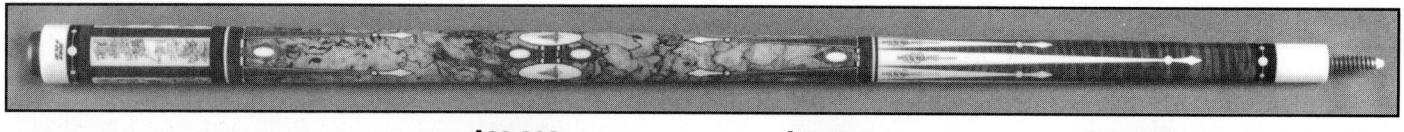

	$20,000	$18,500	$12,000

SECONDARY MARKET MINIMUM VALUES

The following are minimum prices for Schick cues encountered on the secondary market. These prices are representative of cues utilizing basic materials and designs that may not be currently available. Bill also offers one-of-a-kind cues that can command many times these prices due to the use of exotic materials and artistry.

Special construction note: There are many materials and construction techniques that can add value to Schick cues. Inlaid and/or engraved ivory handles can add up to $15,000-20,000+ more to the price of the cue.

For all used Schick cues, except where otherwise noted:
- Add $250+ for each additional original straight playable shaft beyond two.
- Deduct $300 for each missing original straight playable shaft under two.
- Add $350+ for ivory joint.
- Add $450+ for ivory butt cap.
- Add $300+ for leather wrap.
- Add $50+ for each ivory ferrule.
- Deduct 25% for obvious or improper refinish.

	98%	90%	70%
Level 3 - 2-6 points, 0-8 inlays.			
Level 3 cues start at	$2,000	$1,900	$1,300
Level 4 - 4-10 points, 9-25 inlays.			
Level 4 cues start at	$3,100	$2,800	$1,700
Level 5 - 0-12 points, 26-50 inlays.			
Level 5 cues start at	$4,400	$4,000	$2,400
Level 6 - 0-12 points, 51-75 inlays.			
Level 6 cues start at	$6,100	$5,650	$3,300
Level 7 - 0-12 points, 76-125 inlays.			
Level 7 cues start at	$8,800	$8,000	$4,800
Level 8 - 0-12 points, 126-200 inlays.			
Level 8 cues start at	$12,500	$11,350	$7,700

SCHMELKE MANUFACTURING INC.

Maker of pool cues from 1947 to 1969 in Minneapolis, Minnesota, and currently in Rice Lake, Wisconsin.

Jim Schmelke

The Schmelke Manufacturing Company was founded in Minneapolis, Minnesota in 1947 by Duard and Richard Schmelke, two brothers who made a living playing pool in the early 1940s. They saw a need for quality cues in the Twin Cities area and began making custom cues in a small shop in their home. By the late 1940s Duard decided to make two-piece cues on his own; it remained a one-man operation until 1969 when his son, Jim, joined him in making billiard cues. (Richard also made one-piece cues on his own, and eventually sold his end of the business to the Valley Manufacturing Co.)

Duard and Jim formed a partnership and began to expand the business, moving it to Sarona in Northwest Wisconsin. A few employees were hired. Jim concentrated on the manufacturing aspect of the business, while the chatty Duard and his wife, Eva, traveled throughout the Midwest selling their cues. They built a network of dealers, many of whom are still customers today. In the early 1980s Duard and Eva retired, with Jim purchasing the business and changing it to a corporation. In the spring of 1995, Duard Schmelke passed on, leaving James and his wife, Judy, to continue the Schmelke cuemaking tradition of high quality at an affordable price. That year the business made another move to a new manufacturing facility in Rice Lake. With the new building came new manufacturing techniques of higher speed. This new speed and efficiency allowed for greater production without compromising the quality craftsmanship of the original product.

Since 1985 the manufacturing facility has expanded three times. Today, Schmelke sells both one- and two-piece billiard cues, cases and accessories throughout the United States, Europe, and Canada. Schmelke Cues has gone from a one-man shop to a manufacturing plant that employs over 20 people year-round in a 15,000+ square foot manufacturing facility. A new state-of-the-art UV finishing system and a complete climate-control system has since been added. Woods are cured for at least a year to guarantee their consistency and stability. Climate-control allows the wood to stay straight and true throughout the manufacturing process. Throughout the process each cue is checked for straightness five times. Through the 1980s and 1990s Jim and Judy managed the company while raising a family of one son and two daughters. Their son David joined the company after college in 1997, and is now general manager. Daughter Carrie has worked at Schmelke part time since 1994. Her husband, Steve Johnson, joined the business in 1999, when Steve started making cues with David. Steve and David share production responsibilities, with Steve also serving as sales manager. Jim and Judy are now semi-retired, and come into the office several times a week. They hope to maintain Schmelke Cues as a family-owned business and continue to provide their customers with the same quality, value, and customer service as Schmelke has done for over 50 years and three generations.

Schmelke cues can be easily identified by the "Schmelke" logo on the butt sleeve, which they started to put on their cues in the early 1980s. Some early cues were sold under the name "True Stroke," and this logo will appear on them. Schmelke's most identifying feature is their original brass-to-brass joint with a wide 9/16 screw; older cues will have a shorter screw than the 24 thread used on their current cues. Around 1992, three more joint types were designed and offered on all their cue lines. All joints are available with a variety of colors of pearlized rings at a small extra charge. Laminated shafts were used on Schmelke cues as early as the 1970s, and are still offered as an option. Schmelke offers these and other custom options, and can fill most orders within two weeks. The D-Series cues with decals replaced earlier hand-painted cues. The M-Series and S-series were in production for a number of years with slight changes. Other current two-piece cue lines are the T-series and the BW-series of black and white cues.

Schmelke cues are guaranteed against construction defects that are not the result of warpage or abuse. If you have an old Schmelke cue that needs repair, or would like to order a new one, contact Schmelke Manufacturing Inc., listed in the Trademark Index.

SPECIFICATIONS

Butt material: select hardwoods or fiberglass
Shaft material: rock maple
Standard length: 58 in.
Lengths available: 52 to 62 in.
Standard finish: UV
Joint screw: four styles available
Standard joint: brass 9/16-24
Joint type: flat-faced metal-to-metal
Balance point: varies depending on joint
Point construction: full splice
Standard wrap: linen, nylon or leather
Standard butt cap: pearlized acrylic
Standard number of shafts: one
Standard taper: 10 in. pro
Standard ferrules: Tweeten fiber
Standard tip: Elk Master
Tip widths available: 11 to 13.5 mm

OPTIONS (FOR NEW CUES ONLY)

Special length or weight (under 17 or over 22 oz.): $20
Stainless steel joint: $12
Leather wrap (black only): $60
Linen wrap: $16
Nylon wrap: $12
Extra shaft: $60+
Flat laminated shaft: $20

GRADING	100%	95%	70%

Pearl butt spacer (1 1/2 in.) : $28
Layered tip: $6
Personalized decal lettering: $3 per letter

REPAIRS

Repairs done on all makes with joints compatible with the Schmelke joints. (Add 50% if not a Schmelke cue.)
Refinish: $76 + wrap
Rewrap (nylon): $12
Rewrap (linen): $18
Rewrap (leather): $70
Repalce butt cap: $50+
Replace shaft: $60+
Replace ferrule: $14+ plus tip
Replace tip: $7
Replace layered tip: $12

CURRENT SCHMELKE CUES

Schmelke currently manufactures the Fiber Glass Cues which consists of nine models, the Legion Cues which consists of two models, the BW Series which consists of nine models, the D Series which consists of ten models, the L Series which consists of seven models (shown), the S Series which consists of eight models, the Sneaky Petes which consists of four models, the M Series which consists of ten models, and the T Series which consists of eight models. Schmelke also makes a break cue. The current delivery time for a Schmelke cue is a few days for standard models and two weeks for cues with custom options.

CURRENT EXAMPLES

The following Schmeleke cues are all seven examples of the current L Series, Also known as the Signature Series.

Level 4 L20 - Bird's-eye maple forearm, three long and three short floating ebony-bordered malachite phenolic points, ebony butt sleeve with three long and three short reverse floating bird's-eye maple-bordered malachite phenolic points.

| MSR | $275 | $215-275 | $175 | $130 |

Level 3 L30 - Cocobolo forearm, four bird's-eye maple points with a turqoise diamond-shaped inlay in each, cocobolo butt sleeve with four bird's-eye maple reverse points with a turqoise diamond-shaped inlay in each.

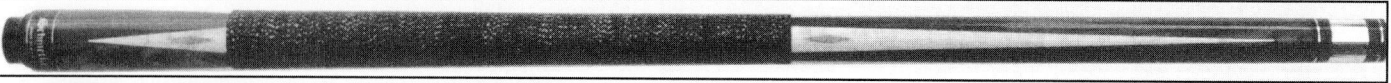

| MSR | $280 | $220-280 | $180 | $135 |

Level 4 L40 - Bird's-eye maple forearm, four long and four short ebony points with a bird's-eye maple diamond-shaped inlay in each, ebony butt sleeve with eight bird's-eye maple diamond-shaped inlays.

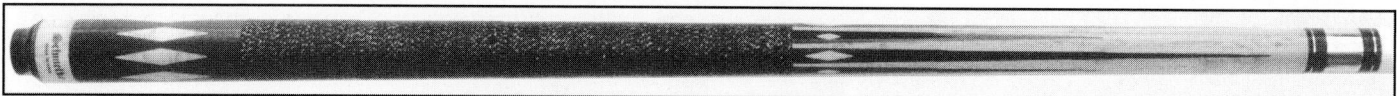

| MSR | $322 | $250-322 | $205 | $150 |

Level 4 L50 - Stained bird's-eye maple forearm, four long and four short ebony points with a pearlized plastic diamond-shaped inlay in each, stained bird's-eye maple butt sleeve with eight ebony diamond-shaped inlays.

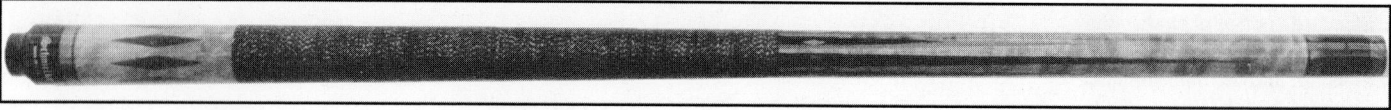

| MSR | $348 | $265-348 | $215 | $160 |

Level 4 L60 - Bird's-eye maple forearm, four ebony points with an ebony-bordered synthetic ivory spear-shaped inlay at the tip of each, ebony butt sleeve with four reverse ebony points with veneers and a veneer-bordered synthetic ivory spear-shaped inlay at the tip of each above an ebony dash ring at bottom.

| MSR | $365 | $275-365 | $225 | $170 |

GRADING	100%	95%	70%

Level 5 L70 - Bird's-eye maple forearm, four ebony points with an ebony spear-shaped inlay at the tip of each point alternating with four sets of ebony diamond-shaped inlays within opposing redwood spear-shaped inlays above and below, bird's-eye maple butt sleeve with eight sets of ebony diamond-shaped inlays within opposing redwood spear-shaped inlays above and below above a nickel silver ring at bottom.

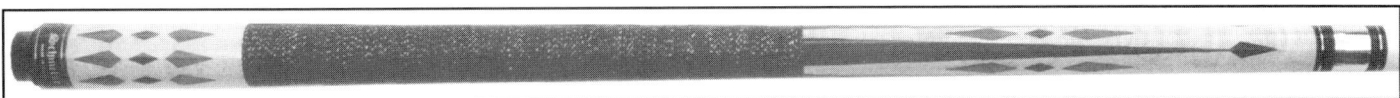

MSR	$387	$290-387	$240	$180

Level 5 L80 - Bird's-eye maple forearm, four floating bocote points with a synthetic ivory diamond-shaped inlay within an ebony oval-shaped inlay in each point alternating with four ebony diamond-shaped inlays, bird's-eye maple butt sleeve with four reverse floating bocote points with a synthetic ivory diamond-shaped inlay within an ebony oval-shaped inlay in each point alternating with four ebony diamond-shaped inlays above a nickel silver ring at bottom.

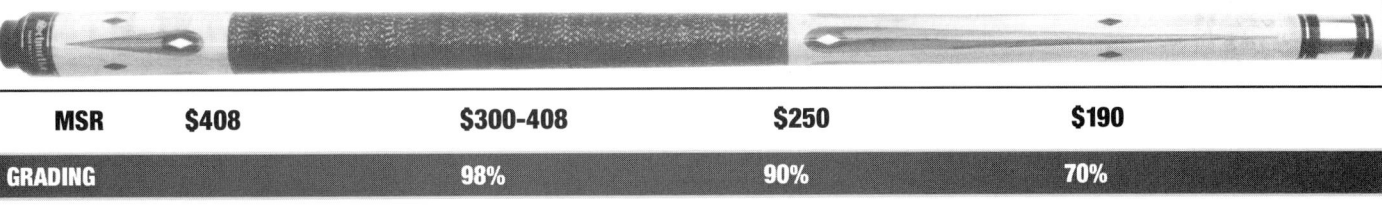

MSR	$408	$300-408	$250	$190

GRADING	98%	90%	70%

DISCONTINUED EXAMPLES

Level 1 R1-W - Maple forearm, four walnut points and butt sleeve.

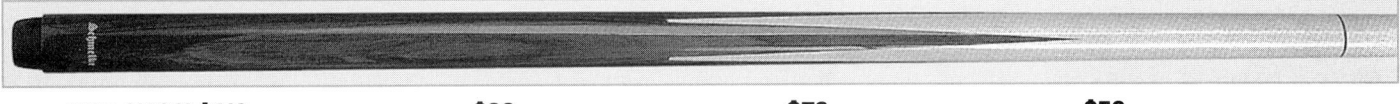

MSR (1996) $110	$90	$70	$50

Level 2 M1-H - Hackberry forearm, hackberry butt sleeve.

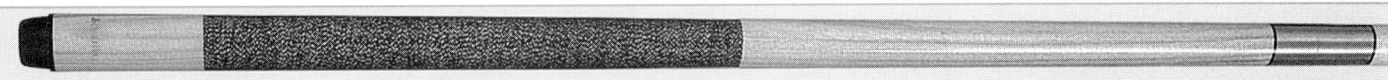

MSR (1996) $68	$60	$50	$30

Level 2 M1-C - Curapay forearm, curapay butt sleeve.

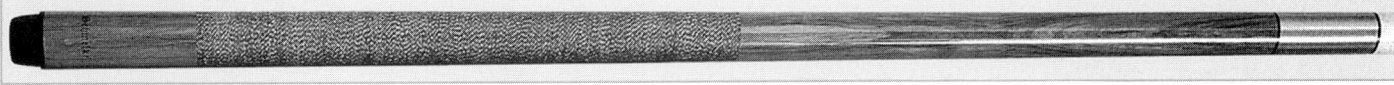

MSR (1996) $68	$60	$50	$30

Level 2 M7 - Rosewood or bocote forearm and butt sleeve with long pearl triangle inlaid above "Schmelke" logo on pearl between brass rings above butt cap (M7-R rosewood shown).

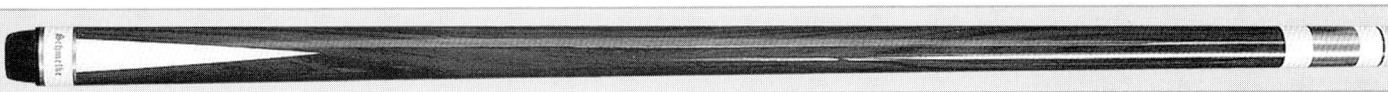

MSR (1999) $160	$150	$115	$75

Level 2 M8 - Ebony or cocobolo forearm, pearl rings at joint, ebony or cocobolo butt sleeve with "Schmelke" logo on pearl between brass rings above butt cap, linen wrap standard (M8-E ebony shown).

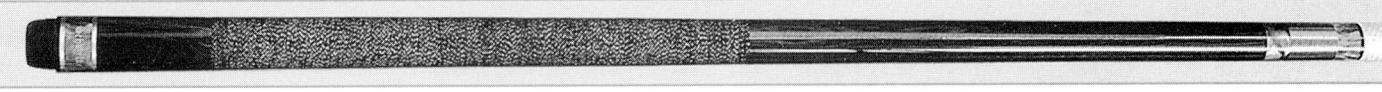

MSR (1999) $180	$165	$125	$80

Level 2 M3 - Rosewood or bocote forearm and butt sleeve with pearl butt spacer (M3-R rosewood shown).

MSR (2000) $100	$85	$65	$40

| GRADING | 98% | 90% | 70% |

2004 SCHMELKE CUES

The following 2004 Schmelke cues are very similar to current cues, except for slight changes, and possible price increases.

The following cues were priced with a linen wrap. For nylon wrap deduct $10, for no wrap deduct $16. Stained shafts were no extra charge.

The following "S" Series (S1 through S13) cues were all available with a pearl butt spacer for $28 extra, as seen on model S1P. The "S" series was available in 8 colors, including plum, brown, wine, blue, gray, black and white.

Level 2 S1 – S13 - Stained maple forearm, stained maple butt sleeve, with linen wrap (S6 wine stain shown).

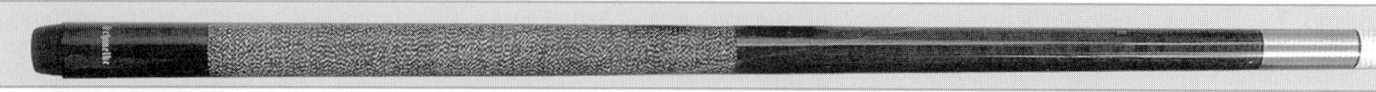

| MSR (2004) $110 | $100 | $75 | $45 |

Level 2 S1P – S13P - Same as above with 1 1/2 in. pearl butt spacer (S1P plum stain shown).

| MSR (2004) $120 | $95 | $75 | $45 |

Level 1 R1 - Maple forearm, four bocote or rosewood points and butt sleeve (R1-B bocote shown).

| MSR (2004) $100 | $85 | $65 | $40 |

Level 2 M1-S - Shedua forearm, shedua butt sleeve. Also available in stained maple as a model M1-N.

| MSR (2004) $74 | $65 | $50 | $30 |

Level 2 M2 - Rosewood or bocote forearm and butt sleeve (M2-R rosewood shown).

| MSR (2004) $84 | $70 | $50 | $30 |

Level 2 M4-R - Rosewood forearm with natural maple butterfly splice, shedua or rosewood butt sleeve with pearl butt spacer (also available as M4-S in shedua).

| MSR (2004) $104 | $85 | $65 | $40 |

Level 2 M6 - Curly maple forearm and butt sleeve, "Schmelke" logo on pearl ring between brass rings above butt cap.

| MSR (2004) $120 | $95 | $75 | $45 |

SECONDARY MARKET MINIMUM VALUES

The following are minimum prices for other Schmelke cues encountered on the secondary market. These prices are representative of cues utilizing basic materials and designs that are not currently available. Early models and limited editions are becoming collectible, and can also command many times these prices. Discontinued Schmelke cues will be further covered in future editions.

Special construction note: There are many materials and construction techniques that can add value to Schmelke cues. The following are the most important examples.

GRADING	98%	90%	70%

Add $5+ for nylon wrap.
Add $15+ for Irish linen.
Add $10+ for pearl joint rings.
For all used Schmelke cues, except where otherwise noted:
Add $40+ for each additional original straight playable shaft (standard with one).
Deduct $50 for missing original straight playable shaft.
Deduct 20% for obvious or improper non-lacquer refinish.

	98%	90%	70%
Level 1 - 4 points, hustler.			
Level 1 cues start at	$65	$50	$30
Level 2 - 0 points, 0-25 inlays.			
Level 2 cues start at	$70	$55	$30
Level 3 - 2-6 points, 0-8 inlays.			
Level 3 cues start at	$90	$70	$40
Level 4 - 4-10 points, 9-25 inlays.			
Level 4 cues start at	$115	$95	$50
Level 5 - 0-12 points, 26-50 inlays.			
Level 5 cues start at	$145	$110	$65

E. SCHMIDT

Maker of pool cues until the early 1970s in Columbia, Missouri.

Although A. E. Schmidt is better known these days for their pool tables, the Schmidt factory made cues for decades under 'AES' label. During the 1970s they discontinued cue manufacturing at their facility in Columbia, Missouri and instead had a line of cues made by other cue manufacturers such as Viking, McDermott, and Huebler. A.E. Schmidt is still family owned and operated with Kurt and Fred Schmidt as the latest generation to take the reins. One of their former cuemakers, Bill Van Hoos, still works in the factory making tables.

SCHON CUES

Maker of pool cues from 1981 to present in Milwaukee, Wisconsin.

Schon Cues was started by Terry Romine and Bob Runde in the back of what was then Romine's High Pocket billiard parlor in downtown Milwaukee, Wisconsin. Bob had more than ten years of cuemaking experience at the time, and Terry also had previous experience with cuemaking. They chose the name "Schon" for their cues, which is German for beautiful. The obvious approach was to build a cue like the best that was available at the time, i.e. Balabushka and Szamboti. The result was highly successful, and to this day they continue to build a Balabushka-style cue, but over the last twenty years have made a myriad of improvements in performance, construction, and design. Schon Cues feels that they are now making the best cue they have ever made.

The basic cue is constructed as a three-piece butt. The center section, or "under the wrap," as they call it, is a laminated unit of various woods which helps maintain straightness and consistent play from cue to cue. The cost of this piece is astronomical in comparison to the standard maple under the wrap, but nothing is sacrificed for performance. The top of the cue, in 85% of all instances, is bird's-eye maple. The rest of the time exotic wood tops are used which are drilled and cored with laminated maple to maintain weight, consistency of hit, and straightness. Their stainless steel joint has a phenolic core, which they pioneered over 25 years ago, and has since been adopted by many of the well-known cuemakers. This construction helps reduce weight and also softens and transfers the sensitivity of the hit. The bottom of the cue is made from various materials such as bird's-eye maple, ebony, or other exotic woods, terminated by a Delrin butt plate which yields the best durability for a section of the cue which takes much abuse from day to day. A little cosmetic quality is sacrificed because they can't finish over the Delrin, but it is infinitely more repairable and maintainable. The primary objectives at Schon Cues are good play, performance, and durability.

All inlay work is made from what Schon Cues calls "high integrity" materials. Black stuff is all ebony, white stuff is elephant ivory, etc. In some small instances, they substitute high tensile synthetics in the ringwork where the structural integrity of the cue is best served. Shafts are Northern hard maple with their own proprietary ferrule and their own water buffalo tip. They tend to resort to the form over function rule regarding the cosmetics of shaft wood. In recent years, there has been a trend to promote squaky white homogenous

| GRADING | 98% | 90% | 70% |

maple as the best shaft. They hit with every cue and shaft that they have ever made, and after all these years cannot make any correlation between tight grain, color, weight, and good hit. The proof is in the hit, and since they make a very small amount of cues, they have the luxury of being able to tune each piece that leaves their shop. They can produce shafts in any length, from 27 to 32 inches in any particular length increment, and any diameter from 11 to 14 mm in any diameter increment. They also offer ivory ferrules as an option for an additional fee.

Schon cues are easily identifiable by the Schon logo which appears on the butt caps. In 1981, the first year of production, all Schon cues had brown phenolic joint rings. By 1982, the first line of sixteen cues was introduced in a brochure. These cues had maple dashes in the joint and spliced points. From 1985 to 1987, the high end Schon cues had nickel silver rings, and by 1988, all Schons had nickel silver joint rings. By the 1990s, Schon cues had inlaid points.

In 1992, Bob Runde retired and Evan Clark took over cuemaking operations. In 1993, Evan saw some Schon shafts for sale that were adequate to deceive the unwitting buyer, so he started marking "Schon" on the shafts that same year. Shafts made in 1993 have "Schon" in gold lettering on the collar, and since then they have been vertically marked on the wood. Evan tries to create a new Limited Edition Schon every week, and no more than twelve of a single design are made. These cues are marked "Schon Ltd." and sometimes include the cue's number, and number of identical cues made. He makes Elite cues, seven per design and Unique cues. These cues are marked "Schon Elite" and "Schon Unique" respectively.

If you have a Schon cue that needs further identification or repair, or would like to talk to someone about ordering a new Schon cue, contact Schon Cues, listed in the Trademark Index.

SPECIFICATIONS

Butt material: hardwoods
Shaft material: rock maple
Standard length: 58 in.
Lengths available: 56 to 61 in.
Balance point: custom
Standard butt cap: Delrin
Standard wrap: Irish linen
Point construction: inlaid
Standard joint: stainless
Joint type: piloted
Joint screw: 5/16-14
Standard taper: 12 in. straight
Standard ferrules: custom
Standard tip: Schon
Standard number of shafts: one

OPTIONS (FOR NEW CUES ONLY)

Leather wrap: $50
Special length: $100
Ivory ferrule: $65
Extra shaft: $160

REPAIRS

Repairs done only on Schon cues.

Refinish (with wrap): $160
Rewrap (Irish linen): $50
Rewrap (leather): $100
Replace Delrin butt cap: $30
Replace shaft: $160
Replace ivory ferrule: $65

CURRENT SCHON CUES

Schon currently specializes in one-of-a-kind cues and limited editions. They are available for quick delivery. Schon also manufactures the STL Series which has 21 models priced from $595 to over $2,000, the CX Series which are available from Cuestix Internatinal, and the Elite Series.

DISCONTINUED SCHON CUES

The following cues are from Schon's first catalogue, circa 1982. They had full-spliced points, and are shown with the maple dashed joint rings Schon used on all of their cues from 1982 to 1985. Later examples will have nickel silver joint rings.

Level 2 R1 - Stained bird's-eye maple forearm with a maple dash ring at bottom, stained bird's-eye maple butt sleeve with maple dash rings at top and bottom.

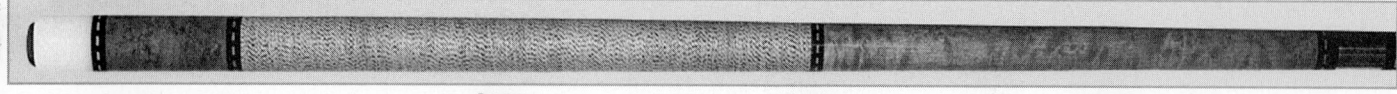

| $600 | $450 | $290 |

SCHON CUES, cont. 707

GRADING	98%	90%	70%

Level 3 R2 - Stained bird's-eye maple forearm, four ebony points, ebony butt sleeve.

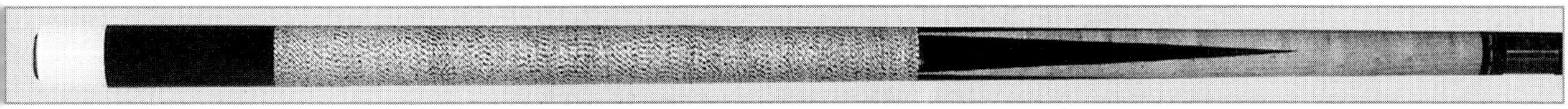

$850 $640 $415

Level 3 R3 - Stained bird's-eye maple forearm, four stained bird's-eye maple points with thick ebony veneers, stained bird's-eye maple butt sleeve.

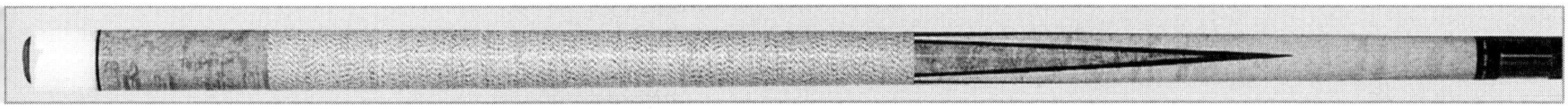

$875 $665 $425

Level 3 R4 - Stained bird's-eye maple forearm, four ebony points, ebony butt sleeve with a row of maple squares towards bottom.

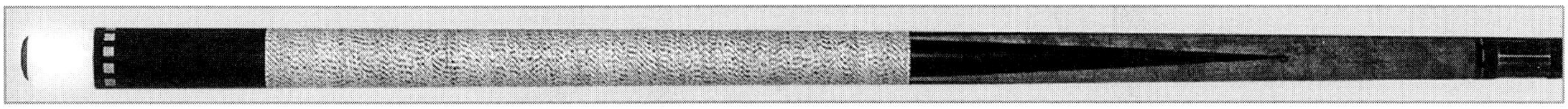

$900 $675 $435

Level 3 R5 - Stained bird's-eye maple forearm, four ebony points, ebony butt sleeve with tall stained bird's-eye maple windows.

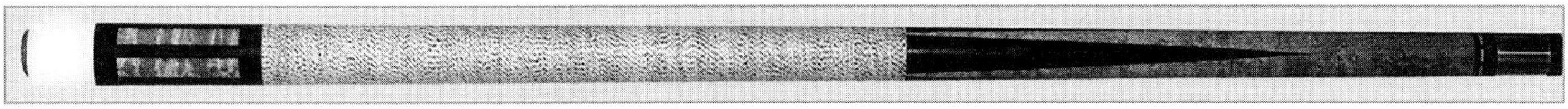

$950 $715 $455

Level 3 R6 - Stained bird's-eye maple forearm, four ebony points with two colored veneers, ebony butt sleeve.

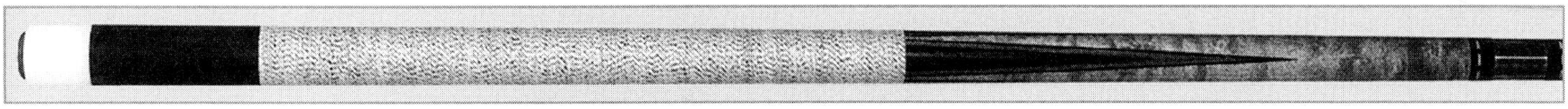

$1,050 $800 $500

Level 3 R7 - Stained bird's-eye maple forearm with ivory dashes at bottom, six ebony points, ebony butt sleeve with ivory dashes at top and bottom.

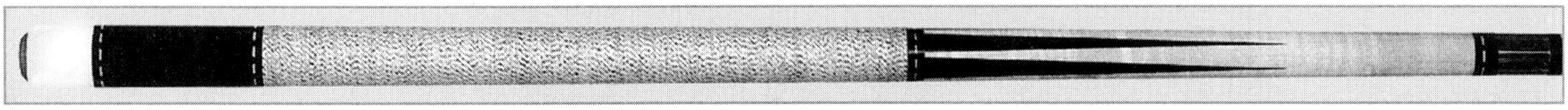

$1,100 $825 $525

Level 4 R8 - Stained bird's-eye maple forearm, four ebony points with two colored veneers, ebony butt sleeve with ebony and ivory dice-shaped inlays set in ivory-bordered windows above and below.

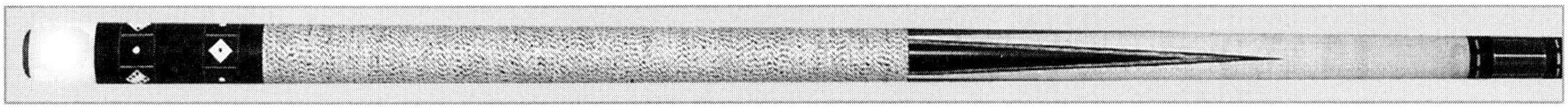

$2,000 $1,500 $950

Level 3 R9 - Stained bird's-eye maple forearm, four hardwood points with four colored veneers, ebony butt sleeve with tall hardwood windows.

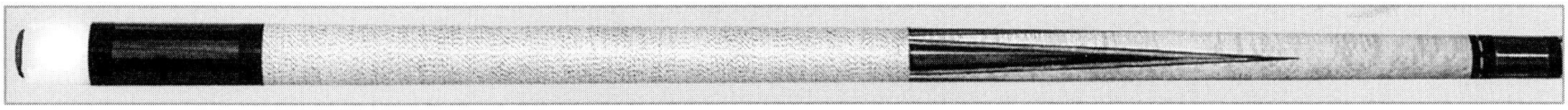

$1,000 $750 $475

Level 3 R10 - Ebony forearm, four ebony points with four colored veneers, ebony butt sleeve with veneer rings at top and bottom.

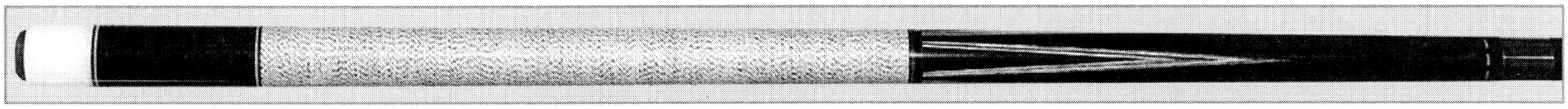

$1,100 $875 $525

708 SCHON CUES, cont.

GRADING	98%	90%	70%

Level 3 R11 - Stained bird's-eye maple forearm, four ebony points with four colored veneers, ebony butt sleeve with four veneer-bordered stained bird's-eye maple windows between veneer rings above and below.

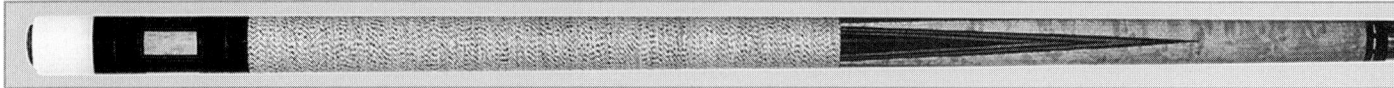

	$1,200	$900	$575

Level 4 R12 - Stained bird's-eye maple forearm with a maple dash ring at bottom, four ebony points with three colored veneers and an ivory diamond-shaped inlay in each point, ebony butt sleeve with four ivory diamond-shaped inlays set in colored veneer-bordered ebony windows between ivory dashes above and below.

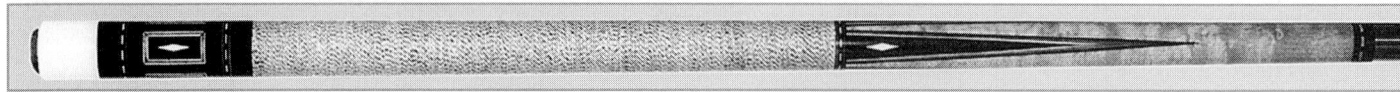

	$1,400	$1,045	$665

Level 4 R13 - Ebony forearm with a red veneer ring at bottom, four ebony points with single red veneers and an ivory diamond-shaped inlay in each point, ebony butt sleeve with ivory bars alternating with ivory diamond-shaped inlays set in red veneer-bordered windows.

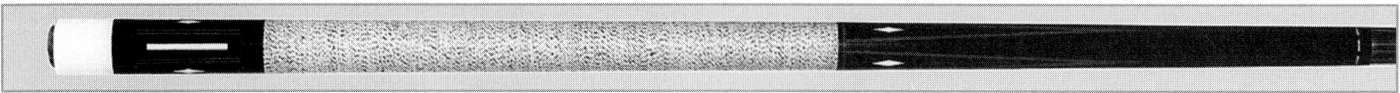

	$1,650	$1,250	$800

Level 4 R14 - Stained bird's-eye maple forearm with maple dashes at bottom, four ebony points with two colored veneers and a red veneer line piercing an ivory oval in each point, ebony butt sleeve with four red veneer lines piercing ebony ovals set in ivory windows between maple dash rings above and below.

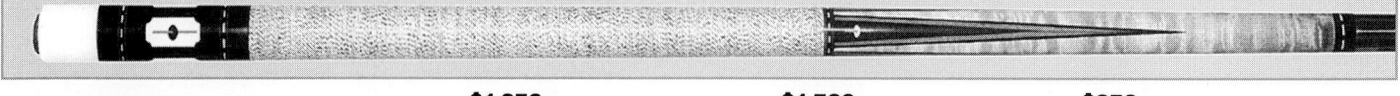

	$1,950	$1,500	$950

Level 4 R15 - Stained bird's-eye maple forearm with an ebony ring at bottom, six ebony points with two colored veneers and a large ivory spear-shaped inlay in each point, ebony butt sleeve with six large ivory bars set in red veneer-bordered ebony windows.

	$2,200	$1,650	$1,000

Level 4 R16 - Stained bird's-eye maple forearm with a nickel silver ring at bottom, three ebony points with a large ivory spear-shaped inlay in each point alternating with three ebony points with an ivory diamond-shaped inlay in each point, ebony butt sleeve with three pairs of opposing ivory triangle-shaped inlays alternating with three ivory diamond-shaped inlays between nickel silver rings at top and bottom.

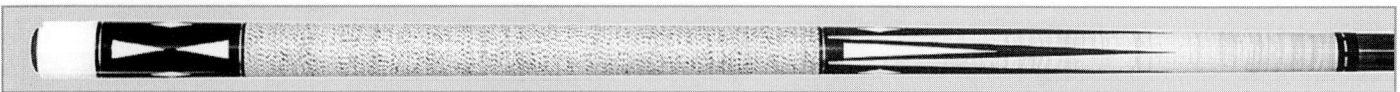

	$2,400	$1,785	$1,100

The following 1999 "STL" Series cues were available in a variety of stains, wraps, and hardwoods.

Level 2 STL1 - Stained bird's-eye maple forearm with nickel silver ring above wrap, stained bird's-eye maple butt sleeve with décor rings at top and bottom and above the wrap.

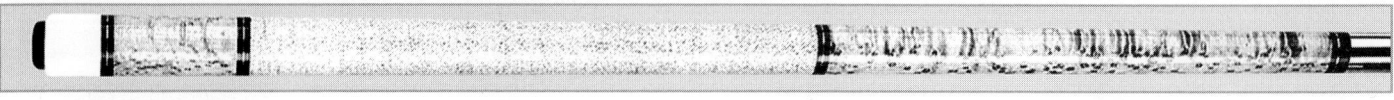

MSR (1999) $555	$525	$395	$250

Level 3 STL2 - Stained bird's-eye maple forearm, four inlaid ebony points, ebony butt sleeve with décor rings at top and bottom and above wrap.

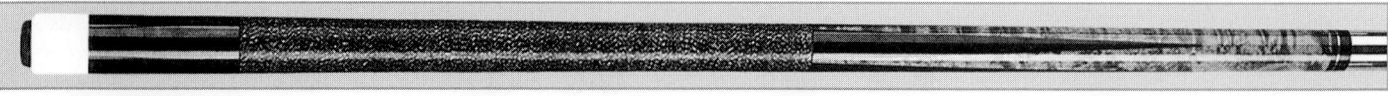

MSR (1999) $578	$550	$415	$265

| GRADING | 98% | 90% | 70% |

Level 3 STL3 - Stained bird's-eye maple forearm with nickel silver ring above wrap, four stained bird's-eye maple points with ebony veneer, stained bird's-eye maple butt sleeve with nickel silver ring at top and bottom.

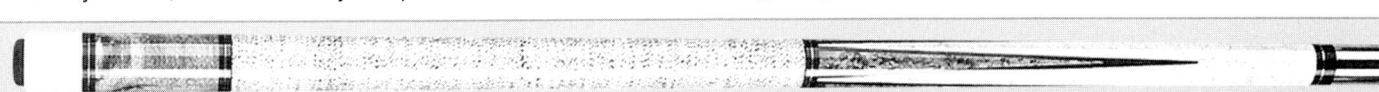

| MSR (1999) $555 | $525 | $395 | $250 |

Level 3 STL4 - Stained bird's-eye maple forearm, four ebony points, ebony butt sleeve.

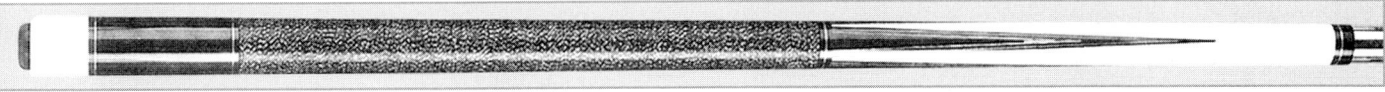

| MSR (1999) $667 | $600 | $450 | $285 |

Level 4 STL5 - Stained bird's-eye maple forearm, four hardwood points with veneers, ebony butt sleeve with décor ring at top and bottom and above wrap.

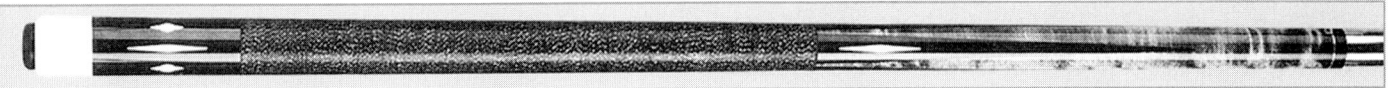

| MSR (1999) $734 | $650 | $500 | $310 |

Level 3 STL6 - Stained bird's-eye maple forearm with nickel silver rings at bottom, four ebony points, ebony butt sleeve with silver rings at top and bottom.

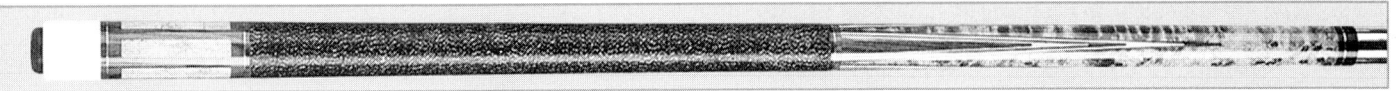

| MSR (1999) $734 | $650 | $500 | $310 |

Level 4 SL7 - Stained bird's-eye maple forearm, four ebony points with ivory diamond-shaped inlay in each point, ebony butt sleeve with four large and four small ivory diamond-shaped inlays.

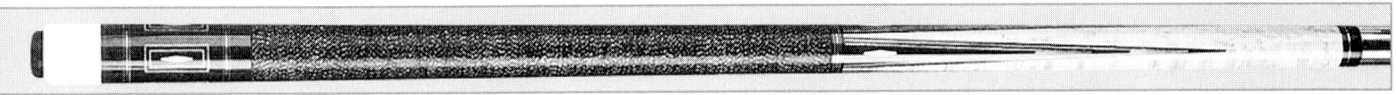

| MSR (1999) $833 | $735 | $550 | $350 |

Level 4 SL8 - Stained bird's-eye maple forearm with checks set within nickel silver rings at bottom, four ebony points with four colored veneers and an ivory diamond-shaped inlay in each point, ebony butt sleeve with pairs of ivory diamond-shaped inlays connected by ivory bars within nickel silver rings and checks set in nickel silver rings above and below.

| MSR (1999) $922 | $800 | $600 | $385 |

Level 4 SL9 - Stained bird's-eye maple forearm with nickel silver ring at bottom, four ebony points with four colored veneers and an ivory notched diamond-shaped inlay in each point alternating with four ivory four-point star-shaped inlays set in ebony ovals, ebony butt sleeve with four ivory-notched diamond-shaped inlays set in ebony ovals alternating with ivory four-point star-shaped inlays set in a thick hardwood ring with hardwood squares set in nickel silver rings above and below.

| MSR (1999) $944 | $835 | $635 | $400 |

Level 4 SL10 - Stained bird's-eye maple forearm with ivory checks set in nickel silver rings at bottom, four ebony points with four colored veneers and an ivory diamond-shaped inlay in each point, ebony butt sleeve with four ivory diamond-shaped inlays alternating with four larger ivory diamond-shaped inlays between ivory checks set in nickel silver rings above and below.

| MSR (1999) $967 | $850 | $650 | $410 |

SCHON CUES, cont.

GRADING	98%	90%	70%

Level 4 SL11 - Stained bird's-eye maple forearm with nickel silver ring at bottom, four floating ebony points with an ivory scalloped diamond-shaped inlay in each point alternating with four ebony ovals, ebony butt sleeve with four ivory scalloped diamond-shaped inlays between nickel silver rings above and below.

MSR (1999) $967	$850	$650	$410

Level 4 SL12 - Stained bird's-eye maple forearm, four ebony points with four colored veneers and an ivory notched diamond-shaped inlay in each point, ebony butt sleeve with four ivory diamond-shaped inlays alternating with four smaller ivory notched diamond-shaped inlays.

MSR (1999) $967	$850	$650	$410

GRADING	100%	95%	70%

Level 4 SL13 - Stained bird's-eye maple forearm with checks set in nickel silver rings at bottom, six ebony points with two colored veneers and an ivory diamond-shaped inlay in each point, ebony butt sleeve with six ivory diamond-shaped inlays with hardwood caps between hardwood checks set in nickel silver rings above and below.

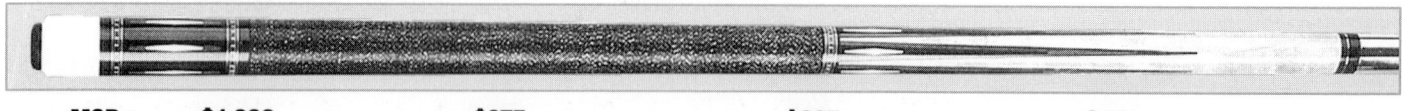

MSR	$1,000	$875	$665	$415

Level 4 SL14 - Stained bird's-eye maple forearm with ivory checks set in nickel silver rings at bottom, six ebony points with an ivory diamond-shaped inlay in each point, ebony butt sleeve with six ivory diamond-shaped inlays between ivory checks set in nickel silver rings above and below.

MSR	$1,000	$875	$665	$415

Level 4 SL15 - Stained bird's-eye maple forearm with a hardwood ring set in nickel rings at bottom, six hardwood points with an ivory diamond-shaped inlay in each point, hardwood butt sleeve with six large ivory diamond-shaped inlays alternating with six smaller ivory diamond-shaped inlays between hardwood rings set in nickel silver rings at top and bottom.

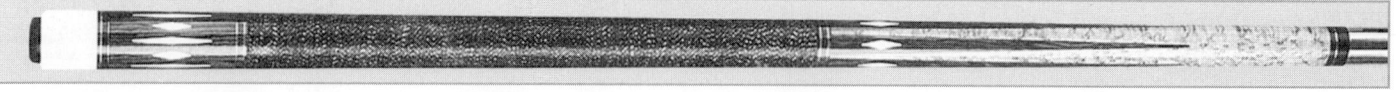

MSR	$1,089	$945	$715	$455

Level 4 SL16 - Stained bird's-eye maple forearm with ivory checks set in nickel silver rings at bottom, four ebony points with four veneers and an ivory notched diamond-shaped inlay in each point, ebony butt sleeve with four ebony-bordered ivory diamond-shaped inlays set in stained bird's-eye maple windows alternating with four ivory notched diamond-shaped inlays between ivory checks set in nickel silver rings at top and bottom.

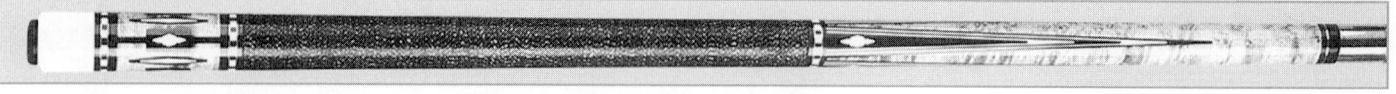

MSR	$1,134	$985	$750	$475

Level 4 SL17 - Stained bird's-eye maple forearm with ivory dashes set in nickel silver rings at bottom, six ebony points with two colored veneers and an ivory spear-shaped inlay in each point, ebony butt sleeve with six colored veneer-bordered ivory windows between ivory dashes set in nickel silver rings above and below.

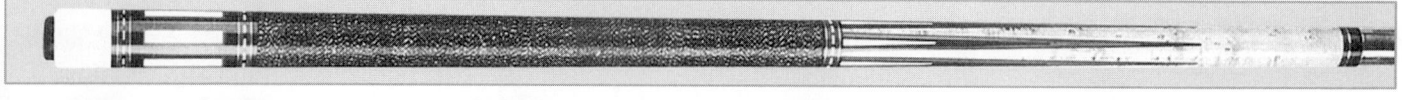

MSR	$1,200	$1,050	$800	$500

SCHON CUES, cont. 711

GRADING	98%	90%	70%

Level 4 SL18 - Stained bird's-eye maple forearm with hardwood squares set in nickel silver rings at bottom, four ebony points with two colored veneers and an ivory diamond-shaped inlay in each, stained bird's-eye maple butt sleeve with four ebony reverse point-shaped inlays with an ivory diamond-shaped inlay in each below hardwood squares set in nickel silver rings at top.

MSR	$1,200	$1,050	$800	$500

Level 5 SL19 - Stained bird's-eye maple forearm with ivory dashes set in nickel silver rings at bottom, four ebony points with two veneers and a large three-piece intricate ivory inlay in each point, stained bird's-eye maple butt sleeve with four ivory ovals set in intricate ebony windows within ivory borders between ivory dashes set in nickel silver rings in ebony at top and bottom.

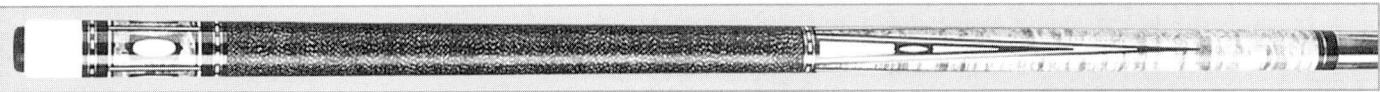

MSR	$1,312	$1,125	$845	$535

Level 5 SL20 - Ebony forearm with ivory dashes set in nickel silver rings at bottom, four floating hardwood points with single veneers and an ivory notched diamond-shaped inlay in each point alternating with four triangular hardwood inlays, ebony butt sleeve with four ivory diamond-shaped inlays set in intricate bordered hardwood windows alternating with intricate bordered triangular barbells between ivory dashes set in nickel silver rings at top and bottom.

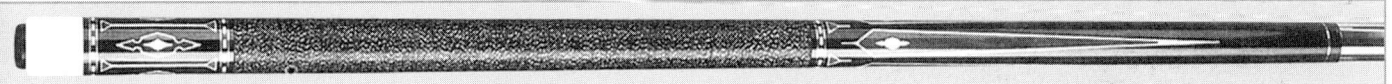

MSR	$1,778	$1,400	$1,045	$675

Level 5 SL21 - Stained bird's-eye maple forearm with hardwood squares set in nickel silver rings at bottom, four ebony points with two veneers and a large three-piece intricate ivory inlay in each point alternating with four ebony-bordered ivory diamond-shaped inlays, ebony butt sleeve with four ebony-bordered ivory diamond-shaped inlays set in hardwood windows alternating with smaller ivory diamond-shaped inlays within opposing ivory triangles between hardwood squares set in nickel silver rings at top and bottom.

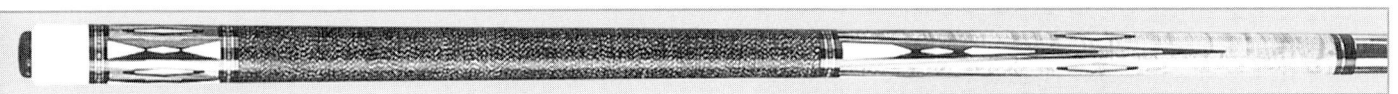

MSR	$1,800	$1,450	$1,100	$700

Level 5 SL22 - Stained bird's-eye maple forearm with nickel silver ring at bottom, four long ebony points with an intricate ivory inlay in each point alternating with four short ivory points with an intricate ebony inlay at the tip of each, ebony butt sleeve with four intricate ebony inlays set in ivory windows alternating with four intricate ivory inlays between nickel silver rings at top and bottom.

MSR	$2,200	$1,850	$1,395	$875

Level 5 SL23 - Stained bird's-eye maple forearm with wood ring set in nickel silver rings at bottom, four ivory points with hardwood borders alternating with four hardwood notched diamond-shaped inlays set in ivory ovals, hardwood butt sleeve with eight ivory notched diamond-shaped inlays alternating with eight ivory scalloped windows within hardwood rings set in nickel silver rings at top and bottom.

MSR	$2,445	$2,100	$1,600	$1,000

Level SL24 - Ebony forearm with ivory dashes set in nickel silver rings at bottom, four floating ivory points with single veneers and a hardwood notched diamond-shaped inlay in each point alternating with four triangular hardwood inlays, ebony butt sleeve with four hardwood diamond-shaped inlays set in intricate bordered ivory windows alternating with intricate ivory-bordered triangular barbells between ivory dashes set in nickel silver rings at top and bottom.

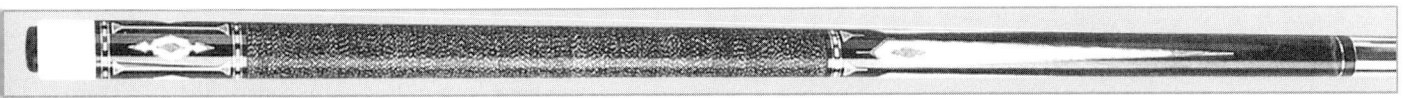

MSR	$2,935	$2,500	$1,900	$1,200

712 SCHON CUES, cont.

GRADING	98%	90%	70%

SECONDARY MARKET MINIMUM VALUES

The following are minimum prices for other Schon cues encountered on the secondary market. These prices are representative of cues utilizing basic materials and designs that may not be currently available. Schon also offers one-of-a-kind cues that can command many times these prices due to the use of exotic materials and artistry.

Special construction note: There are many materials and construction techniques that can add value to Schon cues.

For other Schon cues:
- Add 50%+ for early schon cues with short spliced blanks.
- Add $125 for each original straight playable shaft beyond one.
- Deduct $160 for missing original straight playable shaft.
- Add $50 for each ivory ferrule.
- Deduct 20% for obvious or improper refinish.

Level 2 - 0 points, 0-25 inlays.
Level 2 cues start at	$450	$340	$220

Level 3 - 2-6 points, 0-8 inlays.
Level 3 cues start at	$550	$420	$265

Level 4 - 4-10 points, 9-25 inlays.
Level 4 cues start at	$650	$500	$315

Level 5 - 0-12 points, 26-50 inlays.
Level 5 cues start at	$1,000	$750	$475

Level 6 - 0-12 points, 51-75 inlays.
Level 6 cues start at	$1,400	$1,050	$650

SCHRAGER CUES

Maker of pool cues from 1964 to present, starting in North Hollywood, California.

Bert Schrager grew up in Chicago, in a family that enjoyed billiards. Bert became more interested in the game while he was in the Navy in World War II. A mediocre three-cushion billiards player, Bert did manage to play Willie Hoppe at an exhibition in 1945. After the war, Bert eventually had a custom woodworking business in Chicago. Through his interest in billiards, he came to know Herman Rambow.

In 1962, Bert moved from Chicago to Los Angeles, and was soon working at "The Pool Table Store." In 1962, a customer brought in six cues that needed repair. With his background in custom woodworking, Bert agreed to fix the cues, one of which was split in two. He repaired this cue with glue and two hose clamps and re-tipped the others. After that experience, he knew he wanted to work on cues for a living.

He soon met Harvey Martin, who became Bert's friend and inspiration. Harvey helped him build his first tipping lathe, and he was soon replacing tips for 25 cents each. By 1964, Bert made his first cue. With a bird's-eye maple forearm and butt sleeve, it was very similar to Harvey Martin's most popular cue. Bert continued to make this style of cue for years. When Bert decided to start making cues with spliced forearms, he spent four years perfecting his four-point, four-veneer blanks before he used one in a cue. Soon Bert was making six-point cues, a design for which he is credited with originating. Bert had not learned how to do inlay work, as Harvey believed it weakened the integrity of a cue. The inlays on early Schrager cues were done by a man named Howard Vermillion. But soon Bert was doing his own inlays.

Once Lou Butera started playing on the tour with a custom Schrager cue in the 1970s, Bert's work became popular with pros around the world. Working in North Hollywood, Bert has also made cues for many top celebrities. One of the first to sell cues in Japan, he is recognized as a living legend there.

Pat and Bert Schrager

1986 to Present Day

Although his early cues are unmarked, cues made since 1986 will have "By Schrager" written in an ivory oval for identification. Four-, five-, six-, eight-, and nine-point cues are available, and Bert likes to make longer points than most other cuemakers. Schrager cues are

GRADING	98%	90%	70%

famous for featuring lots of ivory, and the inlays are deeper than most. Bert's wife, Pat, does all of the inlay work by hand on a manual pantograph. They have been married since 1972, and she has always been very supportive of the business.

Bert has twice come very close to buying a CNC machine, but could not bring himself to do it. His cues are designed with playability as the most important aspect, and he prefers the hit of a 3/8-10 flat-faced micarta or ivory joint. He does not like to use stainless steel on this type of joint as he says it makes too much noise. Stainless steel is available on his piloted 5/16-14 joint, which he feels provides more of a stiff East Coast-style hit. Wood joints are available for billiards players. In 1998, he changed from micarta ferrules to Ivorine-3 ferrules because he didn't like the way that micarta ferrules yellowed with age. Bert has carried on with the inspiration of Harvey Martin, and has inspired many of the new generation of cuemakers. He loves to see his cues in the hands of players. His cues are extremely popular in Japan and demand for his work there continues to rise every year. However, Bert has slowed down his cuemaking in recent years.

Schrager cues are guaranteed indefinitely against construction defects that are not the result of warpage or abuse. If you have a Schrager or Martin cue that needs further identification or repair, or would like to talk to Bert about the design of a new custom cue, contact Bert Schrager, listed in the trademark index.

SPECIFICATIONS

Butt material: hardwoods
Shaft material: rock maple
Standard length: 58 in.
Lengths available: any
Standard finish: secret
Joint screw: 3/8-10
Standard joint: Ivorine-3
Joint type: flat faced
Balance point: 1 in. above wrap
Point construction: short splice
Standard wrap: Irish linen
Standard butt cap: Delrin
Standard number of shafts: two
Standard taper: custom
Standard ferrules: Ivorine
Standard tip: Le Pro
Tip widths available: any
Annual production: fewer than 50 cues

CURRENT SCHRAGER CUES

The delivery time for a Schrager cue is entirely dependent on the design and construction of the cue.

SECONDARY MARKET MINIMUM VALUES

The following are minimum prices for Schrager cues encountered on the secondary market. These prices are representative of cues utilizing basic materials and designs that may not be currently available. Bert also offers one-of-a-kind cues that can command many times these prices due to the use of exotic materials and artistry.

Special construction note: There are many materials and construction techniques that can add value to Schrager cues. The following are the most important examples:

Add $750+ for ivory points.
Add $1,000+ for ivory butt sleeve.

For all used Schrager cues:

Add $100+ for each additional original straight playable shaft beyond two.
Deduct $125 for each missing original straight playable shaft under two.
Add $150+ for ivory joint.
Add $75+ for leather wrap.
Deduct 30% for obvious or improper refinish.

	98%	90%	70%
Level 2 - 0 points, 0-25 inlays.			
Level 2 cues start at	$700	$540	$365
Level 3 - 2-6 points, 0-8 inlays.			
Level 3 cues start at	$1,100	$850	$585
Level 4 - 4-10 points, 9-25 inlays.			
Level 4 cues start at	$1,400	$1,095	$750
Level 5 - 0-12 points, 26-50 inlays.			
Level 5 cues start at	$2,000	$1,585	$1,100
Level 6 - 0-12 points, 51-75 inlays.			
Level 6 cues start at	$3,000	$2,345	$1,600
Level 7 - 0-12 points, 76-125 inlays.			
Level 7 cues start at	$4,500	$3,550	$2,400

SCHULER CUE

Maker of pool cues from 1975 to present, currently in Palatine, Illinois.

Ray Schuler grew up in Chicago, learning to play pool at the age of fourteen. His first real cue was made by Herman Rambow, who became a good friend of Ray's for many years. Ray continued to play while he attended John Carroll University in Cleveland, and then the University Of Detroit, where he received a degree in engineering.

In 1975, after spending 25 years as an engineer, Ray was approached by a friend to make him a cue. Ray had been doing repairs for his friends for some years, but this would be his first cue. Shortly after this first cue, he began to make cues from his home. Ray's primary concern was the playability of his cue, and he was constantly searching for ways to enhance the performance of the product. Eight different shaft tapers are available to suit an individual's style of play, and Ray hand-signed each cue as a display of his personal pride and as a seal of quality.

The most noteworthy feature of the Schuler cue is its joint. Ray was able to draw on his engineering experience to produce a unique joining mechanism for his cue, which provides his product with an interchangeable joint system, the first ever in pool cues. The Schuler joint adds as little weight at the joint as possible, for a metal connection. The joint utilizes a 5/16-14 hollow stud with an aircraft aluminum, deep reverse pilot. Half of the connection is recessed; thus, the stud protrudes just slightly from the end of the cue.

In 1988 Ray hired Ivan Lee to learn the cuemaking art, and Ivan became the general manager of the company, as well as a highly skilled cuemaker. Ivan upgraded the joinery of the cue to enhance its playability and longevity, and directed the inlay work to make the cue more visually appealing. He kept an open ear to the player, and provided changes and modifications to the cues as needed.

Ray and Ivan also worked with Jerry Powers. Jerry is a BCA certified Master-level instructor, who designed and sold a specially made Schuler cue under the name Schuler/Jerico. His constant contact with BCA instructors gives Jerry a window into what the serious players want in a cue.

Terry Trim purchased the company in 1999, and Ray continued to run the company. Ray Schuler died in November of 2002. Terry took over the company and continues making cues in the tradition of Ray Schuler.

Terry Trim now heads a five-man shop that includes his son Bryan Trim. The precise tolerances and uniformity from cue to cue have remained consistent for over 30 years. The Schuler cue is made completely in-house, so any type of custom work is available.

Ray Schuler cues are easily identifiable by the "Ray Schuler" signature that appears on every cue. Until he died in 2002, Ray personally signed every Schuler cue "By Ray Schuler." Every Schuler cue since then is hand-signed "Ray Schuler S L C." S L C stands for Schuler Legacy Cue.

The Schuler cue is popular around the world, not only with pool players, but snooker and billiard players as well. The Schuler cue is guaranteed for two years against defects in material and workmanship. If you have a Schuler cue that needs repair, identification, renewal, etc., or you would like to talk to Terry Trim about a new cue, contact Schuler Cue, listed in the Trademark Index.

1980 to 2002

SPECIFICATIONS

Butt material: hardwoods
Shaft material: rock maple
Standard length: 58 in.
Lengths available: any
Standard finish: high tech
Joint screw: 5/16-14
Standard joint: any available
Joint type: piloted and flat faced
Balance point: 18 in. from butt
Point construction: pantographed
Standard wrap: Irish linen
Standard butt cap: Delrin
Standard number of shafts: one
Standard taper: ten available
Standard ferrules: Aegis 2
Standard tip: Triangle
Tip widths available: any
Annual production: fewer than 800 cues

OPTIONS (FOR NEW CUES ONLY)

Leather wrap: $125
Ivory joint: $175
Pair of Delrin joint protectors: $15
Ivory ferrules: $50 each
Extra shaft: $125+

| GRADING | 98% | 90% | 70% |

REPAIRS
Repairs done on all fine cues, most prices for Schuler cues only.
- Refinish (with no wrap): $100
- Refinish (with Irish linen wrap): $125
- Rewrap (linen): $60
- Replace butt cap: $35
- Replace wood butt cap: $50
- Replace ivory joint: $175
- Replace shaft: $120+
- Replace Aegis 2 ferrule: $35 + tip
- Replace ivory ferrule: $80 + tip
- Replace Triangle tip: $15

CURRENT SCHULER CUES
Schuler currently manufactures several models of cues that start at $350 and go to $1,200. One-of-a-kind Schuler cues start at $1,000. Most Schuler cues are available for immediate delivery. The current delivery time for a custom Schuler cue is approximately four to six months or longer depending on the intricacy of the cue.

DISCONTINUED EXAMPLES

Level 2 SC-130 - Stained rock maple forewrap, stained rock maple afterwrap.

| MSR (1996) $255 | $400 | $310 | $210 |

Level 2 SC-180 - Stained bird's-eye maple forewrap, stained bird's-eye maple afterwrap.

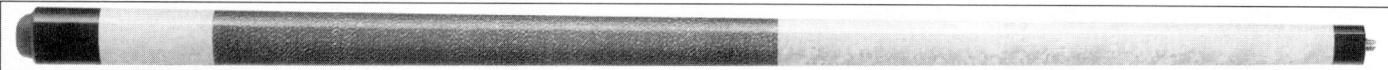

| MSR (1996) $375 | $500 | $390 | $265 |

Level 3 SC-240 - Bird's-eye maple forewrap, four thick bocote-bordered ebony points with a bocote diamond-shaped inlay in each and an ebony spear-shaped inlay at the end of each, ebony afterwrap with four stylized bocote windows.

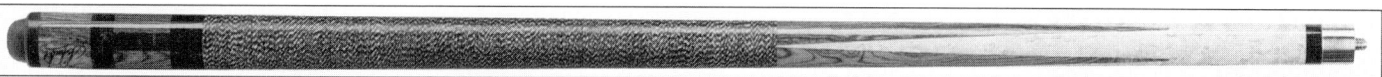

| MSR (1996) $625 | $800 | $615 | $415 |

Level 3 SC-300 - Bird's-eye maple forewrap with maple and cocobolo checks within silver rings above wrap, four cocobolo points with an ebony spear-shaped inlay at the end of each, ebony afterwrap with six cocobolo flame-shaped inlays between maple and cocobolo checks within silver rings above and below.

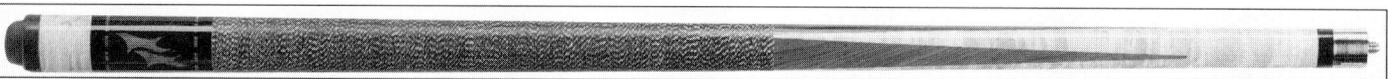

| MSR (1996) $825 | $1,050 | $815 | $545 |

The following cues are representations of the work of Schuler cues in 1999. Maple stains were available in five different colors.

Level 2 SC-150 - Purpleheart forewrap, purpleheart afterwrap.

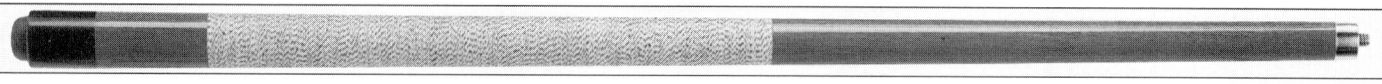

| MSR (1999) $325 | $425 | $325 | $215 |

Level 3 SC-200 - Cocobolo joint, bird's-eye maple forewrap, four cocobolo points with a spear-shaped inlay on the end of each, cocobolo afterwrap.

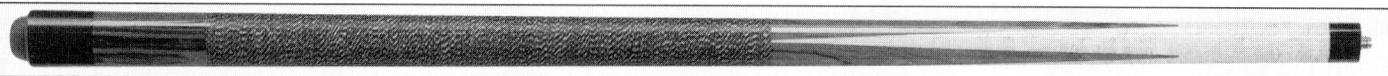

| MSR (1999) $545 | $650 | $505 | $340 |

SCHULER CUE, cont.

GRADING	98%	90%	70%

Level 2 SC-220 - Cocobolo joint, bird's-eye maple forewrap with a thin gold-colored ring above an ebony ring above wrap, cocobolo afterwrap with a thin gold-colored ring below an ebony ring at top.

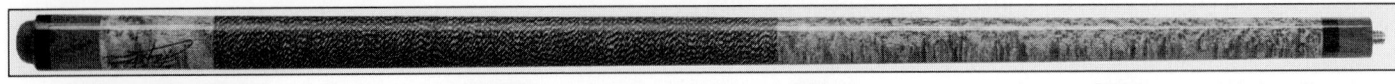

MSR (1999) $475	$600	$465	$315

Level 3 SC-225 - Cocobolo joint, bird's-eye maple forewrap with a thin brass ring above an ebony ring above wrap, two floating ebony points alternating above two floating cocobolo points, cocobolo afterwrap with a thin brass ring below an ebony ring at top.

MSR (1999) $595	$750	$580	$395

Level 3 SC-230 - Stained bird's-eye maple forewrap with a thin silver ring above an ebony ring above wrap, four ebony points with a spear-shaped inlay at the end of each, ebony afterwrap with a thin silver ring below an ebony ring at top.

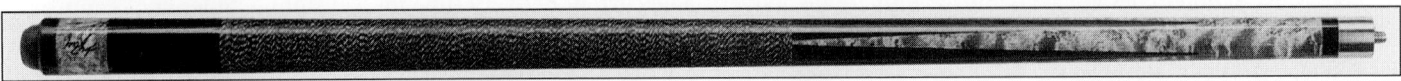

MSR (1999) $575	$735	$370	$385

Level 3 SC-250 - Cocobolo joint, bird's-eye maple forewrap with a thin silver ring above a cocobolo ring above wrap, four ebony-bordered cocobolo points with ebony spear-shaped inlays at the ends of each, ebony afterwrap with four cocobolo oval-shaped inlays.

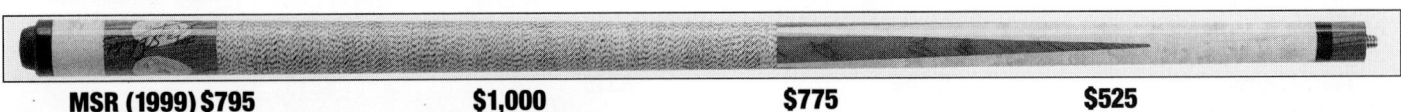

MSR (1999) $795	$1,000	$775	$525

SECONDARY MARKET MINIMUM VALUES

The following are minimum prices for other Schuler cues encountered on the secondary market. These prices are representative of cues utilizing basic materials and designs that are not currently available. Schuler Cues also offers one-of-a-kind cues that can command many times these prices due to the use of exotic materials and artistry. Early models and limited editions are becoming collectible, and can also command many times these prices. Current and discontinued Schuler cues will be further covered in future editions.

Special construction note: There are many materials and construction techniques that can add value to Schuler cues. The following are the most important examples:

- Add $500+ for ivory points.
- Add $500+ for 14k gold joint.
- Add $225+ for each spliced shaft.
- Add 40% for early cues personally signed "By Ray Schuler".

For all used Schuler cues, except where otherwise noted:

- Add $100+ for each additional original straight playable shaft (standard with one).
- Deduct $125+ for missing original straight playable shaft.
- Add $120+ for ivory joint.
- Add $95+ for leather wrap.
- Add $45+ for each ivory ferrule.
- Deduct 25% for obvious or improper refinish.

Level 1 - 4 points, hustler.

Level 1 cues start at	$300	$235	$160

Level 2 - 0 points, 0-25 inlays.

Level 2 cues start at	$315	$245	$165

Level 3 - 2-6 points, 0-8 inlays.

Level 3 cues start at	$450	$350	$235

Level 4 - 4-10 points, 9-25 inlays.

Level 4 cues start at	$600	$465	$320

Level 5 - 0-12 points, 26-50 inlays.

Level 5 cues start at	$1,050	$815	$550

Level 6 - 0-12 points, 51-75 inlays.

Level 6 cues start at	$1,450	$1,145	$750

Level 7 - 0-12 points, 76-125 inlays.

Level 7 cues start at	$2,150	$1,650	$1,100

GRADING	98%	90%	70%

ANTHONY SCIANELLA

Maker of Black Boar Cues. For information, refer to the Black Boar listing.

SCORPION CUES

Line of cues manufactured in China from 1990 to present and distributed by CueStix International in Lafayette, Colorado.

Scorpion Cues are manufactured in China under specifications determined by CueStix International, Inc. They are then imported and inventoried in Colorado, to be exclusively distributed to authorized retailers by CueStix.

At the initial construction stage Johnny Archer was consulted to provide feedback on playability issues; style of joint, balance point, tip, etc. These results were used to modify Scorpion cues and improve performance for both himself and the eventual consumer. Each subsequent year Johnny is consulted on the designs of new models, at least one of which he approves personally.

Scorpion cues are easily identified by the name "Scorpion" written on the butt cap and the Scorpion logo located on the forearm under the joint. If you need a new cue or have a cue that needs repair, contact Cuestix International, listed in the Trademark Index.

SPECIFICATIONS

- Butt material: fiberglass matrix over maple
- Shaft material: Canadian hard rock maple with fiberglass matrix coating
- Standard length: 58 in.
- Lengths available: 58 in. only
- Standard finish: polyurethane
- Balance point: 10 in. from joint
- Standard wrap: Irish linen or genuine leather
- Point construction: overlay
- Standard joint: Implex
- Joint type: stainless steel flat faced
- Joint screw thread: 3/8-14
- Joint protectors: standard
- Standard number of shafts: one
- Standard taper: 14 in. pro
- Standard ferrules: fiber
- Standard tip: Le Pro
- Standard tip width: 13 mm
- Tip widths available: 13 or 12 mm

CURRENT SCORPION CUES

CueStix currently offers forty-five models of Scorpion cues priced from $89 to $229

SECONDARY MARKET MINIMUM VALUES

The following are minimum values for Scorpion cues encountered on the secondary market. These prices are representative of cues utilizing basic materials and designs that are not necessarily available at present.

For all used Scorpion cues, except where otherwise noted:
- Deduct 50% for missing original straight playable shaft.
- Deduct 20% for obvious or improper refinish.

Level 1 - Hustler.

	98%	90%	70%
Level 1 cues start at	$70	$50	$30

Level 2 - 0 points, 0-25 inlays.

	98%	90%	70%
Level 2 cues start at	$80	$60	$35

TIM SCRUGGS CUSTOM CUES, INC.

Maker of pool cues from 1978 to present in Baltimore, Maryland.

Tim Scruggs became a master machinist at a young age while working at Davis and Hemphill for three years in the early 1960s. His true love was pool, and he resigned from the machinist job to run one of the pool halls in Baltimore. Dan Janes was running another pool hall in town at that time, and the two were in constant communication about the road players coming through town. One of these players was Bill Stroud, and in a few years, Dan and Bill were making Joss cues in Baltimore.

As a pool player and friend of Bill and Dan, Tim was one of the first to buy a Joss cue. When he visited the Joss shop, he ended up showing them how to sharpen drill bits. It was immediately apparent to Bill and Dan that Tim knew his way around a machine shop, so they offered him a full-time job with Joss. Tim worked for them for three months in 1970, then returned to the pool hall where he had been working.

For the next couple of years, Tim began to grow tired of running the pool hall, realizing that cuemaking could offer him a brighter long-term future. When Bill Stroud left Joss in 1972, Dan called Tim to see if he would come back. Tim accepted the offer, and told himself that this was what he wanted to do for the rest of his life. This time at Joss, Tim worked much harder, learning every aspect of cuemaking. For the next six years, Dan and Tim made Joss cues together.

In 1978, Tim decided to start making cues of his own. He went to visit with another young cuemaker, and friend, for many years. After this visit, Tim returned to Baltimore to set up shop. Bob Fry, a friend of Tim's since the sixth grade, offered to help Tim to start making cues. That same year, Tim Scruggs Custom Cues was founded in an old meat storage building on the outer edge of Baltimore.

Early Tim Scruggs cues were similar to the cues he was making at Joss, but they were unmarked. Soon his cues developed their own unique style, and began a series of ongoing improvements. By the early 1980s, an intertwined "TS" was being stamped on the Delrin butt caps. All of Tim's cues had ivory ferrules until 1985, when he started experimenting with other materials, eventually settling on melamine, with ivory being an option until 1997, when it became standard again. Linen-based ferrules are available for those who prefer them. In 1988, Tim stopped stamping his logo on cues, and started engraving it with a pantograph. This resulted in a much clearer, more uniform logo. Some of these cues will also have a date below the logo. In 1990, Tim switched from using a lacquer finish to a much better looking polyurethane. Delrin was used for standard butt caps until 1995, when it was replaced with Ivorine 3. In 1996, Tim started adding the last two digits of the year of completion around his identification marks.

1996 to Present Day

Tim Scruggs Custom Cues makes a few cues a month, in the modern two-man shop he moved into in 1996. He moved from the original location that was founded in 1978. Tim makes everything except the tips, screws, and bumpers in house, with the help of Mike Cochran, who has worked for Tim for over twenty years. Mike is starting to make his own cues, which he signs, and may take over the business when Tim retires.

1996 to Present Day

Tim tries to balance a cue before it is assembled so that weight does not have to be added at completion. He does a lot of ivory inlay work, and any kind of joint is available. The steel joint with radial pin Tim uses has become very popular because of its increased contact and more forward balance. Lately Tim has been specializing in building one-of-a-kind cues of his own design costing over $2,500 and offering them for sale on his website. He also likes to make custom cues for players, and what's even better is that they like using them.

If you have a Tim Scruggs cue that needs further identification or repair, or would like to talk to Tim about ordering a new cue, contact Tim Scruggs Custom Cues, listed in the Trademark Index.

SPECIFICATIONS

Butt material: hardwoods
Shaft material: rock maple
Standard length: 58 in.
Standard finish: automotive clear coat
Standard joint screw: radial pin
Standard joint: stainless steel
Joint type: flat faced
Balance point: varies
Point construction: short splice
Standard wrap: Irish linen
Standard butt cap: Ivorine-3
Standard number of shafts: two
Standard taper: 10 in. straight
Standard ferrules: ivory
Standard tip: Triangle
Annual production: fewer than 120 cues

OPTIONS

Options are priced individually on a per-cue basis.

REPAIRS

Repairs done on Tim Scruggs cues only. Price on request.

CURRENT SCRUGGS CUES

One-of-a-kind custom Scruggs cues start at $2,500. The current delivery time for a custom Tim Scruggs cue is approximately three years.

PAST EXAMPLES

The following cues are representations of the late nineties work of Tim Scruggs Custom Cues. These cues can be encountered as shown or modified to suit the desires of the customer.

TIM SCRUGGS CUSTOM CUES, INC., cont.

GRADING	98%	90%	70%

The following Tim Scruggs came with two shafts with ivory ferrules, and a set of black Delrin joint protectors. Bird's-eye maple could be stained six different colors at no extra charge.

Level 2 #1 - Bird's-eye maple forearm, bird's-eye maple butt sleeve (available with Hoppe-style or conventional butt).

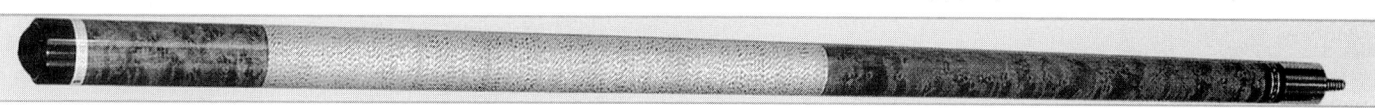

MSR (1999) $600	$900	$715	$500

Level 3 #2 - Bird's-eye maple forearm, four ebony points, ebony butt sleeve (points and butt sleeve available in several different exotic woods at no extra charge, available with Hoppe style or conventional butt).

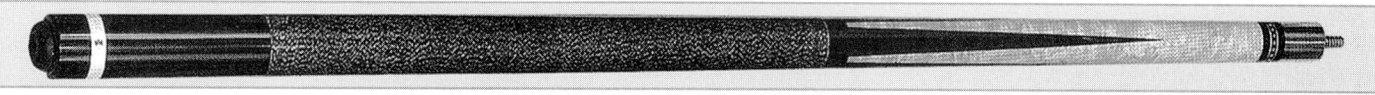

MSR (1999) $750	$1,100	$875	$600

Level 3 #3 - Bird's-eye maple forearm, four kingwood points with four colored veneers, kingwood butt sleeve (points and butt sleeve available in several different exotic woods at no extra charge, available with Hoppe-style or conventional butt).

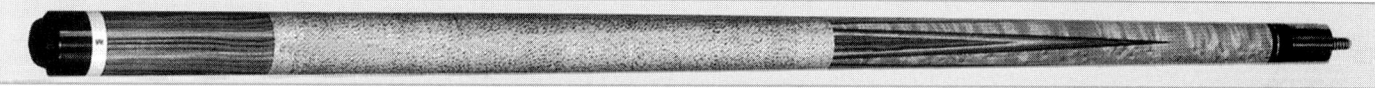

MSR (1999) $950	$1,400	$1,100	$750

Level 3 #4 - Bird's-eye maple forearm, four ebony points, ebony butt sleeve with four maple rectangles alternating with four abalone notched diamond-shaped inlays between ebony and maple rings above and below.

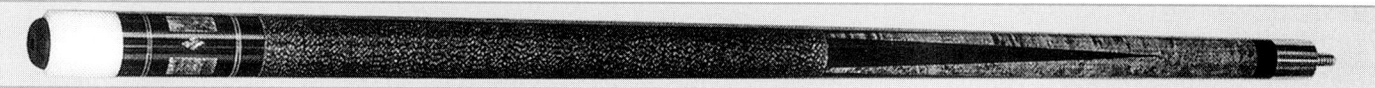

MSR (1999) $975	$1,450	$1,125	$775

Level 3 #5 - Bird's-eye maple forearm with four abalone notched diamond-shaped inlays above wrap between the points, four ebony points, ebony butt sleeve with four abalone notched diamond-shaped inlays at base that extend into butt cap.

MSR (1999) $1,075	$1,600	$1,250	$850

Level 3 #6 - Bird's-eye maple forearm, four ebony points with four colored veneers, solid ebony butt sleeve and cap with eight ivory notched diamond-shaped inlays below ebony and ivory checks within nickel silver rings.

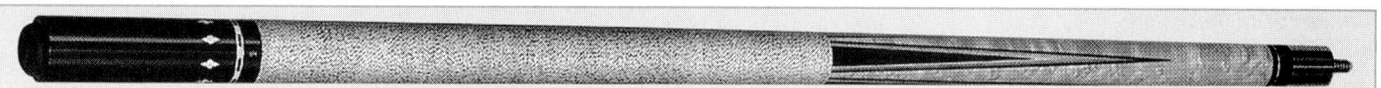

MSR (1999) $1,175	$1,750	$1,350	$900

Level 3 #7 - Bird's-eye maple forearm with maple dashes set in ebony within brass rings above wrap, four ebony points with a stylized ivory arrowhead in each, ebony butt sleeve with four pairs of opposing stylized ivory arrowheads between maple dashes set in ebony within brass rings above and below.

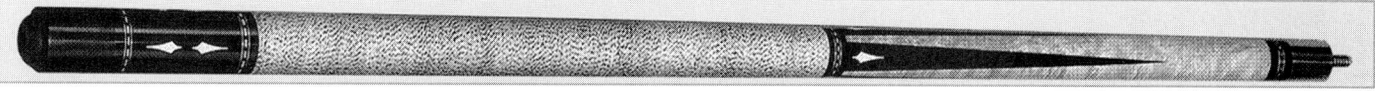

MSR (1999) $1,255	$1,850	$1,325	$950

Level 4 #8 - Bird's-eye maple forearm, four ebony points with four colored veneers and an ivory six-point star in each point, bird's-eye maple butt sleeve with four ivory six-point stars each set in ebony ovals between inward-pointing ebony rings above and below.

MSR (1999) $1,345	$2,000	$1,625	$1,100

TIM SCRUGGS CUSTOM CUES, INC., cont.

GRADING	98%	90%	70%

Level 4 #9 - Bird's-eye maple forearm, four ebony points with four colored veneers and an ivory stylized arrowhead in each, ebony butt sleeve with four ivory diamond-shaped inlays set in tulipwood ovals alternating with four pairs of inward-pointing tulipwood stylized arrowheads.

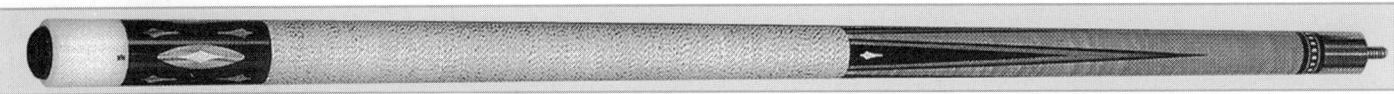

MSR (1999) $1,350	$2,000	$1,625	$1,100

Level 5 #10 - Bird's-eye maple forearm, four zircote points with four colored veneers and an ivory notched diamond-shaped inlay between an ivory dot above and two ivory dots below in each point, zircote butt sleeve with four ivory-bordered zircote rectangles with an ivory notched diamond-shaped inlay between two ivory dots above and below in each.

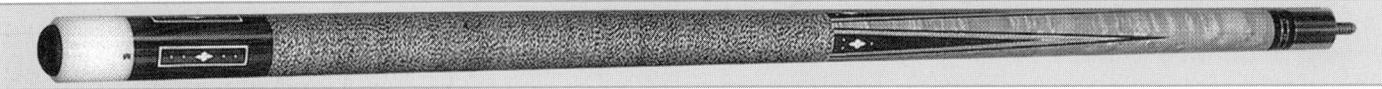

MSR (1999) $1,600	$2,350	$1,850	$1,250

Level 4 #11 - Bird's-eye maple forearm with maple dashes set in ebony within nickel silver rings above wrap, four cocobolo points with four colored veneers and an ivory diamond-shaped inlay in each, cocobolo butt sleeve with four ivory diamond-shaped inlays alternating with four ivory-bordered cocobolo diamond-shaped inlays between maple dashes set in ebony within nickel silver rings above and below, cocobolo butt cap.

MSR (1999) $1,725	$2,475	$1,925	$1,300

Level 4 #12 - Bird's-eye maple forearm with maple dashes set in ebony within brass rings above wrap, four cocobolo points with a stylized ivory spear in each, cocobolo butt sleeve with eight pairs of opposing stylized ivory spears between maple dashes set in ebony within brass rings at top and below, cocobolo butt cap.

MSR (1999) $1,800	$2,550	$2,000	$1,350

Level 4 #13 - Bird's-eye maple forearm with ivory dashes set in ebony within nickel silver rings above wrap, four ebony points with four colored veneers and a stylized ivory spear in each, ebony butt sleeve with eight scrimshawed ivory diamond-shaped inlays between ivory dashes set in ebony within nickel silver rings at top and bottom.

MSR (1999) $2,000	$2,800	$2,200	$1,550

Level 4 #14 - Bird's-eye maple forearm, four ebony points with four colored veneers and a stylized ivory spear in each, ebony butt sleeve with four pairs of opposing stylized ivory arrowheads within ivory-bordered ebony rectangles alternating with four 14-karat gold diamond-shaped inlays.

MSR (1999) $2,150	$3,000	$2,400	$1,600

Level 4 #15 - Bird's-eye maple forearm with an ebony ring above wrap, four ebony points with four colored veneers that border ebony ring and a stylized ivory spear in each point that extends in to ebony ring, Ivorine 3 butt sleeve with eight pairs of opposing stylized ivory arrowheads within ebony rectangles with ivory dashes set in ebony within nickel silver rings above.

MSR (1999) $2,175	$3,050	$2,450	$1,635

GRADING	98%	90%	70%

Level 4 #16 - Bird's-eye maple forearm with a 14-karat gold ring set in ebony within ivory rings above wrap, four ebony points with four colored veneers and a stylized ivory spear in each point, ebony butt sleeve with four 14-karat gold notched diamond-shaped inlays alternating with four ivory notched diamond-shaped inlays set in ivory-bordered ebony ovals between 14-karat gold rings set in ebony within ivory rings above and below.

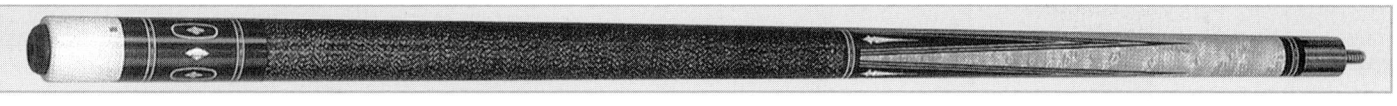

MSR (1999) $2,200	$3,100	$2,475	$1,650

SECONDARY MARKET MINIMUM VALUES

The following are minimum prices for other Tim Scruggs cues encountered on the secondary market. These prices are representative of cues utilizing basic materials and designs that may not be currently available. Tim also offers one-of-a-kind cues that can command many times these prices due to the use of exotic materials and artistry.

Special construction note: There are many materials and construction techniques that can add value to Tim Scruggs cues. The following are the most important examples:

- Add $550+ for ivory points.
- Add 100%+ for precious metals or stones.
- Add 100%+ for ivory handles (usually sectioned, with inlay work).
- Add 20% for early "TS" stamp.

For all used Tim Scruggs cues, unless otherwise noted:

- Add $125+ for each additional original straight playable shaft beyond two.
- Deduct $175 for each missing original straight playable shaft under two.
- Deduct $75+ each for non-ivory ferrules.
- Add $100+ for leather wrap.
- Deduct 25% for obvious or improper refinish.

Level 1 - 4 points, hustler.

Level 1 cues start at	$350	$275	$185

Level 2 - 0 points, 0-25 inlays.

Level 2 cues start at	$800	$625	$425

Level 3 - 2-6 points, 0-8 inlays.

Level 3 cues start at	$1,000	$785	$535

Level 4 - 4-10 points, 9-25 inlays.

Level 4 cues start at	$1,250	$985	$650

Level 5 - 0-12 points, 26-50 inlays.

Level 5 cues start at	$2,000	$1,635	$1,095

Level 6 - 0-12 points, 51-75 inlays.

Level 6 cues start at	$2,800	$2,200	$1,500

DENNIS SEARING CUSTOM CUES

Maker of pool cues 1991 to 1993 in Hollywood, Florida, relocated in 1993 to Wellington, Florida.

Dennis Searing was a semi-professional player who always liked cues. His favorite cues were made by Gus Szamboti, and he always had at least one of Gus's cues on order. He also spent a lot of time on the phone with Gus, talking about cuemaking. After Gus died, Dennis tried playing with other cues but he couldn't find what he was looking for. Finally Dennis decided to try to make cues himseif. He had a background in woodworking and had built custom wood decks, fences, and staircases. Dennis had also worked as an electrician. He built his first cue in his garage in 1991. When he moved to Wellington, Florida Dennis built a shop specifically for making cues.

Dennis Searing

Dennis makes everything in his cues except for the tips, the screws, and the bumpers in his one-man shop. He has made all of the components himself, but for example, Dennis believes it is hard to make a tip that is better than the best tip you can buy. Dennis prefers to concentrate on the wood in his cues. He believes that by selecting the right piece of wood and using the proper building techniques, he can achieve the best hit and playability. He understands the reason for coring cues, but believes traditional methods inspired by George Balabushka and Gus Szamboti are superior. He makes his own short-spliced blanks and refuses to do inlaid points. Dennis will not construct a cue with designs that adversely affect the integrity of the cue. The whole mid section of a Dennis Searing cue is wood with no metal screws. The handle has wood threads that screw directly into the forearm, wood-to-wood. All components are threaded.

Being a pool player himself, Dennis understands that different players have different tastes and prefer cues with different specifications and different types of hits. He has made several extra long custom cues for professional basketball players in Florida. Dennis uses radial

GRADING	98%	90%	70%

pins and also likes stainless steel joints. He has also developed his own stainless steel half joint. He tries to make a cue that resonates like one piece of wood, and Dennis prefers the balance to be slightly forward.

Dennis Searing cues are easily identifiable by the "S" logo that appears on the butt caps. He also signs and dates his cues with "D Searing" if he makes the blanks. Some Searing hustler cues were made from existing full-spliced blanks, and therefore not signed. Dennis no longer makes hustler cues.

Dennis offers a money-back guarantee upon delivery for playability and satisfaction. Searing cues are guaranteed for life against construction defects that are not the result of warpage or abuse. If you have a Dennis Searing cue that needs further identification or repair, or would like to order a new Dennis Searing cue, contact Dennis Searing Custom Cues, listed in the Trademark Index.

SPECIFICATIONS

Butt material: hardwoods
Shaft material: rock maple
Standard length: 58 in.
Lengths available: custom
Standard finish: automotive clear coat
Balance point: custom
Standard butt cap: custom
Standard wrap: Irish linen
Point construction: short spliced
Standard joint: stainless steel
Joint type: piloted
Joint screw thread: 5/16-14
Standard number of shafts: two
Standard taper: progressive custom
Standard ferrules: ivory
Standard tip: Triangle
Annual production: fewer than 35 cues

OPTIONS (FOR NEW CUES ONLY)

Options priced on request.

REPAIRS

Repairs done on Searing cues and those made by deceased cue makers. Priced on request.

CURRENT DENNIS SEARING CUES

Basic Dennis Searing cues with wraps and joint rings start at $1,200. Dennis Searing cues with points start at $1,800.

SECONDARY MARKET MINIMUM VALUES

The following are minimum values for Dennis Searing cues encountered on the secondary market. These prices are representative of cues utilizing basic materials and designs that are not necessarily available at present. Dennis has offered one-of-a-kind cues that can command many times these prices due to the use of exotic materials and artistry.

Special construction note: There are many materials and construction techniques that can add value to Dennis Searing cues.

For all used Dennis Searing cues, except where otherwise noted:

Add $150 for each additional original straight playable shaft beyond two.
Deduct $200 for each missing original straight playable shaft under two.
Deduct $65 each for non ivory ferrules.
Add $150 for leather wrap.
Deduct 25% for obvious or improper refinish.

Level 2 - 0 points, 0-25 inlays.

	98%	90%	70%
Level 2 cues start at	$1,250	$985	$675

Level 3 - 2-6 points, 0-8 inlays.

Level 3 cues start at	$2,000	$1,635	$1,200

Level 4 - 4-10 points, 9-25 inlays.

Level 4 cues start at	$2,500	$2,000	$1,350

Level 5 - 0-12 points, 26-50 inlays.

Level 5 cues start at	$3,500	$2,750	$1,850

Level 6 - 0-12 points, 51-75 inlays.

Level 6 cues start at	$5,000	$3,900	$2,700

SHAMAN CUES

Maker of pool cues from 1995 to 2001 in Las Cruces, New Mexico and from 2001 to present in Winston-Salem, North Carolina.

Bob Smith started playing pool as a kid while growing up in North Carolina. After a career in civil service, working in photography, film and video production, Bob took early retirement in New Mexico. He continued to play pool, eventually becoming a BCA certified instructor, and teaching pocket billiards at New Mexico State University.

In 1992, Bob opened a billiard pro shop specializing in cues. He developed a strong interest in how the cues were made, and decided he should make his own. Bob had woodworking experience as a hobby to help in this endeavor, and after studying cuemaking for a year, he started building Shaman Custom Cues. "Shaman" is another word for the American Indian term "Medicine Man." Bob liked something he had read using this word: "In order to ask the gods for divine intervention, one must seek the aid of a Shaman" (author unknown).

Bob Smith

In 2001, Bob and his wife Judy moved to Winston-Salem, North Carolina. He now makes less than one Shaman cue a week. He loves southwestern art, and some of the inlay work on his cues incorporates Native American designs and materials found there. Bob prefers not to use elephant ivories, with shed antler and prehistoric ivories being his favorite alternatives. Playability is Bob's primary concern, and extra steps are taken toward this goal. Shafts are turned once every two weeks, at least ten times, and feature a custom taper which Bob developed. No taper bar is used to make the shafts, so small changes in the taper can easily be incorporated, upon request. Bob has developed his own hardness grading system for tips to further help the customer achieve a desired hit. The scale runs from less than 10, which is the hardest, to over 30, which is the softest. A flat-faced, radial pin joint is recommended to customers for a great hit, but most common joints are available at no extra charge. Uni-Loc joints and Predator shafts are options on Shaman Cues.

All Shaman cues are easily identifieable by the "Shaman" logo on the butt cap, either engraved or inlaid on a cast piece of silver. Each cue has a two-digit date and serial number under the bumper and under the wrap along with Bob's signature. All Shaman cues come standard with one shaft. Shaman Cues are guaranteed for one year on material and workmanship.

If you have a Shaman cue that needs further identification or repair, or would like to talk to Bob about ordering a new Shaman cue, contact Shaman Cues, listed in the Trademark Index.

SPECIFICATIONS

Butt material: hardwoods
Shaft material: hard maple
Standard length: 58 in.
Lengths available: any up to 60 in.
Standard finish: furniture grade finish
Joint screw: 3/8 radial Uni-Loc
Standard joint: linen phenolic
Joint type: wood-to-wood
Balance point: 18 in. above wrap
Point construction: short splice or inlaid
Standard wrap: Irish linen
Standard butt cap: ivory-colored Delrin
Standard number of shafts: one
Standard taper: custom
Standard ferrules: Aegis
Standard tip: Triangle
Tip widths available: 12 to 14 mm
Annual production: fewer than 30 cues

OPTIONS (FOR NEW CUES ONLY)

Special lengths: snooker $25+
Leather wrap: $30
Uni-Loc joint: $50
Extra shaft: $100
Custom joint protectors: $30+
Layered tip: $20+

REPAIRS

Repairs done on most fine cues.
Refinish with linen wrap: $140
Refinish with leather wrap: $160
Rewrap (leather): $60

GRADING	98%	90%	70%

Rewrap (linen): $45
Clean and press linen wrap: $20
Replace butt cap: $40+
Replace shaft: $100
Replace fiber/linen ferrule: $25+
Replace tip: $15+
Replace layered tip: $25+

CURRENT SHAMAN CUES

Two-piece Shaman bar cues start at $175. Basic Shaman cues with wraps and joint rings start at $300. Shaman cues with points start at $450. One-of-a-kind custom Shaman cues start at $700. The current delivery time for a Shaman cue is approximately two to three months.

SECONDARY MARKET MINIMUM VALUES

The following are minimum prices for Shaman cues encountered on the secondary market. These prices are representative of cues utilizing basic materials and designs that may not be currently available. Bob also offers one-of-a-kind cues that can command many times these prices due to the use of exotic materials and artistry.

Special construction note: There are many materials and construction techniques that can add value to Shaman cues.

For all used Shaman cues, except where otherwise noted:

- Add $85+ for each additional original straight playable shaft beyond one.
- Deduct $100 for missing original straight playable shaft.
- Deduct 20% for obvious or improper refinish.

Level 1 - 4 points, hustler.

Level 1 cues start at	$165	$130	$85

Level 2 - 0 points, 0-25 inlays.

Level 2 cues start at	$285	$220	$145

Level 3 - 2-6 points, 0-8 inlays.

Level 3 cues start at	$400	$315	$215

Level 4 - 4-10 points, 9-25 inlays.

Level 4 cues start at	$625	$485	$325

Level 5 - 0-12 points, 26-50 inlays.

Level 5 cues start at	$1,250	$975	$645

SCOT SHERBINE CUSTOM CUES

Maker of pool cues from 2002 to present in Lancaster County, Pennsylvania.

After graduation from high school, Scot Sherbine went to work for his father in construction for about 10 years before working on cues. Scot's full-time job is cue repair and refinishing. Scot got into cue repairs in 1998 when he found himself tired of construction work on the road. Cue restoration began for Scot with an old Meucci Gambler cue that had its share of war wounds. He decided to try to fix the cue. With his background in woodworking, and hobby in painting cars, he was able to restore the old cue. After showing it to a local cue collector, there was plenty of cue work for Scot to start with. Scot immediately bought his first lathe.

In 2001 Scot started making Sneaky Petes when time allowed, and players who bought them liked the way they hit. Scot's business, Proficient Billiards, began taking off in 2002. It meant less time for cuemaking until friend and co-creator of Proficient, Matt Haines, joined the business full time. In 2003, Proficient launched an all-billiard-related auction site specifically designed for cues. While the office is very high tech, the shop is very low tech, with no computerized equipment. Matt has become an essential part of every aspect of Proficient, and as a result, Scot has more time to devote to cuemaking. Scot specializes in turning full-spliced bar cue blanks and Brunswick Titlist blanks into custom two-piece cues. Sherbine cues are easily identifiable by the Scot Sherbine signature and date on the cues.

If you are interested in talking to Scot Sherbine about a new cue or cue that needs to be repaired, you can contact him at Scot Sherbine Custom Cues, listed in the Trademark Index.

Scot Sherbine

Present Day

SCOT SHERBINE CUSTOM CUES, cont.

GRADING	98%	90%	70%

SPECIFICATIONS
Butt material: hardwoods
Shaft material: rock maple
Standard length: 58 in.
Lengths available: 57 to 61 in.
Standard finish: urethane
Balance point: 17 in. from butt
Standard butt cap: Delrin
Standard wrap: Irish linen
Point construction: full splice
Standard joint: linen based
Joint type: piloted
Joint screw thread: 5/16-14
Standard number of shafts: two
Standard taper: 12 in. straight
Standard ferrules: ivory
Standard tip: Moori
Standard tip width: 13 mm
Tip widths available: any up to 14 mm
Annual production: fewer than 20 cues

OPTIONS (FOR NEW CUES ONLY)
Layered tip: $25
Ivory butt cap: $200
Ivory joint: $150
Leather wrap: $100
Extra shaft: $115

REPAIRS
Repairs done on all fine cues.
Refinish (with Irish linen wrap): $110
Refinish (with leather wrap): $175
Rewrap (Irish linen): $35
Rewrap (leather): $100
Clean and press linen wrap: $15
Replace shaft: $135+
Replace ivory ferrule: $75
Replace butt cap: $40
Replace ivory butt cap: $200
Replace tip: $10+
Replaced layered tip: $17+
Replace fiber/linen ferrule: $20+

CURRENT SCOT SHERBINE CUES
Two-piece Scot Sherbine bar cues start at $285. Two-piece Scot Sherbine bar cues with linen wraps start at $310. Scot Sherbine Titlist conversion cues start at $1,100. The current delivery time for a Scot Sherbine cue is about two to four weeks.

SECONDARY MARKET MINIMUM VALUES
The following are minimum values for other Scot Sherbine cues encountered on the secondary market. These prices are representative of cues utilizing basic materials and designs that are not necessarily available at present.

Special construction note: There are many materials and construction techniques that can add value to Scot Sherbine cues.

For all used Scot Sherbine cues, except where otherwise noted:
Add $95 for each additional original straight playable shaft beyond two.
Deduct $135 for each missing original straight playable shaft under two.
Deduct $30 each for non ivory ferrules.
Add $45 for leather wrap.
Deduct 20% for obvious or improper refinish.

	98%	90%	70%
Level 1 - Hustler.			
Level 1 cues start at	$200	$155	$105
Level 3 - 2-6 points, 0-8 inlays.			
Level 3 cues start at	$250	$195	$130

SHERM CUES

Maker of pool cues from 1980 to present in Cincinnati, Ohio.

1994 to Present Day

Sherm Adamson

Sherm Adamson began making pool cues in 1980. He had been replacing tips and doing minor repairs for some of the players in his area. A pool nut since he was very young, Sherm (short for "Sherman") started making hustler cues in the auto repair shop he was running at the time. He had come to the realization that his game was not strong enough for him to "make his mark" in the billiards world as a player, so he decided to do it as a cuemaker instead. Sherm is proud to have been a member of the American Cuemakers Association for about 10 years. He was also featured in Inside Pool magazine, March 2005.

Sherm had a partner, Richard Neighbors, from 1993 to 1994 (who now makes R.H.N. Custom Cues). Most of the 75 or so cues made during this time are identifiable by an "S" on the butt cap. Cues made from October 1994 (when Sherm started making cues full-time) to 2000 will have a 5/16-12 joint screw. These unique 5/16-12 screws were custom made to his specifications. In 2000 Sherm began using mostly a 3/8-10 pin with no insert. In 2003 Sherm started using the 3/8-8 radial style pin that he uses today. In 2004 he started applying a UV finish to all of his cues. Sherm started engraving the radial joint pin "Sherm" in 2005.

Sherm is constantly getting more creative with his designs. He began using the 4th axis technology to do "wrap around" engraving and inlays. Inlay work on Sherm cues can be done by hand or with the use of CNC. Points can be inlaid, although Sherm prefers to make them short spliced. He likes linen phenolic joints for their playability, which is the most important aspect of Sherm cues. He also likes to weigh and balance his cues without the use of artificial weights when possible. Sherm's wife Jenneth helps out in the family business mostly with encouragement and organizational help, and answers the phone. Sherm's two sons, Scott and Seth, have both been apprenticing in the shop when possible, but they will likely follow their own dreams of the future. Since 1994 almost all Sherm cues are signed "Sherm Adamson" with the month and year on the forearms or butt sleeves.

Although Sherm does not guarantee ivory joints or ivory ferrules, he guarantees all construction defects that are not the result of warpage or abuse. If you have a Sherm cue that needs repair, or would like to talk to Sherm about the design of a one-of-a-kind custom cue, contact Sherm Cues, listed in the Trademark Index.

SPECIFICATIONS

- Butt material: hardwoods
- Shaft material: rock maple
- Standard length: 58 in.
- Lengths available: 40 to 63 in.
- Standard finish: UV catalyzed and automotive clearcoat
- Joint screw: 3/8-8 radial style engraved "Sherm"
- Standard joint: linen phenolic
- Joint type: flat faced
- Balance point: 1 1/4 in. above wrap
- Point construction: short splice or inlaid
- Standard wrap: Irish linen
- Standard butt cap: linen phenolic
- Standard number of shafts: one
- Standard taper: 10 in. pro
- Standard ferrules: linen phenolic
- Standard tip: water buffalo
- Tip widths available: any up to 14 mm
- Annual production: approximately 75 cues

OPTIONS (FOR NEW CUES ONLY)

- Leather wrap: $100
- Ivory joint: $135
- Stainless steel joint: $25
- Joint protectors: por
- 5/16-14 joint: no charge
- Delrin butt cap: $25
- Ivory butt cap: $250
- Extra shaft: $100
- Ivory ferrules: $50 each

SHERM CUES, cont. 727

GRADING	100%	95%	70%

REPAIRS

Repairs done on all cues.
 Refinish (with linen wrap): $100
 Rewrap (linen): $40
 Rewrap (leather): $100
 Replace shaft: $100
 Replace ivory ferrule: $75
 Replace linen phenolic ferrule: $35
 Replace linen phenolic butt cap: $40
 Replace delrin butt cap: $40

CURRENT SHERM CUES

Basic two-piece Sherm hustler cues start at $300. Basic two-piece Sherm cues with wraps and joint rings start at $350. Sherm cues with points start at $500. One-of-a-kind Sherm custom cues start at $1,000. The current delivery time for a new Sherm cue is approximately four to six months.

CURRENT EXAMPLES

The following Sherm cues can be ordered as shown, modified to suit the desires of the customer, or new designs can be created.

Level 5 - Ivory joint, bird's-eye maple forearm with red coral and ebony blocks set in ebony rings above wrap, four laminated ebony and pink ivory points, ebony butt sleeve with intricate red coral/ivory/pink ivory inlay work between red coral and ebony blocks set in ebony rings at top and bottom.

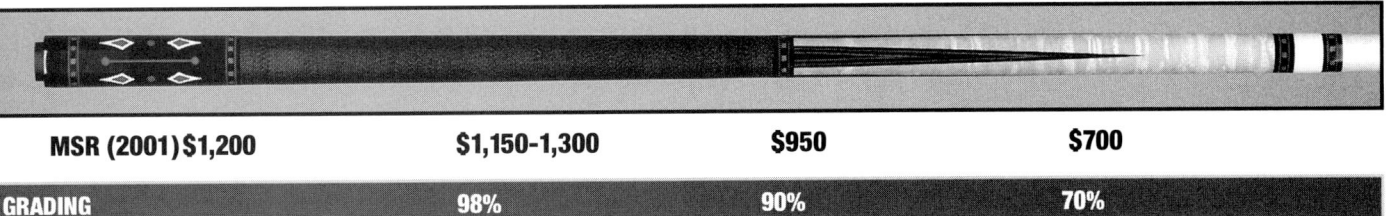

MSR (2001) $1,200	$1,150-1,300	$950	$700

GRADING	98%	90%	70%

PAST EXAMPLES

The following Sherm cues may be encountered as shown, modified to suit the desires of the original customer, or new designs can be encountered.

Level 6 - Cocobolo forearm with cocobolo and ivory checks set in silver rings above wrap, three four ebony points with turquoise and red coral inlay work, cocobolo butt sleeve with intricate turquoise and red coral inlay work between cocobolo and ivory checks set in silver rings at top and bottom.

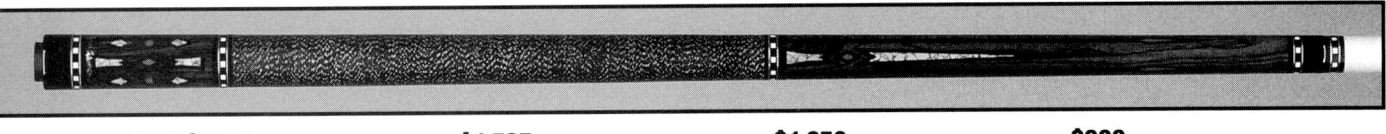

MSR (2001) $1,100	$1,525	$1,250	$900

Level 6 - Ivory joint, ebony forearm with ebony and ivory checks set in silver rings above wrap, three two-piece long ivory floating points with ivory and malachite inlay work in the center alternating with three short malachite two-piece floating points, ebony butt sleeve with intricate ivory and malachite inlay work between ebony and ivory checks set in silver rings at top and bottom.

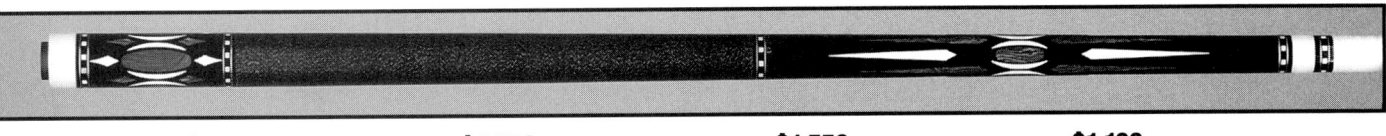

MSR (2001) $1,695	$1,950	$1,550	$1,100

Level 6 - Ivory joint, pink ivory forearm with ebony and turquoise checks set in silver rings above wrap, three two-piece long ivory floating points with ivory and turquoise inlay work in the center alternating with three short turquoise two-piece floating points, pink ivory butt sleeve with intricate ivory and turquoise inlay work between ebony and turquoise checks set in silver rings at top and bottom.

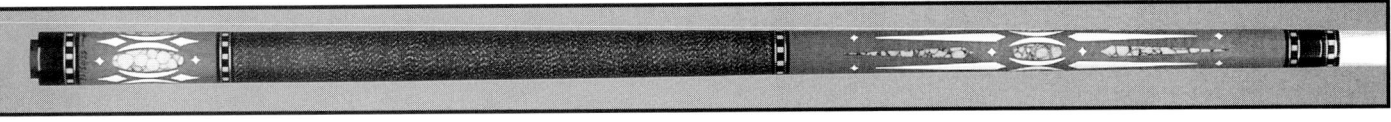

MSR (2001) $2,495	$2,950	$2,350	$1,700

GRADING	98%	90%	70%

SECONDARY MARKET MINIMUM VALUES

The following are minimum prices for other Sherm cues encountered on the secondary market. These prices are representative of cues utilizing basic materials and designs that may not be currently available. Sherm also offers one-of-a-kind cues that can command many times these prices due to the use of exotic materials and artistry.

Special construction note: There are many materials and construction techniques that can add value to Sherm cues.

For all used Sherm cues:
- Add $85+ for each additional original straight playable shaft beyond one.
- Deduct $100 for each missing original straight playable shaft.
- Add $100+ for ivory joint.
- Add $65+ for leather wrap.

Level 1 - 4 points, hustler.

Level 1 cues start at	$275	$215	$145

Level 2 - 0 points, 0-25 inlays.

Level 2 cues start at	$325	$245	$165

Level 3 - 2-6 points, 0-8 inlays.

Level 3 cues start at	$425	$330	$220

Level 4 - 4-10 points, 9-25 inlays.

Level 4 cues start at	$600	$465	$315

Level 5 - 0-12 points, 26-50 inlays.

Level 5 cues start at	$900	$695	$475

Level 6 - 0-12 points, 51-75 inlays.

Level 6 cues start at	$1,400	$1,100	$750

SHOWCASE CUSTOM CUES

Maker of pool cues from 1980 to present in Westminster, Colorado.

Clay Etheridge opened Showcase Billiards in 1980 to retail pool tables and billiard accessories. Clay loved cues, and had made cues while working for a cue manufacturer in the 1970s. He started making cues the year he opened, in a 1,100 square foot shop within his 7,000 square foot building. His custom cues were the perfect complement to the 300+ cues by other makers he kept in stock. Clay marked his cues with a block letter "S" on the butt cap. In the late 1980s Clay hired Ernie Martinez to make Showcase cues. Ernie made Showcase cues for several years before going out on his own. Showcase cues made by Ernie Martinez are identifiable by an "S" within a diamond on the top of the joint screw. Other cuemakers have since worked for Clay making cues. Gale Clark made Showcase cues in the mid-1990s, and marked them with an italic "S" on the butt caps.

Today, Clay owns Showcase and his son Mike Etheridge is the main cuemaker. Mike's cues are identifiable by a small "S" within a larger "C" on the butt caps. Bruce Ryan has also been with the company since 1997, and has been the head cuemaker since 1999. In 2000, Willie Balintucas had been a cuemaker and repairman, but has since moved on. Most Showcase cues have been hustler cues, but one-of-a-kind custom cues have always been available. Low-end Showcase cues with transfer designs, called "onlays," instead of inlays, are also available. The "onlay" artwork was designed and created by Matt Warmoth, who has also since moved on.

Bill Howes, Clay Etheridge (back), Mike Etheridge and Bruce Ryan

Showcase cues are priced from $190 to many thousands of dollars. The majority of the one-of-a-kind cues are custom orders, and they will also create original designs to stock in the store. Showcase cues are designed and executed using the latest CNC technology. "Buster" break cues and "Jumpster" jump cues are available as well. Showcase has also developed their own segmented "Tru-Hit" shaft.

Showcase cues are guaranteed for life against manufacturing defects that are not the result of warpage or abuse. If you have a Showcase cue that needs further identification or repair, or would like to order a new Showcase cue, contact Showcase Custom Cues, listed in the Trademark Index.

SPECIFICATIONS

Butt material: hardwoods
Shaft material: rock maple
Standard length: 58 in.
Lengths available: any
Standard finish: automotive clear coat
Standard butt cap: linen phenolic
Standard wrap: Irish linen
Point construction: CNC

GRADING	100%	95%	70%

Standard joint: linen phenolic
Joint type: flat faced
Joint screw: 3/8-10 stainless
Standard number of shafts: one
Standard taper: pro
Standard ferrules: fiber
Standard tip width: 13 mm
Standard tip: Triangle
Annual production: approximately 250 cues

OPTIONS (FOR NEW CUES ONLY)

Leather wrap: $150+
Special length: no charge
Ivory butt cap: $250+
Ivory joint: $125+
Ivory ferrule: $100+
Extra shaft: $95+

REPAIRS

Repairs done on all fine cues.
Refinish (with linen wrap): $165
Rewrap (Irish linen): $55
Replace shaft: $95+
Replace ivory ferrule: $100+

CURRENT SHOWCASE CUES

Two-piece Showcase bar cues start at $190. Basic Showcase cues with wraps and joint rings start at $350. Showcase cues with points start at $550. Showcase cues priced over $1,000 come with two shafts. The current delivery time for a Showcase custom cue is about three to six months.

CURRENT EXAMPLES

The following cues are representations of the work of Showcase Custom Cues. These cues can be ordered as shown, modified to suit the desires of the customer, or new designs can be created.

Level 4 - Ebony forearm with a bloodwood ring set in silver rings above wrap, four three-piece bloodwood points with maple veneers, ebony butt sleeve with four three-piece bloodwood windows with maple veneers between bloodwood rings set in silver rings at top and bottom.

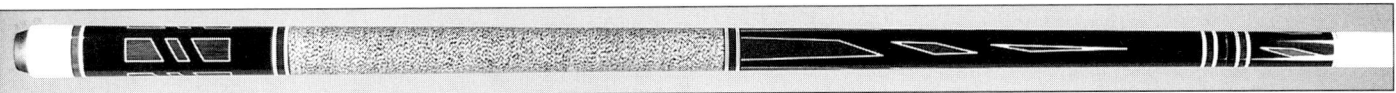

MSR	$1,850	$1,750-2,000	$1,425	$1,050

Level 5 - Ivory joint, bird's-eye maple forearm, eight cocobolo two-piece points with a pair of opposing ivory spear-shaped inlays seperated by ebony and ivory ringwork in each point and an ebony-bordered ivory spear-shaped inlay at the tip of each point, cocobolo butt sleeve with multiple pairs of opposing ivory spear-shaped inlays and ivory dots below ivory spear-shaped inlays set in ebony seperated by malachite dashes set in ebony.

MSR	$3,700	$3,400-3,850	$2,800	$2,150

SECONDARY MARKET MINIMUM VALUES

The following are minimum values for other Showcase Custom Cues encountered on the secondary market. These prices are representative of cues utilizing basic materials and designs that are not currently available. Clay, Ernie, Gale, and Mike have offered one-of-a-kind cues that can command many times these prices due to the use of exotic materials and artistry.

Special construction note: There are many materials and construction techniques that can add value to Showcase cues. The following are the most important examples:

Add 25% for ivory inlay work.

For all used Showcase cues, except where otherwise noted:
Add $80 for each additional original straight playable shaft beyond one.
Deduct $95 for missing original straight playable shaft..
Add $75 each for ivory ferrules.
Add $85 for leather wrap.

GRADING	98%	90%	70%
Deduct 20% for obvious or improper refinish.			
Level 1 - 4 points, hustler.			
Level 1 cues start at	$175	$135	$90
Level 2 - 0 points, 0-25 inlays.			
Level 2 cues start at	$300	$235	$165
Level 3 - 2-6 points, 0-8 inlays.			
Level 3 cues start at	$500	$385	$265
Level 4 - 4-10 points, 9-25 inlays.			
Level 4 cues start at	$700	$550	$375
Level 5 - 0-12 points, 26-50 inlays.			
Level 5 cues start at	$1,000	$795	$550
Level 6 - 0-12 points, 51-75 inlays.			
Level 6 cues start at	$1,450	$1,135	$775

SHOWMAN CUSTOM CUES

Maker of pool cues from 1992 to present in Safety Harbor, Florida.

John L. Showman grew up in Sharpsville, Pennsylvania. He started playing pool as a teenager, and by age 15 John was putting on his own tips. Soon he was putting on tips for his friends as well. John liked the custom cues he saw in the local pool rooms, but he couldn't afford one. In 1989, John moved to Florida and became friends with Rocky Tillis. John learned basic cue construction techniques while helping out in Rocky's shop. John made his first cue in 1992.

Now John makes less than thirty cues a year in his spare time in the one-car garage he has turned into a shop. He also works full time as a machine operator. He is a fan of the great cuemakers of the past, and Showman cues are inspired by traditional cues. All work is done by hand, primarily on antique equipment, and John makes everything except the tips, screws, and bumpers. All inlays are done by hand, but John has plans to get a manual pantograph. John is very proud of his blanks, which have long and even points that are plain or have five veneers. John tapers his shafts for a very stiff hit. Showman cues are identifiable by "Showman" stamped in super small letters on the joint screw and usually on one of the rings. John can even stamp the customer's name on a ring in this manner if they wish.

Showman Cues are guaranteed for life against manufacturing defects that are not the result of warpage or abuse. If you have a Showman cue that needs further identification or repair, or would like to order a new Showman cue, contact Showman Custom Cues, listed in the Trademark Index.

John Showman

Present Day
SHOWMAN 2002 lofl

SPECIFICATIONS

Butt material: hardwoods
Shaft material: rock maple
Standard length: 58 1/2 in.
Lengths available: any
Standard finish: automotive clear coat
Balance point: custom
Standard butt cap: Delrin
Standard wrap: Irish linen
Point construction: short splice
Standard joint: stainless steel
Joint type: piloted
Joint screw: 5/16-14
Standard number of shafts: two
Standard taper: 8 in. straight
Standard ferrules: ivory
Standard tip width: 13 mm
Standard tip: Triangle
Annual production: fewer than 30 cues

GRADING	98%	90%	70%

OPTIONS (FOR NEW CUES ONLY)
Option prices available by request.

REPAIRS
Repairs done only on Showman and Rocky Tillis cues, or cues by legendary cuemakers of the past. Repair prices available by request.

SECONDARY MARKET MINIMUM VALUES
The following are minimum values for Showman Custom Cues encountered on the secondary market. These prices are representative of cues utilizing basic materials and designs that are not necessarily available at present. John Showman has offered one-of-a-kind cues that can command many times these prices due to the use of exotic materials and artistry.

Special construction note: There are many materials and construction techniques that can add value to Showman cues.

For all used Showman cues, except where otherwise noted:
- Add $125 for each additional original straight playable shaft beyond two.
- Deduct $175 for each missing original straight playable shaft under two.
- Deduct 25% for obvious or improper refinish.

Level 1 - 4 points, hustler.
Level 1 cues start at	$350	$275	$185

Level 2 - 0 points, 0-25 inlays.
Level 2 cues start at	$500	$390	$265

Level 3 - 2-6 points, 0-8 inlays.
Level 3 cues start at	$750	$575	$385

Level 4 - 4-10 points, 9-25 inlays.
Level 4 cues start at	$950	$715	$445

Level 5 - 0-12 points, 26-50 inlays.
Level 5 cues start at	$1,450	$1,115	$750

Level 6 - 0-12 points, 51-75 inlays.
Level 6 cues start at	$4,000	$3,300	$2,500

SHURTZ CUSTOM CUES

Maker of pool cues from 1983 to present in Wichita, Kansas.

Shurtz Custom Cues began in 1983 in Jack's garage located in Wichita, Kansas. Jack has been in the billiard business since 1968, traveling five states recovering pool tables and selling billiard supplies. He was also a partner in a retail outlet for pool tables and supplies. Jack learned his trade from the late Verl Horn in Mooreland, Oklahoma. In 1994, a partnership with Bob Owen of Wichita, Kansas was formed. This resulted in the need to move out of the garage. A larger building was found, and again outgrown in a few years. Now, Shurtz Custom Cues, Inc. is in a larger facility with room for pool tables in the front and the shop in the back.

Shurtz cues are made of the finest materials available. Shafts are cut and dried at intervals for six months before being put on a cue. Jack and Bob specialize in custom cues, made to the customer's specifications. Designs and inlay work are done in the shop using exotic woods, ivory, gems and metals. Macines include lathes and CNC. Shurtz has a professional paint room with the latest technology. Shurtz Custom Cues is a small shop which produced one-of-a-kind and limited production cues.

From 1983 to 1994, there were no identification marks on Shurtz cues. In 1995, all cues were engraved with the name SHURTZ just above the butt cap. By 1996, the name was moved into the butt cap and in 1997 the year was added, just under the name.

Shurtz cues are guaranteed for a lifetime against any defect or problem that arises due to the manufacturing. They are not responsible for any cue with abnormal exposure or use.

If you are interested in talking to Jack Shurtz or Bob Owen about a new cue or cue that needs to be repaired, you can contact them at Shurtz Custom Cues, listed in the Trademark Index.

SPECIFICATIONS
Butt material: hardwoods
Shaft material: rock maple
Standard length: 58 in.
Lengths available: any
Standard finish: polyrethane
Balance point: 18 to 19.5 in. from butt
Standard butt cap: phenolic
Standard wrap: Irish linen
Point construction: short splice or inlaid
Standard joints: phenolic, steel, or wood
Joint type: piloted
Joint screw: 5/16-14
Standard number of shafts: one
Standard taper: modified pro

GRADING	100%	95%	70%

Standard ferrules: Ivor-X
Tip widths available: 12 to 13.5 mm
Standard tip: Le Pro
Annual production: 150 to 200 cues

OPTIONS (FOR NEW CUES ONLY)
Ivory ferrule: $60
Ivory butt cap: $200 per inch
Ivory joint: $250
Extra shaft: $100

REPAIRS
Repairs done on all fine cues.
Refinish (with Irish linen wrap): $100
Refinish (with leather wrap): $160
Rewrap (Irish linen): $40
Rewrap (leather): $100
Replace butt cap: $40
Replace tip: $10+
Replace melamine ferrule: $20

CURRENT SHURTZ CUES
Basic two-piece Shurtz cues with wraps and joint rings start at $250. Shurtz cues with points start at $300. One-of-a-kind custom Shurtz cues start at $2,000. The current delivery time for a Shurtz cue is three to four months.

CURRENT EXAMPLES
The following Shurtz cues can be ordered as shown, modified to suit the desires of the customer, or new designs can be created.

Level 4 #410A - Bird's-eye maple forearm with a silver ring above handle, five floating cocobolo points with an ivory-bordered malachite spear-shaped inlay at the base of each point, cocobolo handle, bird's-eye maple butt sleeve with five floating reverse cocobolo points with an ivory-bordered malachite spear-shaped inlay at the base of each point between silver rings at top and bottom.

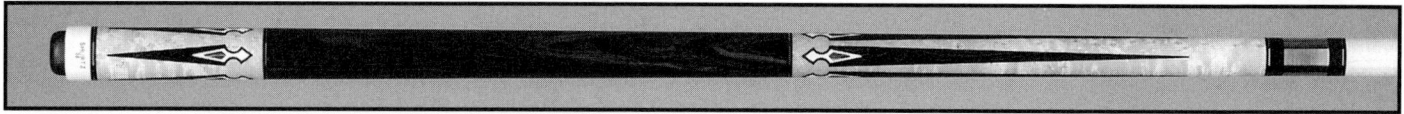

MSR	$1,000	$900-1,250	$765	$600

Level 4 #142A - Stabilized maple joint, bird's-eye maple forearm with a silver ring above wrap, three long and three short ebony points with an intricate two-piece stabilized maple inlay in each point, bird's-eye maple butt sleeve with three large and three small ebony windows with an intricate two-piece stabilized maple inlay in each between silver rings at top and bottom.

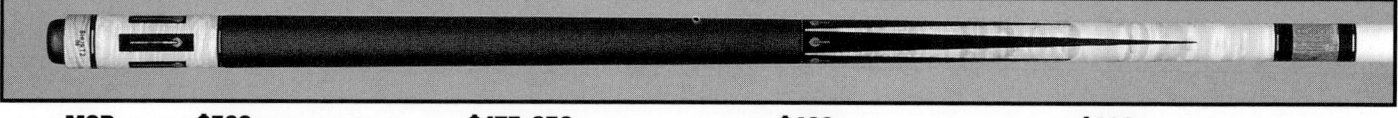

MSR	$500	$475-650	$400	$300

Level 5 - Stabilized maple forearm with a silver ring above wrap, three long and three short ebony points with an intricate three-piece ivory diamond-shaped inlay and an ivory inlaid tip in each point, bird's-eye maple butt sleeve with three long and three short reverse ebony points with an intricate three-piece ivory diamond-shaped inlay and an ivory inlaid tip in each point between silver rings at top and bottom.

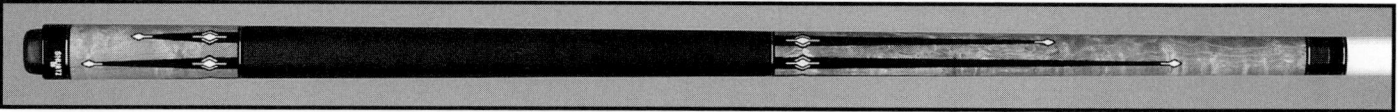

MSR	$1,100	$1,000-1,300	$850	$650

Level 5 #419A - Stabilized maple joint, bird's-eye maple forearm with a silver ring above handle, three long and three short ebony-bordered floating cocobolo points with two ivory diamond-shaped inlays in each point alternating with six intricate ebony-bordered ivory diamond-shaped inlays between the points, cocobolo handle, bird's-eye maple butt sleeve with three long and three short ebony-bordered floating cocobolo points with two ivory diamond-shaped inlays in each point alternating with six intricate ebony-bordered ivory diamond-shaped inlays between silver rings at top and bottom.

MSR	$1,400	$1,275-1,650	$1,050	$775

SHURTZ CUSTOM CUES, cont. 733

| GRADING | 100% | 95% | 70% |

Level 6 #417B - Champhor burl forearm with an ivory ring above handle, three long and three short ebony-bordered floating five-piece ivory points, champhor burl butt sleeve with three large intricate ebony-bordered seven-piece ivory windows alternating with three small intricate ebony-bordered four-piece ivory windows between ivory rings at top and bottom.

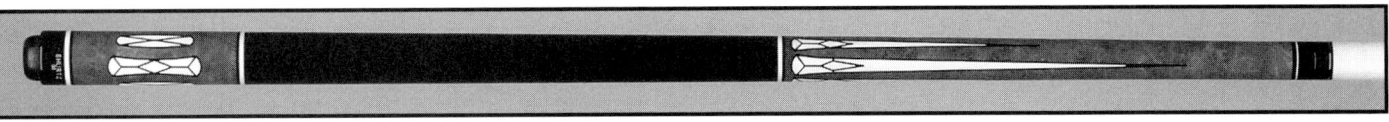

| MSR | $3,000 | $2,600-3,150 | $2,150 | $1,650 |

Level 7 #4122A - Stabilized maple joint, stabilized bird's-eye maple forearm with a silver ring above handle, four intricate hollow ebony-bordered floating seven-piece ivory interwoven points, ebony butt sleeve with intricate interwoven inlays of fiddle-back maple- and ebony-bordered ivory between silver rings at top and bottom.

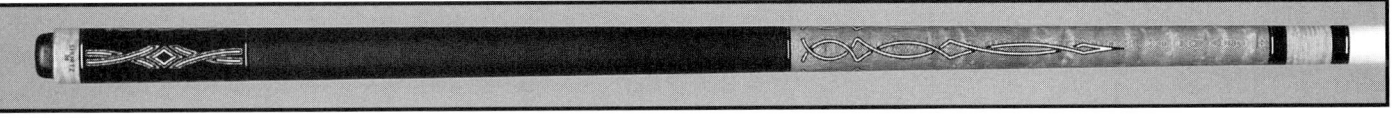

| MSR | $2,500 | $2,400-2,850 | $1,900 | $1,350 |

Level 7 #420A - Masur birch forearm with a silver ring above handle, four intricate ebony-bordered seven-piece ivory points alternating with intricate ebony criss-crossing lines bordering pairs of ivory diamond-shaped inlays, masur birch butt sleeve with four intricate ebony-bordered reverse seven-piece ivory points alternating with intricate ebony criss-crossing lines bordering pairs of ivory diamond-shaped inlays between silver rings at top and bottom.

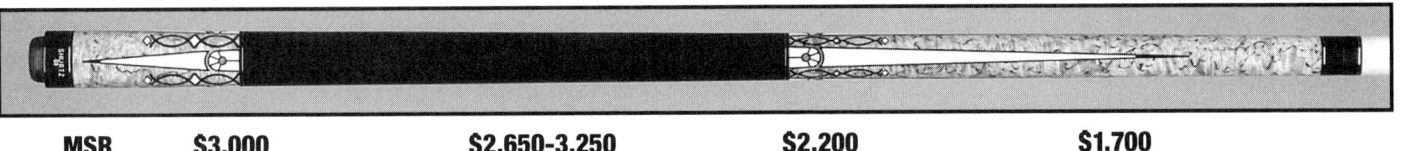

| MSR | $3,000 | $2,650-3,250 | $2,200 | $1,700 |

SECONDARY MARKET MINIMUM VALUES

The following are minimum values for other Shurtz cues encountered on the secondary market. These prices are representative of cues utilizing basic materials and designs that are not necessarily available at present. Bob has offered one-of-a-kind cues that can command many times these prices due to the use of exotic materials and artistry.

Special construction note: There are many materials and construction techniques that can add value to Shurtz cues.

For all used Shurtz cues, except where otherwise noted:
- Add $80 for each additional original straight playable shaft beyond one.
- Deduct $100 for missing original straight playable shaft.
- Add $50 each for ivory ferrules.
- Add $75 for leather wrap.
- Deduct 20% for obvious or improper refinish.

Level 2 - 0 points, 0-25 inlays.
| Level 2 cues start at | $235 | $185 | $125 |

Level 3 - 2-6 points, 0-8 inlays.
| Level 3 cues start at | $285 | $225 | $150 |

Level 4 – 4-10 points, 9-25 inlays.
| Level 4 cues start at | $400 | $310 | $210 |

Level 5 - 0-12 points, 26-50 inlays.
| Level 5 cues start at | $700 | $545 | $370 |

Level 6 - 0-12 points, 51-75 inlays.
| Level 6 cues start at | $1,100 | $875 | $600 |

SIERRA CUSTOM CUE

Maker of pool cues from 1993 to present, currently in Tempe, Arizona.

Sierra Custom cue was founded in 1992 by Eric Niemira and Dave Corbett. They began as avid pool players, each with an interest in cuemaking, each possessing certain talents that helped them get started. Eric had machining skills and technical background in engineering while Dave had experience with engineering and AutoCAD. Each operation in the building of a cue was analyzed and then mastered. From the beginning, Sierra Custom Cue makers have had their own opinion as to how a cue should play, and they have made constant improvements in their construction. Sierra cues are painstakingly handmade with extreme attention to detail and playability. All Sierra cues are constructed using the finest exotic hardwoods and select maple shafts. Highlights of assembly include bored and cut threads over drilled and tapped threads to improve thread strength and playability. Shafts are thoroughly aged and have threaded capped ferrules and cut threads at the joint for a solid connection when the cue is assembled.

GRADING	98%	90%	70%

Playability of the cue is of utmost importance to Sierra Custom Cues. In an effort to achieve this goal, only woods that they feel "play well" are used. Some of the woods used include rosewood, ebony and padauk. The use of two different handle woods is also incorporated, a heavy one and a light one, consisting of purpleheart and padauk respectively. This allows them to minimize the long connecting pins to try to compensate for weight not made from wood. Weight and balance are built into the cue and no adjustment is allowed by means of a weight bolt due to the feeling that no adjustment will ever be necessary and balance is more critical than weight.

Eric Niemira and Dave Corbett

Sierra Custom Cues has some of the most advanced technology in the industry with regards to inlay. A machining center, coupled with the latest in CAM software, allows them to inlay cues with aerospace precision and intricacy. This flexibility allows them to take a conceptual idea to an inlaid cue in a very short amount of time, making their cues unique. Sierra Custom Cues welcomes the opportunity to work with customers on designing their cues. Sierra design style may be characterized by its neo-tribal look accented by silver and materials such as turquoise and malachite. All Sierra cues are then sprayed with a very durable and high gloss finish and then hand-polished. Sierra cues are easily identifiable by their unique Sierra bumpers which have the year of completion molded into them.

If you have a Sierra cue that needs further identification or repair, or would like to order a new Sierra cue, contact Sierra Custom Cues, listed in the Trademark Index.

SPECIFICATIONS

Butt material: hardwoods
Shaft material: rock maple
Standard length: 57 1/2 in.
Standard wrap: Irish linen
Joint screw: 3/8-10
Standard joint: linen phenolic
Standard ferrules: linen melamine
Finish: Dupont V 7600S
Annual production: approximately 250 cues

SECONDARY MARKET MINIMUM VALUES

The following are minimum values for Sierra cues encountered on the secondary market. These prices are representative of cues utilizing basic materials and designs that are not necessarily available at present. Sierra has offered one-of-a-kind cues that can command many times these prices due to the use of exotic materials and artistry.

Special construction note: There are many materials and construction techniques that can add value to Sierra cues.

For all used Sierra cues, except where otherwise noted:
- Add $95 for each additional original straight playable shaft beyond one.
- Deduct $125 for missing original straight playable shaft.
- Add $50 each for ivory ferrules.
- Deduct 20% for obvious or improper refinish.

Level 2 - 0 points, 0-25 inlays.
| Level 2 cues start at | $350 | $275 | $185 |

Level 3 - 2-6 points, 0-8 inlays.
| Level 3 cues start at | $550 | $435 | $295 |

Level 4 - 4-10 points, 9-25 inlays.
| Level 4 cues start at | $700 | $565 | $390 |

Level 5 - 0-12 points, 26-50 inlays.
| Level 5 cues start at | $1,000 | $785 | $545 |

Level 6 - 0-12 points, 51-75 inlays.
| Level 6 cues start at | $1,400 | $1,095 | $750 |

SIGEL'S CUES

Maker of pool cues from 1994 to present, currently in Winter Garden, Florida.

Mike Sigel started playing pool at the age of thirteen, when his parents bought a pool table for the family home. He fell in love with the game, and went on to become one of the greatest all-around pool players. As a professional player, Mike endorsed several cues, and worked for several cuemakers, either helping to make cues or advising how to make their cues play better. Mike made cues for about three years in the late 1970s and early 1980s with Joss cues in Baltimore.

In addition to many television appearances, Mike appeared as himself in the movie "Baltimore Bullet" and performed many of the trick shots for the opening sequences in that film. Mike was the technical advisor, choreographer and instructor of the movie "The Color of Money" starring Paul Newman (who won the Academy Award for Best Actor for his role in the movie) and co-starring Tom Cruise. Mike coached both Newman and Cruise to look like they were professional pool players.

Mike Sigel

One-of-a-kind custom

After playing professionally for over twenty years, and winning 101 professional titles during the past 13 years, including six U.S Open and five World Championships, Mike decided to retire. He then chose to channel his love of the game towards crafting cues of his own design. He spent a year and a half purchasing the necessary equipment and experimenting with design and construction techniques.

By the summer of 1995, Mike was making cues. He feels that his background as a world class player helps him to understand a cue's playability better than other makers. Sigel cues are a little lighter and slimmer than most cues, as this is his preference. Mike hand-signs every cue he makes on the butt caps, so they are easy to identify. He currently specializes in intricate cues, using only exotic hardwoods, stones and ivories, inlaid using the latest CNC technology. Mike is always experimenting with new exotic materials. He refuses to use any imitation materials or plastics. Mike is always creating new designs, and usually makes less than 10 of each.

Mike feels that the hit is the most important aspect of a cue, so he hand selects every tip, and he hits with every cue before they leave the shop. Shafts are cut and dipped in stabilizer every couple of months at least six or seven times. If they warp, Mike throws them out. All cues are weighed before completion, and then Mike uses stainless steel or titanium joint screws to help attain the final weight and balance. Cues with any flaws end up in the trash can, as Mike will only sell cues that he believes are perfect.

Mike has also introduced a line of production cues that bear his name. They feature the "Mike Sigel" signature on the forearm, and an "S" logo on the butt caps. Ten different series of cue models are available.

Custom-made Sigel cues are guaranteed indefinitely against construction defects that are not the result of warpage or abuse. If you have a Sigel cue that needs further identification or repair, or would like to talk to Mike about ordering a new Sigel cue, contact Sigel's Cues, listed in the Trademark Index.

CUSTOM CUE SPECIFICATIONS

Butt material: hardwoods
Shaft material: rock maple
Standard length: 58 in.
Standard finish: PPG
Standard joint: linen phenolic
Joint screw: 3/8-10
Joint type: flat faced
Balance point: 1 1/2 in. above wrap
Point construction: inlaid
Standard wrap: Irish linen
Standard number of shafts: one
Standard taper: custom
Standard ferrules: micarta melamine blend
Standard tip: Le Pro

CURRENT SIGEL'S CUES

Sigel's cues offers four models in the Gambler Series, four models in the Shark Series, four models in the Prowler Series, four models in the Intimidator Series, three models in the Hustler Series, four models in the Traditional Series, four models in the Hook Series, five models in the 3 In 1 Series, three models in the Elite Series, and two models in the Ambassador Series. One-of-a-kind custom cues made by Mike Sigel cost thousands of dollars. The current delivery time for a custom Sigel cue is one week to three months.

SECONDARY MARKET MINIMUM VALUES

The following are minimum values for Sigel's cues encountered on the secondary market. These prices are representative of cues utilizing basic materials and designs that are not necessarily available at present.

GRADING	98%	90%	70%

Special construction note: There are many materials and construction techniques that can add value to Sigel's cues. For all used Sigel's cues, except where otherwise noted:
- Add $45 for each additional original straight playable shaft beyond one.
- Deduct 50% for missing original straight playable shaft.
- Deduct 15% for obvious or improper refinish.

Level 1 - Hustler.

	98%	90%	70%
Level 1 cues start at	$65	$50	$30

Level 2 - 0 points, 0-25 inlays.

Level 2 cues start at	$85	$65	$40

Level 3 - 2-6 points, 0-8 inlays.

Level 3 cues start at	$110	$85	$50

Level 4 - 4-10 points, 9-25 inlays.

Level 4 cues start at	$135	$100	$60

SECONDARY MARKET MINIMUM VALUES (HANDMADE BY MIKE SIGEL)

The following are minimum values for Sigel Custom Cues encountered on the secondary market. These prices are representative of cues utilizing basic materials and designs that are not necessarily available at present. These cues are hand signed by Mike Sigel on the butt caps and have Sterling silver stitch rings. Mike has offered one-of-a-kind cues that can command many times these prices due to the use of exotic materials and artistry.

Special construction note: There are many materials and construction techniques that can add value to Mike Sigel cues.

For all used Mike Sigel cues, except where otherwise noted:
- Add $100 for each additional original straight playable shaft beyond one.
- Deduct $175 for missing original straight playable shaft.
- Add $60 each for ivory ferrules.
- Deduct 25% for obvious or improper refinish.

Level 4 - 4-10 points, 9-25 inlays.

	98%	90%	70%
Level 4 cues start at	$1,500	$1,200	$850

Level 5 - 0-12 points, 26-50 inlays.

Level 5 cues start at	$2,000	$1,600	$1,100

Level 6 - 0-12 points, 51-75 inlays.

Level 6 cues start at	$3,000	$2,400	$1,650

SILVER FOX

Maker of pool cues from 1988 to present in Bellingham, Washington.

Larry Brengman started his own Ohio business as a cue manufacturer sales representative in 1981. In 1988, after these and previous years of experience in the billiard industry, Larry started Silver Fox in Bellingham, Washington. His mission with Silver Fox has been to bring new and innovative products and concepts to the billiard industry.

Silver Fox cues may feature laminated hardwood butts, applied images of the works of Northwestern artists, or titanium shafts. The 725 series cues are identifiable by a dot of pure silver in the butt caps, and come in a special gift box. Other Silver Fox cues are easily recognized by the "Silver Fox" logo on the butt caps. You can even send in a picture which can be put on the butt sleeve of a new cue which costs $330. Silver Fox also offers a line of cue cases.

Silver Fox cues are guaranteed indefinitely against construction defects that are not the result of warpage or abuse. If you have a Silver Fox cue that needs further identification or repair, or would like to talk to someone about ordering a new Silver Fox cue, contact Silver Fox, listed in the Trademark Index.

SPECIFICATIONS

Butt material: hardwoods
Shaft material: rock maple and titanium
Standard length: 58 in.
Joint screw: 3/8-10 or 5/16-18
Standard joint: micarta or ABS
Joint type: flat faced
Balance point: 2 in. above

SILVER FOX, cont.

GRADING	98%	90%	70%

Standard wrap: Irish linen
Standard butt cap: micarta or ABS
Standard number of shafts: one
Standard ferrules: micarta or ABS
Standard tip: Triangle or Le Pro

OPTIONS (FOR NEW CUES ONLY)

Extra maple shaft: $53+

CURRENT SILVER FOX CUES

Silver fox currently carries three different lines of cues starting at $280. The current delivery time for a Silver Fox cue is approximately 30 to 60 days.

SECONDARY MARKET MINIMUM VALUES

The following are minimum prices for Silver Fox cues encountered on the secondary market. These prices are representative of cues utilizing basic materials and designs that may not be currently available.

Special construction note: There are many materials and construction techniques that can add value to Silver Fox cues. The following are the most important examples:

Add $220+ for titanium shaft.
Add $65+ for pure silver dot in butt cap.
Add $35+ for original gift box.

For all used Silver Fox cues, except where otherwise noted:

Add $40+ for each additional original straight playable maple shaft beyond one.
Deduct $53+ for missing original straight playable maple shaft.
Deduct 25% for obvious or improper refinish.

Level 2 - 0 points, 0-25 inlays.

Level 2 cues start at	$200	$150	$90

GREG SIRCA

Maker of GS Cues. For information, refer to the listing for GS Cue.

SMITH HANDCRAFTED CUES

Maker of pool cues from 1989 to present in Charlotte, North Carolina.

Howard Smith enjoys playing pool. As a player, he has always searched for a better cue. He has worked to make great playing cues that fit the individual player. His goal is to make the best playing cue he can make. He is always looking for ways to improve his cues for better playability. He also strives to make cues that look great, so the player and those who see the cue will appreciate its look.

Howard owns The Silvertime Company, a multi-faceted business that does many things. All of his cues are sold through Silvertime Billiards and Darts. Most of Howard's equipment was not intended to be used for cuemaking, and he uses a lot of metal working to get the tolerance needed. He has modified existing tools to accomplish specific jobs.

Early Howard Smith cues have the name "Smith" written on the butt plate with a pen and sealed in. Howard is now engraving his name for a better look that will last forever. He uses gold, silver, white, black, and sometimes other color inlays to fill the engraved name.

Smith makes nearly all of his cues for specific customer needs. He does make one cue per year for himself. The closest thing to a "model" cue would be his "Thunder Chicken" break cue. According to Smith, "When you hit with it, it sounds like thunder, and the balls run like chickens." Smith cues are easily identified by a hand engraved "Smith" that appears on the butt plate of about every cue made since 1998. The engraving is filled in gold leaf, or whatever color best goes with the cue. Earlier Smith cues were marked with a pen.

Smith hopes his cues will outlast the player. If there is anything wrong with the cue, due to something in the manufacturing of it, it will be replaced or repaired.

If you are interested in talking to Howard Smith about a new cue or cue that needs to be repaired, you can contact him at Smith Handcrafted Cues, listed in the Trademark Index.

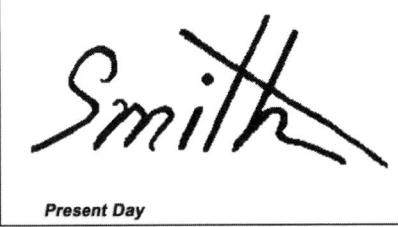

Howard Smith

Smith — Present Day

SPECIFICATIONS

Butt material: hardwoods
Shaft material: hard rock maple
Standard length: 58 in.
Standard wrap: Irish linen
Standard ferrules: Aegis

GRADING	100%	95%	70%

Standard tip: layered Talisman
Annual production: fewer than 100 cues

OPTIONS (FOR NEW CUES ONLY)

Ivory ferrule: $55
Leather wrap: $100
Extra shaft: $150

REPAIRS

Repairs done on all fine cues.
Refinish with Irish linen wrap: $150
Rewrap with Irish linen: $40
Replace shaft: $150
Replace tip: $10+

CURRENT SMITH CUES

Two-piece bar cues made by Howard Smith start at $150. Basic Smith cues with wraps and joint rings start at $400. Smith cues with inlaid points start at $600, ones with spliced points start at $700. The current delivery time for a Smith cue is about six months.

CURRENT EXAMPLES

The following Howard Smith cue can be ordered as shown, modified to suit the desires of the customer, or new designs can be created.

Level 5 "King Snake" - Bird's-eye maple forearm with an ivory staggered inlaid zig-zag ring above ivory ringwork above wrap, four ebony points with three colored veneers, boa constrictor wrap, ebony butt sleeve with four ivory diamond-shaped inlays between sets of eight inward-pointing ivory triangle-shaped inlays above and below within ivory ringwork at top and bottom.

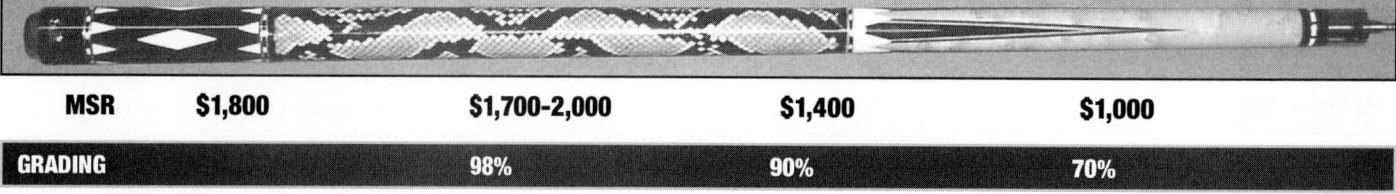

MSR	$1,800	$1,700-2,000	$1,400	$1,000
GRADING		98%	90%	70%

SECONDARY MARKET MINIMUM VALUES

The following are minimum values for other Smith cues encountered on the secondary market. These prices are representative of cues utilizing basic materials and designs that are not necessarily available at present. Howard has offered one-of-a-kind cues that can command many times these prices due to the use of exotic materials and artistry.

Special construction note: There are many materials and construction techniques that can add value to Smith cues.

For all used Smith cues, except where otherwise noted:

Add $115 for each additional original straight playable shaft beyond one.
Deduct $150 for missing original straight playable shaft.
Add $45 each for ivory ferrules.
Add $75 for leather wrap.
Deduct 20% for obvious or improper refinish.

Level 1 - Hustler.
Level 1 cues start at	$125	$100	$65

Level 2 - 0 points, 0-25 inlays.
Level 2 cues start at	$350	$275	$185

Level 3 - 2-6 points, 0-8 inlays.
Level 3 cues start at	$500	$390	$265

Level 4 - 4-10 points, 9-25 inlays.
Level 4 cues start at	$650	$525	$350

Level 5 - 0-12 points, 26-50 inlays.
Level 5 cues start at	$900	$725	$500

JEFF SMITH

Maker of J. Alan Cues. For information, refer to the listing for J. Alan.

GRADING	100%	95%	70%

MARK SMITH CUSTOM CUES

Maker of pool cues from 1997 to present in Russellville, Arkansas.

Mark Smith began building cues in 1997 as a result of an interest in machinery and building. He strives to make each cue better than the last one. Mark's cues are identified by being signed and serialized prior to being finished. Mark's serial numbering includes the year and the number of cue for that year. For example, 2005-4 would mean the 4th cue made in 2005.

Mark's small shop is in a heated and cooled basement. He has extra humidity control to keep his shop at 52% humidity all the time. His equipment includes a digital readout lathe, Porper lathe, and various saws and other cuemaking machinery. He also has an Align-rite CNC setup.

Mark Smith guarantees his cues for his working lifetime against defects that are not caused by warpage or abuse. If you are interested in talking to Mark Smith about a new cue or cue that needs to be repaired, you can contact him at Mark Smith Custom Cues, listed in the Trademark Index.

SPECIFICATIONS

Butt material: hardwoods
Shaft material: maple
Standard length: 58 in.
Standard wrap: linen or leather
Standard ferrules: Ivor-X
Standard tip: pressed Le Pro or Moori
Annual production: fewer than 20 cues

OPTIONS (FOR NEW CUES ONLY)

Ivory ferrule: $50
Leather wrap: $50
Extra shaft: $75

REPAIRS

Repairs done on all fine cues.
Refinish with Irish linen wrap: $75
Rewrap with Irish linen: $25
Replace shaft: $75
Replace tip: $7+

CURRENT MARK SMITH CUES

Basic Mark Smith cues with wraps and joint rings start at $350. Mark Smith cues with points start at $450. One-of-a-kind custom Mark Smith cues start at $700. The current delivery time for a Mark Smith custom cue is at least two months, depending on the design of the cue.

CURRENT EXAMPLES

The following Mark Smith cues can be ordered as shown, modified to suit the desires of the customers, or new designs can be created.

Level 5 - Bird's-eye maple forearm with a silver ring above wrap, four long and four short cocobolo points with a turquoise diamond-shaped inlay in each point, bird's-eye maple butt sleeve with eight turquoise diamond-shaped inlays within pairs of opposing cocobolo spear-shaped inlays between silver rings at top and bottom.

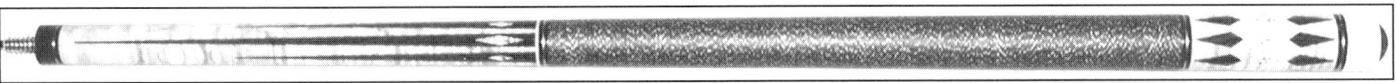

MSR	$650	$625-725	$515	$375

Level 4 - Cocobolo forearm with four turquoise diamond-shaped inlays over double silver rings between forearm and handle, four floating tiger maple points with a turquoise spear-shaped inlay in each point, tiger maple handle, cocobolo butt sleeve with four tiger maple diamond-shaped inlays between double silver rings at bottom and four turquoise diamond-shaped inlays over double silver rings between butt sleeve and handle.

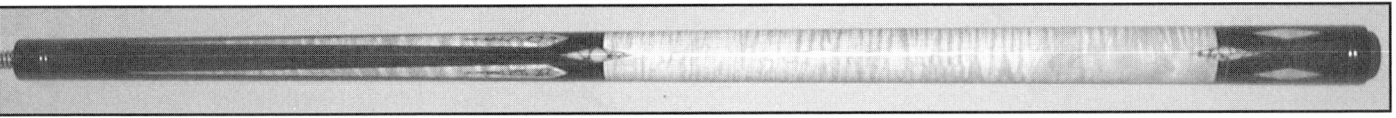

MSR	$700	$675-785	$550	$400

GRADING	100%	95%	70%

Level 4 - Bird's-eye maple forearm with double silver rings above wrap, four long and four short ebony points with an ivory diamond-shaped inlay in each point, ebony butt sleeve with four ivory diamond-shaped inlays between double silver rings at top and bottom.

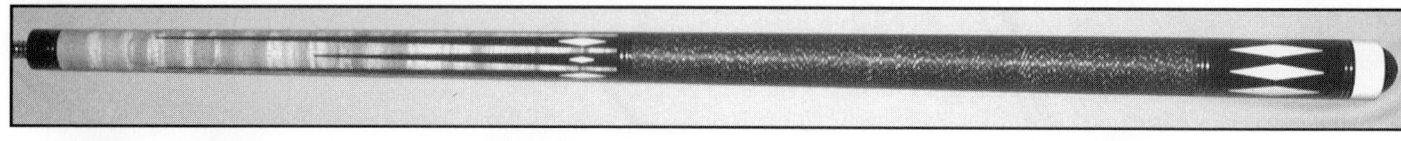

MSR	$700	$675-785	$550	$400

Level 5 - Ebony forearm with a silver ring above wrap, four floating purpleheart points with a turquoise diamond-shaped inlay set in an ivory oval in each point alternating with four turquoise diamond-shaped inlays, ebony butt sleeve with four floating purpleheart reverse points with a turquoise diamond-shaped inlay set in an ivory oval in each point alternating with four turquoise diamond-shaped inlays between silver rings at top and bottom.

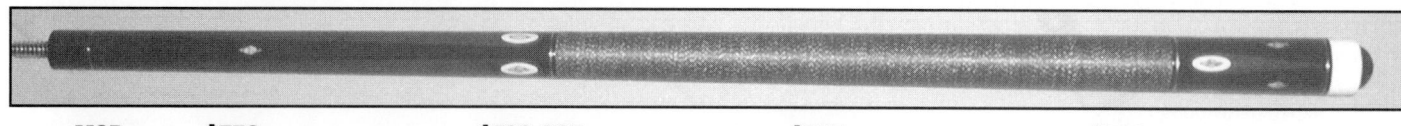

MSR	$750	$700-835	$625	$530

Level 4 - Redheart forearm with double silver rings above wrap, four wormy chestnut points with two veneers alternating with four sterling silver diamond-shaped inlays, ebony butt sleeve with four large redstone diamond-shaped windows with two veneers alternating with four sterling silver diamond-shaped inlays between double silver rings at top and bottom.

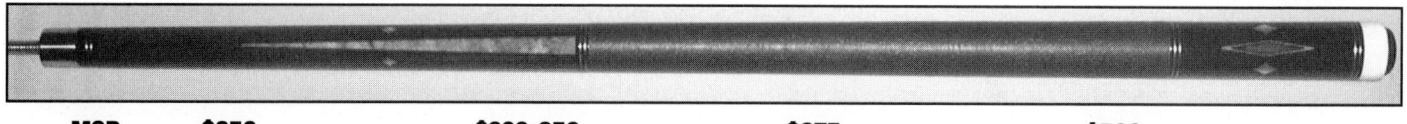

MSR	$850	$800-950	$675	$500

Level 4 - Bird's-eye maple forearm with double silver rings above wrap, four long snakewood points with ebony veneers alternating with four short ebony points with an ivory diamond-shaped inlay in each point, ebony butt sleeve with four ivory diamond-shaped inlays alternating with four snakewood razor blade-shaped windows between double silver rings at top and bottom.

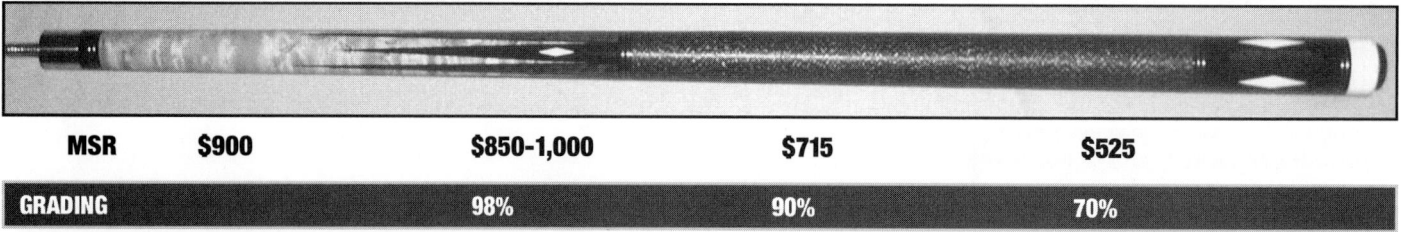

MSR	$900	$850-1,000	$715	$525

GRADING	98%	90%	70%

SECONDARY MARKET MINIMUM VALUES

The following are minimum values for other Mark Smith cues encountered on the secondary market. These prices are representative of cues utilizing basic materials and designs that are not necessarily available at present. Mark has offered one-of-a-kind cues that can command many times these prices due to the use of exotic materials and artistry.

Special construction note: There are many materials and construction techniques that can add value to Mark Smith cues.

For all used Mark Smith cues, except where otherwise noted:
- Add $65 for each additional original straight playable shaft beyond one.
- Deduct $75 for missing original straight playable shaft.
- Add $40 each for ivory ferrules.
- Add $45 for leather wrap.
- Deduct 20% for obvious or improper refinish.

Level 2 - 0 points, 0-25 inlays.
Level 2 cues start at	$300	$240	$165

Level 3 - 2-6 points, 0-8 inlays.
Level 3 cues start at	$400	$315	$215

Level 4 - 4-10 points, 9-25 inlays.
Level 4 cues start at	$500	$390	$270

Level 5 - 0-12 points, 26-50 inlays.
Level 5 cues start at	$850	$665	$445

Level 6 - 0-12 points, 51-75 inlays.
Level 6 cues start at	$1,100	$885	$600

GRADING	98%	90%	70%

ROBERT SMITH

Maker of Shaman cues. For information, refer to listing for Shaman.

SMITH & WESSON BILLIARDS

Distributor of Chinese-made pool cues in Wayne, New Jersey.

Leisure Pursuits Sales and Marketing licensed the Smith & Wesson name for a line of billiard products. The first cues were introduced on January 17, 2005.

Smith & Wesson cues are designed to be warp and damage resistant to temperatures ranging from minus 113 degrees Farenheit to plus 167 degrees Farhenheit. They are easily identifiable by the "Smith & Wesson" name on the butt caps. Smith & Wesson cues are guaranteed for one year against warpage and construction defects that are not the result of abuse.

If you are interested in talking to someone about a new Smith & Wesson cue or cue that needs to be repaired, you can contact them at Smith & Wesson Cues, listed in the Trademark Index.

SPECIFICATIONS

Butt material: fiberglass-cored hardwoods
Shaft material: maple or graphite
Standard length: 58 in.
Standard wrap: Irish linen
Standard joint: stainless steel
Standard number of shafts: one
Standard ferrules: titanium
Standard tip: laminated

CURRENT SMITH & WESSON CUES

Smith & Wesson Billiards currently offers the Player Series, the Performance Series, the Break/Jump Cues, One Piece Cues, and the Heritage Series. Most models are available for immediate delivery.

SECONDARY MARKET MINIMUM VALUES

The following are minimum values for other Smith & Wesson cues encountered on the secondary market. These prices are representative of cues utilizing basic materials and designs that are not necessarily available at present.

For all used Smith & Wesson cues, except where otherwise noted:
Add $50 for each additional original straight playable shaft beyond one.
Deduct 50% for missing original straight playable shaft.
Deduct 15% for obvious or improper refinish.

Level 2 - 0 points, 0-25 inlays.

	98%	90%	70%
Level 2 cues start at	$65	$50	$30

Level 3 - 2-6 points, 0-8 inlays.

	98%	90%	70%
Level 3 cues start at	$100	$75	$45

RICHARD SMITHLIN

Maker of pool cues from mid-1980s to present in Las Vegas, Nevada.

SOUTH EAST CUES

Maker of pool cues from 1992 to present in Clarksville, Tennessee.

Nat Green has played pool for almost all of his life. He liked cues, so in 1985 he bought a lathe to do repair work. He enjoyed it so much that in 1992 he bought a nicer lathe and started making two-piece hustler cues. Two years later in 1994 Nat bought CNC equipment and started making custom cues. Nat enjoys working with wood in his one-man shop. He is self-taught, and makes everything in-house except for the joint screws and the rubber bumpers. Every cue is built one at a time.

South East cues are easily identifiable by the "SE" logo on the butt caps. Nat considers himself a perfectionist and will only sell cues that he considers perfect. Quality is priority number one, and the playability has to be very good as well. South East Cues has a standard line of 21 models, and Nat builds one-of-a-kind custom cues to the designs of the customers. He enjoys creating a piece of art from raw pieces of wood. Nat believes that all South East cues should look good as well. All South East cues have rings at the joints, above and below the wraps, and above the butt caps unless they are hustler cues or are custom ordered otherwise. Irish linen or leather wraps are available.

South East Cues are guaranteed for life, to the original owner, against manufacturing defects that are not the result of warpage or abuse. If you have a South East cue that needs further identification or repair, or would like to order a new South East cue, contact South East Cues, listed in the Trademark Index.

SPECIFICATIONS

Butt material: hardwoods
Shaft material: rock maple
Standard length: 58 in.

GRADING	98%	90%	70%

Lengths available: custom up to 64 in.
Standard wrap: Irish linen
Point construction: inlaid
Joint type: flat faced
Joint screw: 3/8-10
Standard joint: linen phenolic
Standard number of shafts: one
Standard taper: custom
Standard ferrules: linen based phenolic
Tip widths available: 10 to 14 mm

OPTIONS (FOR NEW CUES ONLY)

Weight bolt: $5
Extra shaft: $100
Ivory ferrule: $75
Moori tip: $60
Ivory joint: $150
Ivory butt cap: $250
Leather wrap: $125

REPAIRS

Repairs done on all fine cues.
Refinish with linen wrap: $175
Refinish with leather wrap: $250
Rewrap Irish linen: $40
Replace shaft: $100
Rewrap leather: $125
Replace ivory ferrule: $75
Replace Le Pro tip: $10
Replace layered tip: $30+
Replace linen-based phenolic ferrule: $20

CURRENT SOUTH EAST CUES

Two-piece South East bar cues start at $150. Basic South East cues with wraps and joint rings start at $450. points and inlays start at $12.50 each.

SECONDARY MARKET MINIMUM VALUES

The following are minimum values for South East cues encountered on the secondary market. These prices are representative of cues utilizing basic materials and designs that are not necessarily available at present. South East Cues has offered one-of-a-kind cues that can command many times these prices due to the use of exotic materials and artistry.

Special construction note: There are many materials and construction techniques that can add value to South East cues.

For all used South East cues, except where otherwise noted:
Add $85 for each additional original straight playable shaft beyond one.
Deduct $100 for missing original straight playable shaft.
Add $60 each for ivory ferrules.
Add $85 for leather wrap.
Deduct 20% for obvious or improper refinish.

Level 1 - 4 points, hustler.

	98%	90%	70%
Level 1 cues start at	$135	$105	$70

Level 2 - 0 points, 0-25 inlays.

Level 2 cues start at	$400	$310	$210

Level 3 - 2-6 points, 0-8 inlays.

Level 3 cues start at	$450	$350	$235

Level 4 - 4-10 points, 9-25 inlays.

Level 4 cues start at	$650	$515	$345

Level 5 - 0-12 points, 26-50 inlays.

Level 5 cues start at	$950	$745	$495

SOUTH WEST CUES

Maker of pool cues from 1982 to present in Las Vegas, Nevada.

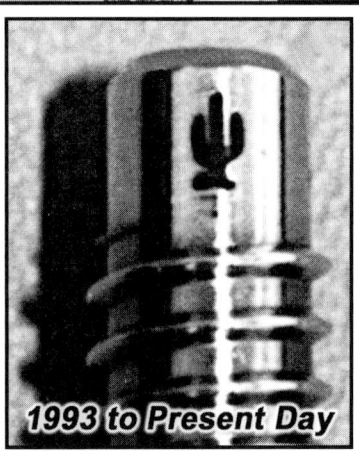

Jerry W. Franklin, founder of South West Cues, was inducted posthumously into the American Cuemakers Association Hall of Fame in March 2005.

Born in Great Bend, Kansas in 1953, Jerry came from a classic midwestern family. Hard work and hard play brought them to a tiny desert boomtown in 1982: Las Vegas, Nevada.

Mechanical aptitude surfaced early for Jerry. By the time he was 10 years old, he was building go-carts from scrap bicycle parts. The day his dad discovered the lawnmower dismantled and the missing motor mounted on his son's "dragster," he knew that the boy was an achiever.

While pursuing a college degree in accounting, his talents and aspirations found a meeting place. In 1976, he repaired David Kersenbrock's car in exchange for a custom pool cue. Shortly thereafter, while setting up a bookkeeping system for Kersenbrock Cue Service, Jerry became intrigued with the machinations of building a pool cue. Soon, he was helping on the machines and learning how to make cues. In 1978, Kersenbrock briefly relocated to Arizona, and Jerry, remaining in Las Vegas, worked in the refrigeration business for the next two years.

In 1980, Jerry started to do cue repairs on his own, and began assembling the equipment necessary to make cues. By 1982, South West Cues was founded. "South West Cues" was the name Jerry selected because it was a collaboration of many hands, minds and passions. From the early years, family members pitched in intermittently. Jerry's nephew and successor Mike Bunker explains, "He gave everyone input into the business. We all had opportunity to develop."

As Franklin's shop in Las Vegas grew, Kersenbrock returned to contribute inlaid artwork while the two jointly developed a new cutting technique. What began as an idea inspired by a hobby magazine became an important innovation in the cuemaking industry. A table saw with mounted jig for tapered cuts shortened a 20-minute job to five minutes. There were many months of experimentation and fine-tuning. Today those same machines still achieve a phenomenally smooth cut, saving important time and labor while avoiding human error in over-sanding.

As South West Cue's popularity grew, so did the number of visitors to the shop. Often described as a true gentleman, Jerry always took the time to stop and talk, share and explain. He was equally forthcoming with information for other cuemakers as well as cue enthusiasts.

Based on outward appearance, there has been confusion between Kersenbrock cues and early South West cues. Although Jerry maintained the six-point and brass joint screw designs from David, he changed the doweling technique of the butt section at his own shop in 1980. The grip section was extended three inches, doweling in two directions; up into the nose and down into the base.

South West cues are easily identifiable by their design and construction. The joint is the most recognizable aspect of the cue. With its long brass 3/8-11 screw and 3/8 in. micarta collar on both the butt and the shaft, it used to be that you could identify a South West cue from across a room. Now that several other makers have adopted the basic design, identification requires closer inspection. For instance, South West cues have a rubber bumper that pops in and out, as opposed to many of the copies which have bumpers held in place with a typical screw. Although the early cues are unmarked, cues made since 1993 feature the cactus symbol stamped into the joint screw, followed by the serial number (which begins each year with 300) and the year of manufacture. The company recommends a Certificate of Authenticity for pre-1993 cues.

On May 11, 1996, just when Jerry was starting to get enough free time to do some of the activities he really enjoyed, he died suddenly of a heart attack, at the age of 42. His wife Laurie and the other workers in the shop have continued making South West cues with the same pursuit of excellence that Jerry started 14 years earlier.

If you order a South West cue today, it will take approximately eight years to arrive. There are two reasons for this. The first has to do with the time required for the scientific approach used in making a South West cue. For example, the shafts start as long, one-inch square pieces of rock maple. They are turned down by a series of twelve cuts that remove less than a sixteenth of an inch at a time, with a minimum of two weeks between each cut. The densities of the materials used in the three sections of the butt are calculated with a computer to determine the weight and balance point of a cue. Added weight or adjustment of balance comes from the aluminum or steel threaded rods that connect the three sections together. Once the butt is assembled, it is turned down with a series of cuts that are several weeks apart. The urethane gloss finish requires a minimum of five coats depending on the species of wood. Each spray requires a minimum 24 hour drying time, and then re-sanding. With a staff of five to seven, South West can only make about 250 cues per year.

Today the demand for new and old South West cues continues to rise. General manager and Jerry's nephew, Michael Bunker, has carried on for his uncle. Machinish Alvin Lawrence, an essential employee of the shop, has been on board since 1988. Jerry's wife, Laurie, has worked with nearly all phases of cuemaking, and handles all the office responsibilities. A former, but important, contributor to their success was Jerry's brother Gary, who did pantograph work on fancy cues.

Because of the limited availability and popularity of South West cues, those available today on the secondary market are bringing a premium. To minimize speculation, South West Cues allows an individual to order no more than two cues per year. Collectors are paying premiums for cues made while Jerry was still in the shop, especially the very early cues and the very fancy cues.

South West cues are guaranteed indefinitely against construction defects that are not the result of warpage or abuse. If you have a South West cue that needs repair or further identification, or you would like to talk to Laurie about the design of a new cue, contact South West Cues, listed in the Trademark Index.

SPECIFICATIONS

Butt material: hardwoods
Shaft material: rock maple
Standard length: 58 in.
Lengths available: 57 to 62 in.
Standard finish: urethane gloss
Joint screw: 3/8-11
Standard joint: micarta
Joint type: flat faced
Balance point: 18 to 18 1/2 in.
Point construction: short splice
Standard wrap: Irish linen
Standard butt cap: micarta
Standard number of shafts: two
Standard taper: custom
Standard ferrules: melamine
Standard tip: Triangle
Tip widths available: any
Annual production: approximately 250 cues

OPTIONS (FOR NEW CUES ONLY)

Leather wrap: $175
Special butt diameter: $75
Joint protectors: $200+
Special length (57, 59 or 60 in.): $75
Special length (61 or 62 in.): $200
Extra shaft: $275
Extra long shaft: $325
Ivory ferrule: $85
Extra ring in base: $50
Extra rings above and below wrap: $225

REPAIRS

Repair prices for South West cues only. Repairs can be done on most fine cues at an additional cost.

Refinish (standard six-point): $275
Refinish (special inlaid): $375
Rewrap (leather): $175
Rewrap (linen): $45
Replace hardwood butt cap: $75
Repair joint: $80+
Replace joint ring: $85
Replace shaft ring: $35
Replace shaft: $275
Replace extra long shaft: $325
Re-cut shaft: $50

GRADING	100%	95%	70%

Refinish shaft (with tip): $35
Replace ivory ferrule: $85
Replace standard tip: $10
Certificate of authenticity (standard): $50
Certificate of authenticity (special inlaid): $70

CURRENT SOUTH WEST CUES

Basic South West cues with wraps and joint rings start at $1,100. South West cues with three long and three short points start at $1,300. Veneers are $100 each. Fancy South West cues which normally start at $2,400 are not available at this time. The current delivery time for a South West cue is approximately eight years.

CURRENT EXAMPLES

The following cues are representations of the work of South West Cues. These cues can be ordered as shown, modified to suit the desires of the customer, or new designs can be created. They are priced with two shafts. Exotic wood refers to your choice of pau ferro, cocobolo, goncolo alves, ebony, and many other exotic woods available.

Level 2 - Bird's-eye maple forearm, bird's-eye maple butt.

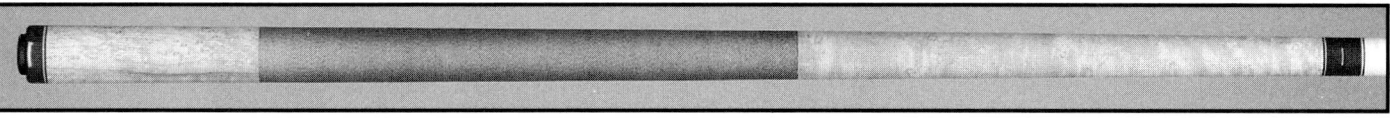

MSR	$1,100	$1,100-1,500	$1,265	$895

Level 2 - Exotic wood forearm, exotic wood butt.

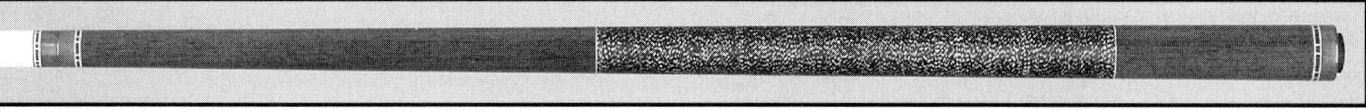

MSR	$1,100	$1,100-1,600	$1,335	$975

Level 3 - Exotic wood forearm, three long and three short bird's-eye maple points, exotic wood butt.

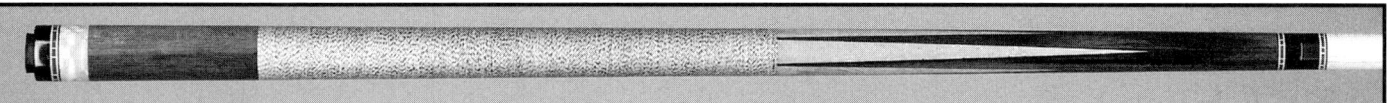

MSR	$1,300	$1,300-2,000	$1,650	$1,150

Level 3 - Exotic wood forearm, three long and three short exotic wood points with one veneer, exotic wood butt.

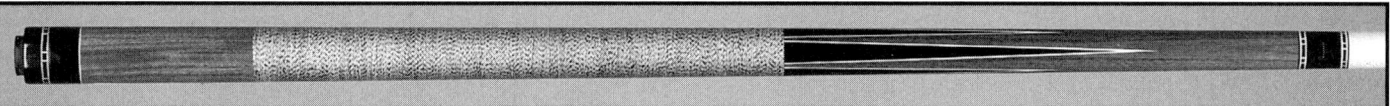

MSR	$1,400	$1,400-2,100	$1,700	$1,200

Level 3 - Exotic wood forearm, three long and three short exotic wood points with two veneers, exotic wood butt.

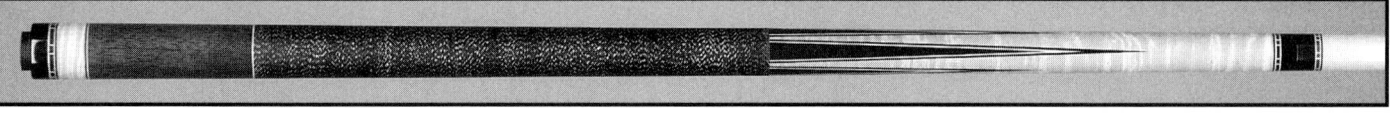

MSR	$1,500	$1,500-2,250	$1,800	$1,250

Level 3 - Bird's-eye maple forearm, three long and three short exotic wood points with two colored veneers, exotic wood butt, ringwork at A,B,C, and D.

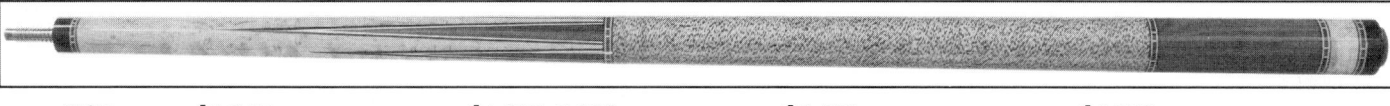

MSR	$1,645	$1,645-2,600	$2,100	$1,550

PAST EXAMPLES

The following cues are representations of past work of South West Cues. These cues can be encountered as shown, modified to suit the desires of the customer, or new designs can be encountered. They are priced with two shafts. Exotic wood refers to pau ferro, cocobolo, goncolo alves, ebony, and many other exotic woods that have been used.

GRADING	98%	90%	70%

Level 2 - Exotic wood forearm, exotic wood butt.

MSR (1999) $855	$1,650	$1,350	$1,000

Level 3 - Bird's-eye maple forearm, three long and three short exotic wood points, exotic wood butt.

MSR (1999) $930	$2,100	$1,795	$1,350

Level 3 - Bird's-eye maple forearm, three long and three short exotic wood points with single exotic wood or colored veneers, exotic wood butt, A+B rings.

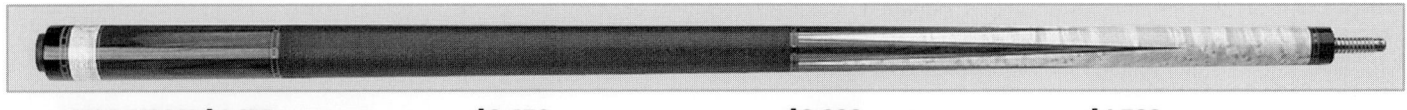

MSR (1999) $1,155	$2,450	$2,000	$1,500

FANCY SOUTH WEST CUES

The following cues are representations of past work of South West Cues. Cues with inlay work or ivory points are rare, and not currently available from South West Cues. These cues can be encountered as shown, modified to suit the desires of the original customer, or different designs can be encountered. They are priced with two shafts. Exotic wood refers to pau ferro, cocobolo, goncolo alves, ebony, and many other exotic woods that have been used.

Level 5 "Ivory points" - Exotic wood forearm, three long scrimshawed ivory points alternating with three short ivory points, exotic wood butt with scrimshawed ivory ovals, ivory ringwork at A,B,C, and D.

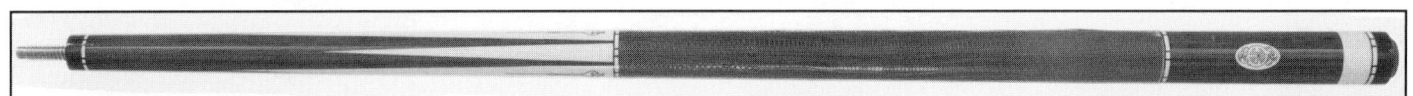

MSR (1998) $3,000	$8,000	$6,500	$4,500

Level 4 "The Dove" - Exotic wood forearm, three two-piece long points with inlay work in the center alternating with three short exotic wood points with veneers, exotic wood butt with ivory dove inlays between exotic wood windows with veneers.

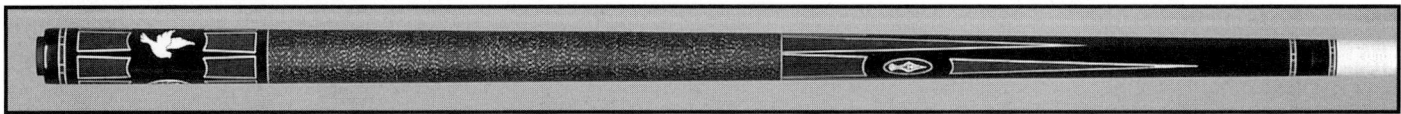

MSR (1990) $2,300	$9,500	$7,750	$5,500

Level 5 - Ebony forearm, three three-piece long ivory floating points with ivory inlay work in the center alternating with three short exotic wood points with veneers and ivory inlay work, ebony butt with ivory inlays alternating with ivory-bordered exotic wood windows between ivory windows with veneers alternating with exotic wood windows with veneers.

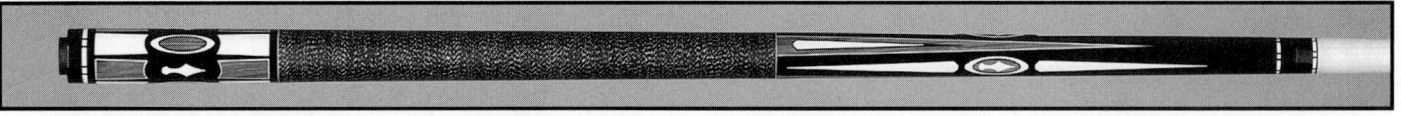

MSR (1998) $4,000	$10,000	$8,200	$6,000

Level 5 "Ivory Handle" - Bird's-eye maple forearm, three two-piece long scrimshawed ivory points with veneers and scrimshawed ivory inlay work in the center alternating with three short scrimshawed ivory points with veneers, three-piece ivory handle, bird's-eye maple butt with scrimshawed ivory inlays between ivory windows with veneers.

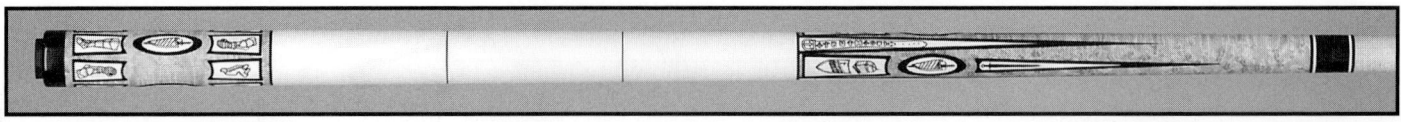

MSR (1998) $10,000	$25,000	$21,000	$15,000

GRADING	98%	90%	70%

SECONDARY MARKET MINIMUM VALUES

The following are minimum prices for other South West cues encountered on the secondary market. These prices are representative of cues utilizing basic materials and designs that may not be currently available. South West also offers one-of-a-kind cues that can command many times these prices due to the use of exotic materials and artistry.

Special construction note: There are many materials and construction techniques that can add value to South West cues. The following are the most important examples:

- Add $10,000+ for ivory handle (only a handful were made by Jerry Franklin).
- Add $2,000+ for ivory points.
- Add 20%+ for level 2 or 3 Jerry Franklin-era cues.
- Add 40%+ for level 4 or higher Jerry Franklin-era cues.

For all used South West cues:

- Add $200 for each additional original straight playable shaft beyond two.
- Deduct $275 for each missing original straight playable shaft.
- Add $250+ for extra rings above and below wrap.
- Add $200+ for original leather wrap (virtually all are black).
- Add $100+ for each ivory ferrule.
- Add $85+ each for original matching joint protectors.
- Add $65+ for extra ring in base.
- Deduct 25% for obvious or improper refinish.

Level 2 - 0 points, 0-25 inlays.
Level 2 cues start at	$1,500	$1,195	$800

Level 3 - 2-6 points, 0-8 inlays.
Level 3 cues start at	$2,000	$1,745	$1,400

Level 4 - 4-10 points, 9-25 inlays.
Level 4 cues start at	$3,000	$2,500	$1,800

Level 5 - 0-12 points, 26-50 inlays.
Level 5 cues start at	$5,000	$4,150	$3,000

Level 6 - 0-12 points, 51-75 inlays.
Level 6 cues start at	$7,500	$6,450	$5,000

SOWDER CUSTOM CUES

Maker of pool cues from 1996 to present in Vancouver, Washington

Gregory Sowder

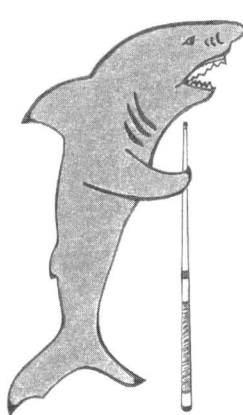

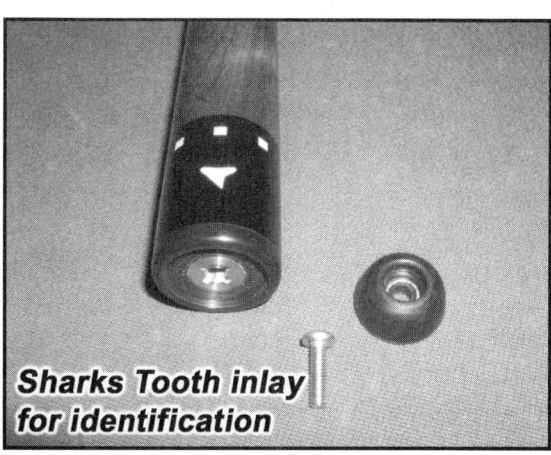
Sharks Tooth inlay for identification

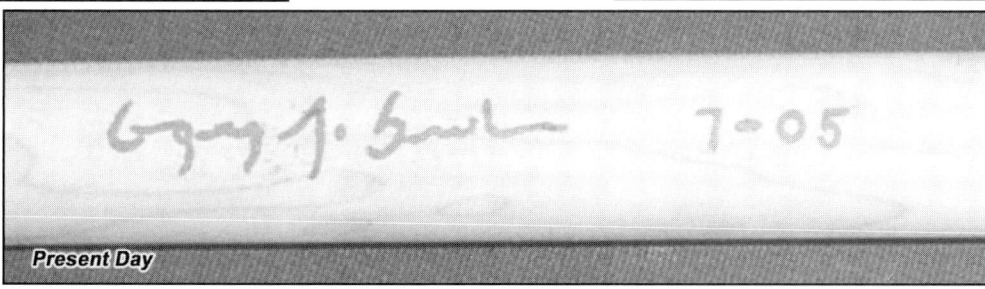
Present Day

Gregory Sowder began doing cue repairs in 1992. This business naturally evolved into cue building. He builds only one-of-a-kind custom cues made to customer specifications in his home-based shop. As a pool player for a number of years, he understands the importance of

GRADING	100%	95%	70%

building cues that feel balanced and solid. Sowder cues have 1/8 in. rings on all shafts and extra long "short splice" points. Matching joint protectors are included on every new cue. Gregory uses 3/8-10 bronze, titanium, or stainless steel joint pins.

Sowder cues are easily identifiable by the shark's tooth that is inlaid in every cue. Gregory's signature and the date the cue was finished is under the wrap and will show up if the cue is x-rayed with the shark's tooth facing up.

If you are interested in talking to Gregory Sowder about a new cue or cue that needs to be repaired, you can contact him at Sowder Cues, listed in the Trademark Index.

SPECIFICATIONS
Butt material: hardwoods
Shaft material: rock maple
Annual production: fewer than 20 cues

REPAIRS
Refinish with Irish linen wrap: $100+
Rewrap with Irish linen: $40
Rewrap with leather: $100
Replace shaft: $100+
Replace tip: $10

CURRENT SOWDER CUES
Basic two-piece Sowder cues with wraps and joint rings start at $650.

CURRENT EXAMPLES
The following Sowder cues can be ordered as shown, modified to suit the desires of the customer, or new designs can be created.

Level 2 - Bird's-eye maple forearm with an ivory dash ring above handle, cocobolo handle, bird's-eye maple butt sleeve with ivory dash rings at top and bottom.

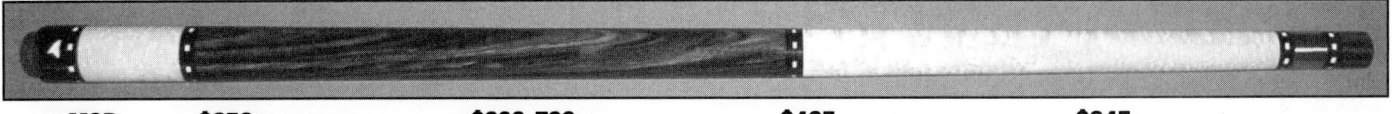

MSR	$650	$600-700	$485	$345

Level 3 - Ivory joint, striped maple forearm, four rosewood points, rosewood butt sleeve.

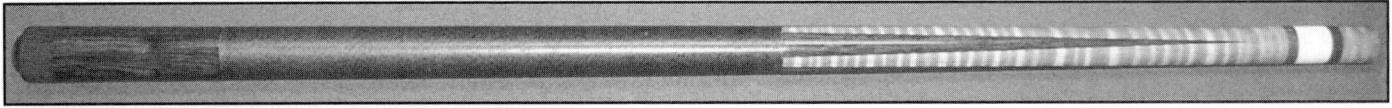

MSR	$750	$700-800	$565	$385

Level 3 - Purpleheart forearm with an ivory dash ring above wrap, four ebony points, leather wrap, purpleheart butt sleeve with four reverse ebony points between ivory dash rings at top and bottom.

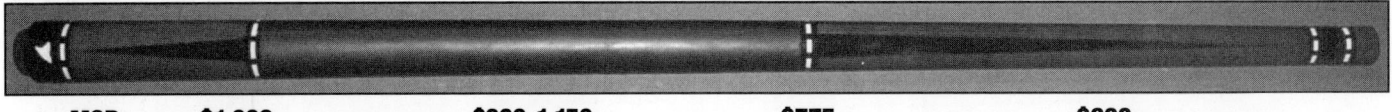

MSR	$1,000	$900-1,150	$775	$600

Level 4 - Ivory joint, ebony forearm with double silver rings above wrap, four figured maple points alternating with four ivory dots, leather wrap, ebony butt sleeve with rings of maple and ivory and ivory dots alternating with silver rings from top to bottom.

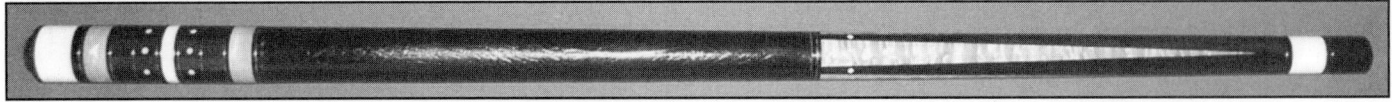

MSR	$1,400	$1,350-1,500	$1,100	$800

Level 4 - Ivory joint, stained figured maple forearm with ebony and ivory blocks set in silver rings above wrap, four ebony points with an ivory diamond-shaped inlay in each, leather wrap, ebony butt sleeve with four large ivory diamond-shaped inlays alternating with four mother-of-pearl notched diamond-shaped inlays between ebony and ivory blocks set in silver rings at top and ebony and ivory blocks set in silver rings below.

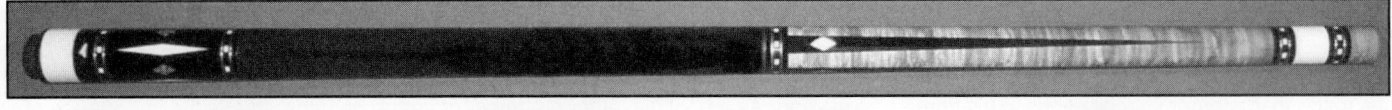

MSR	$1,500	$1,400-1,650	$1,150	$850

GRADING	100%	95%	70%

Level 5 - Ivory joint, olivewood forearm with olivewood and kingwood rings above wrap, four kingwood points with an ivory dot-shaped inlay in each alternating with four short reverse kingwood points with an ivory dot-shaped inlay at the tip of each, leather wrap, olivewood butt sleeve with a ring of ivory dot-shaped inlays set in kingwood between a kingwood ring at top and a kingwood ring below with a rosewood and ivory stitch ring set in silver rings at bottom.

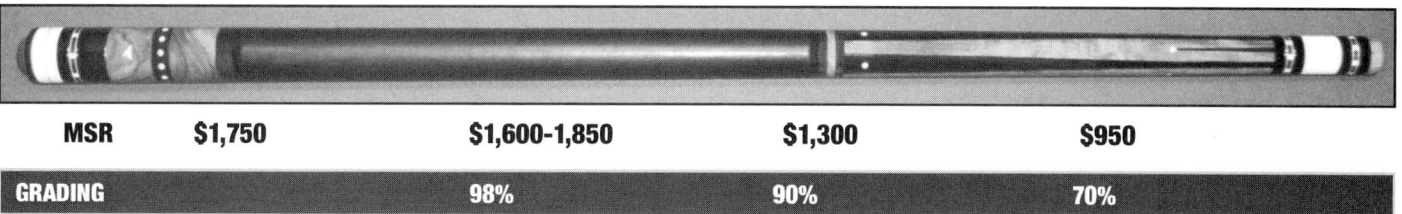

MSR	$1,750	$1,600-1,850	$1,300	$950
GRADING		98%	90%	70%

SECONDARY MARKET MINIMUM VALUES

The following are minimum values for other Sowder cues encountered on the secondary market. These prices are representative of cues utilizing basic materials and designs that are not necessarily available at present. Gregory has offered one-of-a-kind cues that can command many times these prices due to the use of exotic materials and artistry.

Special construction note: There are many materials and construction techniques that can add value to Sowder cues.

For all used Sowder cues, except where otherwise noted:
- Add $75 for each additional original straight playable shaft beyond one.
- Deduct $100 for missing original straight playable shaft.
- Add $45 each for ivory ferrules.
- Add $65 for leather wrap.
- Deduct 20% for obvious or improper refinish.

Level 2 - 0 points, 0-25 inlays.
Level 2 cues start at	$550	$410	$245

Level 3 - 2-6 points, 0-8 inlays.
Level 3 cues start at	$650	$515	$345

Level 4 - 4-10 points, 9-25 inlays.
Level 4 cues start at	$800	$630	$435

Level 5 - 0-12 points, 26-50 inlays.
Level 5 cues start at	$1,100	$875	$600

BURTON SPAIN

Maker of pool cues from 1965 to 1994 in Chicago, Illinois.

Burton Spain

Burton Spain was a Chicago native who enjoyed pool and billiard games. In 1964, at the age of 24, he began playing at Howard-Paulina Billiards in the city. It was there that he met and became friends with Craig Petersen, who was making cues at the age of 18. At Craig's shop, early in 1965, Burton saw a Titlist forearm that was split down the middle, and became fascinated in the construction of the splice. He could see how it was made, and convinced himself that he too could splice woods. Burton started going to a public woodworking shop at a Chicago park every evening, and, before long, he made his first four-point spliced blank. He kept turning it down, trying to make it perfect. When he was done, he had a blank that was thinner than a shaft, and only thirteen inches long. But he knew he could master blank making.

On June 1, 1965, he rented a storefront in Chicago and set out to make cues. Very soon, he was making blanks for his cues that were superior to what was available from Brunswick. At this time, some custom cuemakers did not make their own spliced blanks. They purchased them from Brunswick. When "Tex" Fitzgerald and "Whitey" Stovall, of Ace Cue Service in Chicago, saw that Burton was making his own high-quality blanks, they wanted to buy them. Burton had intended to use them only in his own cues, so he did not know what to say. Soon afterwards, Tex went down to the Jansco Jamboree tournament in Johnson City where he told some cuemakers about what Burton was doing. Soon there was demand for Spain spliced blanks. As a result, Burton began selling blanks to some of the top cuemakers of the time, including Frank Paradise, Gordon Hart, Craig Petersen, and George Balabushka.

In June of 1970, Burton had the opportunity to buy and restore some gray stone row houses in one of the better neighborhoods in Chicago. He sold his equipment to John Davis, a tool and die maker who had been helping him for a few years. John moved the business to a building that he owned on Division Street in Chicago. In 1974, Burton returned as a partner, and bought the business and building a couple of years later. Burton kept his shop at this location until the end of his career.

Burton had experimented with several joint designs for his own cues over the years, and in 1977, he found one with which he adopted for good. Although cues made before 1977 may feature a variety of joints, Burton Spain cues made after this time have a unique joint with the screw in the shaft.

In the late 1970s, Burton called Craig Petersen, who had been living in California for several years, and convinced him to come back to Chicago to help him. Craig worked off and on for Burton for the next several years. Through the late 1970s to mid-1980s, Burton continued to make blanks for other cuemakers, along with making cues of his own. In 1987, Burton stopped all cue work, except for servicing cues that he had already made, and went to school to learn computer programming. Burton finished school in 1988, and although he quickly discovered that he did not like computer programming, he was unable to return to serious cue work until 1991.

When he finally returned to cuemaking, he set out to make full-spliced blanks that were to his satisfaction. Although his early blanks featured a full splice, they were not long enough to continue all the way into the butt sleeve. This was because the ebony in the points and lower piece of the blank was too heavy and too expensive. Burton solved this problem in 1992 with an ingenious full-spliced blank featuring ebony points that were spliced onto maple for the handle area. For blanks with points lighter than ebony, the lower splice simply continued to the butt sleeve. Burton Spain was truly a gifted cuemaker, in fact he has been called a cuemaker's cuemaker in the industry. Burton was inducted into the ACA Cuemakers Hall of Fame in 1993 and into the International Cuemakers Association Hall of Fame in 2005. Building cues, however, was not Burton's only gift. Burton had a very high IQ and was a member of Mensa and the ISPE (International Society of Philosophical Enquiry). To be a member of ISPE your IQ must must into the top 1% of the population. In 1982 during a mid-month meeting of Mensa, Burton gave a speech titled "Everything You Never Wanted To Know About Billiard Cues And Were Afraid I'd Tell You" The following is the text of that speech:

When I was a teenager, one of my haunts was Sheridan Recreation, a bowling alley and pool hall in the heart of Uptown – sleazy, down-and-out Uptown. Back in 1920 or so, when the building was new, it had been called Leffingwell's and it had been large and rather grand. In the late 1950s, it was still large, but time had eroded much of the grandeur. To give you an idea: the billiard rooms were on the third floor and entered by a staircase that came from the street to offices on the second floor, then on to the billiards on the third. In that rough and ready neighborhood it was impossible to leave that downstairs door open after the offices had closed and so, in the evening and on the week-end, the pool and billiard players went through the bowling alley and up an inside staircase to the third floor, and from there through the only room that connected the landing with the billiard rooms. That connecting room was one of the foulest smelling men's toilets in God's creation – and it gave you a pretty good idea of what you were getting into.

At least it gave you an idea of what the poolroom was like, but beyond that was a separate room where three-cushion billiards was played. Played by old-timers – men who had been boys when Willie Hoppe, Jake Schaefer and Welker Cochran were boys, men who had learned the game when this had been Leffingwell's and the grandeur had been intact. Now the game had been in long decline, and there were few such as myself just learning the game new. But I didn't mind.

I was charmed by those old-timers, Runyonesque as they were. Steeped in a lifetime of billiard room etiquette with their ritual phrases, worn and polished banter, sly witticisms – I thought them grand.

My special heroes were the men who played best – performed the sleight-of-hand that makes ivory billiard balls do magic. As the royalty of this ancient kingdom, they had special privileges. They could swagger; they could speak small sarcasms; they could carry their own private two-piece cues. Cues with style and elegance; four-prong inlaid cues; cues with mother-of-pearl designs and cues with ivory butt plates. Cues engraved with the owner's name, and cues bearing the name of some prior owner, some Johnny Layton or Otto Reisalt, legendary names they were. Cues made of ebony and Brazilian rosewood by the great Herman Rambow. Cues in tooled leather cases with small brass nameplates. Magic instruments no less than those created by Stradivarius and Guarnerius long ago in Cremona.

Years passed from that first introduction to billiards, and I presumed to own a cue or two of my own in that time. But mine were new-bought and meager. The cues that had fired my imagination had been made in the glory days of billiards. They had been made at a time when the Brunswick-Balke-Collender Co. could boast that their consumption of maple for cues was so great that it would deplete the open market, and for that reason, they had bought their own forest. Now quoting from their 1923 catalog: "Following this purchase, we erected a saw-mill and lumber camp, consisting of a little city, including dwelling-houses, general store, boarding house, a hotel for superintendents, repair shops, standard railroad locomotives, freight cars for logging many miles of railroad track, steam derrick and innumerable incidentals, such as horses, oxen, log-truck and steam launch." Now those were times – times when the making of billiard cues got the respect it deserved.

Well, in 1965 my father gave me some money to get started. I rented a store, bought some equipment and began to teach myself what I needed to know. It was hard going for a long time, but everything is good now although I still own neither forest nor oxen, either one.

Burton Spain Died in 1994 at the age of 54 from complications of cancer. Before Burt passed, he sold his cuemaking business to Chicago area cuemaker Joel Hercek. Along with the sale of the equipment, Burton stayed on as long as he could to train Joel in all aspects of cuemaking. Burton Spain truly was a cuemaker's cuemaker.

If you have a Burton Spain cue or a cue with a Burton Spain blank that needs repair or further identification, contact Hercek Fine Billiard Cues, listed in the Trademark Index.

SPECIFICATIONS

Butt material: hardwoods
Shaft material: rock maple
Standard length: 58 in.
Lengths encountered: 56 to 64 in.
Standard finish: lacquer-conversion varnish
Joint screws: 5/16-18 or 5/16-14
Standard joint: Delrin
Joint type: flat faced
Point construction: full splice or short splice
Standard wrap: Irish linen
Standard butt cap: Delrin
Standard number of shafts: one
Standard taper: short pro
Standard ferrules: Cyro
Standard tip: Le Pro
Total production: approximately 800 to 900 cues

BURTON SPAIN, cont. 751

| GRADING | 98% | 90% | 70% |

OPTIONS ENCOUNTERED (FOR NEW CUES ONLY)
Leather wrap
Stainless steel joint

BURTON SPAIN CUES

The following cues are representations of the work of Burton Spain. These cues can be encountered as shown, modified to suit the desires of the original customer, or entirely different designs can be encountered. Burton specialized in one-of-a-kind cues.

Level 2 #21 - Bird's-eye maple forearm, bird's-eye maple butt sleeve, possibly with ringwork.

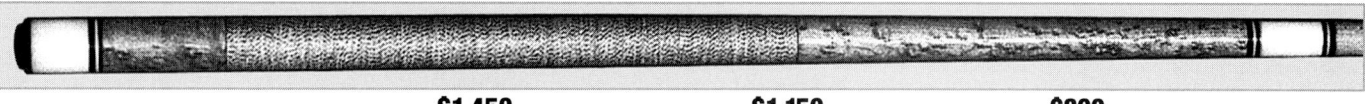

| | $1,450 | $1,150 | $800 |

Level 2 Solid rosewood nose with rosewood backend. White Delrin joint with brass trim rings bordered by black linen. Double brass rings below the wrap with black linen spacers. White Delrin butt cap, linen wrap.

| MSR (1970s) $150 | $1,700 | $1,550 | $1,175 |

Level 2 - Bird's-eye maple nose with bird's-eye maple backend. White Delrin joint with black white black trim. 12 ebony dots with three micarta dots bordered in black inlaid below the wrap. White Delrin butt cap, black linen wrap.

| MSR (1970s) $225 | $2,000 | $1,800 | $1,400 |

Level 3 #24 - Bird's-eye maple forearm, four ebony points with veneers, ebony butt sleeve, possibly with ringwork.

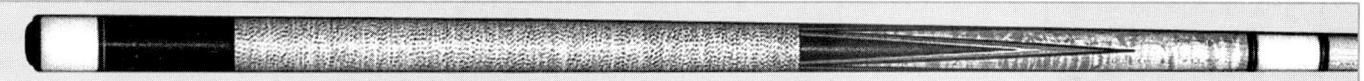

| | $2,200 | $1,900 | $1,550 |

Level 3 - Bird's-eye nose with two padauk butterfly points (one of only four). Three dots of micarta between each butterfly. White Delrin joint with black trim. Cue signed BT Spain 30/92. Padauk backend. White Delrin butt cap, Linen wrap.

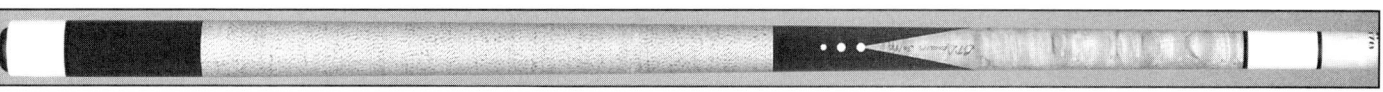

| MSR (1992) $600 | $2,500 | $2,250 | $1,800 |

Level 3 Bird's-eye nose with four ebony points and colored veneers. Full-splice Delrin joint with stainless sleeve. White, blue, red trim at joint and backend. Ebony backend with white Delrin butt cap, linen wrap.

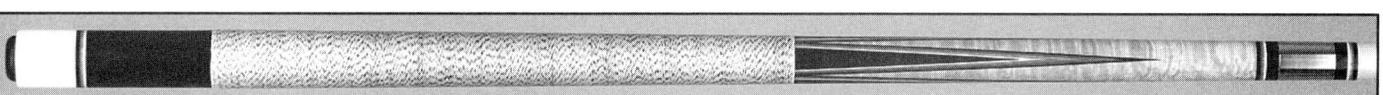

| MSR (1980s) $400 | $3,000 | $2,800 | $1,700 |

Level 4 #32 - Bird's-eye maple forearm, three long and three short ebony points with four colored veneers and possibly inlays, ebony butt sleeve with checked rings and inlays.

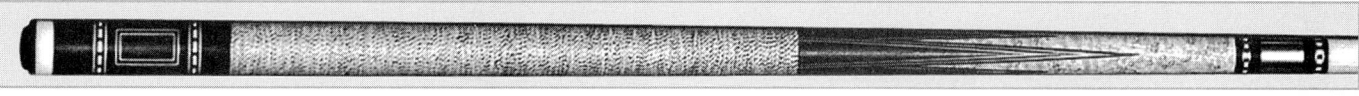

| | $3,150 | $2,850 | $1,800 |

Level 5 - Bird's-eye nose with four ebony points and colored veneers. Full-splice Delrin joint with stainless sleeve. Micarta dot trim at joint and below the wrap. "Moon Cue" short black Delrin butt cap, linen wrap.

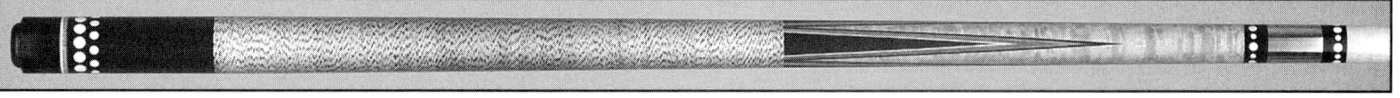

| MSR (1993) $700 | $3,500 | $3,250 | $1,900 |

GRADING	98%	90%	70%

Level 5 #34 - Bird's-eye maple forearm, three long and three short ebony points with four colored veneers and dot and diamond-shaped inlays, ebony butt sleeve with dot and diamond-shaped inlays alternating with veneered windows between checked rings.

	$4,500	$3,650	$2,500

Level 8 - Bird's-eye nose with four ebony points and colored veneers. Full-splice Delrin joint with stainless sleeve. Micarta dot trim at joint. Ebony backend with Argyle micarta dot pattern. "Argyle Cue" small black Delrin butt cap, linen wrap.

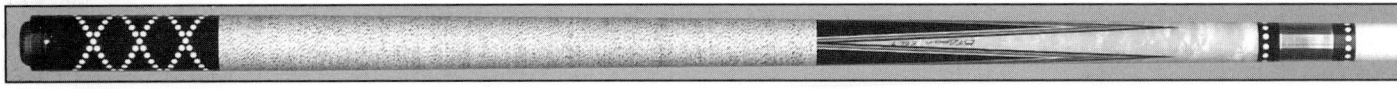

MSR (1993) $900	$8,000	$7,250	$4,500

Level 6 - Bird's-eye nose with four ebony points and colored vinyl veneers. Full-splice Delrin joint with green and yellow trim. 10 ebony dots inlaid at in the nose of the cue with four micarta dots in triangle pattern in each point. Micarta dot pattern below wrap with linen butt cap. Linen wrap with finish applied.

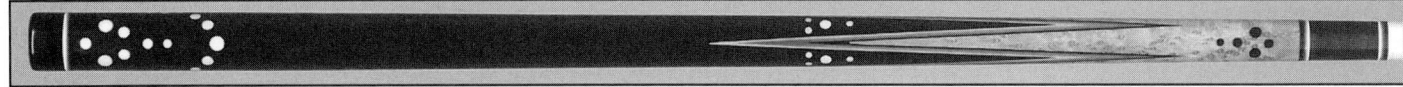

MSR (1980s) $400	$6,000	$5,550	$3,200

Level 7 - Bird's-eye nose with six ebony points and colored veneers. Delrin joint with stainless sleeve. Micarta block trim at joint. Veneer bars inlaid below wrap between micarta block trim. Small black Delrin butt cap, linen wrap.

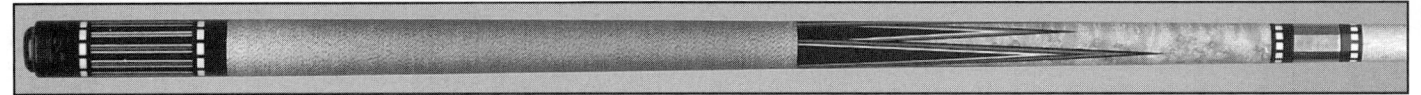

MSR (1970s-80s) $500	$6,500	$6,000	$3,500

Level 7 - Bird's-eye nose with six ebony points and colored veneers. Delrin joint with micarta block trim with brass ring borders. Ivory/micarta diamonds inlaid in each long point with three ivory/micarta dots inlaid in each short point. Four ivory/micarta diamonds with veneered rectangle below wrap with four sets of ivory/micarta dots between patterns. Inlays are bordered with micarta block trim with brass rings and red vinyl. " Model 34" short black Delrin butt cap, linen wrap.

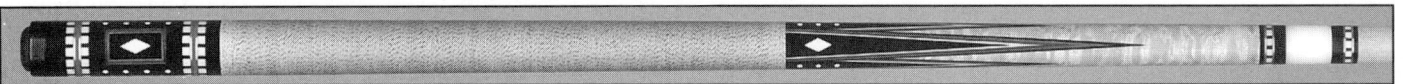

MSR (1970s-80s) $550	$7,500	$6,900	$4,100

Level 5 - Bird's-eye nose with six ebony points and colored veneers on longer points. Delrin joint with brass and white trim. Ivory/micarta diamond inlaid in each long point with three dots of ivory/micarta inlaid in each short point. Four diamond A-Ray pattern inlaid below the wrap set in veneered rectangles. Brass and white trim borders patterns. Short Delrin butt cap, linen wrap.

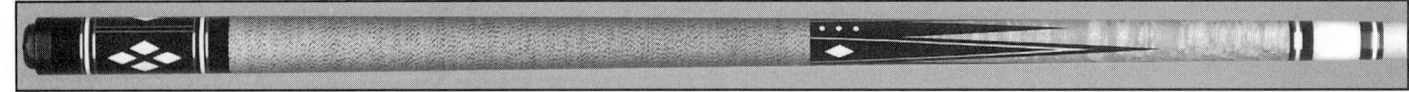

MSR (1970s-80s) $600	$6,000	$5,500	$3,200

Level 5 - Bird's-eye nose with four ebony points and colored veneers. Full splice Delrin joint with stainless sleeve. Orange trim at the joint and below the wrap. Cue signed "BT Spain EOL 6" (end of line number six). This was the last cue made by Burton Spain. Ebony back ends with white Delrin butt cap. Cork wrap.

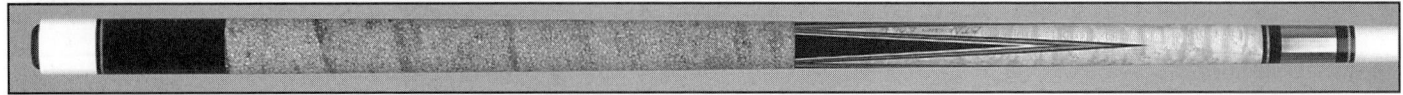

MSR (1993) $600	$11,000	$10,000	$6,200

SECONDARY MARKET MINIMUM VALUES

The following are minimum prices for other Burton Spain cues encountered on the secondary market. These prices are representative of cues utilizing the most basic materials and designs that were available. Burton specialized in one-of-a-kind cues that can command many times these prices due to the use of exotic materials and artistry. Early variations are becoming very collectible, and can also command many times these prices. Burton Spain cues will be further covered in future editions.

GRADING	98%	90%	70%

Note: Due to the rarity of Burton Spain cues and increasing interest, prices are on the rise. Fewer original examples are surfacing, and collectors are holding on to the ones they have. Unique examples with pedigree are bringing the highest prices. Special construction note: There are many materials and construction techniques that can add value to Burton Spain cues. For all used Burton Spain cues, except where otherwise noted:

- Add $850+ for signed, full-spliced cues (1992-1993).
- Add $300+ for each additional original straight playable shaft (standard with one).
- Deduct $300 for missing original straight playable shaft.
- Add $300+ for original leather wrap.
- Deduct up to 40% for obvious or improper refinish.
- Add $1000+ for nickel-silver piloted joint with pin in butt.
- Add $500+ for a floating joint.
- Add $100+ for each original ivory ferrule.
- Add $500+ for use of vinyl veneers.

Level 2 - 0 points, 0-25 inlays.

	98%	90%	70%
Level 2 cues start at	$1,500	$1,350	$1,050

Level 3 - 2-6 points, 0-8 inlays.

Level 3 cues start at	$3,000	$2,700	$2,100

Level 4 - 4-10 points, 9-25 inlays.

Level 4 cues start at	$3,550	$3,150	$2,450

Level 5 - 0-12 points, 26-50 inlays.

Level 5 cues start at	$4,500	$4,050	$3,150

Level 6 - 0-12 points, 51-75 inlays.

Level 6 cues start at	$5,500	$4,950	$3,850

Level 7 - 0-12 points, 76-125 inlays.

Level 7 cues start at	$6,500	$5,850	$4,550

Level 8 - 0-12 points, 126+ inlays.

Level 8 cues start at	$8,000	$7,200	$5,600

SPIDER WEB CUES

Maker of pool cues from 1990 in Seattle, Washington and Hardy, Arkansas.

Billy Webb became interested in cuemaking in Houston in the early 1980s. He had purchased several of Richard Black's cues and had visited his shop on several occasions. He experiment with one of the cues and was able to see, first hand, the "full-splice" construction. What began as a hobby is now a full-time occupation. Webb relocated to Seattle, Washington in the late 1980s but currently lives in Hardy, Arkansas.

Billy's first cues were short spliced forearms for other cuemakers. Billy prefers to make six-point mitered veneered cues. He has been influenced and inspired by such cuemakers as Roger Pettit, Ted Harris, Jerry McWorter, Mike Bender, Ron Haley, Jerry Franklin, and Andy Gilbert.

Spider Web cues can be identified by the "Spider Web" logo on butts and "Webb" on joint screws. Billy does not make two-piece bar cues. He usually builds six-pointed cues with veneers or butterflies.

If you are interested in talking to Billy Webb about a new cue or cue that needs to be repaired, you can contact him at Spider Web Cues, listed in the Trademark Index.

Present Day

SPECIFICATIONS

Butt material: hardwoods
Shaft material: hard rock maple
Standard length: 58.5 in.
Lengths available: up to 60 in.
Standard finish: Dupont clearcoat
Balance point: 18 in. from butt
Standard butt cap: phenolic
Standard wrap: Irish linen
Point construction: short splice
Standard joint: linen based
Joint type: flat faced
Joint screw thread: 3/8-10

| GRADING | 98% | 90% | 70% |

Joint protectors: standard
Standard number of shafts: two
Standard taper: pro
Standard ferrules: linen based
Standard tip: Le Pro
Standard tip width: 12.75 mm
Annual production: 45 to 65 cues

OPTIONS (FOR NEW CUES ONLY)

Ivory butt cap: $200
Ivory joint: $100
Ivory ferrule: $70
Extra shaft: $125

SPIDER WEB CUES

The current delivery time for a Spider Web cue is about six months.

SECONDARY MARKET MINIMUM VALUES

The following are minimum values for other Spider Web cues encountered on the secondary market. These prices are representative of cues utilizing basic materials and designs that are not necessarily available at present. Billy has offered one-of-a-kind cues that can command many times these prices due to the use of exotic materials and artistry.

Special construction note: There are many materials and construction techniques that can add value to Spider Web cues.

For all used Spider Web cues, except where otherwise noted:

Add $90 for each additional original straight playable shaft beyond two.
Deduct $125 for each missing original straight playable shaft under two.
Add $55 each for ivory ferrules.
Deduct 20% for obvious or improper refinish.

	98%	90%	70%
Level 2 - 0 points, 0-25 inlays.			
Level 2 cues start at	$300	$240	$170
Level 3 - 2-6 points, 0-8 inlays.			
Level 3 cues start at	$450	$350	$235
Level 4 - 4-10 points, 9-25 inlays.			
Level 4 cues start at	$550	$475	$285
Level 5 - 0-12 points, 26-50 inlays.			
Level 5 cues start at	$800	$615	$420

M. STACEY CUES

Maker of pool cues from 1992 to 1993 in Muncie, Indiana, from 1993 to 1998 in Fort Wayne, Indiana, and from 1998 to present in Noblesville, Indiana.

Mike Stacey started his cuemaking business in Muncie, Indiana, while majoring in criminal justice in college. It started as a repair business at age 19 at Indiana tournaments, using some of the skills he learned in his high school wood shop class. Mike loved playing in pool tournaments since high school and enjoyed working with his hands. He also worked at a pool hall while in college. When friends saw Mike working on his own cues, they opted to bring him theirs to work on as well. Jobs became more complex, and finally it evolved into a part-time cuemaking business. Mike still works full time as a restaurant manager.

Mike Stacey

Present Day

Mike is self-taught, and he strives to make the best cue that he can. He also tries to improve upon his cues every time. Mike's shop is in his two-and-a-half-car garage, attached to his house. It is very convenient for him to work anytime. He has several lathes for both metal and wood, band saws, table saw, drill press, mill, spray booth, and a CNC for inlays only. He makes his own short-spliced blanks, and prefers cues with six or eight points. His four-point cues have more traditional designs, usually with stainless 5/16-14 piloted joints. He prefers cues that are forward balanced. Mike does all of the work in his one-man shop except when Mike's wife, Kelley, signs and dates all of his cues, as Mike doesn't like his handwriting. His goal is to make a good hitting cue at a good price.

Mike is also known for his repair work. His specialty is repairing damaged or broken cues. He gets a lot of referrals from other cuemakers to repair cues that require a lot of work. He enjoys getting a cue that is in pieces and being able to make it playable again.

M. STACEY CUES, cont. **755**

GRADING	98%	90%	70%

M. Stacey cues are guaranteed for life against all manufacturer's defects and warpage. If you are interested in talking to Mike Stacey about a new cue or cue that needs to be repaired, you can contact him at M. Stacey Cues, listed in the Trademark Index.

SPECIFICATIONS

Butt material: hardwoods
Shaft material: rock maple
Standard length: 58 in.
Lengths available: any up to 60 in.
Standard finish: acrylic urethane
Standard butt cap: linen phenolic
Standard wrap: Irish linen
Point construction: short splice
Standard joint: linen phenolic
Joint type: flat faced
Joint screw: 3/8-11
Standard number of shafts: one
Standard taper: 12 in. straight
Standard ferrules: melamine
Standard tip: Hercules
Annual production: fewer than 60 cues

OPTIONS (FOR NEW CUES ONLY)

Special length: no charge
Ivory ferrule: $75
Ivory joint: $75+
Extra shaft: $125

REPAIRS

Repairs done on all fine cues.
Refinish (with Irish linen wrap): $125
Rewrap (Irish linen): $35
Replace shaft: $125+
Replace melamine ferrule: $25

CURRENT M. STACEY CUES

Two-piece M. Stacey bar cues start at $285. Basic M. Stacey cues with wraps and joint rings start at $475. M. Stacey cues with points start at $600. One-of-a-kind custom M. Stacey cues start at $800. The current delivery time is about four months.

SECONDARY MARKET MINIMUM VALUES

The following are minimum values for other M. Stacey cues encountered on the secondary market. These prices are representative of cues utilizing basic materials and designs that are not necessarily available at present. Mike has offered one-of-a-kind cues that can command many times these prices due to the use of exotic materials and artistry.

Special construction note: There are many materials and construction techniques that can add value to M. Stacey cues.

For all used M. Stacey cues, except where otherwise noted:
Add $100 for each additional original straight playable shaft beyond one.
Deduct $125 for missing original straight playable shaft.
Add $60 each for ivory ferrules.
Deduct 20% for obvious or improper refinish.

Level 1 - Hustler.
	98%	90%	70%
Level 1 cues start at	$225	$175	$115

Level 2 - 0 points, 0-25 inlays.
Level 2 cues start at	$350	$275	$185

Level 3 - 2-6 points, 0-8 inlays.
Level 3 cues start at	$500	$385	$265

Level 4 - 4-10 points, 9-25 inlays.
Level 4 cues start at	$600	$570	$325

Level 5 - 0-12 points, 26-50 inlays.
Level 5 cues start at	$900	$725	$500

Level 6 - 0-12 points, 51-75 inlays.
Level 6 cues start at	$1,200	$965	$675

STADUM

GRADING	98%	90%	70%

Maker of cues for Samsara. For information, refer to the listing for Samsara.

JULIO STAMBOULINI CUES

Line of pool cues made by Adam in the 1980s, with a new line distributed by Competition Sports from 1998 until 2001.

The Julio Stamboulini line of pool cues was introduced by Adam in the 1980s. There were 12 cues in the first series, which have since been discontinued. A new series of six cues was introduced in 1998.

If you have a Julio Stamboulini cue that needs repair, contact Competition Sports, listed in the Trademark Index.

SPECIFICATIONS

Butt material: hardwoods
Shaft material: rock maple
Standard length: 58 in.
Standard wrap: Irish linen
Point construction: short splice or full splice
Joint type: flat faced
Standard number of shafts: one
Standard tip: Le Pro

DISCONTINUED EXAMPLES

The following line of Julio Stamboulini cues was available from Adam Custom Cues from 1998 until the line was discontinued in 2001. The following Julio Stamboulini cues came with one shaft; extra shafts were $75.00 each.

For all used Julio Stamboulini cues:

Add $75 for each additional original straight playable shaft beyond one.
Deduct $100 for missing original straight playable shaft.
Deduct 25% for obvious or improper refinish.

Level 2 JS-1 - Bocote forearm, bocote butt sleeve with a row of blue checks set in black rings at top and bottom.

| MSR (2001) $100 | $90 | $70 | $40 |

Level 2 JS-2 - Bocote forearm, bocote butt sleeve with four white notched diamond-shaped inlays between a row of blue checks set in black rings at top and bottom.

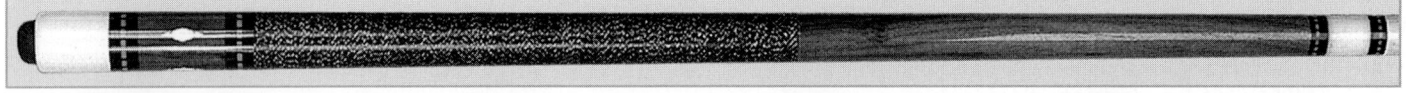

| MSR (2001) $145 | $125 | $95 | $60 |

Level 2 JS-3 - Purpleheart forearm, purpleheart butt sleeve with four white notched diamond-shaped inlays set in white-bordered purpleheart windows alternating with white and purpleheart-bordered white ovals between a row of blue checks set in black rings at top and bottom.

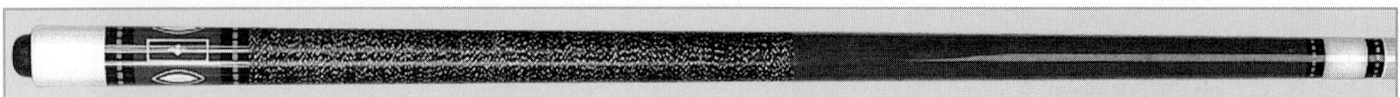

| MSR (2001) $220 | $200 | $150 | $90 |

Level 4 JS-4 - Stained maple forearm, four ebony points with two colored veneers, ebony butt sleeve with four white X-shaped inlays surrounded by pearlized plastic dots between a row of blue checks set in black rings at top and bottom.

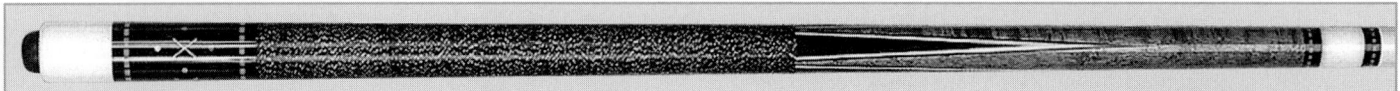

| MSR (2001) $240 | $225 | $175 | $105 |

JULIO STAMBOULINI CUES, cont.

GRADING	98%	90%	70%

Level 3 JS-5 - Stained maple forearm, four ebony points with two colored veneers and a pearlized plastic notched diamond-shaped inlay in each, ebony butt sleeve with four pearlized plastic notched diamond-shaped inlays between a row of blue checks set in black rings at top and bottom.

MSR (2001) $260 $235 $185 $110

Level 4 JS-6 - Stained maple forearm, four floating ebony points with two colored veneers and a pearlized plastic notched diamond-shaped inlay in each, ebony butt sleeve with four pearlized plastic and ebony-bordered pearlized plastic windows between a row of blue checks set in black rings at top and bottom.

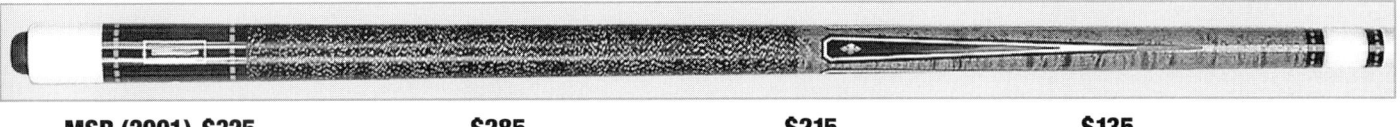

MSR (2001) $325 $285 $215 $135

JULIO STAMBOULINI CUES – 1980S

The following cues were from the first line of Julio Stambolini cues. They had 3/8-10 flat faced joints, linen fiber ferrules, and Delrin butt caps.

Level 2 Julio-1 - One-piece ebony butt with a row of white plastic checks at bottom.

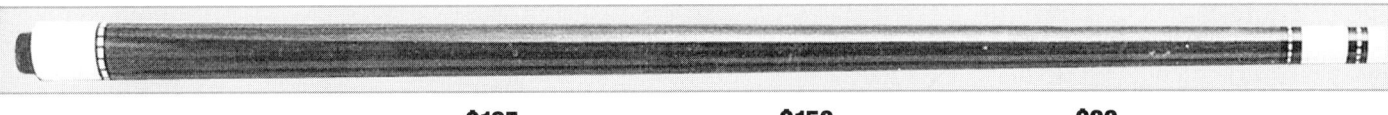

$195 $150 $90

Level 2 Julio-2 - Padauk forearm, padauk butt sleeve with a row of white plastic checks at bottom.

$210 $165 $100

Level 2 Julio-3 - Rosewood forearm, ebony butt sleeve with a row of white plastic checks at bottom.

$210 $165 $100

Level 2 Julio-4 - Stained maple forearm, stained maple butt sleeve with a row of white plastic checks at bottom.

$210 $165 $100

Level 3 Julio-5 - Maple forearm, four full-spliced padauk points with four colored veneers, padauk butt sleeve with a row of white plastic checks at bottom.

$400 $300 $190

Level 3 Julio-6 - Smoke-stained maple forearm, four ebony points with four colored veneers, ebony butt sleeve with a row of white plastic checks at bottom.

$265 $200 $125

JULIO STAMBOULINI CUES, cont.

GRADING	98%	90%	70%

Level 3 Julio-7 - Stained maple forearm with pearlized plastic floral-shaped inlays set in an ebony ring above wrap, stained maple butt sleeve with pearlized plastic floral-shaped inlays set in an ebony ring above center.

	$340	$255	$160

Level 3 Julio-8 - Rosewood forearm, four ebony points with two colored veneers, rosewood butt sleeve with figure-eight pattern in two colored veneers.

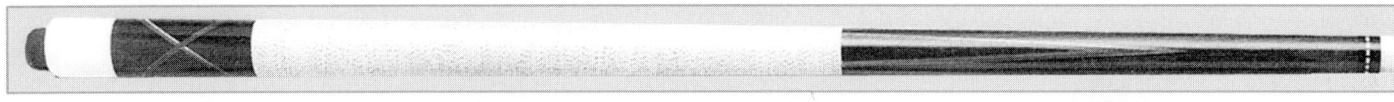

	$450	$345	$210

Level 5 Julio-9 - Smoke-stained maple forearm, four padauk points with an intricately inlaid ebony oval in each point set in an ebony ring, padouk butt sleeve with intricately inlaid ebony ovals set in an ebony ring in center.

	$420	$320	$200

Level 3 Julio-10 - Stained maple forearm, four ebony butterfly points with four colored veneers, rosewood butt sleeve with a pair of figure-eight patterns in two colored veneers.

	$485	$375	$230

Level 4 Julio-11 - Smoke-stained maple forearm, four ebony points with four colored veneers and a pearlized plastic notched diamond-shaped inlay in each, rosewood butt sleeve with four pearlized plastic notched diamond-shaped inlays set in two colored veneer-bordered windows between a row of white plastic checks at top and bottom.

	$460	$350	$220

Level 4 Julio-12 - Stained maple forearm, four floating ebony points with a pearlized plastic dot and notched diamond-shaped inlay in each, stained maple butt sleeve with four pearlized plastic notched diamond-shaped inlays set in ebony ovals with ebony half ovals above and below between a row of white plastic checks at top and bottom.

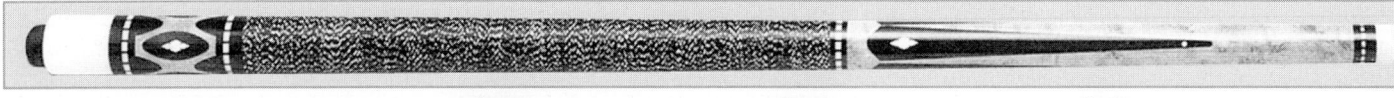

	$695	$520	$330

STAR CITY CUES

Maker of pool cues from 1992 to present in Roanoke, Virginia.

Al "Link" Beckelhimer started playing pool at age 16. He now plays in a league and competes in local tournaments. As an adult, he went through many different cues. He was always interested in cues so he decided to start repairing them on a part-time basis. After a year doing many different types of repairs, he had repaired every major cue component so he decided to make cue sticks as a hobby. The hobby later became a business.

Star City Cues is a one-man shop at Al's home, and all work is done by him. Al spends many hours perfecting each cue, completing them with a hand-rubbed finish. Star City Cues feature traditional designs that stress playability. All cues are one-of-a-kind. They are easily identifiable by the small ivory star in the butt sleeve or butt cap.

Star City cues are guaranteed against construction defects that are not the result of warpage or abuse. If you have a Star City cue that needs further identification or repair, or would like to talk to Al about ordering a new cue, contact Star City Cues, listed in the Trademark Index.

Al Beckelhimer

SPECIFICATIONS

Butt material: hardwoods

STAR CITY CUES, cont.

GRADING	98%	90%	70%

Shaft material: rock maple
Standard length: 58 in.
Lengths available: 57 to 60 in.
Standard finish: polyurethane
Balance point: 1 in. above wrap
Standard butt cap: linen phenolic
Standard wrap: Irish linen
Point construction: short splice
Standard joint: linen phenolic
Joint type: flat faced
Joint screw: 3/8-10
Standard number of shafts: one
Standard taper: 12 in. pro
Standard ferrules: LB melamine
Tip widths available: 12 ½ to 14 mm
Standard tip: Triangle
Annual production: fewer than 30 cues

CURRENT STAR CITY CUES

Two-piece Star City bar cues start at $325. Basic Star City cues with wraps and joint rings start at $550. Star City cues with points start at $675. One-of-a-kind custom Star City cues start at $1,200 The current delivery time for a Star City cue is six to twelve months, depending on the intricacy of the cue.

PAST EXAMPLES

The following cues are past works from Star City Cues. They can be encountered as shown, or modified to suit the design and specifications of the original customer. The following Star City cues come with one shaft with a linen phenolic ferrule.

Level 3 #1 - Stained bird's-eye maple forearm with an ebony ring at bottom, six bloodwood points with ebony veneers, bloodwood butt sleeve with nickel silver rings set in ebony at top and bottom.

MSR (1999) $450	$525	$395	$230

Level 2 #2 - Kingwood forearm with ebony and ivory checks within nickel silver rings towards bottom, kingwood butt sleeve with ebony and ivory checks within nickel silver rings towards top and bottom.

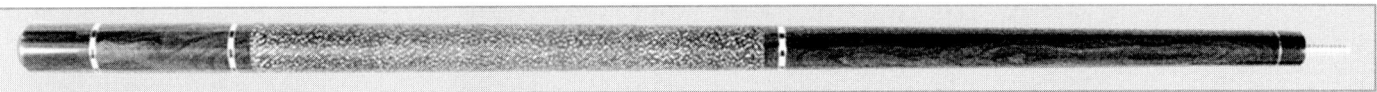

MSR (1999) $500	$595	$465	$315

Level 3 #3 - Stained bird's-eye maple forearm with ebony and ivory checks within gold colored rings at bottom, five ebony points with three colored veneers, ebony butt sleeve with ebony and ivory checks set in gold colored rings towards top and an ebony ring set in gold colored rings at bottom.

MSR (1999) $550	$650	$515	$345

Level 3 #4 - Stained bird's-eye maple forearm, four long and four short ebony points with three colored veneers, ebony butt sleeve with four ivory diamond-shaped inlays between ebony and ivory checks within red veneer rings above and below.

MSR (1999) $750	$875	$675	$450

Level 4 #5 - Stained curly maple forearm, four long ebony points with two colored veneers and an ivory spear-shaped inlay in each point alternating with four short ebony points with two colored veneers and an ivory diamond-shaped inlay in each point, ebony butt sleeve with four ivory spear-shaped inlays alternating with four ivory diamond-shaped inlays above ebony and ivory checks within ivory rings at bottom.

MSR (1999) $900	$1,050	$825	$550

| GRADING | 98% | 90% | 70% |

SECONDARY MARKET MINIMUM VALUES

The following are minimum values for other Star City cues encountered on the secondary market. These prices are representative of cues utilizing basic materials and designs that are not necessarily available at present. Al has offered one-of-a-kind Star City cues that can command many times these prices due to the use of exotic materials and artistry.

Special construction note: There are many materials and construction techniques that can add value to Star City cues.

For all used Star City cues, except where otherwise noted:
- Add $70 for each additional original straight playable shaft beyond one.
- Deduct $85 for missing original straight playable shaft.
- Add $55 each for ivory ferrules.
- Add $75 for leather wrap.
- Deduct 20% for obvious or improper refinish.

Level 2 - 0 points, 0-25 inlays.

	98%	90%	70%
Level 2 cues start at	$400	$315	$215

Level 3 - 2-6 points, 0-8 inlays.

Level 3 cues start at	$465	$365	$245

Level 4 - 4-10 points, 9-25 inlays.

Level 4 cues start at	$750	$575	$390

Level 5 - 0-12 points, 26-50 inlays.

Level 5 cues start at	$1,100	$875	$595

STAR CUE COMPANY

Maker of pool cues from 1973 to present in Miami, Florida.

Abe Rich has a deep heritage in the craft of cuemaking that recalls a time when a wood-turner's shop had little more than a simple lathe and an extensive selection of tools. He is the third master cuemaker from a family whose tradition spans nearly one hundred years.

Abe credits his uncle Isadore Rutzisky ("The Professor") as his greatest teaching influence. Rutzisky, a Lithuanian immigrant who arrived in 1911, was a talented wood-turner. Abe learned his trade as an apprentice in his uncle's company,

Abe Rich

Shop in South Beach, Miami

The New York Billiard Table Company, founded in 1912 and located on the Bowery. Though no tables were made there, the company supplied the brisk demand for "custom" two-piece cues. Abe recalled one of the company's big breaks when it sold a special three-piece cue to Fred Astaire. An excellent player himself, Mr. Astaire wanted a cue that could be stowed inside his suitcase. A special cue was made and the publicity that followed drew many successful and famous people. Celebrities like Sammy Davis Jr., Tony Curtis, Jack Lemmon and Milton Berle patronized the shop.

While the New York Billiard Table Company made some of the best two-piece cues for that time, it was also well known for turning ivory billiard balls. Speaking about his uncle's mastery of the art, Abe would say admiringly, "My Uncle was the best." Samuel Blatt, a successful cuemaker and respected expert at making ivory billiard balls, learned the trade from Isadore Rutzisky. Blatt's family business still thrives today in New York City.

As an adult, Abe Rich worked for the Rich Cue Company with his cousin Saul. Saul Rich's business had an established reputation for making quality cues and Abe eventually took what he learned there to Florida, where, in 1965, he and his brother Morris made cues under the name "Florida Cues." Abe worked with his brother for about eight years before moving into his own shop in March of 1973. Abe chose the name "Star Cue Mfg." instead of using his own name to prevent any confusion with his cousin Saul's company.

Star Cues are still made today by Abe Rich, in a time honored "old-fashioned" way, by hand, in his one-man shop. Abe's shop is small, 20 ft. by 100 ft., but the available space is utilized with a degree of thought and care that allows for separation of the various areas required for making quality cues. Abe has an 8 ft. wide, 12 ft. high stack of wood and materials in the center of the room. The wood has aged there for more than 25 years and when asked about it, Abe will say simply, "You have to make sure the wood is dry." Ferrules are threaded on.

Abe no longer makes cues with points, favoring cues that are designed simply, with an emphasis on playability and exact player specifications. Abe also has a cue area where he keeps finished cues that are ready for customer selection. He still works in the shop six days a week, but his cuemaking has slowed down. Additionally, he offers a variety of other cues, cases and equipment. He loves to make customers happy.

Star cues can be identified by the Abe Rich signature on each and have been made with a variety of different joints, including wood screws. Each was constructed with great pride and displays a care and attention to detail that can only come from a true craftsman.

GRADING	98%	90%	70%

Abraham Rich has been described as a man of deep convictions and extraordinary insight, yet like a cue with masterful construction and simple design, he chooses to remain humble and down-to-earth. In this way, Abe's character lives in his work; his business card echoes this tradition: "Star Cue Mfg…Manufacturer of two-piece custom cues…Hand made by A. Rich."

If you have a Star cue that needs identification or repair, or you would like to talk to Abe Rich about the design of a new Star cue, contact Star Cue Company, listed in the Trademark Index.

SPECIFICATIONS

- Butt material: hardwoods
- Shaft material: rock maple
- Standard length: 58 in.
- Lengths available: any
- Standard finish: lacquer
- Joint screw: 5/16-14
- Standard joint: stainless steel
- Joint type: piloted
- Point construction: short splice
- Standard wrap: Irish linen
- Standard ferrules: Ivorine-3
- Standard number of shafts: one
- Standard taper: 10 in. pro
- Standard ferrules: fiber

OPTIONS (FOR NEW CUES ONLY)

Option prices are given on an individual basis.

REPAIRS

Repairs done on all fine cues, repair prices are given on an individual basis..

CURRENT STAR CUES

Two-piece Star bar cues start at $150. The current delivery time for a Star depends on the intricacy of the cue.

SECONDARY MARKET MINIMUM VALUES

The following are minimum prices for Star cues encountered on the secondary market. These prices are representative of cues utilizing basic materials and designs that may not be currently available. Abe also offers one-of-a-kind cues that can command many times these prices due to the use of exotic materials and artistry.

Special construction note: There are many materials and construction techniques that can add value to Star cues.

For all used Star cues:
- Add $85+ for each additional original straight playable shaft beyond one.
- Deduct $100 for missing original straight playable shaft.
- Deduct 30% for obvious or improper refinish.

Level 2 - 0 points, 0-25 inlays.

Level 2 cues start at	$350	$275	$185

Level 3 - 2-6 points, 0-8 inlays.

Level 3 cues start at	$650	$525	$345

STEALTH CUES

Maker of pool cues from 1992 in Cary, Illinois, currently in Arizona.

Stealth Cues makes maple cues with custom graphics in a variety of designs and sizes. In 2001 they introduced the patented "Dooley" handle, which is an alternating diameter handle that get its name from off road courses. Stealth cues are easily identifiable by the Stealth logo on the butt caps.

If you have a Stealth cue that needs further identification or repair, or would like to talk to someone about ordering a new Stealth cue, contact Stealth Cues, listed in the Trademark Index.

SPECIFICATIONS

- Butt material: maple
- Shaft material: rock maple
- Standard length: 58 in.
- Lengths available: 48 to 90 in.
- Standard wrap: Irish linen
- Standard joint: stainless steel
- Standard number of shafts: one

GRADING	100%	95%	70%

CURRENT STEALTH CUES

The 2005 Lineup from Stealth cues features several models with Dooley handles priced at $159.95, Stealth Crypt cues consist of four models priced from $88 to $159,95, the Childrens series consists of several models priced from $48 to $69, as well as Specialty cues priced from $100 to $115. Most Stealth cues are available for immediate delivery.

CURRENT EXAMPLES

The following examples of models within Stealth lines are available in several different models with different colors, woods, and graphics.

Level 2 "2005 Lineup" - Hardwood forearm with applied graphics, Dooley handle, hardwood butt sleeve with applied graphics.

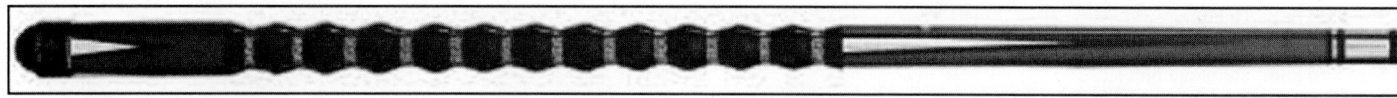

MSR	$159.95	$100-159.95	$90	$75

Level 2 "Children's Series" - Hardwood forearm with applied graphics, Irish linen wrap, hardwood butt sleeve with applied graphics. Available in 48 in. or 52 in. lengths.

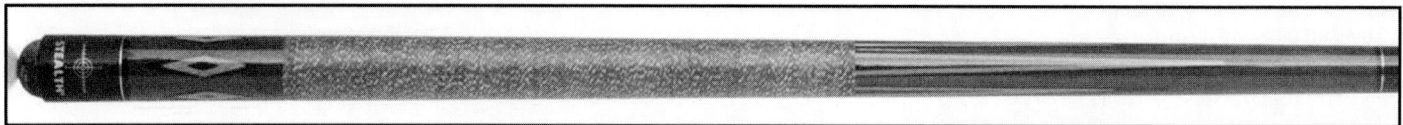

MSR	$48	$35-48	$30	$20

Level 2 "Dooley Handle Children's Series" - Hardwood forearm with applied graphics, Dooley handle, hardwood butt sleeve with applied graphics. Available in 48 in. or 52 in. lengths.

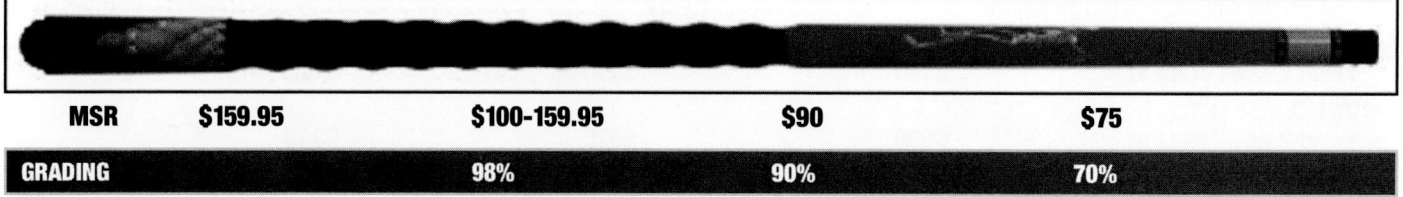

MSR	$69	$50-69	$40	$30

Level 2 "Crypt Cue" - Hardwood forearm with applied horror graphics, hardwood butt sleeve with applied horror graphics.

MSR	$88	$65-88	$55	$40

Level 2 "Dooley Handle Crypt Cue" - Hardwood forearm with applied horror graphics, Dooley handle, hardwood butt sleeve with applied horror graphics.

MSR	$159.95	$100-159.95	$90	$75

GRADING	98%	90%	70%

SECONDARY MARKET MINIMUM VALUES

The following are minimum values for other Stealth cues encountered on the secondary market. These prices are representative of Stealth cues utilizing basic materials and designs that are not necessarily available at present. Stealth Cues has offered unique cues that can command higher prices due to artistry.

Special construction note: There are materials and designs that can add value to Stealth cues.

For all used cues, except where otherwise noted:
- Add $15+ for each additional original straight playable shaft beyond one.
- Deduct $25+ for missing original straight playable shaft.
- Add 60% for 58 in. length.
- Add 30% for "Dooley" handle.
- Deduct 10% for obvious or improper refinish.

Level 2 - 0 points, 0-25 inlays.

Level 2 cues start at	$35	$25	$15

Level 3 - 2-6 points, 0-8 inlays.

Level 3 cues start at	$55	$45	$25

GRADING	98%	90%	70%

FRANK STELLMAN

Maker of Sailor Cues. For information, refer to the listing for Sailor.

BILL STELZENMULLER

Maker of One on One Cue Sticks. For information, refer to the listing for One on One.

STONIER'S CUSTOM CUES

Maker of pool cues from the early 1970s to 2001 in Sacramento, California.

As a kid, Terry Stonier learned to play three-cushion billiards at his next-door neighbor's house. He continued to play the game, and became one of the better billiard players in the Sacramento area. Terry worked at his father's restaurant, and dreamed of opening his own restaurant someday. In 1967, he opened Jointed Cue Billiards, a 19-table pool room famous for its cheeseburgers.

Terry continued to play pool, but was dissatisfied with the cues he was using. So, in the early 1970s, he started making his own. Since then, Stonier's cues have gone through constant improvements for the sake of playability, which is the most important factor. Stonier's cues are identifiable by their unique joint screw, which Terry custom made to his specifications. They are marked "Stonier's Cues, Sacramento" under the wrap for positive identification.

Terry was making less than 100 cues per year with the help of his son, Dave, who also did the repairs. They promoted tournaments in their pool room where they also sold commercial cues and tables. Then Terry Stonier died in 2001. Dave continues to do repair work but has not yet started making cues. He hopes to start making Stonier's Custom cues again in the next few years.

Stonier's cues were guaranteed indefinitely against construction defects that are not the result of warpage or abuse. Dave will still honor this guarantee. If you have a Stonier cue that needs further identification or repair, contact Stonier's Custom Cues, listed in the Trademark Index.

SPECIFICATIONS

Butt material: hardwoods
Shaft material: rock maple
Standard length: 58 in.
Lengths available: 58 to 59 in.
Joint screw: custom
Standard joint: stainless steel
Joint type: flat faced
Point construction: short splice
Standard wrap: Irish linen
Standard number of shafts: one
Standard ferrules: linen phenolic
Standard tip: Le Pro
Total production: approximately 500 cues

SECONDARY MARKET MINIMUM VALUES

The following are minimum prices for Stonier's cues encountered on the secondary market. These prices are representative of cues utilizing basic materials and designs that may not be currently available. Terry also offers one-of-a-kind cues that can command many times these prices due to the use of exotic materials and artistry.

Special construction note: There are many materials and construction techniques that can add value to Stonier's cues.

For all used Stonier's cues, except where otherwise noted:
Add $75+ for each additional original straight playable shaft (standard with one).
Deduct $100 for missing original straight playable shaft.
Deduct 25% for obvious or improper refinish.

Level 1 - 4 points, hustler.

Level 1 cues start at	$100	$75	$45

Level 2 - 0 points, 0-25 inlays.

Level 2 cues start at	$350	$265	$160

Level 3 - 2-6 points, 0-8 inlays.

Level 3 cues start at	$500	$375	$240

Level 4 - 4-10 points, 9-25 inlays.

Level 4 cues start at	$650	$515	$355

Level 5 - 0-12 points, 26-50 inlays.

Level 5 cues start at	$950	$725	$465

| GRADING | 98% | 90% | 70% |

OLIVER STOPS ORIGINAL

Maker of pool cues starting in 1995 in Germany. Distributed in the United States from Alpharetta, Georgia from 1995 to 1997.

Oliver Stops was a hobby chemist who enjoyed playing pool in the "Bundesliga" (German National Pool League). He and his partner had more than twenty years of combined cuemaking experience in Germany, when they set out to invent a new cue material in 1993. After a couple of years of experimentation in Oliver's garage, the result was "Wingopas," a synthetic that was forty times harder to scratch than wood. Oliver also developed his own materials for his ferrules and tip pads, and a unique joint, with a very deep long pilot, and a recessed screw. Basic model cues were available, as well as more intricate limited editions that were introduced regularly. They were easily identifiable by the "OS" logo that appears on the butt caps.

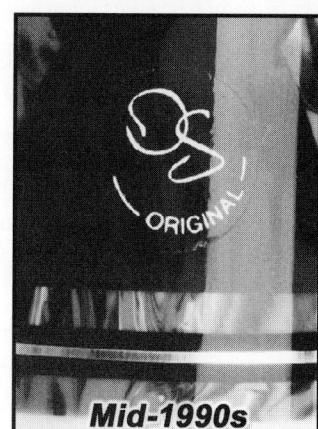
Mid-1990s

SPECIFICATIONS

No examples were made available for publication in this edition.

Butt material: Wingopas
Shaft material: rock maple
Standard length: 59 1/2 in.
Lengths available: any
Joint type: piloted
Balance point: 19 in. from butt
Standard wrap: Irish linen
Standard number of shafts: two
Standard taper: modified pro
Std. Ferrules: epoxy resin or nylon texture
Standard tip: Le Pro or Triangle

SECONDARY MARKET MINIMUM VALUES

The following are minimum values for Oliver Stops Original Cues encountered on the secondary market. These prices are representative of cues utilizing basic materials and designs that were available. Oliver Stops offered one-of-a-kind cues that can command many times these prices due to the use of exotic materials and artistry.

Special construction note: There are many materials and construction techniques that can add value to Oliver Stops cues.

For all used Oliver Stops cues, except where otherwise noted:

Add $125 for each additional original straight playable shaft beyond two.
Deduct $200 for each missing original straight playable shaft under two.
Deduct 30% for obvious or improper refinish.

Level 2 - 0 points, 0-25 inlays.
| Level 2 cues start at | $600 | $450 | $285 |

Level 3 - 2-6 points, 0-8 inlays.
| Level 3 cues start at | $850 | $650 | $400 |

Level 4 - 4-10 points, 9-25 inlays.
| Level 4 cues start at | $1,050 | $800 | $500 |

STOUT STICKS

Maker of pool cues from 1988 to present in Asheboro, North Carolina.

If you have a Stout Sticks cue that needs further identification or repair, or would like to talk to someone about ordering a new Stout cue, contact Stout Cue Manufacturing, listed in the Trademark Index.

Present Day

SPECIFICATIONS

Butt material: hardwoods
Shaft material: rock maple
Standard length: 58 in.
Balance point: 2 1/4 in. above wrap
Standard wrap: Irish linen
Point construction: short splice
Standard number of shafts: two
Standard taper: 11 1/4 straight
Annual production: approximately 100 cues

GRADING	98%	90%	70%

SECONDARY MARKET MINIMUM VALUES

The following are minimum values for other Stout cues encountered on the secondary market. These prices are representative of cues utilizing basic materials and designs that are not necessarily available at present. Stout has offered one-of-a-kind cues that can command many times these prices due to the use of exotic materials and artistry.

Special construction note: There are many materials and construction techniques that can add value to Stout cues.

For all used Stout cues, except where otherwise noted:
- Add $75 for each additional original straight playable shaft beyond one.
- Deduct $100 for missing original straight playable shaft.
- Add $50 each for ivory ferrules.
- Add $65 for leather wrap.
- Deduct 20% for obvious or improper refinish.

Level 2 - 0 points, 0-25 inlays.

	98%	90%	70%
Level 2 cues start at	$350	$270	$185

Level 3 - 2-6 points, 0-8 inlays.

Level 3 cues start at	$500	$390	$270

Level 4 - 4-10 points, 9-25 inlays.

Level 4 cues start at	$600	$470	$320

Level 5 - 0-12 points, 26-50 inlays.

Level 5 cues start at	$950	$710	$440

STRADER CUSTOM CUES

Maker of pool cues from 1995 to present in Danville, Virginia.

David Strader

David Strader began playing pool at the age of 14 and quickly developed a love for the game and an appreciation of fine custom cues. He tried several times at a young age to make his own cue, but was unsuccessful. He didn't let this discourage him and he spent three or more years studying the techniques of past and present cuemakers. During that time, he was also designing and building the machinery he felt he needed to build cues. It was almost four years after deciding he wanted to become a cuemaker that David built his first cue. Time was of no concern. He was only interested in the quality of the work and building a reputation that would stand the test of time.

Strader is continuously improving his craft and techniques to make a cue that is not only beautiful but has excellent playability. He has been building custom cues ever since, and has developed a style that is uniquely his own. An engineer by trade, David has several patents pending for improvements on shaft construction and splicing techniques. His method of short and full splice construction is original, offers greater stability, and a look that cannot be achieved using traditional methods. Using these proprietary construction methods, he is able to create beautiful and functional works of art with the classic and complex styling of past cuemakers and classic cues, like the rare Brunswick model 360. This type of attention to detail is given to every cue he makes. All of David's cues are handmade from the finest materials. He welcomes inquiries on new custom cues and reproduction cues of rare classics that would normally be out of the reach of typical collectors.

Although he has full CNC capability, he prefers to build each cue by hand. He believes this adds to the beauty, character, and value of a cue. However, he does offer retro-fit conversion kits and full technical support to cuemakers who wish to take advantage of CNC technology. In addition, he also offers custom inlay patterns based upon the customer's requirements. Quotes and programming time are offered free of charge on inlay patterns. All of Strader's cues are easily identifiable by his signature and date of completion on the forearm and/or engraving on the butt.

Each Strader cue has a lifetime guarantee for the original owner against construction defects that are not the result of warpage or abuse. They also have a money-back guarantee of satisfaction (the cue must be returned in new condition). If you have a Strader cue that needs further identification or repair, or would like to order a new Strader cue, contact Strader Custom Cues, listed in the Trademark Index.

SPECIFICATIONS

Butt material: hardwoods
Shaft material: rock maple
Standard length: 58 in.
Lengths available: any
Standard finish: proprietary
Balance point: custom
Standard butt cap: linen phenolic
Standard wrap: Irish linen
Point construction: short splice, full splice, or inlaid
Standard joint: stainless steel
Joint type: flat faced

GRADING	98%	90%	70%

Joint screw: 5/16-14
Standard number of shafts: one
Standard taper: custom
Standard ferrules: melamine
Tip widths available: any
Standard tip: Triangle
Annual production: fewer than 30 cues

OPTIONS (FOR NEW CUES ONLY)

Options are priced depending on the intricacy of the cue.

REPAIRS

Repairs done on most fine cues.
- Refinish: $50
- Rewrap (Irish linen): $35
- Rewrap (leather): $70
- Replace melamine ferrule: $20
- Replace shaft: $80
- Replace Triangle tip: $8

CURRENT STRADER CUES

Two-piece Strader bar cues start at $250. Basic Strader cues with wraps and joint rings start at $400. Strader cues with points start at $650. One-of-a-kind custom Strader cues start at $750. The current delivery time for a Strader custom cue is six to eighteen weeks depending on the intricacy of the cue.

SECONDARY MARKET MINIMUM VALUES

The following are minimum values for Strader cues encountered on the secondary market. These prices are representative of cues utilizing basic materials and designs that are not necessarily available at present. David Strader has offered one-of-a-kind cues that can command many times these prices due to the use of exotic materials and artistry.

Special construction note: There are many materials and construction techniques that can add value to Strader cues.

For all used Strader cues, except where otherwise noted:
- Add $65 for each additional original straight playable shaft beyond one.
- Deduct $80 for missing original straight playable shaft.
- Add $70 for leather wrap.
- Deduct 20% for obvious or improper refinish.

Level 1 - 4 points, hustler.

	98%	90%	70%
Level 1 cues start at	$225	$175	$115

Level 2 - 0 points, 0-25 inlays.

Level 2 cues start at	$350	$275	$190

Level 3 - 2-6 points, 0-8 inlays.

Level 3 cues start at	$600	$465	$315

Level 4 - 4-10 points, 9-25 inlays.

Level 4 cues start at	$700	$550	$375

Level 5 - 0-12 points, 26-50 inlays.

Level 5 cues start at	$1,000	$785	$545

BILL STROUD

Maker of Joss West cues, for more information see Joss West.

SWEETWATER CUES, USA

Maker of pool cues starting in 1998 in Olive Branch, Mississippi.

Jeff Bonner is an engineer who has played pool since he was a kid. He owned a manufacturing business that did precision metal turning to extremely close tolerances. He likes to build things as a hobby, such as the car he drag races. In 1998 he set up a modern high tech shop with CNC machines and eight lathes to make a line of pool cues. He designed a cue with weights that fit in the deep drilled butt caps and allow for adjusting the weight and balance.

Jeff called this company Sweetwater Cues, USA, and the cues have "Sweetwater Cues" on the bumpers of his hustler cues, and on the bumpers and butt caps of his other cues. Jeff manufactured a line of cues (no customs) and his shop was set up to produce 500 cues a week at full capacity.

SWEETWATER CUES, USA, cont.

| GRADING | 98% | 90% | 70% |

Sweetwater Cues are guaranteed for life against manufacturing defects that are not the result of warpage or abuse. If you have a Sweetwater cue that needs further identification or repair, or would like to order a new Sweetwater cue, contact Sweetwater Cues, USA, listed in the Trademark Index.

SPECIFICATIONS

Butt material: hardwoods
Shaft material: rock maple
Standard length: 58 in.
Lengths available: 58 or 60 in.
Standard finish: UV topcoat
Balance point: adjustable
Standard wrap: Irish linen
Point construction: full splice
Standard joint: Implex
Joint screw: 5/16-18 quick release
Joint type: piloted
Standard number of shafts: one
Standard tip width: 13 mm
Standard taper: pro
Standard ferrules: proprietary
Standard tip: Le Pro

REPAIRS

Repairs done on Sweetwater cues only, call for pricing.

PAST EXAMPLES

The following Sweetwater cues had an adjustable weight and balance point feature.

Level 1 "Sneaky Pete" - Maple forearm, rosewood points and butt sleeve.

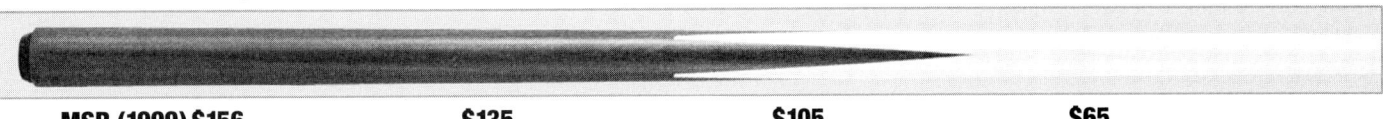

| MSR (1999) $156 | $135 | $105 | $65 |

Level 2 "Jump Break" - Stained maple forearm.

| MSR (1999) $220 | $185 | $145 | $90 |

Level 2 "R99 Rainbow" - Stained maple forearm.

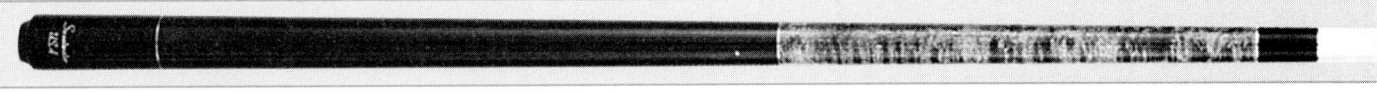

| MSR (1999) $220 | $185 | $145 | $90 |

Level 2 "Hustler" - Stained maple forearm, stained maple handle.

| MSR (1999) $198 | $170 | $130 | $80 |

Level 2 "Diamond with Stain" - Stained curly maple forearm with long ebony spear-shaped inlays above handle, stained maple handle.

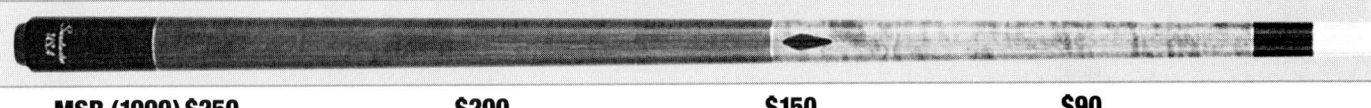

| MSR (1999) $250 | $200 | $150 | $90 |

Level 2 "Diamond with Wrap" - Stained curly maple forearm with long ebony spear-shaped inlays above wrap.

| MSR (1999) $270 | $215 | $165 | $100 |

GRADING	98%	90%	70%

Level 2 "C303 Indonesian Rosewood" - Stained curly maple forearm, Indonesian rosewood handle, stained curly maple butt sleeve.

MSR (1999) $320	$250	$190	$115

Level 2 "C302 Jatoba" - Stained curly maple forearm, jatoba handle, stained curly maple butt sleeve.

MSR (1999) $320	$250	$190	$115

Level 2 "C301 Cocobolo" - Stained curly maple forearm, cocobolo handle, stained curly maple butt sleeve.

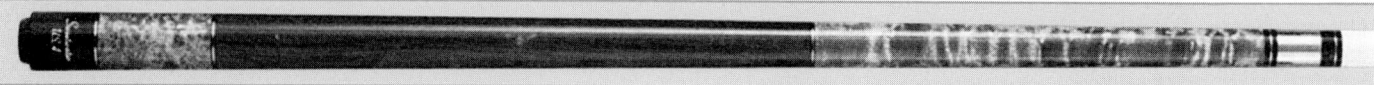

MSR (1999) $320	$250	$190	$115

Level 2 "C300 Ebony" - Stained curly maple forearm, ebony handle, stained curly maple butt sleeve.

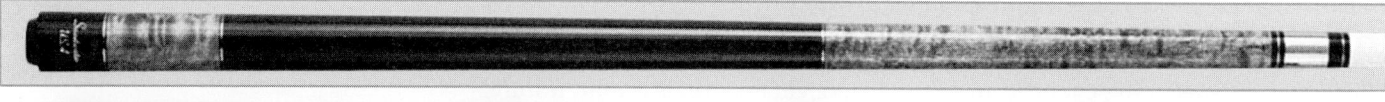

MSR (1999) $320	$250	$190	$115

SECONDARY MARKET MINIMUM VALUES

The following are minimum values for other Sweetwater cues encountered on the secondary market. These prices are representative of cues utilizing basic materials and designs that are not necessarily available at present.

Special construction note: There are many materials and construction techniques that can add value to sweetwater cues.
For all used sweetwater cues, except where otherwise noted:
Add $75 for each additional original straight playable shaft beyond one.
Deduct $125 for missing original straight playable shaft.
Deduct 25% for obvious or improper refinish.

Level 1 - 4 points, hustler.
Level 1 cues start at	$95	$75	$45

Level 2 - 0 points, 0-25 inlays.
Level 2 cues start at	$145	$110	$65

Level 3 - 2-6 points, 0-8 inlays.
Level 3 cues start at	$230	$175	$105

SYRA-CUES BY R.K.

Maker of pool cues from 1989 to present in Camillus, New York, a suburb of Syracuse.

Ron Kadey

Early Cues

Present Day

Ron Kadey grew up in a household with a father who was an excellent woodworker. When Ron was ten, his father built a small pool table for the family home. Ron and his brother soon taught themselves to play. Three years later, Ron's father built a full-sized table to replace the smaller one. Ron became much more serious about the game at this point. Soon he was playing in a league, and competing in local tournaments. But he realized that he did not quite have the talent to make it on the pro tour, so he started working in the insurance business, eventually becoming part owner of an agency in Liverpool, New York.

Ron continued to play pool, and was always intrigued with cues, so he decided to start repairing them on a part time basis in 1988. Using woodworking skills he learned from his father, Ron did more and more types of repair work. After one year, he had repaired every major cue component, so he decided to it was time to make one to see if it would sell.

Ron completed this first cue in October of 1989, and soon sold it for $250. The name "Syra-Cues" was chosen to tell what Ron does, and also, the area from where he works. He has continued to make cues ever since, working in the evenings and on the weekends at the small shop he built in his home. Syra-Cues cues are easily identifiable by the "RK" logo on the butt cap. Ron is proud that all of his work is done by hand, without the aid of CNC. In 1993, Ron started working with a jeweler, and can now inlay most custom designs in gold or silver.

Ron's cues are guaranteed indefinitely against construction defects that are not the result of warpage or abuse. If you have a Syra-Cues cue that needs further identification or repair, or would like to talk to Ron about ordering a new cue, contact Syra-Cues, listed in the Trademark Index.

SPECIFICATIONS

- Butt material: hardwoods
- Shaft material: rock maple
- Standard length: 58 in.
- Lengths available: 57 to 60 in.
- Standard finish: two-part urethane
- Joint screw: 5/16-14
- Standard joint: stainless steel
- Point construction: short splicc
- Balance point: 10 1/2 in. from joint
- Standard butt cap: alternate ivory
- Standard wrap: Irish linen
- Standard taper: 12 in. pro
- Standard number of shafts: one
- Standard tip: Chandivert
- Standard ferrules: Aegis
- Annual production: fewer than 25 cues

OPTIONS (FOR NEW CUES ONLY)

- Leather wrap: $50
- Ivory joint: $150
- Joint protectors: included for butt
- Ivory ferrules: $45 each
- Extra shaft: $100
- Extra shaft (with ivory ferrule): $145

REPAIRS

Repairs done on most fine cues.

- Refinish: $100
- Replace standard butt cap: $35
- Rewrap (leather): $70
- Rewrap (linen): $30
- Replace standard ferrule: $25
- Replace ivory ferrule: $70+
- Replace shaft: $100
- Retaper shaft: $20

CURRENT SYRA-CUES CUES

Basic two-piece Syra-Cues bar cues start at $190. Syra-Cues bar cues with jump/break joints start at $220. Basic Syra-Cues cues with wraps and joint rings start at $350. Syra-Cues cues with points start at $425. One-of-a-kind custom Syra-Cues cues start at $600. Syra-Cues cues over $600 come with two shafts.

SECONDARY MARKET MINIMUM VALUES

The following are minimum prices for Syra-Cues cues encountered on the secondary market. These prices are representative of cues utilizing basic materials and designs that may not be currently available. Ron also offers one-of-a-kind cues that can command many times these prices due to the use of exotic materials and artistry.

Special construction note: There are many materials and construction techniques that can add value to Syra-Cues cues.

For all used Syra-Cues cues:

- Add $85+ for each additional original straight playable shaft beyond one.
- Deduct $100 for each missing original straight playable shaft.

GRADING	98%	90%	70%

Add $135+ for ivory joint.
Add $50+ for leather wrap.
Add $40+ for each ivory ferrule.
Deduct 25% for obvious or improper refinish.

	98%	90%	70%
Level 1 - Hustler.			
Level 1 cues start at	$175	$135	$90
Level 2 - 0 points, 0-25 inlays.			
Level 2 cues start at	$325	$250	$170
Level 3 - 2-6 points, 0-8 inlays.			
Level 3 cues start at	$400	$315	$215
Level 4 - 4-10 points, 9-25 inlays.			
Level 4 cues start at	$625	$515	$375
Level 5 - 0-12 points, 26-50 inlays.			
Level 5 cues start at	$1,150	$895	$600
Level 6 - 0-12 points, 51-75 inlays.			
Level 6 cues start at	$1,750	$1,385	$950

SZAMBOTI CUES

Maker of pool cues from 1989 to present currently in Feasterville, Pennsylvania.

Barry Szamboti

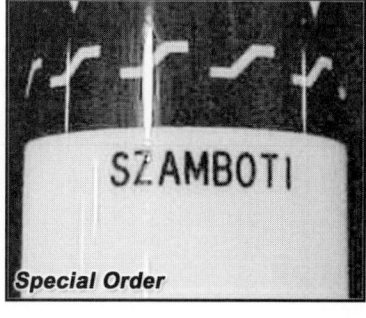
Special Order

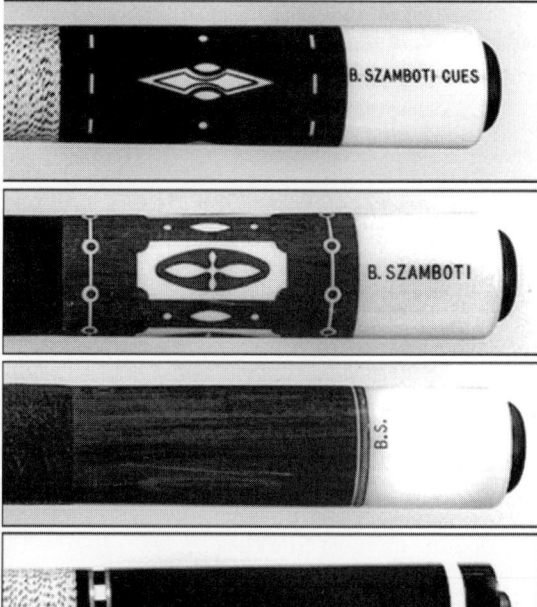
Markings that may appear

Barry Szamboti grew up in the household of his father, Gus Szamboti, one of the greatest cuemakers that ever lived. As a teenager Barry started helping out in the shop. At first, it was basic tasks, like sweeping the floor, cutting wood, and gluing veneers. As the years passed and the backlog of orders increased, Barry was able to help with more and more aspects of creating Szamboti cues. Ultimately, although he had never completed a cue, he had experience in making every single component of one. After the untimely death of his father from heart disease in 1988, he did not officially start selling cues until he felt they were worthy of the Szamboti name. This was in the spring of 1989, when the first three cues were finished in April. Quite a bit of his early work involved refinishing and restoring cues his father had made. Working with these cues made him even more familiar with what makes a great cue. The first cues Barry made were all marked "BS" on the butt cap. Soon, he was not marking his cues, unless the customer requested it. In 2001 he started marking high end cues with "SZAMBOTI."

The cues that are not marked are identifiable by the style and craftsmanship typical of all Szamboti cues. Like his father, Barry is very proud that his cues are made by hand, without the help of CNC machines.

Barry's cues reflect the tradition of his father's work, but incorporate subtle design differences so that they won't be mistaken. For instance, Barry will alter the number of stitches in rings from what his father used. As with cues made by his father, the shafts on a Barry Szamboti cue are of utmost importance in the construction of a cue. Barry discards more shaft wood than most cuemakers today. Over time he continues to become more critical and more selective of materials in order to make even better cues. His shafts always weigh a minimum of four ounces, and usually have 1 1/16 in. ivory ferrules. Most of Barry's cues have bird's-eye maple forearms, with four, six, or eight points of ebony or rosewood. He is sure to use only the finest materials available. Stainless steel joints are most common, but ivory joints are available, as are ivory butt caps.

Propellers, bar bells, and spears are common inlay themes, in the tradition of Gus Szamboti cues. Barry has taken these designs a step further, as well as creating new ones. He feels driven to continue, and add to, the designs of Szamboti cues, as he knows his father would be doing if he was still working today. Recently Barry started using gold and silver in his cues. Barry rarely makes simple cues, because so many of his custom orders are for elaborately inlaid works. Only six plain Szamboti cues without points have ever been made, and five of them went to Japan. Due to this, the restoration work on Balabushkas and Szambotis that has been keeping him very

GRADING	100%	95%	70%

busy, and because of heart disease, Barry's production has decreased in the last few years. He has made less than twenty cues per year for the past few years, and his goal is to make twenty cues in a year soon.

Although anyone who has seen a Barry Szamboti cue will agree that it is truly a work of art, his utmost importance is their playability. He is somewhat disappointed when he knows a cue has been put into a collection without ever having hit a ball. He loves to make cues for players, even the most basic ones, so that he can hear feedback as to how well they play. Barry offers three different tips for different types of play, and he hand-selects the finest tips from his supply.

If you would like to have a Gus Szamboti cue authenticated or restored, or would like to talk to Barry about the design of a new custom made Szamboti cue, contact Szamboti Cues, listed in the Trademark Index.

SPECIFICATIONS

Butt material: hardwoods
Shaft material: rock maple
Standard length: 58 in.
Lengths available: any
Standard finish: lacquer
Joint screw: 5/16-14
Standard joint: stainless steel
Joint type: piloted
Balance point: 2 in. above wrap
Point construction: short splice
Standard wrap: Irish linen
Standard butt cap: Delrin
Standard number of shafts: two
Standard taper: 10 in. pro
Standard ferrules: ivory
Standard tip: Le Pro
Tip widths available: any
Annual production: fewer than 50 cues

OPTIONS (FOR NEW CUES ONLY)

Leather wrap: $200
Lizard wrap: $250
Ivory joint: $250
Joint protector for butt: standard
Extra shaft: $225
Special length: no charge
Ivory butt cap: $550

REPAIRS

Repairs done only on Szamboti or Balabushka cues.
Refinish (with leather wrap): $450+
Refinish (with linen wrap): $400+
Rewrap (leather): $200
Rewrap (linen): $100
Replace shaft: $225+
Replace ivory ferrule (with Le Pro tip): $100
Replace Delrin butt cap: $100
Replace ivory butt cap: $600

CURRENT BARRY SZAMBOTI CUES

Szamboti cues with four points start at $2,200. Fancy ebony or rosewood forearm cues with ebony or rosewood points start at $8,500. Fancy eight-point custom cues start at $12,000. The current delivery time for a barry szamboti cue is many years.

CURRENT EXAMPLES

The following Barry Szamboti cues can be ordered as shown, modified to suit the desires of the customer, or new designs can be created.

Level 3 - Bird's-eye maple forearm, four ebony points with four veneers, ebony butt sleeve.

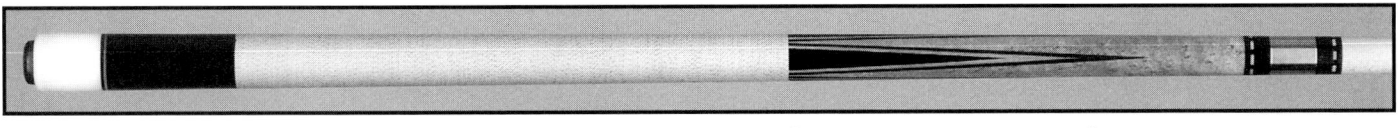

MSR	$2,200	$2,200-3,150	$2,100	$1,600

SZAMBOTI CUES, cont.

GRADING	100%		95%	70%

Level 3 "Titlist" - Maple forearm, four rosewood full-spliced Titlist points with four veneers, rosewood butt sleeve.

MSR	$2,200	$2,200-3,000	$2,000	$1,600

Level 3 "Hoppe" - Bird's-eye maple forearm, four ebony points with four veneers, ebony butt sleeve with an ivory ring at bottom.

MSR	$2,200	$2,200-3,000	$2,000	$1,600

Level 3 - Ivory joint, bird's-eye maple forearm, four amboyna burl points with four veneers, lizard wrap, amboyna burl butt sleeve.

MSR	$2,700	$2,700-3,650	$2,500	$2,000

Level 4 - Bird's-eye maple forearm, four snakewood points with four veneers and an ivory spear-shaped inlay in each point, leather wrap, snakewood butt sleeve with four ivory diamond-shaped inlays alternating with four ivory dots between ivory dash rings above and below.

MSR	$3,600	$3,600-5,500	$4,400	$3,000

Level 5 - Bird's-eye maple forearm, four rosewood points with four veneers and an ivory diamond-shaped inlay within ivory dots in each point, rosewood butt sleeve with four ivory diamond-shaped inlays surrounded by ivory dots between ivory dash rings above and below.

MSR	$3,200	$3,200-5,000	$3,950	$2,750

Level 5 - Ivory joint, bird's-eye maple forearm, four ebony points with four veneers and an ivory peacock shaped inlay in each point and an ebony-bordered ivory diamond-shaped inlay at the tip of each point, ebony butt sleeve with four ivory propeller-shaped inlays within hollow ivory razor blade windows alternating with ivory dots between intricate ivory rings above and below.

MSR	$5,500	$5,500-10,000	$8,250	$6,000

Level 5 "Ebony on Ebony" - Ivory joint, ebony forearm with an ivory Bushka ring above wrap, four ebony points with four veneers and an ivory spear-shaped inlay in each point, ebony butt sleeve with four three-piece ivory diamond-shaped inlays surrounded by ivory dots between ivory dash rings above and below.

MSR	$8,500	$8,500-10,000	$7,750	$6,750

Level 5 "Rosewood on Rosewood" - Ivory joint, rosewood forearm, four rosewood points with four veneers and an ivory peacock shaped inlay in each point, lizard wrap, rosewood butt sleeve with four ivory propeller-shaped inlays within pairs of ivory dots alternating with four scrimshawed ivory windows between ivory dash rings above and below.

MSR	$9,000	$9,000-10,500	$8,150	$7,150

GRADING	100%	95%	70%

Level 5 - Ivory joint, bird's-eye maple forearm with a ring of ivory dots set in ebony above wrap, four long ebony points with an ivory peacock-shaped inlay below an ivory dot in each point and an ebony-bordered ivory diamond-shaped inlay at the tip of each point alternating with four short ebony points with an ivory spear-shaped inlay in each point and an ebony-bordered ivory diamond-shaped inlay at the tip of each point below an ebony-bordered ivory dot above each point, leather wrap, ebony butt sleeve with four ivory three-piece diamond-shaped inlays alternating with four intricate ivory columns between intricate ivory rings above and below.

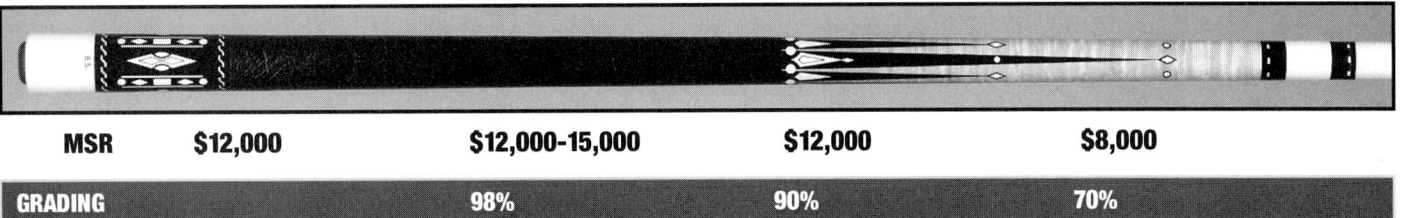

MSR	$12,000	$12,000-15,000	$12,000	$8,000
GRADING		98%	90%	70%

SECONDARY MARKET MINIMUM VALUES

The following are minimum prices for other Barry Szamboti cues encountered on the secondary market. These prices are representative of cues utilizing basic materials and designs that may not be currently available. Barry also offers one-of-a-kind cues that can command many times these prices due to the use of exotic materials and artistry.

Special construction note: There are many materials and construction techniques that can add value to Barry Szamboti cues. The following are the most important examples:

Add $3,500+ for ebony cues with four ivory windows instead of points.

For all used Barry Szamboti cues:

Add $200+ for each additional original straight playable shaft beyond two.
Deduct $225 for each missing original straight playable shaft under two.
Add $275+ for ivory joint.
Add $250+ for leather wrap.
Deduct 30% for obvious or improper refinish.

Level 2 - 0 points, 0-25 inlays.
Level 2 cues start at	$1,750	$1,350	$900

Level 3 - 2-6 points, 0-8 inlays.
Level 3 cues start at	$2,500	$2,000	$1,400

Level 4 - 4-10 points, 9-25 inlays.
Level 4 cues start at	$2,850	$2,185	$1,600

Level 5 - 0-12 points, 26-50 inlays.
Level 5 cues start at	$4,000	$3,150	$2,250

Level 6 - 0-12 points, 51-75 inlays.
Level 6 cues start at	$6,500	$5,150	$3,500

GUS SZAMBOTI

Maker of pool cues from 1969 to 1988 in Penndel, Pennsylvania, a suburb of Philadelphia.

Gus Szamboti circa 1954

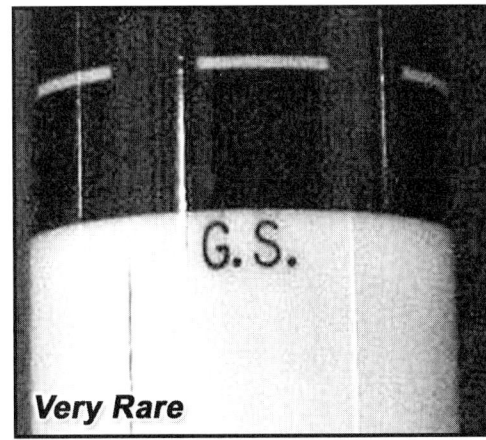
Very Rare

Very Rare

Cues by Gus Szamboti have become among the most sought-after items in the field of cue collecting. A master draftsman and designer for RCA in the late 1960s, he had a passion for pool that began at the age of eight. Gus started repairing cues in 1969, after selling his Harley Davidson to buy his first batch of wood, and using the same year's tax refund check to buy a lathe and other necessary supplies.

By the end of the year, he had made his first cue. This cue was not of the standards of his later cues, and when he saw it again, years later, in a Philadelphia pool room, he purchased it, took it home and destroyed it.

Early on, Gus met and became friends with Doc Fry, a pharmacist who had been making cues for some time in the Philadelphia area. Fry was influential in Gus's work, and soon Gus was making parts for him. The first ten or twelve cues with points Gus made had blanks that were made by WICO of Chicago. These blanks had four ebony or rosewood points with four colored vinyl veneers. The known examples have forearms of rosewood or bird's-eye maple. Gus also made a few cues during this period with Titlist blanks which were the only full-spliced cues he ever made. These first cues had ebony or rosewood butt sleeves and, if inlaid, had mother-of-pearl notched diamonds and dots. Very early cues did not have bumpers.

His son, Barry, remembers the night in 1972 when Gus figured out how to make a spliced blank of his own. Gus sent his two sons on several trips to Sears that night to get more tools and equipment. Gus was soon making blanks so well that George Balabushka became his first customer that same year. Balabushka continued to use Szamboti blanks until his death in 1975.

Early Szamboti cues usually had bird's-eye maple forearms, with ebony butt sleeves and four ebony points, although rosewood was also available instead of ebony. Mother-of-pearl notched diamonds or dots were common inlays, as were maple windows. Most cues had four colored veneers on the points with matching colored stitching in the joint rings, or nickel silver joint rings. In 1976, Gus introduced his "barbell" inlays, which were done in a variety of sizes and materials. Ivory joints were always an option, with the early ones being flat-faced but after 1977, they were all piloted. From the years 1975 to 1977 Gus liked to use two black outer veneers on his cues. These veneers were so well executed that they appear to be one thick black outer veneer. It was after this time that he became much more innovative in his designs, and Gus started using ivory more often in his inlays.

In the late 1970s, he made his first eight-point cue. About 60 of these cues were made, most with ebony points, and one even had veneers. Even more difficult to make were six-point cues, of which he made between 25 and 30. Another rarity was four ebony points on an ebony forearm, of which only about 25 were made. These cues appear to be a solid piece of ebony, with only the veneers revealing the splices. Rare Gus Szamboti cues such as these are among the most valuable cues in the field of cue collecting.

Gus reached his peak in the 1980s. The cues of this time period were the most playable, and the high-end cues were the most elaborate. Propellers, spears, and chain links, all inlaid in ivory, were common themes. By this time, customers had to wait years to receive a cue, and when they got it they could resell it for far more than what they paid. Many customers ordered cues specifically for resale. Gus Szamboti cues were recognized and sought after by players around the world. Since his cues were so popular and so hard to get, some competitors tried to imitate his work. A few even used his blanks to do so.

To this day, the demand for Gus Szamboti cues is so great that buyers are in danger of fakes, frauds, or misrepresentations. On genuine cues, the points will usually come to within 2 1/4 in. of the joint collar and will always be within 3 in. Gus's points and veneers were perfectly executed with razor-sharp ends. The thickness of the veneers is also a factor, as many of the fakes have thinner ones. Original shafts should always weigh at least four ounces, and since he finished them by hand, they should have minimal taper waves. Original paperwork, and/or an original box, add credibility to a cue being genuine.

Before you buy, be sure to get a money-back guarantee, and have an expert authenticate the cue as soon as possible. Barry Szamboti is the best choice, as he has probably seen and worked on more Gus Szamboti cues than anyone. Barry is also the best choice for restoration or extra shafts. For more information, contact Barry Szamboti, listed in the Trademark Index.

SPECIFICATIONS

- Butt materials: hardwoods
- Shaft material: rock maple
- Standard length: 58 in.
- Standard taper: 10 in. pro
- Standard joint: stainless steel
- Joint type: piloted
- Standard wrap: Irish linen
- Point construction: short splice
- Standard butt cap: Delrin
- Standard ferrules: ivory
- Balance point: 2 in. above wrap
- Standard number of shafts: two
- Total production: 1,200-1,300

OPTIONS ENCOUNTERED (FOR NEW CUES ONLY)

- Ivory joint (rare)
- Ivory butt cap (extremely rare)
- Leather wrap
- Silver rings

KNOWN GUS SZAMBOTI EXAMPLES

The following cues are known representations of the work of Gus Szamboti. Gus made a total of 1,200 to 1,300 cues in his lifetime. No two are exactly alike, the following are representative examples:

EARLY CUES

The following cues were mostly made between 1969 and 1972, before Gus was making his own blanks. These cues used plain forearms (very rare), Titlist blanks, or WICO blanks with vinyl veneers (rare). Inlay work in the points tends to be more desirable than inlays in the butt sleeve.

GRADING	98%	90%	70%

Level 3 "Titlist Blank" - Maple forearm, four rosewood points with four colored veneers, rosewood butt sleeve.

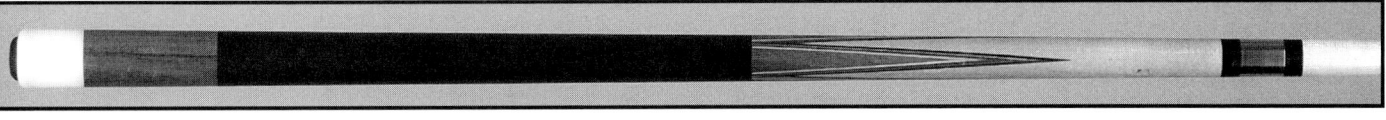

$5,000	$4,150	$3,050

Level 3 "Titlist Blank" - Maple forearm, four rosewood points with four colored veneers and a mother-of-pearl dot in each point, rosewood butt sleeve with mother-of-pearl rings at top and bottom.

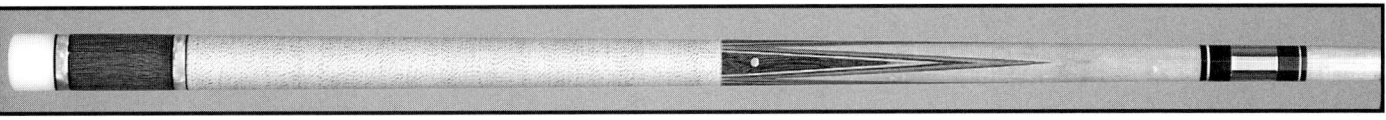

$5,500	$6,000	$3,250

Level 3 "Wico Blank" - Paduak forearm, four ebony points with four colored vinyl veneers and a mother-of-pearl notched diamond-shaped inlay between two mother-of-pearl dots in each point, ebony butt sleeve with four mother-of-pearl notched diamond-shaped inlays between pairs of mother-of-pearl dots and mother-of-pearl rings above and below.

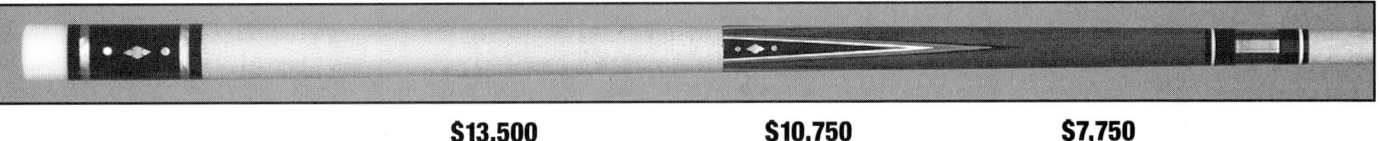

$13,500	$10,750	$7,750

FOUR-POINT CUES

The following cues were mostly made between 1972 and 1988 out of Gus's four-point blanks. Most were four points with four veneers into bird's-eye maple, but there were also cues made with no veneers, and cues with rosewood or ebony forearms (rare). Ivory inlaid cues tend to be more desirable than mother-of-pearl inlaid cues. Mother-of-pearl inlays tend to be notched diamonds and dots or barbells. Ivory inlays graduated from diamonds and dots to spears, gambler themes, peacocks, propellers, scrimshawed windows, etc. No two are exactly alike, the following are representative examples:

Level 3 - Ivory joint, bird's-eye maple forearm, four ebony points without veneers, ebony butt sleeve (usually with steel joint).

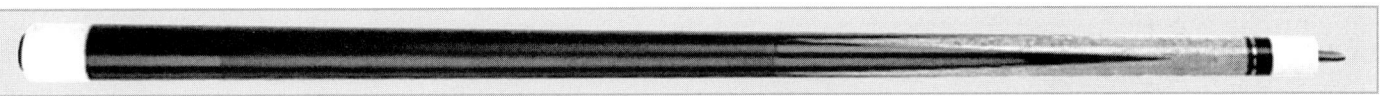

$6,000	$5,000	$3,850

Level 3 "Four Window" - Bird's-eye maple forearm, four ebony points with four colored veneers, ebony butt sleeve with four bird's-eye maple windows.

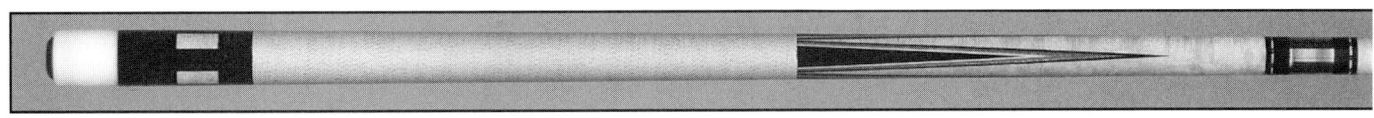

$7,500	$6,250	$4,500

Level 3 "Stitched Ring" - Ivory joint, bird's-eye maple forearm, four rosewood points with four colored veneers, rosewood butt sleeve with a stitched ring towards bottom (usually with steel joint, also encountered in ebony).

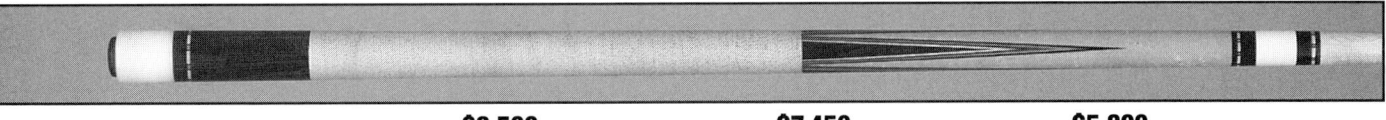

$8,500	$7,450	$5,800

Level 4 - Bird's-eye maple forearm, four ebony points with four colored veneers, ebony butt sleeve, inlays of mother-of-pearl dots and/or notched diamonds and maple rectangles in butt sleeve.

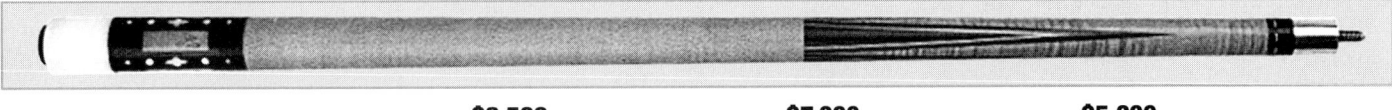

$8,500	$7,000	$5,200

| GRADING | 98% | 90% | 70% |

Level 4 - Ivory joint, bird's-eye maple forearm, four ebony points with four colored veneers, ebony butt sleeve, inlays of ivory diamonds and dots.

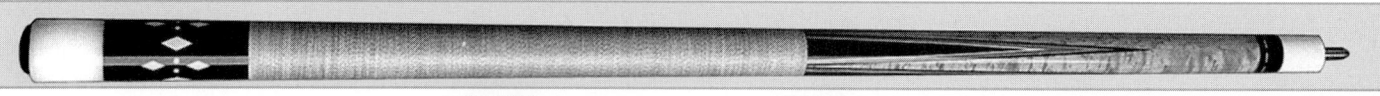

| | $8,750 | $7,200 | $5,400 |

Level 3 "Big Block Ring" - Ivory joint, bird's-eye maple forearm, four ebony points with four colored veneers, leather wrap, ebony butt sleeve with maple blocks within veneer rings at bottom (usually with steel joint).

| | $9,000 | $7,800 | $6,150 |

Level 4 "Hoppe Style" - Bird's-eye maple forearm with mother-of-pearl dots within metal rings above wrap, four rosewood points with four colored veneers and mother-of-pearl dots and a notched diamond-shaped inlay in each point, rosewood butt sleeve with inlays of mother-of-pearl dots and notched diamond-shaped inlays above an ivory ring at bottom, thin butt cap (no bumper).

| | $10,500 | $8,500 | $6,000 |

Level 5 "Barbell Cue" - Bird's-eye maple forearm, four ebony points with four colored veneers and mother-of-pearl and veneer barbells in the points, ebony butt sleeve with inlays of mother-of-pearl and veneer barbells between dash rings above and below.

| | $11,500 | $9,500 | $6,800 |

Level 4 "Gambler Cue" - Bird's-eye maple forearm, four ebony points with four colored veneers, ebony butt sleeve with inlays of an ivory heart/spade/club/diamond in ebony windows with veneers.

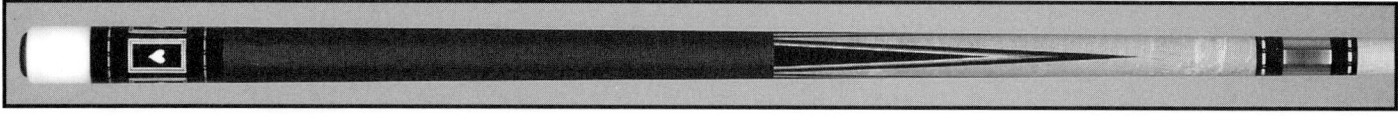

| | $11,500 | $9,250 | $6,500 |

Level 4 "Bird's-eye Maple Butt Sleeve" - Bird's-eye maple forearm, four ebony points with four colored veneers, bird's-eye maple butt sleeve with inlays of mother-of-pearl notched diamonds in ebony rectangles between ebony rings at top and bottom.

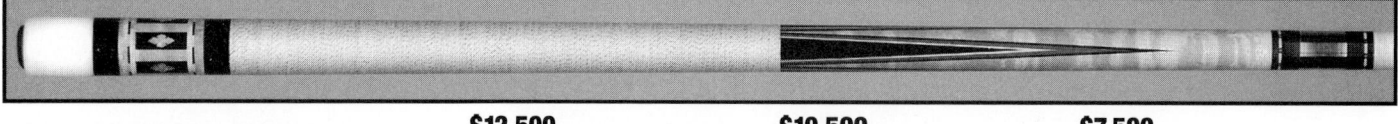

| | $12,500 | $10,500 | $7,500 |

Level 6 "9-Ball Pattern" - Bird's-eye maple forearm with check rings above wrap, four ebony points with four colored veneers and mother-of-pearl dots in the points, ebony butt sleeve with inlays of mother-of-pearl dots in a nin-ball pattern between maple dash rings above and below.

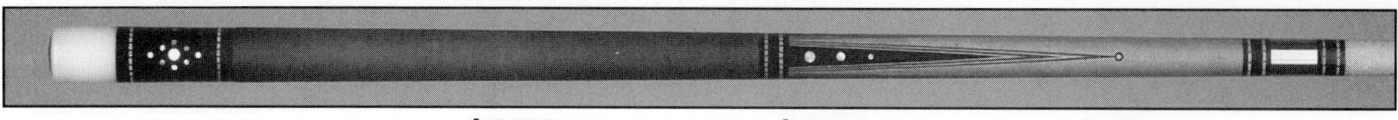

| | $13,500 | $11,000 | $8,000 |

Level 5 "Barbell Cue" - Bird's-eye maple forearm, four ebony points with four colored veneers and mother-of-pearl and veneer barbells in the points, ebony butt sleeve with inlays of mother-of-pearl and veneer barbells alternating with ebony barbells set in maple windows.

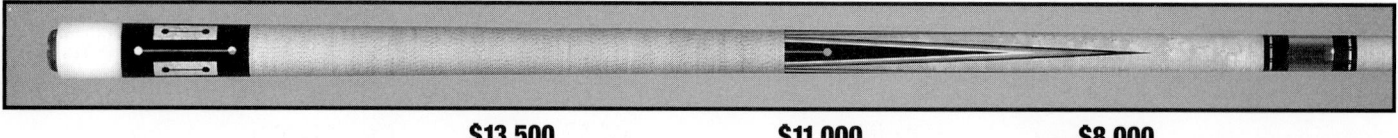

| | $13,500 | $11,000 | $8,000 |

GRADING	98%	90%	70%

Level 4 "Gambler Cue" - Ivory joint, bird's-eye maple forearm, four ebony points with four colored veneers, ebony butt sleeve with inlays of ivory dice and colored nine-balls.

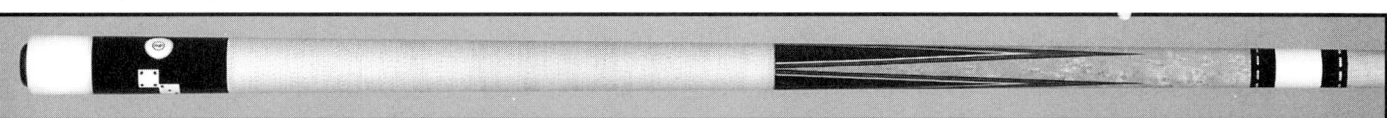

	$14,500	$11,500	$8,000

Level 4 "Ebony Forearm" - Ivory joint, ebony forearm, four ebony points with four colored veneers, ebony butt sleeve with inlays of ivory diamonds and dots (also seen with steel joint).

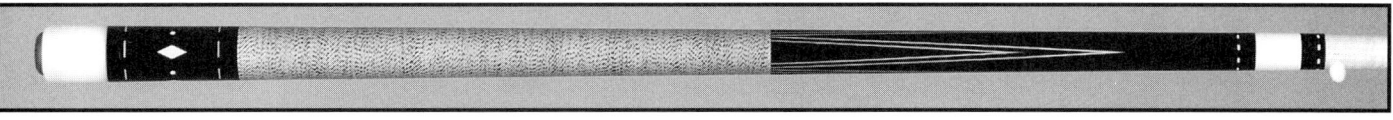

	$15,000	$12,500	$9,250

Level 4 - Bird's-eye maple forearm, four ebony points with four colored veneers and an ivory diamond-shaped inlay in each point, ebony butt sleeve with sets of four ivory diamond-shaped inlays of alternating with ivory dots.

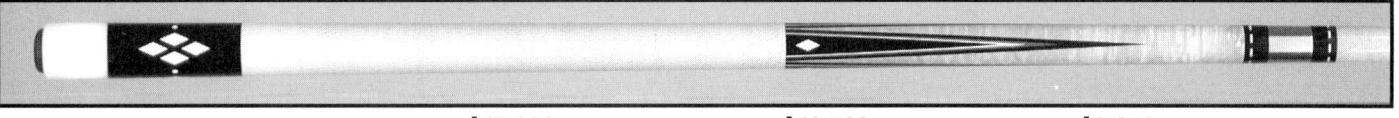

	$15,000	$12,500	$9,250

Level 5 "Hoppe with Ivory Spears" - Bird's-eye maple forearm with ebony and ivory checks within silver rings above wrap, four ebony points with four colored veneers and an ivory spear-shaped inlay within each point and an ebony-bordered ivory dot at the tip of each point, ebony butt sleeve with three-piece ivory diamond-shaped inlays and ivory dots within veneer trimmed ebony windows.

	$15,000	$12,500	$9,000

Level 5 "Ivory Spear Inlays" - Bird's-eye maple forearm, four ebony points with four colored veneers and an ivory spear-shaped inlay and ivory dots in each point, ebony butt sleeve with inlays of opposing ivory spears and ivory dots.

	$17,500	$14,000	$9,500

Level 4 "Ivory Propeller inlays." - Bird's-eye maple forearm, four ebony points with four colored veneers and an ivory propellar-shaped inlay in each point, ebony butt sleeve with inlays of ivory propellers and dots between ivory dash rings above and below.

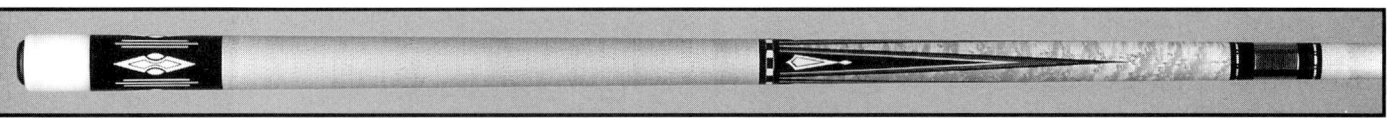

	$19,500	$16,000	$12,000

Level 5 "Ivory Peacock inlays." - Bird's-eye maple forearm with ebony and ivory check rings above wrap, four ebony points with four colored veneers and an ivory peacock-shaped inlay in each point, ebony butt sleeve with intricate three-piece ivory diamond-shaped inlays alternating with ivory lines.

	$20,000	$16,500	$12,000

Level 4 "Ebony T inlays. in Maple" - Bird's-eye maple forearm with ebony and maple checks within silver rings above wrap, four ebony points with four colored veneers and ivory triangles and dots in the points, ebony butt sleeve with ebony-bordered scrimmed ivory windows between ebony T-shaped inlays above and below, "G.S." in butt cap.

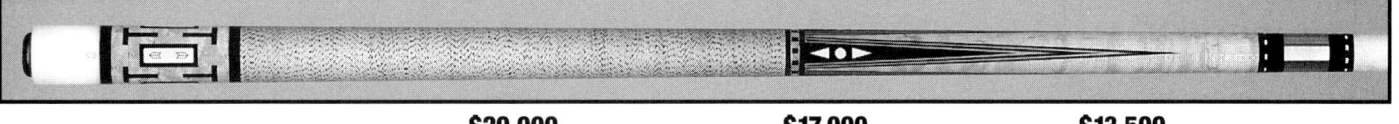

	$20,000	$17,000	$13,500

| GRADING | 98% | 90% | 70% |

Level 5 "Ivory Peacock inlays." - Bird's-eye maple forearm, four ebony points with four colored veneers and an ivory peacock-shaped inlay and ivory dots within each point, ebony butt sleeve with three-piece ivory diamond-shaped inlays and ivory dots.

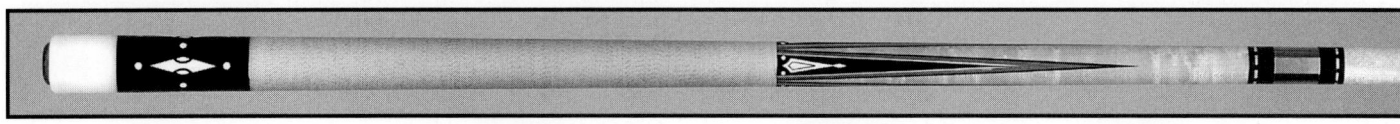

| | $21,500 | $18,000 | $13,500 |

Level 5 - Bird's-eye maple forearm with an ivory Bushka ring above wrap, four ebony points with four colored veneers and an ivory propeller-shaped inlay in each point, ebony butt sleeve with inlays of ivory propellers and dots and scrimmed ivory windows between ivory dash rings above and below.

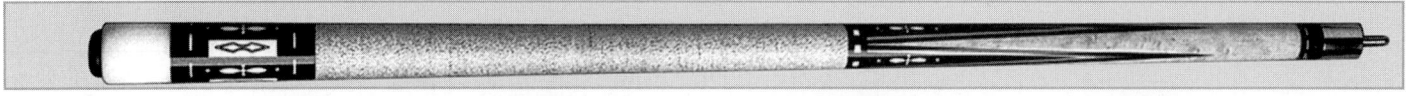

| | $27,500 | $23,000 | $17,250 |

Level 5 "Ebony Forearm" - Ebony forearm with ebony and ivory blocks set within silver rings above wrap, four ebony points with four colored veneers and opposing ivory triangle-shaped inlays around ivory dots, ebony butt sleeve with inlays of ivory triangles and dots around scrimmed ivory windows between ivory dash rings above and below, "G.S." engraved in butt cap.

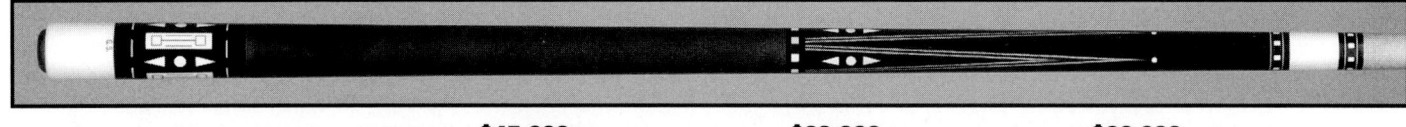

| | $45,000 | $39,000 | $30,000 |

Level 4 "Rosewood Forearm" - Rosewood forearm, four rosewood points with four colored veneers, rosewood butt sleeve, inlays of ivory propellers and dots and possibly scrimmed ivory windows in butt sleeve (extremely rare).

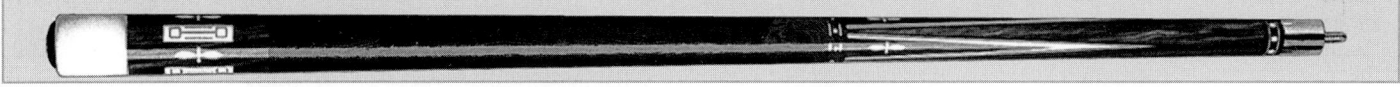

| | $45,000 | $38,000 | $30,000 |

Level 7 "Rosewood Forearm Barbell Cue" - Rosewood forearm with mother-of-pearl and veneer barbells and mother-of-pearl notched diamond-shaped inlays above mother-of-pearl dots in ebony within silver rings above wrap, rosewood butt sleeve with mother-of-pearl and veneer barbell patterns around mother-of-pearl notched diamond-shaped inlays between maple stitched rings above and below.

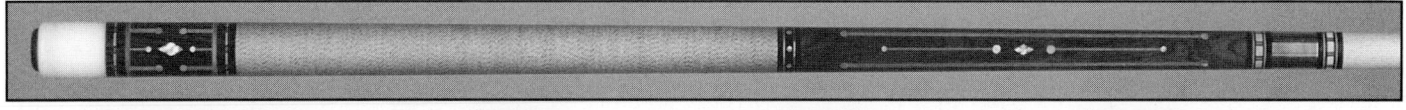

| | $55,000 | $45,000 | $30,000 |

SPECIALTY CUES

The following cues were mostly made between 1975 and 1988 out of solid forearms, six-point, or eight-point blanks. No two are exactly alike, and the following are representative examples:

Level 6 "Six Point With Ivory Spear Inlays" - Ivory joint, bird's-eye maple forearm, three long ebony points with four colored veneers and an ivory spear-shaped inlay in each and an ebony dot at the tip of each alternating with three short ebony points with four colored veneers and an ivory dot in each and an ebony-bordered ivory diamond-shaped inlay at the tip of each, ebony butt sleeve with intricate patterns of ivory diamond-shaped inlays and dots and lines and blocks alternating with three-piece ivory diamond-shaped inlays.

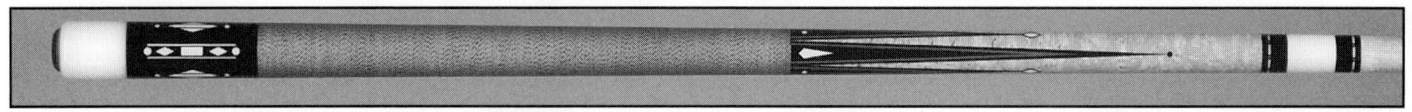

| | $85,000 | $72,500 | $55,000 |

| GRADING | 98% | 90% | 70% |

Level 5 "Six Point With Ivory Spear inlays. and Bushka Ring" - Ivory joint, bird's-eye maple forearm with a Bushka ring above wrap, three long ebony points with four colored veneers and an ivory spear-shaped inlay in each and an ebony dot at the tip of each alternating with three short ebony points with four colored veneers and an ivory dot in each and an ebony dot at the tip of each, ebony butt sleeve with inlays of ivory spears and dots between ivory dash rings above and below.

| $95,000 | $80,000 | $60,000 |

Level 5 "Eight Point with Ivory Spear &Peacock Inlays" - Bird's-eye maple forearm possibly with silver or ivory patterned rings above wrap, eight ebony points without veneers, ebony butt sleeve, inlays of ivory spears and dots and probably scrimmed ivory windows and possibly ivory dash rings in butt sleeve (about 60 of these cues are known to have been made).

| $70,000 | $60,000 | $45,000 |

Level 6 "Eight Point With Ivory Spear & Peacock & Propeller Inlays" - Ivory joint, bird's-eye maple forearm with ivory dots set in ebony above wrap, four long ebony points with an ivory peacock-shaped inlay below an ivory dot in each and an ebony dot at the tip of each alternating with four short ebony points with an ivory spear-shaped inlay in each and an ebony-bordered ivory diamond-shaped inlay at the tip of each, ebony butt sleeve with inlays of ivory propellers within ivory cameo razor blade windows and ivory dots, "G.S." in ivory butt cap (this example was Gus's last personal cue).

| $80,000 | $77,000 | $51,500 |

Level 5 "Ebony Window Forearm" - Bird's-eye maple forearm with ebony and maple checks within silver rings above wrap, ebony windows alternating with ebony barbells, ebony butt sleeve with ebony barbells set in maple windows between maple check rings above and below.

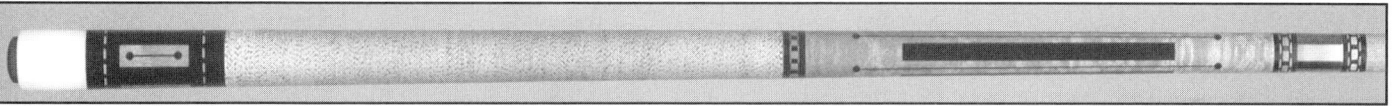

| $18,500 | $15,000 | $10,500 |

Level 6 "Ebony Window Forearm" - Bird's-eye maple forearm with ebony and ivory checks within silver rings above wrap, ebony windows with opposing ivory spear-shaped inlays around ivory dots in each window alternating with ebony barbells, bird's-eye maple butt sleeve with ebony-bordered ivory windows alternating with ebony barbells between maple check rings above and below.

| $22,500 | $18,000 | $12,500 |

Level 4 "Ivory Window Forearm with Ivory Butt Cap" - Ebony forearm with ebony and ivory block rings above wrap, floating ivory rectangles with veneers and smaller ivory hexagons, ivory butt sleeve with ivory hexagons within ebony windows with veneers and ebony and ivory dashes within silver rings above and below.

| $50,000 | $41,500 | $30,000 |

Level 5 "Ivory Window Forearm with Propellers" - Ebony forearm with ebony and ivory block rings above wrap, floating ivory rectangles with veneers and floating ivory propellers, ebony butt sleeve with ivory rectangles with veneers and ivory propellers between ebony and ivory dashes within silver rings above and below.

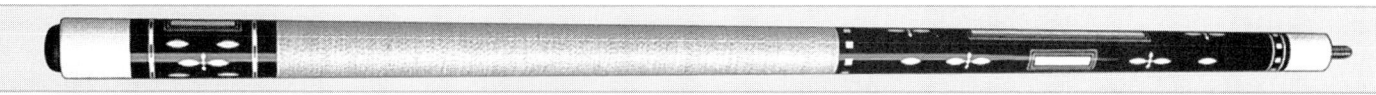

| $65,000 | $55,000 | $40,000 |

GRADING	98%	90%	70%

SECONDARY MARKET MINIMUM VALUES

The following are minimum values for other Gus Szamboti cues encountered on the secondary market. These prices are representative of cues utilizing the most basic materials and designs that were available. Gus specialized in one-of-a-kind cues that can command many times these prices due to the use of exotic materials and artistry. Early variations are becoming very collectible, and can also command many times these prices. Gus Szamboti cues will be further covered in future editions.

Note: Due to the rarity of Gus Szamboti cues and increasing interest, prices are on the rise. Fewer original examples are surfacing, and collectors are holding on to the ones they have. Unique examples with pedigree, and cues made for top professional players are bringing the highest prices.

There are several options that can add value to Gus Szamboti cues. The following are the most important examples.

- Add $2,500+ for Gus's name or initials on butt cap (very rare - make sure they are original).
- Add $1,200+ for ivory butt cap.
- Add $1,500 for ivory chain link rings.
- Add 20% for ivory joint.
- Add $500 for leather wrap.
- Add $250 for silver joint rings.

For all used Gus Szamboti cues, except where otherwise noted:

- Add $550+ for excellent original Fellini case (a $100+ option with cues from the 1970s).
- Add 30%+ for original box.
- Add $600 for each original straight playable shaft beyond two.
- Deduct $850 for each missing original straight playable shaft under two.
- Add 20% for totally original finish, wrap, shafts, and ferrules.
- Deduct 35% for obvious or improper restoration.

Level 2 - 0 points, 0-25 inlays.

Level 2 cues start at	$5,500	$4,500	$3,000

Level 3 - 2-6 points, 0-8 inlays.

Level 3 cues start at	$5,000	$4,100	$2,800

Level 4 - 4-10 points, 9-25 inlays.

Level 4 cues start at	$7,000	$4,400	$3,300

Level 5 - 0-12 points, 26-50 inlays.

Level 5 cues start at	$12,000	$10,000	$7,500

Level 6 - 0-12 points, 51-75 inlays.

Level 6 cues start at	$20,000	$16,000	$11,500

T SECTION

TAD'S CUSTOM CUE

Maker of pool cues from 1963 to present, currently in Stanton, California.

1978 to Present Day

Tad Kohara

Tad Kohara was born in California, the son of first-generation Japanese immigrants. When his father retired in the early 1940s, Tad went to Japan to study cabinetmaking in Hiroshima. In 1945, the school he was attending was destroyed by the atomic bomb. Tad returned to the United States in 1949, and made his living as an automotive mechanic. With hard work, Tad was eventually able to buy his own gas station. In 1963, during the post-"Hustler" billiards boom, he opened Tad´s Family Billiards in Los Angeles. Tad, an experienced woodworker, decided to purchase a lathe to maintain his house cues, and offer repairs to his customers. Within that year, Tad was making his own cues.

The first Tad cues were Brunswick Titlists cut in half, to which he added a joint. He then began making cues from scratch, with solid bird´s-eye maple forearms and butt sleeves, similar to what Harvey Martin was making at the time. Martin was a friend and an influence, and Tad bought his equipment when Harvey retired. A couple of years later Tad sold his poolroom and started making cues full time. Some of Tad's cues of this era (1960s and early 1970s) reflect the influence of other cuemakers such as Ernie Gutierrez, Gene Balner (Palmer) and Doc Fry, all of whom were making cues during that time. Early examples of Tad's cues may have plastic rings or, more rarely, plastic windows in the butt sleeve, and even plastic handles.

Tad was never really a pool player, so he didn't know much about how cues should play. By relying on the advice of players like Willie Mosconi, Jimmy Caras, and Joe Balsis, Tad produced cues which, early on, became known for their playability. Tad even made the cues for Willie Mosconi's pool school in North Hollywood.

From 1963 until 1977, Tad cues were not marked with a logo. In 1978, he started engraving the butt cap of every Tad cue with the "Tad" logo, used to this day. Also in the late 1970s, Tad experimented with different tips and developed his own tip hardness tester. He was unable to find tips that were consistent enough for him, so he started making his own single-layer tips.

In 2000, after four moves in nearly 25 years, Tad settled into the shop he is in today, in Stanton, California. The workshop has 18 lathes and three pantographs. Tad has customized his machinery as he has deemed necessary. Virtually everything in Tad's cues is made in the workshop, except for the bumpers. All ferrules, butt caps, and collars are threaded on. Finished cues hang for several months before delivery, to ensure that all of the materials have settled.

Tad's Custom Cues produces less than 100 cues per year. This is truly a family business. Tad's wife, Susie, does much of the pantograph work. His son, Fred, has been taking on much of the cuemaking responsibility in recent years. All work is done by hand, with the aid of CNC machines. Since a large number of Tad cues go to Japan, ivory is rarely used, due to the ban on export items containing ivory. Consequently, ivory points, joints, and butt caps are extremely rare.

After 40 years in the business, Tad is acknowledged as a master cuemaker. He was honored by his peers and collectors from all over the world at the "Showcase at the Ritz" in Marina del Rey, California in November, 2003.

If you have a Tad cue that needs further identification or repair, or would like to talk to Tad about ordering a new custom cue, contact Tad's Custom Cue, listed in the Trademark Index.

SPECIFICATIONS

- Butt material: hardwoods
- Shaft material: rock maple
- Standard length: 58 in.
- Lengths available: 58 in. only
- Standard finish: lacquer
- Joint screw: 5/16-18
- Standard joint: stainless steel
- Joint type: piloted
- Balance point: custom
- Point construction: short splice
- Standard wrap: Irish linen
- Standard butt cap: Delrin
- Standard number of shafts: two
- Standard taper: 10 in. pro

GRADING	100%	95%	70%

Standard ferrules: fiber
Standard tip: Tad
Tip widths available: any
Annual production: fewer than 100 cues

OPTIONS (FOR NEW CUES ONLY)

Leather wrap: $200
Ivory joint: $200+
3/8-12 Implex joint: no charge
Joint protectors: standard on high-end cues
Extra shaft: $225
Ivory ferrules: $50+ each

REPAIRS

Repairs done on Tad cues only.
Refinish (with leather wrap): $250+
Refinish (with linen wrap): $225+
Rewrap (linen): $125
Replace shaft: $225
Replace ivory joint: $200+

CURRENT TAD CUES

The current delivery time for a Tad cue is approximately one year.

CURRENT EXAMPLES

The following Tad cues are available from J And J America. Some cues are available for immediate delivery; for most there is a waiting list.

Level 2 "Tad-1" - Tigerwood forearm, tigerwood butt sleeve with ringwork at bottom.

MSR	$1,800	$1,800-2,000	$1,650	$1,200

Level 3 "Tad-4" - Stained bird's-eye maple forearm, four ebony points with four veneers, ebony butt sleeve with a micarta ring at bottom.

MSR	$2,800	$2,800-3,200	$2,650	$1,800

Level 4 "Tad-41" - Stained bird's-eye maple forearm with intricate micarta block and dash ringwork set in ebony above wrap, four ebony points with four veneers and a micarta notched diamond-shaped inlay in each point, bird's-eye maple butt sleeve with four micarta notched diamond-shaped inlays set in ebony windows with four veneers between intricate micarta block and dash ringwork set in ebony at top and bottom.

MSR	$4,000	$4,000-5,000	$3,900	$2,700

Level 5 "Tad-82" - Stained bird's-eye maple forearm with intricate micarta and mother-of-pearl block ringwork set in ebony above wrap, four long ebony points with a mother-of-pearl notched diamond-shaped inlay in each point and an intricate ebony and mother-of-pearl cloverleaf-shaped inlay at the tip of each point alternating with four short ebony points with an ebony-bordered mother-of-pearl dot at the tip of each point, ebony butt sleeve with eight mother-of-pearl notched diamond-shaped inlays and dots set in an intricate micarta hollow ring between intricate micarta and mother-of-pearl block ringwork set in ebony at top and bottom.

MSR	$5,600	$5,600-6,650	$5,400	$3,500

Level 6 "Tad-43" - Stained bird's-eye maple forearm with intricate micarta block and dash ringwork set in ebony above wrap, four intricate floating ebony points with veneers and intricate ebony and micarta inlays alternating with four maple notched diamond-shaped inlays set in ebony and micarta ovals, stained bird's-eye maple butt sleeve with four maple notched diamond-shaped inlays set in intricate micarta and ebony windows alternating with intricate ebony columns with intricate ebony and micarta inlays between intricate micarta block and dash ringwork set in ebony at top and bottom.

MSR	$7,000	$7,000-8,500	$6,900	$5,200

Level 6 "Tad-42" - Ebony forearm, four intricate floating micarta points with veneers and intricate ebony and micarta inlays alternating with four micarta notched diamond-shaped inlays set in micarta ovals, ebony butt sleeve with four micarta notched diamond-shaped inlays set in intricate micarta and ebony windows alternating with intricate micarta columns with intricate ebony and micarta inlays between intricate micarta block ringwork set in ebony at top and bottom.

MSR	$8,000	$8,000-9,500	$7,950	$6,000

PAST EXAMPLES

The following Tad cues can be encountered as shown, or modified to suit the desires of the original customer. Many Tad cues encountered will be one-of-a-kind.

TAD'S CUSTOM CUE, cont.

GRADING	98%	90%	70%

Level 2 "Martin Style" - Bird's-eye maple forearm, cork wrap, bird's-eye maple butt sleeve.

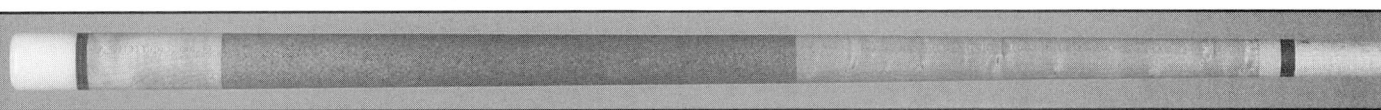

MSR (1968) $85	$2,500	$2,050	$1,500

Level 3 "Titlist" - Maple forearm, four rosewood points with four colored veneers, ebony butt sleeve with Tad identification markings and/or possibly the original owner's name under a clear plastic window in center.

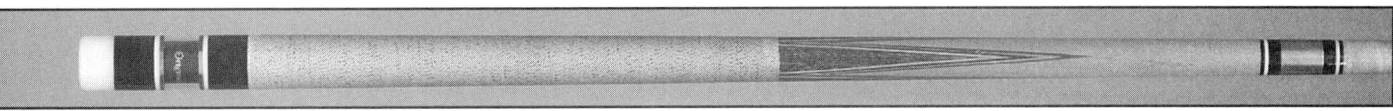

MSR (1964) $100	$3,000	$2,450	$1,800

Level 3 "Titlist with Plastic Handle" - Maple forearm with plastic ringwork above handle, four rosewood points with four colored veneers, plastic handle, butt sleeve of plastic rings with Tad identification markings and/or possibly the original owner's name under a clear plastic window in center.

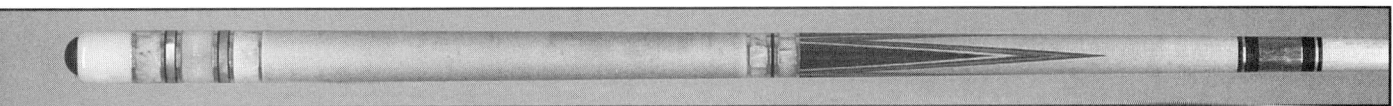

MSR (1965) $150	$8,000	$6,750	$5,000

Level 4 "Katz Butterfly" - Maple forearm, two long ebony butterfly points with two colored veneers, stained bird's-eye maple butt sleeve with windows and inlay work between intricate ringwork set in ebony at top and bottom.

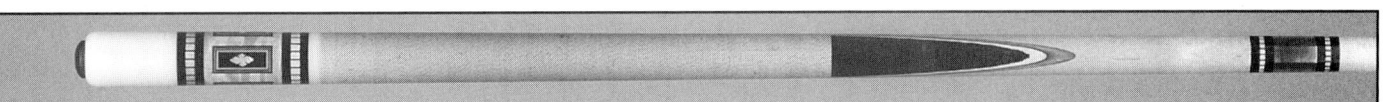

MSR (1965) $125	$4,500	$3,650	$2,600

Level 4 "Tadpole" - Stained bird's-eye maple forearm with intricate ringwork set in ebony above wrap, two long and two short ebony tadpole-shaped points with a mother-of-pearl notched diamond-shaped inlay in each, stained bird's-eye maple butt sleeve with windows and inlay work between intricate ringwork set in ebony at top and bottom.

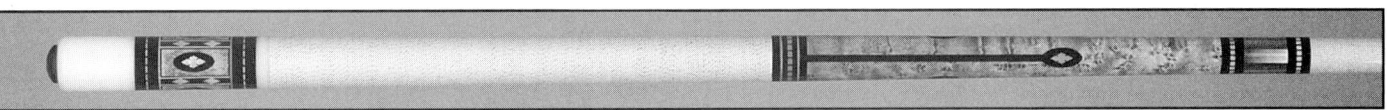

MSR (1973) $225	$5,000	$4,000	$2,850

Level 8 "Ivory Eight Point" - Ivory joint, stained bird's-eye maple forearm with intricate ivory ringwork set in ebony above wrap, four long scrimshawed ivory points with an intricate ebony and ivory cloverleaf-shaped inlay at the tip of each point alternating with four short ivory points with an ebony-bordered ivory dot at the tip of each point, ivory butt sleeve with intricate scrimshawed ivory and ebony inlays between intricate ivory ringwork set in ebony at top and bottom.

MSR (2001) $19,000	$30,000	$25,000	$18,500

SECONDARY MARKET MINIMUM VALUES

The following are minimum prices for other Tad cues encountered on the secondary market. These prices are representative of cues utilizing basic materials and designs that may not be currently available. Tad currently specializes in one-of-a-kind cues that can command many times these prices due to the use of exotic materials and artistry.

Special construction note: There are many materials and construction techniques that can add value to Tad cues. The following are the most important examples:

- Add $5,000+ for ivory points (very rare).
- Add 50%+ for ivory inlay work, as opposed to micarta.
- Add $750+ for ivory butt cap (very rare).
- Add $500+ for trim rings above and below wrap that match the joint rings.

For all used Tad cues:
- Add $200+ for each additional original straight playable shaft beyond two.

GRADING	98%	90%	70%

Deduct $225 for each missing original straight playable shaft under two.
Add $50 for each ivory ferrule.
Deduct 25% for obvious or improper refinish.

	98%	90%	70%
Level 2 - 0 points, 0-25 inlays.			
Level 2 cues start at	$1,750	$1,400	$1,000
Level 3 - 2-6 points, 0-8 inlays.			
Level 3 cues start at	$2,650	$2,250	$1,800
Level 4 - 4-10 points, 9-25 inlays.			
Level 4 cues start at	$3,500	$3,000	$2,400
Level 5 - 0-12 points, 26-50 inlays.			
Level 5 cues start at	$5,000	$4,150	$3,000
Level 6 - 0-12 points, 51-75 inlays.			
Level 6 cues start at	$7,000	$5,650	$4,000
Level 7 - 0-12 points, 76-125 inlays.			
Level 7 cues start at	$10,000	$8,100	$5,800
Level 8 - 4 or more points, 126 or more inlays.			
Level 8 cues start at	$14,500	$11,850	$8,500

TAMPA BILLIARDS

Maker of pool cues from 1964 to present, originally in Tampa, now in Thonotosassa, Florida and named Gunn Cues. Refer to Gunn Cues for information.

TASCARELLA CUSTOM CUES

Maker of pool cues from 1976 to present, currently in Massapequa Park, New York.

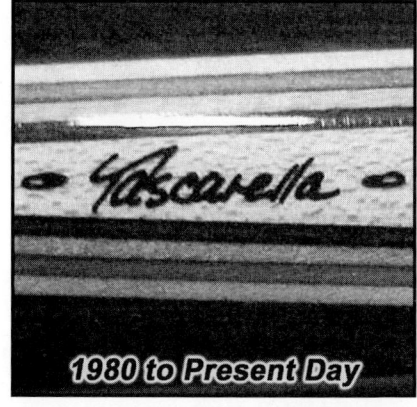
1980 to Present Day

Pete Tascarella is an accomplished player who has run over 200 balls in straight pool. He was a police detective in Brooklyn and spent a lot of time in the neighborhood where George Balabushka lived and made cues. Pete bought his first cue from George in 1971 for $125, and the two became friends. Pete started to visit George regularly, and bring him coffee in the mornings. Although George never formally trained Pete in cuemaking, George worked while Pete was in his shop and he let Pete see what he was doing. When George died in 1975 Pete bought his equipment and materials. Utilizing what he had seen in George's shop, using George's materials, methods, and equipment, Pete made his first cue in fall of 1976.

Pete's early cues could easily be mistaken for Balabushkas so in 1980 Pete began signing his cues "Tascarella" on the forearms to avoid confusion. He has continued to make cues in the tradition of George Balabushka. Pete has retired from the Police Department and he owned a couple of upscale pool rooms in New York in the 1990s. Now Pete's son, a full-time New York State Court Officer, works with him. They thread all components and use traditional gluing methods as opposed to epoxies or super glues. Points are short or full spliced and ferrules are capped. Any kind of joint is available, including a unique ivory joint with a steel bushing that they developed. Their goal is to make the perfect cue, with playability being the primary concern. They still work on the Atlas lathe that George Balabushka customized for his own shop.

If you are interested in talking to Pete Tascarella about a new cue or cue that needs to be repaired, you can contact him at Tascarella Custom Cues, listed in the Trademark Index.

SPECIFICATIONS

Butt material: hardwoods
Shaft material: rock maple
Standard length: 58 in.
Lengths available: any
Standard wrap: Irish linen
Point construction: short splice or full splice
Standard joint: stainless steel
Joint type: piloted
Joint screws: 5/16-14 or 3/8-10
Standard number of shafts: two
Standard ferrules: ivory
Standard Tip: Le Pro
Annual production: very limited

OPTIONS (FOR NEW CUES ONLY)

Options priced on a per cue basis.

GRADING	100%	95%	70%

REPAIRS
Repairs done on all fine cues. Repair prices given on a per cue basis.

CURRENT TASCARELLA CUES
Basic Tascarella cues with wraps and joint rings start at $1,750. Tascarella cues with four points and four veneers start at $2,000. The current delivery time for a Tascarella cue is four years.

CURRENT EXAMPLES
The following Tascarella cue can be ordered as shown, modified to suit the desires of the customer, or new designs can be created.

Level 4 - Ivory joint, bird's-eye maple forearm, four rosewood points with four colored veneers and an ivory diamond-shaped inlay in each point, rosewood butt sleeve four ivory diamond-shaped inlays alternating with four ivory dots around center.

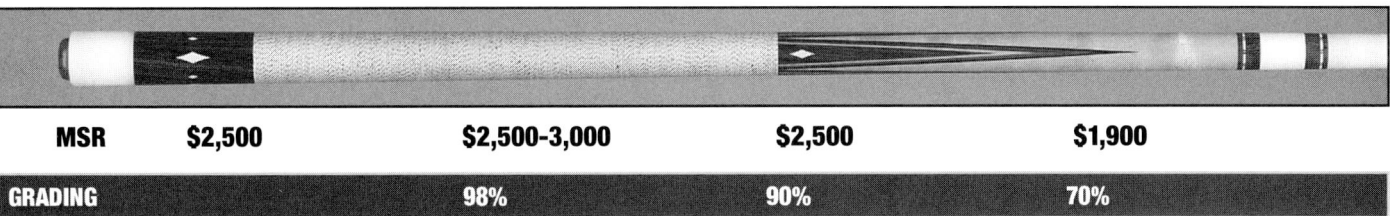

MSR	$2,500	$2,500-3,000	$2,500	$1,900
GRADING	98%	90%		70%

SECONDARY MARKET MINIMUM VALUES
The following are minimum values for Tascarella cues encountered on the secondary market. These prices are representative of cues utilizing basic materials and designs that are not necessarily available at present. Tascarella has offered one-of-a-kind cues that can command many times these prices due to the use of exotic materials and artistry.

Special construction note: There are many materials and construction techniques that can add value to Tascarella cues. For all used Tascarella cues, except where otherwise noted:

- Add $185 for each additional original straight playable shaft beyond two.
- Deduct $250 for each missing original straight playable shaft under two.
- Add $85 for leather wrap.
- Deduct 25% for obvious or improper refinish.

Level 2 - 0 points, 0-25 inlays.
Level 2 cues start at	$1,800	$1,450	$1,000

Level 3 - 2-6 points, 0-8 inlays.
Level 3 cues start at	$2,500	$2,000	$1,450

Level 4 - 4-10 points, 9-25 inlays.
Level 4 cues start at	$3,000	$2,450	$1,750

Level 5 - 0-12 points, 26-50 inlays.
Level 5 cues start at	$4,000	$3,350	$2,400

Level 6 - 0-12 points, 51-75 inlays.
Level 6 cues start at	$5,500	$4,400	$3,000

TAYLOR CUE COMPANY

Maker of pool cues from 1985 to present, currently in Edmond, Oklahoma.

Kent Taylor bought his first lathe at the age of 14 and began refinishing bowling pins for a local bowling alley in Southeastern Kansas. Kent's step-father was a tool and die maker with whom Kent worked part time during his school years, learning to run various types of machine tools and at the same time developing an interest in woodworking and cabinet making. In the mid-1980s, Kent started a cue repair business in the Dallas/Fort Worth area and began making custom cues. Moving to Colorado in 1990, he later resurrected his cue business in 1998. The early cues are not marked and are difficult to identify. All cues completed after July 1998 are signed and dated.

Present Day

Kent Taylor

TAYLOR CUE COMPANY, cont.

Kent moved his cue shop to Edmond, OK, in October 2000. He needed to get away from the thin air in Colorado that was aggravating his emphysema, and he wanted to move closer to his mother. He built a new climate-controlled and humidity-controlled shop that included five lathes, two pantographs, and a full spectrum of woodworking equipment. Kent Taylor creates one-of-a-kind cues with the help of his sons Joey and Zach. All Taylor Cues are hand-fabricated without the aid of CNC, and no plastics are used. Taylor Cues are players' cues based on Kent's 40+ years of professional playing experience.

Taylor Cues are guaranteed against manufacturing defects that are not the result of warpage or abuse. If you have a Taylor Cue that needs further identification or repair, or would like to order a new Taylor Cue, contact Taylor Cue Company, listed in the Trademark Index.

SPECIFICATIONS

Butt material: hardwoods
Shaft Material: hard rock maple
Standard length: 58 in.
Lengths Available: 55 to 60 in.
Standard finish: urethane
Balance Point: 18 in. to 19 in. from butt
Standard butt cap: phenolic
Standard wrap: Irish linen
Point construction: short splice
Standard joint: linen base phenolic
Joint type: true pilot
Joint Screw Thread: 5/16-14
Joint protectors: standard
Standard number of shafts: two
Standard taper: custom pro
Standard ferrules: melamine
Standard tip: Triangle
Standard tip width: 13 mm
Tip widths available: 11 to 14 mm
Annual production: fewer than 50 cues

OPTIONS (FOR NEW CUES ONLY)

Special length: $65
Layered tip: $16
Ivory butt cap: $290
Ivory butt sleeve: $590
Ivory joint: $135
Ivory ferrule: $40
Ivory points: $200 each
Leather wrap: $80
Joint protectors: $100
Extra shaft: $135

REPAIRS

Repairs done on all fine cues.
Refinish (with Irish linen wrap): $150
Refinish (with leather wrap): $210
Rewrap (Irish linen): $40
Rewrap (leather): $100
Clean and press linen wrap: $25
Restore leather wrap: $40+
Replace shaft: $130
Replace ivory ferrule: $75
Replace butt cap: $60
Replace ivory butt cap: $350
Replace ivory joint: $195
Replace tip: $10
Replaced layered tip: $25
Replace fiber/linen/ferrule and tip: $35

SECONDARY MARKET MINIMUM VALUES

The following are minimum values for Taylor cues encountered on the secondary market. These prices are representative of cues utilizing basic materials and designs that are not currently available. Kent Taylor has offered one-of-a-kind cues that can command many times these prices due to the use of exotic materials and artistry.

Special construction note: There are many materials and construction techniques that can add value to Taylor cues.

For all used Taylor cues, except where otherwise noted:

Add $100 for each additional original straight playable shaft beyond one.
Deduct $130 for missing original straight playable shaft.

GRADING	98%	90%	70%

Add $35 each for ivory ferrules.
Add $60 for leather wrap.
Deduct 20% for obvious or improper refinish.

	98%	90%	70%
Level 3 - 2-6 points, 0-8 inlays.			
Level 3 cues start at	$700	$525	$345
Level 4 - 4-10 points, 9-25 inlays.			
Level 4 cues start at	$900	$675	$440
Level 5 - 0-12 points, 26-50 inlays.			
Level 5 cues start at	$1,400	$1,050	$675
Level 6 - 0-12 points, 51-75 inlays.			
Level 6 cues start at	$1,750	$1,350	$850

TC CUES

Maker of pool cues from 1998 to present in Orange, France.

Thierry Chevron began making cues in Orange France in 1998. His sister is a good lady player in France. Theirry wanted to make her a cue. What began as a part-time job is now a full-time occupation, even though he was already working with wood. His work is inspired by Jerry Franklin, Dennis Searing, and Kersenbrock. Thierry makes all his cue components, and all of his cues are handmade.

If you are interested in talking to Thierry Chevron about a new cue or cue that needs to be repaired, you can contact him at TC Cues, listed in the Trademark Index.

Thierry Chevron

Present Day

SPECIFICATIONS

Butt material: hardwoods
Shaft material: rock maple
Standard length: 58 in.
Lengths available: any
Standard finish: catalized urethane
Balance point: 1 to 2 in. above wrap
Standard butt cap: linen phenolic
Standard wrap: Irish linen
Point construction: traditional
Joint type: flat faced
Joint screw thread: radial pin
Standard number of shafts: two
Standard taper: custom
Standard ferrules: Ivorine-3
Standard tip: Triangle
Standard tip width: 13 mm
Annual production: fewer than 50 cues

OPTIONS (FOR NEW CUES ONLY)

Special length: $50 per inch
Layered tip: $30
Ivory butt cap: $200+
Ivory joint: $100
Ivory ferrule: $70
Joint protectors: $200+
Extra shaft: $100

REPAIRS

Repairs done on all fine cues.
Refinish (with Irish linen wrap): $120
Refinish (with leather wrap): $180
Rewrap (Irish linen): $45
Rewrap (leather): $100
Clean and press linen wrap: $20
Replace shaft: $150
Replace ivory ferrule: $70
Replace butt cap: $40
Replace ivory butt cap: $200
Replace tip: $20+
Replace fiber/linen ferrule: $40

GRADING	98%	90%	70%

CURRENT TC CUES

Two-piece TC bar cues start at $400. Basic TC cues with wraps and joint rings start at $500. TC cues with points start at $700. One-of-a-kind custom TC cues start at $1,000. The current delivery time for a TC cue is at least six months, depending on the intricacy of the cue.

SECONDARY MARKET MINIMUM VALUES

The following are minimum values for TC cues encountered on the secondary market. These prices are representative of cues utilizing basic materials and designs that are not necessarily available at present. Thierry has offered one-of-a-kind cues that can command many times these prices due to the use of exotic materials and artistry.

Special construction note: There are many materials and construction techniques that can add value to TC cues.

For all used TC cues, except where otherwise noted:
- Add $75 for each additional original straight playable shaft beyond two.
- Deduct $100 for each missing original straight playable shaft under two.
- Add $55 each for ivory ferrules.
- Add $75 for leather wrap.
- Deduct 20% for obvious or improper refinish.

	98%	90%	70%
Level 1 - Hustler.			
Level 1 cues start at	$375	$295	$195
Level 2 - 0 points, 0-25 inlays.			
Level 2 cues start at	$450	$350	$240
Level 3 - 2-6 points, 0-8 inlays.			
Level 3 cues start at	$650	$515	$350
Level 4 - 4-10 points, 9-25 inlays.			
Level 4 cues start at	$750	$575	$395
Level 5 - 0-12 points, 26-50 inlays.			
Level 5 cues start at	$1,000	$790	$550
Level 6 - 0-12 points, 51-75 inlays.			
Level 6 cues start at	$1,400	$1,100	$750

DALE TEAGUE

Maker of L.T.D. Custom Cues. For further information refer to L.T.D. Cues.

TERBROCK CUES

Maker of pool cues from 1993 to present in Manchester, Missouri.

Jerry Terbrock is one of the best players in the St. Louis area. He opened Chesterfield Billiards in St. Louis in 1991, and he started doing cue repairs in the room. In 1993 Jerry made his first cue. In 2001 Jerry sold the pool room and built a shop in his house. Before that his cues were not marked, but in 2001 he started putting a "T" on the butt caps for identification. Playability is most important for Jerry. All of his cues are one-of-a-kind. He makes his cues in a one-man shop that includes a pantogrph and CNC equipment. Jerry makes everything except for the bumpers, screws, and tips, and all components are threaded together. Points can be inlaid or short spliced. Jerry prefers wood handles, which also provide more room for inlays.

Terbrock cues are guaranteed for the original owner against construction defects that are not the result of warpage or abuse.

If you are interested in talking to Jerry about a new cue or cue that needs to be repaired, you can contact him at Terbrock Cues, listed in the Trademark Index.

SPECIFICATIONS

Butt material: hardwoods
Shaft material: rock maple
Standard length: 58 in.
Lengths available: any
Standard finish: acrylic urethane
Balance point: custom
Standard butt cap: phenolic
Standard handle: wood
Point construction: short splice
Standard joint: phenolic
Joint type: flat faced
Joint screw: radial pin
Standard number of shafts: one
Standard taper: 14 in. straight

GRADING	98%	90%	70%

Standard ferrules: Aegis
Standard tip: Talisman
Annual production: fewer than 40 cues

OPTIONS (FOR NEW CUES ONLY)

Special length: no charge
Ivory ferrule: $75
Ivory butt cap: $150
Ivory joint: $100
Leather wrap: $80
Extra shaft: $100

REPAIRS

Repairs done on all fine cues.
Refinish (with Irish linen wrap): $150
Refinish (with leather wrap): $200
Rewrap (Irish linen): $40
Rewrap (leather): $80
Replace Talisman tip: $20
Replace Aegis ferrule with Talisman tip: $35

CURRENT TERBROCK CUES

Two-piece Terbrock bar cues start at $175. Basic Terbrock cues with wraps and joint rings start at $375. Terbrock cues with points start at $475. One-of-a-kind custom Terbrock cues start at $900. Terbrock cues over $1,000 come with two shafts. The current delivery time for a Terbrock cue is six to eight weeks.

SECONDARY MARKET MINIMUM VALUES

The following are minimum values for Terbrock cues encountered on the secondary market. These prices are representative of cues utilizing basic materials and designs that are not necessarily available at present. Jerry has offered one-of-a-kind cues that can command many times these prices due to the use of exotic materials and artistry.

Special construction note: There are many materials and construction techniques that can add value to Terbrock cues.

For all used Terbrock cues, except where otherwise noted:
Add $75 for each additional original straight playable shaft beyond two.
Deduct $100 for each missing original straight playable shaft under two.
Add $60 each for ivory ferrules.
Add $50 for leather wrap.
Deduct 20% for obvious or improper refinish.

	98%	90%	70%
Level 1 - Hustler.			
Level 1 cues start at	$150	$115	$70
Level 2 - 0 points, 0-25 inlays.			
Level 2 cues start at	$275	$210	$135
Level 3 - 2-6 points, 0-8 inlays.			
Level 3 cues start at	$400	$300	$190
Level 4 - 4-10 points, 9-25 inlays.			
Level 4 cues start at	$500	$375	$235
Level 5 - 0-12 points, 26-50 inlays.			
Level 5 cues start at	$750	$565	$360
Level 6 - 0-12 points, 51-75 inlays.			
Level 6 cues start at	$1,000	$745	$465

JOE THOMAS CUES

Maker of pool cues from 1960 to present in Toledo, Ohio.

Joe "Toledo Joe" Thomas is one of the few old-school cuemakers that are still making cues. When he started, his main competition was Paradise, Rambow, and Martin. Balabushka and Ginacue were just getting started. Joe had taken machine shop in high school and worked for his family's shoe stores. He later worked for a military contractor making parts for bomb sights. Joe was a very good pool player so he decided to start making cues in 1960. He liked the way Paradise cues were identified, so in the 1960s he started putting "Joe Thomas Custom Cues Toledo, Ohio" under a clear plastic window in the butt sleeve. He still does this today.

Joe can make all of his own components. In the shoe business he learned how to mold rubber soles and work with leather. He has used this knowledge to mold rubber bumpers and make leather tips which he sometimes uses. Joe also makes his own joint screws. When he started he used Titlist blanks. Then he started buying blanks from Burton Spain. Now he prefers solid wood forearms, usually cocobolo. Joe likes decorative rings of colored plastics and he used to do mother-of-pearl inlays by hand. He also prefers hand-carved French

| GRADING | 98% | 90% | 70% |

fluted wood handles instead of wraps. Early cues usually had aluminum joints but now brass is most common. Stainless steel and ivory are other options which have been available. Joe has also experimented with buckhorn for ferrules, joints, and butt caps.

Today Joe owns a small pool room with just one table and his one-man shop. He has slowed down his cuemaking, building less than ten cues a year. All work is done by hand without the aid of CNC. Shafts are hand sanded and butts are finished with five coats of hand-rubbed lacquer. He also makes unique red, white, and blue cue cases out of newspapers and duct tape.

If you are interested in talking to Joe Thomas about a new cue or cue that needs to be repaired, you can contact him at Joe Thomas Cues, listed in the Trademark Index.

SPECIFICATIONS

Butt material: hardwoods
Shaft material: rock maple
Standard length: 57 in.
Lengths available: any
Standard finish: lacquer
Standard handle: French fluted
Point construction: short splice
Standard joint: brass
Joint type: piloted
Joint screw: 5/16-18
Standard number of shafts: one
Standard taper: custom
Standard tip: Le Pro
Annual production: fewer than 10 cues

OPTIONS (FOR NEW CUES ONLY)

Special length: no charge
Extra shaft: $100+

REPAIRS

Repairs done on all fine cues.
Refinish (with Irish linen wrap): $125
Rewrap (Irish linen): $40

CURRENT JOE THOMAS CUES

Basic two-piece Joe Thomas hustler cues start at $100. Basic two-piece Joe Thomas cues with wraps and joint rings start at $300. One-of-a-kind custom Joe Thomas cues start at $500. The current delivery time for a Joe Thomas cue is about six weeks.

SECONDARY MARKET MINIMUM VALUES

The following are minimum values for other Joe Thomas cues encountered on the secondary market. These prices are representative of cues utilizing basic materials and designs that are not necessarily available at present. Joe has offered one-of-a-kind cues that can command many times these prices due to the use of exotic materials and artistry.

Special construction note: There are many materials and construction techniques that can add value to Joe Thomas cues.

For all used Joe Thomas cues, except where otherwise noted:

Add $75 for each additional original straight playable shaft beyond one.
Deduct $100 for missing original straight playable shaft.
Deduct 25% for obvious or improper refinish.

Level 2 - 0 points, 0-25 inlays.
	98%	90%	70%
Level 2 cues start at	$300	$225	$145

Level 3 - 2-6 points, 0-8 inlays.
	98%	90%	70%
Level 3 cues start at	$450	$340	$220

Level 4 - 4-10 points, 9-25 inlays.
	98%	90%	70%
Level 4 cues start at	$700	$525	$340

Level 5 - 0-12 points, 26-50 inlays.
	98%	90%	70%
Level 5 cues start at	$1,200	$900	$575

GRADING	100%	95%	70%

THOMPSON CUES U.S.A.

Maker of pool cues from 1992 to present in Fort Worth, Texas.

Hank Thompson began making cues as a hobby in 1992 in Fort Worth, Texas. Hank has been a pool player for over 40 years, and he has worked on cues and sold cues almost all of his life. He was inspired by Richard Black and Schon Cues.

If you are interested in talking to Hank Thompson about a new cue or cue that needs to be repaired, you can contact him at Thompson Cues U.S.A., listed in the Trademark Index.

Hank Thompson

SPECIFICATIONS

- Butt material: hardwoods
- Shaft material: rock maple
- Standard length: 58 in.
- Lengths available: any up to 60 in.
- Standard finish: urethane
- Balance point: custom
- Standard butt cap: fiber
- Standard wrap: Irish linen
- Point construction: short splice
- Standard joint: fiber
- Joint type: flat faced
- Joint screw thread: 3/8-10
- Standard nunber of shafts: one
- Standard Taper: 10 to 15 in.
- Standard ferrules: fiber
- Standard tip: water buffalo
- Standard tip width: 13 mm
- Annual production: 40 cues

OPTIONS (FOR NEW CUES ONLY)

- Layered tip: $35
- Ivory butt cap: $220
- Ivory butt sleeve: $220
- Ivory joint: $110
- Ivory ferrule: $55
- Joint protectors: $35
- Extra shaft: $60+

REPAIRS

Repairs done on all fine cues.
- Refinish (with Irish linen wrap): $125
- Rewrap (Irish linen): $40
- Clean and press linen wrap: $20
- Replace shaft: $60+
- Replace ivory ferrule: $55
- Replace butt cap: $30
- Replace ivory butt cap: $220
- Replace tip: $10
- Replaced layered tip: $35
- Replace fiber/linen ferrule: $15

CURRENT THOMPSON CUES USA CUES

Two-piece Thompson bar cues start at $150. Basic Thompson cues with wraps and joint rings, with or without points, start at $200. One-of-a-kind custom Thompson cues start at $500. The current delivery time for a Thompson cue is from one week to three months depending on the intricacy of the cue.

CURRENT EXAMPLES

The following Thompson cues can be ordered as shown, modified to suit the desires of the customer, or new designs can be created.

Level 1 - Maple forearm, four full-spliced rosewood points and handle.

MSR	$175	$150-200	$125	$95

GRADING	100%	95%	70%

Level 1 - Maple forearm, four full-spliced ebony points and handle.

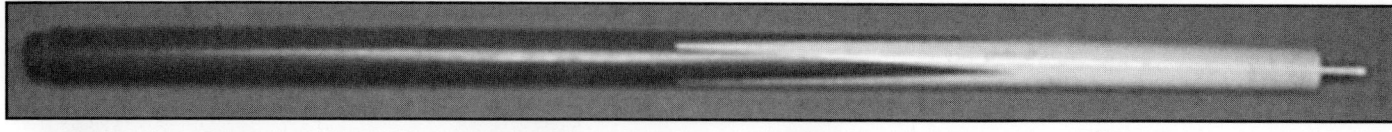

MSR	$250	$200-250	$170	$135

Level 2 - Curly maple forearm, bocote handle, cocobolo butt sleeve with ivory rings at top and bottom.

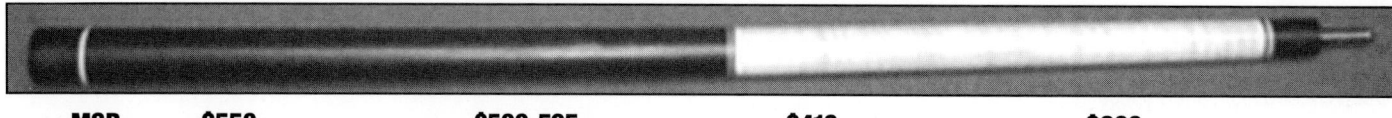

MSR	$500	$450-550	$375	$285

Level 2 - Curly maple forearm, ebony handle and butt sleeve with an ivory ring at bottom.

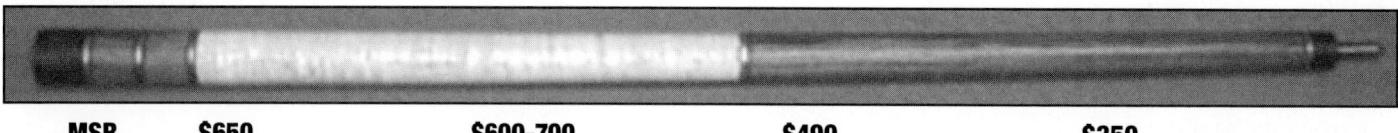

MSR	$550	$500-595	$410	$300

Level 2 - Cocobolo forearm with silver rings above handle, curly maple handle, cocobolo butt sleeve with silver rings in center and at top and bottom.

MSR	$650	$600-700	$490	$350

Level 3 - Ivory joint, cherry forearm, four full-spliced rosewood points and handle, ivory butt cap.

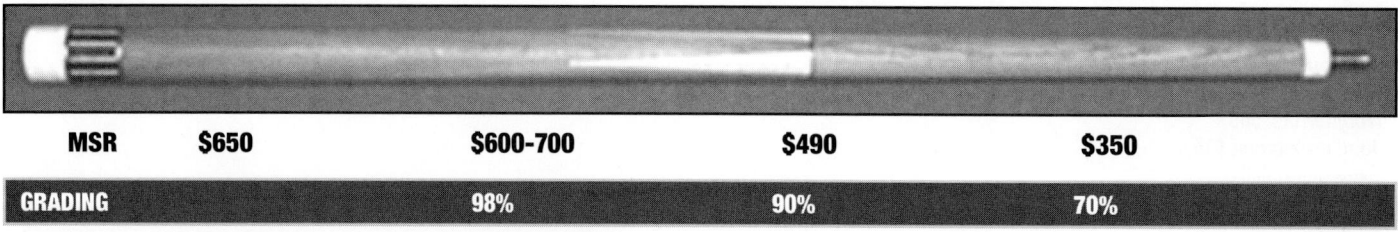

MSR	$650	$600-700	$490	$350

GRADING	98%	90%	70%

SECONDARY MARKET MINIMUM VALUES

The following are minimum values for other Thompson cues encountered on the secondary market. These prices are representative of cues utilizing basic materials and designs that are not necessarily available at present. Hank Thompson has offered one-of-a-kind cues that can command many times these prices due to the use of exotic materials and artistry.

Special construction note: There are many materials and construction techniques that can add value to Thompson cues.

For all used Thompson cues, except where otherwise noted:

- Add $50 for each additional original straight playable shaft beyond one.
- Deduct $60 for missing original straight playable shaft.
- Add $50 each for ivory ferrules.
- Deduct 15% for obvious or improper refinish.

Level 1 - Hustler.

Level 1 cues start at	$140	$115	$80

Level 2 - 0 points, 0-25 inlays.

Level 2 cues start at	$180	$145	$100

Level 3 - 2-6 points, 0-8 inlays.

Level 3 cues start at	$190	$150	$105

Level 4 - 4-10 points, 9-25 inlays.

Level 4 cues start at	$300	$235	$170

Level 5 - 0-12 points, 26-50 inlays.

Level 5 cues start at	$500	$395	$275

DANNY TIBBITTS CUSTOM CUES

Maker of pool cues from 1985 to present in Woodstock, Georgia.

Danny Tibbitts began playing pool as a boy in the Atlanta area, at Warren Memorial Boy's Club. He was also interested in woodworking, and began to do handcarving by age 14. At 17, Danny got a job doing carpentry. He showed a talent for custom cabinetry and eventually specialized in doing high-end, one-of-a-kind custom-made staircases. He continued to play pool, and decided he would prefer to use his skills making cues, instead of doing custom woodwork in homes.

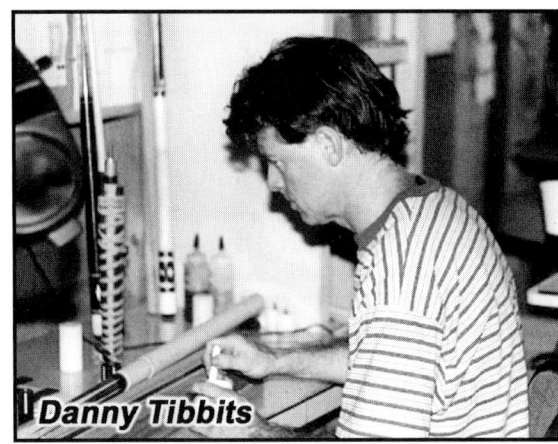
Danny Tibbits

In 1985, Danny made his first cue. Over the next three or four years, Danny made very few cues. These early cues are identifiable by the initials "D.T." in block letters on the cues. Soon, he switched to a stylized "D.T." logo in italic letters, which appeared on almost every cue until 2000. That year Danny started to sign his cues in metallic ink. These signatures are either his full name, or his last name and the year of completion. As Danny is a strong player, playability has always been a very important factor in his cues. Danny has made two "Grecian" cues with gold wire inlaid into ivory columns. All gold work was done freehand.

The most unique features of Tibbitts cues are the points, which are among the longest any cuemakers make. They feature a shorter handle area, so the points start about one inch further back than on most cues, and they go to within two inches of the joint collar. Danny puts the joint screw in the blank before the points are started, so that the points begin on center. This ensures even points, and Danny also makes them razor-sharp. Danny sometimes uses CNC equipment but he also does inlays on a manual pantograph, and achieves the kind of close tolerances that normally require CNC work. This is also true of the rings, collars, and joints, which Danny spends the extra time to perfectly align. Danny makes every component of his cues, except for the tips and the bumpers. He is currently developing his own laminated tip.

Danny Tibbitts Cues is a one-man, 800-square-foot shop behind Danny's house, and all work is done by him. He makes cues full time and currently only makes one-of-a-kind fancy cues. A few construction techniques have changed over the years to improve the playability and strength of Danny Tibbitts cues. All shafts are cut 14 times over the course of three years to prevent warpage, and feature Danny's unique taper, which he personally developed. All ivory has been seasoned and aged at least 14 years. For the forearms he prefers straight-grained maple for its playability and durability over highly figured maple. Danny spends many hours perfecting each cue, completing them with a hand-rubbed finish. In 20 years, he has made less than 100 cues.

If you have a Danny Tibbitts cue that needs further identification or repair, or would like to talk to Danny about ordering a new custom cue, contact Danny Tibbitts Custom Cues, listed in the Trademark Index.

SPECIFICATIONS

- Butt material: hardwoods
- Shaft material: rock maple
- Standard length: 58 in.
- Lengths available: any
- Standard finish: Imron
- Standard joint screw: 5/16-14
- Standard joint: stainless steel
- Standard joint type: piloted
- Balance point: custom
- Point construction: short splice
- Standard wrap: Irish linen
- Standard butt cap: Delrin
- Standard number of shafts: two
- Standard taper: custom
- Standard ferrules: ivory
- Standard tip: anything customer wants
- Tip widths available: any
- Annual production: fewer than 20 cues

OPTIONS (FOR NEW CUES ONLY)

- Leather wrap: $125
- Ivory joint: $125
- Joint protectors: $90+ per set
- Ivory butt cap: $250
- Extra shaft: $175+

REPAIRS

Repairs done on all fine cues.

- Refinish (with leather wrap): $325
- Refinish (with Irish linen wrap): $250
- Rewrap (leather): $150
- Rewrap (linen): $45+

GRADING	98%	90%	70%

Rewrap (Courtland linen): $75
Replace Delrin butt cap: $85
Replace ivory butt cap: P.O.R.
Replace ivory ferrule: $85
Replace chandivert tip (with pad): $20
Replace layered tip: $25+
Replace shaft: $175+

CURRENT DANNY TIBBITTS CUES

One-of-a-kind Danny Tibbits cues start at $3,000. The current delivery time for a Tibbitts custom cue is a long time.

SECONDARY MARKET MINIMUM VALUES

The following are minimum prices for Tibbitts cues encountered on the secondary market. These prices are representative of cues utilizing basic materials and designs that may not be currently available. Danny currently specializes in one-of-a-kind cues that can command many times these prices due to the use of exotic materials and artistry.

Special construction note: There are many materials and construction techniques that can add value to Danny Tibbitts cues.

For all used Danny Tibbitts cues:

Add $150+ for each additional original straight playable shaft over two.
Deduct $175+ for each missing original straight playable shaft under two.
Deduct 25% for obvious or improper refinish.

Level 3 - 2-6 points, 0-8 inlays.

Level 3 cues start at	$2,250	$1,850	$1,400

Level 4 - 4-10 points, 9-25 inlays.

Level 4 cues start at	$2,800	$2,300	$1,700

Level 5 - 0-12 points, 26-50 inlays.

Level 5 cues start at	$4,000	$3,300	$2,400

Level 6 - 0-12 points, 51-75 inlays.

Level 6 cues start at	$6,000	$4,900	$3,500

Level 7 - 0-12 points, 76-125 inlays.

Level 7 cues start at	$8,500	$6,950	$5,000

DAVID TICE CUSTOM CUES

Maker of pool cues from 1970 to present in Leavenworth, Washington.

David Tice started playing pool as a kid. As an adult, he went through many different cues, but was never able to find one he was totally satisfied with. David went to the University of Washington, where he earned his degree in electrical engineering. After school, he landed a job with Intel as a design engineer. In his spare time, he set out to make the perfect pool cue, completing his first cue in 1970.

For the next 20 years, David made cues off and on at the rate of about one per month, constantly experimenting with different designs and construction techniques. He dreamed of making cues full-time for years, and in 1990, he left Intel to do so. David now makes about 20 cues per year in his one-man shop. He makes everything except for the tips, bumpers, and screws, and all work is done by hand without the aid of CNC. David also holds several patents, including one for a golf club.

David Tice cues feature traditional designs, and he prefers simple cues that stress playability. Although David Tice cues are unmarked, they are easily recognizable to those who know his work. They can be identified by his fancy trim rings with small intricate inlays. David refuses to use ivory or elk horn in his cues because he is opposed to poaching, and he believes there are superior synthetics available. David specializes in making one-of-a-kind custom cues to the design and specifications of the specific customer. Lengths, weights, diameters, handle dimensions, joint types, point and inlay designs, etc. can all be tailored to the customer. David has developed a computer modeling program that allows him to input all of these specifications, and he can weigh and balance the cue using the normal construction materials. If a Tice cue has points it will have no less than six. David likes to make 12-point cues and has put as many as 80 two-layered points in a cue.

In 1997 he started using wood stabilizer on all his shafts to virtually eliminate shaft warpage due to environmental variables. David has developed a pendulum mechanism that tests each individual shaft for deflection. It hangs from a ceiling over a table and hits shots with accuracy to within one twentieth of an inch. He used the knowledge from years of experimenting with this device to develop a new low-deflection shaft in 1999. According to his own tests, it is as accurate as any modern low-deflection shaft he has tried. David now likes to make laminated shafts and handles for his cues, which he started doing in 2004.

Dave Tice cues are guaranteed indefinitely against construction defects that are not the result of warpage or abuse. If you have a David Tice cue that needs further identification or repair, or would like to talk to David about ordering a new custom cue, contact David Tice Custom Cues, listed in the Trademark Index.

SPECIFICATIONS

Butt material: hardwoods
Shaft material: laminated rock maple
Standard length: 58 in.
Lengths available: any

DAVID TICE CUSTOM CUES, cont. 795

GRADING	98%	90%	70%

- Standard finish: polyurethane
- Standard balance point: 18.5 in. from butt
- Standard butt cap: double black linen phenolic 0.8 in.
- Standard Wrap: Irish linen
- Point construction: short splice
- Standard joint: black linen phenolic
- Joint type: flat faced
- Joint screw thread: 3/8-10
- Standard number of shafts: two
- Standard taper: complex equation
- Standard ferrules: Aegis I
- Standard tip: Le Pro
- Standard tip width: 13 mm
- Tip widths available: any
- Annual production: fewer than 25 cues

OPTIONS (FOR NEW CUES ONLY)

- Special length: no charge
- Layered tip: $10
- Leather wrap: $100
- Joint protectors: $45
- Extra shaft: $125

REPAIRS

Repairs done on David Tice cues only.
- Replace tip: $15
- Replaced layered tip: $25
- Replace fiber/linen ferrule: $20

CURRENT DAVID TICE CUES

Basic David Tice cues with wraps and joint rings start at $325. David Tice cues with points start at $600. The current delivery time for a David Tice cue is about three to four months.

SECONDARY MARKET MINIMUM VALUES

The following are minimum prices for David Tice cues encountered on the secondary market. These prices are representative of cues utilizing basic materials and designs that may not be currently available. David also offers one-of-a-kind cues that can command many times these prices due to the use of exotic materials and artistry.

Special construction note: There are many materials and construction techniques that can add value to David Tice cues.

For all used David Tice cues, except where otherwise noted:
- Add $100+ for each additional original straight playable shaft over two.
- Deduct $125 for each missing original straight playable shaft under two.
- Deduct 20% for obvious or improper refinish.

	98%	90%	70%
Level 1 - 4 points, hustler.			
Level 1 cues start at	$300	$245	$175
Level 2 - 0 points, 0-25 inlays.			
Level 2 cues start at	$550	$475	$295
Level 3 - 2-6 points, 0-8 inlays.			
Level 3 cues start at	$700	$565	$385
Level 4 - 4-10 points, 9-25 inlays.			
Level 4 cues start at	$1,000	$795	$550
Level 5 - 0-12 points, 26-50 inlays.			
Level 5 cues start at	$1,750	$1,400	$950

ROCKY TILLIS

Maker of pool cues from the 1960s to the early 1990s in Tampa, Florida.

Rocky Tillis was a railroad engineer who lived in Tampa, Florida. Rocky decided to use the equipment and experience gained from his woodworking hobby to make his son a pool cue. The second cue Rocky made was similar to a friend's Balabushka. Many people got to see this cue when it was finished, since Tampa is a city with a great demand for custom cues and repairs. Players who saw this cue were impressed, and repair work soon followed. Rocky was also being asked to make custom cues for local players.

Rocky Tillis cues were not marked, but they are easily recognizable to those who know his work. He worked on one lathe, and had very little equipment, so many of his inlays were dots. He very often put dots in a clover-leaf pattern at the tips of the points, and his fancy

| GRADING | 98% | 90% | 70% |

cues had many more dots. He also liked to cut up old snooker balls and pool balls to use for inlay material, and red, black, or pink windows and dots from these are also encountered. He liked to use African boquiva wood for butt sleeves. He was an absolute perfectionist, and threw away many cues that weren't to his satisfaction. He also made many two-piece bar cues, and he made cues from Titlist blanks and Burton Spain blanks.

Rocky made what was called a half joint, which was 5/8 in. long. He was using super hard stainless steel from used railroad components. These cues were nicknamed "Choo-choo cues."

Rocky took a short break from cuemaking after suffering a stroke in 1983. He later made a few more cues before he died in the 1990s.

If you have a Rocky Tillis cue that needs further identification or repair, contact Wayne Gunn or Terry McEniry of Gunn Cues, listed in the Trademark Index.

SPECIFICATIONS

Butt material: hardwoods
Shaft material: rock maple
Standard length: 58 in.
Standard wrap: Irish linen
Point construction: short splice
Standard joint: stainless
Standard number of shafts: two
Standard ferrules: ivory

PAST EXAMPLES

The following Rocky Tillis cues can be encountered as shown, or modified to suit the desires of the original customer. Almost all Rocky Tillis cues encountered will be one-of-a-kind.

Level 2 - Stainless steel "half joint" bird's-eye maple forearm, ebony butt sleeve with six bird's-eye maple windows.

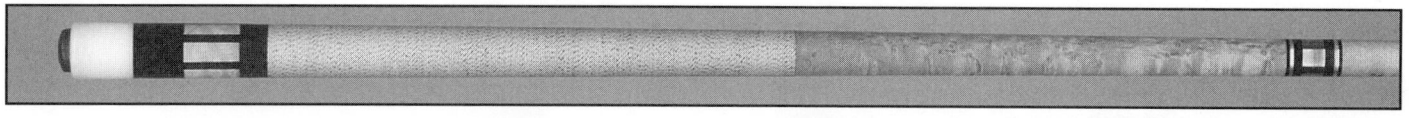

| $1,000 | $790 | $550 |

Level 4 - Bird's-eye maple forearm, six ebony points with maple dots between the bases of the points, bird's-eye maple butt sleeve with ebony windows between ebony arched rings at top and bottom.

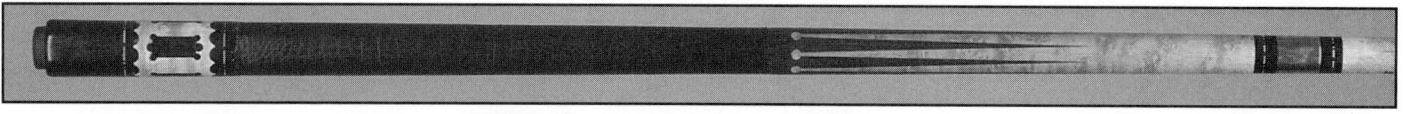

| $2,000 | $1,650 | $1,200 |

Level 5 "Titlist" - Maple forearm, four rosewood points with four colored veneers and inlay work, ebony butt sleeve with inlay work under a clear plastic window in center.

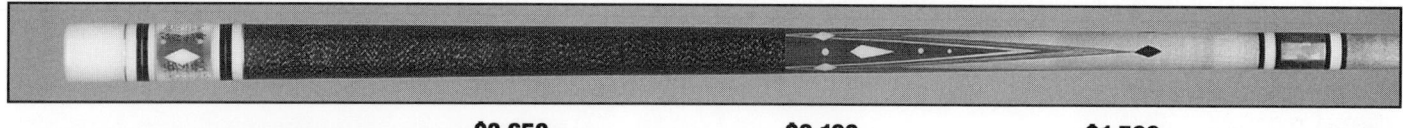

| $2,650 | $2,100 | $1,500 |

SECONDARY MARKET MINIMUM VALUES

The following are minimum values for other Rocky Tillis cues encountered on the secondary market. These prices are representative of cues utilizing basic materials and designs. Rocky Tillis cues can command many times these prices due to the use of exotic materials and artistry.

Special construction note: There are many materials and construction techniques that can add value to Rocky Tillis cues. The following are the most important examples:

Add $650 for red windows (made from three-balls).
For all used Rocky Tillis cues:
Add $200 for each additional original straight playable shaft beyond two.
Deduct $250 for each missing original straight playable shaft under two.
Deduct 30% for obvious or improper refinish.

Level 1 - 4 points, hustler.
  Level 1 cues start at $350 $285 $200
Level 2 - 0 points, 0-25 inlays.
  Level 2 cues start at $850 $685 $500

GRADING	98%	90%	70%
Level 3 - 2-6 points, 0-8 inlays.			
Level 3 cues start at	$1,500	$1,250	$900
Level 4 - 4-10 points, 9-25 inlays.			
Level 4 cues start at	$2,000	$1,650	$1,200
Level 5 - 0-12 points, 26-50 inlays.			
Level 5 cues start at	$2,500	$2,100	$1,500

TING CUSTOM CUES

Maker of pool cues from 1994 to present in Burlington, New Jersey.

Gus Pinca started playing pool in the 1970s. He made his first cue in 1994. A full-time custom furniture maker, Gus specializes in custom oak interior work on new homes. At night he makes cues as a hobby in the shop he has at home. Most Ting cues are one-of-a-kind designs. Inlay work can be done by hand or on the CNC machine that Gus modified. Gus also has a metal lathe so he can make any type of screw thread himself, from metals or exotic materials like G-10 epoxy. He can make any type of flat-faced or piloted joint. Gus prefers handles of exotic woods or leather as opposed to Irish linen.

Ting cues are easily identified by a "Gus Pinca" signature or the initials "TP" engraved on the tip of the joint screw or on the butt cap. Gus guarantees his cues against construction defects that are not the result of abuse, and they are guaranteed against warpage for one year. If you are interested in talking to Gus about a new cue or cue that needs to be repaired, you can contact him at Ting Custom Cues, listed in the Trademark Index.

Gus Pinca

SPECIFICATIONS

Butt material: hardwoods
Shaft material: rock maple
Standard length: 58 in.
Lengths available: any up to 60 in.
Standard finish: urethane
Balance point: 1 in. above wrap
Standard butt cap: linen phenolic
Standard wrap: Irish linen
Point construction: short splice
Standard joint: linen phenolic
Joint type: flat faced
Joint screw: 3/8-10
Standard number of shafts: one
Standard taper: 12 in. straight
Standard ferrules: linen based
Standard tip: Elk Master
Annual production: fewer than 30 cues

OPTIONS (FOR NEW CUES ONLY)

Special length: no charge
Extra shaft: $75+
Leather wrap: $50

REPAIRS

Repairs done on all fine cues.
Refinish (with Irish linen wrap): $100
Refinish (with leather wrap): $150
Rewrap (Irish linen): $35
Rewrap (leather): $50
Replace Elk Master tip: $10

CURRENT TING CUSTOM CUES

Two-piece Ting bar cues start at $125. Basic Ting cues with wraps and joint rings start at $225. Ting cues with points start at $300. One-of-a-kind custom Ting cues start at $375. The current delivery time is about two months or more, depending on the intricacy of the cue.

SECONDARY MARKET MINIMUM VALUES

The following are minimum values for other Ting cues encountered on the secondary market. These prices are representative of cues utilizing basic materials and designs that are not necessarily available at present. Gus has offered one-of-a-kind cues that can command many times these prices due to the use of exotic materials and artistry.

GRADING	98%	90%	70%

Special construction note: There are many materials and construction techniques that can add value to Ting cues. For all used Ting cues, except where otherwise noted:
- Add $60 for each additional original straight playable shaft beyond one.
- Deduct $75 for missing original straight playable shaft.
- Add $35 for leather wrap.
- Deduct 20% for obvious or improper refinish.

Level 1 - Hustler.

	98%	90%	70%
Level 1 cues start at	$100	$85	$60

Level 2 - 0 points, 0-25 inlays.

Level 2 cues start at	$200	$165	$115

Level 3 - 2-6 points, 0-8 inlays.

Level 3 cues start at	$275	$215	$150

Level 4 - 4-10 points, 9-25 inlays.

Level 4 cues start at	$350	$275	$185

Level 5 - 0-12 points, 26-50 inlays.

Level 5 cues start at	$600	$465	$310

Level 6 - 0-12 points, 51-75 inlays.

Level 6 cues start at	$850	$650	$400

TNS CUES

Maker of pool cues from 1996 to present in Rockland County, New York.

Tommy Migliore was brought up in Bridgeport, Connecticut. He started playing pool in his early teens but did not take it seriously at that time. After high school and college, he began working as a machinist in a large corporation making medical products. Tommy started playing pool again, and he bought his first two-piece cue. He noted the plastic joint protectors on cues owned by his pool league team members and decided to make his own joint protectors out of aluminum. Tommy's aluminum joint protectors became a popular item.

Tommy began doing cue repairs and experimented with making shafts. The owner of a pool room asked him to make a cue; this is how his cue making business began. Since that time, Tommy's cues have changed from very simple designs to more complex custom cue orders. Tommy's cues are unique in that he uses different metals to make the collars, pins, and other components so that the user will always find the right balance without having to take anything out of the wood.

If you are interested in talking to Tommy Migliore about a new cue or cue that needs to be repaired, you can contact him at TNS Cues, listed in the Trademark Index.

Tommy Migliore

SPECIFICATIONS

Butt material: hardwoods
Shaft material: rock maple
Standard finish: two-part Dupont clear coat
Standard wrap: Irish linen
Standard ferrules: linen based

REPAIRS

Repairs done on all fine cues.
Refinish (with Irish linen wrap): $125
Refinish (with leather wrap): $150
Rewrap (Irish linen): $45
Rewrap (leather): $75
Clean and press linen wrap: $20
Restore leather wrap: $20
Replace ivory ferrule: $150
Replace butt cap: $50
Replace ivory butt cap: $200
Replace tip: $15
Replaced layered tip: $40
Replace fiber/linen ferrule: $100

CURRENT TNS CUES

TNS CUES, cont.

GRADING	100%	95%	70%

Two-piece TNS bar cues start at $300. Basic TNS cues with wraps and joint rings start at $450. TNS cues with points start at $600. One-of-a-kind custom TNS cues start at $1,000. The current delivery time for a TNS cue is three to four months.

CURRENT EXAMPLES

The following TNS cue can be ordered as shown, modified to suit the desires of the customer, or new designs can be created.

Level 3 - African blackwood forearm with ringwork above wrap, three long and three short snakewood points with maple veneers, leather wrap, African blackwood butt sleeve with ringwork at top and bottom.

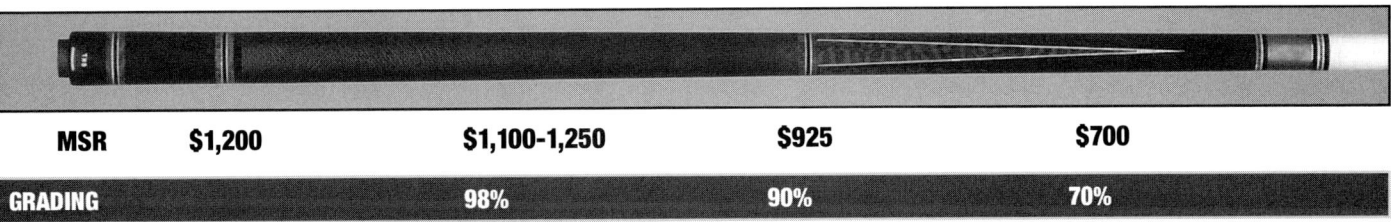

MSR	$1,200	$1,100-1,250	$925	$700
GRADING		98%	90%	70%

SECONDARY MARKET MINIMUM VALUES

The following are minimum values for other TNS cues encountered on the secondary market. These prices are representative of cues utilizing basic materials and designs that are not necessarily available at present. Tommy has offered one-of-a-kind cues that can command many times these prices due to the use of exotic materials and artistry.

Special construction note: There are many materials and construction techniques that can add value to TNS cues.

For all used TNS cues, except where otherwise noted:
- Add $100 each for ivory ferrules.
- Add $50 for leather wrap.
- Deduct 20% for obvious or improper refinish.

Level 1 - Hustler.
Level 1 cues start at	$250	$200	$140

Level 2 - 0 points, 0-25 inlays.
Level 2 cues start at	$400	$315	$215

Level 3 - 2-6 points, 0-8 inlays.
Level 3 cues start at	$600	$470	$325

Level 4 - 4-10 points, 9-25 inlays.
Level 4 cues start at	$750	$575	$395

Level 5 - 0-12 points, 26-50 inlays.
Level 5 cues start at	$1,000	$800	$575

TODD CUES

Maker of pool cues from 2001 to present in Federal Way, Washington.

Jessi Nester grew up on a farm in Oklahoma with one sister and three brothers. It was on the farm that she first learned to work with machinery, and that she discovered her love of working with wood. Jessi wanted to take shop and auto classes in high school, but girls were steered away from them at the time. She began playing pool and was inspired to begin a business with a retail billiards store. The business, Beads and Billiards, is located in Federal Way, Washington. Having a retail store where cues were being sold made it necessary to do cue repairs. Jessi began making her own cues in her one-woman shop in 2001. Today she manages the store, makes Todd cues, and continues to play pool.

Present Day

Jessi Nester

Todd cues is named after Jessi's partner, Courtney Nester's grandfather, Franklin Todd. When the store got robbed of everything, Franklin offered financial help to rebuild the business. Todd Cues is also the inventor and manufacturer of the Original Pocket Chalker and Qclaw Cue Holder. Jessi makes the "Todd Hoppa," a jump cue that retails for $125. Jessi tries to make good playing cues that local league players can afford. Todd cues are usually fairly simple, with very few inlays. No CNC is used. Jessi has her own layered tip, called "Apache." She also makes her own full-spliced blanks for hustler cues. She hopes to be making more cues in the future. Jessi likes to use buffalo horn for ferrules, joint collars, and butt caps. Since Asian water buffalo are raised locally, she also stocks it for sale to other cuemakers at a low cost.

Todd cues were finished with auto clear coat until 2004 when Jessi developed her own way of applying super glue finish. She prefers it for its looks and hardness. She has experimented with all of the brands and techniques and is now working on an injection applicator.

Todd cues are easily identifiable by the "Todd" marking that has appeared on the forearms or butt sleeves of every Todd cue since the beginning. Todd cues are guaranteed for life to the original owner against construction defects that are not the result of warpage or abuse. If you are interested in talking to Jessi Nester about a new cue or cue that needs to be repaired, you can contact her at Todd Cues, listed in the Trademark Index.

SPECIFICATIONS

Butt material: hardwoods
Shaft material: rock maple
Standard length: 58 in.
Lengths available: any
Standard finish: cynocrylate
Balance point: approximately 18 in. from the butt
Standard butt cap: linen phenolic
Standard handle: wood
Point construction: short splice
Standard joint: phenolic
Joint type: flat faced
Joint screw thread: 3/8-10
Standard number of shafts: one
Standard taper: custom
Standard ferrule: linen phenolic
Standard tip: Triangle
Standard tip width: 12.75 mm
Tip widths available: any
Annual production: fewer than 40 cues

OPTIONS (FOR NEW CUES ONLY)

Special length: no charge
Apache tip: $20
Ivory butt cap: $ 75+
Buffalo horn butt cap: no charge
Ivory joint: $100
Buffalo horn joint: no charge
Ivory ferrule: $75
Joint protectors: $20+
Extra shaft: $90+

REPAIRS

Repairs done on all fine cues.
Refinish (with Irish linen wrap): $130
Rewrap (Irish linen): $35
Clean and press linen wrap: $10
Replace shaft: $90
Replace tip and ivory ferrule: $75
Replace phenolic/buffalo horn butt cap: $35
Replace Triangle tip: $15
Replaced Apache tip: $20
Replace fiber/linen/ferrule: $25

CURRENT TODD CUES

Two-piece Todd bar cues start at $175. Basic Todd cues with wraps and joint rings start at $250. Todd cues with points and one-of-a-kind Todd cues start at $350. The current delivery time for a Todd cue is about two to three months.

SECONDARY MARKET MINIMUM VALUES

The following are minimum values for other Todd cues encountered on the secondary market. These prices are representative of cues utilizing basic materials and designs that are not necessarily available at present. Jesse has offered one-of-a-kind cues that can command many times these prices due to the use of exotic materials and artistry.

Special construction note: There are many materials and construction techniques that can add value to Todd cues.

For all used Todd cues, except where otherwise noted:

Add $75 for each additional original straight playable shaft beyond one.
Deduct $90 for missing original straight playable shaft.
Add $60 each for ivory ferrules.
Deduct 25% for obvious or improper refinish.

Level 1 - Hustler.

Level 1 cues start at	$150	$115	$70

GRADING	98%	90%	70%
Level 2 - 0 points, 0-25 inlays.			
Level 2 cues start at	$225	$170	$110
Level 3 - 2-6 points, 0-8 inlays.			
Level 3 cues start at	$300	$225	$140
Level 4 - 4-10 points, 9-25 inlays.			
Level 4 cues start at	$400	$295	$185

TOEBOY

Marking that often appears on Rikard cues.

Refer to Rikard Custom Cues. If you have a Toeboy-marked Rikard cue that needs further identification or repair, contact Rikard Custom Cues, listed in the Trademark Index.

TOEDT CUSTOM CUES

Maker of pool cues in Tulsa, Oklahoma.

No further information was made available for publication in this edition. If you have a Toedt cue that needs further identification or repair, contact Toedt Custom Cues, listed in the Trademark Index.

TONKIN CUSTOM CUES

Maker of pool cues from 2000 to present in Willow Creek, California.

Arthur E. Tonkin Jr. (Pete) was born in 1960 in Willow Creek, California. He began playing pool at a young age. At 16, he began working for his family's construction company and later became interested in machine work. He learned the trade from a friend who had a shop. Pete worked as a machinist for 20 years, with 10 years in CAD/CAM design. He worked in sawmill country in the northwest and he designed machinery for the sawmills.

Because Pete enjoys the game of pool, he wanted a custom cue but could not afford to buy the ones he liked. He decided to build his own. After he got that first cue done in 2000, he entered a pool tournament at the local pub. By the time the tournament was over, two of his friends ordered cues. From that moment on, his cue orders have grown. He went from making a dozen or more cues a year, part time after work, to making over 40 cues a year full time in 2003. Pete has slowly bought equipment for his shop and was doing inlays on a manual pantograph for about a year. Then in January of 2004 he bought a CNC machine. His cues are known in northern California and expanding further. Although self-taught, Pete's work is inspired by David Kikel. He has one apprentice, Damien Sienkiewicz, who comes in about twice a month to his shop which is in Pete's pool room, P&J Billiards. Damien is the nephew of cuemaker David Whitsell.

A cue's playability is the most important part of the cue for Pete Tonkin. In 2003 he began coring some cues with an eight-piece radial spliced rod through the butt, leaving only a 1/16 in. sleeve on the outside. This option is available for an extra $300. Flat laminated wood handles with a wrap are used on cues that are not cored. Pete likes to use black or grey elephant ear for an exotic wrap with a great feel. Tonkin cues are also available with radial laminated shafts. He makes his own short-spliced blanks and sells some forearms to other cuemakers. Pete enjoys the artistry and design in cuemaking and finds working in his shop relaxing. All of his cues are one-of-a-kind. Although some are similar, he always changes details like veneer colors, etc. Pete can micro-engrave a radial inscription of up to nine letters on the end of the joint screw for identification.

Tonkin cues are guaranteed for life to the original owner against construction defects that are not the result of warpage or abuse. If you are interested in talking to Arthur E. (Pete) Tonkin Jr. about a new cue or cue that needs to be repaired, you can contact him at Tonkin Custom Cues, listed in the Trademark Index.

SPECIFICATIONS

Butt material: hardwoods
Shaft material: rock maple
Standard length: 58 in.
Lengths available: any
Standard finish: urethane
Balance point: 18 in. from butt
Standard butt cap: linen phenolic
Standard wrap: Irish linen
Point construction: short splice
Joint type: flat faced
Joint screw thread: 3/8-10
Standard number of shafts: one
Standard taper: 12 in. pro
Standard ferrules: melamine
Standard tip: Le Pro or Triangle
Standard tip eidth: 13 mm
Tip widths available: any
Annual production: 40+

TONKIN CUSTOM CUES, cont.

GRADING	98%	90%	70%

OPTIONS (FOR NEW CUES ONLY)
Special length: no charge
Layered tip: $10
Ivory butt cap: $200
Ivory butt sleeve: $800
Ivory joint: $125
Name on joint screw: $50
Ivory ferrule: $75
Ivory points: $150 each
Ivory handle: $2500
Leather wrap: $150
Lizard wrap: $200
Elephant ear wrap: $300
Joint protectors: $50+
Extra shaft: $125
Radial laminate shaft: $185

REPAIRS
Repairs done on all fine cues.
Refinish (with Irish linen wrap): $200
Refinish (with leather wrap): $310
Rewrap (Irish linen): $40
Rewrap (leather): $150
Clean and press linen wrap: $15
Replace shaft: $125
Replace ivory ferrule: $75
Replace phenolic butt cap: $40
Replace ivory butt cap: $200
Replace tip: $10+
Replaced layered tip: $20+
Replace fiber/linen/ferrule: $40

CURRENT TONKIN CUES
Two-piece Tonkin bar cues start at $325. Basic Tonkin cues with wraps and joint rings start at $450. Tonkin cues with points start at $550. Tonkin cues with points with four veneers start at $850. One-of-a-kind custom Tonkin cues start at $2,000. Tonkin cues over $1,000 come with two shafts. The current delivery time for a Tonkin cue is six months. Tonkin Custom Cues always has some cues in stock for immediate delivery.

SECONDARY MARKET MINIMUM VALUES
The following are minimum values for Tonkin cues encountered on the secondary market. These prices are representative of cues utilizing basic materials and designs that are not necessarily available at present. Pete has offered one-of-a-kind cues that can command many times these prices due to the use of exotic materials and artistry.

Special construction note: There are many materials and construction techniques that can add value to Tonkin cues.

For all used Tonkin cues, except where otherwise noted:
Add $100 for each additional original straight playable shaft beyond one.
Deduct $125 for missing original straight playable shaft.
Add $60 each for ivory ferrules.
Add $75 for leather wrap.
Deduct 20% for obvious or improper refinish.

	98%	90%	70%
Level 1 - Hustler.			
Level 1 cues start at	$200	$150	$95
Level 2 - 0 points, 0-25 inlays.			
Level 2 cues start at	$400	$300	$190
Level 3 - 2-6 points, 0-8 inlays.			
Level 3 cues start at	$600	$445	$285
Level 4 - 4-10 points, 9-25 inlays.			
Level 4 cues start at	$800	$590	$380
Level 5 - 0-12 points, 26-50 inlays.			
Level 5 cues start at	$1,200	$885	$575
Level 6 - 0-12 points, 51-75 inlays.			
Level 6 cues start at	$1,500	$1,150	$700

DAN TROGDON CUSTOM CUES

Maker of pool cues from 1994 to present in Waterford, Ohio.

Dan Trogdon had been doing woodworking for 30 years and decided to make his first pool cue. He showed the cue to a dealer, who then ordered his first year's production. So Dan began making cues in 1994, in Waterford, Ohio. He's been making cues full time in his one-man shop ever since. After making cues for the dealer, customers started to come direct.

Dan's work has been influenced by Dennis Deickman. He tries to make a quality custom cue at a reasonable price, and most are one-of-a-kind. Playability is most important to Dan. He also makes "Sharpshooter" laminated shafts for American Cowboy Billiards which is out of Missouri.

Dan is a member of the International Cuemakers Association and the VNEA pool league.

Trogdon cues are easily identifiable by the "Trogdon" logo that has been engraved on the butt cap in one of several styles on almost every cue Dan has made since he started. If Dan has the wood in stock, the average order time for one of his cues is six months. If the wood is not in stock, the wait is about one year.

Dan Trogdon cues are guaranteed for life against construction defects that are not the result of warpage or abuse. If you are interested in talking to Dan Trogdon about a new cue or cue that needs to be repaired, you can contact him at Dan Trogdon Custom Cues, listed in the Trademark Index.

Dan Trogdon

Present Day

SPECIFICATIONS

Butt material: hardwoods
Shaft material: rock maple
Standard length: 58 in.
Standard finish: cynocrylite
Lengths available: any
Balance point: 18 in. from the butt
Standard butt cap: phenolic
Standard wrap: Irish linen
Point construction: inlaid
Standard joint: phenolic
Joint type: flat faced
Joint screw thread: radial pin
Standard number of shafts: one
Standard taper: custom
Standard ferrules: Aegis II
Standard tip: Triangle
Standard tip width: 13 mm
Annual production: 30 cues

OPTIONS (FOR NEW CUES ONLY)

Special length: no charge
Layered tip: $8+
Ivory butt cap: $150
Ivory joint: $100
Ivory ferrule: $40
Ivory points: $50 each
Leather wrap: $75
Custom joint protectors: $25+
Extra shaft: $90

REPAIRS

Repairs done on all fine cues.

Refinish (with linen wrap): $110
Refinish (with leather wrap): $165
Rewrap (linen): $35
Rewrap (leather): $75
Restore leather wrap: $25
Replace shaft: $90
Replace ivory ferrule: $40
Replace butt cap: $30
Replace ivory butt cap: $150
Replace tip: $8+
Replaced layered tip: $15+
Replace fiber/linen ferrule: $20

GRADING	98%	90%	70%

CURRENT TROGDON CUES

Two-piece Dan Trogdon bar cues start at $275. Basic Trogdon cues with wraps and joint rings start at $325. Dan Trogdon cues with points start at $500. One-of-a-kind Trgdon cues start at $400. The average delivery time for a special order Trogdon cue is about six months.

SECONDARY MARKET MINIMUM VALUES

The following are minimum values for Trogdon cues encountered on the secondary market. These prices are representative of cues utilizing basic materials and designs that are not necessarily available at present. Dan has offered one-of-a-kind cues that can command many times these prices due to the use of exotic materials and artistry.

Special construction note: There are many materials and construction techniques that can add value to Trogdon cues.

For all used Trogdon cues, except where otherwise noted:
- Add $75 for each additional original straight playable shaft beyond one.
- Deduct $90 for missing original straight playable shaft.
- Add $35 each for ivory ferrules.
- Add $50 for leather wrap.
- Deduct 15% for obvious or improper refinish.

Level 1 - Hustler.
Level 1 cues start at	$150	$115	$70

Level 2 - 0 points, 0-25 inlays.
Level 2 cues start at	$275	$210	$135

Level 3 - 2-6 points, 0-8 inlays.
Level 3 cues start at	$400	$300	$190

Level 4 - 4-10 points, 9-25 inlays.
Level 4 cues start at	$500	$375	$235

Level 5 - 0-12 points, 26-50 inlays.
Level 5 cues start at	$750	$575	$350

Level 6 - 0-12 points, 51-75 inlays.
Level 6 cues start at	$1,100	$850	$500

TUCKER CUSTOM CUES

Maker of pool cues from 1999 to present in Leesburg, Florida.

Murray Tucker III began building custom cues in 1999 in Leesburg, Florida. This part-time business started when, as a pool player for over twenty years, Murray wondered if he could build a good cue for himself. He always liked and collected nice cues. Murray has a background in machining and works in a large machine shop. In 1998 he started buying wood and modifying his equipment so that he could build a cue. He has been addicted to making cues ever since. Murray now works full time as a machinist making custom forms for the concrete industry, then he makes cues part time in his home shop as a hobby.

Early cues were in the style of David Kersenbrock and Southwest, but now Murray likes to make more traditional four-point, four-veneer cues inspired by Rambow, Balabushka, and Szamboti, and he likes Hoppe rings. Murray prefers to make what he likes and then offer it for sale. He will only take orders for cues he wants to make. He has a small circle of customers and he only makes about a dozen cues a year. Playability is most important, so he won't sacrifice the hit for looks. He usually uses 5/16-14 piloted stainless steel joints, but he also likes 3/8-11 flat faced joints. Murray makes his own full-splice hustler blanks and is working on full splices with veneers.

Murray Tucker

Murray Tucker III has signed and dated almost every cue since the beginning, usually between the points. A couple of his cues have a "3" decal on the butt cap under the finish. The average delivery time for a Tucker custom cue is currently about two years. Tucker cues are guaranteed for life to the original owner against construction defects that are not the result of warpage or abuse. If you are interested in talking to Murray Tucker III about a new cue or cue that needs to be repaired, you can contact him at Tucker Custom Cues, listed in the Trademark Index.

SPECIFICATIONS

Butt material: hardwoods
Shaft material: rock maple
Standard length: 58 in.
Lengths available: any up to 62 in.
Standard finish: polyurethane
Balance point: 19 in. from butt
Standard butt cap: phenolic
Standard wrap: Irish linen

TUCKER CUSTOM CUES, cont. 805

GRADING	100%	95%	70%

Point construction: short splice
Standard joint type: piloted
Standard joint: stainless steel
Joint screw: 5/16-14
Standard number of shafts: two
Standard taper: custom
Standard ferrules: ivory
Other ferrule options: micarta
Standard tip: Le Pro
Standard tip width: 13 mm
Tip widths available: any up to 13.75
Standard bumper: black rubber
Annual production: fewer than 12 cues

OPTIONS (FOR NEW CUES ONLY)

Special length: no charge
Layered tip: $10+
Ivory butt cap: $150
Ivory joint: $100
Ivory ferrule: $35
Leather wrap: no charge
Extra shaft: $75
Lizard or other exotic wraps: $150+
Ivory Hoppe-style ring: $40

REPAIRS

Repairs done on Tucker cues only. Repairs priced on an individual basis.

CURRENT TUCKER CUES

Two-piece Tucker bar cues start at $325. Basic Tucker cues with wraps and joint rings start at $450. Tucker cues with points start at $750. One-of-a-kind custom Tucker cues start at $1,000. The current delivery time for a Tucker Custom cue is about two years.

CURRENT EXAMPLES

The following Tucker Custom Cue can be ordered as shown, or modified to suit the desires of the customer.

Level 3 - Purpleheart forearm, three long camphor burl-bordered ebony points alternating with three short camphor burl points, lizard wrap, purpleheart butt sleeve with three long reverse camphor burl-bordered ebony points alternating with three short reverse camphor burl points.

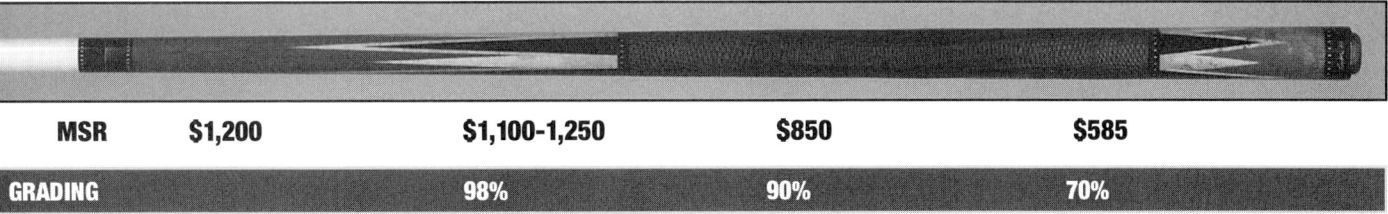

MSR	$1,200	$1,100-1,250	$850	$585
GRADING	98%	90%	70%	

SECONDARY MARKET MINIMUM VALUES

The following are minimum values for other Tucker cues encountered on the secondary market. These prices are representative of cues utilizing basic materials and designs that are not necessarily available at present. Murray has offered one-of-a-kind cues that can command many times these prices due to the use of exotic materials and artistry.

Special construction note: There are many materials and construction techniques that can add value to Tucker cues.

For all used Tucker cues, except where otherwise noted:
  Add $65 for each additional original straight playable shaft beyond two.
  Deduct $75 for each missing original straight playable shaft under two.
  Add $35 each for ivory ferrules.
  Add $100 for lizard wrap.
  Deduct 15% for obvious or improper refinish.

Level 1 - Hustler.
    Level 1 cues start at $200 $150 $95

Level 2 - 0 points, 0-25 inlays.
    Level 2 cues start at $400 $300 $190

GRADING	98%	90%	70%
Level 3 - 2-6 points, 0-8 inlays.			
Level 3 cues start at	$700	$525	$335
Level 4 - 4-10 points, 9-25 inlays.			
Level 4 cues start at	$850	$650	$400
Level 5 - 0-12 points, 26-50 inlays.			
Level 5 cues start at	$1,100	$850	$500
Level 6 - 0-12 points, 51-75 inlays.			
Level 6 cues start at	$1,450	$1,100	$700

TUNDER CUE CO.

Maker of pool cues in the mid-1990s in Olathe, Kansas.

Tunder cues were made by Mike Kinder and Dan Tull, who owns the famous "Shooter's" pool room in Olathe, Kansas. The name was created by combining their last two names. Some cues made by Mike are easily identifiable by the letters "MWK" stamped into the cues.

V SECTION

KYLE VAN DEN BOSCH

Maker of Mariposa cues. For information, refer to Mariposa Cue Co.

VAN HALL CUES

Maker of pool cues from 1993 to 2004 in Berkley, Michigan, a suburb of Detroit.

Herbert Van Hall's lifelong interest in pool began when he was a young boy. He would regularly go see Irving Crane practice in his hometown of Rochester, New York. After high school, Herbert attended a four-year tech school to learn drafting and machining. This led to a job with General Motors, repairing equipment used on their assembly lines in Detroit. Herbert spent many years repairing machinery, and custom making many parts necessary to make repairs.

He always dreamed of making pool cues, and was able to start after his retirement from General Motors in 1993. With his background in custom repair, Herbert went right into repair of custom cues. He designed and built his own equipment specifically for custom cue work. Because of the reputation he has earned for high-quality repairs at very competitive prices, Herbert has not been able to make many cues. Van Hall cues have been primarily two-piece hustler cues that he custom made one at a time, to the specifications of the customer. They are easily identified by either a "Herbert Van Hall" signature, or an "H.V.H." stamp. Cues came with one shaft, and extra shafts could be ordered for $75 each. His standard ferrules were melamine with ivory ferrules available as an option for $55.

Herbert Van Hall

1990s to 2004

Van Hall Cues

Herbert developed a space age shaft insert for the joints in his cues. He specialized in repairs, and made about 10 custom hustler cues a year in his one-man shop. Herbert passed away in early 2004.

SPECIFICATIONS

Butt material: hardwoods
Shaft material: rock maple
Standard length: 57 in.
Lengths available: any
Standard finish: acrylic
Standard joint screw: 5/16-14
Standard joint type: piloted
Point construction: full splice
Standard number of shafts: one
Standard ferrules: melamine
Total production: approximately 100 cues

GRADING

	98%	90%	70%

SECONDARY MARKET MINIMUM VALUES

The following are minimum prices for Van Hall cues encountered on the secondary market. These prices are representative of cues utilizing basic materials that may not be currently available.

Special construction note: There are many materials and construction techniques that can add value to cues.

For all used Van Hall cues:
- Add $75 for each additional original straight playable shaft (standard with one).
- Add $50 for each ivory ferrule.
- Deduct $85 for missing original straight playable shaft.
- Deduct 25% for obvious or improper refinish.

Level 1 - 4 points, hustler.

	98%	90%	70%
Level 1 cues start at	$185	$150	$110

| GRADING | 98% | 90% | 70% |

NICK VARNER CUES & CASES

Distributor of pool cues from 1999 to present in Owensboro, Kentucky.

Nick Varner began making cues in 1999. He is located in Owensboro, Kentucky. He has won many championships in the billiard world and is a member of the BCA Hall of Fame. His cue designs reflect his many accomplishments over the last 25 years. Nick Varner cues are often named after Nick's favorite places or favorite tournaments. One-piece Nick Varner house cues are available in five lengths from 36 in. to 57 in. Nick Varner cues are easily identifiable by the "NV" logo that appears on the butt caps and or the "Nick Varner" signature on the forearms.

If you are interested in talking to Nick Varner about a new cue or cue that needs to be repaired, you can contact him at Nick Varner Cues & Cases, listed in the Trademark Index.

SPECIFICATIONS

- Butt material: exotic woods
- Shaft material: hard rock maple
- Standard length: 58 in.
- Lengths available: 29 in.
- Standard finish: UV finish
- Balance point: 18.5
- Standard butt cap:
- Standard Wrap: Irish linen
- Point construction: handmade and CNC
- Standard joints: stainless steel, Implex or linen based
- Standard joint screw thread: 5/16-18
- Standard number of shafts: one
- Standard taper: long professional taper
- Standard ferrules: linen based fiber
- Standard tip: Le Pro
- Tip width: 13 mm
- Standard bumper: screw-on rubber bumper

OPTIONS (FOR NEW CUES ONLY)

- Joint protectors: $9.99
- Extra shaft: $25+

CURRENT NICK VARNER CUES

There are several models in each of several lines of Nick Varner cues. Lines include the Reno Series, the Chicago Series, the Kentucky Series, etc. Most Nick Varner cues are available for immediate delivery.

SECONDARY MARKET MINIMUM VALUES

The following are minimum values for Nick Varner cues encountered on the secondary market. These prices are representative of cues utilizing basic materials and designs that are not necessarily available at present.

Special construction note: There are many materials and construction techniques that can add value to Nick Varner cues.

For all used Nick Varner cues, except where otherwise noted:
- Add $20+ for each additional original straight playable shaft beyond one.
- Deduct $25+ for missing original straight playable shaft.
- Deduct 15% for obvious or improper refinish.

Level 1 - Hustler.
	98%	90%	70%
Level 1 cues start at	$65	$50	$30

Level 2 - 0 points, 0-25 inlays.
Level 2 cues start at	$80	$60	$35

Level 3 - 2-6 points, 0-8 inlays.
Level 3 cues start at	$110	$85	$50

Level 4 - 4-10 points, 9-25 inlays.
Level 4 cues start at	$130	$100	$60

FRED VELTEN CUES

Maker of pool cues from 1985 to 1994 Corte Madera, California.

Manfred "Fred" Velten was born in Karlsruhe, Germany in 1935. As a young man he fell in love with American Big Band music and enjoyed attending the concerts by the great jazz artists such as Sidney Bechet and Ella Fitzgerald who toured Europe during the 1950s. After serving an apprenticeship as a cabinetmaker and taking English lessons at Berlitz he emigrated to Canada in 1958 to seek his fortune. Fred settled in Toronto where he found work first as a carpenter, then refurbishing pianos, and finally as a designer and installation supervisor for a manufacturer of retail display cases. While living in Toronto, he was introduced to some "classy" pool salons and developed a love for billiards that lasted the rest of his life.

FRED VELTEN CUES, cont.

GRADING	98%	90%	70%

In 1968 Fred decided to move to sunny California. He went to Detroit, bought a Ford Mustang, and drove to San Francisco, where he had a cabinetmaker job waiting. A year later he opened his own business, Golden Gate Coins and Stamps, in Marin County. He soon moved the shop to a building he purchased in Corte Madera, and this is the building he later converted to his billiard supply store, Fred's Cue Shop. This was during the 1980s when Fred was an active player in local tournaments and eight-ball leagues, winning many trophies proudly displayed in his shop. He had taught himself to repair cues, and around 1985 built his first cue. Like everything Fred did, it was meticulously crafted; everything from building the short splice blanks to making the décor rings was done by hand. Some cues were sold to his friends in the pool leagues, and some were sold in his shop.

Then in 1994, Fred suffered a severe stroke affecting one side of his body, which sadly ended his cue building and pool playing. Not one to be discouraged for long, he adapted to his decreased mobility by remodeling his offices and moving into his shop. He customized his lathe so he could continue to repair cues one-handed, with an occasional extra hand from a friend and fellow cuemaker, Don Lim. He remained cheerful and optimistic even through continued health problems, battling cancer and heart trouble, until he finally succumbed in July of 2004.

Fred Velten cues can be identified by the script "V" logo used on early cues, or the "F" on top of a larger "V" used on later cues.

SPECIFICATIONS

Butt material: hardwoods
Shaft material: rock maple
Standard length: 58 in.
Standard wrap: Irish linen
Point construction: short splice
Total production: a few hundred cues

SECONDARY MARKET MINIMUM VALUES

The following are minimum values for Fed Velton cues encountered on the secondary market. These prices are representative of cues utilizing the most basic materials and designs that were available. Fred offered one-of-a-kind cues that can command many times these prices due to the use of exotic materials and artistry.

Special construction note: There are many materials and construction techniques that can add value to Fred Velton cues.

For all used Fred Velton cues, except where otherwise noted:
Add $145 for each additional original straight playable shaft beyond one.
Deduct $175 for missing original straight playable shaft.
Add $50 each for ivory ferrules.
Add $100 for leather wrap.
Deduct 30% for obvious or improper refinish.

Level 1 - Hustler.
   Level 1 cues start at $250 $195 $120

Level 2 - 0 points, 0-25 inlays.
   Level 2 cues start at $450 $345 $215

Level 3 - 2-6 points, 0-8 inlays.
   Level 3 cues start at $700 $525 $325

Level 4 - 4-10 points, 9-25 inlays.
   Level 4 cues start at $1,000 $750 $450

Level 5 - 0-12 points, 26-50 inlays.
   Level 5 cues start at $1,400 $1,075 $600

VIATTORRE CUSTOM CUES

Maker of pool cues from 2000 to present, currently in Quezon City, Phillippines.

Viattorre Custom Cues was founded in 2000 in Manila by Jackson Tan together with Noli Alejandro and Arnold Macompas. Each partner has nearly a decade of cuemaking experience and a unique area of expertise in the different stages of cuemaking. Jackson also has bachehelors degrees in electronics and communications engineering. They founded Viattorre Custom Cues on the principle that it is possible to have both integrity and beauty without sacrificing one for the other. Among the cuemakers who influenced and inspired them are Jerry Franklin, David Kersenbrock, Gus Szamboti, Ernie Gutierrez and Tad Kohara.

Viattorre specializes in solid hitting, affordable custom-made pool cues. All woods are hand-selected and constantly checked for flaws between each stage of construction to ensure the highest quality cue possible. Parts are both threaded and glued to ensure superior playability and life. Every part of a Viattorre cue is made in-house except for the tip, ferrule and rubber bumper. While inlays are done by hand without the use of CNC machines, they constantly search for new ways to improve their cues. Cues can be identified by the "Viattorre" logo.

Viattorre Cuemakers

| GRADING | 98% | 90% | 70% |

Viattorre Cues also prides itself on being one of the top cue repair facilities in Asia. People from all over the world have used their repair services regardless of the make of cue. Viattorre takes pride in repairing cues thought to be beyond repair by others.

If you have a cue requiring identification or repair, or would like to talk to Viattorre about ordering a new cue, please contact Jackson Tan at Viattorre Cues, listed in the Trademark Index.

SPECIFICATIONS

Butt material: hardwoods
Shaft material: rock maple
Standard length: 58 in.
Standard finish: hi-solids urethane
Joint screw thread: brass 3/8-11
Standard joint: flat-faced linen fiber
Other joints offered: stainless steel
Balance point: 18 ½ to 19 ½"= in. from the butt
Point construction: short splice or inlaid
Standard butt cap: linen fiber
Standard number of shafts: Two
Standard wrap: Irish Linen
Standard ferrules: Ivorine III
Other ferrule option: Ivor-X, Aegis
Standard tip width: 12.75 mm
Tip widths available: 12 to 14mm
Standard tip: Triangle
Annual production: approximately 100 cues

CURRENT VIATTORRE CUES

Basic Viattorre cues with wraps and joint rings start at $450. One-of-a-kind custom Viattorre cues start at $800. The current delivery time for a Viattorre cue is from seven to twelve months, depending upon the intricacy of the custom order.

SECONDARY MARKET MINIMUM VALUES

The following are minimum values for other Viattorre cues encountered on the secondary market. These prices are representative of cues utilizing basic materials and designs that are not necessarily available at present. Viattorre has offered one-of-a-kind cues that can command many times these prices due to the use of exotic materials and artistry.

Special construction note: There are many materials and construction techniques that can add value to Viattorre cues.

For all used Viattorre cues, except where otherwise noted:

Add $95 for each additional original straight playable shaft beyond two.
Deduct $125 for each missing original straight playable shaft under two.
Add $50 each for ivory ferrules.
Deduct 20% for obvious or improper refinish.

Level 2 - 0 points, 0-25 inlays.
| Level 2 cues start at | $350 | $270 | $180 |

Level 3 - 2-6 points, 0-8 inlays.
| Level 3 cues start at | $500 | $385 | $260 |

Level 4 - 4-10 points, 9-25 inlays.
| Level 4 cues start at | $600 | $470 | $320 |

Level 5 - 0-12 points, 26-50 inlays.
| Level 5 cues start at | $850 | $655 | $445 |

ADRIAN VIGUERA

Maker of Hadrianus cues. See listing for Hadrianus Cue Company.

VIKING CUE MANUFACTURING INC.

Maker of pool cues from 1965 to present, currently in Madison, Wisconsin.

Gordon Hart started playing "Carom," a board game similar to billiards, in the fourth grade. He was unable to play outdoors at the time, because of an unknown virus that he had for a couple of years. By the seventh grade, with the help of his father and grandfather, Gordon was able to acquire a pool table for the family home. Eventually, Gordon was working in his father's paint contracting business, but a big portion of his time was devoted to his passion of playing pool.

Gordon left his father's business and opened his own pool room in Stoughton, Wisconsin. Because of Stoughton's Norwegian heritage, he named it The Viking. He soon had more rooms in other towns. Eventually, he started experimenting with making cues in the basement of The Viking, hence the birth of the Viking cue. Around this time, Gordon married his wife, Nancy, who has been very active in the company ever since.

During these years, Viking cues were sold at tournaments such as the famous Hustlers Jamboree in Johnston City, Illinois, and the Stardust Tournaments in Vegas, run by the Jansco brothers, George and Paulie. The cues became a favorite of many of the top tournament players at that time. Gordon moved the cue business to its present location in Madison, Wisconsin. With lifelong friend Fred Schulze, Gordon and Nancy expanded production capabilities and began selling cues all over the U.S.

From these humble beginnings Viking became one of the biggest manufacturers of pool cues. Since then, Viking has greatly expanded their domestic and international market. They have employed as many as 92 people at one time, running three shifts. An accomplishment they have taken pride in is elevating their reputation from that of a low-priced cue to that of an impeccable quality cue with prices ranging from $150 to $10,000. With the passing of time they have also grown to become one of the foremost repair facilities in the country for quality, timeliness, and reasonably priced repairs on cues of all brands.

Most Viking cues are easily identifiable by the Viking logo on the butt cap. Some early cues will have the Viking logo under a clear plastic window in the butt sleeve. Viking cues continue to go through constant improvements. Early cues had European tapered shafts, which has progressed to a long professional taper.

As the 1980s came to a close, Gordon invested heavily in research and development in order to construct better hitting cues. As a result of this research, he updated machinery and invested in state-of-the-art equipment. Since 1990, Gordon and Nancy have worked at achieving an aggressive promotional program and quality improvement plan. The results are better playing cues with the top-of-the-line quality. They have even broken into the high-end custom cues just to show what they are capable of. In 1996 Viking started an annual Design-A-Cue Contest, with the winner having their design made into a cue. They introduced their "VM" (Viking Millennium) Series in the summer of 1999.

With the introduction of the Millenium series came several new developments for Viking cues. The current interchangeable weight bolt system, which had been developed over the course of many years, was introduced on the Millenium Series. At the same time, the current finger joint for attaching the handle section to the forearm replaced the earlier metal pin. And Viking introduced their new capped and threaded ferrule, made from a proprietary material which they have never seen crack after seven years of use on thousands of cues.

Gordon was the first cuemaker honored with a Lifetime Achievement Award from the American Cuemakers Association. Nancy was the first woman to serve on the board of the Billiard and Bowling Institute of America, going on to become the first woman president of that institute. She also was an active member who has served on the board of the Billiard Congress of America for almost ten years.

Viking Cue Mfg. Inc. is a very successful family business. Although Gordon and Nancy still spend time at the company, their son and two daughters have taken over day-to-day management. Their son, Barry, is vice president. He manages the production facilities and is involved in marketing. His sister Robin (Hart) Kneebone is Chief Financial Officer and she manages the office area. Viking continues to employ many skilled craftsmen for custom and production cues. Some of these craftsmen have been with Viking Cue for more than 30 years. Eveything is made in-house in the USA except for the tips.

Viking stocks thousands of standard model cues, so immediate delivery is possible. Viking also maintains a custom shop, allowing for any dimensions, designs, materials, tips, etc. to be possible. Most custom orders can be filled within three weeks.

If you have a Viking cue that needs further identification or repair, or would like to talk to someone about ordering a new Viking cue, contact Viking Cue Mfg. Inc., listed in the trademark index.

SPECIFICATIONS

Butt material: hardwoods
Shaft material: rock maple
Standard length: 58 in.
Lengths available: any
Standard finish: UV
Joint screw: several available
Standard joint: several available
Joint type: several available
Balance point: varies
Standard wrap: Irish linen
Standard butt cap: high impact plastic
Standard number of shafts: one
Standard taper: 12 to 14 in. pro
Standard ferrules: high-impact plastic
Standard tip: Le Pro
Tip widths available: 12 to 13 mm no charge

OPTIONS (FOR NEW CUES ONLY)

Leather wrap: $80
Ivory joint: by quote
Name engraving: $25+
Joint protectors: $12 each
Special joint: $15+
Extra shaft: $75+
Special length: $15+

REPAIRS

Repair prices for Viking cues only. For cues not manufactured by Viking, add 50%.

Refinish (with wrap): $100
Refinish/clean shaft: $15+
Rewrap (Irish linen): $35

GRADING	100%	95%	70%

Rewrap (leather): $80
Replace butt cap: $30+
Replace rubber bumper: $1
Replace shaft: $75+
Replace ferrule: $15+
Replace tip: $15+

CURRENT VIKING CUES

Viking currently manufactures 112 models of the F Series, which are shown following. Viking also manufactures the F112 Break/Jump cue which retails for $260. The current delivery time for a standard Viking cue can be as soon as the next day.

CURRENT EXAMPLES

The following F Series Viking cues are representations of the work of Viking Cue Manufacturing Inc. These cues can be ordered as shown, or modified to suit the desires of the customer. F Series cues come with one shaft, and a quick-release joint is standard. A variety of joints and standard Irish linen wraps are available in 27 different color combinations. Butt caps are available in black or white. Pearlized plastic is available in eight different colors. Stained bird's-eye maple is available in twelve different stain colors. And plastic joint rings are available in six different colors.

VIKING F SERIES

Level 5 "F00" - Stained bird's-eye maple forearm, multiple ebony-bordered synthetic ivory floating points alternating with multiple synthetic ivory-bordered snakewood points, stained bird's-eye maple butt sleeve with multiple ebony-bordered synthetic ivory floating diamond-shaped inlays alternating with multiple synthetic ivory-bordered snakewood diamond-shaped inlays.

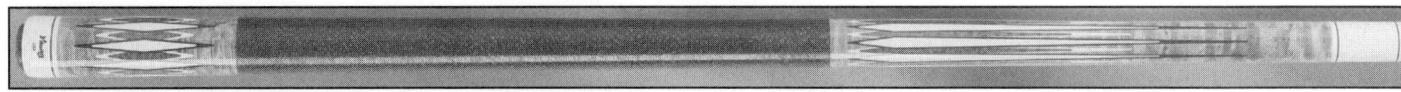

MSR	$1,300	$900-1,300	$775	$625

Level 5 "F01" - Stained bird's-eye maple butt, multiple intricate ebony-bordered synthetic ivory floating inlays alternating with multiple intricate ebony-bordered turquoise inlays.

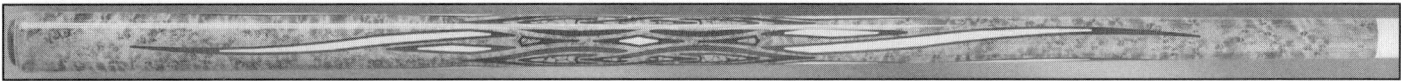

MSR	$1,200	$825-1,200	$710	$575

Level 3 "F02" - Stained bird's-eye maple forearm, ebony-bordered pearlized plastic floating points, pearlized plastic butt sleeve with intricate scrimshaw engraving.

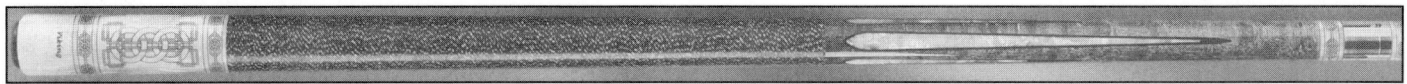

MSR	$1,100	$750-1,100	$650	$535

Level 4 "F03" - Stained bird's-eye maple forearm, multiple ebony-bordered synthetic ivory points with a vermillion diamond-shaped inlay in each alternating with multiple synthetic ivory and vermillion rainbows, stained bird's-eye maple butt sleeve with multiple ebony-bordered synthetic ivory reverse point-shaped inlays with a vermillion diamond-shaped inlay in each alternating with multiple synthetic ivory and vermillion rainbows.

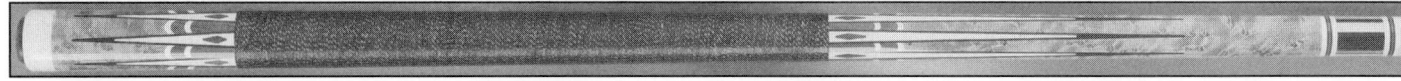

MSR	$900	$625-900	$535	$435

Level 4 "F04" - Ebony forearm, multiple synthetic ivory-bordered ebony floating diamond-shaped points with arrowhead-shaped tips at top and bottom alternating with vermillion-bordered diamond-shaped ebony floating points with arrowhead-shaped tips at top and bottom, ebony butt sleeve with multiple synthetic ivory-bordered ebony floating diamond-shaped windows with arrowhead-shaped tips at top and bottom alternating with vermillion-bordered diamond-shaped ebony floating windows with arrowhead-shaped tips at top and bottom .

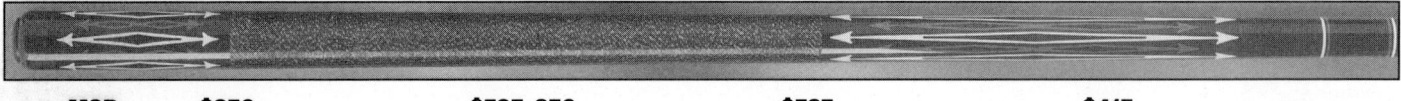

MSR	$850	$595-850	$525	$415

GRADING	100%	95%	70%

Level 4 "F05" - Stained bird's-eye maple forearm, intricate ebony-bordered four-piece synthetic ivory and vermillion floating points alternating with vermillion-bordered synthetic ivory diamond-shaped inlays, stained bird's-eye maple butt sleeve with intricate ebony-bordered three-piece synthetic ivory and vermillion floating point-shaped inlays alternating with vermillion-bordered synthetic ivory diamond-shaped inlays.

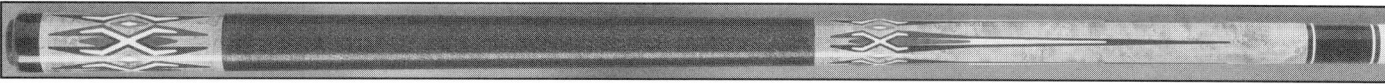

MSR	$800	$565-800	$485	$390

Level 4 "F06" - Ebony forearm, multiple maple-bordered snakewood floating points, ebony butt sleeve with multiple maple-bordered snakewood diamond-shaped inlays between maple ringwork at top and bottom.

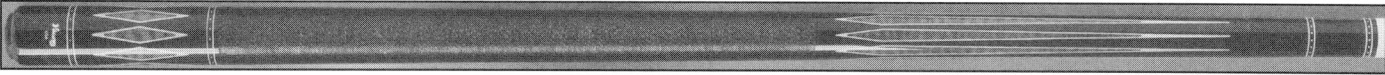

MSR	$775	$550-775	$470	$385

Level 4 "F07" - Stained bird's-eye maple butt, multiple intricate ebony-bordered blue pearlized plastic floating points and inlays.

MSR	$750	$535-750	$455	$370

Level 5 "F08" - Ebony forearm with a ring of synthetic ivory X-shaped inlays alternating with synthetic malachite diamond-shaped inlays above wrap, three two-piece floating stained curly maple points with a synthetic ivory X-shaped inlay in the center of each alternating with three short two-piece floating stained curly maple point-shaped inlays with a synthetic ivory X-shaped inlay in the center of each and synthetic malachite diamond-shaped inlays, ebony butt sleeve with six short two-piece floating stained curly maple point-shaped inlays with a synthetic ivory X-shaped inlay in the center of each alternating with synthetic malachite diamond-shaped inlays.

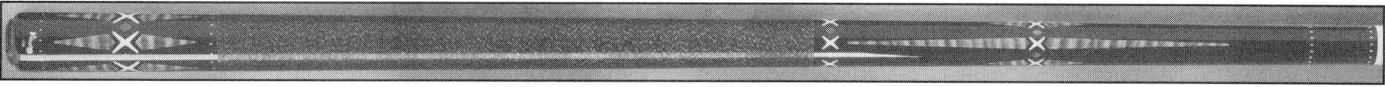

MSR	$725	$520-725	$445	$360

Level 4 "F09" - Ebony forearm, three vermillion points with an intricate pearlized plastic inlay in each alternating with three short two-piece vermillion points with an intricate pearlized plastic inlay in each, ebony butt sleeve with three reverse vermillion point-shaped inlays with an intricate pearlized plastic inlay in each alternating with three short reverse two-piece vermillion point-shaped inlays with an intricate pearlized plastic inlay in each.

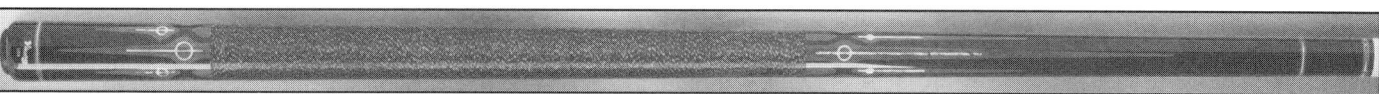

MSR	$700	$505-700	$430	$345

Level 5 "F10" - Stained bird's-eye maple forearm, multiple intricate ebony-bordered blue pearlized plastic floating points and inlays, stained bird's-eye maple butt sleeve with multiple intricate ebony-bordered blue pearlized plastic windows and inlays.

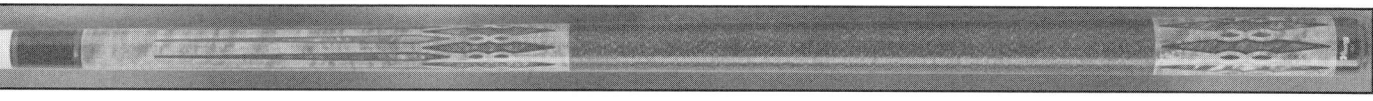

MSR	$650	$475-650	$400	$320

Level 5 "F11" - Ebony forearm, multiple intricate synthetic ivory-bordered blue pearlized plastic floating points and inlays, ebony butt sleeve with multiple intricate synthetic ivory-bordered blue pearlized plastic windows and inlays.

MSR	$630	$460-630	$390	$310

Level 5 "F12" - Stained bird's-eye maple forearm, four intricate synthetic ebony and green pearlized plastic points, synthetic ebony butt sleeve with intricate green pearlized plastic inlays forming the images of lizards.

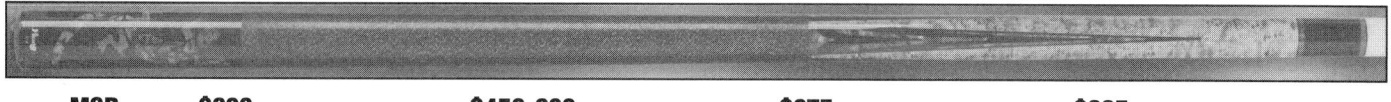

MSR	$600	$450-600	$375	$295

GRADING	100%	95%	70%

Level 5 "F13" - Ebony forearm, multiple intricate five-piece synthetic ivory and vermillion floating points alternating with vermillion dot-shaped inlays, ebony butt sleeve with multiple intricate five-piece synthetic ivory and vermillion inlaid patterns alternating with vermillion dot-shaped inlays.

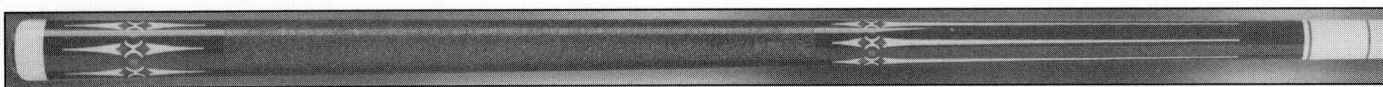

MSR	$590	$440-590	$370	$290

Level 4 "F14" - Stained bird's-eye maple forearm, intricate ebony-bordered two-piece pearlized plastic floating points alternating with ebony-bordered purple pearlized plastic eliptical inlays, stained bird's-eye maple butt sleeve with intricate ebony-bordered two-piece pearlized plastic windows alternating with ebony-bordered purple pearlized plastic eliptical inlays.

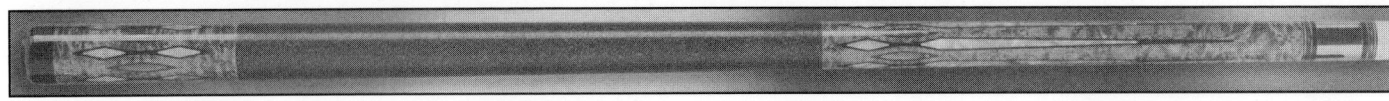

MSR	$580	$430-580	$360	$285

Level 4 "F15" - Ebony forearm, three long and three short smoke-stained bird's-eye maple points with intricate synthetic ivory borders that form into cross-shaped inlays at the tips, ebony butt sleeve with three long and three short smoke-stained bird's-eye maple reverse points with intricate synthetic ivory borders that form into cross-shaped inlays at the tips.

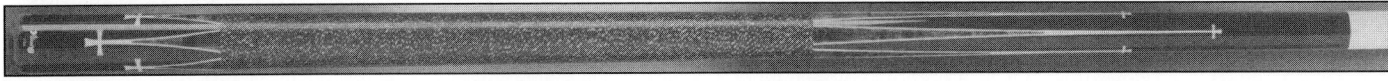

MSR	$570	$420-570	$355	$280

Level 1 "F16" - Bird's-eye maple forearm, four intricately twisted full-spliced rosewood points and handle, four "Viking" logo inlays of bird's-eye maple.

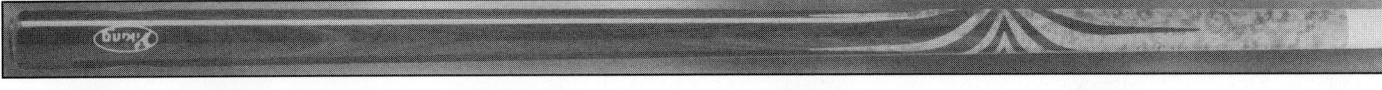

MSR	$560	$410-560	$345	$275

Level 3 "F17" - Bird's-eye maple forearm, ebony points with scrimshaw-engraved synthetic ivory elliptical inlays, ebony butt sleeve with scrimshaw-engraved synthetic ivory elliptical inlays.

MSR	$550	$400-550	$340	$270

Level 5 "F18" - Goncalo alves forearm, four intricate ebony-bordered pearlized plastic multi-piece floating points and inlays, goncalo alves butt sleeve with multiple intricate ebony-bordered pearlized plastic multi-piece diamond-shaped inlays.

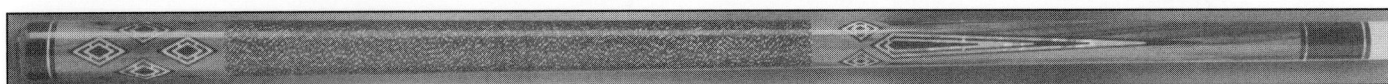

MSR	$540	$395-540	$335	$265

Level 4 "F19" - Ebony forearm, four intricate five-piece vermillion-bordered bird's-eye maple floating points with vermillion-bordered bird's-eye maple notched diamond-shaped inlays in the centers, ebony butt sleeve with four intricate five-piece vermillion-bordered bird's-eye maple windows with vermillion-bordered bird's-eye maple notched diamond-shaped inlays in the centers between bird's-eye maple dashes set in vermillion rings above and below.

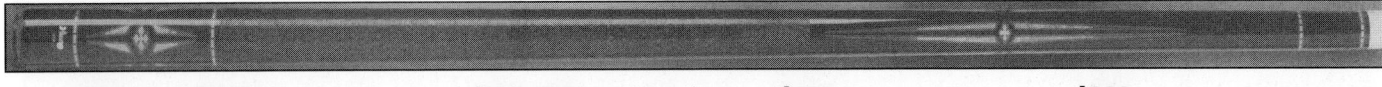

MSR	$530	$385-530	$325	$260

Level 4 "F20" - Bird's-eye maple forearm, six floating ebony-bordered snakewood points alternating with six synthetic ivory elliptical inlays, bird's-eye maple butt sleeve with six ebony-bordered snakewood windows alternating with six synthetic ivory elliptical inlays.

MSR	$520	$375-520	$320	$255

VIKING CUE MANUFACTURING INC., cont.

GRADING	100%	95%	70%

Level 4 "F21" - Bird's-eye maple forearm, four ebony points with ebony and maple veneers and four graduated sized maple diamond-shaped inlays in each point, ebony butt sleeve with four sets of four ebony-bordered maple diamond-shaped inlays set over ebony and silver colored rings.

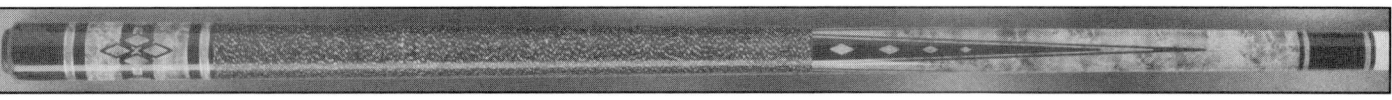

MSR	$520	$375-520	$320	$255

Level 5 "F22" - Bird's-eye maple forearm, four ebony points with an intricate synthetic ivory and maple eight-piece inlay in each point, ebony butt sleeve with four intricate synthetic ivory and maple eight-piece inlays.

MSR	$510	$365-510	$310	$250

Level 4 "F23" - Bird's-eye maple forearm, pairs of intricate ebony-bordered vermillion and maple opposing floating points with intricate ebony and vermillion twist inlays in the centers, bird's-eye maple butt sleeve with intricate ebony and vermillion twist inlays.

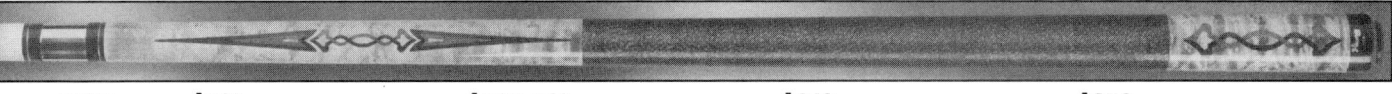

MSR	$510	$365-510	$310	$250

Level 4 "F24" - Ebony forearm, multiple intricate bird's-eye maple and ebony floating points and inlays, ebony butt sleeve with multiple intricate bird's-eye maple and ebony windows and inlays.

MSR	$500	$355-500	$305	$245

Level 3 "F25" - Bird's-eye maple forearm, ebony-bordered blue pearlized plastic floating points, synthetic ebony butt sleeve with blue pearlized plastic windows set between silver colored rings above and below.

MSR	$500	$355-500	$305	$245

Level 4 "F26" - Bird's-eye maple forearm, four ebony points with four colored veneers, ebony butt sleeve with four intricate maple and vermillion hollow six-point star-shaped inlays.

MSR	$490	$345-490	$295	$240

Level 4 "F27" - Bird's-eye maple forearm, intricate ebony-bordered two-piece synthetic ivory floating opposing points, bird's-eye maple butt sleeve with intricate ebony-bordered two-piece synthetic ivory windows.

MSR	$490	$345-490	$295	$240

Level 4 "F28" - Bird's-eye maple forearm, ebony-bordered purple pearlized plastic points with ebony-bordered purple pearlized plastic diamond-shaped tips and three graduated sized maple diamond-shaped inlays in each point, bird's-eye maple butt sleeve with sets of intricate ebony and purple pearlized plastic inlaid patterns.

MSR	$480	$335-480	$290	$235

Level 4 "F29" - Bird's-eye maple forearm, four rosewood points with ebony and synthetic ivory veneers and pairs of graduated sized pearlized plastic notched diamond-shaped inlays and dots in each point, rosewood butt sleeve with four sets of pearlized plastic notched diamond-shaped inlays within pairs of dots alternating with four pearlized plastic dots set over ebony and pearlized plastic rings.

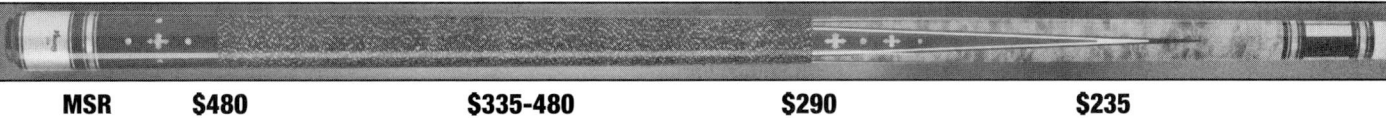

MSR	$480	$335-480	$290	$235

GRADING	100%	95%	70%

Level 4 "F30" - Bird's-eye maple forearm, three intricate ebony-bordered two-piece synthetic ivory points with ebony-bordered vermillion diamond-shaped inlays in the center of each alternating with three short ebony points, bird's-eye maple butt sleeve with three intricate ebony-bordered two-piece synthetic ivory windows with ebony-bordered vermillion diamond-shaped inlays in the center of each alternating with three short ebony reverse points.

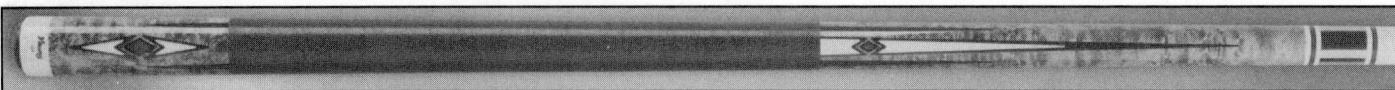

MSR	$470	$325-470	$280	$230

Level 4 "F31" - Ebony forearm, four intricate two-piece blue pearlized plastic hollow floating points with pearlized plastic cross-shaped inlays in the center of each, ebony butt sleeve with four intricate two-piece blue pearlized plastic hollow windows with pearlized plastic cross-shaped inlays in the center of each above a blue pearlized plastic ring set in silver colored rings below.

MSR	$470	$325-470	$280	$230

Level 4 "F32" - Bird's-eye maple forearm, four intricate seven-piece vermillion/osage orangewood/synthetic ebony floating points with a synthetic ivory diamond-shaped inlay in the center of each, bird's-eye maple butt sleeve with four intricate seven-piece vermillion/osage orangewood/ synthetic ebony windows with a synthetic ivory diamond-shaped inlay in the center of each.

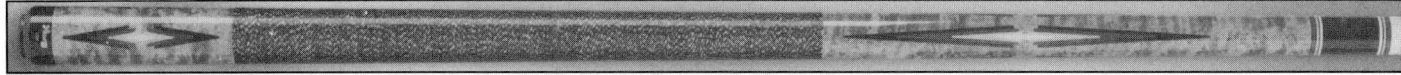

MSR	$460	$315-460	$275	$225

Level 6 "F33" - Bird's-eye maple forearm, four intricate ebony-bordered seven-piece synthetic ivory/vermillion/bird's-eye maple floating points, bird's-eye maple butt sleeve with four intricate ebony-bordered four-piece synthetic ivory/vermillion/bird's-eye maple reverse points.

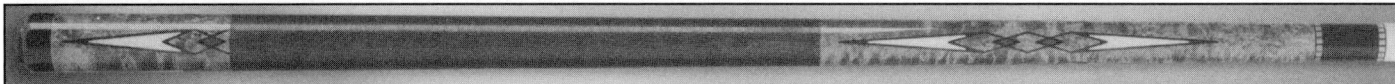

MSR	$460	$315-460	$275	$225

Level 6 "F34" - Stained bird's-eye maple forearm, four ebony points with eight-piece stained bird's-eye maple/vermillion/synthetic ebony elliptical inlays, ebony butt sleeve with four eight-piece stained bird's-eye maple/vermillion/synthetic ebony elliptical inlays.

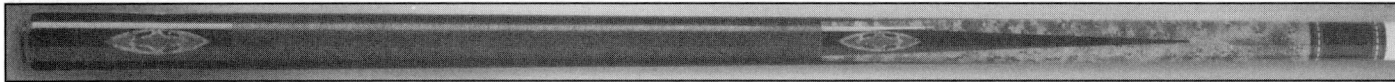

MSR	$450	$310-450	$270	$220

Level 4 "F35" - Stained bird's-eye maple forearm, four ebony points with synthetic ivory crosses over synthetic pearl inlays, ebony butt sleeve with synthetic ivory crosses over synthetic pearl inlays.

MSR	$450	$310-450	$270	$220

Level 6 "F36" - Bird's-eye maple forearm, four intricate ebony-bordered three-piece green pearlized plastic floating points with five stained maple dot-shaped inlays in each, bird's-eye maple butt sleeve with four intricate ebony-bordered three-piece green pearlized plastic windows with five stained maple dot-shaped inlays in each.

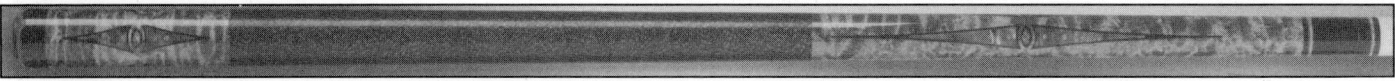

MSR	$440	$300-440	$260	$215

Level 5 "F37" - Bird's-eye maple forearm, four intricate two-piece ebony-bordered synthetic ivory opposing floating points with an intricate three-piece black synthetic inlay in the center of each, bird's-eye maple butt sleeve with four intricate two-piece ebony-bordered synthetic ivory opposing windows with an intricate three-piece black synthetic inlay in the center of each.

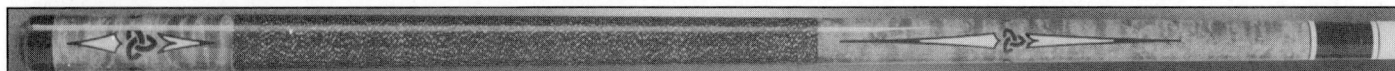

MSR	$440	$300-440	$260	$215

VIKING CUE MANUFACTURING INC., cont. 817

GRADING	100%	95%	70%

Level 3 "F38" - Bird's-eye maple forearm, four intricate ebony-bordered vermillion points that create a striped effect, bird's-eye maple butt sleeve with four intricate ebony-bordered vermillion reverse points that create a striped effect.

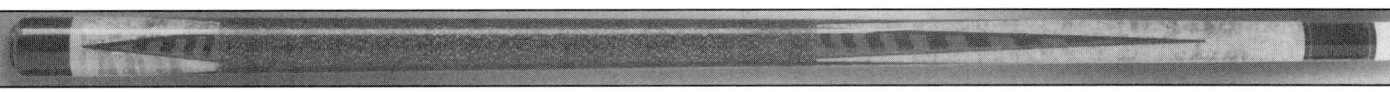

MSR	$430	$295-430	$255	$210

Level 4 "F39" - Bird's-eye maple forearm, four intricate ebony and synthetic ivory three-piece points alternating with four intricate ebony and synthetic ivory three-piece semi-circles, bird's-eye maple butt sleeve with four intricate ebony and synthetic ivory three-piece reverse points alternating with four intricate ebony and synthetic ivory three-piece circles.

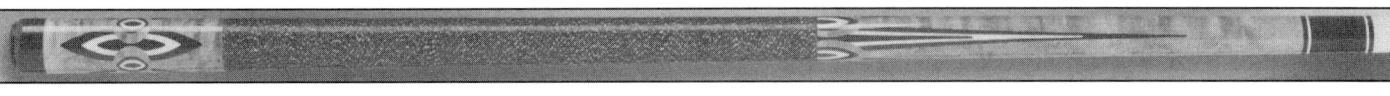

MSR	$430	$295-430	$255	$210

Level 4 "F40" - Stained bird's-eye maple forearm, four ebony points with a vermillion circle between a pair of osage orangewood circles all pierced by a synthetic ivory ellipse-shaped inlay in each point, ebony butt sleeve with four vermillion circles between pairs of osage orangewood circles all pierced by four synthetic ivory ellipse-shaped inlays.

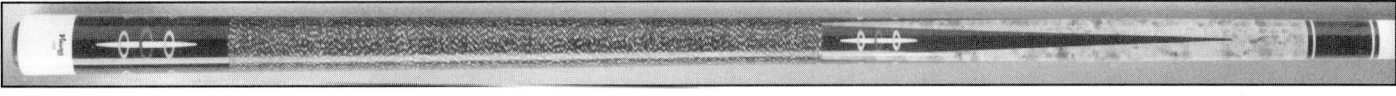

MSR	$420	$290-420	$250	$205

Level 4 "F41" - Stained bird's-eye maple forearm, four floating synthetic ebony-bordered vermillion points with a two-piece synthetic ebony-bordered synthetic ivory oval-shaped inlay at the base of each point, stained bird's-eye maple butt sleeve with four floating synthetic ebony-bordered vermillion reverse points with a two-piece synthetic ebony-bordered synthetic ivory oval-shaped inlay at the base of each point.

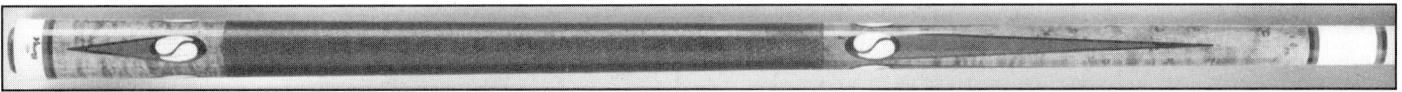

MSR	$420	$290-420	$250	$205

Level 3 "F42" - Ebony forearm, four floating red-stained bird's-eye maple flame-shaped two-piece points, ebony butt sleeve with four red-stained bird's-eye maple flame-shaped reverse points.

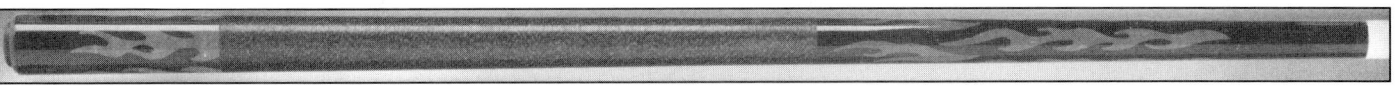

MSR	$420	$290-420	$250	$205

Level 4 "F43" - Stained bird's-eye maple forearm, four intricate synthetic ebony-bordered pearlized plastic points with a synthetic ebony-bordered stained bird's-eye maple cross-shaped inlay in each point, pearlized plastic butt sleeve with four sets of intricate synthetic ebony-bordered stained bird's-eye maple three-piece inlaid patterns.

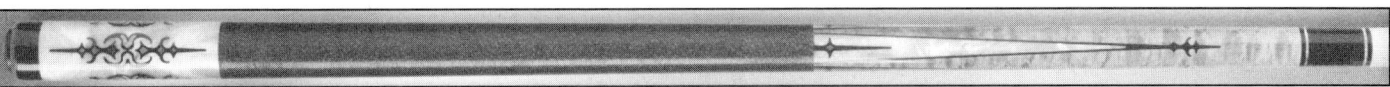

MSR	$420	$290-420	$250	$205

Level 4 "F44" - Stained bird's-eye maple forearm, four rosewood points with synthetic ebony-bordered rosewood and maple veneers, stained bird's-eye maple butt sleeve with four sets of intricate synthetic ebony-bordered maple and rosewood five-piece windows.

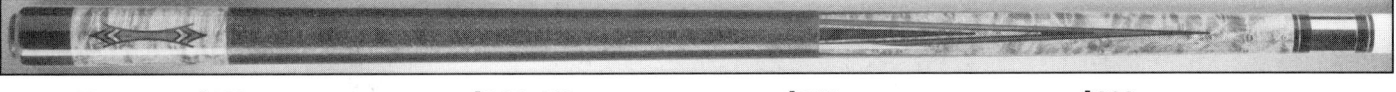

MSR	$410	$280-410	$245	$200

Level 4 "F45" - Stained bird's-eye maple forearm, four intricate synthetic ebony-bordered green pearlized plastic three-piece floating points alternating with four green pearlized plastic circles, stained bird's-eye maple butt sleeve with four intricate synthetic ebony-bordered green pearlized plastic three-piece windows alternating with four green pearlized plastic ovals.

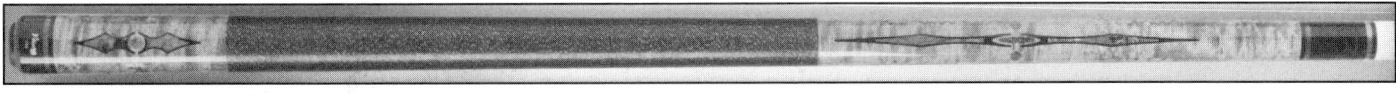

MSR	$410	$280-410	$245	$200

GRADING	100%	95%	70%

Level 3 "F46" - Stained bird's-eye maple forearm, four synthetic ebony-bordered red pearlized plastic floating points alternating with four pearlized plastic triangles, red pearlized plastic butt sleeve with black and white pearlized plastic rings.

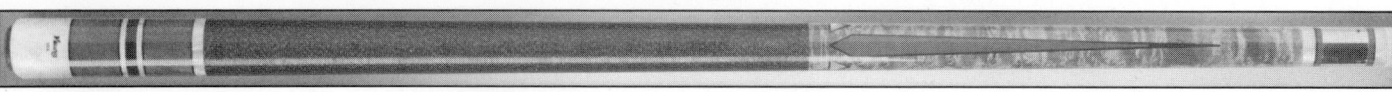

MSR	$410	$280-410	$245	$200

Level 3 "F47" - Stained bird's-eye maple forearm, four intricate synthetic ebony-bordered synthetic ivory two-piece floating points with cross-shaped bottom pieces, stained bird's-eye maple butt sleeve with four intricate synthetic ebony-bordered synthetic ivory cross-shaped windows.

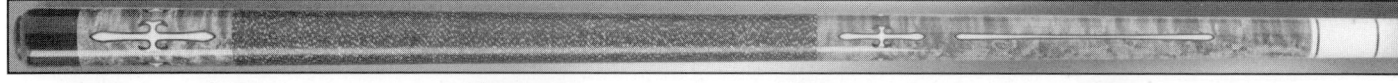

MSR	$400	$275-400	$240	$195

Level 5 "F48" - Stained bird's-eye maple forearm, four synthetic ebony-bordered blue pearlized plastic floating points with an eight-piece pearlized plastic inlaid pattern in each point, stained bird's-eye maple butt sleeve with four synthetic ebony-bordered blue pearlized plastic windows with an eight-piece pearlized plastic inlaid pattern in each.

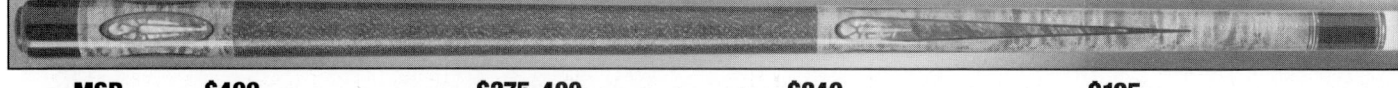

MSR	$400	$275-400	$240	$195

Level 4 "F49" - Stained bird's-eye maple forearm, four intricate synthetic ebony-bordered pearlized plastic points with an intricate synthetic ebony-bordered pearlized plastic spear-shaped inlay in each point and above the tip of each point, stained bird's-eye maple butt sleeve with four intricate synthetic ebony-bordered pearlized plastic reverse points with an intricate synthetic ebony-bordered pearlized plastic spear-shaped inlay in each point and below the tip of each point.

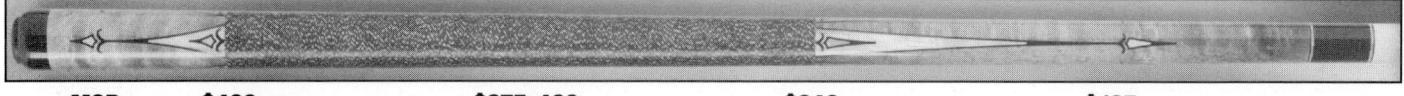

MSR	$400	$275-400	$240	$195

Level 5 "F50" - Stained bird's-eye maple forearm, four synthetic ebony floating points with a four-piece purple pearlized plastic inlaid pattern in each point, stained bird's-eye maple butt sleeve with four synthetic ebony windows with a four-piece purple pearlized plastic inlaid pattern in each.

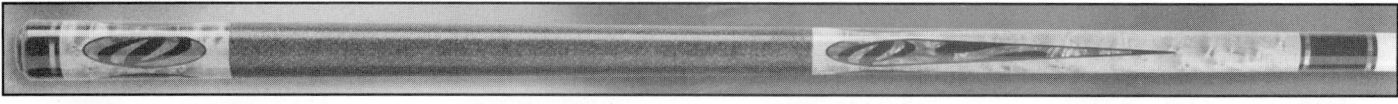

MSR	$400	$275-400	$240	$195

Level 5 "F51" - Stained bird's-eye maple forearm, four synthetic ebony-bordered rosewood points with two three-piece synthetic ebony-bordered bird's-eye maple inlays in each point, rosewood butt sleeve with four pairs of three-piece synthetic ebony-bordered bird's-eye maple windows.

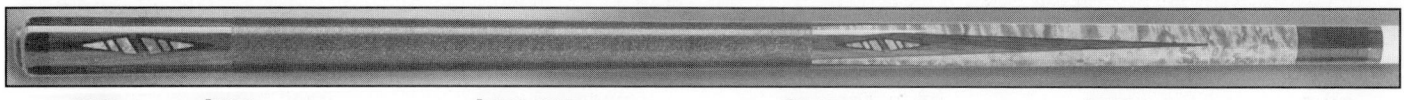

MSR	$390	$270-390	$235	$190

Level 3 "F52" - Stained bird's-eye maple forearm, six stained bird's-eye maple points with synthetic ebony-bordered green pearlized plastic veneers, stained bird's-eye maple butt sleeve with six stained bird's-eye maple eight-sided windows with synthetic ebony-bordered green pearlized plastic veneers.

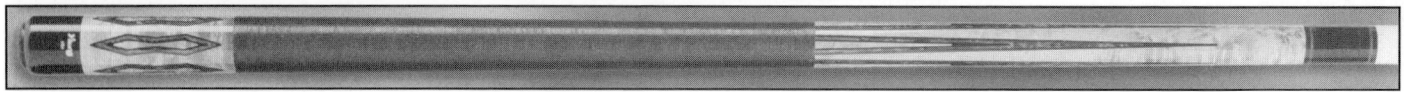

MSR	$390	$270-390	$235	$190

Level 4 "F53" - Stained bird's-eye maple forearm, four two-piece synthetic ebony points with a synthetic ebony-bordered stained bird's-eye maple cross-shaped inlay in the center of each, synthetic ebony butt sleeve with four stained bid's-eye maple cross-shaped inlays set in stained bird's-eye maple-bordered synthetic ebony diamond-shaped windows.

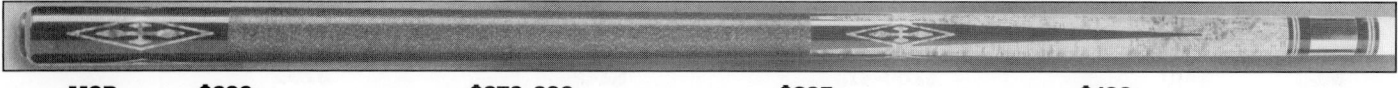

MSR	$390	$270-390	$235	$190

GRADING	100%	95%	70%

Level 5 "F54" - Stained bird's-eye maple forearm, four synthetic ebony-bordered blue pearlized plastic floating points above intricate eight-piece woven synthetic ebony-bordered blue pearlized plastic four-point star-shaped inlays, stained bird's-eye maple butt sleeve with four sets of intricate eight-piece woven synthetic ebony-bordered blue pearlized plastic four-point star-shaped inlays.

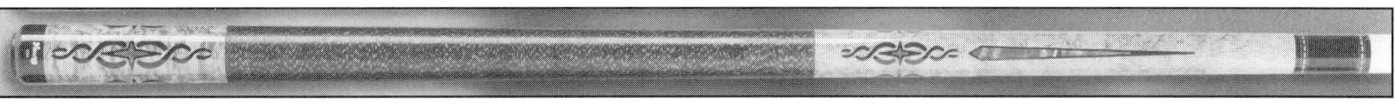

MSR	$390	$270-390	$235	$190

Level 4 "F55" - Stained bird's-eye maple forearm, four synthetic ebony points with a three-piece pearlized plastic striped pattern inlaid in each point, stained bird's-eye maple butt sleeve with four synthetic ebony reverse points with a three-piece pearlized plastic striped pattern inlaid in each point.

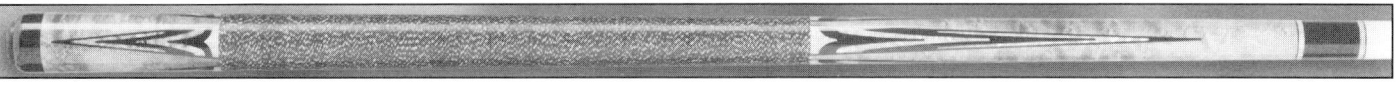

MSR	$380	$265-380	$230	$185

Level 3 "F56" - Stained bird's-eye maple forearm, four stained bird's-eye maple points with intricate synthetic ebony and vermillion veneers, stained bird's-eye maple butt sleeve with four stained bird's-eye maple diamond-shaped windows with intricate synthetic ebony and vermillion veneers.

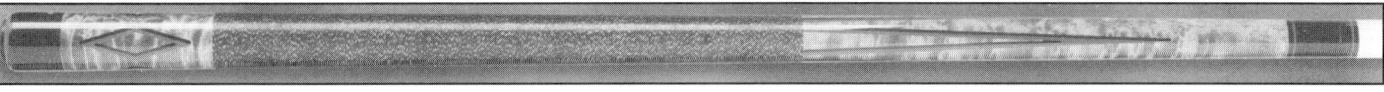

MSR	$380	$265-380	$230	$185

Level 4 "F57" - Stained bird's-eye maple forearm, four synthetic ebony four-piece points with an intricate hollow pearlized plastic inlay in the center of each point, stained bird's-eye maple butt sleeve with four synthetic ebony four-piece windows with an intricate hollow pearlized plastic inlay in the center of each window.

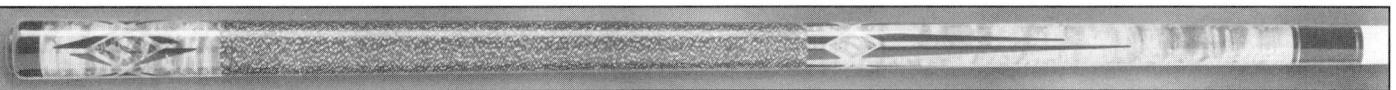

MSR	$380	$265-380	$230	$185

Level 1 "F58" - Bird's-eye maple forearm, four full spliced black-stained bird's-eye maple points and butt with a spiral textured handle.

MSR	$380	$265-380	$230	$185

Level 4 "F59" - Stained bird's-eye maple forearm, four synthetic ebony-bordered wenge floating points with a synthetic ivory hollow diamond-shaped inlay in each point, stained bird's-eye maple butt sleeve with four synthetic ebony-bordered wenge floating points with a synthetic ivory hollow diamond-shaped inlay in each window.

MSR	$370	$260-370	$225	$180

Level 4 "F60" - Stained bird's-eye maple forearm, four synthetic ebony-bordered green pearlized plastic points with a synthetic ebony-bordered pearlized plastic inlay below each point, stained bird's-eye maple butt sleeve with four synthetic ebony-bordered white and green pearlized plastic three-piece windows.

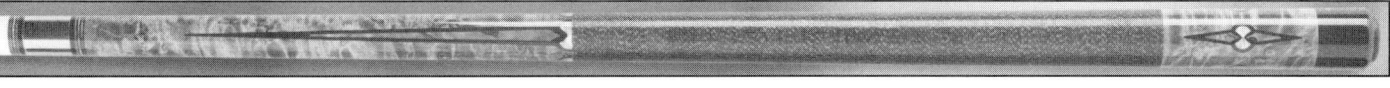

MSR	$370	$260-370	$225	$180

Level 5 "F61" - Rosewood forearm, four intricate eight-piece bird's-eye maple points, rosewood butt sleeve with four intricate two-piece bird's-eye maple reverse points.

MSR	$370	$260-370	$225	$180

GRADING	100%	95%	70%

Level 5 "F62" - Rosewood forearm, four intricate six-piece osage orangewood and synthetic ivory floating points, rosewood butt sleeve with four intricate six-piece osage orangewood and synthetic ivory inlay patterns.

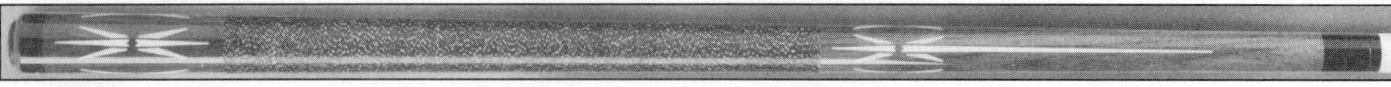

MSR	$360	$250-360	$220	$175

Level 4 "F63" - Stained bird's-eye maple forearm, blue three-piece pearlized plastic points with synthetic ebony-bordered pearlized plastic centers, stained bird's-eye maple butt sleeve with blue three-piece pearlized plastic reverse points with synthetic ebony-bordered pearlized plastic centers.

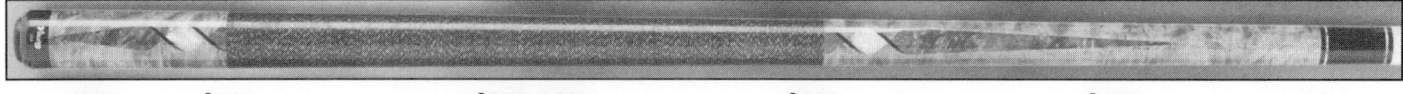

MSR	$360	$250-360	$220	$175

Level 3 "F64" - Rosewood forearm, four intricate synthetic ivory hollow floating points, rosewood butt sleeve with four intricate synthetic ivory hollow inlays.

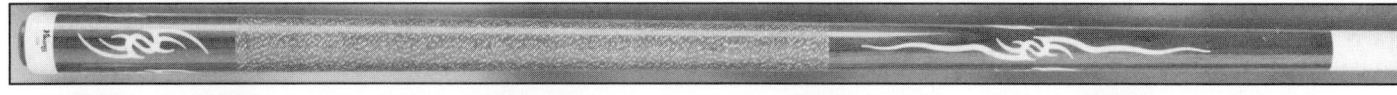

MSR	$360	$250-360	$220	$175

Level 3 "F65" - Black-stained maple forearm, four yellow pearlized plastic points with an intricate synthetic ebony cross-shaped inlay in each point, yellow pearlized plastic butt sleeve with four synthetic ebony cross-shaped inlays.

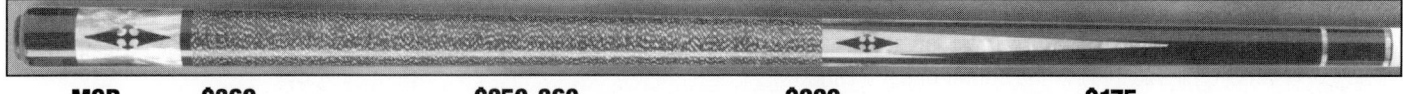

MSR	$360	$250-360	$220	$175

Level 3 "F66" - Stained bird's-eye maple forearm, four synthetic ebony-bordered pearlized plastic wave points, stained bird's-eye maple butt sleeve with four ebony-bordered pearlized plastic reverse wave points.

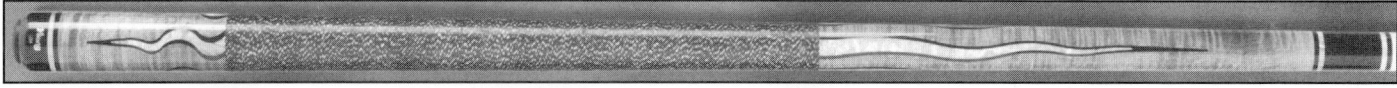

MSR	$360	$250-360	$220	$175

Level 5 "F67" - Stained bird's-eye maple forearm, four intricate five-piece floating purpleheart points, stained bird's-eye maple butt sleeve with four intricate five-piece purpleheart windows.

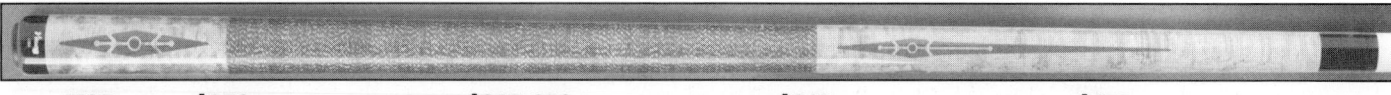

MSR	$350	$245-350	$210	$170

Level 3 "F68" - Stained bird's-eye maple forearm, four synthetic ebony points with a vermillion swirl inlay through the center of each point, stained bird's-eye maple butt sleeve with four synthetic ebony reverse points with a vermillion swirl inlay through the center of each point.

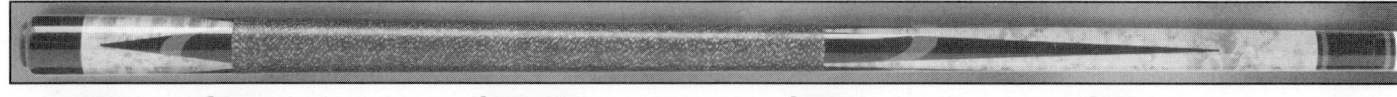

MSR	$350	$245-350	$210	$170

Level 3 "F69" - Stained bird's-eye maple forearm, four synthetic ebony and grey pearlized plastic-bordered stained bird's-eye maple points, grey pearlized plastic butt sleeve with a synthetic ebony ring below wrap.

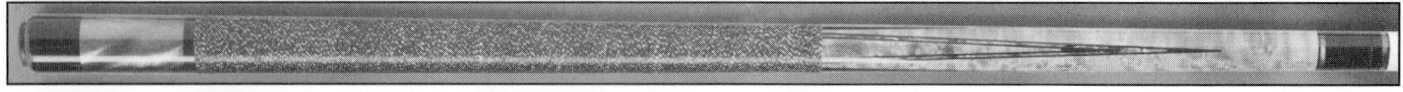

MSR	$340	$240-340	$205	$165

Level 3 "F70" - Stained bird's-eye maple forearm, four synthetic ebony and red vinyl-bordered synthetic ebony points, black-stained maple butt sleeve with red vinyl rings at bottom.

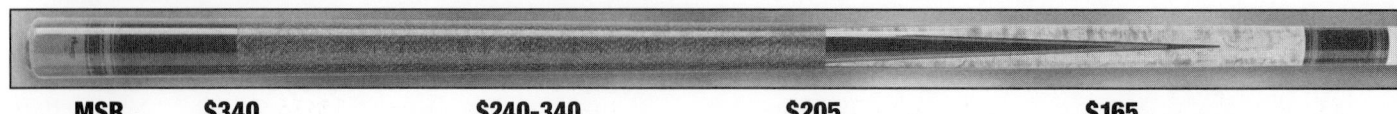

MSR	$340	$240-340	$205	$165

GRADING	100%	95%	70%

Level 2 "F71" - Rosewood forearm with four sets of pearlized plastic four-point star-shaped inlays between pairs of pearlized plastic dots, rosewood butt sleeve with four pearlized plastic four-point star-shaped inlays alternating with four pearlized plastic dots.

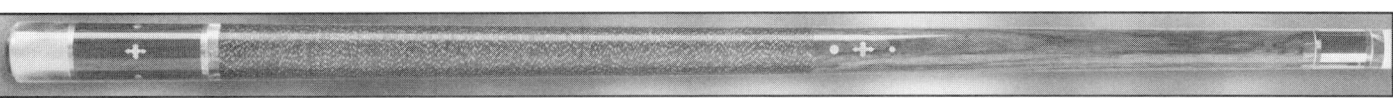

MSR	$340	$240-340	$205	$165

Level 5 "F72" - Rosewood forearm, four intricate eleven-piece stained bird's-eye maple points, rosewood butt sleeve, stained bird's-eye maple butt cap.

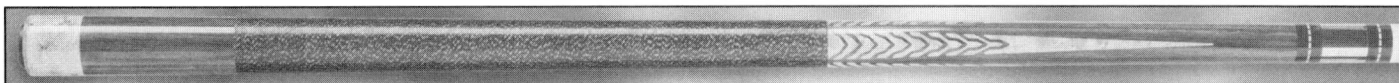

MSR	$330	$235-330	$200	$160

Level 3 "F73" - Stained bird's-eye maple forearm, four synthetic ebony-bordered purple pearlized plastic points, purple pearlized plastic butt sleeve with synthetic ebony rings at top and bottom.

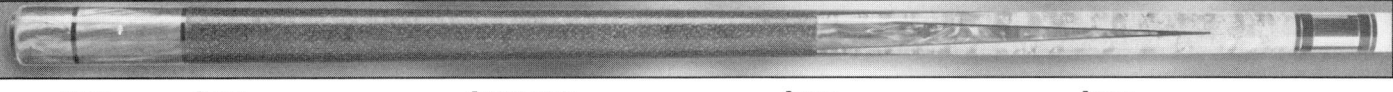

MSR	$320	$225-320	$195	$155

Level 3 "F74" - Rosewood forearm, two-piece pearlized plastic floating zig-zag points, rosewood butt sleeve with two-piece pearlized plastic zig-zag inlays.

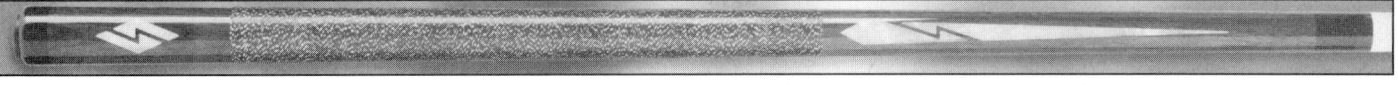

MSR	$310	$220-310	$190	$150

Level 3 "F75" - Rosewood forearm, four intricate stained bird's-eye maple points with a hollow swirl pattern in the center of each point, rosewood butt sleeve with four intricate stained bird's-eye maple reverse points with a hollow swirl pattern in the center of each point.

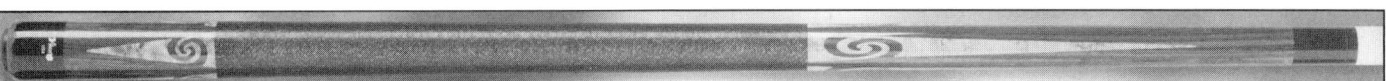

MSR	$310	$220-310	$190	$150

Level 4 "F76" - Rosewood forearm, four intricate synthetic ivory floating points with a pair of rosewood triangle-shaped inlays towards the base of each point, rosewood butt sleeve with four intricate synthetic ivory windows with a pair of rosewood triangle-shaped inlays in the center of each window.

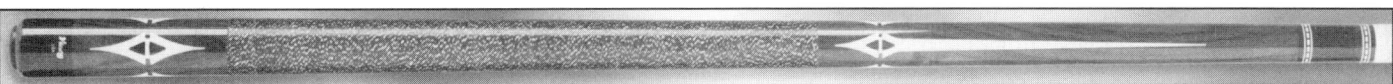

MSR	$300	$210-300	$180	$145

Level 3 "F77" - Stained bird's-eye maple forearm, four synthetic ebony and green vinyl-bordered pearlized plastic points, pearlized plastic butt sleeve with a green vinyl ring at bottom.

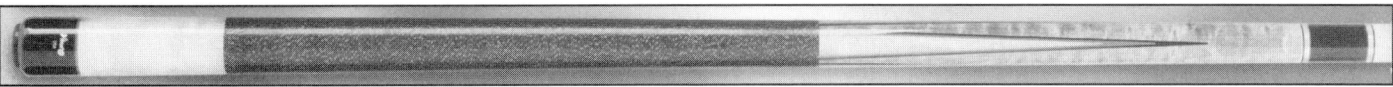

MSR	$290	$205-290	$175	$140

Level 1 "F78" - Bird's-eye maple forearm, four synthetic ebony-bordered black stained bird's-eye maple full-spliced points and handle.

MSR	$280	$200-280	$170	$135

Level 2 "F79" - Black-stained maple forearm, synthetic ebony butt sleeve with four maple-bordered vermillion diamond-shaped inlays set in maple-bordered vermillion four-point star-shaped windows.

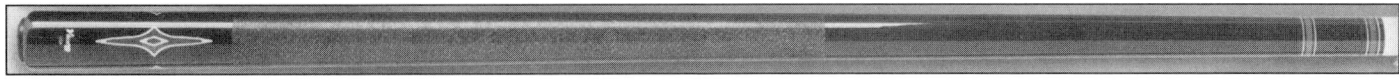

MSR	$275	$195-275	$165	$135

VIKING CUE MANUFACTURING INC., cont.

GRADING	100%	95%	70%

Level 2 "F80" - Black-stained maple forearm, synthetic ebony butt sleeve with four intricate maple hollow four-point star-shaped windows with seven synthetic ebony center pieces in each.

MSR	$270	$190-270	$165	$130

Level 3 "F81" - Rosewood forearm, four stained bird's-eye maple-bordered rosewood points, rosewood butt sleeve, stained bird's-eye maple butt cap.

MSR	$260	$185-260	$160	$125

Level 3 "F82" - Bird's-eye maple forearm, four synthetic ebony-bordered blue-stained bird's-eye maple points, blue-stained bird's-eye maple butt sleeve.

MSR	$260	$185-260	$160	$125

Level 2 "F83" - Orange-stained bird's-eye maple forearm, synthetic ebony butt sleeve with vinyl dash rings above and below.

MSR	$255	$180-255	$155	$125

Level 2 "F84" - Black-stained bird's-eye maple forearm, black-stained bird's-eye maple butt sleeve with a pair of pearlized plastic rings at bottom.

MSR	$250	$180-250	$155	$120

Level 2 "F85" - Green-stained bird's-eye maple forearm, green pearlized plastic butt sleeve with pearlized plastic rings at center and top and bottom.

MSR	$245	$175-245	$150	$120

Level 2 "F86" - Stained bird's-eye maple forearm, stained bird's-eye maple butt sleeve with a synthetic ebony ring and blue pearlized plastic ring at bottom.

MSR	$240	$175-240	$150	$115

Level 2 "F87" - Rosewood forearm, rosewood butt sleeve with white/black/silver rings at bottom.

MSR	$235	$170-235	$145	$115

Level 2 "F88" - Red-stained bird's-eye maple forearm, red-stained bird's-eye maple butt sleeve with black/red/yellow vinyl rings at bottom.

MSR	$230	$170-230	$145	$110

VIKING CUE MANUFACTURING INC., cont.

GRADING	100%	95%	70%

Level 2 "F89" - Rosewood forearm, synthetic ivory butt sleeve with green vinyl rings at top and bottom.

MSR	$225	$165-225	$140	$110

Level 2 "F90" - Black-stained bird's-eye maple forearm, grey pearlized plastic butt sleeve with a synthetic ebony ring at top.

MSR	$220	$165-220	$140	$105

Level 2 "F91" - Blue-stained bird's-eye maple forearm, blue-stained bird's-eye maple butt sleeve.

MSR	$215	$160-215	$135	$105

Level 2 "F92" - Green-stained bird's-eye maple forearm, green-stained bird's-eye maple butt sleeve.

MSR	$210	$160-210	$135	$100

Level 2 "F93" - Grey-stained bird's-eye maple forearm, grey-stained bird's-eye maple butt sleeve.

MSR	$205	$155-205	$130	$100

Level 2 "F94" - Rainbow-stained bird's-eye maple forearm, rainbow-stained bird's-eye maple butt sleeve.

MSR	$200	$155-200	$130	$95

Level 2 "F95" - Green-stained bird's-eye maple forearm, green-stained bird's-eye maple butt sleeve.

MSR	$190	$150-190	$125	$90

Level 2 "F96" - Red-stained bird's-eye maple forearm, red-stained bird's-eye maple butt sleeve.

MSR	$180	$140-180	$115	$85

Level 2 "F97" - Purple-stained bird's-eye maple forearm, purple-stained bird's-eye maple butt sleeve.

MSR	$170	$135-170	$110	$80

Level 2 "F98" - Black-stained maple forearm, black-stained maple butt sleeve.

MSR	$160	$125-160	$105	$75

VIKING CUE MANUFACTURING INC., cont.

GRADING	100%	95%	70%

Level 2 "F99" - Goncalo alves forearm, goncalo alves butt sleeve.

MSR	$150	$120-150	$100	$70

"DECUE" SERIES

The most of the following "DeCue" line cues featured art by John Schmelzer.

Level 2 "F100 Feathers and Leather" - Purple-stained bird's-eye maple forearm with applied image of a beautiful woman scantily clad in leather and spider webbing with a feather headdress, white pearlized plastic butt sleeve etched with a spider web pattern.

MSR	$330	$235-330	$200	$160

Level 2 "F101 Eagle" - Black-stained bird's-eye maple forearm with applied image of an eagle, blue pearlized plastic butt sleeve with applied image of an eagle flying from a branch.

MSR	$330	$235-330	$200	$160

Level 2 "F102 Leopard Lady" - Black-stained bird's-eye maple forearm with applied image of a leopard lady, black-stained bird's-eye maple butt sleeve with applied image of leopard lady face.

MSR	$310	$220-310	$190	$150

Level 2 "F103 Wolves" - Black-stained bird's-eye maple forearm with applied image of wolves under a full moon, black-stained bird's-eye maple butt sleeve with applied image of a wolf howling in front of a full moon.

MSR	$310	$220-310	$190	$150

Level 2 "F104 Skeleton" - Red-stained bird's-eye maple forearm with applied image of a skeleton filled with numbered pool balls rising above flames, red-stained bird's-eye maple butt sleeve with applied image of a dagger piercing a bleeding nine-ball.

MSR	$310	$220-310	$190	$150

Level 2 "F105 Viking Lady" - Black-stained bird's-eye maple forearm with applied image of a Viking lady holding a cue behind a wolf, black-stained bird's-eye maple butt sleeve with applied image of a Viking hat over a horned nine-ball.

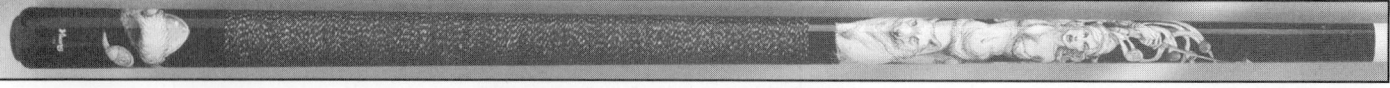

MSR	$310	$220-310	$190	$150

Level 2 "F106 The Dragon" - Green-stained bird's-eye maple forearm with applied image of a dragon, green-stained bird's-eye maple butt sleeve with applied image of a dragon.

MSR	$310	$220-310	$190	$150

VIKING CUE MANUFACTURING INC., cont. 825

GRADING	100%	95%	70%

Level 2 "F107 Leopard" - Black-stained bird's-eye maple forearm with applied image of a stalking leopard, black-stained bird's-eye maple butt sleeve with applied image of a bloody nine-ball.

MSR	$310	$220-310	$190	$150

Level 2 "F108 Wizard" - Blue-stained bird's-eye maple forearm with applied image of stars and planets circling from wrap to joint, blue-stained bird's-eye maple butt sleeve with applied image of a smiling wizard with a pool cue.

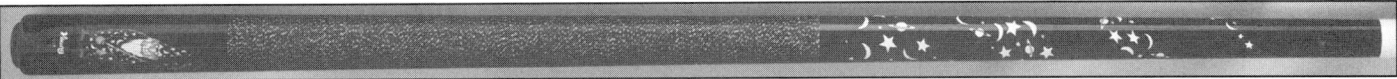

MSR	$310	$220-310	$190	$150

Level 2 "F109 Snake" - Black-stained bird's-eye maple forearm, black-stained bird's-eye maple butt sleeve with applied image of a coiled snake.

MSR	$210	$160-210	$135	$100

Level 2 "F110 Snarling Wolf" - Black-stained bird's-eye maple forearm, black-stained bird's-eye maple butt sleeve with applied image of a snarling wolf.

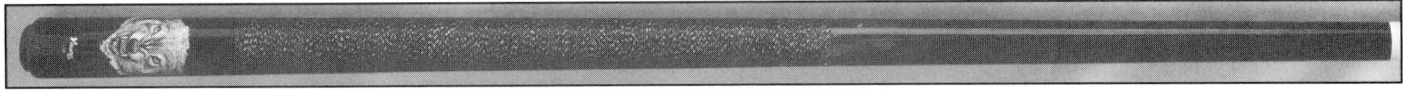

MSR	$210	$160-210	$135	$100

Level 2 "F111 Skull" - Black-stained bird's-eye maple forearm, black-stained bird's-eye maple butt sleeve with applied image of a skull with eight-ball eyes sticking its tongue out.

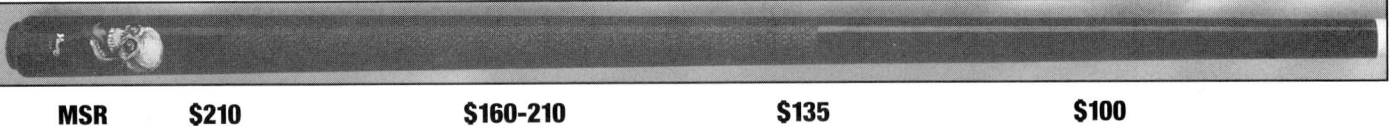

MSR	$210	$160-210	$135	$100

GRADING	98%	90%	70%

DISCONTINUED EXAMPLES

The following cues were from Viking's first line, circa 1967-1968. All had brass joints, and full-spliced butts. A variety of wraps were available, and screw-on ferrules were an option.

Level 3 "20B" - Maple forearm, four rosewood points, rosewood butt sleeve.

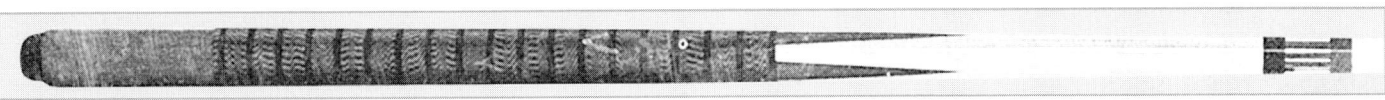

Orig. MSR (1967) $20	$250	$185	$110

Level 3 "V30" - Maple forearm, four rosewood points, rosewood butt sleeve with "The Viking Cue Company" under a clear plastic window at bottom.

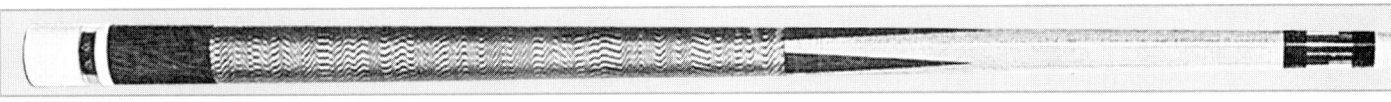

Orig. MSR (1967) $30	$400	$300	$180

Level 3 "40B" - Maple forearm, four rosewood points with four colored veneers, pearlized plastic butt sleeve.

Orig. MSR (1967) $40	$445	$335	$200

GRADING	98%	90%	70%

Level 3 "HR" - Maple forearm, four rosewood points with four colored veneers, rosewood butt sleeve.

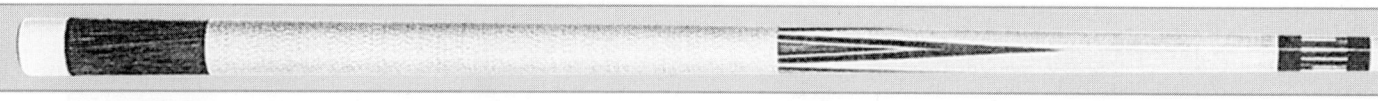

Orig. MSR (1967) $50	$385	$285	$170

Level 3 "V50" - Maple forearm, four rosewood points with four colored veneers, rosewood butt sleeve with "The Viking Cue Company" under a clear plastic window at bottom.

Orig. MSR (1967) $55	$675	$500	$300

Level 2 "V55" - Bocote forearm, bocote butt sleeve with "The Viking Cue Company" under a clear plastic window set in blue pearlized plastic at bottom.

Orig. MSR (1967) $55	$675	$500	$295

Level 2 "V70" - Bocote forearm with a white pearlized plastic ring above wrap, bocote butt sleeve with a white pearlized plastic ring below wrap and "The Viking Cue Company" under a clear plastic window set in white pearlized plastic at bottom.

Orig. MSR (1967) $70	$690	$425	$320

Level 3 "P75" - Maple forearm, four rosewood points with four colored veneers, ebony butt sleeve with "The Viking Cue Company" under a clear plastic window within white plastic rings in middle.

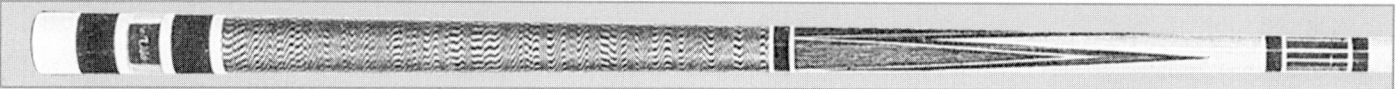

Orig. MSR (1967) $75	$825	$625	$395

Level 2 "V80" - Bocote forearm with a red pearlized plastic ring above wrap, bocote butt sleeve with a red pearlized plastic ring below wrap and "The Viking Cue Company" under a clear plastic window set in red pearlized plastic at bottom.

Orig. MSR (1967) $80	$835	$635	$400

Level 3 "V90" - Maple forearm with a black pearlized plastic ring above wrap, four ebony points with four colored veneers, ebony butt sleeve with a black pearlized plastic ring below wrap and "The Viking Cue Company" under a clear plastic window set in black pearlized plastic at bottom.

Orig. MSR (1967) $90	$865	$650	$405

Level 2 "Onyx" - Ebony forearm with a black pearlized plastic ring above wrap, ebony butt sleeve with a black pearlized plastic ring below wrap and "The Viking Cue Company" under a clear plastic window set in black pearlized plastic at bottom.

Orig. MSR (1967) $100	$895	$675	$420

VIKING CUE MANUFACTURING INC., cont.

GRADING	98%	90%	70%

Level 5 "V.I.P." - Maple forearm with a white plastic ring above wrap, four rosewood points with four white dots in each point, ebony butt sleeve with three rows of four white dots within white plastic rings above and below with "The Viking Cue Company" under a clear plastic window set in white plastic at bottom.

Orig. MSR (1967) $110	$975	$730	$450

Level 2 "R150" - Rosewood forearm with a rosewood ring set within gold rings above wrap, rosewood butt sleeve with a rosewood ring set within gold rings below wrap and "The Viking Cue Company" under a clear plastic window set within gold rings at bottom.

Orig. MSR (1967) $150	$1,000	$750	$470

Level 5 "Champion" - Maple forearm with black-bordered white dots between the points and "The Viking Cue Company" under a clear plastic window above wrap, four rosewood points with four colored veneers and three black-bordered white dots in each point and a black-bordered white dot at the tip of each point, rosewood butt sleeve with three rows of black-bordered white dots between clear plastic windows at top and bottom.

Orig. MSR (1967) $150	$1,150	$865	$540

Level 3 "Black Palm" - Ebony forearm with a green pearlized plastic ring above wrap, four ebony points with four colored veneers, ebony butt sleeve with vertical colored veneers set within a green pearlized plastic ring below wrap and "The Viking Cue Company" under a clear plastic window set in green pearlized plastic at bottom.

Orig. MSR (1967) $150	$1,150	$865	$540

Level 7 "Deluxe Champion" - Maple forearm with "The Viking Cue Company" under a clear plastic window above wrap, four ebony points with four colored veneers and a pattern of white dots in each, ebony butt sleeve with a pattern of white dots within "Deluxe Champion" under a clear plastic window above and a clear plastic window at bottom.

Orig. MSR (1967) $175	$1,750	$1,300	$800

Level 5 "R200" - Ebony forearm with a series of mother-of-pearl dots set above and within pearlized plastic rings above wrap, ebony butt sleeve with a series of mother-of-pearl dots set above and within pearlized plastic rings above and "The Viking Cue Company" under a clear plastic window below.

Orig. MSR (1967) $200	$1,750	$1,300	$800

VIKING'S SECOND LINE

The following cues were from Viking's second line, circa 1969-1972. All had brass or stainless steel joints, and full spliced butts. A variety of wraps were available, and screw-on ferrules were an option.

Level 2 "W30" - Rosewood forearm, rosewood butt sleeve with a clear plastic window at bottom.

Orig. MSR (1972) $30	$165	$125	$80

GRADING	98%	90%	70%

Level 2 "W35" - Rosewood forearm, rosewood butt sleeve with a clear plastic window set in green pearlized plastic at bottom.

Orig. MSR (1972) $35	$175	$135	$85

Level 2 "W40" - Rosewood forearm, rosewood butt sleeve with "Viking Cue" under a clear plastic window set in red pearlized plastic at bottom.

Orig. MSR (1972) $40	$295	$240	$145

Level 2 "W45" - Rosewood forearm, rosewood butt sleeve with "Viking Cue" under a clear plastic window set in black plastic at bottom.

Orig. MSR (1972) $45	$225	$170	$110

Level 3 "HR" - Maple forearm, four full-spliced rosewood points with four colored veneers, rosewood butt sleeve.

Orig. MSR (1972) $50	$235	$185	$115

Level 2 "W55" - Rosewood forearm, rosewood butt sleeve with "Viking Cue" under a clear plastic window set in gold pearlized plastic at bottom.

Orig. MSR (1972) $55	$375	$275	$155

Level 3 "W60" - Maple forearm, four full-spliced rosewood points with four colored veneers, rosewood butt sleeve with "Viking Cue" under a clear plastic window set in black plastic at bottom.

Orig. MSR (1972) $60	$545	$410	$260

Level 2 "W65" - Bocote forearm, black plastic butt sleeve with "Viking Cue" under a clear plastic window set in middle.

Orig. MSR (1972) $65	$570	$430	$265

Level 2 "W70" - Rosewood forearm with white pearlized plastic ring above wrap, rosewood butt sleeve with white pearlized plastic ring below wrap above "Viking Cue" under a clear plastic window set in white pearlized plastic at bottom.

Orig. MSR (1972) $70	$575	$440	$270

Level 3 "P75" - Maple forearm with a white-bordered black plastic ring above wrap, four full-spliced ebony points with four colored veneers, black plastic butt sleeve with "Viking Cue" under a clear plastic window set in middle.

Orig. MSR (1972) $75	$765	$565	$350

GRADING	98%	90%	70%

Level 2 "W80" - Bocote forearm with a blue pearlized plastic ring above wrap, bocote butt sleeve with a blue pearlized plastic ring below wrap and "Viking Cue" under a clear plastic window set within blue pearlized plastic rings at bottom.

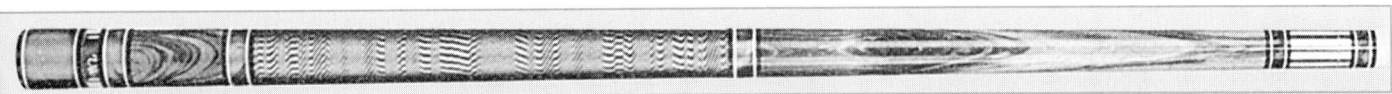

Orig. MSR (1972) $80	$785	$585	$360

Level 3 "W90" - Maple forearm with a white-bordered silver pearlized plastic ring above wrap, four full-spliced ebony points with four colored veneers, ebony butt sleeve with a white-bordered silver pearlized plastic ring below wrap and "Viking Cue" under a clear plastic window set below a white-bordered silver pearlized plastic ring at bottom.

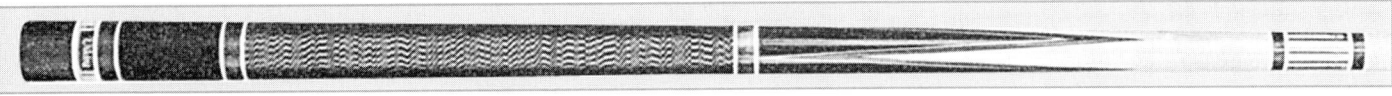

Orig. MSR (1972) $90	$795	$590	$370

Level 5 "VIP" - Maple forearm with a white ring above wrap, four full-spliced ebony points with four colored veneers and four white dots in each, ebony butt sleeve with three rows of white dots above "Viking Cue" under a clear plastic window set below a white plastic ring at bottom.

Orig. MSR (1972) $110	$910	$685	$430

Level 4 "W125" - Maple forearm, four full-spliced rosewood points with four colored veneers and a mother-of-pearl notched diamond-shaped inlay between two mother-of-pearl dots in each, rosewood butt sleeve with four mother-of-pearl notched diamond-shaped inlays alternating with four mother-of-pearl dots above "Viking Cue" under a clear plastic window set below black and white pearlized plastic rings at bottom.

Orig. MSR (1972) $125	$1,100	$835	$490

Level 5 "W150" - Maple forearm with white and black rings above wrap, four full-spliced ebony points with four colored veneers and five white dots in each, ebony butt sleeve with three rows of white dots above "Viking Cue" under a clear plastic window set below a white plastic ring at bottom.

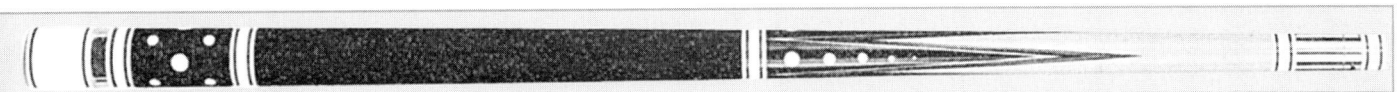

Orig. MSR (1972) $150	$1,250	$940	$550

Level 5 "Champion" - Maple forearm with black-bordered white dots between points and "Viking Cue" under a clear plastic window above wrap, four full-spliced bocote points with three black-bordered white dots in each point and a black-bordered white dot at the tip of each, bocote butt sleeve with three rows of black-bordered white dots between "Champion" under a clear plastic window at top and a clear plastic window at bottom.

Orig. MSR (1972) $150	$1,250	$940	$550

Level 3 "Palm" - Ebony forearm with a white pearlized plastic ring above wrap, four ebony points with three veneers, ebony butt sleeve with four rows of three overcall veneers between a white pearlized plastic ring at top and "Viking Cue" under a clear plastic window below a white pearlized plastic ring at bottom.

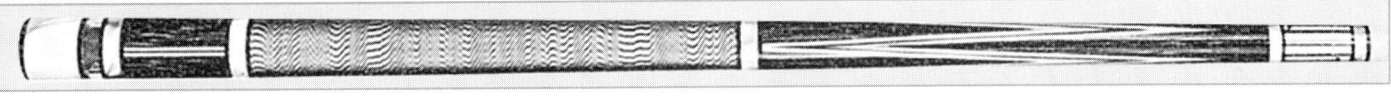

Orig. MSR (1972) $150	$1,150	$850	$520

GRADING	98%	90%	70%

Level 7 "Deluxe Champion" - Maple forearm with a clear plastic window above wrap, four full-spliced ebony points with a pattern of white dots in each point and an ebony dot at the tip of each point, ebony butt sleeve with a pattern of white dots between "Champion" under a clear plastic window at top and a clear plastic window at bottom.

| Orig. MSR (1972) $175 | $1,750 | $1,295 | $750 |

Level 6 "W200" - Cocobolo forearm with a pattern of white dots above intricate rings above wrap, cocobolo butt sleeve with a pattern of white dots between intricate rings at top and a clear plastic window at bottom.

| Orig. MSR (1972) $200 | $1,300 | $985 | $580 |

Level 6 "RDC" - Ebony forearm with "Viking Cue" under a clear plastic window above wrap, four full-spliced maple points with three colored veneers and a pattern of ebony dots in each point and a white dot at the tip of each point, ebony butt sleeve with four patterns of white dots alternating with four vertical rows of three colored veneers between "Champion" under a clear plastic window at top and a clear plastic window at bottom.

| Orig. MSR (1972) $250 | $1,900 | $1,450 | $900 |

VIKING'S THIRD LINE

The following cues were from Viking's third line, circa 1972-1974. All had brass or stainless steel joints, and full spliced butts. A variety of wraps were available, and screw-on ferrules were an option.

Level 2 X30 - Rosewood forearm, rosewood butt sleeve with "Viking Cue" under a clear plastic window at bottom.

| Orig. MSR (1974) $30 | $225 | $165 | $105 |

Level 2 X35 - Cordia forearm, blue pearlized plastic butt sleeve with "Viking Cue" under a clear plastic window in middle.

| Orig. MSR (1974) $35 | $235 | $180 | $110 |

Level 2 X40 - Rosewood forearm, rosewood butt sleeve with "Viking Cue" under a clear plastic window set in red pearlized plastic at bottom.

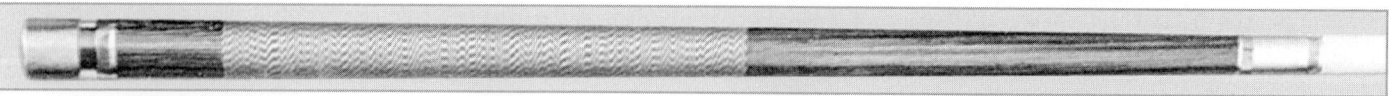

| Orig. MSR (1974) $40 | $245 | $185 | $115 |

Level 2 X45 - Rosewood forearm, rosewood butt sleeve with maple-bordered rosewood dots above "Viking Cue" under a clear plastic window set in black plastic at bottom.

| Orig. MSR (1974) $45 | $260 | $195 | $120 |

Level 2 X50 - Maple forearm, rosewood handle, maple butt sleeve with "Viking Cue" under a clear plastic window set in white plastic at bottom.

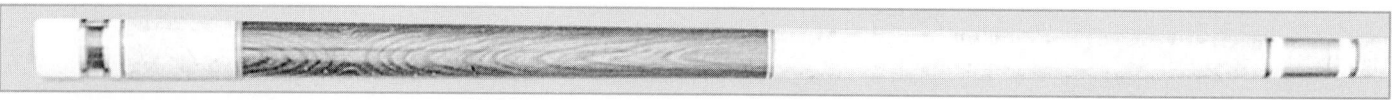

| Orig. MSR (1974) $50 | $270 | $200 | $125 |

VIKING CUE MANUFACTURING INC., cont. 831

GRADING	98%	90%	70%

Level 2 X55 - Rosewood forearm, rosewood butt sleeve with "Viking Cue" under a clear plastic window set in gold pearlized plastic at bottom.

Orig. MSR (1974) $55	$280	$210	$130

Level 3 X60 - Maple forearm, four rosewood points with four colored veneers, rosewood butt sleeve with "Viking Cue" under a clear plastic window set in black plastic at bottom.

Orig. MSR (1974) $60	$450	$345	$210

Level 2 X65 - Rosewood forearm, white plastic butt sleeve with "Viking Cue" under a clear plastic window set between stylized black plastic rings at bottom.

Orig. MSR (1974) $65	$385	$285	$170

Level 2 X70 - Rosewood forearm with a black-bordered blue pearlized plastic ring above wrap, rosewood butt sleeve with a black-bordered blue pearlized plastic ring at top and "Viking Cue" under a clear plastic window below a black-bordered blue pearlized plastic ring at bottom.

Orig. MSR (1974) $70	$420	$315	$180

Level 3 X75 - Maple forearm with black ring at bottom, four full-spliced rosewood points with four colored veneers, black butt sleeve with "Viking Cue" under a clear plastic window within white pearlized plastic rings in center.

Orig. MSR (1974) $75	$575	$425	$255

Level 2 X80 - Rosewood forearm with pearlized plastic ring at bottom below hollow white dots above, rosewood butt sleeve with hollow white dots around center between a grey pearlized plastic ring at top and "Viking Cue" under a clear plastic window below a grey pearlized plastic ring at bottom.

Orig. MSR (1974) $80	$585	$430	$260

Level 2 X85 - Rosewood forearm with rows of three pearlized plastic dots towards bottom, rosewood butt sleeve with mother-of-pearl notched diamond-shaped inlays alternating with mother-of-pearl dots above "Viking Cue" under a clear plastic window within pearlized plastic rings at bottom.

Orig. MSR (1974) $85	$600	$450	$275

Level 2 X90 - Rosewood forearm with pearlized plastic rings at bottom below rows of mother-of-pearl diamond-shaped inlays between mother-of-pearl dots above and below, rosewood butt sleeve with mother-of-pearl notched diamond-shaped inlays alternating with mother-of-pearl dots within pearlized plastic rings above "Viking Cue" under a clear plastic window at bottom.

Orig. MSR (1974) $90	$575	$430	$265

VIKING CUE MANUFACTURING INC., cont.

GRADING	98%	90%	70%

Level 4 X100 - Maple forearm, four full-spliced rosewood points with four colored veneers and three ivory-colored dots in each point, ebony-colored butt sleeve with three rows of ivory-colored dots above "Viking Cue" under a clear plastic window at bottom.

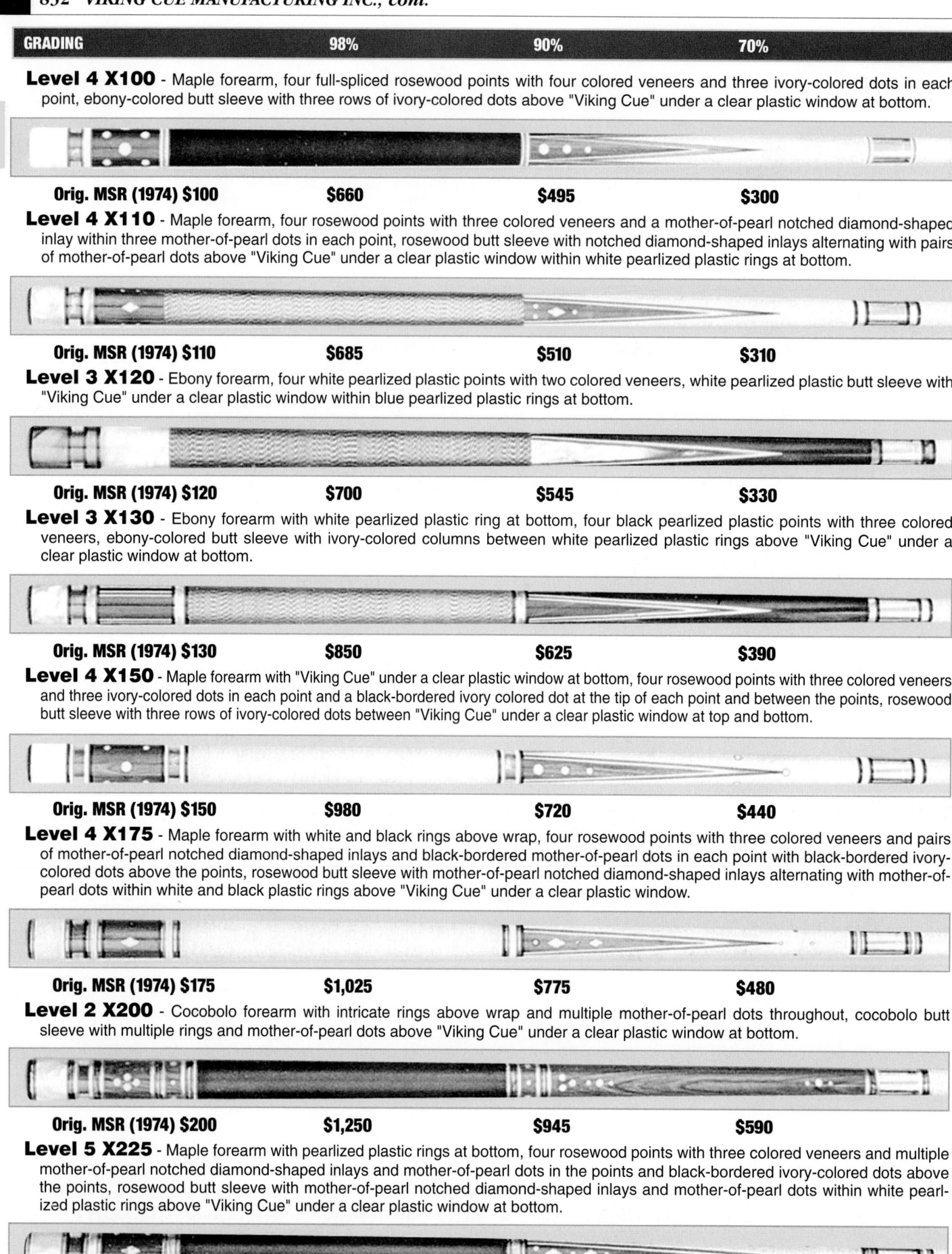

Orig. MSR (1974) $100	$660	$495	$300

Level 4 X110 - Maple forearm, four rosewood points with three colored veneers and a mother-of-pearl notched diamond-shaped inlay within three mother-of-pearl dots in each point, rosewood butt sleeve with notched diamond-shaped inlays alternating with pairs of mother-of-pearl dots above "Viking Cue" under a clear plastic window within white pearlized plastic rings at bottom.

Orig. MSR (1974) $110	$685	$510	$310

Level 3 X120 - Ebony forearm, four white pearlized plastic points with two colored veneers, white pearlized plastic butt sleeve with "Viking Cue" under a clear plastic window within blue pearlized plastic rings at bottom.

Orig. MSR (1974) $120	$700	$545	$330

Level 3 X130 - Ebony forearm with white pearlized plastic ring at bottom, four black pearlized plastic points with three colored veneers, ebony-colored butt sleeve with ivory-colored columns between white pearlized plastic rings above "Viking Cue" under a clear plastic window at bottom.

Orig. MSR (1974) $130	$850	$625	$390

Level 4 X150 - Maple forearm with "Viking Cue" under a clear plastic window at bottom, four rosewood points with three colored veneers and three ivory-colored dots in each point and a black-bordered ivory colored dot at the tip of each point and between the points, rosewood butt sleeve with three rows of ivory-colored dots between "Viking Cue" under a clear plastic window at top and bottom.

Orig. MSR (1974) $150	$980	$720	$440

Level 4 X175 - Maple forearm with white and black rings above wrap, four rosewood points with three colored veneers and pairs of mother-of-pearl notched diamond-shaped inlays and black-bordered mother-of-pearl dots in each point with black-bordered ivory-colored dots above the points, rosewood butt sleeve with mother-of-pearl notched diamond-shaped inlays alternating with mother-of-pearl dots within white and black plastic rings above "Viking Cue" under a clear plastic window.

Orig. MSR (1974) $175	$1,025	$775	$480

Level 2 X200 - Cocobolo forearm with intricate rings above wrap and multiple mother-of-pearl dots throughout, cocobolo butt sleeve with multiple rings and mother-of-pearl dots above "Viking Cue" under a clear plastic window at bottom.

Orig. MSR (1974) $200	$1,250	$945	$590

Level 5 X225 - Maple forearm with pearlized plastic rings at bottom, four rosewood points with three colored veneers and multiple mother-of-pearl notched diamond-shaped inlays and mother-of-pearl dots in the points and black-bordered ivory-colored dots above the points, rosewood butt sleeve with mother-of-pearl notched diamond-shaped inlays and mother-of-pearl dots within white pearlized plastic rings above "Viking Cue" under a clear plastic window at bottom.

Orig. MSR (1974) $225	$1,295	$965	$600

VIKING CUE MANUFACTURING INC., cont. 833

| GRADING | 98% | 90% | 70% |

Level 5 X250 - Ebony forearm with "Viking Cue" under a clear plastic window at bottom, four maple points with three veneers and multiple ebony-colored dots in each point, maple butt sleeve with multiple ebony-colored dots within ebony-colored columns between "Viking Cue" under a clear plastic window at top and bottom.

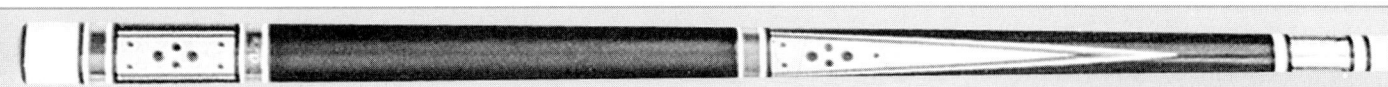

| Orig. MSR (1974) $250 | $1,350 | $995 | $610 |

Level 4 X275 - Maple forearm, three long and three short exotic wood points with black-bordered mother-of-pearl dots at the tips of each point, exotic wood butt sleeve with mother-of-pearl notched diamond-shaped inlays above "Viking Cue" under a clear plastic window at bottom.

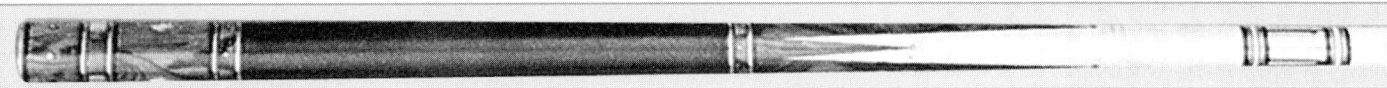

| Orig. MSR (1974) $275 | $1,400 | $1,050 | $650 |

Level 2 X300 - Rosewood forearm with a series of long and short black and white columns, rosewood butt sleeve with four ivory-colored windows within black and white borders and rings above and below.

| Orig. MSR (1974) $300 | $1,550 | $1,150 | $700 |

"Z" SERIES (VIKING'S FIFTH LINE)

The following "Z" Series cues were from Viking's fifth line, circa 1976-1978. Four different types of joints were available, and short-spliced butts were used. A variety of wraps were available, and screw-on ferrules were an option.

Level 2 "S" - Rosewood forearm, rosewood butt sleeve with white rings at top and bottom.

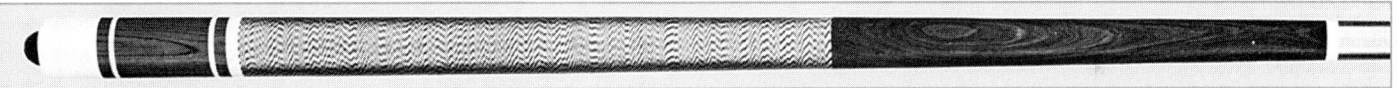

| | $165 | $125 | $75 |

Level 2 Z25 - Rosewood forearm, one-piece rosewood butt sleeve and butt cap.

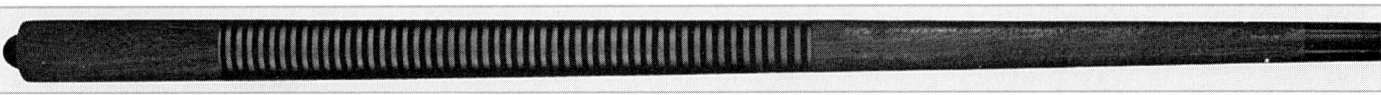

| Orig. MSR (1978) $25 | $185 | $135 | $75 |

Level 2 Z30 - Rosewood forearm, rosewood butt sleeve with "Viking Cue" under a clear plastic window at bottom.

| Orig. MSR (1978) $30 | $195 | $145 | $85 |

Level 2 Z35 - Rosewood forearm, blue pearlized plastic butt sleeve with "Viking Cue" under a clear plastic window in center.

| Orig. MSR (1978) $35 | $205 | $155 | $90 |

Level 2 Z40 - Rosewood forearm, rosewood butt sleeve with "Viking Cue" under a clear plastic window within white and pink pearlized plastic rings at bottom.

| Orig. MSR (1978) $40 | $220 | $165 | $100 |

VIKING CUE MANUFACTURING INC., cont.

GRADING	98%	90%	70%

Level 2 Z45 - Rosewood forearm, ivory-colored butt sleeve with "Viking Cue" within gold bands under a clear plastic window in center.

Orig. MSR (1978) $45	$235	$175	$110

Level 2 Z50 - Rosewood forearm, rosewood butt sleeve with "Viking Cue" under a clear plastic window within purple pearlized plastic rings at bottom.

Orig. MSR (1978) $50	$245	$185	$115

Level 3 Z55 - Stained bird's-eye maple forearm, four rosewood points with three-colored veneers, rosewood butt sleeve with "Viking Cue" under a clear plastic window at bottom.

Orig. MSR (1978) $55	$260	$195	$120

Level 2 Z60 - Rosewood forearm, ebony-colored butt sleeve with "Viking Cue" under a clear plastic window between ivory-colored squares around center.

Orig. MSR (1978) $60	$275	$210	$125

Level 3 Z65 - Stained bird's-eye maple forearm, four rosewood points with three colored veneers, rosewood butt sleeve with "Viking Cue" under a clear plastic window at bottom.

Orig. MSR (1978) $65	$280	$215	$130

Level 2 Z70 - Stained bird's-eye maple forearm, stained bird's-eye maple butt sleeve with a dash ring at bottom.

Orig. MSR (1978) $70	$295	$225	$140

Level 3 Z75 - Rosewood forearm, four rosewood points with four colored veneers and a mother-of-pearl dot in each point, rosewood butt sleeve with white-bordered ebony dots above "Viking Cue" under a clear plastic window within green pearlized plastic rings at bottom.

Orig. MSR (1978) $75	$310	$235	$145

Level 2 Z80 - Rosewood forearm, ebony-colored butt sleeve with a thick red ring between red squares around center.

Orig. MSR (1978) $80	$320	$240	$150

Level 3 Z85 - Stained bird's-eye forearm, four rosewood points with three veneers, rosewood butt sleeve.

Orig. MSR (1978) $85	$330	$245	$155

VIKING CUE MANUFACTURING INC., cont. 835

GRADING	98%	90%	70%

Level 2 Z90 - Rosewood forearm with mother-of-pearl notched diamond-shaped inlays between mother-of-pearl dots above a brown pearlized plastic ring at bottom, rosewood butt sleeve with mother-of-pearl notched diamond-shaped inlays alternating with mother-of-pearl dots between brown pearlized plastic rings above "Viking Cue" under a clear plastic window at bottom.

Orig. MSR (1978) $90	$550	$415	$250

Level 3 Z95 - Rosewood forearm, four black-bordered ivory-colored points with an ebony-colored dot in each point, ivory-colored butt sleeve with "Viking Cue" under a clear plastic window within ebony-colored dots around center.

Orig. MSR (1978) $95	$565	$420	$255

Level 4 Z100 - Stained bird's-eye maple forearm with white and black rings at bottom, four rosewood points with four colored veneers and three ivory-colored dots in each point, rosewood butt sleeve with ivory-colored dots above "Viking Cue" under a clear plastic window at bottom.

Orig. MSR (1978) $100	$575	$435	$260

Level 4 Z110 - Stained bird's-eye maple forearm, four rosewood points with a mother-of-pearl notched diamond-shaped inlay surrounded by three mother-of-pearl dots in each point, rosewood butt sleeve with mother-of-pearl notched diamond-shaped inlays alternating with pairs of mother-of-pearl dots above "Viking Cue" under a clear plastic window within blue pearlized plastic rings at bottom.

Orig. MSR (1978) $110	$585	$440	$265

Level 3 Z120 - Stained bird's-eye maple forearm, four ebony-colored points with black and white veneers, ebony-colored butt sleeve within ivory-colored chain link ring around center.

Orig. MSR (1978) $120	$650	$475	$285

Level 2 Z130 - Rosewood forearm with a series of mother-of-pearl notched diamond-shaped inlays and mother-of-pearl dots, one-piece rosewood butt sleeve and butt cap with a series of mother-of-pearl dots and circles.

Orig. MSR (1978) $130	$550	$405	$245

Level 2 Z140 - Rosewood forearm with ebony and ivory-colored columns, one-piece rosewood butt sleeve and butt cap within ebony- and ivory-colored beveled edge.

Orig. MSR (1978) $140	$595	$445	$270

Level 4 Z150 - Stained bird's-eye maple forearm with black and white rings at bottom, four rosewood points with black and white veneers with three ivory-colored dots in each point and ebony-bordered ivory-colored dots above and between the points, rosewood butt sleeve with ivory-colored dots between "Viking Cue" under a clear plastic window within white rings at top and bottom.

Orig. MSR (1978) $150	$665	$485	$300

| GRADING | 98% | 90% | 70% |

Level 3 Z160 - Ebony forearm with white and black ring above wrap, four rosewood points with three veneers, rosewood butt sleeve with a series of hollow black- and white-bordered windows between black and white rings at top and bottom.

| Orig. MSR (1978) $160 | $750 | $565 | $350 |

Level 4 Z170 - Stained bird's-eye maple forearm with a black-bordered maple ring above wrap, four rosewood points with three colored veneers with pairs of mother-of-pearl notched diamond-shaped inlays and black-bordered mother-of-pearl dots within each point, rosewood butt sleeve with mother-of-pearl notched diamond-shaped inlays between maple rings above "Viking Cue" under a clear plastic window at bottom.

| Orig. MSR (1978) $170 | $775 | $585 | $360 |

Level 3 Z180 - Rosewood forearm, four ebony points with three-colored veneers, ebony-colored butt sleeve with ivory-colored windows between ivory-colored check rings around center.

| Orig. MSR (1978) $180 | $650 | $485 | $300 |

Level 3 Z190 - Stained bird's-eye maple forearm, three long and three short rosewood points with ebony veneers, rosewood butt sleeve with ebony and maple hollow windows between maple and ebony check rings above and below.

| Orig. MSR (1978) $190 | $700 | $525 | $330 |

Level 2 Z200 - Rosewood forearm with a series of mother-of-pearl dots and white pearlized plastic rings, rosewood butt sleeve with a series of mother-of-pearl dots between many white pearlized plastic rings above "Viking Cue" under a clear plastic window at bottom.

| Orig. MSR (1978) $200 | $785 | $580 | $340 |

Level 2 Z210 - Stained bird's-eye maple forearm with three long and three short black-bordered ivory-colored columns above a dash ring at bottom, ebony-colored butt sleeve with black- and white-bordered maple windows with black and white barbell-shaped inlays in each between ivory-colored dash rings above and below.

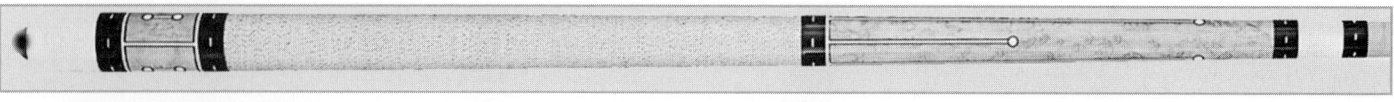

| Orig. MSR (1978) $210 | $775 | $570 | $335 |

Level 4 Z220 - Rosewood forearm, three long and three short ebony points with ivory-colored veneers and a mother-of-pearl dot in each point, one-piece rosewood butt sleeve and butt cap with intricate patterns of mother-of-pearl dots, triangles, and notched diamond-shaped inlays.

| Orig. MSR (1978) $220 | $1,100 | $820 | $500 |

Level 4 Z230 - Stained bird's-eye maple forearm, three long and three short ebony points with three-colored veneers and ebony and mother-of-pearl clover leaf-shaped inlays above the short points, one-piece rosewood butt sleeve and butt cap with ivory-colored backward S shapes within ivory-colored borders between check rings above and below.

| Orig. MSR (1978) $230 | $770 | $570 | $355 |

GRADING	98%	90%	70%

Level 4 Z240 - Ebony forearm, four ivory-colored points with four black and white veneers and a black and white column in each point, one-piece ivory-colored butt sleeve and butt cap with four ebony-colored dominoes alternating with black and white columns.

Orig. MSR (1978) $240	$925	$695	$445

Level 2 Z250 - Stained bird's-eye maple forearm with ivory-colored squared set in black at bottom and four floating ebony inlays within black and white-bordered windows, ebony-colored butt sleeve and butt cap with four ebony floating inlays within black and white-bordered maple windows between white squares around center.

Orig. MSR (1978) $250	$985	$725	$455

Level 4 Z275 - Ebony forearm, three long and three short black pearlized plastic points with three black and white veneers, one-piece black pearlized plastic butt sleeve and butt cap with ivory-colored dominoes within black- and white-bordered windows.

Orig. MSR (1978) $275	$1,095	$815	$495

VIKING'S B LINE

The following cues were from Viking's B line, circa 1981-1983. Four different types of joints were available. A variety of wraps were available, and screw on ferrules were an option.

Level 2 B30 - Bocote forearm, one-piece bocote butt sleeve and butt cap.

Orig. MSR (1981) $30	$95	$75	$45

Level 2 B35 - Bocote forearm, bocote butt sleeve and butt cap.

Orig. MSR (1981) $35	$110	$85	$50

Level 2 B40 - Bocote forearm, bocote butt sleeve with "Viking Cue" under a clear plastic window at bottom.

Orig. MSR (1981) $40	$125	$95	$60

Level 2 B45 - Bocote forearm, bocote butt sleeve with "Viking Cue" under a clear plastic window within gold pearlized plastic rings at bottom.

Orig. MSR (1981) $45	$135	$105	$65

Level 2 B50 - Bocote forearm, blue pearlized plastic butt sleeve with "Viking Cue" under a clear plastic window in center.

Orig. MSR (1981) $50	$145	$110	$70

GRADING	98%	90%	70%

Level 2 B55 - Bocote forearm, bocote butt sleeve with "Viking Cue" under a clear plastic window within green pearlized plastic rings at bottom.

| Orig. MSR (1981) $55 | $160 | $120 | $75 |

Level 2 B60 - Bocote forearm, bocote butt sleeve with "Viking Cue" under a clear plastic window within blue pearlized plastic rings at bottom.

| Orig. MSR (1981) $60 | $170 | $130 | $80 |

Level 3 B65 - Maple forearm, bocote points with ebony veneers, bocote butt sleeve with "Viking Cue" under a clear plastic window within black plastic rings at bottom.

| Orig. MSR (1981) $65 | $185 | $140 | $90 |

Level 2 B70 - Bocote forearm, bocote butt sleeve with a dash ring at bottom.

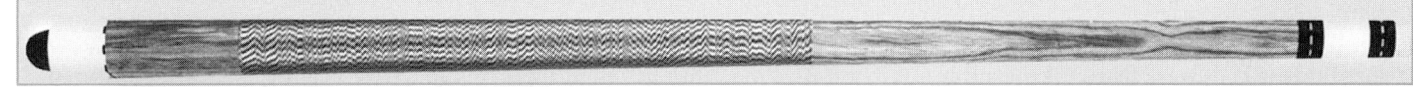

| Orig. MSR (1981) $70 | $200 | $150 | $95 |

Level 3 B75 - Maple forearm, hardwood points with three colored veneers, pink pearlized plastic butt sleeve with "Viking Cue" under a clear plastic window around center.

| Orig. MSR (1981) $75 | $220 | $165 | $105 |

Level 2 B80 - Rosewood forearm, rosewood butt sleeve with "Viking Cue" under a clear plastic window within white pearlized plastic rings at bottom.

| Orig. MSR (1981) $80 | $235 | $175 | $110 |

Level 3 B85 - Bird's-eye maple forearm, rosewood points with four colored veneers, rosewood butt sleeve with "Viking Cue" under a clear plastic window within pairs of metal rings at bottom.

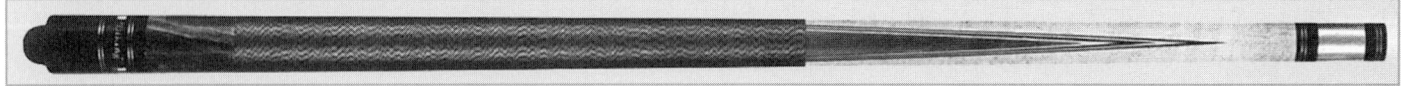

| Orig. MSR (1981) $85 | $245 | $185 | $115 |

Level 2 B90 - Rosewood forearm, ebony-colored butt sleeve with white plastic windows between white plastic check rings above and below.

| Orig. MSR (1981) $90 | $265 | $200 | $125 |

Level 3 B95 - Stained bird's-eye maple forearm, rosewood points with four colored veneers, rosewood butt sleeve.

| Orig. MSR (1981) $95 | $275 | $205 | $130 |

VIKING CUE MANUFACTURING INC., cont. 839

GRADING	98%	90%	70%

Level 2 B100 - Ebony forearm with mother-of-pearl notched diamond-shaped inlays between pairs of mother-of-pearl dots above a brown pearlized plastic ring at bottom, ebony butt sleeve with mother-of-pearl notched diamond-shaped inlays alternating with mother-of-pearl dots between a brown pearlized plastic ring at top and "Viking Cue" under a clear plastic window within brown pearlized plastic rings at bottom.

| Orig. MSR (1981) $100 | $285 | $215 | $135 |

Level 3 B110 - Stained bird's-eye maple forearm, rosewood points with three colored veneers, ebony-colored butt sleeve with "Viking Cue" under a clear plastic window within blue pearlized plastic rings at bottom.

| Orig. MSR (1981) $110 | $300 | $225 | $140 |

Level 2 B120 - Rosewood forearm with mother-of-pearl dots within metal rings towards bottom, rosewood butt sleeve with mother-of-pearl four-point diamond-shaped inlays between mother-of-pearl dots within metal rings above and below.

| Orig. MSR (1981) $120 | $330 | $250 | $155 |

Level 4 B130 - Stained bird's-eye maple forearm, ebony points with three colored veneers and a mother-of-pearl notched diamond-shaped inlay between three mother-of-pearl dots in each point, ebony butt sleeve with mother-of-pearl notched diamond-shaped inlays alternating with pairs of mother-of-pearl dots above "Viking Cue" under a clear plastic window between metal rings at bottom.

| Orig. MSR (1981) $130 | $465 | $355 | $220 |

Level 2 B140 - Rosewood forearm with mother-of-pearl dots at the tops of veneer columns, one-piece rosewood butt sleeve and butt cap with mother-of-pearl dots at bottom of veneer columns alternating with veneer columns.

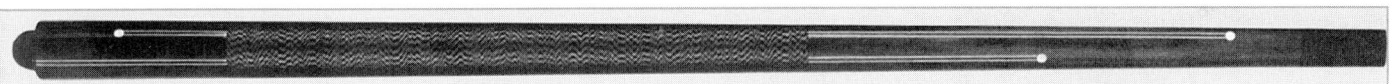

| Orig. MSR (1981) $140 | $385 | $285 | $180 |

Level 4 B150 - Stained bird's-eye maple forearm with black and white rings at bottom, ebony-colored points with black and white veneers and four ivory-colored dots in each point, ebony-colored butt sleeve with three rows of ivory-colored dots between "Viking Cue" under a clear plastic window at top and bottom.

| Orig. MSR (1981) $150 | $465 | $355 | $220 |

Level 4 B160 - Rosewood forearm, ivory-colored points with black and white veneers and an ebony-colored diamond-shaped inlay in each point, one-piece ivory-colored butt sleeve and butt cap with ebony-colored diamond-shaped inlays around center.

| Orig. MSR (1981) $160 | $525 | $400 | $250 |

Level 4 B170 - Stained bird's-eye maple forearm with stained bird's-eye maple ring above wrap, ebony points with three colored veneers and two mother-of-pearl notched diamond-shaped inlays alternating with two mother-of-pearl dots in each point, ebony butt sleeve with mother-of-pearl notched diamond-shaped inlays alternating with mother-of-pearl dots between a stained bird's-eye maple ring at top and "Viking Cue" under a clear plastic window within stained bird's-eye maple rings at bottom.

| Orig. MSR (1981) $170 | $610 | $455 | $285 |

GRADING	98%	90%	70%

Level 2 B180 - Rosewood forearm with patterns of mother-of-pearl dots above a pearlized plastic ring towards bottom, rosewood butt sleeve with mother-of-pearl dots between pearlized plastic rings above and below.

Orig. MSR (1981) $180	$605	$450	$280

Level 2 B190 - Stained bird's-eye maple forearm with ebony-veneered designs above a maple checked ring at bottom, stained bird's-eye maple handle, stained bird's-eye maple butt sleeve with ebony-colored four-point stars between ebony check rings at top and bottom.

Orig. MSR (1981) $190	$600	$445	$275

Level 4 B200 - Bird's-eye maple forearm, three long and three short rosewood points with an ebony dot at the tip of each point, rosewood butt sleeve with intricate ebony ovals within bird's-eye maple and rosewood windows between maple dash rings above and below.

Orig. MSR (1981) $200	$575	$425	$260

Level 2 B225 - Rosewood forearm with intricate pearlized plastic inlays above a white pearlized plastic ring at bottom, rosewood butt sleeve with intricate pearlized plastic inlays between a white pearlized plastic ring at top and "Viking Cue" under a clear plastic window within white pearlized plastic rings at bottom.

Orig. MSR (1981) $225	$655	$495	$325

Level 4 B250 - Stained bird's-eye maple forearm, rosewood points with four veneers with an ivory-colored spear-shaped inlay in each point, ebony-colored butt sleeve with rosewood blocks set in ebony- and ivory-colored windows between maple dash rings above and below.

Orig. MSR (1981) $250	$670	$505	$335

Level 2 B275 - Rosewood forearm with a series of pearlized plastic dots and intricate inlays above intricate pearlized plastic rings at bottom, rosewood butt sleeve with patterns of mother-of-pearl dots within intricate pearlized plastic rings at top and "Viking Cue" under a clear plastic window within pearlized plastic rings at bottom.

Orig. MSR (1981) $275	$880	$665	$410

Level 4 B300 - Stained bird's-eye maple forearm, stained bird's-eye maple points with three colored veneers and an ebony dot at the tip of each point and an ebony dot above an ebony veneer within each point alternating with ebony dots atop ebony veneers, one-piece bird's-eye maple butt sleeve and butt cap with ebony dots at the bottom of colored veneer columns above intricate ebony-colored four-point star-shaped inlays.

Orig. MSR (1981) $300	$900	$680	$430

Level 2 B350 - Ebony forearm with mother-of-pearl dots atop black and white veneers columns above mother-of-pearl dots in a ring at bottom, ebony-colored butt sleeve with white veneer-bordered windows with alternating mother-of-pearl notched diamond-shaped inlays and backwards S-shaped inlays between rings of mother-of-pearl dots above and below.

Orig. MSR (1981) $350	$995	$745	$475

VIKING CUE MANUFACTURING INC., cont. 841

GRADING	98%	90%	70%

Level 5 B400 - Stained bird's-eye maple forearm, ebony points with four-colored veneers and a series of mother-of-pearl notched diamond-shaped inlays and dots and four-point star-shaped inlays in each point, ebony butt sleeve with intricate white pearlized plastic windows within intricate white pearlized plastic rings above and below.

Orig. MSR (1981) $400	$1,200	$895	$550

Level 4 B500 - Ebony forearm, intricate four-piece ivory-colored floating points, ebony butt sleeve with intricate ivory-colored windows alternating with ivory-colored dashes between intricate ivory-colored rings above and below.

Orig. MSR (1981) $500	$1,650	$1,250	$775

VIKING'S A-SERIES LINE

The following cues were from Viking's A-Series line, circa 1983-1989. Four different types of joints were available. A variety of wraps were available, and screw-on ferrules were no longer an option.

Level 2 A40 - Rosewood forearm, one-piece rosewood butt sleeve and butt cap.

Orig. MSR (1983) $40	$90	$70	$40

Level 2 A45 - Rosewood forearm, rosewood butt sleeve.

Orig. MSR (1983) $45	$105	$80	$50

Level 2 A50 - Rosewood forearm, rosewood butt sleeve.

Orig. MSR (1983) $50	$115	$90	$55

Level 2 A55 - Rosewood forearm, rosewood butt sleeve with "Viking Cue" under a clear plastic window at bottom.

Orig. MSR (1983) $55	$125	$95	$60

Level 2 A60 - Rosewood forearm, rosewood butt sleeve with "Viking Cue" under a clear plastic window within gold pearlized plastic rings at bottom.

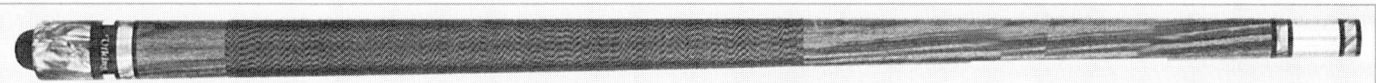

Orig. MSR (1983) $60	$135	$105	$65

Level 2 A65 - Rosewood forearm, orange pearlized plastic butt sleeve with "Viking Cue" under a clear plastic window around center.

Orig. MSR (1983) $65	$145	$110	$70

Level 2 A70 - Rosewood forearm, rosewood butt sleeve with "Viking Cue" under a clear plastic window within green pearlized plastic rings at bottom.

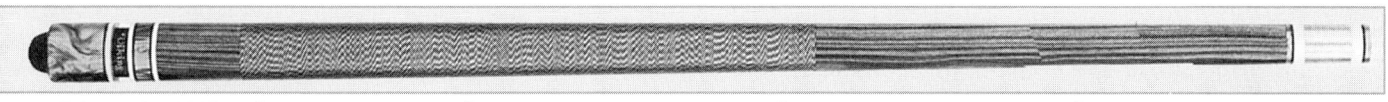

Orig. MSR (1983) $70	$155	$120	$75

GRADING	98%	90%	70%

Level 3 A75 - Maple forearm, rosewood points with ebony veneers, rosewood butt sleeve with "Viking Cue" under a clear plastic window within black plastic rings at bottom.

| Orig. MSR (1983) $75 | $170 | $130 | $80 |

Level 2 A80 - Cocobolo forearm, cocobolo butt sleeve with "Viking Cue" under a clear plastic window within blue pearlized plastic rings at bottom.

| Orig. MSR (1983) $80 | $180 | $135 | $85 |

Level 3A85 - Maple forearm, cocobolo points with three colored veneers, cocobolo butt sleeve with "Viking Cue" under a clear plastic window within red pearlized plastic rings at bottom.

| Orig. MSR (1983) $85 | $195 | $150 | $90 |

Level 2 A90 - Cocobolo forearm with an ebony checked ring at bottom, cocobolo handle, cocobolo butt sleeve with ebony checked rings at top and bottom.

| Orig. MSR (1983) $90 | $205 | $155 | $95 |

Level 3 A95 - Maple forearm, rosewood points with three colored veneers, blue pearlized plastic butt sleeve with "Viking Cue" under a clear plastic window around center.

| Orig. MSR (1983) $95 | $210 | $160 | $100 |

Level 2 A100 - Ebony forearm with mother-of-pearl notched diamond-shaped inlays between pairs of mother-of-pearl dots above purple pearlized plastic ring at bottom, ebony butt sleeve with pearlized plastic notched diamond-shaped inlays alternating with pearlized plastic dots between a purple pearlized plastic ring at top and "Viking Cue" under a clear plastic window within purple pearlized plastic rings at bottom.

| Orig. MSR (1983) $100 | $225 | $170 | $110 |

Level 3 A110 - Stained bird's-eye maple forearm, ebony points with four-colored veneers, ebony butt sleeve.

| Orig. MSR (1983) $110 | $245 | $185 | $120 |

Level 2 A120 - Ebony forearm with intricate ivory-colored four-point stars towards bottom, ebony butt sleeve with intricate ivory-colored four-point stars alternating with ebony- and ivory-colored clover leaf-shaped inlays between ebony- and ivory-colored dash rings above and below.

| Orig. MSR (1983) $120 | $270 | $205 | $130 |

VIKING CUE MANUFACTURING INC., cont. 843

GRADING	98%	90%	70%

Level 3 A130 - Stained bird's-eye maple forearm, ebony points with four colored veneers and a stained bird's-eye maple spear-shaped inlay in each point, ebony butt sleeve with stained bird's-eye maple ovals between maple dash rings above and below.

Orig. MSR (1983) $130	$290	$215	$135

Level 4 A140 - Stained bird's-eye maple forearm, rosewood points with three colored veneers and a mother-of-pearl notched diamond-shaped inlay within three mother-of-pearl dots in each point, rosewood butt sleeve with mother-of-pearl notched diamond-shaped inlays alternating with pairs of mother-of-pearl dots above "Viking Cue" under a clear plastic window below a white pearlized plastic ring at bottom.

Orig. MSR (1983) $140	$315	$235	$145

Level 2 A150 - Rosewood forearm with ivory-colored spear-shaped inlays towards bottom, rosewood butt sleeve with four-piece four-point ivory-colored inlays around center.

Orig. MSR (1983) $150	$385	$290	$180

Level 3 A160 - Stained bird's-eye maple forearm, ebony points with three-colored veneers, ebony butt sleeve with red veneer-bordered stained bird's-eye maple windows within red veneer and maple dash rings above and below.

Orig. MSR (1983) $160	$410	$310	$190

Level 4 A170 - Rosewood forearm, three-piece intricate floating ivory-colored points, rosewood butt sleeve with ivory-colored windows between ebony and ivory-colored dash rings above and below.

Orig. MSR (1983) $170	$495	$375	$230

Level 2 A180 - Rosewood forearm with intricate pearlized plastic inlays above a brown pearlized plastic ring at bottom, rosewood butt sleeve with intricate pearlized plastic inlays between a brown pearlized plastic ring at top and "Viking Cue" under a clear plastic window within brown pearlized plastic rings at bottom.

Orig. MSR (1983) $180	$525	$395	$245

Level 4 A190 - Stained bird's-eye maple forearm, rosewood points with four colored veneers and an ivory-colored six-point star-shaped inlay in each point, rosewood butt sleeve with ivory-colored six-point star-shaped inlays between ebony- and ivory-colored rings above and below.

Orig. MSR (1983) $190	$550	$415	$260

Level 4 A200 - Stained bird's-eye maple forearm with a stained bird's-eye maple ring at bottom, rosewood points with three colored veneers and two mother-of-pearl notched diamond-shaped inlays alternating with two mother-of-pearl dots in each point, rosewood butt sleeve with mother-of-pearl notched diamond-shaped inlays alternating with mother-of-pearl dots between a stained bird's-eye maple ring at top and "Viking Cue" under a clear plastic window within stained bird's-eye maple rings at bottom.

Orig. MSR (1983) $200	$665	$495	$315

844 VIKING CUE MANUFACTURING INC., cont.

GRADING	98%	90%	70%

Level 4 A225 - Cocobolo forearm, cocobolo points with black and white veneers and an intricate ebony inlay in each point, one-piece cocobolo butt sleeve and butt cap with intricate ivory-colored six-point star-shaped inlays set in intricate ebony-colored windows.

Orig. MSR (1983) $225	$685	$510	$325

Level 2 A250 - Rosewood forearm with a series of mother-of-pearl dots above intricate brown pearlized plastic rings at bottom, rosewood butt sleeve with mother-of-pearl dots between an intricate brown pearlized plastic ring at top and "Viking Cue" under a clear plastic window within brown pearlized plastic rings at bottom.

Orig. MSR (1983) $250	$750	$560	$345

Level 4 A275 - Stained bird's-eye maple forearm, ebony points with four veneers, ebony butt sleeve with ivory-colored skull and crossbones within ebony- and ivory-colored windows around center.

Orig. MSR (1983) $275	$750	$560	$345

Level 2 A300 - Stained bird's-eye maple forearm with intricate ebony- and ivory-colored patterns above maple dash rings at bottom, ebony butt sleeve with intricate ebony-bordered ivory-colored four-point star-shaped inlays set in stained bird's-eye maple windows between maple dash rings above and below.

Orig. MSR (1983) $300	$700	$525	$330

Level 4 A350 - Stained bird's-eye maple forearm, ebony points with four colored veneers and intricate two-piece ivory-colored spear-shaped inlays in each point, ebony butt sleeve with intricate ebony-colored inlays set in ivory-colored windows between ebony- and ivory-colored dash rings above and below.

Orig. MSR (1983) $350	$745	$555	$345

Level 4 A400 - Ebony forearm with intricate four-piece floating tulipwood points, one-piece ebony butt sleeve and butt cap with tulipwood windows surrounded by intricate tulipwood inlays.

Orig. MSR (1983) $400	$995	$735	$450

Level 4 A450 - Stained bird's-eye maple forearm, ebony points with three colored veneers and an intricate ivory-colored three-piece spear-shaped inlays in each point, ebony butt sleeve with ivory-colored windows with "Viking" in black letters in center surrounded by intricate ivory inlays.

Orig. MSR (1983) $450	$1,100	$815	$490

Level 5 A500 - Stained bird's-eye maple forearm, ebony points with three colored veneers and a series of mother-of-pearl notched diamond-shaped inlays and dots and intricate four-point stars in each point alternating with mother-of-pearl and ebony clover leaf shapes, ebony butt sleeve with mother-of-pearl and ebony clover leaf shapes in colored veneer-bordered rosewood windows between maple stitch rings above and below.

Orig. MSR (1983) $500	$1,215	$900	$565

GRADING	98%	90%	70%

Level 4 A800 - Ebony forearm, ivory-colored points with black and white veneers and an intricate ebony-colored spear-shaped inlay in each point, ebony-colored butt sleeve with intricate ivory-colored windows with a nine-ball rack set in an ebony-colored oval within each.

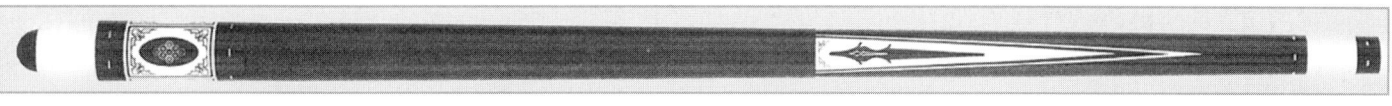

Orig. MSR (1983) $800	$1,650	$1,235	$780

Q LINE

The following Q line cues from 1996 came with a variety of joints and standard Irish linen wraps available in 27 different color combinations. Butt caps were available in black white or brown. Pearlized plastic was available in ten different colors. Stained bird's-eye maple was available in nine different colors. And plastic joint rings were available in six different colors.

Level 4 Q1 - Rosewood forearm with six white-bordered stained bird's-eye maple inlays between points, six floating white-bordered stained bird's-eye maple points, rosewood butt sleeve with six large white-bordered stained bird's-eye maple intricate oval-shaped inlays alternating with six white-bordered stained bird's-eye maple inlays set in round windows hollowed out of the ovals.

MSR (1996) $2,000	$2,150	$1,600	$1,000

Level 4 Q2 - Ebony forearm with two white-bordered two-piece red spears alternating with the points, two floating split tulipwood points with a red cross set in a white oval within each point, ebony butt sleeve with two large split tulipwood hollow diamond-shaped inlays with a red cross set in a white oval within each alternating with two opposing arrowhead-shaped inlays within a single white border.

MSR (1996) $2,000	$2,150	$1,600	$1,000

Level 5 Q3 - Stained bird's-eye maple forearm, four ebony points with four colored veneers, ebony butt sleeve with four stained bird's-eye maple ovals alternating with four spotted red palm ovals set within a complex red and white pattern.

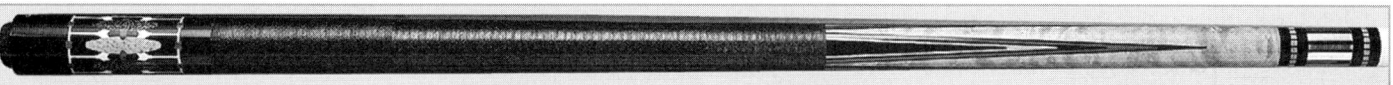

MSR (1996) $2,000	$2,150	$1,600	$1,000

Level 5 Q4 - Stained bird's-eye maple forearm, two floating black-bordered pearlized plastic points with a small arrowhead-shaped inlay and a black-bordered blue and green design within each point, stained bird's-eye maple butt sleeve with two black-bordered blue and green designs set within black-bordered pearlized plastic ovals between nickel silver rings set in ebony at top and bottom.

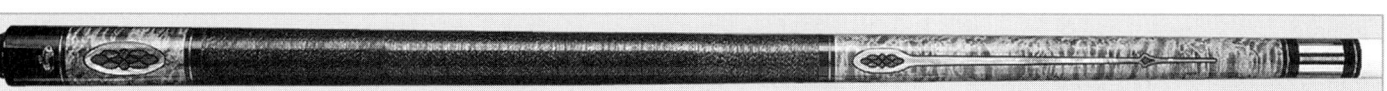

MSR (1996) $1,500	$1,600	$1,175	$725

Level 3 Q5 - Stained bird's-eye maple forearm with an etched vine pattern on a pearlized plastic ring above wrap and at joint, three long and three short floating black-bordered pearlized plastic points, pearlized plastic butt sleeve with three etched windows between etched vine patterns above and below.

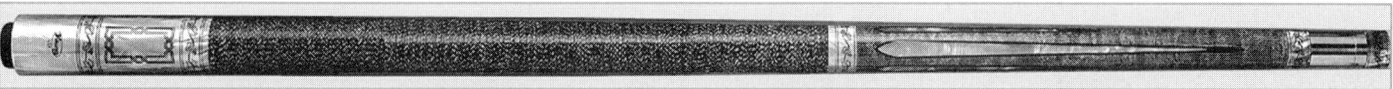

MSR (1996) $1,200	$1,325	$1,000	$650

Level 4 Q6 - Stained bird's-eye maple forearm, four stained bird's-eye maple points with four colored veneers and a black-bordered intricate white oval in each point, stained bird's-eye maple butt sleeve with four black-bordered intricate white ovals alternating with four large black-bordered intricate white designs over rings of black, red, and white.

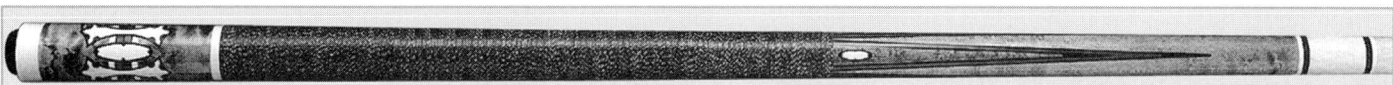

MSR (1996) $1,000	$1,100	$825	$500

GRADING	98%	90%	70%

Level 3 Q7 - Stained bird's-eye maple forearm, four pearlized plastic points with four colored veneers, ebony butt sleeve with four large pearlized plastic windows with three colored veneers.

| MSR (1996) $800 | $875 | $665 | $415 |

Level 4 Q8 - Ebony forearm with an intricate black and white pattern ring above wrap, four floating white points, ebony butt sleeve with four large white downward-pointing triangles below intricate black and white pattern ring at top.

| MSR (1996) $600 | $650 | $590 | $310 |

Level 4 Q8 Ivory - Ebony forearm with an intricate black and ivory pattern ring above wrap, four floating ivory points, ebony butt sleeve with four large ivory downward-pointing triangles below intricate black and ivory pattern ring at top.

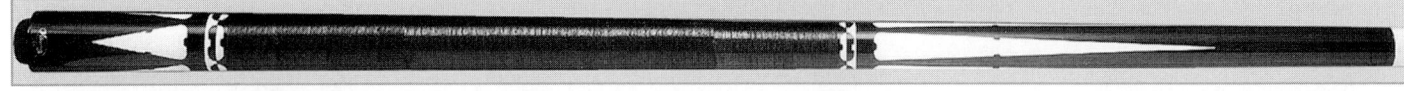

| MSR (1996) $1,100 | $1,400 | $1,050 | $650 |

Level 4 Q11 - Stained bird's-eye maple forearm with stained bird's-eye maple rings within two pearlized plastic rings above wrap and at joint, four rosewood points with two colored veneers and two intricate pearlized plastic four-point inlays alternating with two pearlized plastic dots that upwardly diminish in size in each point, rosewood butt sleeve with four intricate pearlized plastic four point inlays alternating with four pearlized plastic dots between stained bird's-eye maple rings within two pearlized plastic rings at top and bottom.

| MSR (1996) $500 | $465 | $350 | $215 |

Level 6 Q12 - Maple forearm, four floating black-bordered points of multi-colored black-bordered geometric patterns, maple butt sleeve with four black-bordered windows of multi-colored black-bordered geometric patterns.

| MSR (1996) $450 | $400 | $300 | $190 |

Level 4 Q13 - Stained bird's-eye maple forearm, four rosewood points with two colored veneers and an intricate pearlized plastic spear above a small intricate pearlized plastic inlay in each point, rosewood butt sleeve with four intricate hollow pearlized plastic diamond-shaped inlays above rings of black and pearlized plastic.

| MSR (1996) $400 | $375 | $285 | $180 |

Level 4 Q14 - Rosewood forearm with rings of pearlized plastic above wrap and at joint, floating intricate pearlized plastic four-point inlays between opposing intricate pearlized plastic spears, butt sleeve with intricate pearlized plastic four-point inlays within two-piece hollow pearlized plastic diamond-shaped inlays between rings of black and pearlized plastic at top and bottom.

| MSR (1996) $375 | $335 | $255 | $160 |

Level 3 Q15 - Stained bird's-eye maple forearm, six floating black-bordered pearlized plastic points, black butt sleeve with six large pearlized plastic windows between nickel silver rings at top and bottom.

| MSR (1996) $350 | $310 | $235 | $145 |

GRADING	98%	90%	70%

Level 4 Q16 - Stained bird's-eye maple forearm, rosewood points with two colored veneers and a small stained bird's-eye maple diamond-shaped inlay in each point, rosewood butt sleeve with four stained bird's-eye maple diamond-shaped inlays set in long red-bordered cocobolo four-point star-shaped inlays.

MSR (1996) $325	$290	$220	$130

Level 4 Q17 - Stained bird's-eye maple forearm, four intricate floating black-bordered white points with a black border creating a white oval running diagonally through the center of each, stained bird's-eye maple butt sleeve with four intricate black-bordered white ovals with a black border creating a white oval running diagonally through the center of each.

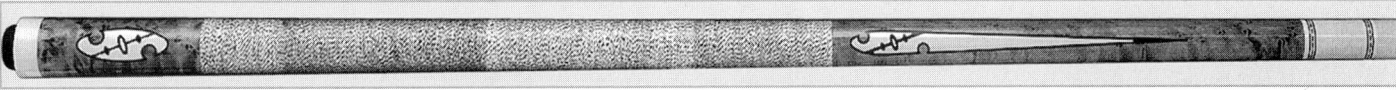

MSR (1996) $300	$275	$210	$125

Level 3 Q18 - Stained bird's-eye maple forearm with black-bordered pearlized plastic triangles between the points, four floating black-bordered pearlized plastic points with veneers, butt sleeve of rings of black and pearlized plastic.

MSR (1996) $275	$245	$185	$115

Level 4 Q21 - Rosewood forearm with a ring of tulipwood triangles above wrap, six floating tulipwood points, rosewood butt sleeve with six tulipwood windows alternating with pairs of opposing tulipwood triangles.

MSR (1996) $250	$225	$170	$105

Level 4 Q22 - Stained bird's-eye maple forearm, floating points with three white four-point inlays running diagonally through each point, stained bird's-eye maple butt sleeve with ovals inlaid with three white four-point inlays running diagonally through each.

MSR (1996) $240	$220	$165	$105

Level 3 Q23 - Stained bird's-eye maple forearm, four black points with two colored veneers, black butt sleeve with six red-bordered stained bird's-eye maple windows between dashes within red rings above and below.

MSR (1996) $230	$210	$160	$100

Level 3 Q24 - Rosewood forearm, four two-piece stained bird's-eye maple points which form a diamond shape within each, rosewood butt sleeve with four two-piece stained bird's-eye maple ovals which form a diamond shape within each.

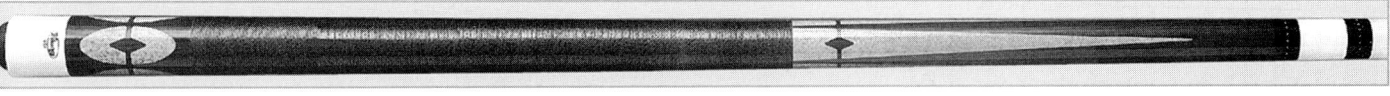

MSR (1996) $220	$200	$150	$95

Level 2 Q25 - Rosewood forearm with intricate pearlized plastic four-point inlays between two pearlized plastic dots above and below, rosewood butt sleeve with intricate pearlized plastic four-point inlays alternating with pearlized plastic dots between pearlized plastic rings at top and bottom.

MSR (1996) $210	$195	$150	$95

VIKING CUE MANUFACTURING INC., cont.

GRADING	98%	90%	70%

Level 3 Q26 - Stained bird's-eye maple forearm, four rosewood points with three colored veneers, rosewood butt sleeve.

MSR (1996) $200	$185	$140	$90

Level 3 Q27 - Rosewood forearm, intricate two-piece stained bird's-eye maple points that form a "Z" through center of each, rosewood butt sleeve with large intricate two-piece stained bird's-eye maple diamond-shaped inlays that form a "Z" through center of each.

MSR (1996) $190	$175	$135	$85

Level 1 Q28 - Maple forearm, stained bird's-eye maple points and butt sleeve inlaid with single black veneers.

MSR (1996) $180	$165	$125	$80

Level 2 Q31 - Stained bird's-eye maple forearm, stained bird's-eye maple butt sleeve with pearlized plastic rings at bottom.

MSR (1996) $170	$155	$120	$75

Level 3 Q32 - Maple forearm, four goncolas alves points with single black veneers, goncolas alves butt sleeve.

MSR (1996) $160	$145	$110	$70

Level 2 Q33 - Stained bird's-eye maple forearm, pearlized plastic butt sleeve.

MSR (1996) $150	$135	$105	$65

Level 2 Q34 - Natural-stained maple forearm, natural-stained maple butt sleeve with black-bordered pearlized plastic ring at bottom.

MSR (1996) $140	$125	$95	$60

Level 2 Q35 - Goncolas alves forearm, goncolas alves butt sleeve.

MSR (1996) $130	$115	$90	$55

Level 2 Q36 - Stained bird's-eye maple forearm, stained bird's-eye maple butt sleeve with a black ring at bottom.

MSR (1996) $120	$105	$80	$50

Level 2 Q37 - Goncolas alves forearm, goncolas alves butt sleeve.

MSR (1996) $110	$95	$75	$45

VIKING CUE MANUFACTURING INC., cont. 849

GRADING	98%	90%	70%

Level 2 Q38 - Goncolas alves forearm, one-piece goncolas alves butt sleeve and cap.

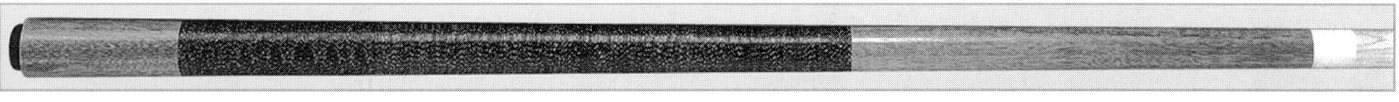

MSR (1996) $100	$85	$65	$40

"DECUE" LINE

The following three "DeCue" line cues came with a variety of joints. DC4 and DC5 featured black nylon wraps. DC7 featured Irish linen wrap. They may feature art by John Schmelzer.

Level 2 DC4 Ball Buster - Red-stained maple forearm with applied image of "Ball Buster" above pieces of a nine-ball, red-stained maple butt sleeve with applied image of a disintegrating nine-ball.

MSR (1996) $195	$170	$130	$80

Level 2 DC5 Hot Stick - Dark-stained maple forearm with applied image of flames circling from wrap to below joint, dark-stained maple butt sleeve with applied image of a smiling devil holding a pool cue.

MSR (1996) $195	$170	$130	$80

Level 2 DC7 Pool Shark - Blue-stained maple forearm with applied image of smiling sharks with cues surrounded by fish that look like numbered pool balls, stained maple butt sleeve with applied image of fish that look like numbered pool balls.

MSR (1996) $245	$215	$160	$100

1999 MILENNIUM SERIES

The following Viking Millennium cues came with one shaft, and a quick-release joint was standard. A variety of joints and standard Irish linen wraps were available in 27 different color combinations. Butt caps were available in black, white or brown. Pearlized plastic was available in ten different colors. Stained bird's-eye maple was available in nine different colors. And plastic joint rings were available in six different colors.

Level 5 VM1 - Ebony forearm, four red-bordered intricate floating ivory points with a five-piece ivory and stained bird's-eye maple diamond shape under each point, ebony butt sleeve with four five-piece ivory and stained bird's-eye maple diamond-shaped inlays between intricate ivory and vermillion rings at top and bottom.

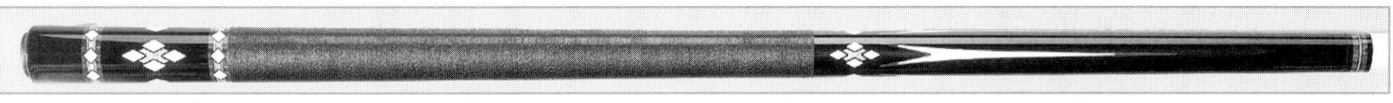

MSR $1,500	$1,200	$900	$575

Level 3 VM2 - Grey-stained bird's-eye maple forearm with an engraved pearlized plastic ring at bottom, three long and three short floating pearlized plastic points, one-piece pearlized plastic butt sleeve and butt cap with intricate engraving patterns.

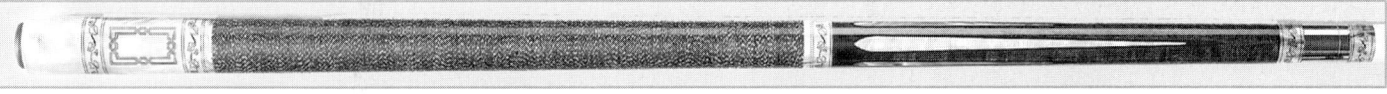

MSR $1,200	$1,000	$750	$480

Level 4 VM3 - Stained bird's-eye maple forearm, four ebony points with four veneers and an ebony-bordered pearlized plastic diamond-shaped inlay set in stained bird's-eye maple in each point and four ebony-bordered pearlized plastic diamond-shaped inlays between the points, ebony butt sleeve with eight pearlized plastic diamond-shaped inlays set in intricate elongated stained bird's-eye maple diamond-shaped inlays between stained bird's-eye maple and ebony rings above and below.

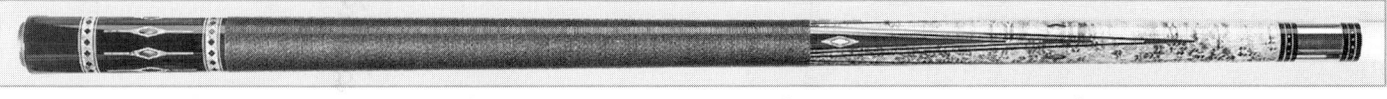

MSR $1,100	$950	$715	$450

GRADING	98%	90%	70%

Level 4 VM4 - Ebony forearm, four intricate two-piece vermillion-bordered ivory points alternating with ivory-bordered vermillion inlays above vermillion dots, one-piece ebony butt sleeve and butt cap with four reverse intricate two-piece vermillion-bordered ivory point-shaped inlays alternating with ivory-bordered vermillion inlays below vermillion dots.

MSR	$1,000	$895	$680	$435

Level 3 VM5 - Stained bird's-eye maple forearm, three long and three short ebony points with four colored veneers and an ivory oval-shaped inlay in each long point, ebony butt sleeve with three ivory oval-shaped inlays within colored veneers in an oval-shaped border.

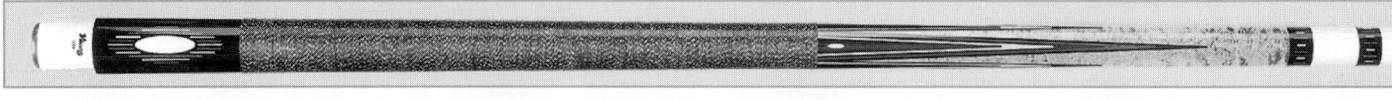

MSR	$900	$850	$645	$400

Level 4 VM6 - Ebony forearm, six white-bordered stained bird's-eye maple floating points alternating with six white-bordered stained bird's-eye maple four point star-shaped inlays, one-piece ebony butt sleeve and butt cap with six intricate white-bordered stained bird's-eye maple scalloped oval-shaped inlays alternating with six white-bordered tained bird's-eye maple four-point star-shaped inlays.

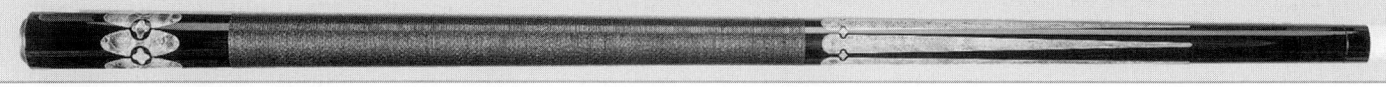

MSR	$800	$745	$560	$355

Level 4 VM7 - Stained bird's-eye maple forearm, ebony-bordered ivory floating points, stained bird's-eye maple butt sleeve with ebony-bordered ivory diamond-shaped inlays between ivory dots within stained bird's-eye maple and ebony rings at top and bottom.

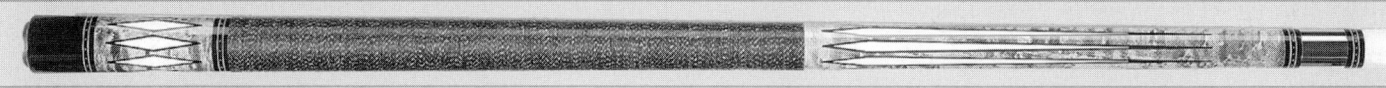

MSR	$700	$635	$485	$305

Level 5 VM8 - Stained bird's-eye maple forearm with a stained bird's-eye maple ring set in ebony and pearlized plastic rings at bottom, four rosewood points with two veneers and pairs of pearlized plastic four-point star-shaped inlays alternating with pairs of pearlized plastic dots in each point, rosewood butt sleeve with four pearlized plastic four-point star-shaped inlays between pearlized plastic dots above and below alternating with pearlized plastic dots between stained bird's-eye maple rings set within ebony and pearlized plastic above and below.

MSR	$650	$595	$455	$280

Level 2 VM9 - Ebony forearm with intricate elongated ivory diamond-shaped inlays in a unique pattern, ebony butt sleeve with intricate elongated ivory diamond-shaped inlays in a similar pattern.

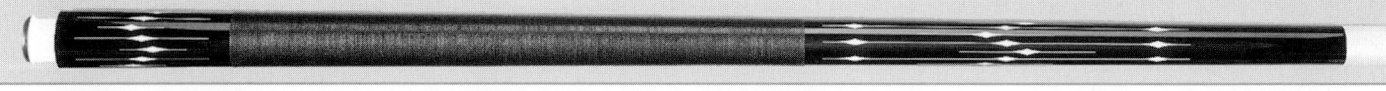

MSR	$600	$535	$400	$255

Level 1 VM10 - Stained bird's-eye maple forearm with four long and four short full-spliced ebony points and butt sleeve with Viking logo inlaid in bird's-eye maple.

MSR	$550	$500	$375	$240

Level 1 VM11 - Stained bird's-eye maple forearm, four intricately twisted full-spliced cocobolo points and butt sleeve with Viking logo inlaid in bird's-eye maple.

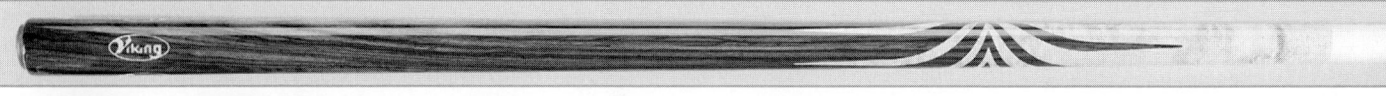

MSR	$500	$450	$340	$215

GRADING	98%	90%	70%

Level 6 VM12 - Stained bird's-eye maple forearm, four ebony points with two colored veneers and an intricate nine-piece ivory-colored inlay in each point, ebony butt sleeve with four intricate nine-piece ivory-colored inlays around center.

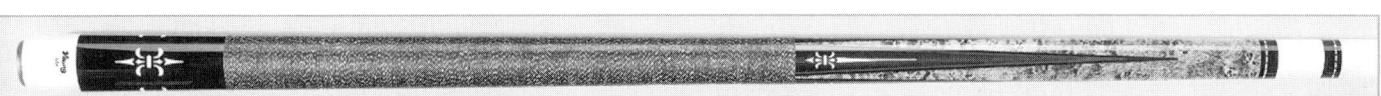

MSR	$475	$435	$330	$205

Level 3 VM13 - Stained bird's-eye maple forearm, six black-bordered pearlized plastic floating points, ebony-colored butt sleeve with six pearlized plastic windows between silver rings above and below.

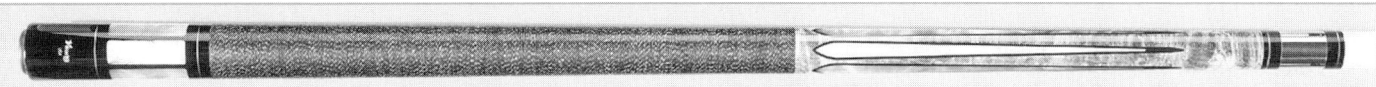

MSR	$450	$415	$315	$200

Level 3 VM14 - Stained bird's-eye maple forearm, four rosewood points with two colored veneers and a pearlized plastic notched diamond-shaped inlay in each point, rosewood butt sleeve with four pearlized plastic notched diamond-shaped inlays above green pearlized plastic rings at bottom

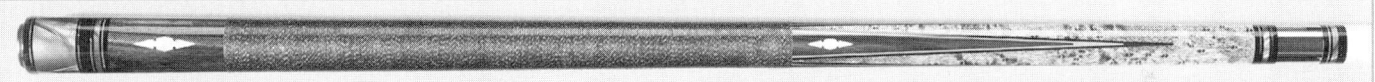

MSR	$425	$400	$300	$190

Level 4 VM15 - Rosewood forearm, six intricate stained bird's-eye maple floating points above a stained bird's-eye maple triangle-shaped inlay alternating with stained bird's-eye maple triangle-shaped inlays, rosewood butt sleeve with six stained bird's-eye maple reverse floating point-shaped inlays below a stained bird's-eye maple triangle alternating with bird's-eye maple triangles.

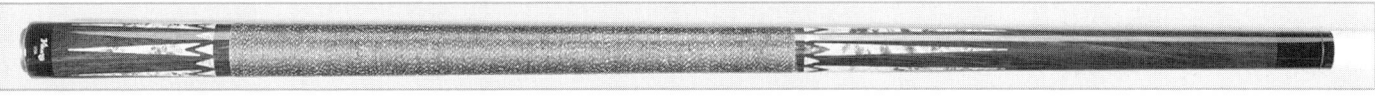

MSR	$400	$375	$285	$180

Level 3 VM16 - Stained bird's-eye maple forearm, stained bird's-eye maple points with three colored veneers, ebony-colored butt sleeve with stained bird's-eye maple windows with colored borders between colored dash rings above and below.

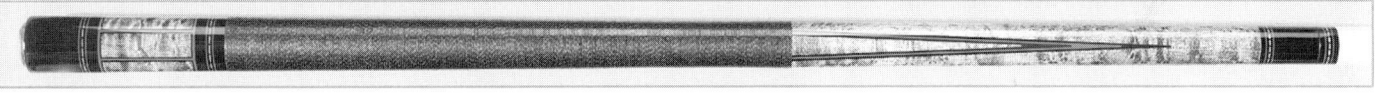

MSR	$390	$365	$275	$175

Level 3 VM17 - Stained bird's-eye maple forearm, four floating black-bordered pearlized points alternating with four black-bordered blue pearlized plastic triangles, blue pearlized plastic butt sleeve with black and pearlized plastic rings at top and around center.

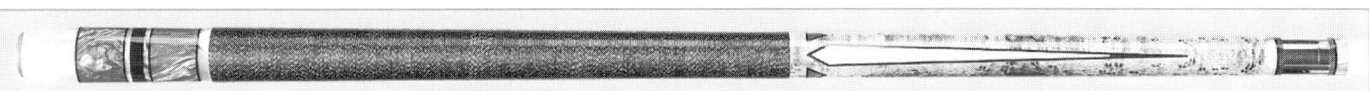

MSR	$375	$355	$265	$170

Level 4 VM18 - Stained bird's-eye maple forearm, three long and three short ebony points with an intricate two-piece ivory-colored diamond-shaped inlay in each point, ebony butt sleeve with three intricate two-piece diamond-shaped inlays alternating with three smaller intricate two-piece diamond-shaped inlays.

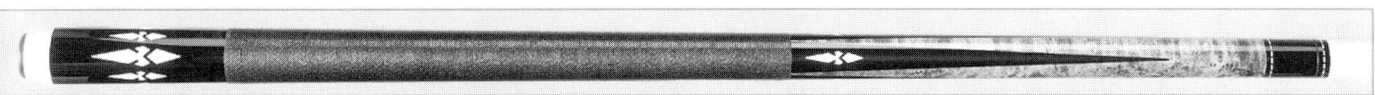

MSR	$360	$345	$260	$165

Level 4 VM19 - Stained bird's-eye maple forearm, four intricate four-piece ebony and ivory-colored floating points, ebony butt sleeve with ivory-colored check rings above and below.

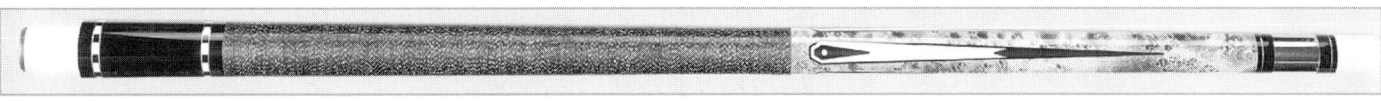

MSR	$345	$335	$255	$160

GRADING	98%	90%	70%

Level 4 VM20 - Stained bird's-eye maple forearm, wedge floating points with three ivory-colored four-point star-shaped inlays overlapping each point, stained bird's-eye maple butt sleeve with large wenge oval-shaped inlays with three ivory-colored four-point star-shaped inlays overlapping each oval.

MSR	$330	$325	$245	$155

Level 3 VM21 - Stained bird's-eye maple forearm, four ebony points with four colored veneers, ebony-colored butt sleeve.

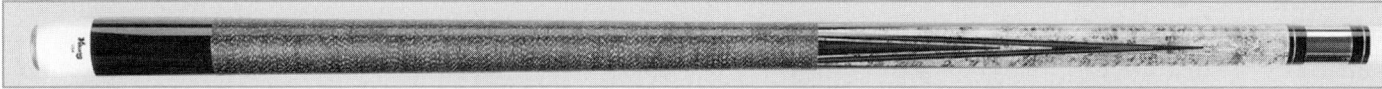

MSR	$315	$300	$230	$145

Level 4 VM22 - Rosewood forearm, four stained bird's-eye maple points with an intricate hollowed ebony diamond-shaped inlay in each point, rosewood butt sleeve with four intricate hollowed ebony diamond-shaped inlays set in stained bird's-eye maple ovals around center.

MSR	$300	$285	$220	$140

Level 2 VM23 - Rosewood forearm with pearlized plastic four-point star-shaped inlays within pairs of pearlized plastic dots, rosewood butt sleeve with pearlized plastic four-point star-shaped inlays alternating with pearlized plastic dots between brown pearlized plastic rings at top and bottom.

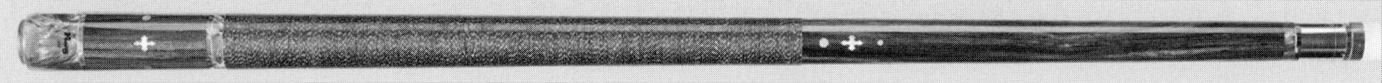

MSR	$290	$275	$210	$135

Level 5 VM24 - Rosewood forearm, four ivory-colored points with seven cocobolo oval-shaped inlays in each point, rosewood butt sleeve with four ivory-colored reverse point-shaped inlays with three cocobolo oval-shaped inlays in each.

MSR	$280	$265	$200	$130

Level 3 VM25 - Stained bird's-eye maple forearm, four black-bordered purple pearlized plastic points, purple pearlized plastic butt sleeve with ebony-colored rings at top and bottom.

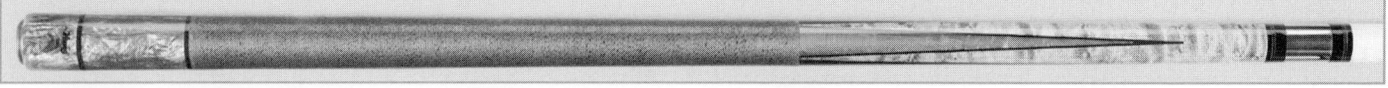

MSR	$270	$255	$190	$125

Level 3 VM26 - Stained bird's-eye maple forearm, rosewood points with three colored veneers, rosewood butt sleeve.

MSR	$260	$245	$185	$120

Level 3 VM27 - Rosewood forearm, intricate two-piece pearlized plastic points, rosewood butt sleeve with intricate two-piece pearlized plastic diamond-shaped inlays around center.

MSR	$250	$235	$180	$115

GRADING	98%	90%	70%

Level 4 VM28 - Goncalo alves forearm, four intricate ivory-colored floating points with a pair of opposing cordia triangle-shaped inlays in each point, goncalo alves butt sleeve with four intricate ivory-colored diamond-shaped inlays with a pair of opposing goncalo alves triangle-shaped inlays in each.

MSR	$240	$225	$175	$110

Level 1 VM29 - Stained bird's-eye maple forearm, four full-spliced stained bird's-eye maple points and butt sleeve with ebony veneers.

MSR	$230	$215	$165	$105

Level 2 VM30 - Green-stained bird's-eye maple forearm, green-stained bird's-eye maple butt sleeve with green pearlized plastic rings at bottom.

MSR	$220	$205	$160	$105

Level 2 VM31 - Red-stained bird's-eye maple forearm, red-stained bird's-eye maple butt sleeve with a red pearlized plastic ring set in pearlized plastic rings at bottom.

MSR	$210	$200	$155	$100

Level 3 VM32 - Stained bird's-eye maple forearm, four goncalo alves points with two colored veneers, goncalo alves butt sleeve.

MSR	$200	$190	$145	$90

Level 2 VM33 - Blue-stained bird's-eye maple forearm, ivory-colored butt sleeve with blue pearlized plastic rings above and below.

MSR	$190	$180	$135	$85

Level 2 VM34 - Ebony-stained bird's-eye maple forearm, grey pearlized plastic butt sleeve with ebony-colored rings at top and bottom.

MSR	$180	$170	$130	$80

Level 2 VM35 - Goncalo alves forearm, goncalo alves butt sleeve with stained maple rings at bottom.

MSR	$170	$160	$120	$75

Level 2 VM36 - Purple-stained bird's-eye maple forearm, purple-stained bird's-eye maple butt sleeve.

MSR	$160	$150	$115	$70

GRADING	98%	90%	70%

Level 2 VM37 - Green-stained bird's-eye maple forearm, green-stained bird's-eye maple butt sleeve.

MSR	$150	$140	$105	$65

Level 2 VM38 - Goncalo alves forearm, goncalo alves butt sleeve.

MSR	$140	$130	$100	$60

Level 2 VM39 - Goncalo alves forearm, goncalo alves butt sleeve.

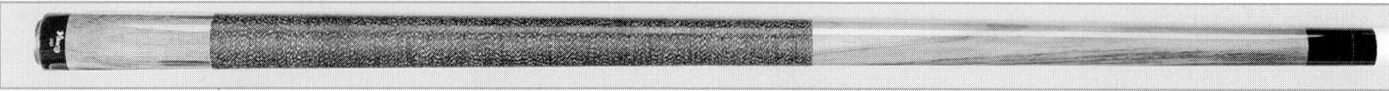

MSR	$130	$120	$95	$55

"DECUE" SERIES

The following "DeCue" line cues came with a variety of joints. DC1 through DC5 featured black nylon wraps. DC7 through DC13 featured Irish linen wraps. Several of the cues featured art by John Schmelzer.

Level 2 DC1 Snake - Green-stained maple forearm, synthetic ivory butt sleeve with applied image of a coiled snake.

MSR	$205	$185	$140	$90

Level 2 DC6 Hustler - Natural-stained bird's-eye maple forearm. Four single black veneered points and butt sleeve of stained bird's-eye maple available in nine different colors with choice of any of the applied images.

MSR	$290	$270	$205	$130

Level 2 DC8 Ride the Nine - Bird's-eye maple forearm with applied image of rodeo cowboys riding nine-balls, bird's-eye maple butt sleeve with applied image of a rodeo cowboy that has been thrown off a nine-ball.

MSR	$290	$270	$205	$130

Level 3 DC13 Skull with points - Natural-stained bird's-eye maple forearm, four rosewood points with three-colored veneers, rosewood butt sleeve with applied image of a skull with eight-ball eyes.

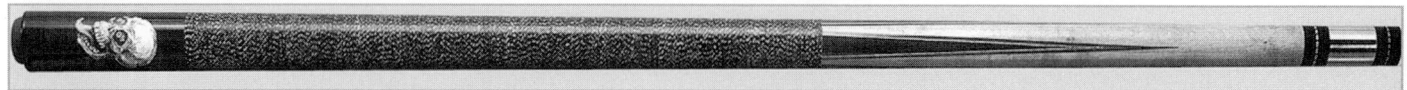

MSR	$290	$270	$205	$130

SECONDARY MARKET MINIMUM VALUES

The following are minimum values for other Viking cues encountered on the secondary market. These prices are representative of cues utilizing basic materials and designs that are not currently available. Viking also offers one- of-a-kind cues that can command many times these prices due to the use of exotic materials and artistry. Early models and limited editions are becoming collectible, and can also command many times these prices. More discontinued Viking cues will be covered in future editions.

Special construction note: There are many materials and construction techniques that can add value to Viking Cues. The following are the most important examples:

Add $500+ for ivory points.
Add 50%+ for ivory inlays

GRADING	98%	90%	70%

For all used Viking cues, except where otherwise noted:
- Add $60+ for each additional original straight playable shaft beyond one.
- Deduct $75+ for missing original straight playable shaft.
- Add $45+ for each ivory ferrule.
- Add $60+ for leather wrap.
- Deduct 20% for obvious or improper refinish.

Level 1 - 4 points, hustler.

	98%	90%	70%
Level 1 cues start at	$100	$75	$45

Level 2 - 0 points, 0-25 inlays.

Level 2 cues start at	$125	$95	$60

Level 3 - 2-6 points, 0-8 inlays.

Level 3 cues start at	$175	$140	$85

Level 4 - 4-10 points, 9-25 inlays.

Level 4 cues start at	$235	$180	$110

Level 5 - 0-12 points, 26-50 inlays.

Level 5 cues start at	$435	$335	$205

Level 6 - 0-12 points, 51-75 inlays.

Level 6 cues start at	$625	$475	$300

NOTES

W SECTION

ARNOT Q WADSWORTH III
Maker of Arnot Q's Custom Cues. For information, refer to Arnot Q.

MICHAEL WAGNER
Maker of Raven Cues. For information, refer to Raven.

NORBERT "NUBS" WAGNER
Maker of Nova Cues. For information, refer to Nova.

RUSS WALDO
Maker of pool cues in Alaska.
If you have a Waldo Cue cue that needs further identification or repair, contact Thomas Wayne Cues, listed in the trademark index.

WARD CUSTOM CUES
Maker of pool cues from 1998 to present in Visalia, California.

Jim Ward started making cues part time out of his glass shop in 1998. His full-time job has been owning and operating AJ Glass which he opened in 1985. He loved to play pool and was always interested in cues. Jim was born in Fresno and raised in the area between Fresno and Bakersfield where he still lives and works today.

Jim likes to take a lot of time building a cue, and he tries to make them the old-fashioned way in his one-man shop. All work is done by Jim, by hand, in a shop that includes five old lathes and an end mill but no CNC. He makes his own short-splice blanks, and enjoys trying different things. He has made just about every joint configuration over the years, including the Uni-Loc. Jim has developed his own taper that is based more on the great cues of the past. He also uses his own capped and threaded "Grice" ferrules.

Jim has made about a couple hundred cues and no two are alike. He likes to make one-of-a-kind cues to the customer's designs. He prefers maple handles on his cues instead of wraps. All Ward cues can be easily identified by the "Jim Ward" signature that has appeared on the forearm or butt of every cue he has made. Cues are also dated.

Jim will take care of servicing his cues for any problem that results from normal use.

If you are interested in talking to Jim about a new cue or cue that needs to be repaired, you can contact him at Ward Custom Cues, listed in the Trademark Index.

SPECIFICATIONS
Butt material: hardwoods
Shaft material: hard rock maple
Standard length: 58 in.
Standard Wrap: Irish Linen, leather, wood
Standard taper: Ward custom
Standard ferrules: Grice or Aegis
Standard tip: Triangle
Annual production: 8 to 10 cues

OPTIONS (FOR NEW CUES ONLY)
Leather wrap: $80
Ivory ferrule: $50
Extra shaft: $150

REPAIRS
Repairs done on all fine cues.
Refinish (with Irish linen wrap): $120
Rewrap (Irish linen): $60
Replace tip: $20
Replace shaft: $150

CURRENT WARD CUES
Two-piece Ward bar cues start at $200. Basic Ward cues with wraps and joint rings start at $250. Ward cues with points start at $400. One-of-a-kind custom cues start at $550. The current delivery time for a Ward custom cue is three to four months.

CURRENT EXAMPLES
The following is an example of a cue currently available from Ward Custom Cues. It can be ordered as shown, modified to suit the desires of the customer, or new designs can be created.

WARD CUSTOM CUES, cont.

GRADING	100%	95%	70%

Level 2 - Tiger maple forearm, stained bird's-eye maple handle, tiger maple butt sleeve.

MSR	$250	$225-275	$175	$120

GRADING	98%	90%	70%

SECONDARY MARKET MINIMUM VALUES

The following are minimum values for other Ward cues encountered on the secondary market. These prices are representative of cues utilizing basic materials and designs that are not necessarily available at present. Jim Ward has offered one-of-a-kind cues that can command many times these prices due to the use of exotic materials and artistry.

Special construction note: There are many materials and construction techniques that can add value to Ward cues.

For all used Ward cues, except where otherwise noted:
- Add $75 for each additional original straight playable shaft beyond one.
- Deduct $90+ for missing original straight playable shaft.
- Add $25 each for ivory ferrules.
- Add $50 for leather wrap.
- Deduct 15% for obvious or improper refinish.

Level 1 - Hustler.
Level 1 cues start at	$185	$140	$90

Level 2 - 0 points, 0-25 inlays.
Level 2 cues start at	$215	$165	$105

Level 3 - 2-6 points, 0-8 inlays.
Level 3 cues start at	$400	$300	$185

Level 4 - 4-10 points, 9-25 inlays.
Level 4 cues start at	$600	$450	$275

Level 5 - 0-12 points, 26-50 inlays.
Level 5 cues start at	$850	$635	$410

Level 6 - 0-12 points, 51-75 inlays.
Level 6 cues start at	$1,100	$825	$525

WAYNE CUSTOM CUES

Maker of pool cues from 1971 to present, currently in Waxhaw, North Carolina.

Wayne Holmes is a second generation cuemaker, having learned from his father, cuemaker Orie Holmes, in the mid-1960s. In 1971, after having served in the military, Wayne attended college to study structural engineering and construction techniques. While in college, he started a small cuemaking and cue repair business to help pay his education expenses. Wayne's early cues were very simple in design, but were quite well known for their quality of hit and expert workmanship. Obviously he had paid close attention to his father's teachings.

Being an avid pool player since the age of 12, Wayne knew exactly how a well-made cue should perform. His education and career in construction and engineering paid off for him when he decided to pursue cuemaking full time. Wayne settled near Charlotte, North Carolina and built a new shop. He then devoted a full three years to research and engineering to improve his methods of constructing his cues, and to developing the pro taper of the shafts. His cues are now even better known for their excellent deflection characteristics, their quality "hit," and superior workmanship.

Wayne now limits the number of cues he makes each year to 100, all of which are constructed without the aid of computerized equipment. Wayne does all of his inlays entirely by hand and has stated, "There will never be a CNC machine in my shop." In 1995, Wayne developed a method of doing the labor-intensive "re-machined points" and brought his cuemaking to an even higher level. Although he is now making cues that sell for several thousand dollars and are being shipped all over the world, he still enjoys making the plain cue for the average player. "Whether it's a three hundred dollar cue, or a three thousand dollar cue, it's still something I love to do."

With Wayne, the search for better and stronger construction methods is never ending. He is credited with the development of a proprietary joint system in 2002 that has proven to significantly improve the hit of his cues. The development of a new and extremely effective taper for the shafts of his cues has come to be very popular among professional and novice players alike. His favorite saying is "...good enough, just isn't good enough."

Wayne Custom Cues are easily identifiable by his signature in gold, silver, or black ink on the forearm. In September 2003, Wayne began signing his one-of-a-kind and limited edition cues in genuine gold or silver leaf.

Wayne Custom Cues are guaranteed for life against manufacturing defects that are not the result of warpage or abuse. If you have a Wayne cue that needs further identification or repair, or would like to order a new Wayne cue, contact Wayne Custom Cues, listed in the Trademark Index.

Wayne Holmes

WAYNE CUSTOM CUES, cont.

| GRADING | 98% | 90% | 70% |

SPECIFICATIONS
- Butt material: hardwoods
- Shaft material: rock maple
- Standard length: 58 in.
- Lengths available: up to 60 in.
- Standard finish: automotive clear coat
- Balance point: 18 to 20 in.
- Standard butt cap: linen base fiber
- Standard wrap: pressed Irish linen
- Point construction: short splice
- Standard joint: stainless steel
- Joint type: flat faced
- Standard number of shafts: one
- Standard taper: 12 in. pro
- Standard ferrules: Ivorine-3
- Standard tip: Triangle
- Annual production: 100 cues

OPTIONS (FOR NEW CUES ONLY)
- Special length: no charge
- Moori tip: $35
- Joint protectors: $30
- Extra shaft: $125

REPAIRS
Repairs done on all fine cues.
- Refinish (with linen wrap): $125
- Rewrap (Irish linen): $35
- Replace butt cap: by quote
- Replace Triangle, Le Pro, or Elkmaster Tip: $12
- Replace Wayne cue shaft: $125
- Refinish shaft: $15

CURRENT WAYNE CUES
Basic Wayne cues with wraps and joint rings start at $319. Wayne cues with points start at $479. One-of-a-kind custom Wayne cues start at $800.

PAST EXAMPLES
The following cues can be encountered as shown or modified to suit the desires of the original owner.

Level 2 - Cocobolo forearm with pairs of silver rings at top and bottom, cocobolo butt sleeve with a silver ring at top and bottom.

| MSR (1999) $390 | $435 | $335 | $220 |

Level 2 - Bird's-eye maple forearm with four long thin micarta inlays between pairs of silver rings at top and bottom, bird's-eye maple butt sleeve with four long thin micarta inlays between pairs of silver rings at top and bottom.

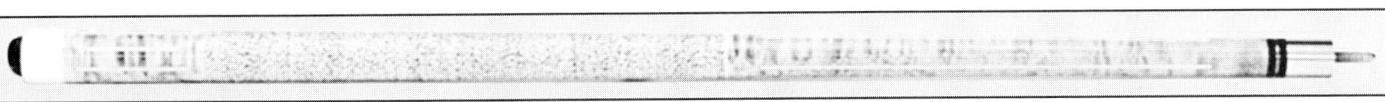

| MSR (1999) $445 | $480 | $380 | $265 |

Level 2 - Ebony forearm with four long thin micarta inlays between pairs of silver rings at top and bottom, ebony butt sleeve with four long thin micarta inlays between pairs of silver rings at top and bottom.

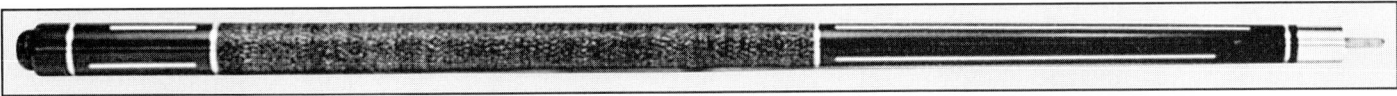

| MSR (1999) $445 | $485 | $385 | $270 |

WAYNE CUSTOM CUES, cont.

GRADING	98%	90%	70%

Level 3 - Curly maple forearm with pairs of silver rings at top and bottom, four lacewood points with four veneers, purpleheart butt sleeve with pairs of silver rings at top and bottom.

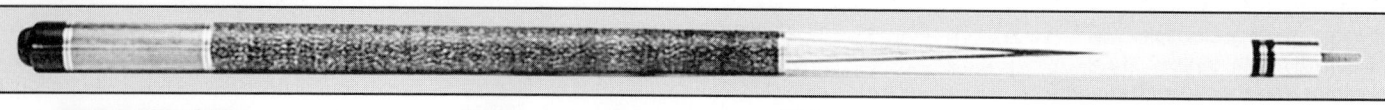

MSR (1999) $445	$495	$395	$275

Level 4 - Maple forearm with pairs of silver rings at top and bottom, four long and four short bocote points, bocote butt sleeve with pairs of silver rings at top and bottom.

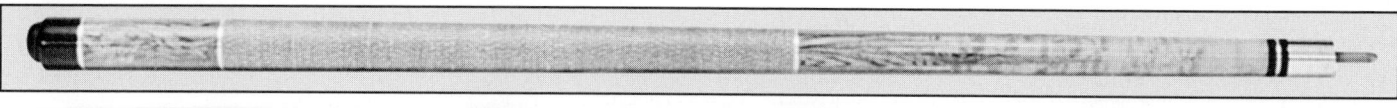

MSR (1999) $495	$550	$435	$300

Level 4 - Bird's-eye maple forearm with pairs of silver rings at top and bottom, four long and four short ebony points with double veneers, ebony butt sleeve with pairs of silver rings at top and bottom.

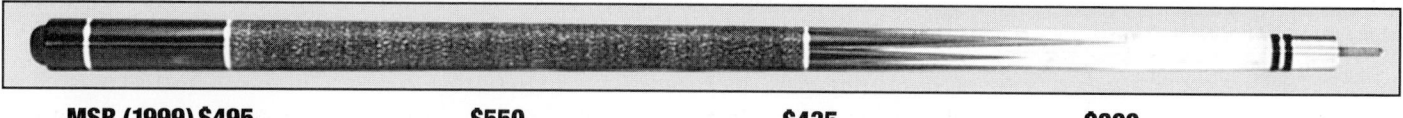

MSR (1999) $495	$550	$435	$300

Level 4 - Ebony forearm with pairs of silver rings at top and bottom, four long and four short ebony points with single tulipwood veneers, ebony butt sleeve with eight tulipwood crescent-shaped inlays within pairs of silver rings at top and bottom.

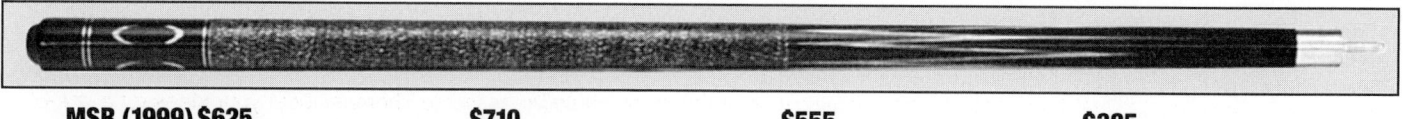

MSR (1999) $625	$710	$555	$385

SECONDARY MARKET MINIMUM VALUES

The following are minimum values for other Wayne cues encountered on the secondary market. These prices are representative of cues utilizing basic materials and designs that are not currently available. Has offered one-of-a-kind cues that can command many times these prices due to the use of exotic materials and artistry.

Special construction note: There are many materials and construction techniques that can add value to Wayne cues.

For all used Wayne cues, except where otherwise noted:
- Add $95 for each additional original straight playable shaft beyond one.
- Deduct $125 for missing original straight playable shaft.
- Deduct 25% for obvious or improper refinish.

Level 1 - 4 points, hustler.
Level 1 cues start at	$150	$120	$85

Level 2 - 0 points, 0-25 inlays.
Level 2 cues start at	$300	$235	$160

Level 3 - 2-6 points, 0-8 inlays.
Level 3 cues start at	$450	$350	$235

Level 4 - 4-10 points, 9-25 inlays.
Level 4 cues start at	$600	$470	$320

THOMAS WAYNE CUES

Maker of pool cues from 1979 to present in Anchorage, Alaska.

Thomas Wayne has been a craftsman for almost as long as he can remember. He has made custom furniture, guitars, knives, jewelry, skateboards, etc. Thomas's formal training was in cabinetry and furniture design and manufacture. He also served an apprenticeship with a world-renowned custom knife maker during his second year in college.

thomas wayne
hand-made custom pool cues

Like many other skilled woodworkers, once he was exposed to the world of custom cues, he had to try it. His first attempts were two-piece house cues in which he added his own inlays. He made his first cue in 1979, and by 1985, he had made approximately five more. It was during this time that his friend, Russ Waldo, a retired machinist, showed Thomas the basics of cue construction and convinced him that he had the talent to pursue cuemaking full-time. Thomas made this commitment in 1985.

The early cues were the only ones he ever made that were not signed. If you believe you have one of these cues, Thomas is the man to contact, as he can identify all his early work. All of his cues made from 1985 to the present are easily recognizable by Thomas Wayne's

GRADING	98%	90%	70%

signature on the forearm. Very special cues were signed in gold leaf, but now gold leaf is used much more often. About 80% of his joints were 5/16-14 stainless, with the other 20% being 3/8-10 flat-faced ivory or phenolic joints. Since about 2001 he has preferred to use ivory joints with the radial pin. That same year Thomas found a great supplier for quality leather and has done mostly leather wraps ever since.

Today, Thomas works out of his spacious one-man hi-tech shop designed especially for creating custom cues, which he has built behind his home in Anchorage. He only makes a couple dozen cues a year, primarily for existing customers that collect his cues. Thomas is currently involved in creating a cue registry to help future generations identify and authenticate contemporary custom cues, including possibly incorporating internal chips in the cues.

Thomas Wayne cues are made of the finest hardwoods, genuine ivories, shells, precious metals, and precious stones, which he personally selects. Almost all cues are one-of-a-kind originals, for Thomas will no longer make two cues that are alike. He is also proud to do all of the work himself. Thomas has no employees or apprentices. Thomas was one of the eight founding members of the American Cuemakers Association and was also one of the cuemakers that was selected to make a cue for the Smithsonian. What makes Thomas Wayne cues unique is the design and intricacy of his inlay work. One of his most famous and creative cues was "The Disintegrating Cue," which is pictured below. This cue has an ebony forearm and butt sleeve, with ivory points and ivory windows that appear to be disintegrating. This effect was achieved by inlaying hundreds of individual pieces of ivory to make up the points and inlays.

He has trademarked the term 4-D Inlay, which refers to the designs he can achieve using fourth axis machining achieved with five-axis programming. Thomas likes computerized solid modeling which subtracts the empty space much like carving a sculpture. 4-D Inlay allows Thomas to create designs that appear three-dimensional, and also to create visual illusions. He enjoys creating designs which appear impossible to assemble, leaving collectors and even other cuemakers studying these cues to try to figure out how he did it. Sometimes he will shorten the wrap areas, resulting in longer forearms, for more artistry. Three different joints are available on Thomas Wayne cues, and shafts are interchangeable, so it is not necessary to send in the butt to get a replacement. Thomas has developed a measuring device for shaft diameters that is about three times more accurate than what is commonly used.

Thomas also makes high end wands for magicians, often using the same kind of intricate inlay work seen on his cues. He is known as the top CNC expert in Alaska and he consults with makers of furniture, souvinirs, guitars, etc. on how to inlay these items. One of Thomas' projects was to train the man who did all of the inlay work on the custom wood judges' benches in a new courthouse in Alaska. He also built and programmed the CNC machines that were necessary for this project. This was funded by "1 Percent for the Arts" which requires that 1% of the budget go towards artistic decoration for publicly funded construction, a program which Thomas supports and participates in. He has also fulfilled military contracts such as a batch of complex wood screws designed to fill above-deck bullet holes on Coast Guard boats that screw in and seal when wet.

If you have a Thomas Wayne cue that needs further identification or repair, or would like to talk to Thomas about your ideas for a one-of-a-kind custom cue, contact Thomas Wayne Cues, listed in the trademark index.

SPECIFICATIONS

Butt material: hardwoods
Shaft material: rock maple
Standard length: 58 1/4 in.
Lengths available: any
Standard joint screw: radial pin
Standard joint: phenolic
Joint type: flat faced
Balance point: 2 1/2 in. above wrap
Standard wrap: leather
Standard number of shafts: two

OPTIONS (FOR NEW CUES ONLY)

Option prices are incorporated into the total price of each cue.

REPAIRS

Repairs done only on Thomas Wayne cues or cues by deceased legends, such as Balabushka or Szamboti. Repairs are priced on an individual basis.

CURRENT THOMAS WAYNE CUES

The following are minimum prices for Thomas Wayne cues encountered on the secondary market. These prices are representative.

PAST EXAMPLES

The following cue is an example of a one-of-a-kind Thomas Wayne cue.

Level 8 "The Disintigrating Cue" - Ebony forearm with pairs of silver rings at top and bottom, four intricate multi-piece ivory disintegrating points, ebony butt sleeve with four intricate ivory disintegrating windows.

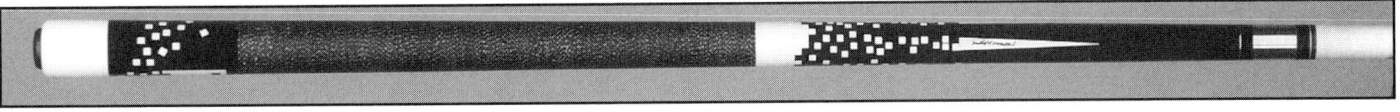

| MSR (1990) $1,400 | $40,000 | $36,000 | $30,000 |

THOMAS WAYNE CUES, cont.

GRADING	98%	90%	70%

SECONDARY MARKET MINIMUM VALUES

The following are minimum prices for Thomas Wayne cues encountered on the secondary market. These prices are representative of cues utilizing basic materials and designs that may not be currently available. Thomas currently specializes in one-of-a-kind cues that can command many times these prices due to the use of exotic materials and artistry.

Special construction note: There are many materials and construction techniques that can add value to Thomas Wayne cues.

For all used Thomas Wayne cues:
Deduct 25% for obvious or improper refinish.

	98%	90%	70%
Level 1 - 4 points, hustler.			
Level 1 cues start at	$600	$480	$345
Level 2 - 0 points, 0-25 inlays.			
Level 2 cues start at	$1,000	$825	$600
Level 3 - 2-6 points, 0-8 inlays.			
Level 3 cues start at	$1,400	$1,125	$800
Level 4 - 4-10 points, 9-25 inlays.			
Level 4 cues start at	$1,850	$1,450	$1,000
Level 5 - 0-12 points, 26-50 inlays.			
Level 5 cues start at	$2,500	$1,900	$1,400
Level 6 - 0-12 points, 51-75 inlays.			
Level 6 cues start at	$3,500	$2,800	$1,900
Level 7 - 0-12 points, 76-125 inlays.			
Level 7 cues start at	$4,500	$3,500	$2,350
Level 8 - 4 or more points, 126 or more inlays.			
Level 8 cues start at	$6,000	$4,700	$3,250

BILLY WEBB

Maker of Spider Web Cues. For information, refer to Spider Web.

MIKE WEBB CUES

Maker of pool cues from 1994 to present in Pawtucket, Rhode Island.

Mike Webb started playing pool in 1986. Just divorced, he joined the Army the same year. Mike had been working in a research and development machine shop in the textile industry. Mike worked as a lineman in the Army, climbing poles and hanging cable. He won "soldier of the year" honors within his platoon four out of five years served. After an honorable discharge Mike left the Army to raise his two children. It was that year, 1991, that Mike met Paul Drexler and became fascinated with pool cues. Mike started replacing tips at pool rooms by hand out of a tackle box that he carried. Mike idolized Paul Drexler and Dave Doucette of Samsara cues, and he tried to learn as much as could from conversations with both of them. He slowly advanced to more difficult repairs and began cutting new shafts for other cuemakers.

Mike would buy cues from players in the pool rooms so that he could take them home and cut them apart. He studied how different cues were constructed, weighted, tapered, etc., and by 1994 he made his first cue. About that time he started setting up at tournaments in the northeast and doing repairs. He learned what players liked about their cues and how materials and construction affected the hit. Mike believes he is good at playing with a cue and being able to make a cue with a similar hit.

Mike still sets up at tournaments doing repairs and he makes cues by hand in his one-man shop. He places the most importance on making cues that look and play the way the customer wants. "Quality is no accident" is Mike's mission statement which he defines as his effort to create the best product possible, always keeping the customer and playability of the cues in mind. Every cue Mike creates he dedicates to his daughter Jamie and son Michael. Without their support he believes none of this could have been possible. Mike prefers the more traditional look and construction methods of the custom cues of the early 1970s. He makes his own short-splice blanks and he does inlays on a manual benchtop pantograph. There is no CNC equipment in his shop. There is a huge stock of exotic hardwoods and rock maple shafts hanging. He stocks his wood years in advance.

Mike makes small cuts on the shafts over the course of two years to achieve the final taper. He also has his own low-deflection shaft design. And Predator shafts are available for those who request them. Many different joints are available on a new Mike Webb cue at no extra cost. Joint protectors are standard. Mike makes everything in his cues except for the bumpers, tips, and screws. He has also made many of the tools in his shop, and he makes his own carbide mandrels. Mike would like to thank the following craftsmen for expanding his understanding of cue construction: Paul Drexler, Chris Hightower, Jeff Prather, Skip Tasker, Dan Janes. For linen wraps he thanks Ted Harris. For finishing he thanks Tony Scianella, Dan Dishaw, Paul Dayton, Leonard Bludworth, Tim Scruggs, Mike Cochran, Paul Mottey, and New Age Auto.

Mike Webb cues are easily identifiable by the name "Webb" which is engraved in the butt cap. Cues made from 1994 to 2001 are engraved in large letters. Cues made in 2001 or later are engraved in smaller letters. Mike Webb cues are warranted for life against manufacturing defects that are not the result of warpage or abuse. Butts are warranted for life against warpage to the original owner.

If you are interested in talking to Mike Webb about a new cue or a cue that needs to be repaired, you can contact him at Mike Webb Cues, listed in the Trademark Index.

MIKE WEBB CUES, cont. **863**

GRADING	98%	90%	70%

SPECIFICATIONS

Butt Material: hardwoods, alternative ivory
Shaft material: rock maple
Standard length: 58 in.
Lengths Available: 42 to 62 in.
Standard finish: PPG urethane
Balance point: 17 1/2 to 17 3/4 in. from bumper
Standard butt cap: phenolic
Standard wrap: Irish Linen, leather
Point construction: short splice
Standard joint: phenolic
Joint type: flat-faced
Joint screw: 5/16-14
Standard number of shafts: one
Standard taper: modified pro
Standard ferrules: melamine, ivory
Tip widths available: any
Standard tip: Triangle
Annual production: 30 cues

OPTIONS (FOR NEW CUES ONLY)

Leather wrap: $100
Lizard wrap: $250
Ivory ferrule: $75
Extra shaft: $125

REPAIRS

Repairs done on all cues.
Refinish (with Irish linen wrap): $150
Refinish (with leather wrap): $200
Refinish (with lizard): $350
Rewrap with Irish linen: $45
Replace shaft: $125
Replace tip: $15

CURRENT MIKE WEBB CUES

Basic Michael Webb cues with wraps and joint rings start at $550. Basic Michael Webb cues with four points start at $700. One-of-a-kind custom Michael Webb cues start at $1,500. Mike Webb cues over $900 come with two shafts.

SECONDARY MARKET MINIMUM VALUES

The following are minimum values for Mike Webb cues encountered on the secondary market. These prices are representative of cues utilizing basic materials and designs that are not necessarily available at present. Mike Webb has offered one-of-a-kind cues that can command many times these prices due to the use of exotic materials and artistry.

Special construction note: There are many materials and construction techniques that can add value to Mike Webb cues.

For all used Mike Webb cues, except where otherwise noted:

Add $100 for each additional original straight playable shaft beyond one.
Add $200 for each additional straight playable Predator shaft
Deduct $125 for missing original straight playable shaft.
Add $50 each for ivory ferrules.
Add $100 for ivory joint.
Deduct 15% for obvious or improper refinish.

Level 2 - 0 points, 0-25 inlays.

	98%	90%	70%
Level 2 cues start at	$500	$390	$265

Level 3 - 2-6 points, 0-8 inlays.

Level 3 cues start at	$600	$465	$315

Level 4 - 4-10 points, 9-25 inlays.

Level 4 cues start at	$700	$545	$375

Level 5 - 0-12 points, 26-50 inlays.

Level 5 cues start at	$900	$700	$485

Level 6 - 0-12 points, 51-75 inlays.

Level 6 cues start at	$1,400	$1,130	$800

ROBERT WEIR CUES

Distributor of pool cues in the early 1980s in Texas.

Robert Weir introduced a line of cues made by Adam in Japan in the early 1980s. There were several standard models that appeared in his catalog. All were easily identifiable by the "Flying W" logo that appeared on every Robert Weir cue. Robert distributed these cues from his business in Texas. It is believed that less than 1,000 were made.

Flying W

SPECIFICATIONS

- Butt material: hardwoods
- Shaft material: rock maple
- Standard length: 58 in.
- Standard wrap: Irish linen
- Point construction: short splice
- Joint type: flat faced
- Standard number of shafts: one
- Total production: approximately 1,000 cues

SECONDARY MARKET MINIMUM VALUES

The following are minimum values for Robert Weir cues encountered on the secondary market. These prices are representative of cues utilizing the basic materials and designs that were available.

Special construction note: There are many materials and construction techniques that can add value to Robert Weir cues.

For all used Robert Weir cues, except where otherwise noted:
- Add $75 for each additional original straight playable shaft beyond one.
- Deduct 50% for missing original straight playable shaft.
- Deduct 25% for obvious or improper refinish.

Grading	98%	90%	70%
Level 2 - 0 points, 0-25 inlays. Level 2 cues start at	$250	$190	$120
Level 3 - 2-6 points, 0-8 inlays. Level 3 cues start at	$350	$265	$165
Level 4 - 4-10 points, 9-25 inlays. Level 4 cues start at	$400	$300	$190
Level 5 - 0-12 points, 26-50 inlays. Level 5 cues start at	$500	$375	$235
Level 6 - 0-12 points, 51-75 inlays. Level 6 cues start at	$600	$450	$285

WESTON CUSTOM CUES

Maker of pool cues from 1982 to present currently in Hot Springs, Arkansas.

Perry Weston started to play pool at the age of 10. Growing up in Wisconsin, Perry liked to play in the local tournaments. He got more serious about the game while attending college. Eventually, he decided to order a cue from a local custom cuemaker.

After a long time waiting for a cue that never arrived, Perry decided to use the knowledge he had received working in a machine shop to make his own custom cue. He got some components from another cuemaker, and completed the cue in 1982. When a friend offered him $50 for the cue, Perry sold it, knowing that he could make another. Soon, more of his friends wanted him to make them custom cues, and the word began to spread. Perry constantly experimented with ways to improve the design and construction of his cues. In 1993, Perry left Wisconsin to make cues in Hot Springs, Arkansas. Perry's cues have been easily identifiable since 1984, when he started

Perry Weston

1984 to 1998

1998 to 2005

engraving "Weston" vertically in cursive on the flared butt caps. In 1998, he started placing them horizontally in block letters. In 2005, he changed to script letters. Around this time Perry switched from piloted stainless steel joints to flat-faced linen phenolic joints. Then he switched from 5/16-14 joint pins to radial pins. In about 2000, Perry sarted coring his butts with a solid piece of rock maple to eliminate the splice.

Sterling silver has become a popular material for inlays and rings on Weston cues, and phenolic and ivory are commonly used to craft the joints. Perry makes every component except the bumpers, tips, and screws, which are custom made to his specifications. Perry offers CNC or traditional veneer points, and he is constantly modernizing his shop with more advanced equipment. Perry was one of a few cuemakers who was selected to make cues for a Smithsonian exhibit in the late 1990s. Recently he trademarked the name "Weston Custom Cues."

Weston cues are indefinitely guaranteed against construction defects that are not the result of abuse. If you have a Weston cue that needs repair, or would like to talk to Perry about the design of a new cue, contact Weston Custom Cues, listed in the trademark index.

SPECIFICATIONS

Butt material: hardwoods
Shaft material: rock maple
Standard length: 58 in.
Lengths available: any up to 60 in.
Standard finish: urethane
Joint screw: radial pin
Standard joint: linen phenolic
Joint type: flat faced
Balance point: 2 in. above wrap
Point construction: short splice or inlaid
Standard wrap: leather
Standard butt cap: linen phenolic
Standard number of shafts: two
Standard taper: custom
Standard ferrules: ivory
Standard tip: Triangle
Tip widths available: any up to 14 mm
Annual production: approximately 30 cues

OPTIONS (FOR NEW CUES ONLY)

Leather wrap: $100+
Lizard wrap: $250
Ivory joint: $250
Uni-Loc joint: $200
Extra shaft: $175+
Special length: no charge

REPAIRS

Repairs done only on Weston Cues.
Refinish (with leather wrap): $250+
Refinish (with linen wrap): $150
Rewrap (leather): $100+
Rewrap (linen): $50
Replace shaft: $150+
Replace ivory ferrule: $75 each
Replace phenolic butt cap: $75
Replace ivory butt cap: $400

CURRENT WESTON CUES

The current delivery time for a Weston cue is in excess of eight months depending on the intricacy of the cue.

SECONDARY MARKET MINIMUM VALUES

The following are minimum prices for Weston cues encountered on the secondary market. These prices are representative of cues utilizing basic materials and designs that may not be currently available. Perry currently specializes in one-of-a-kind cues that can command many times these prices due to the use of exotic materials and artistry.

Special construction note: There are many materials and construction techniques that can add value to Weston cues. The following are the most important examples:

Add $200+ for each ivory point.
Add $1,000+ for solid ivory butt sleeve.

For all used Weston cues, except where otherwise noted:

Add $125+ for each additional original straight playable shaft beyond two.
Deduct $150 for each missing original straight playable shaft under two.
Add $200+ for ivory joint.

WESTON CUSTOM CUES, cont.

GRADING	98%	90%	70%

Add $75+ for leather wrap.
Add $50+ for each ivory ferrule.
Deduct 25% for obvious or improper refinish.

	98%	90%	70%
Level 1 - 4 points, hustler.			
Level 1 cues start at	$300	$225	$145
Level 2 - 0 points, 0-25 inlays.			
Level 2 cues start at	$600	$450	$290
Level 3 - 2-6 points, 0-8 inlays.			
Level 3 cues start at	$1,000	$750	$485
Level 4 - 4-10 points, 9-25 inlays.			
Level 4 cues start at	$1,350	$1,000	$650
Level 5 - 0-12 points, 26-50 inlays.			
Level 5 cues start at	$1,800	$1,350	$850
Level 6 - 0-12 points, 51-75 inlays.			
Level 6 cues start at	$2,500	$2,000	$1,450

SKIP WESTON CUES

Maker of pool cues since 1990 in Haskell, New Jersey.

Skip Weston

Skip Weston has loved to play pool since he was 15 years old. An accomplished player, he has run over a hundred balls more than once and he has won many nine-ball tournaments. Skip has always liked to make things with his hands. Skip completed courses in autocad and mastercam for his employment as a machinist, so it seemed a natural development for him to start repairing and then making pool cues. He made his first cue in 1990. He now makes Skip Weston cues full time. His work has been inspired by Gus Szamboti and Burton Spain.

With over 35 years as a machinist, Skip is proficient on all types of conventional and CNC lathes, millers, grinders, and other machine shop equipment. He makes all of the tooling and fixtures in his one-man shop, and he makes all of the components for his cues except for the tips and bumpers. Skip also has a unique process for making all of his one-piece hardwood veneers which are cut in 90-degree corners instead of mitered. The point veneers therefore have no seam at the tips. And he can make them to match the exotic woods used in the cue instead of dyed sycamore that may look the same color. Usually the outside veneer is the same wood as the point, and he only uses the natural colors of the woods in his cues. Skip is happy to build one-of-a-kind cues around the customers' needs. Many types of joints, ferrules, tips, lengths, etc. are available.

Skip Weston cues are easily identifiable by the "Skip Weston" signature and date on the forearm, which Skip has done since he started making cues. They have an unlimited guarantee to the original owner against defects in construction that are not the result of warpage or abuse.

If you are interested in talking to Skip Weston about a new cue or cue that needs to be repaired, you can contact him at Skip Weston Cues, listed in the Trademark Index.

SPECIFICATIONS

Butt material: hardwoods
Shaft material: rock maple
Standard length: 58 in.
Lengths available: any
Standard finish: acid-catalyzed conversion varnish
Balance point: 18 to 19 in. from bumper
Standard wrap: Irish linen
Point construction: short splice
Standard joint: stainless steel or phenolic
Joint type: piloted
Joint screw: 5/16-14 or flat faced 3/8-10
Standard number of shafts: two
Standard taper: 12 in. straight
Standard ferrules: linen melamine
Standard tip: Triangle
Annual production: approximately 50 cues

OPTIONS (FOR NEW CUES ONLY)

Special length: no charge
Ivory ferrule: $100
Ivory butt cap: $350
Ivory joint: $250

SKIP WESTON CUES, cont.

GRADING	100%	95%	70%

Ivory points: $400 each
Joint protectors: standard
Leather wrap: $100
Lizard/exotic wrap: $200
Extra shaft: $125
Layered tip: $35

REPAIRS

Repairs done on all fine cues.
 Refinish (with Irish linen wrap): $250
 Refinish (with leather wrap): $300
 Rewrap (Irish linen): $50
 Clean and press linen wrap: $20
 Rewrap (leather): $100
 Replace butt cap: $50+
 Replace ferrule: $35+
 Replace Triangle tip: $15
 Replace shaft: $125
 Replace shaft with ivory ferrule: $225

CURRENT SKIP WESTON CUES

Basic Skip Weston cues with four points start at $950. The current delivery time for a Skip Weston Cue is 20 to 24 weeks.

CURRENT EXAMPLES

The following cues are currently available from Skip Weston Cues. They can be ordered as shown, or modified to suit the desires of the customer.

Level 3 - Ebony forearm with a maple dash ring above wrap, four long and four short bird's-eye maple points with three veneers, leather wrap, bird's-eye maple butt sleeve with a thick ebony ring between maple dash rings above and at bottom.

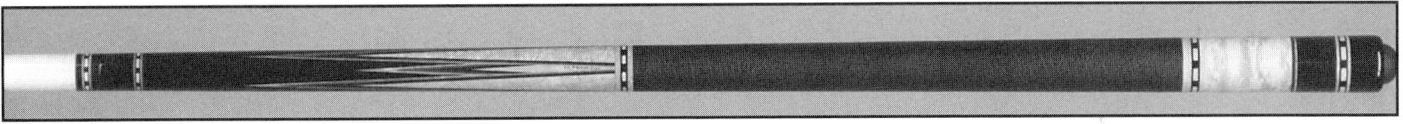

MSR	$1,600	$1,500-1,750	$1,250	$950

Level 3 - Ivory joint, bird's-eye maple forearm with an ivory stitch ring above wrap, four ebony points with four veneers and an ivory spear-shaped inlay in each point, leather wrap, ebony butt sleeve with four ivory spear-shaped inlays within ivory stitch rings between maple rings at top and bottom.

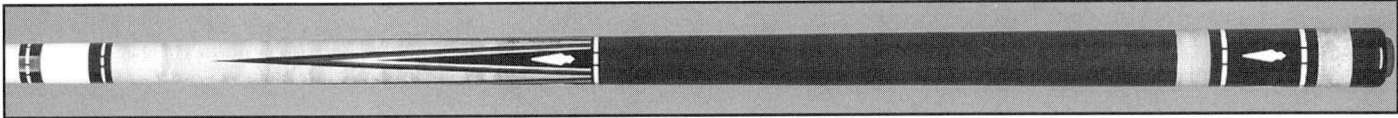

MSR	$2,150	$2,000-2,250	$1,650	$1,200

Level 4 - Ivory joint, bird's-eye maple forearm with an ivory stitch ring above wrap, four kingwood points with four veneers and an ivory diamond-shaped inlay inside an ebony oval in each point, lizard wrap, kingwood butt sleeve with four ivory diamond-shaped inlays set in ebony ovals between ivory stitch rings above and below.

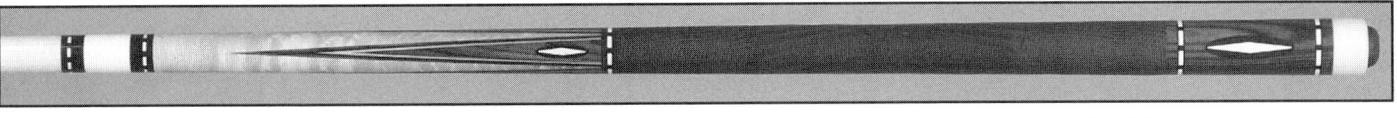

MSR	$2,300	$2,150-2,450	$1,750	$1,300

Level 4 - Ivory joint, bird's-eye maple forearm with an ivory Bushka ring above wrap, four ebony points with four veneers and a mother-of-pearl notched diamond-shaped inlay within four mother-of-pearl dots in each point, lizard wrap, ebony butt sleeve with four mother-of-pearl notched diamond-shaped inlays below two rows of four mother-of-pearl dots.

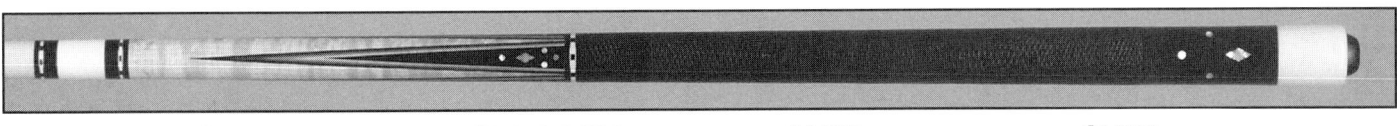

MSR	$2,400	$2,250-2,500	$1,825	$1,350

| GRADING | 100% | 95% | 70% |

Level 4 - Ivory joint, ebony forearm with a snakewood/ebony/ivory dash ring above wrap, four long snakewood points with three veneers and an ebony-bordered ivory heart-shaped inlay in each alternating with four short curly maple points, lizard wrap, snakewood butt sleeve with four ivory heart-shaped inlays set in hollow ebony ovals within snakewood/ebony/ivory columns between snakewood/ebony/ivory dash rings above and below, ivory butt cap.

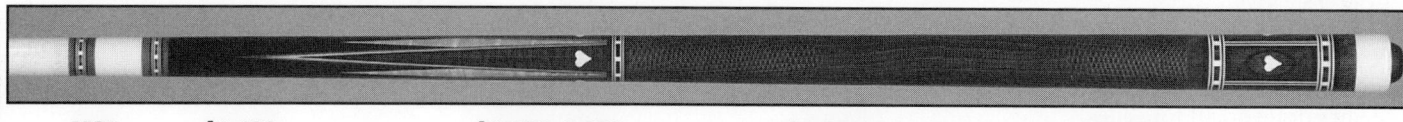

| MSR | $4,100 | $4,000-4,350 | $3,250 | $2,250 |

Level 5 - Ivory joint, bird's-eye maple forearm with an ivory and pink ivory rosary bead ring set in ebony above wrap, four long ebony points with two veneers and a pink ivory-bordered ivory dot between a pair of opposing pink ivory-bordered ivory heart-shaped inlays in each point alternating with four short ebony points, lizard wrap, ebony butt sleeve with four pink ivory-bordered ivory dots between pairs of opposing pink ivory-bordered ivory heart-shaped inlays alternating with pink ivory-bordered ivory columns within pink ivory rings between ivory and pink ivory rosary bead rings set in ebony above and below, ivory butt cap.

| MSR | $4,200 | $4,100-4,450 | $3,375 | $2,300 |

| GRADING | 98% | 90% | 70% |

SECONDARY MARKET MINIMUM VALUES

The following are minimum values for other Skip Weston cues encountered on the secondary market. These prices are representative of cues utilizing basic materials and designs that are not necessarily available at present. Skip Weston has offered one-of-a-kind cues that can command many times these prices due to the use of exotic materials and artistry.

Special construction note: There are many materials and construction techniques that can add value to Skip Weston cues.

For all used Skip Weston cues, except where otherwise noted:

- Add $100 for each additional original straight playable shaft beyond two.
- Deduct $125 for each missing original straight playable shaft under two.
- Add $75 each for ivory ferrules.
- Add $75 for leather wrap.
- Add $200+ for each ivory point
- Deduct 15% for obvious or improper refinish.

Level 1 - Hustler.
| Level 1 cues start at | $300 | $235 | $165 |

Level 2 - 0 points, 0-25 inlays.
| Level 2 cues start at | $400 | $315 | $215 |

Level 3 - 2-6 points, 0-8 inlays.
| Level 3 cues start at | $700 | $545 | $375 |

Level 4 - 4-10 points, 9-25 inlays.
| Level 4 cues start at | $800 | $635 | $435 |

Level 5 - 0-12 points, 26-50 inlays.
| Level 5 cues start at | $1,000 | $790 | $545 |

Level 6 - 0-12 points, 51-75 inlays.
| Level 6 cues start at | $1,400 | $1,095 | $750 |

WHISLER CUSTOM CUES

Maker of pool cues from 1992 to present, currently in Mesa, Arizona.

Scott Whisler grew up in a woodworking household. He also has a strong background in structural engineering. As a pool player, he was disappointed with the quality of many cues and decided to try his hand at cuemaking. He started doing repairs to learn how different cues were made. He cut apart as many cues as he could and repaired broken cues to see internal construction. He learned his favorite methods of making all of the different cue components so that he could incorporate them into his own cues. Scott had been on the road with a friend of Frank Stellman, maker of Sailor Cues. He talked to Sailor on the phone and got many tips about making good cues including what type of lathe to use. Whisler Custom Cues began business in 1992 in Tucson, Arizona. In 1997, the business was relocated to Mesa, Arizona.

Today Scott and his wife, Christine, live in Mesa, Arizona, where Scott still pursues a love of skydiving part time, with 3000 jumps to his credit. Skydiving was his full-time profession when

Christine and Scott Whisler

WHISLER CUSTOM CUES, cont.

he was starting to make cues. Christine helps with designs, glues veneers, does repairs and wraps, handles the paperwork, and manages their website. They like to make one-of-a-kind custom cues designed by customers. All work is done by hand on machinery that Scott has made. He does not use CNC. Whisler cues are built with methods of construction where all parts are threaded with glue releases. When filled with glue and tightened, the result is completely solid interiors, with no airspace, for playability, quality, and durability.

Scott makes a few full-splice cues with veneers, but their production is limited due to the amount of hours required. He can also make full-splice hustler cues from scratch, although most Whisler hustler cues are cut down from one-piece cues. Whisler cues are signed with the year of completion in dark ink somewhere on the lighter woods. Cues made in the first couple of years were signed with the month, date, and year.

Whisler cues are guaranteed for the original owner against construction defects that are not the result of warpage or abuse. If you are interested in talking to Scott Whisler about a new cue or cue that needs to be repaired, you can contact him at Whisler Custom Cues, listed in the Trademark Index.

SPECIFICATIONS

Butt material: hardwoods
Shaft material: rock maple
Standard length: 58 in.
Lengths available: 57 to 59 in.
Standard finish: proprietary
Standard balance point: 17 in. from butt
Standard butt cap: phenolic
Standard wrap: Irish linen
Point construction: short splice
Standard joint: phenolic
Joint type: flat-faced
Joint screw: 3/8-10
Standard number of shafts: one
Standard taper: straight
Standard ferrules: melamine
Tip widths available: 12 to 14 mm
Standard tip: Le Pro
Standard tip width: 13 mm
Standard bumper: custom built
Annual production: 65 cues

OPTIONS (FOR NEW CUES ONLY)

Special length: $40
Ivory butt cap: $200
Ivory joint: $125
Ivory ferrule: $75
Joint protectors: $25+
Extra shaft: $110

REPAIRS

Repairs done on all fine cues.
Refinish (with Irish linen wrap): $150
Rewrap (Irish linen): $50
Clean abd press linen wrap: $15
Replace shaft: $110+
Replace ivory ferrule: $75
Replace butt cap: $40+
Replace ivory butt cap: $200+
Replace tip: $15+
Replace layered tip: $25+
Replace fiber/linen ferrule: $35

CURRENT WHISLER CUES

Two-piece Whisler bar cues start at $125. Basic Whisler cues with wraps and joint rings start at $350. Whisler cues with points start at $450. One-of-a-kind custom Whisler cues start at $650. Whisler cues over $1,000 come with two shafts. Custom Whisler cues can usually be completed in less than six months, depending on intricacy and backlog.

SECONDARY MARKET MINIMUM VALUES

The following are minimum values for other Whisler cues encountered on the secondary market. These prices are representative of cues utilizing basic materials and designs that are not necessarily available at present. Scott and Christine have offered one-of-a-kind cues that can command many times these prices due to the use of exotic materials and artistry.

Special construction note: There are many materials and construction techniques that can add value to Whisler cues.

For all used Whisler cues, except where otherwise noted:

GRADING	98%	90%	70%

Add $95 for each additional original straight playable shaft beyond one.
Deduct $110 for missing original straight playable shaft.
Add $60 each for ivory ferrules.
Deduct 20% for obvious or improper refinish.

	98%	90%	70%
Level 1 - Hustler.			
Level 1 cues start at	$125	$95	$60
Level 2 - 0 points, 0-25 inlays.			
Level 2 cues start at	$325	$250	$155
Level 3 - 2-6 points, 0-8 inlays.			
Level 3 cues start at	$425	$325	$205
Level 4 - 4-10 points, 9-25 inlays.			
Level 4 cues start at	$600	$450	$285
Level 5 - 0-12 points, 26-50 inlays.			
Level 5 cues start at	$950	$725	$455
Level 6 - 0-12 points, 51-75 inlays.			
Level 6 cues start at	$1,400	$1,050	$650

CHRIS WHITAKER

Maker of Chris' Cues. For information, refer to Chris' Cues.

JAMES WHITE CUSTOM CUES

Maker of pool cues from 2000 to present in Pittsburgh, Pennsylvania.

James White knew Paul Mottey from playing pool in the Pittsburgh area. Jim ordered a cue from Paul in the late 1980s. When the cue was taking longer to complete than Jim had hoped, Paul invited him into the shop so he could see how time consuming cuemaking is. Jim was always interested in making cues so he started helping Paul in the shop part time in January of 1992. He started off finishing cues and slowly learned all of the steps necessary to make a pool cue. Jim worked on and off, part time and full time, until 1999 when he bought 49% of Mottey Cues.

Today Jim makes his own cues alongside Paul in their shop in Pittsburgh. He enjoys making one-of-a-kind custom cues designed by customers. Jim makes everything in his cues except for the tips, screws, and bumpers. He tries to make cues with a stiffer hit. Jim has either signed his cues with the month and year since he began or his initials "JMW" will appear on the cue. He hopes to continue the business if or when Paul retires.

Paul and Jim hope to move their shop to "Breakers," the pool room they opened together as equal partners in 2003. It is about a mile from their current shop.

James White cues are guaranteed against manufacturing defects that are not the result of warpage or abuse to the original owner.

If you are interested in talking to James White about a new cue or cue that needs to be repaired, you can contact him at James White Cues, listed in the Trademark Index.

SPECIFICATIONS

Butt material: hardwoods
Shaft material: rock maple
Standard length: 58 in.
Lengths available: any up to 60 in.
Standard finish: automotive clear coat
Balance point: 1 1/2 in. above wrap
Standard wrap: Irish linen
Point construction: any
Standard joint: stainless steel or phenolic
Joint type: piloted or flat
Joint screw: 5/16-14, 3/8-10, 5/16-18, or radial pin
Standard number of shafts: two
Standard taper: custom
Standard ferrules: ivory
Tip widths available: any up to 14 mm
Standard tip: Le Pro or WB
Annual production: fewer than 30 cues

OPTIONS (FOR NEW CUES ONLY)

Special length: no charge
Leather wrap: $100
Lizard wrap: $250
Ivory butt cap: $450+

GRADING	98%	90%	70%

Ivory joint: $250
Black Delrin joint protectors: standard
Extra shaft: $160+

REPAIRS

Repairs done on James White cues or Mottey cues.
- Refinish (with Irish linen wrap): $150
- Refinish (with leather wrap): $175
- Rewrap (Irish linen): $50
- Rewrap (leather): $100
- Replace shaft: $175+
- Replace Le Pro tip: $10
- Replace ivory ferrule: $75

CURRENT JAMES WHITE CUES

The current delivery time for a James White Custom Cue is 8 to 12 months depending on the intricacy of the design.

SECONDARY MARKET MINIMUM VALUES

The following are minimum values for other James White cues encountered on the secondary market. These prices are representative of cues utilizing basic materials and designs that are not necessarily available at present. James White has offered one-of-a-kind cues that can command many times these prices due to the use of exotic materials and artistry.

Special construction note: There are many materials and construction techniques that can add value to James White cues. For all used James White cues, except where otherwise noted:
- Add $150 for each additional original straight playable shaft beyond two.
- Deduct $160 for missing original straight playable shaft under two.
- Deduct $75 each for non-ivory ferrules.
- Add $75 for leather wrap.
- Deduct 20% for obvious or improper refinish.

	98%	90%	70%
Level 2 - 0 points, 0-25 inlays.			
Level 2 cues start at	$700	$540	$365
Level 3 - 2-6 points, 0-8 inlays.			
Level 3 cues start at	$1,100	$850	$575
Level 4 - 4-10 points, 9-25 inlays.			
Level 4 cues start at	$1,300	$915	$685
Level 5 - 0-12 points, 26-50 inlays.			
Level 5 cues start at	$1,500	$1,175	$795
Level 6 - 0-12 points, 51-75 inlays.			
Level 6 cues start at	$1,800	$1,450	$1,000

WHITEY CUES

Name given to two-piece hustler cues made by James Spach from 1980 to 1983 in Mount Pleasant, South Carolina. For more information, refer to Hurricane Cue Co.

If you have a Whitey cue that needs further identification or repair, contact Hurricane Cue Co., listed in the trademark index.

DAVID WHITSELL

Maker of Cues by David. For information, refer to Cues by David.

CHARLES WILHITE

Maker of Rhino Cues. For information, refer to Rhino.

WILLEE CUES

Maker of pool cues from late 2000 to present in Corpus Christi, Texas.

William Lee has been building cues for almost five years. It started because of an interest in the skill required to make a good cue. He also had an appreciation for the craftsmanship involved. He wanted to make cues out of different materials than what are usually available. His acrylic cues are a good example of that.

William strives for perfection, but admits that it is hard to achieve it. He hopes to offer a high quality cue at a value price. He appreciates that his cues will be around longer than he will be.

William also makes some very unique pens. He uses the same kinds of materials in his pens that he uses in his cues. His small shop is equipped with a number of machines designed for special purposes.

William builds less than 30 cues per year, but each one is made one at a time. His first cues had a thick "W" engraved in the butt. Since 2003, he has been engraving the name "WilleeCue" on each one.

GRADING	98%	90%	70%

WilleeCues are warrantied for the life of the cue or the cuemaker. If it can be repaired; there is no charge for repair.

If you are interested in talking to Will about a new cue or cue that needs to be repaired, you can contact him at Willee Cues, listed in the Trademark Index.

SPECIFICATIONS

Butt material: hardwoods
Shaft material: maple or ash
Standard length: 59 in.
Standard wrap: linen
Standard ferrules: LBM
Standard tip: Triangle med.
Annual production: fewer than 30 cues

OPTIONS (FOR NEW CUES ONLY)

Ivory ferrule: $50
Leather wrap: $100
Extra shaft: $80

REPAIRS

Repairs done on all fine cues.
Refinish with Irish Linen Wrap: $140
Rewrap with Irish Linen: $40
Replace shaft: $80+
Replace tip: $15

CURRENT WILLEE CUES:

Basic two-piece Willee bar cues start at about $200. A Willee cue with wrap and joint rings starts at $250. A basic Willee cues with points starts at $300. One-of-a-kind custom Willee cues start at $300.

SECONDARY MARKET MINIMUM VALUES

The following are minimum values for Willee cues encountered on the secondary market. These prices are representative of cues utilizing basic materials and designs that are not necessarily available at present. William Lee has offered one-of-a-kind cues that can command many times these prices due to the use of exotic materials and artistry.

Special construction note: There are many materials and construction techniques that can add value to Willee cues.

For all used Willee cues, except where otherwise noted:
- Add $65 for each additional original straight playable shaft beyond one.
- Deduct $80 for missing original straight playable shaft.
- Add $50 each for ivory ferrules.
- Add $75 for leather wrap.
- Deduct 20% for obvious or improper refinish.

Level 1 - Hustler.

	98%	90%	70%
Level 1 cues start at	$150	$120	$80

Level 2 - 0 points, 0-25 inlays.

Level 2 cues start at	$200	$160	$115

Level 3 - 2-6 points, 0-8 inlays.

Level 3 cues start at	$250	$200	$135

Level 4 - 4-10 points, 9-25 inlays.

Level 4 cues start at	$325	$265	$175

Level 5 - 0-12 points, 26-50 inlays.

Level 5 cues start at	$500	$395	$275

WOODWORTH CUES

Maker of pool cues from 1994 to 2003 in San Antonio, Texas, and from 2003 to present in Dickson, Tennessee.

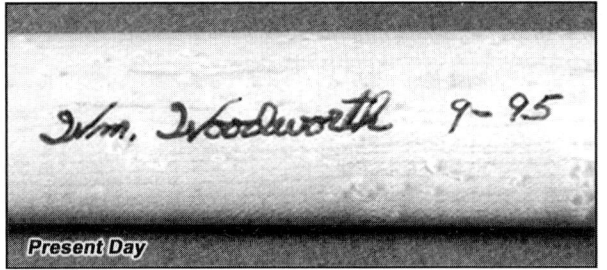

The idea of making cues first occurred to William "Woody" Woodworth in the mid-1980s, but it wasn't until 1994 that he put the lathe to his first cue stick. He was fulfilling a promise he'd made to the 1991 BCA National Team eight-ball champions, of which he was a member. The promise was to make cues for each of the players. None expected the souvenir cues to be replacements for their far more expensive cues until Bill Ryan, the first team member to try a Woodworth Cue, thought the cue was perfectly balanced, feeling as though it didn't have any weight variance. In explaining this feeling, Woody said that he tries to create a fulcrum-like effect when constructing a cue; the balancing weight is put forward of the hand on the butt of the cue, just as it is in a golf club.

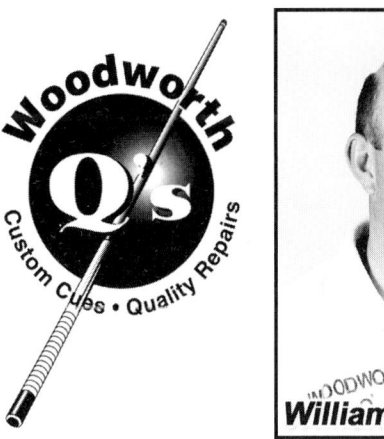

Born in Lackawanna, New York, Woody migrated to the warmer climate in Texas in the mid-1970s, bringing with him over 20 years of experience as a custom furniture maker, three years as a draftsman and two years as a design engineer with a Fortune 500 company. All of this experience has helped him become an accomplished cuemaker, but his love for the game of pool and considerable talent as a player were the catalysts that have earned Woody the most respect.

After 26 years in Texas, Woody moved to Tennesee in 2003. He wanted to be more centrally located for tournaments and shows. It seemed to him that it took at least a day and a half to drive to his favorite events from Texas. Working from his new shop that he built outside Dickson, amidst the drone of country music from his portable radio, you'll find Woody fine-tuning a cue in the main working area or in a separate climate-controlled room. Surrounding him are an arsenal of over one thousand shafts hanging from the ceiling going through the eighteen-month-long curing process and a display of exotic woods from around the world that will be used in several year's worth of future custom cues.

Like all cuemakers, Woody wants to make the perfect cue, but even more important to him are his satisfied customers. What started as a part-time hobby has mushroomed into a full-fledged business. On March 17 2005, Woody started engraving his logo, along with the month and year of production, into the butt caps of his cues.

If you are interested in talking to Woody about a new cue or cue that needs to be repaired, or if you just want to talk shop with him, you can contact him at Woodworth Cues, listed in the Trademark Index.

SPECIFICATIONS

Butt material: hardwoods
Shaft material: rock maple
Standard length: 58 in.
Lengths available: any
Standard finish: UV
Balance point: 2 1/2 to 2 3/4 in. above wrap
Standard butt cap: linen phenolic
Standard wrap: Irish linen
Point construction: short splice
Standard joint: linen phenolic
Joint type: flat faced
Joint screw: radial pin
Standard number of shafts: one
Standard taper: custom
Standard ferrules: melamine
Tip widths available: 12 to 14 mm
Standard tip: Le Pro
Annual production: fewer than 100 cues

OPTIONS (FOR NEW CUES ONLY)

Special length: no charge
Ivory ferrule: $100
Ivory butt cap: $300
Ivory joint: $250
Joint protectors: $20+
Extra shaft: $100

| GRADING | 100% | 95% | 70% |

REPAIRS

Repairs done on all fine cues.
  Refinish (with Irish linen wrap): $100
  Refinish (with leather wrap): $175
  Rewrap (Irish linen): $40
  Rewrap (leather): $80
  Replace butt cap: $35
  Replace Le Pro tip: $10
  Replace melamine ferrule: $30

CURRENT WOODWORTH CUES

Two-piece Woodworth bar cues start at $300. Basic Woodworth cues with wraps and joint rings start at $400. Woodworth cues with points start at $500. One-of-a-kind custom Woodworth cues start at $800. Woodworth Cues over $700.00 come with two shafts. The current delivery time for a Woodworth cue is four to five months.

CURRENT EXAMPLES

The following cues are currently available from Woodworth Cues. They can be ordered as shown, or modified to suit the desires of the customer.

Level 2 - Bird's-eye maple forearm with a purpleheart checked ring at bottom, one-piece bird's-eye handle and butt sleeve.

| MSR | $300 | $275-335 | $215 | $145 |

Level 2 - Bird's-eye maple forearm, cherry wood butt sleeve with four maple windows.

| MSR | $450 | $425-475 | $325 | $200 |

Level 3 - Curly maple forearm with a red veneer ring set in Ivorine-3 rings at bottom, three wenge points with single-colored veneers, wenge butt sleeve with red veneer rings set in Ivorine-3 rings at top and bottom.

| MSR | $500 | $450-535 | $355 | $245 |

Level 3 - Cherrywood forearm with a checked ring at bottom, four bird's-eye maple points with two colored veneers, cherry wood butt sleeve with four bird's-eye maple inlays between checked rings at top and bottom.

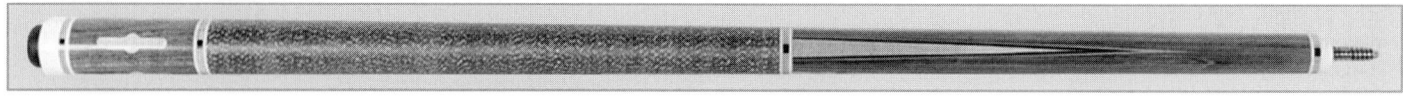

| MSR | $700 | $650-725 | $500 | $315 |

Level 3 - Bird's-eye maple forearm with a checked ring at bottom, five purpleheart points, bird's-eye maple butt sleeve with purpleheart columns between checked rings at top and bottom.

| MSR | $800 | $750-875 | $560 | $345 |

Level 3 - Bird's-eye maple forearm, three long moradilla points with single-colored veneers alternating with three short bubinga points, a butt sleeve of seventeen checked rings arranged in an Aztec design.

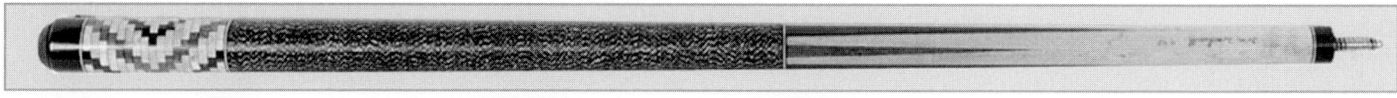

| MSR | $800 | $750-850 | $600 | $385 |

GRADING	100%	95%	70%

Level 3 - Curly maple forearm with a nickel silver ring at bottom, four long paduak points with single-colored veneers alternating with four short ebony points, leather wrap, curly maple butt sleeve with four paduak point-shaped inlays coming down from top alternating with four ebony point-shaped inlays coming up from bottom between nickel silver rings at top and bottom.

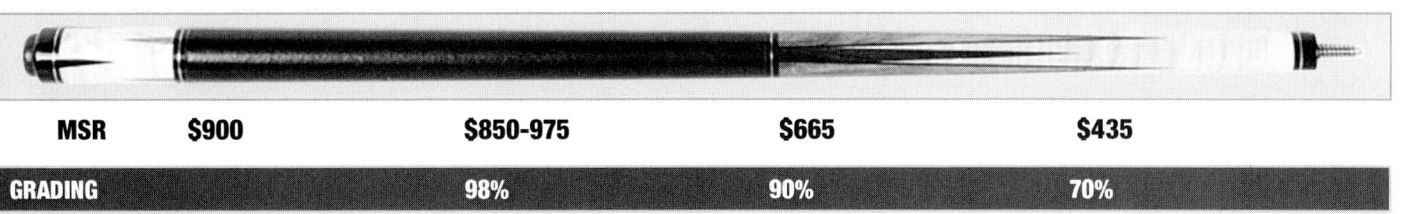

MSR	$900	$850-975	$665	$435

GRADING	98%	90%	70%

SECONDARY MARKET MINIMUM VALUES

The following are minimum values for other Woodworth cues encountered on the secondary market. These prices are representative of cues utilizing basic materials and designs that are not necessarily available at present. Woody has offered one-of-a-kind cues that can command many times these prices due to the use of exotic materials and artistry.

Special construction note: There are many materials and construction techniques that can add value to Woodworth cues. For all used Woodworth cues, except where otherwise noted:
- Add $80 for each additional original straight playable shaft beyond two.
- Deduct $100 for missing original straight playable shaft.
- Add $80 each for ivory ferrules.
- Add $65 for leather wrap.
- Deduct 15% for obvious or improper refinish.

Level 2 - 0 points, 0-25 inlays.
Level 2 cues start at	$300	$240	$170

Level 3 - 2-6 points, 0-8 inlays.
Level 3 cues start at	$500	$385	$260

Level 4 - 4-10 points, 9-25 inlays.
Level 4 cues start at	$650	$500	$335

Level 5 - 0-12 points, 26-50 inlays.
Level 5 cues start at	$1,400	$1,070	$725

Level 6 - 0-12 points, 51-75 inlays.
Level 6 cues start at	$2,000	$1,575	$1,050

HAROLD WORST

Pool cue made by A.E. Schmidt Co. and endorsed by Harold Worst of Grand Rapids, Michigan.

Harold Worst was a champion three-cushion billiards player many years ago. A.E. Schmidt made a Harold Worst signature series cue with his signature engraved on the forearm. These were simple cues with no points or inlays, just some turned rings on the forearm and butt sleeve.

If you have a Harold Worst cue that needs further identification or repair, contact Rubino Cues, listed in the Trademark Index.

SPECIFICATIONS

Butt material: hardwood
Shaft material: rock maple

SECONDARY MARKET MINIMUM VALUES

The following are minimum values for Harold Worst cues encountered on the secondary market.
For all used Harold Worst cues:
- Add $100 for each additional original straight playable shaft beyond one.
- Deduct 50% for missing original straight playable shaft.
- Add $50 each for ivory ferrules.
- Deduct 30% for obvious or improper refinish.

Level 2 - 0 points, 0-25 inlays.
Level 2 cues start at	$400	$300	$185

NOTES

Y SECTION

YAK CUES

Maker of pool cues from 1999 to present in Oklahoma City, Oklahoma.

Dan Goble began building cues in 1999 because of a desire to improve his game of pool with more technical equipment. He spends time in his one-man shop working on research and development. He strives to build a cue with great playability. Yak cues are easily identifiable by the "YAK" signature that appears on Dan's cues.

Yak cues are guaranteed to be replaced if there are problems with manufacturing. If you are interested in talking to Dan Goble about a new cue or cue that needs to be repaired, you can contact him at Yak Cues, listed in the Trademark Index.

SPECIFICATIONS

Butt material: various hardwoods
Shaft material: various
Standard length: 58 in.
Standard wrap: all
Standard number of shafts: one
Standard ferrules: various
Standard tip: various
Annual production: 20 cues

OPTIONS (FOR NEW CUES ONLY)

Ivory ferrule: $85
Leather wrap: $125
Extra shaft: $125

REPAIRS

Repairs done on all fine cues.
Rewrap (Irish linen): $45
Replace shaft: $125
Replace tip: $15+

CURRENT YAK CUES

Two-piece Yak bar cues start at $125. Basic Yak cues with wraps and joint rings start at $250. Yak cues with points start at $400. One-of-a-kind custom Yak cues start at $800. The current delivery time for a Yak cue is about six weeks.

GRADING	98%	90%	70%

SECONDARY MARKET MINIMUM VALUES

The following are minimum values for Yak cues encountered on the secondary market. These prices are representative of cues utilizing basic materials and designs that are not necessarily available at present. Dan has offered one-of-a-kind cues that can command many times these prices due to the use of exotic materials and artistry.

Special construction note: There are many materials and construction techniques that can add value to Yak cues.

For all used Yak cues, except where otherwise noted:
Add $95 for each additional original straight playable shaft beyond one.
Deduct $125 for missing original straight playable shaft.
Add $65 each for ivory ferrules.
Add $85 for leather wrap.
Deduct 15% for obvious or improper refinish.

	98%	90%	70%
Level 1 - Hustler.			
Level 1 cues start at	$100	$80	$55
Level 2 - 0 points, 0-25 inlays.			
Level 2 cues start at	$225	$175	$120
Level 3 - 2-6 points, 0-8 inlays.			
Level 3 cues start at	$350	$275	$185
Level 4 - 4-10 points, 9-25 inlays.			
Level 4 cues start at	$500	$390	$270
Level 5 - 0-12 points, 26-50 inlays.			
Level 5 cues start at	$750	$580	$395

ED YOUNG CUSTOM CUES

Maker of pool cues from 1993 to present in Chicago, Illinois.

Ed Young loved the game of pool since his first experience with it. He enjoyed the action and the environment in the pool rooms, and was fascinated by seeing different cues. By the early 1990s, Ed was buying and selling collectible cues. He became friends with some of the top Chicago area cuemakers, from whom he was buying cues. Ed purchased many cues from Chicago area cuemaker Craig Petersen, and spent a fair amount of time at his shop. After Craig passed away Ed helped Craig's mother sort out his shop. He was fascinated with the work Craig was able to do with such a small shop, which was not much more than a band saw and a lathe.

Another master cuemaker that impressed Ed was Burton Spain. Ed could not believe the complexity of Burton's machinery, especially the machine he had for cutting and tapering shafts. David Kersenbrock told Ed that he had designed a shaft machine in the 1970s that was capable of producing high quality shafts. He also told Ed that he would show him how to make such a machine, and show him how to make cues as well. This was an offer that was too good to turn down.

Although David was still working for Omega, he started living on the weekends in Chicago with Ed and his girlfriend. David would teach Ed the art of cuemaking during his free time and on the weekends when he was in living Chicago. Ed wanted to learn more than basic cuemaking. He wanted to learn everything about cuemaking, from the techniques David used to make his own linen ferrule and joint material to building his own machines and fixtures. Ed opened his shop in 1993, and David helped him make some of the custom machinery. Ed has since learned almost everything he knows about cuemaking from David and Craig Petersen. When Omega closed in 1996, David started working with Ed full time, teaching him advanced techniques, showing him various techniques used by other cuemakers, and making cues of his own. Today, their cues for the most part are built separately from beginning to end. The rough work is shared between the two.

Ed's early cues showed some experimentation with different construction techniques and specifications used by other cuemakers. Ed experimented with radial pins, 3/8-10 pins, Uni-Loc, stainless steel joints with 5/16-14 and 18 screws, threaded wooden dowels, and every other possible joint very early on. He used these on several of his earliest cues. Today Ed strongly prefers the 3/8-11 Kersenbrock joint screw that David designed and made so popular. He and David make the joint screws themselves out of brass, stainless steel, aluminum alloy, or titanium; depending on the desired weight of the cue. David and Ed personally hand select all of the wood they use during the many trips a year they make to purchase materials. There are no shortcuts taken, shafts are cut up to 18 times over a three-year period to insure proper drying, seasoning, and stability to prevent warpage. It is only after this long processing period that materials are selected and used in actual cue construction.

From 1993 to 1998, very few cues had identification marks. The few that were marked were all made for a few Asian customers. Some cues have Ed's initials, the customer's name, and date under the bumper. Ed is now working on a logo to put on every cue he makes. To those who know, Ed's cues are identifiable from the distinctive faceted silver rings that he likes to use, though not all of his cues have these rings. He rarely does inlay work but when he does the inlays are usually hand cut. Ed usually prefers to use old school techniques for inlay work even though he has a pantograph. To date many of his cues are plain, six-, nine-, and twelve-point examples made for playability. He believes his customers appreciate the use of extreamly high-figured woods where the natural beauty of the materials are not overpowered by too many randomly cut inlays and shapes. Ed does not believe a cue has to have hundreds of thoughtless inlays to be fancy or pleasing to the critical eye.

Ed Young Custom Cues are guaranteed for life against manufacturing defects that are not the result of warpage or abuse. If you have an Ed Young cue that needs further identification or repair, or would like to order a new Ed Young cue, contact Ed Young Custom Cues, listed in the trademark index.

SPECIFICATIONS

Butt material: hardwoods
Haft material: rock maple
Standard length: 58 in.
Lengths available: any
Standard finish: part catalyzed urethane
Balance point: 18 in. from butt
Standard butt cap: linen phenolic
Standard wrap: Irish linen
Point construction: short splice
Standard joint: phenolic
Joint screw: 3/8-11 Kersenbrock
Joint type: flat faced
Standard number of shafts: two
Standard taper: Kersenbrock
Standard ferrules: linen
Annual production: fewer than 100 cues

OPTIONS (FOR NEW CUES ONLY)

Leather wrap: $200
Special length: $75
Ivory butt cap: $250+
Ivory joint: $150+
Ivory ferrule: $75
Layered tip: $25+
Ivory points: POR
Ivory handle: POR
Ivory butt sleeve: POR
Custom joint protectors: $100+
Extra shaft: $150+

GRADING	98%	90%	70%

REPAIRS

Repairs done on most fine cues.
- Refinish (with linen wrap): $250+ depending on condition.
- Refinish (with leather wrap): $450+
- Clean and press linen wrap: $25
- Rewrap (Irish linen): $50
- Rewrap (leather): $200
- Replace butt cap: $50+
- Replace shaft: $150+
- Replace linen/fiber ferrule: $45+
- Replace ivory ferrule: $75+
- Replace tip: $15+

CURRENT ED YOUNG CUES

The current delivery time for an Ed Young custom cue is 24 to 48 months.

PAST EXAMPLES

Level 1 - Curly maple butt in one section. Rings are fancy faceted silver stitched. Joint and butt cap are white linen phenolic.

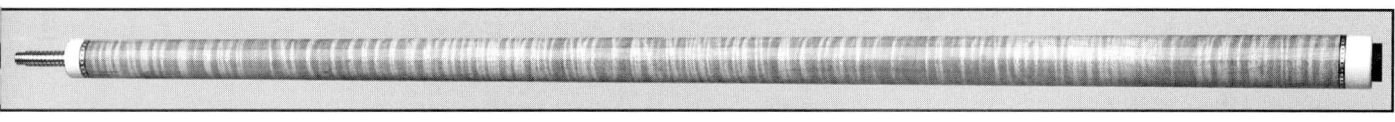

MSR (2003) $750	$1,000	$910	$600

Level 4 - Ebony forearm with short spliced points, high and low, of figured burl wood with white veneers. Inside each point are inlaid ivory diamonds. Wrap is Irish linen. Butt sleeve features large framed windows of burl wood in ebony, and ivory diamonds. Rings are fancy faceted silver stitched. Joint and butt cap are white linen phenolic.

MSR (2004) $1,750	$2,200	$1,900	$1,400

SECONDARY MARKET MINIMUM VALUES

The following are minimum values for Ed Young custom cues encountered on the secondary market. These prices are representative of cues utilizing basic materials and designs that are not currently available. One-of-a-kind cues start at $5000 and can command many times these prices due to the use of exotic materials and artistry.

Special construction note: There are many materials and construction techniques that can add value to Ed Young cues. The following are the most important examples:
- Add $250+ for each ivory point.
- Add $200+ for ivory joint.

For all used Ed Young cues, except where otherwise noted:
- Add $150 for each additional original straight playable shaft beyond two.
- Deduct $150 for each missing original straight playable shaft under two.
- Add $65 each for ivory ferrules.
- Add $125 for leather wrap.
- Deduct 25% for obvious or improper refinish.

Level 1 - 4 points, hustler.
Level 1 cues start at	$750	$700	$375

Level 2 - 0 points, 0-25 inlays.
Level 2 cues start at	$950	$875	$500

Level 3 - 2-6 points, 0-8 inlays.
Level 3 cues start at	$1,200	$1,100	$700

Level 4 - 4-10 points, 9-25 inlays.
Level 4 cues start at	$1,400	$1,300	$800

Level 5 - 0-12 points, 26-50 inlays.
Level 5 cues start at	$1,950	$1,800	$1,050

NOTES

Z SECTION

ZAC CUES

Maker of pool cues from 1996 to present in Sproat Lake, BC Canada.

Scott Zachow has been building cues in his one-man shop located on Sproat Lake, north of Port Alberni, BC since 1996. Dreaming about cue design since he picked up his first cue at the age of 16, Scott purchased his first lathe from a mail-order magazine. The lathe came with an instructional video which Scott watched over and over. For the first year he felt as if he were creating very expensive pieces of firewood. At the time, Scott's full time job was construction, and cuemaking was just a hobby. Self-taught in the fine art of cue design, Scott is now one of Canada's premiere custom cuemakers and has been able to make this his full-time profession. Originally serving only the local market on Vancouver Island, his cues have found their way into the hands of players throughout Canada, the United States and Asia.

Present Day

Scott Zachow

His backyard shop has expanded to include five lathes, milling machines, pantograph, a ventilated spray booth, and many other specialized tools, designed and built by Scott himself. Scott specializes in one-of-a-kind custom cues, which are truly handcrafted. All of the inlays are done with a manual pantograph and no CNC machines will be found in Scott's shop. Materials that are used in the construction include, but are not limited to, exotic hardwoods, ivory, stainless steel, and turquoise, to name just a few. Great pains are taken to create each masterpiece, but only the cues that meet Scott's high standards earn the Zac Cues label. He believes the hit, feel, and playability of the cue is the most important aspect. The craftsmanship and clinical construction techniques applied to every cue have been honed after years of real world experience and playing the game.

Zac cues are easily identifiable by his logo or signature. The standard logo on Scott's cues is "Zac" (the first three letters of Zachow). That logo has appeared on most Zac cues made since 1998. Scott will sign his cues instead if the customer requests.

If you have a Zac cue that needs further identification or repair, or would like to talk to Scott about a new Zac cue, contact Zac Cues listed in the Trademark Index.

SPECIFICATIONS

- Butt material: exotic hardwoods
- Shaft material: Canadian rock maple
- Standard length: 58 in.
- Lengths available: any up to 62 in.
- Standard finish: automotive clear
- Joint screw: 3/10
- Standard joint: phenolic
- Joint type: flat faced
- Balance point: 1 to 2 in. above wrap
- Point construction: short splice
- Standard wrap: Irish linen
- Standard butt cap: phenolic
- Standard number of shafts: two
- Standard taper: Zac taper
- Standard ferrules: Ivorine
- Standard tip: Le Pro
- Other tips available: laminate tips (Hercules, Stingray, Proline, Moray, H2)
- Standard tip width: 13 mm
- Tip widths available: any up to 14 mm
- Annual production: 30 to 40 cues

OPTIONS (FOR NEW CUES ONLY)

- Special length: no charge
- Ivory joint: $150
- Extra shaft: $100
- Ivory ferrule: $75
- Ivory butt cap: $225
- Leather wrap: $125
- Layered tip: $20+

REPAIRS

Repairs done on all fine cues.
- Refinish (with linen wrap): $150

882 ZAC CUES, cont.

GRADING	100%	95%	70%

Refinish (with leather wrap): $225
Rewrap (linen): $50
Rewrap (leather): $100
Clean and press linen wrap: $25
Restore leather wrap: $25
Replace shaft: $100
Replace ivory ferrule: $75
Replace tip: $15+
Replace fiber/linen/ ferrule: $35
Replace butt cap: $75
Replace ivory butt cap: $225
Replace layered tip: $20

CURRENT ZAC CUES

Two-piece Zac bar cues start at $275. Basic Zac cues with wraps and joint rings start at $400. Zac cues with points start at $550. One-of-a-kind custom Zac cues start at $1,200. The current delivery time for a Zac cue is approximately 10 to 12 weeks.

CURRENT EXAMPLES

The following Zac cues can be oedered as shown, modified to suit the desires of the customer, or new designs can be created.

Level 1 "Sneaky Pete Jump/Break" - Maple forearm, four full-spliced rosewood points and handle with a jump/break joint above handle, bird's-eye maple butt sleeve.

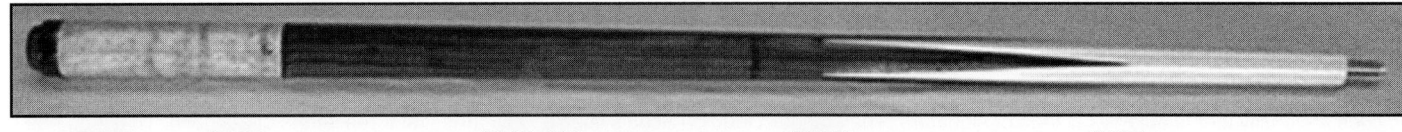

MSR	$275	$265-300	$235	$195

Level 3 - Tiger maple forearm, three long and three short rosewood points, rosewood butt sleeve with ebony within gold rings at bottom.

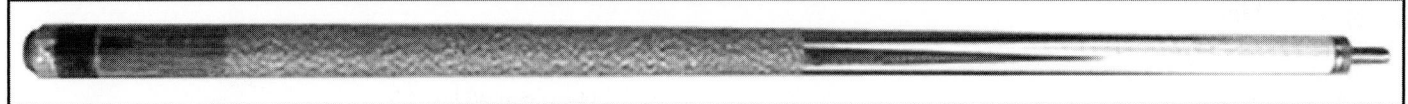

MSR	$500	$475-535	$375	$265

Level 3 - Ebony forearm with a bocote ring set in brass rings above wrap, six bocote points with maple veneers, bocote butt sleeve with a bocote ring set in brass rings below wrap above an ebony ring at bottom.

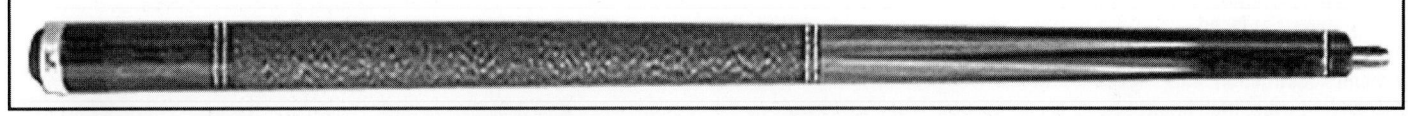

MSR	$700	$675-750	$545	$375

Level 3 - Rosewood forearm with an ebony ring set in brass rings above wrap, four long zebrawood points alternating with four short bird's-eye maple points, zebrawood butt sleeve with four zebrawood oval windows alternating with four bird's-eye maple oval windows between ebony rings set in brass rings at top and bottom.

MSR	$900	$850-1,000	$685	$500

Level 4 - Tiger maple forearm with maple and ebony checks set in silver rings above wrap, four long rosewood points with two veneers alternating with four short ebony points with two veneers, ebony butt sleeve with four sets of two ivory diamond-shaped inlays and two opposing ivory spear-shaped inlays below maple and ebony checks set in silver rings below wrap.

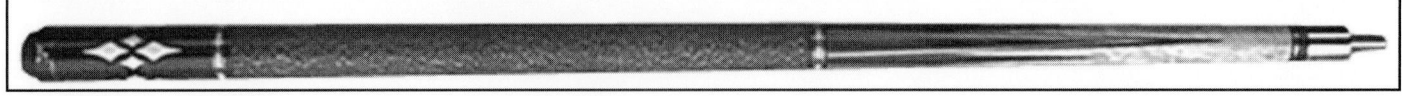

MSR	$1,200	$1,150-1,350	$925	$650

GRADING	100%	95%	70%

Level 3 - Rosewood forearm with maple and ebony checks set in silver rings above wrap, three long and three short ebony points with maple veneers and an ivory diamond-shaped inlay in each point, ebony butt sleeve with six ivory diamond-shaped inlays and twelve rosewood spear-shaped inlays within rings of ivory triangles below maple and ebony checks set in silver rings below wrap.

MSR	$2,200	$2,000-2,350	$1,645	$1,250
GRADING		98%	90%	70%

SECONDARY MARKET MINIMUM VALUES

The following are minimum prices for other Zac cues encountered on the secondary market. These prices are representative of cues utilizing basic materials and designs that may not be currently available. Scott also offers one-of-a-kind cues that can command many times these prices due to the use of exotic materials and artistry.

Special construction note: There are many materials and construction techniques that can add value to Zac cues.

For all used Zac cues:
Add $100+ for each additional original straight playable shaft (standard with one).
Deduct $150 for missing original straight playable shaft.
Deduct 25% for obvious or improper refinish.

Level 1 - 4 points, hustler.
Level 1 cues start at	$200	$165	$110

Level 2 - 0 points, 0-25 inlays.
Level 2 cues start at	$450	$350	$235

Level 3 - 2-6 points, 0-8 inlays.
Level 3 cues start at	$600	$470	$320

ZAR CUES

Maker of pool cues from 1995 to present in Jackson, Michigan.

Dave Czarnecki learned to play pool as a young boy in his grandfather's pool room. His grandfather told him of the stories about the great players of the past to heighten his interest. Dave tried to make his first cue when he was still a boy. As an adult, Dave became a printer, but he still wanted to make cues. In 1993 he started to learn cuemaking from Dennis Dieckman, who lives nearby. He still credits Dennis for teaching him the art, and tries to make every cue just the way Dennis taught him.

In the past, Dave worked two jobs and made cues part time, mainly as a hobby. In October of 2003 he retired from printing. Dave now has more time to spend on making fancier cues. Instead of making custom orders, Dave prefers to make cues of his own design and offer them for sale. He marks his cues with "Zar" logos on the butt caps, and they have their own unique look. Dave prefers to use wood handles on his cues, and refuses to use ivory at all. Most Zar cues utilize bird's-eye maple, ebony, and purpleheart. Dave bought a state-of-the-art CNC machine in 1997, and he is still working on mastering it. All Zar shafts are turned over a dozen times over the course of two years to prevent warpage and ensure optimum playability, which is Dave's primary concern.

Dave donates approximately three to four cues per year to charitable causes in the Jackson, Michigan area. He enjoys being able to use his hobby to benefit his community.

New Zar cues can be returned upon delivery if the customer is not satisfied. Zar cues are guaranteed for life against construction defects that are not the result of warpage or abuse to the original owner. If you have a Zar cue that needs further identification or repair, or would like to talk to Dave about ordering a new Zar cue, contact Zar Cues, listed in the trademark index.

SPECIFICATIONS

Butt material: hardwoods
Shaft material: rock maple
Standard length: 58 in.
Lengths available: any
Standard finish: polyurethane
Joint screw: 3/8-10
Standard joint: stainless steel
Joint type: flat faced
Balance point: varies
Point construction: short splice
Standard wrap: Irish linen

GRADING	98%	90%	70%

Standard butt cap: linen phenolic
Standard number of shafts: one
Standard taper: custom
Standard ferrules: Ivorine-3
Standard tip: Triangle
Tip widths available: any
Annual production: fewer than 15 cues

OPTIONS (FOR NEW CUES ONLY)

Leather wrap: $100
Extra shaft: $100

REPAIRS

Repairs done on most fine cues.
Refinish: $75
Rewrap (linen): $75
Rewrap (leather): $110
Replace shaft: $100
Replace ferrule: $10+
Replace tip: $10+

CURRENT ZAR CUES

Basic two-piece Zar bar cues start at $100. Basic two-piece Zar cues with wraps and joint rings start at $200. Zar cues with points start at $300. The current delivery time for a Zar cue is approximately one year.

SECONDARY MARKET MINIMUM VALUES

The following are minimum prices for Zar cues encountered on the secondary market. These prices are representative of cues utilizing basic materials and designs that may not be currently available. Dave also offers one-of-a-kind cues that can command many times these prices due to the use of exotic materials and artistry.

Special construction note: There are many materials and construction techniques that can add value to Zar cues.

For all used Zar cues:
Add $60+ for each additional original straight playable shaft (standard with one).
Deduct $75 for missing original straight playable shaft.
Deduct 25% for obvious or improper refinish.

	98%	90%	70%
Level 1 - 4 points, hustler.			
Level 1 cues start at	$85	$70	$45
Level 2 - 0 points, 0-25 inlays.			
Level 2 cues start at	$225	$175	$120
Level 3 - 2-6 points, 0-8 inlays.			
Level 3 cues start at	$325	$265	$175

KERRY ZEILER

Maker of Zylr Cues. For information, refer to Zylr.

BOB ZIDE CUES

Maker of pool cues from 2001 to 2003 in Margate, Florida, and from 2003 to present in Pompano Beach, Florida.

Bob Zide learned about cues from his father, who did cue repair work in California. Bob later became interested in cuemaking after he had relocated to Florida. He bought equipment from Arnot Wadsworth and, after learning from Arnot, Bob started making cues in 2001. Bob's cues are traditional designs with block work and veneers, and no inlays as he does not have a pantograph or CNC machine. He has learned a lot from Dennis Searing, and he helps Dennis a couple of days a week.

Bob makes cues part time while working full time as a baker. He specializes in repair work and does many repairs. Bob Zide cues are not marked, but are recognizable to those who are familiar with his work.

Bob Zide cues are guaranteed for life against construction defects that are not the result of warpage or abuse to the original owner.

If you are interested in talking to Bob about a new cue or cue that needs to be repaired, you can contact him at Bob Zide Cues, listed in the Trademark Index.

Bob Zide

BOB ZIDE CUES, cont. 885

| GRADING | 98% | 90% | 70% |

SPECIFICATIONS
- Butt material: hardwoods
- Shaft material: rock maple
- Standard length: 58 in.
- Lengths available: any
- Standard finish: polyurethane
- Balance point: 19 in. from butt
- Standard butt cap: Delrin
- Standard wrap: Irish linen
- Point construction: short splice
- Standard joint: Ivorine 3
- Joint type: flat faced
- Joint screw: radial pin
- Standard number of shafts: one
- Standard ferrules: Ivorine 3
- Standard tip: Triangle
- Annual production: fewer than 20 cues

OPTIONS (FOR NEW CUES ONLY)
- Special length: no charge
- Ivory ferrule: $90
- Extra shaft: $125+

REPAIRS
Repairs done on all fine cues.
- Refinish (with Irish linen wrap): $140
- Refinish (with leather wrap): $200
- Rewrap (Irish linen): $45
- Rewrap (leather): $90
- Replace Triangle tip: $15
- Replace Ivorine 3 ferrule: $40

CURRENT BOB ZIDE CUES
Basic two-piece bar cues start at $200. Basic two-piece Bob Zide cues with wraps and joint rings start at $400. Cues with points start at $500. Bob Zide cues with veneered points start at $800. The current delivery time for a Bob Zide cue is about four to six months.

SECONDARY MARKET MINIMUM VALUES
The following are minimum values for Bob Zide cues encountered on the secondary market. These prices are representative of cues utilizing basic materials and designs that are not necessarily available at present. Bob has offered one-of-a-kind cues that can command many times these prices due to the use of exotic materials and artistry.

There are many materials and construction techniques that can add value to Bob Zide cues.

For all used Bob Zide cues, except where otherwise noted:
- Add $100 for each additional original straight playable shaft beyond one.
- Deduct $125 for missing original straight playable shaft.
- Add $70 each for ivory ferrules.
- Deduct 20% for obvious or improper refinish.

Level 1 - Hustler.

	98%	90%	70%
Level 1 cues start at	$185	$145	$95

Level 2 - 0 points, 0-25 inlays.

	98%	90%	70%
Level 2 cues start at	$350	$275	$185

Level 3 - 2-6 points, 0-8 inlays.

	98%	90%	70%
Level 3 cues start at	$450	$350	$235

ZYLR CUES

Maker of pool cues from 1982 to present in Santa Ana, California.

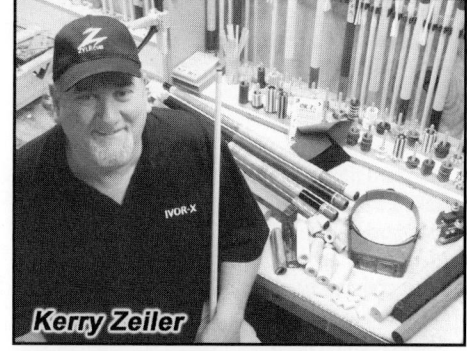
Kerry Zeiler

Kerry Zeiler was born in New Kensington, PA and lived there for thirteen years before moving to Orange County, CA where he still resides. He has been playing pool since the age of ten, has been a very avid and competitive player for 45 years, and has taught the game for 31 years. The progression to becoming a cuemaker was very natural for him.

Kerry has been a licensed radiologic technologist for 29 years. He has studied how to manufacture a well shooting and hitting cue from some of the best. His background in the medical field led him to become one of the first to x-ray the tooling mechanics and structure of cues manufactured by cuemakers such as Szamboti, Balabushka, Billy Stroud, Tad and Martin. Some of the cues he x-rayed were from more than fifty years ago and this collection of x-rays has opened many doors for Zeiler. The combined interest of Ron Sakahara and Roy Yamane, with the availability of their vast cue collections, was just the beginning of the work he has applied to his endless learning and knowledge of cue construction. Working with a large collection of exotic and custom cues, Kerry has been able to scrutinize many variables in the internal construction of a cue. He believes he has found the "why" of some cues hitting great and some not so great.

1997 to Present Day

Although he has inlaid cues in the past, he no longer does inlays, and he only puts rings right above the butt cap. Kerry believes that adding rings between the tip and the handle deadens the resonance of the cue, which negatively affects the hit. Kerry has tried different joints, including the Uni-Loc. Now he believes buckhorn-to-buckhorn joints play best, and he listens to the tones of his shafts to match them in pairs to his cues. Kerry says the quality of the wood used is the most important factor in building great playing cues. He strives to make two-piece cues that play like one-piece cues.

Zeiler has been building cues part time from 1982 to 1998, and full time from 1998 to present. His first exposure to custom cuemaking was by studying under the craftsmanship of the late Hank Korsiak, of "Corsair Cues" in Orange County, CA. In the past, he made a few "Black Beauty" tribute cues out of paper-based black phenolic blanks from Hank. He was also influenced by other well-known and respected cuemakers. Early cues with points were made from Verl Horn short spliced blanks. The unique quality and never-ending innovation Zeiler brings to cuemaking has resulted in a high quality cue with minimum deflection. Kerry's last name, having been misspelled and pronounced incorrectly more often that not, over the years, has led to Zylr Hand-Crafted Cues.

"Elegance through Simplicity," which translates to "the beauty of the woods is the beauty of the cue," has become the motto for Zylr cues. The selection of materials used in producing a soundly constructed cue includes a variety of hardwoods from all over the world. Kerry keeps an open mind and is constantly looking for new ways to develop the use of the natural appearance in the grain of different woods. As an environmentalist, and therefore a respecter of wildlife, Zeiler does not use ivory in his cues. Instead, buck horn, naturally shed yearly, from whitewall and mule deer, caribou, Indian stag and moose add a unique and natural appearance to the joint, butt cap, and rings. Kerry believes this material is superior to ivory since it is very dense and resilient, providing a distinctly solid hit. Kerry can bleach buck horn to look almost identical to ivory. He started using Ivor-X for ferrules in 2003 after a 23-year search for the perfect ivory ferrule replacement.

Since Zeiler is 60 inches tall, he has also become an expert in making a solid hitting well proportioned 60-inch cue, which has been difficult, if not impossible, to locate until now. His standard cue has buck horn joint rings and Ivor-X ferrules, and is available in a variety of exotic hardwoods for $1,050 retail with two matched shafts. These cues have no points or inlays. The only metal is the joint screw, and everything else is threaded on to wood tenons. The cues are weighted based on the woods used. Zylr cues are easily idenifiable by the "Z" lightning bolt logo on the butt cap that has appeared since 1997. Kerry keeps a record of original owner's cues in case a Zylr cue is stolen or needs to be identified.

Zylr cues are guaranteed for life against manufacturing defects that are not the result of warpage or abuse. If you have a Zylr cue that needs further identification or repair, or would like to order a new Zylr cue, contact Zylr Handcrafted Cues, listed in the trademark index.

SPECIFICATIONS

Butt material: hardwoods
Shaft material: rock maple
Standard length: 58 in.
Lengths available: 57 to 60 in.
Standard finish: Dupont Hyper Cure
Balance point: varies
Standard butt cap: Delrin
Standard wrap: Irish linen
Standard joint: buck horn
Joint screw: 3/8-11
Standard number of shafts: two
Standard taper: custom
Standard ferrules: Ivor-X
Standard tip width: 13 mm
Standard tip: Triangle
Annual production: fewer than 50 cues

ZYLR CUES, cont.

GRADING	100%	95%	70%

OPTIONS (FOR NEW CUES ONLY)
Special length: no charge
Leather wrap: $150
Wood handle: $100
Buck horn Butt Cap: $150
Extra shaft with Ivor-X ferrule and buckhorn joint: $175
Buck horn ferrule: $75

REPAIRS
Repairs done on most fine cues. Repair prices are for Zylr cues only.
Refinish: $200
Rewrap (Irish linen): $45
Replace ferrule (buck horn): $75
Replace butt cap (buck horn): $150
Replace joint (linen phenolic): $30
Replace joint (buck horn): $60
Replace shaft with Ivor-X ferrule: $150
Replace shaft with buck horn ferrule: $225

CURRENT ZYLR CUES
Basic two-piece Zylr hustler cues start at $450. Basic two-piece Zylr cues with wraps and joint rings start at $1,050. The current delivery time for a Zylr cue is two-and-a-half years.

CURRENT EXAMPLES

Level 2 - Buck horn joint, bocote forearm, bocote butt sleeve with buck horn dashes between silver rings at bottom.

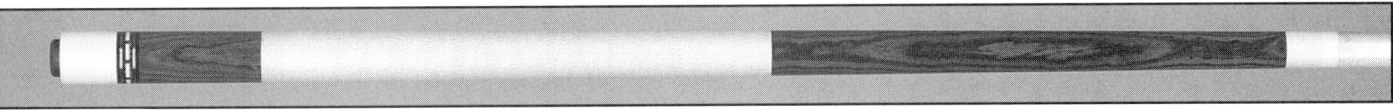

MSR	$1,050	$1,000-1,100	$775	$500

Level 2 - Buck horn joint, bird's-eye maple forearm, bird's-eye maple butt sleeve with cocobolo checks between silver rings at bottom.

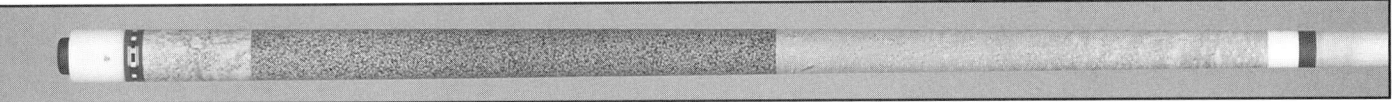

MSR	$1,050	$1,000-1,100	$775	$500

Level 2 - Mule deer joint, bird's-eye maple forearm, pigskin wrap, maple burl butt sleeve with maple burl ring between brass rings at bottom, moose antler butt cap.

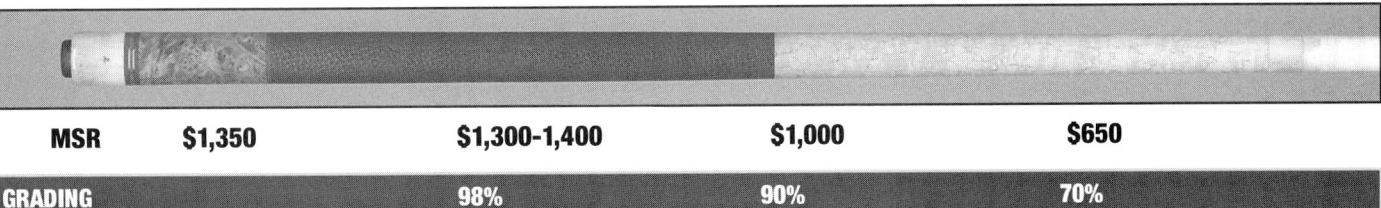

MSR	$1,350	$1,300-1,400	$1,000	$650

GRADING	98%	90%	70%

PAST EXAMPLES

Level 2 "Tribute to Hank Corsair" Buck horn joint, black phenolic forearm, stained fiddle back maple handle, black phenolic butt sleeve with buckhorn dashes between silver rings within buckhorn at bottom.

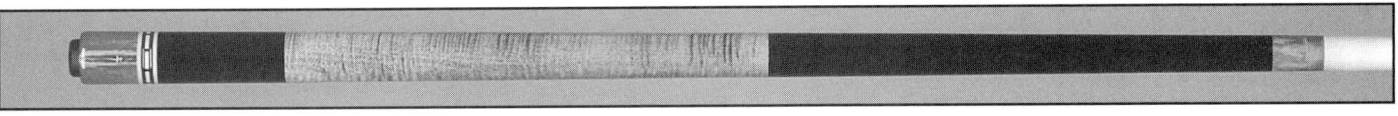

MSR (2003) $1,200	$1,750	$1,300	$800

GRADING	98%	90%	70%

Level 3 "Titlist" Buck horn joint, maple forearm, four full-spliced rosewood points with four colored veneers, rosewood handle and butt with buckhorn ring at bottom (originally sold with matching jump butt).

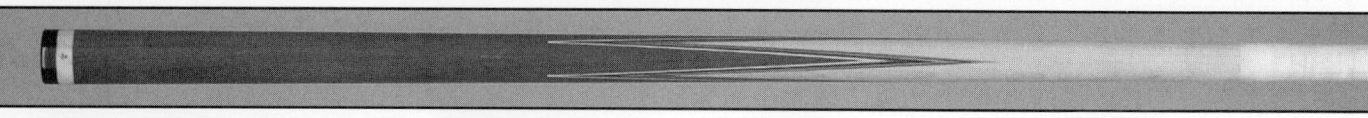

MSR (2003) $2,500	$3,000	$2,250	$1,450

SECONDARY MARKET MINIMUM VALUES

The following are minimum values for Zylr cues encountered on the secondary market. Zylr cues may be found in a variety of exotic hardwoods that can increase the value.

Special construction note: There are exotic materials that can add value to Zylr cues.

For all used cues, except where otherwise noted:
  Add $150 for each additional original straight playable shaft beyond two.
  Deduct $175 for each missing original straight playable shaft under two.
  Deduct 25% for obvious or improper refinish.

Level 1 - 4 points, hustler.
Level 1 cues start at	$400	$300	$195

Level 2 - 0 points, 0-25 inlays.
Level 2 cues start at	$800	$600	$375

Level 3 - 2-6 points, 0-8 inlays.
Level 3 cues start at	$900	$715	$500

TRADEMARK INDEX

ADVANCED ACCURACY CUES
Mr. Mark Wilson
8561 Prairietown Rd.
Dorsey, IL 62021
618-888-2333
618-346-0325
www.playgreatpool.com
mark@playgreatpool.com

AE CUES
Mr. Bruce Kuhn
Mr. Jeff Fugal 261-B Airport Blvd
Aurora, CO 80011
303-341-9202
Fax: 303-341-9337
www.aecues.com
aecues@aol.com

AKERS CUES
Mr. Bill Akers
PO Box 702
Mediapolis, IA 52637
319-394-3209
Fax: 319-394-3209
www.akerscues.com
akers_cues@yahoo.com

J. ALAN CUES
Mr. Jeff Smith
Jonesboro, AR 72404
870-802-4563
www.jalancues.com
jeff@jalancues.com

CHIP ALBERY CUES
Mr. Richard "Chip" Albery Jr.
9202 E. Emerald Drive
Sun Lakes, AZ 85248
623-570-3821
www.rvalbery.com
chip@rvalbery.com

ALDREN CUES
Mr. Jim Aldren
4600 Mill Road
Rapid City, SD 57702
605-787-6118
jaldren@rapidnet.com

ALLEN'S CUSTOM CUES
Mr. Gary Allen
14810 Kornblum Ave
Hawthorne, CA 90250
310-675-4005

AMOS CUES & REPAIRS
Mr. Richard Amos
1 S. 448 Monterey Ave
Oak Brook Terrace, IL 60181

A O CUSTOM CUES
Ms. Anne Mayes
9208 Rasmus Dr, Ste 1
Houston, TX 77063
832-251-0055
www.annieosproshop.com
ramayes@annieosproshop.com

AP CUES
Mr. Andrew Park
918 Honeywood Rd
Los Angeles, CA 90049
310-666-1411
apcues@hotmail.com

ARNOT Q'S CUSTOM CUE
Mr. Arnot Wadsworth
3717 Jeanne Ave
Lake Worth, FL 33461
561-439-0441
www.arnotq.com
www.terminator.com
arnot@arnotq.com

AUERBACH CUSTOM CUES
Mr. John Parker
4136-E S. 70th E. Ave
Tulsa, OK 74145
918-381-9364
www.auerbachcustomcues.com
ceebee@sbcglobal.net

AXIOM BILLIARD SUPPLIES, INC
David T. Miller
35235 US Hwy 19 North
Palm Harbor, FL 34684
727-773-1819
800-980 2837
Fax: 727-773-1917
www.axiombilliards.com
axiombilliards@aol.com

BAKER CUSTOM CUES
Mr. Buddy Baker
1311 Southwest 95th St
Oklahoma City, OK 73159
405-692-1604
405-590-3789
www.bakercustomcues.com
stickbkb2001@aol.com

BARENBRUGGE CUES
Mr. Dave Barenbrugge
PO Box 5591
Apache Junction, AZ 85278
480-213-5416
Fax: 480-982-1995
agentcue@earthlink.net

BARKLEY CUSTOM CUES
Mr. Jim Barkley
2520 West 20th St
Joplin, MO 64801
417-781-2532
www.barkleycustomcues.com
info@barkleycustomcues.com

BARNET CUES
Mr. Jerry Barnet
% Shooters
810 W Hwy 56
Olathe, KS 66061
913-780-5740

BARNHART CUES
Mr. Cory Barnhart
6731 Arden Nollville Rd
Martinsburg WV 25401
304-671-6811
corybarnhart@msn.com

BARRINGER CUES
Mr. Joe Barringer
joe@barringercues.com

BCM CUES
Mr. Bryan C. Mordt
17425 N 19th Ave #2102
Phoenix, AZ 85023
602-625-1042
www.bcmcue.com
bryanmordt@cox.net

MARK BEAR CUSTOM CUES
Mr. Mark Bear
2800 Princess Anne St.
Fredericksburg, VA 22401
540-424-0780
www.bearcues.com
bearcues@hotmail.com

BECKER CUSTOM CUES
Mr. Roland Becker
44050 Priddy Ave
Pierce, CO 80565
970-443-2777
970-493-5513

BELLA SERA CUSTOM CUES LLC
Mr. Wayne Anderson
Mr. Mike "Cosmo" Gray
178 Ardmore Street
PO Box 5172
Shreveport, LA 71105
318-868-6050
www.bellaseracues.com
info@bellaseracues.com
sales@bellaseracues.com

BENDER CUES
Mr. Michael Bender
Ms. Tracy Dunham
HC60 Box 3890
Delta Junction, AK
99737-9454
907-895-4725
bendercues@wildak.net

BENSON CUE
Mr. Richard Benson
PO Box 6563
Kennewick, WA 99336
509-586-7277
877-845-6740
www.bensoncues.com
bensoncue@juno.com

BLACK BOAR CUES
Mr. Anthony Scianella
Mr. Raymond Scianella
5110 College Ave
College Park, MD 20740
301-277-3236
Fax: 301-927-1847

BLACKCREEK CUSTOM CUES
Mr. Travis Niklich
407 S. Smith St.
Smithton, IL 62285
618-604-3158
niklich@yahoo.com

BLACK HAWK CUSTOM CUES INC.
Mr. Stan Hawkins
6700 Kimberly Dr
Black Hawk, SD 57718
605-787-7678
www.blackhawkcustomcues.com
hawkeye@rapidnet.com

BLACK HEART CUSTOM CUES
Mr. Jerry Eick
822 Schuyler St
Peru, IL 61354
815-223-8774
blkhrt4@insightbb.com

RICHARD BLACK CUSTOM CRAFTED CUES
Mr. Richard Black
PO Box 1886
Humble, TX 77347
281-852-5025
Fax: 281-852-7936
www.blackcues.com
Richard@blackcues.com

BLUDWORTH CUES
Mr. Leonard Bludworth
Mr. Donald Bludworth
PO Box 809
Leakey, TX 78873
830-232-5991
Cell: 830-796-1610 Leonard
Cell: 830-483-1018 Donald
Fax: 830-232-6181
www.bludworth.com
poolcues@hctc.net

BLUE GRASS CUES
Mr. Richard Harris
1025 Redkey Rd
Winchester, OH 45697
937-927-0025
www.poolcues.net
sales@poolcues.net

BOB'S CUES
Robert Parsons
589 Castlebury Dr
Saline MI 48176
rparson1@comcast.net
734-945-4425

BOURQUE CUES
Mr. Dan Bourque
9 Brompton St
Sanford, ME 04073
207-324-3889
www.bourques.com
cuemaker@psouth.net

BOURQUE CUSTOM MADE CUES
Mr. Douglas Bourque
4012 Venice Rd. Lot 100
Sandusky, OH 44870
419-626-9723
419-684-9499
www.dbcustomcues.com
db@dbcustomcues.com

BRADEN CUES
Mr. Brady Andresen
3000 Paseo Mercado #106
Oxnard, CA 93036-7960
805-981-1551
bradencues@dslextreme.com

BRELAND CUES
Mr. Dale Breland
17139 Phlox Drive
Fort Myers, FL 33908
239-633-3642
brelandcues@earthlink.net

BRICK CUE CO.
Mr. Alex Brick
326 Matterhorn Drive
Old Hickory, TN 37138
615-758-6557
615-868-4270 JOB Billiards
www.jobbilliards.com
alex@brickcues.com

BRUNSWICK BILLIARDS
Mr. John Stransky
8663 196th Ave
Bristol, WI 53014-0068
800-336-8764
Fax: 414-857-7489
www.brunswick-billiards.com
jstransky@brunblrds.com

BRYLES CUSTOM CUES
Mr. Joseph Bryles
6556 Delta Road
Delta, PA 17314

JIM BUSS CUSTOM CUES
Mr. Jim Buss
9319-A Midland Blvd
Overland, MO 63114
314-423-6122
www.jimbuss.com
jimbuss@jimbuss.com

CHRIS BYRNE CUSTOM CUES
Mr. Chris Byrne
3201 S. Bryant St
Englewood, CO 80110
720-206-4034

CADILLAC CUSTOM CUES
Mr. Joe Mazlewski
515 Ruxton Drive
Wilmington, DE 19809
302-762-1821

CAM CUSTOM CUES
Mr. Chad McLennan
1156 S. Douglas Blvd.
Midwest City, OK 73130
405-412-5350
www.camcustomcues.com
info@camcustomcues.com
sales@camcustomcues.com
billiardking@itlnet.net

CAMERON CUSTOM CUES
Mr. Barry Cameron
PO Box 19
Clinton, CT 06413
860-669-8498
www.cameroncues.com
barryc@cameroncues.com

PETE CAMPBELL CUES
Mr. Courtney Campell
56 Sheldon Rd.
Wrentham, MA 02093
508-384-2260
poolcue@att.net

CANTANDO CUSTOM CUES
Mr. Arthur W. Cantando
652 Moredon Rd.
Huntington Valley, PA 19006
215-947-2449
Fax: 215-947-4792
a.cantando@comcast.net

CAPONE CUSTOM CUES
Mr. Michael Capone Jr.
PO Box 886
Poolesville, MD 20837
301-349-2187
Fax: 301-349-2188
www.caponecues.com
mike@caponecues.com

CARMELI CUSTOM CUES
Mr. Ariel Carmeli
1136 E. 17th St.
Santa Ana, CA 92701
714-543-5700
www.accues.com
accues@aol.com

CARTER CUSTOM CUES
Mr. Chad Carter
515 Ford Av
Owensboro, KY 42301
270-689-9878
270-993-2005
ccarter@southcentralbank.net

CASANOVA CUSTOM CUES
Mr. Paul Casanova
4533 Brighton
Corona Del Mar, CA 92625
949-721-8947
www.casanovacues.com
paul@casanovacues.com

JOE CHILDS CUSTOM POOL CUES
Mr. Joe Childs
2651 Stephens Hwy.
Mt. Holly, AR 71758
870-554-2311

CHILTON CUSTOM CUES
Mr. Dale Chilton
135 11th Avenue South
South St. Paul, MN 55075
651-457-0527
651-470-0127
www.chiltoncue.com
dale@chiltoncue.com

TRADEMARK INDEX, cont. 891

CHRIS' CUES
Mr. Chris Whitaker
155 Miller Lane
Anna, IL 62906
618-833-3170
bkk9@midwest.net

CHUDY CUSTOM CUES
Mr. Richard Chudy
1867 Lucille Ln.
Pleasant Hill, CA 94523
925-798-4369
Fax: 925-798-3763
www.rc3cues.com
rc3@pacbell.net

CK CUSTOM CUES
Mr. Chester Krick
272 East Spring Lane
East Peoria, IL 61611
309-694-6796
www.ckcues.com
cueman@mtco.com

GALE CLARK CUES
Mr. Gale Clark
6843 Vance Street
Arvada CO 80003
303-403-9898
mjs449@aol.com

CLASSIC CUSTOM CUE
Mr. William Charles Gibbs
149 Manchester Road
Fairfield Glade, TN 38558
931-484-2288

COGNOSCENTI CUES
Mr. Joe Gold
3701 N. Ravenswood Ave
Chicago, IL 60613
773-348-7154
Fax: 773-348-7170
cognoscenti@att.net

COKER CUES
Mr. Tom Coker
Michi Coker
Mr. Grady Coker
8101 Elder Creek Rd. Suite D/E
Sacramento, CA 95824
916-383-4410
Fax: 916-383-4410
cokercues@acninc.net

COMPETITION SPORTS CORP
Mr. Don Spetkar
168 Milbar Blvd
Farmingdale, NY 11735
800-645-2162
www.competitionsports.com
info@competitionsports.com

CORLISS CUE
Mr. Neil Corliss, Sr.
2068 Ardley Rd.
Juno Isles, FL 33408
561-626-3186
corlissque@aol.com

CORSAIR CUSTOM CUES
Mr. Roger Korsiak
18627 Brookhurst St. #150
Fountain Valley, CA 92708
714-968-8566
www.corsaircustomcues.com
corsaircues@cs.com

COUSINS CUSTOM CUES
Mr. Gary Wright
4918 Mirrill
Liverpool, NY 13088
250-846-9206
www.cousins-pool-cues.com
ed@cousins-pool-cues.com

CRAMER CUSTOM CUES
Mr. Jeff Cramer
PO Box 3046
Albany, OR 97321
541-981-9815
www.cramercues.com
jeffcramer@cramercues.com

CRYSTAL LEISURE INC
6880 South Emporia Street
Englewood, CO 80112
800-525-7059
Fax: 800-261-GAME
303-790-0885
Fax: 303-790-0746
www.crystalleisure.com
game@amusemp.com

CUE & CASE SALES
Mr. Mike Baggett
190 Cumberland Park Dr
St Augustine, FL 800-835-7665
www.cueandcase.com

CUE MASTER
Mr. James Wough
2422 E. 37th Ave.
Spokane, WA 99223

THE CUE MASTERS
Mr. Tom Haskin
Mr. Jimmy Haskin
223 Co. Rd. 305
Calliham, TX 78007
361-274-3336
361-449-7736
thaskin@granderiver.net
jnchaskin@fnbnet.net

CUES BY DAVID
Mr. David Whitsell
Pool Tools
821 W. 15th St. Unit 3B
Newport Beach, CA 92663
949-515-2159
nowhitse@aol.com

CUESTIX INTERNATIONAL
Dba Action Cues, 5280 Cues, Scorpion Cues
Ms. Kathy McFarland
1380 Overlook Drive #104
Lafayette, CO 80026
800-645-9803
Fax: 303-926-2679
www.cuestix.com
info@cuestix.com

JOHN DAVIS CUES
Mr. John Davis
Chicago, IL
773-545-2170

DAYTON CUSTOM CUES
Mr. Paul Dayton
5145 Turtle Creek Place
Fort Pierce, FL 34981
772-489-0577
www.daytoncues.com
paul@daytoncues.com

DG CUES
Mr. Don Gaudreau
16 Reservoir Road
Rockaway, NJ 07866
973-980-8680
dgcues@optonline.net

DIECKMAN CUSTOM CUE
Mr. Dennis Dieckman
PO Box 369
Manchester, MI 48158
734-428-1161
www.cuemaker.com
www.xuanloc.org
cuebuilder@cuemaker.com

DISHAW CUSTOM CUES
Mr. Dan Dishaw
2608 Bellevue Ave
Syracuse, NY 13219
315-472-4712
Fax: 315-472-1181
dan@dishawcues.com
www.dishawcues.com

DIVENEY CUES
Mr. Pat Diveney
110 West Gibson St
West Liberty, IA 52776
319-627-6574
www.diveneycue.com
patd@Lcom.net

DMI SPORTS, INC./G CUE
375 Commerce Drive
Fort Washington PA 19034
Contact: Graham Bowe
215-283-0153 ex 131
Fax: 215-283-9573

DOMINIAK CUES
Mr. William Dominiak
Mr. Aaron Dominiak
6305 E. Bethany Le Roy Rd
Stafford, NY 14143
585-768-7838
Fax: 585-768-2975
www.dominiak.com
dominiak@rochester.rr.com

DOWNEY CUSTOM CUES
% Mueller Sporting Goods
Mr. Troy Downey
4825 S. 16th St
Lincoln, NE 68512
402-423-8888
Fax: 402-423-5964
www.poolndarts.com
downeycues@poolndarts.com

DON DOYON CUSTOM CUES
Mr. Don Doyon
733 Riverside Dr.
Augusta, ME 04330
207-623-3589
Fax: 207-623-0499
Ddoyon1@adelphia.net

DP CUSTOM CUES
Mr. Dale Perry
26 Industrial Loop #171
Orange Park, FL 32073
904-215-7161
Fax: 904-215-7162
www.dpcues.com
dale@dpcues.com

DURBIN CUSTOM CUES
Mr. J. Michael Durbin
RR2 Box 145
Sullivan, IL 61951
217-728-8912
jmdurbin@one-eleven.net

DZ CUES
Mr. Bob Dzuricky
1922 E. 2nd St
Erie, PA 16511
814-455-5601
www.dzcues.com
bob@dzcues.com
dzcues@ma.rr.com

ERWIN CUSTOM CUES
Mr. Mike Erwin
3829 Hwy 4 W
Sarah, MS 38665
662-562-9009
www.erwincues.com
erwincue@erwincues.com

ESCALADE SPORTS
Mosconi Cues
Mr. Randy Beckum
817 Maxwell Avenue
Evansville, IN 47711
812-467-1200
Fax: 812-467-1300
www.escaladesports.com
randybeckum@escaladesports.com

ESPIRITU CUSTOM CUES
Mr. Russ Espiritu
6162 Hwy 18
Brandon, MS 39042
601-825-7077
Fax: 601-824-1962
www.omnicue.com
espiritucues@att.net

EUROWEST CUES GBR
Mr. Markus Funk
Mr. Andreas Stahl
Messenhauserstrasse 49
D-63322 Roedermark Germany
+49-6074-211 60 50
Fax: +49-6074-211 60 49
www.eurowest-cues.de
service@eurowest-cues.de

EYE CUES
Mr. Jeff Lipp
571 Jadine Drive
Defiance, OH 43512
419-784-4120
goodwin64@earthlink.net

FALCON CUES, LTD
2556 Meadowpine Blvd
Mississauga, Ontario
Canada L5N 6P9
800-371-6299
905-812-5555
Fax: 905-812-8822
www.falconcues.com

FANELLI CUES
Mr. Paul Fanelli
Clifton, NJ
973-473-7721
pauliecue@yahoo.com

FARRIS CUES
Mr. Eddie L. Farris
6313 So. 126th West Ave
Sapulpa, OK 74066
918-227-1308
Cell: 918-521-0521
efarris1@swbell.net

FIERCE EAGLE CUES
Mr. Paddy Sheya
4014 Tennyson St
Denver CO 80212
303-455-1412
Fax: 303-456-0771
www.fierceeagle.com

FRANK FISHER CUSTOM CUES
Mr. Frank Fisher
429 W Maple
Johnson City, TN 37604
frankfisher@ziplip.com

ADAM FRANKS CUSTOM CUES (OJO)
Mr. Adam Franks
2419 Lead Avenue SE
Albuquerque, NM 87106
www.afcues.com
adam@afcues.com

FURY CUES
877-283-7444
www.fury-cues.com

GARDNER CUES
Mr. Mike Gardner
148 Franklin Road
Mercer, PA 16137
724-662-9225
www.gbccues.com
mikegardner@gbccues.com

GATZKE'S CUSTOM CUES
Mr. Mike Gatzke
2025 Avalon
Las Cruces, NM 88005
505-523-5131
www.gatzkecues.com
mike@gatzkecues.com

G. B. CUSTOM CUES
Mr. George Buss
9319A Midland Blvd
Overland, MO 63144
314-423-6122
Fax: 314-423-6122*51
www.georgebuss.com
georgebuss@georgebuss.com

GD CUES
Mr. Gary Dawkins
4097 Briarwood Dr
Martinez, GA 30907
Cell: 706-799-2346
706-210-0395 (M-Sat)
yrag47@knology.net

GEM CUES
Mr. Gary Medlin
2505 Bonito Drive
Lake Charles, LA 70605
337-474-3044
www.gemcues.com
gemcues@cox-internet.com

GEPPETTO CUSTOM CUES
Mr. Steven Hopper
532 Turner Ave.
Glen Ellyn, IL 60137
630-858-8117
kmac.hopper@sbcglobal.net

GILBERT CUSTOM CUES
Mr. Andy Gilbert
827 Frazier Rd
Clever, MO 65631
417-743-2759
gilbertcues@msn.com

GINACUE
Mr. Ernie Gutierrez
5424 Vineland Ave
North Hollywood, CA 91601
818-509-0454
Fax: 818-509-1231
ginacue@yahoo.com

GOLDENROD CUES
Mr. Bill Hughes
302 11th St
Lincoln, IL 62656
217-732-7688
grcues@hotmail.com

GREG'S KUES
Mr. Greg Kucharski
Southington, CT 06489

GRIFFIN & SON CUSTOM CUES
Mr. "Madison" Bob Griffin
5883N 933W
Deputy, IN 47230
812-873-7745
www.madisonbobs.com
dagriffin@seidata.com

GS CUE
Mr. Greg Sirca
Oakley, CA 94561
925-625-5855
Fax: 925-625-5855
www.gscue.com
gsirca@yahoo.com
gsirca@sbcglobal.net

TRADEMARK INDEX, cont. 893

JOHN GUFFEY CUSTOM CUES
Mr. John Guffey
2422 Cedar Oak Dr
Edmond, OK 73013
405-359-2045

GUGINO'S CUSTOM CUES
Mr. Tony Gugino
7425 Beryl Street
Lemon Grove, CA 91945
619-464-0212
puppy103@cox.net

GULYASSY CUES
Mr. Mike Gulyassy
Baby's Pro Shop
1161 Miller Road
Greenville, SC 29607
864-458-7662
864-430-7797
Fax: 864-234-6883
www.babysproshop.com
mike@babysproshop.com

GUNN CUES
Mr. Wayne Gunn
Mr. Terry McEniry
11612 Jefferson Road
Thonotosassa, FL 33592
813-986-6978
Fax: 813-986-6978
www.tampabilliards.com
mullet.man@verizon.net

HADRIANUS CUE CO.
Mr. Adrian Viguera
3701 South 60th Court
Cicero, IL 60804
708-652-5952

HAGAN CUE
Mr. Bill Hagan
331 N Corinne Dr
Gilbert AZ 85234

RON HALEY CUSTOM CUES
Mr. Ron Haley
892 Apple Blossom Ln
Springdale, AR 72762
479-361-5054
rhaley@shilohsteel.com

HAMILTON CUES
Mr. Al Hamilton
601 SE US Hwy 19 S
Crystal River, FL 34429
352-382-3900 (M-F)
352-795-4569
hunterdm@gowebco.com
poolschool9@aol.com

HAMMER CUSTOM CUES
Mr. Travis Frakes
3804 S. 142nd E. Ave
Tulsa, OK 74134
918-439-3665
www.hammercues.com
info@hammercues.com

HARPER'S PERSONALIZED CUES
Mr. Bud Harper
403 N. Poplar
Creston, IA 50801
515-782-5476
harperbilliards@yahoo.com

TED HARRIS CUSTOM CUES
Mr. Ted Harris
808 South Dixie Highway
Hollywood, FL 33020
305-677-3434
www.tedharris.com
poolcues@tedharris.com

TOM HARRIS CUES
Mr. Tom Harris
PO Box 120036
East Haven, CT 06512
203-483-5777

HAWKINS CUES
Mr. Hal Hawkins
W3940 Box 50, Mitchell
Eau Claire, WI 54701
Fax: 715-836-9196
hhawk1ns@yahoo.com

HERCEK FINE BILLIARD CUES
Mr. Joel Hercek
1352 Armour Blvd
Mundelein, IL 60060
847-680-7498
Fax: 847-816-6333
www.hercek.com
joel@hercek.com

HICKS STICKS
Mr. Jeff Hicks
Rt 1 Box 175
Stronghurst, IL 61480
309-924-1127

HIGHTOWER CUSTOM CUES
Mr. Chris Hightower
444 Flint Hill Rd.
Aragon, GA 30104
770-684-7004
www.hightowercues.com
www.cuesmith.com
cueman@cuesmith.com

HUEBLER INDUSTRIES, INC.
Mr. Paul Huebler
600 Jefferson St
Linn, MO 65051
573-897-2062
Fax: 573-897-2805
www.hueblercue.com
info@hueblercue.com

HUNTER CLASSIC CUSTOM CUES
Mr. Wes Hunter
172 La Luz Gate Rd
Alamagordo, NM 88310
505-437-1972
Fax: 505-439-8506
www.hunterclassics.com
hunterclassics@netMDC.com

HUNTER CUSTOM CUES
Mr. Bob Hunter
4825 Convair Dr #20
Carson City, NV 89706
775-884-2837
www.huntercues.com
bob@huntercues.com

IMPERIAL INTERNATIONAL
621 W. Route 46
Hasbrouck Heights, NJ 07604
800-526-6261
201-288-9199
Fax: 201-288-8990
www.imperialusa.com
contact@imperialusa.com

INGRAM CUE
Mr. Jimmy L. Ingram
7000 S. Pennsylvania Ave
Oklahoma City, OK 71359
405-685-2199
405-502-9926 (Pager)
ingramq@yahoo.com

J & J AMERICA BILLIARDS INC
14130 E. Alondra Blvd, Suite B
Santa Fe Springs, CA 90670
562-229-9688
Fax: 562-229-9906
www.jjcue.com
info@jjcue.com

J. B. CUSTOM CUES
Mr. James Brumfield
1020 Newman Lane
Lexington, KY 40515

JACKSON CUSTOM CUE
Tony & Karen Muesch
Mike & Diane Weyer
120-B W. Commerce Blvd (Hwy 60)
Slinger, WI 53086
262-644-0200
262-644-0022
Fax: 262-644-4499
www.jacksoncue.com
info@jacksoncue.com
sales@jacksoncue.com

JACOBY CUSTOM CUES
Mr. David Jacoby
309 Market Street
Nekoosa, WI 54457
800-461-6060
715-886-2900
Fax: 715-886-4449
www.jacobycue.com
jacobycc@wctc.net

JENSEN CUSTOM CUES
Mr. Mike Johnson
9135 Cuyhanga Parkway
Baton Rouge, LA 70815
225-924-4517
www.jensencues.com
jensencues@cox.net

JERICO CUES
Mr. Jerry Powers
205 Field Street
Clyde, TX 79510
325-893-2393
www.jericocuesales.com
jjcue@direcway.com

JOBO POOL STICKS & ACCESSORIES
Mr. Joel Jose
Mr. Bong Nicdao
Don Juico St. Field Avenue
Balibago, Angeles City
Philippines
0921-350-6160 Joel
0919-687-9234 Bong
jobo_cues@yahoo.com

CHRIS JONES CUSTOM CUES
Mr. Chris Jones
813 Garden Grove
Yukon, OK 73099
405-350-1671
twocardchris@yahoo.com

DAVE JONES CUSTOM CUES
Mr. Dave Jones
2322 236 St. SW
Lynnwood, WA 98036
425-485-6242
Fax: 425-398-4439
www.djcues.com
djcues@comcast.net

JOSEPH FULL SPLICE CUES
Mr. Joseph Franke
45-35 218th St
Bayside NY 11361
646-522-0266
josephcustomcues@aol.com

JOSEY CUSTOM CUES
Mr. Keith Josey
Mrs. Sherri Josey
12 Wymberly Way
Savannah, GA 31406
800-514-CUES
912-356-1816
Fax: 912-355-1893
www.joseycues.com
info@joseycues.com

JOSS CUES LTD
Mr. Dan Janes
8749 Mylander Ln
Towson, MD 21286
410-821-0064
800-245-JOSS
Fax: 410-821-8321
www.josscues.com
info@josscues.com

JOSSWEST
Mr. Bill Stroud
PO Box 1085
Ruidoso Downs, NM 88346
505-378-5677
505-378-1678
www.cues.com
bill@cues.com

J-S SALES COMPANY, INC.
CueTec
5 South Fulton Ave
Mt. Vernon, NY 10550
800-431-2944
Fax: 914-668-8735
www.cuetec.net
www.j-ssales.com

JUDD'S CUSTOM CUES
Mr. Garland "Judd" Fuller
20911 Hwy 666
Yellow Jacket, CO 81335
888-909-7833
Fax: 970-562-4290
www.juddcues.com
juddcues@fone.net

JUSTIS CUES
Mr. Jack Justis
4031 N. W. 4th Street
Coconut Creek, FL 33066
954-974-5614
Fax: 954-974-5614
Jjustis4@aol.com

KELLY CUES
Mr. Ned Kelly
2615 Ryan Dr
Indianapolis, IN 46220
317-251-0684
ndkelly@aol.com

MR. DAVID PAUL KERSENBROCK
% Ed Young Cues
429 West Ohio St. #117
Chicago, IL 60610
312-519-2505
artisian@comcast.net

KIKEL CUES
Mr. David Kikel
35 Tierra de Casa
Pueblo, CO 81005
719-564-2396

KILBY CUES
Mr. Ronald Kilby
990 Donaldson Way
Medford, OR 97501
541-245-4530
www.caromcues.com
zozzl@charter.net

KLEIN CUSTOM CUES
Mr. Steven A. Klein
www.kleincues.com
sales@kleincues.com

KLICKCUE
Mr. Chris Klindt
3215 W. 9th
Lawrence, KS 66049
785-749-4633
www.klickcue.com
chris@klickcue.com

KORNELE CUSTOM CUES
Mr. Steve Kornele
PO Box 81
Mooreland, OK 73852
580-994-2798
www.kornelepoolcues.com
steve@kornelepoolcues.com

LAMBROS CUES, INC.
Mr. Michael Lambros
154 Willard St
Baltimore, MD 21223
410-233-6300
www.lambroscues.com
mlambros@ix.netcom.com

LANZ CUSTOM CUES
Mr. Richard Lanz
4816 N. Arvilla Drive
Toledo, OH 43623
419-882-0870
lanzcustomcues@aol.com

CUES BY LARUE
Mr. Larry LaRue
1811 N. Tampa St
Tampa, FL 33602

LAWHEAD CUES
Mr. Jerry Lawhead
106 11th Street SE
Winter Haven, FL 33880
863-299-5446
www.lawheadcues.com
jerry@lawheadcues.com

LAYANI CUES
Mr. Alain Gendron
Mr. Thierry Layani
70 St-Jean, Longueuil
Quebec Canada
J4H 2W9
888-651-7381
514-836-2837
www.layanicues.com
info@layanicues.com

LEBOW CUSTOM CUES
Mr. Sheldon Lebow
1090 Linda Ln
Springfield, OR 97478
541-741-1947
www.sheldoncue.com
mail@sheldoncue.com

LINEAR Q
Hyper-Designs
621 Brademas Ct
Simi Valley, CA 93065
877-4-HYPER-D
www.Hyper-Designs.com
customerservice@hyper-designs.com

LOMAX CUSTOM CUES
Mr. Steve Lomax
PO Box 414
Cornelia GA 30531
706-776-1252
706-499-0803
Fax: 775-514-0524
stevenl@alltel.net

LONGONI CUES
Mr. Pierluigi Longoni
Mr. Renzo Longoni
Via Cappelletti 56
Mariano Comense
22066 Italy
+39-031-746542
Fax: +39-031-3551044
www.longonicues.com
longoni@norditalia.it

L. T. D. CUES
Mr. Dale Teague
PO Box 88
Sultan, WA 98284
Fax 360-793-0172
ltdcue@ix.netcom.com

LUDWIG CUES
Mr. Todd Ludwig
qmaker@cox.net

MACE CUES
Mr. Rick Howard
8246 Verano
Navarre, FL 32566
850-939-1454
www.macecues.com
rick@macecues.com

JOHN MADDEN CUES
Mr. John Madden
6913 Allard Road
St. Ignatius, MT 59865
406-745-3562
www.johnmaddencues.com
cuemaker@johnmaddencues.com

MALI CO. INC.
257 Park Avenue South
New York, NY 10010
800-223-6468
www.malicloth.com
info@malicloth.com

MANZINO CUSTOM POOL CUES
Mr. Bob Manzino
414 N.E. 28th St
Boca Raton, FL 33431
561-393-9146
bobmanzinocom@msn.com

MARIPOSA CUE CO
Kyle Van den Bosch
% Chicago Billiard Café
5935 Irving Park Rd
Chicago IL 60634
847-989-5953
mariposacues@aol.com

MIKE MARTIN CUSTOM CUES
Mr. Mike Martin
4220 Mahoning Ave
Austintown OH 44515
330-519-6292
billiardemporium@sbcglobal.net

MARTINEZ CUSTOM CUES
Mr. Ernie Martinez
981 East 70th St, Unit G
Denver, CO 80229
303-287-1660

MAZZCO
500 Eastern Ave
Bensenville IL 60106
800-292-4491
www.mazzco.com

MCDANIEL CUSTOM CUES
Mr. Bill McDaniel
586 Airways Blvd.
Jackson, TN 38301
731-424-4455
Fax: 731-424-4459
www.billmcdaniel.com
bill@billmcdaniel.com

MCDERMOTT CUE MFG CO.
W146 N9560 Held Dr
Menomonee Falls, WI 53051
800-666-2283
262-251-4090
Fax: 262-251-9290
www.mcdermottcue.com
info@mcdermottcue.com

MCWORTER CUES
Mr. Jerry McWorter
82 S. Anacapa St.
Ventura, CA 93001
805-648-2225
Fax: 805-648-3442
www.mcwortercues.com
jmcworter1@aol.com

MEISTER CUES
Mr. Fred Meister
114 Evernia Street
Jupiter, FL 33458
561-747-5175
fqmeister@bellsouth.net

MEUCCI ORIGINALS, INC.
Mr. Bob Meucci
1 Meucci Center Drive
Sledge, MS 38670
800-563-8224
Fax: 662-382-7001
www.meuccicues.com
sales@meuccicues.com

MEZZ CUES
Miki Co Ltd
Kazunori Miki
Japan
www.miki-mezz.com

MICHAELANGELO CUSTOM CUES
Mr. Michael Givens
21424 Judy Circle
McCloud, OK 74851
214-223-5231
www.customq.com
michaelg@customq.com

MICHAEL MORGAN CUSTOM CUES
Mr. Michael Miller
216 N. Chestnut
Massapequa, NY 11758
516-799-8203
mmcue@aol.com

MICHAEL'S CUSTOM CUES
Mr. Michael Kratochvill
1729 St. Claire
Racine, WI 53402
262-633-7657
mcustomcues@wi.net

MIDWEST CUSTOM CUES
Mr. Steve Morris
720 1st Ave. South
South St. Paul, MN 55075
651-455-3435
stevemorris@attbi.com

MILTONIO CUSTOM CUES
Mr. Milt Hyman
1504 Brengle Way
Vista, CA 92084
760-630-4631
www.miltoniocues.com
cuesbymilt@cox.net

MISTER BILLIARD
1515 Britannia Rd East, Unit 1
Mississauga, Ontario
Canada
800-661-0106
Fax: 905-696-0605
www.mrbilliard.com
sales@mrbilliard.com

HAROLD MOREY CUES
Mr. Harold Morey
703 King Settlement Rd
Alpena, MI 49707
989-379-3683

MORRIS CUE
Mr. Ned Morris
Mr. Mark Schwenson
10720 Santa Cruz
Desert Hot Springs, CA 92240
760-329-3224
morriscue@earthlink.net

MOTTEY CUSTOM CUES
Mr. Paul Mottey
1628 Saw Mill Run Blvd
Pittsburgh, PA 15210
412-881-9211
Fax: 412-531-7390
www.motteycues.com
motteycues@aol.com

MUELLER SPORTING GOODS
Mr. Troy Downey
Mr. Ryan Theewen
4825 S. 16th St
Lincoln, NE 68512
402-423-8888
Fax: 402-423-5964
www.poolndarts.com

MURRELL CUSTOM CUES
Mr. Kenneth Murrell
1212 Roger Ave
Swansea, IL 62226
618-257-8490
ktmurrell@msn.com

MICHAEL NEAL CUSTOM CUES
Mr. Mike Neal
PO Box 67142
Lincoln, NE 68506
402-450-1175
www.cueman.com
mike@cueman.com

NEWPORT CUSTOM CUES
Mr. Gene Newport
1620 Shore Drive
Edgewater, MD 21037
410-956-2609
www.newportcustomcues.com
cues@newportcustomcues.com

NITTI CUES
Mr. Chris Nitti
706 Bridlewood Ave
Orlando, FL 32825
407-380-6121
Fax: 407-380-7284
www.nitticues.com
chris@nitticues.com

NORTHERN CUE
Mr. Ray Gurgall
PO Box 153
Norway, MI 49870
906-498-2118

NORWELA CUES
Mr. Jim Griffin
4312 Greenwood Rd
Shreveport, LA 71109
318-294-4566
www.norwelacues.com
norwelacues@hotmail.com

NOVA CUES, INC.
Mr. Norbert "Nubs" Wagner
2100 Northwestern Ave
West Bend, WI 53090
414-335-2600
novacues@nconnect.net

ODOM CUES
Mr. Jim Odom
3300 Minot St
Fort Worth, TX 76133
817-370-2931
djodom@ev1.net

JERRY OLIVIER CUSTOM CUES
Mr. Jerry Olivier
2302 County Rd #124
Pearland, TX 77581
281-996-8030
www.jocues.com
jocues@flash.net

JIM OLMS BILLIARD EQUIPMENT
J. O. B. E.
Mr. Jim Olms
Genoa, OH

OLNEY CUES
Mr. Jeff Olney
2016 Benton
Boone, IA 50036
515-432-7708 daytime
515-432-2511 evenings
www.galynx.com/jolney/index.htm
olneycues@yahoo.com

OMEGA BILLIARDS
Mr. Michael Hoang
6712 Cambrian Way
Fort Worth, TX 76137
817-232-4494
Fax: 817-232-4920
www.omegabilliards.com
mike@omegabilliards.com

OMEN CUSTOM CUES
Mr. Peter Ohman
7591 Pinecrest Ave
Melbourne, FL 32904
321-951-8123
www.omencues.com
pohman@cfl.rr.com

ONE ON ONE CUE STICKS
Mr. Bill Stelzenmuller
7505 Carpenter Fire Station Rd
Cary, NC 27519
919-467-3096
billstelz@aol.com

ORCHID U.S.A. CUSTOM CUES
25 Hutcheson Pl.
Lynbrook, NJ 11563
800-645-2162
Fax: 818-782-1713

GUIDO ORLANDI CUSTOM CUES
Mr. Guido Orlandi
PO Box 4-N12
620 Sawyer Lake Rd
Channing, MI 49815
906-542-7069
www.guidoorlandicues.com
guido@guidoorlandicues.com

PADGETT CUSTOM CUES
Mr. Tim Padgett
401 N 1st Ave #E
Arcadia, CA 91006
626-445-8444
padgettcues@sbcglobal.net

PADISHAN INTERNATIONAL CO. LTD.
Mr. Jack Lin
1F, No. 26 Lo Li Road
Taipei, Taiwan R.O.C.
+886-2-2736-6114
Fax: +886-2-2736-2312
www.padishan.com
padico@padishan.com.tw
padico.tw@msa.hinet.net

PANCERNY CUSTOM CUES
Mr. Mike Pancerny
29173 Rachid Lae
Chesterfield, MI 48047
586-598-4643
Fax: 586-598-4643
www.customcuemaker.com
mike@customcuemaker.com

PARROT CUE
Mr. Todd Elkins
2125 Staples Mill Rd
Richmond, VA 23230
804-358-7665
Fax: 804-358-0292
www.parrotcue.com
todd.elkins@parrotcue.com
jeff.martin@parrotcue.com

PATRICK CUSTOM CUES
Mr. Doug Patrick
7350 Geradini
Hazelwood MO 63042
618-709-2615
patrickcustomcues@yahoo.com

CUSTOM CUES BY DALE PATTEN
Mr. Dale Patten
411 Emerald
Redondo Beach, CA 90277
310-372-0479

J. PECHAUER CUSTOM CUES
Mr. Jerry Pechauer
Mr. Joe Pechauer
4140 Velp Ave
Green Bay, WI 54313
800-934-7735
920-434-7755
Fax: 920-434-7757
www.pechauer.com
joe@pechauer.com
questions@pechauer.com

PENROSE CUES
Mr. Tom Penrose
Sweelincklaan 426
5012BD Tilburg
Netherlands
+31-622866 525
www.penrosecues.com
info@penrosecues.com

PETREE CUSTOM CUES
Mr. J. W. Petree
11408 N 132 East Ave
Owasso OK 74055
918-398-3600
petreecustomcues.com
www.oklahomabilliards.com
info@oklahomabilliards.com

PFD STUDIOS
Mr. Paul F. Drexler
Ms. Ellen Drexler
213 Flood Rd
Marlborough, CT 06447
860-295-8500
Fax: 860-295-8212
www.pfdcues.com
paul@pfdcues.com

PHILLIPPI CUSTOM CUES
Mr. Richard W. Phillippi
182 11th St
Pasadena, MD 21122
410-437-2386
www.phillippicustomcues.com
phillippiq@aol.com

PICONE CUES
Mr. Joe Picone
630 SW 12th Street
Fort Lauderdale, FL 33315
954-767-9004
www.piconecues.com
joe@piconecues.com

PORCUPINE CUES
Mr. Glen Sadler
PO Box 588
Meridianville, AL 35759
800-232-3654
thesadlers@bellsouth.net

JOE PORPER'S CREATIVE INVENTIONS
Mr. Joe Porper
9142-44 Jordan Ave
Chatsworth, CA 91311
818-727-7966
800-388-5132
Fax: 818-727-9076
www.porperoriginals.com
joeporper@hotmail.com

TRADEMARK INDEX, cont. **897**

PRATHER CUE
Mr. Jeff Prather
200 S. Main
PO Box 7
Mooreland, OK 73852
580-994-2414
Fax: 580-994-2700
www.prathercue.com
sales@prathercue.com

PREDATOR CUES
Mr. Allan McCarty
5055-5 St. Augustine Rd
Jacksonville, FL 32207
904-448-8748
888-314-4111
Fax: 904-448-9151
www.predatorcues.com
info@predatorcues.com

PREWITT CUSTOM CUES
Mr. Ed Prewitt
Santa Monica, CA 310-305-9202
prewittcues@hotmail.com

PRINCE CUES
Mr. Tim Prince
437 Benden Ave
Glendale Hts, IL 60139
630-661-7805
princecue@comcast.net

PUTNAM CUES
Mr. Shawn Putnam
422 Wesley Ave
Youngstown, OH 44509
330-518-7550

QUEST ASP CUSTOM CUES
Mr. Don Moyer
762 Highland St
Enhaut, PA 11713
717-985-9050

Q-WORKS
Mr. Bob Burgoyne
3530 Hicks Lane
Chico, CA 95973
530-345-7909

RAT CUES
% Mueller Recreational Products
Mr. Ryan Theewen
4825 S. 16th Street
Lincoln, NE 68512
402-423-8888
800-925-7665
Fax: 402-423-5964
www.poolndarts.com
cuerepair@poolndarts.com

RATHBUN CUES
Mr. William Rathbun
1167 Outlook Dr
Deltona, FL 32725
386-574-5950

RAUENZAHN CUSTOM CUES
Mr. Jerry Rauenzahn
1608 Pennsylvania Ave E
Warren, PA 16365
814-723-8322
www.rauenzahncues.com
rauenzahncue@atlanticbb.net

RAVEN CUES
Mr. Michael Wagner
1083 6th Street
Marion, IA 52302
319-373-2917
www.ravencues.com
contact-us@ravencues.com

REEVES CUSTOM CUES
Mr. Jimmy Reeves
1004 Pope Field Rd
Easley, SC 29642
864-442-9911
Cell 864-313-4832
www.reevescues.com
info@reevescues.com

RENIS CUES
Mr. Bob Renis
Quality Billiards
930 West Washington, Ste #1
San Diego, CA 92103
619-260-0820
800-848-7665
www.westcoastcues.com
info@westcoastcues.com

EDWIN REYES CUSTOM HAND-CRAFTED CUES
% Alpha Billiards
Mr. Edwin Reyes
#97 Maningning St.
Quezon City
Philippines 1101
(63917)357-8524
www.edwinreyescues.com

RHINO CUES
Mr. Charlie Wilhite
1414 Avenue C
Danbury, TX 77534
409-922-8670
rhinowhilhite@netscape.net

R. H. N. CUSTOM CUES
Mr. Richard Neighbors
318 Linden Street
Cincinnati, OH 45216
Fax: 513-528-3500
www.dickiecues.com
rhncue@aol.com

RICCO CUSTOM CUES
Mr. Marco Cervantes
21W537 Kensington Rd
Glen Ellyn, IL 60137
630-881-8353
philo1219@sbcglobal.net

HARRY RICHARDS CUSTOM CUES
Mr. Harry Richards
617 Williamsburg Dr
Daytona Beach, FL 32117
386-255-3770
www.hrcues.com
hrcues@yahoo.com

RIKARD CUSTOM CUES
Mr. William Rikard
1008 12th Street
Galena Park, TX 77547

R J. H. CUSTOM CUES
Mr. Richard Hsu
% Action Billiards
5430 Avenue N
Brooklyn, NY 11204
917-603-6630
www.rjhcustomcues.com
rjhcues@aol.com

ROBINSON CUSTOM CUES
Mr. John Robinson
13634 N. 51st Way
Scottsdale, AZ 85254
602-996-5022
www.robinsoncues.com
john@robinsoncues.com
robinsoncues@cox.net

ROMERO CUES
Mr. Al Romero
% Hardtimes Billiards
17450 Bellflower Blvd.
Bellflower, CA 90706
562-867-3580
www.romerocue.com
brook@hardtimesbellflower.com

PAUL RUBINO CUSTOM CUES
Mr. Paul Rubino
316 Lynden Ave
New Windsor, NY 12553
845-496-3795
www.rubinocues.com
paul@rubinocues.com

BOB RUNDE CUES
Mr. Bob Runde
21751 65th St
Bristol, WI 53104
262-857-6533

SAILOR CUES
Mr. Frank Stellman
1650 Taylor Avenue
Racine, WI 53403

SAMSARA CUES
Mr. David Doucette
Mr. Jim Stadum
601 First Street NE
Rugby, ND 58368
701-776-7240
Fax: 701-776-7242
www.samsaracues.com
sales@samsaracues.com

SANKO CUSTOM CUES
Mr. Joe Sanko
2364 E.Tamiami Tr.
Naples, FL 34112
866-732-1300
Fax: 239-732-1300
www.sankocues.com
sankocues@yahoo.com

BILL SCHICK ORIGINALS
Mr. Bill Schick
8101 Kingston Rd. Suite 112
Shreveport, LA 71108
318-688-8070
Fax: 318-688-8272
www.billschickoriginals.net
info@billschickoriginals.net

SCHMELKE MFG INC.
Mr. James Schmelke
1879 28th Ave
Rice Lake, WI 54868
715-234-6553
schmelke@charterinternet.net

SCHON CUES
Mr. Evan Clark
3812 W Burnham St
Milwaukee, WI 53215
414-383-9661
Fax: 414-383-6086
www.schoncues.com
info@schoncues.com

SCHRAGER CUE CO.
Mr. Bert Schrager
Mrs. Pat Schrager
PO Box 893
Lake Isabella, CA 93240
760-379-2999
bertschr@earthlink.net

SCHULER CUE
Mr. Bryan Trim
540 West Colfax #2
Palatine, IL 60067
847-776-7768
888-843-1283
Fax: 847-520-7899
www.schulercue.com
info@schulercue.com

TIM SCRUGGS CUSTOM CUES, INC.
Mr. Tim Scruggs
900 Leeds Ave
Baltimore, MD 21229
410-247-1231
Fax: 410-247-7459
www.timscruggs.com
cueman@webtv.net

SEARING PRECISION CUSTOM CUES
Mr. Dennis Searing
11586 Pierson Rd, Suite L-7
Wellington, FL 33414
561-792-3222
Fax: 561-792-3792
www.searingcues.com
searing@aol.com

SHAMAN CUES
Mr. Robert Smith
3130 Fraternity Church Rd
Winston-Salem, NC 27127
336-650-0185
www.shamancues.com
bobsmith@shamancues.com

SCOT SHERBINE CUSTOM CUES
Mr. Scot Sherbine
202 South State Street
Ephrata, PA 17522
717-721-9000
www.proficientbilliards.com
sales@proficientbilliards.com

SHERM CUES
Mr. Sherman Adamson
3352 Nine Mile Rd
Cincinnati, OH 45255
Shop: 513-553-2172
Cell: 513-509-9152
www.shermcue.com
sherm@shermcue.com

SHOWCASE CUSTOM CUES
Mr. Mike Etheridge
12031 N. Tejon St
Westminster, CO 80234
303-457-2501
800-783-STIX
www.showcasebilliards.com
vettelinc@prodigy.net

SHOWMAN CUES
Mr. John Showman
215 6th St North
Safety Harbor, FL 34695
727-724-0520
Fax: 727-724-0520
showmancues@hotmail.com

SHURTZ CUSTOM CUES INC.
Mr. Jack Shurtz
Mr. Bob Owen
2006 S. Washington
Wichita, KS 67216
316-269-3844
www.shurtzcue.com
bob@shurtzcue.com

SIERRA CUES
Mr. Eric Niemira
130 W. Hampton, Suite 5
Mesa, AZ 85210
www.sierracue.com
eric@sierracue.com

SIGEL'S UNLIMITED CUES & ACCESS
Sigel's World Class Cues
Mr. Mike Sigel
PO Box 914
Oakland, FL 34760
407-656-2837
www.sigelscues.com
www.sigelsunlimited.com
sigelcues@msn.com

MR. MIKE SIGEL
PO Box 914
Oakland, FL 34760
407-656-2837
www.sigelscues.com
sigelcues@msn.com

SILVER FOX
Mr. Larry Brengman
3233 Sunset Way
Bellingham, WA 98226
800-545-5912
360-758-7304
Fax: 360-758-2300
www.silverfoxcues.com
silverfoxcue@earthlink.net

SMITH HANDCRAFTED CUSTOM CUES
Mr. Howard Smith
The Silvertime Company
2410 W Sugar Creek Rd
Charlotte, NC 28262
704-597-1376
www.silvertime.org
hcsilvert@aol.com

MARK SMITH CUSTOM CUES
Mr. Mark Smith
224 N. Shamrock Blvd
Russellville, AR 72802
Pool Room: 479-968-3559
479-968-8781 (evenings)
Cell: 479-970-0056
www.marksmithcues.com
mark@marksmithcues.com

SMITH & WESSON BILLIARDS
Leisure Pursuits Sales and Marketing, LLC
50 Oakley Way
Wayne, NJ 07470
973-703-4637
Fax: 973-305-0090
www.smithandwessonbilliards.com
jack.mulvihill@leisurepursuitsales.com

SMITHLIN CUSTOM CUES
Mr. Richard Smithlin
5419 East Owens Ave
Las Vegas, NV 89110
702-453-7693
cuemakerrich@cox.net

SOUTH EAST CUES
Mr. Nat Green
404 N Second Street
Clarksville, TN 37040
931-647-8424
Fax: 931-553-8222
931-553-6822
www.southeastcues.com
secues@southeastcues.com

SOUTH WEST CUES
Mrs. Laurie Franklin
4608 Nolan Ln
Las Vegas, NV 89107
702-870-9615
swcue@aol.com

SOWDER CUES
Mr. Gregory J Sowder
Sharkshooter Billiards
8309 N W 6th Avenue
Vancouver, WA 98665
360-573-1322
shootsowdercue@comcast.net

SPIDER WEB CUES
Mr. Billy Webb
PO Box 903
Hardy, AR 72542
billy023@centurytel.net

M. STACEY CUES
Mr. Mike Stacey
7708 Mistflower Lane
Noblesville, IN 46062
317-773-5401
www.mstaceycues.com
mstaceycues@sbcglobal.net

STAR CITY CUES
Mr. Al Beckelhimer
3338 Overhill Trail
Roanoke, VA 24018
540-776-3559
awbeck@msn.com

STAR CUE MFG.
Mr. Abe Rich
428 Jefferson Ave (rear)
Miami Beach, FL 33139
305-673-1133

STEALTH CUE
Mr. Mark Stoller
21618 N. 9th Ave Ste 1
Pheonix, AZ 85027
623-215-0425
Fax: 623-215-0502
www.stealthcues.com
stealthcues@msn.com

STONIER'S CUES
Mr. Dave Stonier
% The Jointed Cue
2375 Fruitridge Rd
Sacramento, CA 95822
916-456-2284
davestobro@comcast.net

STOUT STICKS
Mr. Danny Stout
692 Back Creek Rd
Asheboro, NC 27205
336-629-0449

STRADER CUES
Mr. David Strader
219 Norwood Drive
Danville, VA 24540
919-451-9760
www.stradercues.com
sccues@hotmail.com

SWEETWATER CUES USA
Mr. Jeff Bonner
8341 Industrial Drive
Olive Branch, MS 38654
888-828-2837
mjbonner@memphisline.com

SYRA CUES BY RK
Mr. Ron Kadey
105 Hillside Way
Camillias, NY 13031
315-488-6621
rkadey@yahoo.com

SZAMBOTI CUES INC.
Mr. Barry Szamboti
1914 Midfield Rd
Feasterville, PA 19053
215-357-5032
blscues@comcast.net

TAD'S CUSTOM CUE
Mr. Tad Kohara
Mr. Fred Kohara
8101 Electric Ave
Stanton, CA 90680
714-995-1644
Fax: 714-828-8287

TASCARELLA CUSTOMCUES
Mr. Peter Tascarella Sr.
Mr. Peter Tascarella Jr.
PO Box 66
Massapequa Park, NY 11762
516-799-8477
tascarellacues@optonline.net

TAYLOR CUE COMPANY
Mr. Kent Taylor
Mr. Joey Taylor
Mr. Zach Taylor
PO Box 21693
Oklahoma City, OK 73156-1693
Orders: 888-231-9988
Shop: 405-340-9779
www.taylorcuecompany.com
taylorcues@prodigy.net

TC CUES
Mr. Thierry Chevron
Quart des Cremades
1 lot les Girbes
84100 Orange
France
+33 6 80 61 98 43
www.tccues.com
info@tccues.com

TERBROCK CUES
Mr. Jerry Terbrock
1221 Priest Dr
Manchester, MO 63021
636-861-3350
www.terbrockcues.com
jterbrock@earthlink.net

JOE THOMAS CUES
Mr. Joe "Toledo Joe" Thomas
2750 Lagrange Street
Toledo, OH 43608
419-917-4813

THOMPSON CUES U.S.A.
Mr. Hank Thompson
7321 Cottonwood Creek Rd
Fort Worth, TX 76135
817-238-9869
thompsoncues@hotmail.com

DANNY TIBBITTS CUSTOM CUES
Mr. Danny Tibbits
112 Golden Hill Dr
Woodstock, GA 30189
770-926-0475
www.tibbittscustomcues.com
tibbitt1@bellsouth.net

TICE CUSTOM CUES
Mr. David Tice
16441 Lakeview Drive
Leavenworth, WA 98826
509-763-3020
ticecues@genext.net
ticecues@wmconnect.com

TING CUSTOM CUES
Mr. Augusto "Gus" Pinca
29 Steeplechase Blvd
Burlington, NJ 08016
609-747-0840
ping@snip.net

TNS CUES
Mr. Tommy Migliore
89 Woodbury Rd
Highland Mills, NY 10930
845-928-1708
www.tnscues.com
info@tnscues.com
qnhand34@optonline.net

TODD CUES
Jessi Nester
29408 Pacific Hwy S
Federal Way, WA 98003
253-945-1888
Fax: 253-941-8904
www.beadsandbilliards.com
info@beadsandbilliards.com

TOEDT CUSTOM CUES
Mr. Chris Toedt
3415 S. Peoria Ave
Tulsa, OK 74105
918-744-5843

TONKIN CUSTOM CUES
Mr. Pete Tonkin
PO Box 891
39078 Hwy 299
Willow Creek, CA 95573
530-629-3313
www.tonkincustomcues.com
pete@tonkincustomcues.com

TROGDON CUSTOM CUES
Mr. Dan Trogdon
954 Luke Chute Road
Waterford, OH 45786
888-288-0330
740-984-4287
www.trogdoncues.com
dan@trogdoncues.com

TUCKER CUSTOM CUES
Mr. Murray Tucker III
8020 Gibson Terrace
Leesburg, FL 34748
352-551-7171
www.murraytucker.com
iii@tuckerbilt.com

VARNER CUES
Mr. Nick Varner
1400-B Triplett St
Owensboro, KY 42303
270-926-4248
Fax: 270-686-7833
www.nickvarner.com
nvcues@mindspring.com

VIATTORRE CUES
Mr. Jackson Tan
24 Sanso Street
Corinthian Gardens
Quezon City, 1110
Philippines
www.viattorre.com
cues@viattorre.com

TRADEMARK INDEX, cont.

VIKING CUE MFG INC.
Ms Robin Kneebone
Mr. Barry Hart
2710 Syene Rd
Madison, WI 53713
800-397-0122
608-271-5155
Fax: 608-271-5157
www.vikingcue.com
info@vikingcue.com

WARD CUSTOM CUES
Mr. Jim Ward
642 N Ben Maddox Way Ste H
Visalia, CA 93292
559-625-2592
jimbob8712@aol.com

WAYNE CUSTOM CUES
Mr. Wayne Holmes
4507 Bigham Road
Waxhaw, NC 28173
704-843-1888
877-843-1888
www.waynecustomcues.com
wayne@waynecustomcues.com

THOMAS WAYNE CUES
Mr. Thomas Wayne
3705 Arctic Blvd #1806
Anchorage, AK 99503
907-349-3743
twcues@ptialaska.net

MICHAEL WEBB CUES
Mr. Mike Webb
388 East Avenue
Pawtucket, RI 02860
401-724-4476
www.webbcues.com
webbcues@cox.net

WESTON CUSTOM CUES
Mr. Perry Weston
266 Cobb Lane
Hot Springs, AR 71901
501-624-7164
www.westoncues.com
Weston@direclynx.net

SKIP WESTON CUES
Mr. Skip Weston
157 Jackson St
Haskell, NJ 07420
973-831-6809
www.skipwestoncues.com
westongm@bellatlantic.net

WHISLER CUES
Mr. Scott Whisler
Mesa, AZ
480-655-1528
www.whislercues.com
whislercues@cox.net

JIM WHITE CUSTOM CUES
% Mottey Cues
1413 Potomac Ave
Pittsburgh, PA 15216
412-881-9211 shop
724-825-2898 mobile
www.motteycues.com
motteycues@aol.com

WILLEE CUE
Mr. William Lee
1325 Nile Drive
Corpus Christi, TX 78412
361-563-1303
www.willeecue.com
willeecue@willeecue.com

WOODWORTH CUES
Mr. William Woodworth
720 Plunder Creak Road
Dickson, TN 37055
615-740-1790
www.woodworthcues.com
William@woodworthcues.com

YAK POOL CUES
Mr. Dan Goble
3020 SW 100th Street
Oklahoma City, OK 73159
405-850-1555
www.yakcues.com
dangoble@cox.net

ED YOUNG CUSTOM CUES
Mr. Ed Young
Mr. David Paul Kersenbrock
429 West Ohio St. #117
Chicago, IL 60610
312-519-2505
artisian@comcast.net

ZAC CUES
Mr. Scott Zachow
8718 Faber Road
Sproat Lake
Port Alberni, BC
Canada
V9Y 9B7
250-724-9822
www.zaccues.com
scott@zaccues.com

ZAR CUES
Mr. David W. Czarnecki
1337 Maguire St
Jackson, MI 49202
517-784-4844
djczar@jcisd.k12.mi.us

BOB ZIDE CUES
Mr. Bob Zide
1451 SW 12th Ave Suite D
Pompano Beach FL 33069
954-755-2152

ZYLR HANDCRAFTED CUES
Mr. Kerry Zeiler
761 S. Park Vine St
Orange, CA 92868
714-750-2837
zylrcue@yahoo.com

ORGANIZATIONS

No doubt you have more than a casual interest in pool, billiards, cues, tournaments, etc. Here is a short listing of organizations that support the sport and craft, and offer information that may be of interest.

POOL CUE ORGANIZATIONS

The American Cuemaker's Association
Mr. Dan Dishaw, President
2608 Bellevue Avenue
Syracuse, New York 13219
Ph. 315-472-4712   Fax 315-472-1181
www.cuemakers.org
aca@cuemakers.org

Associate Membership is $50 per year (open to anyone who wishes to support the art of cuemaking). Merchandising Membership is $100 per year. Probationary Voting Membership is $200 per year (a probationary member has three years to be approved by the A.C.A. Board). Voting Membership is $300 per year, and is open only to established cuemakers (quality of work must be approved by the A.C.A. Board).

International Cuemakers Association
Mr. Chris Hightower, President
444 Flint Hill Road
Aragon, Georgia 30104
www.internationalcuemakers.com
ica@internationalcuemakers.com

BILLIARD ORGANIZATIONS

The Billiard Congress of America
4345 Beverly Street, Suite D
Colorado Springs, CO 80918
Ph. 719-264-8300 Fax 719-264-0900
www.bca-pool.com
bca@netins.net

Non Profit Recreation Center Membership is $60 per year. Affiliate Membership or Room Operator Membership is $150 per year, Retail Membership is $200 per year, Associate Membership is $500 per year (open to all business categories within the billiard industry). Voting Membership is $1,000 per year (open to all business categories within the billiard industry).

PERIODICALS

BILLIARDS DIGEST
122 S. Michigan Ave. #1506
Chicago, IL 60603
Phone: 888-313-7665
Fax: 312-341-1469
Website: www.billiardsdigest.com
Subscription - 12 issues for $30

CUE TIMES BILLIARD NEWS
Phone: 303-433-5553
Website: www.cuetimes.com
Email: info@cuetimes.com
Published monthly and online
Subscription - 12 issues for $22

CUESPORT
Global Snooker Pool Magazine
Phone: 011-44-1457-873223
Website: www.cuesport.org
Published 9 times per year
U.S. subscription - £44 per year

INSIDE POOL MAGAZINE
220 S. Jefferson Street
Kittanning, PA 16201
Phone: 866-961-7665
Fax: 877-349-2119
Website: www.insidepoolmag.com
Subscription - 8 issues for $19.99

ON THE WIRE
Newspaper and free online news source
371 E. Columbia River Hwy
Troutdale, OR 97060
Phone: 503-674-8300
Fax: 503-674-8330
Website: www.onthewirebilliards.com
Email: onthewire@aol.com

PROFESSOR-Q-BALL
1662 Rocky Hollow Road
Germantown, TN 38138
Phone: 901-756-2594
Website: www.professorqball.com
Published bi-monthly
Subscription - $15 per year

POOL & BILLIARD MAGAZINE
115 S. Main Street
Summerville, SC 29483
Phone: 888-766-5624
Fax: 843-875-5171
Website: www.poolmag.com
Subscription - 12 issues for $34.95

THE BREAK
P.O. Box 100
Three Forks, MT 59752
Phone: 406-285-3099
Website: www.onthebreaknews.com
Email: otbnews@aol.com
Published monthly
Subscription - $25 (US delivery) or $35 (Canadian delivery)

ULTIMATE POOL PLAYER MAGAZINE
Phone: 541-890-1906
Website: www.ultimatepoolplayer.com
Email: theultimatepoolplayer@hotmail.com
Free online magazine

BUY – SELL – TRADE

The following is an index of reputable dealers in pool cues who were supportive of this project. They are listed for buy-sell-trade inquiries only, and prefer not to field questions or offer over-the-phone appraisals. For appraisal/identification inquiries, refer to page 26.

AAA NIELSEN'S BILLIARDS
Mr. Joe Nielsen
2601 Taylor Avenue
Springfield, IL 62703
217-585-1660
Fax: 217-585-8077
joerackem@aol.com

AAM LIMITED
Mr. Tony Martino
1015 Westwood Drive
Ashtabula, OH 44004
440-964-6974
Cell: 440-862-0346
wincue@alltel.net

ALPHA INTERNATIONAL, INC.
Mr. Charles Takahashi
Marugen Bldg. 3F, 2-17-11
Jiyugaoka, Meguro-ku, Tokyo
Japan 152
03-3723-6311
Fax: 81-3-3723-6313

DENO J. ANDREWS
312- 735-8841
www.3cushion.com
denoandrews@sbcglobal.net

BEADS & BILLIARDS
Ms. Jesse Nestor
29408 Pacific Hwy S
Federal Way, WA 98003
253-945-1888
Fax: 253-941-8904
www.beadsandbilliards.com
info@beadsandbilliards.com

BILLIARDCUE.COM
Mr. Dick Abbott
6521 Sugar Ridge Dr.
Roanoke, VA 24018
540-772-7827
www.billiardcue.com
dick@billiardcue.com

BILLIARDS & BAGELS
Mr. Jim Oswald
31 N.E. 3rd. Street
Gresham, OR 97030
503-666-5338
Fax: 503-667-1980

BLATT BILLIARDS
Mr. Victor Stein
809 Broadway
New York, New York 10003
212-674-8855
www.blattbilliards.com
victor@blattbilliards.com
vs@billiardencyclopedia.com

CORNERSTONE CUSTOM CUES
Mr. William Grassley
Ida, MI 48140
734-693-3177
www.cornerstonecustomcues.com
wg@cornerstonecustomcues.com

CUESTIX INTERNATIONAL
Mrs. Kathy McFarland
1380 Overlook Drive #104
Lafayette, CO 80026
303-926-2670
Fax: 303-926-2679
www.cuestixint.com
info@cuestixint.com

EXCLUSIVELY BILLIARDS
Mr. Len "De Pole" Jaszewski
2723 George Street
La Crosse, WI 54603
608-781-7665
Fax: 608-783-7765
www.exclusivelybilliards.com
info@exclusivelybilliards.com

FLYIN' LION ANTIQUES
Mr. Mark & Mrs. Connie Stellinga
416 Sierra Trail
Coralville, IA 52241
319-354-7287
www.avalon.net/~billiard/welcome.html
billiard@avalon.net

GO BILLIARDS
Mr. Tom Peck
Galesburg, IL 61401
877-882-2295
www.gobilliards.com
sales@gobilliards.com

GROVER'S BILLIARDS
Mr. Blair Thein
122 North Military Trail
West Palm Beach, FL 33415
561-478-1680

HAMMERHEAD BILLIARD SUPPLY
Mr. Sean Granahan and Mr. Lucky Slay
8685 A Fort Smallwood Road
Pasadena, MD 21122
410-255-6329
Fax: 410-255-6329
www.hammerheadbilliards.com
info@hammerheadbilliards.com

BUY – SELL – TRADE, cont.

HAWAIIAN BRIAN'S
Mr. Richard Akimoto
1680 Kapiolani Blvd.
Honolulu, HI 96814
808-946-1343
Fax: 808-943-8574
www.hawaiianbrians.com
info@hawaiianbrians.com

I LOVE CUES
Mr. Iwao "Lucky" Hishinuma
Japan
www.ilovecues.com

INDY Q SHOP
Mr. Roy E. Malott
2608 S. Madison Ave.
Indianapolis, IN 46225-2111
317-780-0042
www.INDYQ.com
INDYQ@sbcglobal.net

insidepool.COM
Mr. Scott Taylor
3372 Smith Farm Rd
Matthews, NC 28104
877-283-7444
Fax: 704-821-1006
www.insidepool.com
orders@sterling-gaming.com

ERIK LEE CUES
Mr. Erik Lee
www.erikleecues.com
erik@erikleecues.com

MUELLER RECREATIONAL PRODUCTS
Mr. Rory Mueller
4825 S. 16th. St.
Lincoln, NE 68512
800-627-8888
Fax: 402-423-5964
www.poolndarts.com
info@poolndarts.com

ON THE HILL POOL SALES
Mr. Troy Oldham
1295 Ivy Drive
Greenville, IL 62246
618-623-2761
www.onthehill.net
Sales@onthehill.net

POOL TABLE MAGIC
Mr. Mark Kulungian
75 Ella Grasso Turnpike
Windsor Locks, CT 06096
860-627-8494
www.classiccues.com
www.pooltablemagic.com
MarkPTM@aol.com

SIMPSON LTD.
Mr. Brad Simpson
140 S. Seminary Street
Galesburg, IL 61401
309-342-5800
Fax: 309-342-5730
Cell: 309-335-0440
Thailand: 011-669-918-9895
www.simpsonltd.com
brad@simpsonltd.com
bradinbangkok@yahoo.com

SPECIALIZED SPORTS
Mr. Don Weathersby
2970 Shed Road Suite E
Bossier City, LA 71111
800-942-1002
Fax: 318-741-0027
www.specializedsports.com

MR. JAMES GERMANY
PO Box 277
Oakhurst, OK 74050
918-834-7653
Fax: 918-227-0997
www.JamesGermany.com
jamesgermany@att.net

TIME AFTER TIME
Mr. Ed O'Connell
32 Stony Hill
Bethel, CT 06801
203-743-2801
Fax: 203-743-2801
www.tatpool.com
tatpool@snet.net

WALTON'S CUE SALES
Mr. Keith Walton
407 Ambriance Drive
Burr Ridge, IL 60521
630-887-0419
Fax: 630-887-0438
www.waltoncues.com
waltoncues@aol.com

WE LOVE POOL
Mr. Tony Norella
1710 N 32nd Street
Boise, ID 83703
208-344-8108
866-414-1904
www.welovepool.com
admin@welovepool.com

INDEX

Title Page	1
Publisher's Note & Copyright	2
Table of Contents	3
Acknowledgements & Dedication/About the Cover & Credits	4
Contributing Editors	5
BBP General Information	6
Meet the Staff	7
Publisher's Overview	8
Foreword & A Word About the Author	9
The PCIII Overview by Carol Simpson	10
How To Use This Book	11-12
Tracking Your Cue Through the Book	13
Collecting Pool Cues by Deno Andrews.	14-17
Scuffers & Cue Accessories by Tom Shaw	18-21
The Hustler Cue by James Yonge	22-25
Wanted Dead or Alive/Correspondence & Appraisals	26
Glossary	27-28
Condition Factors	29
Levels of Intricacy	30
How to Use the Level of Intricacy Grading	31
The Pool Cue Catscan	32
Cue Gallery	33-96
A-Z sections	97-888

-A-

ABEAR CUES	97
AC CUES	97
ACTION CUES	97
ADAM CUSTOM CUES	98
MID-1970S TO EARLY 1980S CUES	101
TWIN JOINT PROFESSIONAL CUES	106
HELMSTETTER H SERIES CUES	110
HELMSTETTER 97 SERIES CUES	112
HELMSTETTER 98 SERIES	114
HELMSTETTER TJ SERIES	115
ADAM CUSTOM SERIES CUES	116
SECONDARY MARKET MINIMUM VALUES	117
GUS ADAMS	118
SHERM ADAMSON	118
ADVANCED ACCURACY CUES	118
AE CUES	119
AKERS CUES	122
J. ALAN CUES	123
CHIP ALBERY CUSTOM CUES	124
ALDREN CUES	125
ALLEN'S CUSTOM CUES	127
AMOS CUES & REPAIRS	128
BRADY ANDRESEN	128
AO CUSTOM CUES	128
AP CUES	130
ARNOT Q'S CUSTOM CUES	131
AUERBACH CUSTOM CUES	133
AXIOM CUES	135

-B-

BAKER CUSTOM CUES	137
GEORGE BALABUSHKA	139
KNOWN BALABUSHKA EXAMPLES	140
TITLIST BLANK CUES (1959-1975)	140
BURTON SPAIN/JOHN DAVIS BLANK CUES (1966-1971)	142
GUS SZAMBOTI BLANK CUES	143
TITLIST BLANK GEORGE BALABUSHKA CUES (1959-1975)	144
BURTON SPAIN/JOHN DAVIS BLANK GEORGE BALABUSHKA CUES (1966-1972)	144
GUS SZAMBOTI BLANK GEORGE BALABUSHKA CUES (1973-1975)	144
BALICINI CUES	145
FRANK BALL CUSTOM CUES	145
BARBER CUSTOM CUES	146
BARENBRUGGE CUES	148
BARKLEY CUSTOM CUES	149
BARNET CUES	150
BARNHART CUES	150
BARRINGER CUES	153
BCM CUES	155
MARK BEAR CUSTOM CUES	156
AL BECKELHIMER	157
BECKER CUSTOM CUES	157
BELLA SERA CUSTOM CUES, LLC	159
BENDER CUES	161
MATT K. BENDER	164
BENSON CUE	164
BLACK BOAR INDUSTRIES	165
BLACKCREEK CUSTOM CUES	167
BLACK HAWK CUSTOM CUES	169
BLACK HEART CUSTOM CUES	171
RICHARD BLACK CUSTOM CRAFTED CUES	172
SAMUEL BLATT	177
LES BLEVINS	177
BLUDWORTH CUES	178

INDEX, cont.

BLUE GRASS CUES 180
BOB'S CUES 182
BourQue CUES 182
BOURQUE CUSTOM MADE CUES 183
BRADEN CUES 186
BRELAND CUES 186
BRICK CUE CO. 187
OLIVER BRIGGS 189
JAMES BRUMFIELD 189
BRUNSWICK BILLIARDS 189
   CURRENT BRUNSWICK CUES 190
   DISCONTINUED EXAMPLES 190
   MAJESTIC SERIES 191
   EWA MATAYA LAWRENCE SERIES 191
   JIMMY CARAS SERIES 191
   CORVETTE SERIES 192
   MAGNUM SERIES 193
   DIAMOND SERIES 193
   OPAL SERIES 194
   SECONDARY MARKET MINIMUM VALUES 194
   SPECIAL INTEREST CUES: BRUNSWICK BALKE
   COLLENDER MODELS C. PRE-1900 195
   SPECIAL INTEREST CUES: BRUNSWICK MODELS C. 1912 - 1929 .197
   SPECIAL INTEREST CUES: BRUNSWICK BALKE
   COLLENDER MODELS C. 1950 - 1965 198

BRYLES CUES 199
BOB BURGOYNE 199
GEORGE BUSS 199
JIM BUSS CUSTOM CUES 199

-C-

CHRIS BYRNE CUSTOM CUES 203
CADILLAC CUSTOM CUES 205
CAM CUSTOM CUES 206
CAMERON CUSTOM CUES 207
PETE CAMPBELL CUES 209
CANTANDO CUSTOM CUES 210
CAPONE CUES 212
ARIEL CARMELI CUSTOM CUES 214
CARTER CUSTOM CUES 216
CASANOVA CUES 217
MARCO CERVANTES 218
RICCO CERVANTES 218
THIERRY CHEVRON 218
JOE CHILDS CUSTOM POOL CUES 218
CHILTON CUSTOM CUES 218
CHRIS' CUES 220
RICHARD CHUDY CUSTOM CUES 221
CK CUSTOM CUES 224
GALE CLARK CUES 226
CLASSIC CUSTOM CUE 227

CLAWSON CUES 228
COGNOSCENTI CUES 228
COKER CUES 231
COMPETITION SPORTS CORP 232
CORLISS CUE 234
CORSAIR CUSTOM CUES 236
   CURRENT CORSAIR CUES 237
   CURRENT EXAMPLES 237
   PAST EXAMPLES (BY HANK KORSIAK) 238
   PAST EXAMPLES (BY ROGER KORSIAK) 239
   SECONDARY MARKET MINIMUM VALUES
   (BY HANK KORSIAK) 239
   SECONDARY MARKET MINIMUM VALUES
   (BY ROGER KORSIAK) 239

FRANK COSTER 239
COUSIN'S CUSTOM CUES 242
CRAMER CUES 242
CRYSTAL LEISURE 242
CUE MASTER 242
THE CUE MASTERS 243
CUES BY DAVID 245
CUESPORT 246
CUETEC 246

-D-

DAVID CZARNECKI 247
DANBUILT CUSTOM CUES 249
JOHN DAVIS CUSTOM CUES 249
GARY DAWKINS 250
DAYTON CUSTOM CUES 250
DG CUES 253
DIAMOND CUE CO. 254
DENNIS DIECKMAN 255
DAN DISHAW HANDCRAFTED CUES 257
DIVENEY CUES 260
DAVE DOUCETTE 262
DOWNEY CUSTOM CUES 262
DON DOYON CUSTOM CUES 265
DP CUSTOM CUES 267
PAUL DREXLER 270
DUFFERIN CUES 270
DURBIN CUSTOM CUES 271
DZ CUSTOM CUES 273

-E-

ECKES CUES INC. 277
JERRY EICK 278
ELIMINATOR CUES 278

ELITE CUSTOM CUES, INC.	279
TODD ELKINS	279
EMBASSY CUES	279
ERWIN CUSTOM CUES	280
ESPIRITU HAND CRAFTED CUSTOM CUES	281
MIKE ETHERIDGE	285
EUROWEST	285
EYE CUE	290

-F-

FALCON CUES LTD	293
FANELLI CUES	294
FARRIS CUES	296
FIERCE EAGLE CUES	297
5280 CUES	297
FRANK FISHER CUSTOM CUES	298
RITCHIE FLORENCE CUES	298
TRAVIS FRAKES	298
JOSEPH FRANKE	298
JERRY and LAURIE FRANKLIN	298
ADAM FRANKS CUSTOM CUES	298
DOC FRY	299

-G-

GARLAND "JUDD" FULLER	300
FURY CUES	300
GARDNER CUES	303
GATZKE'S CUSTOM CUES	304
DAN GAUDREAU	305
G.B. CUSTOM CUES	305
GCUE	307
GD CUES	307
GEM CUES	309
GEPPETTO CUSTOM CUES	310
WILLIAM CHARLES GIBBS	310
GILBERT CUSTOM CUES	310
GINACUE	312
CURRENT GINACUE CUES	314
CURRENT EXAMPLES	314
PAST EXAMPLES	317
SPECIAL INTEREST GINACUE CUES	317
SECONDARY MARKET MINIMUM VALUES (EARLY CUES)	318
SECONDARY MARKET MINIMUM VALUES (LATER CUES)	318
GIONNI POOL CUES	319
MICHAEL GIVENS	319
JOE GOLD	319
GOLDENROD CUES	319
MIKE "COSMO" GRAY	319
NAT GREEN	319
GREG'S KUES	319
GRIFFIN and SON CUSTOM CUES	320
JIM GRIFFIN	321
GSCUE	322
JOHN GUFFEY CUSTOM CUES/J.G. CUSTOM CUE	324
GUGINO'S CUSTOM CUES	326
GULYASSY CUES	328
GUNN CUES	329
RAY GURGALL	330
ERNIE GUTIERREZ	330

-H-

HADRIANUS CUE COMPANY - HAND-MADE CUES BY ADRIAN VIGUERA	331
HAGAN CUE	332
RON HALEY HANDMADE CUES	333
HAMILTON CUE	334
HAMMER CUSTOM CUES	335
HARPER'S PERSONALIZED CUES	336
RICHARD HARRIS	337
TED HARRIS CUSTOM CUES	337
TOM HARRIS CUES	340
TIM & JIM HASKIN	341
STAN HAWKINS	341
HAWKINS CUES	341
STEVE HEBERT	341
RICHARD HELMSTETTER	341
HERCEK FINE BILLIARD CUES	342
HICKS STICKS	346
HIGHTOWER CUSTOM CUES	347
DAVID HODGES	348
ORIE HOLMES CUSTOM CUES	349
WAYNE HOLMES	349
VERL HORN CUES	349
HOWARD CUES	350
RICK HOWARD	351
RICHARD HSU	351
HUBBART CUES	351
HUEBLER INDUSTRIES, INC.	352
CURRENT HUEBLER CUES	353
CURRENT EXAMPLES	353
"STAINED MAPLE" SERIES	353
"ANNIVERSARY" SERIES	354
DISCONTINUED HUEBLER CUES	355
"FAST EDDIE PARKER SIGNATURE" SERIES	356
"25TH ANNIVERSARY SILVER JUBILEE" SERIES	357
"ELITE" SERIES	357
THE JEAN BALUKAS SIGNATURE SERIES	358

INDEX, cont.

- "ANNIVERSARY" SERIES 359
- "HS" SERIES 359
- HUEBLER CUSTOM SHOP 360
- SECONDARY MARKET MINIMUM VALUES 363

BILL HUGHES 363
HUNTER CLASSICS CUSTOM CUES 363
HUNTER CUSTOM CUES 364
HURRICANE CUE CO. 366
MILT HYMAN 367

-I-

IMPERIAL INTERNATIONAL 369
INGRAM CUES 369
IT'S GEORGE 370

-J-

J & J AMERICA 371
J.B. CUSTOM CUES 371
JACKSON CUSTOM CUE 372
JACOBY CUSTOM CUES 375
DAN JANES 385
JENSEN CUSTOM CUES 386
JERICO CUES 387
JOBO CUES 388
MIKE JOHNSON 388
CHRIS JONES CUSTOM CUES 388
DAVE JONES CUSTOM CUES 389
JOSEPH FULL SPLICE CUES 390
JOSEY CUSTOM CUES 392
JOSS CUES LTD. 395
- CURRENT EXAMPLES 396
- DISCONTINUED JOSS CUES 397
- 2000 SERIES 399
- "EDDIE TAYLOR SPECIAL EDITION" SERIES ... 402
- SECONDARY MARKET MINIMUM VALUES (EARLY CUES) 403
- SECONDARY MARKET MINIMUM VALUES (1972-PRESENT CUES) 403

JOSSWEST 404
JOUST GRAPHITE CUES 406
JUDD'S CUSTOM CUES 406
JUSTIS CUES 409

-K-

RON KADEY 411
KAIZEN CUSTOM CUES 411
KARELLA CUES 412
KEITH KUSTOM KUES 412
KELLY CUES 413

DAVID PAUL KERSENBROCK 413
KIKEL CUSTOM CUES 416
RONALD KILBY CUES 418
RON KITZMILLER CUES 419
KLEIN CUSTOM CUES 419
KLICKCUE CUES 421
TAD KOHARA 422
KORNELE CUSTOM CUES 422
MICHAEL KRATOCHVILL 424
CHESTER KRICK 424
GREG KUCHARSKI 424

-L-

LAMBROS CUES, INC. 425
LANZ CUSTOM CUES 428
CUES BY LARUE 430
EDDIE LAUBE CUES 430
LAWHEAD CUES 431
LAYANI CUES 431
LEBOW CUSTOM CUES 434
WILLIAM LEE 435
LEGACY CUES 435
LEGEND CUES 436
LIBRA CUES 436
LINEAR Q 436
JEFF LIPP 437
LOMAX CUSTOM CUES 437
LONGONI CUSTOM CUES 438
L.T.D. CUES 440
LUCASI CUE 440
LUDWIG CUSTOM CUES 441
MACE CUES BY RICK HOWARD 443
THE MACE 445
JOHN MADDEN CUES 446

-M-

MADISON BOB'S CUSTOM CUES 447
MALI CUES 447
- CURRENT MALI CUES 448
- CURRENT EXAMPLES 448
- 2005 MALI VINTAGE 448
- DISCONTINUED EXAMPLES 450
- 1996 "SPECTRUM SERIES" 450
- "386 IN. SERIES 450
- "CLASSIC" SERIES 452
- "REGALIA" SERIES 452
- 1999 SERIES" 453
- SECONDARY MARKET MINIMUM VALUES 455

MANZINO CUSTOM POOL CUES 456

JOE MARCHANT	458
MARIPOSA CUE CO.	459
MARQUETRY BILLIARD CUES	460
HARVEY MARTIN	461
MIKE MARTIN CUSTOM CUES	463
ERNIE MARTINEZ CUSTOM CUES	464
ANNIE MAYES	467
MAXIMUM CUE	467
JOE MAZLEWSKI	467
KARL MEYER CUE	467
BILL MCDANIEL CUES	468
MCDERMOTT CUE MANUFACTURING INC.	471
CURRENT CUES	472
"PRESTIGE" SERIES	473
"ELITE" SERIES	473
"PROFESSIONAL" SERIES	475
"TOURNAMENT" SERIES	479
"COMPETITOR" SERIES	483
"LICENSED" SERIES	484
DISCONTINUED CUES	485
A-LINE SERIES	485
B-LINE SERIES	486
C-LINE SERIES	488
D-LINE SERIES	490
"WILDLIFE SERIES"	494
HD-LINE (HARLEY DAVIDSON SERIES)	494
E-A SERIES	495
"E-B" SERIES	496
"E-C" SERIES	498
"E-D" SERIES	498
"E-F" SERIES	499
"E-G" SERIES	499
"E-H" SERIES	500
"E-I" SERIES	501
"E-J" SERIES	501
"E-K" SERIES	502
"E-L" SERIES	502
"E-M" (MASTERPIECE SERIES)	503
"E-N" SERIES	504
"M7 IN. COLLEGIATE SERIES	505
"RS" (REVIVAL SERIES)	506
GENESIS SERIES CUES	508
"M-8" SERIES	508
"M-7" SERIES	509
"M8 PROFESSIONAL" SERIES	509
"E-I" SERIES	510
"E-L" SERIES	511
HARLEY DAVIDSON SERIES	511
"E-F" SERIES	511
"E-H" SERIES	511
"E-B" SERIES	512
HARLEY DAVIDSON SERIES	512
SPECIAL INTEREST MCDERMOTT CUES	512
COMMEMORATIVE SERIES	513
SECONDARY MARKET MINIMUM VALUES	513
CHAD MCLENNAN	513
MCWORTER CUES	513
GARY MEDLIN	516
MEISTER CUES	516
MEUCCI ORIGINALS INC.	517
CURRENT EXAMPLES	519
HI-PRO SERIES	521
DISCONTINUED MEUCCI CUES	521
1990'S CUES	522
SPECIAL INTEREST MEUCCI CUES	526
SECONDARY MARKET MINIMUM VALUES	526
MEZZ CUES	527
MICHAELANGELO CUSTOM CUES	528
MICHAEL MORGAN CUES	530
MICHAEL'S CUSTOM CUES	532
MID WEST CUSTOM CUES	533
TOMMY MIGLIORE	535
MIKI CO. LTD	535
S.C. MILLER CUSTOM CUES	535
MICHAEL MILLER	536
MILTONIO CUSTOM CUES	536
MINNESOTA FATS CUES	538
MISTER BILLIARD CUES	539
RANDY MOBLEY	539
MOHAWK CUES	539
BRYAN MORDT	539
HAROLD MOREY CUES	539
MORRIS CUSTOM CUES	540
STEVE MORRIS	542
STU MORTENSON	542
MOSCONI CUES	542
MOTTEY CUSTOM CUES	542
DON MOYER	545
RAY MUDDER	546
MUELLER SPORTING GOODS	546
KENNETH MURRELL CUSTOM CUES	547
MYSTYQUE	549

-N-

NATIONAL CUES	551
MIKE NEAL CUSTOM CUES	551
RICHARD H. NEIGHBORS	553
JESSI NESTER	553
NEWPORT CUSTOM CUES	553
NEW YORK BILLIARD TABLE CO.	554
TRAVIS NIKLICH	554
NITTI CUES	554
NORTHERN CUE	556
NORWELA CUES	557
NOVA CUES INC.	559

-O-

ODOM CUES 561
OJO CUES 562
JERRY OLIVIER HAND CRAFTED
  CUSTOM CUES 562
JIM OLMS CUES 566
OLNEY CUSTOM CUES 567
OMEGA CUES 568
OMEGA CUE COMPANY, LATER
  OMEGA/DPK 569
OMEN CUSTOM CUES 570
ONE ON ONE CUE STICKS 572
ORCHID U.S.A. 573
GUIDO ORLANDI CUSTOM CUES 574

-P-

PADGETT CUSTOM CUES 575
PADISHAN INTERNATIONAL 576
PALMER CUSTOM CUES COMPANY 576
PANCERNY CUSTOM CUES 580
PANTHER CUSTOM CUES 583
FRANK PARADISE 583
ANDREW PARK 586
JOHN PARKER 586
PARROT CUES 586
ROBERT PARSONS 587
PATRICK CUSTOM CUES 587
CUSTOM CUES BY DALE PATTEN 589
J. PECHAUER CUSTOM CUES 590
  CURRENT J PECHAUER CUES 591
  CURRENT EXAMPLES 591
  "JP" SERIES 592
  PROFESSIONAL SERIES 594
  DISCONTINUED EXAMPLES 597
  1980'S "JP" SERIES 597
  1992 "JP" SERIES 598
  1995 "JP" SERIES 600
  "PROFESSIONAL" SERIES 602
  "JP USA" SERIES 608
  "JP" SERIES 608
  "J. PECHAUER PROFESSIONAL" SERIES 610
  SECONDARY MARKET MINIMUM VALUES (JP SERIES) ... 613
  SECONDARY MARKET MINIMUM VALUES
    (PROFESSIONAL SERIES) 613
JOSEPH PECHAUER CUSTOM CUES 614
PENROSE CUES 615
DALE PERRY 616
CRAIG PETERSEN 616
PETREE CUSTOM CUES 618
pfd STUDIOS 620

PHILLIPPI CUSTOM CUES 623
ALBERT PICK COMPANY 626
PICONE CUES 627
PIERCE CUES 629
AUGUSTO "GUS" PINCA 629
PLAYER'S CUES 629
PORCUPINE CUES 630
JOE PORPER'S CREATIVE INVENTIONS 632
JERRY POWERS 633
PRATHER CUE 634
  CURRENT PRATHER CUES 635
  CURRENT EXAMPLES 635
  DISCONTINUED EXAMPLES 636
  P-SERIES 636
  201, 301, AND 401 SERIES 637
  SECONDARY MARKET MINIMUM VALUES 640
PRECISION CUE DESIGN 640
PREDATOR CUES 640
  CURRENT EXAMPLES 642
  PREDATOR BREAK CUES 642
  PREDATOR SNEAKY PETES 642
  PREDATOR 4K SERIES 642
  PREDATOR P2 CUES 643
  PREDATOR P2 "10TH ANNIVERSARY" 644
  DISCONTINUED EXAMPLES 644
  PREDATOR 1996 SERIES 644
  1999 PREDATOR 2 645
  PREDATOR 1999 SERIES 645
  2000 2K SERIES 646
  2002 3K SERIES 647
  SPECIAL INTEREST PREDATOR CUES 648
  LE4 LIMITED EDITION 648
  LE5 LIMITED EDITION 648
  SE1 AND SE2 SPECIAL EDITION 648
  SE3 SPECIAL EDITION 648
  SE5 SPECIAL EDITION 649
  SECONDARY MARKET MINIMUM VALUES 649
PREWITT CUSTOM CUES 649
PRINCE CUES 650
PROFICIENT BILLIARDS 651
SHAWN PUTNAM CUES 651

-Q-

QUEST ASP CUSTOM CUES 653
Q-WORKS 654

-R-

HERMAN RAMBOW 655
RAT CUES 657
RATHBUN CUES 658
RAUENZAHN CUSTOM CUES 659
RAVEN CUSTOM CUES 661

REEVES CUSTOM CUES	664
BOB RENIS	665
EDWIN REYES CUSTOM HANDCRAFTED CUES	665
RHINO CUES	666
R.H.N. CUSTOM CUES	667
RICCO CUSTOM CUES	668
ABE RICH	669
RICH CUE	669
HARRY RICHARDS CUSTOM CUES	671
RIEPER MANUFACTURING CO.	673
RIKARD CUSTOM CUES	676
RJH CUSTOM CUES	677
ROBINSON CUES	678
ROMERO CUES	680
RUBINO CUES	681
BOB RUNDE CUES	683
RUTZISKY, ISADORE	684

-S-

SAILOR CUES	685
SAMPAIO BILLIARD CUES	686
SAMSARA CUES	688
CURRENT SAMSARA CUES	690
CURRENT EXAMPLES	690
DISCONTINUED EXAMPLES	691
DISCONTINUED EXAMPLES	693
SECONDARY MARKET MINIMUM VALUES	694
SANKO CUSTOM CUES	695
BILL SCHICK ORIGINALS	698
SCHMELKE MANUFACTURING INC.	701
E. SCHMIDT	705
SCHON CUES	705
SCHRAGER CUES	712
SCHULER CUE	714
ANTHONY SCIANELLA	717
SCORPION CUES	717
TIM SCRUGGS CUSTOM CUES, INC.	717
DENNIS SEARING CUSTOM CUES	721
SHAMAN CUES	723
SCOT SHERBINE CUSTOM CUES	724
SHERM CUES	726
SHOWCASE CUSTOM CUES	728
SHOWMAN CUSTOM CUES	730
SHURTZ CUSTOM CUES	731
SIERRA CUSTOM CUE	733
SIGEL'S CUES	735
SILVER FOX	736
GREG SIRCA	737
SMITH HANDCRAFTED CUES	737
JEFF SMITH	738
MARK SMITH CUSTOM CUES	739
ROBERT SMITH	741
SMITH & WESSON BILLIARDS	741
RICHARD SMITHLIN	741
SOUTH EAST CUES	741
SOUTH WEST CUES	743
SOWDER CUSTOM CUES	747
BURTON SPAIN	749
SPIDER WEB CUES	753
M. STACEY CUES	754
STADUM	756
JULIO STAMBOULINI CUES	756
STAR CITY CUES	758
STAR CUE COMPANY	760
STEALTH CUES	761
FRANK STELLMAN	763
BILL STELZENMULLER	763
STONIER'S CUSTOM CUES	763
OLIVER STOPS ORIGINAL	764
STOUT STICKS	764
STRADER CUSTOM CUES	765
BILL STROUD	766
SWEETWATER CUES, USA	766
SYRA-CUES BY R.K.	768
SZAMBOTI CUES	770
GUS SZAMBOTI	773

-T-

TAD'S CUSTOM CUE	781
TAMPA BILLIARDS	784
TASCARELLA CUSTOM CUES	784
TAYLOR CUE COMPANY	785
TC CUES	787
DALE TEAGUE	788
TERBROCK CUES	788
JOE THOMAS CUES	789
THOMPSON CUES U.S.A.	791
DANNY TIBBITTS CUSTOM CUES	793
DAVID TICE CUSTOM CUES	794
ROCKY TILLIS	795
TING CUSTOM CUES	797
TNS CUES	798
TODD CUES	799
TOEBOY	801
TOEDT CUSTOM CUES	801
TONKIN CUSTOM CUES	801

DAN TROGDON CUSTOM CUES 803
TUCKER CUSTOM CUES 804
TUNDER CUE CO. 806

-V-

KYLE VAN DEN BOSCH 807
VAN HALL CUES 807
NICK VARNER CUES & CASES 808
FRED VELTEN CUES 808
VIATTORRE CUSTOM CUES 809
ADRIAN VIGUERA 810
VIKING CUE MANUFACTURING INC. 810
   CURRENT VIKING CUES 812
   CURRENT EXAMPLES 812
   VIKING F SERIES 812
   "DECUE" SERIES 824
   DISCONTINUED EXAMPLES 825
   VIKING'S SECOND LINE 827
   VIKING'S THIRD LINE 830
   "Z" SERIES (VIKING'S FIFTH LINE) 833
   VIKING'S B LINE 837
   VIKING'S A-SERIES LINE 841
   Q LINE 845
   "DECUE" LINE 849
   1999 MILENNIUM SERIES 849
   "DECUE" SERIES 854
   SECONDARY MARKET MINIMUM VALUES .. 854

-W-

ARNOT Q WADSWORTH III 857
MICHAEL WAGNER 857
NORBERT "NUBS" WAGNER 857
RUSS WALDO 857
WARD CUSTOM CUES 857
WAYNE CUSTOM CUES 858
THOMAS WAYNE CUES 860
BILLY WEBB 862
MIKE WEBB CUES 862
ROBERT WEIR CUES 864
WESTON CUSTOM CUES 864
SKIP WESTON CUES 866
WHISLER CUSTOM CUES 868
CHRIS WHITAKER 870
JAMES WHITE CUSTOM CUES 870
WHITEY CUES 871
DAVID WHITSELL 871
CHARLES WILHITE 871
WILLEE CUES 871
WOODWORTH CUES 873
HAROLD WORST 875

-Y-

YAK CUES 877
ED YOUNG CUSTOM CUES 878

-Z-

ZAC CUES 881
ZAR CUES 883
KERRY ZEILER 884
BOB ZIDE CUES 884
ZYLR CUES 886

Trademark Index 889-900
Organizations 901
Periodicals Listing 902
Buy/Sell/Trade 903-904
Index 905-912